SYMBOLS

RELIEF

METRES		FEET
6000		19686
5000		16404
4000		13124
3000		9843
2000		6562
1000		3281
500		1640
200		656
SEA		LEVEL
200		656
2000		6562
4000		13124
6000		19686

Additional bathymetric contour layers are shown at scales greater than 1:2 million. These are labelled on an individual basis.

213 △ Summit *height in metres*

BOUNDARIES

- International
- International disputed
- Ceasefire line
- Main administrative (U.K.)
- Main administrative
- Main administrative through water

COMMUNICATIONS

- Motorway
- Motorway tunn

Motorways are classified separately at scales greate. 1:5 million. At smaller scales motorways are classified with main roads.

- Main road
- Main road under construction
- Main road tunnel
- Other road
- Other road under construction
- Other road tunnel
- Track
- Main railway
- Main railway under construction
- Main railway tunnel
- Other railway
- Other railway under construction
- Other railway tunnel
- ⊕ Main airport
- ⊹ Other airport

- Seasonal saltwater lake
- Dry salt lake *or* Salt pan
- Marsh
- River
- Waterfall
- Dam or Barrage
- Seasonal river *or* Wadi
- Canal
- Flood dyke
- Reef
- ▲ Volcano
- Lava field
- Sandy desert
- Rocky desert
- Oasis
- Escarpment
- ≍ 923 Mountain pass *height in metres*
- Ice cap *or* Glacier

STYLES OF LETTERING

Country name	**FRANCE**	Island	*Gran Canaria*
	BARBADOS	Lake	*LAKE ERIE*
Main administrative name	HESSEN	Mountain	*ANDES*
Area name	*ARTOIS*	River	*Zambeze*

OTHER FEATURES

- National park
- Reserve
- Ancient wall
- ∴ Historic or Tourist site

SETTLEMENTS

POPULATION	NATIONAL CAPITAL	ADMINISTRATIVE CAPITAL	CITY OR TOWN
Over 5 million	▣ **Beijing**	◉ **Tianjin**	◉ **New York**
1 to 5 million	▣ **Seoul**	◉ **Lagos**	◉ **Barranquilla**
500000 to 1 million	▣ **Bangui**	◉ **Douala**	◉ **Memphis**
100000 to 500000	▢ Wellington	○ Mansa	○ Mara
50000 to 100000	▢ Port of Spain	○ Lubango	○ Tuzla
10000 to 50000	▫ Malabo	○ Chinhoyi	○ El Tigre
Less than 10000	▫ Roseau	○ Ati	○ Soledad

Urban area

C000049016

COLLINS
ILLUSTRATED
ATLAS
OF THE WORLD

HarperCollinsPublishers

ILLUSTRATED
ATLAS
OF THE WORLD

Collins Illustrated Atlas of the World

Collins
An Imprint of HarperCollins*Publishers*
77-85 Fulham Palace Road
London W6 8JB

First Published 1995
Second Edition 1997
Reprinted with revisions 1997
Reprinted 1998,1999
Revised Edition 2000

Copyright ©HarperCollins*Publishers* Ltd 2000
Maps © Bartholomew Ltd 2000
Collins® is a registered trademark
of HarperCollins*Publishers* Ltd

Printed in Italy

ISBN 0 00 448937 3

Photo credits:
Jacket and pages 16-19: Tony Stone Images
All other photos: Pictor International - London

MH10307 Imp 001

www.**fire**and**water**.com
Visit the book lover's website

CONTENTS

SYMBOLS
Endpapers

THE WORLD

COUNTRIES *4-5*
PHYSICAL FEATURES *6-7*
ENVIRONMENT *8-9*
CLIMATE *10-11*
ATLANTIC OCEAN 1:58M *12*
INDIAN OCEAN 1:58M *13*
PACIFIC OCEAN 1:58M *14-15*

NORTH AMERICA

COUNTRIES : POPULATION
16-17
RELIEF : CLIMATE
18-19

Western CANADA
1:7M *20-21*

Eastern CANADA
1:7M *22-23*

Western USA
1:7M *24-25*

Central USA
1:7M *26-27*

Eastern USA
1:7M *28-29*

THE GREAT LAKES
1:3.5M *30-31*

Northeastern USA
1:3.5M *32-33*

Southwestern USA 1:3.5M
(inset) HAWAII 1:6M *34-35*

CENTRAL AMERICA
and the CARIBBEAN
1:14M *36-37*

SOUTH AMERICA

COUNTRIES : POPULATION
38-39

RELIEF : CLIMATE
40-41

Northern SOUTH AMERICA
1:15M *42-43*

Southern SOUTH AMERICA
1:15M *44*

VENEZUELA and
COLOMBIA
1:7.5M *45*

Southeastern BRAZIL
1:7.5M *46*

URUGUAY, Central CHILE
and Central ARGENTINA
1:7.5M *47*

EUROPE

COUNTRIES : POPULATION
48-51

RELIEF : CLIMATE
52-53

SCANDINAVIA
and the BALTIC STATES
1:5M *54-55*

BRITISH ISLES 1:5M *56*

SCOTLAND 1:2M *57*

ENGLAND and WALES
1:2M *58-59*

IRELAND 1:2M *60*

BELGIUM and
NETHERLANDS
1:2M *61*

North Central EUROPE
1:5M *62-63*

FRANCE 1:5M *64*

SPAIN and PORTUGAL 1:5M *65*

ITALY and the BALKANS
1:5M *66-67*

Western RUSSIA,
BELARUS and UKRAINE
1:7M *68-69*

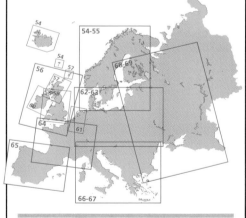

ASIA

COUNTRIES : POPULATION
70-73

RELIEF : CLIMATE
74-75

RUSSIAN FEDERATION
1:21M *76-77*

Southwestern ASIA
and the MIDDLE EAST
1:12.5M *78-79*

Eastern MEDITERRANEAN
1:5M *80-81*

Southern ASIA 1:14M *82-83*

Northern INDIA, Eastern PAKISTAN
and BANGLADESH 1:7M *84-85*

CHINA 1:15M *86-87*

Central CHINA 1:7.5M *88-89*

JAPAN 1:4M *90-91*

SOUTHEAST ASIA 1:15M *92-93*

PHILIPPINES 1:7M *94*

THAILAND, CAMBODIA and
Peninsular MALAYSIA 1:7.5M *95*

AFRICA

COUNTRIES : POPULATION
96-97

RELIEF : CLIMATE
98-99

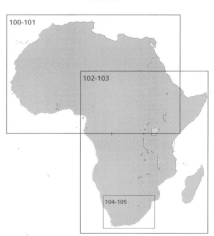

Northern AFRICA 1:16M *100-101*

Central and Southern AFRICA
1:16M *102-103*

REPUBLIC OF SOUTH AFRICA
1:5M *104-105*

OCEANIA

COUNTRIES : POPULATION
106-107

RELIEF : CLIMATE
108-109

AUSTRALIA and
Southwestern PACIFIC
1:20M *110-111*

AUSTRALIA
1:12M *112-113*

Southeastern AUSTRALIA
1:5M *114-115*

Northeastern AUSTRALIA
1:5M *116*

NEW ZEALAND 1:5M *117*

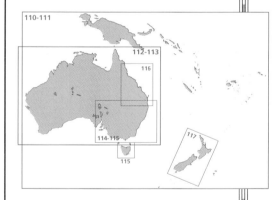

POLAR

THE ARCTIC 1:32M *118*

ANTARCTICA 1:32M *119*

ABBREVIATIONS
and GLOSSARY *120*

INDEX *121-184*

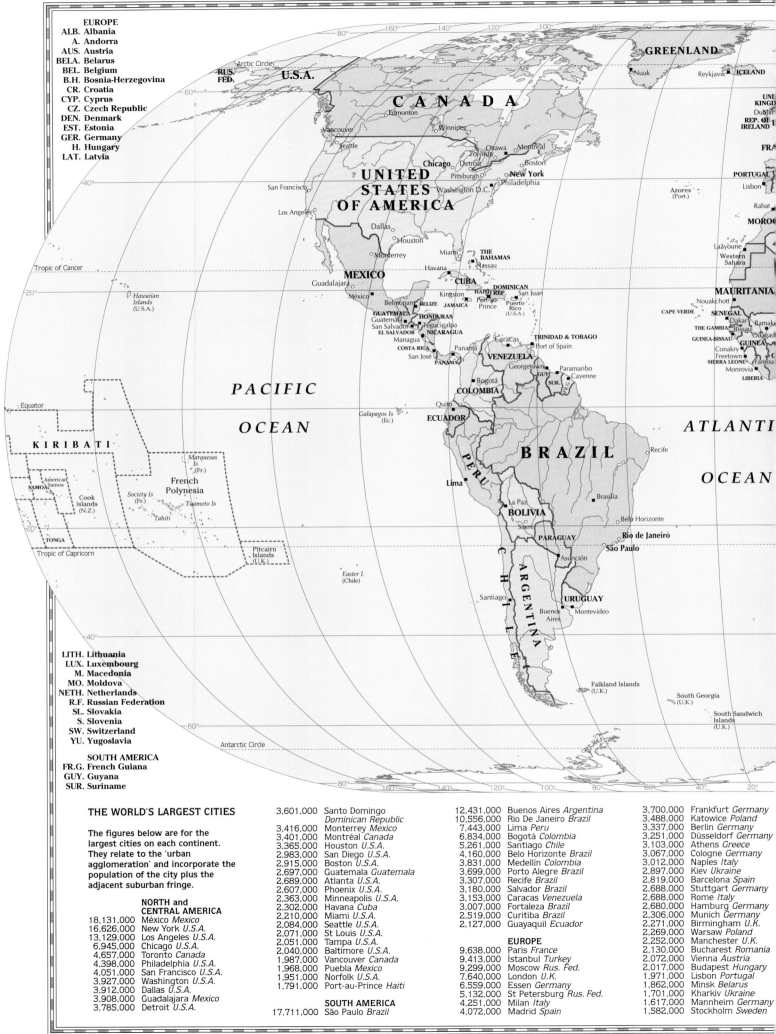

EUROPE
ALB. Albania
A. Andorra
AUS. Austria
BELA. Belarus
BEL. Belgium
B.H. Bosnia-Herzegovina
CR. Croatia
CYP. Cyprus
CZ. Czech Republic
DEN. Denmark
EST. Estonia
GER. Germany
H. Hungary
LAT. Latvia

LITH. Lithuania
LUX. Luxembourg
M. Macedonia
MO. Moldova
NETH. Netherlands
R.F. Russian Federation
SL. Slovakia
S. Slovenia
SW. Switzerland
YU. Yugoslavia

SOUTH AMERICA
FR.G. French Guiana
GUY. Guyana
SUR. Suriname

THE WORLD'S LARGEST CITIES

The figures below are for the
largest cities on each continent.
They relate to the 'urban
agglomeration' and incorporate the
population of the city plus the
adjacent suburban fringe.

**NORTH and
CENTRAL AMERICA**
18,131,000	México *Mexico*
16,626,000	New York *U.S.A.*
13,129,000	Los Angeles *U.S.A.*
6,945,000	Chicago *U.S.A.*
4,657,000	Toronto *Canada*
4,398,000	Philadelphia *U.S.A.*
4,051,000	San Francisco *U.S.A.*
3,927,000	Washington *U.S.A.*
3,912,000	Dallas *U.S.A.*
3,908,000	Guadalajara *Mexico*
3,785,000	Detroit *U.S.A.*
3,601,000	Santo Domingo *Dominican Republic*
3,416,000	Monterrey *Mexico*
3,401,000	Montréal *Canada*
3,365,000	Houston *U.S.A.*
2,983,000	San Diego *U.S.A.*
2,915,000	Boston *U.S.A.*
2,697,000	Guatemala *Guatemala*
2,689,000	Atlanta *U.S.A.*
2,607,000	Phoenix *U.S.A.*
2,363,000	Minneapolis *U.S.A.*
2,302,000	Havana *Cuba*
2,210,000	Miami *U.S.A.*
2,084,000	Seattle *U.S.A.*
2,071,000	St Louis *U.S.A.*
2,051,000	Tampa *U.S.A.*
2,040,000	Baltimore *U.S.A.*
1,987,000	Vancouver *Canada*
1,968,000	Puebla *Mexico*
1,951,000	Norfolk *U.S.A.*
1,791,000	Port-au-Prince *Haiti*

SOUTH AMERICA
17,711,000	São Paulo *Brazil*
12,431,000	Buenos Aires *Argentina*
10,556,000	Rio De Janeiro *Brazil*
7,443,000	Lima *Peru*
6,834,000	Bogotá *Colombia*
5,261,000	Santiago *Chile*
4,160,000	Belo Horizonte *Brazil*
3,831,000	Medellín *Colombia*
3,699,000	Porto Alegre *Brazil*
3,307,000	Recife *Brazil*
3,180,000	Salvador *Brazil*
3,153,000	Caracas *Venezuela*
3,007,000	Fortaleza *Brazil*
2,519,000	Curitiba *Brazil*
2,127,000	Guayaquil *Ecuador*

EUROPE
9,638,000	Paris *France*
9,413,000	İstanbul *Turkey*
9,299,000	Moscow *Rus. Fed.*
7,640,000	London *U.K.*
6,559,000	Essen *Germany*
5,132,000	St Petersburg *Rus. Fed.*
4,251,000	Milan *Italy*
4,072,000	Madrid *Spain*
3,700,000	Frankfurt *Germany*
3,488,000	Katowice *Poland*
3,337,000	Berlin *Germany*
3,251,000	Düsseldorf *Germany*
3,103,000	Athens *Greece*
3,067,000	Cologne *Germany*
3,012,000	Naples *Italy*
2,897,000	Kiev *Ukraine*
2,819,000	Barcelona *Spain*
2,688,000	Stuttgart *Germany*
2,688,000	Rome *Italy*
2,680,000	Hamburg *Germany*
2,306,000	Munich *Germany*
2,271,000	Birmingham *U.K.*
2,269,000	Warsaw *Poland*
2,252,000	Manchester *U.K.*
2,130,000	Bucharest *Romania*
2,072,000	Vienna *Austria*
2,017,000	Budapest *Hungary*
1,971,000	Lisbon *Portugal*
1,862,000	Minsk *Belarus*
1,701,000	Kharkiv *Ukraine*
1,617,000	Mannheim *Germany*
1,582,000	Stockholm *Sweden*

Eckert IV Projection

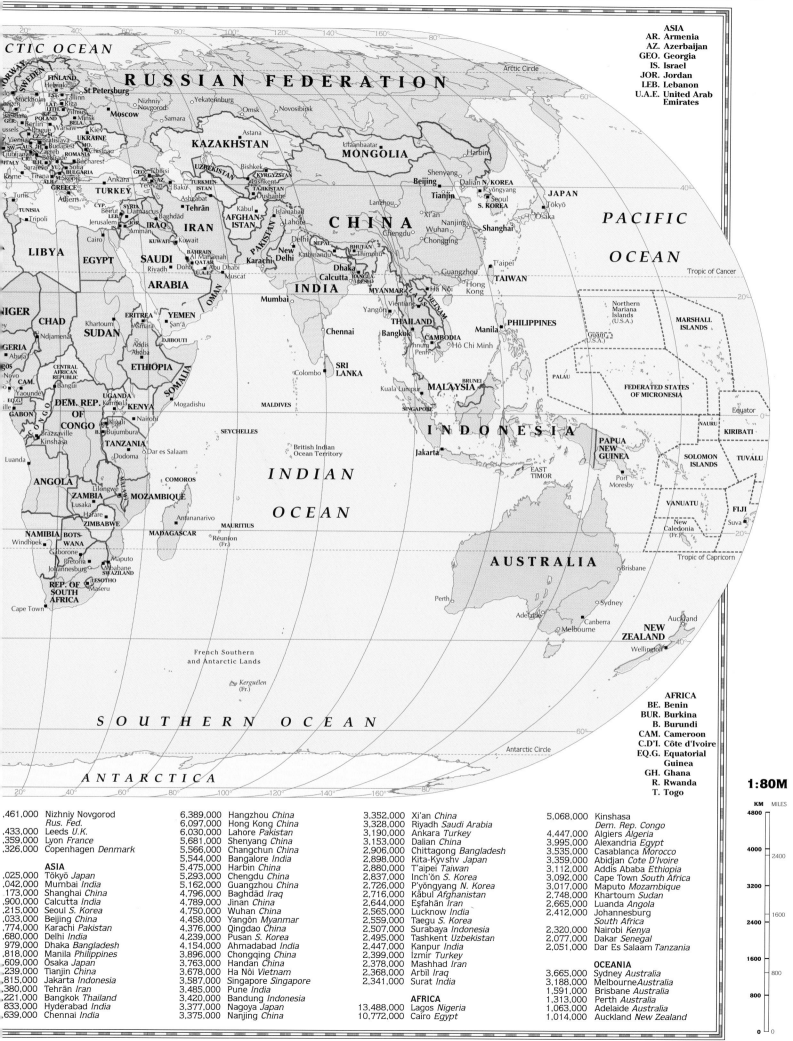

ASIA
AR. Armenia
AZ. Azerbaijan
GEO. Georgia
IS. Israel
JOR. Jordan
LEB. Lebanon
U.A.E. United Arab Emirates

AFRICA
BE. Benin
BUR. Burkina
B. Burundi
CAM. Cameroon
C.D'I. Côte d'Ivoire
EQ.G. Equatorial Guinea
GH. Ghana
R. Rwanda
T. Togo

1:80M

,461,000 Nizhniy Novgorod *Rus. Fed.*	6,389,000 Hangzhou *China*	3,352,000 Xi'an *China*	5,068,000 Kinshasa *Dem. Rep. Congo*
,433,000 Leeds *U.K.*	6,097,000 Hong Kong *China*	3,328,000 Riyadh *Saudi Arabia*	4,447,000 Algiers *Algeria*
,359,000 Lyon *France*	6,030,000 Lahore *Pakistan*	3,190,000 Ankara *Turkey*	3,995,000 Alexandria *Egypt*
,326,000 Copenhagen *Denmark*	5,681,000 Shenyang *China*	3,153,000 Dalian *China*	3,535,000 Casablanca *Morocco*
	5,566,000 Changchun *China*	2,906,000 Chittagong *Bangladesh*	3,359,000 Abidjan *Cote D'Ivoire*
ASIA	5,544,000 Bangalore *India*	2,898,000 Kita-Kyvshv *Japan*	3,112,000 Addis Ababa *Ethiopia*
,025,000 Tōkyō *Japan*	5,475,000 Harbin *China*	2,880,000 T'aipei *Taiwan*	3,092,000 Cape Town *South Africa*
,042,000 Mumbai *India*	5,293,000 Chengdu *China*	2,837,000 Inch'ŏn *S. Korea*	3,017,000 Maputo *Mozambique*
173,000 Shanghai *China*	5,162,000 Guangzhou *China*	2,726,000 P'yŏngyang *N. Korea*	2,748,000 Khartoum *Sudan*
,900,000 Calcutta *India*	4,796,000 Baghdad *Iraq*	2,716,000 Kābul *Afghanistan*	2,665,000 Luanda *Angola*
,215,000 Seoul *S. Korea*	4,789,000 Jinan *China*	2,644,000 Eşfahān *Iran*	2,412,000 Johannesburg *South Africa*
,033,000 Beijing *China*	4,750,000 Wuhan *China*	2,565,000 Lucknow *India*	2,320,000 Nairobi *Kenya*
,774,000 Karachi *Pakistan*	4,458,000 Yangôn *Myanmar*	2,559,000 Taegu *S. Korea*	2,077,000 Dakar *Senegal*
,680,000 Delhi *India*	4,376,000 Qingdao *China*	2,507,000 Surabaya *Indonesia*	2,051,000 Dar Es Salaam *Tanzania*
979,000 Dhaka *Bangladesh*	4,239,000 Pusan *S. Korea*	2,495,000 Tashkent *Uzbekistan*	
,818,000 Manila *Philippines*	4,154,000 Ahmadabad *India*	2,447,000 Kanpur *India*	**OCEANIA**
,609,000 Ōsaka *Japan*	3,896,000 Chongqing *China*	2,399,000 İzmir *Turkey*	3,665,000 Sydney *Australia*
,239,000 Tianjin *China*	3,763,000 Handan *China*	2,378,000 Mashhad *Iran*	3,188,000 Melbourne *Australia*
,815,000 Jakarta *Indonesia*	3,678,000 Ha Nôi *Vietnam*	2,368,000 Arbīl *Iraq*	1,591,000 Brisbane *Australia*
,380,000 Tehrān *Iran*	3,587,000 Singapore *Singapore*	2,341,000 Surat *India*	1,313,000 Perth *Australia*
,221,000 Bangkok *Thailand*	3,485,000 Pune *India*		1,063,000 Adelaide *Australia*
833,000 Hyderabad *India*	3,420,000 Bandung *Indonesia*	**AFRICA**	1,014,000 Auckland *New Zealand*
639,000 Chennai *India*	3,377,000 Nagoya *Japan*	13,488,000 Lagos *Nigeria*	
	3,375,000 Nanjing *China*	10,772,000 Cairo *Egypt*	

KM MILES
4800
4000
3200
2400
1600
800
0
2400
1600
800

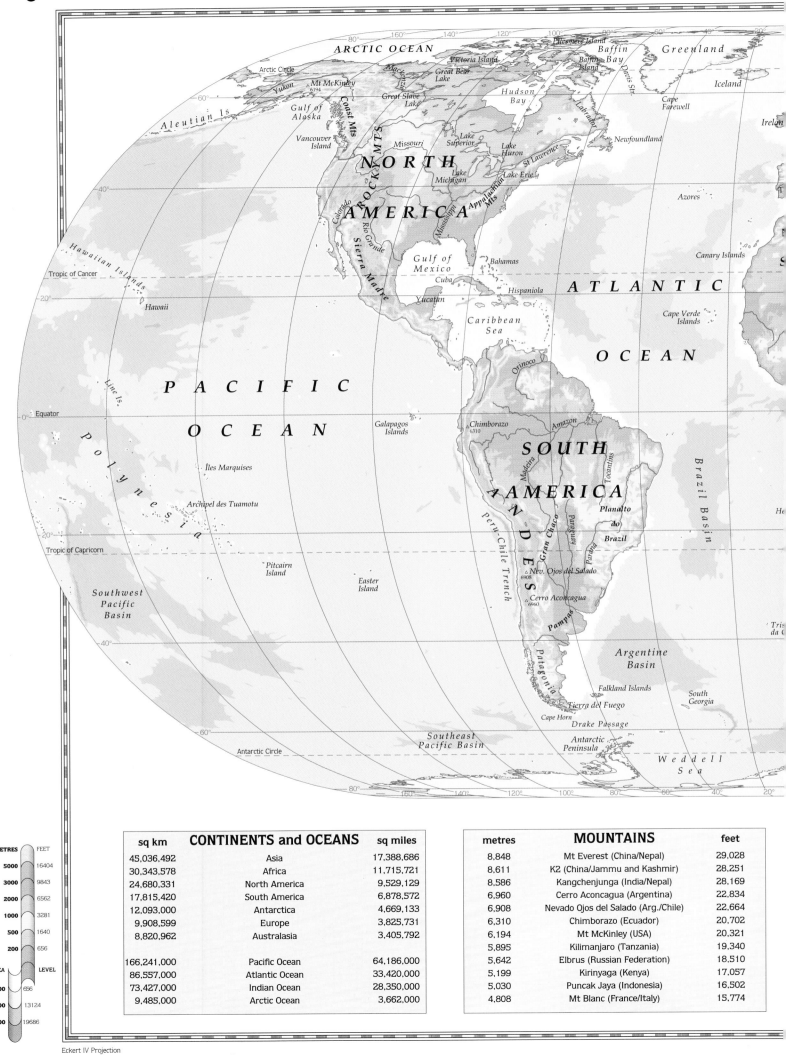

METRES	FEET
5000	16404
3000	9843
2000	6562
1000	3281
500	1640
200	656
SEA	LEVEL
200	656
4000	13124
6000	19686

sq km	CONTINENTS and OCEANS	sq miles
45,036,492	Asia	17,388,686
30,343,578	Africa	11,715,721
24,680,331	North America	9,529,129
17,815,420	South America	6,878,572
12,093,000	Antarctica	4,669,133
9,908,599	Europe	3,825,731
8,820,962	Australasia	3,405,792
166,241,000	Pacific Ocean	64,186,000
86,557,000	Atlantic Ocean	33,420,000
73,427,000	Indian Ocean	28,350,000
9,485,000	Arctic Ocean	3,662,000

metres	MOUNTAINS	feet
8,848	Mt Everest (China/Nepal)	29,028
8,611	K2 (China/Jammu and Kashmir)	28,251
8,586	Kangchenjunga (India/Nepal)	28,169
6,960	Cerro Aconcagua (Argentina)	22,834
6,908	Nevado Ojos del Salado (Arg./Chile)	22,664
6,310	Chimborazo (Ecuador)	20,702
6,194	Mt McKinley (USA)	20,321
5,895	Kilimanjaro (Tanzania)	19,340
5,642	Elbrus (Russian Federation)	18,510
5,199	Kirinyaga (Kenya)	17,057
5,030	Puncak Jaya (Indonesia)	16,502
4,808	Mt Blanc (France/Italy)	15,774

Eckert IV Projection

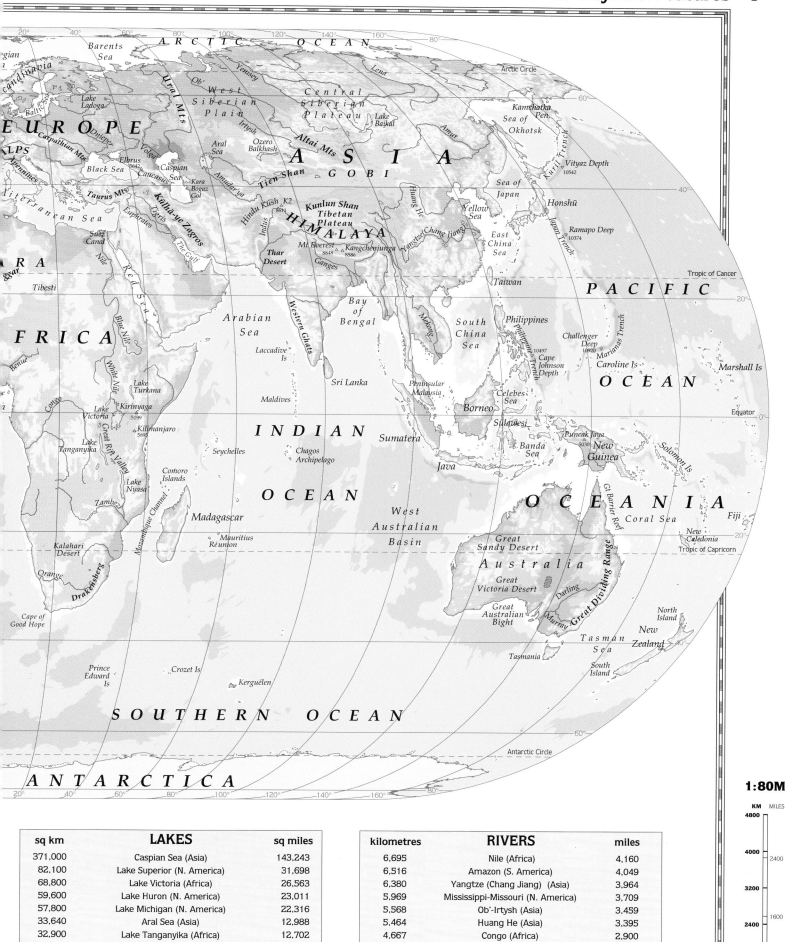

1:80M

sq km	LAKES	sq miles
371,000	Caspian Sea (Asia)	143,243
82,100	Lake Superior (N. America)	31,698
68,800	Lake Victoria (Africa)	26,563
59,600	Lake Huron (N. America)	23,011
57,800	Lake Michigan (N. America)	22,316
33,640	Aral Sea (Asia)	12,988
32,900	Lake Tanganyika (Africa)	12,702
31,328	Great Bear Lake (N. America)	12,095
30,500	Lake Baikal (Asia)	11,776
28,568	Great Slave Lake (N. America)	11,030
25,700	Lake Erie (N. America)	9,922
30,044	Lake Nyasa (Africa)	11,600

kilometres	RIVERS	miles
6,695	Nile (Africa)	4,160
6,516	Amazon (S. America)	4,049
6,380	Yangtze (Chang Jiang) (Asia)	3,964
5,969	Mississippi-Missouri (N. America)	3,709
5,568	Ob'-Irtysh (Asia)	3,459
5,464	Huang He (Asia)	3,395
4,667	Congo (Africa)	2,900
4,425	Mekong (Asia)	2,749
4,416	Amur (Asia)	2,744
4,400	Lena (Asia)	2,734
4,241	Mackenzie (N. America)	2,635
4,090	Yenisey (Asia)	2,541

ICE CAP

Areas of permanent ice cap around the north and south poles. The intense cold, dry weather and the ice cover render these regions almost lifeless. In Antarctica, tiny patches of land free of ice have a cover of mosses and lichens which provide shelter for some insects and mites.

TUNDRA and MOUNTAIN

Sub-arctic areas or mountain tops which are usually frozen. Tundra vegetation is characterized by mosses, lichens, rushes, grasses and flowering herbs; animals include the arctic fox and reindeer. Mountain vegetation is also characterized by mosses and lichens, and by low growing birch and willow.

TAIGA (NORTHERN FOREST)

Found only in the high latitudes of the northern hemisphere where winters are long and very cold, and summers are short. The characteristic vegetation is coniferous trees, including spruce and fir; animals include beavers, squirrels and deer.

MIXED and DECIDUOUS FOREST

Typical of both temperate mid-latitude regions and of eastern subtropical regions. The vegetation is a mixture of broadleaf and coniferous trees, including oak, beech and maple. Humankind has had a major impact on these regions, and in many areas little natural vegetation remains.

MEDITERRANEAN SCRUB

Long, hot, dry summers and short, warm, wet winters characterize these areas. A variety of herbaceous plants grow beneath shrub thickets with pine, oak and gorse.

GRASSLAND

Areas of long grasslands (prairies) and short grasslands (steppe) in both the northern and southern hemispheres. These grasslands have hot summers, cold winters and moderate rainfall.

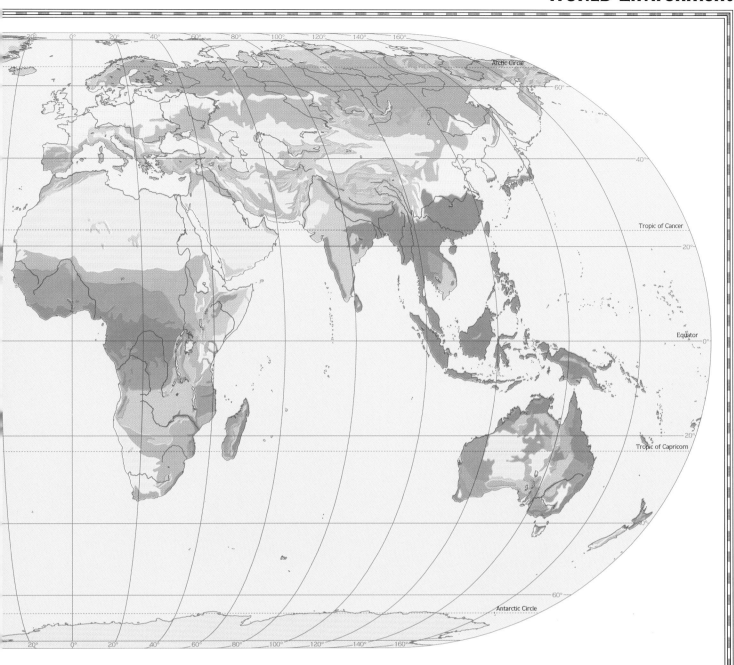

1:100M

SAVANNA
Tropical grasslands with a short rainy season; areas of grassland are interspersed with thorn bushes and deciduous trees such as acacia and eucalyptus.

RAINFOREST
Dense evergreen forests found in areas of high rainfall and continuous high temperatures. Up to three tree layers grow above a variable shrub layer: high trees, the tree canopy and the open canopy.

DRY TROPICAL FOREST and SCRUB
Low to medium size semi-deciduous trees and thorny scrub with thick bark and long roots characterize the forest areas; in the scrub areas the trees are replaced by shrubs, bushes and succulents.

DESERT
Little vegetation grows in the very hot, dry climate of desert areas. The few shrubs, grasses and cacti have adapted by storing water when it is available.

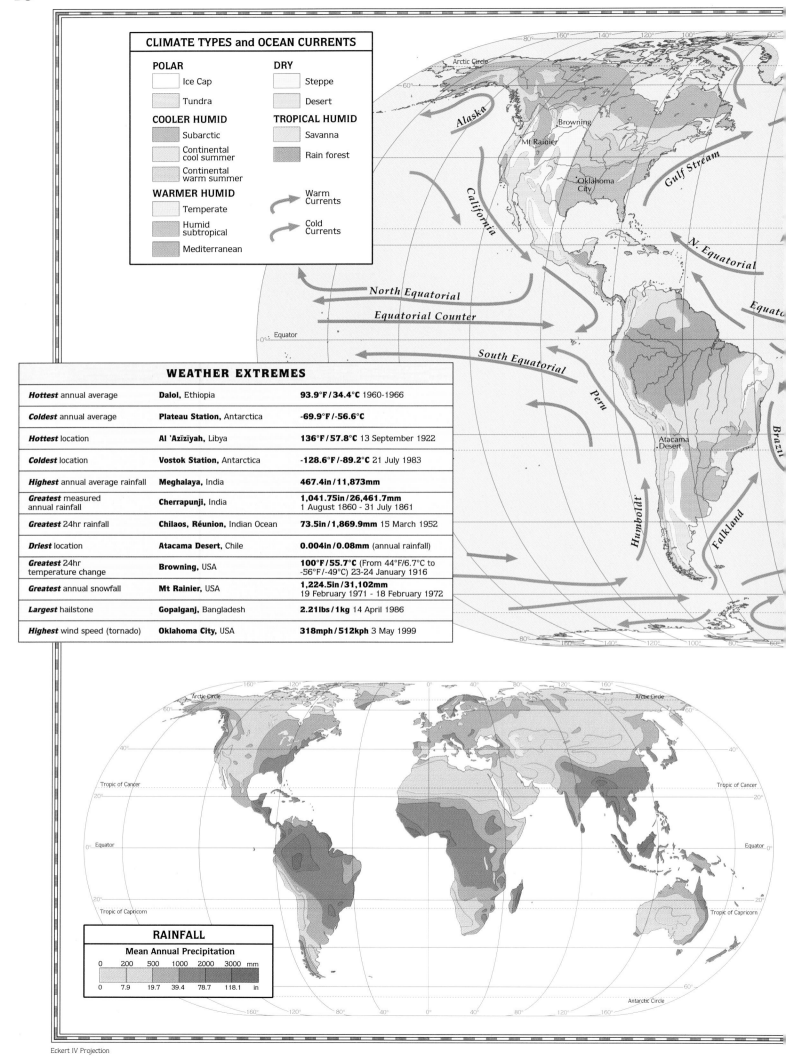

CLIMATE TYPES and OCEAN CURRENTS

POLAR
- Ice Cap
- Tundra

COOLER HUMID
- Subarctic
- Continental cool summer
- Continental warm summer

WARMER HUMID
- Temperate
- Humid subtropical
- Mediterranean

DRY
- Steppe
- Desert

TROPICAL HUMID
- Savanna
- Rain forest

→ Warm Currents
→ Cold Currents

WEATHER EXTREMES

Hottest annual average	**Dalol**, Ethiopia	**93.9°F / 34.4°C** 1960-1966
Coldest annual average	**Plateau Station**, Antarctica	**-69.9°F / -56.6°C**
Hottest location	**Al 'Azīzīyah**, Libya	**136°F / 57.8°C** 13 September 1922
Coldest location	**Vostok Station**, Antarctica	**-128.6°F / -89.2°C** 21 July 1983
Highest annual average rainfall	**Meghalaya**, India	**467.4in / 11,873mm**
Greatest measured annual rainfall	**Cherrapunji**, India	**1,041.75in / 26,461.7mm** 1 August 1860 - 31 July 1861
Greatest 24hr rainfall	**Chilaos, Réunion**, Indian Ocean	**73.5in / 1,869.9mm** 15 March 1952
Driest location	**Atacama Desert**, Chile	**0.004in / 0.08mm** (annual rainfall)
Greatest 24hr temperature change	**Browning**, USA	**100°F / 55.7°C** (From 44°F/6.7°C to -56°F/-49°C) 23-24 January 1916
Greatest annual snowfall	**Mt Rainier**, USA	**1,224.5in / 31,102mm** 19 February 1971 - 18 February 1972
Largest hailstone	**Gopalganj**, Bangladesh	**2.21lbs / 1kg** 14 April 1986
Highest wind speed (tornado)	**Oklahoma City**, USA	**318mph / 512kph** 3 May 1999

RAINFALL

Mean Annual Precipitation

0	200	500	1000	2000	3000	mm
0	7.9	19.7	39.4	78.7	118.1	in

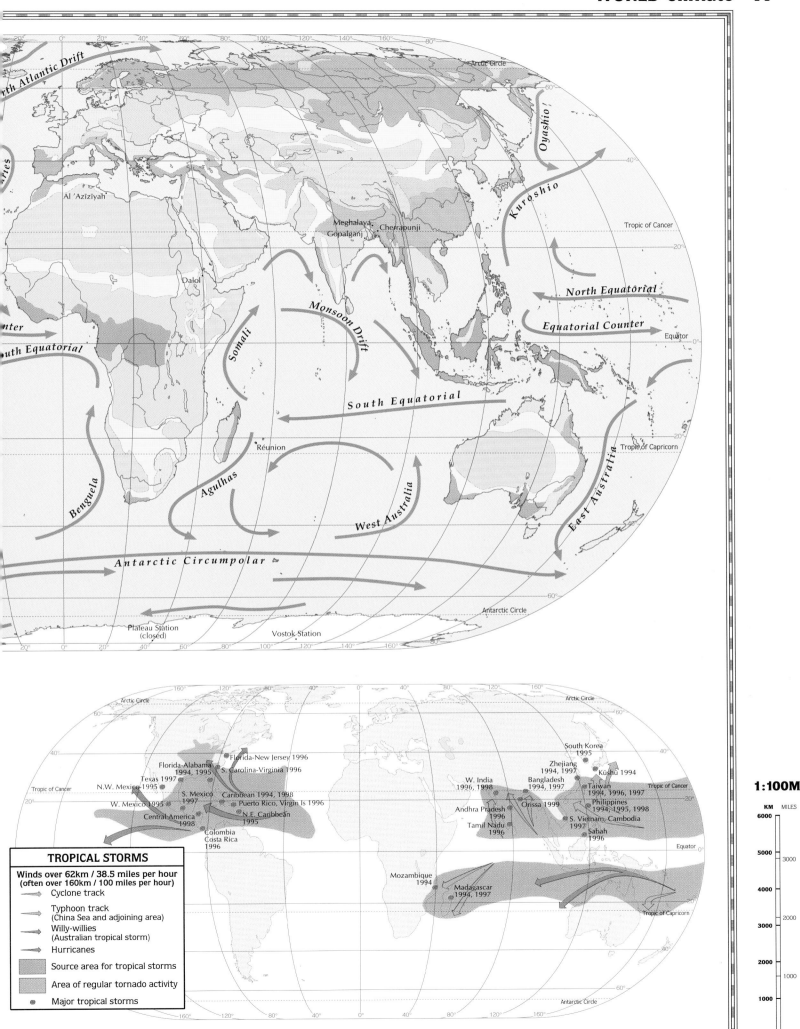

North Atlantic Drift
Arctic Circle
Al 'Azīzīyah
South Equatorial
Dalol
Meghalaya
Gopalganj Cherrapunji
Tropic of Cancer
Oyashio
Kuroshio
North Equatorial
Equatorial Counter
Equator
Monsoon Drift
Somali
South Equatorial
Réunion
Tropic of Capricorn
Agulhas
West Australia
East Australia
Benguela
Antarctic Circle
Antarctic Circumpolar
Plateau Station (closed)
Vostok Station
Arctic Circle

TROPICAL STORMS

Winds over 62km / 38.5 miles per hour
(often over 160km / 100 miles per hour)

→ Cyclone track

→ Typhoon track
(China Sea and adjoining area)

→ Willy-willies
(Australian tropical storm)

→ Hurricanes

▨ Source area for tropical storms

▨ Area of regular tornado activity

• Major tropical storms

Florida-New Jersey 1996
Florida-Alabama 1994, 1995
S. Carolina-Virginia 1996
Texas 1997
N.W. Mexico 1995
S. Mexico 1997
Caribbean 1994, 1998
Puerto Rico, Virgin Is 1996
W. Mexico 1995
Central America 1998
N.E. Caribbean 1995
Colombia Costa Rica 1996
South Korea 1995
Zhejiang 1994, 1997
Kūshū 1994
W. India 1996, 1998
Bangladesh 1994, 1997
Taiwan 1994, 1996, 1997
Andhra Pradesh 1996
Orissa 1999
Philippines 1994, 1995, 1998
S. Vietnam, Cambodia 1997
Tamil Nadu 1996
Sabah 1996
Tropic of Cancer
Equator
Mozambique 1994
Madagascar 1994, 1997
Tropic of Capricorn
Antarctic Circle

1:100M

KM	MILES
6000	
5000	3000
4000	2000
3000	
2000	1000
1000	
0	

© Bartholomew Ltd

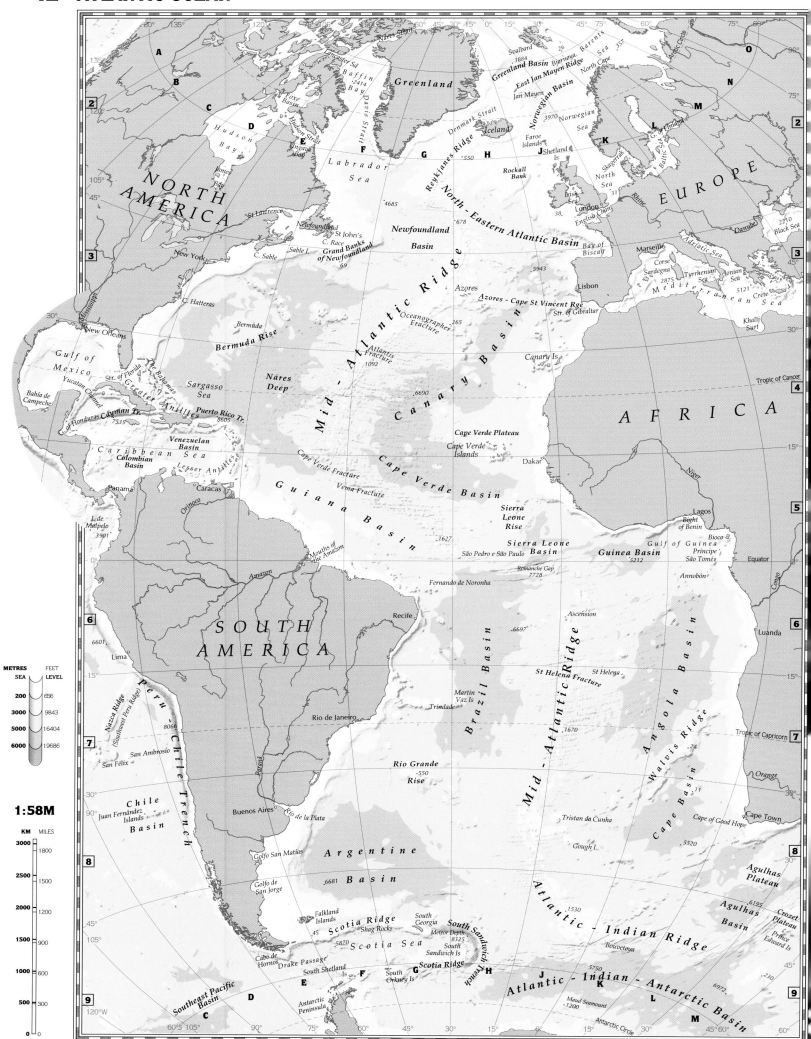

NORTH AMERICA

EUROPE

AFRICA

SOUTH AMERICA

Greenland

Iceland

Baffin Bay

Hudson Bay

James Bay

Ungava Bay

Foxe Basin

Labrador Sea

Greenland Basin

Norwegian Basin

Norwegian Sea

Barents Sea

Svalbard

Bjørnøya

Jan Mayen

East Jan Mayen Ridge

North Cape

Faroe Islands

Shetland Is

Rockall Bank

North Sea

Skagerrak

Irish Sea

London

English Chan.

Bay of Biscay

Lisbon

Marseille

Corse

Sardegna

Tyrrhenian Sea

Ionian Sea

Adriatic Sea

Mediterranean Sea

Crete

Khalīj Surt

Black Sea

Danube

Rhine

Denmark Strait

Reykjanes Ridge

North-Eastern Atlantic Basin

Newfoundland Basin

Grand Banks of Newfoundland

St John's

C. Race

C. Sable

Sable I.

Newfoundland

St Lawrence

New York

C. Hatteras

Bermuda

Bermuda Rise

New Orleans

Gulf of Mexico

Bahía de Campeche

Yucatán Channel

Str. of Florida

The Bahamas

Greater Antilles

Cayman Tr.

G. of Honduras

Panama

Colombian Basin

Venezuelan Basin

Caribbean Sea

Lesser Antilles

Puerto Rico Tr.

Sargasso Sea

Nares Deep

Mid - Atlantic Ridge

Atlantis Fracture

Oceanographer Fracture

Azores

Azores - Cape St Vincent Rge

Str. of Gibraltar

Canary Is

Canary Basin

Cape Verde Plateau

Cape Verde Islands

Dakar

Niger

Lagos

Bight of Benin

Bioco

Príncipe

São Tomé

Gulf of Guinea

Annobón

Guinea Basin

Equator

Congo

Luanda

Cape Verde Fracture

Cape Verde Basin

Vema Fracture

Guiana Basin

Sierra Leone Rise

Sierra Leone Basin

São Pedro e São Paulo

Romanche Gap

Fernando de Noronha

Recife

Caracas

Orinoco

Mouths of the Amazon

Amazon

L. de Malpelo

Lima

Nazca Ridge

(Southwest Peru Ridge)

Peru - Chile Trench

San Ambrosio

San Félix

Juan Fernández Islands

Chile Basin

Buenos Aires

Rio de la Plata

Paraná

Golfo San Matías

Golfo de San Jorge

Argentine Basin

Falkland Islands

Cabo de Hornos

Drake Passage

South Shetland Is

Southeast Pacific Basin

Antarctic Peninsula

Scotia Ridge

Scotia Sea

Shag Rocks

South Georgia

South Orkney Is

South Sandwich Is

South Sandwich Trench

Meteor Depth 8325

Rio de Janeiro

Trindade

Martin Vaz Is

Brazil Basin

Ascension

St Helena

St Helena Fracture

Rio Grande Rise

Mid - Atlantic Ridge

Walvis Ridge

Angola Basin

Cape Basin

Cape Town

Cape of Good Hope

Tristan da Cunha

Gough I.

Bouvetøya

Atlantic - Indian Ridge

Atlantic - Indian - Antarctic Basin

Maud Seamount

Agulhas Plateau

Agulhas Basin

Crozet Plateau

Prince Edward Is

Antarctic Circle

Tropic of Cancer

Tropic of Capricorn

Arctic Circle

METRES
SEA

METRES SEA	FEET LEVEL
200	656
3000	9843
5000	16404
6000	19686

1:58M

KM	MILES
3000	1800
2500	1500
2000	1200
1500	900
1000	600
500	300
0	0

Lambert Azimuthal Equal Area Projection

© Bartholomew Ltd

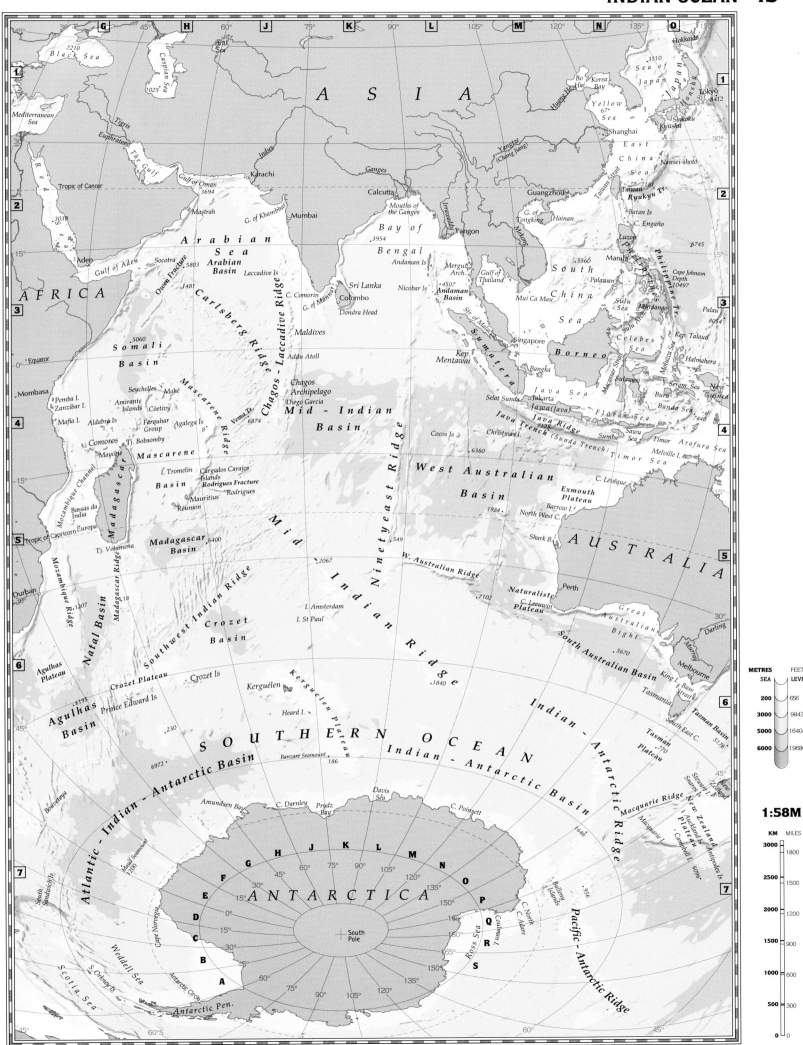

A S I A

Black Sea
2210
Caspian Sea
1025
Aral Sea
Sea of Japan
Hokkaido
Tôkyô
8412
Honshu
Shikoku
Kyushu
Korea Bay
Bo Hai
Hwang He
Yellow Sea
67'
Shanghai
East China Sea
Nansei-shotō
Guangzhou
Yangtze (Chang Jiang)
Taiwan
7191
G. of Tongking
Hainan
Taiwan Strait
Ryukyu Tr.

Mediterranean Sea
Tigris
Euphrates
Red Sea
3039
The Gulf
Tropic of Cancer
Gulf of Oman
3694
Masīrah
G. of Khambhat
Karachi
Indus
Ganges
Mouths of the Ganges
3954
Calcutta
Irrawaddy
Yangon
Mekong
Batan Is
C. Engaño
Luzon
6745
Manila
Philippine Tr.
Cape Johnson Depth
10497
Palau
8054

AFRICA

Aden
Gulf of Aden
Socotra
Owen Fracture
5803
1481
Carlsberg Ridge
Chagos - Laccadive Ridge
Laccadive Is
C. Comorin
G. of Mannar
Sri Lanka
Colombo
Dondra Head
Andaman Is
Mergui Arch.
4507
Andaman Basin
Nicobar Is
Gulf of Thailand
5560
South China Sea
Palawan
Mui Ca Mau
Sulu Sea
Mindanao
Sulu Arch.
Kep. Talaud
Celebes Sea
Halmahera

Arabian Sea
Arabian Basin

Somali Basin
5060

Mombasa
Pemba I.
Zanzibar I.
Mafia I.
Aldabra Is
Comoros
Mayotte
Seychelles
Amirante Islands
Cöetivy
Farquhar Group
Agalega Is
8'
Mahé
Mascarene Ridge
Vema Tr.
6874
Tj. Bobaomby
Mascarene
Maldives
Addu Atoll
Chagos Archipelago
Diego Garcia
Mid - Indian Basin
6360
Selat Sunda
Jakarta
Jawa (Java)
Java Ridge
Cocos Is
Christmas I.
Java Trench (Sunda Trench)
7125
Sumba
Sawu Sea
Timor
Melville I.
Timor Sea
Arafura Sea
440
New Guinea
Banda Sea
Seram Sea
Buru
Molucca Sea
Sulawesi
Makassar Strait
Borneo
Bangka
Singapore
Str. of Malacca
Sumatra
Kep. Mentawai
Equator

Madagascar Ridge
Madagascar
Mozambique Channel
Bassas da India
Mayotte
Mascarene Basin
I. Tromelin
Cargados Carajos Islands
Rodrigues Fracture
Rodrigues
Mauritius
Réunion
Tropic of Capricorn
Bassas da India Europa
West Australian Basin
1924
North West C.
Exmouth Plateau
Barrow I.
C. Lévêque
AUSTRALIA
Shark B.

Durban
Mozambique Ridge
1207
Natal Basin
Madagascar Ridge
18
Madagascar Basin
6400
Southwest Indian Ridge
Crozet Basin
2067
Mid Indian Ridge
Ninetyeast Ridge
549
W. Australian Ridge
South Australian Basin
5670
Naturaliste Plateau
C. Leeuwin
Perth
7102
Great Australian Bight
Darling
Murray
Melbourne
King I.
Bass Strait
Tasmania
Tasman Basin
Tasman Plateau
770
South East C.
5176
Macquarie Ridge
Macquarie I.
New Zealand
Stewart I.
Snares Is
Auckland Is
Antipodes Is
Campbell I.
609'

Agulhas Plateau
6195
Agulhas Basin
Crozet Plateau
Crozet Is
Prince Edward Is
Heard I.
Kerguélen
Kerguelen Plateau
1840
I. Amsterdam
I. St Paul
Indian - Antarctic Ridge
Indian - Antarctic Basin

SOUTHERN OCEAN

Atlantic - Indian - Antarctic Basin
Maud Seamount
1200
230
6972
Banzare Seamount
186
Bouvetøya
Cape Norvegia
South Sandwich Is
South Orkney Is
Scotia Sea
Weddell Sea
Antarctic Pen.
Antarctic Circle
Amundsen Bay
C. Darnley
Prydz Bay
Davis Sea
C. Poinsett
1646
Balleny Islands
956
Ross Sea
C. North
C. Adare
Coulman I.
Pacific - Antarctic Ridge

ANTARCTICA

South Pole

METRES SEA | FEET LEVEL
200 | 656
3000 | 9843
5000 | 16404
6000 | 19686

1:58M

KM | MILES
3000 | 1800
2500 | 1500
2000 | 1200
1500 | 900
1000 | 600
500 | 300
0 | 0

Lambert Azimuthal Equal Area Projection

© Bartholomew Ltd

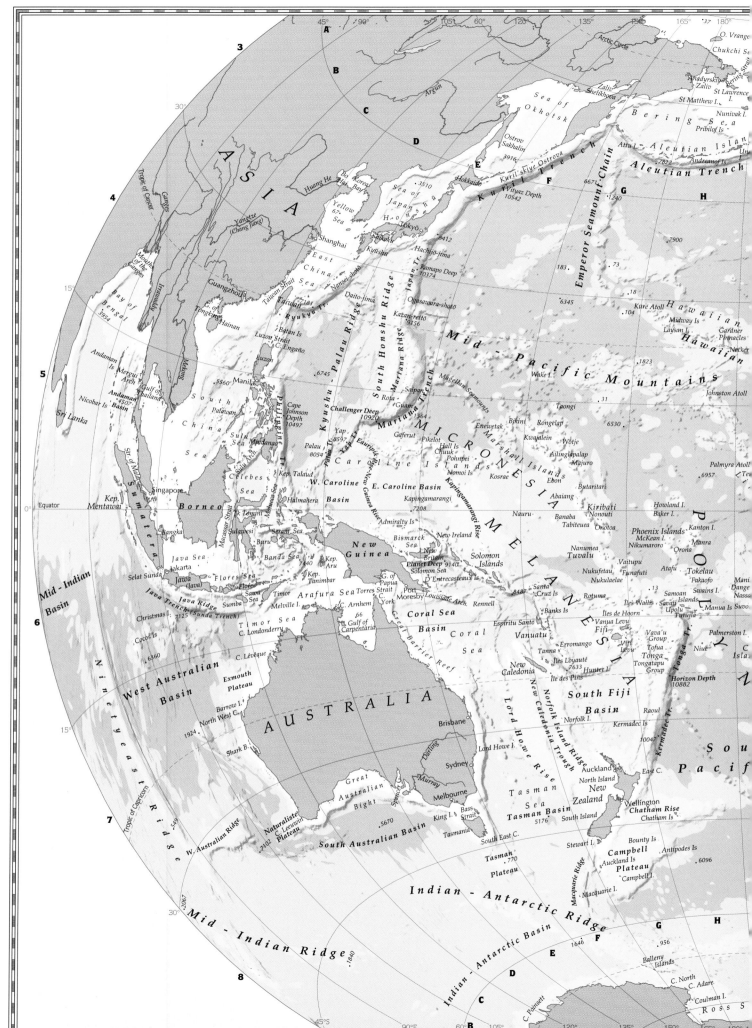

METRES
SEA

FEET
LEVEL

METRES	FEET
200	656
3000	9843
5000	16404
6000	19686

Lambert Azimuthal Equal Area Projection

1:58M

KM MILES

3000 1800

2500 1500

2000 1200

1500 900

1000 600

500 300

0 0

Barrow
Mackenzie
Gulf of Alaska
Kodiak I.
Alexander Archipelago
Queen Charlotte Islands
Vancouver Island
Vancouver
Columbia
Missouri
NORTH AMERICA
Hudson Bay
James Bay
Newfoundland
C. Sable I.
New York
C. Hatteras
Bermuda
Bermuda Rise
Mid - Atlantic Ridge
Nares Deep
Rio Grande
New Orleans
Gulf of Mexico
The Bahamas
Greater Antilles
Puerto Rico Tr.
8605
St. of Florida
Yucatan Channel
Bahía de Campeche
Cayman Tr. 7535
G. de Honduras
Venezuelan Basin
Caribbean Sea
Colombian Basin
Lesser Antilles
Caracas
Panamá
Orinoco
Guiana Basin
Mouths of the Amazon
San Francisco
Los Angeles
Colorado
Golfo de California
Guadalupe
2733 C. Mendocino
Erben Tablemount 412
Murray Seascarp
6217
Molokai Fracture Zone
Maui
Hawaii
7022
Clarion Fracture Zone
Is Revillagigedo
I. Clarión
I. Socorro
G. de Tehuantepec
Tehuantepec Ridge
Middle America Trench
6662
Clipperton Fracture Zone
Clipperton I.
East Pacific Rise
I. de Coco
Cocos Ridge
I. de Malpelo
3901
.20
.10
Galapagos Is (Islas Galápagos)
Carnegie Ridge
G. de Guayaquil
Amazon
SOUTH AMERICA
Kiritimati
Malden I.
Starbuck I.
Tongareva
Caroline I.
Nuku Hiva
Îles Marquises
Hiva Oa
Flint I.
Îles du Roi Georges
Îles de Désappointement
Archipel des Tuamotu
4385
Bora Bora Ura
Rhiatea
Tahiti
Anaa
Raroia
Hao
Arch. de la Société
Hervey Is
Hétéhérétué
Tonga
Îles Maria
Mururoa
Groupe Actéon
Gaia
Îles Gambier
Tubuai
Raivavae
Henderson I.
Îles Australes
Rapa
Pitcairn I.
Ducie I.
6601
Lima
1929
East Pacific Ridge
Peru Basin
5470
Nazca Ridge (Southeast Peru Ridge)
Peru - Chile Trench
.1344
Easter Island Fracture Zone
Easter I.
I. Sala y Gómez
571
San Félix
San Ambrosio
8066
15°
SIA
west Basin
5420
Challenger Fracture Zone
Chile Basin
.2743
Juan Fernández, Islands
Robinson Crusoe
Santiago
Río de Janeiro
Paraná
K L M
Pacific - Antarctic Ridge
Eltanin Fracture Zone
Buenos Aires
Río de la Plata
Golfo San Matías
K L M N O P
5230
Southeast Pacific Basin
Golfo de San Jorge
Argentine Basin
6681
Amundsen Sea
Peter I Øy
Antarctic Circle
Cape Horn
Drake Passage
Scotia Sea
5870
Scotia Ridge
Falkland Islands

R
3
4
Q
P
O
N
M
K L
5
6
7
8

50° 135° 120° 105° 90° 75° 60° 45° 45°
69°
30°
15°
0°
15°
30°
45° 60°

U.S.A.
ALASKA

St Lawrence I.
Bering Str.
Kotzebue Sd
Nome
Point Hope
Barrow

Aleutian Islands
Bristol Bay
Alaska Pen.
Kodiak I.
Gulf of Alaska
Seward
Valdez
Anchorage
Mt McKinley
Fairbanks
Tanacross
Dawson

Queen Charlotte Islands
Prince Rupert
Juneau
Alexander Archipelago

C A N A D A

BRITISH COLUMBIA
Vancouver Island
Victoria
Vancouver
Kamloops
Fraser

YUKON TERRITORY
Whitehorse

NORTHWEST TERRITORIES
Inuvik
Mackenzie
Great Bear Lake
Simpson
Port Liard
Great Slave L.
Yellowknife
Uranium City

ALBERTA
Grande Prairie
Peace
Edmonton
Calgary
Medicine Hat
La Ronge
Lake Athabasca

SASKATCHEWAN
Saskatoon
Regina

MANITOBA
The Pas
Lake Winnipeg
Winnipeg
Churchill
Nelson

NUNAVUT
Banks Island
Victoria Island
Cambridge Bay
Prince of Wales Island
King William I.
Queen Maud Gulf
Gulf of Boothia
Bathurst Inlet
Dubawnt L.
Chesterfield Inlet
Ivujivik
Southampton Island

Queen Elizabeth Islands
Parry Islands
Melville Island
Devon Island
Somerset Island
Bylot I.
Pond Inlet
Brodeur Pen.
Hall Beach
Prince Charles I.
Foxe Basin

Ellesmere Island
Kane Basin
Hayes Peninsula
Dundas
Clyde River

Greenland (Denmark)
Scoresbysund
Scoresby Sound
King Frederik IX Land
Christian X Land
King Frederik VI Coast
Nuuk (Godthåb)
Frederikshåb
C. Farewell

Baffin Bay
Baffin Island
Davis Strait
Cumberland Sd

Hudson Strait
Ungava Bay
Kuujjuaq
Inukjuak

ONTARIO
L. Nipigon
Thunder Bay
Sudbury
Ottawa

QUÉBEC
Rouyn
Chicoutimi
Québec
Montréal
Septîles
Caniapiscau Res.
Schefferville
James Bay
Belcher Is

NEWFOUNDLAND
LABRADOR
Goose Bay
Gander
Corner Brook
Anticosti I.
St Lawrence
Cabot Str.
Str. of Belle Isle
Newfoundland
St John's
C. Ray

Hudson Bay

UNITED STATES OF AMERICA

WASHINGTON
Seattle
Olympia
Columbia

OREGON
Portland
Salem
Eureka

IDAHO
Boise
Snake

MONTANA
Helena
Billings
Yellowstone

NORTH DAKOTA
Bismarck

SOUTH DAKOTA
Pierre

WYOMING
Casper
Cheyenne

NEVADA
Reno
Carson City
Las Vegas
Great Salt L.
Salt Lake City

CALIFORNIA
Sacramento
San Francisco
Fresno
Los Angeles
San Diego

UTAH
Salt Lake City

COLORADO
Denver
Colorado Springs

NEBRASKA
Omaha
Lincoln

ARIZONA
Phoenix
Tucson

NEW MEXICO
Santa Fe
Albuquerque

MINNESOTA
Duluth
Minneapolis
St Paul

WISCONSIN
Madison
Milwaukee

MICHIGAN
Lansing
Detroit
Lake Michigan
L. Huron

IOWA
Des Moines

KANSAS
Kansas City
Topeka

MISSOURI
St Louis
Jefferson City

ILLINOIS
Chicago
Springfield

INDIANA
Indianapolis

OHIO
Columbus
Cleveland
Cincinnati

OKLAHOMA
Oklahoma City

ARKANSAS
Little Rock
Red
Arkansas

TEXAS
Ft Worth
Dallas
Austin
Houston
San Antonio
El Paso
Rio Grande

LOUISIANA
Baton Rouge
New Orleans

MISSISSIPPI
Jackson

ALABAMA
Birmingham
Montgomery

GEORGIA
Atlanta
Columbia

TENNESSEE
Nashville

KENTUCKY
Frankfort

NEW YORK
Albany
New York
Buffalo

PENNSYLVANIA
Pittsburgh
Harrisburg
Philadelphia

MAINE
Augusta
Portland

VERMONT
Montpelier

NEW HAMPSHIRE
Concord

MASSACHUSETTS
Boston

RHODE ISLAND
Providence

CONNECTICUT
Hartford

NEW JERSEY
Trenton

DELAWARE
Dover

MARYLAND
Annapolis

WEST VIRGINIA
Charleston

VIRGINIA
Richmond

NORTH CAROLINA
Charlotte
Raleigh
C. Hatteras

SOUTH CAROLINA
Columbia
Charleston

FLORIDA
Tallahassee
Jacksonville
Tampa
Miami

Washington D.C.

L. Erie
L. Ontario
Lake Superior

ATLANTIC OCEAN
Bermuda (U.K.)

MEXICO
Mexicali
Hermosillo
Guadalupe (Mex.)
Revillagigedo Is. (Mex.)
Ciudad Juárez
Chihuahua
Culiacán
Nuevo Laredo
Saltillo
Monterrey
Ciudad Victoria
Guadalajara
León
Querétaro
México
Puebla
Veracruz
Campeche
Acapulco
Bahía de Campeche
G. of Tehuantepec
Gulf of California

GULF OF MEXICO

PACIFIC OCEAN

BELIZE
Belmopan

GUATEMALA
Guatemala
Puerto Barrios

HONDURAS
Tegucigalpa

EL SALVADOR
San Salvador

NICARAGUA
Managua
L. Nicaragua

COSTA RICA
San José
Puntarenas
Limón

PANAMA
Panama City
Colón
Golfo del Darién

Yucatán Channel

THE BAHAMAS
Nassau

CUBA
Havana
Camagüey
Santiago de Cuba
Str. of Florida

Cayman Is (U.K.)
Turks and Caicos Is (U.K.)

JAMAICA
Kingston

HAITI
Port-au-Prince

DOMINICAN REP.
Santo Domingo

Puerto Rico (U.S.A.)
San Juan

Virgin Is (U.K.)
Virgin Is (U.S.A.)
Anguilla (U.K.)

ANTIGUA AND BARBUDA
ST KITTS AND NEVIS
Montserrat (U.K.)
Guadeloupe (Fr.)
DOMINICA
Martinique (Fr.)
ST LUCIA
ST VINCENT AND THE GRENADINES
BARBADOS
GRENADA
TRINIDAD AND TOBAGO

Aruba (Neth.)
Neth. Antilles (Neth.)

CARIBBEAN SEA

Greater Antilles
Lesser Antilles

Caracas
Port of Spain

VENEZUELA
Orinoco

COLOMBIA
Bogotá

Georgetown
GUYANA

ST LUCIA
MONARCHY

Area: 616 sq km (238 sq mls)
Population: 150,000
Capital: Castries
Language: English, French Creole
Religion: R.Catholic, Protestant
Currency: E.Carib.Dollar

CONTINENTAL FACTS

TOTAL POPULATION
472,518,000

LARGEST COUNTRY POPULATION
U.S.A. 274,028,000

LARGEST COUNTRY AREA
CANADA
9,970,610 sq km 3,849,674 sq miles

LARGEST CITY POPULATION
MÉXICO, Mexico 18,131,000

 CANADA
FEDERATION

Area: 9,970,610 sq km
(3,849,674 sq mls)
Population: 30,563,000
Capital: Ottawa
Language: English, French,
Amerindian
Languages,
Inuktitut
Religion: R.Catholic,
Protestant,
Greek Orthodox
Currency: Dollar

 **UNITED STATES
OF AMERICA** (USA)
REPUBLIC

Area: 9,809,378 sq km
(3,787,422 sq mls)
Population: 274,028,000
Capital: Washington
Language: English, Spanish,
Amerindian
Languages
Religion: Protestant,
R.Catholic,
Muslim, Jewish
Currency: Dollar

 MEXICO
REPUBLIC

Area: 1,972,545 sq km
(761,604 sq mls)
Population: 95,831,000
Capital: México (Mexico City)
Language: Spanish, Amerindian
Languages
Religion: R.Catholic,
Protestant
Currency: Peso

THE BAHAMAS
MONARCHY

Area: 13,939 sq km
(5,382 sq mls)
Population: 296,000
Capital: Nassau
Language: English, Creole,
French Creole
Religion: Protestant,
R.Catholic
Currency: Dollar

CUBA
REPUBLIC

Area: 110,860 sq km
(42,803 sq mls)
Population: 11,116,000
Capital: Havana (La Habana)
Language: Spanish
Religion: R.Catholic,
Protestant
Currency: Peso

JAMAICA
MONARCHY

Area: 10,991 sq km
(4,244 sq mls)
Population: 2,538,000
Capital: Kingston
Language: English, Creole
Religion: Protestant,
R.Catholic,
Rastafarian
Currency: Dollar

York. Covering an area of 777 sq km, the city is made up of five boroughs, of
only one, the Bronx, is on the mainland.

 GUATEMALA
REPUBLIC

Area: 108,890 sq km
(42,043 sq mls)
Population: 10,801,000
Capital: Guatemala
(Guatemala City)
Language: Spanish
Mayan Languages
Religion: R.Catholic,
Protestant
Currency: Quetzal

BELIZE
MONARCHY

Area: 22,965 sq km
(8,867 sq mls)
Population: 230,000
Capital: Belmopan
Language: English, Creole,
Spanish, Mayan
Religion: R.Catholic,
Protestant, Hindu
Currency: Dollar

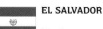 **EL SALVADOR**
REPUBLIC

Area: 21,041 sq km
(8,124 sq mls)
Population: 6,032,000
Capital: San Salvador
Language: Spanish
Religion: R.Catholic,
Protestant
Currency: Colón

**DOMINICAN
REPUBLIC**
REPUBLIC

Area: 48,442 sq km
(18,704 sq mls)
Population: 8,232,000
Capital: Santo Domingo
Language: Spanish,
French Creole
Religion: R.Catholic,
Protestant
Currency: Peso

HAITI
REPUBLIC

Area: 27,750 sq km
(10,714 sq mls)
Population: 7,952,000
Capital: Port-au-Prince
Language: French,
French Creole
Religion: R.Catholic,
Protestant, Voodoo
Currency: Gourde

 HONDURAS
REPUBLIC

Area: 112,088 sq km
(43,277 sq mls)
Population: 6,147,000
Capital: Tegucigalpa
Language: Spanish,
Amerindian
Languages
Religion: R.Catholic,
Protestant
Currency: Lempira

NICARAGUA
REPUBLIC

Area: 130,000 sq km
(50,193 sq mls)
Population: 4,807,000
Capital: Managua
Language: Spanish, Amerindian
Languages
Religion: R.Catholic,
Protestant
Currency: Córdoba

 COSTA RICA
REPUBLIC

Area: 51,100 sq km
(19,730 sq mls)
Population: 3,841,000
Capital: San José
Language: Spanish
Religion: R.Catholic,
Protestant
Currency: Colón

PANAMA
REPUBLIC

Area: 77,082 sq km
(29,762 sq mls)
Population: 2,767,000
Capital: Panamá (Panama
City)
Language: Spanish, English
Creole, Amerindian
Languages
Religion: R.Catholic,
Protestant, Sunni
Muslim, Baha'i
Currency: Balboa

**ANTIGUA AND
BARBUDA**
MONARCHY

Area: 442 sq km
(171 sq mls)
Population: 67,000
Capital: St John's
Language: English, Creole
Religion: Protestant,
R.Catholic
Currency: E.Carib.Dollar

POPULATION

Sayil, Yucatan, Mexico. Mayan
palace of about 85 rooms built
between 6thC and 9thC AD.

 **DOMINICA**
REPUBLIC

Area: 750 sq km
(290 sq mls)
Population: 71,000
Capital: Roseau
Language: English, French Creole
Religion: R.Catholic, Protestant
Currency: E.Carib.dollar

BARBADOS
MONARCHY

Area: 430 sq km
(166 sq mls)
Population: 268,000
Capital: Bridgetown
Language: English, Creole
(Bajan)
Religion: Protestant,
R.Catholic
Currency: Dollar

 **ST KITTS AND
NEVIS**
MONARCHY

Area: 261 sq km
(101 sq mls)
Population: 39,000
Capital: Basseterre
Language: English, Creole
Religion: Protestant,
R.Catholic
Currency: E.Carib.Dollar

**ST VINCENT AND
THE GRENADINES**
MONARCHY

Area: 389 sq km
(150 sq mls)
Population: 112,000
Capital: Kingstown
Language: English, Creole
Religion: Protestant,
R.Catholic
Currency: E.Carib.Dollar

**TRINIDAD AND
TOBAGO**
REPUBLIC

Area: 5,130 sq km
(1,981 sq mls)
Population: 1,283,000
Capital: Port of Spain
Language: English, Creole,
Hindi
Religion: R.Catholic, Hindu,
Protestant, Muslim
Currency: Dollar

GRENADA
MONARCHY

Area: 378 sq km
(146 sq mls)
Population: 93,000
Capital: St George's
Language: English, Creole
Religion: R.Catholic,
Protestant
Currency: E.Carib.Dollar

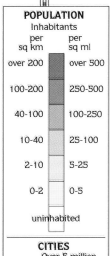

POPULATION
Inhabitants

per sq km	per sq ml
over 200	over 500
100-200	250-500
40-100	100-250
10-40	25-100
2-10	5-25
0-2	0-5
uninhabited	

CITIES
■ Over 5 million
population
● 2.5 - 5 million
population

© Bartholomew Ltd

St Lawrence I.

Nunivak I.
Norton
Sound
Seward
Pen.
Alaska Pen.
Pt Barrow
Brooks Range
Mt McKinley
Alaska Range
Nushagak
Kuskokwim
Yukon
Kodiak I.
Gulf of Alaska
Alexander Archipelago
Dixon Entrance
Queen Charlotte Islands
Hecate Str.
Vancouver Island
C. Blanco

Beaufort Sea

Banks I.
Prince Patrick Island
Melville I.
Parry Islands
Devon I.

Ellef Ringnes I.
Axel Heiberg Island
Borden I.

Queen Elizabeth Islands

Ellesmere Island

Greenland

King Frederik VIII Land
Lauge Koch Land
Shannon
King Oscar Fj.
Scoresby Sound
King Christian X Land
King Christian IX Land
King Frederik VI Coast
C. Farewel

Victoria Island

Prince of Wales I.
Somerset I.
Boothia Pen.
G. of Boothia
King William I.

Bylot I.
Baffin Bay
Qeqertarsuaq (Disko)
Davis Strait
Home B.

Mackenzie Mts
Selwyn Mts
Great Bear L.
Mackenzie
Great Slave L.
Liard
Caribou Mts
Peace
Dubawnt L.

Melville Peninsula
Prince Charles I.
Foxe Basin
Nettilling L.
Cumberland Pen.
Cumberland Sd
Frobisher B.

Cassiar Mts
Coast Mountains
Fraser
Cascade Ra.
Columbia

Lake Athabasca
Reindeer L.
Wollaston L.
Southern Indian L.
Churchill

Southampton I.
Coats I.
Mansel I.

Hudson Bay

Hudson Strait
C. Chidley

Ungava Bay

Labrador Sea

R O C K Y   M O U N T A I N S

L. Winnipegosis
Lake Winnipeg
Nelson
Severn

Belcher Is
James Bay

Labrador

L. Bienville
Caniapiscau Res.
La Grande Res.
Smallwood Res.

F. D. Roosevelt L.
Bitterroot Ra.
Fort Peck Res.
L. Sakakawea
Lake of the Woods

L. Nipigon
Lake Superior

St Lawrence
Anticosti I.
Gulf of St Lawrence
Str. of Belle Isle
Newfoundland
Cabot Str.
St Pierre and Miquelon
Cape Breton I.
C. Ray

Coast Range
Sierra Nevada
Great Basin
Great Salt L.
Snake
Yellowstone
L. Oahe
Missouri

L. Michigan
L. Huron
L. Ontario
Erie

B. of Fundy
Massachusetts Bay
C. Sable

Colorado Plateau
Grand Canyon
Colorado
Arkansas
Ozark Plateau
Red

Ohio
Allegheny Mts
Appalachian Mts

Chesapeake B.
C. Cod
Long I.
C. Hatteras

Llano Estacado
Rio Grande
Edwards Plateau
Mississippi

C. Fear

Bermuda

A T L A N T I C   O C E A N

Baja California
Gulf of California
Sierra Madre Occidental
Sierra Madre Oriental

C. Canaveral
Gd Bahama
Gt Abaco

G U L F   O F
M E X I C O

Str. of Florida
Andros
Acklins I.
Turks and Caicos Is

I. Socorro
Bahía de Campeche
Yucatán
Yucatán Channel
Cayman Is
Gt Inagua

C u b a
G r e a t e r   A n t i l l e s
Jamaica

Hispaniola
Puerto Rico
Virgin Is
Anguilla
Guadeloupe

Dominica
Martinique
St Lucia

Sa Madre del Sur
G. of Honduras
Bahía de Campeche

C A R I B B E A N
S E A

Aruba
Neth. Antilles
L e s s e r   A n t i l l e s
Trinidad

P A C I F I C
O C E A N
L. Nicaragua
Pen. de Nicoya

Golfo del Darién
Orinoco

CONTINENTAL FACTS
TOTAL AREA
24,680,331 sq km 9,529,129 sq miles
HIGHEST PEAK, MT McKINLEY
6,194 m 20,321 ft
LARGEST LAKE, SUPERIOR
82,100 sq km 31,698 sq miles
LONGEST RIVER, MISSISSIPPI-MISSOURI
5,969 km 3,709 miles

Guatemala. Deforestation as a result of pressure for land to sustain families and their crops.

Mt McKinley, Alaska. The highest peak in North America can generate its own weather system due to its comparative height and isolation.

CLIMATE

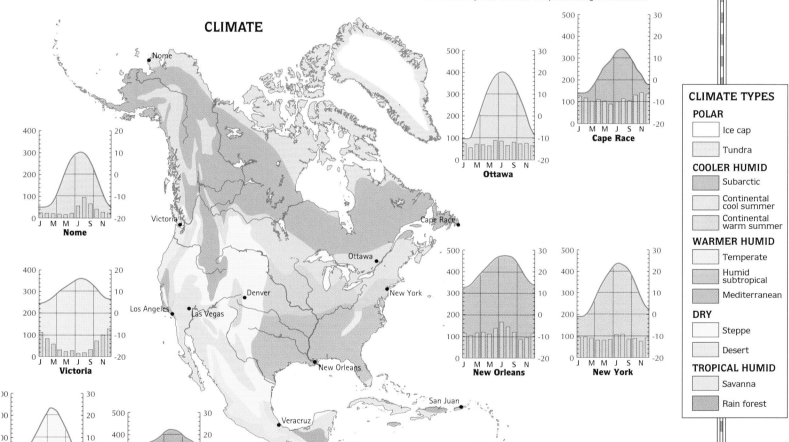

Nome

Nome

Victoria

Denver

Los Angeles

Las Vegas

Rain mm

average monthly temperature

colour refers to climate type shown on map

average monthly rainfall

Temp °C

Veracruz

Ottawa

Cape Race

New Orleans

New York

San Juan

CLIMATE TYPES

POLAR
- Ice cap
- Tundra

COOLER HUMID
- Subarctic
- Continental cool summer
- Continental warm summer

WARMER HUMID
- Temperate
- Humid subtropical
- Mediterranean

DRY
- Steppe
- Desert

TROPICAL HUMID
- Savanna
- Rain forest

St Lucia. Stunning scenery and a tropical climate have helped make the Caribbean a popular holiday destination.

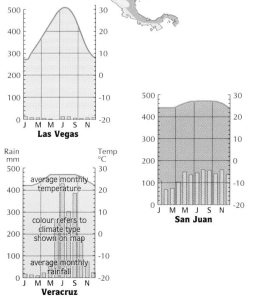

Bryce Canyon, Utah. Weathered sandstone formations in canyons up to 300m deep.

Transverse Mercator Projection

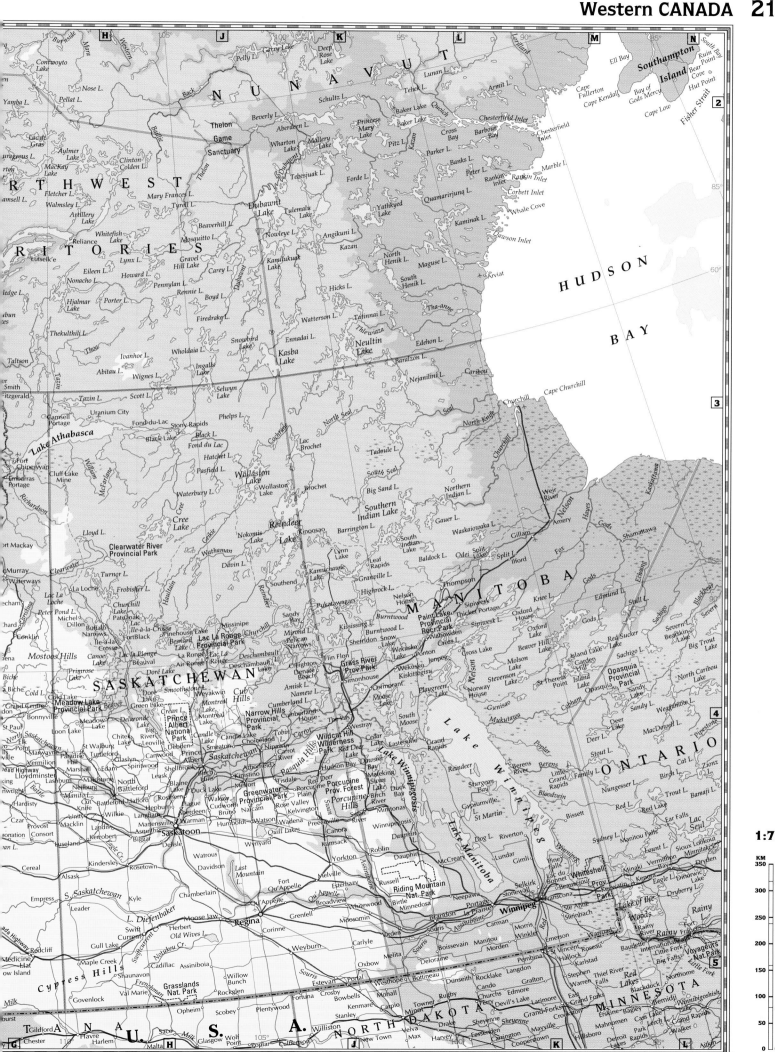

1:7M

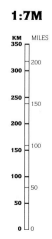

KM / MILES
350
300 / 200
250 / 150
200
150 / 100
100
50
0 / 0

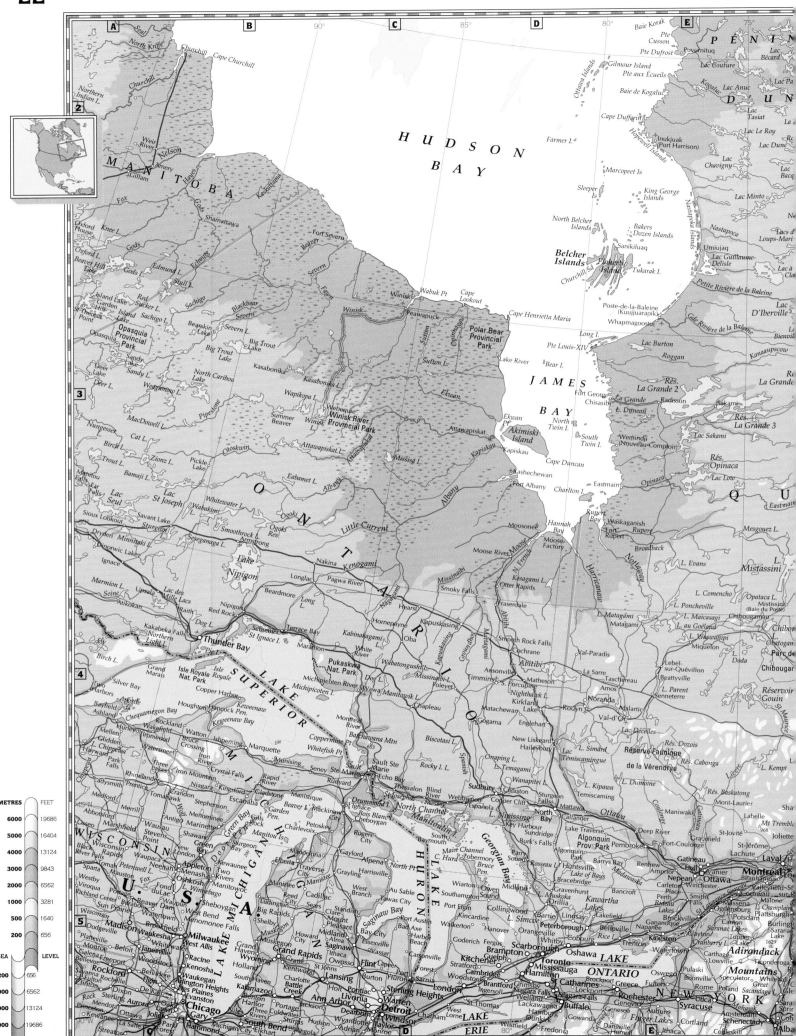

Transverse Mercator Projection

1:7M

Lambert Conformal Conic Projection

1:7M

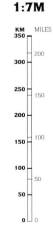

KM	MILES
350	
	200
300	
250	150
200	
	100
150	
100	
	50
50	
0	0

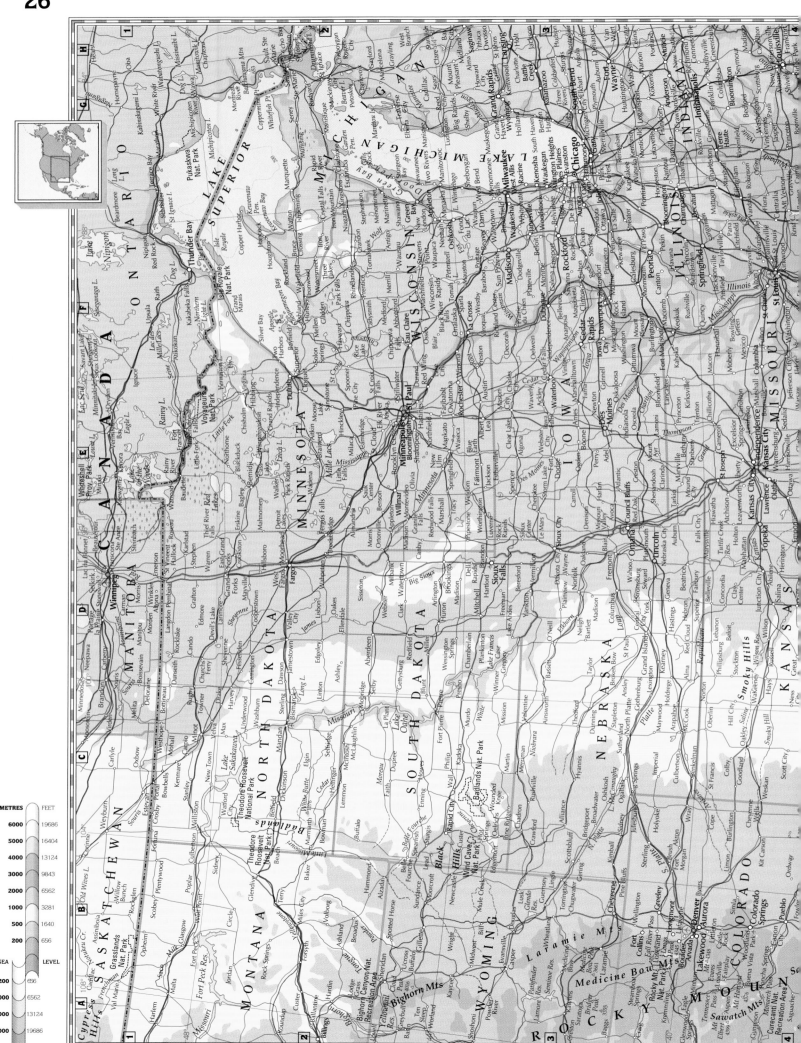

Lambert Conformal Conic Projection

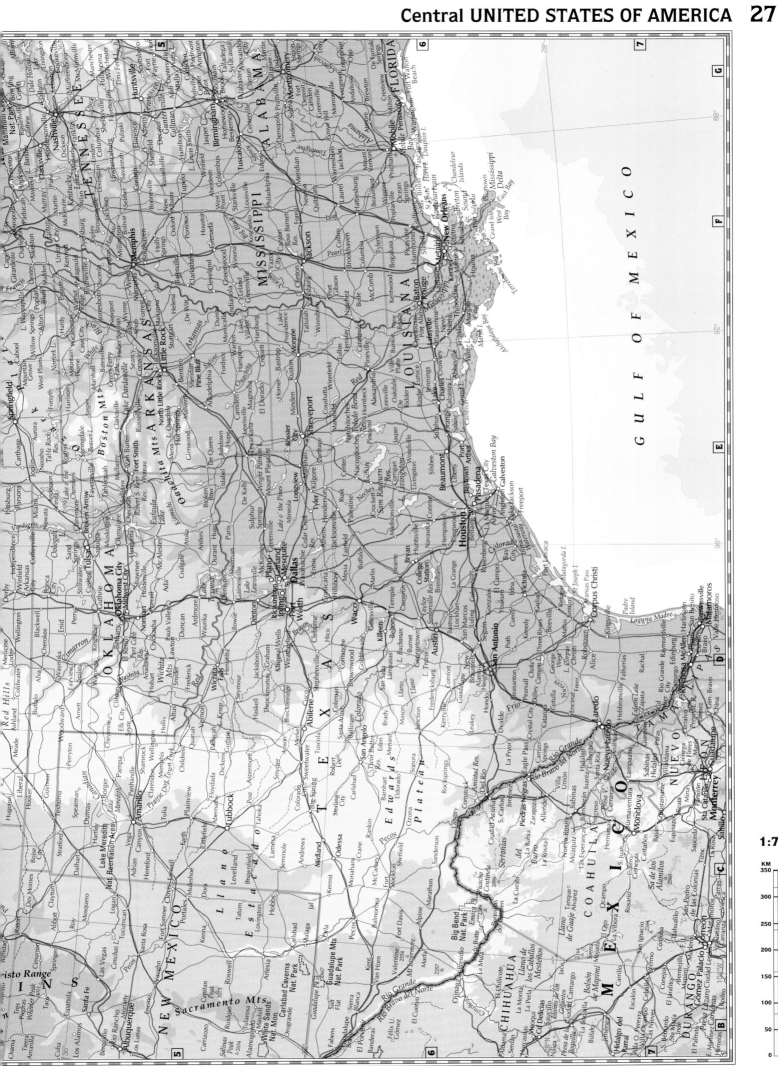

1:7M

KM   MILES
350
300   200
250
      150
200

150   100

100
      50
50

0   0

1:7M

KM   MILES
350   200
300
250   150
200
150   100
100
50
0

© Bartholomew Ltd

MINNESOTA

LAKE SUPERIOR

Isle Royale
National Park

Michipicoten
Bay

MICHIGAN

WISCONSIN

LAKE MICHIGAN

IOWA

ILLINOIS

U.S.

MISSOURI

INDIANA

METRES	FEET
6000	19686
5000	16404
4000	13124
3000	9843
2000	6562
1000	3281
500	1640
200	656
SEA	LEVEL
200	656
2000	6562
4000	13124
6000	19686

Lambert Conformal Conic Projection

1:3.5M

© Bartholomew Ltd

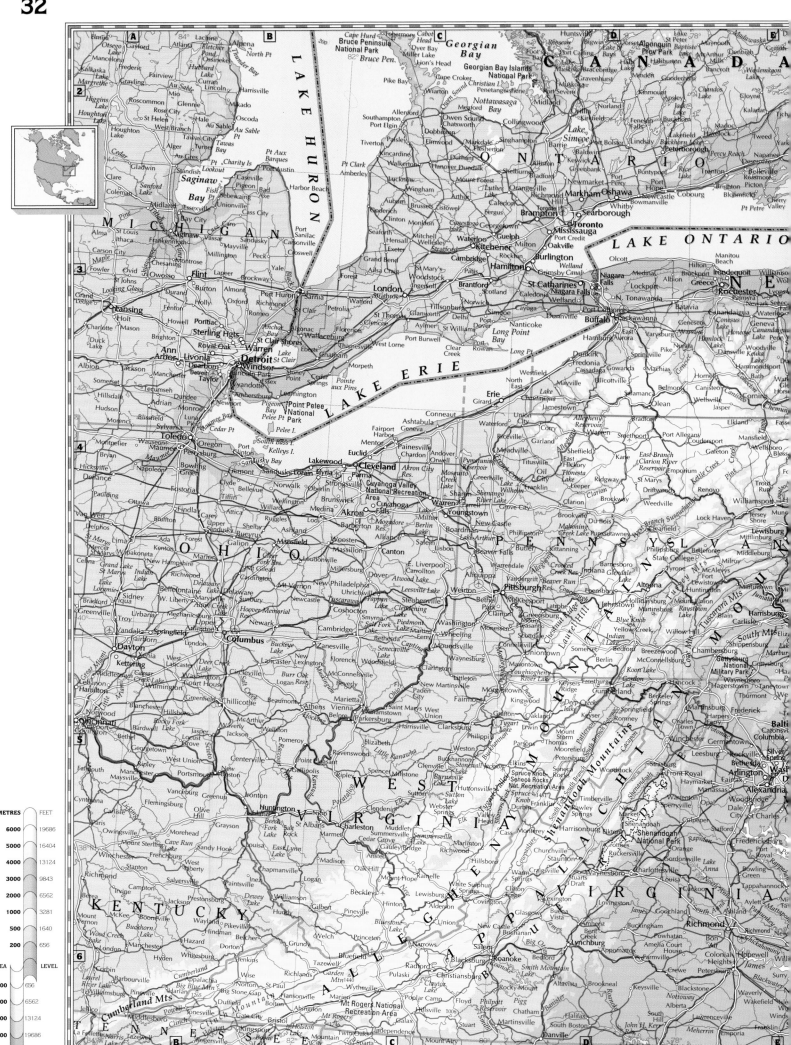

Lambert Conformal Conic Projection

1:3.5M

KM   MILES
175
          100
150
          75
125
100
          50
75
50   25
25
0   0

continuation at the same scale

© Bartholomew Ltd

PACIFIC OCEAN

OAHU
(Hawaii) 1:1.5M

HAWAIIAN ISLANDS
(Main group)
(U.S.A.)
160°W 1:6M

Lambert Conformal Conic Projection

METRES	FEET
6000	19686
5000	16404
4000	13124
3000	9843
2000	6562
1000	3281
500	1640
200	656
SEA	LEVEL
200	656
2000	6562
4000	13124
6000	19686

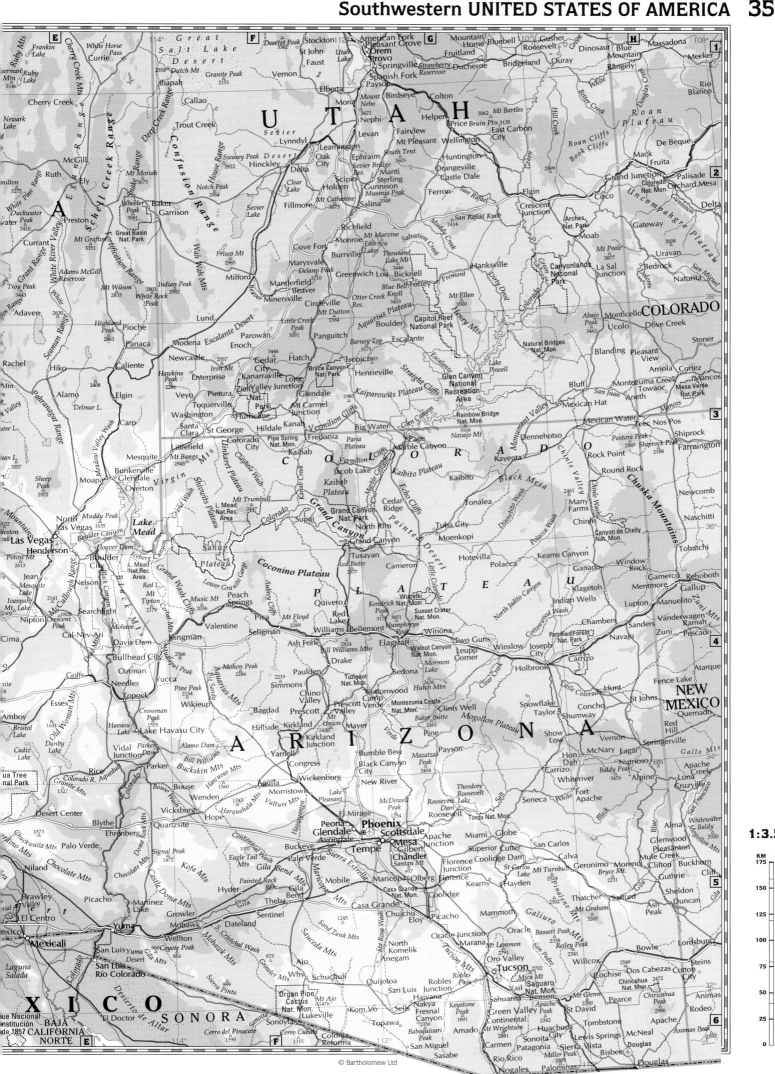

1:3.5M

KM 175   MILES

150   100

125   75

100

75   50

50

25   25

0   0

© Bartholomew Ltd

Lambert Azimuthal Equal Area Projection

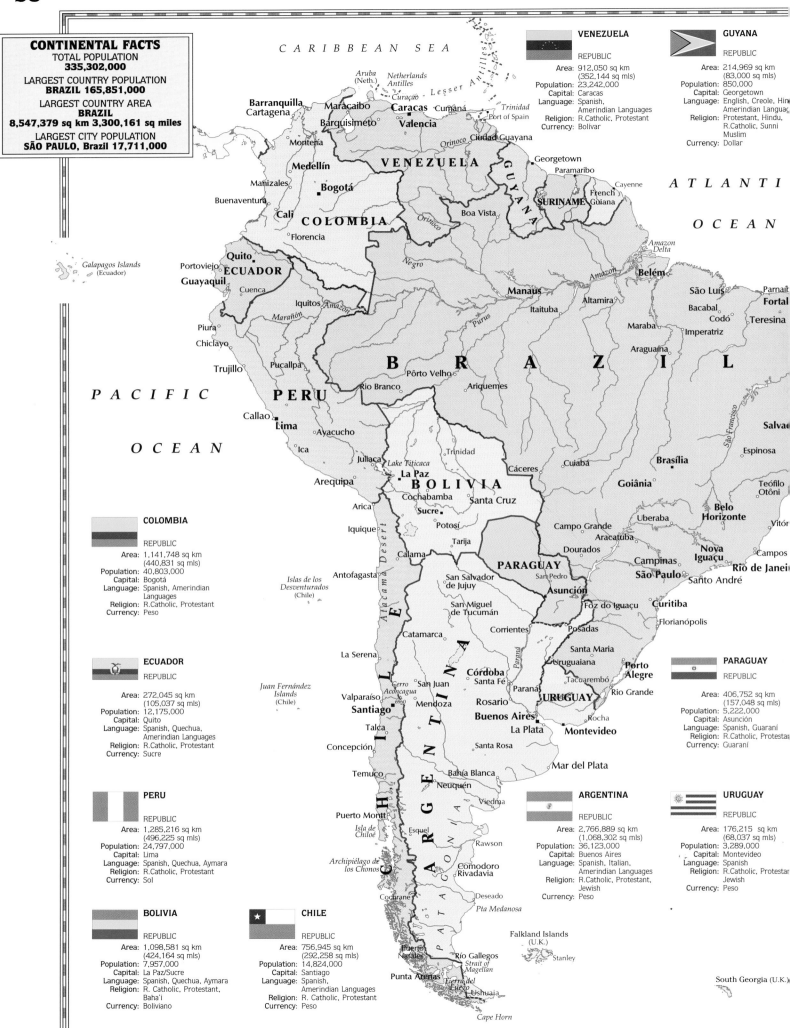

CONTINENTAL FACTS
TOTAL POPULATION
335,302,000
LARGEST COUNTRY POPULATION
BRAZIL 165,851,000
LARGEST COUNTRY AREA
BRAZIL
8,547,379 sq km 3,300,161 sq miles
LARGEST CITY POPULATION
SÃO PAULO, Brazil 17,711,000

VENEZUELA
REPUBLIC
Area: 912,050 sq km
(352,144 sq mls)
Population: 23,242,000
Capital: Caracas
Language: Spanish,
Amerindian Languages
Religion: R.Catholic, Protestant
Currency: Bolívar

GUYANA
REPUBLIC
Area: 214,969 sq km
(83,000 sq mls)
Population: 850,000
Capital: Georgetown
Language: English, Creole, Hindi,
Amerindian Languages
Religion: Protestant, Hindu,
R.Catholic, Sunni
Muslim
Currency: Dollar

COLOMBIA
REPUBLIC
Area: 1,141,748 sq km
(440,831 sq mls)
Population: 40,803,000
Capital: Bogotá
Language: Spanish, Amerindian
Languages
Religion: R.Catholic, Protestant
Currency: Peso

ECUADOR
REPUBLIC
Area: 272,045 sq km
(105,037 sq mls)
Population: 12,175,000
Capital: Quito
Language: Spanish, Quechua,
Amerindian Languages
Religion: R.Catholic, Protestant
Currency: Sucre

PERU
REPUBLIC
Area: 1,285,216 sq km
(496,225 sq mls)
Population: 24,797,000
Capital: Lima
Language: Spanish, Quechua, Aymara
Religion: R.Catholic, Protestant
Currency: Sol

BOLIVIA
REPUBLIC
Area: 1,098,581 sq km
(424,164 sq mls)
Population: 7,957,000
Capital: La Paz/Sucre
Language: Spanish, Quechua, Aymara
Religion: R. Catholic, Protestant,
Baha'i
Currency: Boliviano

CHILE
REPUBLIC
Area: 756,945 sq km
(292,258 sq mls)
Population: 14,824,000
Capital: Santiago
Language: Spanish,
Amerindian Languages
Religion: R. Catholic, Protestant
Currency: Peso

PARAGUAY
REPUBLIC
Area: 406,752 sq km
(157,048 sq mls)
Population: 5,222,000
Capital: Asunción
Language: Spanish, Guaraní
Religion: R.Catholic, Protestant
Currency: Guaraní

ARGENTINA
REPUBLIC
Area: 2,766,889 sq km
(1,068,302 sq mls)
Population: 36,123,000
Capital: Buenos Aires
Language: Spanish, Italian,
Amerindian Languages
Religion: R.Catholic, Protestant,
Jewish
Currency: Peso

URUGUAY
REPUBLIC
Area: 176,215 sq km
(68,037 sq mls)
Population: 3,289,000
Capital: Montevideo
Language: Spanish
Religion: R.Catholic, Protestant,
Jewish
Currency: Peso

Peru. Local Uros Indians make fishing boats by collecting and tying together the reeds found around Lake Titicaca.

Rio de Janeiro. Sugar Loaf Mountain stands at the entrance to the harbour in one of Brazil's major ports.

Natal

João Pessoa

Recife

Maceió

u

 SURINAME

REPUBLIC

Area: 163,820 sq km
(63,251 sq mls)
Population: 414,000
Capital: Paramaribo
Language: Dutch, Surinamese,
English, Hindi, Javanese
Religion: Hindu, R.Catholic,
Protestant, Sunni
Muslim
Currency: Guilder

FRENCH GUIANA

FRENCH TERRITORY

Area: 90,000 sq km
(34,749 sq mls)
Population: 167,000
Capital: Cayenne
Language: French, French Creole
Religion: R.Catholic, Protestant
Currency: French Franc

 BRAZIL

REPUBLIC

Area: 8,547,379 sq km
(3,300,161 sq mls)
Population: 165,851,000
Capital: Brasília
Language: Portuguese, German,
Japanese, Italian,
Amerindian Languages
Religion: R. Catholic, Spiritist,
Protestant
Currency: Real

POPULATION

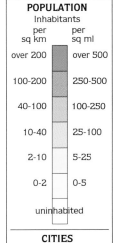

POPULATION
Inhabitants

per sq km	per sq ml
over 200	over 500
100-200	250-500
40-100	100-250
10-40	25-100
2-10	5-25
0-2	0-5
uninhabited	

CITIES
- Over 5 million population
- 2.5 - 5 million population

La Parva, Chile. A resort in the Andes near Santiago where skiing is possible to over 3600m.

CARIBBEAN SEA

ATLANTIC OCEAN

L. Nicaragua
Gallinas Pt.
Aruba
Netherlands Antilles
Curaçao
Margarita
Lesser Antilles
Trinidad
G. of Darién
L. Maracaibo
Orinoco Delta
Waini Point
Orinoco
Llanos
Pointe Isère
Meta
Guaviare
Cabo Orange
Cordillera Occidental
Cordillera Central
Cordillera Oriental
Caquetá
Branco
Negro
Essequibo
Mucuri
Amazon Delta
I. de Marajó
Cotopaxi 5896
Chimborazo 6310
Putumayo
Japurá
Balbina Resr.
Amazon
Huascarán 6768
Cordillera Central
Ucayali
Amazon
Juruá
Purus
Madeira
Tapajós
Iriri
Xingu
Tocantins
Tucuruí Resr.
Parnaíba
Selvas
Jiparana
Teles Pires
Juruena
Arinos
Araguaia
São Francisco
Cordillera Oriental
Cordillera Occidental
Guaporé
Lago de San Luis
Beni
Planalto do Mato Grosso
Tocantins
Planalto do Brasil
Lake Titicaca
San Miguel
Yungas
Altiplano
Izozog Marshes
Cordillera Central
Paraguay
Paraíba
Grande
Tietê
L. Poopó
Gran Chaco
Pilcomayo
Teuco
Paraná
Paranapanema
Iguaçu Falls
Cabo de São Tomé
Cabo Frio

PACIFIC OCEAN

Pta Tetas
Atacama Desert
Islas de los Desventurados (Chile)
Pta Ballena
Pta Morro
Salado
Desaguadero
Salinas Grandes
Sierras de Córdoba
Paraná
Uruguay
Lagoa dos Patos
Lagoa Mirim
Pampas

ATLANTIC OCEAN

Juan Fernández Islands (Chile)
Cerro Aconcagua
Colorado
Rio de la Plata
Bahía Blanca
Negro
Golfo San Matías
Península Valdés
Isla de Chiloé
Archipiélago de los Chonos
Golfo de San Jorge
Golfo de Penas
Pta Medanosa
L. San Martín
L. Argentino
Strait of Magellan
Tierra del Fuego
I. de los Estados
Cape Horn

ANDES

PATAGONIA

Falkland Islands
West Falkland
East Falkland

Iguaçu Falls. These spectacular waterfalls on the border of Brazil and Argentina plunge between 60 and 80 m.

Jaguar. Found in Amazonia and the Gran Chaco, these big cats vary from the colour of the one in the photograph to plain black or white coats.

CONTINENTAL FACTS
TOTAL AREA
17,815,420 sq km   6,878,572 sq miles
HIGHEST PEAK, CERRO ACONCAGUA
6,960 m   22,834 ft
LARGEST LAKE, TITICACA
8,340 sq km   3,220 sq miles
LONGEST RIVER, AMAZON
6,516 km   4,049 miles

CLIMATE

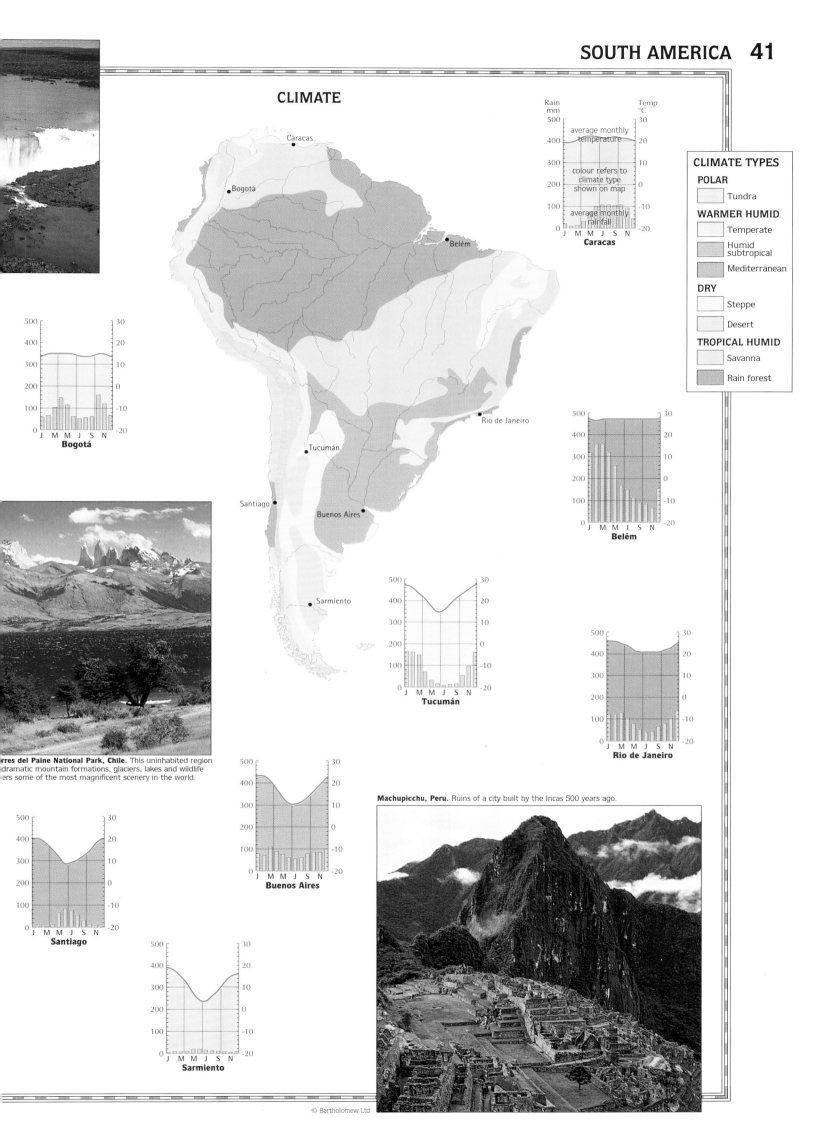

Caracas

Rain mm — Temp °C
- average monthly temperature
- colour refers to climate type shown on map
- average monthly rainfall

CLIMATE TYPES

POLAR
- Tundra

WARMER HUMID
- Temperate
- Humid subtropical
- Mediterranean

DRY
- Steppe
- Desert

TROPICAL HUMID
- Savanna
- Rain forest

Bogotá

Belém

Tucumán

Rio de Janeiro

Buenos Aires

Santiago

Sarmiento

Torres del Paine National Park, Chile. This uninhabited region of dramatic mountain formations, glaciers, lakes and wildlife offers some of the most magnificent scenery in the world.

Machupicchu, Peru. Ruins of a city built by the Incas 500 years ago.

© Bartholomew Ltd

METRES	FEET
6000	19686
5000	16404
4000	13124
3000	9843
2000	6562
1000	3281
500	1640
200	656
SEA	LEVEL
200	656
2000	6562
4000	13124
6000	19686

GALAPAGOS IS
(Ecuador)
at the same scale

Lambert Azimuthal Equal Area Projection

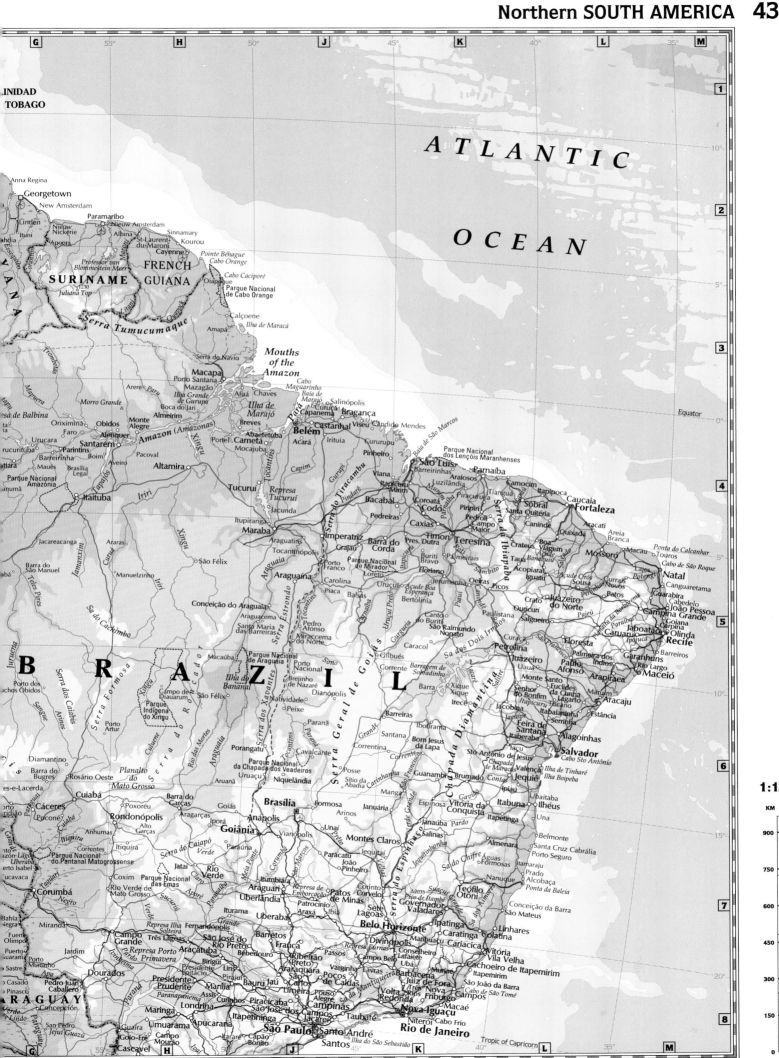

NIDAD
TOBAGO

Anna Regina
Georgetown
New Amsterdam
Linden
Ituni
Nieuw
Nickerie
Paramaribo
Albina
St-Laurent-
du-Maroni
Apoora
Nieuw Amsterdam
Sinnamary
Kourou
Cayenne

Professor van
Blommestein Meer
SURINAME
**FRENCH
GUIANA**
Juliana Top
Pointe Béhague
Cabo Orange
Oiapoque

Serra Tumucumaque
Cabo Caciporé
Parque Nacional
de Cabo Orange

Calçoene

A T L A N T I C

O C E A N

Serra do Navio
Ilha de Maracá

**Mouths
of the
Amazon**

Equator

Macapá
Amapá
Porto Santana
Mazagão
Cabo
Maguarinho

Morro Grande
Afuá
Chaves

Ilha Grande
de Gurupá
Boca do Jari

Ilha de
Marajó

Baía de
Marajó

Salinópolis

Orixmina
Almeirim

Breves

Capanema
Bragança
Viseu
Candido Mendes

Obidos
Alenquer
Santarém
Portel
Abaetetuba
Acará
Irituia
Pinheiro
Cururupu

Parque Nacional
dos Lençóis Maranhenses

Boim
Barreirinha
Aveiro
Pacoval
Altamira

Mocajuba
Cametá
Belém
Castanhal

Baía de São Marcos

Parintins
Amazon (Amazonas)

Xingu

São Luís
Barreirinhas
Araiosos
Parnaíba
Luzilândia
Camocim
Itapipoca
Caucaia
Fortaleza

Barra do
São Manuel

Sa do Cachimbo

Tucuruí
Represa
Tucuruí

Viana
Itapicuru
Mirim
Bacabal
Coroatá
Codó
Pinpiri
Piracuruca
Tianguá
Sobral
Santa Quitéria
Aracati

Itupiranga
Pedreiras
Caxias
Timon
Pres.
Dutra
Campo
Maior
Canindé
Quixadá

Maraba
Araguatins
Imperatriz
Barra do
Corda
Grajau
Teresina
Crateús
Boa
Viagem
Taua
Acopiara
Iguatú
Mossoró
Macau
Natal
Canguaretama

Conceição do Araguaia
Porto
Franco
Carolina
Parque Nacional
de Mirador
Loreto
Buriti
Bravo
Palmeiras
Floriano
Oeiras
Picos
Crato
Juazeiro
do Norte
Sousa
Patos
Campina Grande

B R A Z I L

Rio de Janeiro

1:15M

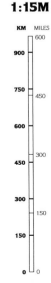

KM   MILES

© Bartholomew Ltd

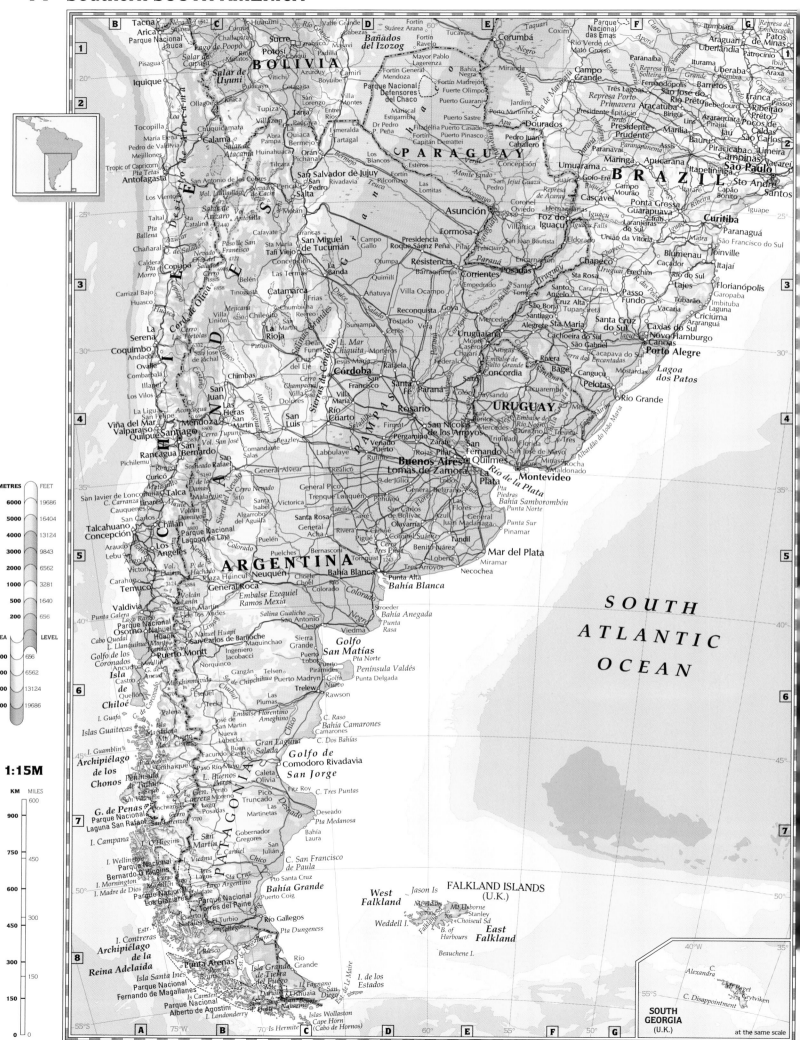

© Bartholomew Ltd

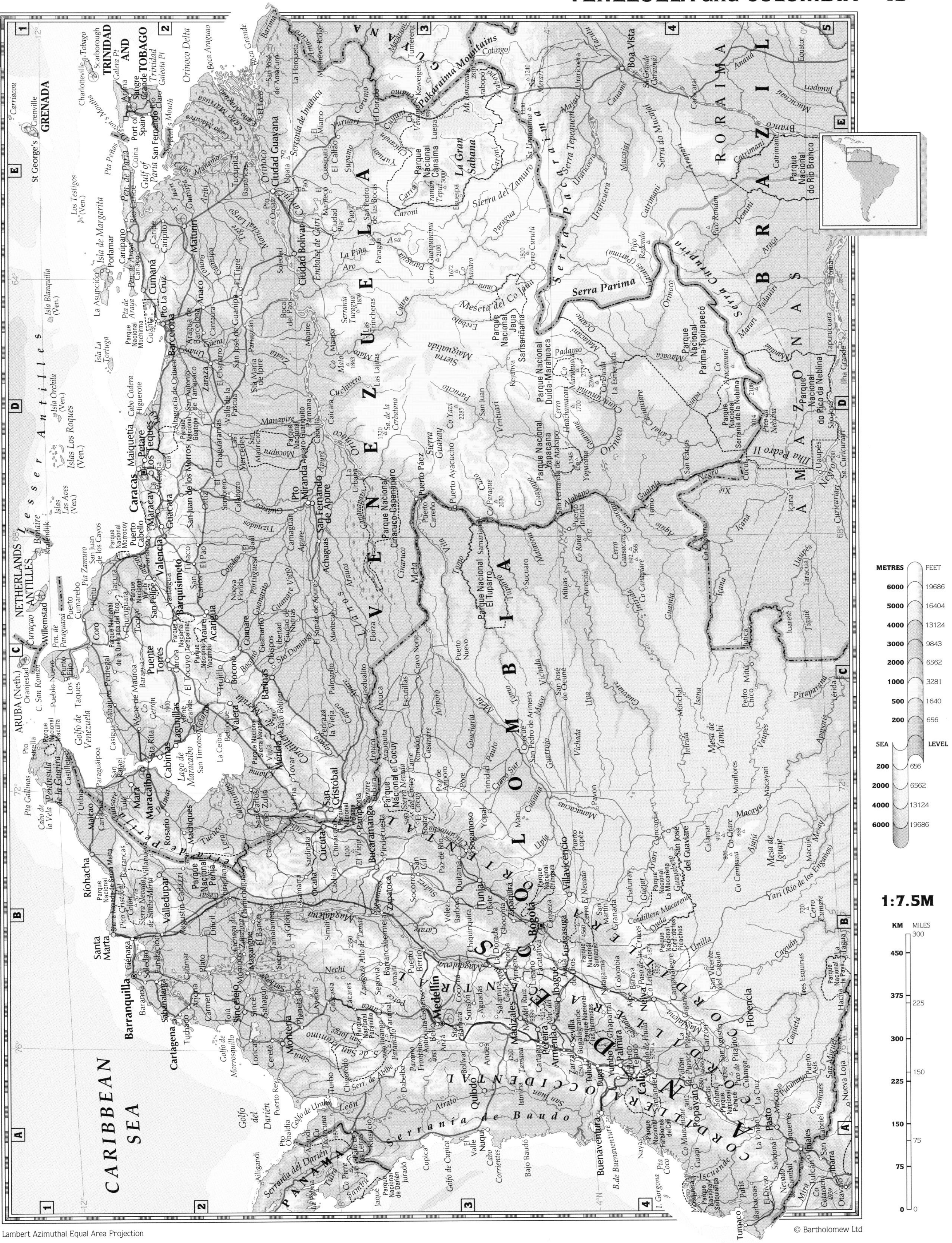

CARIBBEAN SEA

GRENADA
St George's · Grenville · Carriacou

TRINIDAD AND TOBAGO
Scarborough · Port of Spain · Trinidad

NETHERLANDS ANTILLES
ARUBA (Neth.) · Oranjestad
Curaçao · Willemstad · Bonaire

Lesser Antilles

VENEZUELA

Caracas · Maracaibo · Valencia · Barquisimeto · Maracay · Maiquetía · Los Teques · Barcelona · Cumaná · Maturín · Ciudad Guayana · Ciudad Bolívar · San Cristóbal · Mérida · Valera · Barinas · Acarigua · San Fernando de Apure · Puerto Ayacucho

Orinoco Delta · Golfo de Venezuela · Lago de Maracaibo · Isla de Margarita · Porlamar

La Gran Sabana · Pakáraima Mountains · Serra Parima · Meseta del Cerro Jaua

COLOMBIA

Bogotá · Medellín · Cali · Barranquilla · Cartagena · Cúcuta · Bucaramanga · Santa Marta · Valledupar · Ríohacha · Montería · Sincelejo · Ibagué · Manizales · Pereira · Armenia · Villavicencio · Pasto · Popayán · Neiva · Florencia · Yopal · Tunja · Buenaventura · Quibdó

Cordillera Oriental · *Cordillera Central* · *Cordillera Occidental*

Río Magdalena · Río Meta · Río Guaviare · Río Orinoco · Río Negro

PANAMA

Golfo del Darién · Serranía del Darién

BRAZIL (RORAIMA · AMAZONAS)
Boa Vista · Branco

Lambert Azimuthal Equal Area Projection

© Bartholomew Ltd

1:7.5M

METRES	FEET
6000	19686
5000	16404
4000	13124
3000	9843
2000	6562
1000	3281
500	1640
200	656
SEA	LEVEL
200	656
2000	6562
4000	13124
6000	19686

KM / MILES
0 · 75 · 150 · 225 · 300 · 375 · 450
0 · 75 · 150 · 225 · 300

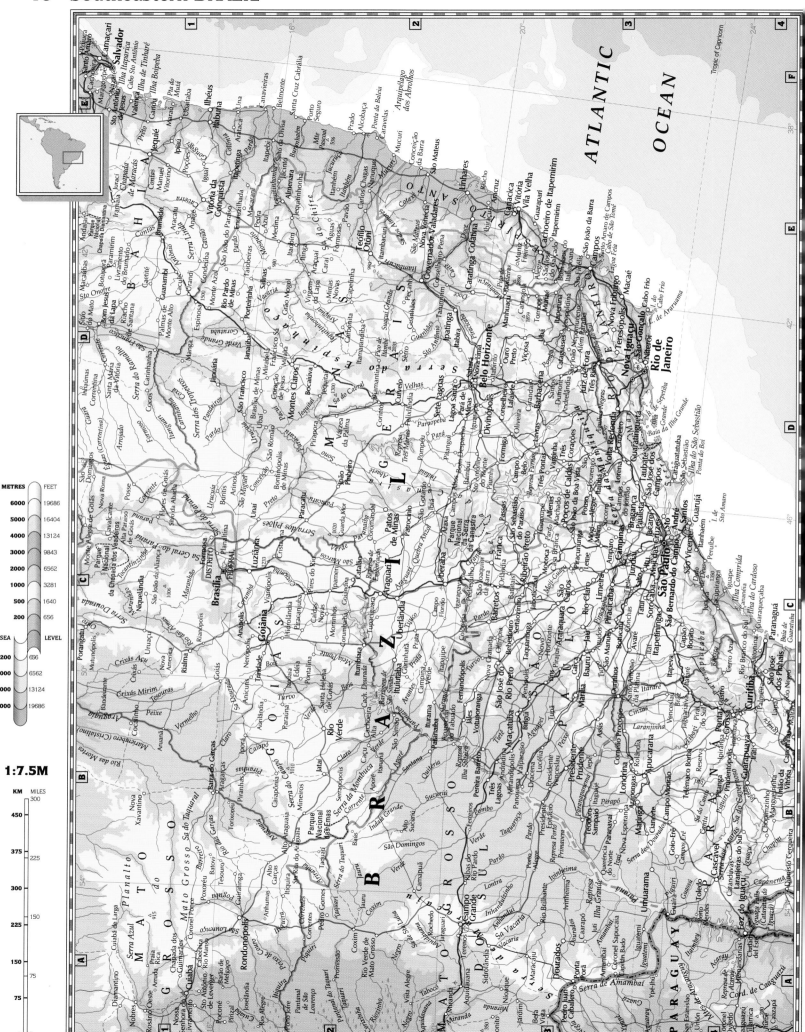

1:7.5M

Lambert Azimuthal Equal Area Projection

© Bartholomew Ltd

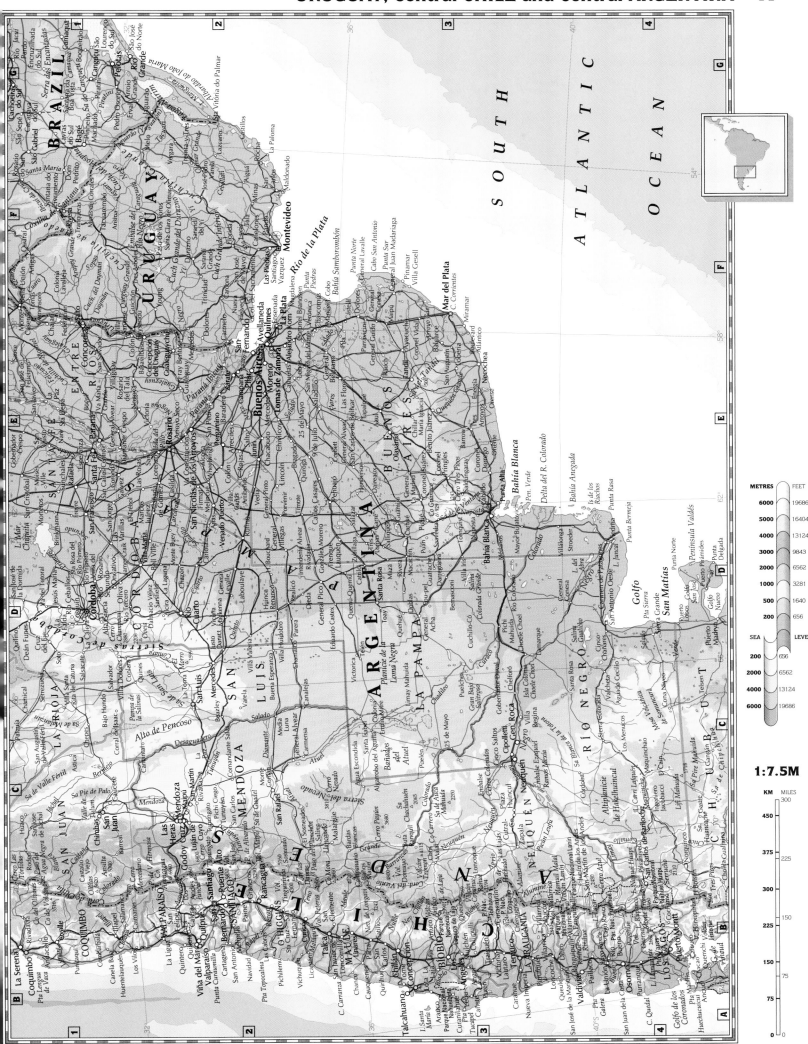

1:7.5M

METRES		FEET
6000		19686
5000		16404
4000		13124
3000		9843
2000		6562
1000		3281
500		1640
200		656
SEA		LEVEL
200		656
2000		6562
4000		13124
6000		19686

KM	MILES
450	300
375	225
300	150
225	75
150	
75	
0	0

Lambert Azimuthal Equal Area Projection

© Bartholomew Ltd

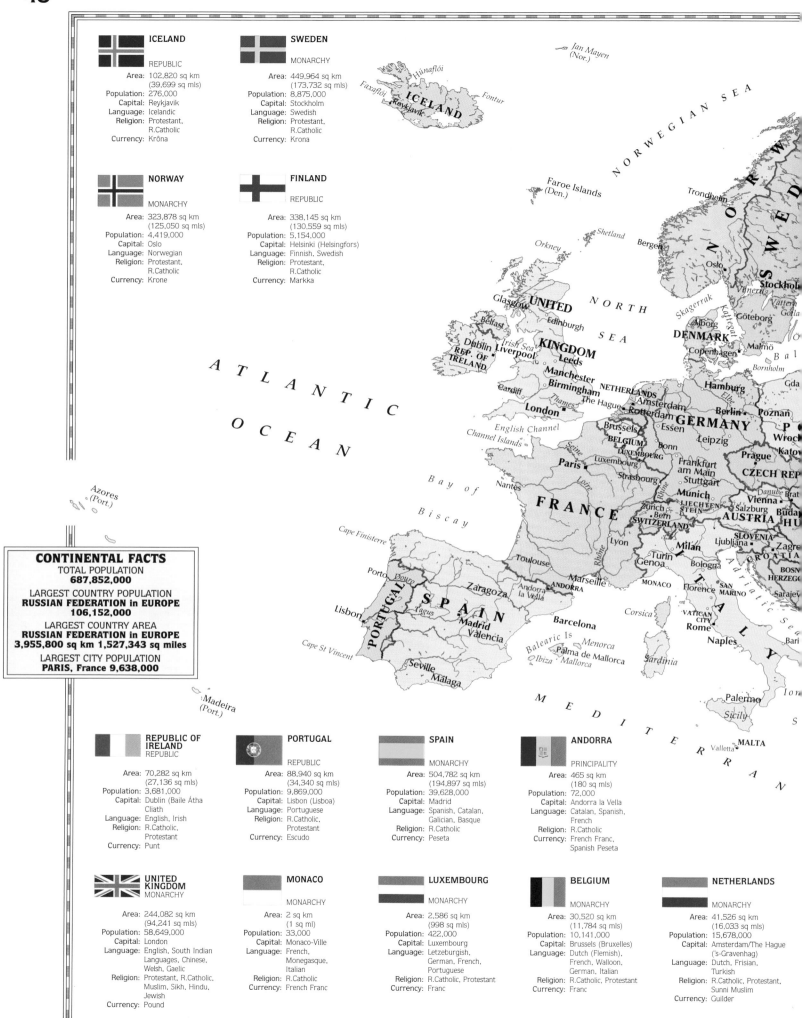

ICELAND
REPUBLIC

Area: 102,820 sq km
(39,699 sq mls)
Population: 276,000
Capital: Reykjavik
Language: Icelandic
Religion: Protestant,
R.Catholic
Currency: Krôna

SWEDEN
MONARCHY

Area: 449,964 sq km
(173,732 sq mls)
Population: 8,875,000
Capital: Stockholm
Language: Swedish
Religion: Protestant,
R.Catholic
Currency: Krona

NORWAY
MONARCHY

Area: 323,878 sq km
(125,050 sq mls)
Population: 4,419,000
Capital: Oslo
Language: Norwegian
Religion: Protestant,
R.Catholic
Currency: Krone

FINLAND
REPUBLIC

Area: 338,145 sq km
(130,559 sq mls)
Population: 5,154,000
Capital: Helsinki (Helsingfors)
Language: Finnish, Swedish
Religion: Protestant,
R.Catholic
Currency: Markka

CONTINENTAL FACTS
TOTAL POPULATION
687,852,000

LARGEST COUNTRY POPULATION
**RUSSIAN FEDERATION in EUROPE
106,152,000**

LARGEST COUNTRY AREA
**RUSSIAN FEDERATION in EUROPE
3,955,800 sq km 1,527,343 sq miles**

LARGEST CITY POPULATION
PARIS, France 9,638,000

REPUBLIC OF IRELAND
REPUBLIC

Area: 70,282 sq km
(27,136 sq mls)
Population: 3,681,000
Capital: Dublin (Baile Átha
Cliath
Language: English, Irish
Religion: R.Catholic,
Protestant
Currency: Punt

PORTUGAL
REPUBLIC

Area: 88,940 sq km
(34,340 sq mls)
Population: 9,869,000
Capital: Lisbon (Lisboa)
Language: Portuguese
Religion: R.Catholic,
Protestant
Currency: Escudo

SPAIN
MONARCHY

Area: 504,782 sq km
(194,897 sq mls)
Population: 39,628,000
Capital: Madrid
Language: Spanish, Catalan,
Galician, Basque
Religion: R.Catholic
Currency: Peseta

ANDORRA
PRINCIPALITY

Area: 465 sq km
(180 sq mls)
Population: 72,000
Capital: Andorra la Vella
Language: Catalan, Spanish,
French
Religion: R.Catholic
Currency: French Franc,
Spanish Peseta

UNITED KINGDOM
MONARCHY

Area: 244,082 sq km
(94,241 sq mls)
Population: 58,649,000
Capital: London
Language: English, South Indian
Languages, Chinese,
Welsh, Gaelic
Religion: Protestant, R.Catholic,
Muslim, Sikh, Hindu,
Jewish
Currency: Pound

MONACO
MONARCHY

Area: 2 sq km
(1 sq ml)
Population: 33,000
Capital: Monaco-Ville
Language: French,
Monegasque,
Italian
Religion: R.Catholic
Currency: French Franc

LUXEMBOURG
MONARCHY

Area: 2,586 sq km
(998 sq mls)
Population: 422,000
Capital: Luxembourg
Language: Letzeburgish,
German, French,
Portuguese
Religion: R.Catholic, Protestant
Currency: Franc

BELGIUM
MONARCHY

Area: 30,520 sq km
(11,784 sq mls)
Population: 10,141,000
Capital: Brussels (Bruxelles)
Language: Dutch (Flemish),
French, Walloon,
German, Italian
Religion: R.Catholic, Protestant
Currency: Franc

NETHERLANDS
MONARCHY

Area: 41,526 sq km
(16,033 sq mls)
Population: 15,678,000
Capital: Amsterdam/The Hague
('s-Gravenhag)
Language: Dutch, Frisian,
Turkish
Religion: R.Catholic, Protestant,
Sunni Muslim
Currency: Guilder

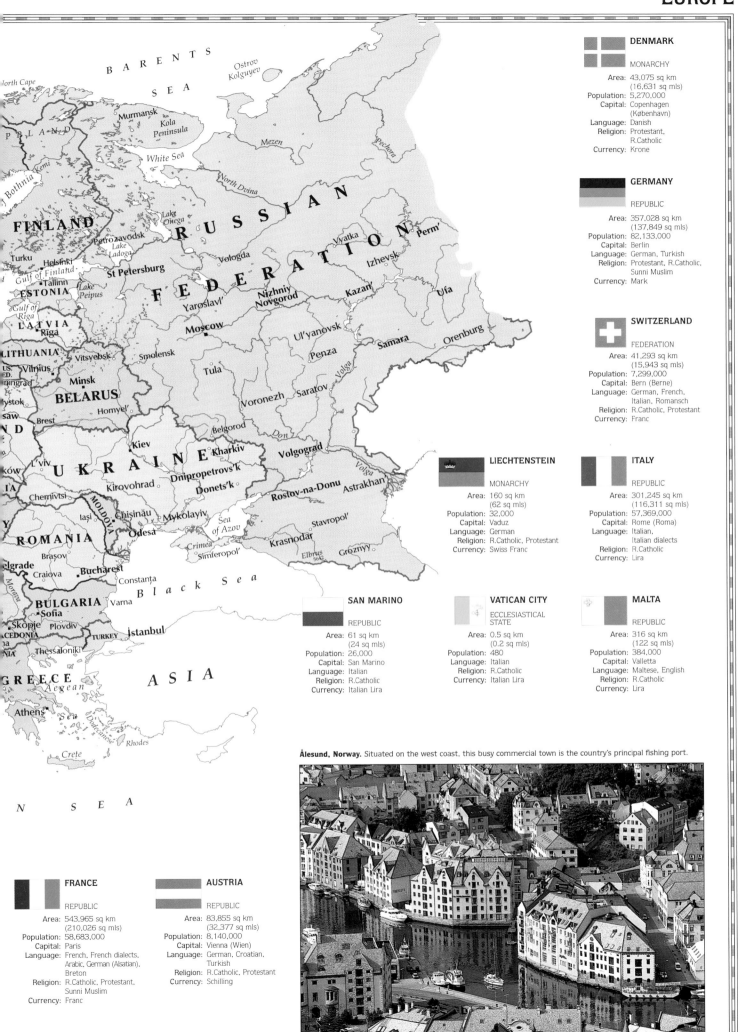

Map labels

BARENTS SEA

North Cape

Ostrov Kolguyev

Murmansk

Kola Peninsula

Mezen

Pechora

White Sea

North Devina

LAPLAND

Kemi

G. of Bothnia

FINLAND

Turku

Helsinki

Gulf of Finland

Lake Onega

Petrozavodsk

Lake Ladoga

St Petersburg

Tallinn

ESTONIA

Lake Peipus

Gulf of Riga

LATVIA

Riga

LITHUANIA

Vilnius

RUS. FED.

Kaliningrad

Vitsyebsk

Smolensk

Minsk

BELARUS

Homyel'

Brest

Bialystok

Warsaw

POLAND

Kraków

Vyatka

Perm'

Vologda

Izhevsk

Ufa

RUSSIAN FEDERATION

Yaroslavl'

Nizhniy Novgorod

Kazan'

Moscow

Ul'yanovsk

Samara

Orenburg

Penza

Volga

Tula

Saratov

Voronezh

Don

Belgorod

Kiev

Kharkiv

UKRAINE

Dnipropetrovs'k

Volgograd

Volga

Astrakhan

Kirovohrad

Donets'k

Rostov-na-Donu

L'viv

Chernivtsi

Iasi

MOLDOVA

Chisinau

Mykolayiv

Odesa

Sea of Azov

Stavropol'

Krasnodar

Crimea

Simferopol'

Elbrus 5642

Groznyy

ROMANIA

Brasov

Craiova

Bucharest

Constanta

Black Sea

Belgrade

Morava

BULGARIA

Varna

Sofia

MACEDONIA

Skopje

Plovdiv

ALBANIA

Thessaloniki

TURKEY

Istanbul

GREECE

Athens

Aegean Sea

Dodecanese

Rhodes

Crete

ASIA

N SEA A

© Bartholomew Ltd

Country data

DENMARK

MONARCHY

Area: 43,075 sq km (16,631 sq mls)
Population: 5,270,000
Capital: Copenhagen (København)
Language: Danish
Religion: Protestant, R.Catholic
Currency: Krone

GERMANY

REPUBLIC

Area: 357,028 sq km (137,849 sq mls)
Population: 82,133,000
Capital: Berlin
Language: German, Turkish
Religion: Protestant, R.Catholic, Sunni Muslim
Currency: Mark

SWITZERLAND

FEDERATION

Area: 41,293 sq km (15,943 sq mls)
Population: 7,299,000
Capital: Bern (Berne)
Language: German, French, Italian, Romansch
Religion: R.Catholic, Protestant
Currency: Franc

LIECHTENSTEIN

MONARCHY

Area: 160 sq km (62 sq mls)
Population: 32,000
Capital: Vaduz
Language: German
Religion: R.Catholic, Protestant
Currency: Swiss Franc

ITALY

REPUBLIC

Area: 301,245 sq km (116,311 sq mls)
Population: 57,369,000
Capital: Rome (Roma)
Language: Italian, Italian dialects
Religion: R.Catholic
Currency: Lira

SAN MARINO

REPUBLIC

Area: 61 sq km (24 sq mls)
Population: 26,000
Capital: San Marino
Language: Italian
Religion: R.Catholic
Currency: Italian Lira

VATICAN CITY

ECCLESIASTICAL STATE

Area: 0.5 sq km (0.2 sq mls)
Population: 480
Language: Italian
Religion: R.Catholic
Currency: Italian Lira

MALTA

REPUBLIC

Area: 316 sq km (122 sq mls)
Population: 384,000
Capital: Valletta
Language: Maltese, English
Religion: R.Catholic
Currency: Lira

FRANCE

REPUBLIC

Area: 543,965 sq km (210,026 sq mls)
Population: 58,683,000
Capital: Paris
Language: French, French dialects, Arabic, German (Alsatian), Breton
Religion: R.Catholic, Protestant, Sunni Muslim
Currency: Franc

AUSTRIA

REPUBLIC

Area: 83,855 sq km (32,377 sq mls)
Population: 8,140,000
Capital: Vienna (Wien)
Language: German, Croatian, Turkish
Religion: R.Catholic, Protestant
Currency: Schilling

Ålesund, Norway. Situated on the west coast, this busy commercial town is the country's principal fishing port.

50

Budapest, Hungary. The picturesque old part of the city (Buda) shown in the photograph is separated from the administrative and commercial centre (Pest) by the River Danube.

 POLAND
REPUBLIC
Area: 312,683 sq km
(120,728 sq mls)
Population: 38,718,000
Capital: Warsaw (Warszawa)
Language: Polish, German
Religion: R.Catholic,
Polish Orthodox
Currency: Złoty

SLOVAKIA
REPUBLIC
Area: 49,035 sq km
(18,933 sq mls)
Population: 5,377,000
Capital: Bratislava
Language: Slovak, Hungarian,
Czech
Religion: R.Catholic, Protestant,
Orthodox
Currency: Koruna

 SLOVENIA
REPUBLIC
Area: 20,251 sq km
(7,819 sq mls)
Population: 1,993,000
Capital: Ljubljana
Language: Slovene, Serbian,
Croatian
Religion: R.Catholic, Protestant
Currency: Tólar

 CROATIA
REPUBLIC
Area: 56,538 sq km
(21,829 sq mls)
Population: 4,481,000
Capital: Zagreb
Language: Croatian, Serbian
Religion: R.Catholic, Orthodox,
Sunni Muslim
Currency: Kuna

 BOSNIA-HERZEGOVINA
REPUBLIC
Area: 51,130 sq km
(19,741 sq mls)
Population: 3,675,000
Capital: Sarajevo
Language: Bosnian, Serbian,
Croatian
Religion: Sunni Muslim,
Serbian Orthodox,
R.Catholic, Protestant
Currency: Dinar

YUGOSLAVIA
REPUBLIC
Area: 102,173 sq km
(39,449 sq mls)
Population: 10,635,000
Capital: Belgrade (Beograd)
Language: Serbian, Albanian
Religion: Serbian Orthodox,
Montenegrin Orthodox,
Sunni Muslim
Currency: Dinar

 MACEDONIA (F.Y.R.O.M.)
REPUBLIC
Area: 25,713 sq km
(9,928 sq mls)
Population: 1,999,000
Capital: Skopje
Language: Macedonian, Albanian,
Croatian, Serbian,
Turkish, Romany
Religion: Macedonian Orthodox,
Sunni Muslim,
R.Catholic
Currency: Denar

 GREECE
REPUBLIC
Area: 131,957 sq km
(50,949 sq mls)
Population: 10,600,000
Capital: Athens (Athína)
Language: Greek, Macedonian
Religion: Greek Orthodox,
Sunni Muslim
Currency: Drachma

BULGARIA
REPUBLIC
Area: 110,994 sq km
(42,855 sq mls)
Population: 8,336,000
Capital: Sofia (Sofiya)
Language: Bulgarian, Turkish,
Romany, Macedonian
Religion: Bulgarian Orthodox,
Sunni Muslim
Currency: Lev

ROMANIA
REPUBLIC
Area: 237,500 sq km
(91,699 sq mls)
Population: 22,474,000
Capital: Bucharest (Bucureşti)
Language: Romanian,
Hungarian
Religion: Romanian Orthodox,
R.Catholic, Protestant
Currency: Leu

Ronda, Spain. The town is precariously situated on a rocky shelf which falls on three sides to a depth of 120m.

 MOLDOVA
REPUBLIC
Area: 33,700 sq km
(13,012 sq mls)
Population: 4,378,000
Capital: Chisinău (Kishinev)
Language: Romanian, Russian,
Ukrainian, Gagauz
Religion: Moldovan Orthodox,
Russian Orthodox
Currency: Leu

 CZECH REPUBLIC
REPUBLIC
Area: 78,864 sq km
(30,450 sq mls)
Population: 10,282,000
Capital: Prague (Praha)
Language: Czech, Moravian,
Slovak
Religion: R.Catholic, Protestant
Currency: Koruna

 UKRAINE
REPUBLIC
Area: 603,700 sq km
(233,090 sq mls)
Population: 50,861,000
Capital: Kiev (Kyiv)
Language: Ukrainian, Russian,
Regional Languages
Religion: Ukrainian Orthodox,
R.Catholic
Currency: Hryvnia

 HUNGARY
REPUBLIC
Area: 93,030 sq km
(35,919 sq mls)
Population: 10,116,000
Capital: Budapest
Language: Hungarian, Romany,
German, Slovak
Religion: R.Catholic, Protestant
Currency: Forint

 LITHUANIA
REPUBLIC
Area: 65,200 sq km
(25,174 sq mls)
Population: 3,694,000
Capital: Vilnius
Language: Lithuanian, Russian,
Polish
Religion: R.Catholic, Protestant,
Russian Orthodox
Currency: Litas

 BELARUS
REPUBLIC
Area: 207,600 sq km
(80,155 sq mls)
Population: 10,315,000
Capital: Minsk
Language: Belorussian,
Russian, Ukrainian
Religion: Belorussian Orthodox,
R.Catholic
Currency: Rouble

ALBANIA
REPUBLIC
Area: 28,748 sq km
(11,100 sq mls)
Population: 3,119,000
Capital: Tirana (Tiranë)
Language: Albanian (Gheg, Tosk
dialects), Greek
Religion: Sunni Muslim, Greek
Orthodox, R.Catholic
Currency: Lek

 ESTONIA
REPUBLIC
Area: 45,200 sq km
(17,452 sq mls)
Population: 1,429,000
Capital: Tallinn
Language: Estonian, Russian
Religion: Protestant,
Russian Orthodox
Currency: Kroon

POPULATION

St Petersburg

Moscow

Hamburg

Berlin

London

Essen-Dortmund
Düsseldorf
Cologne

Paris

Frankfurt am Main
Stuttgart

Katowice

Kiev

Madrid

Barcelona

Rome

Naples

Istanbul

Athens

POPULATION
Inhabitants

per sq km	per sq ml
over 200	over 500
100-200	250-500
50-100	130-250
10-50	25-130
1-10	2.5-25
0-1	0-2.5

uninhabited

CITIES
■ Over 5 million population

● 2.5 - 5 million population

Grindelwald, Switzerland. A resort popular with skiers and climbers, as it is spread across an expanse of Alpine meadows and is near many majestic peaks and glaciers.

LATVIA
REPUBLIC

Area: 63,700 sq km
(24,595 sq mls)
Population: 2,424,000
Capital: Rīga
Language: Latvian, Russian
Religion: Protestant, R.Catholic, Russian Orthodox
Currency: Lat

RUSSIAN FEDERATION
REPUBLIC   in Europe

Area: 17,075,400 sq km   3,955,800 sq km
(6,592,849 sq mls)   (1,527,343 sq mls)
Population: 147,434,000   106,152,000
Capital: Moscow (Moskva)
Language: Russian, Tatar, Ukrainian, Local Languages
Religion: Russian Orthodox, Sunni Muslim, Other Christian, Jewish
Currency: Rouble

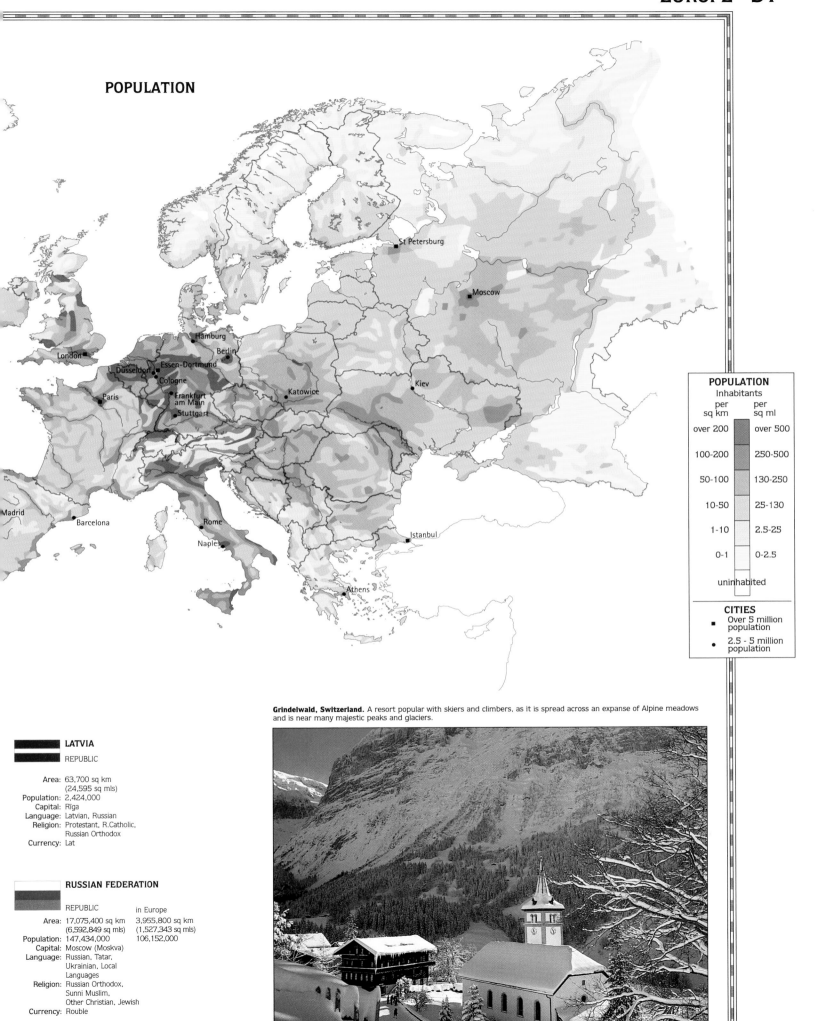

Faxaflói
Vestmannaeyjar
Fontur
Vatnajökull
Iceland

ATLANTIC
OCEAN

NORWEGIAN SEA

North Cape

Ostrov
Kolguyev
C. Kanin
Cheshskaya Guba

Lofoten
Vesterålen
Vestfjorden

Lappland

Inarijärvi
Oz.
Imandra
Kola
Peninsula

Mezen

White Sea

SCANDINAVIA

Lule
Kemi

North Dvina

Faroe
Islands

Shetland

Ume

Indals

Gulf of Bothnia

Lake
Onega

North Sea

Vyc

Outer Hebrides
Orkney

Mälaren

Åland

Lake
Ladoga

NORTH
SEA

Skagerrak
Kattegat

Vänern
Vättern

Gotland

Gulf of Finland

Lake
Peipus

Rybinsk
Reservoir

Ben Nevis

British
Isles

Baltic Sea

Gulf of
Riga

Valdai
Hills

Galway Bay
Shannon
Ireland
Irish Sea

Pennines
Snowdon

Great
Britain

Zealand
Fyn
Bornholm

Öland

Vol
Upla

English Channel
Channel Islands

Thames
Strait of Dover

Maas

Weser
Elbe

North European Plain

Pripet
Marshes

Dnieper

Central Russian Uplands

Seine
Marne
Ardennes
Rhine
Moselle

Elbe
Oder
Warta

Wisla

Bug

Don

Kiev
Resr.

Bay of
Biscay

Loire
Vienne

Vosges
Jura

Danube
Bodensee
Inn

Ore Mts
Bohemian Forest

Sudeten Mts

Wisla

Dniester

Tsimlyans
Reservoir

Cape
Finisterre

Gironde
Gulf of
Gascony

Allier
L. Geneva
Mont Blanc

ALPS
Matterhorn

Danube

Carpathian Mts

Dniester

Sea
of Azov

Do

Cantabrian Mts
Douro
Duero

Massif
Central

Rhône
Saône

Dolomites
Po

Balaton

Tisza

Mures

Dnieper

Crimea

Pyrenees
Pico de
Aneto

Golfe
du Lion

Ligurian
Sea

Apennines

Adriatic Sea

Dinaric Alps
Sava

Transylvanian Alps

Danube

Black Sea

Tagus

Ebro

Corsica

Morava

Balkan Mts
Rhodope Mts

ASIA

Sierra Morena
Guadalquivir

Balearic Is
Menorca
Mallorca
Ibiza

Sardinia

Tyrrhenian
Sea

Vesuvius

Aegean

Sea of
Marmara

Cape
St Vincent

Sierra Nevada

Stromboli

Ionian

Pindus Mts

Sea

Dodecanese

MEDITERRANEAN

Sicily
Mt Etna

Sea

Rhodes

Malta

Crete

SEA

CONTINENTAL FACTS
TOTAL AREA
9,908,599 sq km   3,825,731 sq miles

HIGHEST PEAK, ELBRUS
5,642 m   18,510 ft

LARGEST LAKE, LADOGA
18,390 sq km   7,100 sq miles

LONGEST RIVER, VOLGA
3,688 km   2,291 miles

Venice, Italy. Boats are the primary mode of transport as the town is built on 118 islands and traversed by over 100 canals.

Strokkur Geyser, Iceland. This hot spring erupts every 3 minutes, throwing steam clouds up to 20m high.

CLIMATE

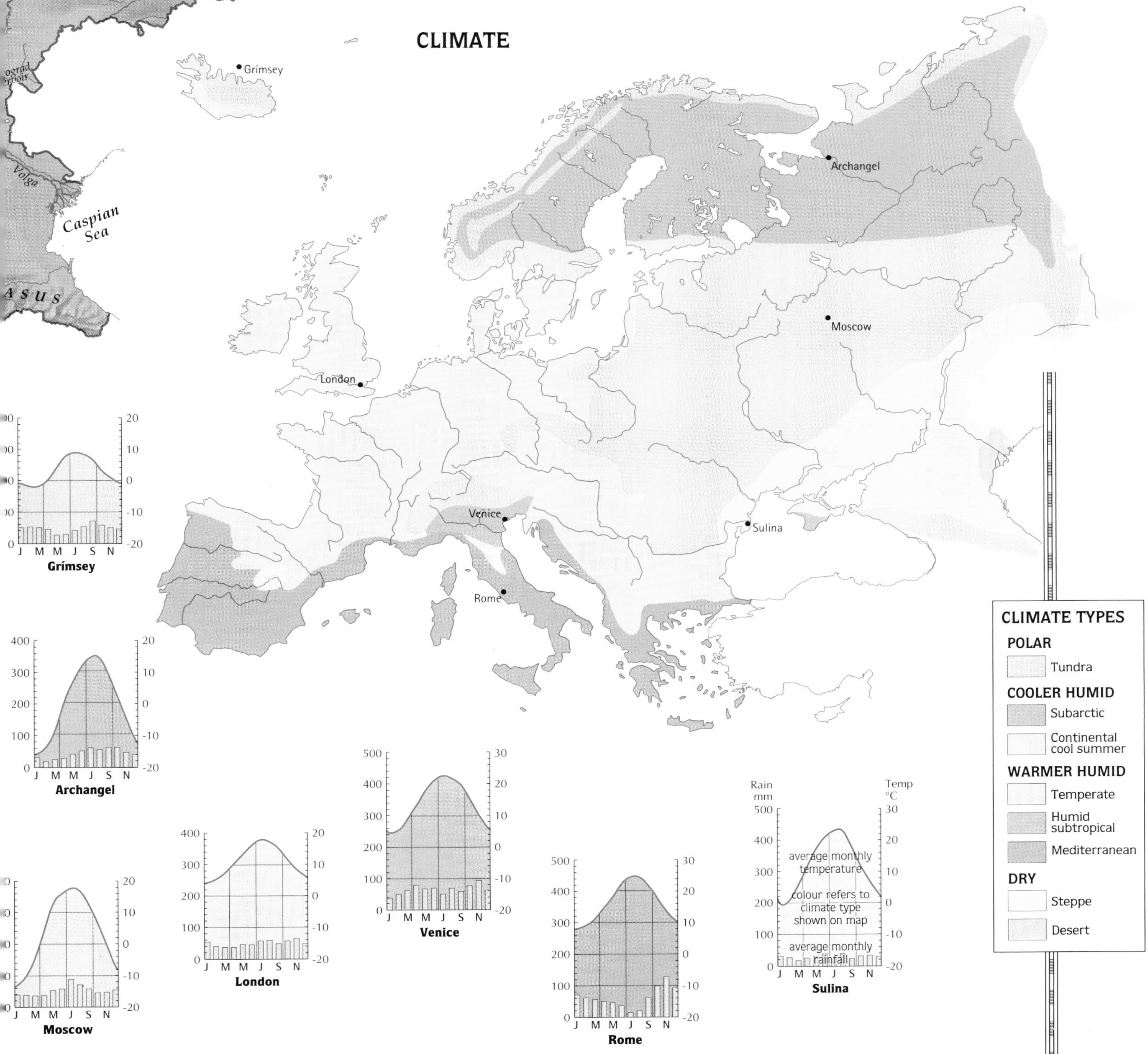

Usa
Ural Mountains
Koma
Pechora
Kamskoye Reservoir
Votkinsk Reservoir
Kuybyshev Reservoir
ograd voir
Volga
Caspian Sea
A S U S

Grimsey

Archangel

Moscow

London

Venice

Sulina

Rome

Grímsey

J M M J S N

Archangel

400
300
200
100
20
10
0
-10
-20
J M M J S N

Moscow

20
10
0
-10
-20
J M M J S N

London

400
300
200
100
20
10
0
-10
-20
J M M J S N

Venice

500
400
300
200
100
30
20
10
0
-10
-20
J M M J S N

Rome

500
400
300
200
100
20
10
0
-10
-20
J M M J S N

Sulina

Rain mm
500
400
300
200
100

Temp °C
30
20
10
0
-10
-20

average monthly temperature

colour refers to climate type shown on map

average monthly rainfall

J M M J S N

CLIMATE TYPES

POLAR

Tundra

COOLER HUMID

Subarctic

Continental cool summer

WARMER HUMID

Temperate

Humid subtropical

Mediterranean

DRY

Steppe

Desert

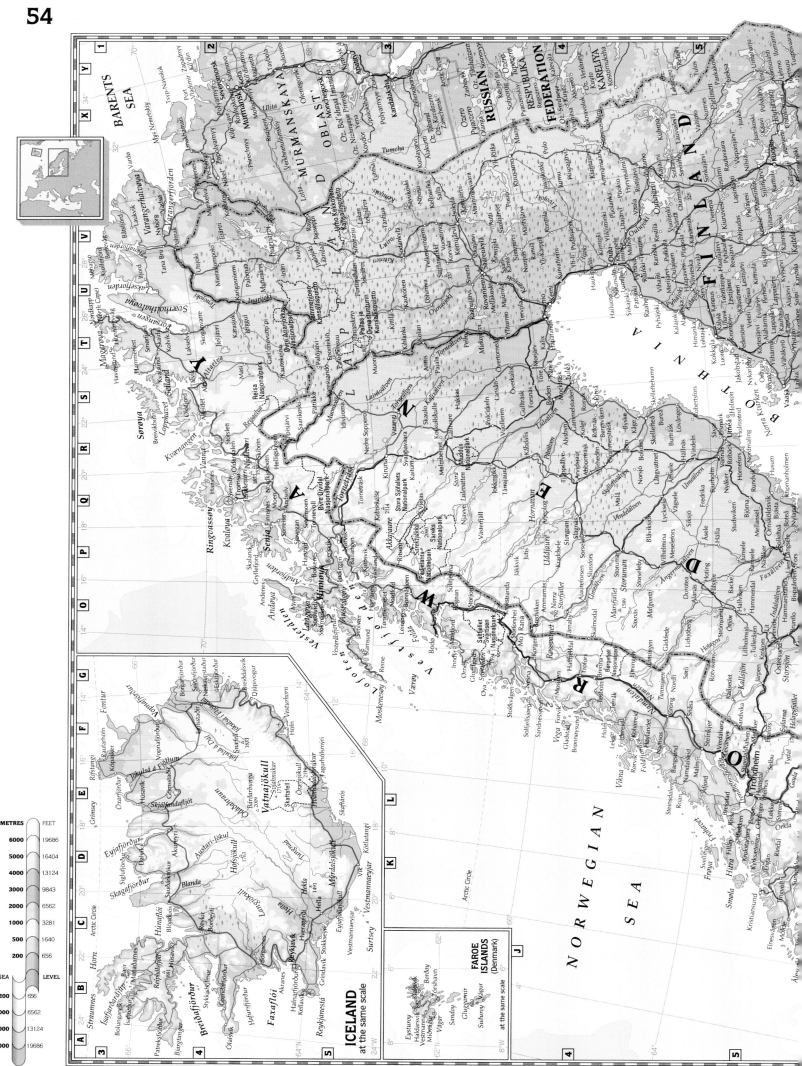

ICELAND
at the same scale

FAROE ISLANDS
(Denmark)
at the same scale

Conic Equidistant Projection

1:5M

© Bartholomew Ltd

© Bartholomew Ltd

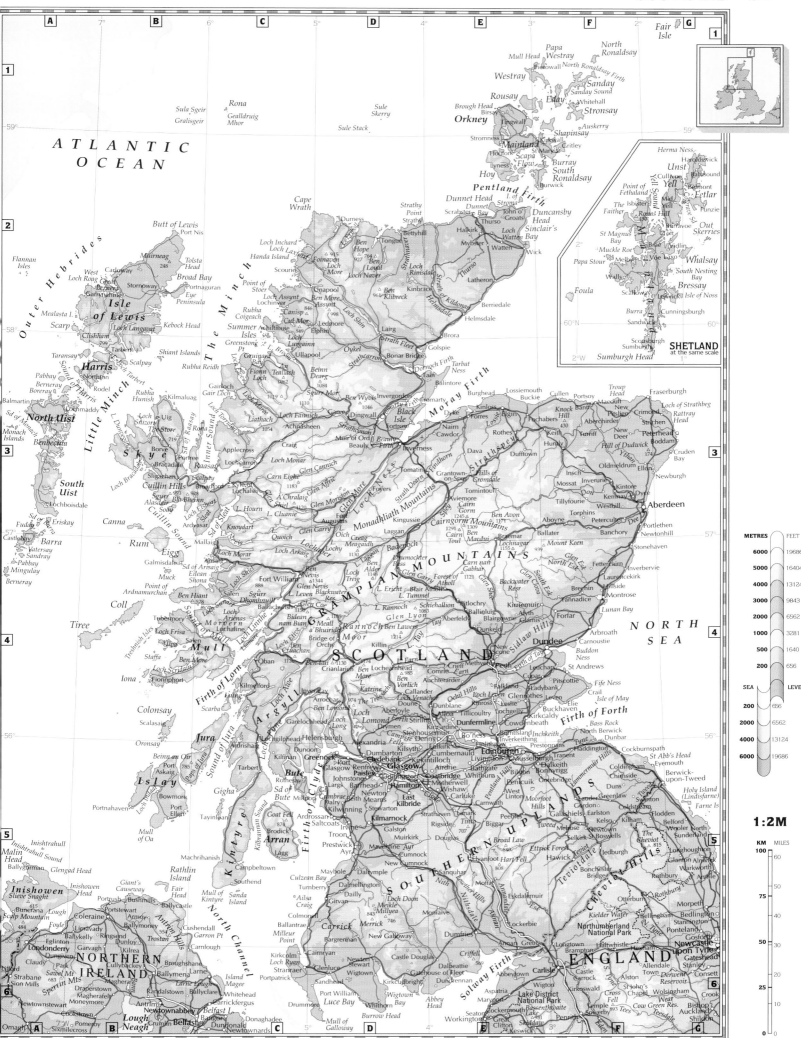

SHETLAND
at the same scale

1:2M

METRES		FEET
6000		19686
5000		16404
4000		13124
3000		9843
2000		6562
1000		3281
500		1640
200		656
SEA		LEVEL
200		656
2000		6562
4000		13124
6000		19686

KM	MILES
100	60
75	50
	40
50	30
	20
25	10
0	0

Conic Equidistant Projection

© Bartholomew Ltd

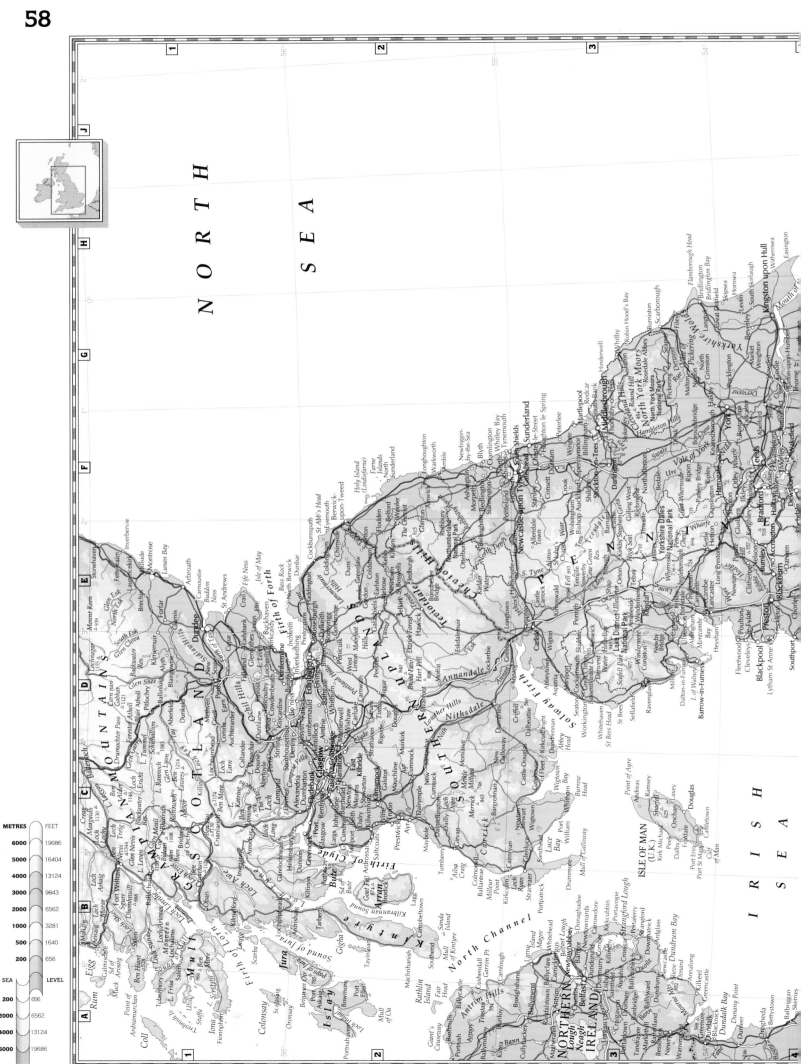

Conic Equidistant Projection

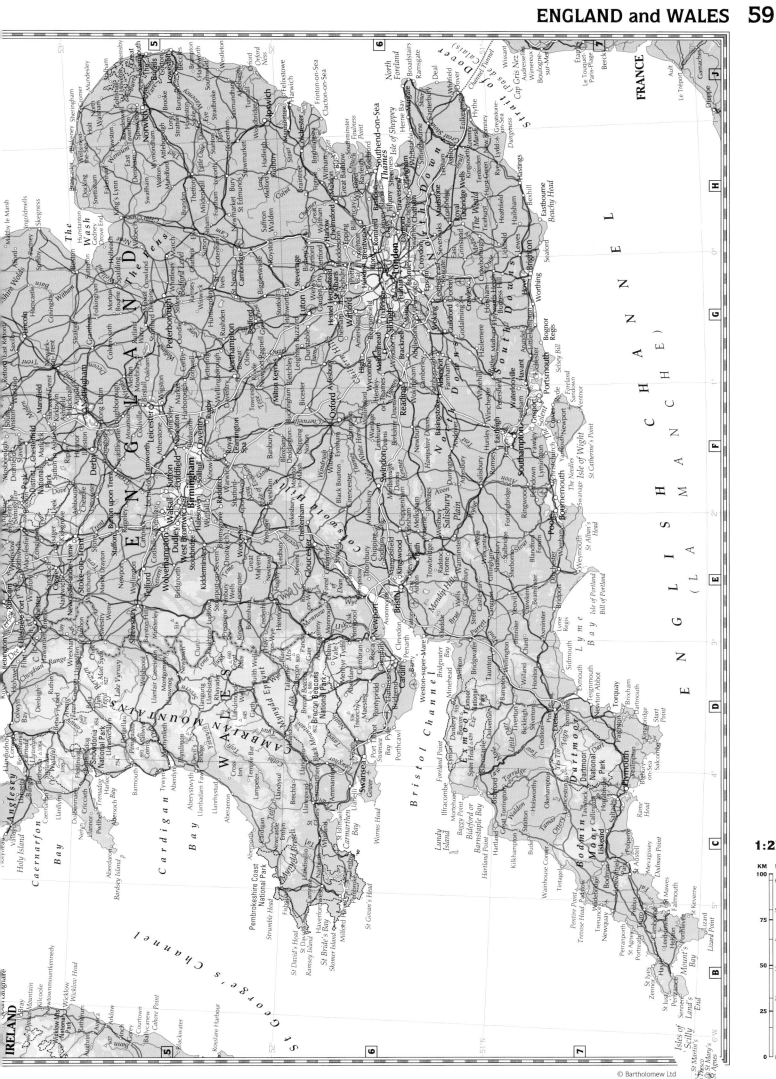

1:2M

1:2M

Conic Equidistant Projection

1:5M

KM   MILES
                200
300
                150
250
                100
200
150
                50
100
50
0

© Bartholomew Ltd

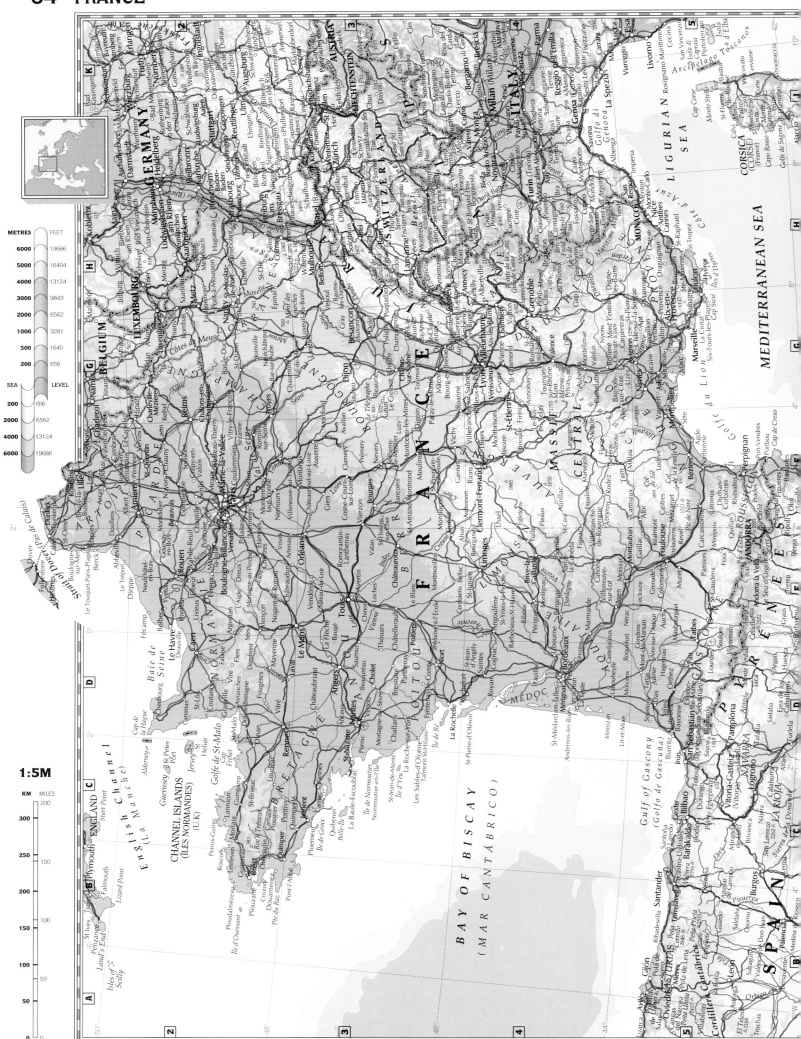

1:5M

Conic Equidistant Projection

© Bartholomew

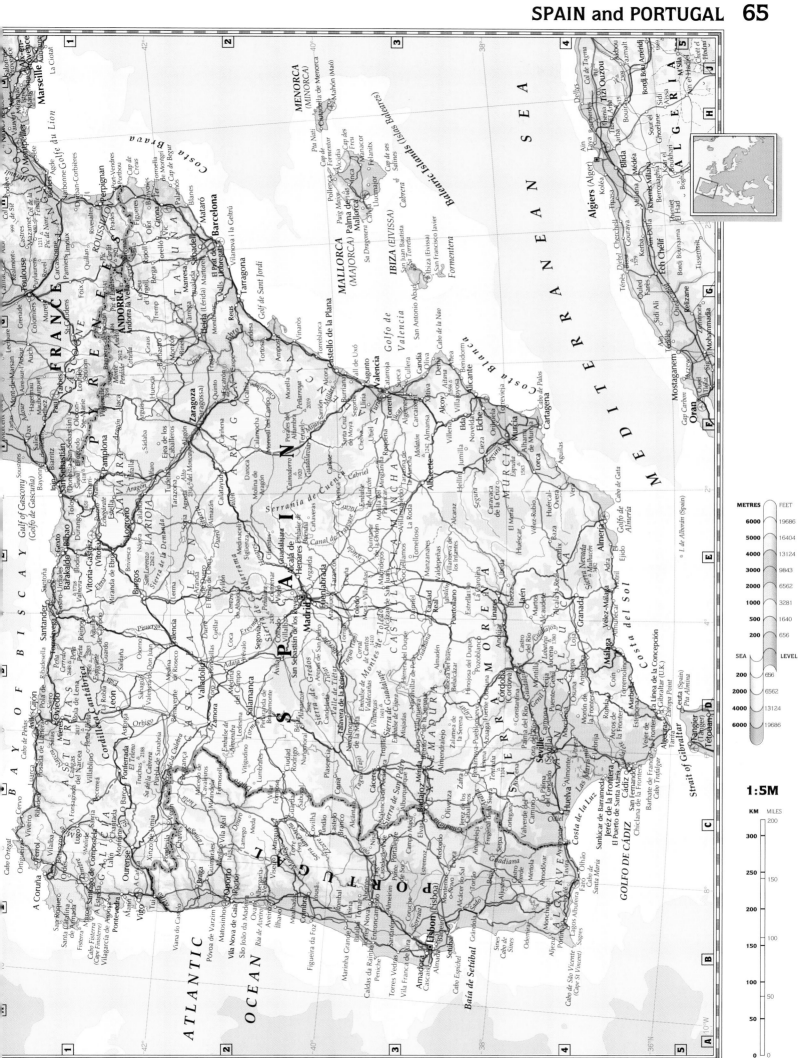

METRES   FEET

6000   19686
5000   16404
4000   13124
3000   9843
2000   6562
1000   3281
500   1640
200   656
SEA   LEVEL
200   656
2000   6562
4000   13124
6000   19686

1:5M

KM   MILES

Equidistant Projection   © Bartholomew Ltd

Conic Equidistant Projection

1:5M

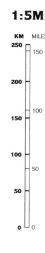

KM	MILES
250	150
200	100
150	
	50
100	
50	
0	0

Divides of Rus. Fed. not named on map

1. RESP. ADYGEYA (G6)
2. RESP. SEVERNAYA OSETIYA (H7)
3. INGUSHSKAYA RESP. (H7)

1:7M

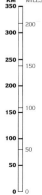

KM   MILES
350
          200
300
250   150
200
150   100
100
          50
50
0

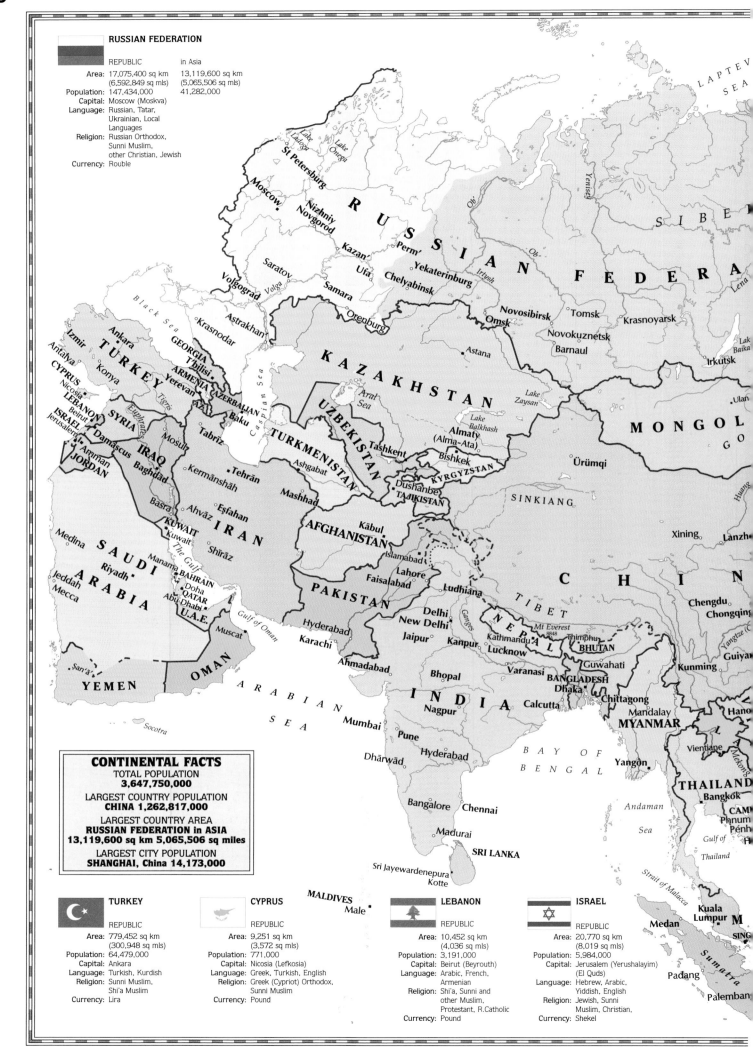

RUSSIAN FEDERATION

REPUBLIC in Asia

Area: 17,075,400 sq km 13,119,600 sq km
(6,592,849 sq mls) (5,065,506 sq mls)
Population: 147,434,000 41,282,000
Capital: Moscow (Moskva)
Language: Russian, Tatar, Ukrainian, Local Languages
Religion: Russian Orthodox, Sunni Muslim, other Christian, Jewish
Currency: Rouble

CONTINENTAL FACTS

TOTAL POPULATION
3,647,750,000

LARGEST COUNTRY POPULATION
CHINA 1,262,817,000

LARGEST COUNTRY AREA
RUSSIAN FEDERATION in ASIA
13,119,600 sq km 5,065,506 sq miles

LARGEST CITY POPULATION
SHANGHAI, China 14,173,000

TURKEY

REPUBLIC

Area: 779,452 sq km
(300,948 sq mls)
Population: 64,479,000
Capital: Ankara
Language: Turkish, Kurdish
Religion: Sunni Muslim, Shi'a Muslim
Currency: Lira

CYPRUS

REPUBLIC

Area: 9,251 sq km
(3,572 sq mls)
Population: 771,000
Capital: Nicosia (Lefkosia)
Language: Greek, Turkish, English
Religion: Greek (Cypriot) Orthodox, Sunni Muslim
Currency: Pound

LEBANON

REPUBLIC

Area: 10,452 sq km
(4,036 sq mls)
Population: 3,191,000
Capital: Beirut (Beyrouth)
Language: Arabic, French, Armenian
Religion: Shi'a, Sunni and other Muslim, Protestant, R.Catholic
Currency: Pound

ISRAEL

REPUBLIC

Area: 20,770 sq km
(8,019 sq mls)
Population: 5,984,000
Capital: Jerusalem (Yerushalayim) (El Quds)
Language: Hebrew, Arabic, Yiddish, English
Religion: Jewish, Sunni Muslim, Christian,
Currency: Shekel

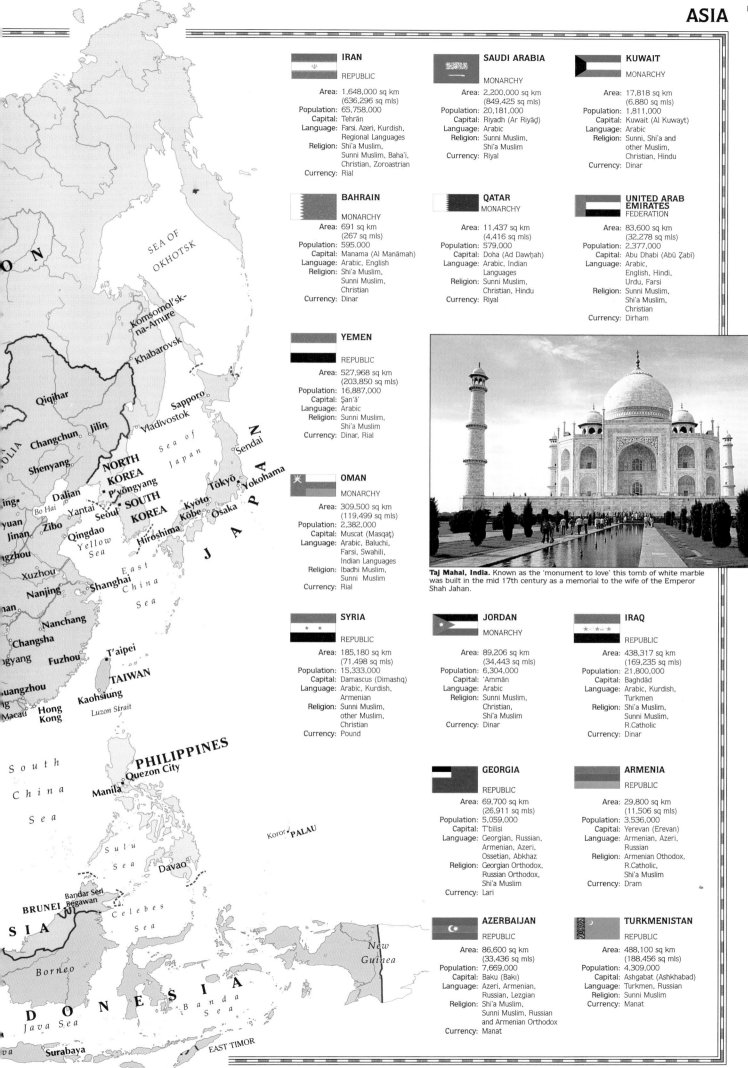

IRAN
REPUBLIC

Area: 1,648,000 sq km
(636,296 sq mls)
Population: 65,758,000
Capital: Tehrān
Language: Farsi, Azeri, Kurdish,
Regional Languages
Religion: Shi'a Muslim,
Sunni Muslim, Baha'i,
Christian, Zoroastrian
Currency: Rial

SAUDI ARABIA
MONARCHY

Area: 2,200,000 sq km
(849,425 sq mls)
Population: 20,181,000
Capital: Riyadh (Ar Riyāḍ)
Language: Arabic
Religion: Sunni Muslim,
Shi'a Muslim
Currency: Riyal

KUWAIT
MONARCHY

Area: 17,818 sq km
(6,880 sq mls)
Population: 1,811,000
Capital: Kuwait (Al Kuwayt)
Language: Arabic
Religion: Sunni, Shi'a and
other Muslim,
Christian, Hindu
Currency: Dinar

BAHRAIN
MONARCHY

Area: 691 sq km
(267 sq mls)
Population: 595,000
Capital: Manama (Al Manāmah)
Language: Arabic, English
Religion: Shi'a Muslim,
Sunni Muslim,
Christian
Currency: Dinar

QATAR
MONARCHY

Area: 11,437 sq km
(4,416 sq mls)
Population: 579,000
Capital: Doha (Ad Dawḥah)
Language: Arabic, Indian
Languages
Religion: Sunni Muslim,
Christian, Hindu
Currency: Riyal

UNITED ARAB EMIRATES
FEDERATION

Area: 83,600 sq km
(32,278 sq mls)
Population: 2,377,000
Capital: Abu Dhabi (Abū Ẓabī)
Language: Arabic,
English, Hindi,
Urdu, Farsi
Religion: Sunni Muslim,
Shi'a Muslim,
Christian
Currency: Dirham

YEMEN
REPUBLIC

Area: 527,968 sq km
(203,850 sq mls)
Population: 16,887,000
Capital: Ṣan'ā'
Language: Arabic
Religion: Sunni Muslim,
Shi'a Muslim
Currency: Dinar, Rial

Taj Mahal, India. Known as the 'monument to love' this tomb of white marble
was built in the mid 17th century as a memorial to the wife of the Emperor
Shah Jahan.

OMAN
MONARCHY

Area: 309,500 sq km
(119,499 sq mls)
Population: 2,382,000
Capital: Muscat (Masqaṭ)
Language: Arabic, Baluchi,
Farsi, Swahili,
Indian Languages
Religion: Ibadhi Muslim,
Sunni Muslim
Currency: Rial

SYRIA
REPUBLIC

Area: 185,180 sq km
(71,498 sq mls)
Population: 15,333,000
Capital: Damascus (Dimashq)
Language: Arabic, Kurdish,
Armenian
Religion: Sunni Muslim,
other Muslim,
Christian
Currency: Pound

JORDAN
MONARCHY

Area: 89,206 sq km
(34,443 sq mls)
Population: 6,304,000
Capital: 'Ammān
Language: Arabic
Religion: Sunni Muslim,
Christian,
Shi'a Muslim
Currency: Dinar

IRAQ
REPUBLIC

Area: 438,317 sq km
(169,235 sq mls)
Population: 21,800,000
Capital: Baghdād
Language: Arabic, Kurdish,
Turkmen
Religion: Shi'a Muslim,
Sunni Muslim,
R.Catholic
Currency: Dinar

GEORGIA
REPUBLIC

Area: 69,700 sq km
(26,911 sq mls)
Population: 5,059,000
Capital: T'bilisi
Language: Georgian, Russian,
Armenian, Azeri,
Ossetian, Abkhaz
Religion: Georgian Orthodox,
Russian Orthodox,
Shi'a Muslim
Currency: Lari

ARMENIA
REPUBLIC

Area: 29,800 sq km
(11,506 sq mls)
Population: 3,536,000
Capital: Yerevan (Erevan)
Language: Armenian, Azeri,
Russian
Religion: Armenian Othodox,
R.Catholic,
Shi'a Muslim
Currency: Dram

AZERBAIJAN
REPUBLIC

Area: 86,600 sq km
(33,436 sq mls)
Population: 7,669,000
Capital: Baku (Bakı)
Language: Azeri, Armenian,
Russian, Lezgian
Religion: Shi'a Muslim,
Sunni Muslim, Russian
and Armenian Orthodox
Currency: Manat

TURKMENISTAN
REPUBLIC

Area: 488,100 sq km
(188,456 sq mls)
Population: 4,309,000
Capital: Ashgabat (Ashkhabad)
Language: Turkmen, Russian
Religion: Sunni Muslim
Currency: Manat

KAZAKHSTAN
REPUBLIC

Area: 2,717,300 sq km
(1,049,155 sq mls)
Population: 16,319,000
Capital: Astana (Akmola)
Language: Kazakh, Russian,
German, Ukrainian,
Uzbek, Tatar
Religion: Sunni Muslim, Russian
Orthodox, Protestant
Currency: Tanga

KYRGYZSTAN
REPUBLIC

Area: 198,500 sq km
(76,641 sq mls)
Population: 4,643,000
Capital: Bishkek (Frunze)
Language: Kirghiz, Russian,
Uzbek
Religion: Sunni Muslim,
Russian Orthodox
Currency: Som

AFGHANISTAN
REPUBLIC

Area: 652,225 sq km
(251,825 sq mls)
Population: 21,354,000
Capital: Kābul
Language: Dari, Pushtu,
Uzbek, Turkmen
Religion: Sunni Muslim,
Shi'a Muslim
Currency: Afghani

UZBEKISTAN
REPUBLIC

Area: 447,400 sq km
(172,742 sq mls)
Population: 23,574,000
Capital: Tashkent
Language: Uzbek, Russian,
Tajik, Kazakh
Religion: Sunni Muslim
Russian Orthodox
Currency: Som

TAJIKISTAN
REPUBLIC

Area: 143,100 sq km
(55,251 sq mls)
Population: 6,015,000
Capital: Dushanbe
Language: Tajik, Uzbek,
Russian
Religion: Sunni Muslim
Currency: Rouble

PAKISTAN
REPUBLIC

Area: 803,940 sq km
(310,403 sq mls)
Population: 148,166,000
Capital: Islamabad
Language: Urdu (official),
Punjabi, Sindhi,
Pushtu, English
Religion: Sunni Muslim,
Shi'a Muslim,
Christian, Hindu
Currency: Rupee

Great Wall of China. Stretching 3460 km, this is the longest wall in
the world and dates from the 3rdC BC.

MYANMAR
REPUBLIC

Area: 676,577 sq km
(261,228 sq mls)
Population: 44,497,000
Capital: Yangôn (Rangoon)
Language: Burmese, Shan,
Karen, Local Languages
Religion: Buddhist, Sunni Muslim,
Protestant, R.Catholic
Currency: Kyat

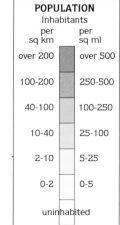

St. Petersburg
Moscow
Ankara
Baghdād
Tehrān
Eşfahan
Kābul
Riyadh
Lahore
Delhi
Lucknow
Karachi
Ahmadabad
Calcutta
Mumbai
Chittag
Pune
Hyderabad
Bangalore
Chennai

Japan. The speedy 'Bullet train' travels past Mount Fuji, a volcano which last erupted in 1707.

INDIA
REPUBLIC

Area: 3,065,027 sq km
(1,183,414 sq mls)
Population: 982,223,000
Capital: New Delhi
Language: Hindi, English (official),
Many Regional Languages
Religion: Hindu, Sunni Muslim,
Sikh, Christian,
Buddhist, Jain
Currency: Rupee

NEPAL
MONARCHY

Area: 147,181 sq km
(56,827 sq mls)
Population: 22,847,000
Capital: Kathmandu
Language: Nepali, Maithili,
Bhojpuri, English,
Many Local Languages
Religion: Hindu, Buddhist,
Sunni Muslim
Currency: Rupee

SRI LANKA
REPUBLIC

Area: 65,610 sq km
(25,332 sq mls)
Population: 18,455,000
Capital: Sri Jayewardenepura
Kotte
Language: Sinhalese, Tamil,
English
Religion: Buddhist, Hindu,
Sunni Muslim,
R. Catholic
Currency: Rupee

BHUTAN
MONARCHY

Area: 46,620 sq km
(18,000 sq mls)
Population: 2,004,000
Capital: Thimphu
Language: Dzongkha, Nepali
Assamese, English
Religion: Buddhist, Hindu
Currency: Ngultrum,
Indian Rupee

MALDIVES
REPUBLIC

Area: 298 sq km
(115 sq mls)
Population: 271,000
Capital: Male
Language: Divehi (Maldivian)
Religion: Sunni Muslim
Currency: Rufiyaa

BANGLADESH
REPUBLIC

Area: 143,998 sq km
(55,598 sq mls)
Population: 124,774,000
Capital: Dhaka (Dacca)
Language: Bengali, Bihari,
Hindi, English,
Local Languages
Religion: Sunni Muslim, Hindu,
Buddhist, Christian
Currency: Taka

POPULATION
Inhabitants

per sq km	per sq ml
over 200	over 500
100-200	250-500
40-100	100-250
10-40	25-100
2-10	5-25
0-2	0-5
uninhabited	

CITIES
• Over 5 million
population
• 2.5 - 5 million
population

THAILAND
MONARCHY
Area: 513,115 sq km
(198,115 sq mls)
Population: 60,300,000
Capital: Bangkok (Krung Thep)
Language: Thai, Lao, Chinese,
Malay,
Mon-Khmer Languages
Religion: Buddhist,
Sunni Muslim
Currency: Baht

LAOS
REPUBLIC
Area: 236,800 sq km
(91,429 sq mls)
Population: 5,163,000
Capital: Vientiane (Viangchan)
Language: Lao, Local Languages
Religion: Buddhist,
Trad. Beliefs,
R.Catholic,
Sunni Muslim
Currency: Kip

CAMBODIA
MONARCHY
Area: 181,000 sq km
(69,884 sq mls)
Population: 10,716,000
Capital: Phnum Pénh
(Phnom Penh)
Language: Khmer,
Vietnamese
Religion: Buddhist, R.Catholic,
Sunni Muslim
Currency: Riel

VIETNAM
REPUBLIC
Area: 329,565 sq km
(127,246 sq mls)
Population: 77,562,000
Capital: Ha Nôi (Hanoi)
Language: Vietnamese, Thai,
Khmer, Chinese, Many
Local Languages
Religion: Buddhist, Taoist,
R.Catholic, Cao Dai
Currency: Dong

CHINA
REPUBLIC
Area: 9,584,492 sq km
(3,700,593 sq mls)
Population: 1,262,817,000
Capital: Beijing (Peking)
Language: Chinese (Mandarin
official), Many
Regional Languages
Religion: Confucian, Taoist, Buddhist,
Sunni Muslim, R.Catholic
Currency: Yuan

OPULATION

MONGOLIA
REPUBLIC
Area: 1,565,000 sq km
(604,250 sq mls)
Population: 2,579,000
Capital: Ulaanbaatar
(Ulan Bator)
Language: Khalka (Mongolian),
Kazakh, Local Languages
Religion: Buddhist, Sunni Muslim,
Trad. Beliefs
Currency: Tugrik

NORTH KOREA
REPUBLIC
Area: 120,538 sq km
(46,540 sq mls)
Population: 23,348,000
Capital: P'yŏngyang
Language: Korean
Religion: Trad. Beliefs,
Chondoist, Buddhist,
Confucian, Taoist
Currency: Won

SOUTH KOREA
REPUBLIC
Area: 99,274 sq km
(38,330 sq mls)
Population: 46,109,000
Capital: Seoul (Sŏul)
Language: Korean
Religion: Buddhist, Protestant,
R.Catholic, Confucian,
Trad. Beliefs
Currency: Won

JAPAN
MONARCHY
Area: 377,727 sq km
(145,841 sq mls)
Population: 126,281,000
Capital: Tōkyō
Language: Japanese
Religion: Shintoist, Buddhist,
Christian
Currency: Yen

TAIWAN
REPUBLIC
Area: 36,179 sq km
(13,969 sq mls)
Population: 21,908,000
Capital: T'aipei
Language: Chinese (Mandarin
official, Fukien,
Hakka), Local Languages
Religion: Buddhist, Taoist,
Confucian, Christian
Currency: Dollar

Harbin
Changchun
Shenyang
Pyŏngyang Tōkyō
Beijing
Dalian Seoul Nagoya
Tianjin Inch'ŏn Taegu
Handan Jinan Osaka
Pusan
Qingdao Kita-Kyūshū
Xi'an
Nanjing
Chengdu Shanghai
Wuhan Hangzhou
Chongqing
T'aipei
Guangzhou
Hong Kong
Ha Nôi
gon
Bangkok
Manila

Singapore

Jakarta Surabaya
Bandung

Hong Kong. A traditional Chinese sailing ship, known as a junk, sails in the spectacular harbour.

BRUNEI
MONARCHY
Area: 5,765 sq km
(2,226 sq mls)
Population: 315,000
Capital: Bandar Seri Begawan
Language: Malay, English,
Chinese
Religion: Sunni Muslim,
Buddhist, Christian
Currency: Dollar (Ringgit)

PHILIPPINES
REPUBLIC
Area: 300,000 sq km
(115,831 sq mls)
Population: 72,944,000
Capital: Manila
Language: English, Filipino
(Tagalog), Cebuano
Religion: R.Catholic, Aglipayan,
Sunni Muslim,
Protestant
Currency: Peso

PALAU
REPUBLIC
Area: 497 sq km
(192 sq mls)
Population: 19,000
Capital: Koror
Language: Palauan, English
Religion: R.Catholic, Protestant,
Trad. Beliefs
Currency: US Dollar

MALAYSIA
FEDERATION
Area: 332,965 sq km
(128,559 sq mls)
Population: 21,410,000
Capital: Kuala Lumpur
Language: Malay, English,
Chinese, Tamil,
Local Languages
Religion: Sunni Muslim,
Buddhist, Hindu,
Christian, Trad. Beliefs
Currency: Dollar (Ringgit)

SINGAPORE
REPUBLIC
Area: 639 sq km
(247 sq mls)
Population: 3,476,000
Capital: Singapore
Language: Chinese, English,
Malay, Tamil
Religion: Buddhist, Taoist,
Sunni Muslim,
Christian, Hindu
Currency: Dollar

INDONESIA
REPUBLIC
Area: 1,919,445 sq km
(741,102 sq mls)
Population: 206,338,000
Capital: Jakarta
Language: Indonesian (official),
Many Local Languages
Religion: Sunni Muslim, Protestant,
R.Catholic, Hindu,
Buddhist
Currency: Rupiah

Vietnam. Rice is grown in irrigated paddy fields throughout lowland equatorial Asia.

CONTINENTAL FACTS
TOTAL AREA
45,036,492 sq km   17,388,686 sq miles
HIGHEST PEAK, MT EVEREST
8,848 m   29,028 ft
LARGEST LAKE, CASPIAN SEA (salt)
371,000 sq km   143,243 sq miles
LONGEST RIVER, YANGTZE (CHANG JIANG)
6,380 km   3,964 miles

ARCTIC OCEAN

Franz Josef Land

Severnaya Zemlya

New Siberia Islands

Wrangel I.

LAPTEV SEA

Kolyma Range

Novaya Zemlya

Taymyr Peninsula

Verkhoyansk Range

SEA OK

Lake Ladoga

Lake Onega

Ural Mountains

West Siberian Plain

Central Siberian Plateau

Dzhugdzhur Range

Central Russian Uplands

Irtysh

Ob'

Yenisey

Lena

Stanovoy Range

Don

Volga

Black Sea

Lake Baikal

Da Hinggan Ling

Elbrus Caucasus

Caspian Sea

Aral Sea

Yenisey

Taurus Mts

L. Zaysan

Lake Balkhash

Altai Mts

GOBI

Tien Shan

Huang He

Taihang Shan

Bo Hai

Yellow Sea

Tigris

Euphrates

Elburz Mts

Amudar'ya

Zagros Mountains

Dasht-e Kavir

Hindu Kush

Karakoram

K2

Taklimakan Desert

Kunlun Shan

Plateau of Tibet

East Chi Se

An Nafud

Helmand

Sulaiman Ranges

Indus

Sutlej

HIMALAYA

Annapurna I

Mt. Everest

Yangtze (Chang Jiang)

Hijaz

'Asir

Makran

Thar Desert

Narmada

Ganges

Brahmaputra

Nan Ling

Xi Jiang

Taiwa

The Gulf

Gulf of Oman

Rub'al Khali

Maşirah

Mouths of the Ganges

Irrawaddy

Hainan

Luzon

ARABIAN SEA

Western Ghats

Eastern Ghats

Bay of Bengal

South China Sea

Socotra

Laccadive Is

Andaman Islands

Andaman Sea

Mekong

Luzon Strait

Sri Lanka

Gulf of Thailand

Palawan

Sulu Sea

Maldives

Nicobar Islands

Strait of Malacca

Peninsular Malaysia

Cele S

INDIAN OCEAN

Mentawai Islands

Sumatra

Borneo

Sula

Chagos Archipelago

Java Sea

Java

Bali

Lombok

Mt Everest. Rising to 8848m, this peak is the Earth's highest point.

CLIMATE

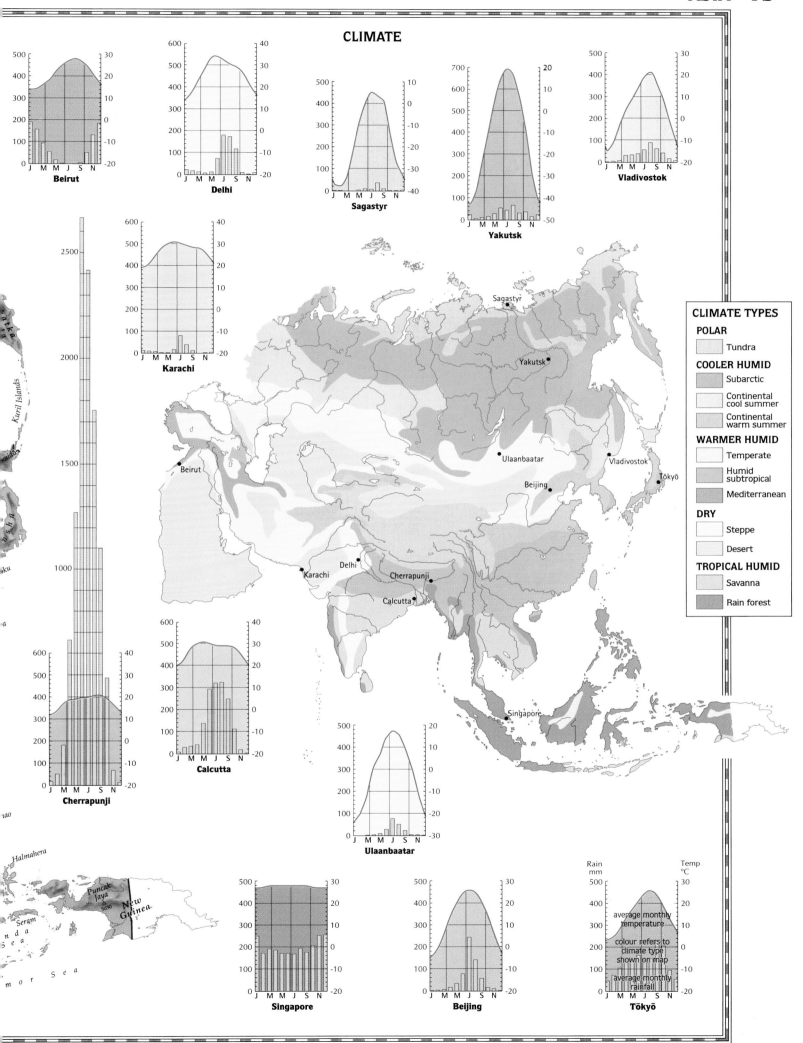

Beirut

Delhi

Sagastyr

Yakutsk

Vladivostok

Karachi

CLIMATE TYPES

POLAR
Tundra

COOLER HUMID
Subarctic
Continental cool summer
Continental warm summer

WARMER HUMID
Temperate
Humid subtropical
Mediterranean

DRY
Steppe
Desert

TROPICAL HUMID
Savanna
Rain forest

Cherrapunji

Calcutta

Ulaanbaatar

Singapore

Beijing

Rain mm
Temp °C

average monthly temperature

colour refers to climate type shown on map

average monthly rainfall

Tōkyō

© Bartholomew Ltd

1:21M

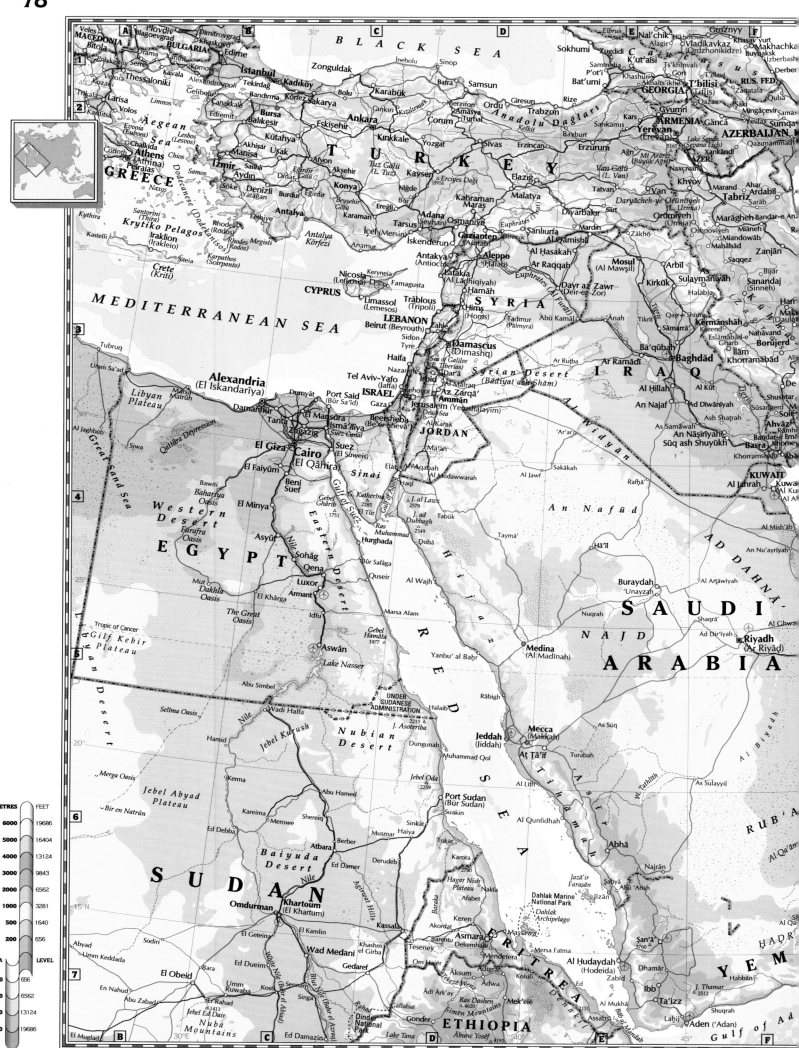

Albers Equal Area Conic Projection

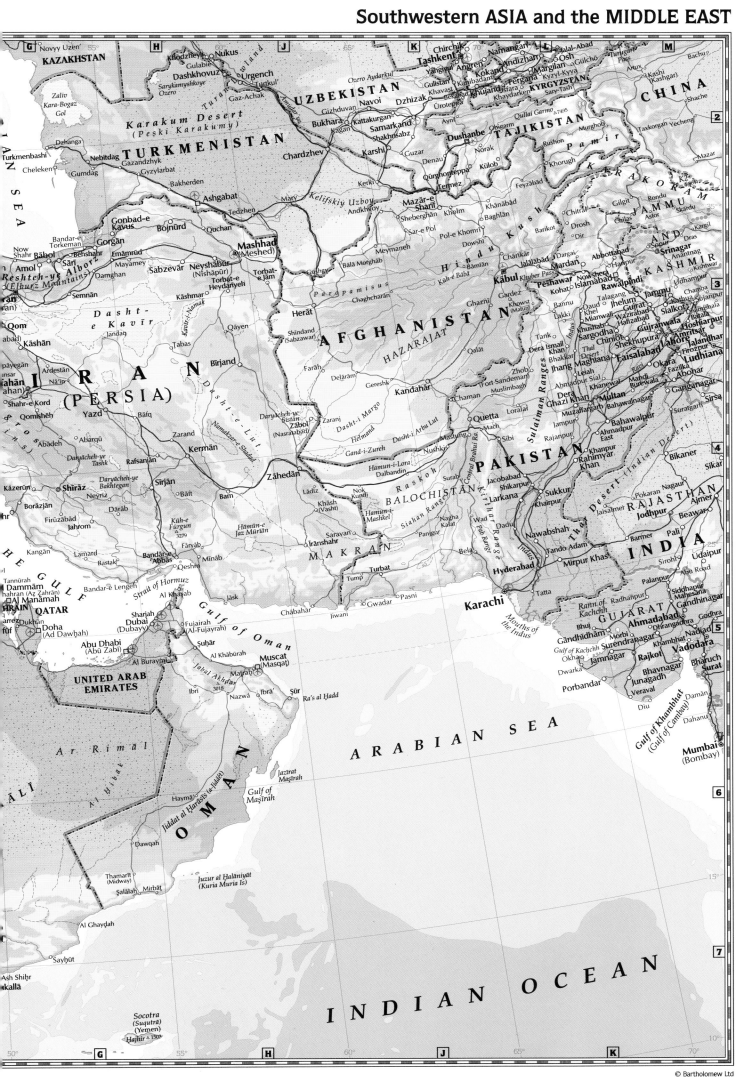

KAZAKHSTAN

Novyy Uzen'
Gulabie
Khodzheyli Nukus
Dashkhovuz Urgench
Sarykamyshkoye Turkul'
Zaliv Ozero
Kara-Bogaz Gaz-Achak
Gol
Dzhanga

Turkmenbashi
Cheleken
Nebitdag Gazandzhyk
Gumdag Gyzylarbat
Bakherden
Bandar-e Ashgabat
Torkeman Tedzhen
Now Gonbad-e Mary Kelifskiy Uzboy
Shahr Kavus Quchan
Amol Gorgan Bojnūrd
Behshahr Mayamey
Sārī Emāmrūd
Reshteh-ye Damghan Sabzevār Neyshābūr
Alborz (Nishāpūr)
(Elburz Mountains) Semnān Kāshmar Torbat-e
Heydarīyeh

TURKMENISTAN

Karakum Desert
(Peski Karakumy)

Chardzhev
Kerki

UZBEKISTAN

Gizhduvan
Bukhara Navoi
Kagan Kattakurgan
Karshi Samarkand
Shakhrisabz
Guzar
Denau
Termez

Chirchik Namangan
Tashkent Andizhan
Yangiyūl Angren Kokand Osh
Gulistan Kambadam Fergana
Khavast Khūjand Isfara Margilan KYRGYZSTAN
Dzhizak Bekabad Khaydarken Sary-Tash
Ürotepp Ayni Obigarm Qullai Garmo ▲7495
Norak Pamir
Dushanbe TAJIKISTAN Murghob
Qŭrghonteppa Kūlob Khorugh Rushon

CHINA

Bachu
Jalal-Abad
Turugart Artux Kashi
Pass (Kashgar)
Shache

Mazar

Karshi
Sheberghan Khānābād
Sar-e Pol Baghlān
Dowshi Pol-e Khomrī
Pol-e Khomrī
Meymaneh Chārīkār
Bālā Morghāb

HINDU KUSH

Feyzābād
Khānābād
Kholm
Mazār-e Sharīf
Andkhvoy

Chitral Drosh
Barikot
Chilas Astor
Gilgit Skardu
Rondu K2
Kargil
Kishtwar

Mashhad (Meshed)

Torbat-e Jām

IRAN (PERSIA)

Qom
Kāshān
Ardestān
Nā'īn
Yazd Bāfq
Zarand
Kermān
Rafsanjān
Sirjān Bāft
Bam
Kūh-e Fūrgūn 3279
Bandar-e Mīnāb
Abbās Qeshm
Bandar-e Lengeh Jāsk

Dasht-e Kavīr
Jandaq
Tabas
Bīrjand

Chaghcharān

AFGHANISTAN
HAZARAJAT

Herāt
Shindand (Sabzawar)
Farāh Delārām
Gereshk
Kandahār
Zaranj Chaman
Dasht-i Margo
Helmand
Gand-i-Zureh

Kūh-e Bābā
Ghaznī
Gardēz
Khōst (Matūn)
Qalāt

Kabul Klyber Pass
Bāmīān Peshawar
Jalālābād Mardan
Charikar Kohat
Daud Bannu
Khel Lakki
Tank
Dera Ismail
Khan
Mianwali
Sargodha
Chiniot

Srinagar
Anantnag
KASHMIR
Abbottabad Udhampur
Talagang Jammu
Islāmābād Kathua
Rāwalpindi Sialkot
Gujrat Gujranwala
Hāfizābād Lahore
Shekhupura Amritsar
Faisalabad Jalandhar
Okara Ludhiana

Parapamisus

Qalāt
Zhob
(Fort Sandeman)
Muslimbagh Loralai

PAKISTAN

Quetta Mach
Nushki
Mastung

Sulaiman Ranges

Dera Jhang Maghiana
Ghazi Khan Khānewāl
Muzaffargarh Multan
Jampur Bahawalnagar
Rajanpur Bahawalpur
Ahmadpur
East

Khānpur
Rahīmyār Bīkaner
Khan

RAJASTHAN

Sīkar
Nāgaur Ajmer
Pokaran Beawar
Jaisalmer Jodhpur Pali
Barmer Sirohi
Udaipur

Ardestān
Shahr-e Kord
Kāzerūn
Borūjān
Borāzjān Firūzābād
Jahrom
Kangān Lamard Bastak
Fāryāb
Lār

Darāb
Neyrīz
Daryācheh-ye Bakhtegān
Daryācheh-ye Tashk

Daryācheh-ye Sīstān
(Nasrābād) Zābol
Dasht-i Arbu Lut
Nok Dalbandin
Kundi
Khāsh Hamun-i-Mashkel
(Vasht)
Lādīz Hamun-i-Lora

Zāhedān
Īrānshahr Saravan
MAKRAN Tump
Turbat

Sūrāb
Raskoh Kalat
Panjgur Bela
Gwadar Pasni
Jiwani Chābahār
Jāsk

Siahan Range

Central Brahui Ra
Kīrthar Range
Kalat
Wad
Pab Range
Nāl
Nagha

Khārān

Jacobabad
Shikarpur
Larkana Sukkur
Khairpur
Dadu
Nawabshah Khanpur

Thar Desert (Indian Desert)

Sūratgarh
Sirsa
Gangānagar
Abohar
Fāzilka
Mandi
Burewala

INDIA

Hyderabad
Tando Adam
Mirpur Khas

Karachi
Tatta Mouths of the Indus

Rann of Kachchh
Radhanpur
Gāndhīdhām Siddhapur Mahesana
Bhuj Mōrbi Gandhinagar
Dhrāngadhra Nadiad Godhra
Surendranagar Ahmadabad
Okha Khambhat Vadodara
Dwarka Rajkot Bharuch
Jāmnagar Bhavnagar Surat
Porbandar Junagadh
Veraval Diu Damān
Gulf of Kachchh
GUJARAT
Gulf of Khambhat Dahanu
(Gulf of Cambay)

Mumbai (Bombay)

THE GULF

Ra's Tannūrah
Ad Dammām (Az Zahrān)
Dhahran (Az Zahrān)
Al Manāmah
BAHRAIN
QATAR
Dukhān
Doha (Ad Dawhah)
Abu Dhabi (Abū Zabī)
Al Buraymī

Strait of Hormuz
Al Khasab
Shārjah Dubai (Dubayy)
Fujairah (Al-Fujayrah)
Suhār
Al Khābūrah
Muscat (Masqat)
Matrah

UNITED ARAB EMIRATES

Ibrī
Jabal Akhdar 3018
Nazwā Ibrā'
Sūr
Ra's al Hadd

OMAN

Ar Rimāl

Al Hibak

Haymā'
Jazīrat Masīrah
Gulf of Masīrah

Dawqah

Thamarīt (Midway)
Tiddat al Harāsīs (al-Jiddah)
Salālah Mirbāt
Juzur al Halānīyāt (Kuria Muria Is)

Al Ghaydah

Sayhūt

Ash Shihr
kalla

ARABIAN SEA

INDIAN OCEAN

Socotra (Suqutrā) (Yemen)
Hajhir ▲1503

© Bartholomew Ltd

1:12.5M

KM MILES
750 450
600 300
450 300
300 150
150
0 0

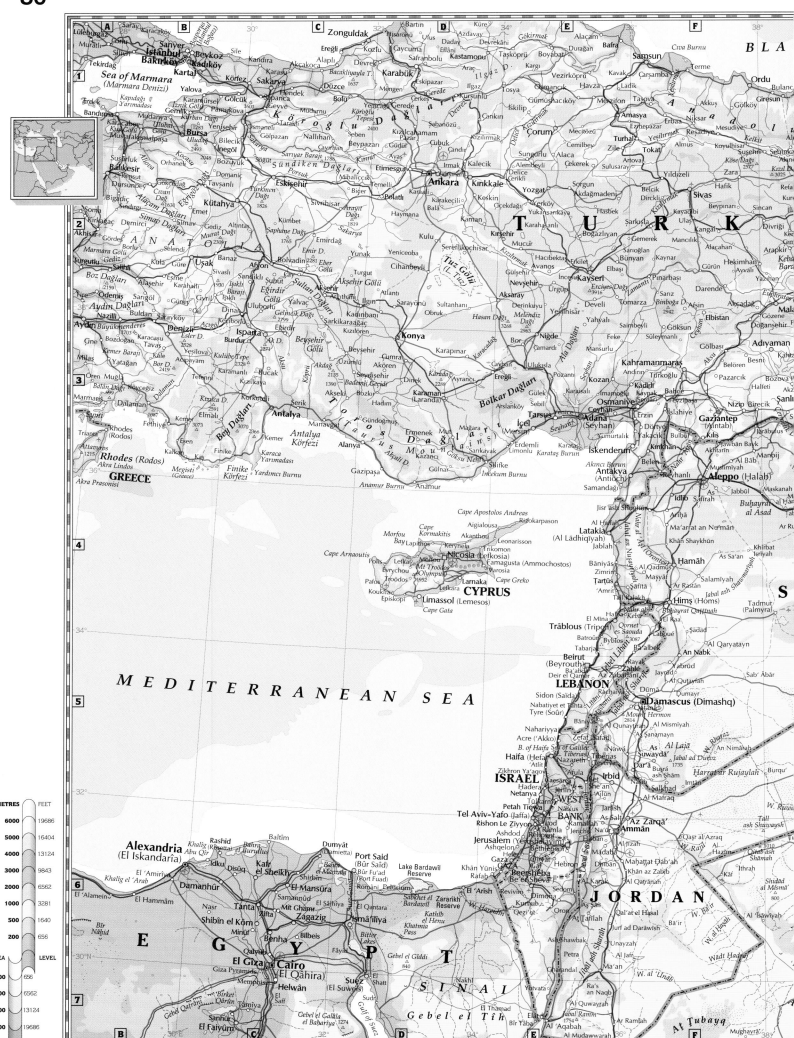

Conic Equidistant Projection

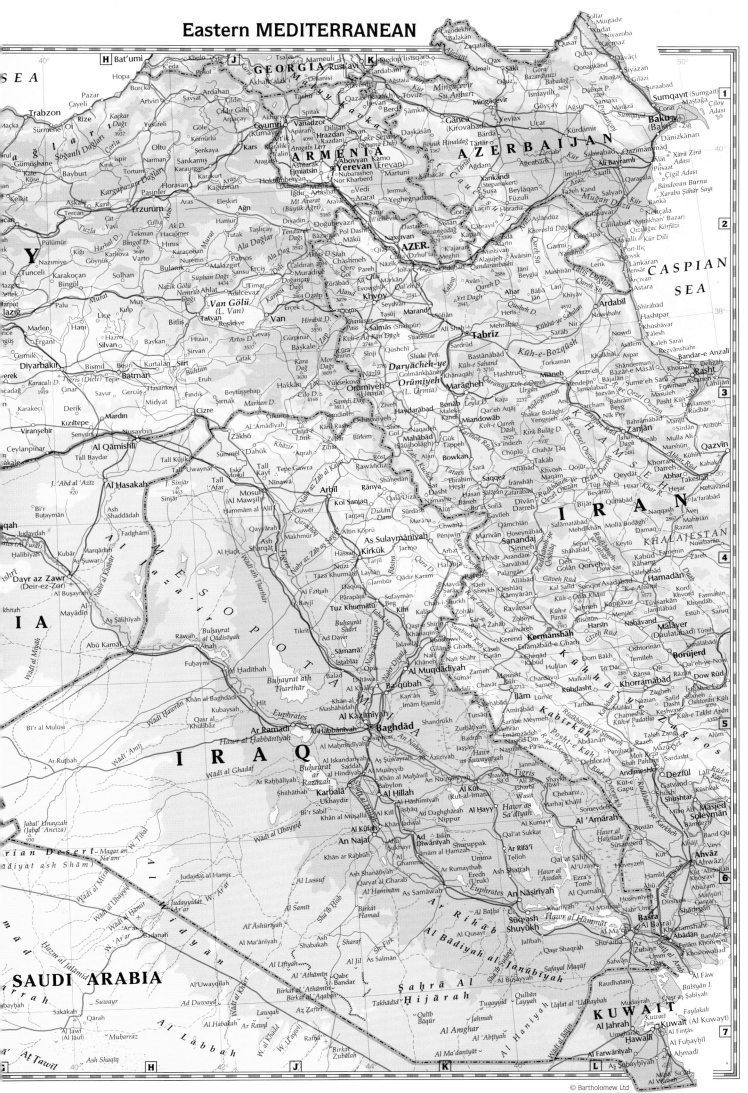

1:5M

KM MILES
300 — 200
— 150
250 —
200 — 100
150 —
100 — 50
50 —
0 — 0

© Bartholomew Ltd

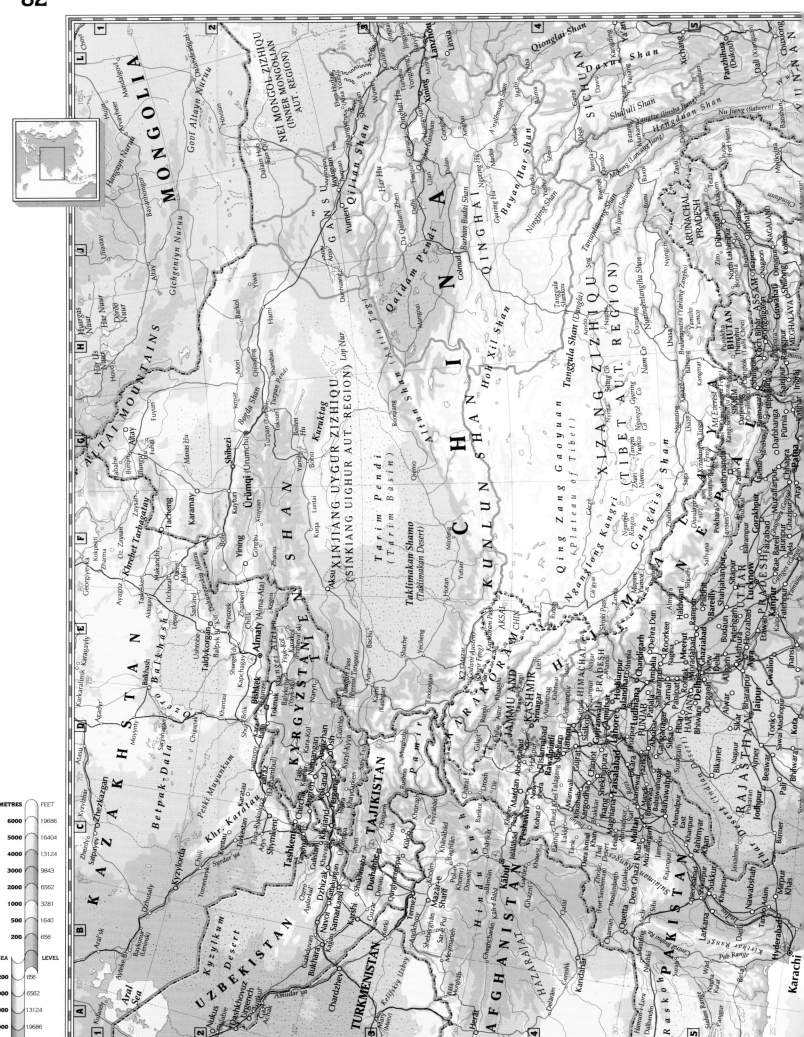

1:14M

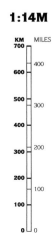

KM	MILES
700	
	400
600	
500	300
400	200
300	
200	100
100	
0	0

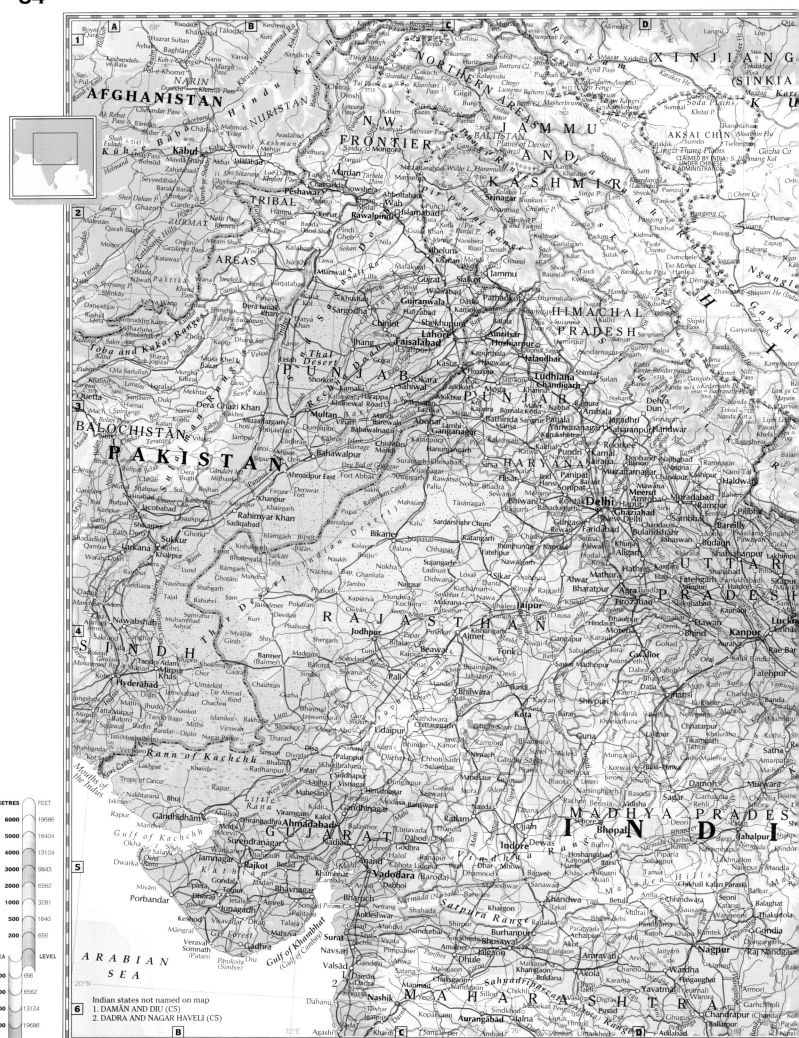

Conic Equidistant Projection

1:7M

Albers Equal Area Conic Projection

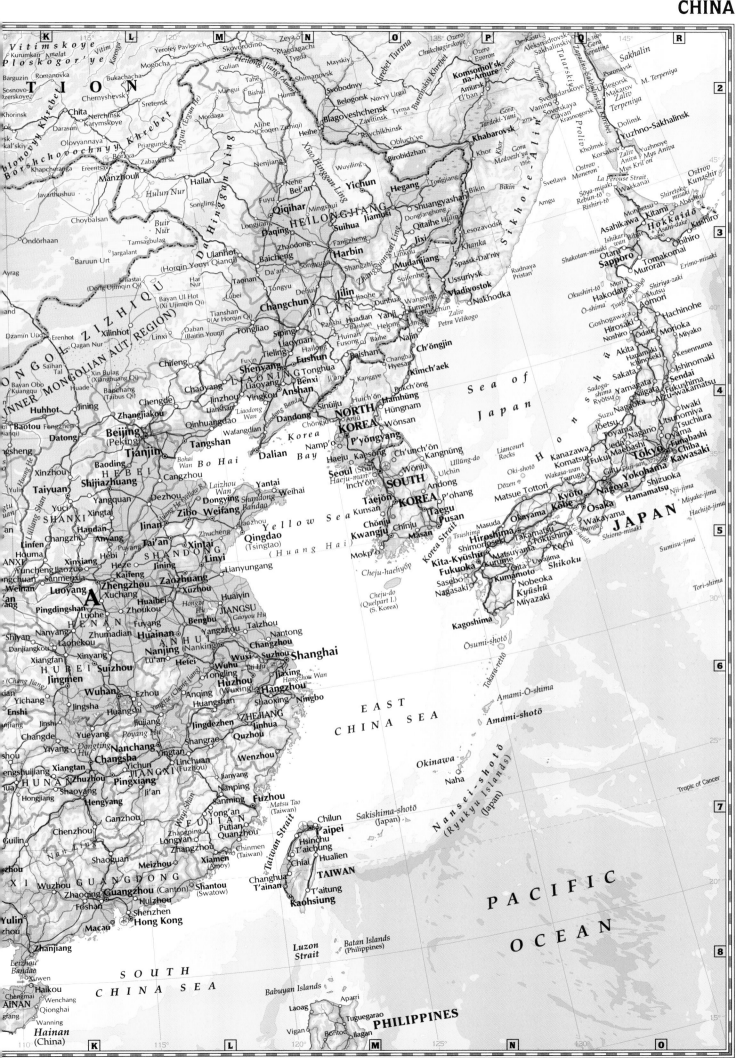

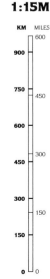

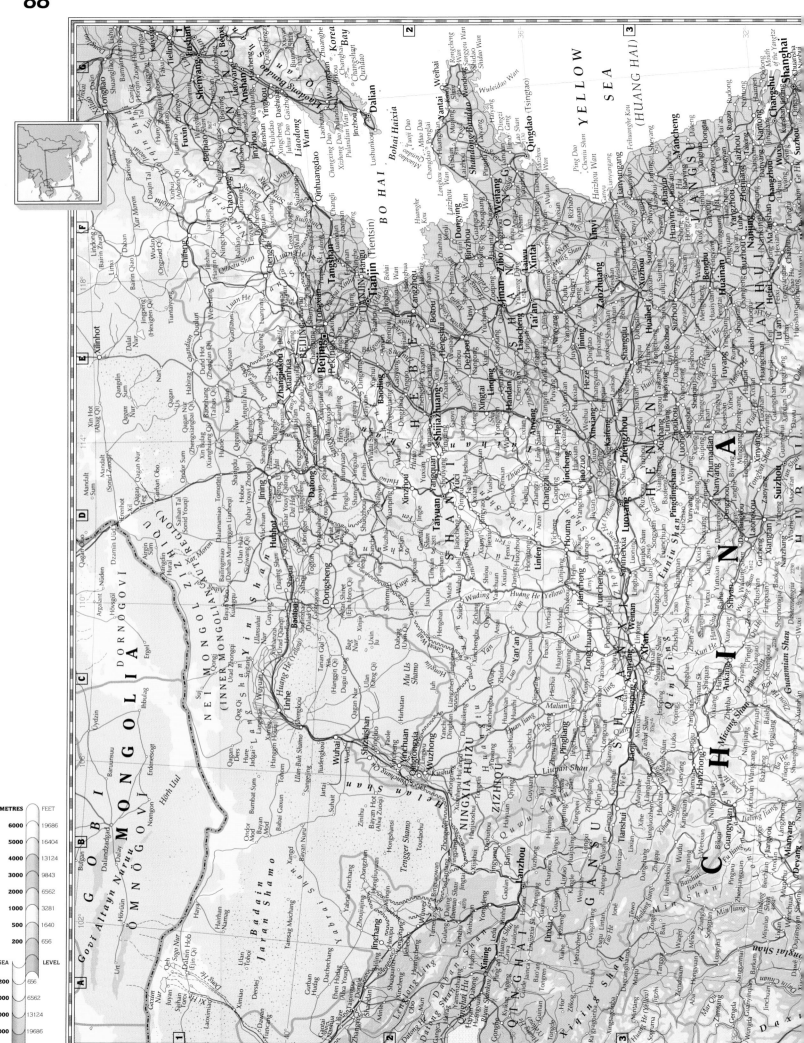

Conic Equidistant Projection

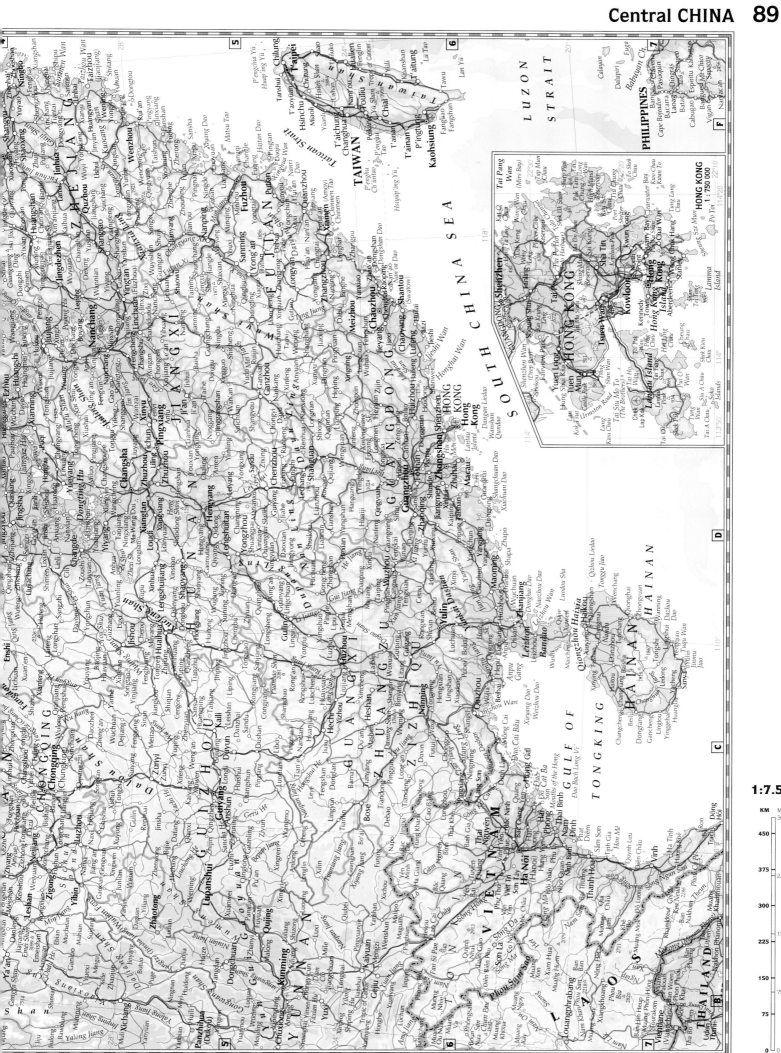

1:7.5M

KM	MILES
	300
450	
	225
375	
	150
300	
225	
	150
150	
	75
75	
0	0

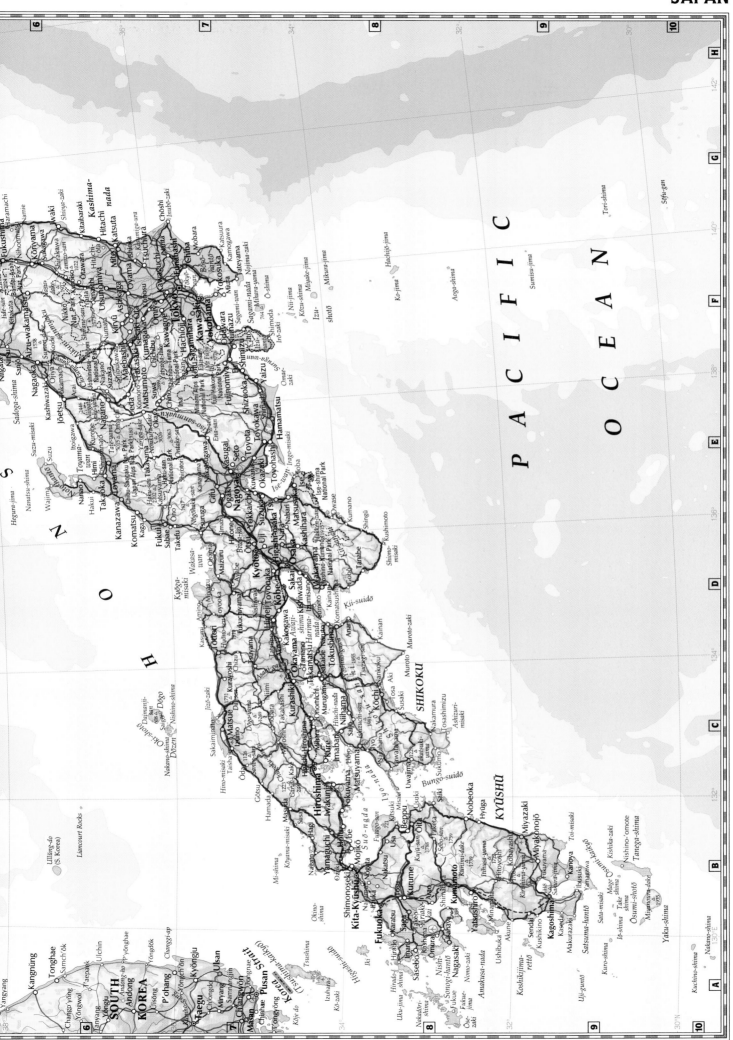

1:5M

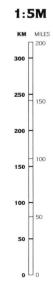

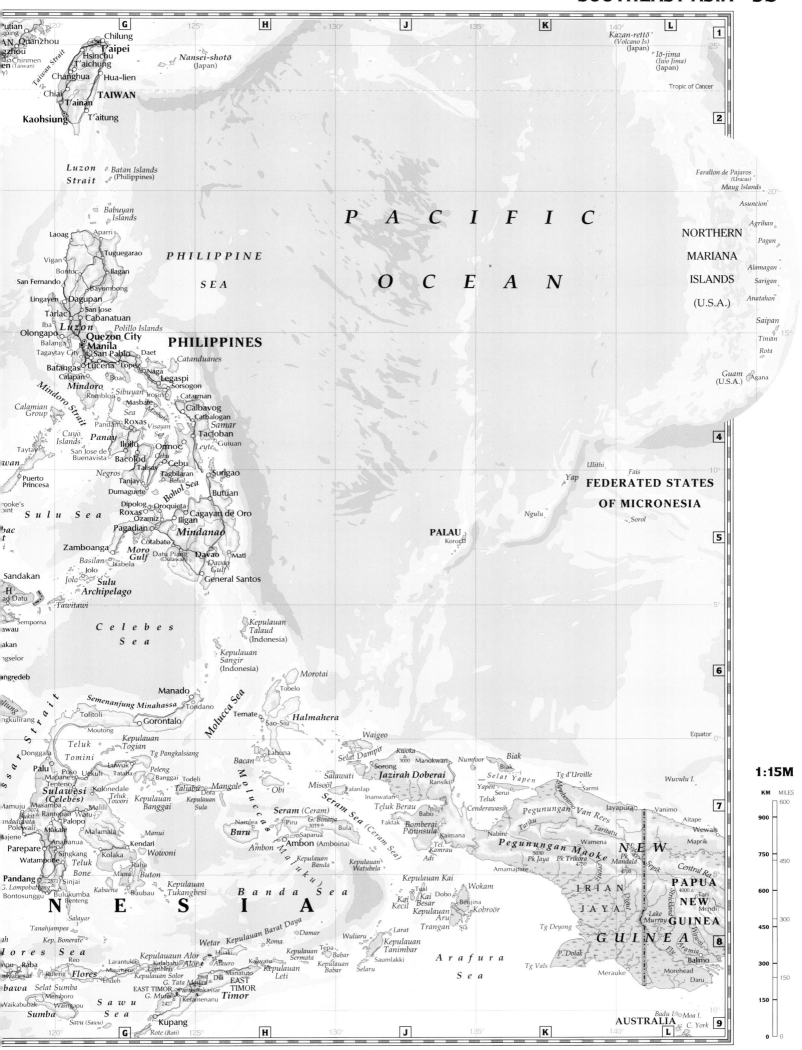

G H J K L

1

Chilung
T'aipei
Hsinchu
T'aichung Hua-lien
Changhua
Chiai
T'ainan T'aitung
TAIWAN
Kaohsiung

Quanzhou
Chinmen
(Taiwan)
Taiwan Strait

Nansei-shotō
(Japan)

Kazan-rettō
(Volcano Is)
(Japan)

Iō-jima
(Iwo Jima)
(Japan)

Tropic of Cancer

2

Luzon
Strait

Batan Islands
(Philippines)

Farallon de Pajaros
(Uracas)

Maug Islands

Asuncion

P A C I F I C

Babuyan
Islands

Laoag Aparri
Vigan Tuguegarao
Bontoc Ilagan
San Fernando
Lingayen Dagupan
Tarlac San Jose
Iba Cabanatuan
Olongapo **Luzon**
Balanga **Quezon City**
Tagaytay City **Manila**
Batangas **San Pablo** Daet
Calapan **Lucena** Lopez
Boac Naga

PHILIPPINE
SEA

Agrihan
Pagan

NORTHERN

MARIANA

Alamagan
Sarigan

O C E A N

ISLANDS

Anatahan

(U.S.A.)

Saipan

Tinian
Rota

Guam
(U.S.A.) Agana

3

Polillo Islands

PHILIPPINES

Catanduanes

Legaspi
Sorsogon
Irosin
Catarman
Calbayog
Catbalogan
Samar
Tacloban
Guiuan

Mindoro
Romblon *Sibuyan*
Pandan *Sea*
Masbate
Masbate

Calamian
Group

Taytay

Cuyo
Islands

Roxas
Panay
San Jose de
Buenavista
Iloilo Ormoc
Bacolod Cebu
Talisay *Cebu*
Negros Tagbilaran
Tanjay Bohol
Dumaguete *Bohol Sea*
Dipolog Oroquieta
Roxas
Ozamiz Iligan
Pagadian

Surigao
Butuan

Ulithi *Fais*

Yap

FEDERATED STATES

4

Ngulu

OF MICRONESIA

Sorol

Puerto
Princesa

Brooke's
Point

Sulu Sea

Sandakan

Cagayan de Oro

Mindanao

Zamboanga
Basilan Isabela
Moro
Gulf

Cotabato
Datu Piang
(Dulawan) **Davao** Mati

Davao
Gulf

General Santos

PALAU
Koror

5

Ngaregur

Jolo
Sulu
Archipelago

ad Datu

Semporna

Tawitawi

C e l e b e s
S e a

Kepulauan
Talaud
(Indonesia)

6

Sandakan
ngredeb

ngselor
akan

Kepulauan
Sangir
(Indonesia)

Equator

Manado

Semenanjung Minahassa
Tolitoli Tondano
Moutong
Gorontalo

Molucca Sea

Morotai

Tobelo

Ternate
Sao-Siu *Halmahera*

Waigeo

1:15M

7

Teluk
Tomini

Donggala
Palu
Poso Uekuli
Tentena Tataba
Kolonedale
Sulawesi
(Celebes)

Kepulauan
Togian
Luwuk
Banggai

Kepulauan
Banggai

Mapane
Mamuju
Masamba
Malili Wotu
Rantepao
Palopo
Makale
Malamala
Paloppo

Kendari
Wowoni

Kwoka
3000
Selat Dampir
Salawati
Sorong
Misool **Jazirah Doberai**
Ranski
Fafanlap
Inanwatan

Manokwari
Numfoor
Yapen
Serui

Biak
Biak

Tg d'Urville
Sarmi

Pegunungan Van Rees
Tariku Jayapura
Taritatu

KM MILES

900 *600*

750 *450*

Parepare
Watampone

Pandang
G. Lompobattang
Bontosunggu

Singkang
Kolaka
Teluk
Bone
Sinjai
Raha
Muna
Buton

Selat Yapen
Teluk Berau
Babo Kaimana
Faktak
Bomberai
Peninsula

Nabire
Pegunungan Maoke

Wamena

N E W

Vanimo

Aitape
Wewak
Maprik

600 *300*

Seram (Ceram)
Piru G. Binatja
3019
Namlea Bula
Buru
Ambon (Amboina)

Seram Sea
(Ceram Sea)

Tel.
Kamrau

Adi
Amamapare

5030
Pk Jaya Pk Trikora
Pk Mandala
4750 *4500*

Lake
Murray

PAPUA

NEW

Mandala

Mendi

750 *450*

8

Kabaena Baubau
Kepulauan
Tukangbesi

B a n d a S e a

Kepulauan
Watubela

Kepulauan Kai
Tual
Kai
Kecil *Kai* Dobo
Besar *Kepulauan*
Benjina *Aru*
Kobroör

Wokam

I R I A N
J A Y A

Central Ra.

Strickland

Fly

G U I N E A

450 *300*

N E S I A

Tanahjampea
Kep. Bonerate
Bontosunggu

Wetar

Kepulauan Barat Daya

Roma
Wuliaru

Larat
Trangan

Sia

Tg Deyong

P. Dolak

Kepulauan
Tanimbar

A r a f u r a
S e a

Tg Vals

Merauke

300 *150*

Morehead

Daru

9

F l o r e s S e a
Reo
Larantuka
Maumere
Flores
Endeh

Kepulauan Alor
Kalabahi
Lomblen *Alor*
G. Tata Mailau
G. Mutis
2427

Huaki

Manatuto
Dili
Pantemakassar
EAST
TIMOR

Kepulauan
Sermata Tepa

Kepulauan
Leti

Kepulauan
Babar

Saumlakki
Selaru

Badu I. *Moa I.*

AUSTRALIA
Saibai

150

Sumba
Waingapu
Selat Sumba
Memboro
Waikabubak

Sawu
Sea
Savu (Sawu)
Savu

Kupang
Rote (Roti)

Timor
EAST TIMOR
Kefamenanu

C. York

0 *0*

120° 125° 130° 135° 140°

© Bartholomew Ltd

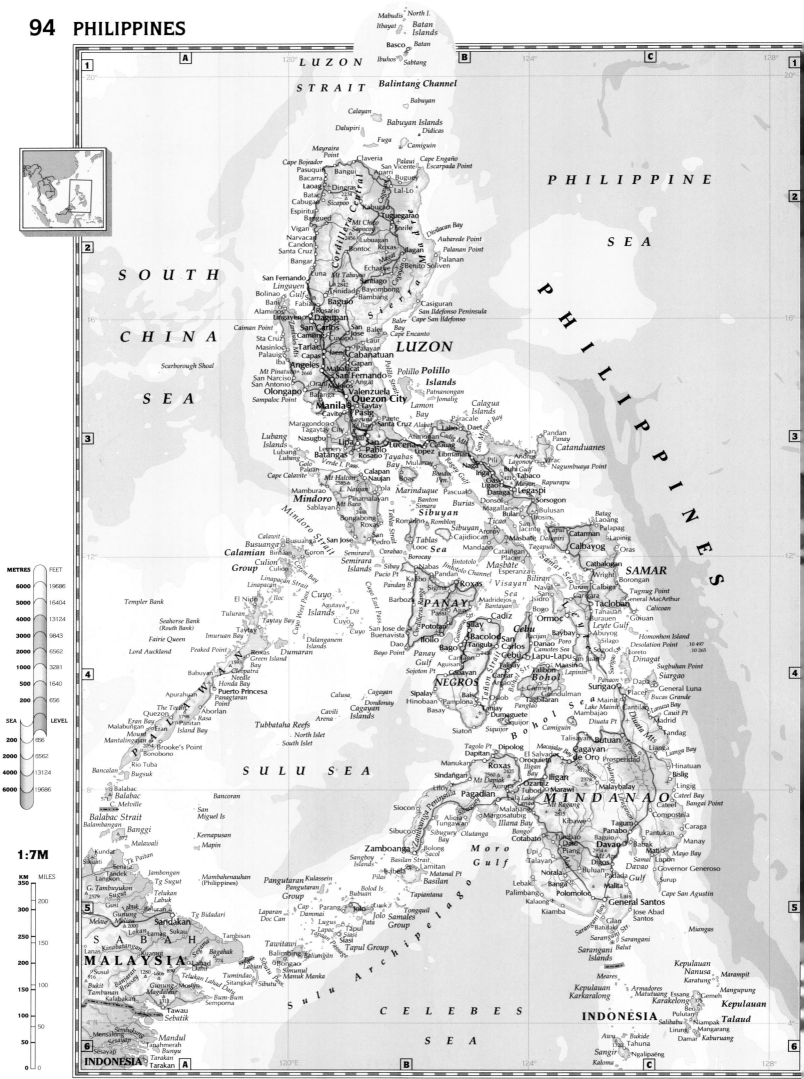

Mabudis · North I.
Itbayat · Batan Islands
Basco · Batan
Ibuhos · Sabtang

LUZON STRAIT
Balintang Channel

Babuyan
Calayan
Babuyan Islands
Dalupiri · Didicas
Fuga · Camiguin

Mayraira Point
Cape Bojeador · Claveria
Pasuquin · Bangui
Bacarra · Aparri · Buguey
Laoag · Dingras · Lal-Lo
Batac · Sicapoo
Cabugao · Espiritu
Bangued
Vigan · Mt Chico · Tuguegarao
Sapocoy · Enrile
Narvacan · Candon
Santa Cruz · Bontoc · Ilagan
Bangar · Echague
Benito Soliven
Luna · Mt Tabayo · La · Santiago
San Fernando · Lingayen · Trinidad · Bayombong
Bolinao · Gulf · Fabian · Bambang
Bani · Dagupan · Baguio
Alaminos · Lingayen · Rosario
Caiman Point · Sta Cruz · Casiguran
San Narciso · Masinloc · Palayan
Palauig · Cuyapo · Baler
Iba · Capas · Tarlac · San Jose · Baler Bay
Mt Pinatubo · Cabanatuan · Cape Encanto
Angeles · Malabacat · Gapan
San Antonio · San Fernando · Angat
Olongapo · Oran · Malolos
Balanga · Valenzuela
Sampaloc Pt · Quezon City
Manila · Pasig
Cavite · Taytay
Maragondon · Santa Cruz
Tagaytay City · Paete
Nasugbu · Calamba · Lucena
Lubang Islands · Lemery · Lipa · San Pablo
Lubang · Batangas · Lopez
Lubang · Rosario · Libmanan
Golo · Calapan · Naga
Paluan · Cape Calavite · Naujan · Buhi Gulf
Mamburao · Mt Halcon · Pola · Iriga
Mindoro · Boac · Oas · Ligao · Tabaco
Sablayan · Mt Baco · Daraga · Mayon
Bongabong · Marinduque · Legaspi
Roxas · Sorsogon
San Jose · Romblon · Bulusan
Calawit · Bongabong · Masbate · Bulan · Irosin
Busuanga · San Pedro · Sibuyan Sea · Batag
Coron · Tablas · Laoang · Palapag
Calamian Group · Semirara Islands · Masbate · Calbayog
Culion · Nabas · Catarman
Linapacan Strait · Pucio Pt · Catbalogan · SAMAR
El Nido · Sibay · Roxas · Borongan
Tuluran · Cuyo Islands · PANAY · Visayan Sea · Wright · Tugnug Point
Taytay · Dit · Passi · Tacloban
Iloc · Agutaya · Cuyo · Silay · Tanauan · General MacArthur
Cagayan · Iloilo · Cebu · Ormoc · Guiuan
Apurahuan · Peaked Point · Dumaran · San Jose de Buenavista · Bacolod · Homonhon Island
PALAWAN · Roxas · Bago · San Carlos · Lapu-Lapu · Desolation Point
Puerto Princesa · Dao · Panay Gulf · Cebu · Maasin · Dinagat
Quezon · Babuyan · Calusa · Bayo Point · Talisay · Bohol · Siargao
Eran Bay · Sojoton Pt · NEGROS · Carcar · General Luna
Malabuñgan · Aborlan · Sipalay · Bais · Tagbilaran · Surigao
Mount · Cagayan Islands · Hinoban · Pamplona · Dumaguete · Carmen · Placer
Bonobono · Cavili · Basay · Tanjay · Siquijor · Cantilan
Rio Tuba · North Islet · Siaton · Guindulman · Butuan
Bugsuk · Tubbataha Reefs · South Islet · Camiguin · Talisayan
Bancalan · Tagolo Pt · Dipolog · Macajalar Bay · Lianga
Balabac · Dapitan · El Salvador · Cagayan de Oro · Prosperidad
C. Melville · Manukan · Oroquieta · Iligan · Hinatuan
Balabac Strait · Sindangan · Iligan Bay · MINDANAO · Bislig
Banggi · Roxas · Ozamiz · Aurora · Mt Ragang · Lingig
Malawali · Lloy · Pagadian · Tubod · Marawi · Lianga Bay
San Miguel Is · Siocon · Lake Lanao · Malaybalay · Cateel
Keenapusan · Alicia · Sibuco · Malabang · Kibawe · Caraga
Mapin · Tungawan · Margosatubig · Tumbao · Tagum · Compostela
Zamboanga · Illana Bay · Dato · Panabo · Pantukan
Sikuti · Bongo · Baguio · Davao · Manay
Mambahenauhan · Cotabato · Upi · Babak · Mati
Pangutaran Group · Bolong · Talayan · Samal · Davao · Mayo Bay
Bolod Is · Sacol · Moro Gulf · Piang · Lupon
Bubuan · Basilan Strait · Talayan · Digos · Governor Generoso
Tapiantana · Isabela · Lamitan · Lebak · Norala · Malita
Jolo · Matanal Pt · Basilan · Palimbang · Banga · Cape San Agustin
Pilas · Tongquil · Kalaong · Polomolok · Surup
Cap · Parang · Luuk · Kiamba · General Santos · Padada Gulf
Tapul Group · Jolo Samales Group · Lais · Jose Abad Santos
Siasi · Pata · Glan · Miangas
Tandek · Lapac · Tapul · Batulaki · Sarangani Str.
Siasi · Tongkil · Sarangani · Sarangani Islands · Balut
Tawitawi · Tumindao · Sibutu · Simunul · Manuk Manka · Balimbing · Meares
Balimbing · Bongao · Mensalong · Tarakan

Scale / Elevation Legend

METRES · FEET
6000 · 19686
5000 · 16404
4000 · 13124
3000 · 9843
2000 · 6562
1000 · 3281
500 · 1640
200 · 656
SEA · LEVEL
200 · 656
2000 · 6562
4000 · 13124
6000 · 19686

1:7M

KM · MILES
350
300 · 200
250 · 150
200 · 100
150
100 · 50
50
0 · 0

Seas and regions

LUZON
PHILIPPINE SEA
PHILIPPINES
SOUTH CHINA SEA
SULU SEA
CELEBES SEA
Moro Gulf
Scarborough Shoal
Templer Bank
Seahorse Bank (Routh Bank)
Fairie Queen
Lord Auckland
Mindoro Strait
Verde I. Pass.
Tablas Strait
Sibuyan Sea
Visayan Sea
Samar Sea
Bohol Sea
Camotes Sea
Sulu Archipelago
Cuyo West Pass
Cuyo East Pass
Linapacan Strait

SABAH
MALAYSIA
Sandakan
Lahad Datu
Tawau · Sebatik
INDONESIA
Mandul
Tarakan

Mercator Projection

© Bartholomew L

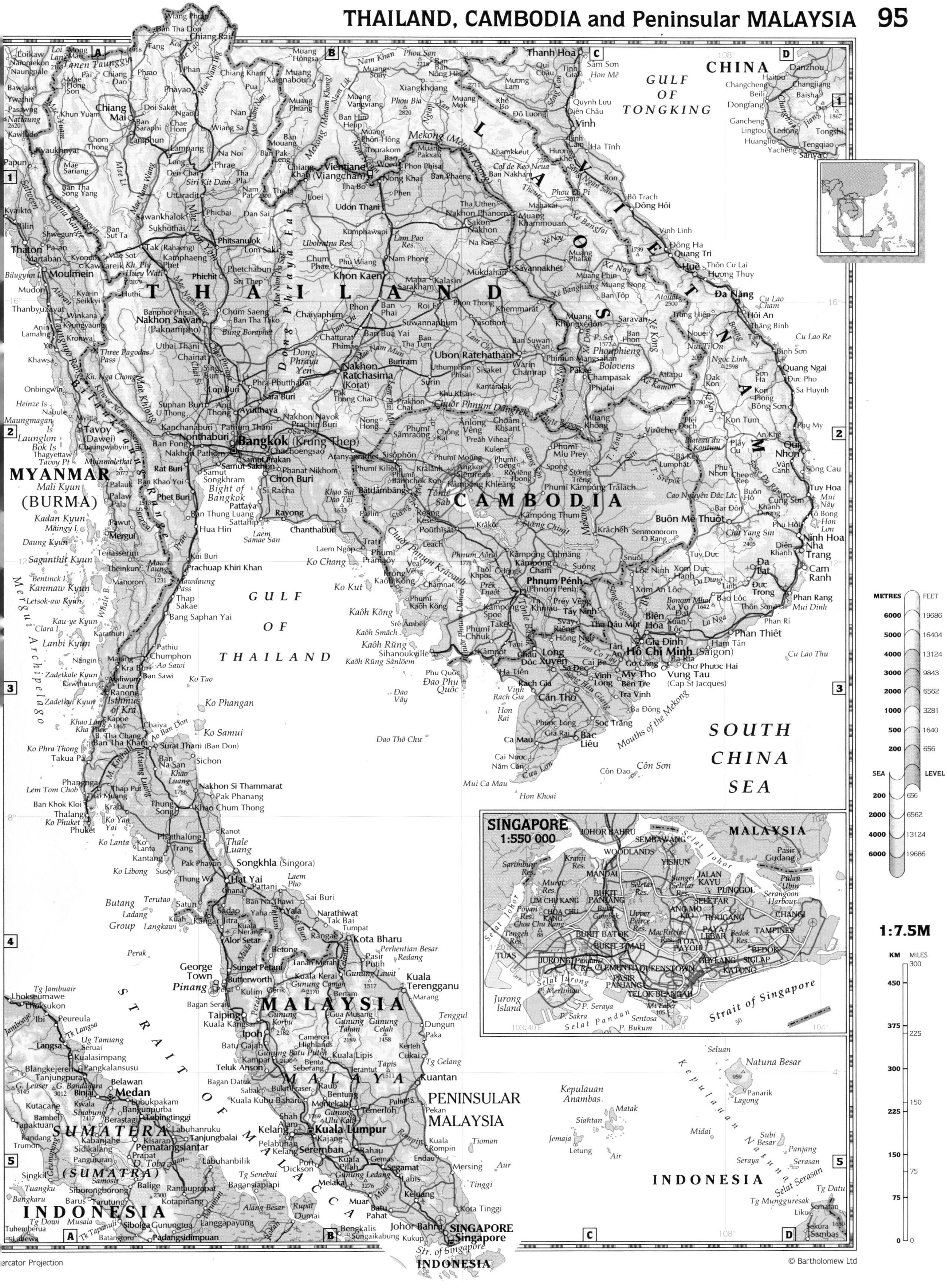

CHINA

GULF OF TONGKING

THAILAND

MYANMAR (BURMA)

LAOS

VIETNAM

CAMBODIA

GULF OF THAILAND

MALAYSIA

MALAYA

PENINSULAR MALAYSIA

SOUTH CHINA SEA

STRAIT OF MALACCA

SUMATERA (SUMATRA)

INDONESIA

Mercator Projection

© Bartholomew Ltd

Singapore inset

SINGAPORE 1:550 000

JOHOR BAHRU

MALAYSIA

Strait of Singapore

1:7.5M

Elevation scale

METRES	FEET
6000	19686
5000	16404
4000	13124
3000	9843
2000	6562
1000	3281
500	1640
200	656
SEA	LEVEL
200	656
2000	6562
4000	13124
6000	19686

KM / MILES scale: 450, 375, 300, 225, 150, 75, 0 (300, 225, 150, 75, 0)

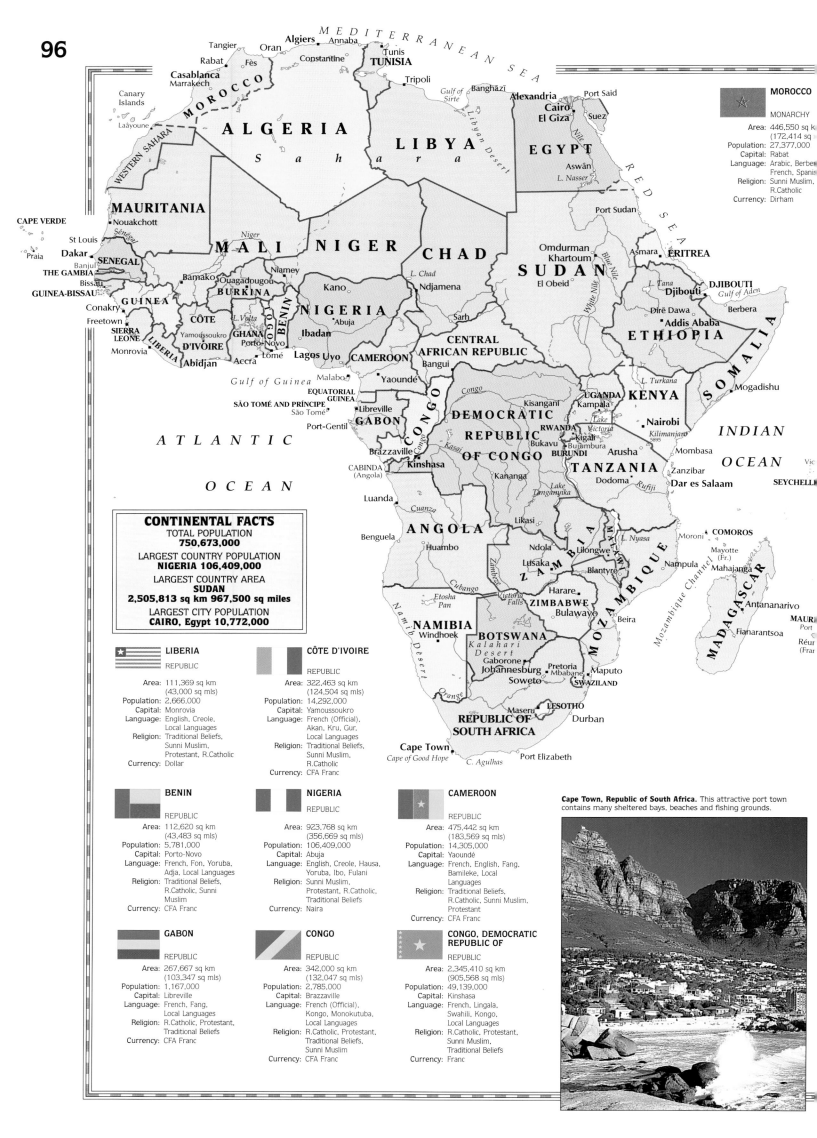

MEDITERRANEAN SEA

Tangier
Algiers · Annaba
Oran · Constantine
Rabat · Fès
Casablanca · Tunis · **TUNISIA**
Marrakech
Tripoli
Canary Islands
MOROCCO
Gulf of Sirte · Banghāzī
Laâyoune
ALGERIA
Alexandria
WESTERN SAHARA
LIBYA
Cairo · Port Said
El Gîza · Suez
Sahara
EGYPT
Aswān
L. Nasser
Libyan Desert

MAURITANIA
Nouakchott
Port Sudan
CAPE VERDE
St Louis
Niger
Asmara · **ERITREA**
Dakar
MALI · **NIGER** · **CHAD**
Omdurman
SENEGAL
Khartoum
L. Tana
Praia
Banjul
THE GAMBIA
Bamako · Niamey
SUDAN
L. Chad
El Obeid
Djibouti · **DJIBOUTI**
Bissau
Ouagadougou
Gulf of Aden
GUINEA-BISSAU
BURKINA
Kano
Ndjamena
Dirē Dawa · Berbera
Conakry · **GUINEA**
Sarh
NIGERIA
Blue Nile
Freetown
CÔTE · L. Volta
Abuja
Addis Ababa
SIERRA LEONE
Yamoussoukro
Ibadan
ETHIOPIA
D'IVOIRE
Porto-Novo
White Nile
Monrovia
GHANA
Lagos · Uyo
CAMEROON
L. Turkana
Abidjan · Accra · Lomé
CENTRAL
LIBERIA
BENIN
AFRICAN REPUBLIC
Bangui
SOMALIA
Gulf of Guinea
Malabo
Yaoundé
Congo
UGANDA
Mogadishu
EQUATORIAL GUINEA
Kisangani
Kampala
KENYA
SÃO TOMÉ AND PRÍNCIPE
Libreville
DEMOCRATIC
GABON
REPUBLIC
Lake Victoria
Nairobi
São Tomé
Port-Gentil
CONGO
RWANDA
Kilimanjaro 5895
OF CONGO
Kigali
Bukavu · Bujumbura
Mombasa
INDIAN
Brazzaville
Kasai
BURUNDI
Arusha
OCEAN
ATLANTIC
CABINDA
Kananga
TANZANIA
Zanzibar
(Angola)
Kinshasa
Dodoma
Dar es Salaam
SEYCHELL
OCEAN
Luanda
Lake Tanganyika
Rufiji
Cuanza
Likasi
L. Nyasa
COMOROS
Benguela
Moroni · Mayotte (Fr.)
ANGOLA
Ndola
ZAMBIA
Nampula · Mahajanga
Huambo
Lilongwe
MALAWI
Lusaka · Blantyre
Cubango
Zambezi
MOZAMBIQUE
MADAGASCAR
Harare
MAUR
Etosha Pan
Victoria Falls
Antananarivo
NAMIBIA
ZIMBABWE
Beira
Port
Windhoek
Bulawayo
Réu
Namib Desert
Kalahari Desert
BOTSWANA
Fianarantsoa
(Fran
REPUBLIC OF
Gaborone
Pretoria
Mozambique Channel
Johannesburg
Mbabane · Maputo
Soweto
SWAZILAND
Orange
Maseru · **LESOTHO**
SOUTH AFRICA
Durban
Cape Town
Cape of Good Hope
Port Elizabeth
C. Agulhas

RED SEA

CONTINENTAL FACTS

TOTAL POPULATION
750,673,000

LARGEST COUNTRY POPULATION
NIGERIA 106,409,000

LARGEST COUNTRY AREA
SUDAN
2,505,813 sq km 967,500 sq miles

LARGEST CITY POPULATION
CAIRO, Egypt 10,772,000

MOROCCO
MONARCHY
Area: 446,550 sq k
(172,414 sq
Population: 27,377,000
Capital: Rabat
Language: Arabic, Berber French, Spanis
Religion: Sunni Muslim, R.Catholic
Currency: Dirham

LIBERIA
REPUBLIC
Area: 111,369 sq km
(43,000 sq mls)
Population: 2,666,000
Capital: Monrovia
Language: English, Creole, Local Languages
Religion: Traditional Beliefs, Sunni Muslim, Protestant, R.Catholic
Currency: Dollar

CÔTE D'IVOIRE
REPUBLIC
Area: 322,463 sq km
(124,504 sq mls)
Population: 14,292,000
Capital: Yamoussoukro
Language: French (Official), Akan, Kru, Gur, Local Languages
Religion: Traditional Beliefs, Sunni Muslim, R.Catholic
Currency: CFA Franc

BENIN
REPUBLIC
Area: 112,620 sq km
(43,483 sq mls)
Population: 5,781,000
Capital: Porto-Novo
Language: French, Fon, Yoruba, Adja, Local Languages
Religion: Traditional Beliefs, R.Catholic, Sunni Muslim
Currency: CFA Franc

NIGERIA
REPUBLIC
Area: 923,768 sq km
(356,669 sq mls)
Population: 106,409,000
Capital: Abuja
Language: English, Creole, Hausa, Yoruba, Ibo, Fulani
Religion: Sunni Muslim, Protestant, R.Catholic, Traditional Beliefs
Currency: Naira

CAMEROON
REPUBLIC
Area: 475,442 sq km
(183,569 sq mls)
Population: 14,305,000
Capital: Yaoundé
Language: French, English, Fang, Bamileke, Local Languages
Religion: Traditional Beliefs, R.Catholic, Sunni Muslim, Protestant
Currency: CFA Franc

GABON
REPUBLIC
Area: 267,667 sq km
(103,347 sq mls)
Population: 1,167,000
Capital: Libreville
Language: French, Fang, Local Languages
Religion: R.Catholic, Protestant, Traditional Beliefs
Currency: CFA Franc

CONGO
REPUBLIC
Area: 342,000 sq km
(132,047 sq mls)
Population: 2,785,000
Capital: Brazzaville
Language: French (Official), Kongo, Monokutuba, Local Languages
Religion: R.Catholic, Protestant, Traditional Beliefs, Sunni Muslim
Currency: CFA Franc

CONGO, DEMOCRATIC REPUBLIC OF
REPUBLIC
Area: 2,345,410 sq km
(905,568 sq mls)
Population: 49,139,000
Capital: Kinshasa
Language: French, Lingala, Swahili, Kongo, Local Languages
Religion: R.Catholic, Protestant, Sunni Muslim, Traditional Beliefs
Currency: Franc

Cape Town, Republic of South Africa. This attractive port town contains many sheltered bays, beaches and fishing grounds.

ALGERIA

REPUBLIC
Area: 2,381,741 sq km
(919,595 sq mls)
Population: 30,081,000
Capital: Algiers (Alger)
Language: Arabic, French, Berber
Religion: Sunni Muslim,
R.Catholic
Currency: Dinar

TUNISIA

REPUBLIC
Area: 164,150 sq km
(63,379 sq mls)
Population: 9,335,000
Capital: Tunis
Language: Arabic, French
Religion: Sunni Muslim
Currency: Dinar

LIBYA
REPUBLIC
Area: 1,759,540 sq km
(679,362 sq mls)
Population: 5,339,000
Capital: Tripoli (Ţarābulus)
Language: Arabic, Berber
Religion: Sunni Muslim,
R.Catholic
Currency: Dinar

EGYPT

REPUBLIC
Area: 1,000,250 sq km
(386,199 sq mls)
Population: 65,978,000
Capital: Cairo (El Qâhira)
Language: Arabic, French
Religion: Sunni Muslim,
Coptic Christian
Currency: Pound

MAURITANIA
REPUBLIC
Area: 1,030,700 sq km
(397,955 sq mls)
Population: 2,529,000
Capital: Nouakchott
Language: Arabic, French,
Local Languages
Religion: Sunni Muslim
Currency: Ouguiya

Harare. Following Zimbabwe's independence in 1980 this city became the focus for the population and the economy.

MALI

REPUBLIC
Area: 1,240,140 sq km
(478,821 sq mls)
Population: 10,694,000
Capital: Bamako
Language: French, Bambara,
Local Languages
Religion: Sunni Muslim,
Traditional Beliefs,
R.Catholic
Currency: CFA Franc

BURKINA
REPUBLIC
Area: 274,200 sq km
(105,869 sq mls)
Population: 11,305,000
Capital: Ouagadougou
Language: French, More (Mossi),
Fulani, Local Languages
Religion: Traditional Beliefs,
Sunni Muslim,
R.Catholic
Currency: CFA Franc

NIGER

REPUBLIC
Area: 1,267,000 sq km
(489,191 sq mls)
Population: 10,078,000
Capital: Niamey
Language: French (Official),
Hausa, Fulani,
Local Languages
Religion: Sunni Muslim,
Traditional Beliefs
Currency: CFA Franc

CHAD
REPUBLIC
Area: 1,284,000 sq km
(495,755 sq mls)
Population: 7,270,000
Capital: Ndjamena
Language: Arabic, French,
Local Languages
Religion: Sunni Muslim,
Traditional Beliefs,
R.Catholic
Currency: CFA Franc

SUDAN

REPUBLIC
Area: 2,505,813 sq km
(967,500 sq mls)
Population: 28,292,000
Capital: Khartoum
Language: Arabic, Dinka, Nubian,
Beja, Nuer,
Local Languages
Religion: Sunni Muslim, Traditional
Beliefs, R.Catholic,
Protestant
Currency: Dinar

ERITREA

REPUBLIC
Area: 117,400 sq km
(45,328 sq mls)
Population: 3,577,000
Capital: Asmara
Language: Tigrinya, Arabic,
Tigre, English
Religion: Sunni Muslim,
Coptic Christian
Currency: Nakfa

ETHIOPIA

REPUBLIC
Area: 1,133,880 sq km
(437,794 sq mls)
Population: 59,649,000
Capital: Addis Ababa
(Ādīs Ābeba)
Language: Amharic, Oromo,
Local Languages
Religion: Ethiopian Orthodox,
Sunni Muslim,
Traditional Beliefs
Currency: Birr

DJIBOUTI
REPUBLIC
Area: 23,200 sq km
(8,958 sq mls)
Population: 623,000
Capital: Djibouti
Language: Somali, French,
Arabic, Issa, Afar
Religion: Sunni Muslim,
R.Catholic
Currency: Franc

SENEGAL

REPUBLIC
Area: 196,720 sq km
(75,954 sq mls)
Population: 9,003,000
Capital: Dakar
Language: French (Official),
Wolof, Fulani,
Local Languages
Religion: Sunni Muslim,
R.Catholic,
Traditional Beliefs
Currency: CFA Franc

THE GAMBIA

REPUBLIC
Area: 11,295 sq km
(4,361 sq mls)
Population: 1,229,000
Capital: Banjul
Language: English (Official),
Malinke, Fulani,
Wolof
Religion: Sunni Muslim,
Protestant
Currency: Dalasi

GUINEA-BISSAU

REPUBLIC
Area: 36,125 sq km
(13,948 sq mls)
Population: 1,161,000
Capital: Bissau
Language: Portuguese,
Portuguese Creole,
Local Languages
Religion: Traditional Beliefs,
Sunni Muslim,
R.Catholic
Currency: Peso

GUINEA
REPUBLIC
Area: 245,857 sq km
(94,926 sq mls)
Population: 7,337,000
Capital: Conakry
Language: French, Fulani,
Malinke, Local
Languages
Religion: Sunni Muslim,
Traditional Beliefs,
R.Catholic
Currency: Franc

SIERRA LEONE
REPUBLIC
Area: 71,740 sq km
(27,699 sq mls)
Population: 4,568,000
Capital: Freetown
Language: English, Creole,
Mende, Temne,
Local Languages
Religion: Traditional Beliefs,
Sunni Muslim,
Protestant, R.Catholic
Currency: Leone

GHANA

REPUBLIC
Area: 238,537 sq km
(92,100 sq mls)
Population: 19,162,000
Capital: Accra
Language: English (Official),
Hausa, Akan,
Local Languages
Religion: Protestant, R.Catholic,
Sunni Muslim,
Traditional Beliefs
Currency: Cedi

TOGO

REPUBLIC
Area: 56,785 sq km
(21,925 sq mls)
Population: 4,397,000
Capital: Lomé
Language: French, Ewe, Kabre,
Local Languages
Religion: Traditional Beliefs,
R.Catholic,
Sunni Muslim,
Protestant
Currency: CFA Franc

POPULATION

Algiers
Casablanca
Alexandria
Cairo
Khartoum
Addis Ababa
Abidjan
Lagos
Kinshasa
Luanda
Maputo
Cape Town

CENTRAL AFRICAN REPUBLIC

REPUBLIC
Area: 622,436 sq km
(240,324 sq mls)
Population: 3,485,000
Capital: Bangui
Language: French, Sango, Banda,
Baya, Local Languages
Religion: Protestant, R.Catholic,
Traditional Beliefs,
Sunni Muslim
Currency: CFA Franc

EQUATORIAL GUINEA
REPUBLIC
Area: 28,051 sq km
(10,831 sq mls)
Population: 431,000
Capital: Malabo
Language: Spanish, Fang
Religion: R.Catholic,
Traditional Beliefs
Currency: CFA Franc

UGANDA

REPUBLIC
Area: 241,038 sq km
(93,065 sq mls)
Population: 20,554,000
Capital: Kampala
Language: English, Swahili
(Official), Luganda,
Local Languages
Religion: R.Catholic, Protestant,
Sunni Muslim,
Traditional Beliefs
Currency: Shilling

KENYA

REPUBLIC
Area: 582,646 sq km
(224,961 sq mls)
Population: 29,008,000
Capital: Nairobi
Language: Swahili (Official),
English,
Local Languages
Religion: R.Catholic,
Protestant,
Traditional Beliefs,
Currency: Shilling

CITIES
■ Over 5 million population
● 2.5 - 5 million population

POPULATION
Inhabitants

per sq km	per sq ml
over 200	over 500
100-200	250-500
40-100	100-250
10-40	25-100
2-10	5-25
0-2	0-5
uninhabited	

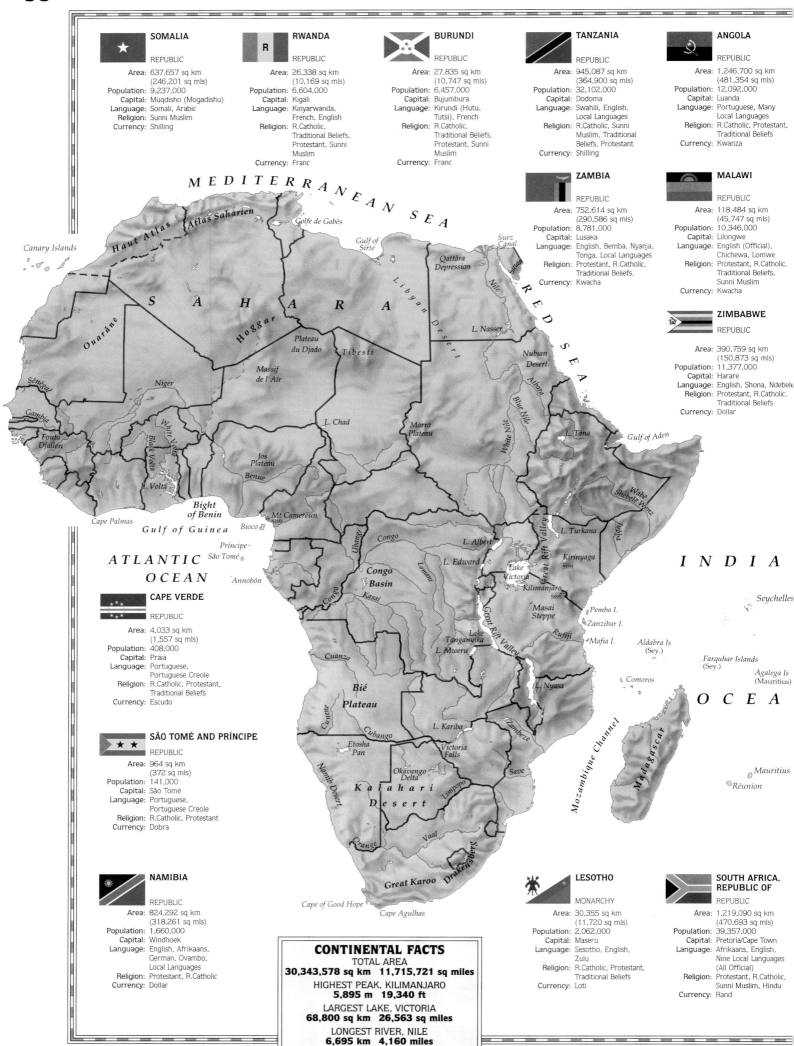

SOMALIA
REPUBLIC
Area: 637,657 sq km
(246,201 sq mls)
Population: 9,237,000
Capital: Muqdisho (Mogadishu)
Language: Somali, Arabic
Religion: Sunni Muslim
Currency: Shilling

RWANDA
REPUBLIC
Area: 26,338 sq km
(10,169 sq mls)
Population: 6,604,000
Capital: Kigali
Language: Kinyarwanda,
French, English
Religion: R.Catholic,
Traditional Beliefs,
Protestant, Sunni
Muslim
Currency: Franc

BURUNDI
REPUBLIC
Area: 27,835 sq km
(10,747 sq mls)
Population: 6,457,000
Capital: Bujumbura
Language: Kirundi (Hutu,
Tutsi), French
Religion: R.Catholic,
Traditional Beliefs,
Protestant, Sunni
Muslim
Currency: Franc

TANZANIA
REPUBLIC
Area: 945,087 sq km
(364,900 sq mls)
Population: 32,102,000
Capital: Dodoma
Language: Swahili, English,
Local Languages
Religion: R.Catholic, Sunni
Muslim, Traditional
Beliefs, Protestant
Currency: Shilling

ANGOLA
REPUBLIC
Area: 1,246,700 sq km
(481,354 sq mls)
Population: 12,092,000
Capital: Luanda
Language: Portuguese, Many
Local Languages
Religion: R.Catholic, Protestant,
Traditional Beliefs
Currency: Kwanza

ZAMBIA
REPUBLIC
Area: 752,614 sq km
(290,586 sq mls)
Population: 8,781,000
Capital: Lusaka
Language: English, Bemba, Nyanja,
Tonga, Local Languages
Religion: Protestant, R.Catholic,
Traditional Beliefs.
Currency: Kwacha

MALAWI
REPUBLIC
Area: 118,484 sq km
(45,747 sq mls)
Population: 10,346,000
Capital: Lilongwe
Language: English (Official),
Chichewa, Lomwe
Religion: Protestant, R.Catholic,
Traditional Beliefs,
Sunni Muslim
Currency: Kwacha

ZIMBABWE
REPUBLIC
Area: 390,759 sq km
(150,873 sq mls)
Population: 11,377,000
Capital: Harare
Language: English, Shona, Ndebele
Religion: Protestant, R.Catholic,
Traditional Beliefs
Currency: Dollar

CAPE VERDE
REPUBLIC
Area: 4,033 sq km
(1,557 sq mls)
Population: 408,000
Capital: Praia
Language: Portuguese,
Portuguese Creole
Religion: R.Catholic, Protestant,
Traditional Beliefs
Currency: Escudo

SÃO TOMÉ AND PRÍNCIPE
REPUBLIC
Area: 964 sq km
(372 sq mls)
Population: 141,000
Capital: São Tomé
Language: Portuguese,
Portuguese Creole
Religion: R.Catholic, Protestant
Currency: Dobra

NAMIBIA
REPUBLIC
Area: 824,292 sq km
(318,261 sq mls)
Population: 1,660,000
Capital: Windhoek
Language: English, Afrikaans,
German, Ovambo,
Local Languages
Religion: Protestant, R.Catholic
Currency: Dollar

LESOTHO
MONARCHY
Area: 30,355 sq km
(11,720 sq mls)
Population: 2,062,000
Capital: Maseru
Language: Sesotho, English,
Zulu
Religion: R.Catholic, Protestant,
Traditional Beliefs
Currency: Loti

SOUTH AFRICA,
REPUBLIC OF
REPUBLIC
Area: 1,219,090 sq km
(470,693 sq mls)
Population: 39,357,000
Capital: Pretoria/Cape Town
Language: Afrikaans, English,
Nine Local Languages
(All Official)
Religion: Protestant, R.Catholic,
Sunni Muslim, Hindu
Currency: Rand

CONTINENTAL FACTS
TOTAL AREA
30,343,578 sq km   11,715,721 sq miles
HIGHEST PEAK, KILIMANJARO
5,895 m   19,340 ft
LARGEST LAKE, VICTORIA
68,800 sq km   26,563 sq miles
LONGEST RIVER, NILE
6,695 km   4,160 miles

CLIMATE

COMOROS

REPUBLIC

Area: 1,862 sq km
(719 sq mls)
Population: 658,000
Capital: Moroni
Language: Comorian, French,
Arabic
Religion: Sunni Muslim,
R.Catholic
Currency: Franc

SEYCHELLES

REPUBLIC

Area: 455 sq km
(176 sq mls)
Population: 76,000
Capital: Victoria
Language: Seychellois (Seselwa,
French Creole),
English
Religion: R.Catholic, Protestant
Currency: Rupee

MAURITIUS

REPUBLIC

Area: 2,040 sq km
(788 sq mls)
Population: 1,141,000
Capital: Port Louis
Language: English, French Creole,
Hindi, Indian Languages
Religion: Hindu, R.Catholic,
Sunni Muslim,
Protestant
Currency: Rupee

MADAGASCAR

REPUBLIC

Area: 587,041 sq km
(226,658 sq mls)
Population: 15,057,000
Capital: Antananarivo
Language: Malagasy, French
Religion: Traditional Beliefs,
R.Catholic, Protestant,
Sunni Muslim,
Currency: Franc

MOZAMBIQUE

REPUBLIC

Area: 799,380 sq km
(308,642 sq mls)
Population: 18,880,000
Capital: Maputo
Language: Portuguese, Makua,
Tsonga, Local Languages
Religion: Traditional Beliefs,
R.Catholic,
Sunni Muslim
Currency: Metical

BOTSWANA

REPUBLIC

Area: 581,370 sq km
(224,468 sq mls)
Population: 1,570,000
Capital: Gaborone
Language: English, Setswana,
Shona, Local Languages
Religion: Traditional Beliefs,
Protestant, R.Catholic
Currency: Pula

SWAZILAND

MONARCHY

Area: 17,364 sq km
(6,704 sq mls)
Population: 952,000
Capital: Mbabane
Language: Swazi (Siswati),
English
Religion: Protestant, R.Catholic,
Traditional Beliefs
Currency: Emalangeni

CLIMATE TYPES

WARMER HUMID
Temperate
Mediterranean

DRY
Steppe
Desert

TROPICAL HUMID
Savanna
Rain forest

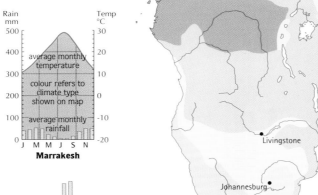

Marrakesh

average monthly
temperature

colour refers to
climate type
shown on map

average monthly
rainfall

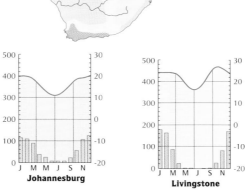

Freetown

Johannesburg

Livingstone

Zanzibar

Aswân

Botswana. Elephants are one of the many types of native
wildlife to be found in the Chobe National Park.

River Nile, Egypt. 96% of Egypt's population live in the Nile Delta and a 20km wide
strip along the river.

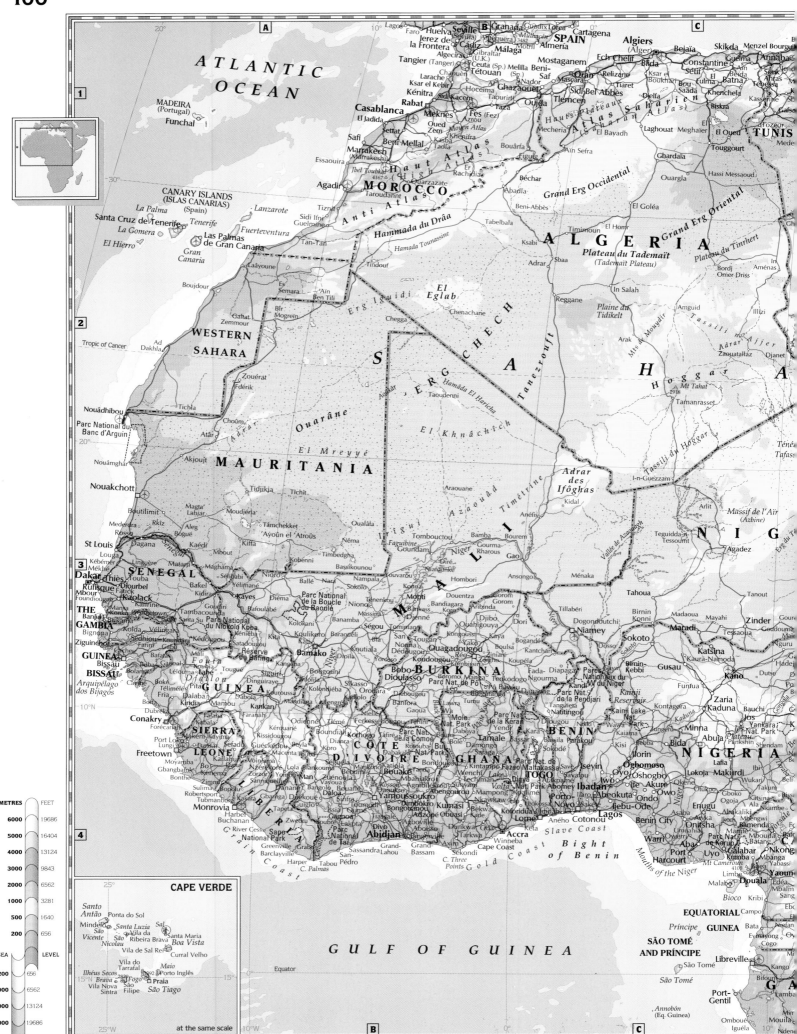

ATLANTIC
OCEAN

MADEIRA
(Portugal)
Funchal

CANARY ISLANDS
(ISLAS CANARIAS)
(Spain)
La Palma
Santa Cruz de Tenerife
La Gomera
El Hierro
Tenerife
Fuerteventura
Gran
Canaria
Las Palmas
de Gran Canaria
Lanzarote

Tropic of Cancer

WESTERN
SAHARA

MAURITANIA

Nouâdhibou
Parc National du
Banc d'Arguin
Nouâmghâr
Nouakchott

SENEGAL
Dakar
THE
GAMBIA
GUINEA
BISSAU
BISSAU
Arquipélago
dos Bijagós

GUINEA
Conakry

SIERRA
LEONE
Freetown

LIBERIA
Monrovia

CÔTE
D'IVOIRE

MALI

BURKINA

GHANA
TOGO
BENIN

Accra

Gold Coast
C. Three
Points

SPAIN
Algiers
(Alger)

MOROCCO
Casablanca
Rabat

ALGERIA

Grand Erg Occidental
Grand Erg Oriental

TUNIS

S   A   H   A   R   A

NIG

NIGERIA
Abuja
Lagos
Ibadan

Bight
of Benin

Slave Coast

GULF OF GUINEA

Equator

EQUATORIAL
GUINEA
Libreville

SÃO TOMÉ
AND PRÍNCIPE

GA

METRES	FEET
6000	19686
5000	16404
4000	13124
3000	9843
2000	6562
1000	3281
500	1640
200	656
SEA	LEVEL
200	656
2000	6562
4000	13124
6000	19686

CAPE VERDE
Santo
Antão
Mindelo
São
Vicente
Santa Luzia
São
Nicolau
Sal
Vila da
Ribeira Brava
Santa Maria
Boa Vista
Curral Velho
Vila do
Tarrafal
Ilhéus Secos
Brava
Vila Nova
Sintra
São
Filipe
Fogo
Maio
Porto Inglês
Praia
São Tiago
at the same scale

Lambert Azimuthal Equal Area Projection

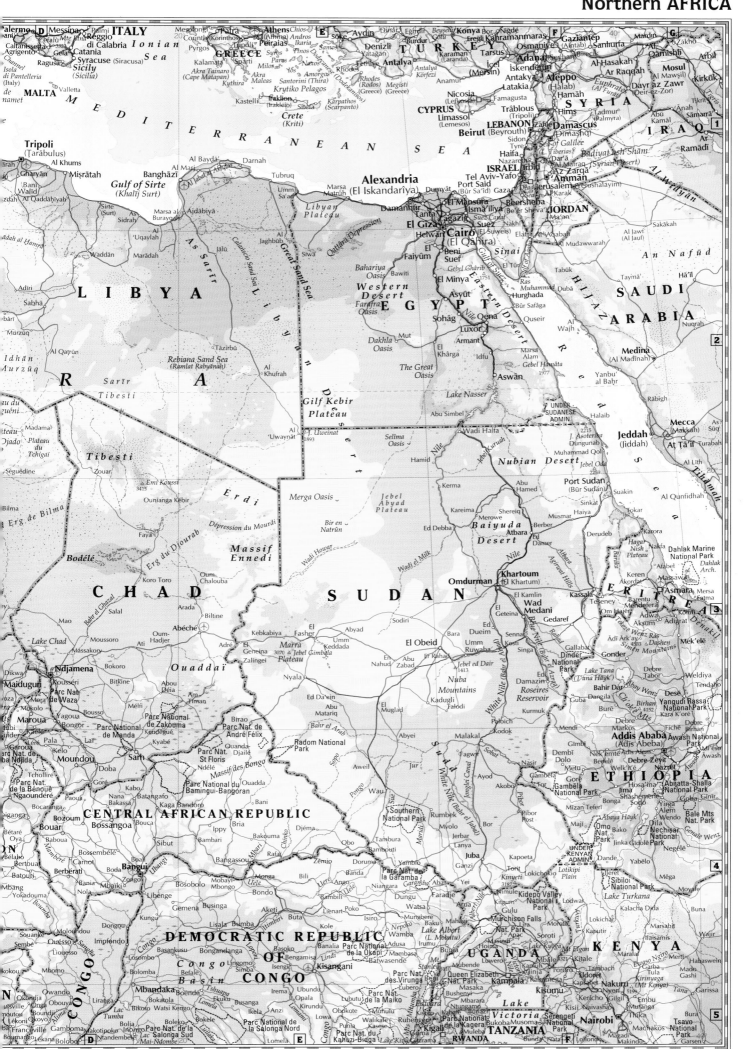

1:16M

KM   MILES
1000   600

800   500

600   400

400   200

200   100

0   0

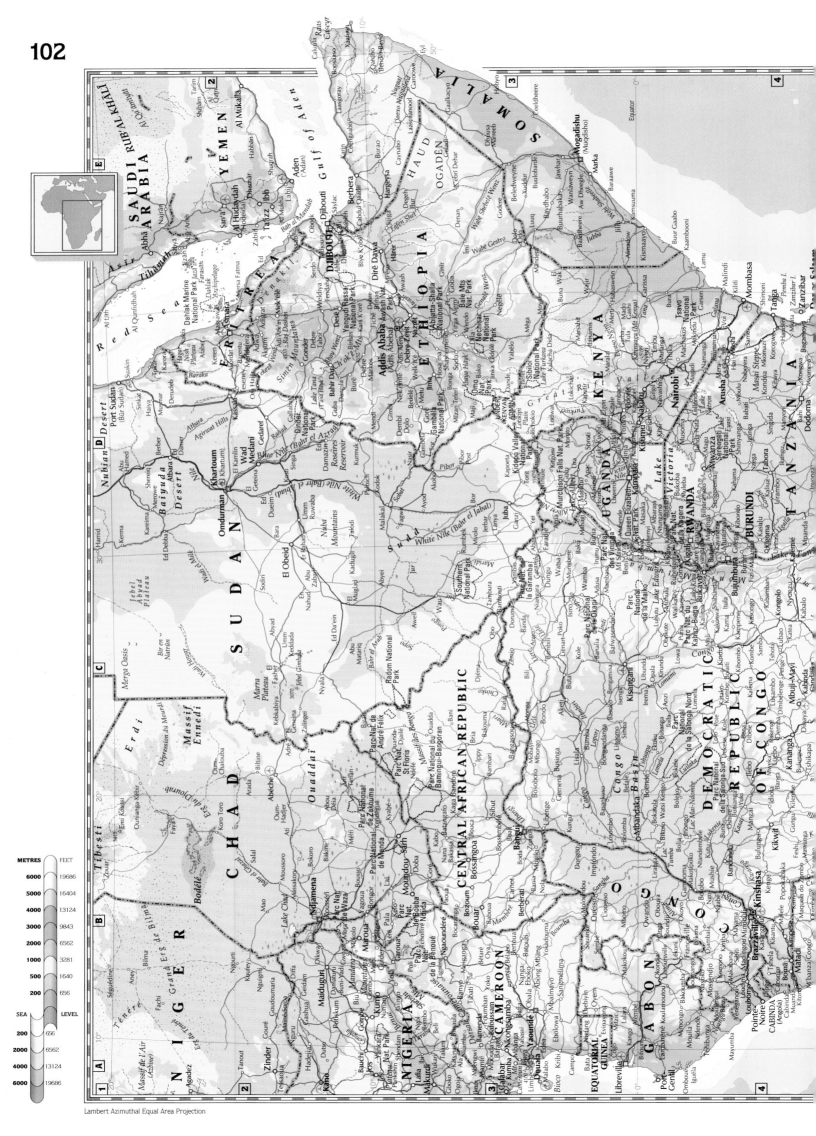

Lambert Azimuthal Equal Area Projection

MADAGASCAR

COMOROS

MAYOTTE (France)

MOZAMBIQUE

MALAWI

ZAMBIA

ZIMBABWE

BOTSWANA

NAMIBIA

ANGOLA

REPUBLIC OF SOUTH AFRICA

LESOTHO

SWAZILAND

ANGOLA

INDIAN OCEAN

ATLANTIC OCEAN

Mozambique Channel

Cape of Good Hope

Cape Agulhas

Tropic of Capricorn

Aldabra Islands (Seychelles)

1:16M

KM	MILES
1000	600
	500
800	
	400
600	300
400	200
	100
200	
0	0

© Bartholomew Ltd

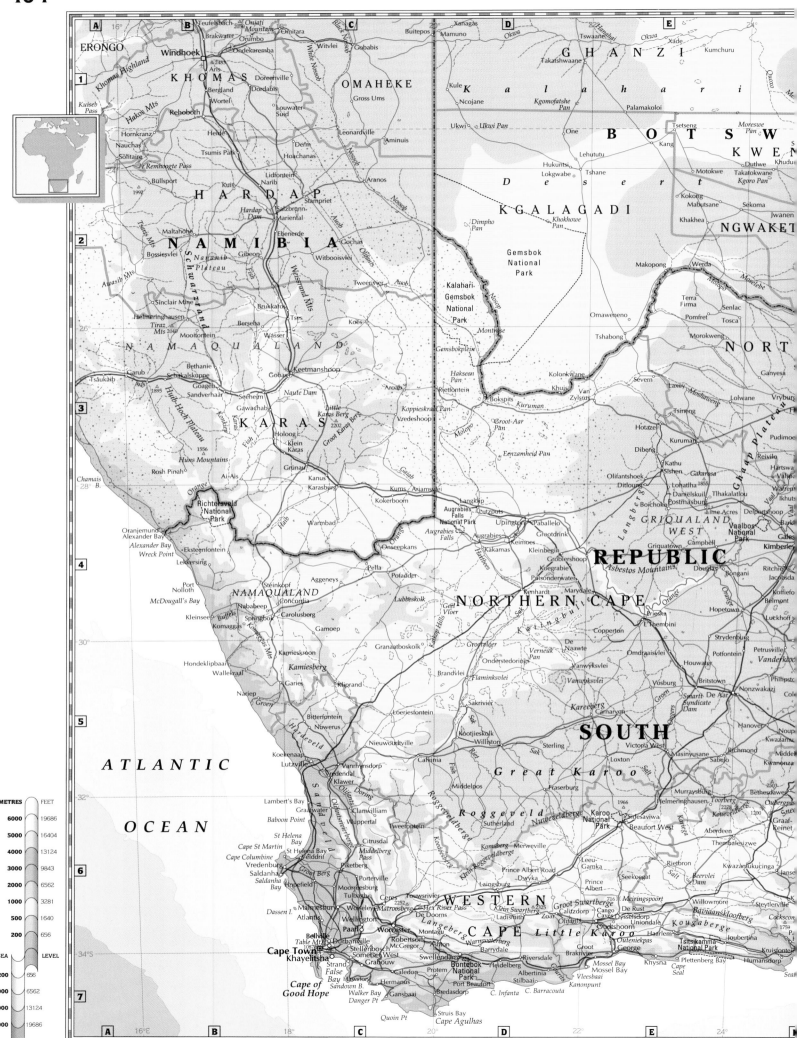

Lambert Azimuthal Equal Area Projection

1:5M

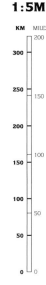

© Bartholomew Ltd

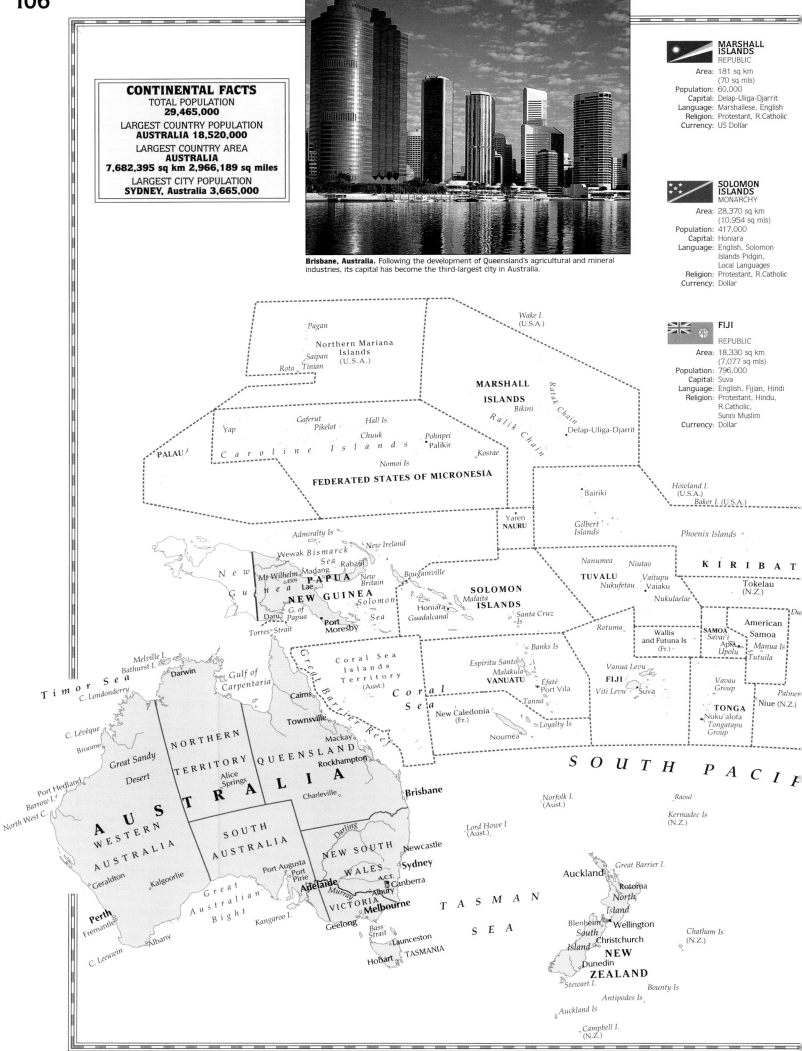

CONTINENTAL FACTS
TOTAL POPULATION
29,465,000
LARGEST COUNTRY POPULATION
AUSTRALIA 18,520,000
LARGEST COUNTRY AREA
AUSTRALIA
7,682,395 sq km 2,966,189 sq miles
LARGEST CITY POPULATION
SYDNEY, Australia 3,665,000

Brisbane, Australia. Following the development of Queensland's agricultural and mineral industries, its capital has become the third-largest city in Australia.

MARSHALL ISLANDS
REPUBLIC
Area: 181 sq km
(70 sq mls)
Population: 60,000
Capital: Delap-Uliga-Djarrit
Language: Marshallese, English
Religion: Protestant, R.Catholic
Currency: US Dollar

SOLOMON ISLANDS
MONARCHY
Area: 28,370 sq km
(10,954 sq mls)
Population: 417,000
Capital: Honiara
Language: English, Solomon
Islands Pidgin,
Local Languages
Religion: Protestant, R.Catholic
Currency: Dollar

FIJI
REPUBLIC
Area: 18,330 sq km
(7,077 sq mls)
Population: 796,000
Capital: Suva
Language: English, Fijian, Hindi
Religion: Protestant, Hindu,
R.Catholic,
Sunni Muslim
Currency: Dollar

FED. STATES OF MICRONESIA
REPUBLIC
Area: 701 sq km
(271 sq mls)
Population: 114,000
Capital: Palikir
Language: English, Trukese, Pohnpeian, Local Languages
Religion: Protestant, R.Catholic
Currency: US Dollar

PAPUA NEW GUINEA
MONARCHY
Area: 462,840 sq km
(178,704 sq mls)
Population: 4,600,000
Capital: Port Moresby
Language: English, Tok Pisin (Pidgin), Local Languages
Religion: Protestant, R.Catholic, Traditional Beliefs
Currency: Kina

NAURU
REPUBLIC
Area: 21 sq km
(8 sq mls)
Population: 11,000
Capital: Yaren
Language: Nauruan, Kiribati (Gilbertese,) English
Religion: Protestant, R.Catholic
Currency: Australian Dollar

KIRIBATI
REPUBLIC
Area: 717 sq km
(277 sq mls)
Population: 81,000
Capital: Bairiki
Language: Kiribati (Gilbertese), English
Religion: R.Catholic, Protestant, Baha'i, Mormon
Currency: Australian Dollar

TONGA
MONARCHY
Area: 748 sq km
(289 sq mls)
Population: 98,000
Capital: Nuku'alofa
Language: Tongan, English
Religion: Protestant, R.Catholic, Mormon
Currency: Pa'anga

TUVALU
MONARCHY
Area: 25 sq km
(10 sq mls)
Population: 11,000
Capital: Vaiaku
Language: Tuvaluan, English (official)
Religion: Protestant
Currency: Dollar

VANUATU
REPUBLIC
Area: 12,190 sq km
(4,707 sq mls)
Population: 182,000
Capital: Port Vila
Language: English, Bislama (English Creole), French (all official)
Religion: Protestant, R.Catholic, Traditional Beliefs
Currency: Vatu

SAMOA
MONARCHY
Area: 2,831 sq km
(1,093 sq mls)
Population: 174,000
Capital: Apia
Language: Samoan, English
Religion: Protestant, R.Catholic, Sunni Muslim
Currency: Tala

POPULATION

POPULATION	
Inhabitants	
per sq km	per sq ml
over 200	over 500
100-200	250-500
40-100	100-250
10-40	25-100
2-10	5-25
0-2	0-5
uninhabited	

CITIES
■ Over 5 million population
● 2.5 - 5 million population

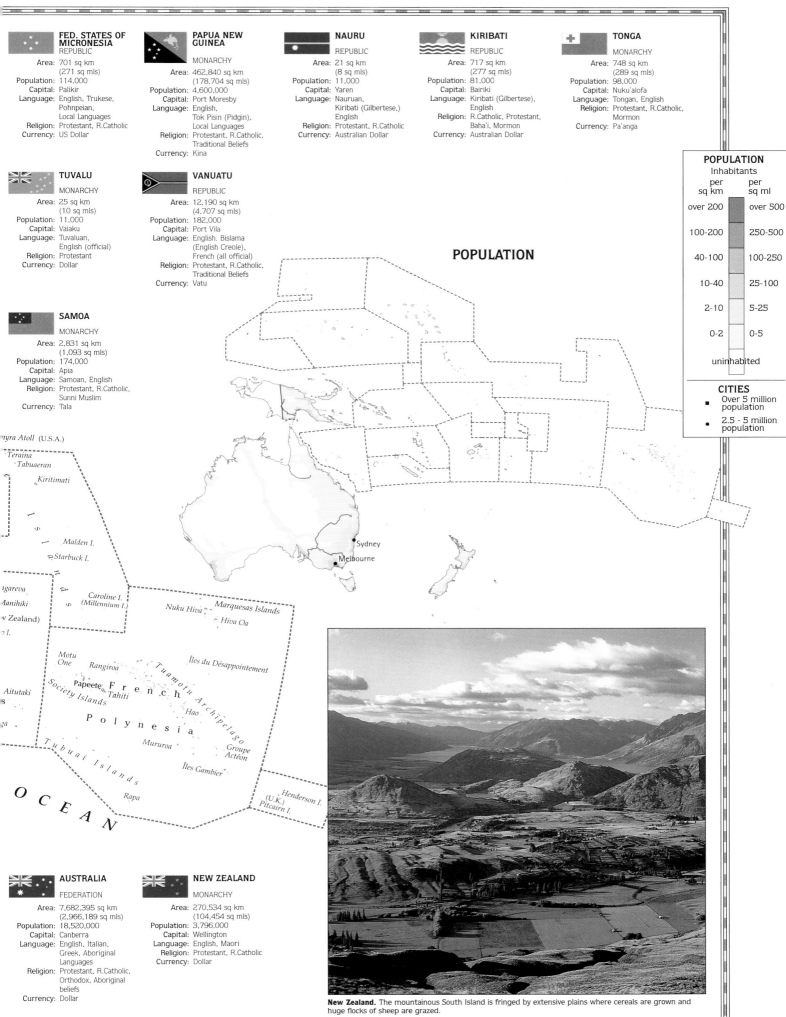

yra Atoll (U.S.A.)
Teraina
Tabuaeran
Kiritimati
Malden I.
Starbuck I.
gareva
Manihiki
Zealand)
I.
Caroline I.
(Millennium I.)
Nuku Hiva · Marquesas Islands
· Hiva Oa
Motu One
Rangiroa
Îles du Désappointement
Papeete · French
Society Islands · Tahiti
Aitutaki
Hao
Polynesia
Tuamotu Archipelago
Mururoa
Groupe Actéon
Tubuai Islands
Îles Gambier
Rapa
Henderson I.
(U.K.)
Pitcairn I.
O C E A N

Sydney
Melbourne

AUSTRALIA
FEDERATION
Area: 7,682,395 sq km
(2,966,189 sq mls)
Population: 18,520,000
Capital: Canberra
Language: English, Italian, Greek, Aboriginal Languages
Religion: Protestant, R.Catholic, Orthodox, Aboriginal beliefs
Currency: Dollar

NEW ZEALAND
MONARCHY
Area: 270,534 sq km
(104,454 sq mls)
Population: 3,796,000
Capital: Wellington
Language: English, Maori
Religion: Protestant, R.Catholic
Currency: Dollar

New Zealand. The mountainous South Island is fringed by extensive plains where cereals are grown and huge flocks of sheep are grazed.

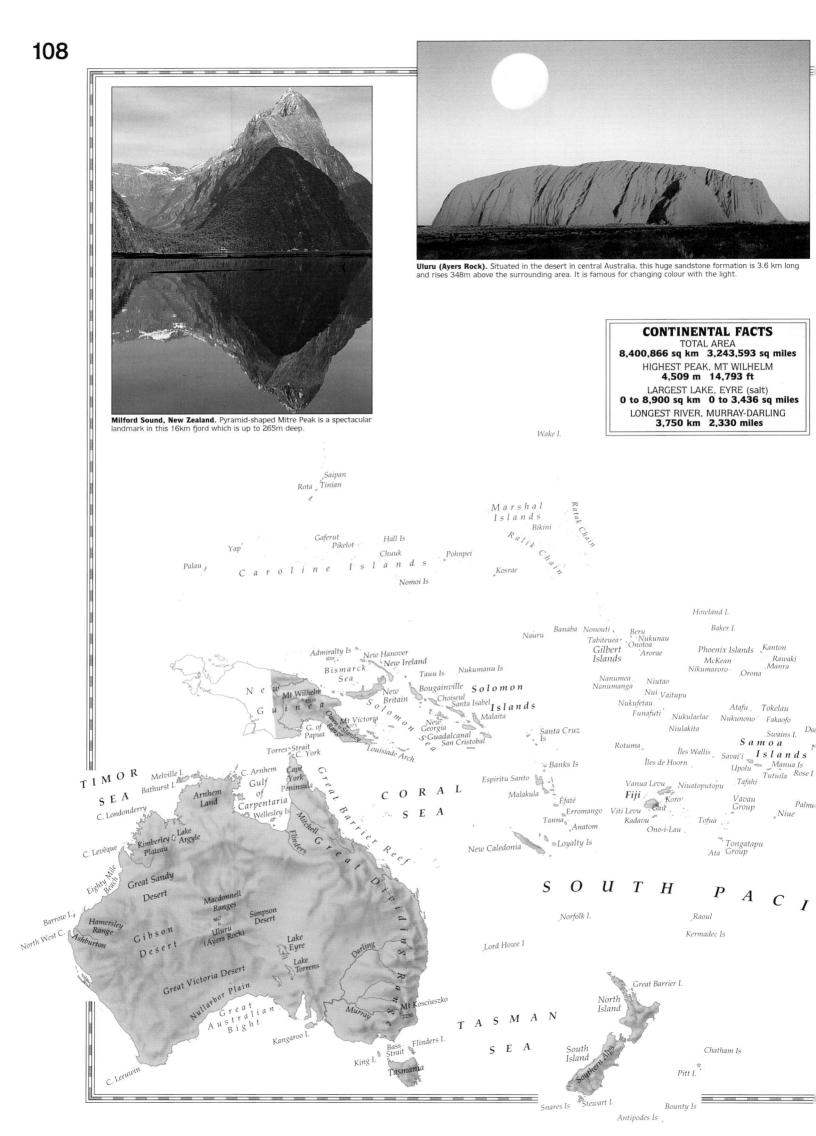

Milford Sound, New Zealand. Pyramid-shaped Mitre Peak is a spectacular landmark in this 16km fjord which is up to 265m deep.

Uluru (Ayers Rock). Situated in the desert in central Australia, this huge sandstone formation is 3.6 km long and rises 348m above the surrounding area. It is famous for changing colour with the light.

CONTINENTAL FACTS
TOTAL AREA
8,400,866 sq km   3,243,593 sq miles
HIGHEST PEAK, MT WILHELM
4,509 m   14,793 ft
LARGEST LAKE, EYRE (salt)
0 to 8,900 sq km   0 to 3,436 sq miles
LONGEST RIVER, MURRAY-DARLING
3,750 km   2,330 miles

Wake I.

Saipan
Rota Tinian

Marshal Islands

Bikini

Ratak Chain

Gaferut
Yap' Pikelot Hall Is
  Chuuk Pohnpei

Ralik Chain

Palau *C a r o l i n e   I s l a n d s* Kosrae

Nomoi Is

Howland I.

Nauru Banaba Nonouti Beru Baker I.
  Tabiteuea Nukunau
  Onotoa
  Arorae Phoenix Islands Kanton
  Gilbert Islands McKean Rawaki
  Nikumaroro Orona Manra

Admiralty Is New Hanover
  New Ireland Nukumanu Is Nanumea Niutao
  Bismarck Sea Tauu Is Nanumanga Nui Vaitupu
  New Bougainville *Solomon* Nukufetau
  Britain Choiseul Santa Isabel *Islands* Funafuti Nukulaelae Atafu Tokelau
  New New Malaita Niulakita Nukunono Fakaofo
Mt Wilhelm Georgia *S o l o m o n* Swains I.
N e w 4509 Guadalcanal Santa Cruz *S a m o a*
Mt Victoria *S e a* San Cristobal Is Rotuma *I s l a n d s* Da
G u i n e a 3073 Íles Wallis Savai'i Manua Is
  G. of Louisiade Arch. Banks Is Íles de Hoorn Upolu Tutuila Rose I.
  Papua Tafahi
Torres Strait Espiritu Santo Niuatoputapu Palme
  C. York *C O R A L* Malakula Vanua Levu Niuatoputapu Vavau
TIMOR Melville I. C. Arnhem Cape Éfaté *Fiji* Koro Group Niue
SEA Bathurst I. York *Great* *S E A* Erromango Viti Levu Gau
C. Londonderry Arnhem Peninsula Tanna Kadavu Tofua
  Land Gulf Anatom Ono-i-Lau Tongatapu
C. Levêque of Wellesley Is New Caledonia Loyalty Is Ata Group
  Kimberley Carpentaria
Eighty Mile Plateau Lake *Michell* *Great*
Barrow I. Argyle *S O U T H   P A C I*
Hamersley *Flinders* *Barrier*
North West C. Range Great Sandy *Reef* Norfolk I. Raoul
Ashburton Desert Macdonnell *Dividing* Kermadec Is
  Gibson Ranges Simpson Lord Howe I
  867 Desert *Range*
  Desert Uluru Lake *Great Barrier I.*
  (Ayers Rock) Eyre Darling
  Great Victoria Desert Lake North
  Torrens Mt Kosciuszko Island
  Nullarbor Plain Murray 2230 *T A S M A N*
C. Leeuwin *Great* *S E A* South
  Australian Island Chatham Is
  Bight Kangaroo I. Bass Flinders I. *Southern Alps* Pitt I.
  King I. Strait
  Tasmania
  Snares Is Stewart I. Bounty Is
  Antipodes Is

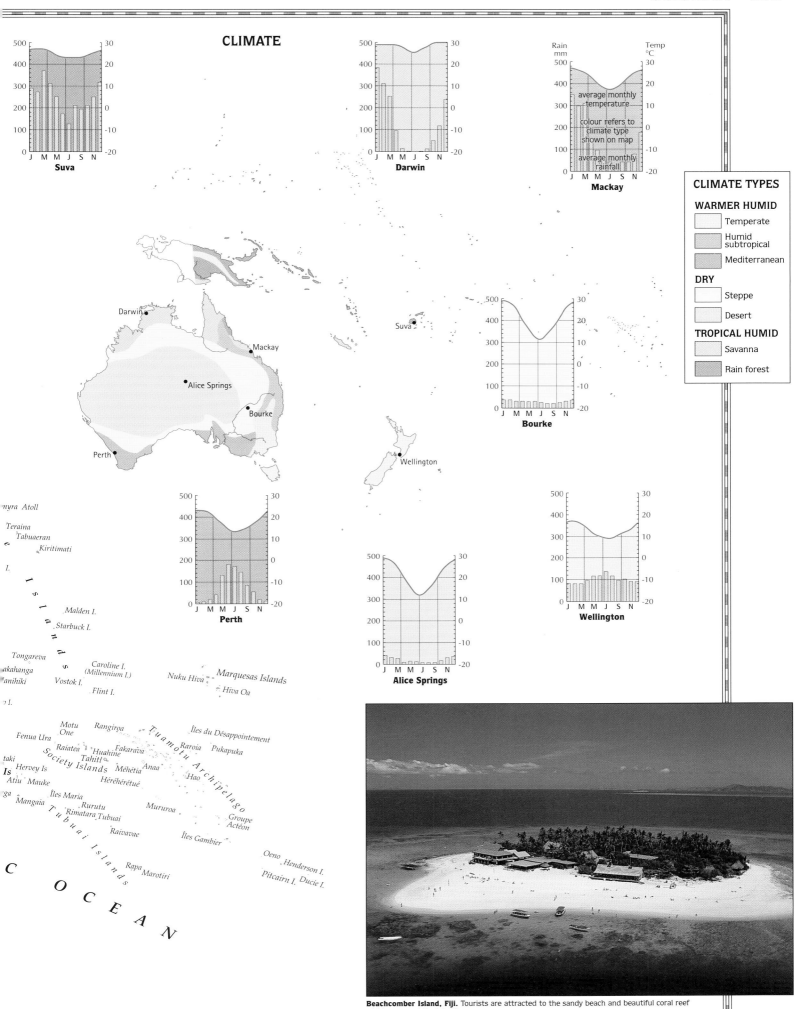

CLIMATE

Suva

Darwin

Rain mm — Temp °C

average monthly temperature

colour refers to climate type shown on map

average monthly rainfall

Mackay

CLIMATE TYPES

WARMER HUMID

Temperate

Humid subtropical

Mediterranean

DRY

Steppe

Desert

TROPICAL HUMID

Savanna

Rain forest

Darwin

Mackay

Alice Springs

Bourke

Bourke

Suva

Wellington

Perth

Perth

Wellington

Alice Springs

nyra Atoll

Teraina
Tabuaeran
Kiritimati

I.

Islands

Malden I.

Starbuck I.

Tongareva
akahanga
anihiki   Vostok I.   Caroline I.
                                (Millennium I.)
                Flint I.

Nuku Hiva   Marquesas Islands

                                Hiva Oa

Motu   Rangiroa   Îles du Désappointement
One
Fenua Ura   Raroia   Pukapuka
        Raiatea   Huahine   Fakarava
taki   Hervey Is   Tahiti   Méhétia   Anaa   Hao
Is   Atiu   Mauke   Héréhérétué
ga   Îles Maria
    Mangaia   Rurutu   Mururoa   Groupe
                Rimatara Tubuai   Actéon
            Raivavae   Îles Gambier

Tubuai Islands

O C E A N   Rapa Marotiri   Oeno
                                              Henderson I.
                            Pitcairn I. Ducie I.

Society Islands

Tuamotu Archipelago

Beachcomber Island, Fiji. Tourists are attracted to the sandy beach and beautiful coral reef which surround the island.

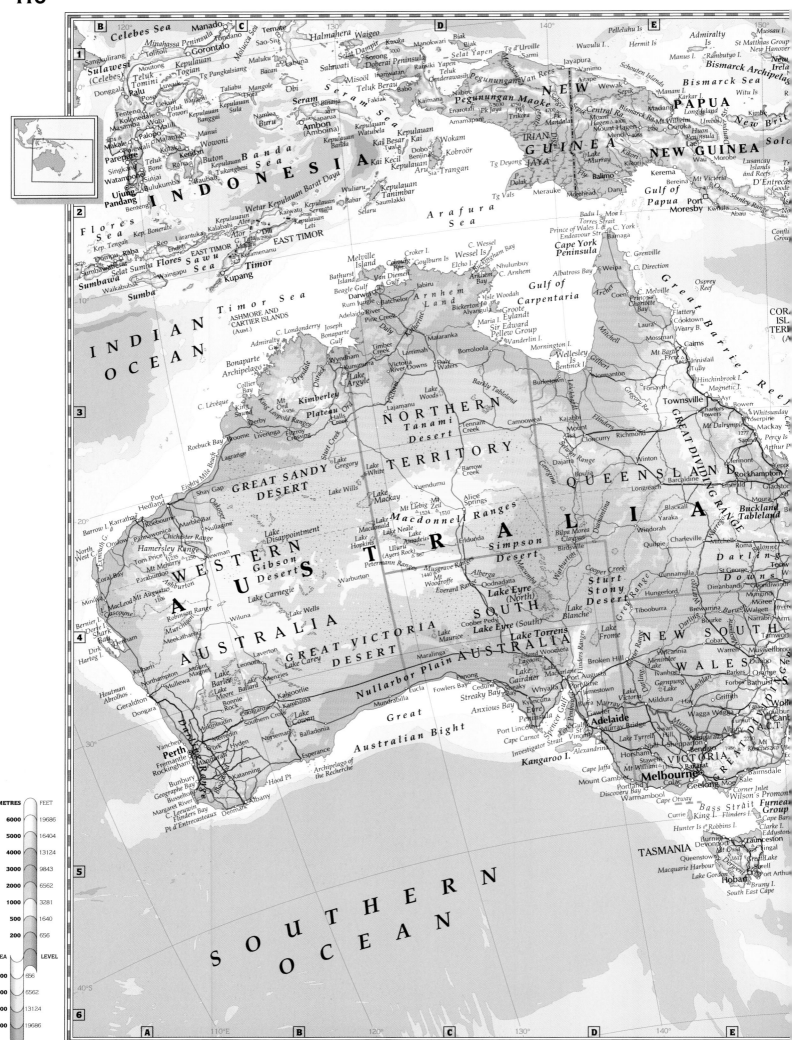

METRES | FEET
6000 | 19686
5000 | 16404
4000 | 13124
3000 | 9843
2000 | 6562
1000 | 3281
500 | 1640
200 | 656
SEA | LEVEL
200 | 656
2000 | 6562
4000 | 13124
6000 | 19686

Lambert Azimuthal Equal Area Projection

1:20M

KM   MILES

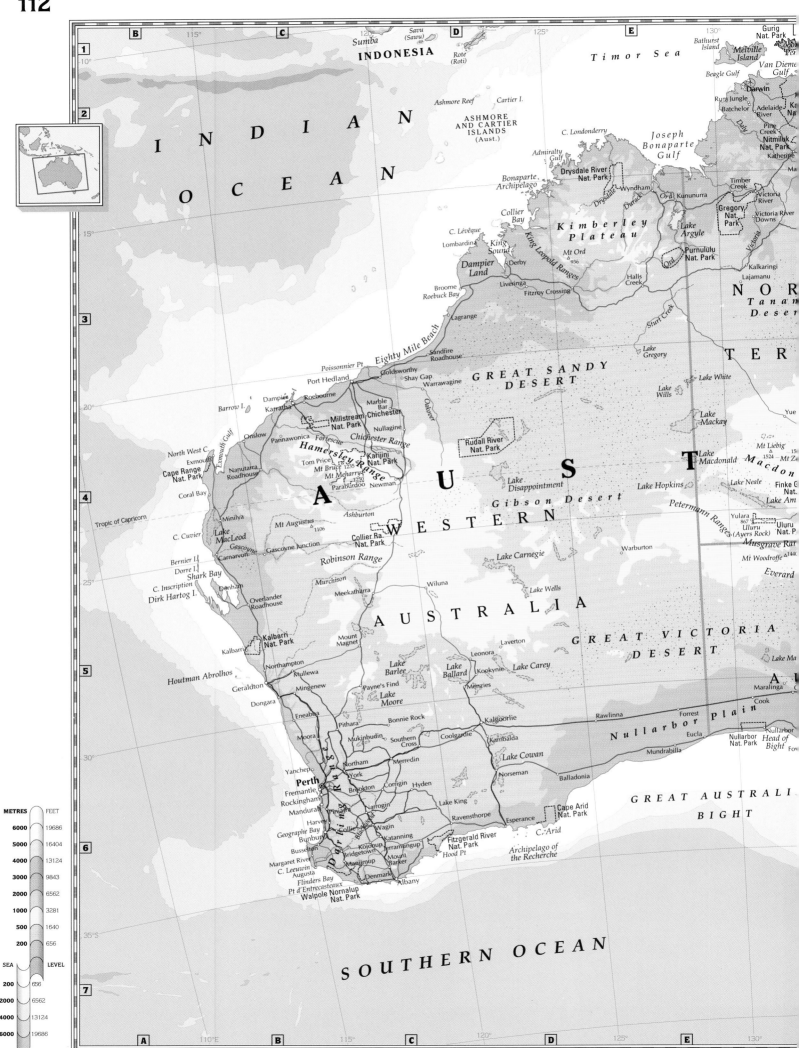

Lambert Azimuthal Equal Area Projection

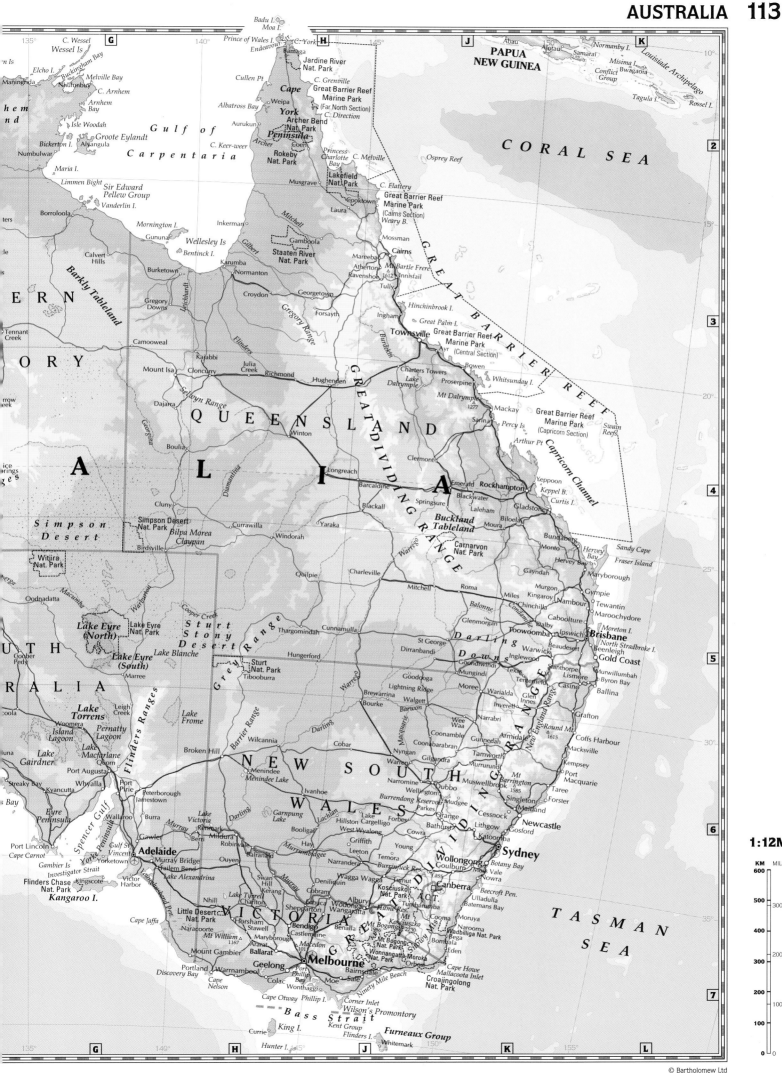

1:12M

KM   MILES
600

500   300

400
       200
300

200
       100
100

0   0

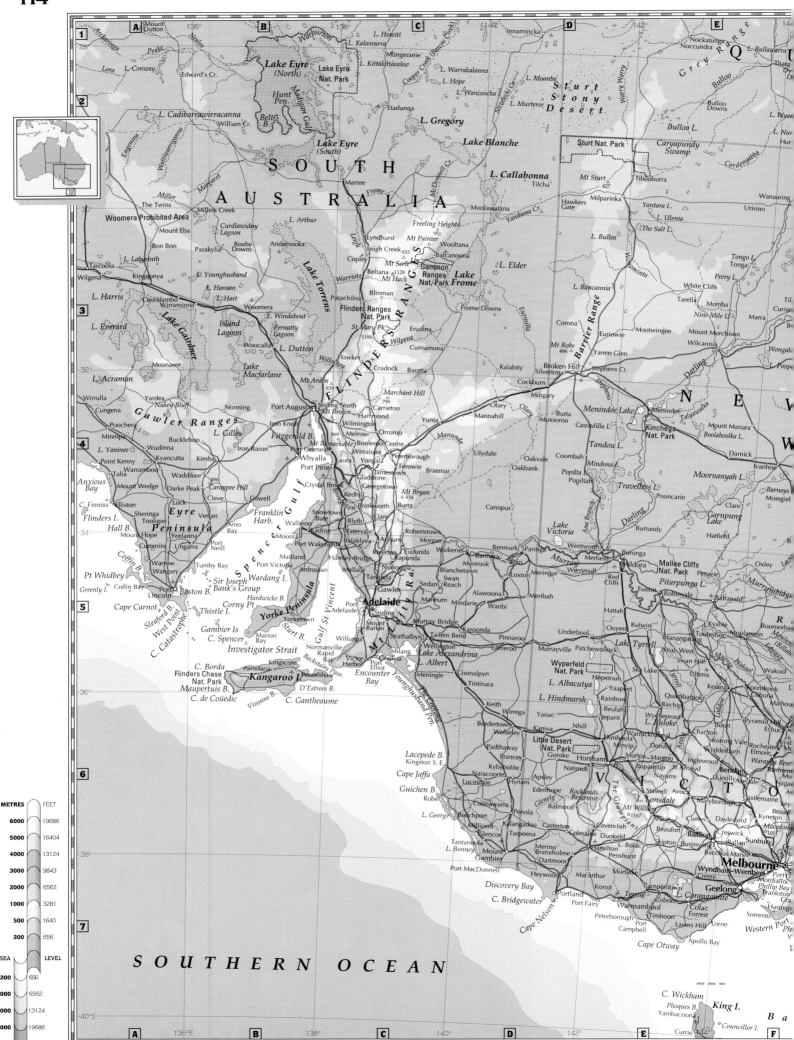

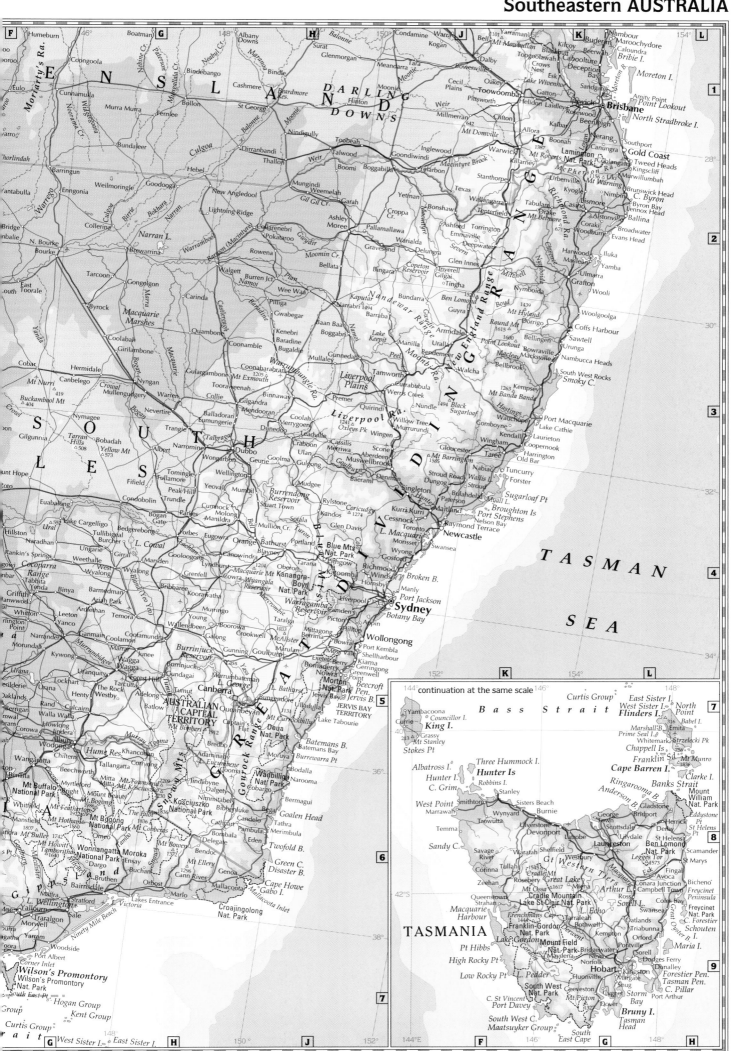

1:5M

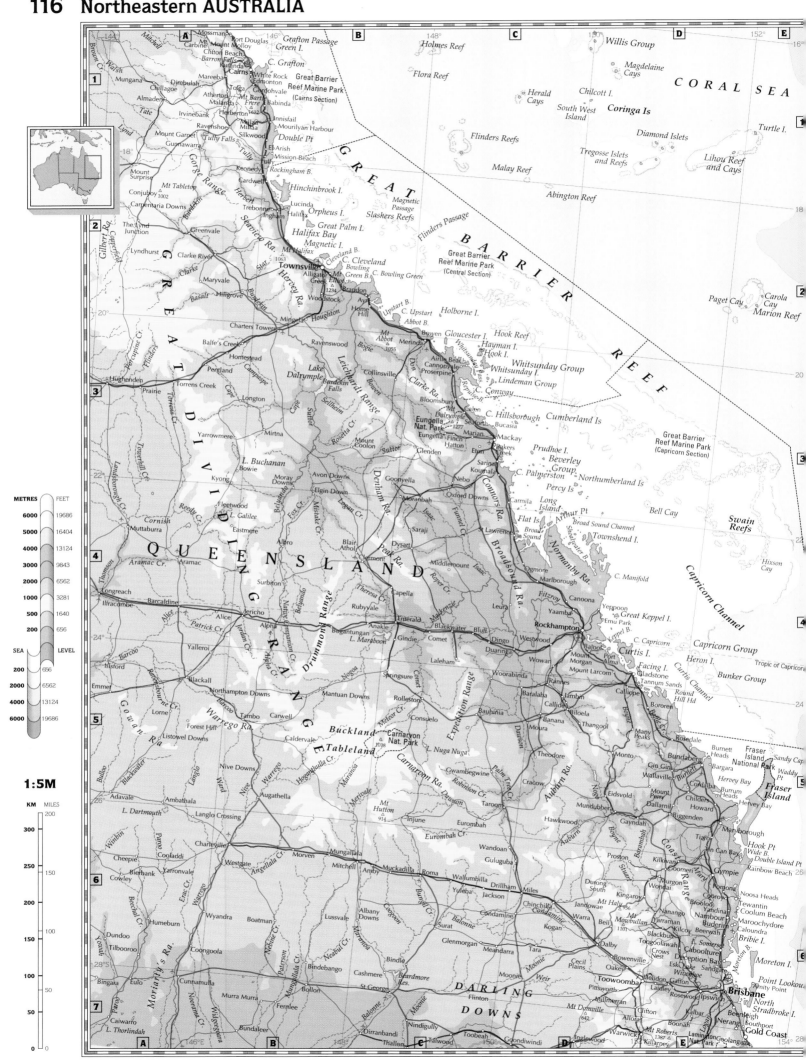

1:5M

Lambert Azimuthal Equal Area Projection

© Bartholomew

TASMAN SEA

NORTH ISLAND

SOUTH ISLAND

SOUTH PACIFIC OCEAN

Three Kings Is

Cape Reinga — North Cape
Cape Maria van Diemen
Te Paki
Parengarenga Harbour
Rangaunu Bay — C. Karikari
Doubtless Bay
Awanui — Kaeo — Bay of Islands — Cape Brett
Ahipara Bay — Kaitaia — Ahipara — Kerikeri — Russell
Tauroa Pt — Broadwood
Poor Knights Is
Hokianga Harbour — Taheke — Pakotai — Whangarei
Donnellys Crossing
Dargaville — Mokohinau Is
Tangaehe — Maumaturoro — Bream Bay — Port Fitzroy — Great Barrier Island
North Head — Warkworth — Leigh — Little Barrier
Kaipara Harbour — East Coast Bays — Colville Chan — Mercury Islands
Takapuna — Coromandel Peninsula — Whitianga
Auckland — Manukau — The Aldermen Is
Manukau Harbour — Thames — Whangamata
Pukekohe — Waihi — Mayor I. — Cape Runaway — Hicks Bay
Port Waikato — Te Aroha — Matakana I. — White I. — Waikawa Pt — Te Araroa
Glen Afton — Huntly — Waihi — Tauranga — Puke — **Bay of Plenty** — East Cape
Ngaruawahia — Waito — Katikati — Whakatane — Opotiki — Ruatoria
Hamilton — Waiharoa — Cambridge — Rotorua — Tokomaru Bay
Kawhia — Te Awamutu — Rotorua — Mawhai Pt — Tolaga Bay
Kawhia Harbour — Otorohanga — Mangakino — Murupara — Hikurangi
Te Kuiti — Tokoroa — Urewera Nat. Park
Awakino — Aria — Taupo — Poverty Bay
North Taranaki Bight — Mokau — Okahukura — Hauhungaroa — **Gisborne**
Waitara — Ohura — Lake Taupo — Wairoa — Frasertown
New Plymouth — Whangamomona — Turangi — Mohaka — Mahia Pen.
Cape Egmont — Egmont Nat. Park — Tongariro Nat. Park — Kaimanawa Mts — Nuhaka — Portland I. — Table Cape
Mt Taranaki — Stratford — Kaweka Range — Bay View — **Hawke Bay**
Opunake — Raetihi — Ohakune — Taihape — **Napier**
Hawera — Ripiriki — Waiouru — Hastings — Havelock North — C. Kidnappers
South Taranaki Bight — Patea — Waikaremoana — Waimarama
Wanganui — Turakina — Marton — Feilding — Kimbolton — Takapau — Waipawa — Waipukurau
Foxton — **Palmerston North** — Woodville — Dannevirke — Wanstead — Porangahau
Levin — Pahiatua — Cape Turnagain
Otaki — Eketahuna

Cape Farewell — Farewell Spit
Collingwood — Cape Stephens — Kapiti I. — Paraparaumu — Mitre — Castlepoint
Kahurangi Pt — **Golden Bay** — Separation Pt — D'Urville I. — Porirua — Masterton
Takaka — French Pass — Upper Hutt — Carterton
Abel Tasman Nat. Park — Tasman Bay — **Wellington** — Lower Hutt — Te Wharau
Upper Takaka — Riwaka — Nelson — Flat Point
Mts Richmond — Canvastown — Cloudy B. — Palliser Bay — Mt Ross
Karamea — Wakefield — Blenheim — Clifford B. — Cape Palliser
Karamea Bight — Owen River — Richmond — Seddon — Cape Campbell
Seddonville — Hope Saddle — Wairau
Waimangaroa — Westport — Bullet — Pinnacle
Cape Foulwind — Inangahua Junction — St Arnaud Range
Charleston — Reefton — Mt Travers
Runanga — Ahaura — Lewis P.
Greymouth — Springs Junction — Hanmer Springs — Kaikoura
Hokitika — L. Brunner — Mt Ajax — Hope — Inland Kaikoura Range — Clarence — Kaikoura Peninsula
Kowhitirangi — Reefton — Rotherham — Oaro
Ross — Kaniere — Mt Crossley — Culverden — Cheviot
Kumara — Arthur's Pass Nat. Park — Parnassus
Abut Head — Harihari — Waikari — Waipara — Pegasus Bay
Franz Josef Glacier — Mt Arrowsmith — Oxford — Rangiora — Kaiapoi — Belfast
Fox Glacier — Coleridge — Sheffield — **Christchurch** — Sumner
Southern Alps — Aoraki — Mt Cook — Te Pirita — Rolleston — Banks Peninsula
Westland Nat. Park — Mt Cook Nat. Park — Canterbury Plains — Ashburton — Akaroa
Haast — Mt Ward — Mt Cook — Mayfield — Southbridge Lake — Ellesmere — Akaroa Harb.
Jackson Head — Paringa — Lake Tekapo — Geraldine
Cascade Pt — Mt Aspiring Nat. Park — **Canterbury Bight**
Awarua Pt — Mt Aspiring — Pukaki — Temuka — Timaru
Milford Sd — Lake Pukaki — Fairlie — Pleasant Pt — Pareora
Milford Sound — Hawea — Benmore — Otematata — Oamaru
George Sd — Wanaka — Lake Wanaka — Kurow — Waimate — Studholme Junction
Caswell Sd — Fiordland National Park — Glenavy
Secretary I. — Queenstown — Cromwell — Duntroon — Pukeuri Junction — C. Wanbrow
Doubtful Sd — Te Anau — Alexandra — Hyde — Palmerston — Shag Pt
Breaksea Sd — Lake Manapouri — Ranfurly — Hampden — Waikouaiti
Resolution — Mt Ward — Kingston — Obelisk — Mosgiel — **Dunedin** — Otago Peninsula
Dusky Sd — Lumsden — Roxburgh — Port Chalmers — Brighton
Chalky In. — Athol — Mandeville — Beaumont — Warrington
Cape Providence — Tuatapere — Waikoikoi — Henley
Puysegur Pt — Winton — Waipahi — Milton
Orepuki — Edendale — Balclutha
Solander I. — Riverton — Gore — Kaitangata
Foveaux Strait — Invercargill — Mataura — Owaka — Nugget Pt
Codfish I. — Bluff — Otatara — Fortrose — Tokanui — Long Pt — Chaslands Mistake
Mason B. — Halfmoon Bay — Waipapa Pt
Stewart Island — Ruapuke I.
Muttonbird Is — South West Cape — Shelter Pt

Elevation Scale

METRES	FEET
6000	19686
5000	16404
4000	13124
3000	9843
2000	6562
1000	3281
500	1640
200	656
SEA	LEVEL
200	656
2000	6562
4000	13124
6000	19686

1:5M

KM	MILES
300	200
	150
250	
200	100
150	
	50
100	
0	0

Conic Equidistant Projection

© Bartholomew Ltd

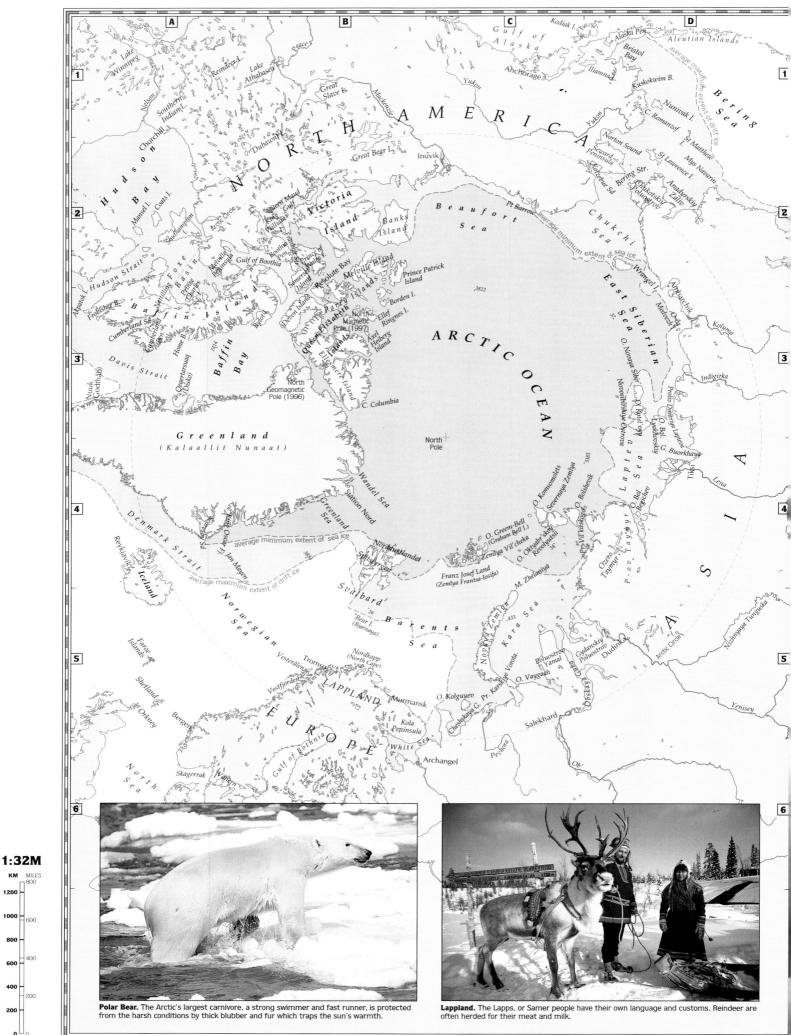

Polar Bear. The Arctic's largest carnivore, a strong swimmer and fast runner, is protected from the harsh conditions by thick blubber and fur which traps the sun's warmth.

Lappland. The Lapps, or Samer people have their own language and customs. Reindeer are often herded for their meat and milk.

1:32M

KM MILES

1200 — 800

1000 — 600

800 — 400

600

400 — 200

200

0 — 0

Polar Stereographic Projection

© Bartholomew

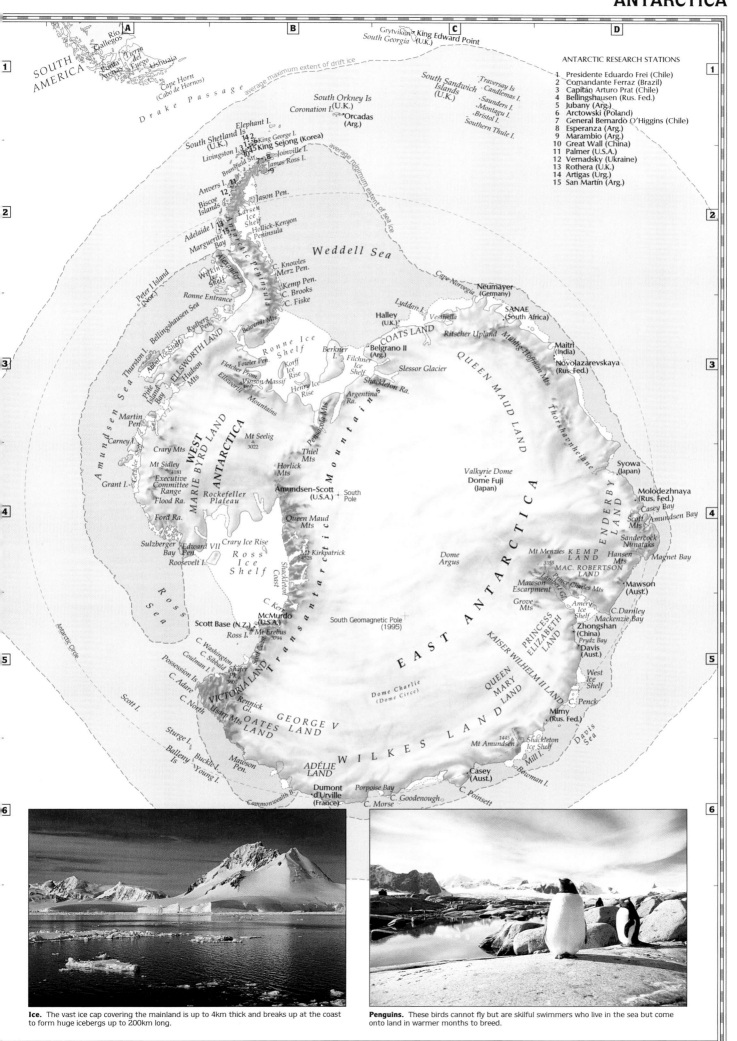

SOUTH AMERICA
Rio Gallegos
Punta Arenas
Tierra del Fuego
Ushuaia
Cape Horn (Cabo de Hornos)

Drake Passage

average maximum extent of drift ice

average minimum extent of sea ice

South Sandwich Islands (U.K.)
Traversay Is
Candlemas I.
Saunders I.
Montagu I.
Bristol I.
Southern Thule I.

South Orkney Is
Coronation I. (U.K.)
Orcadas (Arg.)

Elephant I.
South Shetland Is (U.K.)
King George I.
Livingston I.
King Sejong (Korea)
Joinville I.
James Ross I.
Bransfield Str.

Anvers I.
Biscoe Islands
Jason Pen.

Adelaide I.
Marguerite Bay
Larsen Ice Shelf
Hollick-Kenyon Peninsula

Weddell Sea

Peter I Island (Nor.)
Alexander I.
Wilkins Ice Shelf

Bellingshausen Sea

C. Knowles
Merz Pen.
Kemp Pen.
C. Brooks
C. Fiske

Cape Norvegia
Neumayer (Germany)

Lyddan I.
Vestfjella
SANAE (South Africa)

Halley (U.K.)
COATS LAND
Ritscher Upland
Mühlig-Hofmann Mts

Maitri (India)
Novolazarevskaya (Rus. Fed.)

Ronne Entrance
Rydberg Pen.
Thurston I.
Abbot Ice Shelf
Pine Island Bay

ELLSWORTH LAND
Behrendt Mts
Ronne Ice Shelf
Berkner I.
Fowler Pen.
Korff Ice Rise
Filchner Ice Shelf
Belgrano II (Arg.)
Shackleton Ra.
Slessor Glacier

QUEEN MAUD LAND

Thorshavnheiane

Fletcher Prom.
Vinson Massif
Henry Ice Rise
Pensacola Mts
Argentina Ra.

Martin Pen.
Carney I.
Grant I.
Crary Mts
Mt Sidley
Executive Committee Range
Flood Ra.
Ford Ra.

WEST ANTARCTICA
MARIE BYRD LAND
ELLSWORTH LAND
Hudson Mts
Ellsworth Mountains

Mt Seelig 3022
Thiel Mts
Horlick Mts

Rockefeller Plateau

Transantarctic Mountains

Amundsen-Scott (U.S.A.)
+ South Pole

Queen Maud Mts

Valkyrie Dome
Dome Fuji (Japan)

Syowa (Japan)

ENDERBY LAND
Molodezhnaya (Rus. Fed.)
Casey Bay
Scott Mts
Amundsen Bay
Sandercock Nunataks
Magnet Bay

Dome Argus

Mt Menzies 3355
Hansen Mts
KEMP LAND
MAC. ROBERTSON LAND
Mawson Escarpment
Prince Charles Mts
Grove Mts
Lambert Gl.
Amery Ice Shelf

Mawson (Aust.)
C. Darnley
Mackenzie Bay

Sulzberger Bay
Edward VII Pen.
Roosevelt I.
Crary Ice Rise
Ross Ice Shelf
Mt Kirkpatrick 4528
Shackleton Coast

Ross Sea

Antarctic Circle

C. Kerr
Scott Base (N.Z.)
McMurdo (U.S.A.)
Ross I.
Mt Erebus 3794
C. Washington
C. Sibbald
Coulman I.
Possession Is
C. Adare
C. North
Rennick Gl.
Shafer Pk. 3600
Usarp Mts

VICTORIA LAND

South Geomagnetic Pole (1995)

EAST ANTARCTICA

KAISER WILHELM II LAND
PRINCESS ELIZABETH LAND
Zhongshan (China)
Prydz Bay
Davis (Aust.)
West Ice Shelf
C. Penck

QUEEN MARY LAND

Dome Charlie (Dome Circe)

Mirny (Rus. Fed.)

Davis Sea

Scott I.

Sturge I.
Balleny Is
Buckle I.
Young I.

OATES LAND
GEORGE V LAND
Mawson Pen.

WILKES LAND
Mt Amundsen 1445
Shackleton Ice Shelf
Mill I.

ADÉLIE LAND
Dumont d'Urville (France)
Porpoise Bay
C. Goodenough
C. Poinsett
Casey (Aust.)
Bowman I.
Commonwealth B.
C. Morse

ANTARCTIC RESEARCH STATIONS
1 Presidente Eduardo Frei (Chile)
2 Comandante Ferraz (Brazil)
3 Capitán Arturo Prat (Chile)
4 Bellingshausen (Rus. Fed.)
5 Jubany (Arg.)
6 Arctowski (Poland)
7 General Bernardo O'Higgins (Chile)
8 Esperanza (Arg.)
9 Marambio (Arg.)
10 Great Wall (China)
11 Palmer (U.S.A.)
12 Vernadsky (Ukraine)
13 Rothera (U.K.)
14 Artigas (Urg.)
15 San Martín (Arg.)

Ice. The vast ice cap covering the mainland is up to 4km thick and breaks up at the coast to form huge icebergs up to 200km long.

Penguins. These birds cannot fly but are skilful swimmers who live in the sea but come onto land in warmer months to breed.

1:32M
KM   MILES
1200   800
1000   600
800
600   400
400   200
200
0   0

Stereographic Projection

© Bartholomew Ltd

THE INDEX includes the names on the maps in the ATLAS. The names are generally indexed to the largest scale map on which they appear, and can be located using the grid reference letters and numbers around the map frame. Names on insets have a symbol: □, followed by the inset number.

Abbreviations used to describe features in the index and on the maps are explained below.

ABBREVIATIONS AND GLOSSARY

A.   Alp Alpen Alpi *alp*
    Alt *upper*
A.C.T.   Australian Capital Territory
Afgh.   Afghanistan
Afr.   Africa African
Aig.   Aiguille *peak*
AK   Alaska
AL   Alabama
Alg.   Algeria
Alta   Alberta
AR   Arkansas
Arch.   Archipelago
Arg.   Argentina
Arr.   Arrecife *reef*
Austr.   Australia
AZ   Arizona
Azer.   Azerbaijan

B.   Bad *spa*
    Ban *village*
    Bay
Bangl.   Bangladesh
B.C.   British Columbia
Bg   Berg *mountain*
Bge.   Barragem *reservoir*
Bgt   Bight Bugt *bay*
Bj   Burj *hills*
Bol.   Bolivia
Bos.-Herz.   Bosnia Herzegovina
Br.   Burun Burnu *point, cape*
Bt   Bukit *bay*
Bü.   Büyük *big*
Bulg.   Bulgaria

C.   Cape
    Col *high pass*
Ç.   Çay *river*
CA   California
Cabo   Cabeço *summit*
Can.   Canada
    Canal Canale *canal, channel*
    Cañon Canyon *canyon*
C.A.R.   Central African Republic
Cat.   Cataract
    Catena *mountains*
Cd   Ciudad *town city*
Ch.   Chaung *stream*
    Chott *salt lake, marsh*
Chan.   Channel
Che   Chaîne *mountain chain*
Cma   Cima *summit*
Cno   Corno *peak*
Co   Cerro *hill, peak*
CO   Colorado
Col.   Colombia
Cord.   Cordillera *mountain chain*
Cr.   Creek
CT   Connecticut
Cuch.   Cuchilla *chain of mountains*

D.   Da *big, river*
    Dag Dagh Dağı *mountain*
    Dağları *mountains*
-d.   -dake *peak*
DE   Delaware
Dem. Rep. Congo   Democratic Republic of Congo
Dj.   Djebel *mountain*
Dom. Rep.   Dominican Republic

Eil.   Eiland *island*
    Eilanden *islands*
Emb.   Embalse *reservoir*
Equat.   Equatorial
Escarp.   Escarpment
Est.   Estuary
Eth.   Ethiopia
Etg   Etang *lake, lagoon*

F.   Firth

Fin.   Finland
Fj.   Fjell *mountain*
    Fjord Fjördur *fjord*
Fl.   Fleuve *river*
FL   Florida
Fr.   French
F.Y.R.O.M.   Former Yugoslav Republic of Macedonia

G.   Gebel *mountain*
    Göl Gölö Göl *lake*
G.   Golfe Golfo Gulf Guba *gulf, bay*
    Gunung *mountain*
-g.   -gawa *river*
GA   Georgia
Gd   Grand *big*
Gde   Grande *big*
Geb.   Gebergte *mountain range*
    Gebirge *mountains*
Gl.   Glacier
Ger.   Germany
Gr.   Graben *trench, ditch*
    Gross Grosse
    Grande *big*
Grp   Group
Gt   Great Groot Groote *big*
Gy   Góry Gory *mountains*

H.   Hawr *lake*
    Hill Hills
    Hoch *high*
    Hora *mountain*
    Hory *mountains*
Harb.   Harbour
Hd   Head
Hgts   Heights
HI   Hawaii
Ht   Haut *high*
Hte   Haute *high*

I.   Île Ilha Insel Isla Island Isle *island, isle*
    Isola Isole *island*
IA   Iowa
ID   Idaho
IL   Illinois
IN   Indiana
Indon.   Indonesia
Is   Islas Îles Ilhas Islands Isles *islands, isles*
Isr.   Israel
Isth.   Isthmus

J.   Jabal Jebel *mountain*
    Jibāl *mountains*
    Jrvi Jaure Jezero
    Jezioro *lake*
    Jökull *glacier*

K.   Kaap Kap Kapp *cape*
    Kaikyō *strait*
    Kato Káto *lower*
    Kiang *river or stream*
    Ko *island, lake, inlet*
    Koh Küh Kühha *island*
    Kolpos *gulf*
    Kopf *hill*
    Kuala *estuary*
    Kyst *coast*
    Küçük *small*
Kan.   Kanal Kanaal *canal*
Kazak.   Kazakhstan
Kep.   Kepulauan *archipelago, islands*
Kg   Kampong *village*
Khr.   Khrebet *mountain range*
Kl.   Klein Kleine *small*
Kör.   Körfez Körfezi *bay, gulf*
KS   Kansas
KY   Kentucky
Kyrg.   Kyrgyzstan

L.   Lac Lago Lake
    Liqen Loch Lough *lake, loch*
    Lam *stream*

LA   Louisiana
Lag.   Lagoon Laguna
    Lagôa *lagoon*
Lith.   Lithuania
Lux.   Luxembourg

M.   Mae *river*
    Me *great, chief, mother*
    Meer *lake, sea*
    Muang *kingdom, province, town*
    Muong *town*
    Mys *cape*
    Maloye *small*
MA   Massachusetts
Madag.   Madagascar
Man.   Manitoba
Maur.   Mauritania
MD   Maryland
ME   Maine
Mex.   Mexico
Mf   Massif *mountains, upland*
Mgna   Montagna *mountain*
Mgne   Montagne *mountain*
Mgnes   Montagnes *mountains*
MI   Michigan
MN   Minnesota
MO   Missouri
Mon.   Monasterio Monastery *monastery*
    Monument *monument*
Moz.   Mozambique
MS   Mississippi
Mt   Mont Mount *mountain*
Mt.   Mountain
MT   Montana
Mte   Monte *mountain*
Mtes   Montes *mountains*
Mti   Monti Munți *mountains*
Mtii   Munţii *mountains*
Mth   Mouth
Mths   Mouths
Mtn   Mountain
Mts   Monts Mountains

N.   Nam *south(ern), river*
    Neu Ny *new*
    Nevado *peak*
    Nudo *mountain*
    Noord Nord Nörre
    Nørre North *north(ern)*
    Nos *spit, point*
Nac.   Nacional *national*
Nat.   National
N.B.   New Brunswick
NC   North Carolina
ND   North Dakota
NE   Nebraska
Neth.   Netherlands
Nfld   Newfoundland
NH   New Hampshire
Nic.   Nicaragua
Nizh.   Nizhneye Nizhniy Nizhnyaya *lower*
Nizm.   Nizmennost' *lowland*
NJ   New Jersey
NM   New Mexico
N.O.   Noord Oost Nord Ost *northeast*
Nov.   Novyy Novaya Noviye Novoye *new*
N.S.   Nova Scotia
N.S.W.   New South Wales
N.T.   Northern Territory
NV   Nevada
Nva   Nueva *new*
N.W.T.   Northwest Territories
NY   New York
N.Z.   New Zealand

O.   Oost Ost *east*
    Ostrov *island*
Ø   Østre *east*
Ob.   Ober *upper, higher*
Oc.   Ocean
Ode   Oude *old*
Ogl.   Oglat *well*
OH   Ohio
OK   Oklahoma
Ont.   Ontario
Or.   Óri Óros Ori *mountains*
    Oros *mountain*
OR   Oregon
Orm.   Ormos *bay*
O-va   Ostrova *islands*
Ot   Olet *mountain*

Öv.   Över Övre *upper*
Oz.   Ozero *lake*
    Ozera *lakes*

P.   Pass
    Pic Pico Piz *peak, summit*
    Pou *mountain*
    Pulau *island*
PA   Pennsylvania
Pak.   Pakistan
Para.   Paraguay
Pass.   Passage
Peg.   Pegunungan *mountain range*
P.E.I.   Prince Edward Island
Pen.   Peninsula Penisola *peninsula*
Per.   Pereval *pass*
Phil.   Philippines
Phn.   Phnom *hill, mountain*
Pgio   Poggio *hill*
Pl.   Planina Planinski *mountain(s)*
Pla   Playa *beach*
Plat.   Plateau
Plosk.   Ploskogor'ye *plateau*
P.N.G.   Papua New Guinea
Pno   Pantano *reservoir, swamp*
Pol.   Poland
Por.   Porog *rapids*
Port.   Portugal
P-ov   Poluostrov *peninsula*
P.P.   Pulau-pulau *islands*
Pr.   Proliv *strait*
    Przylądek *cape*
Presq.   Presqu'île *peninsula*
Prom.   Promontory
Prov.   Province Provincial
Psa   Presa *dam*
Pso   Passo *dam*
Pt   Point
    Pont *bridge*
    Petit *small*
Pta   Ponta Punta *cape, point*
    Puerta *narrow pass*
Pte   Pointe *cape, point*
    Ponte Puente *bridge*
Pto   Porto Puerto *harbour, port*
Pzo   Pizzo *mountain peak, mountain*

Qld.   Queensland
Que.   Quebec

R.   Reshteh *mountain range*
    Rio Río Rivière Rüd *river*
Ra.   Range
Rca   Rocca *rock, fortress*
Reg.   Region
Rep.   Republic
Res.   Reserve
Resr   Reservoir
Resp.   Respublika *republic*
Rf   Reef
Rge   Ridge
RI   Rhode Island
Riba   Ribeira *coast, bottom of the river valley*
Rte   Route
Rus. Fed.   Russian Federation

S.   Salar Salina *salt pan*
    San São *saint*
    See *lake*
    Seto *strait, channel*
    Sjö *lake*
    Sör Süd Sud Syd *south*
    sur *on*
Sa   Serra Sierra *mountain range*
S.A.   South Australia
Sab.   Sabkhat *salt flat*
Sask.   Saskatchewan
SC   South Carolina
Sc.   Scoglio *rock, reef*
Sd   Sound Sund *sound*
SD   South Dakota
Seb.   Sebjet Sebkhat Sebkra *salt flat*
Serr.   Serranía *mountain range*
Sev.   Severnaya Severnyy *north(ern)*
Sh.   Shā'ib *watercourse*
    Shaţţ *river (-mouth)*
    Shima *island*
    Shankou *pass*

Si   Sidi *lord, master*
Sing.   Singapore
Sk.   Shuiku *reservoir*
Skt   Sankt *saint*
Smt   Seamount
Snra   Senhora *Mrs, lady*
Snro   Senhoro *Mr, gentleman*
Sp.   Spain Spanish
    Spitze *peak*
Sr   Sönder Sönder *southern*
Sr.   Sredniy Srednyaya *middle*
St   Saint Sint
    Staryy *old*
St.   Stor Store *big*
    Stung *river*
Sta   Santa *saint*
Ste   Sainte *saint*
    Store *big*
Sto   Santo *saint*
Str.   Strait Stretta *strait*
Sv.   Svätý Sveti *holy, saint*
Switz.   Switzerland

T.   Tal *valley*
    Tall Tell *hill*
    Tepe Tepesi *hill, peak*
Tajik.   Tajikistan
Tanz.   Tanzania
Tas.   Tasmania
Terr.   Territory
Tg   Tanjung Tanjong *cape, point*
Thai.   Thailand
Tk   Teluk *bay*
Tmt   Tablemount
TN   Tennessee
Tr.   Trench Trough
Tre   Torre *tower, fortress*
Tte   Teniente *lieutenant*
Turkm.   Turkmenistan
TX   Texas

U.A.E.   United Arab Emirates
Ug   Ujung *point, cape*
U.K.   United Kingdom
Ukr.   Ukraine
Unt.   Unter *lower*
Upr   Upper
Uru.   Uruguay
U.S.A.   United States of America
UT   Utah
Uzbek.   Uzbekistan

V.   Val Valle Valley *valley*
    Väster Vest Vester *west(ern)*
    Vatn *lake*
    Ville *town*
Va   Vila *small town*
VA   Virginia
Venez.   Venezuela
Vic.   Victoria
Volc.   Volcán Volcan
    Volcano *volcano*
Vdkhr.   Vodokhranilishche *reservoir*
Vdskh.   Vodoskhovyshche Vodaskhovishcha *reservoir*
Vel.   Velikiy Velikaya Velikiye *big*
Verkh.   Verkhniy Verkhneye Verkhne *upper* Verkhnyaya *upper*
Vost.   Vostochnyy *eastern*
Vozv.   Vozvyshennost' *hills, upland*
VT   Vermont

W.   Wadi *watercourse*
    Wald *forest*
    Wan *bay*
    Water *water*
WA   Washington
W.A.   Western Australia
Wr   Wester
WV   West Virginia
WY   Wyoming

-y   -yama *mountain*
Yt.   Ytre Ytter Ytri *outer*
Yugo.   Yugoslavia
Yuzh.   Yuzhnaya Yuzhno Yuzhnyy *southern*

Zal.   Zaliv *bay*
Zap.   Zapadnyy Zapadnaya Zapadno Zapadnoye *western*
Zem.   Zemlya *land*

A

62 C5 Aachen Ger.
62 E6 Aalen Ger.
61 C2 Aalsmeer Neth.
61 C4 Aalst Belgium
61 C4 Aarschot Belgium
88 A3 Aba China
102 D3 Aba Dem. Rep. Congo
100 C4 Aba Nigeria
81 M6 Ābādān Iran
79 G3 Ābādeh Iran
100 B1 Abadla Alg.
46 D2 Abaeté r. Brazil
43 J4 Abaetetuba Brazil
25 E4 Abajo Pk summit U.S.A.
100 C4 Abakaliki Nigeria
86 F1 Abakan Rus. Fed.
86 F1 Abakanskiy Khrebet mts Rus. Fed.
69 E7 Abana Turkey
42 C5 Abancay Peru
79 G3 Abarqū Iran
90 J2 Abashiri Japan
90 J2 Abashiri-wan b. Japan
110 E3 Abau P.N.G.
102 D3 Abaya Hāyk' l. Eth.
    Ābay Wenz r. see Blue Nile
86 F1 Abaza Rus. Fed.
66 C4 Abbasanta Italy
30 C2 Abbaye, Pt pt U.S.A.
65 A5 Abbaye de Chaalis France
61 D5 Abbaye d'Orval Belgium
102 E2 Abbe, L. l. Eth.
64 L1 Abbeville France
27 E6 Abbeville LA U.S.A.
29 D5 Abbeville SC U.S.A.
60 B5 Abbeyfeale Rep. of Ireland
57 E6 Abbey Head hd U.K.
60 D5 Abbeyleix Rep. of Ireland
58 D3 Abbeytown U.K.
54 Q4 Abborrträsk Sweden
116 B3 Abbot, Mt mt Austr.
116 B2 Abbot B. b. Austr.
119 A3 Abbot Ice Shelf ice feature Antarctica
20 E5 Abbotsford Can.
30 B3 Abbotsford U.S.A.
25 H4 Abbott U.S.A.
84 C2 Abbottabad Pak.
81 H3 'Abd al 'Azīz, J. h. Syria
81 L5 Abdānān Iran
101 E3 Abéché Chad
117 D4 Abel Tasman National Park nat. park N.Z.
100 B4 Abengourou Côte d'Ivoire
55 L9 Åbenrå Denmark
100 C4 Abeokuta Nigeria
59 C5 Aberaeron U.K.
57 F3 Aberchirder U.K.
115 H5 Abercrombie r. Austr.
59 D6 Aberdare U.K.
59 C5 Aberdaron U.K.
115 J4 Aberdeen Austr.
21 H4 Aberdeen Can.
89 □ Aberdeen China
104 E6 Aberdeen S. Africa
57 F3 Aberdeen U.K.
33 E5 Aberdeen MD U.S.A.
27 F5 Aberdeen MS U.S.A.
26 D2 Aberdeen SD U.S.A.
24 B2 Aberdeen WA U.S.A.
21 J2 Aberdeen Lake l. Can.
57 E4 Aberdyfi U.K.
57 E4 Aberfeldy U.K.
58 F4 Aberford U.K.
57 D4 Aberfoyle U.K.
59 D6 Abergavenny U.K.
27 C5 Abernathy U.S.A.
59 C5 Aberporth U.K.
59 C5 Abersoch U.K.
59 C5 Aberystwyth U.K.
78 E6 Abhā Saudi Arabia
81 M3 Abhar Iran
81 M4 Abhar Rūd r. Iran
    Abiad, Bahr el r. see White Nile
45 A2 Abiad, Serranía de mts Col.
100 B4 Abidjan Côte d'Ivoire
84 B2 Ab-i-Istada l. Afgh.
102 D3 Abijatta-Shalla National Park nat. park Eth.
26 D4 Abilene KS U.S.A.
27 D5 Abilene TX U.S.A.
59 F6 Abingdon U.K.
30 B5 Abingdon IL U.S.A.
32 C6 Abingdon VA U.S.A.
116 C2 Abington Reef rf Coral Sea Is. Terr.
69 F6 Abinsk Rus. Fed.
42 C5 Abiseo, Parque Nacional nat. park Peru
21 H2 Abitau Lake l. Can.
22 E4 Abitibi r. Can.
22 E4 Abitibi, Lake l. Can.
81 K5 Āb Naft r. Iraq
84 C3 Abohar India
100 B4 Aboisso Côte d'Ivoire
100 C4 Abomey Benin
101 D4 Abong Mbang Cameroon
94 A4 Aborlan Phil.
101 D3 Abou Déia Chad
81 K1 Abovyan Armenia
57 F3 Aboyne U.K.
79 F4 Abqaiq Saudi Arabia
47 K2 Abra, L. del l. Arg.
65 B3 Abrantes Port.
44 C2 Abra Pampa Arg.

46 E2 Abrolhos, Arquipélago dos is Brazil
24 E2 Absaroka Range mts U.S.A.
78 E6 Abū 'Arīsh Saudi Arabia
79 G5 Abu Dhabi U.A.E.
101 F3 Abu Hamed Sudan
100 C4 Abuja Nigeria
81 H4 Abū Kamāl Syria
101 E3 Abū Matariq Sudan
42 E6 Abunã r. Bol.
42 E5 Abunã Brazil
78 D7 Ābune Yosēf mt Eth.
80 C6 Abu Qīr, Khalīg b. Egypt
82 D6 Abu Road India
78 C5 Abu Simbel Egypt
81 K6 Abū Şukhayr Iraq
117 C2 Abut Head hd N.Z.
94 C4 Abuyog Phil.
101 E3 Abu Zabad Sudan
    Abū Żabī see Abu Dhabi
81 M6 Abūzām Iran
101 E3 Abyad Sudan
101 E4 Abyei Sudan
33 J2 Acadia Nat. Park nat. park U.S.A.
36 D4 Acambaro Mex.
45 A2 Acandí Col.
65 B1 A Cañiza Spain
36 E5 Acaponeta Mex.
36 E5 Acapulco Mex.
43 J4 Acará Brazil
43 K4 Acaraú r. Brazil
44 E4 Acaray r. Para.
44 E3 Acaray, Represa de resr Para.
45 C2 Acarigua Venez.
36 F5 Acayucán Mex.
100 B4 Accra Ghana
58 E4 Accrington U.K.
45 C3 Achaguas Venez.
84 D5 Achalpur India
77 T3 Achayvayam Rus. Fed.
60 A4 Achill Island i. Rep. of Ireland
60 B4 Achill Sound Rep. of Ireland
57 C2 Achiltibuie U.K.
76 L4 Achinsk Rus. Fed.
57 C2 Achnasheen U.K.
57 C3 A'Chralaig mt U.K.
69 F6 Achuyevo Rus. Fed.
80 B3 Acıgöl l. Turkey
80 B3 Acıpayam Turkey
66 F6 Acireale Italy
26 E3 Ackley U.S.A.
37 K4 Acklins Island i. Bahamas
59 J5 Acle U.K.
47 B2 Aconcagua r. Chile
47 B2 Aconcagua, Cerro mt Arg.
43 L5 Acopiara Brazil
65 B1 A Coruña Spain
66 C2 Acqui Terme Italy
114 A4 Acraman, L. salt flat Austr.
80 E5 Acre Israel
66 G5 Acri Italy
62 J7 Ács Hungary
109 Actéon, Groupe atolls Pac. Oc.
32 D4 Ada OH U.S.A.
27 D5 Ada OK U.S.A.
65 D2 Adaja r. Spain
44 E8 Adam, Mt h. Falkland Is
115 H6 Adaminaby Austr.
33 G3 Adams MA U.S.A.
30 C4 Adams WV U.S.A.
24 B2 Adams, Mt mt U.S.A.
20 F4 Adams L. l. Can.
35 E2 Adams McGill Reservoir resr U.S.A.
20 C3 Adams Mt. mt U.S.A.
    Adam's Peak mt see Sri Pada
34 C2 Adams Peak mt U.S.A.
    'Adan see Aden
80 C2 Adana Turkey
60 C5 Adare Rep. of Ireland
119 A5 Adare, C. c. Antarctica
116 A5 Adavale Austr.
35 E2 Adaven U.S.A.
81 K5 Ad Daghgharah Iraq
78 F5 Ad Dahnā' des. Saudi Arabia
100 A2 Ad Dakhla Western Sahara
79 G4 Ad Dammām Saudi Arabia
    Ad Dawḥah see Doha
81 J4 Ad Dawr Iraq
78 F5 Ad Dir'īyah Saudi Arabia
102 D3 Addis Ababa Eth.
33 K2 Addison U.S.A.
81 K6 Ad Dīwānīyah Iraq
59 G6 Addlestone U.K.
13 J4 Addu Atoll atoll Maldives
81 J6 Ad Duwayd w. Saudi Arabia
29 D6 Adel GA U.S.A.
26 E3 Adel IA U.S.A.
114 C5 Adelaide Austr.
105 G6 Adelaide S. Africa
29 E7 Adelaide Bahamas
119 B2 Adelaide I. i. Antarctica
112 F2 Adelaide River Austr.
34 D4 Adelanto U.S.A.
119 B6 Adélie Land reg. Antarctica
115 H5 Adelong Austr.
78 E7 Aden Yemen
102 E2 Aden, Gulf of g. Somalia/Yemen
93 J7 Adi i. Indon.
102 D2 Ādī Ārk'ay Eth.

102 D2 Ādīgrat Eth.
84 D6 Adilabad India
81 J2 Adilcevaz Turkey
24 B3 Adin U.S.A.
101 D2 Adīrī Libya
33 F2 Adirondack Mountains mts U.S.A.
    Ādīs Ābeba see Addis Ababa
102 D3 Ādīs Alem Eth.
80 G3 Adıyaman Turkey
63 N7 Adjud Romania
23 J3 Adlavik Islands is Can.
112 E2 Admiralty Gulf b. Austr.
20 C3 Admiralty Island i. U.S.A.
20 C3 Admiralty Island National Monument – Kootznoowoo Wilderness res. U.S.A.
110 E2 Admiralty Islands is P.N.G.
119 A5 Admiralty Mts mts Antarctica
83 E7 Adoni India
64 D5 Adour r. France
65 E4 Adra Spain
66 F6 Adrano Italy
100 B2 Adrar Alg.
100 C2 Adrar mts Alg.
101 D3 Adré Chad
31 E5 Adrian MI U.S.A.
27 C5 Adrian TX U.S.A.
52 Adriatic Sea sea Europe
102 C3 Adusa Dem. Rep. Congo
102 D2 Ādwa Eth.
77 P3 Adycha r. Rus. Fed.
69 F6 Adygeya, Respublika div. Rus. Fed.
69 G6 Adygeysk Rus. Fed.
69 H6 Adyk Rus. Fed.
100 B4 Adzopé Côte d'Ivoire
52 Aegean Sea sea Greece/Turkey
65 B1 A Estrada Spain
102 D2 Afabet Eritrea
81 K3 Afan Iran
70 Afghanistan country Asia
54 M5 Åfjord Norway
102 E3 Afmadow Somalia
65 C1 A Fonsagrada Spain
80 F3 'Afrīn, Nahr r. Syria/Turkey
80 F2 Afşin Turkey
61 D2 Afsluitdijk barrage Neth.
24 E3 Afton U.S.A.
43 H4 Afuá Brazil
80 E5 'Afula Israel
80 C2 Afyon Turkey
100 C3 Agadez Niger
100 B1 Agadir Morocco
82 D7 Agadyr' Kazak.
85 G5 Agartala India
84 C4 Agashi India
31 F2 Agate Can.
67 M6 Agathonisi i. Greece
83 D8 Agatti i. India
100 B4 Agboville Côte d'Ivoire
81 L1 Ağcabädi Azer.
81 L2 Ağdam Azer.
64 F5 Agde France
64 E4 Agen France
104 C4 Aggeneys S. Africa
61 F4 Agger r. Ger.
84 D1 Aghil Pass pass China
60 C3 Aghla Mountain h. Rep. of Ireland
67 L7 Agia Vervara Greece
80 C1 Ağın Turkey
67 K6 Agios Dimitrios Greece
67 K6 Agios Efstratios i. Greece
67 M5 Agios Fokas, Akra pt Greece
67 L7 Agios Konstantinos Greece
67 L7 Agios Nikolaos Greece
67 K4 Agiou Orous, Kolpos b. Greece
101 F3 Agirwat Hills h. Sudan
105 F3 Agisanang S. Africa
100 B4 Agnibilékrou Côte d'Ivoire
67 L2 Agnita Romania
88 A2 Agong China
84 D4 Agra India
69 H7 Agrakhanskiy Poluostrov pen. Rus. Fed.
84 B1 Agram Pass pass Pak.
65 F2 Agreda Spain
81 J2 Ağrı Turkey
67 K7 Agria Gramvousa i. Greece
66 E6 Agrigento Italy
93 L3 Agrihan i. N. Mariana Is
67 J5 Agrinio Greece
47 B3 Agrio r. Arg.
66 F4 Agropoli Italy
81 K1 Ağstafa Azer.
81 M1 Ağsu Azer.
45 B3 Aguadas Col.
37 L5 Aguadilla Puerto Rico
47 C3 Agua Dulce Arg.
37 H7 Aguadulce Panama
47 C3 Agua Escondida Arg.
47 B4 Aguanaval r. Mex.
47 C1 Agua Negra, Paso del pass Arg./Chile
46 B3 Aguapei r. Brazil
36 C2 Agua Prieta Mex.
45 D2 Aguaray Guazú r. Para.
45 D2 Aguaro-Guariquito, Parque Nacional nat. park Venez.
36 D4 Aguascalientes Mex.
46 E2 Águas Formosas Brazil

46 C3 Agudos Brazil
35 F5 Aguila U.S.A.
65 D1 Aguilar de Campóo Spain
65 E3 Águilas Spain
94 B4 Aguisan Phil.
104 D7 Agulhas, Cape c. S. Africa
13 F7 Agulhas Basin sea feature Indian Ocean
46 D3 Agulhas Negras mt Brazil
13 F6 Agulhas Plateau sea feature Indian Ocean
92 □ Agung, G. vol. Indon.
94 C4 Agusan r. Phil.
94 B3 Agutaya Phil.
81 L2 Ahar Iran
117 B6 Ahaura N.Z.
61 F2 Ahaus Ger.
117 F3 Ahimanawa Ra. mts N.Z.
117 D1 Ahipara N.Z.
117 D1 Ahipara Bay b. N.Z.
81 J2 Ahlat Turkey
84 C5 Ahmadabad India
83 D7 Ahmadnagar India
84 B3 Ahmadpur East Pak.
79 L3 Ahmadpur Sial Pak.
54 T5 Ähtäri Fin.
55 U7 Ahtme Estonia
81 M6 Āhū Iran
64 F3 Ahun France
117 B6 Ahuriri r. N.Z.
81 M6 Ahvāz Iran
84 C5 Ahwa India
    Ahwāz see Ahvāz
104 B3 Ai-Ais Namibia
88 D1 Aibag Gol r. China
34 □1 Aiea U.S.A.
80 E4 Aigialousa Cyprus
67 K6 Aigina i. Greece
67 J5 Aigio Greece
64 H4 Aigle de Chambeyron mt France
47 F2 Aiguá Uru.
91 F5 Aikawa Japan
29 D5 Aiken U.S.A.
31 G4 Ailsa Craig Can.
57 C5 Ailsa Craig i. U.K.
46 E2 Aimorés, Sa dos h. Brazil
100 C1 Aïn Beïda Alg.
100 B2 Aïn Ben Tili Maur.
65 H5 Aïn Defla Alg.
100 B1 Aïn el Hadjel Alg.
100 B1 Aïn Sefra Alg.
23 H4 Ainslie, Lake l. Can.
26 D3 Ainsworth U.S.A.
    Aintab see Gaziantep
65 H4 Aïn Taya Alg.
65 G5 Aïn Tédélès Alg.
45 B4 Aipe Col.
95 C1 Air i. Indon.
20 G4 Airdrie Can.
57 E5 Airdrie U.K.
64 D5 Aire-sur-l'Adour France
88 D1 Airgin Sum China
116 C3 Airlie Beach Austr.
21 H3 Air Ronge Can.
88 F2 Ai Shan h. China
20 B2 Aishihik Can.
20 B2 Aishihik Lake l. Can.
64 G2 Aisne r. France
65 F3 Aitana mt Spain
110 E2 Aitape P.N.G.
26 E2 Aitkin U.S.A.
63 L7 Aiud Romania
64 G4 Aix-en-Provence France
64 G4 Aix-les-Bains France
85 F5 Aiyar Res. resr India
85 H5 Aizawl India
55 T8 Aizkraukle Latvia
55 R8 Aizpute Latvia
91 F6 Aizu-wakamatsu Japan
66 F6 Ajaccio France
45 B4 Ajajú r. Col.
    Ajanta h. see Sahyadriparvat Range
54 O3 Ajaureforsen Sweden
117 D5 Ajax, Mt mt N.Z.
101 E1 Ajdābiyā Libya
    a-Jiddet gravel area see Harāsīs, Jiddat al
90 G4 Ajigasawa Japan
80 E5 'Ajlūn Jordan
84 C4 Ajmer India
35 F4 Ajo U.S.A.
35 F5 Ajo, Mt mt U.S.A.
94 A3 Ajuy Phil.
90 H3 Akabira Japan
90 J3 Akan National Park Japan
80 D4 Akanthou Cyprus
117 D5 Akaroa N.Z.
117 D5 Akaroa Har. in. N.Z.
84 E3 Akbar Afgh.
85 E4 Akbarpur India
65 J4 Akbou Alg.
76 G4 Akbulak Rus. Fed.
81 G3 Akçakale Turkey
80 C3 Akçakoca Turkey
80 D3 Akçali D. mt Turkey
80 C3 Ak D. mt Turkey
80 C3 Ak D. mt Turkey
80 D3 Akçadağ Turkey
80 H2 Akdağ mt Turkey
80 A2 Akdağ mt Turkey
55 Q7 Åkersberga Sweden
61 C2 Akersloot Neth.
102 C3 Aketi Dem. Rep. Congo
81 J1 Akhalk'alak'i Georgia
69 G7 Akhalts'ikhe Georgia
85 G5 Akhaura Bangl.
101 E1 Akhdar, Al Jabal al mts Libya

79 H5 Akhdar, Jabal mts Oman
80 A2 Akhisar Turkey
80 F3 Akhtarīn Syria
69 H5 Akhtubinsk Rus. Fed.
81 J1 Akhuryan Armenia
91 C8 Aki Japan
22 D3 Akimiski Island i. Can.
80 E3 Akıncı Burun pt Turkey
80 G1 Akıncılar Turkey
90 G5 Akita Japan
100 A3 Akjoujt Maur.
54 P3 Akkajaure l. Sweden
90 J3 Akkeshi Japan
    'Akko see Acre
76 J4 Akkol' Kazak.
80 E1 Akkuş Turkey
84 D4 Akna India
55 R8 Akmenrags pt Latvia
84 D1 Akmeqit China
    Akmola see Astana
91 A7 Akō Japan
101 F4 Akobo Sudan
84 D5 Akola India
102 D2 Akordat Eritrea
80 D3 Akören Turkey
84 D5 Akot India
23 G1 Akpatok Island i. Can.
54 B4 Akranes Iceland
69 C7 Akrathos, Akra pt Greece
55 J7 Åkrehamn Norway
84 A2 Ak Robat Pass pass Afgh.
24 G3 Akron CO U.S.A.
32 C4 Akron OH U.S.A.
32 C4 Akron City Reservoir resr U.S.A.
84 D2 Aksai Chin terr. China/India
80 C2 Aksaray Turkey
69 H6 Aksay Rus. Fed.
84 D2 Aksayqin Hu l. China/Jammu and Kashmir
80 C2 Akşehir Turkey
80 C2 Akşehir Gölü l. Turkey
80 C3 Akseki Turkey
76 H5 Akshiganak Kazak.
82 F2 Aksu China
80 C3 Aksu r. Turkey
102 D2 Āksum Eth.
85 F1 Aktag mt China
81 L2 Aktas D. mt Turkey
76 G5 Aktau Kazak.
82 E1 Aktogay Kazak.
63 O4 Aktsyabrski Belarus
76 G4 Aktyubinsk Kazak.
91 B8 Akune Japan
100 C4 Akure Nigeria
54 D4 Akureyri Iceland
85 Akxokesay China
    Akyab see Sittwe
80 G3 Akziyaret Turkey
55 L6 Ål Norway
29 C5 Alabama div. U.S.A.
29 C6 Alabama r. U.S.A.
29 C5 Alabaster U.S.A.
94 B3 Alabat i. Phil.
81 K7 Al 'Abţīyah w. Iraq
80 E1 Alaca Turkey
80 F2 Alacahan Turkey
80 E1 Alaçam Turkey
80 B2 Alaçam Dağları mts Turkey
81 J2 Ala Dag mt Turkey
81 J2 Ala Dağlar mts Turkey
80 E3 Ala Dağları mts Turkey
69 H7 Alagir Rus. Fed.
43 L6 Alagoinhas Brazil
65 F2 Alagón Spain
94 A3 Alah r. Phil.
54 S5 Alahärmä Fin.
81 L7 Al Aḥmadī Kuwait
54 S5 Alajärvi Fin.
37 H6 Alajuela Costa Rica
81 L2 Alajujeh Iran
84 D3 Alaknanda r. India
82 F1 Alakol', Ozero salt l. Kazak.
54 W3 Alakurtti Rus. Fed.
42 F4 Alalaú r. Brazil
81 J3 Al 'Amādīyah Iraq
93 L3 Alamagan i. N. Mariana Is
81 L6 Al 'Amārah Iraq
85 H3 Alamdo China
81 K7 Al Amghar waterhole Iraq
94 A3 Alaminos Phil.
35 E3 Alamo U.S.A.
35 F4 Alamo Dam dam U.S.A.
25 F5 Alamogordo U.S.A.
25 E6 Alamos Heights U.S.A.
25 E6 Alamos Mex.
25 F4 Alamosa U.S.A.
54 O4 Åland is Fin.
55 Q6 Åland is Fin.
81 K2 Aland r. Iran
95 B5 Alang Besar i. Indon.
30 E3 Alanson U.S.A.
80 D3 Alanya Turkey
80 C1 Alaplı Turkey
    Alappuzha see Alleppey
80 E5 Al 'Aqabah Jordan
65 E3 Alarcón, Embalse de resr Spain
78 F4 Al Arţāwīyah Saudi Arabia
80 B2 Alaşehir Turkey
81 J6 Al 'Āshūrīyah w. Iraq
16 Alaska div. North America
118 C1 Alaska, Gulf of g. U.S.A.
20 D3 Alaska Highway Can./U.S.A.
118 D1 Alaska Peninsula pen. U.S.A.
18 Alaska Range mts U.S.A.
81 M2 Alāt Azer.

81 J6 Al 'Athāmīn h. Iraq
68 H4 Alatyr' Rus. Fed.
68 H4 Alatyr' r. Rus. Fed.
42 C4 Alausí Ecuador
81 K1 Alaverdi Armenia
54 T4 Alavieska Fin.
54 S5 Alavus Fin.
114 D5 Alawoona Austr.
81 L1 Alazani r. Azer./Georgia
81 K5 Al 'Azīzīyah Iraq
66 C2 Alba Italy
80 F3 Al Bāb Syria
65 F3 Albacete Spain
114 D5 Albacutya, L. l. Austr.
81 K6 Al Bādiyah al Janūbīyah h. Iraq
67 K1 Alba Iulia Romania
81 M6 Albājī Iran
22 F3 Albanel, L. l. Can.
49 Albania country Europe
112 C7 Albany Austr.
22 C3 Albany r. Can.
29 C6 Albany GA U.S.A.
30 E5 Albany IN U.S.A.
28 C4 Albany KY U.S.A.
33 G3 Albany NY U.S.A.
24 B2 Albany OR U.S.A.
115 H1 Albany Downs Austr.
47 G2 Albardão do João Maria coastal area Brazil
    Al Başrah see Basra
81 K6 Al Baţḥa' marsh Iraq
113 H2 Albatross Bay b. Austr.
115 F8 Albatross I. i. Austr.
101 E1 Al Baydā' Libya
42 □ Albemarle, Pta pt Ecuador
29 E5 Albemarle Sd chan. U.S.A.
66 C2 Albenga Italy
65 D3 Alberche r. Spain
113 F5 Alberga watercourse Austr.
65 B2 Albergaria-a-Velha Port.
115 G4 Albert Austr.
64 F1 Albert France
114 C5 Albert, Lake l. Austr.
102 D3 Albert, Lake l. Uganda/Dem. Rep. Congo
20 F4 Alberta div. Can.
32 E6 Alberta U.S.A.
20 F4 Alberta, Mt mt Can.
104 D7 Albertinia S. Africa
61 D4 Albert Kanaal canal Belgium
26 E3 Albert Lea U.S.A.
101 F4 Albert Nile r. Sudan/Uganda
44 B8 Alberto de Agostini, Parque Nacional nat. park Chile
105 H3 Alberton S. Africa
64 H4 Albertville France
64 F5 Albi France
43 H3 Albina Suriname
34 A2 Albion CA U.S.A.
33 J2 Albion ME U.S.A.
30 E4 Albion MI U.S.A.
32 D3 Albion NY U.S.A.
65 E5 Alborán, Isla de i. Spain
55 L8 Ålborg Denmark
55 M8 Ålborg Bugt b. Denmark
79 G2 Alborz, Reshteh-ye mts Iran
20 F4 Albreda Can.
116 B4 Albro Austr.
65 B4 Albufeira Port.
25 F5 Albuquerque U.S.A.
79 H5 Al Buraymī Oman
65 C3 Alburquerque Spain
115 G6 Albury Austr.
81 H4 Al Buşayrah Syria
80 G7 Al Busayyā' plain Saudi Arabia
81 L6 Al Buşayyah Iraq
65 B3 Alcácer do Sal Port.
65 E2 Alcalá de Henares Spain
65 E4 Alcalá la Real Spain
66 E6 Alcamo Italy
65 F2 Alcañiz Spain
65 C3 Alcántara Spain
65 E3 Alcaraz Spain
65 D4 Alcaudete Spain
65 E3 Alcázar de San Juan Spain
69 F5 Alchevs'k Ukr.
47 C2 Alcira Spain
46 E2 Alcobaça Brazil
65 F2 Alcora Spain
47 C2 Alcorta Arg.
65 F3 Alcoy Spain
65 H3 Alcúdia Spain
103 E4 Aldabra Islands is Seychelles
27 B6 Aldama Mex.
77 O4 Aldan Rus. Fed.
77 P3 Aldan r. Rus. Fed.
59 J5 Aldeburgh U.K.
56 E7 Alderney i. U.K.
34 B4 Alder Peak summit U.S.A.
59 G6 Aldershot U.K.
32 C6 Alderson U.S.A.
58 D3 Aldingham U.K.
59 F5 Aldridge U.K.
30 B5 Aledo U.S.A.
100 A3 Aleg Maur.
44 E3 Alegre Brazil
44 E3 Alegrete Brazil
47 E2 Alejandro Korn Arg.
68 E2 Alekhovshchina Rus. Fed.
68 F3 Aleksandrov Rus. Fed.

69 J5 Aleksandrov Gay Rus. Fed.
69 H6 Aleksandrovskoye Rus. Fed.
87 Q1 Aleksandrovsk-Sakhalinskiy Rus. Fed.
69 F5 Alekseyevka Rus. Fed.
69 F5 Alekseyevka Rus. Fed.
69 G5 Alekseyevskaya Rus. Fed.
68 F4 Aleksin Rus. Fed.
67 J3 Aleksinac Yugo.
102 B4 Alèmbé Gabon
80 E1 Alembeyli Turkey
46 D3 Além Paraíba Brazil
54 M5 Ålen Norway
64 E2 Alençon France
43 H4 Alenquer Brazil
34 □² Alenuihaha Channel chan. U.S.A.
80 F3 Aleppo Syria
42 D6 Alerta Peru
20 D4 Alert Bay Can.
64 G4 Alès France
63 L7 Aleşd Romania
66 C2 Alessandria Italy
54 K5 Ålesund Norway
15 G2 Aleutian Trench sea feature Pac. Oc.
77 R4 Alevina, Mys c. Rus. Fed.
Alevişik see Samandağı
33 K2 Alexander U.S.A.
20 B3 Alexander Archipelago is U.S.A.
104 B4 Alexander Bay b. Namibia/S. Africa
104 B4 Alexander Bay S. Africa
29 C5 Alexander City U.S.A.
119 A2 Alexander I. i. Antarctica
115 F6 Alexandra Austr.
117 B6 Alexandra N.Z.
44 □ Alexandra, C. c. Atlantic Ocean
67 K4 Alexandreia Greece
Alexandretta see İskenderun
33 F2 Alexandria Can.
78 B3 Alexandria Egypt
67 L3 Alexandria Romania
105 G6 Alexandria S. Africa
57 D5 Alexandria U.K.
30 E5 Alexandria IN U.S.A.
27 E6 Alexandria LA U.S.A.
26 E2 Alexandria MN U.S.A.
32 E5 Alexandria VA U.S.A.
33 F2 Alexandria Bay U.S.A.
114 C5 Alexandrina, L. l. Austr.
67 L4 Alexandroupoli Greece
23 J3 Alexis r. Can.
30 B5 Alexis U.S.A.
20 E4 Alexis Creek Can.
86 D1 Aleysk Rus. Fed.
65 F1 Alfaro Spain
81 L7 Al Farwānīyah Kuwait
81 J4 Al Fatḥah Iraq
81 M7 Al Fāw Iraq
46 D3 Alfenas Brazil
81 M7 Al Finṭās Kuwait
63 K7 Alföld plain Hungary
59 H4 Alford U.K.
33 F2 Alfred Can.
33 H3 Alfred U.S.A.
81 M7 Al Fuḥayḥīl Kuwait
Al-Fujayrah see Fujairah
Al Furāt r. see Euphrates
55 J7 Ålgård Norway
47 C2 Algarrobo del Aguila Arg.
65 G4 Algarve reg. Port.
68 G4 Algasovo Rus. Fed.
65 D4 Algeciras Spain
65 F3 Algemesí Spain
Alger see Algiers
31 E3 Alger U.S.A.
96 Algeria country Africa
81 K6 Al Ghammās Iraq
79 G6 Al Ghaydah Yemen
66 C4 Alghero Italy
78 F4 Al Ghwaybiyah Saudi Arabia
100 C1 Algiers Alg.
105 F6 Algoa Bay b. S. Africa
30 D3 Algoma U.S.A.
26 E3 Algona U.S.A.
31 F4 Algonac U.S.A.
31 H3 Algonquin Park Can.
31 H3 Algonquin Provincial Park res. Can.
81 J7 Al Habakah w. Saudi Arabia
81 J5 Al Ḥabbānīyah Iraq
81 J4 Al Ḥadīthah Iraq
81 J4 Al Ḥadr Iraq
80 F4 Al Ḥaffah Syria
81 G6 Al Ḥamād reg. Jordan/S. Arabia
101 D2 Al Ḥamādah al Ḥamrā' plat. Libya
65 F4 Alhama de Murcia Spain
81 J6 Al Hammām w. Iraq
81 K7 Al Haniyah escarpment Iraq
81 G6 Al Ḥarrah reg. Saudi Arabia
81 H3 Al Ḥasakah Syria
81 K5 Al Hāshimīyah Iraq
81 L5 Al Ḥayy Iraq
80 F6 Al Ḥazim Jordan
79 G6 Al Ḥibāk Saudi Arabia
81 K5 Al Ḥillah Iraq
100 B1 Al Hoceima Morocco
78 E7 Al Ḥudaydah Yemen
79 F4 Al Ḥufūf Saudi Arabia
81 L3 'Alīābād Iran
81 L4 'Alīābād Iran

67 M5 Aliağa Turkey
67 K4 Aliakmonas r. Greece
81 L5 'Alī al Gharbī Iraq
84 B4 Ali Bandar Pak.
81 M2 Āli Bayramlı Azer.
65 F3 Alicante Spain
116 A4 Alice Austr.
116 A4 Alice watercourse Austr.
105 G6 Alice S. Africa
27 D6 Alice U.S.A.
20 D3 Alice Arm Can.
113 F4 Alice Springs Austr.
29 E7 Alice Town Bahamas
94 B5 Alicia Phil.
84 D4 Aligarh India
78 F3 Alīgūdarz Iran
87 M1 Alihe China
102 B4 Alima r. Congo
55 N8 Alingsås Sweden
80 B2 Aliova r. Turkey
84 B3 Alipur Pak.
85 G4 Alipur Duar India
32 C4 Aliquippa U.S.A.
102 E2 Ali Sabieh Djibouti
80 F6 Al 'Īsāwīyah Saudi Arabia
81 K2 Alī Shah Iran
81 K5 Al Iskandarīyah Iraq
67 L5 Aliveri Greece
105 G3 Aliwal North S. Africa
20 G4 Alix Can.
80 F6 Al Jafr Jordan
101 E2 Al Jaghbūb Libya
81 L7 Al Jahra Kuwait
78 D4 Al Jawf Saudi Arabia
101 D1 Al Jawf Libya
81 G3 Al Jazā'ir reg. Iraq/Syria
65 B4 Aljezur Port.
81 J6 Al Jil w. Iraq
80 E6 Al Jīzah Jordan
79 F4 Al Jubayl Saudi Arabia
65 B4 Aljustrel Port.
80 E6 Al Karak Jordan
81 K5 Al Kāẓimīyah Iraq
79 H5 Al Khābūrah Oman
81 K5 Al Khāliṣ Iraq
79 H4 Al Khaṣab Oman
101 E2 Al Khufrah Libya
101 D1 Al Khums Libya
81 K5 Al Kifl Iraq
61 C2 Alkmaar Neth.
81 K5 Al Kūfah Iraq
81 L5 Al Kumayt Iraq
81 K5 Al Kūt Iraq
Al Kuwayt see Kuwait
81 H7 Al Labbah plain Saudi Arabia
Al Lādhiqīyah see Latakia
33 J1 Allagash U.S.A.
33 J1 Allagash r. U.S.A.
33 J1 Allagash Lake l. U.S.A.
85 E4 Allahabad India
80 F5 Al Lajā lava Syria
77 P3 Allakh-Yun' Rus. Fed.
105 G3 Alldays S. Africa
105 H1 Alldays S. Africa
30 E4 Allegan U.S.A.
32 C4 Allegheny r. U.S.A.
32 C6 Allegheny Mountains mts U.S.A.
32 D4 Allegheny Reservoir resr U.S.A.
60 C3 Allen, Lough l. Rep. of Ireland
29 D5 Allendale U.S.A.
58 E3 Allendale Town U.K.
27 C6 Allende Mex.
31 G3 Allenford Can.
33 F4 Allentown U.S.A.
83 E9 Alleppey India
62 D4 Aller r. Ger.
26 C3 Alliance NE U.S.A.
32 C4 Alliance OH U.S.A.
81 J6 Al Lifīyah w. Iraq
116 B2 Alligator Creek Austr.
55 O9 Allinge-Sandvig Denmark
31 H3 Alliston Can.
78 E5 Al Līth Saudi Arabia
57 E4 Alloa U.K.
115 K2 Allora Austr.
81 J6 Al Lussuf w. Iraq
23 F4 Alma Can.
30 E4 Alma MI U.S.A.
26 D3 Alma NE U.S.A.
35 H5 Alma NM U.S.A.
81 J6 Al Ma'ānīyah Iraq
Alma-Ata see Almaty
65 B3 Almada Port.
81 K7 Al Ma'danīyat w. Iraq
116 A1 Almaden Austr.
65 D3 Almadén Spain
81 L6 Al Madīnah Iraq
Al Madīnah see Medina
80 F5 Al Mafraq Jordan
81 K5 Al Maḥmūdīyah Iraq
81 L1 Almalı Azer.
79 G4 Al Manāmah Bahrain
34 B1 Almanor, Lake l. U.S.A.
65 F3 Almansa Spain
65 D2 Almanzor mt Spain
81 L6 Al Ma'qil Iraq
101 E1 Al Marj Libya
46 C1 Almas, Rio das r. Brazil
82 E2 Almaty Kazak.
81 J3 Al Mawṣil Iraq
Al Mawṣil see Al Mawṣil
81 H4 Al Mayādīn Syria
65 E2 Almazán Spain
77 N3 Almaznyy Rus. Fed.
84 H4 Almeirim Brazil
65 B3 Almeirim Port.
61 E2 Almelo Neth.
46 E2 Almenara Brazil

65 C2 Almendra, Embalse de resr Spain
65 D3 Almendralejo Spain
61 D2 Almere Neth.
65 E4 Almería Spain
65 E4 Almería, Golfo de b. Spain
76 G4 Al'met'yevsk Rus. Fed.
55 O8 Älmhult Sweden
65 D5 Almina, Pta pt Morocco
78 F4 Al Mish'āb Saudi Arabia
80 F5 Al Mismīyah Syria
65 B4 Almodôvar Port.
31 F4 Almont U.S.A.
31 J3 Almonte Can.
65 C3 Almonte Spain
82 E5 Almora India
79 F4 Al Mubarrez Saudi Arabia
80 E7 Al Mudawwarah Jordan
79 F7 Al Mukallā Yemen
78 E7 Al Mukhā Yemen
65 E4 Almuñécar Spain
81 K5 Al Muqdādīyah Iraq
80 F1 Almus Turkey
81 K5 Al Musayyib Iraq
67 L7 Almyrou, Ormos b. Greece
34 □¹ Alna Haina U.S.A.
58 F2 Alnwick U.K.
85 H5 Alon Myanmar
85 H3 Along India
67 K5 Alonnisos i. Greece
93 G8 Alor i. Indon.
93 G8 Alor, Kepulauan is Indon.
92 C5 Alor Setar Malaysia
Alost see Aalst
84 C1 Alot India
113 K2 Alotau P.N.G.
54 W4 Alozero Rus. Fed.
34 C4 Alpaugh U.S.A.
31 F3 Alpena U.S.A.
116 B4 Alpha Austr.
116 B4 Alpha Cr. r. Austr.
35 H5 Alpine AZ U.S.A.
27 C6 Alpine TX U.S.A.
24 E3 Alpine WY U.S.A.
52 Alps mts Europe
78 F6 Al Qa'āmīyāt reg. Saudi Arabia
101 D1 Al Qaddāḥīyah Libya
80 F4 Al Qadmūs Syria
81 H3 Al Qāmishlī Syria
80 F4 Al Qaryatayn Syria
78 F6 Al Qaṭn Yemen
80 F6 Al Qaṭrānah Jordan
101 D2 Al Qaṭrūn Libya
80 E5 Al Qunayṭirah Syria
78 E6 Al Qunfidhah Saudi Arabia
81 L6 Al Qurnah Iraq
81 K6 Al Quṣayr Iraq
80 F5 Al Quṭayfah Syria
80 E7 Al Quwayrah Jordan
64 H2 Alsace reg. France
59 E4 Alsager U.K.
81 J6 Al Samīt w. Iraq
21 H4 Alsask Can.
58 E3 Alston U.K.
115 K2 Alstonville Austr.
55 R8 Alsunga Latvia
54 S2 Alta Norway
117 B6 Alta, Mt mt N.Z.
54 S2 Altaelva r. Norway
47 D1 Alta Gracia Arg.
45 D2 Altagracía de Orituco Venez.
74 Altai Mountains mts China/Mongolia
29 D6 Altamaha r. U.S.A.
43 H4 Altamira Brazil
66 G4 Altamura Italy
88 C2 Altan Shiret China
46 C1 Alta Paraíso de Goiás Brazil
25 E6 Altar Mex.
35 E5 Altar, Desierto de des. Mex.
32 D6 Altavista U.S.A.
82 C1 Altay China
86 G2 Altay Mongolia
65 F3 Altea Spain
54 S1 Alteidet Norway
85 H1 Altenqoke China
81 M1 Altıağaç Azer.
84 B2 Altimur Pass pass Afgh.
81 K4 Altın Köprü Iraq
67 M5 Altınoluk Turkey
80 C2 Altıntaş Turkey
42 F2 Altiplano plain Bol.
62 E6 Altmühl r. Ger.
46 B2 Alto Araguaia Brazil
45 F2 Alto del Moncayo mt Spain
47 C2 Alto de Pencoso h. Arg.
45 B3 Alto de Tamar mt Col.
46 B2 Alto Garças Brazil
103 D5 Alto Molócuè Moz.
28 B4 Alton IL U.S.A.
27 F4 Alton MO U.S.A.
33 H3 Alton NH U.S.A.
26 D1 Altona Can.
32 D4 Altoona U.S.A.
46 B2 Alto Sucuriú Brazil
62 F6 Altötting Ger.
59 E4 Altrincham U.K.
82 G3 Altun Shan mts China
24 B3 Alturas U.S.A.
27 D5 Altus U.S.A.
80 C1 Alucra Turkey
55 U8 Alūksne Latvia
81 M5 Alum Iran
32 C4 Alum Creek Lake l. U.S.A.

69 E6 Alupka Ukr.
101 D1 Al 'Uqaylah Libya
69 E6 Alushta Ukr.
81 K4 'Alūt Iran
101 E2 Al 'Uwaynāt Libya
81 J6 Al 'Uwayqīlah Saudi Arabia
81 L6 Al 'Uzayr Iraq
27 D4 Alva U.S.A.
81 M4 Alvand, Kūh-e mt Iran
47 C2 Alvarado, P. de pass Chile
42 F4 Alvarães Brazil
55 M5 Ålvdal Norway
55 O6 Ålvdalen Sweden
55 O8 Alvesta Sweden
55 K6 Ålvik Norway
55 P5 Alvik Sweden
27 E6 Alvin U.S.A.
55 R4 Älvsbyn Sweden
81 L7 Al Wafrah Kuwait
78 D4 Al Wajh Saudi Arabia
84 D4 Alwar India
81 H5 Al Widyān plat. Iraq/S. Arabia
Alxa Youqi see Ehen Hudag
Alxa Zuoqi see Bayan Hot
113 G2 Alyangula Austr.
57 E4 Alyth U.K.
55 T9 Alytus Lith.
24 F2 Alzada U.S.A.
45 E3 Amacuro r. Guyana/Venez.
112 F4 Amadeus, Lake salt flat Austr.
35 G6 Amado U.S.A.
65 B3 Amadora Port.
91 A8 Amakusa-nada b. Japan
55 N7 Åmål Sweden
45 B3 Amalfi Col.
66 F4 Amalfi Italy
104 F3 Amalia S. Africa
67 J6 Amaliada Greece
84 C5 Amalner India
93 K7 Amamapare Indon.
46 A3 Amambaí Brazil
46 A3 Amambaí r. Brazil
46 A3 Amambaí, Serra de h. Brazil/Para.
87 N6 Amami-Ō-shima i. Japan
87 N6 Amami-shotō is Japan
76 H4 Amangel'dy Kazak.
66 G5 Amantea Italy
105 J5 Amanzimtoti S. Africa
43 H3 Amapá Brazil
65 C3 Amareleja Port.
34 D3 Amargosa Desert des. U.S.A.
34 D3 Amargosa Range mts U.S.A.
34 D3 Amargosa Valley U.S.A.
27 C5 Amarillo U.S.A.
66 F3 Amaro, Monte mt Italy
84 E4 Amarpatan India
80 E1 Amasya Turkey
43 H3 Amazon r. S. America
43 J3 Amazon, Mouths of the est. Brazil
45 D4 Amazonas div. Brazil
Amazonas r. see Amazon
43 G4 Amazónia, Parque Nacional nat. park Brazil
84 C6 Ambad India
84 D3 Ambala India
103 E6 Ambalavao Madag.
103 E5 Ambanja Madag.
42 C4 Ambato Ecuador
103 E5 Ambato Boeny Madag.
103 E6 Ambato Finandrahana Madag.
103 E5 Ambatolampy Madag.
103 E5 Ambatomainty Madag.
103 E5 Ambatondrazaka Madag.
62 E6 Amberg Ger.
36 G5 Ambergris Cay i. Belize
64 G4 Ambérieu-en-Bugey France
31 G3 Amberley Can.
85 E4 Ambikapur India
103 E5 Ambilobe Madag.
20 C3 Ambition, Mt mt Can.
58 F2 Amble U.K.
58 E3 Ambleside U.K.
61 D4 Amblève r. Belgium
103 E6 Amboasary Madag.
103 E5 Ambohidratrimo Madag.
103 E6 Ambohimahasoa Madag.
Amboina see Ambon
93 H7 Ambon Indon.
93 H7 Ambon i. Indon.
103 E6 Ambositra Madag.
103 E6 Ambovombe Madag.
35 C4 Amboy CA U.S.A.
30 C5 Amboy IL U.S.A.
33 F3 Amboy Center U.S.A.
103 B4 Ambriz Angola
111 G3 Ambrym i. Vanuatu
92 □ Ambunten Indon.
116 C6 Amby Austr.
85 G2 Amdo China
61 D4 Amel, Étang d' l. France
61 D1 Ameland i. Neth.
32 E6 Amelia Court House U.S.A.
33 G3 Amenia U.S.A.
34 B2 American, North Fork r. U.S.A.
24 D3 American Falls U.S.A.
24 D3 American Falls Res. resr U.S.A.

35 G1 American Fork U.S.A.
29 C5 Americus U.S.A.
61 D2 Amersfoort Neth.
105 H3 Amersfoort S. Africa
59 G6 Amersham U.K.
21 L3 Amery Can.
119 D5 Amery Ice Shelf ice feature Antarctica
26 E3 Ames U.S.A.
59 F6 Amesbury U.K.
33 G3 Amesbury U.S.A.
85 E4 Amethi India
67 K5 Amfissa Greece
77 P3 Amga Rus. Fed.
77 P5 Amga Rus. Fed.
100 C2 Amguid Alg.
77 P4 Amgun' r. Rus. Fed.
23 H4 Amherst Can.
33 G3 Amherst MA U.S.A.
33 J2 Amherst ME U.S.A.
32 D6 Amherst VA U.S.A.
31 F4 Amherstburg Can.
66 D3 Amiata, Monte mt Italy
64 F2 Amiens France
81 H5 'Amīj, Wādī watercourse Iraq
83 D8 Amindivi Islands is India
91 D7 Amino Japan
104 C1 Aminuis Namibia
81 L5 Amīrābād Iran
21 J4 Amisk L. l. Can.
Amistad, Represa de resr see Amistad Reservoir
27 C6 Amistad Reservoir resr Mex./U.S.A.
115 K1 Amity Point Austr.
84 D5 Amla India
55 L7 Åmli Norway
59 C4 Amlwch U.K.
80 E6 'Ammān Jordan
59 D6 Ammanford U.K.
54 V4 Ämmänsaari Fin.
54 P4 Ammarnäs Sweden
62 E7 Ammersee l. Ger.
Ammochostos see Famagusta
84 D4 Amod India
89 B6 Amo Jiang r. China
79 G2 Amol Iran
67 L6 Amorgos i. Greece
22 E4 Amos Can.
Amoy see Xiamen
46 C3 Amparo Brazil
62 E2 Amper r. Ger.
65 G2 Amposta Spain
84 D5 Amravati India
84 B5 Amreli India
84 B4 Amri Pak.
80 E4 'Amrit Syria
84 C3 Amritsar India
84 C3 Amroha India
54 Q4 Åmsele Sweden
61 C2 Amstelveen Neth.
61 C2 Amsterdam Neth.
105 J3 Amsterdam S. Africa
33 F3 Amsterdam U.S.A.
13 K6 Amsterdam Island i. Indian Ocean
62 G6 Amstetten Austria
101 E3 Am Timan Chad
79 J1 Amudar'ya r. Turkm./Uzbek.
119 C5 Amundsen, Mt mt Antarctica
119 D4 Amundsen Bay b. Antarctica
119 B4 Amundsen-Scott U.S.A. Base Antarctica
119 A3 Amundsen Sea sea Antarctica
92 F7 Amuntai Indon.
Amur r. see Heilong Jiang
87 P1 Amursk Rus. Fed.
69 F6 Amvrosiyivka Ukr.
30 E1 Amyot Can.
85 H6 An Myanmar
93 G7 Anabanua Indon.
77 N2 Anabar r. Rus. Fed.
77 N2 Anabarskiy Zaliv b. Rus. Fed.
67 L6 Anafi i. Greece
46 E1 Anagé Brazil
81 H4 'Ānah Iraq
34 D5 Anaheim U.S.A.
20 D4 Anahim Lake Can.
27 C7 Anáhuac Mex.
116 B4 Anakie Austr.
103 E5 Analalava Madag.
42 F4 Anamã Brazil
92 D6 Anambas, Kepulauan is Indon.
30 B4 Anamosa U.S.A.
80 D3 Anamur Turkey
80 D3 Anamur Burnu pt Turkey
91 D8 Anan Japan
84 C5 Anand India
85 E5 Anandapur India
85 F5 Anandpur r. India
84 C2 Anantnag Jammu and Kashmir
84 D4 Anant Peth India

69 D6 Anan'yiv Ukr.
69 F6 Anapa Rus. Fed.
46 C2 Anápolis Brazil
93 L3 Anatahan i. N. Mariana Is
80 D2 Anatolia reg. Turkey
111 G4 Anatom i. Vanuatu
44 D3 Añatuya Arg.
45 E4 Anauá r. Brazil
81 M3 Anbūh Iran
64 D3 Ancenis France
118 C1 Anchorage U.S.A.
31 F4 Anchor Bay b. U.S.A.
66 E3 Ancona Italy
44 B6 Ancud Chile
47 B4 Ancud, Golfo de g. Chile
47 B1 Andacollo Chile
85 F5 Andal India
54 K5 Åndalsnes Norway
65 D4 Andalucía div. Spain
Andalusia div. see Andalucía
27 G6 Andalusia U.S.A.
83 H8 Andaman and Nicobar Islands div. India
13 L3 Andaman Basin sea feature Indian Ocean
83 H8 Andaman Islands is Andaman and Nicobar Is
92 A4 Andaman Sea sea Asia
114 B3 Andamooka Austr.
103 E5 Andapa Madag.
46 E1 Andaraí Brazil
54 P2 Andenes Norway
61 D4 Andenne Belgium
61 C4 Anderlecht Belgium
64 D4 Andernos-les-Bains France
30 E5 Anderson IN U.S.A.
27 E4 Anderson MO U.S.A.
29 D5 Anderson SC U.S.A.
115 G8 Anderson B. b. Austr.
40 Andes S. America
40 Andes mts S. America
54 P2 Andfjorden chan. Norway
83 E7 Andhra Pradesh div. India
103 E5 Andilamena Madag.
103 E5 Andilanatoby Madag.
81 M5 Andīmeshk Iran
80 F3 Andirin Turkey
69 H7 Andiyskoye Koysu r. Rus. Fed.
79 L1 Andizhan Uzbek.
79 K2 Andkhvoy Afgh.
103 E5 Andoany Madag.
42 C4 Andoas Peru
87 N4 Andong S. Korea
91 A6 Andong-ho l. S. Korea
48 Andorra country Europe
65 G1 Andorra la Vella Andorra
59 F6 Andover U.K.
33 H2 Andover ME U.S.A.
32 C4 Andover OH U.S.A.
54 O2 Andøya i. Norway
46 B3 Andradina Brazil
68 E3 Andreapol' Rus. Fed.
58 C3 Andreas U.K.
102 C3 André Félix, Parc National de nat. park C.A.R.
46 D3 Andrelândia Brazil
27 C5 Andrews U.S.A.
66 G4 Andria Italy
103 E6 Androka Madag.
67 L6 Andros i. Greece
29 E7 Andros i. Bahamas
33 H2 Androscoggin r. U.S.A.
29 E7 Andros Town Bahamas
83 D8 Andrott i. India
69 D5 Andrushivka Ukr.
54 Q2 Andselv Norway
65 D2 Andújar Spain
103 B5 Andulo Angola
100 C3 Anéfis Mali
37 M5 Anegada i. Virgin Is
47 D4 Anegada, Bahía b. Arg.
35 F5 Anegam U.S.A.
100 C4 Aného Togo
'Aneiza, Jabal h. see 'Unayzah, Jabal
35 H3 Aneth U.S.A.
65 G1 Aneto mt Spain
101 D3 Aney Niger
89 D5 Anfu China
103 E5 Angadoka, Lohatanjona hd Madag.
86 H3 Angara r. Rus. Fed.
77 M4 Angarsk Rus. Fed.
94 B3 Angat Phil.
55 O5 Ånge Sweden
36 B3 Angel de la Guarda, Isla i. Mex.
94 B3 Angeles Phil.
55 N8 Ängelholm Sweden
116 B6 Angellala Cr. r. Austr.
34 B2 Angels Camp U.S.A.
54 P4 Ångermanälven r. Sweden
64 D3 Angers France
21 K2 Angikuni Lake l. Can.
95 B2 Angkor Cambodia
59 C4 Anglesey i. U.K.
27 E6 Angleton U.S.A.
31 H2 Angliers Can.
95 □ Ang Mo Kio Sing.
102 C3 Ango Dem. Rep. Congo
103 D5 Angoche Moz.
47 B3 Angol Chile
96 Angola country Africa
30 E5 Angola U.S.A.
12 K7 Angola Basin sea feature Atlantic Ocean
64 E4 Angoulême France

79 L1 **Angren** Uzbek.
95 B2 **Ang Thong** Thai.
37 M5 **Anguilla** terr. Caribbean
88 E1 **Anguli Nur** l. China
88 E2 **Anguo** China
46 A3 **Anhandui** r. Brazil
55 M8 **Anholt** i. Denmark
89 D4 **Anhua** China
88 E3 **Anhui** div. China
46 A2 **Anhumas** Brazil
46 C2 **Anicuns** Brazil
68 G3 **Anikovo** Rus. Fed.
35 H6 **Animas** U.S.A.
35 H6 **Animas Peak** summit U.S.A.
95 A2 **Anin** Myanmar
90 H1 **Aniva** Rus. Fed.
90 H1 **Aniva, Mys** c. Rus. Fed.
87 Q2 **Aniva, Zaliv** b. Rus. Fed.
111 G3 **Aniwa** i. Vanuatu
61 B5 **Anizy-le-Château** France
55 U6 **Anjalankoski** Fin.
89 F4 **Anji** China
84 D5 **Anji** India
64 D3 **Anjou** reg. France
103 E5 **Anjouan** i. Comoros
103 E5 **Anjozorobe** Madag.
87 N4 **Anju** N. Korea
103 E6 **Ankaboa, Tanjona** pt Madag.
88 C3 **Ankang** China
80 D2 **Ankara** Turkey
103 E6 **Ankazoabo** Madag.
103 E5 **Ankazobe** Madag.
95 D2 **An Khê** Vietnam
84 C5 **Ankleshwar** India
61 D5 **Anlier, Forêt d'** forest Belgium
89 B5 **Anlong** China
95 C2 **Ânlong Vêng** Cambodia
89 D4 **Anlu** China
33 H3 **Ann, Cape** hd U.S.A.
69 G5 **Anna** Rus. Fed.
32 E5 **Anna, Lake** l. U.S.A.
100 C1 **Annaba** Alg.
80 F4 **An Nabk** Syria
78 E4 **An Nafūd** des. Saudi Arabia
58 A3 **Annahilt** U.K.
81 K5 **An Nahrawān al Qadīm** canal Iraq
81 K6 **An Najaf** Iraq
60 D3 **Annalee** r. Rep. of Ireland
60 F3 **Annalong** U.K.
57 E6 **Annan** U.K.
57 E6 **Annan** r. U.K.
57 E5 **Annandale** v. U.K.
32 E5 **Annapolis** U.S.A.
23 G5 **Annapolis Royal** Can.
85 E3 **Annapurna I** mt Nepal
31 F4 **Ann Arbor** U.S.A.
43 G2 **Anna Regina** Guyana
81 L6 **An Nāşirīyah** Iraq
64 H4 **Annecy** France
64 H3 **Annemasse** France
20 C4 **Annette I.** i. U.S.A.
80 F5 **An Nimārah** Syria
89 B5 **Anning** China
29 C5 **Anniston** U.S.A.
100 C5 **Annobón** i. Equatorial Guinea
64 G4 **Annonay** France
78 F4 **An Nu'ayrīyah** Saudi Arabia
81 K5 **An Nu'māniyah** Iraq
26 E2 **Anoka** U.S.A.
103 E5 **Anorontany, Tanjona** hd Madag.
67 L7 **Ano Viannos** Greece
89 D6 **Anpu** China
89 C6 **Anpu Gang** b. China
89 E4 **Anqing** China
88 F2 **Anqiu** China
89 D5 **Anren** China
88 C2 **Ansai** China
115 G7 **Anser Group** is Austr.
88 C1 **Anshan** China
89 B5 **Anshun** China
47 C1 **Ansilta** mt Arg.
47 F1 **Ansina** Uru.
26 D3 **Ansley** U.S.A.
27 D5 **Anson** U.S.A.
100 C3 **Ansongo** Mali
22 D4 **Ansonville** Can.
32 C5 **Ansted** U.S.A.
84 D4 **Anta** India
42 D6 **Antabamba** Peru
80 F3 **Antakya** Turkey
103 F5 **Antalaha** Madag.
80 C3 **Antalya** Turkey
80 C3 **Antalya Körfezi** g. Turkey
103 E5 **Antananarivo** Madag.
119 B2 **Antarctic Peninsula** pen. Antarctica
57 C3 **An Teallach** mt U.K.
34 D2 **Antelope Range** mts U.S.A.
65 D4 **Antequera** Spain
25 F5 **Anthony** U.S.A.
100 B1 **Anti Atlas** mts Morocco
64 H5 **Antibes** France
23 H4 **Anticosti, Île d'** i. Can.
30 C3 **Antigo** U.S.A.
23 H4 **Antigonish** Can.
37 M5 **Antigua** i. Antigua
36 F6 **Antigua** Guatemala
16 **Antigua and Barbuda** country Caribbean Sea
36 E4 **Antiguo-Morelos** Mex.
67 K7 **Antikythira** i. Greece
67 K7 **Antikythiro, Steno** chan. Greece
Anti Lebanon mts see Sharqī, Jabal ash

Antioch see Antakya
34 B3 **Antioch** CA U.S.A.
30 C4 **Antioch** IL. U.S.A.
45 B3 **Antioquia** Col.
67 L5 **Antipsara** i. Greece
27 E5 **Antlers** U.S.A.
44 B2 **Antofagasta** Chile
44 C3 **Antofalla, Vol.** vol. Arg.
46 C4 **Antonina** Brazil
46 E1 **Antônio** r. Brazil
25 F4 **Antonito** U.S.A.
60 E3 **Antrim** U.K.
60 E2 **Antrim Hills** h. U.K.
103 E5 **Antsalova** Madag.
103 E5 **Antsirabe** Madag.
103 E5 **Antsirañana** Madag.
103 E5 **Antsohihy** Madag.
54 S3 **Anttis** Sweden
55 U6 **Anttola** Fin.
90 A3 **Antu** China
47 B3 **Antuco** Chile
47 B3 **Antuco, Volcán** vol. Chile
61 C3 **Antwerp** Belgium
33 F2 **Antwerp** U.S.A.
Antwerpen see Antwerp
22 C2 **Anuc, Lac** l. Can.
90 C3 **Anuchino** Rus. Fed.
85 F5 **Anugul** India
84 C3 **Anupgarh** India
83 F9 **Anuradhapura** Sri Lanka
Anvers see Antwerp
119 B2 **Anvers I.** i. Antarctica
89 F5 **Anxi** Fujian China
82 J2 **Anxi** Gansu China
88 B4 **Anxian** China
89 D4 **Anxiang** China
88 E2 **Anxin** China
114 A4 **Anxious Bay** b. Austr.
88 E2 **Anyang** China
67 L6 **Anydro** i. Greece
82 J4 **A'nyêmaqên Shan** mts China
89 E4 **Anyi** China
89 E5 **Anyuan** China
89 B4 **Anyue** China
77 S3 **Anyuysk** Rus. Fed.
45 B3 **Anzá** Col.
88 D2 **Anze** China
76 K4 **Anzhero-Sudzhensk** Rus. Fed.
102 C4 **Anzi** Dem. Rep. Congo
66 E4 **Anzio** Italy
111 G3 **Aoba** i. Vanuatu
91 F8 **Aoga-shima** i. Japan
Aohan Qi see Xinhui
90 G4 **Aomori** Japan
84 D3 **Aonla** India
117 C5 **Aoraki** mt N.Z.
95 C2 **Aôral, Phnum** mt Cambodia
117 D4 **Aorere** r. N.Z.
66 B2 **Aosta** Italy
100 B2 **Aoukâr** reg. Mali/Maur.
43 G8 **Apa** r. Brazil
102 D3 **Apac** Uganda
35 H6 **Apache** U.S.A.
35 H5 **Apache Creek** U.S.A.
35 G5 **Apache Junction** U.S.A.
35 G6 **Apache Peak** summit U.S.A.
29 C6 **Apalachee Bay** b. U.S.A.
29 C6 **Apalachicola** U.S.A.
45 C5 **Apaporis** r. Col.
81 K1 **Aparan** Armenia
46 B3 **Aparecida do Tabuado** Brazil
94 B2 **Aparri** Phil.
54 X3 **Apatity** Rus. Fed.
36 D5 **Apatzingán** Mex.
55 U8 **Ape** Latvia
61 D2 **Apeldoorn** Neth.
84 E3 **Api** mt Nepal
111 J3 **Apia** Samoa
117 E3 **Apiti** N.Z.
94 C5 **Apo, Mt** vol. Phil.
43 G2 **Apoera** Suriname
114 E7 **Apollo Bay** Austr.
42 E6 **Apolo** Bol.
29 D6 **Apopka, L.** l. U.S.A.
46 B2 **Aporé** Brazil
46 B2 **Aporé** r. Brazil
28 B2 **Apostle Islands** is U.S.A.
30 B2 **Apostle Islands National Lakeshore** res. U.S.A.
80 E4 **Apostolos Andreas, Cape** c. Cyprus
32 B6 **Appalachia** U.S.A.
18 **Appalachian Mountains** mts U.S.A.
66 E3 **Appennino Abruzzese** mts Italy
66 D2 **Appennino Tosco-Emiliano** mts Italy
66 E3 **Appennino Umbro-Marchigiano** mts Italy
115 J5 **Appin** Austr.
57 C3 **Applecross** U.K.
26 D2 **Appleton** MN U.S.A.
30 C3 **Appleton** WV U.S.A.
34 D4 **Apple Valley** U.S.A.
32 D6 **Appomattox** U.S.A.
66 E4 **Aprilia** Italy
69 F6 **Apsheronsk** Rus. Fed.
114 D6 **Apsley** Austr.
31 H3 **Apsley** Can.
64 G5 **Apt** France
46 B3 **Apucarana** Brazil
94 A4 **Apurahuan** Phil.
45 D3 **Apure** r. Venez.
42 D6 **Apurímac** r. Peru
78 C4 **Aqaba, Gulf of** g. Asia
81 K2 **Aq Chai** r. Iran
81 L3 **Aqdoghmish** r. Iran

81 K3 **Āq Kān Dāgh, Kūh-e** mt Iran
86 E4 **Aqqikkol Hu** salt l. China
81 J3 **'Aqrah** Iraq
35 H4 **Aquarius Mts** mts U.S.A.
35 G3 **Aquarius Plateau** plat. U.S.A.
66 G4 **Aquaviva delle Fonti** Italy
46 A3 **Aquidauana** Brazil
46 A3 **Aquidauana** r. Brazil
45 D3 **Aquio** r. Col.
64 D4 **Aquitaine** reg. France
85 F4 **Ara** India
29 C5 **Arab** U.S.A.
101 E4 **Arab, Bahr el** watercourse Sudan
80 B6 **'Arab, Khalīg el** b. Egypt
13 J3 **Arabian Basin** sea feature Indian Ocean
74 **Arabian Sea** sea Indian Ocean
45 E3 **Arabopó** Venez.
45 E3 **Arabopó** r. Venez.
80 D1 **Araç** Turkey
46 E1 **Araça** r. Brazil
43 L6 **Aracaju** Brazil
45 D4 **Aracamuni, Co** summit Venez.
46 A4 **Aracanguy, Mtes de** h. Para.
43 L4 **Aracati** Brazil
46 E1 **Aracatu** Brazil
46 B3 **Araçatuba** Brazil
65 C4 **Aracena** Spain
46 C2 **Aracruz** Brazil
46 D2 **Araçuaí** Brazil
46 D2 **Araçuaí** r. Brazil
67 J1 **Arad** Romania
101 E3 **Arada** Chad
110 D2 **Arafura Sea** sea Austr./Indon.
46 B1 **Aragarças** Brazil
81 J1 **Aragats** Armenia
81 K1 **Aragats Lerr** mt Armenia
65 F2 **Aragón** div. Spain
65 F1 **Aragón** r. Spain
43 J5 **Araguacema** Brazil
45 D2 **Aragua de Barcelona** Venez.
43 J5 **Araguaia** r. Brazil
43 H6 **Araguaia, Parque Nacional de** nat. park Brazil
43 J5 **Araguaína** Brazil
45 E2 **Araguao, Boca** est. Venez.
46 C2 **Araguari** Brazil
46 C2 **Araguari** r. Brazil
43 J3 **Araguatins** Brazil
69 H7 **Aragvi** r. Georgia
91 F6 **Arai** Japan
43 K4 **Araiosos** Brazil
100 C2 **Arak** Alg.
79 F3 **Arāk** Iran
83 H6 **Arakan Yoma** mts Myanmar
81 K2 **Aralık** Turkey
82 B1 **Aral Sea** salt l. Kazak./Uzbek.
82 B1 **Aral'skoye More** salt l. see Aral Sea
69 D7 **Aralsor, Ozero** l. Kazak.
116 A4 **Aramac** Austr.
116 A4 **Aramac Cr.** watercourse Austr.
93 L8 **Aramia** r. P.N.G.
84 D6 **Aran** r. India
65 E2 **Aranda de Duero** Spain
81 L4 **Arandān** Iran
67 J2 **Aranđelovac** Yugo.
60 C3 **Aran Island** i. Rep. of Ireland
60 B4 **Aran Islands** is Rep. of Ireland
65 E2 **Aranjuez** Spain
103 B6 **Aranos** Namibia
27 D7 **Aransas Pass** U.S.A.
46 B2 **Arantes** r. Brazil
111 H1 **Aranuka** i. Gilbert Is
95 B2 **Aranyaprathet** Thai.
91 B8 **Arao** Japan
100 B3 **Araouane** Mali
26 D3 **Arapahoe** U.S.A.
45 A4 **Arapari** r. Brazil
47 F1 **Arapey Grande** r. Uru.
43 L5 **Arapiraca** Brazil
67 L4 **Arapis, Akra** pt Greece
80 C2 **Arapkir** Turkey
46 B3 **Arapongas** Brazil
85 F4 **A Rapti Doon** r. Nepal
81 H6 **'Ar'ar** Saudi Arabia
81 J6 **'Ar'ar, W.** watercourse Iraq/S. Arabia
44 D3 **Araranguá** Brazil
46 C3 **Araraquara** Brazil
43 H5 **Araras** Brazil
46 B4 **Araras, Serra das** mts Brazil
81 K2 **Ararat** Armenia
114 E6 **Ararat** Austr.
81 K2 **Ararat, Mt** mt Turkey
85 F4 **Araria** India
46 D3 **Araruama, Lago de** lag. Brazil
45 E2 **Arias** Arg.
81 J2 **Aras** Turkey
81 J2 **Aras** r. Turkey
46 E1 **Arataca** Brazil
45 C3 **Arauca** Col.
45 C3 **Arauca** r. Venez.
47 B3 **Arauco** Chile
45 C3 **Arauquita** Col.
45 C2 **Araure** Venez.
Trinidad and Tobago
84 C4 **Aravalli Range** mts India

55 T7 **Aravete** Estonia
111 F2 **Arawa** P.N.G.
46 C2 **Araxá** Brazil
45 D2 **Araya, Pen. de** pen. Venez.
45 D2 **Araya, Pta de** pt Venez.
80 C2 **Arayıt Dağı** mt Turkey
81 M2 **Araz** r. Asia
81 K4 **Arbat** Iraq
68 J3 **Arbazh** Rus. Fed.
81 K3 **Arbīl** Iraq
55 O7 **Arboga** Sweden
21 J4 **Arborfield** Can.
57 F4 **Arbroath** U.K.
34 A2 **Arbuckle** U.S.A.
79 J4 **Arbu Lut, Dasht-e** des. Afgh.
64 D5 **Arcachon** France
29 D7 **Arcadia** U.S.A.
24 A3 **Arcata** U.S.A.
34 D2 **Arc Dome** summit U.S.A.
68 G1 **Archangel** Rus. Fed.
113 H2 **Archer** r. Austr.
113 H2 **Archer Bend National Park** nat. park Austr.
35 H2 **Arches Nat. Park** nat. park U.S.A.
81 M2 **Ärçivan** Azer.
114 A2 **Arckaringa** watercourse Austr.
24 D3 **Arco** U.S.A.
65 D4 **Arcos de la Frontera** Spain
118 C3 **Arctic Ocean**
119 B2 **Arctowski** Pol. Base Antarctica
81 M2 **Ardabīl** Iran
81 J1 **Ardahan** Turkey
55 K6 **Årdalstangen** Norway
60 C3 **Ardara** Rep. of Ireland
67 L4 **Ardas** r. Bulg.
68 G4 **Ardatov** Mordov. Rus. Fed.
68 G4 **Ardatov** Nizheg. Rus. Fed.
31 G3 **Ardbeg** Can.
60 E4 **Ardee** Rep. of Ireland
114 B4 **Arden, Mount** h. Austr.
61 C5 **Ardennes, Canal des** canal France
79 G3 **Ardeştān** Iran
60 F3 **Ardglass** U.K.
65 B3 **Ardila** r. Port.
115 G5 **Ardlethan** Austr.
27 D5 **Ardmore** U.S.A.
57 B4 **Ardnamurchan, Point of** pt U.K.
57 C4 **Ardrishaig** U.K.
114 B5 **Ardrossan** Austr.
57 D5 **Ardrossan** U.K.
57 C4 **Ardvasar** U.K.
47 E2 **Areco** r. Arg.
43 L4 **Areia Branca** Brazil
61 E4 **Aremberg** h. Ger.
94 B4 **Arena** r. Phil.
34 A2 **Arena, Pt** pt U.S.A.
65 D2 **Arenas de San Pedro** Spain
55 L7 **Arendal** Norway
59 D5 **Arenig Fawr** h. U.K.
67 K6 **Areopoli** Greece
42 D7 **Arequipa** Peru
43 H4 **Arere** Brazil
65 D2 **Arévalo** Spain
66 D3 **Arezzo** Italy
80 G6 **'Arfajah** w. Saudi Arabia
88 D1 **Argalant** Mongolia
65 E2 **Arganda** Spain
94 B4 **Argao** Phil.
66 D2 **Argenta** Italy
64 E2 **Argentan** France
66 D3 **Argentario, Monte** h. Italy
66 B2 **Argentera, Cima dell'** mt Italy
38 **Argentina** country S. America
119 B3 **Argentina Range** mts Antarctica
12 F8 **Argentine Basin** sea feature Atlantic Ocean
44 B8 **Argentino, Lago** l. Arg.
67 L2 **Argeş** r. Romania
84 A3 **Arghandāb** r. Afgh.
80 C2 **Argıthanı** Turkey
67 K6 **Argolikos Kolpos** b. Greece
67 K6 **Argos** Greece
67 J5 **Argostoli** Greece
65 F1 **Arguís** Spain
87 M1 **Argun'** r. China/Rus. Fed.
69 H7 **Argun** Rus. Fed.
34 D2 **Argus Range** mts U.S.A.
30 C4 **Argyle** U.S.A.
112 E3 **Argyle, Lake** l. Austr.
57 C4 **Argyll** reg. U.K.
Ar Horqin Qi see Tianshan
55 M8 **Århus** Denmark
117 E3 **Aria** N.Z.
115 G5 **Ariah Park** Austr.
91 B6 **Ariake-kai** b. Japan
103 B6 **Ariamsvlei** Namibia
66 F4 **Ariano Irpino** Italy
45 B4 **Ariari** r. Col.
83 D10 **Ari Atoll** atoll Maldives
45 E2 **Aribí** r. Venez.
100 B3 **Aribinda** Burkina
44 B1 **Arica** Chile
112 D6 **Arid, C.** c. Austr.
57 C4 **Arienas, Loch** l. U.K.
24 A4 **Arikaree** r. U.S.A.
45 E2 **Arima** Trinidad and Tobago
46 C1 **Arinos** Brazil

43 G6 **Arinos** r. Brazil
45 C3 **Aripio** r. Col.
42 F5 **Aripuanã** Brazil
42 F5 **Aripuanã** r. Brazil
42 F5 **Ariquemes** Brazil
46 B2 **Ariranhá** r. Brazil
104 B1 **Aris** Namibia
57 C4 **Arisaig** U.K.
57 C4 **Arisaig, Sound of** chan. U.K.
20 D4 **Aristazabal I.** i. Can.
44 C2 **Arizaro, Salar de** salt flat Arg.
35 G4 **Arizona** div. U.S.A.
25 E6 **Arizpe** Mex.
45 B2 **Arjona** Col.
92 □ **Arjuna, G.** vol. Indon.
69 G5 **Arkadak** Rus. Fed.
27 E5 **Arkadelphia** U.S.A.
57 C4 **Arkaig, Loch** l. U.K.
76 H4 **Arkalyk** Kazak.
27 E5 **Arkansas** div. U.S.A.
27 F5 **Arkansas** r. U.S.A.
27 D4 **Arkansas City** U.S.A.
85 G1 **Arkatag Shan** mts China
Arkhangel'sk see Archangel
68 G2 **Arkhangel'skaya Oblast'** div. Rus. Fed.
68 F4 **Arkhangel'skoye** Rus. Fed.
90 E5 **Arkhipovka** Rus. Fed.
67 M6 **Arkoi** i. Greece
62 F3 **Arkona, Kap** hd Ger.
76 K2 **Arkticheskogo Instituta, Ostrova** is Rus. Fed.
33 F3 **Arkville** U.S.A.
64 G5 **Arles** France
105 G4 **Arlington** S. Africa
24 B2 **Arlington** OR U.S.A.
26 D2 **Arlington** SD U.S.A.
32 E5 **Arlington** VA U.S.A.
30 D4 **Arlington Heights** U.S.A.
100 C3 **Arlit** Niger
61 D5 **Arlon** Belgium
94 **Armadores** i. Indon.
60 E3 **Armagh** U.K.
78 C4 **Armant** Egypt
69 G6 **Armavir** Rus. Fed.
70 **Armenia** country Asia
45 B3 **Armenia** Col.
61 A4 **Armentières** France
45 B3 **Armero** Col.
115 J3 **Armidale** Austr.
21 L2 **Armit Lake** l. Can.
84 E5 **Armori** India
20 B3 **Armour, Mt** mt Can./U.S.A.
60 E2 **Armoy** U.K.
20 F4 **Armstrong** B.C. Can.
22 C3 **Armstrong** Ont. Can.
90 E1 **Armu** r. Rus. Fed.
69 E6 **Armyans'k** Ukr.
80 D4 **Arnaoutis, Cape** c. Cyprus
23 H1 **Arnaud** r. Can.
55 M6 **Ârnes** Norway
27 D4 **Arnett** U.S.A.
61 D3 **Arnhem** Neth.
113 G2 **Arnhem, C.** c. Austr.
113 G2 **Arnhem Bay** b. Austr.
113 F2 **Arnhem Land** reg. Austr.
66 D3 **Arno** r. Italy
114 B4 **Arno Bay** Austr.
59 F4 **Arnold** U.K.
30 D2 **Arnold** U.S.A.
31 H1 **Arnoux, Lac** l. Can.
31 J3 **Arnprior** Can.
62 D5 **Arnsberg** Ger.
31 H3 **Arnstein** Can.
31 H1 **Arntfield** Can.
45 E3 **Aro** r. Venez.
103 B6 **Aroab** Namibia
66 D2 **Arona** Italy
33 K1 **Aroostook** Can.
33 J1 **Aroostook** r. Can./U.S.A.
111 H2 **Arorae** i. Kiribati
94 B3 **Aroroy** Phil.
81 J1 **Arpaçay** Turkey
81 J5 **Ar Raḥḥālīyah** Iraq
81 J5 **Ar Ramādī** Iraq
80 E7 **Ar Ramlah** Jordan
81 G4 **Ar Raqqah** Syria
64 F1 **Arras** France
80 F4 **Ar Rastān** Syria
81 J7 **Ar Rawd** w. Saudi Arabia
45 C4 **Arrecifal** Col.
47 E2 **Arrecifes** Arg.
36 F5 **Arriagá** Mex.
47 E2 **Arribeños** Arg.
81 L6 **Ar Rifā'ī** Iraq
81 K6 **Ar Rihāb** salt flat Iraq
79 K6 **Ar Rimāl** reg. Saudi Arabia
35 H3 **Arriola** U.S.A.
Ar Riyāḍ see Riyadh
47 G2 **Arroio Grande** Brazil
46 D1 **Arrojado** r. Brazil
60 C3 **Arrow, Lough** l. Rep. of Ireland
30 C2 **Arrow Lake** l. Can.
24 D3 **Arrowrock Res.** resr U.S.A.
117 C5 **Arrowsmith, Mt** mt N.Z.
47 F3 **Arroyo Grande** r. Arg.
34 B4 **Arroyo Grande** U.S.A.
47 E2 **Arroyo Seco** Arg.
81 K6 **Ar Rumaythah** Iraq
81 G4 **Ar Ruşāfah** Syria
81 H5 **Ar Ruţbah** Iraq

55 L8 ** Års** Denmark
81 L3 **Ars** Iran
90 C2 **Arsen'yev** Rus. Fed.
68 J3 **Arsk** Rus. Fed.
80 E3 **Arslanköy** Turkey
67 J5 **Arta** Greece
81 K2 **Artashat** Armenia
90 C3 **Artem** Rus. Fed.
69 F5 **Artemivs'k** Ukr.
90 C3 **Artemovskiy** Rus. Fed.
64 E2 **Artenay** France
25 F5 **Artesia** U.S.A.
31 G4 **Arthur** Can.
114 B3 **Arthur, Lake** salt flat Austr.
32 C4 **Arthur, Lake** l. U.S.A.
115 G8 **Arthur** r. Austr.
116 D4 **Arthur Pt** pt Austr.
117 C5 **Arthur's Pass** pass N.Z.
117 C5 **Arthur's Pass National Park** nat. park N.Z.
29 F7 **Arthur's Town** Bahamas
119 B1 **Artigas** Uru. Base Antarctica
47 F1 **Artigas** Uru.
81 J1 **Art'ik** Armenia
21 H2 **Artillery Lake** l. Can.
105 G2 **Artisia** Botswana
64 F1 **Artois** reg. France
81 J2 **Artos D.** mt Turkey
80 F1 **Artova** Turkey
69 D6 **Artsyz** Ukr.
82 E3 **Artux** China
81 H1 **Artvin** Turkey
93 J8 **Aru, Kepulauan** is Indon.
102 D3 **Arua** Uganda
46 B1 **Aruanã** Brazil
37 L6 **Aruba** terr. Caribbean
42 F4 **Arumã** Brazil
85 F4 **Arun** r. Nepal
85 H3 **Arunachal Pradesh** div. India
59 G7 **Arundel** U.K.
102 D4 **Arusha** Tanz.
26 B4 **Arvada** U.S.A.
60 E4 **Arvagh** Rep. of Ireland
88 H2 **Arvayheer** Mongolia
84 D5 **Arvi** India
21 L2 **Arviat** Can.
23 F4 **Arvida** Can.
54 Q4 **Arvidsjaur** Sweden
55 N7 **Arvika** Sweden
34 C4 **Arvin** U.S.A.
77 O2 **Ary** Rus. Fed.
82 C2 **Arys'** Kazak.
68 G4 **Arzamas** Rus. Fed.
65 F5 **Arzew** Alg.
69 H6 **Arzgir** Rus. Fed.
45 E2 **Asa** r. Venez.
100 C4 **Asaba** Nigeria
80 B2 **Asad, Buḩayrat al** resr Syria
84 B2 **Asadābād** Afgh.
81 M4 **Asadābād** Iran
45 A5 **Asahan** r. Indon.
90 H3 **Asahi-dake** vol. Japan
91 C2 **Asahi-gawa** r. Japan
90 H3 **Asahikawa** Japan
81 M3 **Asālem** Iran
85 F5 **Asansol** India
23 F4 **Asbestos** Can.
104 E4 **Asbestos Mountains** mts S. Africa
33 F4 **Asbury Park** U.S.A.
66 F4 **Ascea** Italy
96 **Ascension** island Atlantic Ocean
42 F7 **Ascensión** Bol.
25 E6 **Ascensión** Mex.
62 D6 **Aschaffenburg** Ger.
61 F3 **Ascheberg** Ger.
66 E3 **Ascoli Piceno** Italy
55 O8 **Åseda** Sweden
54 P4 **Åsele** Sweden
67 L3 **Asenovgrad** Bulg.
59 E6 **Ashbourne** U.K.
112 C4 **Ashburton** watercourse Austr.
117 C5 **Ashburton** N.Z.
30 D2 **Ashburton Bay** b. Can.
20 E4 **Ashcroft** Can.
80 E6 **Ashdod** Israel
27 E5 **Ashdown** U.S.A.
29 D5 **Asheboro** U.S.A.
29 D5 **Asheville** U.S.A.
115 J2 **Ashford** Austr.
59 H6 **Ashford** U.K.
35 F4 **Ash Fork** U.S.A.
79 H2 **Ashgabat** Turkm.
90 H3 **Ashibetsu** Japan
91 F6 **Ashikaga** Japan
58 F2 **Ashington** U.K.
68 J3 **Ashit** r. Rus. Fed.
91 C7 **Ashizuri-misaki** pt Japan
32 C5 **Ashland** KS U.S.A.
32 B5 **Ashland** KY U.S.A.
33 J1 **Ashland** ME U.S.A.
24 F2 **Ashland** MT U.S.A.
33 H3 **Ashland** NH U.S.A.
32 B4 **Ashland** OH U.S.A.
24 B3 **Ashland** OR U.S.A.
32 E6 **Ashland** VA U.S.A.
30 B2 **Ashland** WV U.S.A.
115 H2 **Ashley** Austr.
26 D2 **Ashley** U.S.A.
112 D2 **Ashmore and Cartier Islands** terr. Austr.
112 D2 **Ashmore Reef** rf Ashmore and Cartier Is
68 C4 **Ashmyany** Belarus
35 H5 **Ash Peak** U.S.A.
80 E6 **Ashqelon** Israel
81 J6 **Ash Shabakah** Iraq
81 H3 **Ash Shaddādah** Syria

81 K6 **Ash Shanāfīyah** Iraq
81 H7 **Ash Shaqīq** *w.* Saudi Arabia
81 J4 **Ash Sharqāt** Iraq
81 L6 **Ash Shatrah** Iraq
80 E6 **Ash Shawbak** Jordan
79 F7 **Ash Shiḥr** Yemen
32 C4 **Ashtabula** U.S.A.
81 K1 **Ashtarak** Armenia
84 D5 **Ashti** India
104 D6 **Ashton** S. Africa
24 E2 **Ashton** U.S.A.
58 E4 **Ashton-under-Lyne** U.K.
22 F4 **Ashuapmushuan** *r.* Can.
29 C5 **Ashville** U.S.A.
80 F4 **'Āsī, Nahr al** *r.* Asia
85 F6 **Āsika** India
66 C4 **Asinara, Golfo dell'** *b.* Italy
76 K4 **Asino** Rus. Fed.
68 D4 **Asipovichy** Belarus
78 E5 **'Asīr** *reg.* Saudi Arabia
81 H2 **Aşkale** Turkey
55 M7 **Asker** Norway
55 O7 **Askersund** Sweden
55 M7 **Askim** Norway
86 F1 **Askiz** Rus. Fed.
81 L2 **Aşlāndūz** Iran
102 D2 **Asmara** Eritrea
55 O8 **Åsnen** *l.* Sweden
84 C4 **Asop** India
78 D5 **Asoteriba, J.** *mt* Sudan
81 M3 **Aspar** Iran
58 D3 **Aspatria** U.K.
25 C5 **Aspen** U.S.A.
27 C5 **Aspermont** U.S.A.
117 B6 **Aspiring, Mt** *mt* N.Z.
21 H4 **Asquith** Can.
80 F4 **As Sa'an** Syria
102 E2 **Assab** Eritrea
80 E6 **Aş Şāfī** Jordan
80 F3 **As Safīrah** Syria
81 H4 **Aş Şālihīyah** Syria
81 K6 **As Salmān** Iraq
80 E5 **As Salt** Jordan
84 H4 **Assam** *dr.* India
81 K6 **As Samāwah** Iraq
80 F5 **Aş Şanamayn** Syria
101 E2 **As Sarīr** *reg.* Libya
33 F5 **Assateague I.** *i.* U.S.A.
33 F6 **Assateague Island National Seashore** *res.* U.S.A.
61 E1 **Assen** Neth.
61 D4 **Assesse** Belgium
85 F5 **Assia Hills** *h.* India
101 D1 **As Sidrah** Libya
21 H5 **Assiniboia** Can.
21 K5 **Assiniboine** *r.* Can.
20 F4 **Assiniboine, Mt** *mt* Can.
46 B3 **Assis** Brazil
66 E3 **Assisi** Italy
81 L7 **Aş Şubayḩīyah** Kuwait
81 K4 **As Sukhnah** Syria
81 K4 **As Sulaymānīyah** Iraq
78 F5 **As Sulayyil** Saudi Arabia
78 E5 **As Sūq** Saudi Arabia
81 H4 **Aş Şuwar** Syria
80 F5 **As Suwaydā'** Syria
81 K5 **Aş Şuwayrah** Iraq
57 C2 **Assynt, Loch** *l.* U.K.
67 M7 **Astakida** *i.* Greece
76 J4 **Astana** Kazak.
81 M3 **Astaneh** Iran
81 M2 **Astara** Azer.
66 C2 **Asti** Italy
34 A2 **Asti** U.S.A.
47 C1 **Astica** Arg.
Astin Tag *mts see* **Altun Shan**
84 C2 **Astor** Jammu and Kashmir
84 C2 **Astor** *r.* Pak.
65 C1 **Astorga** Spain
32 B2 **Astoria** U.S.A.
55 N8 **Åstorp** Sweden
69 J6 **Astrakhan'** Rus. Fed.
Astrakhan' Bazar *see* **Cälilabad**
69 H6 **Astrakhanskaya Oblast'** *div.* Rus. Fed.
68 C4 **Astravyets** Belarus
65 C1 **Asturias** *div.* Spain
67 M6 **Astypalaia** *i.* Greece
93 L3 **Asuncion** *i.* N. Mariana Is
44 E3 **Asunción** Para.
78 C5 **Aswân** Egypt
78 C4 **Asyût** Egypt
111 J4 **Ata** *i.* Tonga
45 D4 **Atabapo** *r.* Col./Venez.
44 C2 **Atacama, Desierto de** *des.* Chile
44 C2 **Atacama, Salar de** *salt flat* Chile
111 J2 **Atafu** *i.* Tokelau
100 C4 **Atakpamé** Togo
67 K5 **Atalanti** Greece
42 C6 **Atalaya** Peru
100 A2 **Atâr** Maur.
95 A1 **Ataran** *r.* Myanmar
35 H4 **Atarque** U.S.A.
34 B4 **Atascadero** U.S.A.
82 D1 **Atasu** Kazak.
93 H8 **Atauro** *i.* Indon.
101 F3 **Atbara** Sudan
101 F3 **Atbara** *r.* Sudan
76 H4 **Atbasar** Kazak.
27 F6 **Atchafalaya Bay** *b.* U.S.A.
26 E4 **Atchison** U.S.A.
66 E3 **Aterno** *r.* Italy
66 F3 **Atessa** Italy
61 B4 **Ath** Belgium
20 G4 **Athabasca** Can.
21 G3 **Athabasca, Lake** *l.* Can.
60 E4 **Athboy** Rep. of Ireland

60 C4 **Athenry** Rep. of Ireland
31 K3 **Athens** Can.
67 K6 **Athens** Greece
29 C5 **Athens** *AL* U.S.A.
29 D5 **Athens** *GA* U.S.A.
32 B5 **Athens** *OH* U.S.A.
29 C5 **Athens** *TN* U.S.A.
27 E5 **Athens** *TX* U.S.A.
59 F5 **Atherstone** U.K.
116 A1 **Atherton** Austr.
Athina *see* **Athens**
60 C4 **Athleague** Rep. of Ireland
60 D4 **Athlone** Rep. of Ireland
117 B6 **Athol** N.Z.
33 G3 **Athol** U.S.A.
57 E4 **Atholl, Forest of** *reg.* U.K.
67 L4 **Athos** *mt* Greece
60 E5 **Athy** Rep. of Ireland
101 D3 **Ati** Chad
42 D7 **Atico** Peru
22 B4 **Atikokan** Can.
23 H3 **Atikonak L.** *l.* Can.
94 B3 **Atimonan** Phil.
77 R3 **Atka** Rus. Fed.
69 H5 **Atkarsk** Rus. Fed.
29 C5 **Atlanta** *GA* U.S.A.
30 C5 **Atlanta** *IL* U.S.A.
31 E3 **Atlanta** *MI* U.S.A.
80 D2 **Atlantı** Turkey
26 E3 **Atlantic** U.S.A.
33 F5 **Atlantic City** U.S.A.
13 D7 **Atlantic-Indian-Antarctic Basin** *sea feature* Atlantic Ocean
12 J9 **Atlantic-Indian Ridge** *sea feature* Indian Ocean
4 **Atlantic Ocean**
104 C6 **Atlantis** S. Africa
12 G3 **Atlantis Fracture** *sea feature* Atlantic Ocean
100 C1 **Atlas Saharien** *mts* Alg.
20 C3 **Atlin** Can.
20 C3 **Atlin Lake** *l.* Can.
20 C3 **Atlin Prov. Park** Can.
80 E5 **'Atlit** Israel
27 G6 **Atmore** U.S.A.
27 D5 **Atoka** U.S.A.
95 C1 **Atouat** *mt* Laos
85 G4 **Atrai** *r.* India
45 A3 **Atrato** *r.* Col.
33 F5 **Atsion** U.S.A.
80 E6 **At Tafīlah** Jordan
78 E5 **At Ta'if** Saudi Arabia
29 C5 **Attalla** U.S.A.
95 C2 **Attapu** Laos
67 M6 **Attavyros** *mt* Greece
22 D3 **Attawapiskat** Can.
22 C3 **Attawapiskat** *r.* Can.
22 C3 **Attawapiskat L.** *l.* Can.
81 G7 **At Tawil** *mts* Saudi Arabia
62 F7 **Attersee** *l.* Austria
30 D5 **Attica** *IN* U.S.A.
32 B4 **Attica** *OH* U.S.A.
33 H3 **Attleboro** U.S.A.
59 J5 **Attleborough** U.K.
80 F7 **At Tubayq** *reg.* Saudi Arabia
14 G2 **Attu Island** *i.* U.S.A.
47 C2 **Atuel** *r.* Arg.
55 O7 **Åtvidaberg** Sweden
32 C4 **Atwood Lake** *l.* U.S.A.
76 G5 **Atyrau** Kazak.
64 G5 **Aubagne** France
94 B2 **Aubarede Point** *pt* Phil.
64 G4 **Aubenas** France
35 F4 **Aubrey Cliffs** *cliff* U.S.A.
114 C5 **Auburn** Austr.
116 D5 **Auburn** *r.* Austr.
31 G4 **Auburn** Can.
29 C5 **Auburn** *AL* U.S.A.
34 B2 **Auburn** *CA* U.S.A.
30 E5 **Auburn** *IN* U.S.A.
33 H2 **Auburn** *ME* U.S.A.
26 E3 **Auburn** *NE* U.S.A.
32 E3 **Auburn** *NY* U.S.A.
24 B2 **Auburn** *WA* U.S.A.
116 D5 **Auburn Ra.** *h.* Austr.
64 F4 **Aubusson** France
47 C3 **Auca Mahuida, Sa de** *mt* Arg.
64 E4 **Auch** France
57 E4 **Auchterarder** U.K.
117 E2 **Auckland** N.Z.
111 G7 **Auckland Islands** *is* N.Z.
33 H2 **Audet** Can.
59 J7 **Audresselles** France
116 B5 **Augathella** Austr.
60 D3 **Augher** U.K.
60 E3 **Aughnacloy** U.K.
60 C5 **Aughrim** Rep. of Ireland
104 D4 **Augrabies** S. Africa
104 D4 **Augrabies Falls** *waterfall* S. Africa
104 D4 **Augrabies Falls National Park** *nat. park* S. Africa
31 H4 **Au Gres** U.S.A.
62 E6 **Augsburg** Ger.
112 C4 **Augusta** Austr.
66 F6 **Augusta** Italy
29 D5 **Augusta** *GA* U.S.A.
27 D4 **Augusta** *KS* U.S.A.
33 J2 **Augusta** *ME* U.S.A.
30 B3 **Augusta** *WV* U.S.A.
45 B2 **Augustin Cadazzi** Col.
112 C4 **Augustus, Mt** *mt* Austr.
61 B4 **Aulnoye-Aymeries** France
59 J7 **Ault** France
103 B6 **Auob** *r.* Namibia
23 G2 **Aupaluk** Can.
95 C4 **Aur** *i.* Malaysia
55 S6 **Aura** Fin.
84 D4 **Auraiya** India
84 C6 **Aurangābād** India

62 C4 **Aurich** Ger.
46 B2 **Aurilândia** Brazil
64 E4 **Aurillac** France
94 B5 **Aurora** Phil.
24 F4 **Aurora** *CO* U.S.A.
30 C5 **Aurora** *IL* U.S.A.
33 J2 **Aurora** *ME* U.S.A.
27 E4 **Aurora** *MO* U.S.A.
113 H2 **Aurukun** Austr.
103 B6 **Aus** Namibia
31 F3 **Au Sable** U.S.A.
31 E3 **Au Sable** *r.* U.S.A.
33 G2 **Ausable** *r.* U.S.A.
33 G2 **Ausable Forks** U.S.A.
30 D2 **Au Sable Pt** *pt MI* U.S.A.
31 F3 **Au Sable Pt** *pt MI* U.S.A.
57 F1 **Auskerry** *i.* U.K.
54 D4 **Austari-Jökulsá** *r.* Iceland
26 E3 **Austin** *MN* U.S.A.
34 D2 **Austin** *NV* U.S.A.
27 D6 **Austin** *TX* U.S.A.
109 **Australes, Îles** *is* Pac. Oc.
106 **Australia** *country* Australasia
115 H5 **Australian Capital Territory** *div.* Austr.
48 **Austria** *country* Europe
54 O2 **Austvågøy** *i.* Norway
54 U3 **Autti** Fin.
64 G3 **Autun** France
64 F4 **Auvergne** *reg.* France
64 F3 **Auxerre** France
64 G3 **Auxonne** France
33 F3 **Ava** U.S.A.
64 F3 **Avallon** France
34 C5 **Avalon** U.S.A.
23 K4 **Avalon Peninsula** *pen.* Can.
81 L2 **Avān** Iran
80 E2 **Avanos** Turkey
46 C3 **Avaré** Brazil
81 L2 **Āvārsin** Iran
34 D4 **Avawatz Mts** *mts* U.S.A.
43 G4 **Aveiro** Brazil
65 B2 **Aveiro** Port.
65 B2 **Aveiro, Ria de** *est.* Port.
81 M4 **Avej** Iran
47 E2 **Avellaneda** Arg.
66 F4 **Avellino** Italy
34 B3 **Avenal** U.S.A.
114 F4 **Avenel** Austr.
66 F4 **Aversa** Italy
61 B4 **Avesnes-sur-Helpe** France
55 P6 **Avesta** Sweden
64 F4 **Aveyron** *r.* France
66 E3 **Avezzano** Italy
57 E3 **Aviemore** U.K.
66 F4 **Avigliano** Italy
64 G5 **Avignon** France
65 D2 **Ávila** Spain
65 D1 **Avilés** Spain
68 H2 **Avnyugskiy** Rus. Fed.
115 G8 **Avoca** *Tas.* Austr.
114 E6 **Avoca** *Vic.* Austr.
114 E6 **Avoca** *r.* Austr.
60 E5 **Avoca** Rep. of Ireland
26 E3 **Avoca** U.S.A.
66 F6 **Avola** Italy
59 F5 **Avon** *r. Eng.* U.K.
59 F7 **Avon** *r. Eng.* U.K.
30 B5 **Avon** U.S.A.
35 F5 **Avondale** U.S.A.
116 B3 **Avon Downs** Austr.
59 E6 **Avonmouth** U.K.
29 D7 **Avon Park** U.S.A.
64 D2 **Avranches** France
61 A5 **Avre** *r.* France
111 G2 **Avuavu** Solomon Is
91 D7 **Awaji-shima** *i.* Japan
117 E3 **Awakino** N.Z.
117 D1 **Awanui** N.Z.
117 B6 **Awarua Pt** *pt* N.Z.
102 E3 **Āwash** Indon.
102 E2 **Āwash** *r.* Eth.
90 F5 **Awa-shima** *i.* Japan
102 F3 **Awash National Park** *nat. park* Eth.
104 A2 **Awasib Mts** *mts* Namibia
117 D4 **Awatere** *r.* N.Z.
101 D2 **Awbārī** Libya
60 C5 **Awbeg** *r.* Rep. of Ireland
81 L6 **'Awdah, Hawr al** *l.* Iraq
102 E3 **Aw Dheegle** Somalia
57 C4 **Awe, Loch** *l.* U.K.
101 E4 **Aweil** Sudan
100 C4 **Awka** Nigeria
94 C6 **Awu** *mt* Indon.
114 F6 **Axedale** Austr.
118 B3 **Axel Heiberg Island** *i.* Can.
100 B4 **Axim** Ghana
59 E7 **Axminster** U.K.
91 D7 **Ayabe** Japan
47 D3 **Ayacucho** Arg.
42 D6 **Ayacucho** Peru
82 F1 **Ayagoz** Kazak.
86 E4 **Ayakkum Hu** *salt l.* China
65 C4 **Ayamonte** Spain
77 P4 **Ayan** Rus. Fed.
69 E7 **Ayancık** Turkey
45 B2 **Ayapel** Col.
80 C1 **Ayaş** Turkey
42 D6 **Ayaviri** Peru
84 B3 **Aybak** Afgh.
69 F5 **Aydar** *r.* Ukr.
79 K1 **Aydarkul', Ozero** *l.* Uzbek.
80 A2 **Aydın** Turkey
80 A2 **Aydın Dağları** *mts* Turkey
95 □ **Ayer Chawan, P.** *i.* Sing.
95 □ **Ayer Merbau, P.** *i.* Sing.
Ayers Rock *h. see* **Uluru**
77 N3 **Aykhal** Rus. Fed.

68 J2 **Aykino** Rus. Fed.
117 D5 **Aylesbury** N.Z.
59 G6 **Aylesbury** U.K.
32 E6 **Aylett** U.S.A.
65 E2 **Ayllón** Spain
31 G4 **Aylmer** Can.
21 H2 **Aylmer Lake** *l.* Can.
79 K2 **Ayní** Tajik.
80 G3 **'Ayn 'Īsá** Syria
101 F4 **Ayod** Sudan
77 S3 **Ayon, O.** *i.* Rus. Fed.
100 B3 **'Ayoûn el 'Atroûs** Maur.
116 B2 **Ayr** Austr.
57 D5 **Ayr** *r.* U.K.
57 D5 **Ayr** U.K.
80 D3 **Ayrancı** Turkey
58 C3 **Ayre, Point of** *pt* Isle of Man
82 B2 **Ayteke Bi** Kazak.
67 M3 **Aytos** Bulg.
95 B2 **Ayutthaya** Thai.
80 F2 **Ayvacık** Turkey
80 A2 **Ayvalık** Turkey
85 E4 **Azamgarh** India
100 B3 **Azaouâd** *reg.* Mali
100 C3 **Azaouagh, Vallée de** *watercourse* Mali/Niger
Azbine *mts see* **L'Aïr, Massif de**
80 D1 **Azdavay** Turkey
70 **Azerbaijan** *country* Asia
31 G2 **Azilda** Can.
33 H2 **Aziscohos Lake** *l.* U.S.A.
42 C4 **Azogues** Ecuador
76 F3 **Azopol'ye** Rus. Fed.
48 **Azores** *terr.* Port.
12 H3 **Azores - Cape St Vincent Ridge** *sea feature* Atlantic Ocean
69 F6 **Azov** Rus. Fed.
69 F6 **Azov, Sea of** *sea* Rus. Fed./Ukr.
100 B1 **Azrou** Morocco
25 F4 **Aztec** U.S.A.
65 D3 **Azuaga** Spain
44 B3 **Azúcar** *r.* Chile
37 H7 **Azuero, Península de** *pen.* Panama
47 E3 **Azul** Arg.
47 B4 **Azul, Cerro** *mt* Arg.
42 C5 **Azul, Cordillera** *mts* Peru
46 A1 **Azul, Serra** *h.* Brazil
91 G6 **Azuma-san** *vol.* Japan
42 F8 **Azurduy** Bol.
66 B6 **Azzaba** Alg.
80 F5 **Az Zabadānī** Syria
81 J6 **Az Zafīrī** *reg.* Iraq
Az Zahrān *see* **Dhahran**
80 F5 **Az Zarqā'** Jordan
81 L6 **Az Zubayr** Iraq

B

80 E5 **Ba'abda** Lebanon
80 F4 **Ba'albek** Lebanon
115 H3 **Baan Baa** Austr.
102 E3 **Baardheere** Somalia
84 B2 **Bābā, Kūh-e** *mts* Afgh.
67 M5 **Baba Burnu** *pt* Turkey
81 M1 **Babadağ** *mt* Azer.
67 N2 **Babadag** Romania
69 C7 **Babaeski** Turkey
42 C4 **Babahoyo** Ecuador
85 E3 **Babai** *r.* Nepal
88 B1 **Babai Gaxun** China
81 L2 **Bābā Jān** Iran
94 C5 **Babak** Phil.
78 E7 **Bāb al Mandab** *str.* Africa/Asia
93 H8 **Babar** *i.* Indon.
93 H8 **Babar, Kepulauan** *is* Indon.
102 D4 **Babati** Tanz.
68 E3 **Babayevo** Rus. Fed.
69 H7 **Babayurt** Rus. Fed.
30 B2 **Babbitt** U.S.A.
115 H7 **Babel I.** *i.* Austr.
116 A1 **Babinda** Austr.
20 D4 **Babine Lake** *l.* Can.
93 J7 **Babo** Indon.
79 G2 **Bābol** Iran
104 C6 **Baboon Point** *pt* S. Africa
35 G6 **Baboquivari Peak** *summit* U.S.A.
102 B3 **Baboua** C.A.R.
68 D4 **Babruysk** Belarus
84 B4 **Babuhri** India
84 C2 **Babusar Pass** *pass* Pak.
86 J1 **Babushkin** Rus. Fed.
94 A4 **Babuyan** Phil.
94 B2 **Babuyan** *i.* Phil.
89 F7 **Babuyan Channel** *chan.* Phil.
94 B2 **Babuyan Islands** *is* Phil.
81 K5 **Babylon** Iraq
43 K4 **Bacabal** Brazil
80 C1 **Bacakliyayla T.** *mt* Turkey
93 H7 **Bacan** *i.* Indon.
67 N7 **Bacău** Romania
114 F6 **Bacchus Marsh** Austr.
89 C6 **Bắc Giang** Vietnam
25 F6 **Bachiniva** Mex.
89 C6 **Bach Long Vi, Đao** *i.* Vietnam
82 E3 **Bachu** China
21 J1 **Back** *r.* Can.
67 H2 **Bačka Palanka** Yugo.
20 D2 **Backbone Ranges** *mts* Can.

54 P5 **Backe** Sweden
114 B5 **Backstairs Pass.** *chan.* Austr.
57 E4 **Backwater Reservoir** *resr* U.K.
89 B6 **Bac Lac** Vietnam
95 C5 **Bac Liêu** Vietnam
89 C6 **Bắc Ninh** Vietnam
94 B3 **Baco, Mt** *mt* Phil.
94 B4 **Bacolod** Phil.
89 B6 **Bắc Quang** Vietnam
22 F2 **Bacqueville, Lac** *l.* Can.
83 E8 **Badagara** India
88 A1 **Badain Jaran Shamo** *des.* China
42 F4 **Badajós, Lago** *l.* Brazil
65 C3 **Badajoz** Spain
81 H6 **Badanah** Saudi Arabia
85 H4 **Badarpur** India
31 H4 **Bad Axe** U.S.A.
23 H4 **Baddeck** Can.
80 C3 **Bademli Geçidi** *pass* Turkey
62 H6 **Baden** Austria
62 D7 **Baden** Switz.
62 D6 **Baden-Baden** Ger.
57 D4 **Badenoch** *reg.* U.K.
23 J4 **Badger** Can.
62 D5 **Bad Hersfeld** Ger.
62 F7 **Bad Hofgastein** Austria
66 D2 **Badia Polesine** Italy
84 B4 **Badin** Pak.
62 F7 **Bad Ischl** Austria
Bādiyat ash Shām *des. see* **Syrian Desert**
62 E5 **Bad Kissingen** Ger.
62 C6 **Bad Kreuznach** Ger.
26 C3 **Badlands** *reg.* U.S.A.
26 C3 **Badlands Nat. Park** *nat. park* U.S.A.
62 D6 **Bad Mergentheim** Ger.
61 F4 **Bad Neuenahr-Ahrweiler** Ger.
88 D4 **Badong** China
95 D3 **Ba Đông** Vietnam
81 K5 **Badrah** Iraq
62 F7 **Bad Reichenhall** Ger.
84 D3 **Badrinath Peaks** *mts* India
62 E4 **Bad Salzungen** Ger.
62 E4 **Bad Schwartau** Ger.
62 E4 **Bad Segeberg** Ger.
113 H2 **Badu I.** *i.* Austr.
83 F9 **Badulla** Sri Lanka
54 B3 **Bær** Iceland
115 J4 **Baerami** Austr.
65 E4 **Baeza** Spain
100 D4 **Bafang** Cameroon
100 A3 **Bafatá** Guinea-Bissau
118 A3 **Baffin Bay** *b.* Can.
118 A3 **Baffin Island** *i.* Can.
116 D5 **Baffle Cr.** *r.* Austr.
100 D4 **Bafia** Cameroon
100 A3 **Bafing, Réserve du** *nat. park* Mali
100 A3 **Bafoulabé** Mali
100 D4 **Bafoussam** Cameroon
79 H3 **Bāfq** Iran
80 E1 **Bafra** Turkey
69 E7 **Bafra Burnu** *pt* Turkey
79 H4 **Bāft** Iran
102 C3 **Bafwasende** Dem. Rep. Congo
85 F4 **Bagaha** India
94 A5 **Bagahak** *h.* Malaysia
83 E7 **Bagalkot** India
102 D4 **Bagamoyo** Tanz.
92 C6 **Bagan Datuk** Malaysia
103 B5 **Bagani** Namibia
95 B4 **Bagan Serai** Malaysia
95 B5 **Bagansiapiapi** Indon.
35 F4 **Bagdad** U.S.A.
47 F1 **Bagé** Brazil
84 D3 **Bageshwar** India
24 F3 **Baggs** U.S.A.
59 C6 **Baggy Point** *pt* U.K.
84 C5 **Bagh** India
81 K5 **Baghdād** Iraq
84 B1 **Baghlān** Afgh.
26 E2 **Bagley** U.S.A.
85 E3 **Baglung** Nepal
65 G1 **Bagnères-de-Luchon** France
64 F4 **Bagnols-sur-Cèze** France
85 F4 **Bagnuiti** *r.* Nepal
88 C2 **Bag Nur** *l.* China
Bago *see* **Pegu**
94 B4 **Bago** Phil.
63 K3 **Bagrationovsk** Rus. Fed.
94 B2 **Baguio** Phil.
94 B2 **Baguio** Phil.
94 B2 **Baguio** Phil.
84 D3 **Bahadurgarh** India
85 G4 **Baharampur** India
78 B4 **Bahariya Oasis** *oasis* Egypt
92 B7 **Bahau** Malaysia
84 B3 **Bahawalnagar** Pak.
84 B3 **Bahawalpur** Pak.
80 F3 **Bahçe** Turkey
89 B5 **Ba Hẽ** *r.* China
84 D3 **Baheri** India
102 D4 **Bahi** Tanz.
46 E1 **Bahia** *div.* Brazil
47 D3 **Bahía Blanca** Arg.
25 E6 **Bahía Kino** Mex.
44 C7 **Bahía Laura** Arg.
44 C5 **Bahía Negra** Para.
25 D7 **Bahía Tortugas** Mex.
102 D2 **Bahir Dar** Eth.
84 E4 **Bahraich** India
70 **Bahrain** *country* Asia
81 M3 **Bahrāmābād** Iran
81 M3 **Bahrām Beyg** Iran

Bahr el Azraq *r. see* **Blue Nile**
63 L7 **Baia Mare** Romania
87 M2 **Baicheng** China
23 G4 **Baie-Comeau** Can.
Baie du Poste *see* **Mistissini**
23 H4 **Baie-St-Paul** Can.
23 J4 **Baie Verte** Can.
88 E2 **Baigou** *r.* China
84 E5 **Baihar** India
87 N3 **Baihe** *Jilin* China
88 D3 **Baihe** *Shaanxi* China
Baikal, Lake *l. see* **Baykal, Ozero**
67 K2 **Băileşti** Romania
67 K2 **Băileştilor, Câmpia** *plain* Romania
88 D1 **Bailingmiao** China
61 A4 **Bailleul** France
21 H2 **Baillie** *r.* Can.
60 E4 **Baillieborough** Rep. of Ireland
88 B3 **Bailong Jiang** *r.* China
82 K4 **Baima** China
59 G4 **Bain** *r.* U.K.
82 G5 **Bainang** China
29 C6 **Bainbridge** *GA* U.S.A.
33 F3 **Bainbridge** *NY* U.S.A.
85 G3 **Baingoin** China
80 F6 **Bā'ir** Jordan
80 F6 **Bā'ir, Wādī** *watercourse* Jordan
85 E4 **Bairab Co** *l.* China
85 F4 **Bairagnia** India
88 F1 **Bairin Qiao** China
Bairin Youqi *see* **Daban**
Bairin Zuoqi *see* **Lindong**
115 G6 **Bairnsdale** Austr.
94 B4 **Bais** Phil.
89 C7 **Baisha** *Hainan* China
89 D5 **Baisha** *Jiangxi* China
88 C4 **Baisha** *Sichuan* China
87 N3 **Baishan** China
87 N3 **Baishan** China
88 D3 **Baishui Jiang** *r.* China
89 B7 **Bai Thương** Vietnam
88 E1 **Baitle** *r.* China
88 E1 **Baixingt** China
88 B2 **Baiyin** China
101 F3 **Baiyuda Desert** *des.* Sudan
67 H7 **Baja** Hungary
25 D6 **Baja, Punta** *pt* Mex.
36 A2 **Baja California** *pen.* Mex.
35 E6 **Baja California Norte** *div.* Mex.
81 M3 **Bājalān** Iran
27 C7 **Bajan** Mex.
84 E3 **Bajang** Nepal
85 G5 **Baj Baj** India
45 A3 **Bajo Baudó** Col.
47 D3 **Bajo Hondo** Arg.
116 D4 **Bajool** Austr.
100 A3 **Bakel** Senegal
34 D4 **Baker** *CA* U.S.A.
24 F2 **Baker** *MT* U.S.A.
35 E2 **Baker** *NV* U.S.A.
24 C2 **Baker** *OR* U.S.A.
24 B1 **Baker, Mt** *vol.* U.S.A.
35 G4 **Baker Butte** *summit* U.S.A.
20 L3 **Baker I.** *i.* U.S.A.
111 J1 **Baker Island** *i.* Pac. Oc.
21 K2 **Baker Lake** Can.
21 K2 **Baker Lake** *l.* Can.
116 C3 **Bakers Creek** Austr.
22 E2 **Bakers Dozen Islands** *is* Can.
34 C4 **Bakersfield** U.S.A.
95 C2 **Bâ Kêv** Cambodia
84 B4 **Bakhasar** India
69 E6 **Bakhchysaray** Ukr.
79 H2 **Bakherden** Turkm.
69 E5 **Bakhmach** Ukr.
79 G3 **Bakhtegan, Daryācheh-ye** *salt pan* Iran
Bakı *see* **Baku**
80 B1 **Bakırköy** Turkey
102 D3 **Bako** Eth.
102 C3 **Bakouma** C.A.R.
102 B3 **Bakoumba** Gabon
69 G7 **Baksan** Rus. Fed.
81 M1 **Baku** Azer.
102 C3 **Baku** Dem. Rep. Congo
80 D2 **Balâ** Turkey
59 D5 **Bala** U.K.
42 E6 **Bala, Cerros de** *mts* Bol.
94 A4 **Balabac** Phil.
94 A5 **Balabac** *i.* Phil.
94 A5 **Balabac Strait** *str.* Malaysia/Phil.
81 K4 **Balad** Iraq
84 E5 **Balaghat** India
81 L1 **Balakhna** Azer.
114 C5 **Balaklava** Austr.
69 E6 **Balaklava** Ukr.
69 F5 **Balakliya** Ukr.
69 H4 **Balakovo** Rus. Fed.
94 A5 **Balambangan** *i.* Malaysia
79 J2 **Bālā Morghāb** Afgh.
84 B4 **Bāla** India
69 H5 **Balashov** Rus. Fed.
84 C5 **Balasinor** India
62 H7 **Balaton** *l.* Hungary
62 H7 **Balatonboglár** Hungary
62 H7 **Balatonfüred** Hungary
43 G4 **Balbina, Represa de** *resr* Brazil

60 E4 **Balbriggan** Rep. of Ireland
114 C3 **Balcanoona** Austr.
47 E3 **Balcarce** Arg.
67 N3 **Balchik** Bulg.
117 B7 **Balclutha** N.Z.
27 F5 **Bald Knob** U.S.A.
35 E3 **Bald Mtn** *mt* U.S.A.
21 K3 **Baldock Lake** *l.* Can.
31 H3 **Baldwin** Can.
29 D6 **Baldwin** *FL* U.S.A.
30 E4 **Baldwin** *MI* U.S.A.
30 A3 **Baldwin** *WV* U.S.A.
33 E3 **Baldwinsville** U.S.A.
35 H5 **Baldy Peak** *mt* U.S.A.
Baleares, Islas *is see* **Balearic Islands**
65 H3 **Balearic Islands** *is* Spain
46 E2 **Baleia, Ponta da** *pt* Brazil
102 D3 **Bale Mts National Park** *nat. park* Eth.
94 B3 **Baler** Phil.
94 B3 **Baler Bay** *b.* Phil.
85 F5 **Bāleshwar** India
55 K6 **Balestrand** Norway
116 A3 **Balfe's Creek** Austr.
117 B6 **Balfour** N.Z.
92 □ **Bali** *div.* Indon.
92 □ **Bali** *i.* Indon.
92 B6 **Balige** Indon.
85 E5 **Baliguda** India
88 F1 **Balihan** China
80 A2 **Balıkesir** Turkey
92 F7 **Balikpapan** Indon.
94 A5 **Balimbing** Phil.
110 E2 **Balimo** P.N.G.
62 D6 **Balingen** Ger.
94 B2 **Balintang Channel** *chan.* Phil.
57 E3 **Balintore** U.K.
92 F8 **Bali Sea** *g.* Indon.
94 B5 **Baliungan** *i.* Phil.
52 **Balkan Mountains** *mts* Bulg./Yugo.
84 A1 **Balkhab** *r.* Afgh.
82 D1 **Balkhash** Kazak.
82 D1 **Balkhash, Ozero** *l.* Kazak.
69 H6 **Balkuduk** Kazak.
57 C4 **Ballachulish** U.K.
112 D6 **Balladonia** Austr.
115 H3 **Balladoran** Austr.
60 C4 **Ballaghaderreen** Rep. of Ireland
114 F6 **Ballan** Austr.
54 P2 **Ballangen** Norway
24 E2 **Ballantine** U.S.A.
57 D5 **Ballantrae** U.K.
114 E6 **Ballarat** Austr.
112 D5 **Ballard, L.** *salt flat* Austr.
84 D6 **Ballarpur** India
57 E3 **Ballater** U.K.
100 B3 **Ballé** Mali
44 B3 **Ballena, Pta** *pt* Chile
119 A6 **Balleny Is** *is* Antarctica
85 F4 **Ballia** India
115 K2 **Ballina** Austr.
60 B3 **Ballina** Rep. of Ireland
60 C3 **Ballinafad** Rep. of Ireland
60 D4 **Ballinalack** Rep. of Ireland
60 D3 **Ballinamore** Rep. of Ireland
60 C4 **Ballinasloe** Rep. of Ireland
60 C4 **Ballindine** Rep. of Ireland
27 D6 **Ballinger** U.S.A.
57 E4 **Ballinluig** U.K.
60 B4 **Ballinrobe** Rep. of Ireland
33 G3 **Ballston Spa** U.S.A.
60 E3 **Ballybay** Rep. of Ireland
60 A6 **Ballybrack** Rep. of Ireland
60 B5 **Ballybunnion** Rep. of Ireland
60 E5 **Ballycanew** Rep. of Ireland
60 B3 **Ballycastle** Rep. of Ireland
60 E2 **Ballycastle** U.K.
60 F3 **Ballyclare** U.K.
60 A4 **Ballyconneely Bay** *b.* Rep. of Ireland
60 D3 **Ballyconnell** Rep. of Ireland
60 C4 **Ballygar** Rep. of Ireland
60 D3 **Ballygawley** U.K.
60 D2 **Ballygorman** Rep. of Ireland
60 C4 **Ballyhaunis** Rep. of Ireland
60 B5 **Ballyheigue** Rep. of Ireland
60 C5 **Ballyhoura Mts** *h.* Rep. of Ireland
60 D2 **Ballykelly** U.K.
60 D5 **Ballylynan** Rep. of Ireland
60 D5 **Ballymacmague** Rep. of Ireland
60 D4 **Ballymahon** Rep. of Ireland
60 E3 **Ballymena** U.K.
60 E2 **Ballymoney** U.K.
60 C3 **Ballymote** Rep. of Ireland
60 F3 **Ballynahinch** U.K.
60 C3 **Ballyshannon** Rep. of Ireland
60 E5 **Ballyteige Bay** *b.* Rep. of Ireland
60 B4 **Ballyvaughan** Rep. of Ireland
60 E3 **Ballyward** U.K.
57 A3 **Balmartin** U.K.
Balmer *see* **Barmer**
114 D6 **Balmoral** Austr.
27 C6 **Balmorhea** U.S.A.
84 A3 **Balochistān** *reg.* Pak.
84 E5 **Balod** India
85 E5 **Baloda Bazar** India
115 H2 **Balonne** *r.* Austr.
84 C4 **Balotra** India
82 E2 **Balpyk Bi** Kazak.
85 E4 **Balrampur** India
114 E5 **Balranald** Austr.
67 L2 **Balş** Romania
31 H2 **Balsam Creek** Can.
43 J5 **Balsas** Brazil
69 D6 **Balta** Ukr.
68 J3 **Baltasi** Rus. Fed.
57 □ **Baltasound** U.K.
69 C6 **Bălţi** Moldova
52 **Baltic Sea** *g.* Europe
80 C6 **Baltîm** Egypt
105 H1 **Baltimore** S. Africa
32 E5 **Baltimore** U.S.A.
60 E5 **Baltinglass** Rep. of Ireland
84 C2 **Baltistan** *reg.* Jammu and Kashmir
63 J3 **Baltiysk** Rus. Fed.
84 D2 **Baltoro Glacier** *gl.* Pak.
85 G4 **Balurghat** India
94 C5 **Balut** *i.* Phil.
55 U8 **Balvi** Latvia
67 M5 **Balya** Turkey
82 E2 **Balykchy** Kyrgyzstan
79 H4 **Bam** Iran
89 C5 **Bama** China
113 H2 **Bamaga** Austr.
22 B3 **Bamaji L.** *l.* Can.
100 B3 **Bamako** Mali
100 B3 **Bamba** Mali
94 B2 **Bambang** Phil.
102 C3 **Bambari** C.A.R.
95 A5 **Bambel** Indon.
62 E6 **Bamberg** Ger.
29 D5 **Bamberg** U.S.A.
102 C3 **Bambili** Dem. Rep. Congo
105 G5 **Bamboesberg** *mts* S. Africa
102 C3 **Bambouti** C.A.R.
46 D3 **Bambuí** Brazil
81 M6 **Bāmdezh** Iran
100 D4 **Bamenda** Cameroon
84 A2 **Bāmīān** Afgh.
88 G1 **Bamiancheng** China
102 C3 **Bamingui-Bangoran, Parc National du** *nat. park* C.A.R.
84 B2 **Bamiyan** *r.* Afgh.
59 D7 **Bampton** U.K.
111 G2 **Banaba** *i.* Kiribati
43 L5 **Banabuiu, Açude** *resr* Brazil
47 C3 **Bañados del Atuel** *marsh* Arg.
42 F7 **Bañados del Izozog** *swamp* Bol.
60 D4 **Banagher** Rep. of Ireland
102 C3 **Banalia** Dem. Rep. Congo
105 K1 **Banamana, Lagoa** *l.* Moz.
100 B3 **Banamba** Mali
89 C4 **Banan** China
116 D5 **Banana** Austr.
43 H6 **Bananal, Ilha do** *i.* Brazil
85 F6 **Bānapur** India
84 D4 **Banas** *r.* India
80 B2 **Banaz** Turkey
95 B1 **Ban Ban** Laos
85 H3 **Banbar** China
60 E3 **Banbridge** U.K.
95 B2 **Ban Bua Yai** Thai.
59 F5 **Banbury** U.K.
94 A4 **Bancalan** *i.* Phil.
114 D3 **Bancannia, Lake** *salt flat* Austr.
100 A2 **Banc d'Arguin, Parc National du** *nat. park* Maur.
57 F3 **Banchory** U.K.
94 A5 **Bancoran** *i.* Phil.
31 J3 **Bancroft** Can.
102 C3 **Banda** Dem. Rep. Congo
84 E4 **Banda** India
93 H7 **Banda, Kepulauan** *is* Indon.
92 B5 **Banda Aceh** Indon.
115 K3 **Banda Banda, Mt** *mt* Austr.
84 B2 **Banda Daud Shah** Pak.
95 A5 **Bandahara, G.** *mt* Indon.
91 F6 **Bandai-Asahi National Park** Japan
85 H5 **Bandarban** Bangl.
79 H4 **Bandar-e 'Abbās** Iran
81 M3 **Bandar-e Anzalī** Iran
81 M6 **Bandar-e Emām Khomeynī** Iran
79 G4 **Bandar-e Lengeh** Iran
Bandar-e Shāhpūr *see* **Bandar-e Emām Khomeynī**
79 G2 **Bandar-e Torkeman** Iran
84 D3 **Bandarpunch** *mt* India
92 E6 **Bandar Seri Begawan** Brunei
93 H8 **Banda Sea** *sea* Indon.
46 B1 **Bandeirante** Brazil
46 E3 **Bandeiras, Pico de** *mt* Brazil
105 H1 **Bandelierkop** S. Africa
27 B6 **Banderas** Mex.
36 C4 **Banderas, Bahía de** *b.* Mex.
84 C4 **Bandi** *r.* *Rajasthan* India
84 C4 **Bandi** *r.* *Rajasthan* India
84 E6 **Bandia** *r.* India
100 B3 **Bandiagara** Mali
84 A1 **Band-i-Amir** *r.* Afgh.
80 A1 **Bandırma** Turkey
60 C6 **Bandon** Rep. of Ireland
60 C6 **Bandon** *r.* Rep. of Ireland
Ban Don *see* **Surat Thani**
95 A3 **Ban Don, Ao** *b.* Thai.
81 M2 **Bändovan Burnu** *pt* Azer.
81 M6 **Band Qīr** Iran
102 B4 **Bandundu** Dem. Rep. Congo
92 □ **Bandung** Indon.
81 K4 **Bāneh** Iran
37 J4 **Banes** Cuba
20 F4 **Banff** Can.
57 F3 **Banff** U.K.
20 F4 **Banff National Park** *nat. park* Can.
100 B3 **Banfora** Burkina
102 C4 **Banga** Dem. Rep. Congo
94 C5 **Banga** Phil.
94 C5 **Bangai Point** *pt* Phil.
83 E8 **Bangalore** India
84 D4 **Banganga** *r.* India
85 G5 **Bangaon** India
94 B2 **Bangar** Phil.
102 C3 **Bangassou** C.A.R.
85 E2 **Bangdag Co** *salt l.* China
95 C1 **Bangfai, Xé** *r.* Laos
93 G7 **Banggai** Indon.
93 G7 **Banggai, Kepulauan** *is* Indon.
93 F5 **Banggi** *i.* Malaysia
101 E1 **Banghāzī** Libya
95 C1 **Banghiang, Xé** *r.* Laos
92 □ **Bangil** Indon.
92 D7 **Bangka** *i.* Indon.
92 □ **Bangkalan** Indon.
95 A5 **Bangkaru** *i.* Indon.
92 C7 **Bangko** Indon.
85 G3 **Bangkog Co** *salt l.* China
95 B2 **Bangkok** Thai.
95 B2 **Bangkok, Bight of** *b.* Thai.
70 **Bangladesh** *country* Asia
100 B4 **Bangolo** Côte d'Ivoire
84 D2 **Bangong Co** *l.* China
60 F3 **Bangor** *N. Ireland* U.K.
59 C4 **Bangor** *Wales* U.K.
33 J2 **Bangor** *ME* U.S.A.
30 D4 **Bangor** *MI* U.S.A.
33 F4 **Bangor** *PA* U.S.A.
60 B3 **Bangor Erris** Rep. of Ireland
35 F3 **Bangs, Mt** *mt* U.S.A.
95 A3 **Bang Saphan Yai** Thai.
54 M4 **Bangsund** Norway
94 B2 **Bangued** Phil.
102 B3 **Bangui** C.A.R.
94 B2 **Bangui** Phil.
95 A5 **Bangunpurba** Indon.
103 C5 **Bangweulu, Lake** *l.* Zambia
103 D6 **Banhine, Parque Nacional de** *nat. park* Moz.
95 B1 **Ban Hin Heup** Laos
102 C3 **Bani** C.A.R.
94 A2 **Bani** Phil.
102 B3 **Bania** C.A.R.
84 C2 **Banihal Pass and Tunnel** *pass* Jammu and Kashmir
32 D6 **Banister** *r.* U.S.A.
101 D1 **Banī Walīd** Libya
80 E5 **Bāniyās** Syria
80 E4 **Bāniyās** Syria
66 G2 **Banja Luka** Bos.-Herz.
84 D3 **Banjar** India
92 E7 **Banjarmasin** Indon.
100 A3 **Banjul** The Gambia
81 M2 **Bankä** Azer.
85 F4 **Banka** India
113 F3 **Banka Banka** Austr.
100 B3 **Bankass** Mali
95 A2 **Ban Khao Yoi** Thai.
95 A3 **Ban Khok Kloi** Thai.
85 F5 **Banki** India
118 B2 **Banks I.** *i.* Can.
111 G3 **Banks Islands** *is* Vanuatu
24 C2 **Banks L.** *l.* U.S.A.
21 L2 **Banks Lake** *l.* Can.
117 D5 **Banks Peninsula** *pen.* N.Z.
115 H8 **Banks Strait** *chan.* Austr.
85 F5 **Bankura** India
95 B1 **Ban Mouang** Laos
60 E5 **Bann** *r.* Rep. of Ireland
60 E3 **Bann** *r.* U.K.
95 C1 **Ban Nakham** Laos
95 A3 **Ban Na San** Thai.
95 B4 **Ban Na Thawi** Thai.
30 C5 **Banner** U.S.A.
29 E7 **Bannerman Town** Bahamas
34 D5 **Banning** U.S.A.
79 L3 **Bannu** Pak.
47 B3 **Baños Maule** Chile
95 B1 **Ban Pak-Leng** Laos
95 C1 **Ban Phaeng** Thai.
95 B1 **Ban Phai** Thai.
95 C2 **Ban Phon** Laos
95 A2 **Banphot Phisai** Thai.
95 A2 **Ban Pong** Thai.
95 A1 **Ban Saraphi** Thai.
95 A3 **Ban Sawi** Thai.
85 E4 **Bansi** India
63 J6 **Banská Bystrica** Slovakia
95 A1 **Ban Sut Ta** Thai.
95 C2 **Ban Suwan Wari** Thai.
84 C5 **Banswara** India
94 B4 **Bantayan** *i.* Phil.
60 C5 **Banteer** Rep. of Ireland
95 A3 **Ban Tha Chang** Thai.
95 A1 **Ban Tha Don** Thai.
95 A3 **Ban Tha Kham** Thai.
95 A1 **Ban Tha Song Yang** Thai.
95 B2 **Ban Tha Tako** Thai.
95 B2 **Ban Tha Tum** Thai.
95 A2 **Ban Thung Luang** Thai.
94 B3 **Banton** *i.* Phil.
95 C1 **Ban Tôp** Laos
60 B6 **Bantry** Rep. of Ireland
60 B6 **Bantry Bay** *b.* Rep. of Ireland
92 □ **Bantul** Indon.
95 B1 **Ban Woen** Laos
100 D4 **Banyo** Cameroon
65 H1 **Banyoles** Spain
92 □ **Banyuwangi** Indon.
13 J7 **Banzare Seamount** *sea feature* Indian Ocean
88 B3 **Bao'an** China
88 E1 **Baochang** China
88 E2 **Baoding** China
88 D3 **Baofeng** China
88 C3 **Baoji** China
89 C4 **Baojing** China
88 D4 **Baokang** China
90 A2 **Baolin** China
95 C3 **Bao Lôc** Vietnam
90 C1 **Baoqing** China
82 J5 **Baoshan** China
88 D1 **Baotou** China
89 B4 **Baoxing** China
88 F3 **Baoying** China
84 C4 **Bap** India
61 A4 **Bapaume** France
31 H3 **Baptiste Lake** *l.* Can.
85 H3 **Baqên** China
85 H2 **Baqên** China
81 K5 **Ba'qūbah** Iraq
67 H3 **Bar** Yugo.
101 F3 **Bara** Sudan
102 E3 **Baraawe** Somalia
85 F4 **Barabar Hills** *h.* India
30 C4 **Baraboo** U.S.A.
30 B4 **Baraboo** *r.* U.S.A.
37 K4 **Baracoa** Cuba
47 E2 **Baradero** Arg.
115 H3 **Baradine** Austr.
115 H3 **Baradine** *r.* Austr.
30 C2 **Baraga** U.S.A.
85 E5 **Baragarh** India
45 C2 **Baragua** Venez.
37 K5 **Barahona** Dom. Rep.
85 H4 **Barail Range** *mts* India
85 H4 **Barak** *r.* India
102 D2 **Baraka** *watercourse* Eritrea/Sudan
65 E1 **Barakaldo** Spain
84 B2 **Barakī Barak** Afgh.
85 F5 **Bārākot** India
116 C5 **Baralaba** Austr.
84 D2 **Bara Lacha Pass** *pass* India
21 K3 **Baralzon Lake** *l.* Can.
116 D5 **Barambah** *r.* Austr.
84 D4 **Baran** India
84 B4 **Baran** *r.* Pak.
68 C4 **Baranavichy** Belarus
77 S3 **Baranikha** Rus. Fed.
69 C5 **Baranivka** Ukr.
45 B2 **Baranoa** Col.
20 B3 **Baranof Island** *i.* U.S.A.
46 A2 **Barão de Melgaço** Brazil
100 B3 **Baraouéli** Mali
61 D4 **Baraque de Fraiture** *h.* Belgium
93 H8 **Barat Daya, Kepulauan** *is* Indon.
114 C4 **Baratta** Austr.
84 D3 **Baraut** India
45 B4 **Baraya** Col.
46 D3 **Barbacena** Brazil
45 A4 **Barbacoas** Col.
16 **Barbados** *country* Caribbean Sea
65 G1 **Barbastro** Spain
65 D4 **Barbate de Franco** Spain
34 □[1] **Barbers Pt** *pt* U.S.A.
105 J2 **Barberton** S. Africa
32 C4 **Barberton** U.S.A.
64 D4 **Barbezieux-St-Hilaire** France
45 B3 **Barbosa** Col.
21 L2 **Barbour Bay** *b.* Can.
32 B6 **Barbourville** U.S.A.
94 B4 **Barboza** Phil.
37 M5 **Barbuda** *i.* Antigua
116 A4 **Barcaldine** Austr.
65 H2 **Barcelona** Spain
45 D2 **Barcelona** Venez.
42 F4 **Barcelos** Brazil
100 B4 **Barclayville** Liberia
116 A4 **Barcoo** *watercourse* Austr.
66 G2 **Barcs** Hungary
81 L1 **Bärdä** Azer.
54 E4 **Bárðarbunga** *mt* Iceland
47 C2 **Bardas Blancas** Arg.
80 D6 **Bardawîl, Sabkhet el** *lag.* Egypt
85 F5 **Barddhaman** India
63 K6 **Bardejov** Slovakia
95 C2 **Bar Đôn** Vietnam
59 C5 **Bardsey Island** *i.* U.K.
28 C4 **Bardstown** U.S.A.
32 B5 **Bardwell** U.S.A.
84 D3 **Bareilly** India
76 C2 **Barentsburg** Svalbard
76 D2 **Barentsøya** *i.* Svalbard
76 F2 **Barents Sea** *sea* Arctic Ocean
102 D2 **Barentu** Eritrea
84 E3 **Barga** China
116 E5 **Bargara** Austr.
84 D5 **Bargi** India
57 D5 **Bargrennan** U.K.
85 G5 **Barguna** Bangl.
86 E6 **Barh** India
33 J2 **Bar Harbor** U.S.A.
66 G4 **Bari** Italy
95 C3 **Ba Ria** Vietnam
84 C3 **Bari Doab** *lowland* Pak.
79 L2 **Barikot** Afgh.
85 E3 **Barikot** Nepal
45 E2 **Barima** *r.* Venez.
45 C2 **Barinas** Venez.
85 G5 **Barisal** Bangl.
92 C7 **Barisan, Pegunungan** *mts* Indon.
92 E7 **Barito** *r.* Indon.
42 F8 **Baritu, Parque Nacional** *nat. park* Arg.
88 B4 **Barkam** China
55 U8 **Barkava** Latvia
20 E4 **Barkerville** Can.
28 C4 **Barkley, L.** *l.* U.S.A.
20 D5 **Barkley Sd** *in.* Can.
105 G5 **Barkly East** S. Africa
113 G3 **Barkly Tableland** *reg.* Austr.
104 F4 **Barkly West** S. Africa
82 H2 **Barkol** China
84 D3 **Barkot** India
63 N7 **Bârlad** Romania
64 G2 **Bar-le-Duc** France
112 C5 **Barlee, L.** *salt flat* Austr.
66 G4 **Barletta** Italy
115 G5 **Barmedman** Austr.
84 B4 **Barmer** India
114 D5 **Barmera** Austr.
59 C5 **Barmouth** U.K.
84 C3 **Barnala** India
58 F3 **Barnard Castle** U.K.
115 F3 **Barnato** Austr.
76 K4 **Barnaul** Rus. Fed.
33 F5 **Barnegat** U.S.A.
33 F5 **Barnegat Bay** *b.* U.S.A.
32 D4 **Barnesboro** U.S.A.
114 F4 **Barneys Lake** *l.* Austr.
35 G3 **Barney Top** *mt* U.S.A.
27 C6 **Barnhart** U.S.A.
58 F4 **Barnsley** U.K.
59 C6 **Barnstaple** U.K.
Barnstaple Bay *b. see* **Bideford Bay**
29 D5 **Barnwell** U.S.A.
Baroda *see* **Vadodara**
84 C1 **Baroghil Pass** *pass* Afgh.
85 H4 **Barpathar** India
85 G4 **Barpeta** India
30 D3 **Barques, Pt Aux** *pt MI* U.S.A.
31 F3 **Barques, Pt Aux** *pt MI* U.S.A.
45 C2 **Barquisimeto** Venez.
43 K6 **Barra** Brazil
57 A4 **Barra** *i.* U.K.
57 A3 **Barra, Sound of** *chan.* U.K.
115 J3 **Barraba** Austr.
104 D7 **Barracouta, Cape** *hd* S. Africa
43 G6 **Barra do Bugres** Brazil
43 J5 **Barra do Corda** Brazil
46 B1 **Barra do Garças** Brazil
43 G5 **Barra do São Manuel** Brazil
42 C6 **Barranca** *Lima* Peru
42 C4 **Barranca** *Loreto* Peru
45 B3 **Barrancabermeja** Col.
47 C3 **Barrancas** *r.* Arg.
45 B2 **Barrancas** Col.
45 E2 **Barrancas** Venez.
44 E3 **Barranqueras** Arg.
45 B2 **Barranquilla** Col.
33 G2 **Barre** U.S.A.
47 C1 **Barreal** Arg.
43 K6 **Barreiras** Brazil
43 G4 **Barreirinha** Brazil
43 K4 **Barreirinhas** Brazil
46 B1 **Barreiro** *r.* Brazil
65 B3 **Barreiro** Port.
43 L5 **Barreiros** Brazil
46 C3 **Barretos** Brazil
20 G4 **Barrhead** Can.
57 D5 **Barrhead** U.K.
31 H3 **Barrie** Can.
31 F3 **Barrie I** *i.* Can.
20 E4 **Barrière** Can.
114 D3 **Barrier Range** *h.* Austr.
115 J4 **Barrington, Mt** *mt* Austr.
21 J3 **Barrington Lake** *l.* Can.
115 F2 **Barringun** Austr.
30 B3 **Barron** U.S.A.
116 A1 **Barron Falls** *waterfall* Austr.
27 C7 **Barroterán** Mex.
47 E3 **Barrow** Arg.
60 E5 **Barrow** *r.* Rep. of Ireland
113 F4 **Barrow Creek** Austr.
112 C4 **Barrow I.** *i.* Austr.
58 D3 **Barrow-in-Furness** U.K.
59 D6 **Barry** U.K.
104 D6 **Barrydale** S. Africa
31 J3 **Barrys Bay** Can.
84 C3 **Barsalpur** India
84 D5 **Barsi lakli** India
34 D4 **Barstow** U.S.A.
64 G2 **Bar-sur-Aube** France
62 F3 **Barth** Ger.
43 G2 **Bartica** Guyana
80 D1 **Bartın** Turkey
116 A1 **Bartle Frere, Mt** *mt* Austr.
35 G2 **Bartles, Mt** *mt* U.S.A.
26 D3 **Bartlett** *NE* U.S.A.
33 H2 **Bartlett** *NH* U.S.A.
20 F2 **Bartlett Lake** *l.* Can.
33 G2 **Barton** U.S.A.
58 G4 **Barton-upon-Humber** U.K.
63 K3 **Bartoszyce** Pol.
37 H7 **Barú, Volcán** *vol.* Panama
95 B5 **Barumun** *r.* Indon.
92 □ **Barung** *i.* Indon.
95 A5 **Barus** Indon.
88 B1 **Baruunsuu** Mongolia
87 K2 **Baruun Urt** Mongolia
84 D5 **Barwah** India
84 C3 **Barwala** India
84 C5 **Barwani** India
115 H2 **Barwon** *r.* Austr.
68 D4 **Barysaw** Belarus
68 H4 **Barysh** Rus. Fed.
68 H4 **Barysh** *r.* Rus. Fed.
95 C3 **Basăk, Tônlé** *r.* Cambodia
116 A2 **Basalt** *r.* Austr.
34 C2 **Basalt** U.S.A.
102 B3 **Basankusu** Dem. Rep. Congo
67 N2 **Basarabi** Romania
47 E2 **Basavilbaso** Arg.
94 B4 **Basay** Phil.
94 B1 **Basco** Phil.
62 C7 **Basel** Switz.
20 G4 **Bashaw** Can.
105 H6 **Bashee** *r.* S. Africa
84 B2 **Bashgul** *r.* Afgh.
68 G4 **Bashmakovo** Rus. Fed.
69 E6 **Bashtanka** Ukr.
84 D4 **Basi** India
85 F5 **Basia** India
94 B5 **Basilan** *i.* Phil.
94 B5 **Basilan Strait** *chan.* Phil.
59 H6 **Basildon** U.K.
24 E2 **Basin** U.S.A.
59 F6 **Basingstoke** U.K.
81 K4 **Bāsīra** *r.* Iraq
85 G5 **Basirhat** India
33 K2 **Baskahegan Lake** *l.* U.S.A.
81 K2 **Başkale** Turkey
31 K2 **Baskatong, Réservoir** *resr* Can.
69 H5 **Baskunchak, Ozero** *l.* Rus. Fed.
Basle *see* **Basel**
84 D5 **Basoda** India
102 C3 **Basoko** Dem. Rep. Congo
81 L6 **Basra** Iraq
66 D2 **Bassano del Grappa** Italy
100 C4 **Bassar** Togo
103 D6 **Bassas da India** *i.* Indian Ocean
83 H7 **Bassein** Myanmar
58 D3 **Bassenthwaite Lake** *l.* U.K.
100 A3 **Basse Santa Su** The Gambia
37 M5 **Basse-Terre** Guadeloupe
37 M5 **Basseterre** St Kitts-Nevis
26 D3 **Bassett** U.S.A.
35 G5 **Bassett Peak** *summit* U.S.A.
33 J2 **Bass Harbor** U.S.A.
100 B3 **Bassikounou** Maur.
100 C4 **Bassila** Benin
57 F4 **Bass Rock** *i.* U.K.
110 E5 **Bass Strait** *str.* Austr.
30 B1 **Basswood Lake** *l.* U.S.A.
55 N8 **Båstad** Sweden
79 G4 **Bastak** Iran
81 L3 **Bastānābād** Iran
85 E4 **Basti** India
66 C3 **Bastia** France
61 D4 **Bastogne** Belgium
27 F5 **Bastrop** *LA* U.S.A.
27 D6 **Bastrop** *TX* U.S.A.
100 C4 **Bata** Equatorial Guinea
37 H4 **Batabanó, Golfo de** *b.* Cuba
94 B2 **Batac** Phil.
94 C3 **Batag** *i.* Phil.
77 P3 **Batagay** Rus. Fed.
84 B2 **Batai Pass** *pass* Pak.
84 C3 **Batala** India
65 B3 **Batalha** Port.
95 C5 **Batam** *i.* Indon.
77 O3 **Batamay** Rus. Fed.
94 B1 **Batan** *i.* Phil.
82 J4 **Batang** China
102 B3 **Batangafo** C.A.R.
94 B3 **Batangas** Phil.
95 A5 **Batangtoru** Indon.
94 B1 **Batan Islands** *is* Phil.
46 C3 **Batatais** Brazil
Batavia *see* **Jakarta**
30 C5 **Batavia** *IL* U.S.A.
32 D3 **Batavia** *NY* U.S.A.
69 F6 **Bataysk** Rus. Fed.
31 E2 **Batchawana** Can.
31 E2 **Batchawana** *r.* Can.
30 E2 **Batchawana Bay** Can.
22 D4 **Batchawana Mtn** *h.* Can.
112 F2 **Batchelor** Austr.
95 B2 **Bătdâmbâng** Cambodia
115 J5 **Batemans B.** *b.* Austr.
115 J5 **Batemans Bay** Austr.
27 F5 **Batesville** *AR* U.S.A.
27 F5 **Batesville** *MS* U.S.A.
68 D3 **Batetskiy** Rus. Fed.
23 G4 **Bath** *N.B.* Can.
31 J3 **Bath** *Ont.* Can.
59 E6 **Bath** U.K.
33 J3 **Bath** *ME* U.S.A.
32 E3 **Bath** *NY* U.S.A.
57 E5 **Bathgate** U.K.
84 C3 **Bathinda** India
115 H4 **Bathurst** Austr.
23 G4 **Bathurst** Can.
105 G6 **Bathurst** S. Africa
115 H5 **Bathurst, L.** *l.* Austr.
112 F2 **Bathurst Island** *i.* Austr.
81 L6 **Bāţin, Wādī al** *watercourse* Asia
58 F4 **Batley** U.K.
115 H5 **Batlow** Austr.
81 H3 **Batman** Turkey
100 C1 **Batna** Alg.
27 F6 **Baton Rouge** U.S.A.
101 D4 **Batouri** Cameroon

46 B1 Batovi Brazil
80 E4 Batroûn Lebanon
54 V1 Båtsfjord Norway
83 F9 Batticaloa Sri Lanka
66 F4 Battipaglia Italy
21 G4 Battle r. Can.
30 E4 Battle Creek U.S.A.
21 H4 Battleford Can.
24 C3 Battle Mountain U.S.A.
84 C1 Battura Glacier gl. Jammu and Kashmir
92 B7 Batu, Pulau-pulau is Indon.
95 B4 Batu Gajah Malaysia
94 C5 Batulaki Phil.
81 H1 Bat'umi Georgia
92 C6 Batu Pahat Malaysia
95 B4 Batu Puteh, Gunung mt Malaysia
93 G8 Baubau Indon.
100 C3 Bauchi Nigeria
26 E1 Baudette U.S.A.
45 A3 Baudo, Serranía de mts Col.
64 D3 Baugé France
116 C5 Bauhinia Austr.
23 K4 Bauld, C. hd Can.
64 H3 Baume-les-Dames France
84 C2 Baundal India
46 C3 Bauru Brazil
46 B2 Baús Brazil
55 T8 Bauska Latvia
62 G5 Bautzen Ger.
104 E6 Baviaanskloofberg mts S. Africa
25 E6 Bavispe r. Mex.
59 J5 Bawdeswell U.K.
92 ☐ Bawean i. Indon.
78 B4 Bawiti Egypt
100 B3 Bawku Ghana
95 A1 Bawlake Myanmar
89 B4 Bawolung China
88 B3 Baxi China
29 D6 Baxley U.S.A.
82 J4 Baxoi China
94 B3 Bay, Laguna de lag. Phil.
37 J4 Bayamo Cuba
84 D4 Bayana India
82 J4 Bayan Har Shan mts China
86 H2 Bayanhongor Mongolia
88 B2 Bayan Hot China
88 B1 Bayan Mod China
88 B1 Bayan Nuru China
88 C1 Bayan Obo Kuangqu China
87 L3 Bayan Ul Hot China
94 C4 Baybay Phil.
81 H1 Bayburt Turkey
31 F4 Bay City MI U.S.A.
27 D6 Bay City TX U.S.A.
76 H3 Baydaratskaya Guba b. Rus. Fed.
102 E3 Baydhabo Somalia
62 F6 Bayerischer Wald mts Ger.
30 B2 Bayfield U.S.A.
67 M5 Bayındır Turkey
81 J4 Bayjī Iraq
87 J1 Baykal, Ozero l. Rus. Fed.
86 H1 Baykal'sk Rus. Fed.
86 J1 Baykal'sky Khr. mts Rus. Fed.
81 K7 Baykan Turkey
82 B1 Baykonur Kazak.
76 G4 Baymak Rus. Fed.
94 B2 Bayombong Phil.
64 D5 Bayonne France
94 B4 Bayo Point pt Phil.
67 M5 Bayramiç Turkey
62 E6 Bayreuth Ger.
33 G4 Bay Shore U.S.A.
27 F6 Bay St Louis U.S.A.
59 E5 Bayston Hill U.K.
27 E6 Baytown U.S.A.
117 F3 Bay View N.Z.
65 E4 Baza Spain
81 L1 Bazardyuzi, Gora mt Azer./Rus. Fed.
81 M3 Bāzār-e Māsāl Iran
81 K2 Bāzārgān Iran
69 H4 Bazarnyy Karabulak Rus. Fed.
103 D6 Bazaruto, Ilha do i. Moz.
88 C4 Bazhong China
88 C4 Bazhou China
95 C3 Be r. Vietnam
26 C2 Beach U.S.A.
31 J3 Beachburg Can.
33 F5 Beach Haven U.S.A.
114 E6 Beachport Austr.
33 F5 Beachwood U.S.A.
59 H7 Beachy Head hd U.K.
33 G4 Beacon U.S.A.
105 G6 Beacon Bay S. Africa
59 G6 Beaconsfield U.K.
44 C8 Beagle, Canal chan. Chile
112 F2 Beagle Gulf b. Austr.
103 E5 Bealanana Madag.
59 F7 Beaminster U.K.
24 E3 Bear r. U.S.A.
21 N2 Bear Cove b. Can.
22 C4 Beardmore Can.
115 H1 Beardmore Res. resr Austr.
30 B5 Beardstown U.S.A.
22 D3 Bear Island Can.
76 C2 Bear Island i. Svalbard
24 E3 Bear L. l. U.S.A.
20 D3 Bear Lake Can.
84 D4 Bearma r. India
24 E1 Bear Paw Mtn mt U.S.A.
22 B3 Bearskin Lake Can.

34 B2 Bear Valley U.S.A.
84 C3 Beas r. India
84 C3 Beas Dam dam India
37 K5 Beata, Cabo c. Dom. Rep.
37 K5 Beata, I. i. Dom. Rep.
26 D3 Beatrice U.S.A.
20 E3 Beatton r. Can.
20 E3 Beatton River Can.
34 D3 Beatty U.S.A.
22 E4 Beattyville Can.
64 G5 Beaucaire France
44 E8 Beauchene I. i. Falkland Is
113 K5 Beaudesert Austr.
114 E6 Beaufort Austr.
29 D5 Beaufort U.S.A.
118 C2 Beaufort Sea sea Can./U.S.A.
104 E6 Beaufort West S. Africa
22 F4 Beauharnois Can.
57 D3 Beauly U.K.
57 D3 Beauly Firth est. U.K.
59 C4 Beaumaris U.K.
61 C4 Beaumont Belgium
117 B6 Beaumont N.Z.
27 F6 Beaumont MS U.S.A.
32 B5 Beaumont OH U.S.A.
27 E6 Beaumont TX U.S.A.
64 G3 Beaune France
64 D3 Beaupréau France
61 C4 Beauraing Belgium
21 K4 Beauséjour Can.
64 F2 Beauvais France
21 H3 Beauval Can.
20 H4 Beaver r. Can.
20 D2 Beaver r. B.C./Y.T. Can.
22 C2 Beaver r. Ont. Can.
35 F2 Beaver r. U.S.A.
35 F2 Beaver r. U.S.A.
20 A2 Beaver Creek Can.
28 C4 Beaver Dam KY U.S.A.
30 C4 Beaver Dam WV U.S.A.
32 C4 Beaver Falls U.S.A.
24 D2 Beaverhead Mts mts U.S.A.
21 J2 Beaverhill L. l. Can.
21 K4 Beaver Hill Lake l. Can.
30 E3 Beaver Island i. U.S.A.
27 E4 Beaver L. resr U.S.A.
20 F3 Beaverlodge Can.
32 D4 Beaver Run Reservoir resr U.S.A.
84 C4 Beawar India
47 C2 Beazley Arg.
46 C3 Bebedouro Brazil
59 D4 Bebington U.K.
22 F1 Bécard, Lac l. Can.
59 J5 Beccles U.K.
67 J2 Bečej Yugo.
65 C1 Becerreá Spain
100 B1 Béchar Alg.
32 C6 Beckley U.S.A.
58 F3 Bedale U.K.
33 J2 Beddington U.S.A.
102 D3 Bedelē Eth.
33 G2 Bedford Can.
105 J4 Bedford S. Africa
59 G5 Bedford U.K.
28 C4 Bedford IN U.S.A.
33 H3 Bedford MA U.S.A.
32 D4 Bedford PA U.S.A.
32 D6 Bedford VA U.S.A.
59 G5 Bedford Level lowland U.K.
115 G4 Bedgerebong Austr.
58 F2 Bedlington U.K.
95 ☐ Bedok Sing.
95 ☐ Bedok Res. resr Sing.
35 H2 Bedrock U.S.A.
59 F5 Bedworth U.K.
116 A6 Beechal Cr. watercourse Austr.
32 B5 Beech Fork Lake l. U.S.A.
30 C2 Beechwood U.S.A.
115 G6 Beechworth Austr.
115 J5 Beecroft Pen. pen. Austr.
115 K1 Beenleigh Austr.
60 A5 Beenoskee h. Rep. of Ireland
80 E6 Beersheba Israel Be'ér Sheva' see Beersheba
104 E6 Beervlei Dam dam S. Africa
115 K1 Beerwah Austr.
27 D6 Beeville U.S.A.
102 C3 Befale Dem. Rep. Congo
103 E5 Befandriana Avaratra Madag.
115 H6 Bega Austr.
84 B3 Begari r. Pak.
65 H2 Begur, Cap de pt Spain
85 F4 Begusarai India
43 H3 Béhague, Pointe pt Fr. Guiana
20 C3 Behm Canal in. U.S.A.
119 B3 Behrendt Mts mts Antarctica
79 G2 Behshahr Iran
84 A2 Behsūd Afgh.
87 N2 Bei'an China
88 B4 Beibei China
89 C6 Beihai China
89 D6 Bei Jiang r. China
88 D2 Beijing China
88 B1 Beijing div. China
89 C7 Beili China
88 D3 Beiliu China
88 F1 Beining China
57 C5 Beinn an Oir h. U.K.
57 D3 Beinn Dearg mt U.K.
88 F1 Beipiao China

103 D5 Beira Moz.
88 E3 Beiru r. China
80 E5 Beirut Lebanon
103 C6 Beitbridge Zimbabwe
57 D5 Beith U.K.
63 L7 Beiuş Romania
65 C3 Beja Port.
100 C1 Béja Tunisia
100 C1 Bejaïa Alg.
65 D2 Béjar Spain
84 B3 Beji r. Pak.
79 K1 Bekabad Uzbek.
92 ☐ Bekasi Indon.
63 K7 Békés Hungary
63 K7 Békéscsaba Hungary
103 E6 Bekily Madag.
90 J3 Bekkai Japan
100 B4 Bekwai Ghana
85 E4 Bela India
79 K4 Bela Pak.
84 B3 Belab r. India
105 H2 Bela-Bela S. Africa
101 D4 Bélabo Cameroon
67 J2 Bela Crkva Yugo.
33 E5 Bel Air U.S.A.
65 D3 Belalcázar Spain
115 F4 Belaraboon Austr.
49 Belarus country Europe
Belau country see Palau
46 A3 Bela Vista Brazil
103 D6 Bela Vista Moz.
95 A5 Belawan Indon.
77 T3 Belaya r. Rus. Fed.
69 G6 Belaya Glina Rus. Fed.
69 G5 Belaya Kalitva Rus. Fed.
68 J3 Belaya Kholunitsa Rus. Fed.
63 J5 Bełchatów Pol.
32 B6 Belcher U.S.A.
80 F2 Belcik Turkey
60 D3 Belcoo U.K.
31 J1 Belcourt Can.
34 B1 Belden U.S.A.
102 E3 Beledweyne Somalia
43 J4 Belém Brazil
44 C3 Belén Arg.
80 F3 Belen Turkey
25 F5 Belen U.S.A.
111 G3 Bélep, Îles is New Caledonia
68 H4 Belev Rus. Fed.
117 D5 Belfast N.Z.
105 J2 Belfast S. Africa
60 F3 Belfast U.K.
33 H2 Belfast U.S.A.
60 F3 Belfast Lough in. U.K.
26 C2 Belfield U.S.A.
58 F2 Belford U.K.
64 H3 Belfort France
83 D7 Belgaum India
48 Belgium country Europe
69 F5 Belgorod Rus. Fed.
69 F5 Belgorodskaya Oblast' div. Rus. Fed.
24 E2 Belgrade U.S.A.
67 J2 Belgrade Yugo.
119 B3 Belgrano II Arg. Base Antarctica
100 D4 Beli Nigeria
66 E6 Belice r. Italy
68 G4 Belinskiy Rus. Fed.
92 D7 Belinyu Indon.
92 D7 Belitung i. Indon.
36 G5 Belize Belize
16 Belize country Central America
90 E2 Belkina, Mys pt Rus. Fed.
77 P2 Bel'kovskiy, O. i. Rus. Fed.
115 J1 Bell Austr.
115 H4 Bell r. Austr.
20 E3 Bella Bella Can.
64 E3 Bellac France
20 D4 Bella Coola Can.
27 E6 Bellaire U.S.A.
83 E7 Bellary India
115 H2 Bellata Austr.
47 F1 Bella Unión Uru.
115 K3 Bellbrook Austr.
116 D3 Bell Cay rf Austr.
32 B4 Bellefontaine U.S.A.
32 E4 Bellefonte U.S.A.
26 C2 Belle Fourche U.S.A.
26 C2 Belle Fourche r. U.S.A.
64 G3 Bellegarde-sur-Valserine France
29 D7 Belle Glade U.S.A.
64 C3 Belle-Île i. France
23 K3 Belle Isle i. Can.
23 J3 Belle Isle, Strait of str. Can.
35 E4 Bellemont U.S.A.
30 A5 Belle Plaine U.S.A.
31 H2 Belleterre Can.
31 J3 Belleville Can.
26 D4 Belleville U.S.A.
30 B4 Bellevue IA U.S.A.
24 D3 Bellevue ID U.S.A.
32 B4 Bellevue OH U.S.A.
24 B2 Bellevue WA U.S.A.
Bellin see Kangirsuk
115 K3 Bellingen Austr.
58 E2 Bellingham U.K.
24 B1 Bellingham U.S.A.
119 B2 Bellingshausen Rus. Fed. Base Antarctica
119 A3 Bellingshausen Sea sea Antarctica
62 D7 Bellinzona Switz.
45 B3 Bello Col.
33 G3 Bellows Falls U.S.A.
84 B3 Bellpat Pak.
33 F5 Belltown U.S.A.
66 E1 Belluno Italy

47 D2 Bell Ville Arg.
104 C6 Bellville S. Africa
57 ☐ Belmont U.K.
46 E1 Belmonte Brazil
36 G5 Belmopan Belize
115 K2 Belmore, Mt h. Austr.
60 B3 Belmullet Rep. of Ireland
33 G2 Beloeil Can.
87 N1 Belogorsk Rus. Fed.
103 E6 Beloha Madag.
46 D2 Belo Horizonte Brazil
26 D4 Beloit KS U.S.A.
30 C4 Beloit WI U.S.A.
68 E2 Belomorsk Rus. Fed.
85 G5 Belonia India
69 F6 Belorechensk Rus. Fed.
80 F3 Belören Turkey
76 G4 Beloretsk Rus. Fed.
Belorussia country see Belarus
103 E5 Belo Tsiribihina Madag.
68 F1 Beloye Rus. Fed.
68 F2 Beloye, Ozero l. Rus. Fed.
Beloye More g. see White Sea
68 F2 Belozersk Rus. Fed.
32 C5 Belpre U.S.A.
24 E2 Belt U.S.A.
114 C3 Beltana Austr.
114 B2 Belt B. salt flat Austr.
34 D3 Belted Range mts U.S.A.
27 D6 Belton U.S.A.
94 A5 Beluran Malaysia
30 C4 Belvidere U.S.A.
116 B4 Belyando r. Austr.
68 H3 Belyshevo Rus. Fed.
68 E4 Belyy Rus. Fed.
76 J2 Belyy, O. i. Rus. Fed.
30 C4 Bement U.S.A.
26 E2 Bemidji U.S.A.
102 C4 Bena Dibele Dem. Rep. Congo
57 D3 Ben Alder mt U.K.
115 F6 Benalla Austr.
66 D6 Ben Arous Tunisia
65 D1 Benavente Spain
57 E3 Ben More mt U.K.
60 B4 Benbaun h. Rep. of Ireland
57 A3 Benbecula i. U.K.
60 C3 Benbulben h. Rep. of Ireland
60 E3 Benburb U.K.
57 C4 Ben Cruachan mt U.K.
24 B2 Bend U.S.A.
105 G5 Bendearg mt S. Africa
115 J3 Bendemeer Austr.
102 E3 Bender-Bayla Somalia
114 F6 Bendigo Austr.
115 H6 Bendoc Austr.
103 D5 Bene Moz.
23 J3 Benedict, Mount h. Can.
33 J2 Benedicta U.S.A.
103 E6 Benenitra Madag.
62 G6 Benešov Czech Rep.
66 F4 Benevento Italy
88 F3 Beng r. China
74 Bengal, Bay of sea Asia
102 C3 Bengamisa Dem. Rep. Congo
88 E3 Bengbu China
95 B5 Bengkalis Indon.
92 C7 Bengkulu Indon.
55 N7 Bengtsfors Sweden
80 C6 Benha Egypt
57 B4 Ben Hiant h. U.K.
57 D2 Ben Hope mt U.K.
42 E6 Beni r. Bol.
102 C3 Beni Dem. Rep. Congo
100 B1 Beni-Abbès Alg.
65 F3 Benidorm Spain
100 B1 Beni Mellal Morocco
96 Benin country Africa
100 C4 Benin, Bight of g. Africa
100 C4 Benin City Nigeria
100 B1 Beni-Saf Alg.
78 C4 Beni Suef Egypt
25 D6 Benito, Islas is Mex.
47 E3 Benito Juárez Arg.
94 B2 Benito Soliven Phil.
42 E4 Benjamim Constant Brazil
36 B2 Benjamín Hill Mex.
93 J8 Benjina Indon.
26 C3 Benkelman U.S.A.
57 D2 Ben Klibreck mt U.K.
57 D4 Ben Lawers mt U.K.
115 J3 Ben Lomond mt Austr.
57 D4 Ben Lomond mt U.K.
115 G8 Ben Lomond Nat. Park nat. park Austr.
57 D4 Ben Loyal h. U.K.
57 D4 Ben Lui mt U.K.
57 E3 Ben Macdui mt U.K.
57 D4 Ben More mt Scot. U.K.
57 B4 Ben More mt Scot. U.K.
117 C6 Benmore, L. l. N.Z.
57 D2 Ben More Assynt mt U.K.
77 Q2 Bennetta, O. i. Rus. Fed.
57 B5 Ben Nevis mt U.K.
33 G3 Bennington U.S.A.
105 H3 Benoni S. Africa
25 E5 Benson AZ U.S.A.
26 E2 Benson U.S.A.
95 B4 Benta Seberang Malaysia
32 D6 Bent Creek U.S.A.
93 H7 Benteng Indon.
113 G3 Bentinck I. i. Austr.
95 A3 Bentinck I. i. Myanmar
58 F4 Bentley U.K.

33 K2 Benton Can.
27 E5 Benton AR U.S.A.
34 C3 Benton CA U.S.A.
28 B4 Benton IL U.S.A.
30 D4 Benton Harbor U.S.A.
95 C3 Bên Tre Vietnam
95 B5 Bentung Malaysia
100 C4 Benue r. Nigeria
57 D4 Ben Vorlich mt U.K.
60 B4 Benwee h. Rep. of Ireland
60 B3 Benwee Head hd Rep. of Ireland
57 D3 Ben Wyvis mt U.K.
88 C5 Benxi China
94 C5 Beo Indon.
Beograd see Belgrade
84 D3 Beohari India
100 B4 Béoumi Côte d'Ivoire
89 C5 Bepian Jiang r. China
91 B8 Beppu Japan
111 H3 Beqa i. Fiji
84 C3 Berach r. India
67 H3 Berane Yugo.
23 G2 Bérard, Lac l. Can.
84 D5 Berasia India
95 A5 Berastagi Indon.
67 H4 Berat Albania
93 J7 Berau, Teluk b. Indon.
101 F3 Berber Sudan
102 E2 Berbera Somalia
102 B3 Berbérati C.A.R.
64 E1 Berck France
81 K1 Berd Armenia
77 O3 Berdigestyakh Rus. Fed.
69 F6 Berdyans'k Ukr.
69 D5 Berdychiv Ukr.
32 A6 Berea U.S.A.
69 B5 Berehove Rus. Fed.
110 E2 Bereina P.N.G.
21 K4 Berens r. Can.
21 K4 Berens River Can.
26 D3 Beresford U.S.A.
69 C5 Berezhany Ukr.
69 D6 Berezivka Ukr.
69 C5 Berezne Ukr.
68 G2 Bereznik Rus. Fed.
76 H3 Berezovo Rus. Fed.
61 D4 Berg Neth.
65 G1 Berga Spain
67 M5 Bergama Turkey
66 C2 Bergamo Italy
55 P6 Bergby Sweden
62 F3 Bergen Ger.
55 J6 Bergen Norway
61 C3 Bergen op Zoom Neth.
64 E3 Bergerac France
62 C5 Bergheim Ger.
61 F4 Bergisch Gladbach Ger.
104 B1 Bergland Namibia
30 C2 Bergland U.S.A.
55 P6 Bergsjö Sweden
54 A3 Bergsviken Sweden
61 E1 Bergumermeer l. Neth.
105 H4 Bergville S. Africa
77 S4 Beringa, O. i. Rus. Fed.
61 D3 Beringen Belgium
77 T3 Beringovskiy Rus. Fed.
77 T4 Bering Sea sea Pac. Oc.
77 V3 Bering Strait str. Rus. Fed./U.S.A.
54 M5 Berkåk Norway
61 E2 Berkel r. Neth.
34 A3 Berkeley U.S.A.
32 C5 Berkeley Springs U.S.A.
61 D2 Berkhout Neth.
119 B3 Berkner I. i. Antarctica
67 K3 Berkovitsa Bulg.
59 F6 Berkshire Downs h. U.K.
54 V1 Berlevåg Norway
62 F4 Berlin Ger.
33 F5 Berlin MD U.S.A.
33 H2 Berlin NH U.S.A.
32 D5 Berlin PA U.S.A.
30 C4 Berlin WV U.S.A.
32 C4 Berlin Lake l. U.S.A.
115 J6 Bermagui Austr.
47 D3 Bermeja, Pta pt Arg.
27 C7 Bermejillo Mex.
47 C1 Bermejo r. Arg.
44 D2 Bermejo r. Arg./Bol.
42 F8 Bermejo Bol.
37 M2 Bermuda terr. Atlantic Ocean
12 E3 Bermuda Rise sea feature Atlantic Ocean
62 C7 Bern Switz.
25 C7 Bernalillo U.S.A.
44 A7 Bernardo O'Higgins, Parque Nacional nat. park Chile
47 D2 Bernasconi Arg.
30 E5 Berne U.S.A.
62 D7 Berner Alpen mts Switz.
57 A4 Berneray i. U.K.
57 A3 Berneray i. U.K.
112 B4 Bernier I. i. Austr.
62 E7 Bernina Pass pass Switz.
61 F5 Bernkastel-Kues Ger.
103 E6 Beroroha Madag.
62 G6 Beroun Czech Rep.
62 G6 Berounka r. Czech Rep.
114 D5 Berri Austr.
57 F2 Berriedale U.K.
115 F5 Berrigan Austr.
65 H4 Berrouaghia Alg.
115 J5 Berrima Austr.
115 H5 Berry Austr.
34 A2 Berryessa, Lake l. U.S.A.
29 E7 Berry Islands is Bahamas
104 D3 Berseba Namibia
69 D5 Bershad' Ukr.
95 A3 Bertam Malaysia
43 K5 Bertolinía Brazil

101 D4 Bertoua Cameroon
60 B4 Bertraghboy Bay b. Rep. of Ireland
111 H2 Beru i. Kiribati
42 F4 Beruri Brazil
114 F7 Berwick Austr.
33 E4 Berwick U.S.A.
58 E2 Berwick-upon-Tweed U.K.
20 E3 Berwyn Can.
59 D5 Berwyn h. U.K.
69 E6 Beryslav Ukr.
103 E5 Besalampy Madag.
64 H3 Besançon France
81 H3 Beşiri Turkey
69 H4 Beslan Rus. Fed.
21 H3 Besnard Lake l. Can.
80 F3 Besni Turkey
60 E3 Bessbrook U.K.
29 C5 Bessemer AL U.S.A.
30 B2 Bessemer MI U.S.A.
103 E6 Betanty Madag.
65 B1 Betanzos Spain
101 D4 Bétaré Oya Cameroon
105 H3 Bethal S. Africa
104 B3 Bethanie Namibia
26 E3 Bethany MO U.S.A.
27 D5 Bethany OK U.S.A.
33 H2 Bethel ME U.S.A.
30 A6 Bethel MO U.S.A.
32 A5 Bethel OH U.S.A.
32 D4 Bethel Park U.S.A.
59 C4 Bethesda U.K.
32 E5 Bethesda MD U.S.A.
32 C4 Bethesda OH U.S.A.
104 F5 Bethesdaweg S. Africa
105 H4 Bethlehem S. Africa
33 H4 Bethlehem U.S.A.
80 E6 Bethlehem West Bank
105 F5 Bethulie S. Africa
61 A4 Béthune France
45 C2 Betijoque Venez.
103 E6 Betioky Madag.
95 B4 Betong Thai.
82 C1 Betpak-Dala plain Kazak.
103 E6 Betroka Madag.
80 E5 Bet She'an Israel
23 G4 Betsiamites Can.
23 G4 Betsiamites r. Can.
103 E5 Betsiboka r. Madag.
30 D3 Betsie, Pt pt U.S.A.
30 E2 Betsy Lake l. U.S.A.
30 B5 Bettendorf U.S.A.
85 E4 Bettiah India
57 D2 Bettyhill U.K.
60 E4 Bettystown Rep. of Ireland
84 D5 Betul India
61 D3 Betuwe reg. Neth.
84 D4 Betwa r. India
59 D4 Betws-y-coed U.K.
114 E5 Beulah Austr.
30 D3 Beulah U.S.A.
59 H6 Beult r. U.K.
58 G4 Beverley U.K.
116 C3 Beverley Group is Austr.
33 H3 Beverly MA U.S.A.
32 C5 Beverly OH U.S.A.
34 C4 Beverly Hills U.S.A.
21 J2 Beverly Lake l. Can.
61 C2 Beverwijk Neth.
59 H7 Bexhill U.K.
81 L4 Beyânlü Iran
80 C3 Bey Dağları mts Turkey
80 B1 Beykoz Turkey
100 B4 Beyla Guinea
81 L2 Beylagan Azer.
80 C1 Beypazarı Turkey
80 F2 Beypınarı Turkey
Beyrouth see Beirut
80 C3 Beyşehir Turkey
80 C3 Beyşehir, Gölü l. Turkey
69 F6 Beysug r. Rus. Fed.
81 J3 Beytüşşebap Turkey
68 J3 Bezbozhnik Rus. Fed.
68 J3 Bezhanitsy Rus. Fed.
68 E3 Bezhetsk Rus. Fed.
64 F5 Béziers France
84 B4 Bhabhar India
85 E4 Bhabua India
84 B5 Bhadar r. India
84 C5 Bhadasar India
85 F4 Bhadgaon Nepal
85 E4 Bhadohi India
84 C3 Bhadra India
84 D5 Bhadravati India
83 E8 Bhadrakh India
85 G5 Bhairab Bazar Bangl.
85 E3 Bhairawa Nepal
79 L3 Bhakkar Pak.
82 J6 Bhamo Myanmar
85 E4 Bhander India
85 F6 Bhanjanagar India
84 D4 Bhanrer Range h. India
84 D3 Bharatpur India
85 H4 Bharatpur India
84 C5 Bharuch India
85 E5 Bhatapara India
83 D8 Bhatkal India
85 G5 Bhatpara India
84 C5 Bhavnagar India
85 E6 Bhawanipatna India
105 J3 Bhekuzulu S. Africa
85 E3 Bheri r. Nepal
84 D4 Bhilwara India
83 F7 Bhima r. India
85 F5 Bhind India
84 C4 Bhindar India

85 E4 Bhinga India
84 C4 Bhinmal India
84 D3 Bhiwani India
85 F4 Bhojpur Nepal
105 H5 Bhongweni S. Africa
84 D5 Bhopal India
85 F5 Bhuban India
85 F5 Bhubaneshwar India
84 B5 Bhuj India
84 C5 Bhusawal India
70 Bhutan country Asia
84 B4 Bhuttewala India
95 B1 Bia, Phou mt Laos
84 C2 Biafo Gl. gl. Pak.
93 K7 Biak Indon.
93 K7 Biak i. Indon.
63 L4 Biała Podlaska Pol.
62 G4 Białogard Pol.
63 L4 Białystok Pol.
100 B4 Biankouma Côte d'Ivoire
84 D5 Biaora India
64 D5 Biarritz France
62 D7 Biasca Switz.
90 G3 Bibai Japan
103 B5 Bibala Angola
115 H6 Bibbenluke Austr.
66 D3 Bibbiena Italy
62 D6 Biberach an der Riß Ger.
85 G4 Bibiyana r. Bangl.
80 C2 Biçer Turkey
59 F6 Bicester U.K.
115 H8 Bicheno Austr.
69 G7 Bichvint'a Georgia
113 G2 Bickerton I. i. Austr.
59 D7 Bickleigh U.K.
35 G2 Bicknell U.S.A.
103 B5 Bicuari, Parque Nacional do nat. park Angola
83 E7 Bid India
100 C4 Bida Nigeria
94 A5 Bidadari, Tg pt Malaysia
83 E7 Bidar India
33 H3 Biddeford U.S.A.
57 C4 Bidean nam Bian mt U.K.
59 C6 Bideford U.K.
59 C6 Bideford Bay b. U.K.
63 L4 Biebrza r. Pol.
62 C7 Biel Switz.
62 H5 Bielawa Pol.
62 D4 Bielefeld Ger.
66 C2 Biella Italy
63 J6 Bielsko-Biała Pol.
63 L4 Bielsk Podlaski Pol.
95 C3 Biên Hoa Vietnam
Bienne see Biel
22 F2 Bienville, Lac l. Can.
102 B5 Bié Plateau plat. Angola
116 A6 Bierbank Austr.
105 F3 Biesiesvlei S. Africa
61 D5 Bièvre Belgium
102 B4 Bifoun Gabon
23 J3 Big r. Can.
34 A2 Big r. U.S.A.
69 C7 Biga Turkey
80 B2 Bigadiç Turkey
67 M5 Biga Yarımadası pen. Turkey
30 D2 Big Bay U.S.A.
30 D3 Big Bay de Noc b. U.S.A.
34 D4 Big Bear Lake U.S.A.
24 E2 Big Belt Mts mts U.S.A.
105 J3 Big Bend Swaziland
27 C6 Big Bend Nat. Park nat. park U.S.A.
27 F5 Big Black r. U.S.A.
59 D7 Bigbury-on-Sea U.K.
29 D7 Big Cypress Nat. Preserve res. U.S.A.
30 C3 Big Eau Pleine Reservoir resr U.S.A.
21 L5 Big Falls U.S.A.
21 H4 Biggar Can.
57 E5 Biggar U.K.
116 E5 Biggenden Austr.
20 B3 Bigger, Mt mt Can.
59 G5 Biggleswade U.K.
24 D2 Big Hole r. U.S.A.
24 F2 Bighorn r. U.S.A.
24 E2 Bighorn Canyon Nat. Recreation Area res. U.S.A.
24 F2 Bighorn Mountains mts U.S.A.
20 F2 Big Island i. Can.
33 K2 Big Lake l. U.S.A.
100 A3 Bignona Senegal
32 D6 Big Otter r. U.S.A.
34 C3 Big Pine U.S.A.
30 E4 Big Rapids U.S.A.
30 C3 Big Rib r. U.S.A.
21 H4 Big River Can.
30 D3 Big Sable Pt pt U.S.A.
20 C2 Big Salmon r. Can.
21 K3 Big Sand Lake l. Can.
35 F4 Big Sandy r. U.S.A.
26 D2 Big Sioux r. U.S.A.
34 D2 Big Smokey Valley v. U.S.A.
27 C5 Big Spring U.S.A.
26 C3 Big Springs U.S.A.
32 B6 Big Stone Gap U.S.A.
34 B3 Big Sur U.S.A.
24 E2 Big Timber U.S.A.
22 C3 Big Trout Lake Can.
22 C3 Big Trout Lake l. Can.
35 G3 Big Water U.S.A.
31 H3 Bigwin Can.
66 F2 Bihać Bos.-Herz.
85 F4 Bihar div. India
85 F4 Bihar Sharif India
63 L7 Bihor, Vârful mt Romania
90 J3 Bihoro Japan
100 A3 Bijagós, Arquipélago dos is Guinea-Bissau
84 C4 Bijainagar India
83 E7 Bijapur India
81 L4 Bījār Iran
67 H2 Bijeljina Bos.-Herz.
67 H3 Bijelo Polje Yugo.
89 B5 Bijie China
85 G4 Bijni India
84 D3 Bijnor India
84 B3 Bijnot Pak.
84 C3 Bikaner India
90 D1 Bikin r. Rus. Fed.
87 O2 Bikin Rus. Fed.
102 B4 Bikoro Dem. Rep. Congo
88 B3 Bikou China
84 C4 Bilara India
85 E5 Bilaspur India
81 M2 Biläsuvar Azer.
69 D5 Bila Tserkva Ukr.
95 A2 Bilauktaung Range mts Myanmar/Thai.
65 E1 Bilbao Spain
80 C6 Bilbeis Egypt
67 H3 Bileća Bos.-Herz.
80 B1 Bilecik Turkey
63 L5 Biłgoraj Pol.
102 D4 Bilharamulo Tanz.
69 D6 Bilhorod-Dnistrovs'kyy Ukr.
102 C3 Bili Dem. Rep. Congo
77 S3 Bilibino Rus. Fed.
95 A1 Bilin Myanmar
94 C4 Biliran i. Phil.
24 F3 Bill U.S.A.
59 H6 Billericay U.K.
58 F3 Billingham U.K.
24 E2 Billings U.S.A.
59 E7 Bill of Portland hd U.K.
35 F4 Bill Williams r. U.S.A.
35 F4 Bill Williams Mtn mt U.S.A.
101 D3 Bilma Niger
116 D5 Biloela Austr.
69 E6 Bilohirs'k Ukr.
63 N5 Bilohir"ya Ukr.
69 F5 Bilolut s'k Ukr.
69 E5 Bilopillya Ukr.
69 F5 Bilovods'k Ukr.
29 B6 Biloxi U.S.A.
113 G5 Bilpa Morea Claypan salt flat Austr.
57 E5 Bilston U.K.
101 E3 Biltine Chad
95 A1 Bilugyun I. i. Myanmar
68 J4 Bilyarsk Rus. Fed.
69 D6 Bilyayivka Ukr.
115 H5 Bimberi, Mt mt Austr.
29 E7 Bimini Is is Bahamas
81 M3 Bināb Iran
84 D4 Bina-Etawa India
93 H7 Binaija, G. mt Indon.
80 F2 Binboğa Daği mt Turkey
115 G1 Bindebango Austr.
85 E4 Bindki India
115 H1 Bindle Austr.
103 B4 Bindu Dem. Rep. Congo
103 D5 Bindura Zimbabwe
65 G2 Binefar Spain
115 J2 Bingara N.S.W. Austr.
115 F2 Bingara Qld. Austr.
88 B2 Bingcaowan China
62 C6 Bingen am Rhein Ger.
100 B4 Bingerville Côte d'Ivoire
33 J2 Bingham U.S.A.
33 E3 Binghamton U.S.A.
81 H2 Bingöl Turkey
81 H2 Bingol D. mt Turkey
89 C6 Binh Gia Vietnam
89 D2 Binh Sơn Vietnam
85 H4 Bini India
85 E5 Binika India
95 A5 Binjai Indon.
115 H3 Binnaway Austr.
95 C5 Bintan i. Indon.
94 B3 Bintuan Phil.
92 C7 Bintuhan Indon.
92 E6 Bintulu Malaysia
88 C3 Binxian China
115 G5 Binya Austr.
89 C6 Binyang China
82 F2 Binzhou China
47 B3 Bióbío div. Chile
47 B3 Bióbío r. Chile
100 C4 Bioco i. Equatorial Guinea
66 F3 Biograd na Moru Croatia
66 G3 Biokovo mts Croatia
81 H5 Bi'r al Mulūsi Iraq
68 F2 Birandozero Rus. Fed.
102 C2 Birao C.A.R.
85 F4 Biratnagar Nepal
81 G3 Bi'r Buţaymān Syria
20 G3 Birch r. Can.
21 H4 Birch Hills Can.
114 E5 Birchip Austr.
20 F4 Birch Island Can.
22 B3 Birch L. l. Can.
30 B2 Birch Lake l. U.S.A.
20 G3 Birch Mountains h. Can.
21 J4 Birch River Can.
35 G2 Birdseye U.S.A.
113 G5 Birdsville Austr.
80 F3 Birecik Turkey
101 E3 Bir en Natrūn w. Sudan
92 B5 Bireun Indon.
85 F4 Birganj Nepal
102 D2 Birhan mt Eth.
46 B3 Birigüi Brazil
79 H3 Bīrjand Iran
81 J6 Birkat al 'Aqabah w. Iraq
81 J6 Birkat al 'Athāmīn w. Iraq
81 K6 Birkāt Hamad w. Iraq
81 J7 Birkat Zubālah waterhole Saudi Arabia
59 D4 Birkenhead U.K.
80 C7 Birket Qârûn l. Egypt
81 K3 Bīrkim Iraq
66 F7 Birkirkara Malta
59 F5 Birmingham U.K.
29 C5 Birmingham U.S.A.
100 A2 Bîr Mogreïn Maur.
80 B6 Bîr Nâḩid oasis Egypt
100 C3 Birnin-Kebbi Nigeria
100 C3 Birnin Konni Niger
87 O2 Birobidzhan Rus. Fed.
60 D4 Birr Rep. of Ireland
115 G2 Birrie r. Austr.
81 J5 Bi'r Sābil Iraq
57 E1 Birsay U.K.
59 F5 Birstall U.K.
80 E7 Bîr Tâba Egypt
21 J4 Birtle Can.
85 H3 Biru China
55 T8 Biržai Lith.
35 H6 Bisbee U.S.A.
52 Biscay, Bay of sea France/Spain
29 D7 Biscayne Nat. Park nat. park U.S.A.
62 F7 Bischofshofen Austria
119 B2 Biscoe Islands is Antarctica
31 F2 Biscotasi Lake l. Can.
31 F2 Biscotasing Can.
89 C4 Bishan China
81 M5 Bīsheh Iran
82 D2 Bishkek Kyrgyzstan
85 F5 Bishnupur India
105 G6 Bisho S. Africa
34 C3 Bishop U.S.A.
58 F3 Bishop Auckland U.K.
59 H6 Bishop's Stortford U.K.
81 G4 Bishrī, Jabal h. Syria
87 M1 Bishui China
100 C1 Biskra Alg.
94 C4 Bislig Phil.
26 C2 Bismarck U.S.A.
110 E2 Bismarck Archipelago is P.N.G.
110 E2 Bismarck Range mts P.N.G.
110 E2 Bismarck Sea sea P.N.G.
81 H3 Bismil Turkey
55 L6 Bismo Norway
81 L4 Bīsotūn Iran
54 P5 Bispgården Sweden
65 G4 Bissa, Djebel mt Alg.
100 A3 Bissau Guinea-Bissau
100 D4 Bissaula Nigeria
21 K4 Bissett Can.
20 F3 Bistcho Lake l. Can.
63 M7 Bistriţa Romania
63 N7 Bistriţa r. Romania
62 C6 Bitburg Ger.
61 F5 Bitche France
101 D3 Bitkine Chad
81 J2 Bitlis Turkey
67 J4 Bitola Macedonia
66 G4 Bitonto Italy
83 D8 Bitra Par rf India
35 H2 Bitter Creek r. U.S.A.
104 C5 Bitterfontein S. Africa
80 D6 Bitter Lakes lakes Egypt
24 D2 Bitterroot Range mts U.S.A.
69 G5 Bityug r. Rus. Fed.
101 D3 Biu Nigeria
91 D7 Biwa-ko l. Japan
88 D3 Biyang China
102 E2 Bīye K'obē Eth.
86 E1 Biysk Rus. Fed.
105 H5 Bizana S. Africa
100 C1 Bizerte Tunisia
54 A4 Bjargtangar hd Iceland
54 Q5 Bjästa Sweden
66 G2 Bjelovar Croatia
54 P2 Bjerkvik Norway
55 L8 Bjerringbro Denmark
55 P6 Björklinge Sweden
55 L5 Bjorli Norway
54 Q5 Björna Sweden
Bjørnøya i. see Bear Island
54 Q5 Bjurholm Sweden
100 B3 Bla Mali
57 B3 Bla Bheinn mt U.K.
27 F5 Black r. AR U.S.A.
35 H5 Black r. AZ U.S.A.
31 F4 Black r. MI U.S.A.
30 B3 Black r. WV U.S.A.
116 A5 Blackall Austr.
30 C1 Black Bay b. Can.
22 B3 Blackbear r. Can.
59 F6 Black Bourton U.K.
58 E4 Blackburn U.K.
115 K1 Blackbutt Austr.
34 A2 Black Butte summit U.S.A.
34 A2 Black Butte L. l. U.S.A.
35 E4 Black Canyon U.S.A.
35 F4 Black Canyon City U.S.A.
26 E2 Blackduck U.S.A.
20 G4 Blackfalds Can.
24 D3 Blackfoot U.S.A.
24 D2 Black Foot r. U.S.A.
26 C2 Black Hills reg. U.S.A.
57 D3 Black Isle i. U.K.
21 H3 Black Lake Can.
21 H3 Black Lake l. Can.
31 E3 Black Lake l. U.S.A.
35 G3 Black Mesa plat. U.S.A.
59 D6 Black Mountain h. U.K.
34 D4 Black Mt mt U.S.A.
59 D6 Black Mts h. U.K.
35 E4 Black Mts mts U.S.A.
104 C1 Black Nossob watercourse Namibia
58 D4 Blackpool U.K.
30 B3 Black River Falls U.S.A.
58 A4 Blackrock Rep. of Ireland
24 C3 Black Rock Desert des. U.S.A.
32 C6 Blacksburg U.S.A.
52 Black Sea sea Asia/Europe
60 A3 Blacksod Bay b. Rep. of Ireland
60 E5 Blackstairs Mountain h. Rep. of Ireland
60 E5 Blackstairs Mountains h. Rep. of Ireland
32 E6 Blackstone U.S.A.
115 J3 Black Sugarloaf mt Austr.
100 B4 Black Volta r. Africa
116 C4 Blackwater Austr.
116 A5 Blackwater watercourse Austr.
60 E5 Blackwater Rep. of Ireland
60 D5 Blackwater r. Rep. of Ireland
60 E4 Blackwater r. Rep. of Ireland
60 E3 Blackwater r. Rep. of Ireland/U.K.
59 H6 Blackwater r. U.K.
32 E6 Blackwater r. U.S.A.
20 E2 Blackwater Lake l. Can.
57 D4 Blackwater Reservoir resr U.K.
27 D4 Blackwell U.S.A.
112 C6 Blackwood r. Austr.
69 G6 Blagodarnyy Rus. Fed.
90 D2 Blagodatnyy Rus. Fed.
67 K3 Blagoevgrad Bulg.
87 N1 Blagoveshchensk Rus. Fed.
32 E4 Blain U.S.A.
24 B1 Blaine U.S.A.
21 H4 Blaine Lake Can.
20 D3 Blair NE U.S.A.
30 B3 Blair WV U.S.A.
116 B4 Blair Athol Austr.
57 E4 Blair Atholl U.K.
57 E4 Blairgowrie U.K.
29 C6 Blakely U.S.A.
59 J5 Blakeney U.K.
30 C1 Blake Pt pt U.S.A.
92 □ Blambangan, Semenanjung pen. Indon.
47 E3 Blanca, Bahía b. Arg.
47 C3 Blanca de la Totora, Sa h. Arg.
25 F4 Blanca Peak summit U.S.A.
114 C2 Blanche, L. salt flat Austr.
32 B5 Blanchester U.S.A.
114 C5 Blanchetown Austr.
47 C1 Blanco r. Arg.
42 F6 Blanco r. Bol.
24 A3 Blanco, C. c. U.S.A.
23 J3 Blanc-Sablon Can.
115 G4 Bland r. Austr.
54 D4 Blanda r. Iceland
59 E7 Blandford Forum U.K.
35 H3 Blanding U.S.A.
65 H2 Blanes Spain
30 E2 Blaney Park U.S.A.
92 A5 Blangkejeren Indon.
61 B3 Blankenberge Belgium
61 E4 Blankenheim Ger.
45 D2 Blanquilla, Isla i. Venez.
62 H6 Blansko Czech Rep.
103 D5 Blantyre Malawi
60 C6 Blarney Rep. of Ireland
54 Q4 Blåviksjön Sweden
115 H4 Blayney Austr.
117 D4 Blenheim N.Z.
60 E4 Blessington Lakes lakes Rep. of Ireland
59 G5 Bletchley U.K.
100 C1 Blida Alg.
61 F5 Blies r. Ger.
111 H3 Bligh Water b. Fiji
31 F2 Blind River Can.
114 C3 Blinman Austr.
24 D3 Bliss U.S.A.
33 F5 Blissfield U.S.A.
33 H4 Block I. i. U.S.A.
33 H4 Block Island Sound chan. U.S.A.
105 G4 Bloemfontein S. Africa
105 F3 Bloemhof S. Africa
105 F3 Bloemhof Dam dam S. Africa
54 C4 Blönduós Iceland
33 E5 Bloodsworth I. i. U.S.A.
21 K4 Bloodvein r. Can.
60 C2 Bloody Foreland pt Rep. of Ireland
31 J4 Bloomfield Can.
30 A5 Bloomfield IA U.S.A.
28 C4 Bloomfield IN U.S.A.
25 E4 Bloomfield NM U.S.A.
30 C5 Bloomington IL U.S.A.
28 C4 Bloomington IN U.S.A.
26 E2 Bloomington MN U.S.A.
33 E4 Bloomsburg U.S.A.
116 C3 Bloomsbury Austr.
92 □ Blora Indon.
32 E4 Blossburg U.S.A.
105 H1 Blouberg S. Africa
59 F5 Bloxham U.K.
35 H5 Blue r. U.S.A.
35 G1 Bluebell U.S.A.
35 G2 Blue Bell Knoll summit U.S.A.
26 E3 Blue Earth U.S.A.
32 C6 Bluefield U.S.A.
37 H6 Bluefields Nic.
33 J2 Blue Hill U.S.A.
31 H5 Blue Knob h. U.S.A.
85 H5 Blue Mountain mt India
35 H1 Blue Mountain U.S.A.
33 F3 Blue Mountain Lake U.S.A.
105 G4 Blue Mountain Pass pass Lesotho
115 J4 Blue Mountains mts Austr.
24 C2 Blue Mountains mts U.S.A.
115 J4 Blue Mountains Nat. Park nat. park Austr.
78 C7 Blue Nile r. Eth./Sudan
29 C5 Blue Ridge U.S.A.
32 D6 Blue Ridge mts U.S.A.
20 F4 Blue River Can.
34 D2 Blue Springs U.S.A.
60 C3 Blue Stack mt Rep. of Ireland
60 C3 Blue Stack Mts h. Rep. of Ireland
32 C6 Bluestone Lake l. U.S.A.
116 C4 Bluff Austr.
117 B7 Bluff N.Z.
35 H3 Bluff U.S.A.
30 E5 Bluffton IN U.S.A.
32 B4 Bluffton OH U.S.A.
44 G3 Blumenau Brazil
26 C2 Blunt U.S.A.
24 B3 Bly U.S.A.
114 C4 Blyth Austr.
58 F2 Blyth Eng. U.K.
59 F4 Blyth Eng. U.K.
35 E5 Blythe U.S.A.
27 F5 Blytheville U.S.A.
55 L7 Bø Norway
100 A4 Bo Sierra Leone
94 B3 Boac Phil.
43 K5 Boa Esperança, Açude resr Brazil
88 D3 Bo'ai Henan China
89 C6 Bo'ai Yunnan China
102 B3 Boali C.A.R.
105 K3 Boane Moz.
32 C4 Boardman U.S.A.
105 F1 Boatlaname Botswana
115 G1 Boatman Austr.
43 L5 Boa Viagem Brazil
45 E4 Boa Vista Brazil
100 □ Boa Vista i. Cape Verde
115 G4 Bobadah Austr.
89 D6 Bobai China
103 E5 Bobaomby, Tanjona c. Madag.
83 F7 Bobbili India
100 B3 Bobo-Dioulasso Burkina
103 C6 Bobonong Botswana
69 G5 Bobrov Rus. Fed.
69 D5 Bobrovytsya Ukr.
69 E5 Bobrynets' Ukr.
103 E6 Boby mt Madag.
45 D2 Boca del Pao Venez.
37 M7 Boca de Macareo Venez.
42 E5 Boca do Acre Brazil
43 H4 Boca do Jari Brazil
45 E2 Boca Grande est. Venez.
46 D2 Bocaiúva Brazil
45 C2 Bocanó r. Venez.
102 B3 Bocaranga C.A.R.
29 D7 Boca Raton U.S.A.
37 H7 Bocas del Toro Panama
63 K6 Bochnia Pol.
62 C5 Bocholt Ger.
62 C5 Bochum Ger.
105 H1 Bochum S. Africa
45 C2 Boconó Venez.
25 F7 Bocoyna Mex.
102 B3 Boda C.A.R.
115 J3 Bodalla Austr.
77 N4 Bodaybo Rus. Fed.
57 G3 Boddam U.K.
34 A2 Bodega Head hd U.S.A.
101 D3 Bodélé reg. Chad
54 R4 Boden Sweden
59 E5 Bodenham U.K.
Bodensee l. see Constance, Lake
59 C7 Bodmin U.K.
59 C7 Bodmin Moor reg. U.K.
54 O3 Bodø Norway
67 M6 Bodrum Turkey
61 C3 Boechout Belgium
102 C4 Boende Dem. Rep. Congo
100 A3 Boffa Guinea
85 H3 Boga India
27 F6 Bogalusa U.S.A.
115 G3 Bogan r. Austr.
100 B3 Bogandé Burkina
115 G4 Bogan Gate Austr.
116 B4 Bogantungan Austr.
68 J3 Bogatye Saby Rus. Fed.
80 E2 Boğazlıyan Turkey
85 F3 Bogcang Zangbo r. China
82 G2 Bogda Shan mts China
115 J2 Boggabilla Austr.
115 J3 Boggabri Austr.
60 B5 Boggeragh Mts h. Rep. of Ireland
65 H5 Boghar Alg.
116 B3 Bogie r. Austr.
59 G7 Bognor Regis U.K.
94 C4 Bogo Phil.
60 D4 Bog of Allen reg. Rep. of Ireland
68 E4 Bogolyubovo Rus. Fed.
115 G6 Bogong, Mt mt Austr.
90 D2 Bogopol' Rus. Fed.
92 □ Bogor Indon.
68 G3 Bogorodsk Rus. Fed.
68 J3 Bogorodskoye Rus. Fed.
45 B3 Bogotá Col.
85 G4 Bogra Bangl.
77 L4 Boguchany Rus. Fed.
69 G5 Boguchar Rus. Fed.
100 A3 Bogué Maur.
88 F2 Bo Hai g. China
88 F2 Bohai Haixia chan. China
64 F2 Bohain-en-Vermandois France
88 E2 Bohai Wan b. China
105 H4 Bohlokong S. Africa
62 F6 Böhmer Wald mts Ger.
69 E5 Bohodukhiv Ukr.
94 C4 Bohol i. Phil.
94 C4 Bohol Sea sea Phil.
94 B4 Bohol Str. chan. Phil.
82 G2 Bohu China
69 D5 Bohuslav Ukr.
46 D3 Boi, Ponta do pt Brazil
33 F4 Boiceville U.S.A.
104 E4 Boichoko S. Africa
105 G3 Boikhutso S. Africa
43 G4 Boim Brazil
85 H5 Boinu r. Myanmar
46 E1 Boipeba, Ilha i. Brazil
46 C2 Bois r. Brazil
31 E3 Bois Blanc I. i. U.S.A.
24 C3 Boise U.S.A.
27 C4 Boise City U.S.A.
21 J5 Boissevain Can.
105 F3 Boitumelong S. Africa
94 B2 Bojeador, Cape c. Phil.
79 H2 Bojnūrd Iran
92 □ Bojonegoro Indon.
85 G1 Bokadaban Feng mt China
85 H4 Bokajan India
85 F5 Bokaro India
102 B4 Bokatola Dem. Rep. Congo
100 A3 Boké Guinea
102 C4 Bokele Dem. Rep. Congo
115 G2 Bokhara r. Austr.
55 J7 Boknafjorden chan. Norway
101 D3 Bokoro Chad
69 G5 Bokovskaya Rus. Fed.
68 E3 Boksitogorsk Rus. Fed.
103 C6 Bokspits Botswana
102 C4 Bolaiti Dem. Rep. Congo
100 A3 Bolama Guinea-Bissau
84 A3 Bolan r. Pak.
84 A3 Bolan Pass pass Pak.
64 E2 Bolbec France
82 F2 Bole China
100 B4 Bole Ghana
102 B4 Boleko Dem. Rep. Congo
100 B3 Bolgatanga Ghana
69 D6 Bolhrad Ukr.
90 B2 Boli China
102 B4 Bolia Dem. Rep. Congo
54 R4 Boliden Sweden
94 A2 Bolinao Phil.
67 L2 Bolintin-Vale Romania
45 A3 Bolívar Col.
42 C5 Bolívar Peru
27 E4 Bolivar MO U.S.A.
29 B5 Bolivar TN U.S.A.
45 C2 Bolívar, Pico mt Venez.
38 Bolivia country S. America
80 E3 Bolkar Dağları mts Turkey
68 F4 Bolkhov Rus. Fed.
31 F1 Bolkow Can.
64 G4 Bollène France
55 P6 Bollnäs Sweden
115 G2 Bollon Austr.
54 P5 Bollstabruk Sweden
55 N8 Bolmen l. Sweden
69 H7 Bolnisi Georgia
102 B4 Bolobo Dem. Rep. Congo
94 B5 Bolod Islands is Phil.
66 D2 Bologna Italy
63 P2 Bologovo Rus. Fed.
68 E3 Bologoye Rus. Fed.
105 F4 Bolokanang S. Africa
102 B3 Bolomba Dem. Rep. Congo
94 B5 Bolong Phil.
76 K4 Bolotnoye Rus. Fed.
95 C2 Bolovens, Phouphieng plat. Laos
85 F5 Bolpur India
66 D3 Bolsena, Lago di l. Italy
63 K3 Bol'shakovo Rus. Fed.
54 X3 Bol'shaya Imandra, Oz. l. Rus. Fed.
69 G6 Bol'shaya Martinovka Rus. Fed.
77 M2 Bol'shevik, Ostrov i. Rus. Fed.
68 H2 Bol'shiye Chirki Rus. Fed.
77 S3 Bol'shoy Aluy r. Rus. Fed.
90 C3 Bol'shoy Kamen' Rus. Fed.
69 J5 Bol'shoy Uzen' r. Rus. Fed.
58 E4 Bolton U.K.
32 B6 Bolton U.S.A.
80 C1 Bolu Turkey
54 B3 Bolungarvík Iceland
89 E6 Boluo China
80 C2 Bolvadin Turkey
66 D1 Bolzano Italy
102 B4 Boma Dem. Rep. Congo
115 J5 Bomaderry Austr.
115 H6 Bombala Austr.
Bombay see Mumbai
93 J7 Bomberai Peninsula pen. Indon.
42 E5 Bom Comércio Brazil
46 D2 Bom Despacho Brazil
85 H4 Bomdila India
85 H3 Bomi China
46 D1 Bom Jesus da Lapa Brazil
46 E3 Bom Jesus do Itabapoana Brazil
55 J7 Bømlo i. Norway
101 D1 Bon, Cap c. Tunisia

81 L3 Bonāb Iran
32 E6 Bon Air U.S.A.
37 L6 Bonaire i. Neth. Ant.
37 H6 Bonanza Nic.
112 D2 Bonaparte Archipelago is Austr.
57 D3 Bonar Bridge U.K.
23 K4 Bonavista Can.
23 K4 Bonavista Bay b. Can.
114 A3 Bon Bon Austr.
57 F5 Bonchester Bridge U.K.
102 C5 Bondo Dem. Rep. Congo
94 B3 Bondoc Peninsula pen. Phil.
100 B4 Bondoukou Côte d'Ivoire
92 □ Bondowoso Indon.
93 G7 Bone, Teluk b. Indon.
30 A3 Bone Lake l. U.S.A.
93 G8 Bonerate, Kepulauan is Indon.
57 E4 Bo'ness U.K.
44 C3 Bonete, Cerro mt Arg.
46 D2 Bonfinópolis de Minas Brazil
102 D3 Bonga Eth.
94 B3 Bongabong Phil.
85 G4 Bongaigaon India
102 C3 Bongandanga Dem. Rep. Congo
104 E4 Bongani S. Africa
94 A5 Bongao Phil.
85 G3 Bong Co l. China
94 C5 Bongo i. Phil.
102 C3 Bongo, Massif des mts C.A.R.
103 E5 Bongolava mts Madag.
101 E3 Bongor Chad
100 B4 Bongouanou Côte d'Ivoire
95 D2 Bồng Sơn Vietnam
61 C3 Bonheiden Belgium
66 C4 Bonifacio France
66 C4 Bonifacio, Strait of str. France/Italy
46 A3 Bonito Brazil
62 C5 Bonn Ger.
54 O3 Bonnåsjøen Norway
24 C1 Bonners Ferry U.S.A.
64 H3 Bonneville France
24 D3 Bonneville Salt Flats salt flat U.S.A.
114 D6 Bonney, L. l. Austr.
112 C6 Bonnie Rock Austr.
57 E5 Bonnyrigg U.K.
21 G4 Bonnyville Can.
94 A4 Bonobono Phil.
95 C3 Bonom Mhai mt Vietnam
66 C4 Bonorva Italy
115 J2 Bonshaw Austr.
104 D7 Bontebok National Park nat. park S. Africa
100 A4 Bonthe Sierra Leone
94 B2 Bontoc Phil.
93 F8 Bontosunggu Indon.
105 F6 Bontrug S. Africa
105 G1 Bonwapitse Botswana
35 H2 Book Cliffs cliff U.S.A.
114 E4 Boolaboolka L. l. Austr.
114 C4 Booleroo Centre Austr.
60 D5 Booley Hills h. Rep. of Ireland
114 F4 Booligal Austr.
115 H2 Boomi Austr.
115 K1 Boonah Austr.
26 E3 Boone IA U.S.A.
29 D4 Boone NC U.S.A.
32 B6 Boone Lake l. U.S.A.
32 B6 Booneville KY U.S.A.
27 F5 Booneville MS U.S.A.
34 A2 Boonville CA U.S.A.
28 C4 Boonville IN U.S.A.
26 E4 Boonville MO U.S.A.
33 F3 Boonville NY U.S.A.
114 F5 Booroorban Austr.
115 H5 Boorowa Austr.
114 E6 Boort Austr.
102 E2 Boosaaso Somalia
33 J3 Boothbay Harbor U.S.A.
118 B2 Boothia Peninsula pen. Can.
59 E4 Bootle U.K.
100 A4 Bopolu Liberia
61 H4 Boppard Ger.
47 G1 Boqueirão Brazil
27 C6 Boquillas del Carmen Mex.
101 F4 Bor Sudan
80 B3 Bor Turkey
67 K2 Bor Yugo.
24 D2 Borah Peak summit U.S.A.
55 N8 Borås Sweden
79 G4 Borāzjān Iran
43 G4 Borba Brazil
43 L5 Borborema, Planalto da plat. Brazil
81 H1 Borçka Turkey
80 B3 Bor D. mt Turkey
114 B5 Borda, C. pt Austr.
64 D5 Bordeaux France
23 H4 Borden Can.
118 B3 Borden I. i. Can.
114 D6 Bordertown Austr.
54 C4 Borðeyri Iceland
65 J4 Bordj Bou Arréridj Alg.
65 G5 Bordj Bounaama Alg.
100 C2 Bordj Omer Driss Alg.
54 □ Borðoy i. Faroe Is
57 A3 Boreray i. U.K.
54 C4 Borgarfjörður Iceland
54 C4 Borgarnes Iceland
54 N4 Børgefjell Nasjonalpark nat. park Norway
27 C5 Borger U.S.A.
55 P8 Borgholm Sweden

66 B2 Borgo San Dalmazzo Italy
66 D3 Borgo San Lorenzo Italy
66 C2 Borgosesia Italy
61 B4 Borinage reg. Belgium
69 G5 Borisoglebsk Rus. Fed.
69 F5 Borisovka Rus. Fed.
68 F3 Borisovo-Sudskoye Rus. Fed.
69 G7 Borjomi Georgia
61 E3 Borken Ger.
54 P2 Borkenes Norway
61 E1 Borken Ger.
61 E1 Borkum Ger.
61 E1 Borkum i. Ger.
55 O6 Borlänge Sweden
80 B2 Borlu Turkey
61 D1 Borndiep chan. Neth.
92 E6 Borneo i. Indon.
55 O9 Bornholm i. Denmark
67 M5 Bornova Turkey
94 B4 Borocay i. Phil.
76 K3 Borodino Rus. Fed.
55 V6 Borodinskoye Rus. Fed.
69 D5 Borodyanka Ukr.
77 P3 Borogontsy Rus. Fed.
68 F3 Borok Rus. Fed.
100 B3 Boromo Burkina
94 C4 Borongan Phil.
116 D5 Bororen Austr.
58 F3 Boroughbridge U.K.
68 E3 Borovichi Rus. Fed.
68 J3 Borovoy Kirovsk. Rus. Fed.
68 K2 Borovoy Komi Rus. Fed.
68 E1 Borovoy Korel. Rus. Fed.
60 C5 Borrisokane Rep. of Ireland
113 G3 Borroloola Austr.
54 M5 Børsa Norway
69 M7 Borşa Romania
69 C5 Borshchiv Ukr.
87 K1 Borshchovochnyy Khrebet mts Rus. Fed.
81 M5 Borūjerd Iran
57 B3 Borve U.K.
69 B5 Boryslav Ukr.
69 D5 Boryspil' Ukr.
69 E5 Borzna Ukr.
87 L1 Borzya Rus. Fed.
66 G2 Bosanska Dubica Bos.-Herz.
66 G2 Bosanska Gradiška Bos.-Herz.
66 G2 Bosanska Krupa Bos.-Herz.
66 G2 Bosanski Novi Bos.-Herz.
66 G2 Bosansko Grahovo Bos.-Herz.
30 B4 Boscobel U.S.A.
89 C6 Bose China
105 F4 Boshof S. Africa
48 Bosnia-Herzegovina country Europe
102 B3 Bosobolo Dem. Rep. Congo
91 G7 Bōsō-hantō pen. Japan
80 B1 Bosporus str. Turkey
102 B3 Bossangoa C.A.R.
102 B3 Bossembélé C.A.R.
27 E5 Bossier City U.S.A.
104 B2 Bossiesvlei Namibia
85 F1 Bostan China
81 L6 Bostān Iran
82 B2 Bosten Hu l. China
59 G5 Boston U.K.
33 H3 Boston U.S.A.
114 A5 Boston B. b. Austr.
31 H1 Boston Creek Can.
33 H3 Boston-Logan International airport U.S.A.
27 E5 Boston Mts mts U.S.A.
58 F4 Boston Spa U.K.
30 D5 Boswell U.S.A.
84 B5 Botad India
115 J4 Botany Bay b. Austr.
54 P5 Boteå Sweden
67 L3 Botev mt Bulg.
67 K3 Botevgrad Bulg.
105 G3 Bothaville S. Africa
52 Bothnia, Gulf of g. Fin./Sweden
115 G9 Bothwell Austr.
69 H5 Botkul', Ozero l. Kazakh./Rus. Fed.
63 N7 Botoşani Romania
88 E2 Botou China
95 C1 Bô Trach Vietnam
105 G2 Botshabelo S. Africa
96 Botswana country Africa
66 G5 Botte Donato, Monte mt Italy
58 G4 Bottesford U.K.
26 C1 Bottineau U.S.A.
62 C5 Bottrop Ger.
46 C3 Botucatu Brazil
46 D1 Botuporã Brazil
23 K4 Botwood Can.
100 B4 Bouaflé Côte d'Ivoire
100 B4 Bouaké Côte d'Ivoire
102 B3 Bouar C.A.R.
100 B1 Bouârfa Morocco
101 D4 Bouba Ndjida, Parc National de nat. park Cameroon
102 B3 Bouca C.A.R.
33 G2 Boucherville Can.
31 K2 Bouchette Can.
23 H4 Bouctouche Can.
111 F2 Bougainville Island i. P.N.G.
100 B3 Bougouni Mali
61 H4 Bouillon Belgium
65 H4 Bouira Alg.
100 A2 Boujdour Western Sahara
24 F3 Boulder CO U.S.A.

24 D2 Boulder MT U.S.A.
35 G3 Boulder UT U.S.A.
35 E3 Boulder Canyon U.S.A.
35 E4 Boulder City U.S.A.
34 D5 Boulevard U.S.A.
47 E3 Boulevard Atlántico Arg.
113 G4 Boulia Austr.
64 F2 Boulogne-Billancourt France
64 E1 Boulogne-sur-Mer France
100 B3 Boulsa Burkina
102 B4 Boumango Gabon
101 D4 Boumba r. Cameroon
65 H4 Boumerdes Alg.
100 B4 Bouna Côte d'Ivoire
33 H2 Boundary Mountains mts U.S.A.
34 C3 Boundary Peak summit U.S.A.
100 B4 Boundiali Côte d'Ivoire
102 B4 Boundji Congo
95 D1 Boung r. Vietnam
89 A6 Boun Nua Laos
24 E3 Bountiful U.S.A.
111 H6 Bounty Islands is N.Z.
100 B3 Bourem Mali
64 E4 Bourganeuf France
64 G3 Bourg-en-Bresse France
64 F3 Bourges France
33 F2 Bourget Can.
31 K1 Bourgmont Can.
64 G3 Bourgogne reg. France
115 F3 Bourke Austr.
31 G1 Bourkes Can.
59 G5 Bourne U.K.
59 F7 Bournemouth U.K.
61 F2 Bourtanger Moor reg. Ger.
100 C1 Bou Saâda Alg.
66 C6 Bou Salem Tunisia
35 E5 Bouse U.S.A.
35 E5 Bouse Wash r. U.S.A.
101 D3 Bousso Chad
100 A3 Boutilimit Maur.
12 K9 Bouvetøya i. Atlantic Ocean
61 E5 Bouzonville France
47 L1 Bovril Arg.
21 G4 Bow r. Can.
26 C1 Bowbells U.S.A.
116 C3 Bowen Austr.
116 B3 Bowen r. Austr.
30 B5 Bowen U.S.A.
115 H6 Bowen, Mt mt Austr.
115 J1 Bowenville Austr.
116 A3 Bowie Austr.
35 H5 Bowie AZ U.S.A.
27 D5 Bowie TX U.S.A.
21 G5 Bow Island Can.
81 L3 Bowkan Iran
28 C4 Bowling Green KY U.S.A.
26 F4 Bowling Green MO U.S.A.
32 B4 Bowling Green OH U.S.A.
32 E5 Bowling Green VA U.S.A.
116 B2 Bowling Green, C. pt Austr.
116 B2 Bowling Green B. b. Austr.
26 C2 Bowman U.S.A.
20 E4 Bowman, Mt mt Can.
119 C6 Bowman I. i. Antarctica
31 H4 Bowmanville Can.
57 B5 Bowmore U.K.
115 J5 Bowral Austr.
115 K3 Bowraville Austr.
20 E4 Bowron r. Can.
20 E4 Bowron Lake Provincial Park res. Can.
88 E2 Boxing China
61 D3 Boxtel Neth.
80 E1 Boyabat Turkey
89 E4 Boyang China
115 K3 Boyd r. Austr.
21 J2 Boyd Lake l. Can.
20 G4 Boyle U.S.A.
60 C4 Boyle Rep. of Ireland
116 D5 Boyne r. Qld. Austr.
116 D5 Boyne r. Qld. Austr.
60 E4 Boyne r. Rep. of Ireland
84 A1 Boyni Qara Afgh.
29 D7 Boynton Beach U.S.A.
24 E3 Boysen Res. resr U.S.A.
42 F8 Boyuibe Bol.
81 K1 Böyük Hinaldağ mt Azer.
67 M5 Bozcaada i. Turkey
67 M5 Bozdağ mt Turkey
80 A2 Boz Dağları mts Turkey
80 B3 Bozdoğan Turkey
59 G5 Bozeat U.K.
24 E2 Bozeman U.S.A.
88 E3 Bozhou China
80 D3 Bozkır Turkey
102 B3 Bozoum C.A.R.
80 G3 Bozova Turkey
80 C2 Bozüyük Turkey
66 B2 Bra Italy
66 G3 Brač i. Croatia
57 B3 Bracadale U.K.
57 B3 Bracadale, Loch b. U.K.
66 E3 Bracciano, Lago di l. Italy
31 H3 Bracebridge Can.
54 O5 Bräcke Sweden
59 G6 Bracknell U.K.
66 E4 Bradano r. Italy
29 D7 Bradenton U.S.A.
31 H3 Bradford Can.
58 F4 Bradford U.K.
32 A4 Bradford OH U.S.A.
32 D4 Bradford PA U.S.A.
33 F3 Bradford VT U.S.A.
27 D6 Brady U.S.A.
20 B3 Brady Gl. gl. U.S.A.

57 □ Brae U.K.
114 C4 Braemar Austr.
57 E4 Braemar U.K.
65 B2 Braga Port.
47 E2 Bragado Arg.
43 J4 Bragança Brazil
65 C2 Bragança Port.
46 C3 Bragança Paulista Brazil
69 D5 Brahin Belarus
85 G5 Brahmanbaria Bangl.
85 F5 Brahmani r. India
83 F7 Brahmapur India
85 G4 Brahmaputra r. Asia
67 M2 Brăila Romania
26 E2 Brainerd U.S.A.
59 H6 Braintree U.K.
105 H1 Brak r. S. Africa
103 B6 Brakwater Namibia
20 E4 Bramberg Can.
55 L9 Bramming Denmark
55 P5 Brämön i. Sweden
31 H4 Brampton Can.
58 E3 Brampton Eng. U.K.
59 H5 Brampton Eng. U.K.
59 H5 Brancaster U.K.
23 K4 Branch Can.
45 C4 Branco r. Brazil
55 M6 Brandbu Norway
55 L9 Brande Denmark
62 F4 Brandenburg Ger.
105 G4 Brandfort S. Africa
116 B2 Brandon Austr.
21 K5 Brandon Can.
59 H5 Brandon U.K.
26 D3 Brandon SD U.S.A.
33 G3 Brandon VT U.S.A.
60 A5 Brandon Head hd Rep. of Ireland
60 A5 Brandon Hill h. Rep. of Ireland
60 A5 Brandon Mountain mt Rep. of Ireland
104 D5 Brandvlei S. Africa
29 D4 Branford U.S.A.
63 J3 Braniewo Pol.
119 B2 Bransfield Str. str. Antarctica
31 G4 Brantford Can.
114 C4 Branxholme Austr.
23 H4 Bras d'Or L. l. Can.
42 F2 Brasileia Brazil
46 C1 Brasília Brazil
46 D2 Brasília de Minas Brazil
43 G4 Brasília Legal Brazil
63 N3 Braslaw Belarus
67 L2 Braşov Romania
94 A5 Brassey, Banjaran mts Malaysia
33 J2 Brassua Lake l. U.S.A.
63 J3 Bratislava Slovakia
77 M4 Bratsk Rus. Fed.
62 F6 Braunau am Inn Austria
62 E4 Braunschweig Ger.
100 □ Brava i. Cape Verde
55 P7 Bråviken in. Sweden
Bravo del Norte, Río r. see Rio Grande
35 E5 Brawley U.S.A.
60 E3 Bray Rep. of Ireland
20 F4 Brazeau r. Can.
38 Brazil country S. America
12 H7 Brazil Basin sea feature Atlantic Ocean
27 D5 Brazos r. U.S.A.
102 B4 Brazzaville Congo
67 H2 Brčko Bos.-Herz.
117 A6 Breaksea Sd in. N.Z.
117 E1 Bream Bay b. N.Z.
117 E1 Bream Head hd N.Z.
92 □ Brebes Indon.
59 C5 Brechfa U.K.
57 F4 Brechin U.K.
61 C3 Brecht Belgium
26 C2 Breckenridge MN U.S.A.
27 D5 Breckenridge TX U.S.A.
62 H6 Břeclav Czech Rep.
59 D6 Brecon U.K.
59 D6 Brecon Beacons h. U.K.
59 D6 Brecon Beacons National Park U.K.
61 C3 Breda Neth.
104 D7 Bredasdorp S. Africa
115 H5 Bredbo Austr.
54 O3 Bredviken Norway
32 D5 Breezewood U.S.A.
62 D7 Bregenz Austria
54 B4 Breiðafjörður b. Iceland
54 B4 Breiðdalsvik Iceland
62 C6 Breisach am Rhein Ger.
54 S1 Breivikbotn Norway
43 J6 Brejinho de Nazaré Brazil
54 L5 Brekstad Norway
62 D5 Bremen Ger.
29 C5 Bremen GA U.S.A.
28 C5 Bremen IN U.S.A.
62 D5 Bremerhaven Ger.
24 B2 Bremerton U.S.A.
27 D6 Brenham U.S.A.
54 N4 Brenna Norway
62 E7 Brenner Pass pass Austria/Italy
31 H2 Brent Can.
66 D2 Brenta r. Italy
59 H6 Brentwood U.K.
33 B3 Brentwood CA U.S.A.
33 G4 Brentwood NY U.S.A.
66 D2 Brescia Italy
66 D1 Bressanone Italy
57 □ Bressay i. U.K.
64 D3 Bressuire France
69 B4 Brest Belarus
64 B2 Brest France
64 C2 Bretagne reg. France

27 F6 Breton Sound b. U.S.A.
117 E1 Brett, Cape c. N.Z.
59 E4 Bretton U.K.
29 D5 Brevard U.S.A.
30 E2 Brevort U.S.A.
115 G2 Brewarrina Austr.
33 J2 Brewer U.S.A.
24 C1 Brewster U.S.A.
27 G6 Brewton U.S.A.
105 H3 Breyten S. Africa
Brezhnev see Naberezhnyye Chelny
63 J6 Brezno Slovakia
66 G2 Brezovo Polje h. Croatia
102 C3 Bria C.A.R.
64 H4 Briançon France
115 G5 Bribbaree Austr.
115 K1 Bribie I. i. Austr.
69 C5 Briceni Moldova
64 H4 Bric Froid mt France/Italy
60 C5 Bride r. Rep. of Ireland
35 G1 Bridgeland U.S.A.
59 D6 Bridgend U.K.
57 D4 Bridge of Orchy U.K.
34 C2 Bridgeport CA U.S.A.
33 G4 Bridgeport CT U.S.A.
26 C3 Bridgeport NE U.S.A.
24 E2 Bridger U.S.A.
24 F3 Bridger Peak summit U.S.A.
33 F5 Bridgeton U.S.A.
112 C6 Bridgetown Austr.
37 N6 Bridgetown Barbados
115 G9 Bridgewater Austr.
23 H5 Bridgewater Can.
33 K1 Bridgewater U.S.A.
114 D7 Bridgewater, C. hd Austr.
59 E5 Bridgnorth U.K.
33 H2 Bridgton U.S.A.
59 D6 Bridgwater U.K.
59 D6 Bridgwater Bay b. U.K.
58 G3 Bridlington U.K.
58 G3 Bridlington Bay b. U.K.
115 G8 Bridport Austr.
59 E7 Bridport U.K.
62 C7 Brig Switz.
58 G3 Brigg U.K.
24 D3 Brigham City U.S.A.
115 G6 Bright Austr.
59 J6 Brightlingsea U.K.
31 J3 Brighton Can.
117 C6 Brighton N.Z.
59 G7 Brighton U.K.
31 F4 Brighton U.S.A.
64 H5 Brignoles France
100 A3 Brikama The Gambia
66 G4 Brindisi Italy
47 D1 Brinkmann Arg.
114 C4 Brinkworth Austr.
23 H4 Brion, Île i. Can.
64 H4 Brioude France
23 F3 Brisay Can.
115 K1 Brisbane Austr.
33 K1 Bristol Can.
59 E6 Bristol U.K.
33 G4 Bristol CT U.S.A.
33 H4 Bristol PA U.S.A.
32 B6 Bristol TN U.S.A.
118 D7 Bristol Bay U.S.A.
59 C6 Bristol Channel est. U.K.
119 C1 Bristol I. i. Atlantic Ocean
35 H3 Bristol Lake l. U.S.A.
20 D3 British Columbia div. Can.
105 G2 Brits S. Africa
104 E5 Britstown S. Africa
Brittany reg. see Bretagne
64 E4 Brive-la-Gaillarde France
65 E1 Briviesca Spain
59 D7 Brixham U.K.
82 D2 Brlik Kazak.
62 H6 Brno Czech Rep.
29 D6 Broad r. U.S.A.
33 F3 Broadalbin U.S.A.
22 F3 Broadback r. Can.
57 B2 Broad Bay b. U.K.
57 F6 Broadford Austr.
60 C5 Broadford Rep. of Ireland
57 C3 Broadford U.K.
57 E5 Broad Law h. U.K.
116 C4 Broad Sound chan. Austr.
116 D4 Broad Sound Channel chan. Austr.
59 J6 Broadstairs U.K.
21 J4 Broadus U.S.A.
21 J4 Broadview Can.
115 K2 Broadwater Austr.
26 C3 Broadwater U.S.A.
117 D1 Broadwood N.Z.
55 S8 Broceni Latvia
21 J3 Brochet Can.
21 J3 Brochet, Lac l. Can.
32 E5 Brockport U.S.A.
33 H3 Brockton U.S.A.
31 K3 Brockville Can.
31 K3 Brockway MI U.S.A.
32 D4 Brockway PA U.S.A.
57 C5 Brodick U.K.
63 J4 Brodnica Pol.
69 C5 Brody Ukr.
27 E4 Broken Arrow U.S.A.
115 J4 Broken B. b. Austr.
26 D3 Broken Bow NE U.S.A.
27 E5 Broken Bow OK U.S.A.
114 D3 Broken Hill Austr.
59 G5 Bromley U.K.
59 E5 Bromsgrove U.K.
55 L8 Brønderslev Denmark
105 H2 Bronkhorstspruit S. Africa
54 N4 Brønnøysund Norway

30 E5 Bronson U.S.A.
59 J5 Brooke U.K.
94 A4 Brooke's Point Phil.
30 C4 Brookfield U.S.A.
27 E6 Brookhaven U.S.A.
24 A3 Brookings OR U.S.A.
26 D2 Brookings SD U.S.A.
33 H3 Brookline U.S.A.
30 A5 Brooklyn IA U.S.A.
30 B5 Brooklyn IL U.S.A.
26 E2 Brooklyn Center U.S.A.
32 D6 Brookneal U.S.A.
21 G4 Brooks Can.
34 A2 Brooks CA U.S.A.
33 J2 Brooks ME U.S.A.
119 B3 Brooks, C. c. Antarctica
18 Brooks Range mts U.S.A.
29 D6 Brooksville U.S.A.
112 C6 Brookton Austr.
32 C4 Brookville U.S.A.
116 E6 Brooloo Austr.
57 C3 Broom, Loch in. U.K.
112 D3 Broome Austr.
57 E2 Brora U.K.
55 O9 Brösarp Sweden
60 D4 Brosna r. Rep. of Ireland
24 B3 Brothers U.S.A.
58 E3 Brough U.K.
57 E1 Brough Head hd U.K.
60 E3 Broughshane U.K.
114 C4 Broughton r. Austr.
115 K4 Broughton Is is Austr.
63 P5 Brovary Ukr.
55 L8 Brovst Denmark
114 C4 Brown, Mt mt Austr.
116 A1 Brown Cr. r. Austr.
27 C5 Brownfield U.S.A.
24 D1 Browning U.S.A.
30 D6 Brownsburg U.S.A.
33 F5 Browns Mills U.S.A.
29 B5 Brownsville TN U.S.A.
27 D7 Brownsville TX U.S.A.
33 J2 Brownville U.S.A.
33 J2 Brownville Junction U.S.A.
27 D6 Brownwood U.S.A.
63 O4 Brozha Belarus
64 F1 Bruay-la-Bussière France
112 C4 Bruce, Mt mt Austr.
30 C2 Bruce Crossing U.S.A.
22 D4 Bruce Pen. pen. Can.
31 G3 Bruce Peninsula National Park nat. park Can.
62 G7 Bruck an der Mur Austria
59 E6 Brue r. U.K.
61 B3 Bruges Belgium
Brugge see Bruges
35 J3 Bruin Pt summit U.S.A.
85 J3 Bruint India
104 C2 Brukkaros Namibia
30 B3 Brule U.S.A.
23 H3 Brûlé, Lac l. Can.
46 E1 Brumado Brazil
55 M6 Brumunddal Norway
24 D3 Bruneau U.S.A.
24 D3 Bruneau r. U.S.A.
71 Brunei country Asia
54 O3 Brunflo Sweden
66 D1 Brunico Italy
117 C5 Brunner, L. l. N.Z.
21 H4 Bruno Can.
62 D4 Brunsbüttel Ger.
29 D6 Brunswick GA U.S.A.
33 J3 Brunswick ME U.S.A.
32 C4 Brunswick OH U.S.A.
44 B8 Brunswick, Península de pen. Chile
115 K2 Brunswick Head Austr.
62 H6 Bruntál Czech Rep.
105 J4 Bruntville S. Africa
115 G9 Bruny I. i. Austr.
24 D3 Brush U.S.A.
61 C4 Brussels Belgium
31 G4 Brussels Can.
30 D3 Brussels U.S.A.
63 O5 Busyliv Ukr.
115 G6 Bruthen Austr.
Bruxelles see Brussels
32 A4 Bryan OH U.S.A.
27 D6 Bryan TX U.S.A.
114 C4 Bryan, Mt mt Austr.
68 E4 Bryansk Rus. Fed.
68 E4 Bryanskaya Oblast' div. Rus. Fed.
69 H6 Bryanskoye Rus. Fed.
35 H5 Bryce, Mt. mt U.S.A.
35 F3 Bryce Canyon Nat. Park nat. park U.S.A.
55 J7 Bryne Norway
69 F6 Bryukhovetskaya Rus. Fed.
62 F6 Brzeg Pol.
111 F2 Buala Solomon Is
100 A3 Buba Guinea-Bissau
81 M7 Būbīyān I. i. Kuwait
94 B5 Bubuan i. Phil.
80 C3 Bucak Turkey
45 B3 Bucaramanga Col.
94 C4 Bucas Grande i. Phil.
116 C3 Bucasia Austr.
115 H6 Buchan Austr.
100 A4 Buchanan Liberia
30 D5 Buchanan MI U.S.A.
32 D6 Buchanan VA U.S.A.
116 A3 Buchanan, L. salt flat Austr.
27 D6 Buchanan, L. l. U.S.A.
23 J4 Buchans Can.
67 M2 Bucharest Romania
34 B4 Buchon, Point pt U.S.A.
63 M7 Bucin, Pasul pass Romania
115 F3 Buckambool Mt h. Austr.
35 F5 Buckeye U.S.A.

32 B5 Buckeye Lake l. U.S.A.
32 C5 Buckhannon U.S.A.
32 C5 Buckhannon r. U.S.A.
57 E4 Buckhaven U.K.
31 H3 Buckhorn Can.
35 H5 Buckhorn U.S.A.
31 H3 Buckhorn Lake l. Can.
32 B6 Buckhorn Lake l. U.S.A.
57 F3 Buckie U.K.
31 K3 Buckingham Can.
59 G5 Buckingham U.K.
32 D6 Buckingham U.S.A.
113 G2 Buckingham Bay b. Austr.
116 B5 Buckland Tableland reg. Austr.
114 B4 Buckleboo Austr.
119 A6 Buckle I. i. Antarctica
35 F4 Buckskin Mts mts U.S.A.
34 B2 Bucks Mt mt U.S.A.
33 J2 Bucksport U.S.A.
București see Bucharest
32 B4 Bucyrus U.S.A.
63 P4 Buda-Kashyalyova Belarus
63 J7 Budapest Hungary
84 D3 Budaun India
114 F3 Budda Austr.
57 F4 Buddon Ness pt U.K.
66 C4 Buddusò Italy
59 C7 Bude U.K.
27 F6 Bude U.S.A.
69 H6 Budennovsk Rus. Fed.
115 K1 Buderim Austr.
84 D5 Budni India
68 E3 Budogoshch' Rus. Fed.
85 H2 Budongquan China
66 C4 Budoni Italy
100 C4 Buea Cameroon
34 B4 Buellton U.S.A.
47 D2 Buena Esperanza Arg.
45 A4 Buenaventura Col.
36 C3 Buenaventura Mex.
45 A4 Buenaventura, B. de b. Col.
25 F4 Buena Vista CO U.S.A.
32 D6 Buena Vista VA U.S.A.
65 E2 Buendia, Embalse de resr Spain
47 B4 Bueno r. Chile
47 E2 Buenos Aires Arg.
47 C3 Buenos Aires div. Arg.
44 B7 Buenos Aires, L. l. Arg./Chile
44 C7 Buen Pasto Arg.
27 B7 Búfalo Mex.
20 G3 Buffalo r. Can.
32 D3 Buffalo NY U.S.A.
27 D4 Buffalo OK U.S.A.
26 C2 Buffalo SD U.S.A.
27 D6 Buffalo TX U.S.A.
30 B3 Buffalo WV U.S.A.
24 F2 Buffalo WY U.S.A.
30 B3 Buffalo r. U.S.A.
115 G6 Buffalo, Mt mt Austr.
20 F3 Buffalo Head Hills h. Can.
20 F2 Buffalo Lake l. Can.
21 H3 Buffalo Narrows Can.
104 B4 Buffels watercourse S. Africa
105 G1 Buffels Drift S. Africa
29 D5 Buford U.S.A.
67 L2 Buftea Romania
63 K4 Bug r. Pol.
45 A4 Buga Col.
45 A3 Bugalagrande Col.
115 H3 Bugaldie Austr.
92 □ Bugel, Tanjung pt Indon.
66 G2 Bugojno Bos.-Herz.
94 A4 Bugsuk i. Phil.
94 B2 Buguey Phil.
103 D5 Buhera Zimbabwe
94 B3 Buhi Phil.
24 D3 Buhl ID U.S.A.
30 A2 Buhl MN U.S.A.
81 J3 Bühtan r. Turkey
63 N7 Buhuși Romania
59 D5 Builth Wells U.K.
100 B4 Bui National Park nat. park Ghana
68 J4 Buinsk Rus. Fed.
81 L4 Bu'in Soflā Iran
87 L2 Buir Nur l. Mongolia
103 B6 Buitepos Namibia
67 J3 Bujanovac Yugo.
102 C4 Bujumbura Burundi
87 L1 Bukachacha Rus. Fed.
111 F2 Buka I. i. P.N.G.
102 C4 Bukavu Dem. Rep. Congo
79 J2 Bukhara Uzbek.
94 C6 Bukide i. Indon.
95 □ Bukit Batok Sing.
95 B5 Bukit Fraser Malaysia
95 □ Bukit Panjang Sing.
95 □ Bukit Timah Sing.
92 C7 Bukittinggi Indon.
102 D4 Bukoba Tanz.
95 □ Bukum, P. i. Sing.
93 J7 Bula Indon.
68 J4 Bula r. Rus. Fed.
115 K4 Bulahdelal Austr.
94 B3 Bulan Phil.
80 G1 Bulancak Turkey
84 D3 Bulandshahr India
81 J2 Bulanık Turkey
103 C6 Bulawayo Zimbabwe
80 F3 Bulbul Syria
80 B2 Buldan Turkey
84 D5 Buldana India
105 J2 Bulembu Swaziland
86 H2 Bulgan Hövsgöl Mongolia
88 B1 Bulgan Ömnögovi Mongolia
49 Bulgaria country Europe

114 E1 Bullawarra, Lake salt flat Austr.
114 D3 Bullea, Lake salt flat Austr.
117 D4 Buller r. N.Z.
115 G2 Buller, Mt mt Austr.
35 E4 Bullhead City U.S.A.
34 D4 Bullion Mts mts U.S.A.
114 E2 Bulloo watercourse Austr.
114 E2 Bulloo Downs Austr.
114 E2 Bulloo L. salt flat Austr.
104 B2 Büllsport Namibia
114 E6 Buloke, Lake l. Austr.
105 G4 Bultfontein S. Africa
94 C5 Buluan Phil.
93 G8 Bulukumba Indon.
77 O2 Bulun Rus. Fed.
102 B4 Bulungu Bandundu Dem. Rep. Congo
102 C4 Bulungu Kasai-Occidental Dem. Rep. Congo
94 C3 Bulusan Phil.
102 C3 Bumba Dem. Rep. Congo
88 B1 Bumbat Sum China
35 F4 Bumble Bee U.S.A.
94 A5 Bum-Bum i. Malaysia
102 B4 Buna Dem. Rep. Congo
102 D3 Buna Kenya
102 D4 Bunazi Tanz.
60 C2 Bunbeg Rep. of Ireland
112 C6 Bunbury Austr.
60 E5 Bunclody Rep. of Ireland
60 D2 Buncrana Rep. of Ireland
102 D4 Bunda Tanz.
116 E5 Bundaberg Austr.
115 G2 Bundaleer Austr.
115 J3 Bundarra Austr.
84 C4 Bundi India
60 C3 Bundoran Rep. of Ireland
85 F5 Bundu India
59 J5 Bungay U.K.
95 B2 Bung Boraphet l. Thai.
115 H5 Bungendore Austr.
116 C6 Bungil r. Austr.
Bungle Bungle National Park nat. park see Purnululu National Park
91 C8 Bungo-suidō chan. Japan
102 D3 Bunia Dem. Rep. Congo
102 C4 Bunianga Dem. Rep. Congo
114 E6 Buninyong Austr.
100 D3 Buni-Yadi Nigeria
84 C2 Bunji Jammu and Kashmir
116 E4 Bunker Group atolls Austr.
35 E3 Bunkerville U.S.A.
27 E6 Bunkie U.S.A.
29 D6 Bunnell U.S.A.
80 E2 Bünyan Turkey
94 A6 Bunyu i. Indon.
95 D2 Buôn Hồ Vietnam
95 D2 Buôn Mê Thuôt Vietnam
77 P2 Buorkhaya, Guba b. Rus. Fed.
102 D4 Bura Kenya
84 B3 Burang China
46 E2 Buranhaém r. Brazil
102 E3 Burao Somalia
94 C4 Burauen Phil.
78 E4 Buraydah Saudi Arabia
34 C4 Burbank U.S.A.
115 G4 Burcher Austr.
116 B3 Burdekin r. Austr.
116 B3 Burdekin Falls waterfall Austr.
80 C3 Burdur Turkey
102 D2 Burē Eth.
59 J5 Bure r. U.K.
54 R4 Bureå Sweden
87 O1 Bureinskiy Khrebet mts Rus. Fed.
80 D6 Bûr Fu'ad Egypt
67 M3 Burgas Bulg.
29 E5 Burgaw U.S.A.
23 J4 Burgeo Can.
105 G5 Burgersdorp S. Africa
105 J2 Burgersfort S. Africa
59 G7 Burgess Hill U.K.
62 F6 Burghausen Ger.
57 E3 Burghead U.K.
66 F6 Burgio, Serra di h. Italy
65 E1 Burgos Spain
55 Q8 Burgsvik Sweden
Burgundy reg. see Bourgogne
82 J3 Burhan Budai Shan mts China
67 M5 Burhaniye Turkey
84 D5 Burhanpur India
85 E5 Burhar-Dhanpuri India
85 F4 Burhi Gandak r. India
94 B3 Burias i. Phil.
85 H4 Buri Dihing r. India
85 E4 Buri Gandak r. Nepal
23 J4 Burin Peninsula pen. Can.
95 B2 Buriram Thai.
43 K5 Buriti Bravo Brazil
46 C1 Buritis Brazil
117 C6 Burke Pass N.Z.
113 G3 Burketown Austr.
96 Burkina country Africa
31 H3 Burk's Falls Can.
24 D3 Burley U.K.
31 H4 Burlington Can.
26 C4 Burlington CO U.S.A.
30 B5 Burlington IA U.S.A.
30 D5 Burlington IN U.S.A.
33 G2 Burlington ME U.S.A.
33 G2 Burlington VT U.S.A.
30 C4 Burlington WV U.S.A.
Burma country see Myanmar

27 D6 Burnet U.S.A.
116 E5 Burnett r. Austr.
116 E5 Burnett Heads Austr.
24 B3 Burney U.S.A.
33 J2 Burnham U.S.A.
115 F8 Burnie Austr.
58 G3 Burniston U.K.
58 E4 Burnley U.K.
24 C3 Burns U.S.A.
21 H1 Burnside r. Can.
32 C5 Burnsville Lake l. U.S.A.
57 E4 Burntisland U.K.
21 K3 Burntwood r. Can.
21 J3 Burntwood Lake l. Can.
114 E5 Buronga Austr.
82 G1 Burqin China
80 G5 Burqu' Jordan
114 C4 Burra Austr.
57 □ Burra i. U.K.
57 □ Burravoe U.K.
57 F2 Burray i. U.K.
67 J4 Burrel Albania
115 H4 Burrendong Reservoir resr Austr.
115 H3 Burren Jct. Austr.
115 J5 Burrewarra Pt pt Austr.
65 F3 Burriana Spain
115 H5 Burrinjuck Austr.
115 H5 Burrinjuck Reservoir resr Austr.
36 D3 Burro, Serranías del mts Mex.
32 B5 Burr Oak Reservoir resr U.S.A.
57 D6 Burrow Head hd U.K.
116 E5 Burrum Heads Austr.
35 G2 Burrville U.S.A.
80 B1 Bursa Turkey
78 C4 Bûr Safâga Egypt
Bûr Sa'îd see Port Said
Bûr Sudan see Port Sudan
114 B4 Burta Austr.
30 E3 Burt Lake l. U.S.A.
31 H4 Burton U.S.A.
22 E3 Burton, Lac l. Can.
60 C3 Burtonport Rep. of Ireland
59 F5 Burton upon Trent U.K.
54 R4 Burträsk Sweden
33 K1 Burtts Corner Can.
114 E4 Burtundy Austr.
93 H7 Buru i. Indon.
80 C6 Burullus, Bahra el lag. Egypt
102 C4 Burundi country Africa
102 C4 Bururi Burundi
20 B2 Burwash Landing Can.
57 F2 Burwick U.K.
59 H5 Bury St Edmunds U.K.
84 C2 Burzil Pass pass Jammu and Kashmir
102 C4 Busanga Dem. Rep. Congo
60 E2 Bush r. U.K.
79 G4 Büshehr Iran
85 E2 Bushêngcaka China
102 D4 Bushenyi Uganda
60 E2 Bushmills U.K.
30 B5 Bushnell U.S.A.
95 □ Busing, P. i. Sing.
102 C3 Businga Dem. Rep. Congo
80 F5 Busrá ash Shām Syria
61 D2 Bussum Neth.
27 C7 Bustamante Mex.
25 F6 Bustillos, Lago l. Mex.
66 C2 Busto Arsizio Italy
94 A3 Busuanga Phil.
94 A3 Busuanga i. Phil.
102 C3 Buta Dem. Rep. Congo
95 A4 Butang Group is Thai.
47 C3 Buta Ranquil Arg.
102 C4 Butare Rwanda
114 B4 Bute Austr.
57 C5 Bute i. U.K.
57 C5 Bute, Sound of chan. U.K.
20 D4 Butedale Can.
20 D4 Bute In. in. Can.
105 H4 Butha Buthe Lesotho
30 D4 Butler IN U.S.A.
32 D4 Butler PA U.S.A.
60 D3 Butlers Bridge Rep. of Ireland
93 G7 Buton i. Indon.
24 D2 Butte U.S.A.
34 B1 Butte Meadows U.S.A.
92 C5 Butterworth Malaysia
105 H6 Butterworth S. Africa
60 C5 Buttevant Rep. of Ireland
20 D5 Buttle L. l. Can.
57 B2 Butt of Lewis hd U.K.
34 C4 Buttonwillow U.S.A.
94 C4 Butuan Phil.
89 B5 Butuo China
69 G5 Buturlinovka Rus. Fed.
85 E4 Butwal Nepal
102 E3 Buulobarde Somalia
102 E4 Buur Gaabo Somalia
102 E3 Buurhakaba Somalia
85 F4 Buxar India
59 F4 Buxton U.K.
68 G3 Buy Rus. Fed.
30 A1 Buyck U.S.A.
69 H7 Buynaksk Rus. Fed.
Büyük Ağrı mt see Ararat, Mt
80 B2 Büyükmenderes r. Turkey
88 D1 Buyun Shan mt China
67 M2 Buzău Romania
103 D5 Búzi Moz.
76 H4 Buzuluk Rus. Fed.
69 G5 Buzuluk r. Rus. Fed.
33 H4 Buzzards Bay b. U.S.A.

113 K2 Bwagaoia P.N.G.
67 L3 Byala Bulg.
67 K3 Byala Slatina Bulg.
63 O4 Byalynichy Belarus
68 D4 Byarezina r. Belarus
68 C4 Byaroza Belarus
80 E4 Byblos Lebanon
62 J4 Bydgoszcz Pol.
68 D4 Byerazino Belarus
24 F4 Byers U.S.A.
63 O3 Byeshankovichy Belarus
55 K7 Bygland Norway
55 K7 Bykhaw Belarus
55 K7 Bykle Norway
118 A3 Bylot I. i. Can.
31 J1 Byng Inlet Can.
55 K6 Byrkjelo Norway
115 G3 Byrock Austr.
30 C4 Byron IL U.S.A.
33 H2 Byron ME U.S.A.
115 K2 Byron, C. hd Austr.
115 K2 Byron Bay Austr.
77 M2 Byrranga, Gory mts Rus. Fed.
54 R4 Byske Sweden
77 P3 Bytantay r. Rus. Fed.
63 J5 Bytom Pol.
62 H3 Bytów Pol.

C

44 E3 Caacupé Para.
46 A4 Caaguazú Para.
46 A4 Caaguazú, Cordillera de h. Para.
46 A3 Caarapó Brazil
46 A4 Caazapá Para.
42 C6 Caballas Peru
42 C6 Caballococha Peru
94 B3 Cabanatuan Phil.
23 G4 Cabano Can.
102 E2 Cabdul Qaadir Somalia
46 A1 Cabeceira Rio Manso Brazil
43 M5 Cabedelo Brazil
65 D3 Cabeza del Buey Spain
42 F7 Cabezas Bol.
47 B3 Cabildo Chile
45 C2 Cabimas Venez.
102 B4 Cabinda Angola
102 B4 Cabinda div. Angola
24 C1 Cabinet Mts mts U.S.A.
45 B3 Cable Way pass Col.
46 D3 Cabo Frio Brazil
46 E3 Cabo Frio, Ilha do i. Brazil
22 E4 Cabonga, Réservoir resr Can.
27 E4 Cabool U.S.A.
115 K1 Caboolture Austr.
43 H3 Cabo Orange, Parque Nacional de nat. park Brazil
42 C4 Cabo Pantoja Peru
36 B2 Caborca Mex.
31 G2 Cabot Head pt Can.
23 J4 Cabot Strait str. Can.
46 D2 Cabral, Serra do mts Brazil
81 L2 Cäbrayıl Azer.
65 F3 Cabrera i. Spain
65 F3 Cabriel r. Spain
45 C3 Cabruta Venez.
94 B2 Cabugao Phil.
44 F3 Caçador Brazil
67 J3 Čačak Yugo.
47 G1 Cacapava do Sul Brazil
32 D5 Cacapon r. U.S.A.
45 B3 Cáceres Col.
66 C4 Caccia, Capo pt Italy
43 G7 Cáceres Brazil
65 C3 Cáceres Spain
24 D3 Cache Peak summit U.S.A.
100 A3 Cacheu Guinea-Bissau
44 C3 Cachi r. Arg.
44 C2 Cachi, Nevados de mt Arg.
43 H5 Cachimbo, Serra do h. Brazil
45 B3 Cáchira Col.
46 E1 Cachoeira Brazil
46 B2 Cachoeira Alta Brazil
47 G1 Cachoeira do Sul Brazil
46 E3 Cachoeiro de Itapemirim Brazil
100 A3 Cacine Guinea-Bissau
43 H3 Caciporé, Cabo pt Brazil
103 B5 Cacolo Angola
102 B4 Caconga Angola
34 B4 Cactus Range mts U.S.A.
46 B2 Caçu Brazil
46 D1 Caculé Brazil
63 J6 Čadca Slovakia
114 A2 Cadibarrawirracanna, L. salt flat Austr.
94 B3 Cadig Mountains mts Phil.
31 H1 Cadillac Que. Can.
21 H5 Cadillac Can.
30 E3 Cadillac U.S.A.
94 B4 Cadiz i. Phil.
65 C4 Cádiz Spain
65 C4 Cádiz, Golfo de g. Spain
35 E4 Cadiz Lake l. U.S.A.
64 D2 Caen France
59 C4 Caernarfon U.K.
59 C4 Caernarfon Bay b. U.K.
59 D6 Caerphilly U.K.
32 B5 Caesar Creek Lake l. U.S.A.
80 E5 Caesarea Israel

46 D1 Caetité Brazil
44 C3 Cafayate Arg.
94 B4 Cagayan Phil.
94 B3 Cagayan r. Phil.
94 C4 Cagayan de Oro Phil.
94 A4 Cagayan Islands is Phil.
66 E3 Cagli Italy
66 C5 Cagliari Italy
66 C5 Cagliari, Golfo di b. Italy
45 B4 Caguán r. Col.
60 B6 Caha h. Rep. of Ireland
29 C5 Cahaba r. U.S.A.
60 B6 Caha Mts h. Rep. of Ireland
60 A6 Cahermore Rep. of Ireland
60 A6 Cahersiveen Rep. of Ireland
60 D5 Cahore Point pt Rep. of Ireland
103 D5 Cahora Bassa, Lago de resr Moz.
60 D5 Cahore Point pt Rep. of Ireland
64 E4 Cahors France
42 C5 Cahuapanas Peru
69 D6 Cahul Moldova
103 D5 Caia Moz.
43 G6 Caiabis, Serra dos h. Brazil
103 C5 Caianda Angola
46 B2 Caiapó r. Brazil
46 B2 Caiapó, Serra do mts Brazil
46 B2 Caiapônia Brazil
37 J4 Caibarién Cuba
89 C6 Cai Bầu, Đao i. Vietnam
95 C3 Cai Be Vietnam
45 D3 Caicara Venez.
37 K4 Caicos Is is Turks and Caicos Is
89 Caidian China
47 B1 Caimanes Chile
94 A3 Caiman Point pt Phil.
65 F2 Caimodorro mt Spain
95 C3 Cai Nước Vietnam
57 E3 Cairn Gorm mt U.K.
57 E3 Cairngorm Mountains mts U.K.
57 C6 Cairnryan U.K.
116 A1 Cairns Austr.
57 E3 Cairn Toul mt U.K.
78 C4 Cairo Egypt
29 C6 Cairo U.S.A.
66 C2 Cairo Montenotte Italy
103 B5 Caiundo Angola
115 F2 Caiwarro Austr.
42 C5 Cajamarca Peru
94 B3 Cajidiocan Phil.
66 G1 Čakovec Croatia
80 B2 Cal Turkey
105 G5 Çala S. Africa
100 C4 Calabar Nigeria
31 J3 Calabogie Can.
45 D2 Calabozo Venez.
67 K3 Calafat Romania
44 B8 Calafate Arg.
94 B3 Calagua Islands is Phil.
65 F1 Calahorra Spain
64 E1 Calais France
33 K2 Calais U.S.A.
42 F5 Calama Brazil
44 C2 Calama Chile
45 B2 Calamar Bolivar Col.
45 B3 Calamar Guaviare Col.
94 A4 Calamian Group is Phil.
65 F2 Calamocha Spain
103 B4 Calandula Angola
101 E2 Calanscio Sand Sea des. Libya
94 B3 Calapan Phil.
67 M2 Călărași Romania
65 F2 Calatayud Spain
94 B3 Calauag Phil.
94 B3 Calavite, Cape pt Phil.
94 A3 Calawit i. Phil.
94 B2 Calayan i. Phil.
94 C4 Calbayog Phil.
94 C4 Calbiga Phil.
47 B4 Calbuco Chile
43 L5 Calcanhar, Ponta do pt Brazil
27 B6 Calcasieu L. l. U.S.A.
43 H3 Calçoene Brazil
85 G5 Calcutta India
65 B3 Caldas da Rainha Port.
46 C2 Caldas Novas Brazil
116 B5 Caldervale Austr.
81 J2 Çaldıran Turkey
24 C3 Caldwell U.S.A.
32 D3 Caledon Can.
105 G5 Caledon r. Lesotho/S. Africa
104 C7 Caledon S. Africa
31 H4 Caledonia Can.
30 D4 Caledonia U.S.A.
116 C3 Calen Austr.
44 C7 Caleta Olivia Arg.
35 E5 Calexico U.S.A.
58 C3 Calf of Man i. U.K.
20 G4 Calgary Can.
29 C5 Calhoun U.S.A.
45 A4 Cali Col.
94 C4 Calicoan i. Phil.
83 E8 Calicut India
34 C3 Caliente CA U.S.A.
35 E3 Caliente NV U.S.A.
34 B3 California dir. U.S.A.
36 B2 California, Golfo de g. Mex.
34 B3 California Aqueduct canal U.S.A.
34 C4 California Hot Springs U.S.A.

81 M2 Cälilabad Azer.
25 D5 Calipatria U.S.A.
34 A2 Calistoga U.S.A.
104 D6 Calitzdorp S. Africa
114 D2 Callabonna, L. salt flat Austr.
34 A2 Callaghan, Mt mt U.S.A.
29 C6 Callahan U.S.A.
60 D5 Callan Rep. of Ireland
31 H2 Callander Can.
57 D4 Callander U.K.
42 C6 Callao Peru
35 F2 Callao U.S.A.
33 F4 Callicoon U.S.A.
116 D5 Callide Austr.
59 C7 Callington U.K.
116 D5 Calliope Austr.
31 G2 Callum Can.
20 G4 Calmar Can.
30 B4 Calmar U.S.A.
35 E4 Cal-Nev-Ari U.S.A.
29 D7 Caloosahatchee r. U.S.A.
115 K1 Caloundra Austr.
34 B2 Calpine U.S.A.
66 F6 Caltanissetta Italy
30 C2 Calumet U.S.A.
103 B5 Calunga Angola
103 B5 Caluquembe Angola
94 B4 Calusa i. Phil.
102 F2 Caluula Somalia
35 G5 Calva U.S.A.
113 G3 Calvert Hills Austr.
20 D4 Calvert I. i. Can.
66 C3 Calvi France
65 H3 Calvià Spain
104 C5 Calvinia S. Africa
66 F4 Calvo, Monte mt Italy
59 H5 Cam r. U.K.
46 E1 Camaçari Brazil
34 E2 Camache Reservoir resr U.S.A.
103 B5 Camacuio Angola
103 B5 Camacupa Angola
45 D2 Camaguán Venez.
37 J4 Camagüey Cuba
37 J4 Camagüey, Arch. de is Cuba
95 B4 Camah, Gunung mt Malaysia
Çamalan see Gülek
42 D7 Camana Peru
103 C5 Camanongue Angola
46 B2 Camapuã Brazil
47 G1 Camaquã Brazil
47 G1 Camaquã r. Brazil
80 E3 Çamardı Turkey
36 E3 Camargo Mex.
44 C6 Camarones Arg.
44 C6 Camarones, Bahía b. Arg.
24 B2 Camas U.S.A.
95 C3 Ca Mau Vietnam
Cambay see Khambhat
Cambay, Gulf of g. see Khambhat, Gulf of
59 G6 Camberley U.K.
70 Cambodia country Asia
59 B7 Camborne U.K.
64 F1 Cambrai France
34 B4 Cambria U.S.A.
59 D5 Cambrian Mountains reg. U.K.
31 G4 Cambridge Can.
117 E2 Cambridge N.Z.
59 H5 Cambridge U.K.
30 B5 Cambridge IL U.S.A.
33 H3 Cambridge MA U.S.A.
33 E5 Cambridge MD U.S.A.
26 E2 Cambridge MN U.S.A.
33 G3 Cambridge NY U.S.A.
32 C4 Cambridge OH U.S.A.
23 G2 Cambrien, Lac l. Can.
115 J5 Camden Austr.
29 C5 Camden AL U.S.A.
27 E5 Camden AR U.S.A.
33 J2 Camden ME U.S.A.
33 F5 Camden NJ U.S.A.
33 F3 Camden NY U.S.A.
29 D5 Camden SC U.S.A.
44 B8 Camden, Isla i. Chile
103 C5 Cameia, Parque Nacional da nat. park Angola
35 G4 Cameron AZ U.S.A.
27 E6 Cameron LA U.S.A.
26 E4 Cameron MO U.S.A.
27 D6 Cameron TX U.S.A.
30 B3 Cameron WV U.S.A.
95 B4 Cameron Highlands Malaysia
20 F3 Cameron Hills h. Can.
34 B2 Cameron Park U.S.A.
96 Cameroon country Africa
100 C4 Cameroun, Mt mt Cameroon
43 J4 Cametá Brazil
94 B2 Camiguin i. Phil.
94 C4 Camiguin i. Phil.
94 B3 Camiling Phil.
29 C6 Camilla U.S.A.
42 F8 Camiri Bol.
43 K4 Camocim Brazil
113 G3 Camooweal Austr.
94 C4 Camotes Sea g. Phil.
47 E2 Campana Arg.
45 A4 Campana, Co h. Col.
44 A7 Campana, I. i. Chile
47 B2 Campanario mt Arg./Chile
20 D4 Campania I. i. Can.
116 B3 Campaspe r. Austr.
104 E4 Campbell S. Africa
117 E4 Campbell, Cape c. N.Z.
14 G9 Campbell Plateau sea feature Pac. Oc.
20 D4 Campbell River Can.
31 J3 Campbells Bay Can.

28 C4 Campbellsville U.S.A.
23 G4 Campbellton Can.
115 G8 Campbell Town Austr.
57 C5 Campbeltown U.K.
36 F5 Campeche Mex.
36 F5 Campeche, Bahía de g. Mex.
114 E7 Camperdown Austr.
67 L2 Câmpina Romania
43 L5 Campina Grande Brazil
46 C3 Campinas Brazil
46 C2 Campina Verde Brazil
100 C4 Campo Cameroon
45 B4 Campoalegre Col.
66 F4 Campobasso Italy
46 D3 Campo Belo Brazil
43 H6 Campo de Diauarum Brazil
46 C2 Campo Florido Brazil
44 D3 Campo Gallo Arg.
46 A3 Campo Grande Brazil
43 K4 Campo Maior Brazil
65 C3 Campo Maior Port.
46 B4 Campo Mourão Brazil
46 E3 Campos Brazil
46 C3 Campos Altos Brazil
46 D3 Campos do Jordão Brazil
57 D4 Campsie Fells h. U.K.
32 B6 Campton KY U.S.A.
33 H3 Campton NH U.S.A.
67 L2 Câmpulung Romania
63 M7 Câmpulung Moldovenesc Romania
35 G4 Camp Verde U.S.A.
95 D3 Cam Ranh Vietnam
20 B4 Camrose Can.
59 B6 Camrose U.K.
21 G2 Camsell Lake l. Can.
21 H3 Camsell Portage Can.
69 C7 Can Turkey
33 G3 Čanaan U.S.A.
16 Canada country North America
47 E2 Cañada de Gómez Arg.
33 J4 Canada Falls Lake l. U.S.A.
27 C5 Canadian r. U.S.A.
45 E3 Canaima, Parque Nacional nat. park Venez.
33 F3 Canajoharie U.S.A.
69 C2 Çanakkale Turkey
Çanakkale Boğazı str. see Dardanelles
47 C2 Canalejas Arg.
32 E3 Canandaigua U.S.A.
32 E3 Canandaigua Lake l. U.S.A.
36 B2 Cananea Mex.
46 C4 Cananéia Brazil
45 C4 Canapiare, Co h. Col.
42 C4 Cañar Ecuador
Canarias, Islas is see Canary Islands
12 G4 Canary Basin sea feature Atlantic Ocean
100 A1 Canary Islands is Atlantic Ocean
33 F3 Canastota U.S.A.
46 C2 Canastra, Serra da mts Brazil
29 D6 Canaveral, Cape c. U.S.A.
65 E2 Cañaveras Spain
46 E1 Canavieiras Brazil
115 G3 Canbelego Austr.
115 H5 Canberra Austr.
24 B3 Canby CA U.S.A.
26 D2 Canby MN U.S.A.
36 G4 Cancún Mex.
25 F6 Candelaria Mex.
65 D2 Candeleda Spain
115 H6 Candelo Austr.
43 J4 Cândido Mendes Brazil
80 D1 Çandır Turkey
21 H4 Candle Lake Can.
21 H4 Candle Lake l. Can.
119 C1 Candlemas I. i. Atlantic Ocean
33 G4 Candlewood, Lake l. U.S.A.
26 D1 Cando U.S.A.
94 B2 Candon Phil.
47 B1 Canela Baja Chile
47 F2 Canelones Uru.
47 B3 Cañete Chile
65 F2 Cañete Spain
42 D6 Cangallo Peru
103 B5 Cangamba Angola
65 C1 Cangas del Narcea Spain
104 E6 Cango Caves caves S. Africa
43 L5 Canguaretama Brazil
47 G1 Canguçu Brazil
47 G1 Canguçu, Sa do h. Brazil
89 D6 Cangwu China
88 E2 Cangzhou China
23 G3 Caniapiscau Can.
23 G2 Caniapiscau r. Can.
23 G3 Caniapiscau, Lac resr Can.
66 E6 Canicattì Italy
20 E4 Canim Lake Can.
20 E4 Canim Lake l. Can.
43 L4 Canindé Brazil
43 K5 Canindé r. Brazil
57 C2 Canisp h. U.K.
32 E3 Canisteo U.S.A.
32 E3 Canisteo r. U.S.A.
80 D1 Çankırı Turkey
94 B4 Canlaon Phil.
20 F4 Canmore Can.
57 B3 Canna i. U.K.
83 E8 Cannanore India

64 H5 Cannes France
59 E5 Cannock U.K.
116 C3 Cannonvale Austr.
115 H6 Cann River Austr.
45 E2 Caño Araguao r. Venez.
44 F3 Canoas Brazil
21 H3 Canoe L. l. Can.
46 B4 Canoinhas Brazil
45 E2 Caño Macareo r. Venez.
45 E2 Caño Manamo r. Venez.
45 E2 Caño Mariusa r. Venez.
25 F4 Canon City U.S.A.
116 D4 Canoona Austr.
114 D4 Canopus Austr.
21 J4 Canora Can.
115 H4 Canowindra Austr.
23 H4 Canso, C. hd Can.
65 D1 Cantábrica, Cordillera mts Spain
Cantábrico, Mar sea see Biscay, Bay of
47 C2 Cantantal Arg.
45 C2 Cantaura Venez.
33 K2 Canterbury Can.
59 J6 Canterbury U.K.
117 C6 Canterbury Bight b. N.Z.
117 C5 Canterbury Plains plain N.Z.
95 C3 Cân Thơ Vietnam
94 C4 Cantilan Phil.
43 K5 Canto do Buriti Brazil
Canton see Guangzhou
30 B5 Canton IL U.S.A.
33 H2 Canton ME U.S.A.
30 B5 Canton MO U.S.A.
27 F5 Canton MS U.S.A.
33 F2 Canton NY U.S.A.
32 C4 Canton OH U.S.A.
32 E4 Canton PA U.S.A.
46 B4 Cantu r. Brazil
46 B4 Cantu, Serra do h. Brazil
47 E2 Cañuelas Arg.
43 G4 Canumã Brazil
115 K2 Canungra Austr.
42 F5 Canutama Brazil
117 D4 Canvastown N.Z.
59 H6 Canvey Island U.K.
21 H4 Canwood Can.
27 C5 Canyon U.S.A.
24 C2 Canyon City U.S.A.
35 H3 Canyon de Chelly National Monument res. U.S.A.
24 D2 Canyon Ferry L. l. U.S.A.
35 H2 Canyonlands National Park nat. park U.S.A.
20 D2 Canyon Ranges mts Can.
24 B3 Canyonville U.S.A.
89 C6 Cao Băng Vietnam
95 D2 Cao Nguyên Đắc Lắc plat. Vietnam
88 B3 Caoxian China
94 B5 Cap i. Phil.
45 D3 Capanaparo r. Venez.
43 J4 Capanema Brazil
46 B4 Capanema r. Brazil
46 C4 Capão Bonito Brazil
45 C3 Caparo r. Venez.
45 C4 Caparro, Co h. Brazil
94 B3 Capas Phil.
23 H4 Cap-aux-Meules Can.
23 F4 Cap-de-la-Madeleine Can.
116 D2 Cape r. Austr.
112 D6 Cape Arid National Park nat. park Austr.
115 H8 Cape Barren Island i. Austr.
12 K8 Cape Basin sea feature Atlantic Ocean
23 H4 Cape Breton Highlands Nat. Pk nat. park Can.
23 H4 Cape Breton Island i. Can.
23 J3 Cape Charles Can.
33 E6 Cape Charles U.S.A.
100 B4 Cape Coast Ghana
33 H4 Cape Cod Bay b. U.S.A.
33 J4 Cape Cod National Seashore res. U.S.A.
29 D7 Cape Coral U.S.A.
31 G3 Cape Croker Can.
18 Cape Farewell c. Greenland
29 E5 Cape Fear r. U.S.A.
27 F4 Cape Girardeau U.S.A.
14 D5 Cape Johnson Depth depth Pac. Oc.
46 D2 Capelinha Brazil
116 C4 Capelle Austr.
33 F5 Cape May U.S.A.
33 F5 Cape May Court House U.S.A.
33 F5 Cape May Pt pt U.S.A.
103 B4 Capenda-Camulemba Angola
112 B4 Cape Range National Park nat. park Austr.
23 J4 Cape St George Can.
23 H4 Cape Tormentine Can.
104 C6 Cape Town S. Africa
96 Cape Verde country Africa
12 G5 Cape Verde Basin sea feature Atlantic Ocean
12 F5 Cape Verde Fracture sea feature Atlantic Ocean
12 F5 Cape Verde Plateau sea feature Atlantic Ocean
33 G2 Cape Vincent U.S.A.
113 H2 Cape York Peninsula pen. Austr.
37 K5 Cap-Haïtien Haiti
43 J4 Capim r. Brazil

119 B2 Capitán Arturo Prat Chile Base Antarctica
46 A3 Capitán Bado Para.
25 C4 Capitan Peak mt U.S.A.
35 G2 Capitol Reef National Park nat. park U.S.A.
66 G3 Čapljina Bos.-Herz.
66 F5 Capo d'Orlando Italy
60 D5 Cappoquin Rep. of Ireland
66 C3 Capraia, Isola di i. Italy
66 F4 Capri, Isola di i. Italy
116 D4 Capricorn, C. pt Austr.
116 D4 Capricorn Channel chan. Austr.
116 E4 Capricorn Group atolls Austr.
103 C5 Caprivi Strip reg. Namibia
Cap St Jacques see Vung Tau
34 □² Captain Cook U.S.A.
115 H5 Captain's Flat Austr.
32 C5 Captina r. U.S.A.
94 C3 Capul i. Phil.
94 B3 Carabao i. Phil.
67 L2 Caracal Romania
45 E4 Caracarai Brazil
45 D2 Caracas Venez.
43 K5 Caracol Brazil
94 C5 Caraga Phil.
47 F2 Caraguatá r. Uru.
46 D3 Caraguatatuba Brazil
47 B3 Carahue Chile
46 E2 Caraí Brazil
46 D3 Carandaí Brazil
46 D3 Carangola Brazil
67 K2 Caransebeş Romania
114 B4 Carappee Hill h. Austr.
23 H4 Caraquet Can.
45 B3 Carare r. Col.
37 H5 Caratasca, Laguna lag. Honduras
46 D2 Caratinga Brazil
42 E4 Carauari Brazil
Carauná mt see Grande, Serra
65 F3 Caravaca de la Cruz Spain
46 E2 Caravelas Brazil
44 F3 Carazinho Brazil
26 D1 Carberry Can.
66 C5 Carbonara, Capo pt Italy
28 B4 Carbondale IL U.S.A.
33 F4 Carbondale PA U.S.A.
23 K4 Carbonear Can.
66 C5 Carbonia Italy
46 D2 Carbonita Brazil
65 F3 Carcaixent Spain
94 B4 Carcar Phil.
47 E2 Carcarañá r. Arg.
64 F5 Carcassonne France
20 C2 Carcross Can.
36 E4 Cárdenas Mex.
114 E2 Cardenyabba watercourse Austr.
44 F7 Cardiel, L. l. Arg.
59 D6 Cardiff U.K.
59 C5 Cardigan U.K.
59 C5 Cardigan Bay b. U.K.
33 F2 Cardinal Can.
32 B4 Cardington U.S.A.
47 F2 Cardona Uru.
46 C4 Cardoso, Ilha do i. Brazil
117 B6 Cardrona N.Z.
20 G5 Cardston Can.
116 B2 Cardwell Austr.
63 L7 Carei Romania
64 D2 Carentan France
32 B4 Carey U.S.A.
112 D5 Carey, L. salt flat Austr.
21 J2 Carey Lake l. Can.
13 J5 Cargados Carajos Islands is Mauritius
64 C2 Carhaix-Plouguer France
47 D3 Carhué Arg.
46 E3 Cariacica Brazil
45 E2 Cariaco Venez.
115 F5 Carrathool Austr.
65 F2 Cariñena Spain
46 D1 Carinhanha Brazil
46 D1 Carinhanha r. Brazil
45 E2 Caripe Venez.
45 E2 Caripito Venez.
60 D3 Cark Mountain h. Rep. of Ireland
31 J3 Carleton Place Can.
105 G3 Carletonville S. Africa
24 C3 Carlin U.S.A.
60 E3 Carlingford Lough in. Rep. of Ireland/U.K.
58 E3 Carlisle U.K.
32 A5 Carlisle KY U.S.A.
32 E4 Carlisle PA U.S.A.
64 C3 Carlit, Pic mt France
47 B2 Carlos Casares Arg.
46 E2 Carlos Chagas Brazil
60 E5 Carlow Rep. of Ireland
57 B2 Carloway U.K.
34 D5 Carlsbad CA U.S.A.
25 F5 Carlsbad NM U.S.A.
27 C6 Carlsbad TX U.S.A.

25 F5 Carlsbad Caverns Nat. Park nat. park U.S.A.
13 J3 Carlsberg Ridge sea feature Indian Ocean
57 E5 Carluke U.K.
21 J5 Carlyle Can.
20 B2 Carmacks Can.
21 K5 Carman Can.
59 C6 Carmarthen U.K.
59 C6 Carmarthen Bay b. U.K.
64 F4 Carmaux France
33 J2 Carmel U.S.A.
59 C4 Carmel Head hd U.K.
47 E2 Carmelo Uru.
45 B2 Carmen Col.
94 C4 Carmen Phil.
35 G6 Carmen U.S.A.
36 B3 Carmen, Isla i. Mex.
47 D4 Carmen de Patagones Arg.
47 C2 Carmensa Arg.
28 B4 Carmi U.S.A.
34 B2 Carmichael U.S.A.
116 C3 Carmila Austr.
65 D4 Carmona Spain
64 C3 Carnac France
112 B4 Carnarvon Austr.
104 E5 Carnarvon S. Africa
116 C5 Carnarvon Nat. Park nat. park Austr.
116 C5 Carnarvon Ra. mts Austr.
60 E4 Carndonagh Rep. of Ireland
59 D4 Carnedd Llywelyn mt U.K.
112 D5 Carnegie, L. salt flat Austr.
15 O6 Carnegie Ridge sea feature Pac. Oc.
57 C3 Carn Eighe mt U.K.
30 D3 Carney U.S.A.
119 A3 Carney I. i. Antarctica
58 E3 Carnforth U.K.
92 A5 Car Nicobar i. Andaman and Nicobar Is
60 F3 Carnlough U.K.
57 E4 Carn nan Gabhar mt U.K.
102 B3 Carnot C.A.R.
114 A5 Carnot, C. hd Austr.
57 F4 Carnoustie U.K.
60 E5 Carnsore Point pt Rep. of Ireland
57 E5 Carnwath U.K.
31 F4 Caro U.S.A.
116 E2 Carola Cay rf Coral Sea Is Terr.
29 D7 Carol City U.S.A.
43 J5 Carolina Brazil
105 J3 Carolina S. Africa
109 Caroline Island i. Pac. Oc.
117 A6 Caroline Pk summit N.Z.
104 B3 Carolusberg S. Africa
45 E2 Caroní r. Venez.
45 C2 Corora Venez.
35 E3 Carp U.S.A.
115 K2 Carp Austr.
45 D4 Carpentaria, Canal r. Venez.
113 G2 Carpentaria, Gulf of g. Austr.
116 A2 Carpentaria Downs Austr.
64 G4 Carpentras France
66 D2 Carpi Italy
43 L5 Carpina Brazil
34 C4 Carpinteria U.S.A.
21 J5 Carpio U.S.A.
20 E4 Carp Lake Prov. Park res. Can.
60 B4 Carra, Lough l. Rep. of Ireland
33 H2 Carrabassett U.S.A.
29 C6 Carrabelle U.S.A.
45 B2 Carraipía Col.
60 B6 Carran h. Rep. of Ireland
60 B6 Carrantuohill mt Rep. of Ireland
47 B2 Carranza, C. pt Chile
45 E3 Carrao r. Venez.
66 D2 Carrara Italy
115 F5 Carrathool Austr.
47 C3 Carrero, Co m Arg.
45 E1 Carriacou i. Grenada
57 D5 Carrick U.K.
60 F3 Carrickfergus U.K.
60 E4 Carrickmacross Rep. of Ireland
60 D3 Carrick-on-Shannon Rep. of Ireland
60 D5 Carrick-on-Suir Rep. of Ireland
114 C4 Carrieton Austr.
60 D4 Carrigallen Rep. of Ireland
60 C6 Carrigtwohill Rep. of Ireland
114 C4 Carri Lafquén, L. l. Arg.
27 B7 Carrillo Mex.
26 D2 Carrington U.S.A.
44 B3 Carrizal Bajo Chile
35 H4 Carrizo AZ U.S.A.
35 G4 Carrizo AZ U.S.A.
34 D5 Carrizo Cr. r. U.S.A.
27 D6 Carrizo Springs U.S.A.
25 F5 Carrizozo U.S.A.
26 E3 Carroll U.S.A.
29 C5 Carrollton GA U.S.A.
28 C4 Carrollton KY U.S.A.
26 E4 Carrollton MO U.S.A.
32 C4 Carrollton OH U.S.A.
21 J4 Carrot r. Can.
21 J4 Carrot River Can.
58 E3 Carrowdore U.K.
60 B3 Carrowmore Lake l. Rep. of Ireland
33 F2 Carry Falls Reservoir resr U.S.A.

80 F1 Çarşamba Turkey
30 E4 Čarson City MI U.S.A.
34 C2 Carson City NV U.S.A.
34 C2 Carson Lake l. U.S.A.
34 C2 Carson Sink l. U.S.A.
31 F4 Carsonville U.S.A.
47 B2 Cartagena Chile
45 B2 Cartagena Col.
65 F4 Cartagena Spain
45 B3 Cartago Col.
37 H7 Cartago Costa Rica
29 C5 Cartersville U.S.A.
30 B5 Carthage IL U.S.A.
27 E5 Carthage MO U.S.A.
33 F2 Carthage NY U.S.A.
27 E5 Carthage TX U.S.A.
31 G2 Cartier Can.
112 D2 Cartier Island i. Ashmore and Cartier Is
58 E3 Cartmel U.K.
23 J3 Cartwright Can.
43 L5 Caruaru Brazil
45 E2 Carúpano Venez.
34 D2 Carvers U.S.A.
61 A4 Carvin France
116 B5 Carwell Austr.
29 E5 Cary U.S.A.
114 E2 Caryapundy Swamp swamp Austr.
100 B1 Casablanca Morocco
46 C3 Casa Branca Brazil
25 E6 Casa de Janos Mex.
35 G5 Casa Grande U.S.A.
35 G5 Casa Grande National Monument res. U.S.A.
66 C2 Casale Monferrato Italy
66 D2 Casalmaggiore Italy
45 C3 Casanare r. Col.
67 H4 Casarano Italy
25 F6 Casas Grandes Mex.
25 E6 Casas Grandes mts Mex.
117 B6 Cascade d. N.Z.
30 A4 Cascade IA U.S.A.
24 C2 Cascade ID U.S.A.
24 E2 Cascade MT U.S.A.
117 B6 Cascade Pt pt N.Z.
24 B3 Cascade Range mts U.S.A.
24 C2 Cascade Res. resr U.S.A.
65 B3 Cascais Port.
46 B4 Cascavel Brazil
33 J3 Casco Bay b. U.S.A.
66 F4 Caserta Italy
31 F4 Caseville U.S.A.
119 C6 Casey Austr. Base Antarctica
119 D4 Casey Bay b. Antarctica
102 F2 Caseyr, Raas c. Somalia
60 D5 Cashel Rep. of Ireland
60 H1 Cashmere Austr.
30 B4 Cashton U.S.A.
45 C2 Casigua Falcón Venez.
45 B2 Casigua Zulia Venez.
94 B2 Casiguran Phil.
47 E2 Casilda Arg.
115 K2 Casino Austr.
45 D4 Casiquiare, Canal r. Venez.
42 C5 Casma Peru
30 E4 Casnovia U.S.A.
34 A2 Caspar U.S.A.
65 F2 Caspe Spain
24 F3 Casper U.S.A.
Caspian Lowland lowland see Prikaspiyskaya Nizmennost'
32 D5 Cass U.S.A.
31 F4 Cass r. U.S.A.
32 D3 Cassadaga U.S.A.
103 C5 Cassai Angola
31 F4 Cass City U.S.A.
33 F2 Casselman Can.
20 D3 Cassiar Can.
20 C3 Cassiar Mountains mts Can.
115 G3 Cassilis Austr.
66 F4 Cassino Italy
26 E2 Cass Lake U.S.A.
43 J4 Castanhal Brazil
47 C3 Castaño r. Arg.
27 C7 Castaños Mex.
47 C3 Castaño Viejo Arg.
66 D2 Castelfranco Veneto Italy
64 E4 Casteljaloux France
66 F4 Castellammare di Stabia Italy
47 F3 Castelli Arg.
65 F3 Castelló de la Plana Spain
65 C3 Castelo Branco Port.
65 C3 Castelo de Vide Port.
66 C6 Castelsardo Italy
66 E6 Casteltermini Italy
66 E6 Castelvetrano Italy
114 D6 Casterton Austr.
23 G2 Castignon, Lac l. Can.
65 E3 Castilla - La Mancha div. Spain
65 D2 Castilla y León div. Spain
45 C2 Castilletes Col.
47 G2 Castillos Uru.
60 B4 Castlebar Rep. of Ireland
57 A4 Castlebay U.K.
60 E4 Castlebellingham Rep. of Ireland
60 E3 Castleblayney Rep. of Ireland
60 E5 Castlebridge Rep. of Ireland
58 E3 Castle Carrock U.K.
59 E6 Castle Cary U.K.
35 G2 Castle Dale U.S.A.
60 D3 Castlederg U.K.

60 E5 Castledermot Rep. of Ireland
35 E5 Castle Dome Mts mts U.S.A.
59 F5 Castle Donington U.K.
57 D6 Castle Douglas U.K.
58 F4 Castleford U.K.
20 F5 Castlegar Can.
60 A5 Castlegregory Rep. of Ireland
60 B5 Castleisland Rep. of Ireland
114 F6 Castlemaine Austr.
60 B5 Castlemaine Rep. of Ireland
60 C6 Castlemartyr Rep. of Ireland
34 D4 Castle Mt mt U.S.A.
117 F4 Castlepoint N.Z.
60 D4 Castlepollard Rep. of Ireland
60 C4 Castlerea Rep. of Ireland
115 H3 Castlereagh r. Austr.
25 F4 Castle Rock U.S.A.
30 B4 Castle Rock Lake l. U.S.A.
58 C3 Castletown Isle of Man
60 D5 Castletown Rep. of Ireland
21 G4 Castor Can.
64 F5 Castres France
61 C2 Castricum Neth.
37 M6 Castries St Lucia
46 C4 Castro Brazil
44 B6 Castro Chile
65 D4 Castro del Río Spain
65 E1 Castro-Urdiales Spain
65 B4 Castro Verde Port.
66 G5 Castrovillari Italy
34 B3 Castroville U.S.A.
117 A6 Caswell Sd in. N.Z.
81 H2 Cat Turkey
42 B5 Catacaos Peru
46 D3 Cataguases Brazil
27 E6 Catahoula L. l. U.S.A.
94 B3 Catal Phil.
81 J3 Çatak Turkey
46 C2 Catalão Brazil
Catalonia div. see Cataluña
65 G2 Cataluña div. Spain
44 C3 Catamarca Arg.
94 C3 Catanduanes i. Phil.
46 B3 Catanduvas Brazil
66 F6 Catania Italy
66 G5 Catanzaro Italy
27 D6 Catarina U.S.A.
94 C3 Catarman Phil.
65 F3 Catarroja Spain
114 A5 Catastrophe, C. hd Austr.
45 C2 Catatumbo r. Venez.
89 C6 Cat Ba, Đao i. Vietnam
94 C4 Catbalogan Phil.
29 E7 Cat Cays is Bahamas
94 C5 Cateel Phil.
94 C5 Cateel Bay b. Phil.
105 K3 Catembe Moz.
115 H6 Cathercart Austr.
105 G6 Cathcart S. Africa
105 H4 Cathedral Peak mt S. Africa
60 A6 Catherdaniel Rep. of Ireland
35 F2 Catherine, Mt mt U.S.A.
43 J3 Catillo Chile
29 E7 Cat Island i. Bahamas
22 B3 Cat L. l. Can.
36 G4 Catoche, C. c. Mex.
32 E5 Catonsville U.S.A.
47 D3 Catriló Brazil
45 E4 Catrimani Brazil
45 E4 Catrimani r. Brazil
61 A4 Cats, Mont des h. France
33 G3 Catskill U.S.A.
33 F4 Catskill Mts mts U.S.A.
105 K3 Catuane Moz.
45 E4 Cauamé r. Brazil
94 B4 Cauayan Phil.
23 H2 Caubvick, Mount mt Can.
45 B3 Cauca r. Col.
43 L4 Caucaia Brazil
45 B3 Caucasia Col.
47 C1 Caucete Arg.
33 J1 Caucomgomoc Lake l. U.S.A.
61 B4 Caudry France
94 C4 Cauit Point pt Phil.
47 B2 Cauquenes Chile
45 D3 Caura r. Venez.
23 H4 Causapscal Can.
64 G5 Cavaillon France
46 C1 Cavalcante Brazil
60 D4 Cavan Rep. of Ireland
27 F4 Cave City U.S.A.
46 E1 Caveira r. Brazil
114 E6 Cavendish Austr.
46 A3 Cavernoso, Serra do mts Brazil
32 B5 Cave Run Lake l. U.S.A.
94 B4 Cavili rf Phil.
94 B3 Cavite Phil.
57 E3 Cawdor U.K.
114 D4 Cawndilla Lake l. Austr.
59 J5 Cawston U.K.
43 K4 Caxias Brazil
44 F3 Caxias do Sul Brazil
103 B4 Caxito Angola
80 C2 Çay Turkey
29 C5 Çayce U.S.A.
80 D1 Çaycuma Turkey
81 H1 Çayeli Turkey
43 H3 Cayenne Fr. Guiana
80 E3 Çayhan Turkey
80 E3 Cayhan Turkey
80 D1 Çayırhan Turkey
37 J5 Cayman Brac i. Cayman Is

37 H5 Cayman Islands terr. Caribbean
102 E3 Caynabo Somalia
31 H4 Cayuga Can.
32 E3 Cayuga U.S.A.
33 F3 Cazenovia U.S.A.
103 C5 Cazombo Angola
27 B7 Ceballos Mex.
47 F2 Ceballatí r. Uru.
94 B4 Cebu Phil.
94 B4 Cebu i. Phil.
30 C3 Cecil U.S.A.
115 J1 Cecil Plains Austr.
66 D3 Cecina Italy
30 A4 Cedar r. IA U.S.A.
26 C2 Cedar r. ND U.S.A.
30 D4 Cedarburg U.S.A.
35 F3 Cedar City U.S.A.
27 D5 Cedar Creek Res. resr U.S.A.
30 A4 Cedar Falls U.S.A.
30 D4 Cedar Grove WV U.S.A.
32 C5 Cedar Grove WV U.S.A.
33 F6 Cedar L. i. Can.
21 J4 Cedar L. l. Can.
30 D5 Cedar Lake l. U.S.A.
32 B4 Cedar Pt pt U.S.A.
30 B5 Cedar Rapids U.S.A.
35 G3 Cedar Ridge U.S.A.
33 F5 Cedar Run U.S.A.
31 F4 Cedar Springs Can.
30 E4 Cedar Springs U.S.A.
29 C5 Cedartown U.S.A.
105 H5 Cedarville S. Africa
30 E3 Cedarville U.S.A.
36 A3 Cedros, Isla i. Mex.
113 F6 Ceduna Austr.
102 E3 Ceeldheere Somalia
102 E2 Ceerigaabo Somalia
66 F5 Cefalù Italy
63 J7 Cegléd Hungary
89 B5 Ceheng China
80 E1 Çekerek Turkey
95 B4 Čelah, Gunung mt Malaysia
36 D4 Celaya Mex.
60 E4 Celbridge Rep. of Ireland
Celebes i. see Sulawesi
93 G6 Celebes Sea sea Indon./Phil.
32 A4 Celina U.S.A.
66 F1 Celje Slovenia
62 E4 Celle Ger.
56 C6 Celtic Sea sea Rep. of Ireland/U.K.
80 E1 Cemilbey Turkey
80 G2 Çemişgezek Turkey
93 K7 Cenderawasih, Teluk b. Indon.
89 C5 Cengong China
35 F5 Centennial Wash r. U.S.A.
27 E6 Center U.S.A.
33 G4 Centereach U.S.A.
29 C5 Center Point U.S.A.
32 B5 Centerville U.S.A.
29 C5 Centerville U.S.A.
105 G1 Central div. Botswana
45 A4 Central, Cordillera mts Col.
42 C5 Central, Cordillera mts Peru
94 B2 Central, Cordillera mts Phil.
96 Central African Republic country Africa
79 K4 Central Brahui Ra. mts Pak.
30 B4 Central City IA U.S.A.
26 D3 Central City NE U.S.A.
28 B4 Centralia IL U.S.A.
24 B2 Centralia WA U.S.A.
30 A2 Central Lakes U.S.A.
24 B3 Central Point U.S.A.
110 E2 Central Ra. mts P.N.G.
Central Russian Upland reg. see Sredne-Russkaya Vozvyshennost'
74 Central Siberian Plateau plat. Rus. Fed.
89 D6 Cenxi China
Cephalonia i. see Kefallonia
Ceram i. see Seram
Ceram Sea g. see Seram Sea
35 E4 Cerbat Mts mts U.S.A.
21 G4 Cereal Can.
44 D3 Ceres Arg.
104 C6 Ceres S. Africa
45 B2 Cereté Col.
65 E2 Cerezo de Abajo Spain
66 F4 Cerignola Italy
80 D2 Çerikli Turkey
80 E1 Çerkeş Turkey
80 G3 Çermelik Deresi r. Syria
81 G2 Çermik Turkey
67 N2 Cernavodă Romania
27 D7 Cerralvo Mex.
36 C4 Cerralvo, Isla i. Mex.
67 H4 Cërrik Albania
36 D4 Cerritos Mex.
46 C4 Cerro Azul Brazil
42 C6 Cerro de Pasco Peru
45 D3 Cerro Jáua, Meseta del plat. Venez.
45 C2 Cerrón, C. mt Venez.
47 C3 Cerros Colorados, Embalse resr Arg.
42 B4 Cerros de Amotape, Parque Nacional nat. park Peru
66 F2 Cervati, Monte mt Italy
66 C3 Cervione France
65 C1 Cervo Spain

45 B2 César r. Col.
66 E2 Cesena Italy
55 T8 Cēsis Latvia
62 G6 České Budějovice Czech Rep.
62 G6 Český Krumlov Czech Rep.
62 F6 Český Les mts Czech Rep./Ger.
67 M5 Çeşme Turkey
115 J4 Cessnock Austr.
67 H3 Cetinje Yugo.
66 F5 Cetraro Italy
65 D5 Ceuta Spain
111 H4 Ceva-i-Ra rf Fiji
64 F4 Cévennes mts France
80 E3 Ceyhan Turkey
80 E3 Ceyhan r. Turkey
81 H3 Ceylanpınar Turkey
79 J4 Chābahār Iran
85 E3 Chabyêr Caka salt l. China
47 E2 Chacabuco Arg.
47 B4 Chacao Chile
47 C3 Chachahuén, Sa mt Arg.
42 C5 Chachapoyas Peru
68 D4 Chachersk Belarus
95 B2 Chachoengsao Thai.
84 B4 Chachro Pak.
20 C4 Chacon, C. c. U.S.A.
96 Chad country Africa
101 D3 Chad, Lake l. Africa
86 H2 Chadaasan Mongolia
86 F1 Chadan Rus. Fed.
105 G1 Chadibe Botswana
47 C3 Chadileo r. Arg.
26 C3 Chadron U.S.A.
95 A1 Chae Hom Thai.
45 B4 Chafurray Col.
85 F2 Chagdo Kangri reg. China
79 K3 Chaghcharān Afgh.
64 G3 Chagny France
13 J4 Chagos Archipelago is British Indian Ocean Territory
13 J4 Chagos-Laccadive Ridge sea feature Indian Ocean
68 J4 Chagra r. Rus. Fed.
45 D2 Chaguaramas Venez.
85 D2 Cha'gyüngoinba China
81 L3 Chāhār Ṭāq Iran
81 K4 Chah-i-Shurkh Iraq
85 F5 Chāībāsa India
23 G3 Chaigneau, Lac l. Can.
95 B2 Chainat Thai.
95 B2 Chai Si r. Thai.
89 □ Chai Wan China
95 A3 Chaiya Thai.
95 B2 Chaiyaphum Thai.
47 F1 Chajari Arg.
84 B3 Chakar r. Pak.
85 H5 Chakaria Bangl.
85 E4 Chakia India
42 D7 Chala Peru
36 G6 Chalatenango El Salvador
23 G4 Chaleur Bay in. Can.
89 D5 Chaling China
84 C5 Chalisgaon India
67 K5 Chalkida Greece
117 A7 Chalky Inlet in. N.Z.
64 D3 Challans France
42 E7 Challapata Bol.
14 E5 Challenger Deep sea feature N. Pacific Ocean
15 M8 Challenger Fracture Zone sea feature Pac. Oc.
15 M8 Challis U.S.A.
64 G2 Châlons-en-Champagne France
64 G3 Chalon-sur-Saône France
62 F6 Cham Ger.
25 F4 Chama U.S.A.
45 C2 Chama r. Venez.
103 D5 Chama Zambia
47 D2 Chamaico Arg.
104 A3 Chamais Bay b. Namibia
79 K3 Chaman Pak.
84 D4 Chambal r. India
23 G3 Chambeaux, Lac l. Can.
21 H4 Chamberlain Can.
26 D3 Chamberlain U.S.A.
33 J1 Chamberlain Lake l. U.S.A.
35 H4 Chambers U.S.A.
32 E5 Chambersburg U.S.A.
64 G4 Chambéry France
103 D5 Chambeshi Zambia
66 C7 Chambi, Jebel mt Tunisia
64 G4 Chamechaude mt France
81 M5 Chameshk Iran
47 C1 Chamical Arg.
85 F4 Chamlang mt Nepal
95 B3 Châmnar Cambodia
85 E5 Champa India
20 B2 Champagne Can.
64 G2 Champagne reg. France
105 H4 Champagne Castle mt S. Africa
64 G3 Champagnole France
30 C5 Champaign U.S.A.
47 D1 Champaqui, Cerro mt Arg.
95 C2 Champasak Laos
85 H5 Champhai India
30 D2 Champion U.S.A.
33 G2 Champlain U.S.A.
33 G2 Champlain, L. l. Can./U.S.A.
36 F5 Champotón Mex.
68 H4 Chamzinka Rus. Fed.
95 A3 Chan, Ko i. Thai.
95 B4 Chana Thai.
44 B3 Chañaral Chile

45 E3 Chanaro, Co mt Venez.
47 B2 Chanco Chile
Chanda see Chandrapur
85 E5 Chandarpur India
84 D3 Chandausi India
27 F6 Chandeleur Islands is U.S.A.
84 E5 Chandia India
84 D3 Chandigarh India
35 G5 Chandler U.S.A.
31 J3 Chandos Lake l. Can.
85 G5 Chandpur Bangl.
84 D3 Chandpur India
85 H5 Chandraghona Bangl.
84 D6 Chandrapur India
84 D3 Chandur India
95 B2 Chang, Ko i. Thai.
103 D6 Changane r. Moz.
103 D5 Changara Moz.
87 N3 Changbai China
89 C7 Changcheng China
119 B1 Chang Cheng (Great Wall) China Base Antarctica
88 F2 Changdao China
89 D4 Changde China
88 D3 Changfeng China
91 A6 Changgi-ap pt S. Korea
88 G2 Changhai China
89 F5 Changhua Taiwan
95 D1 Changhua Jiang r. China
95 □ Changi Sing.
95 □ Changi airport Sing.
89 C7 Changjiang China
Chang Jiang r. see Yangtze
Changjiang Kou est. see Yangtze, Mouth of the
89 F5 Changle China
88 F2 Changli China
89 D5 Changning China
88 E1 Changping China
91 A6 Changp'yŏng S. Korea
89 F4 Changshan China
88 G2 Changshan Qundao is China
89 C4 Changshou China
89 D4 Changshoujie China
88 F4 Changshu China
89 C5 Changshun China
89 E5 Changtai China
89 E5 Changting China
90 A2 Changtu China
88 G1 Changtu China
91 A7 Ch'angwŏn S. Korea
88 C3 Changwu China
88 F2 Changxing Dao i. China
89 D4 Changyang China
88 F2 Changyi China
88 E3 Changyuan China
88 D2 Changzhi China
88 F3 Changzhou China
67 L7 Chania Greece
88 B3 Chankou China
56 E7 Channel Islands is English Channel
34 C5 Channel Islands is U.S.A.
34 B5 Channel Is Nat. Park nat. park U.S.A.
23 J4 Channel-Port-aux-Basques Can.
59 J6 Channel Tunnel tunnel France/U.K.
30 C2 Channing U.S.A.
65 C1 Chantada Spain
95 B2 Chanthaburi Thai.
64 F2 Chantilly France
27 E4 Chanute U.S.A.
76 J4 Chany, Ozero salt l. Rus. Fed.
88 E2 Chaobai Xinhe r. China
88 E4 Chaohu China
88 E4 Chao Hu l. China
95 B2 Chao Phraya r. Thai.
100 B1 Chaouèn Morocco
85 H2 Chaowula Shan mts China
89 E6 Chaoyang Guangdong China
88 F1 Chaoyang Liaoning China
89 E6 Chaozhou China
46 E1 Chapada Diamantina, Parque Nacional nat. park Brazil
46 A1 Chapada dos Guimarães Brazil
46 C1 Chapada dos Veadeiros, Parque Nacional da nat. park Brazil
36 D4 Chapala, L. de l. Mex.
45 B4 Chaparral Col.
76 G4 Chapayevo Kazak.
68 J4 Chapayevsk Rus. Fed.
44 F3 Chapecó Brazil
44 F3 Chapecó r. Brazil
59 F4 Chapel-en-le-Frith U.K.
29 E5 Chapel Hill U.S.A.
59 F4 Chapeltown U.K.
30 D5 Chapin, Lake l. U.S.A.
31 F2 Chapleau Can.
68 F4 Chaplygin Rus. Fed.
69 E6 Chaplynka Ukr.
32 B6 Chapmanville U.S.A.
115 G8 Chappell Is is Austr.
42 E7 Chaqui Bol.
84 D2 Char Jammu and Kashmir
85 H3 Char Chu r. China
21 G3 Chard Can.
59 E7 Chard U.K.
81 L5 Chardāvol Iran
32 C4 Chardon U.S.A.

79 J2 Chardzhev Turkm.
64 E3 Charente r. France
84 B2 Chārīkār Afgh.
28 E3 Chariton r. U.S.A.
31 F3 Charity Is l. U.S.A.
76 G3 Charkayuvom Rus. Fed.
84 D4 Charkhari India
61 C4 Charleroi Belgium
30 A4 Charles City U.S.A.
117 C4 Charleston N.Z.
28 B4 Charleston IL U.S.A.
33 J2 Charleston ME U.S.A.
27 F4 Charleston MO U.S.A.
29 E5 Charleston SC U.S.A.
32 C5 Charleston WV U.S.A.
35 E3 Charleston Peak summit U.S.A.
60 Charlestown Rep. of Ireland
33 G3 Charlestown NH U.S.A.
33 H4 Charlestown RI U.S.A.
32 E5 Charles Town U.S.A.
116 B6 Charleville Austr.
64 G2 Charleville-Mézières France
30 E3 Charlevoix U.S.A.
20 E3 Charlie Lake Can.
30 E4 Charlotte MI U.S.A.
29 D5 Charlotte NC U.S.A.
29 D7 Charlotte Harbor b. U.S.A.
32 D5 Charlottesville U.S.A.
23 H4 Charlottetown Can.
45 E2 Charlotteville Trinidad and Tobago
114 E6 Charlton Austr.
22 E3 Charlton I. i. Can.
68 F2 Charozero Rus. Fed.
84 B2 Charsadda Pak.
116 B3 Charters Towers Austr.
64 E2 Chartres France
47 C1 Chascomús Arg.
20 F4 Chase Can.
68 D4 Chashniki Belarus
117 B7 Chaslands Mistake c. N.Z.
64 D3 Châteaubriant France
64 E3 Château-du-Loir France
64 E2 Châteaudun France
33 F2 Chateaugay U.S.A.
33 G2 Châteauguay Can.
64 B2 Châteaulin France
64 F3 Châteauneuf-sur-Loire France
64 E3 Châteauroux France
64 F2 Château-Thierry France
61 C4 Châtelet Belgium
64 E3 Châtellerault France
30 A4 Chatfield U.S.A.
23 G4 Chatham N.B. Can.
31 F4 Chatham Ont. Can.
59 H6 Chatham U.K.
33 H4 Chatham MA U.S.A.
33 G3 Chatham NY U.S.A.
32 D6 Chatham VA U.S.A.
111 J6 Chatham Islands is N.Z.
20 C4 Chatham Sd chan. Can.
20 C3 Chatham Strait chan. U.S.A.
84 F4 Chatra India
31 G3 Chatsworth Can.
30 C5 Chatsworth U.S.A.
29 C5 Chattanooga U.S.A.
59 H5 Chatteris U.K.
95 B2 Chatturat Thai.
95 C3 Châu Đốc Vietnam
84 B4 Chauhtan India
85 H5 Chauk Myanmar
84 E4 Chauka r. India
64 G2 Chaumont France
95 A2 Chaungwabyin Myanmar
77 S3 Chaunskaya Guba b. Rus. Fed.
64 F2 Chauny France
85 F4 Chauparan India
32 D3 Chautauqua, Lake l. U.S.A.
81 L5 Chavār Iran
43 J4 Chaves Brazil
65 C2 Chaves Port.
22 E2 Chavigny, Lac l. Can.
68 D4 Chavusy Belarus
84 A3 Chawal r. Pak.
89 B6 Chây r. Vietnam
Chāyul see Qayü
47 D2 Chazón Arg.
33 G2 Chazy U.S.A.
59 F5 Cheadle U.K.
32 D5 Cheat r. U.S.A.
62 F5 Cheb Czech Rep.
66 D7 Chebba Tunisia
68 H3 Cheboksary Rus. Fed.
30 E3 Cheboygan U.S.A.
69 H7 Chechen', Ostrov i. Rus. Fed.
69 H7 Chechenskaya Respublika div. Rus. Fed.
27 E5 Checotah U.S.A.
59 E6 Cheddar U.K.
21 G3 Checham Can.
116 A6 Cheepie Austr.
77 V3 Chefornak Alaska
105 K1 Chefu Moz.
100 B2 Chegga Maur.
103 D5 Chegutu Zimbabwe
24 B2 Chehalis U.S.A.
84 B2 Chehardar Pass pass Afgh.
81 L5 Cheharīz Iraq
87 N5 Cheju-do i. S. Korea
87 N5 Cheju-haehyŏp chan. S. Korea
68 F4 Chekhov Rus. Fed.
32 C4 Chelan, L. l. U.S.A.

79 G2 Cheleken Turkm.
47 C3 Chelforó Arg.
65 G4 Chélif, Oued r. Alg.
76 G5 Chelkar Kazak.
63 L5 Chełm Pol.
59 H6 Chelmer r. U.K.
63 J4 Chełmno Pol.
59 H6 Chelmsford U.K.
33 H3 Chelmsford U.S.A.
59 E6 Cheltenham U.K.
65 F3 Chelva Spain
76 H4 Chelyabinsk Rus. Fed.
103 D5 Chemba Moz.
84 D2 Chem Co l. China
62 F5 Chemnitz Ger.
32 E3 Chemung r. U.S.A.
84 B3 Chenab r. Pak.
100 B2 Chenachane Alg.
33 F3 Chenango r. U.S.A.
24 C2 Cheney U.S.A.
27 D4 Cheney Res. resr U.S.A.
88 E2 Cheng'an China
89 D5 Chengbu China
88 E1 Chengde China
89 B4 Chengdu China
88 C3 Chenggu China
89 E6 Chenghai China
88 C3 Chengkou China
89 D7 Chengmai China
88 F3 Cheniu Shan i. China
83 F8 Chennai India
Chennai see Chennai
30 C5 Chenoa U.S.A.
89 D5 Chenxi China
89 D5 Chenzhou China
95 D2 Cheo Reo Vietnam
42 C5 Chepén Peru
47 C1 Chepes Arg.
59 E6 Chepstow U.K.
68 J3 Cheptsa r. Rus. Fed.
81 L5 Cheqād Kabūd Iran
30 B2 Chequamegon Bay b. U.S.A.
64 F3 Cher r. France
29 E5 Cheraw U.S.A.
64 D2 Cherbourg France
65 G4 Cherchell Alg.
68 J4 Cherdakly Rus. Fed.
77 M4 Cheremkhovo Rus. Fed.
90 D2 Cheremshany Rus. Fed.
68 H2 Cherepovets Rus. Fed.
68 H2 Cherevkovo Rus. Fed.
69 E5 Chéria Alg.
69 G6 Cherkasy Ukr.
69 G6 Cherkessk Rus. Fed.
103 C5 Chermenze Angola
76 K2 Chernaya Rus. Fed.
68 J3 Chernaya Kholunitsa Rus. Fed.
90 C2 Chernigovka Rus. Fed.
69 D5 Chernihiv Ukr.
69 F6 Cherninivka Ukr.
69 C5 Chernivtsi Ukr.
86 F1 Chernogorsk Rus. Fed.
68 H3 Chernovskoye Rus. Fed.
Chernoye More sea see Black Sea
69 C6 Chernyakhiv Ukr.
63 K3 Chernyakhovsk Rus. Fed.
69 F5 Chernyanka Rus. Fed.
87 L1 Chernyshevsk Rus. Fed.
77 N3 Chernyshevskiy Rus. Fed.
69 H6 Chernyye Zemli reg. Rus. Fed.
69 H5 Chernyy Yar Rus. Fed.
26 E3 Cherokee IA U.S.A.
27 D4 Cherokee OK U.S.A.
27 C4 Cherokees, Lake o' the l. U.S.A.
29 E7 Cherokee Sound Bahamas
47 B3 Cherquenco Chile
85 G4 Cherrapunji India
35 E2 Cherry Creek U.S.A.
35 E1 Cherry Creek Mts mts U.S.A.
33 K2 Cherryfield U.S.A.
111 G3 Cherry Island i. Solomon Is
31 J4 Cherry Valley Can.
33 F3 Cherry Valley U.S.A.
77 Q3 Cherskogo, Khrebet mts Rus. Fed.
69 G5 Chertkovo Rus. Fed.
68 J2 Cherva Rus. Fed.
67 L3 Cherven Bryag Bulg.
69 C5 Chervonohrad Ukr.
69 E5 Chervonozavods'ke Ukr.
68 C4 Chervyen' Belarus
59 F6 Cherwell r. U.K.
68 D4 Cherykaw Belarus
31 E4 Chesaning U.S.A.
33 E5 Chesapeake U.S.A.
33 E5 Chesapeake Bay b. U.S.A.
59 G6 Chesham U.K.
33 G3 Cheshire U.S.A.
59 E4 Cheshire Plain lowland U.K.
76 F3 Cheshskaya Guba b. Rus. Fed.
59 G6 Cheshunt U.K.
59 E4 Chester U.K.
34 B1 Chester CA U.S.A.
28 B4 Chester IL U.S.A.
24 E1 Chester MT U.S.A.
33 F5 Chester PA U.S.A.
29 D5 Chester SC U.S.A.
33 E5 Chester U.S.A.
59 F4 Chesterfield U.K.
111 F2 Chesterfield, Îles is New Caledonia
21 L2 Chesterfield Inlet Can.
21 L2 Chesterfield Inlet in. Can.
58 F3 Chester-le-Street U.K.

33 E5 Chestertown MD U.S.A.
33 G3 Chestertown NY U.S.A.
33 F2 Chesterville Can.
32 D4 Chestnut Ridge ridge U.S.A.
33 J1 Chesuncook U.S.A.
33 J1 Chesuncook Lake l. U.S.A.
66 B6 Chetaïbi Alg.
23 H4 Chéticamp Can.
83 D8 Chetlat i. India
36 G5 Chetumal Mex.
20 E3 Chetwynd Can.
89 □ Cheung Chau China
117 D5 Cheviot N.Z.
58 E2 Cheviot Hills h. U.K.
24 C1 Chewelah U.S.A.
27 D5 Cheyenne U.S.A.
24 F3 Cheyenne WY U.S.A.
26 C3 Cheyenne r. U.S.A.
26 C4 Cheyenne Wells U.S.A.
20 E4 Chezacut Can.
84 C4 Chhapar India
85 F4 Chhapra India
84 D4 Chhatarpur India
84 B3 Chhatr Pak.
84 D5 Chhindwara India
84 C5 Chhota Udepur India
84 C4 Chhoti Sadri India
85 G4 Chhukha Bhutan
89 F6 Chiai Taiwan
95 A1 Chiang Dao Thai.
95 B1 Chiang Kham Thai.
95 B1 Chiang Khan Thai.
95 A1 Chiang Mai Thai.
95 A1 Chiang Rai Thai.
66 C2 Chiari Italy
91 G7 Chiba Japan
103 B5 Chibia Angola
103 D6 Chiboma Moz.
22 F4 Chibougamau Can.
22 F4 Chibougamau, Parc de res. Can.
22 F4 Chibougamau L. l. Can.
91 E6 Chibu-Sangaku Nat. Park Japan
105 K2 Chibuto Moz.
30 D5 Chicago U.S.A.
30 D5 Chicago Heights U.S.A.
30 C5 Chicago Ship Canal canal U.S.A.
45 B3 Chicamocha r. Col.
45 E3 Chicanán r. Venez.
20 B3 Chichagof U.S.A.
20 B3 Chichagof Island i. U.S.A.
88 E1 Chicheng China
59 G7 Chichester U.K.
112 C4 Chichester Range mts Austr.
91 F7 Chichibu Japan
91 F7 Chichibu-Tama National Park Japan
32 E6 Chickahominy r. U.S.A.
29 C5 Chickamauga L. l. U.S.A.
27 D5 Chickasha U.S.A.
65 C4 Chiclana de la Frontera Spain
42 C5 Chiclayo Peru
44 C6 Chico r. Chubut Arg.
47 B4 Chico r. Chubut/Rio Negro Arg.
44 C7 Chico r. Santa Cruz Arg.
34 B2 Chico U.S.A.
105 L2 Chicomo Moz.
33 G3 Chicopee U.S.A.
94 B2 Chico Sapocoy, Mt mt Phil.
23 H4 Chicoutimi Can.
105 J1 Chicualacuala Moz.
105 L2 Chidenguele Moz.
23 H1 Chidley, C. c. Can.
85 H3 Chido China
105 L2 Chiduacane Moz.
29 D6 Chiefland U.S.A.
62 F7 Chiemsee l. Ger.
61 D5 Chiers r. France
66 F3 Chieti Italy
88 F1 Chifeng China
46 E2 Chifre, Serra do mts Brazil
82 D1 Chiganak Kazak.
23 G4 Chignecto B. b. Can.
45 A3 Chigorodó Col.
103 D6 Chigubo Moz.
85 G3 Chigu Co l. China
27 B6 Chihuahua div. Mex.
36 C3 Chihuahua Mex.
82 C2 Chiili Kazak.
89 D6 Chikan China
68 D3 Chikhachevo Rus. Fed.
84 D5 Chikhali Kalan Parasia India
84 D5 Chikhli India
83 E8 Chikmagalur India
91 F6 Chikuma-gawa r. Japan
20 E4 Chilanko Forks Can.
82 D3 Chilas Jammu and Kashmir
34 B2 Chilcotin r. Can.
116 D1 Chilcott I. i. Coral Sea Is Terr.
116 E3 Childers Austr.
27 C5 Childress U.S.A.
38 Chile country S. America
15 O8 Chile Basin sea feature Pac. Oc.
44 C3 Chilecito Arg.
69 H6 Chilgir Rus. Fed.
82 E2 Chilik Kazak.
85 F6 Chilika Lake l. India
103 C5 Chililabombwe Zambia
20 E4 Chilko r. Can.
20 E4 Chilko L. l. Can.

20 C3 Chilkoot Trail National Historic Site nat. park U.S.A.
116 A1 Chillagoe Austr.
47 B3 Chillán Chile
47 B3 Chillán, Nevado mts Chile
47 E3 Chillar Arg.
26 E4 Chillicothe MO U.S.A.
32 B5 Chillicothe OH U.S.A.
30 C5 Chillicothe U.S.A.
84 C1 Chillinji Pak.
20 E5 Chilliwack Can.
44 B6 Chiloé, Isla de i. Chile
24 B3 Chiloquin U.S.A.
36 E5 Chilpancingo Mex.
115 G6 Chiltern Austr.
59 G6 Chiltern Hills h. U.K.
30 C3 Chilton U.S.A.
89 F5 Chilung Taiwan
84 D2 Chilung Pass pass India
103 D4 Chimala Tanz.
61 C4 Chimay Belgium
61 C4 Chimay, Bois de woodland Belgium
47 C1 Chimbas Arg.
42 C4 Chimborazo mt Ecuador
42 C5 Chimbote Peru
45 B2 Chimichaguá Col.
Chimkent see Shymkent
103 D5 Chimoio Moz.
70 China country Asia
27 D7 China Mex.
45 B3 Chinácota Col.
34 D4 China Lake l. CA U.S.A.
33 J2 China Lake l. ME U.S.A.
36 G6 Chinandega Nic.
34 C5 China Pt pt U.S.A.
42 C6 Chincha Alta Peru
20 F3 Chinchaga r. Can.
116 D6 Chinchilla Austr.
36 G5 Chinchorro, Banco is Mex.
33 F6 Chincoteague B. b. U.S.A.
103 D5 Chinde Moz.
82 J4 Chindu China
82 J6 Chindwin r. Myanmar
84 C2 Chineni Jammu and Kashmir
45 B3 Chingaza, Parque Nacional nat. park Col.
103 C5 Chingola Zambia
103 B5 Chinguar Angola
91 A7 Chinhae S. Korea
103 D5 Chinhoyi Zimbabwe
84 C3 Chiniot Pak.
25 E7 Chinipas Mex.
95 C2 Chinit, Stœng r. Cambodia
87 N4 Chinju S. Korea
102 C3 Chinko r. C.A.R.
35 H3 Chinle U.S.A.
35 H3 Chinle Valley v. U.S.A.
35 H3 Chinle Wash r. U.S.A.
89 F5 Chinmen Taiwan
89 F5 Chinmen Tao i. Taiwan
91 F7 Chino Japan
64 E3 Chinon France
35 F4 Chino Valley U.S.A.
103 D5 Chinsali Zambia
61 D5 Chiny, Forêt de forest Belgium
66 E2 Chioggia Italy
67 M5 Chios Greece
67 L5 Chios i. Greece
103 D5 Chipata Zambia
47 C4 Chipchihua, Sa de mts Arg.
103 B5 Chipindo Angola
103 D6 Chipinge Zimbabwe
83 D7 Chiplun India
59 E6 Chippenham U.K.
30 B3 Chippewa r. U.S.A.
30 B3 Chippewa, Lake l. U.S.A.
30 B3 Chippewa Falls U.S.A.
59 F6 Chipping Norton U.K.
59 E6 Chipping Sodbury U.K.
33 K2 Chiputneticook Lakes lakes U.S.A.
36 G6 Chiquimula Guatemala
45 B3 Chiquinquira Col.
69 G5 Chir r. Rus. Fed.
84 C3 Chirāwa India
79 K1 Chirchik Uzbek.
103 D6 Chiredzi Zimbabwe
35 H5 Chiricahua National Monument res. U.S.A.
35 H6 Chiricahua Peak summit U.S.A.
45 B2 Chiriguaná Col.
37 H7 Chiriqui, Golfo de b. Panama
59 D5 Chirk U.K.
57 F5 Chirnside U.K.
67 L3 Chirpan Bulg.
37 H7 Chirripo mt Costa Rica
103 C5 Chirundu Zambia
22 E3 Chisasibi Can.
30 A2 Chisholm U.S.A.
84 C3 Chishtian Mandi Pak.
89 B4 Chistochina U.S.A.
69 D6 Chişinău Moldova
63 K7 Chişineu-Criş Romania
68 J4 Chistopol' Rus. Fed.
87 K1 Chita Rus. Fed.
103 B5 Chitado Angola
103 D5 Chitambo Zambia
102 C4 Chitato Angola
21 H4 Chitek Lake Can.
103 B5 Chitembo Angola
103 D4 Chitipa Malawi
103 C5 Chitokoloki Zambia
90 G3 Chitose Japan
83 E8 Chitradurga India

79 L2 Chitral Pak.
84 B2 Chitral r. Pak.
37 H7 Chitré Panama
85 G5 Chittagong Bangl.
85 F5 Chittaranjan India
84 C4 Chittaurgarh India
83 E8 Chittoor India
103 D5 Chitungulu Zambia
103 D5 Chitungwiza Zimbabwe
103 C5 Chiume Angola
103 D5 Chivhu Zimbabwe
47 E2 Chivilcoy Arg.
89 D6 Chixi China
91 D7 Chizu Japan
68 G3 Chkalovsk Rus. Fed.
90 C2 Chkalovskoye Rus. Fed.
95 ☐ Choa Chu Kang Sing.
95 ☐ Choa Chu Kang h. Sing.
95 C2 Chŏâm Khsant Cambodia
47 B1 Choapa r. Chile
103 C5 Chobe National Park nat. park Botswana
35 E3 Chocolate Mts mts U.S.A.
45 A3 Chocontá Col.
47 D3 Choele Choel Arg.
84 C2 Chogo Lungma Gl. gl. Pak.
69 H3 Chograyskoye Vdkhr. resr Rus. Fed.
21 J4 Choiceland Can.
111 F2 Choiseul i. Solomon Is
44 E8 Choiseul Sound chan. Falkland Is
62 H4 Chojnice Pol.
90 G5 Chōkai-san vol. Japan
27 D6 Choke Canyon L. l. U.S.A.
102 D2 Ch'ok'ē Mts mts Eth.
85 F3 Choksum India
77 Q2 Chokurdakh Rus. Fed.
103 D6 Chókwé Moz.
64 D3 Cholet France
47 B4 Cholila Arg.
36 G6 Choluteca Honduras
103 C5 Choma Zambia
85 G4 Chomo Lhari mt Bhutan
95 A1 Chom Thong Thai.
62 F5 Chomutov Czech Rep.
77 M3 Chona r. Rus. Fed.
95 B2 Chon Buri Thai.
42 B4 Chone Ecuador
91 A7 Ch'ongdo S. Korea
87 N3 Ch'ŏngjin N. Korea
87 N4 Chŏngju N. Korea
95 B2 Chŏng Kal Cambodia
89 C7 Chongqing China
89 E5 Chongren China
105 K2 Chongoene Moz.
103 C5 Chongwe Zambia
89 D4 Chongyang China
89 F5 Chongyang Xi r. China
89 E5 Chongyi China
89 C6 Chongzuo China
87 N4 Chŏnju S. Korea
85 F5 Cho Oyu mt China
95 C3 Cho Phươc Hai Vietnam
46 B4 Chopim r. Brazil
46 B4 Chopimzinho Brazil
33 F5 Choptank r. U.S.A.
84 B4 Chor Pak.
58 E4 Chorley U.K.
69 D5 Chornobyl' Ukr.
69 E6 Chornomors'ke Ukr.
69 C5 Chortkiv Ukr.
91 G7 Chōshi Japan
47 B3 Chos Malal Arg.
62 G4 Choszczno Pol.
42 C5 Chota Peru
24 D2 Choteau U.S.A.
84 B3 Choti Pak.
100 A2 Choûm Maur.
34 B3 Chowchilla U.S.A.
20 F4 Chown, Mt mt Can.
87 K2 Choybalsan Mongolia
86 J2 Choyr Mongolia
62 H6 Chřiby h. Czech Rep.
30 D6 Chrisman U.S.A.
117 D5 Christchurch N.Z.
59 F7 Christchurch U.K.
105 F3 Christiana S. Africa
31 G3 Christian I. i. Can.
32 C5 Christiansburg U.S.A.
20 C3 Christian Sound chan. U.S.A.
21 G3 Christina r. Can.
13 L4 Christmas Island i. Indian Ocean
62 G6 Chrudim Czech Rep.
67 L7 Chrysi i. Greece
76 H5 Chu r. Kazak.
85 G5 Chuadanga Bangl.
105 K2 Chuali, L. l. Moz.
88 F4 Chuansha China
24 D3 Chubbuck U.S.A.
47 C4 Chubut div. Arg.
44 C6 Chubut r. Arg.
35 E5 Chuckwalla Mts mts U.S.A.
69 D3 Chudniv Ukr.
68 D3 Chudovo Rus. Fed.
Chudskoye Ozero l. see Peipus, Lake
91 C7 Chūgoku-sanchi mts Japan
90 C2 Chuguyevka Rus. Fed.
24 F3 Chugwater U.S.A.
69 F5 Chuhuyiv Ukr.
35 G4 Chuichu U.S.A.
87 P1 Chukchagirskoye, Ozero l. Rus. Fed.
77 V3 Chukchi Sea sea Rus. Fed./U.S.A.
68 G3 Chukhloma Rus. Fed.

77 U3 Chukotskiy Poluostrov pen. Rus. Fed.
68 H1 Chulasa Rus. Fed.
34 D5 Chula Vista U.S.A.
76 K4 Chulym r. Rus. Fed.
85 G4 Chumbi China
44 C3 Chumbicha Arg.
77 P4 Chumikan Rus. Fed.
95 B1 Chum Phae Thai.
95 A3 Chumphon Thai.
95 B2 Chum Saeng Thai.
77 L4 Chuna r. Rus. Fed.
89 F7 Chun'an China
87 N4 Ch'unch'ŏn S. Korea
Chungking see Chongqing
84 B2 Chungur, Koh-i- mt Afgh.
90 B3 Chunhua China
77 M3 Chunya r. Rus. Fed.
95 C2 Chuŏr Phnum Dângrêk mts Cambodia/Thai.
81 L3 Chūplū Iran
42 D7 Chuquibamba Peru
44 C2 Chuquicamata Chile
62 D7 Chur Switz.
77 P3 Churapcha Rus. Fed.
21 L3 Churchill Can.
21 K3 Churchill r. Man./Sask. Can.
23 H3 Churchill r. Nfld Can.
21 L3 Churchill, Cape c. Can.
23 H3 Churchill Falls Can.
21 H3 Churchill Lake l. Can.
20 D3 Churchill Peak summit Can.
22 E2 Churchill Sound chan. Can.
26 D1 Churchs Ferry U.S.A.
32 D3 Churchville U.S.A.
85 F4 Churia Ghati Hills mts Nepal
68 H3 Churov Rus. Fed.
84 C3 Churu India
45 C2 Churuguara Venez.
84 D2 Chushul Jammu and Kashmir
35 H3 Chuska Mountains mts U.S.A.
23 F4 Chute-des-Passes Can.
31 J2 Chute-Rouge Can.
31 K2 Chute-St-Philippe Can.
89 F5 Chutung Taiwan
68 H4 Chuvashskaya Respublika div. Rus. Fed.
89 A5 Chuxiong China
95 D2 Chư Yang Sin mt Vietnam
88 F3 Chuzhou China
81 K4 Chwārtā Iraq
69 D6 Ciadâr-Lunga Moldova
92 ☐ Ciamis Indon.
92 ☐ Cianjur Indon.
46 B3 Cianorte Brazil
25 E6 Cibuta Mex.
66 F2 Čičarija mts Croatia
80 E2 Çiçekdağı Turkey
92 ☐ Cidaun Indon.
69 E7 Cide Turkey
63 K4 Ciechanów Pol.
37 J4 Ciego de Avila Cuba
45 B2 Ciénaga Col.
45 B2 Ciénaga de Zapatoza l. Col.
27 C7 Ciénega de Flores Mex.
37 H4 Cienfuegos Cuba
65 F3 Cieza Spain
65 E2 Cifuentes Spain
81 M2 Cigil Adası i. Azer.
65 E3 Cigüela r. Spain
80 D2 Çihanbeyli Turkey
65 D3 Cijara, Embalse de resr Spain
92 ☐ Cikalong Indon.
92 ☐ Cilacap Indon.
81 J1 Çıldır Turkey
81 J1 Çıldır Gölü l. Turkey
89 D4 Cili China
81 K3 Cilo D. mt Turkey
81 N1 Çıloy Adası i. Azer.
35 E4 Cima U.S.A.
92 ☐ Cimahi Indon.
25 F4 Cimarron U.S.A.
27 D4 Cimarron r. U.S.A.
69 D6 Cimişlia Moldova
66 D2 Cimone, Monte mt Italy
81 H3 Çınar Turkey
45 C3 Cinaruco r. Venez.
45 D3 Cinaruco-Capanaparo, Parque Nacional nat. park Venez.
65 G2 Cinca r. Spain
32 A5 Cincinnati U.S.A.
33 F3 Cincinnatus U.S.A.
47 C3 Cinco Chañares Arg.
47 C3 Cinco Saltos Arg.
59 E6 Cinderford U.K.
80 B3 Çine Turkey
61 D4 Ciney Belgium
64 J5 Cinto, Monte mt France
46 B3 Cinzas r. Brazil
24 F2 Cipolletti Arg.
32 B5 Circleville OH U.S.A.
35 F2 Circleville UT U.S.A.
92 ☐ Cirebon Indon.
59 F6 Cirencester U.K.
66 D2 Ciriè Italy
66 G5 Cirò Marina Italy
32 H2 Cirque Mtn mt Can.
30 C6 Cisco IL U.S.A.
27 D5 Cisco TX U.S.A.
35 H2 Cisco UT U.S.A.
45 B3 Cisneros Col.
29 E7 Cistern Point pt Bahamas

66 G3 Čitluk Bos.-Herz.
104 C6 Citrusdal S. Africa
66 E3 Città di Castello Italy
67 L2 Ciucaş, Vârful mt Romania
36 D3 Ciudad Acuña Mex.
36 D5 Ciudad Altamirano Mex.
45 E3 Ciudad Bolívar Venez.
36 C3 Ciudad Camargo Mex.
46 A4 Ciudad del Carmen Mex.
36 C3 Ciudad del Este Para.
36 E4 Ciudad de Valles Mex.
45 E2 Ciudad Guayana Venez.
36 D5 Ciudad Guerrero Mex.
36 D5 Ciudad Guzmán Mex.
36 E5 Ciudad Ixtepec Mex.
36 C2 Ciudad Juárez Mex.
27 C7 Ciudad Lerdo Mex.
36 E4 Ciudad Mante Mex.
36 C3 Ciudad Obregón Mex.
45 E3 Ciudad Piar Venez.
65 E3 Ciudad Real Spain
27 D7 Ciudad Río Bravo Mex.
65 C2 Ciudad Rodrigo Spain
36 E4 Ciudad Victoria Mex.
65 H2 Ciutadella de Menorca Spain
80 F1 Civa Burnu pt Turkey
80 B2 Cıvan Dağ mt Turkey
66 E1 Cividale del Friuli Italy
66 E3 Civita Castellana Italy
66 E3 Civitanova Marche Italy
66 D3 Civitavecchia Italy
80 B2 Çivril Turkey
89 F4 Cixi China
88 E2 Cixian China
81 J3 Cizre Turkey
59 J6 Clacton-on-Sea U.K.
60 D3 Clady r. U.K.
21 G3 Claire, Lake l. Can.
24 B3 Clair Engle L. resr U.S.A.
32 D4 Clairton U.S.A.
64 F3 Clamecy France
34 D2 Clan Alpine Mts mts U.S.A.
60 E4 Clane Rep. of Ireland
29 C5 Clanton U.S.A.
104 C6 Clanwilliam S. Africa
60 D4 Clara Rep. of Ireland
95 A3 Clara i. Myanmar
114 E4 Clare N.S.W. Austr.
114 C4 Clare S.A. Austr.
60 C4 Clare r. Rep. of Ireland
30 E4 Clare U.S.A.
60 C5 Clarecastle Rep. of Ireland
60 A4 Clare Island i. Rep. of Ireland
33 G3 Claremont U.S.A.
27 E4 Claremore U.S.A.
60 C4 Claremorris Rep. of Ireland
115 K2 Clarence r. Austr.
117 D5 Clarence r. N.Z.
20 C3 Clarence Str. chan. U.S.A.
29 F7 Clarence Town Bahamas
27 C5 Clarendon U.S.A.
23 K4 Clarenville Can.
20 G5 Claresholm Can.
26 E3 Clarinda U.S.A.
32 C5 Clarington U.S.A.
32 D4 Clarion U.S.A.
32 D4 Clarion r. U.S.A.
15 L4 Clarion Fracture Zone sea feature Pac. Oc.
26 D2 Clark, Pt pt Can.
31 G3 Clark, Pt pt Can.
116 A2 Clarke r. Austr.
105 H5 Clarkebury S. Africa
115 H8 Clarke I. i. Austr.
116 E3 Clarke Range mts Austr.
116 A2 Clarke River Austr.
29 D5 Clark Hill Res. resr U.S.A.
35 E4 Clark Mt mt U.S.A.
32 C5 Clarksburg U.S.A.
27 F5 Clarksdale U.S.A.
33 F4 Clarks Summit U.S.A.
24 C2 Clarkston U.S.A.
27 E5 Clarksville AR U.S.A.
30 A4 Clarksville IA U.S.A.
29 C4 Clarksville TN U.S.A.
46 B2 Claro r. Goiás Brazil
46 B1 Claro r. Goiás Brazil
60 D5 Clashmore Rep. of Ireland
60 D3 Claudy U.K.
94 B2 Claveria Phil.
33 G2 Claysburg U.S.A.
26 D4 Clay Center U.S.A.
35 F3 Clayhole Wash r. U.S.A.
29 D5 Clayton GA U.S.A.
25 G4 Clayton NM U.S.A.
33 F2 Clayton NY U.S.A.
33 J1 Clayton Lake U.S.A.
32 C6 Claytor Lake l. U.S.A.
60 B6 Clear, Cape c. Rep. of Ireland
31 G4 Clear Creek Can.
35 G4 Clear Creek r. U.S.A.
32 D4 Clearfield PA U.S.A.
24 E3 Clearfield UT U.S.A.
32 B4 Clear Fork Reservoir resr U.S.A.
20 F3 Clear Hills mts Can.
26 E3 Clear Lake IA U.S.A.
30 A3 Clear Lake WV U.S.A.
34 A2 Clear Lake l. CA U.S.A.
35 F2 Clear Lake l. U.S.A.
24 B3 Clear L. Res. resr U.S.A.
20 F4 Clearwater r. Alta. Can.
21 H4 Clearwater r. Sask. Can.
29 D7 Clearwater U.S.A.
89 ☐ Clearwater Bay b. China

24 D2 Clearwater Mountains mts U.S.A.
21 H3 Clearwater River Provincial Park res. Can.
27 D5 Cleburne U.S.A.
24 D2 Cle Elum U.S.A.
58 G4 Cleethorpes U.K.
95 ☐ Clementi Sing.
32 C5 Clendenin U.S.A.
32 C4 Clendening Lake l. U.S.A.
94 A4 Cleopatra Needle mt Phil.
31 H1 Cléricy Can.
116 B4 Clermont Austr.
61 A5 Clermont France
29 D6 Clermont U.S.A.
64 F3 Clermont-Ferrand France
61 E4 Clervaux Lux.
66 D1 Cles Italy
114 B4 Cleve Austr.
59 E6 Clevedon U.K.
27 F5 Cleveland MS U.S.A.
32 C4 Cleveland OH U.S.A.
29 C5 Cleveland TN U.S.A.
116 B2 Cleveland, C. hd Austr.
20 E5 Cleveland, Mt mt U.S.A.
116 B2 Cleveland B. b. Austr.
30 D2 Cleveland Cliffs Basin l. U.S.A.
58 F3 Cleveland Hills h. U.K.
58 D4 Cleveleys U.K.
60 B4 Clew Bay b. Rep. of Ireland
29 D7 Clewiston U.S.A.
60 A4 Clifden Rep. of Ireland
35 H5 Cliff U.S.A.
60 C3 Cliffonoy Rep. of Ireland
117 E4 Clifford Bay b. N.Z.
115 J1 Clifton Austr.
35 H5 Clifton U.S.A.
116 A1 Clifton Beach Austr.
32 C6 Clifton Forge U.S.A.
32 B6 Clinch r. U.S.A.
32 B6 Clinch Mountain mts U.S.A.
20 E4 Clinton B.C. Can.
31 G4 Clinton Ont. Can.
33 G4 Clinton CT U.S.A.
30 B5 Clinton IA U.S.A.
30 C5 Clinton IL U.S.A.
33 H3 Clinton MA U.S.A.
33 J2 Clinton ME U.S.A.
26 E4 Clinton MO U.S.A.
27 F5 Clinton MS U.S.A.
29 E5 Clinton NC U.S.A.
27 D5 Clinton OK U.S.A.
21 H2 Clinton–Colden Lake l. Can.
30 C5 Clinton Lake l. U.S.A.
30 C5 Clintonville U.S.A.
35 G4 Clints Well U.S.A.
36 C6 Clipperton, Île terr. Pac. Oc.
15 L5 Clipperton Fracture Zone sea feature Pac. Oc.
57 B3 Clishham h. U.K.
58 E4 Clitheroe U.K.
105 G4 Clocolan S. Africa
60 D3 Cloghan Rep. of Ireland
60 C6 Clonakilty Rep. of Ireland
60 C6 Clonakilty Bay b. Rep. of Ireland
60 C4 Clonbern Rep. of Ireland
113 H4 Cloncurry Austr.
60 C4 Clones Rep. of Ireland
60 D5 Clonmel Rep. of Ireland
60 D4 Clonygowan Rep. of Ireland
60 B5 Cloonbannin Rep. of Ireland
60 D4 Clooneagh Rep. of Ireland
30 A2 Cloquet U.S.A.
24 E2 Cloud Peak summit U.S.A.
117 E4 Cloudy Bay b. N.Z.
31 K1 Clova Can.
57 F5 Clova U.K.
34 A2 Cloverdale U.S.A.
27 C5 Clovis U.S.A.
31 J3 Cloyne Can.
57 D5 Cluanie, Loch l. U.K.
21 H3 Cluff Lake Mine Can.
63 L2 Cluj-Napoca Romania
59 D5 Clun U.K.
114 E6 Clunes Austr.
113 G4 Cluny Austr.
64 F4 Cluses France
59 D5 Clwydian Range h. U.K.
20 G4 Clyde Can.
57 D5 Clyde r. U.K.
32 E3 Clyde NY U.S.A.
32 B4 Clyde OH U.S.A.
57 D5 Clyde, Firth of est. U.K.
57 D5 Clydebank U.K.
25 C5 Coachella U.S.A.
27 C7 Coahuila div. Mex.
30 C5 Coal City U.S.A.
34 D3 Coaldale U.S.A.
27 D5 Coalgate U.S.A.
34 B3 Coalinga U.S.A.
20 D3 Coal River Can.
59 F5 Coalville U.K.
42 F4 Coari Brazil
42 F4 Coari r. Brazil
29 C6 Coastal Plain plain U.S.A.
20 D4 Coast Mountains mts Can.
116 E5 Coast Ra. h. Austr.
34 B3 Coast Ranges mts U.S.A.
34 B3 Coast Ranges mts U.S.A.
57 D5 Coatbridge U.K.
33 F5 Coatesville U.S.A.
22 F4 Coaticook Can.
118 A2 Coats I. i. Can.
119 C3 Coats Land coastal area Antarctica

36 F5 Coatzacoalcos Mex.
31 H2 Cobalt Can.
36 F5 Cobán Guatemala
115 F2 Cobar Austr.
115 H6 Cobargo Austr.
115 H6 Cobberas, Mt mt Austr.
114 E7 Cobden Austr.
31 J3 Cobden Can.
60 C6 Cóbh Rep. of Ireland
21 K4 Cobham r. Can.
42 E8 Cobija Bol.
33 F3 Cobleskill U.S.A.
31 H4 Cobourg Can.
112 F2 Cobourg Peninsula pen. Austr.
115 G4 Cobram Austr.
62 E5 Coburg Ger.
65 D2 Coca Spain
46 B1 Cocalinho Brazil
42 E7 Cochabamba Bol.
47 B5 Cochamó Chile
61 F4 Cochem Ger.
83 E9 Cochin India
35 H5 Cochise U.S.A.
20 G4 Cochrane Alta. Can.
22 D4 Cochrane Ont. Can.
21 J3 Cochrane r. Can.
44 B7 Cochrane Chile
114 D4 Cockburn Austr.
31 F3 Cockburn I. i. Can.
57 F5 Cockburnspath U.K.
29 F7 Cockburn Town Bahamas
Cockburn Town see Grand Turk
58 D3 Cockermouth U.K.
104 F6 Cockscomb summit S. Africa
37 H6 Coco r. Honduras/Nic.
36 G7 Coco, Isla de i. Col.
45 A4 Coco, Pta pt Venez.
35 F4 Coconino Plateau plat. U.S.A.
115 G4 Cocoparra Range h. Austr.
45 B3 Cocorná Col.
46 D1 Cocos Brazil
13 L3 Cocos Is is Indian Ocean
15 O5 Cocos Ridge sea feature Pac. Oc.
45 B3 Cocuy, Sierra Nevada del mt Col.
33 H4 Cod, Cape c. U.S.A.
42 F4 Codajás Brazil
45 D2 Codera, C. pt Venez.
117 A7 Codfish I. i. N.Z.
66 E2 Codigoro Italy
23 H2 Cod Island i. Can.
67 L2 Codlea Romania
43 K4 Codó Brazil
59 E5 Codsall U.K.
60 A6 Cod's Head hd Rep. of Ireland
24 E3 Cody U.S.A.
113 H2 Coen Austr.
13 H4 Coëtivy i. Seychelles
24 C2 Coeur d'Alene U.S.A.
24 C2 Coeur d'Alene L. l. U.S.A.
105 H5 Coffee Bay S. Africa
27 E4 Coffeyville U.S.A.
114 A5 Coffin B. b. Austr.
114 A5 Coffin Bay Austr.
115 K3 Coffs Harbour Austr.
105 G6 Cofimvaba S. Africa
30 B4 Coggon U.S.A.
64 D4 Cognac France
100 C4 Cogo Equatorial Guinea
32 E3 Cohocton r. U.S.A.
33 G3 Cohoes U.S.A.
114 F5 Cohuna Austr.
37 H7 Coiba, Isla i. Panama
44 C8 Coig r. Arg.
57 C2 Coigeach, Rubha pt U.K.
44 B7 Coihaique Chile
83 E8 Coimbatore India
65 B2 Coimbra Port.
65 D4 Coin Spain
42 E7 Coipasa, Salar de salt flat Bol.
45 C2 Cojedes r. Venez.
24 E3 Cokeville U.S.A.
114 E7 Colac Austr.
46 E2 Colatina Brazil
26 C4 Colby U.S.A.
42 D7 Colca r. Peru
59 H6 Colchester U.K.
30 B5 Colchester U.S.A.
57 F5 Coldingham U.K.
21 G4 Cold L. l. Can.
21 G4 Cold Lake Can.
57 F5 Coldstream U.K.
27 D4 Coldwater KS U.S.A.
30 E5 Coldwater MI U.S.A.
30 D1 Coldwell Can.
33 H2 Colebrook U.S.A.
30 E4 Coleman MI U.S.A.
27 D6 Coleman TX U.S.A.
105 H4 Colenso S. Africa
114 D6 Coleraine Austr.
60 E2 Coleraine U.K.
117 C5 Coleridge, L. l. N.Z.
115 H9 Coles Bay Austr.
104 F6 Colesberg S. Africa
34 B2 Colfax CA U.S.A.
24 C2 Colfax WA U.S.A.
57 ☐ Colgrave Sound chan. U.K.
105 G3 Coligny S. Africa
36 D5 Colima Mex.
36 D5 Colima, Nevado de vol. Mex.
57 B4 Coll i. U.K.
65 E2 Collado Villalba Spain
115 H2 Collarenebri Austr.
29 C5 College Park U.S.A.

27 D6 College Station U.S.A.
115 G2 Collerina Austr.
115 H3 Collie N.S.W. Austr.
112 C6 Collie W.A. Austr.
112 D3 Collier Bay b. Austr.
112 C4 Collier Range National Park nat. park Austr.
31 G3 Collingwood Can.
117 D4 Collingwood N.Z.
27 F6 Collins U.S.A.
116 B3 Collinsville Austr.
28 B4 Collinsville U.S.A.
47 B3 Collipulli Chile
60 C3 Collooney Rep. of Ireland
64 H2 Colmar France
65 E2 Colmenar Viejo Spain
57 C5 Colmonell U.K.
59 H6 Colne r. U.K.
115 J4 Colo r. Austr.
62 C5 Cologne Ger.
30 C3 Coloma U.S.A.
46 C3 Colômbia Brazil
27 D7 Colombia Mex.
45 B4 Colombia Col.
38 Colombia country S. America
83 K4 Colombo Sri Lanka
64 E5 Colomiers France
47 E2 Colón Buenos Aires Arg.
47 E2 Colón Entre Ríos Arg.
37 H4 Colón Cuba
37 J7 Colón Panama
112 F6 Colona Austr.
25 C6 Colonet, C. c. Mex.
46 E1 Colônia r. Brazil
47 D3 Colonia Choele Choel, Isla i. Arg.
47 F2 Colonia del Sacramento Uru.
47 C3 Colonia Emilio Mitre Arg.
47 F1 Colonia Lavalleja Uru.
32 E6 Colonial Heights U.S.A.
35 F6 Colonia Reforma Mex.
66 G5 Colonna, Capo pt Italy
60 E1 Colonsay i. U.K.
47 C3 Colorada Grande, Salina l. Arg.
47 D3 Colorado r. La Pampa/Río Negro Arg.
47 C1 Colorado r. San Juan Arg.
35 E5 Colorado r. Mex./U.S.A.
25 F4 Colorado div. U.S.A.
27 D6 Colorado r. U.S.A.
47 D3 Colorado, Delta del Río delta Arg.
35 F3 Colorado City AZ U.S.A.
27 C5 Colorado City TX U.S.A.
34 D5 Colorado Desert des. U.S.A.
35 H2 Colorado National Monument res. U.S.A.
35 G3 Colorado Plateau plat. U.S.A.
35 E4 Colorado River Aqueduct canal U.S.A.
25 F4 Colorado Springs U.S.A.
59 G5 Colsterworth U.K.
59 J5 Coltishall U.K.
34 D4 Colton CA U.S.A.
33 F2 Colton NY U.S.A.
35 G2 Colton UT U.S.A.
24 B2 Columbia r. Can./U.S.A.
32 E5 Columbia MD U.S.A.
26 E4 Columbia MO U.S.A.
27 F6 Columbia MS U.S.A.
32 E4 Columbia PA U.S.A.
29 D5 Columbia SC U.S.A.
29 C5 Columbia TN U.S.A.
118 B3 Columbia, Cape c. Can.
32 E5 Columbia, District of div. U.S.A.
20 F4 Columbia, Mt mt Can.
30 E5 Columbia Falls U.S.A.
33 K2 Columbia Falls ME U.S.A.
24 D1 Columbia Falls MT U.S.A.
20 F4 Columbia Mountains mts Can.
24 C2 Columbia Plateau plat. U.S.A.
104 B6 Columbine, Cape pt S. Africa
29 C5 Columbus GA U.S.A.
28 C4 Columbus IN U.S.A.
27 F5 Columbus MS U.S.A.
24 E2 Columbus MT U.S.A.
26 D3 Columbus NE U.S.A.
25 F6 Columbus NM U.S.A.
32 B5 Columbus OH U.S.A.
27 D6 Columbus TX U.S.A.
30 C4 Columbus WV U.S.A.
30 B5 Columbus Jct U.S.A.
29 F7 Columbus Pt pt Bahamas
34 D2 Columbus Salt Marsh salt marsh U.S.A.
34 A2 Colusa U.S.A.
117 E2 Colville N.Z.
24 C1 Colville U.S.A.
117 E2 Colville Channel chan. N.Z.
59 D4 Colwyn Bay U.K.
66 D2 Comacchio Italy
66 E2 Comacchio, Valli di lag. Italy
85 G3 Comai China
47 B4 Comallo r. Arg.
27 D6 Comanche U.S.A.
119 B1 Comandante Ferraz Brazil Base Antarctica
47 C4 Comandante Salas Arg.
63 N7 Comăneşti Romania
47 B1 Combarbalá Chile
60 F3 Comber U.K.
31 J3 Combermere Can.
85 H6 Combermere Bay b. Myanmar

105 K1 Combomune Moz.
115 K3 Comboyne Austr.
22 E3 Comencho, L. l. Can.
60 D5 Comeragh Mountains h. Rep. of Ireland
116 C4 Comet Austr.
116 C5 Comet r. Austr.
27 D6 Comfort U.S.A.
85 G5 Comilla Bangl.
66 C4 Comino, Capo pt Italy
36 F5 Comitán de Domínguez Mex.
33 G4 Commack U.S.A.
31 H3 Commanda Can.
119 B6 Commonwealth B. b. Antarctica
66 C2 Como Italy
66 C2 Como, Lago di l. Italy
85 G3 Como Chamling l. China
44 C4 Comodoro Rivadavia Arg.
96 Comoros country Africa
64 F2 Compiègne France
36 D4 Compostela Mex.
94 C5 Compostela Phil.
46 C4 Comprida, Ilha i. Brazil
30 C5 Compton U.S.A.
69 D6 Comrat Moldova
57 E4 Comrie U.K.
27 C6 Comstock U.S.A.
95 C1 Con, Sông r. Vietnam
85 H4 Cona China
100 A4 Conakry Guinea
47 C4 Cona Niyeo Arg.
115 G8 Conara Jct. Austr.
46 D2 Conceição r. Brazil
46 E2 Conceição da Barra Brazil
43 J5 Conceição do Araguaia Brazil
44 C3 Concepción Arg.
42 F7 Concepción Bol.
47 B3 Concepción Chile
37 H7 Concepción Panama
44 E2 Concepción Para.
47 E2 Concepción del Uruguay Arg.
34 B4 Conception, Pt pt U.S.A.
23 K4 Conception Bay South Can.
29 F7 Conception I. i. Bahamas
46 C3 Conchas Brazil
25 F5 Conchas L. l. U.S.A.
35 H4 Concho U.S.A.
36 D3 Conchos r. Chihuahua Mex.
36 E4 Conchos r. Tamaulipas Mex.
34 A3 Concord CA U.S.A.
29 D5 Concord NC U.S.A.
33 H3 Concord NH U.S.A.
47 F1 Concordia Arg.
45 B4 Concordia Col.
104 B4 Concordia S. Africa
26 D4 Concordia U.S.A.
115 J1 Condamine Austr.
116 D6 Condamine r. Austr.
95 C3 Côn Đao Vietnam
46 E1 Condeúba Brazil
115 G4 Condobolin Austr.
64 E5 Condom France
24 B2 Condon U.S.A.
61 D4 Condroz reg. Belgium
29 C6 Conecuh r. U.S.A.
66 E2 Conegliano Italy
27 C7 Conejos Mex.
32 C4 Conemaugh r. U.S.A.
31 G4 Conestogo Lake l. Can.
32 E3 Conesus Lake l. U.S.A.
33 G4 Coney I. i. U.S.A.
Coney I. i. see Serangoon, P.
110 F3 Conflict Group is P.N.G.
64 E3 Confolens France
35 F2 Confusion Range mts U.S.A.
89 D6 Conghua China
89 C5 Congjiang China
59 E4 Congleton U.K.
96 Congo country Africa
102 B4 Congo r. Congo/Dem. Rep. Congo
96 Congo, Democratic Republic of country Africa
102 C3 Congo Basin basin Dem. Rep. Congo
35 F4 Congress U.S.A.
47 B3 Conguillo, Parque Nacional nat. park Chile
59 G4 Coningsby U.K.
22 D3 Coniston Can.
58 D3 Coniston U.K.
116 A2 Conjuboy Austr.
21 G3 Conklin Can.
47 D2 Conlara Arg.
47 D2 Conlara r. Arg.
60 B3 Conn, Lough l. Rep. of Ireland
32 C4 Conneaut U.S.A.
33 G4 Connecticut div. U.S.A.
28 F3 Connecticut r. U.S.A.
32 C4 Connellsville U.S.A.
60 B4 Connemara reg. Rep. of Ireland
33 J1 Conners Can.
28 C4 Connersville U.S.A.
116 C3 Connors Ra. h. Austr.
114 F4 Conoble Austr.
89 B6 Co Nôi Vietnam
33 E5 Conowingo U.S.A.
24 E1 Conrad U.S.A.
27 E6 Conroe U.S.A.
46 D3 Conselheiro Lafaiete Brazil
46 E2 Conselheiro Pena Brazil

58 F3 Consett U.K.
95 C3 Côn Sơn i. Vietnam
21 G4 Consort Can.
62 D7 Constance, Lake l. Ger./Switz.
42 F5 Constância dos Baetas Brazil
67 N2 Constanţa Romania
65 D4 Constantina Spain
100 C1 Constantine Alg.
30 E5 Constantine U.S.A.
35 E6 Constitución de 1857, Parque Nacional nat. park Mex.
116 C5 Consuelo Austr.
24 D3 Contact U.S.A.
42 C5 Contamana Peru
46 E1 Contas r. Brazil
33 G6 Continental U.S.A.
33 H3 Contoocook r. U.S.A.
44 B8 Contreras, I. i. Chile
21 G1 Contwoyto Lake l. Can.
27 E5 Conway AR U.S.A.
33 H3 Conway NH U.S.A.
29 E5 Conway SC U.S.A.
116 C3 Conway, C. pt Austr.
114 A2 Conway, L. salt flat Austr.
59 D4 Conwy U.K.
59 D4 Conwy r. U.K.
113 F5 Coober Pedy Austr.
116 C6 Coogoon r. Austr.
112 F6 Cook Austr.
30 A2 Cook U.S.A.
20 A2 Cook, C. c. Can.
29 C4 Cookeville U.S.A.
105 F6 Cookhouse S. Africa
33 F3 Cooksburg U.S.A.
23 J3 Cook's Harbour Can.
60 E3 Cookstown U.K.
117 E4 Cook Strait str. N.Z.
113 J3 Cooktown Austr.
115 G3 Coolabah Austr.
116 A6 Cooladdi Austr.
115 H3 Coolah Austr.
115 K2 Coolangatta Austr.
112 D6 Coolgardie Austr.
35 G5 Coolidge U.S.A.
35 G5 Coolidge Dam U.S.A.
116 E6 Coolum Beach Austr.
115 H6 Cooma Austr.
60 A6 Coomacarrea h. Rep. of Ireland
114 D4 Coombah Austr.
115 H3 Coonabarabran Austr.
114 C5 Coonalpyn Austr.
115 H3 Coonamble Austr.
114 D6 Coonawarra Austr.
114 A3 Coondambo Austr.
115 F1 Coongoola Austr.
114 C2 Cooper Creek watercourse Austr.
115 K3 Coopernook Austr.
33 J2 Coopers Mills U.S.A.
29 E7 Cooper's Town Bahamas
26 D2 Cooperstown ND U.S.A.
33 F3 Cooperstown NY U.S.A.
116 E6 Cooroy Austr.
24 A3 Coos Bay U.S.A.
115 H5 Cootamundra Austr.
60 D3 Cootehill Rep. of Ireland
47 B3 Copahue, Volcán mt Chile
24 G4 Cope U.S.A.
55 N9 Copenhagen Denmark
115 J2 Copeton Reservoir resr Austr.
95 C1 Cô Pi, Phou mt Laos/Vietnam
44 B3 Copiapó Chile
44 B3 Copiapó r. Chile
114 C3 Copley Austr.
66 D2 Copparo Italy
31 G2 Copper Cliff Can.
116 A2 Copperfield r. Austr.
30 D2 Copper Harbor U.S.A.
30 E2 Coppermine Pt pt Can.
104 E4 Copperton S. Africa
85 F3 Coqên China
47 B3 Coquimbo Chile
47 B1 Coquimbo div. Chile
67 L3 Corabia Romania
46 D2 Coração de Jesus Brazil
Coracesium see Alanya
42 D7 Coracora Peru
115 K2 Coraki Austr.
112 B4 Coral Bay Austr.
29 D7 Coral Gables U.S.A.
111 F3 Coral Sea sea Coral Sea Is Austr.
14 E6 Coral Sea Basin sea feature Pac. Oc.
106 Coral Sea Islands Territory terr. Pac. Oc.
30 B5 Coralville Reservoir resr U.S.A.
114 E7 Corangamite, L. l. Austr.
43 G3 Corantijn r. Suriname
81 M1 Corat Azer.
47 E2 Corbett Arg.
21 L2 Corbett Inlet in. Can.
61 A5 Corbie France
32 A5 Corbin U.S.A.
59 G5 Corby U.K.
34 C3 Corcoran U.S.A.
44 B6 Corcovado, G. de b. Chile
116 E5 Cordalba Austr.
29 E5 Cordele U.S.A.
45 B4 Cordillera de los Picachos, Parque Nacional nat. park Col.
94 B4 Cordilleras Range mts Phil.

47 D1 Córdoba Arg.
47 C4 Córdoba div. Arg.
47 D2 Córdoba div. Arg.
36 D3 Córdoba Durango Mex.
36 E5 Córdoba Vera Cruz Mex.
65 D4 Córdoba Spain
47 D2 Córdoba, Sierras de mts Arg.
Cordova see Córdoba
20 C4 Cordova Bay b. U.S.A.
33 K2 Corea U.S.A.
67 H5 Corfu i. Greece
65 C3 Coria Spain
115 J4 Coricudgy mt Austr.
66 G5 Corigliano Calabro Italy
116 D1 Coringa Is is Coral Sea Is Terr.
115 F8 Corinna Austr.
33 J2 Corinna U.S.A.
21 J4 Corinne Can.
27 F5 Corinth MS U.S.A.
33 G3 Corinth NY U.S.A.
46 D2 Corinto Brazil
43 G7 Corixa Grande r. Bol./Brazil
46 A2 Corixinha r. Brazil
60 C6 Cork Rep. of Ireland
66 E6 Corleone Italy
80 A1 Çorlu Turkey
21 J4 Cormorant Can.
105 H3 Cornelia S. Africa
46 B3 Cornélio Procópio Brazil
30 B3 Cornell U.S.A.
23 J4 Corner Brook Can.
115 G7 Corner Inlet b. Austr.
61 C5 Cornillet, Mont h. France
34 A2 Corning CA U.S.A.
32 E3 Corning NY U.S.A.
116 A4 Cornish watercourse Austr.
Corn Islands is see Maíz, Islas del
66 D3 Corno, Monte mt Italy
22 F4 Cornwall Can.
114 B5 Corny Pt pt Austr.
45 C2 Coro Venez.
43 K4 Coroatá Brazil
42 E7 Corocoro Bol.
60 B5 Corofin Rep. of Ireland
42 E7 Coroico Bol.
46 C2 Coromandel Brazil
83 F8 Coromandel Coast coastal area India
117 E2 Coromandel Peninsula pen. N.Z.
117 E2 Coromandel Range h. N.Z.
94 B3 Coron Phil.
114 D3 Corona Austr.
34 D5 Corona U.S.A.
37 H7 Coronado, Bahía de b. Costa Rica
21 G4 Coronation Can.
119 B1 Coronation I. i. Atlantic Ocean
20 C3 Coronation Island i. U.S.A.
94 B4 Coron Bay b. Phil.
47 E1 Coronda Arg.
47 E2 Coronel Brandsen Arg.
47 E3 Coronel Dorrego Arg.
44 E3 Coronel Oviedo Para.
46 A1 Coronel Ponce Brazil
47 E3 Coronel Pringles Arg.
46 A3 Coronel Sapucaia Brazil
47 E3 Coronel Suárez Arg.
47 F3 Coronel Vidal Arg.
67 J4 Çorovodë Albania
115 G5 Corowa Austr.
27 D7 Corpus Christi U.S.A.
27 D6 Corpus Christi, L. l. U.S.A.
42 E7 Corque Bol.
65 D3 Corral de Cantos mt Spain
47 C1 Corral de Isaac Arg.
43 J6 Corrente Brazil
46 D1 Corrente r. Bahia Brazil
46 B2 Corrente r. Goiás Brazil
46 C1 Corrente r. Brazil
46 A2 Correntes Brazil
46 A2 Correntes r. Brazil
46 D1 Correntina Brazil
Correntina r. see Éguas
60 B4 Corrib, Lough l. Rep. of Ireland
44 E3 Corrientes Arg.
44 E4 Corrientes r. Arg.
47 F3 Corrientes, C. hd Arg.
36 C4 Corrientes, C. c. Mex.
45 A3 Corrientes, Cabo hd Col.
27 E6 Corrigan U.S.A.
112 C6 Corrigin Austr.
59 D5 Corris U.K.
32 D4 Corry U.S.A.
115 G6 Corryong Austr.
66 C3 Corse, Cap hd France
Corse i. see Corsica
59 E6 Corsham U.K.
64 J5 Corsica i. France
27 D5 Corsicana U.S.A.
66 C3 Corte France
65 C4 Cortegana Spain
35 H3 Cortez U.S.A.
34 D1 Cortez Mts mts U.S.A.
66 E1 Cortina d'Ampezzo Italy
33 E3 Cortland U.S.A.
59 J5 Corton U.K.
66 D3 Cortona Italy
65 B3 Coruche Port.
81 H1 Çoruh r. Turkey
80 E1 Çorum Turkey
43 G7 Corumbá r. Brazil

46 C2 Corumbá r. Brazil
46 C2 Corumbaíba Brazil
45 E3 Corumo r. Venez.
24 B2 Corvallis U.S.A.
59 D5 Corwen U.K.
66 G5 Cosenza Italy
32 C4 Coshocton U.S.A.
64 F3 Cosne-Cours-sur-Loire France
47 D1 Cosquín Arg.
65 F3 Costa Blanca coastal area Spain
65 H2 Costa Brava coastal area France/Spain
65 C4 Costa de la Luz coastal area Spain
65 D4 Costa del Sol coastal area Spain
37 H6 Costa de Mosquitos coastal area Nic.
16 Costa Rica country Central America
36 C4 Costa Rica Mex.
67 L2 Costeşti Romania
33 J2 Costigan U.S.A.
94 C5 Cotabato Phil.
45 A4 Cotacachi, Co mt Ecuador
42 E8 Cotagaita Bol.
46 E2 Cotaxé r. Brazil
20 C3 Cote, Mt mt U.S.A.
64 H5 Côte d'Azur coastal area France
96 Côte d'Ivoire country Africa
64 G2 Côtes de Meuse ridge France
59 D5 Cothi r. U.K.
65 G1 Cotiella mt Spain
45 E3 Cotingo r. Brazil
100 C4 Cotonou Benin
42 C4 Cotopaxi, Volcán vol. Ecuador
59 E5 Cotswold Hills h. U.K.
24 B3 Cottage Grove U.S.A.
62 G5 Cottbus Ger.
59 H5 Cottenham U.K.
35 H5 Cotton City U.S.A.
35 H5 Cottonwood U.S.A.
35 G4 Cottonwood Wash r. U.S.A.
27 D6 Cotulla U.S.A.
32 D4 Coudersport U.S.A.
114 B6 Cŏuedic, C. de c. Austr.
64 F2 Coulommiers France
31 J2 Coulonge r. Can.
34 B3 Coulterville U.S.A.
24 C2 Council U.S.A.
26 E3 Council Bluffs U.S.A.
114 F7 Councillor Island i. Austr.
21 G2 Courageous Lake l. Can.
55 R9 Courland Lagoon lag. Lith./Rus. Fed.
20 E5 Courtenay Can.
60 C5 Courtmacsherry Rep. of Ireland
60 D5 Courtown Rep. of Ireland
Courtrai see Kortrijk
27 E5 Coushatta U.S.A.
64 D2 Coutances France
22 E2 Couture, Lac l. Can.
61 C4 Couvin Belgium
35 F2 Cove Fort U.S.A.
31 G3 Cove I. i. Can.
32 E5 Cove Mts h. U.S.A.
59 F5 Coventry U.K.
33 E5 Cove Point U.S.A.
65 C2 Covilhã Port.
29 D5 Covington GA U.S.A.
30 D5 Covington IN U.S.A.
32 A5 Covington KY U.S.A.
29 B5 Covington TN U.S.A.
32 D6 Covington VA U.S.A.
31 F2 Cow r. Can.
115 G4 Cowal, L. l. Austr.
112 D6 Cowan, L. salt flat Austr.
33 G2 Cowansville Can.
57 E4 Cowdenbeath U.K.
114 B4 Cowell Austr.
114 F7 Cowes Austr.
59 F7 Cowes U.K.
58 E3 Cow Green Reservoir resr U.K.
116 A6 Cowley Austr.
32 D5 Cowpasture r. U.S.A.
115 H4 Cowra Austr.
46 D1 Coxá r. Brazil
47 F1 Coxilha de Santana h. Brazil/Uru.
46 A2 Coxim Brazil
46 A2 Coxim r. Brazil
33 G3 Coxsackie U.S.A.
85 H5 Cox's Bazar Bangl.
34 D4 Coyote Lake l. U.S.A.
35 E5 Coyote Peak summit AZ U.S.A.
34 C3 Coyote Peak summit CA U.S.A.
85 F2 Cozhê China
67 L2 Cozia, Vârful mt Romania
25 D5 Cozón, Co mt Mex.
36 G4 Cozumel Mex.
36 G4 Cozumel, I. de i. Mex.
115 H4 Craboon Austr.
116 D5 Cracow Austr.
115 G8 Cradle Mountain Lake St Clair Nat. Park nat. park Austr.
115 G8 Cradle Mt mt Austr.
114 C3 Cradock Austr.
105 F6 Cradock S. Africa
57 C3 Craig U.K.
20 C3 Craig AK U.S.A.

24 F3 Craig CO U.S.A.
60 E3 Craigavon U.K.
114 F6 Craigieburn Austr.
32 D5 Craigsville U.S.A.
57 F4 Crail U.K.
62 E6 Crailsheim Ger.
67 K2 Craiova Romania
58 F2 Cramlington U.K.
33 F2 Cranberry L. l. U.S.A.
33 F2 Cranberry Lake U.S.A.
114 F7 Cranbourne Austr.
20 F5 Cranbrook Can.
30 C3 Crandon U.S.A.
24 C3 Crane OR U.S.A.
27 C6 Crane TX U.S.A.
30 A1 Crane Lake U.S.A.
33 H4 Cranston U.S.A.
119 B4 Crary Ice Rise ice feature Antarctica
119 A4 Crary Mts mts Antarctica
24 B3 Crater L. l. U.S.A.
24 B3 Crater Lake Nat. Pk nat. park U.S.A.
24 D3 Craters of the Moon Nat. Mon. res. U.S.A.
43 K5 Crateús Brazil
43 L5 Crato Brazil
45 C3 Cravo Norte Col.
45 C3 Cravo Sur r. Col.
26 C3 Crawford U.S.A.
30 D5 Crawfordsville U.S.A.
29 C6 Crawfordville U.S.A.
59 G6 Crawley U.K.
24 E2 Crazy Mts mts U.S.A.
57 D4 Creag Meagaidh mt U.K.
21 H4 Crean L. l. Can.
59 E5 Credenhill U.K.
59 D7 Crediton U.K.
21 H3 Cree r. Can.
25 F7 Creel Mex.
21 H3 Cree Lake l. Can.
21 J4 Creighton Can.
61 A5 Creil France
66 D2 Cremona Italy
64 F2 Crépy-en-Valois France
66 F2 Cres i. Croatia
24 A3 Crescent City U.S.A.
35 H2 Crescent Junction U.S.A.
34 B1 Crescent Mills U.S.A.
35 E4 Crescent Peak summit U.S.A.
30 A4 Cresco U.S.A.
47 E2 Crespo Arg.
114 E7 Cressy Austr.
20 F5 Creston Can.
30 A4 Creston IA U.S.A.
24 F3 Creston WY U.S.A.
29 C6 Crestview U.S.A.
33 F5 Crestwood Village U.S.A.
114 E6 Creswick Austr.
67 L7 Crete i. Greece
65 H1 Creus, Cap de pt Spain
64 E3 Creuse r. France
59 E4 Crewe U.K.
32 D6 Crewe U.S.A.
59 E7 Crewkerne U.K.
57 D4 Crianlarich U.K.
59 C5 Criccieth U.K.
44 G3 Criciúma Brazil
57 E4 Crieff U.K.
57 E6 Criffell h. U.K.
66 F2 Crikvenica Croatia
69 E6 Crimea pen. Ukr.
57 G3 Crimond U.K.
33 F6 Crisfield U.S.A.
46 C2 Cristalina Brazil
Cristalino r. see Mariembero
45 B2 Cristóbal Colón, Pico mt Col.
46 C1 Crixás Brazil
46 C1 Crixás Açu r. Brazil
46 B1 Crixás Mirim r. Brazil
Crna Gora div. see Montenegro
66 F2 Črnomelj Slovenia
60 B4 Croagh Patrick h. Rep. of Ireland
115 H6 Croajingolong Nat. Park nat. park Austr.
48 Croatia country Europe
27 E6 Crockett U.S.A.
33 F3 Croghan U.S.A.
110 D3 Croker I. i. Austr.
57 D3 Cromarty U.K.
57 D3 Cromarty Firth est. U.K.
57 D3 Cromdale, Hills of h. U.K.
59 J5 Cromer U.K.
117 B6 Cromwell N.Z.
58 F3 Crook U.K.
32 D4 Crooked Creek Reservoir resr U.S.A.
37 K4 Crooked I. Passage chan. Bahamas
37 K4 Crooked Island i. Bahamas
30 B1 Crooked Lake l. Can./U.S.A.
26 D2 Crookston U.S.A.
115 H5 Crookwell Austr.
60 C5 Croom Rep. of Ireland
115 J2 Croppa Creek Austr.
58 D4 Crosby U.K.
21 J5 Crosby U.S.A.
21 L2 Cross Bay b. Can.
29 D6 Cross City U.S.A.
33 K1 Cross Creek Can.
27 E5 Crossett U.S.A.
58 E3 Cross Fell h. U.K.
60 F3 Crossgar U.K.
60 C6 Crosshaven Rep. of Ireland
59 C5 Cross Inn U.K.
21 K4 Cross Lake Can.

21 K4 Cross Lake *l.* Can.
32 E3 Cross Lake U.S.A.
60 E3 Crossmaglen U.K.
35 E4 Crossman Peak *summit* U.S.A.
20 B3 Cross Sound *chan.* U.S.A.
30 E3 Cross Village U.S.A.
29 C5 Crossville U.S.A.
31 F4 Croswell U.S.A.
66 G5 Crotone Italy
59 H6 Crouch *r.* U.K.
115 G3 Crowal *watercourse* Austr.
59 H6 Crowborough U.K.
115 F4 Crowl *watercourse* Austr.
59 G5 Crowland U.K.
27 E6 Crowley U.S.A.
34 C3 Crowley, Lake *l.* U.S.A.
30 D5 Crown Point *IN* U.S.A.
33 G3 Crown Point *NY* U.S.A.
115 K1 Crows Nest Austr.
20 U5 Crowsnest Pass Can.
113 H3 Croydon Austr.
59 G6 Croydon U.K.
13 H6 Crozet Basin *sea feature* Indian Ocean
13 H7 Crozet Islands *is* Indian Ocean
13 G6 Crozet Plateau *sea feature* Indian Ocean
64 B2 Crozon France
57 G3 Cruden Bay U.K.
60 E3 Crumlin U.K.
60 C5 Crusheen Rep. of Ireland
37 J5 Cruz, Cabo *c.* Cuba
44 F3 Cruz Alta Brazil
47 D1 Cruz del Eje Arg.
46 D3 Cruzeiro Brazil
42 D5 Cruzeiro do Sul Brazil
35 H5 Cruzville U.S.A.
20 E3 Crysdale, Mt *mt* Can.
114 C4 Crystal Brook Austr.
27 D6 Crystal City U.S.A.
30 C2 Crystal Falls U.S.A.
30 C4 Crystal Lake U.S.A.
63 K7 Csongrád Hungary
81 K5 Ctesiphon Iraq
45 D2 Cúa Venez.
95 C3 Cua Lon *r.* Vietnam
103 C5 Cuando *r.* Angola/Zambia
103 B5 Cuangar Angola
102 B4 Cuango *r.* Angola/Dem. Rep. Congo
103 B4 Cuanza *r.* Angola
45 D3 Cuao *r.* Venez.
47 F1 Cuaro *r.* Uru.
47 D2 Cuarto *r.* Arg.
27 C7 Cuatro Ciénegas Mex.
36 C3 Cuauhtémoc Mex.
16 Cuba *country* Caribbean Sea
30 B5 Cuba *IL* U.S.A.
25 F4 Cuba *NM* U.S.A.
35 F6 Cubabi, Cerro *summit* Mex.
103 B4 Cubal Angola
103 B5 Cubango *r.* Angola/Namibia
45 B3 Cubara Col.
21 J4 Cub Hills *h.* Can.
80 D1 Çubuk Turkey
47 F1 Čuchilla Grande *h.* Uru.
47 F1 Cuchilla Grande Inferior *h.* Uru.
47 D3 Cuchillo-Có Arg.
45 D3 Cuchivero *r.* Venez.
32 E6 Cuckoo U.S.A.
45 D4 Cucuí Brazil
45 B3 Cúcuta Col.
83 E8 Cuddalore India
83 E8 Cuddapah India
21 H4 Cudworth Can.
65 D2 Cuéllar Spain
103 B5 Cuemba Angola
42 C4 Cuenca Ecuador
65 E2 Cuenca Spain
65 E2 Cuenca, Serranía de *mts* Spain
36 E5 Cuernavaca Mex.
27 D6 Cuero U.S.A.
34 B4 Cuesta Pass *pass* U.S.A.
67 K2 Cugir Romania
43 G5 Cuiabá *Amazonas* Brazil
46 A1 Cuiabá *Mato Grosso* Brazil
46 A2 Cuiabá *r.* Brazil
46 A1 Cuiabá de Larga Brazil
60 D3 Cuilcagh *h.* Rep. of Ireland/U.K.
57 B3 Cuillin Hills *mts* U.K.
57 B3 Cuillin Sound *chan.* U.K.
103 B4 Cuilo Angola
46 E2 Cuité *r.* Brazil
103 B5 Cuito *r.* Angola
103 B5 Cuito Cuanavale Angola
95 B4 Cukai Malaysia
81 J3 Çukurca Turkey
95 D3 Cu Lao Cham *i.* Vietnam
95 D2 Cu Lao Re *i.* Vietnam
95 D3 Cu Lao Thu *i.* Vietnam
24 F1 Culbertson *MT* U.S.A.
26 C3 Culbertson *NE* U.S.A.
115 G5 Culcairn Austr.
81 K2 Culfa Azer.
115 G2 Culgoa *r.* Austr.
36 C4 Culiacán Mex.
94 A4 Culion Phil.
94 A4 Culion *i.* Phil.
57 F3 Cullen U.K.
113 H2 Cullen Pt *pt* Austr.
65 F3 Cullera Spain
57 ☐ Cullivoe U.K.
29 C5 Cullman U.S.A.
81 H2 Çullu Turkey
60 E3 Cullybackey U.K.

57 C2 Cul Mor *h.* U.K.
32 D5 Culpeper U.S.A.
42 ☐ Culpepper, Isla *i.* Ecuador
43 H6 Culuene *r.* Brazil
117 D5 Culverden N.Z.
57 D5 Culzean Bay *b.* U.K.
45 D2 Cumaná Venez.
45 B4 Cumare, Cerro *h.* Col.
45 A4 Cumbal, Nevado de *mt* Col.
32 D5 Cumberland *MD* U.S.A.
30 A3 Cumberland *WV* U.S.A.
28 C4 Cumberland *r.* U.S.A.
21 J4 Cumberland House Can.
116 C3 Cumberland Is *is* Austr.
21 J4 Cumberland Lake *l.* Can.
32 B6 Cumberland Mts *mts* U.S.A.
118 A3 Cumberland Peninsula *pen.* Can.
28 C4 Cumberland Plateau *plat.* U.S.A.
30 C2 Cumberland Pt *pt* U.S.A.
118 A3 Cumberland Sound *sound* Can.
57 E5 Cumbernauld U.K.
34 A2 Cummings U.S.A.
114 A5 Cummins Austr.
115 H4 Cumnock Austr.
57 D5 Cumnock U.K.
25 E6 Cumpas Mex.
80 D3 Çumra Turkey
103 B5 Čunene *r.* Angola
66 B2 Cuneo Italy
114 A4 Cungena Austr.
95 D2 Cung Son Vietnam
81 G2 Çüngüş Turkey
115 F2 Čunnamulla Austr.
57 ☐ Cunningsburgh U.K.
45 D4 Cunucunuma *r.* Venez.
66 B2 Cuorgnè Italy
57 E4 Cupar U.K.
45 A3 Cupica Col.
45 A3 Cupica, Golfo de *b.* Col.
43 L5 Curaçá Brazil
37 L6 Curaçao *i.* Neth. Ant.
47 B3 Curacautín Chile
47 D3 Curacó *r.* Arg.
47 B3 Curanilahue Chile
42 D4 Curaray *r.* Ecuador
47 B3 Curaumilla, Punta *pt* Chile
114 B3 Curdlawidny Lagoon *salt flat* Austr.
25 F4 Curecanti Nat. Rec. Area *res.* U.S.A.
47 B2 Curicó Chile
45 D5 Curicuriari, Sa. *h.* Brazil
45 D5 Curicuriari *r.* Brazil
46 C4 Curitiba Brazil
114 A4 Curnamona Austr.
115 J3 Currabubula Austr.
43 L5 Currais Novos Brazil
100 ☐ Curral Velho Cape Verde
31 F3 Currant U.S.A.
60 A6 Currane, Lough *l.* Rep. of Ireland
35 E2 Currant U.S.A.
114 F3 Curranyalpa Austr.
113 H5 Currawilla Austr.
29 E7 Current Bahamas
115 E7 Currie Austr.
35 E1 Currie U.S.A.
115 J5 Currockbilly, Mt *mt* Austr.
116 E5 Curtis Channel *chan.* Austr.
115 G7 Curtis Group *is* Austr.
116 D4 Curtis I. *i.* Austr.
43 H5 Curuá *r.* Brazil
43 J4 Curuçá Brazil
92 C7 Curup Indon.
45 D4 Curupira, Serra *mts* Brazil/Venez.
43 K4 Cururupu Brazil
45 E3 Curutú, Cerro *mt* Venez.
46 D2 Curvelo Brazil
42 D6 Cusco Peru
60 E2 Cushendall U.K.
60 E2 Cushendun U.K.
27 D4 Cushing U.S.A.
45 C3 Cusiana *r.* Col.
25 F6 Cusihuiráchic Mex.
29 C5 Cusseta U.S.A.
30 A1 Cusson U.S.A.
22 E1 Cusson, Pte *pt* Can.
24 F2 Custer *MT* U.S.A.
26 C3 Custer *SD* U.S.A.
45 A4 Cutanga, Pico de *mt* Col.
24 D1 Cut Bank U.S.A.
29 C6 Cuthbert U.S.A.
21 H4 Cut Knife Can.
35 K2 Cutler U.S.A.
29 D7 Cutler Ridge U.S.A.
47 C3 Cutral-Co Arg.
85 F5 Cuttack India
35 ☐ Cutter U.S.A.
112 B4 Cuvier, C. *hd* Austr.
62 D4 Cuxhaven Ger.
32 C4 Cuyahoga Falls U.S.A.
32 C4 Cuyahoga Valley National Recreation Area *res.* U.S.A.
34 C4 Cuyama *r.* U.S.A.
94 B3 Cuyapo Phil.
94 B4 Cuyo Phil.
94 B4 Cuyo *i.* Phil.
94 B4 Cuyo East Pass. *chan.* Phil.
94 B4 Cuyo Islands *is* Phil.
94 B4 Cuyo West Pass. *chan.* Phil.
45 E3 Cuyuni *r.* Guyana
Cuzco *see* Cusco

59 D6 Cwmbran U.K.
102 C4 Cyangugu Rwanda
67 L6 Cyclades *is* Greece
115 G9 Cygnet Austr.
32 A5 Cynthiana U.S.A.
21 G5 Cypress Hills *mts* Can.
71 Cyprus *country* Asia
21 G4 Czar Can.
48 Czech Republic *country* Europe
62 H4 Czersk Pol.
63 J5 Częstochowa Pol.

D

89 B6 Đa, Sông *r.* Vietnam
87 M2 Da'an China
45 C2 Dabajuro Venez.
100 B4 Dabakala Côte d'Ivoire
88 F1 Daban China
88 A2 Daban Shan *mts* China
88 B5 Daba Shan *mts* China
45 A3 Dabeiba Col.
84 C5 Dabhoi India
88 E4 Dabie Shan *mts* China
84 D4 Daboh India
100 A3 Dabola Guinea
100 B4 Daboya Ghana
88 C2 Dabqig China
84 D4 Dabra India
63 J7 Dąbrowa Górnicza Pol.
89 E5 Dabu China
Dacca *see* Dhaka
62 H4 Dachau Ger.
88 A2 Dachechang China
88 F1 Dachengzi China
88 C4 Dachuan China
31 J3 Dacre Can.
80 D1 Daday Turkey
29 D6 Dade City U.S.A.
84 C5 Dadra India
84 C5 Dadra and Nagar Haveli *div.* India
84 A4 Dadu Pak.
89 B4 Dadu He *r.* China
95 C3 Da Dung *r.* Vietnam
93 B4 Daet Phil.
89 B5 Dafang China
88 F3 Dafeng China
85 H4 Dafla Hills *mts* India
100 A3 Dagana Senegal
83 B3 Dagcanglhamo China
69 H7 Dagestan, Respublika *div.* Rus. Fed.
88 F2 Dagu *r.* China
89 B5 Daguan China
94 B2 Dagupan Phil.
85 H1 Dagur China
85 G3 Dagzê China
85 F3 Dagzê Co *salt l.* China
84 C6 Dahanu India
88 D1 Dahei *r.* China
90 C1 Dahezhen China
87 M3 Da Hinggan Ling *mts* China
102 E2 Dahlak Archipelago *is* Eritrea
102 E2 Dahlak Marine National Park *nat. park* Eritrea
66 C7 Dahmani Tunisia
84 C5 Dāhod India
84 D2 Dahongliutan China/Jammu and Kashmir
81 J3 Dahūk Iraq
88 D1 Dai Hai *l.* China
57 D5 Dailly U.K.
91 C6 Daimanji-san *h.* Japan
65 E3 Daimiel Spain
47 E3 Daireaux Arg.
30 A2 Dairyland U.S.A.
91 C7 Dai-sen *vol.* Japan
89 G4 Daishan China
89 F5 Daiyun Shan *mts* China
113 G4 Dajarra Austr.
88 A4 Dajin Chuan *r.* China
88 B2 Dajing China
85 H1 Da Juh China
100 A3 Dakar Senegal
85 G3 Dakelangsi China
85 G5 Dakhin Shahbazpur Island *i.* Bangl.
78 B4 Dakhla Oasis *oasis* Egypt
95 D2 Dak Kon Vietnam
68 D4 Dakol'ka *r.* Belarus
26 D3 Dakota City U.S.A.
67 J3 Đakovica Yugo.
67 H2 Đakovo Croatia
103 C5 Dala Angola
100 A3 Dalaba Guinea
Dalad Qi *see* Shulinzhao
88 A1 Dalain Hob China
88 E1 Dalai Nur *l.* China
81 L4 Dālā Khānī, Kūh-e *h.* Iraq
88 D2 Dalamamiao China
80 B3 Dalaman Turkey
80 B3 Dalaman *r.* Turkey
86 H3 Dalandzadgad Mongolia
94 B4 Dalanganem Islands *is* Phil.
95 D3 Đa Lat Vietnam
88 B1 Dalay Mongolia
79 J4 Dalbandin Pak.
57 E6 Dalbeattie U.K.
115 J1 Dalby Austr.
58 D3 Dale *Hordaland* Norway
55 J6 Dale *Sogn og Fjordane* Norway
32 E5 Dale City U.S.A.

27 G4 Dale Hollow Lake *l.* U.S.A.
85 H6 Dalet Myanmar
85 H5 Daletme Myanmar
55 O6 Dalfors Sweden
115 H6 Dalgety Austr.
27 C4 Dalhart U.S.A.
23 H4 Dalhousie Can.
88 D3 Dali *Shaanxi* China
82 K5 Dali *Yunnan* China
88 F2 Dalian China
89 B4 Daliang Shan *mts* China
88 G1 Dalin China
88 F1 Daling *r.* China
57 E5 Dalkeith U.K.
85 F4 Dālkola India
116 E5 Dalkon Austr.
33 H4 Dallas *PA* U.S.A.
27 D5 Dallas *TX* U.S.A.
30 B5 Dallas City U.S.A.
20 C4 Dall I. *i.* U.S.A.
47 D2 Dalmacio Vélez Sarsfield Arg.
84 E4 Dalman India
66 G3 Dalmatia *reg.* Croatia
57 D5 Dalmellington U.K.
90 D2 Dal'negorsk Rus. Fed.
90 C2 Dal'nerechensk Rus. Fed.
100 B4 Daloa Côte d'Ivoire
89 B4 Dalou Shan *mts* China
57 D5 Dalry U.K.
57 D5 Dalrymple U.K.
116 B3 Dalrymple, L. *l.* Austr.
116 C3 Dalrymple, Mt *mt* Austr.
85 F4 Daltenganj India
31 E1 Dalton Can.
105 J4 Dalton S. Africa
29 C5 Dalton *GA* U.S.A.
33 G3 Dalton *MA* U.S.A.
58 D3 Dalton-in-Furness U.K.
31 E1 Dalton Mills Can.
60 C1 Dalua *r.* Rep. of Ireland
94 B2 Dalupiri *i.* Phil.
94 C3 Dalupiri *i.* Phil.
54 D4 Dalvík Iceland
112 F2 Daly *r.* Austr.
34 A3 Daly City U.S.A.
113 F3 Daly Waters Austr.
84 C5 Damān India
84 C5 Damān and Diu *div.* India
78 C3 Damanhûr Egypt
81 M4 Damaq Iran
88 E1 Damaqun Shan *mts* China
94 C6 Damar Indon.
93 H8 Damar *i.* Indon.
47 B2 Damas, P. de las *pass* Arg./Chile
80 F5 Damascus Syria
100 D3 Damaturu Nigeria
79 H2 Damghan Iran
88 E2 Daming China
89 C6 Daming Shan *mt* China
85 H2 Damjong China
94 B5 Damiani *i.* Phil.
84 D5 Damoh India
100 B4 Damongo Ghana
112 C4 Dampier Austr.
112 D3 Dampier Land *reg.* Austr.
110 E2 Dampier Strait *chan.* P.N.G.
93 J7 Dampir, Selat *chan.* Indon.
Damqoq Zangbo *r. see* Maquan He
85 H3 Damroh India
82 H4 Damxung China
100 B4 Danané Côte d'Ivoire
95 D1 Đa Nang Vietnam
94 B4 Danao Phil.
84 A4 Danba China
33 G3 Danbury *CT* U.S.A.
33 H3 Danbury *NH* U.S.A.
33 G3 Danby U.K.
35 E4 Danby Lake *l.* U.S.A.
88 B3 Dancheng China
102 D3 Dande Eth.
114 F6 Dandenong Austr.
87 M3 Dandong China
59 E4 Dane *r.* U.K.
33 K2 Danforth U.S.A.
89 E6 Dangan Liedao *is* China
85 G3 Dangbe La *pass* China
90 B2 Dangbizhen Rus. Fed.
88 B3 Dangchang China
104 C7 Danger Pt *pt* S. Africa
102 D2 Dangila Eth.
Dangla *mts see* Tanggula Shan
85 G3 Danggên China
36 G5 Dangriga Belize
88 E3 Dangshan China
89 D4 Dangtu China
88 C3 Dangyang China
24 E3 Daniel U.S.A.
104 E4 Daniëlskuil S. Africa
68 G3 Danilov Rus. Fed.
69 H5 Danilovka Rus. Fed.
68 G3 Danilovskaya Vozvyshennost' *reg.* Rus. Fed.
88 D2 Daning China
81 M1 Dänizkänarı Azer.
88 D3 Danjiangkou China
88 D3 Danjiangkou Sk. *resr* China
84 D2 Dankhar India
68 F4 Dankov Rus. Fed.
88 A2 Danleng China
36 G6 Danlí Honduras
33 G2 Dannemora U.S.A.

117 F4 Dannevirke N.Z.
105 J4 Dannhauser S. Africa
95 B1 Dan Sai Thai.
32 E3 Dansville U.S.A.
84 C4 Danta India
67 M3 Danube *r.* Europe
30 D5 Danville *IL* U.S.A.
30 D6 Danville *IN* U.S.A.
28 C4 Danville *KY* U.S.A.
31 J5 Danville *PA* U.S.A.
32 D6 Danville *VA* U.S.A.
88 F4 Danyang China
89 C5 Danzhai China
89 C7 Danzhou China
94 B4 Dao Phil.
100 B4 Daoukro Côte d'Ivoire
89 D5 Daoxian China
89 C4 Daozhen China
94 C2 Dapa Phil.
100 C3 Dapaong Togo
85 J4 Daphabum *mt* India
94 B4 Dapiak, Mt *mt* Phil.
94 B4 Dapitan Phil.
82 J3 Da Qaidam Zhen China
87 N2 Daqing China
88 D2 Daqing Shan *mts* China
88 F1 Daqin Tal China
89 F5 Daqiu China
81 K4 Dāqūq Iraq
89 A4 Daqu Shan *i.* China
80 F5 Dar'ā Syria
79 M4 Dārāb Iran
94 B3 Daraga Phil.
63 O4 Darahanava Belarus
100 D1 Daraj Libya
94 C4 Daram *i.* Phil.
95 D2 Đa Răng, Sông *r.* Vietnam
87 K1 Darasun Rus. Fed.
85 F4 Darbhanga India
34 C2 Dardanelle U.S.A.
27 E5 Dardanelle, Lake *l.* U.S.A.
67 M4 Dardanelles *str.* Turkey
80 F2 Darende Turkey
102 D4 Dar es Salaam Tanz.
66 D2 Darfo Boario Terme Italy
84 B2 Dargai Pak.
117 D1 Dargaville N.Z.
115 G6 Dargo Austr.
86 J2 Darhan Mongolia
Darhan Muminggan Lianheqi *see* Bailingmiao
29 D6 Darien U.S.A.
45 A2 Darién, Golfo del *g.* Col.
37 J7 Darién, Parque Nacional de *nat. park* Panama
45 A2 Darién, Serranía del *mts* Panama
85 G4 Därjiling India
114 B4 Darke Peak Austr.
82 J4 Darlag China
114 E4 Darling *r.* Austr.
115 H1 Darling Downs *reg.* Austr.
112 C6 Darling Range *h.* Austr.
58 F3 Darlington U.K.
30 B4 Darlington U.S.A.
115 G5 Darlington Point Austr.
62 H3 Darłowo Pol.
62 D6 Darmstadt Ger.
84 C5 Darna *r.* India
101 E1 Darnah Libya
105 J4 Darnall S. Africa
114 E4 Darnick Austr.
119 D5 Darnley, C. *c.* Antarctica
65 F2 Daroca Spain
68 G3 Darovka Rus. Fed.
68 H3 Darovskoy Rus. Fed.
47 D3 Darregueira Arg.
84 B2 Darreh-ye Shekārī *r.* Afgh.
59 D7 Dart *r.* U.K.
59 H6 Dartford U.K.
114 D7 Dartmoor Austr.
59 C7 Dartmoor *reg.* U.K.
59 D7 Dartmoor National Park U.K.
23 H5 Dartmouth Can.
59 D7 Dartmouth U.K.
116 A6 Dartmouth, L. *salt flat* Austr.
58 F4 Darton U.K.
110 E2 Daru P.N.G.
100 A4 Daru Sierra Leone
85 G3 Darum Tso *l.* China
84 A3 Daruvar Croatia
84 A3 Darwazgai Afgh.
58 E4 Darwen U.K.
112 F2 Darwin Austr.
44 C8 Darwin, Mte *mt* Chile
84 B3 Darya Khan Pak.
88 D4 Dashennongjia *mt* China
88 B1 Dashiqiao China
79 H1 Dashkhovuz Turkm.
88 C2 Dashuikeng China
88 B3 Dashuitou China
84 C2 Daska Pak.
81 L1 Daşkäsän Azer.
84 C1 Daspar *mt* Pak.
104 C6 Dassen Island *i.* S. Africa
81 L2 Dastakert Armenia
90 B3 Da Suifen *r.* China
67 M6 Datça Turkey
90 G3 Date Japan
35 F5 Dateland U.S.A.
84 D4 Datia India
88 E5 Datian China
88 A2 Datong *Qinghai* China
88 D1 Datong *Shanxi* China
88 F4 Datong He *r.* China
88 A2 Datong Shan *mts* China
95 D5 Datu, Tanjung *c.* Indon./Malaysia

94 C5 Datu Piang Phil.
79 L3 Daud Khel Pak.
68 C5 Daugava *r.* Belarus/Latvia
55 U9 Daugavpils Latvia
84 C6 Daulatabad India
Daulatabad *see* Malāyer
61 E4 Daun Ger.
95 A2 Daung Kyun *i.* Myanmar
21 J4 Dauphin Can.
64 G4 Dauphiné *reg.* France
27 F6 Dauphin I. *i.* U.S.A.
21 K4 Dauphin L. *l.* Can.
84 D4 Dausa India
57 E3 Dava U.K.
81 M1 Däväçi Azer.
83 E8 Davangere India
94 C5 Davao Phil.
94 C5 Davao Gulf *b.* Phil.
105 H3 Davel S. Africa
34 A3 Davenport *CA* U.S.A.
30 B5 Davenport *IA* U.S.A.
59 F5 Daventry U.K.
105 H3 Daveyton S. Africa
37 H7 David Panama
21 H7 David Can.
21 J3 Davin Lake *l.* Can.
119 D5 Davis *Austr. Base* Antarctica
34 B2 Davis U.S.A.
35 E4 Davis Dam U.S.A.
23 H2 Davis Inlet Can.
119 D3 Davis Sea *sea* Antarctica
118 A3 Davis Strait *str.* Can./Green.
62 D7 Davos Switz.
88 A1 Dawan China
85 F3 Dawaxung China
88 B4 Dawê China
Dawei *see* Tavoy
88 E3 Dawen *r.* China
95 A1 Dawna Range *mts* Myanmar/Thai.
79 G6 Dawqah Oman
116 C3 Dawson *r.* Austr.
29 C6 Dawson *GA* U.S.A.
26 D2 Dawson *ND* U.S.A.
21 J4 Dawson Bay *b.* Can.
20 E3 Dawson Creek Can.
21 L2 Dawson Inlet *in.* Can.
20 B2 Dawson Range *mts* Can.
88 A4 Dawu *Hubei* China
82 K4 Dawu *Sichuan* China
64 D5 Dax France
89 D4 Daxin China
88 E2 Daxing China
89 A4 Daxue Shan *mts* China
85 H4 Dayang *r.* India
89 D6 Dayao Shan *mts* China
89 D6 Daye China
89 B4 Dayi China
114 F6 Daylesford Austr.
34 D3 Daylight Pass *pass* U.S.A.
47 F1 Daymán *r.* Uru.
47 F1 Daymán, Cuchilla del *h.* Uru.
89 D4 Dayong China
81 H4 Dayr az Zawr Syria
32 A5 Dayton *OH* U.S.A.
29 C5 Dayton *TN* U.S.A.
24 C2 Dayton *WA* U.S.A.
29 D6 Daytona Beach U.S.A.
89 D5 Dayu China
89 D5 Dayu Ling *mts* China
88 F3 Da Yunhe *r.* China
24 C2 Dayville U.S.A.
89 D7 Dazhou Dao *i.* China
89 C4 Dazhou China
89 B4 Dazu China
104 F5 De Aar S. Africa
30 D2 Dead *r.* Can.
33 H2 Dead *r.* U.S.A.
29 F7 Deadman's Cay Bahamas
35 H4 Dead Mts *mts* U.S.A.
80 E6 Dead Sea *salt l.* Asia
59 J6 Deal U.K.
105 F4 Dealesville S. Africa
20 D4 Dean *r.* Can.
89 E4 De'an China
59 E6 Dean, Forest of *forest* U.K.
47 D1 Deán Funes Arg.
31 F4 Dearborn U.S.A.
20 D3 Dease *r.* Can.
20 C3 Dease Lake Can.
34 D3 Death Valley *v.* U.S.A.
34 D3 Death Valley Junction U.S.A.
34 D3 Death Valley National Park *res.* U.S.A.
64 E2 Deauville France
92 E6 Debak Malaysia
89 C6 Debao China
67 J4 Debar Macedonia
21 H4 Debden Can.
59 J5 Debenham U.K.
35 H2 De Beque U.S.A.
61 C3 De Biesbosch, Nationaal Park *nat. park* Neth.
33 J2 Deblois U.S.A.
102 D3 Debre Birhan Eth.
63 K7 Debrecen Hungary
102 D2 Debre Markos Eth.
102 D2 Debre Tabor Eth.
102 D3 Debre Zeyit Eth.
29 C5 Decatur *AL* U.S.A.
29 C5 Decatur *GA* U.S.A.
30 C6 Decatur *IL* U.S.A.
30 D5 Decatur *IN* U.S.A.
30 E4 Decatur *MI* U.S.A.
83 E7 Deccan *plat.* India
31 H2 Decelles, Lac *resr* Can.
115 K1 Deception Bay Austr.
62 G5 Děčín Czech Rep.
30 B4 Decorah U.S.A.

59 F6 Deddington U.K.
46 C4 Dedo de Deus *mt* Brazil
104 C6 De Doorns S. Africa
81 L1 Dedop'listsqaro Georgia
100 B3 Dédougou Burkina
68 D3 Dedovichi Rus. Fed.
103 D5 Dedza Malawi
59 D4 Dee *est.* U.K.
59 E4 Dee *r.* England/Wales U.K.
57 F3 Dee *r.* Scot. U.K.
60 C5 Deel *r.* Rep. of Ireland
60 D3 Deele *r.* Rep. of Ireland
32 D5 Deep Creek Lake *l.* U.S.A.
35 F2 Deep Creek Range *mts* U.S.A.
31 J2 Deep River Can.
33 G4 Deep River U.S.A.
21 K1 Deep Rose Lake *l.* Can.
34 D3 Deep Springs U.S.A.
115 J2 Deepwater Austr.
32 B5 Deer Creek Lake *l.* U.S.A.
33 K2 Deer I. *i.* Can.
33 J2 Deer I. *i.* U.S.A.
33 J2 Deer Isle U.S.A.
22 B3 Deer L. *l.* Can.
23 J4 Deer Lake Nfld Can.
22 B3 Deer Lake Ont. Can.
24 D2 Deer Lodge U.S.A.
44 D2 Defensores del Chaco, Parque Nacional *nat. park* Para.
32 A4 Defiance U.S.A.
29 C6 De Funiak Springs U.S.A.
82 J4 Dêgê China
102 E3 Degeh Bur Eth.
85 G3 Dêgên China
62 F6 Deggendorf Ger.
84 C3 Degh *r.* Pak.
61 D3 De Groote Peel, Nationaal Park *nat. park* Neth.
81 N3 Dehgāh Iran
81 L4 Deh Golān Iran
81 L5 Dehlorān Iran
84 D3 Dehra Dun India
85 F4 Dehri India
81 K4 Deh Sheykh Iran
89 F5 Dehua China
87 N3 Dehui China
61 B4 Deinze Belgium
80 E5 Deir el Qamer Lebanon
Deir-ez-Zor *see* Dayr az Zawr
63 L7 Dej Romania
89 C4 Dejiang China
30 C5 De Kalb IL U.S.A.
27 E5 De Kalb TX U.S.A.
33 F2 De Kalb Junction U.S.A.
87 Q1 De-Kastri Rus. Fed.
78 D6 Dekemhare Eritrea
102 C4 Dekese Dem. Rep. Congo
34 C4 Delano U.S.A.
35 F2 Delano Peak *summit* U.S.A.
79 J3 Delārām Afgh.
105 F3 Delareyville S. Africa
21 H4 Delaronde Lake *l.* Can.
30 C5 Delavan IL U.S.A.
30 C4 Delavan WI U.S.A.
32 B4 Delaware U.S.A.
33 F5 Delaware *div.* U.S.A.
33 F4 Delaware *r.* U.S.A.
33 F5 Delaware Bay *b.* U.S.A.
32 B4 Delaware Lake *l.* U.S.A.
33 F4 Delaware Water Gap National Recreational Area *res.* U.S.A.
115 H6 Delegate Austr.
62 C7 Delémont Switz.
61 C2 Delft Neth.
61 E1 Delfzijl Neth.
103 E5 Delgado, Cabo *pt* Moz.
31 G4 Delhi Can.
82 J3 Delhi China
84 D3 Delhi India
25 F4 Delhi CO U.S.A.
33 F3 Delhi NY U.S.A.
92 □ Deli *i.* Indon.
81 J2 Deli *r.* Turkey
80 E2 Delice Turkey
80 E1 Delice *r.* Turkey
20 E1 Déline Can.
21 H4 Delisle Can.
26 D3 Dell Rapids U.S.A.
65 H4 Dellys Alg.
34 D5 Del Mar U.S.A.
35 E3 Delmar L. *l.* U.S.A.
62 D4 Delmenhorst Ger.
77 R2 De-Longa, O-va *is* Rus. Fed.
21 J5 Deloraine Can.
30 D5 Delphi U.S.A.
32 A4 Delphos U.S.A.
104 F4 Delportshoop S. Africa
29 D7 Delray Beach U.S.A.
25 E6 Del Río Mex.
27 C6 Del Rio U.S.A.
55 P6 Delsbo Sweden
35 H2 Delta CO U.S.A.
30 A5 Delta IA U.S.A.
35 F2 Delta UT U.S.A.
33 F3 Delta Reservoir *resr* U.S.A.
29 D6 Deltona U.S.A.
115 J2 Delungra Austr.
60 D4 Delvin Rep. of Ireland
67 J5 Delvinë Albania
102 C4 Demba Dem. Rep. Congo
102 D3 Dembī Dolo Eth.
68 D4 Demidov Rus. Fed.
25 F5 Deming U.S.A.
45 E4 Demini *r.* Brazil
80 B2 Demirci Turkey
67 M4 Demirköy Turkey
62 F4 Demmin Ger.
29 C5 Demopolis U.S.A.
30 D5 Demotte U.S.A.
92 C7 Dempo, G. *vol.* Indon.
84 D2 Dêmqog China/India
68 H2 Dem'yanovo Rus. Fed.
68 E3 Demyansk Rus. Fed.
104 D5 De Naawte S. Africa
102 E2 Denakil *reg.* Eritrea
102 E3 Denan Eth.
21 J4 Denare Beach Can.
79 K2 Denau Uzbek.
31 J3 Denbigh Can.
59 D4 Denbigh U.K.
61 C1 Den Burg Neth.
95 B1 Den Chai Thai.
61 D2 Den Dolder Neth.
105 H1 Dendron S. Africa
91 C1 Dengkou China
85 H3 Dêngqên China
88 D3 Dengzhou China
Den Haag *see* The Hague
112 B5 Denham Austr.
116 B3 Denham Ra. *mts* Austr.
61 C2 Den Helder Neth.
65 G3 Denia Spain
114 F5 Deniliquin Austr.
24 C3 Denio U.S.A.
26 E3 Denison IA U.S.A.
27 D5 Denison TX U.S.A.
80 B3 Denizli Turkey
115 J4 Denman Austr.
112 C6 Denmark Austr.
48 Denmark *country* Europe
118 A4 Denmark Strait *str.* Greenland/Iceland
35 H3 Dennehotso U.S.A.
33 H4 Dennis Port U.S.A.
57 E4 Denny U.K.
33 K2 Dennysville U.S.A.
92 □ Denpasar Indon.
33 F5 Denton MD U.S.A.
27 D5 Denton TX U.S.A.
112 C6 D'Entrecasteaux, Point *pt* Austr.
111 G3 D'Entrecasteaux, Récifs *rf* New Caledonia
110 F2 D'Entrecasteaux Islands *is* P.N.G.
24 F4 Denver U.S.A.
85 F4 Deo India
84 D3 Deoband India
85 F5 Deogarh India
85 E5 Deogarh *mt* India
85 F4 Deoghar India
84 D5 Deori India
85 E4 Deoria India
84 C2 Deosai, Plains of *plain* Pak.
85 E5 Deosil India
61 D3 De Peel *reg.* Neth.
30 C3 De Pere U.S.A.
33 F3 Deposit U.S.A.
31 J2 Depot-Forbes Can.
31 J2 Depot-Rowanton Can.
30 C5 Depue U.S.A.
77 P3 Deputatskiy Rus. Fed.
82 J5 Dêqên China
89 D6 Deqing *Guangdong* China
89 F4 Deqing *Zhejiang* China
27 E5 De Queen U.S.A.
84 B3 Dera Bugti Pak.
84 B3 Dera Ghazi Khan Pak.
84 B3 Dera Ismail Khan Pak.
84 B3 Derawar Fort Pak.
69 J7 Derbent Rus. Fed.
115 G8 Derby *Tas.* Austr.
112 D3 Derby *W.A.* Austr.
59 F5 Derby U.K.
33 G4 Derby CT U.S.A.
27 D4 Derby KS U.S.A.
60 D3 Derg *r.* Rep. of Ireland/U.K.
60 C5 Derg, Lough *l.* Rep. of Ireland
69 J5 Dergachi Rus. Fed.
69 F5 Derhachi Ukr.
27 E6 De Ridder U.S.A.
81 H3 Derik Turkey
80 E2 Derinkuyu Turkey
69 F5 Derkul *r.* Rus. Fed./Ukr.
104 C1 Derm Namibia
60 D4 Derravaragh, Lough *l.* Rep. of Ireland
60 E5 Derry *r.* Rep. of Ireland
33 H3 Derry U.S.A.
60 C3 Derryveagh Mts *h.* Rep. of Ireland
88 A1 Derstei China
101 F3 Derudeb Sudan
104 E6 De Rust S. Africa
66 G2 Derventa Bos.-Herz.
115 G9 Derwent *r.* Austr.
58 G4 Derwent *r.* U.K.
57 G6 Derwent Reservoir *resr* U.K.
58 D3 Derwent Water *l.* U.K.
76 H4 Derzhavinsk Kazak.
47 C2 Desaguadero *r.* Arg.
42 E7 Desaguadero *r.* Bol.
34 D2 Desatoya Mts *mts* U.S.A.
31 F2 Desbarats Can.
21 J3 Deschambault L. *l.* Can.
21 J4 Deschambault Lake Can.
24 B2 Deschutes *r.* U.S.A.
102 D2 Desē Eth.
44 C7 Deseado Arg.
44 C7 Deseado *r.* Arg.
25 D6 Desemboque Mex.
35 F1 Deseret Peak *summit* U.S.A.
31 J3 Deseronto Can.
84 B3 Desert Canal *canal* Pak.
35 E5 Desert Center U.S.A.
26 E3 Des Moines IA U.S.A.
25 G4 Des Moines NM U.S.A.
30 A5 Des Moines *r.* U.S.A.
68 E5 Desna *r.* Rus. Fed.
69 D5 Desna Ukr.
68 E4 Desnogorsk Rus. Fed.
94 C4 Desolation Point *pt* Phil.
30 D4 Des Plaines U.S.A.
62 F5 Dessau Ger.
31 H1 Destor Can.
114 B5 D'Estrees B. *b.* Austr.
20 B2 Destruction Bay Can.
67 J2 Deta Romania
20 G2 Detah Can.
103 C5 Dete Zimbabwe
62 D5 Detmold Ger.
30 D3 Detour, Pt *pt* U.S.A.
31 F3 De Tour Village U.S.A.
31 F4 Detroit U.S.A.
26 E2 Detroit Lakes U.S.A.
115 H5 Deua Nat. Park *nat. park* Austr.
66 F1 Deutschlandsberg Austria
31 H2 Deux-Rivières Can.
67 K2 Deva Romania
80 E2 Develi Turkey
61 E2 Deventer Neth.
62 H6 Devét Skal *h.* Czech Rep.
84 B4 Devikot India
60 D5 Devil's Bit Mountain *h.* Rep. of Ireland
59 D5 Devil's Bridge U.K.
34 C4 Devils Den U.S.A.
34 C2 Devils Gate *pass* U.S.A.
30 B2 Devil's Island *i.* U.S.A.
26 D1 Devil's Lake U.S.A.
34 C3 Devil's Peak *summit* U.S.A.
34 C3 Devils Postpile National Monument *res.* U.S.A.
29 F7 Devil's Pt Bahamas
59 F6 Devizes U.K.
84 C4 Devli India
67 M3 Devnya Bulg.
20 G4 Devon Can.
59 G5 Devon *r.* U.K.
118 B3 Devon I. *i.* Can.
115 G8 Devonport Austr.
80 C1 Devrek Turkey
80 D1 Devrekâni Turkey
80 E1 Devrez *r.* Turkey
85 D5 Dewas India
61 E2 De Weerribben, Nationaal Park *nat. park* Neth.
105 G4 Dewetsdorp S. Africa
32 B6 Dewey Lake *l.* U.S.A.
27 F5 De Witt AR U.S.A.
30 B5 De Witt IA U.S.A.
58 F4 Dewsbury U.K.
89 E4 Dexing China
32 J3 Dexter ME U.S.A.
27 F4 Dexter MO U.S.A.
33 E2 Dexter NY U.S.A.
88 B4 Deyang China
81 M3 Deylaman Iran
93 K8 Deyong, Tanjung *pt* Indon.
81 M6 Dez *r.* Iran
81 M5 Dezfūl Iran
88 E2 Dezhou China
79 G4 Dhahran Saudi Arabia
85 G5 Dhaka Bangl.
85 G5 Dhaleswari *r.* Bangl.
85 H4 Dhaleswari *r.* India
78 E7 Dhamār Yemen
85 F5 Dhāmara India
84 C5 Dhamnod India
85 E5 Dhamtari India
84 B3 Dhana Sar Pak.
85 F5 Dhanbad India
84 C5 Dhandhuka India
85 E3 Dhang Ra. *mts* Nepal
85 C5 Dhar India
85 F4 Dharan Bazar Nepal
84 B5 Dhari India
83 E8 Dharmavaram India
84 D2 Dharmshala India
83 E7 Dhārwād India
84 D4 Dhasan *r.* India
85 E3 Dhaulagiri *mt* Nepal
84 D4 Dhaulpur India
84 C4 Dhebar L. *l.* India
85 H4 Dhekiajuli India
80 E6 Dhībān Jordan
85 H4 Dhing India
84 B5 Dhoraji India
84 B5 Dhrangadhra India
84 C5 Dhule India
85 F4 Dhulian India
85 F4 Dhunche Nepal
84 D4 Dhund *r.* India
102 E3 Dhuusa Marreeb Somalia
67 L7 Dia *i.* Greece
34 B3 Diablo, Mt *mt* U.S.A.
25 D6 Diablo, Picacho del *mt* Mex.
34 B3 Diablo Range *mts* U.S.A.
47 E2 Diamante Arg.
47 C2 Diamante *r.* Arg.
113 H4 Diamantina *watercourse* Austr.
46 D2 Diamantina Brazil
43 K6 Diamantina, Chapada *plat.* Brazil
46 A1 Diamantino Brazil
34 □1 Diamond Head *hd* U.S.A.
116 D1 Diamond Islets *is* Coral Sea Is Terr.
35 E2 Diamond Peak *summit* U.S.A.
89 D6 Dianbai China
89 B5 Dian Chi *l.* China
89 C4 Dianjiang China
43 J6 Dianópolis Brazil
100 B4 Dianra Côte d'Ivoire
90 B2 Diaoling China
100 C3 Diapaga Burkina
102 C4 Dibaya Dem. Rep. Congo
104 E3 Dibeng S. Africa
22 F2 D'Iberville, Lac *l.* Can.
105 G1 Dibete Botswana
85 H4 Dibrugarh India
27 C5 Dickens U.S.A.
33 J1 Dickey U.S.A.
26 C2 Dickinson U.S.A.
29 C4 Dickson U.S.A.
33 F4 Dickson City U.S.A.
Dicle *r. see* Tigris
94 B2 Didicas *i.* Phil.
84 C4 Didwana India
67 M4 Didymoteicho Greece
64 G4 Die France
100 B3 Diébougou Burkina
21 H4 Diefenbaker, L. *l.* Can.
13 J4 Diego Garcia *i.* British Indian Ocean Territory
61 E5 Diekirch Lux.
100 B3 Diéma Mali
89 B6 Điện Biên Phu Vietnam
95 C1 Diên Châu Vietnam
95 D2 Diên Khanh Vietnam
64 E2 Dieppe France
88 C2 Di'er Nonchang Qu *r.* China
61 D3 Diessen Neth.
61 D4 Diest Belgium
62 D7 Dietikon Switz.
101 D3 Diffa Niger
23 G5 Digby Can.
85 F5 Digha India
64 H4 Digne-les-Bains France
64 F3 Digoin France
94 C5 Digos Phil.
84 D5 Digras India
84 B4 Digri Pak.
93 K8 Digul *r.* Indon.
100 B4 Digya National Park *nat. park* Ghana
64 G3 Dijon France
102 E2 Dikhil Djibouti
67 M5 Dikili Turkey
61 A3 Diksmuide Belgium
76 K2 Dikson Rus. Fed.
101 D3 Dikwa Nigeria
102 D3 Dīla Eth.
93 H8 Dili Indon.
81 K1 Dilijan Armenia
95 D3 Di Linh Vietnam
27 D6 Dilley U.S.A.
62 E6 Dillingen an der Donau Ger.
21 H3 Dillon Can.
24 D2 Dillon MT U.S.A.
29 E5 Dillon SC U.S.A.
103 C5 Dilolo Dem. Rep. Congo
81 K5 Diltāwa Iraq
85 H4 Dimapur India
Dimashq *see* Damascus
102 C4 Dimbelenge Dem. Rep. Congo
100 B4 Dimbokro Côte d'Ivoire
114 E6 Dimboola Austr.
116 A1 Dimbulah Austr.
67 L3 Dimitrovgrad Bulg.
68 J4 Dimitrovgrad Rus. Fed.
80 E6 Dīmona Israel
104 D2 Dimpho Pan *salt pan* Botswana
94 C4 Dinagat *i.* Phil.
85 G4 Dinajpur Bangl.
64 C2 Dinan France
84 C2 Dinanagar India
61 C4 Dinant Belgium
85 F4 Dinapur India
80 C2 Dinar Turkey
66 G2 Dinara Planina *mts* Croatia
102 D2 Dinder National Park *nat. park* Sudan
83 E8 Dindigul India
105 K1 Dindiza Moz.
84 E5 Dindori India
80 D3 Dinek Turkey
85 H4 Dingba Qu *r.* India
88 C2 Dingbian China
102 B4 Dinge Angola
85 F4 Dingla Nepal
60 A5 Dingle Rep. of Ireland
60 A5 Dingle Bay *b.* Rep. of Ireland
89 E5 Dingnan China
116 C4 Dingo Austr.
94 B2 Dingras Phil.
88 E3 Dingtao China
100 A3 Dinguiraye Guinea
57 D3 Dingwall U.K.
88 B3 Dingxi China
88 E2 Dingxing China
88 E3 Dingyuan China
88 E2 Dingzhou China
88 F2 Dingzi Gang *harbour* China
89 C6 Dinh Lâp Vietnam
35 G3 Dinnebito Wash *r.* U.S.A.
85 F3 Dinngyê China
105 G1 Dinokwe Botswana
21 L5 Dinorwic Lake U.S.A.
35 H1 Dinosaur U.S.A.
24 E3 Dinosaur Nat. Mon. *res.* U.S.A.
100 B3 Dioïla Mali
46 B4 Dionísio Cerqueira Brazil
100 A3 Diourbel Senegal
85 H4 Diphu India
84 B4 Diplo Pak.
94 B4 Dipolog Phil.
117 B6 Dipton N.Z.
79 L2 Dir Pak.
80 F2 Dirckli Turkey
100 B3 Diré Mali
113 H2 Direction, C. *c.* Austr.
102 E3 Dirē Dawa Eth.
103 C5 Dirico Angola
112 B5 Dirk Hartog I. *i.* Austr.
115 H2 Dirranbandi Austr.
81 M6 Dīrsīyeh Iran
35 G2 Dirty Devil *r.* U.S.A.
84 C4 Dīsa India
44 □ Disappointment, C. *c.* Atlantic Ocean
24 A2 Disappointment, C. *c.* U.S.A.
112 D4 Disappointment, L. *salt flat* Austr.
115 H6 Disaster B. *b.* Austr.
114 D7 Discovery Bay *b.* Austr.
Disko *i. see* Qeqertarsuaq
33 E6 Dismal Swamp *swamp* U.S.A.
85 G4 Dispur India
59 J5 Diss U.K.
46 C1 Distrito Federal *div.* Brazil
80 C6 Disûq Egypt
94 B4 Dit *i.* Phil.
104 E4 Ditloung S. Africa
66 F6 Dittaino *r.* Italy
84 B5 Diu India
94 C4 Diuata Mountains *mts* Phil.
94 C4 Diuata Pt *pt* Phil.
81 L4 Dīvān Darreh Iran
68 G4 Diveyevo Rus. Fed.
94 B2 Divilacan Bay *b.* Phil.
46 D3 Divinópolis Brazil
69 G6 Divnoye Rus. Fed.
100 B4 Divo Côte d'Ivoire
80 G2 Divriği Turkey
33 H2 Dixfield U.S.A.
33 J2 Dixmont U.S.A.
34 B2 Dixon CA U.S.A.
30 C5 Dixon IL U.S.A.
20 C4 Dixon Entrance *chan.* Can./U.S.A.
29 F7 Dixon's Bahamas
20 F3 Dixonville Can.
33 H2 Dixville Can.
81 J2 Diyadin Turkey
81 K5 Diyālā, Nahr *r.* Iraq
81 H3 Diyarbakır Turkey
84 B4 Diyodar India
101 D2 Djado Niger
101 D2 Djado, Plateau du *plat.* Niger
102 B4 Djambala Congo
100 C2 Djanet Alg.
100 C1 Djelfa Alg.
102 C3 Djéma C.A.R.
100 B3 Djenné Mali
100 B3 Djibo Burkina
96 Djibouti *country* Africa
102 E2 Djibouti Djibouti
60 E4 Djouce Mountain *h.* Rep. of Ireland
100 C4 Djougou Benin
54 F4 Djúpivogur Iceland
55 O6 Djurås Sweden
81 K1 Dmanisi Georgia
77 Q2 Dmitriya Lapteva, Proliv *chan.* Rus. Fed.
90 C2 Dmitriyevka Rus. Fed.
68 G4 Dmitriyevka Rus. Fed.
69 E4 Dmitriyev-L'govskiy Rus. Fed.
68 F3 Dmitrov Rus. Fed.
Dnepr *r. see* Dnieper
63 P5 Dnieper *r.* Europe
63 P3 Dnieper *r.* Rus. Fed.
76 E5 Dnieper *r.* Ukr.
63 N6 Dniester *r.* Ukr.
Dnipro *r. see* Dnieper
69 E5 Dniprodzerzhyns'k Ukr.
69 E5 Dnipropetrovs'k Ukr.
69 E6 Dniprorudne Ukr.
68 D3 Dno Rus. Fed.
Dnyapro *r. see* Dnieper
101 D4 Doba Chad
31 G3 Dobbinton Can.
55 S8 Dobele Latvia
93 J7 Doberai Peninsula *pen.* Indon.
47 D3 Doblas Arg.
93 J8 Dobo Indon.
67 H2 Doboj Bos.-Herz.
67 M3 Dobrich Bulg.
69 G4 Dobrinka Rus. Fed.
69 D4 Dobrush Belarus
94 A5 Doc Can *rf* Phil.
46 E2 Doce *r.* Brazil
59 H5 Docking U.K.
25 F6 Doctor Belisario Domínguez Mex.
67 M6 Dodecanese *is* Greece
Dodekanisos *is see* Dodecanese
24 C2 Dodge U.S.A.
30 A3 Dodge Center U.S.A.
27 C4 Dodge City U.S.A.
115 G9 Dodges Ferry Austr.
30 B4 Dodgeville U.S.A.
59 C7 Dodman Point *pt* U.K.
102 D4 Dodoma Tanz.
61 E3 Doetinchem Neth.
93 H7 Dofa Indon.
85 G2 Dogai Coring *salt l.* China
85 G2 Dogaicoring Qangco *salt l.* China
81 J2 Doğançay Dağı *mt* Turkey
80 F2 Doğanşehir Turkey
20 E4 Dog Creek Can.
85 G3 Dogên Co *l.* China
23 H2 Dog Island *i.* Can.
21 K4 Dog L. *l.* Can.
31 E1 Dog Lake *l.* Can.
91 C6 Dōgo *i.* Japan
100 C3 Dogondoutchi Niger
91 C7 Dōgo-yama *mt* Japan
81 K2 Doğubeyazıt Turkey
85 F3 Dogxung Zangbo *r.* China
85 G3 Do'gyaling China
79 G4 Doha Qatar
Dohad *see* Dāhod
85 H5 Dohazari Bangl.
85 G3 Doilungdêqên China
95 A1 Doi Saket Thai.
43 K5 Dois Irmãos, Serra dos *h.* Brazil
67 K4 Dojran, Lake *l.* Greece/Macedonia
55 M6 Dokka Norway
61 D1 Dokkum Neth.
84 B4 Dokri Pak.
63 N3 Dokshytsy Belarus
69 F6 Dokuchayevs'k Ukr.
93 K8 Dolak, Pulau *i.* Indon.
23 F4 Dolbeau Can.
59 C5 Dolbenmaen U.K.
64 D2 Dol-de-Bretagne France
64 G3 Dole France
59 D5 Dolgellau U.K.
33 F3 Dolgeville U.S.A.
69 F4 Dolgorukovo Rus. Fed.
69 F4 Dolgoye Rus. Fed.
66 C5 Dolianova Italy
87 Q2 Dolinsk Rus. Fed.
66 D1 Dolomiti *mts* Italy
102 E3 Dolo Odo Eth.
47 F3 Dolores Arg.
47 E2 Dolores Uru.
35 H2 Dolores *r.* U.S.A.
89 B7 Đô Lương Vietnam
69 B5 Dolyna Ukr.
80 B2 Domaniç Turkey
84 E2 Domar China
62 F6 Domažlice Czech Rep.
85 H2 Domba China
81 L5 Dom Bākh Iran
55 L5 Dombås Norway
62 J7 Dombóvár Hungary
119 C4 Dome Argus *ice feature* Antarctica
119 C5 Dome Charlie *ice feature* Antarctica
Dome Circe *ice feature see* Dome Charlie
20 E4 Dome Creek Can.
119 C4 Dome Fuji *Japan Base* Antarctica
20 D2 Dome Pk *summit* Can.
35 E5 Dome Rock Mts *mts* U.S.A.
64 D2 Domfront France
16 Dominica *country* Caribbean Sea
16 Dominican Republic *country* Caribbean Sea
95 C2 Dom Noi, L. *r.* Thai.
66 C1 Domodossola Italy
67 K5 Domokos Greece
47 F1 Dom Pedrito Brazil
93 F8 Dompu Indon.
47 B3 Domuyo, Volcán *vol.* Arg.
115 J2 Domville, Mt *h.* Austr.
116 C3 Don *r.* Austr.
69 G5 Don *r.* Rus. Fed.
57 F3 Don *r.* U.K.
95 C2 Don, Xé *r.* Laos
60 F3 Donaghadee U.K.
60 E3 Donaghmore U.K.
114 E6 Donald Austr.
Donau *r. see* Danube
62 D7 Donaueschingen Ger.
62 E6 Donauwörth Ger.
65 D3 Don Benito Spain
58 F4 Doncaster U.K.
103 B4 Dondo Angola
103 D5 Dondo Moz.
94 B4 Dondonay *i.* Phil.
60 C3 Donegal Rep. of Ireland
60 C3 Donegal Bay *g.* Rep. of Ireland
69 F6 Donets'k Ukr.
69 F5 Donets'kyy Kryazh *h.* Rus. Fed./Ukr.
89 D5 Dong'an China
112 B5 Dongara Austr.
84 E5 Dongargarh India
89 B5 Dongchuan China
85 F2 Dongco China
89 C7 Dongfang China
90 C1 Dongfanghong China
93 F7 Donggala Indon.
89 E5 Donggu China
89 D6 Dongguan China
95 C1 Đông Ha Vietnam
88 F3 Donghai China
89 D6 Donghai Dao *i.* China
88 C4 Dong He *r.* China
88 A1 Dong He *watercourse* China
95 C1 Đông Hôi Vietnam
90 A2 Dongjingcheng China
85 H3 Dongjug *Xizang Zizhiqu* China
85 H3 Dongjug *Xizang Zizhiqu* China
89 D5 Dongkou China
85 G4 Dongkya La *pass* India
89 C5 Donglan China
88 A2 Dongle China

88 G1 Dongliao r. China
90 B3 Dongning China
103 B5 Dongo Angola
102 B3 Dongou Congo
95 B1 Dong Phraya Fai mts Thai.
95 B2 Dong Phraya Yen escarpment Thai.
89 D6 Dongping Guangdong China
88 E3 Dongping Shandong China
85 G3 Dongqiao China
89 E6 Dongshan China
89 E6 Dongshan Dao i. China
88 D2 Dongsheng China
88 F3 Dongtai China
88 F3 Dongtai r. China
89 D4 Dongting Hu l. China
89 F5 Dongtou China
Dong Ujimqin Qi see Uliastai
89 E4 Dongxiang China
89 F4 Dongyang China
88 F2 Dongying China
88 B2 Dongzhen China
89 E4 Dongzhi China
20 B2 Donjek r. Can.
85 G5 Donmanick Islands is Bangl.
23 F4 Donnacona Can.
20 F3 Donnelly Can.
117 D1 Donnellys Crossing N.Z.
34 B2 Donner Pass pass U.S.A.
Donostia-San Sebastián see San Sebastián
67 L6 Donoussa i. Greece
68 F4 Donskoy Rus. Fed.
69 G6 Donskoye Rus. Fed.
94 B3 Donsol Phil.
60 A4 Dooagh Rep. of Ireland
57 D5 Doon, Loch l. U.K.
60 B5 Doonbeg r. Rep. of Ireland
30 D3 Door Peninsula pen. U.S.A.
102 E3 Dooxo Nugaaleed v. Somalia
27 C5 Dora U.S.A.
66 C2 Dora Baltea r. Italy
59 E7 Dorchester U.K.
103 B6 Dordabis Namibia
64 E4 Dordogne r. France
61 C3 Dordrecht Neth.
105 G5 Dordrecht S. Africa
104 C1 Doreenville Namibia
21 H4 Doré L. l. Can.
21 H4 Doré Lake Can.
66 C4 Dorgali Italy
100 B3 Dori Burkina
104 C5 Doring r. S. Africa
59 G6 Dorking U.K.
57 D3 Dornoch Firth est. U.K.
88 C1 Dornogovĭ div. Mongolia
68 E4 Dorogobuzh Rus. Fed.
63 N7 Dorohoi Romania
86 F2 Döröö Nuur salt l. Mongolia
54 P4 Dorotea Sweden
112 B5 Dorre I. i. Austr.
115 K3 Dorrigo Austr.
24 B3 Dorris U.S.A.
100 D4 Dorsale Camerounaise slope Cameroon/Nigeria
31 H3 Dorset Can.
62 C5 Dortmund Ger.
61 F3 Dortmund-Ems-Kanal canal Ger.
32 B6 Dorton U.S.A.
80 F3 Dörtyol Turkey
102 C3 Doruma Dem. Rep. Congo
44 C6 Dos Bahías, C. pt Arg.
35 H5 Dos Cabezas U.S.A.
42 C5 Dos de Mayo Peru
89 C6 Đo Son Vietnam
34 B3 Dos Palos U.S.A.
100 C3 Dosso Niger
29 C6 Dothan U.S.A.
64 F1 Douai France
100 C4 Douala Cameroon
64 B2 Douarnenez France
116 E5 Double Island Pt pt Austr.
34 C4 Double Peak summit U.S.A.
116 B1 Double Pt pt Austr.
64 H3 Doubs r. France
117 A6 Doubtful Sound in. N.Z.
117 D1 Doubtless Bay b. N.Z.
100 B3 Douentza Mali
58 C3 Douglas Isle of Man
104 E4 Douglas S. Africa
57 E5 Douglas U.K.
20 C3 Douglas AK U.S.A.
35 H6 Douglas AZ U.S.A.
29 D6 Douglas GA U.S.A.
24 F3 Douglas WY U.S.A.
20 D4 Douglas Chan. chan. Can.
35 H2 Douglas Creek r. U.S.A.
64 F1 Doullens France
57 D4 Doune U.K.
46 C2 Dourada, Cach. waterfall Brazil
46 B2 Dourada, Serra h. Brazil
46 C1 Dourada, Serra mts Brazil
46 A3 Dourados Brazil
46 A3 Dourados r. Brazil
46 B3 Dourados, Serra dos h. Brazil
65 C2 Douro r. Port.
59 F4 Dove r. Eng. U.K.
59 J5 Dove r. Eng. U.K.
23 J3 Dove Brook Can.
35 H3 Dove Creek U.S.A.
115 G9 Dover Austr.
59 J6 Dover U.K.
33 F5 Dover DE U.S.A.
33 H3 Dover NH U.S.A.
33 F4 Dover NJ U.S.A.
32 C4 Dover OH U.S.A.
59 J7 Dover, Strait of str. France/U.K.
33 J2 Dover-Foxcroft U.S.A.
81 M6 Doveyrīch, Rūd-e r. Iran/Iraq
30 D5 Dowagiac U.S.A.
95 A5 Dowi, Tg pt Indon.
34 B2 Downieville U.S.A.
60 F3 Downpatrick U.K.
33 F3 Downsville U.S.A.
81 M5 Dow Rūd Iran
81 L4 Dow Sar Iran
79 K2 Dowshī Afgh.
34 B1 Doyle U.S.A.
33 F4 Doylestown U.S.A.
91 C6 Dōzen is Japan
31 J2 Dozois, Réservoir resr Can.
46 B3 Dracena Brazil
61 E1 Drachten Neth.
67 L2 Drăgănești-Olt Romania
67 L2 Drăgășani Romania
45 E2 Dragon's Mouths str. Trinidad/Venez.
55 S6 Dragsfjärd Fin.
64 H5 Draguignan France
69 C4 Drahichyn Belarus
115 K2 Drake Austr.
35 F4 Drake AZ U.S.A.
21 J5 Drake ND U.S.A.
105 H5 Drakensberg mts Lesotho/S. Africa
105 J2 Drakensberg mts S. Africa
119 A1 Drake Passage str. Antarctica
67 L4 Drama Greece
55 M7 Drammen Norway
55 L7 Drangedal Norway
60 E3 Draperstown U.K.
84 C2 Dras Jammu and Kashmir
62 F7 Drau r. Austria
20 G4 Drayton Valley Can.
66 B6 Dréan Alg.
62 F5 Dresden Ger.
68 D4 Dretun' Belarus
64 E2 Dreux France
55 N6 Drevsjø Norway
32 D4 Driftwood U.S.A.
116 D6 Drillham Austr.
60 B6 Drimoleague Rep. of Ireland
66 G3 Drniš Croatia
67 K2 Drobeta - Turnu Severin Romania
60 E4 Drogheda Rep. of Ireland
69 B5 Drohobych Ukr.
Droichead Átha see Drogheda
59 E5 Droitwich U.K.
85 G4 Drokung India
60 D4 Dromod Rep. of Ireland
60 E3 Dromore Co. Down U.K.
60 D3 Dromore Co. Tyrone U.K.
59 F4 Dronfield U.K.
119 C3 Dronning Maud Land reg. Antarctica
84 B2 Drosh Pak.
69 F5 Droskovo Rus. Fed.
115 F7 Drouin Austr.
44 D2 Dr Pedro P. Peña Para.
20 G4 Drumheller Can.
24 D2 Drummond MT U.S.A.
30 B2 Drummond WV U.S.A.
31 F3 Drummond Island i. U.S.A.
116 B5 Drummond Range h. Austr.
23 F4 Drummondville Can.
57 D6 Drummore U.K.
57 D4 Drumochter Pass pass U.K.
55 T10 Druskininkai Lith.
77 Q3 Druzhina Rus. Fed.
67 L3 Dryanovo Bulg.
83 B3 Dry Bay b. U.S.A.
21 L5 Dryberry L. l. Can.
30 E2 Dryburg U.S.A.
22 B4 Dryden Can.
34 D2 Dry Lake l. U.S.A.
57 D4 Drymen U.K.
112 E3 Drysdale r. Austr.
112 E3 Drysdale River National Park nat. park Austr.
81 M4 Dūāb r. Iran
89 C6 Du'an China
33 F2 Duane U.S.A.
116 C4 Duaringa Austr.
85 G4 Duars reg. India
78 D4 Ḍubā Saudi Arabia
79 H4 Dubai U.A.E.
21 J2 Dubawnt r. Can.
21 J2 Dubawnt Lake l. Can.
Dubayy see Dubai
78 D4 Dubbagh, J. ad mt Saudi Arabia
115 H4 Dubbo Austr.
30 D1 Dublin Can.
60 E4 Dublin Rep. of Ireland
29 D5 Dublin U.S.A.
68 F3 Dubna Rus. Fed.
69 C5 Dubno Ukr.
24 D2 Dubois ID U.S.A.
24 E3 Dubois WY U.S.A.
32 D4 Du Bois U.S.A.
69 H5 Dubovka Rus. Fed.
69 G6 Dubovskoye Rus. Fed.
81 M1 Dübrar P. pass Azer.
100 A4 Dubréka Guinea
67 H3 Dubrovnik Croatia
69 C5 Dubrovytsya Ukr.
68 D4 Dubrowna Belarus
30 B4 Dubuque U.S.A.
55 S9 Dubysa r. Lith.
89 E4 Duchang China
35 G1 Duchesne U.S.A.
29 C5 Duck r. U.S.A.
21 J4 Duck Bay Can.
21 H4 Duck Lake Can.
30 E4 Duck Lake U.S.A.
35 E2 Duckwater U.S.A.
35 E2 Duckwater Peak summit U.S.A.
95 D2 Đưc Pho Vietnam
95 D3 Đưc Trong Vietnam
45 B4 Duda r. Col.
85 E4 Dudhi India
85 G4 Dudhnai India
76 K3 Dudinka Rus. Fed.
59 E5 Dudley U.K.
84 D6 Dudna r. India
57 F3 Dudwick, Hill of h. U.K.
100 B4 Duékoué Côte d'Ivoire
65 C2 Duero r. Spain
31 H1 Dufault, Lac l. Can.
22 E2 Dufferin, Cape hd Can.
32 B6 Duffield U.S.A.
111 G2 Duff Is is Solomon Is
57 E3 Dufftown U.K.
22 E1 Dufrost, Pte pt Can.
66 F3 Dugi Otok i. Croatia
82 F3 Dugui Qarag China
88 D3 Du He r. China
45 D4 Duida, Co mt Venez.
42 E3 Duida-Marahuaca, Parque Nacional nat. park Venez.
62 C5 Duisburg Ger.
45 B3 Duitama Col.
105 J1 Duiwelskloof S. Africa
88 B4 Dujiangyan China
81 K4 Dukān Dam dam Iraq
105 G5 Dukathole S. Africa
20 C4 Duke I. i. U.S.A.
79 G4 Dukhān Qatar
63 Q3 Dukhovshchina Rus. Fed.
83 B3 Duki Pak.
55 U9 Dūkštas Lith.
82 J3 Dulan China
Dulawan see Datu Piang
44 D3 Dulce r. Arg.
85 E2 Dulishi Hu salt l. China
105 J2 Dullstroom S. Africa
61 F3 Dülmen Ger.
67 M3 Dulovo Bulg.
30 A2 Duluth U.S.A.
30 A2 Duluth/Superior airport U.S.A.
59 D6 Dulverton U.K.
80 F5 Dūmā Syria
94 B4 Dumaguete Phil.
92 C6 Dumai Indon.
94 B4 Dumaran i. Phil.
27 F5 Dumas AR U.S.A.
27 C5 Dumas TX U.S.A.
80 F5 Ḍumayr Syria
57 D5 Dumbarton U.K.
105 J3 Dumbe S. Africa
63 J6 Ďumbier mt Slovakia
84 D2 Dumchele Jammu and Kashmir
85 H4 Dum Duma India
57 E5 Dumfries U.K.
85 F4 Dumka India
22 E4 Dumoine, L. l. Can.
119 B6 Dumont d'Urville France Base Antarctica
119 B6 Dumont d'Urville Sea sea Antarctica
78 C3 Dumyâṭ Egypt
Duna r. see Danube
62 H7 Dunajská Streda Slovakia
63 J7 Dunakeszi Hungary
115 G9 Dunalley Austr.
60 E4 Dunany Point pt Rep. of Ireland
67 N2 Dunării, Delta delta Romania
63 J7 Dunaújváros Hungary
Dunav r. see Danube
69 C5 Dunayivtsi Ukr.
117 C6 Dunback N.Z.
57 F4 Dunbar U.K.
57 E4 Dunblane U.K.
60 E4 Dunboyne Rep. of Ireland
20 E5 Duncan Can.
35 H5 Duncan AZ U.S.A.
27 D5 Duncan OK U.S.A.
22 D3 Duncan, Cape c. Can.
22 E3 Duncan, L. l. Can.
32 E4 Duncannon U.S.A.
57 E2 Duncansby Head hd U.K.
30 B5 Duncans Mills U.S.A.
60 E5 Duncormick Rep. of Ireland
55 S8 Dundaga Latvia
31 G3 Dundalk Can.
60 E3 Dundalk Rep. of Ireland
32 E5 Dundalk U.S.A.
60 E4 Dundalk Bay b. Rep. of Ireland
20 C4 Dundas I. i. Can.
Dun Dealgan see Dundalk
105 J4 Dundee S. Africa
57 F4 Dundee U.K.
31 F5 Dundee MI U.S.A.
32 E3 Dundee NY U.S.A.
88 E1 Dund Hot China
60 F3 Dundonald U.K.
115 F1 Dundoo Austr.
57 E6 Dundrennan U.K.
60 F3 Dundrum U.K.
60 F3 Dundrum Bay b. U.K.
85 E4 Dundwa Range mts India/Nepal
22 F2 Dune, Lac l. Can.
117 C6 Dunedin N.Z.
29 D6 Dunedin U.S.A.
115 H4 Dunedoo Austr.
57 E4 Dunfermline U.K.
60 E3 Dungannon U.K.
84 C5 Dungarpur India
60 D5 Dungarvan Rep. of Ireland
59 H7 Dungeness hd U.K.
44 C8 Dungeness, Pta pt Arg.
60 E3 Dungiven U.K.
60 C3 Dungloe Rep. of Ireland
115 J4 Dungog Austr.
102 C3 Dungu Dem. Rep. Congo
92 C6 Dungun Malaysia
101 F2 Dungunab Sudan
87 N3 Dunhua China
82 H2 Dunhuang China
114 E6 Dunkeld Austr.
57 E4 Dunkeld U.K.
Dunkerque see Dunkirk
59 D6 Dunkery Beacon h. U.K.
64 F1 Dunkirk France
32 D3 Dunkirk U.S.A.
100 B4 Dunkwa Ghana
60 E4 Dún Laoghaire Rep. of Ireland
60 E4 Dunlavin Rep. of Ireland
60 E4 Dunleer Rep. of Ireland
60 E2 Dunloy U.K.
60 B6 Dunmanus Bay b. Rep. of Ireland
60 B6 Dunmanway Rep. of Ireland
60 C4 Dunmore Rep. of Ireland
29 E7 Dunmore Town Bahamas
34 D3 Dunmovin U.S.A.
60 F3 Dunmurry U.K.
29 E5 Dunn U.S.A.
57 E2 Dunnet Bay b. U.K.
57 E2 Dunnet Head hd U.K.
34 B2 Dunnigan U.S.A.
26 C3 Dunning U.S.A.
31 H4 Dunnville Can.
114 E6 Dunolly Austr.
57 D5 Dunoon U.K.
57 F5 Duns U.K.
26 C1 Dunseith U.S.A.
24 B3 Dunsmuir U.S.A.
59 G6 Dunstable U.K.
117 B6 Dunstan Mts mts N.Z.
117 C6 Duntroon N.Z.
57 B3 Dunvegan, Loch in. U.K.
84 B3 Dunyapur Pak.
88 E1 Duolun China
89 D5 Dupang Ling mts China
31 H1 Duparquet, Lac l. Can.
67 K3 Dupnitsa Bulg.
26 C2 Dupree U.S.A.
28 B4 Du Quoin U.S.A.
112 E3 Durack r. Austr.
Dura Europos see Aş Şālihīyah
80 E1 Durağan Turkey
64 G5 Durance r. France
31 F4 Durand MI U.S.A.
30 B3 Durand WV U.S.A.
27 B7 Durango div. Mex.
36 D4 Durango Mex.
65 E1 Durango Spain
25 F4 Durango U.S.A.
27 D5 Durant U.S.A.
47 F2 Durazno Uru.
47 F1 Durazno, Cuchilla Grande del h. Uru.
105 J4 Durban S. Africa
64 F5 Durban-Corbières France
104 C6 Durbanville S. Africa
32 D5 Durbin U.S.A.
61 D4 Durbuy Belgium
61 E4 Düren Ger.
84 E5 Durg India
85 F5 Durgapur India
31 G3 Durham Can.
58 F3 Durham U.K.
34 B2 Durham CA U.S.A.
29 E4 Durham NC U.S.A.
33 H3 Durham NH U.S.A.
69 D6 Durleşti Moldova
67 H3 Durmitor mt Yugo.
57 D2 Durness U.K.
116 D6 Durong South Austr.
67 H4 Durrës Albania
59 F6 Durrington U.K.
60 A6 Dursey Island i. Rep. of Ireland
80 B2 Dursunbey Turkey
80 F5 Durūz, Jabal ad mt Syria
93 K7 D'Urville, Tanjung pt Indon.
117 D4 D'Urville Island i. N.Z.
89 C5 Dushan China
79 K2 Dushanbe Tajik.
69 H7 Dushet'i Georgia
117 A6 Dusky Sound in. N.Z.
62 C5 Düsseldorf Ger.
35 F1 Dutch Mt mt U.S.A.
104 E1 Dutlwe Botswana
100 C3 Dutse Nigeria
114 B3 Dutton, Lake salt flat Austr.
35 F2 Dutton, Mt mt U.S.A.
68 H3 Duvannoye Rus. Fed.
23 F2 Duvert, Lac l. Can.
89 C5 Duyun China
80 C1 Düzce Turkey
Dvina, Western r. see Zapadnaya Dvina
69 F5 Dvorichna Ukr.
90 B2 Dvoryanka Rus. Fed.
84 B5 Dwarka India
105 G2 Dwarsberg S. Africa
30 C5 Dwight U.S.A.
61 E2 Dwingelderveld, Nationaal Park nat. park Neth.
24 C2 Dworshak Res. resr U.S.A.
104 D6 Dwyka S. Africa
68 E4 Dyat'kovo Rus. Fed.
57 F3 Dyce U.K.
30 D5 Dyer IN U.S.A.
34 C3 Dyer NV U.S.A.
31 G3 Dyer Bay Can.
29 B4 Dyersburg U.S.A.
30 B4 Dyersville U.S.A.
59 D5 Dyfi r. U.K.
57 E3 Dyke U.K.
69 G7 Dykh Tau mt Georgia/Rus. Fed.
63 J4 Dylewska Góra h. Pol.
114 F2 Dynevor Downs Austr.
105 H5 Dyoki S. Africa
116 C4 Dysart Austr.
30 A4 Dysart U.S.A.
104 E6 Dysselsdorp S. Africa
87 K3 Dzamïn Üüd Mongolia
103 E5 Dzaoudzi Africa
68 G3 Dzerzhinsk Rus. Fed.
63 N5 Dzerzhyns'k Ukr.
Dzhambul see Taraz
79 G1 Dzhanga Turkm.
69 E6 Dzhankoy Ukr.
69 H5 Dzhanybek Rus. Fed.
77 R3 Dzhigudzhak Rus. Fed.
79 K1 Dzhizak Uzbek.
77 P4 Dzhugdzhur, Khrebet mts Rus. Fed.
Dzhul'fa see Culfa
82 E2 Dzhungarskiy Alatau, Khr. mts China/Kazak.
82 B1 Dzhusaly Kazak.
63 K4 Działdowo Pol.
Dzungarian Basin basin see Junggar Pendi
86 J2 Dzuunmod Mongolia
68 C4 Dzyaniskavichy Belarus
68 C4 Dzyarzhynsk Belarus
63 N4 Dzyatlavichy Belarus

E

22 C3 Eabamet L. l. Can.
35 H4 Eagar U.S.A.
23 J3 Eagle r. Can.
25 F4 Eagle U.S.A.
33 F3 Eagle Bay U.S.A.
21 H4 Eagle Cr. r. Can.
34 D4 Eagle Crags summit U.S.A.
21 L5 Eagle L. l. Can.
24 B3 Eagle L. l. U.S.A.
33 J1 Eagle Lake U.S.A.
33 J1 Eagle Lake l. U.S.A.
30 B2 Eagle Mtn h. U.S.A.
27 C6 Eagle Pass U.S.A.
30 C2 Eagle River MI U.S.A.
30 C3 Eagle River WV U.S.A.
20 F3 Eaglesham Can.
35 F5 Eagle Tail Mts mts U.S.A.
22 B3 Ear Falls Can.
34 C4 Earlimart U.S.A.
57 F5 Earlston U.K.
31 H2 Earlton Can.
57 E4 Earn r. U.K.
57 D4 Earn, L. l. U.K.
27 C5 Earth U.S.A.
58 H4 Easington U.K.
29 D5 Easley U.S.A.
119 C5 East Antarctica reg. Antarctica
33 F4 East Ararat U.S.A.
32 D3 East Aurora U.S.A.
27 F6 East Bay b. U.S.A.
33 G2 East Berkshire U.S.A.
59 H7 Eastbourne U.K.
32 D4 East Branch Clarion River Reservoir resr U.S.A.
33 H4 East Brooklyn U.S.A.
117 G2 East Cape c. N.Z.
35 G2 East Carbon City U.S.A.
30 D5 East Chicago U.S.A.
87 M6 East China Sea sea Asia
33 G2 East Corinth U.S.A.
59 H5 East Dereham U.K.
15 M7 Easter Island is Pac. Oc.
15 M7 Easter Island Fracture Zone sea feature Pac. Oc.
105 G5 Eastern Cape div. S. Africa
78 C4 Eastern Desert des. Egypt
85 E6 Eastern Ghats mts India
84 B4 Eastern Nara canal Pak.
Eastern Transvaal div. see Mpumalanga
21 K4 Easterville Can.
44 E8 East Falkland i. Falkland Is
33 H4 East Falmouth U.S.A.
62 C4 East Frisian Islands is Ger.
34 D2 Eastgate U.S.A.
26 D2 East Grand Forks U.S.A.
59 G6 East Grinstead U.K.
33 G3 East Hampton U.S.A.
33 G3 Easthampton U.S.A.
32 D4 East Hickory U.S.A.
33 G3 East Jamaica U.S.A.
12 K1 East Jan Mayen Ridge sea feature Atlantic Ocean
30 E3 East Jordan U.S.A.
57 D5 East Kilbride U.K.
30 D3 East Lake U.S.A.
59 F7 Eastleigh U.K.
32 C4 East Liverpool U.S.A.
57 B3 East Loch Tarbert b. U.K.
105 G6 East London S. Africa
32 B5 East Lynn Lake l. U.S.A.
22 E3 Eastmain Can.
22 F3 Eastmain r. Can.
33 G2 Eastman Can.
29 D5 Eastman U.S.A.
116 A4 Eastmere Austr.
33 J2 East Millinocket U.S.A.
30 B5 East Moline U.S.A.
30 C5 Easton IL U.S.A.
33 E5 Easton MD U.S.A.
33 F4 Easton PA U.S.A.
15 M8 East Pacific Ridge sea feature Pac. Oc.
15 N5 East Pacific Rise sea feature Pac. Oc.
34 A2 East Park Res. resr U.S.A.
23 H4 East Point pt Can.
29 C5 East Point U.S.A.
33 K2 Eastport ME U.S.A.
30 E3 Eastport MI U.S.A.
34 D1 East Range mts U.S.A.
East Retford see Retford
77 Q2 East Siberian Sea sea Rus. Fed.
115 H7 East Sister I. i. Austr.
28 B4 East St Louis U.S.A.
85 F4 East Tons r. India
115 F3 East Toorale Austr.
30 C4 East Troy U.S.A.
33 F6 Eastville U.S.A.
34 C2 East Walker r. U.S.A.
33 G3 East Wallingford U.S.A.
29 D5 Eatonton U.S.A.
30 B3 Eau Claire U.S.A.
30 B3 Eau Claire r. U.S.A.
14 E5 Eauripik Rise-New Guinea Rise sea feature Pac. Oc.
36 E4 Ebano Mex.
59 D6 Ebbw Vale U.K.
100 D4 Ebebiyin Equatorial Guinea
104 B2 Ebenerde Namibia
32 D4 Ebensburg U.S.A.
80 C2 Eber Gölü l. Turkey
62 F4 Eberswalde-Finow Ger.
31 F4 Eberts Can.
90 G3 Ebetsu Japan
89 B4 Ebian China
86 D3 Ebinur Hu salt l. China
66 F4 Eboli Italy
100 D4 Ebolowa Cameroon
81 K3 Ebrāhim Ḩeşār Iran
65 G2 Ebro r. Spain
67 M4 Eceabat Turkey
94 B2 Echague Phil.
65 E1 Echarri-Aranaz Spain
100 C1 Ech Chélif Alg.
65 E1 Echegárate, Puerto pass Spain
115 G9 Echo, L. l. Austr.
20 F1 Echo Bay N.W.T. Can.
31 F2 Echo Bay Ont. Can.
35 G3 Echo Cliffs cliff U.S.A.
22 B3 Echoing r. Can.
31 K2 Échouani, Lac l. Can.
61 E5 Echternach Lux.
114 F6 Echuca Austr.
65 D4 Écija Spain
30 E2 Eckerman U.S.A.
62 D3 Eckernförde Ger.
38 Ecuador country S. America
22 E2 Écueils, Pte aux pt Can.
102 E2 Ed Eritrea
55 M7 Ed Sweden
21 H4 Edam Can.
57 F1 Eday i. U.K.
101 E3 Ed Da'ein Sudan
78 C7 Ed Dair, Jebel mt Sudan
101 F3 Ed Damazin Sudan
101 F3 Ed Damer Sudan
101 F3 Ed Debba Sudan
101 F3 Ed Dueim Sudan
115 H8 Eddystone Pt pt Austr.
100 D4 Edéa Cameroon
21 K2 Edehon Lake l. Can.
46 C2 Edéia Brazil
115 H6 Eden Austr.
58 E3 Eden r. U.K.
27 D6 Eden U.S.A.
105 F4 Edenburg S. Africa
117 B7 Edendale N.Z.
60 D4 Edenderry Rep. of Ireland
114 D6 Edenhope Austr.
29 E4 Edenton U.S.A.
105 G3 Edenville S. Africa
67 K4 Edessa Greece
33 H4 Edgartown U.S.A.
26 D2 Edgeley U.S.A.
26 C3 Edgemont U.S.A.
30 C4 Edgerton U.S.A.
60 D4 Edgeworthstown Rep. of Ireland
30 A5 Edina U.S.A.
27 D7 Edinburg U.S.A.
57 E5 Edinburgh U.K.
69 C7 Edirne Turkey
20 F4 Edith Cavell, Mt mt Can.
24 B2 Edmonds U.S.A.
116 A1 Edmonton Austr.
20 G4 Edmonton Can.
21 K5 Edmore U.S.A.
30 B4 Edmund U.S.A.
21 L4 Edmund L. l. Can.
23 G4 Edmundston Can.
27 D6 Edna U.S.A.
20 C3 Edna Bay U.S.A.
67 M5 Edremit Turkey
55 O6 Edsbyn Sweden
20 F4 Edson Can.

47 D2 Eduardo Castex Arg.
114 F5 Edward r. Austr.
102 C4 Edward, Lake l. Uganda/Dem. Rep. Congo
30 C1 Edward I. i. Can.
33 F2 Edwards U.S.A.
114 A2 Edward's Cr. Austr.
27 C6 Edwards Plateau plat. U.S.A.
28 B4 Edwardsville U.S.A.
119 A4 Edward VII Pen. pen. Antarctica
20 C3 Edziza Pk mt Can.
34 A1 Eel r. U.S.A.
34 A2 Eel, South Fork r. U.S.A.
61 E1 Eemshaven pt Neth.
104 D3 Eenzamheid Pan salt pan S. Africa
111 G3 Éfaté i. Vanuatu
28 B4 Effingham U.S.A.
80 D1 Eflâni Turkey
35 E2 Egan Range mts U.S.A.
31 J3 Eganville Can.
63 K7 Eger Hungary
55 K7 Egersund Norway
54 F4 Egilsstaðir Iceland
80 C3 Eğirdir Turkey
80 C3 Eğirdir Gölü l. Turkey
64 F4 Égletons France
60 D2 Eglinton U.K.
61 C2 Egmond aan den Hoef Neth.
117 D3 Egmont, Cape c. N.Z.
Egmont, Mt vol. see Taranaki, Mt
117 E3 Egmont National Park nat. park N.Z
80 B2 Eğrigöz Dağı mts Turkey
58 G3 Egton U.K.
46 D1 Éguas r. Brazil
77 V3 Egvekinot Rus. Fed.
96 Egypt country Africa
88 A2 Ehen Hudag China
62 D6 Ehingen (Donau) Ger.
35 E5 Ehrenberg U.S.A.
61 E2 Eibergen Neth.
55 K6 Eidfjord Norway
116 D5 Eidsvold Austr.
55 M6 Eidsvoll Norway
61 E4 Eifel reg. Ger.
57 B4 Eigg i. U.K.
83 D9 Eight Degree Channel chan. India/Maldives
112 D3 Eighty Mile Beach beach Austr.
115 F6 Eildon Austr.
115 F6 Eildon, Lake l. Austr.
21 H2 Eileen Lake l. Can.
61 D3 Eindhoven Neth.
62 D7 Einsiedeln Switz.
42 E5 Eirunepé Brazil
103 C5 Eiseb watercourse Namibia
62 E5 Eisenach Ger.
62 G4 Eisenhüttenstadt Ger.
62 H7 Eisenstadt Austria
57 C3 Eishort, Loch in. U.K.
Eivissa see Ibiza
Eivissa i. see Ibiza
65 F1 Ejea de los Caballeros Spain
103 E6 Ejeda Madag.
Ejin Horo Qi see Altan Shiret
Ejin Qi see Dalain Hob
81 K1 Ejmiatsin Armenia
55 S7 Ekenäs Fin.
61 C3 Ekeren Belgium
117 E4 Eketahuna N.Z.
76 J4 Ekibastuz Kazak.
77 M3 Ekonda Rus. Fed.
55 N6 Ekshärad Sweden
55 O8 Eksjö Sweden
104 B4 Eksteenfontein S. Africa
102 C4 Ekuku Dem. Rep. Congo
22 D3 Ekwan r. Can.
22 D3 Ekwan Point pt Can.
67 K6 Elafonisou, Steno chan. Greece
80 B6 El 'Alamein Egypt
80 B6 El 'Âmirîya Egypt
105 H2 Elands r. S. Africa
105 H2 Elandsdoorn S. Africa
66 B7 El Aouinet Alg.
25 D6 El Arco Mex.
116 B1 El Arish Austr.
80 D6 El 'Arîsh Egypt
67 K5 Elassona Greece
80 E7 Elat Israel
81 G2 Elazığ Turkey
66 D3 Elba, Isola d' i. Italy
87 P1 El'ban Rus. Fed.
45 B2 El Banco Col.
67 J4 Elbasan Albania
80 E2 Elbaşı Turkey
45 C2 El Baúl Venez.
100 C1 El Bayadh Alg.
62 E4 Elbe r. Ger.
25 F4 Elbert, Mount mt U.S.A.
30 D3 Elberta MI U.S.A.
35 G2 Elberta UT U.S.A.
29 D5 Elberton U.S.A.
64 E2 Elbeuf France
80 F2 Elbistan Turkey
63 J3 Elbląg Pol.
47 B4 El Bolsón Arg.
29 F7 Elbow Cay i. Bahamas
69 G7 Elbrus mt Rus. Fed.
65 E2 El Burgo de Osma Spain
Elburz Mountains mts see Alborz, Reshteh-ye
47 C4 El Cain Arg.
34 D5 El Cajon U.S.A.
45 E3 El Callao Venez.
27 D6 El Campo U.S.A.
35 E5 El Centro U.S.A.
42 F7 El Cerro Bol.
45 D2 El Chaparro Venez.
65 F3 Elche Spain
27 B6 El Chilicote Mex.
113 G2 Elcho I. i. Austr.
45 B3 El Cocuy Col.
45 B3 El Cocuy, Parque Nacional nat. park Col.
27 B6 El Cuervo Spain
65 F3 Elda Spain
31 H2 Eldee Can.
114 D3 Elder, Lake salt flat Austr.
45 B2 El Difícil Col.
77 P3 El'dikan Rus. Fed.
45 A4 El Diviso Col.
35 E6 El Doctor Mex.
30 A5 Eldon IA U.S.A.
26 E4 Eldon MO U.S.A.
44 F3 Eldorado Arg.
36 C4 El Dorado Mex.
27 E5 El Dorado AR U.S.A.
27 D4 El Dorado KS U.S.A.
27 C6 Eldorado U.S.A.
45 E3 El Dorado Venez.
102 D3 Eldoret Kenya
24 E2 Electric Peak summit U.S.A.
100 B2 El Eglab plat. Alg.
65 E4 El Ejido Spain
70 F4 Elektrostal' Rus. Fed.
42 D4 El Encanto Col.
25 F5 Elephant Butte Res. resr U.S.A.
119 B1 Elephant I. i. Antarctica
85 H5 Elephant Point pt Bangl.
81 J2 Eleşkirt Turkey
100 C1 El Eulma Alg.
29 E7 Eleuthera i. Bahamas
66 C6 El Fahs Tunisia
78 C4 El Faiyûm Egypt
101 E3 El Fasher Sudan
101 E3 El Geneina Sudan
101 F3 El Geteina Sudan
57 E3 Elgin U.K.
30 C4 Elgin IL U.S.A.
26 C2 Elgin ND U.S.A.
35 E3 Elgin NV U.S.A.
35 G2 Elgin UT U.S.A.
116 B4 Elgin Down Austr.
77 Q3 El'ginskiy Rus. Fed.
78 C4 El Gîza Egypt
100 C1 El Goléa Alg.
25 D6 El Golfo de Santa Clara Mex.
102 D3 Elgon, Mount mt Uganda
66 B6 El Hadjar Alg.
80 B6 El Hammâm Egypt
100 A2 El Hierro i. Canary Is
100 C2 El Homr Alg.
57 F4 Elie U.K.
117 C5 Elie de Beaumont mt N.Z.
77 V3 Elim Alaska
23 H2 Eliot, Mount mt Can.
65 F1 Elizondo Spain
El Iskandarîya see Alexandria
69 H6 Elista Rus. Fed.
30 B4 Elizabeth IL U.S.A.
33 F4 Elizabeth NJ U.S.A.
32 C5 Elizabeth WV U.S.A.
29 E4 Elizabeth City U.S.A.
33 H4 Elizabeth Is is U.S.A.
29 D4 Elizabethton U.S.A.
28 C4 Elizabethtown KY U.S.A.
29 E5 Elizabethtown NC U.S.A.
33 G2 Elizabethtown NY U.S.A.
32 E4 Elizabethtown PA U.S.A.
100 B1 El Jadida Morocco
27 B7 El Jaralito Mex.
66 D7 El Jem Tunisia
20 G4 Elk r. Can.
63 L4 Ełk Pol.
34 A2 Elk U.S.A.
32 C5 Elk r. U.S.A.
80 F4 El Kaa Lebanon
66 C6 El Kala Alg.
101 F3 El Kamlin Sudan
27 D5 Elk City U.S.A.
34 A2 Elk Creek U.S.A.
34 B2 Elk Grove U.S.A.
78 C4 El Khârga Egypt
30 E5 Elkhart U.S.A.
El Khartum see Khartoum
100 B2 El Khnâchîch escarpment Mali
30 C4 Elkhorn U.S.A.
26 D3 Elkhorn r. U.S.A.
78 E1 El'khotovo Rus. Fed.
67 M3 Elkhovo Bulg.
32 D5 Elkins U.S.A.
20 G4 Elk Island Nat. Park nat. park Can.
31 G2 Elk Lake Can.
30 E3 Elk Lake l. U.S.A.
32 E4 Elkland U.S.A.
20 F5 Elko Can.
24 D3 Elko U.S.A.
21 G4 Elk Point Can.
26 E2 Elk River U.S.A.
33 F5 Elkton MD U.S.A.
32 D5 Elkton VA U.S.A.
21 M2 Ell Bay b. Can.
118 B3 Ellef Ringnes I. i. Can.
35 G2 Ellen, Mt mt U.S.A.
84 C3 Ellenabad India
26 D2 Ellendale U.S.A.
24 B2 Ellensburg U.S.A.
33 F4 Ellenville U.S.A.
115 H6 Ellery, Mt mt Austr.
117 D5 Ellesmere, Lake l. N.Z.
118 B3 Ellesmere Island i. Can.
59 E4 Ellesmere Port U.K.
32 D3 Ellicottville U.S.A.
105 G5 Elliot S. Africa
116 B2 Elliot, Mt mt Austr.
105 H5 Elliotdale S. Africa
31 F2 Elliot Lake Can.
24 D2 Ellis U.S.A.
105 G1 Ellisras S. Africa
114 A4 Elliston Austr.
57 F3 Ellon U.K.
33 J2 Ellsworth ME U.S.A.
30 A3 Ellsworth WV U.S.A.
119 A3 Ellsworth Land reg. Antarctica
119 B3 Ellsworth Mountains mts Antarctica
80 B3 Elmalı Turkey
34 D6 El Maneadero Mex.
78 C3 El Mansûra Egypt
45 E3 El Manteco Venez.
100 C1 El Meghaïer Alg.
45 E3 El Miamo Venez.
80 E4 El Mîna Lebanon
78 C4 El Minya Egypt
30 E3 Elmira MI U.S.A.
32 E3 Elmira NY U.S.A.
35 F5 El Mirage U.S.A.
65 E4 El Moral Spain
114 F6 Elmore Austr.
47 D2 El Morro mt Arg.
100 B2 El Mreyyé reg. Maur.
62 D4 Elmshorn Ger.
101 E3 El Muglad Sudan
31 G3 Elmwood Can.
30 C5 Elmwood IL U.S.A.
30 A3 Elmwood WV U.S.A.
54 K5 Elnesvågen Norway
45 B3 El Nevado, Cerro mt Col.
94 A4 El Nido Phil.
101 F3 El Obeid Sudan
27 C7 El Oro Mex.
45 C3 Elorza Venez.
100 C1 El Oued Alg.
35 G5 Eloy U.S.A.
27 B7 El Palmito Mex.
45 E2 El Pao Bolívar Venez.
45 C2 El Pao Cojedes Venez.
30 C5 El Paso IL U.S.A.
25 F6 El Paso TX U.S.A.
57 C2 Elphin U.K.
34 C3 El Portal U.S.A.
27 B6 El Porvenir Panama
65 H2 El Prat de Llobregat Spain
65 C4 El Puerto de Santa María Spain
El Qâhira see Cairo
80 D6 El Qantara Egypt
27 D5 El Reno U.S.A.
30 B4 Elroy U.S.A.
20 B2 Elsa Can.
80 C7 El Saff Egypt
80 D6 El Sâlhîya Egypt
36 C4 El Salto Mex.
16 El Salvador country Central America
94 C4 El Salvador Phil.
45 C3 El Samán de Apure Venez.
31 F1 Elsas Can.
25 F6 El Sauz Mex.
85 H2 Elsen Nur l. China
80 D7 El Shatt Egypt
34 D5 Elsinore U.S.A.
25 D6 El Socorro Mex.
45 D2 El Sombrero Venez.
47 C2 El Sosneado Arg.
25 F6 El Sueco Mex.
El Suweis see Suez
45 B3 El Tama, Parque Nacional nat. park Venez.
66 C6 El Tarf Alg.
65 C1 El Teleno mt Spain
80 E7 El Thamad Egypt
45 D2 El Tigre Venez.
45 C2 El Tocuyo Venez.
69 H5 El'ton Rus. Fed.
69 H5 El'ton, Ozero l. Rus. Fed.
24 C2 Eltopia U.S.A.
45 E2 El Toro Venez.
47 E2 El Trébol Arg.
45 C3 El Tuparro, Parque Nacional nat. park Col.
78 C4 El Tûr Egypt
44 B8 El Turbio Chile
83 F7 Eluru India
55 U7 Elva Estonia
45 A3 El Valle Col.
57 E5 Elvanfoot U.K.
65 C3 Elvas Port.
55 M6 Elverum Norway
45 B3 El Viejo mt Col.
45 C2 El Vigía Venez.
42 D5 Elvira Brazil
102 E3 El Wak Kenya
30 E5 Elwood U.S.A.
59 H5 Ely U.K.
30 B2 Ely MN U.S.A.
35 E2 Ely NV U.S.A.
32 B4 Elyria U.S.A.
111 G3 Émaé i. Vanuatu
79 G2 Emāmrūd Iran
81 L5 Emāmzādeh Naşrod Dīn Iran
55 O8 Emån r. Sweden
46 B2 Emas, Parque Nacional das nat. park Brazil
76 G5 Emba Kazak.
105 H3 Embalenhle S. Africa
21 G3 Embarras Portage Can.
46 C2 Emborcação, Represa de resr Brazil
33 F2 Embrun Can.
102 D4 Embu Kenya
62 C4 Emden Ger.
89 B4 Emeishan China
89 B4 Emei Shan mt China
116 C4 Emerald Qld. Austr.
114 F6 Emerald Vic. Austr.
23 G3 Emeril Can.
21 K5 Emerson Can.
80 B2 Emet Turkey
105 J2 eMgwenya S. Africa
35 E3 Emigrant Valley v. U.S.A.
105 J2 eMijindini S. Africa
101 D3 Emi Koussi mt Chad
27 B7 Emiliano Martínez Mex.
67 M3 Emine, Nos pt Bulg.
67 M3 Eminska Planina h. Bulg.
80 C2 Emir D. mt Turkey
80 C2 Emirdağ Turkey
115 G8 Emita Austr.
55 O8 Emmaboda Sweden
55 S7 Emmaste Estonia
115 J2 Emmaville Austr.
61 D2 Emmeloord Neth.
61 E2 Emmen Neth.
62 D7 Emmen Switz.
116 A5 Emmet Austr.
27 C6 Emory Pk summit U.S.A.
36 B3 Empalme Mex.
105 J4 Empangeni S. Africa
44 E3 Empedrado Arg.
14 G3 Emperor Seamount Chain sea feature Pac. Oc.
66 D3 Empoli Italy
26 D4 Emporia KS U.S.A.
32 E6 Emporia VA U.S.A.
32 D4 Emporium U.S.A.
21 G4 Empress Can.
62 C4 Ems r. Ger.
31 H3 Emsdale Can.
61 F1 Ems-Jade-Kanal canal Ger.
61 F2 Emsland reg. Ger.
116 D4 Emu Park Austr.
105 H3 Emzinoni S. Africa
54 N5 Enafors Sweden
110 D2 Enarotali Indon.
91 E7 Ena-san mt Japan
47 G1 Encantadas, Serra das h. Brazil
94 B3 Encanto, Cape pt Phil.
44 E3 Encarnación Para.
27 D6 Encinal U.S.A.
34 D5 Encinitas U.S.A.
25 F5 Encino U.S.A.
114 C5 Encounter Bay b. Austr.
46 E1 Encruzilhada Brazil
47 G1 Encruzilhada do Sul Brazil
20 D4 Endako Can.
95 B5 Endau Malaysia
113 H2 Endeavour Strait chan. Austr.
93 G8 Endeh Indon.
119 D4 Enderby Land reg. Antarctica
33 E3 Endicott U.S.A.
20 C3 Endicott Arm in. U.S.A.
112 C5 Eneabba Austr.
47 E3 Energía Arg.
69 E6 Enerhodar Ukr.
66 D6 Enfidaville Tunisia
33 G3 Enfield U.S.A.
32 E2 Engadine U.S.A.
54 L5 Engan Norway
94 B2 Engaño, Cape c. Phil.
Engaños, Río de los r. see Yari
90 H2 Engaru Japan
105 G5 Engcobo S. Africa
29 F5 Engelhard U.S.A.
69 H5 Engel's Rus. Fed.
61 C1 Engelschmangat chan. Neth.
114 A2 Engenina watercourse Austr.
92 C8 Enggano i. Indon.
56 E5 England div. U.K.
23 J3 Englee Can.
31 H2 Englehart Can.
56 E6 English Channel str. France/U.K.
69 G7 Enguri r. Georgia
105 J4 Enhlalakahle S. Africa
27 D4 Enid U.S.A.
90 G3 Eniwa Japan
61 D2 Enkhuizen Neth.
55 P7 Enköping Sweden
66 F6 Enna Italy
21 J2 Ennadai Lake l. Can.
101 E3 En Nahud Sudan
101 E3 Ennedi, Massif mts Chad
60 D4 Ennell, Lough l. Rep. of Ireland
115 F2 Enngonia Austr.
26 C2 Enning U.S.A.
60 C5 Ennis Rep. of Ireland
24 E2 Ennis MT U.S.A.
27 D5 Ennis TX U.S.A.
60 E5 Enniscorthy Rep. of Ireland
60 D3 Enniskillen U.K.
60 B5 Ennistymon Rep. of Ireland
62 G7 Enns r. Austria
54 W5 Eno Fin.
35 F3 Enoch U.S.A.
54 S2 Enontekiö Fin.
89 D6 Enping China
94 B2 Enrile Phil.
115 G6 Ensay Austr.
61 E2 Enschede Neth.
47 F2 Ensenada Arg.
36 A2 Ensenada Mex.
89 C4 Enshi China
20 F2 Enterprise N.W.T. Can.
31 J3 Enterprise Ont. Can.
29 C6 Enterprise AL U.S.A.
24 C2 Enterprise OR U.S.A.
35 F3 Enterprise UT U.S.A.
20 F4 Entrance Can.
47 E2 Entre Ríos div. Arg.
42 F8 Entre Ríos Bol.
65 B3 Entroncamento Port.
100 C4 Enugu Nigeria
77 V3 Enurmino Rus. Fed.
42 D5 Envira Brazil
42 D5 Envira r. Brazil
117 C5 Enys, Mt mt N.Z.
91 F7 Enzan Japan
61 B5 Épernay France
35 G2 Ephraim U.S.A.
33 E4 Ephrata PA U.S.A.
24 C2 Ephrata WA U.S.A.
111 G3 Épi i. Vanuatu
64 H2 Épinal France
80 D4 Episkopi Cyprus
66 E4 Epomeo, Monte h. Italy
59 H6 Epping U.K.
59 D5 Eppynt, Mynydd h. U.K.
59 G6 Epsom U.K.
47 D3 Epu-pel Arg.
96 Equatorial Guinea country Africa
45 E3 Equeipa Venez.
116 A6 Erac Cr. watercourse Austr.
94 A4 Eran Phil.
94 A4 Eran Bay b. Phil.
80 F1 Erbaa Turkey
62 C6 Erbeskopf h. Ger.
81 J2 Erçek Turkey
81 J2 Erciş Turkey
80 E2 Erciyes Dağı mt Turkey
63 J7 Érd Hungary
85 H2 Erdaogou China
80 A1 Erdek Turkey
80 E3 Erdemli Turkey
88 C1 Erdenetsogt Mongolia
101 E3 Erdi reg. Chad
69 H6 Erdniyevskiy Rus. Fed.
46 B4 Eré, Campos reg. Brazil
45 D3 Erebato r. Venez.
119 B5 Erebus, Mt vol. Antarctica
81 K6 Erech Iraq
44 F3 Erechim Brazil
87 L2 Ereentsav Mongolia
80 E3 Ereğli Konya Turkey
80 C1 Ereğli Zonguldak Turkey
66 F6 Erei, Monti mts Italy
88 D1 Erenhot China
65 D2 Eresma r. Spain
67 K5 Eretria Greece
Erevan see Yerevan
62 E5 Erfurt Ger.
81 G2 Ergani Turkey
100 B2 'Erg Chech sand dunes Alg./Mali
101 D3 Erg du Djourab sand dunes Chad
100 D3 Erg du Ténéré des. Niger
88 C1 Ergel Mongolia
67 M4 Ergene r. Turkey
100 B2 Erg Iguidi sand dunes Alg./Maur.
55 T8 Ērgļi Latvia
90 A1 Ergu China
Ergun He r. see Argun'
57 D2 Eriboll, Loch in. U.K.
57 D4 Ericht, Loch l. U.K.
30 B5 Erie IL U.S.A.
27 E4 Erie KS U.S.A.
32 C3 Erie PA U.S.A.
31 F5 Erie, Lake l. Can./U.S.A.
90 H3 Erimo Japan
90 H4 Erimo-misaki c. Japan
57 A3 Eriskay i. U.K.
96 Eritrea country Africa
80 E2 Erkilet Turkey
62 E6 Erlangen Ger.
113 F5 Erldunda Austr.
90 A3 Erlong Shan mt China
105 H3 Ermelo S. Africa
80 D3 Ermenek Turkey
67 L6 Ermoupoli Greece
83 E9 Ernakulam India
83 E8 Erode India
104 B1 Erongo div. Namibia
61 D3 Erp Neth.
100 B1 Er Rachidia Morocco
101 F3 Er Rahad Sudan
103 D5 Errego Moz.
66 D7 Er Remla Tunisia
60 C2 Errigal h. Rep. of Ireland
60 A3 Erris Head hd Rep. of Ireland
33 H2 Errol U.S.A.
111 G3 Erromango i. Vanuatu
67 J4 Ersekë Albania
26 D2 Erskine U.S.A.
54 R5 Ersmark Sweden
69 G5 Ertil' Rus. Fed.
114 C3 Erudina Austr.
81 J3 Eruh Turkey
47 G2 Erval Brazil
32 D5 Erwin U.S.A.
62 F5 Erzgebirge mts Czech Rep./Ger.
80 F3 Erzin Turkey
81 G2 Erzincan Turkey
81 H2 Erzurum Turkey
90 G4 Esan-misaki pt Japan
90 H2 Esashi Japan
90 G4 Esashi Japan
55 L9 Esbjerg Denmark
35 G3 Escalante U.S.A.
35 G3 Escalante r. U.S.A.
35 F3 Escalante Desert des. U.S.A.
27 B7 Escalón Mex.
30 D3 Escanaba U.S.A.
36 F5 Escárcega Mex.
94 B2 Escarpada Point pt Phil.
65 F2 Escatrón Spain
61 B4 Escaut r. France/Belgium
61 D3 Esch Neth.
61 D5 Esch-sur-Alzette Lux.
61 E4 Eschweiler Ger.
34 D5 Escondido U.S.A.
45 C3 Escutillas Col.
80 B3 Eşen Turkey
61 F1 Esens Ger.
79 G3 Eşfahān Iran
105 J4 Eshowe S. Africa
103 C6 Esigodini Zimbabwe
105 K4 Esikhawini S. Africa
115 K1 Esk Austr.
115 G8 Esk r. Austr.
58 D2 Esk r. U.K.
57 E5 Eskdalemuir U.K.
23 G3 Esker Can.
54 F4 Eskifjörður Iceland
55 P7 Eskilstuna Sweden
81 J3 Eski Mosul Iraq
80 D1 Eskipazar Turkey
80 C2 Eskişehir Turkey
65 D1 Esla r. Spain
81 L4 Eslāmābād-e Gharb Iran
80 B3 Esler D. mt Turkey
55 N9 Eslöv Sweden
80 B2 Eşme Turkey
42 C3 Esmeraldas Ecuador
30 E1 Esnagi Lake l. Can.
64 F4 Espalion France
31 G2 Espanola Can.
25 F4 Espanola U.S.A.
42 □ Española, Isla i. Ecuador
34 A2 Esparto U.S.A.
112 D6 Esperance Austr.
119 B2 Esperanza Arg. Base Antarctica
47 E1 Esperanza Arg.
36 C3 Esperanza Mex.
94 C4 Esperanza Phil.
65 B3 Espichel, Cabo hd Port.
65 D1 Espigüete mt Spain
27 C7 Espinazo Mex.
46 D2 Espinhaço, Serra do mts Brazil
46 D1 Espinosa Brazil
46 E2 Espírito Santo div. Brazil
94 B2 Espiritu Phil.
111 G3 Espíritu Santo i. Vanuatu
55 T6 Espoo Fin.
65 F4 Espuña mt Spain
44 B6 Esquel Arg.
20 E5 Esquimalt Can.
94 C5 Essang Indon.
100 B1 Essaouira Morocco
100 A2 Es Semara Western Sahara
62 C5 Essen Ger.
43 G2 Essequibo r. Guyana
31 F4 Essex Can.
35 E4 Essex U.S.A.
33 G2 Essex Junction U.S.A.
31 F4 Essexville U.S.A.
77 R4 Esso Rus. Fed.
31 G2 Estaire Can.
43 L6 Estância Brazil
65 G1 Estats, Pic d' mt France/Spain
105 H4 Estcourt S. Africa
65 E1 Estella Spain
65 D4 Estepa Spain
65 D4 Estepona Spain
21 J4 Esterhazy Can.
34 B4 Estero Bay b. U.S.A.
44 D2 Esteros Para.
21 J5 Estevan Can.
26 E3 Estherville U.S.A.
29 D5 Estill U.S.A.
49 Estonia country Europe
65 C2 Estrela, Serra da mts Port.
65 E3 Estrella mt Spain
35 F5 Estrella, Sierra mts U.S.A.
65 C3 Estremoz Port.
43 J5 Estrondo, Serra h. Brazil
81 M4 Estūh Iran
114 C2 Etadunna Austr.
84 D4 Etah India
61 D5 Étain France
64 F2 Étampes France
64 E1 Étaples France
84 D4 Etawah India
105 J3 eThandakukhanya S. Africa
104 E4 E'Thembini S. Africa
96 Ethiopia country Africa
80 D2 Etimesğut Turkey
57 C4 Etive, Loch in. U.K.
66 F6 Etna, Monte vol. Italy
55 J7 Etne Norway
20 C3 Etolin I. i. U.S.A.
116 C3 Eton Austr.
103 B5 Etosha National Park nat. park Namibia
103 B5 Etosha Pan salt pan Namibia
67 L3 Etropole Bulg.
61 E5 Ettelbruck Lux.
61 C3 Etten-Leur Neth.
57 E5 Ettrick Forest reg. U.K.
115 G4 Euabalong Austr.
Euboea i. see Evvoia
112 E6 Eucla Austr.

32 C4 Euclid U.S.A.
43 L6 Euclides da Cunha Brazil
115 H6 Eucumbene, L. l. Austr.
114 C5 Eudunda Austr.
29 C5 Eufaula U.S.A.
27 E5 Eufaula Lake resr U.S.A.
24 B2 Eugene U.S.A.
36 A3 Eugenia, Pta c. Mex.
115 H4 Eugowra Austr.
115 F2 Eulo Austr.
115 H3 Eumungerie Austr.
116 C3 Eungella Austr.
116 C3 Eungella Nat. Park nat. park Austr.
27 E6 Eunice U.S.A.
81 K6 Euphrates r. Asia
55 S6 Eura Fin.
64 E2 Eure r. France
24 A3 Eureka CA U.S.A.
24 D1 Eureka MT U.S.A.
35 E2 Eureka NV U.S.A.
114 D3 Eurinilla watercourse Austr.
114 D3 Euriowie Austr.
115 F6 Euroa Austr.
116 C5 Eurombah Austr.
116 C5 Eurombah Cr. r. Austr.
103 D6 Europa, Île l. Indian Ocean
65 D4 Europa Point pt Gibraltar
61 C3 Europoort reg. Neth.
61 E4 Euskirchen Ger.
114 E5 Euston Austr.
20 C5 Eustuk Lake l. Can.
29 C5 Eutaw U.S.A.
105 H3 Evander S. Africa
22 E3 Evans, L. l. Can.
25 F4 Evans, Mt mt U.S.A.
20 F4 Evansburg Can.
115 K2 Evans Head Austr.
30 D4 Evanston IL U.S.A.
24 E3 Evanston WY U.S.A.
31 F3 Evansville Can.
28 C4 Evansville IN U.S.A.
30 C4 Evansville WI U.S.A.
24 F3 Evansville WY U.S.A.
30 E4 Evart U.S.A.
105 G3 Evaton S. Africa
30 A2 Eveleth U.S.A.
77 R3 Evensk Rus. Fed.
114 A4 Everard, L. salt flat Austr.
112 F5 Everard Range h. Austr.
61 D3 Everdingen Neth.
85 F4 Everest, Mt mt China
33 K1 Everett Can.
24 B1 Everett U.S.A.
61 B3 Evergem Belgium
29 D7 Everglades swamp U.S.A.
29 D7 Everglades Nat. Park nat. park U.S.A.
27 G6 Evergreen U.S.A.
59 F5 Evesham U.K.
59 F5 Evesham, Vale of reg. U.K.
54 S5 Evijärvi Fin.
100 D4 Evinayong Equatorial Guinea
55 K7 Evje Norway
65 C3 Évora Port.
87 P1 Evoron, Ozero l. Rus. Fed.
81 K2 Evowghlī Iran
64 E2 Évreux France
67 K6 Evrotas r. Greece
80 D4 Evrychou Cyprus
67 L5 Evvoia i. Greece
34 □1 Ewa Beach U.S.A.
102 E3 Ewaso Ngiro r. Kenya
57 C3 Ewe, Loch in. U.K.
42 E6 Exaltación Bol.
105 G4 Excelsior S. Africa
34 C2 Excelsior Mtn mt U.S.A.
34 C2 Excelsior Mts mts U.S.A.
26 E4 Excelsior Springs U.S.A.
59 D6 Exe r. U.K.
119 A4 Executive Committee Range mts Antarctica
115 J5 Exeter Austr.
31 G4 Exeter Can.
59 D7 Exeter U.K.
34 C3 Exeter CA U.S.A.
33 H3 Exeter NH U.S.A.
61 E2 Exloo Neth.
59 D7 Exminster U.K.
59 D6 Exmoor reg. U.K.
59 D6 Exmoor National Park U.K.
33 F6 Exmore U.S.A.
112 B4 Exmouth Austr.
59 D7 Exmouth U.K.
115 H3 Exmouth, Mt mt Austr.
112 B4 Exmouth Gulf b. Austr.
13 M5 Exmouth Plateau sea feature Indian Ocean
116 C5 Expedition Range mts Austr.
65 D3 Extremadura div. Spain
29 E7 Exuma Sound chan. Bahamas
69 F6 Eya r. Rus. Fed.
102 D4 Eyasi, Lake salt l. Tanz.
59 J5 Eye U.K.
57 F5 Eyemouth U.K.
57 B2 Eye Peninsula pen. U.K.
54 D5 Eyjafjallajökull ice cap Iceland
54 D3 Eyjafjörður in. Iceland
102 E3 Eyl Somalia
59 F6 Eynsham U.K.
114 B2 Eyre, Lake salt flat Austr.
114 B2 Eyre, Lake (South) salt flat Austr.
117 B6 Eyre Mountains mts N.Z.

114 A4 Eyre Peninsula pen. Austr.
54 □ Eysturoy i. Faroe Is
105 J4 Ezakheni S. Africa
105 H3 Ezenzeleni S. Africa
47 C3 Ezequiel Ramos Mexía, Embalse resr Arg.
89 E4 Ezhou China
68 J2 Ezhva Rus. Fed.
67 M5 Ezine Turkey
80 F1 Ezinepazar Turkey
81 L6 Ezra's Tomb Iraq

F

83 D9 Faadhippolhu Atoll atoll Maldives
27 B6 Fabens U.S.A.
95 □ Faber, Mt h. Sing.
20 F2 Faber Lake l. Can.
55 M9 Fåborg Denmark
66 E3 Fabriano Italy
45 B3 Facatativá Col.
100 D3 Fachi Niger
116 D4 Facority i. Austr.
33 F4 Factoryville U.S.A.
44 B7 Facundo Arg.
100 C3 Fada-Ngourma Burkina
81 H4 Fadghāmī Syria
66 D2 Faenza Italy
Faeroes terr. see Faroe Islands
93 J7 Fafanlap Indon.
102 E3 Fafen Shet' watercourse Eth.
67 L2 Făgăraş Romania
55 L6 Fagernes Norway
55 O7 Fagersta Sweden
44 C8 Fagnano, L. l. Arg./Chile
61 C4 Fagne reg. Belgium
100 B3 Faguibine, Lac l. Mali
54 E5 Fagurhólsmýri Iceland
101 F4 Fagwir Sudan
32 B5 Fairborn U.S.A.
26 D3 Fairbury U.S.A.
32 E5 Fairfax U.S.A.
34 A2 Fairfield CA U.S.A.
30 B5 Fairfield IA U.S.A.
28 C4 Fairfield OH U.S.A.
27 D6 Fairfield TX U.S.A.
33 G3 Fair Haven U.S.A.
60 E2 Fair Head hd U.K.
94 A4 Fairie Queen sand bank Phil.
57 G1 Fair Isle i. U.K.
26 E3 Fairmont MN U.S.A.
32 C5 Fairmont WV U.S.A.
25 F4 Fairplay U.S.A.
30 D3 Fairport U.S.A.
32 C4 Fairport Harbor U.S.A.
20 F3 Fairview Can.
31 E3 Fairview MI U.S.A.
27 D4 Fairview OK U.S.A.
35 G2 Fairview UT U.S.A.
89 □ Fairview Park China
20 B3 Fairweather, Cape c. U.S.A.
20 B3 Fairweather, Mt mt U.S.A.
93 L5 Fais i. Micronesia
84 C3 Faisalabad Pak.
61 C5 Faissault France
26 C2 Faith U.S.A.
85 E4 Faizabad India
111 J2 Fakaofo i. Tokelau
59 H5 Fakenham U.K.
54 O5 Fåker Sweden
93 J7 Fakfak Indon.
88 G1 Faku China
59 C7 Fal r. U.K.
100 A4 Falaba Sierra Leone
64 D2 Falaise France
85 G4 Falakata India
85 H5 Falam Myanmar
27 D7 Falcon Lake l. Mex./U.S.A.
27 D7 Falfurrias U.S.A.
20 F3 Falher Can.
55 N8 Falkenberg Sweden
57 E5 Falkirk U.K.
57 F4 Falkland U.K.
44 E8 Falkland Islands terr. Atlantic Ocean
44 Falkland Sound chan. Falkland Is
55 N7 Falköping Sweden
34 D3 Fallbrook U.S.A.
34 C2 Fallon U.S.A.
33 H4 Fall River U.S.A.
24 E3 Fall River Pass U.S.A.
26 E3 Falls City U.S.A.
59 B7 Falmouth U.K.
32 A5 Falmouth KY U.S.A.
33 H3 Falmouth ME U.S.A.
30 E3 Falmouth MI U.S.A.
104 C7 False Bay b. S. Africa
55 M9 Falster i. Denmark
63 N7 Fălticeni Romania
55 O6 Falun Sweden
80 D4 Famagusta Cyprus
81 M4 Famenin Iran
61 C4 Famenne v. Belgium
21 K4 Family L. l. Can.
88 C4 Fanchang China
60 E4 Fane r. Rep. of Ireland
95 A1 Fang Thai.
88 D3 Fangcheng China
89 C4 Fangdou Shan mts China
89 F6 Fangliao Taiwan
88 E2 Fangshan Beijing China
88 D2 Fangshan Shanxi China
89 F6 Fangshan Taiwan

88 D3 Fangxian China
90 A2 Fangzheng China
89 □ Fanling China
57 C3 Fannich, Loch l. U.K.
66 E3 Fano Italy
89 F5 Fanshan China
88 D2 Fanshi China
89 B6 Fan Si Pan mt Vietnam
119 B2 Faraday Ukr. Base Antarctica
102 E3 Faradje Dem. Rep. Congo
103 E6 Farafangana Madag.
78 B4 Farafra Oasis oasis Egypt
79 J3 Farāh Afgh.
93 L2 Farallon de Pajaros i. N. Mariana Is
45 A4 Farallones de Cali, Parque Nacional nat. park Col.
100 A3 Faranah Guinea
78 E6 Farasān, Jazā'ir is Saudi Arabia
59 F7 Fareham U.K.
117 D4 Farewell, Cape c. N.Z.
117 D4 Farewell Spit spit N.Z.
55 N7 Färgelanda Sweden
26 D2 Fargo U.S.A.
26 E2 Faribault U.S.A.
23 L7 Faribault, Lac l. Can.
84 D3 Faridabad India
84 C3 Farīdkot India
85 G5 Faridpur Bangl.
100 A3 Farim Guinea-Bissau
55 P8 Färjestaden Sweden
81 M4 Farmahin Iran
30 C5 Farmer City U.S.A.
22 D2 Farmer Island i. Can.
20 E3 Farmington Can.
30 B5 Farmington IA U.S.A.
30 B5 Farmington IL U.S.A.
33 H2 Farmington ME U.S.A.
33 H3 Farmington NH U.S.A.
35 H3 Farmington NM U.S.A.
24 E3 Farmington UT U.S.A.
20 D4 Far Mt. mt Can.
32 D6 Farmville U.S.A.
59 G6 Farnborough U.K.
58 F2 Farne Islands is U.K.
59 G6 Farnham U.K.
20 F4 Farnham, Mt mt Can.
43 L6 Faro Brazil
20 C2 Faro Can.
65 C4 Faro Port.
55 Q8 Fårö i. Sweden
54 □ Faroe Islands terr. Atlantic Ocean
55 Q8 Fårösund Sweden
98 Farquhar Islands is Indian Ocean
32 C4 Farrell U.S.A.
31 K3 Farrellton Can.
Farrukhabad see Fatehgarh
67 K5 Farsala Greece
24 E3 Farson U.S.A.
55 K7 Farsund Norway
27 C5 Farwell U.S.A.
79 H4 Fāryāb Iran
66 G4 Fasano Italy
32 E4 Fassett U.S.A.
69 D5 Fastiv Ukr.
84 D4 Fatehgarh India
84 C4 Fatehpur Rajasthan India
84 E4 Fatehpur Uttar Pradesh India
31 G3 Fathom Five National Marine Park nat. park Can.
100 A3 Fatick Senegal
64 H2 Faulquemont France
105 F4 Fauresmith S. Africa
54 O3 Fauske Norway
35 F1 Faust U.S.A.
66 E6 Favignana, Isola i. Italy
20 G4 Fawcett Can.
59 F7 Fawley U.K.
22 C3 Fawn r. Can.
54 B4 Faxaflói b. Iceland
54 P5 Faxälven r. Sweden
89 B5 Faxian Hu l. China
101 D3 Faya Chad
30 D3 Fayette U.S.A.
27 E4 Fayetteville AR U.S.A.
29 E5 Fayetteville NC U.S.A.
29 C5 Fayetteville TN U.S.A.
80 D6 Fâyid Egypt
81 M7 Faylakah i. Kuwait
100 C4 Fazao Malfakassa, Parc National de nat. park Togo
84 C3 Fazilka India
100 A2 Fdérik Maur.
60 D3 Feale r. Rep. of Ireland
29 E5 Fear, Cape c. U.S.A.
34 B2 Feather, North Fork r. U.S.A.
117 E4 Feather Falls U.S.A.
117 E4 Featherston N.Z.
115 G6 Feathertop, Mt mt Austr.
64 E2 Fécamp France
47 F1 Federación Arg.
44 E4 Federal Arg.
106 Federated States of Micronesia country Pac. Oc.
62 E3 Fehmarn i. Ger.
46 E3 Feia, Lagoa lag. Brazil
88 F3 Feihuanghe Kou est. China
42 D5 Feijó Brazil
117 E4 Feilding N.Z.

89 □ Fei Ngo Shan h. China
43 L6 Feira de Santana Brazil
88 E4 Feixi China
80 E3 Feke Turkey
65 H3 Felanitx Spain
30 D3 Felch U.S.A.
62 D7 Feldberg mt Ger.
62 G7 Feldkirch Austria
62 G7 Feldkirchen in Kärnten Austria
47 E1 Feliciano r. Arg.
83 D10 Felidhu Atoll atoll Maldives
46 D2 Felixlândia Brazil
59 J6 Felixstowe U.K.
27 B6 Félix U. Gómez Mex.
66 D1 Feltre Italy
55 M5 Femunden l. Norway
55 N5 Femundsmarka Nasjonalpark nat. park Norway
88 D2 Fen r. China
66 D3 Fenaio, Punta del pt Italy
31 H3 Fence Lake U.S.A.
31 H3 Fenelon Falls Can.
67 L4 Fengari mt Greece
89 E4 Fengcheng China
88 C4 Fengdu China
89 C5 Fenggang China
89 F4 Fenghua China
89 C5 Fenghuang China
88 C4 Fengjie China
89 D6 Fengkai China
89 F6 Fenglin Taiwan
88 F2 Fengnan China
88 E1 Fengning China
88 E3 Fengqiu China
89 C5 Fengshan China
89 E6 Fengshun China
88 D3 Fengtai China
89 E3 Fengxin China
88 E3 Fengyang China
88 D1 Fengzhen China
85 G5 Feni Bangl.
111 F2 Feni Is is P.N.G.
64 F5 Fenille, Col de la pass France
30 B4 Fennimore U.S.A.
31 F4 Fenton U.S.A.
88 D2 Fenxi China
88 D2 Fenyang China
89 E5 Fenyi China
69 E6 Feodosiya Ukr.
66 B6 Fer, Cap de hd Alg.
79 L1 Fergana Uzbek.
31 G4 Fergus Can.
26 D2 Fergus Falls U.S.A.
110 F2 Fergusson I. i. P.N.G.
66 C7 Fériana Tunisia
100 B4 Ferkessédougou Côte d'Ivoire
66 E3 Fermo Italy
23 G3 Fermont Can.
65 C2 Fermoselle Spain
60 C5 Fermoy Rep. of Ireland
42 □ Fernandina, Isla i. Ecuador
29 D6 Fernandina Beach U.S.A.
44 B8 Fernando de Magallanes, Parque Nacional nat. park Chile
12 G6 Fernando de Noronha i. Atlantic Ocean
46 B3 Fernandópolis Brazil
24 B1 Ferndale U.S.A.
59 F7 Ferndown U.K.
20 F5 Fernie Can.
115 G2 Fernlee Austr.
34 C2 Fernley U.S.A.
33 F4 Fernridge U.S.A.
60 E5 Ferns Rep. of Ireland
24 C2 Fernwood U.S.A.
66 D2 Ferrara Italy
46 B3 Ferreiros Brazil
27 F6 Ferriday U.S.A.
66 C4 Ferro, Capo pt Italy
65 C1 Ferrol Spain
35 G2 Ferron U.S.A.
100 B1 Fès Morocco
102 C4 Feshi Dem. Rep. Congo
21 K5 Fessenden U.S.A.
26 E4 Festus U.S.A.
57 □ Fethaland, Point of pt U.K.
60 D5 Fethard Rep. of Ireland
80 C3 Fethiye Turkey
57 □ Fetlar i. U.K.
57 F4 Fettercairn U.K.
23 F2 Feuilles, Rivière aux r. Can.
80 F3 Fevzipaşa Turkey
79 L2 Feyzābād Afgh.
Fez see Fès
59 D5 Ffestiniog U.K.
103 E6 Fianarantsoa Madag.
102 D3 Fichē Eth.
105 G4 Ficksburg S. Africa
20 F4 Field B.C. Can.
31 G2 Field Ont. Can.
67 H4 Fier Albania
30 E3 Fife Lake U.S.A.
57 F4 Fife Ness pt U.K.
115 G4 Fifield Austr.
30 B3 Fifield U.S.A.
64 F4 Figeac France
65 B2 Figueira da Foz Port.
65 H1 Figueres Spain
100 B1 Figuig Morocco
106 Fiji country Pac. Oc.
44 D2 Filadélfia Para.
119 B3 Filchner Ice Shelf ice feature Antarctica

58 G3 Filey U.K.
67 J5 Filippiada Greece
55 O7 Filipstad Sweden
54 L5 Fillan Norway
34 C3 Fillmore CA U.S.A.
35 F2 Fillmore UT U.S.A.
33 F2 Finch Can.
116 C3 Finch Hatton Austr.
57 E3 Findhorn r. U.K.
81 H3 Findık Turkey
32 B4 Findlay U.S.A.
115 H8 Fingal Austr.
22 E5 Finger Lakes lakes U.S.A.
103 D5 Fingoè Moz.
80 C3 Finike Turkey
80 C3 Finike Körfezi b. Turkey
Finisterre, Cape c. see Fisterra, Cabo
112 F4 Finke Gorge National Park nat. park Austr.
49 Finland country Europe
52 Finland, Gulf of g. Europe
20 D3 Finlay r. Can.
20 D3 Finlay, Mt mt Can.
115 F5 Finley Austr.
114 A4 Finniss, C. pt Austr.
54 P2 Finnsnes Norway
55 O7 Finspång Sweden
60 D3 Fintona U.K.
60 C3 Fintown Rep. of Ireland
57 C3 Fionn Loch l. U.K.
57 B4 Fionnphort U.K.
117 A6 Fiordland National Park nat. park N.Z.
Firat r. see Euphrates
34 D3 Firebaugh U.S.A.
21 J2 Firedrake Lake l. Can.
33 G4 Fire Island National Seashore res. U.S.A.
Firenze see Florence
81 K6 Firk, Sha'ib watercourse Iraq
47 E2 Firmat Arg.
64 G4 Firminy France
63 Q2 Firovo Rus. Fed.
84 B3 Firoza Pak.
84 D4 Firozabad India
84 C3 Firozpur India
33 H2 First Connecticut L. l. U.S.A.
79 G4 Firūzābād Iran
103 B6 Fish r. Namibia
104 D5 Fish r. S. Africa
33 F6 Fisherman I. i. U.S.A.
33 H4 Fishers I. i. U.S.A.
21 N2 Fisher Strait chan. Can.
59 C6 Fishguard U.K.
20 E2 Fish Lake l. Can.
30 A2 Fish Lake l. MN U.S.A.
35 G2 Fish Lake l. UT U.S.A.
31 F4 Fish Pt pt U.S.A.
119 B3 Fiske, C. c. Antarctica
61 B5 Fismes France
65 B1 Fisterra Spain
65 B1 Fisterra, Cabo c. Spain
33 H3 Fitchburg U.S.A.
21 H3 Fitzgerald Can.
29 D6 Fitzgerald U.S.A.
114 B4 Fitzgerald Bay b. Austr.
112 C6 Fitzgerald River National Park nat. park Austr.
44 C7 Fitz Roy Arg.
116 D4 Fitzroy r. Austr.
112 E3 Fitzroy Crossing Austr.
31 G3 Fivewilliam I. i. Can.
60 D3 Fivemiletown U.K.
66 D2 Fivizzano Italy
102 C4 Fizi Dem. Rep. Congo
55 L6 Flå Norway
105 H5 Flagstaff S. Africa
35 G4 Flagstaff U.S.A.
33 H2 Flagstaff Lake l. U.S.A.
22 E3 Flaherty Island i. Can.
30 B3 Flambeau r. U.S.A.
58 G3 Flamborough Head hd U.K.
24 E3 Flaming Gorge Res. l. U.S.A.
104 D5 Flaminksvlei salt pan S. Africa
61 B4 Flandre reg. France
57 A2 Flannan Isles is U.K.
54 O4 Flåsjön l. Sweden
30 E4 Flat r. U.S.A.
24 D2 Flathead L. l. U.S.A.
116 C4 Flat Is is Austr.
117 F4 Flat Point pt N.Z.
113 J2 Flattery, C. pt N.Z.
24 A1 Flattery, C. c. U.S.A.
116 A4 Fleetwood Austr.
58 D4 Fleetwood U.K.
33 F4 Fleetwood U.S.A.
55 K7 Flekkefjord Norway
32 E3 Fleming U.S.A.
32 B5 Flemingsburg U.S.A.
55 P7 Flen Sweden
62 D3 Flensburg Ger.
64 D2 Flers France
30 E3 Flesherton Can.
21 H2 Fletcher Lake l. Can.
31 F3 Fletcher Pond l. U.S.A.
119 B3 Fletcher Prom. hd Antarctica
113 H3 Flinders r. Austr.
112 C6 Flinders Bay b. Austr.
114 B5 Flinders Chase Nat. Park nat. park Austr.
115 H2 Flinders I. i. Austr.
114 A4 Flinders Island i. Austr.
116 C2 Flinders Passage chan. Austr.
114 C3 Flinders Ranges mts Austr.

114 C3 Flinders Ranges Nat. Park nat. park Austr.
116 C1 Flinders Reefs rf Coral Sea Is Terr.
21 J4 Flin Flon Can.
59 D4 Flint U.K.
31 F4 Flint U.S.A.
29 C6 Flint r. GA U.S.A.
31 F4 Flint r. MI U.S.A.
115 H1 Flinton Austr.
55 N6 Flisa Norway
58 E2 Flodden U.K.
119 A4 Flood Ra. mts Antarctica
30 A2 Floodwood U.S.A.
28 B4 Flora U.S.A.
64 F4 Florac France
116 A3 Flora Reef rf Coral Sea Is Terr.
31 H4 Florence Can.
66 D3 Florence Italy
29 C5 Florence AL U.S.A.
35 G5 Florence AZ U.S.A.
26 D4 Florence KS U.S.A.
32 C5 Florence OH U.S.A.
24 A3 Florence OR U.S.A.
29 E5 Florence SC U.S.A.
35 G5 Florence Junction U.S.A.
33 K1 Florenceville Can.
45 B4 Florencia Col.
44 C6 Florentino Ameghino, Embalse resr Arg.
47 E2 Flores r. Arg.
36 G5 Flores Guatemala
93 G8 Flores i. Indon.
46 C1 Flores de Goiás Brazil
93 F8 Flores Sea sea Indon.
43 L5 Floresta Brazil
43 K5 Floriano Brazil
44 C3 Florianópolis Brazil
47 F2 Florida Uru.
29 D7 Florida div. U.S.A.
37 H4 Florida, Straits of str. Bahamas/U.S.A.
29 D7 Florida Bay b. U.S.A.
29 D7 Florida City U.S.A.
111 G2 Florida Is is Solomon Is
67 J4 Florina Greece
55 J6 Florø Norway
31 H3 Flour Lake l. Can.
30 A4 Floyd IA U.S.A.
32 C6 Floyd VA U.S.A.
35 F4 Floyd, Mt mt U.S.A.
27 C5 Floydada U.S.A.
61 D2 Fluessen l. Neth.
110 E2 Fly r. P.N.G.
32 C5 Fly r. P.N.G.
67 H3 Foča Bos.-Herz.
57 E3 Fochabers U.K.
105 G3 Fochville S. Africa
63 M2 Focşani Romania
89 D6 Fogang China
66 F4 Foggia Italy
100 □ Fogo i. Cape Verde
23 K4 Fogo I. i. Can.
57 D2 Foinaven h. U.K.
64 E5 Foix France
54 O3 Folda chan. Norway
54 M4 Foldereid Norway
54 M4 Foldfjorden chan. Norway
67 L6 Folegandros i. Greece
31 F1 Foleyet Can.
66 E3 Foligno Italy
59 J6 Folkestone U.K.
59 G5 Folkingham U.K.
29 D6 Folkston U.S.A.
54 M5 Folldal Norway
66 D3 Follonica Italy
34 B2 Folsom Lake l. U.S.A.
69 H6 Fomin Rus. Fed.
68 J2 Fominskiy Rus. Fed.
21 H3 Fond-du-Lac Can.
21 J3 Fond du Lac r. Can.
30 C4 Fond du Lac U.S.A.
65 B2 Fondevila Spain
66 E4 Fondi Italy
66 E4 Fonni Italy
36 G6 Fonseca, G. de b. Central America
23 F3 Fontanges Can.
20 E3 Fontas Can.
20 E3 Fontas r. Can.
42 E4 Fonte Boa Brazil
64 D3 Fontenay-le-Comte France
54 F3 Fontur pt Iceland
31 H3 Foot's Bay Can.
88 C3 Foping China
115 H4 Forbes Austr.
24 C1 Forbes, Mt mt Can.
62 E6 Forchheim Ger.
23 G2 Ford r. U.S.A.
30 D2 Ford r. U.S.A.
55 J6 Førde Norway
21 K2 Forde Lake l. Can.
59 H5 Fordham U.K.
59 F7 Fordingbridge U.K.
119 A4 Ford Ra. mts Antarctica
115 J2 Fords Bridge Austr.
27 E5 Fordyce U.S.A.
100 A4 Forécariah Guinea
59 F7 Foreland hd U.K.
59 D6 Foreland Point pt U.K.
20 C3 Foresight Mtn mt Can.
31 G4 Forest Can.
27 F5 Forest MS U.S.A.
32 B4 Forest OH U.S.A.
33 G3 Forest Dale U.S.A.
115 G5 Forest Hill N.S.W. Austr.
116 A5 Forest Hill Qld. Austr.
34 B2 Foresthill U.S.A.
115 H9 Forestier, C. hd Antarctica
115 H9 Forestier Pen. pen. Austr.
30 A3 Forest Lake U.S.A.

29 C5	Forest Park U.S.A.	
23 G4	Forestville Can.	
57 F4	Forfar U.K.	
24 A2	Forks U.S.A.	
33 J2	Forks, The U.S.A.	
32 E4	Forksville U.S.A.	
66 E2	Forli Italy	
58 D4	Formby U.K.	
65 G3	Formentera i. Spain	
65 H3	Formentor, Cap de pt Spain	
46 D3	Formiga Brazil	
44 E3	Formosa Arg.	
	Formosa country see Taiwan	
46 C1	Formosa Brazil	
43 G6	Formosa, Serra h. Brazil	
46 D1	Formoso r. Brazil	
57 E3	Forres U.K.	
114 E7	Forrest Vic. Austr.	
112 E6	Forrest W.A. Austr.	
30 C5	Forrest U.S.A.	
27 F5	Forrest City U.S.A.	
30 C4	Forreston U.S.A.	
54 P5	Fors Sweden	
113 H3	Forsayth Austr.	
54 S3	Forsnäs Sweden	
55 S6	Forssa Fin.	
115 K4	Forster Austr.	
27 E4	Forsyth MO U.S.A.	
24 F2	Forsyth MT U.S.A.	
31 J1	Forsythe Can.	
84 C3	Fort Abbas Pak.	
22 D3	Fort Albany Can.	
43 L4	Fortaleza Brazil	
35 H5	Fort Apache U.S.A.	
20 E4	Fort Assiniboine Can.	
30 C4	Fort Atkinson U.S.A.	
30 D3	Fort Augustus U.K.	
105 G6	Fort Beaufort S. Africa	
24 E2	Fort Benton U.S.A.	
21 H3	Fort Black Can.	
34 A2	Fort Bragg U.S.A.	
	Fort-Chimo see Kuujjuaq	
21 G3	Fort Chipewyan Can.	
27 D5	Fort Cobb Res. resr U.S.A.	
24 F3	Fort Collins U.S.A.	
31 J3	Fort-Coulonge Can.	
33 F2	Fort Covington U.S.A.	
27 C6	Fort Davis U.S.A.	
37 M6	Fort-de-France Martinique	
29 C5	Fort Deposit U.S.A.	
26 E3	Fort Dodge U.S.A.	
112 C4	Fortescue r. Austr.	
26 E1	Fort Frances U.S.A.	
22 E3	Fort George Can.	
57 D4	Forth r. U.K.	
57 E4	Forth, Firth of est. U.K.	
	Fort Hertz see Putao	
35 E2	Fortification Range mts U.S.A.	
44 D2	Fortín Capitán Demattei Para.	
44 D2	Fortín General Mendoza Para.	
44 E2	Fortín Madrejón Para.	
44 D2	Fortín Pilcomayo Arg.	
42 F7	Fortín Ravelo Bol.	
42 F7	Fortín Suárez Arana Bol.	
33 J1	Fort Kent U.S.A.	
29 D7	Fort Lauderdale U.S.A.	
20 E2	Fort Liard Can.	
21 G3	Fort Mackay Can.	
20 G5	Fort Macleod Can.	
30 B5	Fort Madison U.S.A.	
30 B3	Fort McCoy U.S.A.	
21 G3	Fort McMurray Can.	
24 G3	Fort Morgan U.S.A.	
29 D7	Fort Myers U.S.A.	
20 E3	Fort Nelson Can.	
20 E3	Fort Nelson r. Can.	
	Fort Norman see Tulít'a	
29 C5	Fort Payne U.S.A.	
24 F1	Fort Peck U.S.A.	
24 F2	Fort Peck Res. resr U.S.A.	
29 D7	Fort Pierce U.S.A.	
26 C2	Fort Pierre U.S.A.	
20 F2	Fort Providence Can.	
21 J4	Fort Qu'Appelle Can.	
20 G2	Fort Resolution Can.	
117 B7	Fortrose N.Z.	
57 D3	Fortrose U.K.	
34 A2	Fort Ross U.S.A.	
22 E3	Fort Rupert Can.	
	Fort Sandeman see Zhob	
20 G4	Fort Saskatchewan Can.	
27 E4	Fort Scott U.S.A.	
22 C2	Fort Severn Can.	
20 E2	Fort Simpson Can.	
21 G2	Fort Smith Can.	
27 E5	Fort Smith U.S.A.	
20 E4	Fort St James Can.	
20 E4	Fort St John Can.	
27 C6	Fort Stockton U.S.A.	
25 F5	Fort Sumner U.S.A.	
24 A3	Fortuna U.S.A.	
26 C1	Fortuna U.S.A.	
23 J4	Fortune B. b. Can.	
20 F3	Fort Vermilion Can.	
29 C6	Fort Walton Beach U.S.A.	
30 E5	Fort Wayne U.S.A.	
57 C4	Fort William U.K.	
27 D5	Fort Worth U.S.A.	
54 N4	Forvik Norway	
89 D6	Foshan China	
89 □	Fo Shek Chau i. China	
66 B2	Fossano Italy	
115 G7	Foster Austr.	
20 B3	Foster, Mt mt Can./U.S.A.	
54 S4	Fostoria U.S.A.	
59 G6	Fotherby U.K.	
64 D2	Fougères France	
57 □	Foula i. U.K.	
59 H6	Foulness Point pt U.K.	
117 C4	Foulwind, Cape c. N.Z.	
100 D4	Foumban Cameroon	
100 A3	Foundiougne Senegal	
30 A4	Fountain U.S.A.	
64 G2	Fourches, Mont des h. France	
34 D4	Four Corners U.S.A.	
105 H4	Fouriesburg S. Africa	
67 M6	Fournoi i. Greece	
30 C2	Fourteen Mile Pt pt U.S.A.	
100 A3	Fouta Djallon reg. Guinea	
117 A7	Foveaux Strait str. N.Z.	
29 E7	Fowl Cay i. Bahamas	
25 F4	Fowler CO U.S.A.	
30 D5	Fowler IN U.S.A.	
30 E4	Fowler MI U.S.A.	
119 B3	Fowler Pen. pen. Antarctica	
112 F6	Fowlers Bay Austr.	
81 M3	Fowman Iran	
21 L3	Fox r. Can.	
30 C4	Fox r. U.S.A.	
116 B4	Fox Cr. r. Austr.	
20 H3	Fox Creek Can.	
20 C4	Fox Lake Can.	
30 C4	Fox Lake U.S.A.	
117 E4	Foxton N.Z.	
57 D3	Foyers U.K.	
60 D3	Foyle r. Rep. of Ireland/U.K.	
60 D2	Foyle, Lough b. Rep. of Ireland/U.K.	
60 B5	Foynes Rep. of Ireland	
103 B5	Foz do Cunene Angola	
46 A4	Foz do Iguaçu Brazil	
65 G2	Fraga Spain	
46 C3	Franca Brazil	
111 G3	Français, Récif des rf New Caledonia	
48	France country Europe	
114 D6	Frances Austr.	
20 E2	Frances r. Can.	
20 D2	Frances Lake l. Can.	
20 D2	Frances Lake Can.	
30 D5	Franceville U.S.A.	
102 B4	Franceville Gabon	
33 H2	Francis, Lake l. U.S.A.	
26 D3	Francis Case, Lake l. U.S.A.	
27 C7	Francisco I. Madero Mex.	
46 D2	Francisco Sá Brazil	
103 C6	Francistown Botswana	
20 D4	François Lake l. Can.	
24 E3	Francs Peak summit U.S.A.	
31 J1	Frankenmuth U.S.A.	
105 H3	Frankfort S. Africa	
30 D5	Frankfort IN U.S.A.	
28 C4	Frankfort KY U.S.A.	
30 D3	Frankfort MI U.S.A.	
62 D5	Frankfurt am Main Ger.	
62 G4	Frankfurt an der Oder Ger.	
35 E1	Frankin Lake l. U.S.A.	
62 E6	Fränkische Alb reg. Ger.	
62 E6	Fränkische Schweiz reg. Ger.	
24 E3	Franklin ID U.S.A.	
28 C4	Franklin IN U.S.A.	
27 F6	Franklin LA U.S.A.	
33 H4	Franklin MA U.S.A.	
29 C5	Franklin NC U.S.A.	
33 H3	Franklin NH U.S.A.	
33 F4	Franklin NJ U.S.A.	
32 A4	Franklin PA U.S.A.	
29 C5	Franklin TN U.S.A.	
28 C4	Franklin VA U.S.A.	
32 D5	Franklin WV U.S.A.	
24 C1	Franklin D. Roosevelt Lake l. U.S.A.	
115 F9	Franklin-Gordon National Park nat. park Austr.	
114 B4	Franklin Harbor b. Austr.	
20 E2	Franklin Mountains mts Can.	
117 A6	Franklin Mts mts N.Z.	
115 G8	Franklin Sd chan. Austr.	
118 B2	Franklin Strait sea chan. Can.	
114 F7	Frankston Austr.	
55 P5	Fränsta Sweden	
30 E1	Franz Can.	
117 C5	Franz Josef Glacier N.Z.	
76 G2	Franz Josef Land is Rus. Fed.	
66 C5	Frasca, Capo della pt Italy	
66 F4	Frascati Italy	
20 E4	Fraser r. B.C. Can.	
23 H2	Fraser r. Nfld Can.	
104 D5	Fraserburg S. Africa	
57 F3	Fraserburgh U.K.	
22 D4	Fraserdale Can.	
116 E5	Fraser Island i. Austr.	
116 E5	Fraser Island National Park Austr.	
20 E4	Fraser Lake Can.	
20 E4	Fraser Plateau plat. Can.	
117 F3	Frasertown N.Z.	
30 E2	Frater Can.	
62 D7	Frauenfeld Switz.	
47 E2	Fray Bentos Uru.	
58 E4	Freckleton U.K.	
30 E4	Frederic MI U.S.A.	
30 A3	Frederic WI U.S.A.	
55 L9	Fredericia Denmark	
32 E5	Frederick MD U.S.A.	
27 D5	Frederick OK U.S.A.	
27 D6	Fredericksburg TX U.S.A.	
32 E5	Fredericksburg VA U.S.A.	
20 C3	Frederick Sound chan. U.S.A.	
27 F4	Fredericktown U.S.A.	
23 G4	Fredericton Can.	
55 M8	Frederikshavn Denmark	
55 N9	Frederiksværk Denmark	
35 F3	Fredonia AZ U.S.A.	
32 D3	Fredonia NY U.S.A.	
54 Q4	Fredrika Sweden	
55 M7	Fredrikstad Norway	
33 H4	Freehold U.S.A.	
33 H4	Freeland U.S.A.	
114 C3	Freeling Heights mt Austr.	
34 C2	Freel Peak summit U.S.A.	
26 D3	Freeman U.S.A.	
30 D5	Freeman, Lake l. U.S.A.	
30 C4	Freeport IL U.S.A.	
33 H3	Freeport ME U.S.A.	
33 G4	Freeport NY U.S.A.	
27 E6	Freeport TX U.S.A.	
29 E7	Freeport City Bahamas	
27 D7	Freer U.S.A.	
105 G4	Free State div. S. Africa	
100 A4	Freetown Sierra Leone	
65 C3	Fregenal de la Sierra Spain	
64 C2	Fréhel, Cap pt France	
62 C6	Freiburg im Breisgau Ger.	
62 E6	Freising Ger.	
62 G6	Freistadt Austria	
64 H5	Fréjus France	
112 C6	Fremantle Austr.	
30 E4	Fremont MI U.S.A.	
26 D3	Fremont NE U.S.A.	
32 B4	Fremont OH U.S.A.	
35 G2	Fremont r. U.S.A.	
32 B6	Frenchburg U.S.A.	
32 C4	French Creek r. U.S.A.	
38	French Guiana terr. S. America	
114 F1	French I. i. Austr.	
21 H5	Frenchman r. Can./U.S.A.	
34 C2	Frenchman U.S.A.	
34 B2	Frenchman L. l. CA U.S.A.	
35 E3	Frenchman L. l. NV U.S.A.	
115 F9	Frenchmans Cap mt Austr.	
60 C4	Frenchpark Rep. of Ireland	
117 D4	French Pass N.Z.	
33 J1	Frenchville U.S.A.	
60 D5	Freshford Rep. of Ireland	
35 G6	Fresnal Canyon U.S.A.	
36 D4	Fresnillo Mex.	
34 C3	Fresno U.S.A.	
34 C3	Fresno r. U.S.A.	
65 H3	Freu, Cap des pt Spain	
62 D6	Freudenstadt Ger.	
115 H9	Freycinet Nat. Park nat. park Austr.	
115 H9	Freycinet Peninsula pen. Austr.	
64 H2	Freyming-Merlebach France	
47 D1	Freyre Arg.	
100 A3	Fria Guinea	
34 D3	Friant U.S.A.	
44 C3	Frias Arg.	
62 C7	Fribourg Switz.	
62 D7	Friedrichshafen Ger.	
33 J3	Friendship U.S.A.	
61 D1	Friese Wad tidal flats Neth.	
59 J6	Frinton-on-Sea U.K.	
27 D6	Frio r. U.S.A.	
57 E4	Frisa, Loch l. U.K.	
35 F2	Frisco Mt mt U.S.A.	
118 A3	Frobisher Bay b. Can.	
21 H3	Frobisher Lake l. Can.	
54 L5	Frohavet b. Norway	
69 G5	Frolovo Rus. Fed.	
68 K2	Frolovskaya Rus. Fed.	
114 C2	Frome watercourse Austr.	
59 E6	Frome U.K.	
114 C3	Frome, Lake salt flat Austr.	
114 C2	Frome Downs Austr.	
36 F5	Frontera Mex.	
25 E6	Fronteras Mex.	
32 D5	Front Royal U.S.A.	
66 E4	Frosinone Italy	
32 D5	Frostburg U.S.A.	
54 L5	Frøya i. Norway	
35 H2	Fruita U.S.A.	
35 G1	Fruitland U.S.A.	
	Frunze see Bishkek	
62 D7	Frutigen Switz.	
63 J6	Frýdek-Místek Czech Rep.	
33 H2	Fryeburg U.S.A.	
89 F5	Fu'an China	
89 D5	Fuchuan China	
89 F4	Fuchun Jiang r. China	
57 A3	Fude U.K.	
89 E5	Fude China	
89 F5	Fuding China	
65 E2	Fuenlabrada Spain	
65 D3	Fuente Obejuna Spain	
44 E2	Fuerte Olimpo Para.	
100 A2	Fuerteventura i. Canary Is	
88 E3	Fugou China	
88 D2	Fugu China	
82 G1	Fuhai China	
81 J4	Fuḩaymī Iraq	
79 H4	Fujairah U.A.E.	
91 F7	Fuji Japan	
89 E5	Fujian div. China	
88 C4	Fu Jiang r. China	
91 F7	Fuji-Hakone-Izu National Park Japan	
90 B1	Fujin China	
91 F7	Fujinomiya Japan	
91 F7	Fuji-san vol. Japan	
90 H3	Fukagawa Japan	
91 D7	Fukuchiyama Japan	
91 A8	Fukue Japan	
91 A8	Fukue-jima i. Japan	
91 E6	Fukui Japan	
91 B8	Fukuoka Japan	
91 G6	Fukushima Japan	
91 B9	Fukuyama Japan	
62 D5	Fulda Ger.	
59 G6	Fulham U.K.	
88 E3	Fuliji China	
89 C4	Fuling China	
21 M2	Fullerton, Cape hd Can.	
30 B5	Fulton IL U.S.A.	
28 B4	Fulton KY U.S.A.	
27 F4	Fulton MO U.S.A.	
33 E3	Fulton NY U.S.A.	
105 K2	Fumane Moz.	
61 C5	Fumay France	
91 F7	Funabashi Japan	
111 H2	Funafuti i. Tuvalu	
100 A1	Funchal Port.	
45 B2	Fundación Col.	
65 C2	Fundão Port.	
23 G4	Fundy, Bay of g. Can.	
23 G4	Fundy Nat. Park nat. park Can.	
34 D3	Funeral Peak summit U.S.A.	
103 D6	Funhalouro Moz.	
88 F3	Funing Jiangsu China	
89 B6	Funing Yunnan China	
88 D3	Funiu Shan mts China	
116 D2	Funnel Cr. r. Austr.	
100 C3	Funtua Nigeria	
89 F5	Fuqing China	
90 H3	Furano Japan	
79 E4	Fūrgun, Kūh-e mt Iran	
68 G3	Furmanov Rus. Fed.	
90 D7	Furmanovo Rus. Fed.	
34 D3	Furnace Creek U.S.A.	
46 C3	Furnas, Represa resr Brazil	
113 J7	Furneaux Group is Austr.	
62 E6	Fürstenwalde Ger.	
62 E6	Fürth Ger.	
90 G3	Furubira Japan	
90 E7	Furukawa Japan	
45 B3	Fusagasugá Col.	
89 C7	Fushan China	
88 G1	Fushun Liaoning China	
89 B4	Fushun Sichuan China	
87 N3	Fusong China	
89 C6	Fusui China	
91 B8	Futago-san vol. Japan	
111 H3	Futuna i. Vanuatu	
89 E5	Futun Xi r. China	
88 C3	Fuxian China	
88 M3	Fuxin Liaoning China	
88 F1	Fuxin Liaoning China	
90 F5	Fuya Japan	
88 E2	Fuyang Anhui China	
89 F4	Fuyang Zhejiang China	
88 E2	Fuyang r. China	
87 M2	Fuyu China	
89 B5	Fuyuan China	
82 G1	Fuyun China	
89 F5	Fuzhou China	
	Fuzhou see Linchuan	
81 L2	Füzuli Azer.	
55 M9	Fyn i. Denmark	
57 D3	Fyne, Loch in. U.K.	
	F.Y.R.O.M. country see Macedonia	

G

66 C6	Gaâfour Tunisia	
102 E3	Gaalkacyo Somalia	
105 F2	Gabane Botswana	
34 D2	Gabbs U.S.A.	
34 C2	Gabbs Valley Range mts U.S.A.	
103 B5	Gabela Angola	
100 D1	Gabès Tunisia	
101 D1	Gabès, Golfe de g. Tunisia	
115 H6	Gabo I. i. Austr.	
96	Gabon country Africa	
103 C6	Gaborone Botswana	
67 L3	Gabrovo Bulg.	
100 A3	Gabú Guinea-Bissau	
83 E7	Gadag India	
54 O4	Gädede Sweden	
84 B5	Gadhra India	
84 B4	Gadra Pak.	
29 C5	Gadsden U.S.A.	
83 E7	Gadwal India	
100 C1	Gafsa Tunisia	
68 E4	Gagarin Rus. Fed.	
68 H4	Gagino Rus. Fed.	
100 B4	Gagnoa Côte d'Ivoire	
23 G3	Gagnon Can.	
69 G7	Gagra Georgia	
81 L4	Gahväreh Iran	
104 C4	Gaiab watercourse Namibia	
84 G4	Gaibandha Bangl.	
64 E5	Gaillac France	
29 D6	Gainesville FL U.S.A.	
29 D5	Gainesville GA U.S.A.	
27 D5	Gainesville TX U.S.A.	
59 G4	Gainsborough U.K.	
114 A3	Gairdner, Lake salt flat Austr.	
57 C3	Gairloch U.K.	
57 C3	Gair Loch in. U.K.	
88 G1	Gaizhou China	
104 E3	Gakarosa mt S. Africa	
84 C1	Gakuch Jammu and Kashmir	
85 G3	Gala China	
80 C7	Galāla al Baḩarîya, Gebel el plat. Egypt	
102 D4	Galana r. Kenya	
57 F5	Galashiels U.K.	
67 M3	Galata, Nos pt Bulg.	
67 N2	Galaţi Romania	
67 H4	Galatina Italy	
32 C6	Galax U.S.A.	
60 C5	Galbally Rep. of Ireland	
55 L6	Galdhøpiggen summit Norway	
30 B4	Galena U.S.A.	
45 E2	Galeota Pt pt Trinidad and Tobago	
47 B4	Galera, Punta pt Chile	
45 E2	Galera Pt pt Trinidad and Tobago	
30 B5	Galesburg U.S.A.	
104 E4	Galeshewe S. Africa	
30 B3	Galesville U.S.A.	
32 E4	Galeton U.S.A.	
69 G7	Gali Georgia	
68 G3	Galich Rus. Fed.	
68 G2	Galichskaya Vozvyshennost' reg. Rus. Fed.	
65 C1	Galicia div. Spain	
116 A4	Galilee, L. salt flat Austr.	
80 E5	Galilee, Sea of l. Israel	
32 B4	Galion U.S.A.	
35 G5	Galiuro Mts mts U.S.A.	
101 F3	Gallabat Sudan	
29 C5	Gallatin U.S.A.	
24 E2	Gallatin r. U.S.A.	
83 F9	Galle Sri Lanka	
44 B8	Gallegos r. Arg.	
45 C1	Gallinas, Pta pt Col.	
66 H4	Gallipoli Italy	
32 B5	Gallipolis U.S.A.	
54 R3	Gällivare Sweden	
54 O5	Gällö Sweden	
33 G3	Gallo I. i. U.S.A.	
35 H4	Gallo Mts mts U.S.A.	
35 H4	Gallup U.S.A.	
57 B4	Galmisdale U.K.	
115 H5	Galong Austr.	
57 D5	Galston U.K.	
34 B2	Galt U.S.A.	
100 A2	Galtat Zemmour Western Sahara	
60 C5	Galtee Mountains h. Rep. of Ireland	
60 C5	Galtymore h. Rep. of Ireland	
30 B5	Galva U.S.A.	
27 E6	Galveston U.S.A.	
27 E6	Galveston Bay b. U.S.A.	
47 E2	Galvez Arg.	
85 E3	Galwa Nepal	
60 B4	Galway Rep. of Ireland	
60 B4	Galway Bay g. Rep. of Ireland	
89 B6	Gâm r. Vietnam	
59 J8	Gamaches France	
105 J5	Gamalakhe S. Africa	
45 B2	Gamarra Col.	
85 G3	Gamba China	
102 D3	Gambēla Eth.	
102 D3	Gambēla National Park nat. park Eth.	
84 D4	Gambhir r. India	
109	Gambier, Îles is Pac. Oc.	
114 B5	Gambier Is is Austr.	
23 K4	Gambo Can.	
102 B4	Gamboma Congo	
113 H4	Gamboola Austr.	
35 H4	Gamerco U.S.A.	
55 P8	Gamleby Sweden	
54 S4	Gammelstaden Sweden	
114 C3	Gammon Ranges Nat. Park nat. park Austr.	
90 D2	Gamova, Mys pt Rus. Fed.	
35 H4	Ganado U.S.A.	
31 J3	Gananoque Can.	
81 L1	Gäncä Azer.	
89 C7	Gancheng China	
93 C7	Gandadiwata, Bukit mt Indon.	
85 G3	Gandaingoin China	
102 C4	Gandajika Dem. Rep. Congo	
85 E4	Gandak Dam dam Nepal	
84 B3	Gandari Mountain mt Pak.	
84 A3	Gandava Pak.	
23 K4	Gander Can.	
65 G2	Gandesa Spain	
84 B5	Gāndhīdhām India	
84 B5	Gandhinagar India	
84 C4	Gāndhī Sāgar resr India	
84 C4	Gāndhī Sāgar Dam dam India	
65 F3	Gandía Spain	
79 J4	Gand-i-Zureh plain Afgh.	
46 E1	Gandu Brazil	
	Ganga r. see Ganges	
47 C4	Gangán Arg.	
84 D3	Ganganagar India	
84 D4	Gangapur India	
85 H5	Gangaw Myanmar	
88 A2	Gangca China	
84 E3	Gangdisê Shan mts China	
64 F5	Ganges France	
85 G4	Ganges r. India	
85 G5	Ganges, Mouths of the est. Bangl./India	
84 D3	Gangoh India	
84 D3	Gangotri mt India	
85 G4	Gangtok India	
88 B3	Gangu China	
83 G2	Ganjam India	
89 E4	Gan Jiang r. China	
88 G1	Ganjig China	
89 B4	Ganluo China	
115 G5	Ganmain Austr.	
64 F3	Gannat France	
24 E3	Gannett Peak summit U.S.A.	
84 D3	Ganora India	
88 C2	Ganquan China	
104 C7	Gansbaai S. Africa	
88 B3	Gansu div. China	
88 B2	Gantang China	
114 B6	Gantheaume, C. hd Austr.	
69 G7	Gant'iadi Georgia	
89 F3	Ganxian China	
88 F3	Ganyu China	
89 F5	Ganzhou China	
101 E3	Ganzi Sudan	
100 B3	Gao Mali	
89 F4	Gao'an China	
88 E2	Gaocheng China	
88 F1	Gaochun China	
89 E4	Gaohebu China	
88 B2	Gaolan China	
88 F2	Gaomi China	
89 D5	Gaomutang China	
88 B3	Gaoping China	
88 A2	Gaotai China	
88 E2	Gaotang China	
88 C2	Gaotouyao China	
100 B3	Gaoua Burkina	
100 A3	Gaoual Guinea	
89 B4	Gaoxian China	
88 E2	Gaoyang China	
88 F2	Gaoyi China	
88 F3	Gaoyou China	
88 F3	Gaoyou Hu l. China	
89 D6	Gaozhou China	
64 F3	Gap France	
94 B3	Gapan Phil.	
65 F5	Gap Carbon hd Alg.	
84 E2	Gar China	
60 C4	Gara, Lough l. Rep. of Ireland	
115 H2	Garah Austr.	
102 C3	Garamba r. Dem. Rep. Congo	
43 L5	Garanhuns Brazil	
105 G2	Ga-Rankuwa S. Africa	
102 D3	Garba Tula Kenya	
34 A1	Garberville U.S.A.	
62 D4	Garbsen Ger.	
46 C3	Garça Brazil	
46 B1	Garças, Rio das r. Brazil	
85 G2	Garco China	
66 D2	Garda, Lago di l. Italy	
81 K1	Gardabani Georgia	
66 B6	Garde, Cap de hd Alg.	
26 C4	Garden City U.S.A.	
30 D3	Garden Corners U.S.A.	
34 C5	Garden Grove U.S.A.	
21 L4	Garden Hill Can.	
30 D3	Garden I. i. U.S.A.	
28 C2	Garden Pen. pen. U.S.A.	
84 B2	Gardez Afgh.	
33 J2	Gardiner ME U.S.A.	
24 E2	Gardiner MT U.S.A.	
33 G4	Gardiners I. i. U.S.A.	
30 C5	Gardner U.S.A.	
33 K2	Gardner Lake l. U.S.A.	
14 H4	Gardner Pinnacles is U.S.A.	
34 C2	Gardnerville U.S.A.	
57 D3	Garelochhead U.K.	
30 E2	Gargantua, Cape c. Can.	
81 M6	Gargar Iran	
55 R9	Gargždai Lith.	
84 D5	Garhakota India	
84 E5	Garhchiroli India	
84 A3	Garhi Khairo Pak.	
84 D4	Garhi Malehra India	
20 E5	Garibaldi, Mt mt Can.	
20 E5	Garibaldi Prov. Park nat. park Can.	
105 G5	Gariep Dam resr S. Africa	
104 B5	Garies S. Africa	
66 F4	Garigliano r. Italy	
102 D4	Garissa Kenya	
55 T8	Garkalne Latvia	
32 D4	Garland PA U.S.A.	
27 D5	Garland TX U.S.A.	
81 M2	Garmī Iran	
62 E7	Garmisch-Partenkirchen Ger.	
79 G2	Garmo, Qullai mt Tajik.	
26 E4	Garnett U.S.A.	
114 E4	Garnpung Lake l. Austr.	
85 G4	Gāro Hills h. India	
64 E4	Garonne r. France	
102 E3	Garoowe Somalia	
44 G3	Garopaba Brazil	
101 D4	Garoua Cameroon	
47 D3	Garré Arg.	
35 E1	Garrison U.S.A.	
60 F2	Garron Point pt U.K.	
57 D4	Garry, Loch l. U.K.	
21 J1	Garry Lake l. Can.	
57 B2	Garrynahine U.K.	
102 B4	Garsen Kenya	
59 D5	Garth U.K.	
57 D3	Garve U.K.	

30 D5 Gary U.S.A.
84 E3 Garyarsa China
91 C7 Garyū-zan mt Japan
84 D2 Gar Zangbo r. China
82 J4 Garzê China
45 B4 Garzón Col.
64 D5 Gascogne reg. France
26 E4 Gasconade r. U.S.A.
Gascony reg. see Gascogne
64 C5 Gascony, Gulf of g. France/Spain
112 B4 Gascoyne r. Austr.
112 C5 Gascoyne Junction Austr.
Gascuña, Golfo de g. see Gascony, Gulf of
84 D2 Gasherbrum mt China/Jammu and Kashmir
100 D3 Gashua Nigeria
23 H4 Gaspé Can.
23 H4 Gaspé, C. c. Can.
23 G4 Gaspé, Péninsule de pen. Can.
23 G4 Gaspésie, Parc de la nat. park Can.
Gasteiz see Vitoria-Gasteiz
29 D5 Gastonia U.S.A.
47 C4 Gastre Arg.
65 E4 Gata, Cabo de c. Spain
80 D4 Gata, Cape c. Cyprus
68 D3 Gatchina Rus. Fed.
32 B6 Gate City U.S.A.
57 D6 Gatehouse of Fleet U.K.
58 F3 Gateshead U.K.
27 D6 Gatesville U.S.A.
35 H2 Gateway U.S.A.
33 F4 Gateway National Recreational Area res. U.S.A.
31 K3 Gatineau Can.
31 K2 Gatineau r. Can.
115 K1 Gatton Austr.
81 M1 Gatvand Iran
111 H3 Gau i. Fiji
21 K3 Gauer Lake l. Can.
54 M5 Gaula r. Norway
32 C5 Gauley Bridge U.S.A.
61 D5 Gaume reg. Belgium
85 F4 Gauri Sankar mt China
105 G3 Gauteng div. S. Africa
67 L7 Gavdos i. Greece
81 L4 Gäveh Rūd r. Iran
46 E1 Gavião r. Brazil
81 L4 Gavīleh Iran
34 B4 Gaviota U.S.A.
55 P6 Gävle Sweden
68 F3 Gavrilov-Yam Rus. Fed.
104 B3 Gawachab Namibia
114 C5 Gawler Austr.
114 A4 Gawler Ranges h. Austr.
88 A1 Gaxun Nur salt l. China
90 A3 Gaya r. China
85 F4 Gaya India
100 C3 Gaya Niger
30 E3 Gaylord U.S.A.
116 D5 Gayndah Austr.
80 E6 Gaza terr. Asia
80 E6 Gaza Gaza
105 K1 Gaza div. Moz.
79 J1 Gaz-Achak Turkm.
79 H2 Gazandzhyk Turkm.
84 B2 Gazdarra Pass pass Afgh.
80 F3 Gaziantep Turkey
80 D3 Gazipaşa Turkey
100 A4 Gbangbatok Sierra Leone
100 B4 Gbarnga Liberia
100 C4 Gboko Nigeria
63 J3 Gdańsk Pol.
63 J3 Gdańsk, Gulf of g. Pol./Rus. Fed.
68 C3 Gdov Rus. Fed.
63 J3 Gdynia Pol.
57 C1 Gealldruig Mhor i. U.K.
101 F3 Gedaref Sudan
80 B2 Gediz Turkey
80 A2 Gediz r. Turkey
59 H5 Gedney Drove End U.K.
55 M9 Gedser Denmark
61 D3 Geel Belgium
114 F7 Geelong Austr.
104 D4 Geel Vloer salt pan S. Africa
115 G9 Geeveston Austr.
82 F4 Gê'gyai China
88 F4 Ge Hu l. China
100 D3 Geidam Nigeria
21 J3 Geikie r. Can.
61 E4 Geilenkirchen Ger.
55 L6 Geilo Norway
55 K5 Geiranger Norway
30 E6 Geist Reservoir resr U.S.A.
89 B6 Gejiu China
66 F6 Gela Italy
102 E3 Geladī Eth.
95 B4 Gelang, Tanjong pt Malaysia
61 E3 Geldern Ger.
69 F6 Gelendzhik Rus. Fed.
63 L3 Gelgaudiškis Lith.
69 C7 Gelibolu Turkey
80 C2 Gelincik Dağı mt Turkey
62 C5 Gelsenkirchen Ger.
95 B5 Gemas Malaysia
94 C5 Gemeh Indon.
102 B3 Gemena Dem. Rep. Congo
80 F2 Gemerek Turkey
80 B1 Gemlik Turkey
66 E1 Gemona del Friuli Italy
103 C6 Gemsbok National Park nat. park Botswana

104 D3 Gemsbokplein w. S. Africa
102 E3 Genalē Wenz r. Eth.
47 D3 General Acha Arg.
47 E3 General Alvear Buenos Aires Arg.
47 E1 General Alvear Entre Rios Arg.
47 C2 General Alvear Mendoza Arg.
47 E2 General Belgrano Arg.
119 B2 General Bernardo O'Higgins Chile Base Antarctica
27 D7 General Bravo Mex.
44 B7 General Carrera, L. l. Chile
47 D3 General Conesa Buenos Aires Arg.
47 D4 General Conesa Río Negro Arg.
47 F3 General Guido Arg.
47 F3 General Juan Madariaga Arg.
47 F3 General La Madrid Arg.
47 F3 General Lavalle Arg.
47 D2 General Levalle Arg.
94 C4 General Luna Phil.
94 C4 General MacArthur Phil.
47 D2 General Pico Arg.
47 E2 General Pinto Arg.
47 C3 General Roca Arg.
119 B2 General San Martín Arg. Base Antarctica
94 C5 General Santos Phil.
47 D2 General Villegas Arg.
32 D3 Genesee r. U.S.A.
30 B5 Geneseo IL U.S.A.
32 E3 Geneseo NY U.S.A.
105 G3 Geneva r. S. Africa
30 C5 Geneva IL U.S.A.
26 D3 Geneva NE U.S.A.
32 E3 Geneva NY U.S.A.
32 C4 Geneva OH U.S.A.
Geneva, Lake l. see Léman, Lac
30 C4 Geneva, Lake l. U.S.A.
62 C7 Genève Switz.
88 A3 Gengda China
65 D4 Genil r. Spain
61 D4 Genk Belgium
115 H6 Genoa Austr.
66 C2 Genoa Italy
Genova see Genoa
66 C2 Genova, Golfo di g. Italy
61 B3 Gent Belgium
92 □ Genteng Indon.
92 □ Genteng i. Indon.
112 C6 Geographe Bay b. Austr.
23 G2 George r. Can.
104 E6 George S. Africa
115 H5 George, L. l. N.S.W. Austr.
114 C6 George, L. l. S.A. Austr.
29 D6 George, L. l. U.S.A.
33 G3 George, Lake l. U.S.A.
117 A6 George Sd in. N.Z.
113 H3 Georgetown Qld. Austr.
114 C4 Georgetown S.A. Austr.
115 G8 George Town Austr.
31 H4 Georgetown Can.
43 G2 Georgetown Guyana
92 C5 George Town Malaysia
29 F7 George Town Bahamas
100 A3 Georgetown The Gambia
33 F5 Georgetown DE U.S.A.
30 D6 Georgetown IL U.S.A.
28 C4 Georgetown KY U.S.A.
32 B5 Georgetown OH U.S.A.
29 E5 Georgetown SC U.S.A.
27 D6 Georgetown TX U.S.A.
119 B5 George V Land reg. Antarctica
27 D6 George West U.S.A.
70 Georgia country Asia
29 D5 Georgia div. U.S.A.
20 E5 Georgia, Strait of chan. Can.
31 G3 Georgian Bay l. Can.
31 H3 Georgian Bay Islands National Park nat. park Can.
113 G4 Georgina watercourse Austr.
82 F1 Georgiyevka Kazak.
69 G6 Georgiyevsk Rus. Fed.
68 H3 Georgiyevskoye Rus. Fed.
62 F5 Gera Ger.
61 B4 Geraardsbergen Belgium
43 J6 Geral de Goiás, Serra h. Brazil
117 C6 Geraldine N.Z.
46 C1 Geral do Paraná, Serra h. Brazil
112 B5 Geraldton Austr.
81 H3 Gercüş Turkey
80 D1 Gerede Turkey
80 D1 Gerede r. Turkey
79 J3 Gereshk Afgh.
95 B4 Gerik Malaysia
26 C3 Gering U.S.A.
24 C3 Gerlach U.S.A.
20 E3 Germansen Landing Can.
32 E5 Germantown U.S.A.
48 Germany country Europe
62 D6 Germersheim Ger.
105 H3 Germiston S. Africa
61 E4 Gerolstein Ger.
35 G5 Geronimo U.S.A.
115 J5 Gerringong Austr.
85 F2 Gêrzê China
69 E7 Gerze Turkey
61 D4 Gete r. Belgium
32 E5 Gettysburg PA U.S.A.
26 D2 Gettysburg SD U.S.A.

32 E5 Gettysburg National Military Park res. U.S.A.
89 D7 Getu He r. China
119 A4 Getz Ice Shelf ice feature Antarctica
95 A5 Geumapang r. Indon.
115 H4 Geurie Austr.
81 J2 Gevaş Turkey
67 K4 Gevgelija Macedonia
65 E1 Gexto Spain
95 □ Geylang Sing.
105 F3 Geysdorp S. Africa
80 C1 Geyve Turkey
104 E2 Ghaap Plateau plat. S. Africa
81 J5 Ghadaf, Wādī al watercourse Iraq
100 C1 Ghadāmis Libya
84 C3 Ghaggar, Dry Bed of watercourse Pak.
84 F4 Ghaghara r. India
85 F5 Ghaghra India
96 Ghana country Africa
84 C4 Ghanliala India
103 C6 Ghanzi Botswana
104 E1 Ghanzi div. Botswana
80 E6 Gharandal Jordan
100 C1 Ghardaïa Alg.
78 C4 Ghârib, Gebel mt Egypt
101 D3 Gharyān Libya
100 D2 Ghāt Libya
84 B3 Ghauspur Pak.
101 C5 Ghazal, Bahr el watercourse Chad
100 B1 Ghazaouet Alg.
84 D3 Ghaziabad India
85 E4 Ghazipur India
84 A3 Ghazluna Pak.
84 B2 Ghaznī Afgh.
84 B2 Ghazni r. Afgh.
Ghent see Gent
63 M7 Gheorgheni Romania
63 L7 Gherla Romania
66 C3 Ghisonaccia France
84 C1 Ghizar Pak.
85 G4 Ghoraghat Bangl.
84 B2 Ghorband r. Afgh.
84 B2 Ghorband Pass pass Afgh.
84 B4 Ghotāru India
84 B4 Ghotki Pak.
85 F4 Ghuari r. India
84 D6 Ghugus India
84 B4 Ghulam Mohammed Barrage barrage Pak.
95 C3 Gia Đinh Vietnam
69 G6 Giaginskaya Rus. Fed.
67 K4 Giannitsa Greece
105 H4 Giant's Castle mt S. Africa
60 D2 Giant's Causeway U.K.
92 F8 Gianyar Indon.
95 C3 Gia Rai Vietnam
66 F6 Giarre Italy
104 B2 Gibeon Namibia
65 D4 Gibraltar terr. Europe
65 C5 Gibraltar, Strait of str. Morocco/Spain
30 C5 Gibson City U.S.A.
112 D4 Gibson Desert des. Austr.
86 F2 Gichgeniyn Nuruu mts Mongolia
83 E7 Giddalur India
80 D5 Giddi, Gebel el h. Egypt
102 D3 Gidole Eth.
64 F3 Gien France
62 D5 Gießen Ger.
20 F3 Gift Lake Can.
91 E7 Gifu Japan
45 B4 Gigante Col.
57 C5 Gigha i. U.K.
65 D1 Gijón Spain
35 F5 Gila r. U.S.A.
35 F5 Gila Bend U.S.A.
35 F5 Gila Bend Mts mts U.S.A.
35 F5 Gila Mts mts U.S.A.
81 K4 Gīlān-e Gharb Iran
81 M1 Gilāzi Azer.
113 H3 Gilbert r. Austr.
35 G5 Gilbert AZ U.S.A.
32 C6 Gilbert WV U.S.A.
111 H2 Gilbert Is is Kiribati
116 A2 Gilbert Ra. mts Austr.
43 J5 Gilbués Brazil
24 E1 Gildford U.S.A.
20 D4 Gilford I. i. Can.
115 J2 Gilgai Austr.
115 H3 Gilgandra Austr.
102 D4 Gilgil Kenya
115 H2 Gil Gil Cr. r. Austr.
84 C2 Gilgit Jammu and Kashmir
84 C2 Gilgit r. Jammu and Kashmir
115 G4 Gilgunnia Austr.
20 D4 Gil Island i. Can.
21 L3 Gillam Can.
114 B4 Gilles, L. salt flat Austr.
30 C3 Gillett U.S.A.
24 F2 Gillette U.S.A.
59 H6 Gillingham Eng. U.K.
59 E6 Gillingham Eng. U.K.
58 F3 Gilling West U.K.
30 D3 Gills Rock U.S.A.
30 D5 Gilman IL U.S.A.
30 B3 Gilman WV U.S.A.
22 E2 Gilmour Island i. Can.
34 B3 Gilroy U.S.A.
33 G3 Gilsum U.S.A.
101 E3 Gimbala, Jebel mt Sudan
102 D3 Gimbī Eth.
21 K4 Gimli Can.

116 C4 Gindie Austr.
42 E6 Ginebra, Laguna l. Bol.
116 D5 Gin Gin Austr.
102 E3 Gīnīr Eth.
66 G4 Ginosa Italy
66 G4 Gioia del Colle Italy
115 G6 Gippsland reg. Austr.
84 B4 Girab India
32 C3 Girard U.S.A.
84 B3 Girdao Pak.
80 G1 Giresun Turkey
85 B5 Gir Forest forest India
85 F4 Girīdīh India
115 G3 Girilambone Austr.
65 H2 Girona Spain
64 D3 Gironde est. France
115 G4 Girral Austr.
57 D5 Girvan U.K.
68 E5 Girvas Rus. Fed.
84 E4 Girwan India
117 G3 Gisborne N.Z.
20 E4 Giscome Can.
55 N8 Gislaved Sweden
102 C4 Gitarama Rwanda
102 C4 Gitega Burundi
66 E3 Giulianova Italy
67 L3 Giurgiu Romania
67 L2 Giuvala, Pasul pass Romania
61 C4 Givet France
64 G4 Givors France
105 J1 Giyani S. Africa
80 C7 Giza Pyramids Egypt
81 L4 Gīzeh Rūd r. Iran
79 J1 Gizhduvan Uzbek.
77 S3 Gizhiga Rus. Fed.
67 J4 Gjirokastër Albania
54 L5 Gjøra Norway
55 M6 Gjøvik Norway
23 J4 Glace Bay Can.
20 B3 Glacier B. b. U.S.A.
20 B3 Glacier Bay National Park and Preserve nat. park U.S.A.
20 F4 Glacier Nat. Park nat. park Can.
24 D1 Glacier Nat. Park nat. park U.S.A.
24 B1 Glacier Peak vol. U.S.A.
54 M4 Gladstad Norway
116 D4 Gladstone Qld. Austr.
114 C4 Gladstone S.A. Austr.
115 H8 Gladstone Tas. Austr.
30 D3 Gladstone U.S.A.
30 E4 Gladwin U.S.A.
57 E4 Glamis U.K.
61 F5 Glan r. Ger.
94 C5 Glan Phil.
60 B5 Glanaruddery Mts h. Rep. of Ireland
58 F2 Glanton U.K.
31 G4 Glanworth Can.
57 D5 Glasgow U.K.
28 C4 Glasgow KY U.S.A.
24 F1 Glasgow MT U.S.A.
32 D6 Glasgow VA U.S.A.
21 H4 Glaslyn Can.
34 C3 Glass Mt mt U.S.A.
59 E6 Glastonbury U.K.
76 G4 Glazov Rus. Fed.
63 P3 Glazunovka Rus. Fed.
33 H2 Glen U.S.A.
57 C4 Glen Affric v. U.K.
31 G2 Glen Afton Can.
117 E2 Glen Afton N.Z.
105 H1 Glen Alpine Dam dam S. Africa
60 C4 Glenamaddy Rep. of Ireland
30 E3 Glen Arbor U.S.A.
117 C6 Glenavy N.Z.
57 C3 Glen Cannich v. U.K.
25 E4 Glen Canyon gorge U.S.A.
35 G3 Glen Canyon National Recreation Area res. U.S.A.
57 E4 Glen Clova v. U.K.
114 D6 Glencoe Austr.
31 G4 Glencoe Can.
105 J4 Glencoe S. Africa
57 C4 Glen Coe v. U.K.
31 E2 Glendale Can.
35 F5 Glendale AZ U.S.A.
34 C4 Glendale CA U.S.A.
35 E3 Glendale NV U.S.A.
35 F3 Glendale UT U.S.A.
32 D4 Glendale Lake l. U.S.A.
115 J4 Glen Davis Austr.
116 C3 Glenden Austr.
24 F2 Glendive U.S.A.
21 G4 Glendon Can.
114 D6 Glenelg r. Austr.
57 F4 Glen Esk v. U.K.
57 A5 Glengad Head hd Rep. of Ireland
57 D4 Glen Garry v. Scot. U.K.
57 C4 Glen Garry v. Scot. U.K.
60 D3 Glengavlen Rep. of Ireland
115 J2 Glen Innes Austr.
57 D6 Glenluce U.K.
57 D4 Glen Lyon v. U.K.
57 D3 Glen More v. U.K.
57 H1 Glenmorgan Austr.
57 D4 Glen Moriston v. U.K.
57 G6 Glenn, Mt mt U.S.A.
57 E4 Glen Nevis v. U.K.
31 F3 Glennie U.S.A.
57 E4 Glenns U.S.A.
20 D4 Glenora Can.
114 D6 Glenora Austr.
57 E4 Glenrothes U.K.

33 G3 Glens Falls U.S.A.
57 E4 Glen Shee v. U.K.
57 C3 Glen Shiel v. U.K.
60 C3 Glenties Rep. of Ireland
60 D2 Glenveagh National Park nat. park Rep. of Ireland
32 C5 Glenville U.S.A.
27 E5 Glenwood AR U.S.A.
35 H5 Glenwood NM U.S.A.
25 F4 Glenwood Springs U.S.A.
30 B2 Glidden U.S.A.
63 J5 Gliwice Pol.
35 G5 Globe U.S.A.
62 H5 Głogów Pol.
54 N3 Glomfjord Norway
55 M5 Glomma r. Norway
103 E5 Glorieuses, Îles is Indian Ocean
115 J3 Gloucester Austr.
59 E6 Gloucester U.K.
33 H3 Gloucester MA U.S.A.
32 E6 Gloucester VA U.S.A.
116 C3 Gloucester I. i. Austr.
33 F3 Gloversville U.S.A.
90 D1 Glubinnoye Rus. Fed.
69 G6 Glubokiy Rus. Fed.
86 D1 Glubokoye Kazak.
54 □ Gluggarnir h. Faroe Is
58 F4 Glusburn U.K.
69 H5 Gmelinka Rus. Fed.
62 G6 Gmünd Austria
62 F7 Gmunden Austria
55 P5 Gnarp Sweden
62 H4 Gniezno Pol.
67 J3 Gnjilane Yugo.
83 D7 Goa div. India
104 B3 Goageb Namibia
115 J6 Goalen Head hd Austr.
85 G4 Goalpara India
57 C5 Goat Fell h. U.K.
102 E3 Goba Eth.
103 B6 Gobabis Namibia
104 C3 Gobas Namibia
74 Gobi des. Mongolia
91 D8 Gobō Japan
61 E3 Goch Ger.
103 B6 Gochas Namibia
95 C3 Go Công Vietnam
59 G6 Godalming U.K.
83 F7 Godavari, Mouths of the est. India
23 G4 Godbout Can.
34 C3 Goddard, Mt mt U.S.A.
102 E3 Godere Eth.
31 G4 Goderich Can.
84 C5 Godhra India
47 C2 Godoy Cruz Arg.
21 L3 Gods r. Can.
21 L4 Gods Lake l. Can.
21 M2 Gods Mercy, Bay of b. Can.
Godthåb see Nuuk
Godwin Austen mt see K2
61 D3 Goedereede Neth.
22 E4 Goéland, Lac au l. Can.
23 H2 Goélands, Lac aux l. Can.
61 B3 Goes Neth.
31 E2 Goetzville U.S.A.
35 E4 Goffs U.S.A.
31 G2 Gogama Can.
30 C2 Gogebic, Lake l. U.S.A.
30 C2 Gogebic Range h. U.S.A.
Gogra r. see Ghaghara
84 D4 Gohad India
43 M5 Goiana Brazil
46 C2 Goiandira Brazil
46 C2 Goiânia Brazil
46 B1 Goiás Brazil
46 B3 Goiás div. Brazil
46 B4 Goio-Erê Brazil
84 C3 Gojra Pak.
69 C7 Gökçeada i. Turkey
80 E1 Gökirmak r. Turkey
80 F2 Göksun Turkey
80 E3 Göksu Nehri r. Turkey
103 C5 Gokwe Zimbabwe
55 L6 Gol Norway
84 D3 Gola India
85 H4 Golaghat India
80 F1 Gölbaşı Turkey
76 K2 Gol'chikha Rus. Fed.
80 B1 Gölcük Turkey
63 L3 Gołdap Pol.
115 K2 Gold Coast Austr.
100 B4 Gold Coast coastal area Ghana
20 F4 Golden Can.
117 D4 Golden Bay b. N.Z.
34 A3 Golden Gate National Recreation Area res. U.S.A.
20 D5 Golden Hinde mt Can.
60 D5 Golden Vale lowland Rep. of Ireland
34 D3 Goldfield U.S.A.
34 D3 Gold Point U.S.A.
29 E5 Goldsboro U.S.A.
112 C4 Goldsworthy Austr.
27 D6 Goldthwaite U.S.A.
81 J1 Göle Turkey
81 K3 Golmänkhänen Iran
86 B4 Golmud China
85 H1 Golmud He r. China
94 B3 Golo i. Phil.

90 J3 Golovnino Rus. Fed.
79 G3 Golpāyegān Iran
80 C1 Gölpazarı Turkey
57 E3 Golspie U.K.
67 L4 Golyama Syutkya mt Bulg.
67 L4 Golyam Persenk mt Bulg.
102 C4 Goma Dem. Rep. Congo
85 G3 Gomang Co salt l. China
84 E4 Gomati r. India
95 □ Gombak, Bukit h. Sing.
100 D3 Gombe Nigeria
102 D4 Gombe r. Tanz.
101 D3 Gombi Nigeria
25 F6 Gómez Farías Mex.
36 D3 Gómez Palacio Mex.
85 F2 Gomo Co salt l. China
37 K5 Gonaïves Haiti
105 J1 Gonarezhou National Park nat. park Zimbabwe
79 H2 Gonbad-e Kavus Iran
85 E4 Gonda India
84 B5 Gondal India
102 D2 Gonder Eth.
84 E5 Gondia India
80 A1 Gönen Turkey
89 D5 Gong'an China
89 A4 Gongga Shan mt China
88 A2 Gonghe China
88 E1 Gonghui China
82 F2 Gongliu China
46 E1 Gongogi r. Brazil
100 D4 Gongola r. Nigeria
115 G3 Gongolgon Austr.
89 B5 Gongwang Shan mts China
89 B4 Gongxian China
88 D3 Gongyi China
105 H6 Gonubie S. Africa
34 B3 Gonzales CA U.S.A.
27 D6 Gonzales TX U.S.A.
47 D2 González Moreno Arg.
32 D5 Goochland U.S.A.
119 C6 Goodenough, C. c. Antarctica
110 F2 Goodenough I. i. P.N.G.
31 H3 Gooderham Can.
30 E3 Good Harbor Bay b. U.S.A.
104 C7 Good Hope, Cape of c. S. Africa
24 D3 Gooding U.S.A.
26 C4 Goodland U.S.A.
115 G2 Goodooga Austr.
58 G4 Goole U.K.
115 F5 Goolgowi Austr.
115 H4 Goolma Austr.
115 H4 Gooloogong Austr.
114 C5 Goolwa Austr.
115 F2 Goombalie Austr.
116 E6 Goomeri Austr.
115 J2 Goondiwindi Austr.
116 B3 Goonyella Austr.
23 H3 Goose r. Can.
24 B3 Goose L. l. U.S.A.
62 D6 Göppingen Ger.
85 E4 Gorakhpur India
67 H3 Goražde Bos.-Herz.
68 G3 Gorchukha Rus. Fed.
29 E7 Gorda Cay i. Bahamas
80 B2 Gördes Turkey
63 P4 Gordeyevka Rus. Fed.
115 F9 Gordon r. Austr.
57 F5 Gordon U.K.
115 G9 Gordon, L. l. Austr.
20 G2 Gordon Lake l. Can.
32 D5 Gordon Lake l. U.S.A.
32 D5 Gordonsville U.S.A.
116 A1 Gordonvale Austr.
101 D4 Goré Chad
102 D3 Gorē Eth.
117 B7 Gore N.Z.
31 F3 Gore Bay Can.
57 F5 Gorebridge U.K.
60 E5 Gorey Rep. of Ireland
79 G2 Gorgān Iran
116 A2 Gorge Range mts Austr.
45 A4 Gorgona, I. i. Col.
33 H2 Gorham U.S.A.
69 H7 Gori Georgia
61 C3 Gorinchem Neth.
81 L4 Goris Armenia
66 E2 Gorizia Italy
Gor'kiy see Nizhniy Novgorod
69 H5 Gor'ko-Solenoye, Ozero l. Rus. Fed.
68 G3 Gor'kovskoye Vdkhr. resr Rus. Fed.
63 K6 Gorlice Pol.
62 G5 Görlitz Ger.
84 D4 Gormi India
67 L3 Gorna Oryakhovitsa Bulg.
67 J2 Gornji Milanovac Yugo.
66 G3 Gornji Vakuf Bos.-Herz.
86 E1 Gorno-Altaysk Rus. Fed.
90 G1 Gornozavodsk Rus. Fed.
86 D1 Gornyak Rus. Fed.
90 G1 Gornye Klyuchi Rus. Fed.
90 C2 Gornyy Rus. Fed.
69 J5 Gornyy Rus. Fed.
69 H5 Gornyy Balykley Rus. Fed.
68 G3 Gorodets Rus. Fed.
69 H5 Gorodishche Rus. Fed.
69 G6 Gorodovikovsk Rus. Fed.
110 E2 Goroka P.N.G.
114 D6 Goroke Austr.
68 G3 Gorokhovets Rus. Fed.
100 B3 Gorom Gorom Burkina
103 D5 Gorongosa Moz.
93 G6 Gorontalo Indon.
69 F5 Gorshechnoye Rus. Fed.
60 C4 Gort Rep. of Ireland

60 C2 **Gortahork** Rep. of Ireland
46 D1 **Gorutuba** r. Brazil
69 F6 **Goryachiy Klyuch** Rus. Fed.
62 G4 **Gorzów Wielkopolski** Pol.
115 J4 **Gosford** Austr.
58 F2 **Gosforth** U.K.
30 E5 **Goshen** IN U.S.A.
33 F4 **Goshen** NY U.S.A.
90 M4 **Goshogawara** Japan
66 F2 **Gospić** Croatia
59 F7 **Gosport** U.K.
67 J4 **Gostivar** Macedonia
Göteborg see **Gothenburg**
55 N7 **Götene** Sweden
62 E5 **Gotha** Ger.
55 M8 **Gothenburg** Sweden
26 C3 **Gothenburg** U.S.A.
55 Q8 **Gotland** i. Sweden
67 K4 **Gotse Delchev** Bulg.
55 O7 **Gotska Sandön** i. Sweden
91 C7 **Gōtsu** Japan
62 D5 **Göttingen** Ger.
20 E4 **Gott Peak** summit Can.
Gottwaldov see **Zlín**
61 C2 **Gouda** Neth.
61 C3 **Gouderak** Neth.
100 A3 **Goudiri** Senegal
100 D3 **Goudoumaria** Niger
30 E1 **Goudreau** Can.
12 J8 **Gough Island** i. Atlantic Ocean
22 F4 **Gouin, Réservoir** resr Can.
30 E2 **Goulais River** Can.
115 H5 **Goulburn** Austr.
115 J4 **Goulburn** r. N.S.W. Austr.
114 F6 **Goulburn** r. Vic. Austr.
113 F2 **Goulburn Is** is Austr.
30 E2 **Gould City** U.S.A.
100 B3 **Goundam** Mali
65 G4 **Gouraya** Alg.
100 D3 **Gouré** Niger
104 D7 **Gourits** r. S. Africa
100 B3 **Gourma-Rharous** Mali
64 E2 **Gournay-en-Bray** France
115 H6 **Gourock Range** mts Austr.
33 F2 **Gouverneur** U.S.A.
21 H5 **Govenlock** Can.
46 E2 **Governador Valadares** Brazil
94 C5 **Governor Generoso** Phil.
29 E7 **Governor's Harbour** Bahamas
86 G3 **Govĭ Altayn Nuruu** mts Mongolia
85 E4 **Govind Ballash Pant Sāgar** resr India
84 D3 **Govind Sagar** resr India
32 D3 **Gowanda** U.S.A.
116 A5 **Gowan Ra.** h. Austr.
59 C6 **Gower** pen. U.K.
31 G2 **Gowganda** Can.
60 D4 **Gowna, Lough** l. Rep. of Ireland
44 E3 **Goya** Arg.
81 L1 **Göyçay** Azer.
81 H2 **Göynük** Turkey
90 G5 **Goyō-zan** mt Japan
81 M2 **Göytäpä** Azer.
80 G2 **Gözene** Turkey
84 E2 **Gozha Co** salt l. China
66 F6 **Gozo** i. Malta
104 F6 **Graaf-Reinet** S. Africa
104 C6 **Graafwater** S. Africa
100 B4 **Grabo** Côte d'Ivoire
104 C7 **Grabouw** S. Africa
66 F2 **Gračac** Croatia
31 J2 **Gracefield** Can.
115 K2 **Grafton** Austr.
26 D1 **Grafton** ND U.S.A.
32 C5 **Grafton** WV U.S.A.
30 D4 **Grafton** WV U.S.A.
116 A1 **Grafton, C.** pt Austr.
35 H5 **Grafton, Mt** mt U.S.A.
116 B1 **Grafton Passage** chan. Austr.
27 D5 **Graham** U.S.A.
35 H5 **Graham, Mt** mt U.S.A.
Graham Bell Island i. see **Greem-Bell, Ostrov**
20 C4 **Graham Island** i. Can.
33 J2 **Graham Lake** l. U.S.A.
105 G6 **Grahamstown** S. Africa
60 E5 **Graigue** Rep. of Ireland
100 A4 **Grain Coast** coastal area Liberia
43 J5 **Grajaú** Brazil
57 B1 **Graisgeir** i. U.K.
67 J4 **Grámmos** mt Greece
57 D4 **Grampian Mountains** mts U.K.
114 E6 **Grampians, The** mts Austr.
45 B4 **Granada** Col.
37 G6 **Granada** Nic.
65 E3 **Granada** Spain
26 C4 **Granada** U.S.A.
60 D4 **Granard** Rep. of Ireland
47 C3 **Gran Bajo Salitroso** salt flat Arg.
22 F4 **Granby** Can.
100 A2 **Gran Canaria** i. Canary Is
44 D3 **Gran Chaco** reg. Arg./Para.
28 C3 **Grand** r. MI U.S.A.
26 E3 **Grand** r. MO U.S.A.
29 E7 **Grand Bahama** i. Bahamas
23 J4 **Grand Bank** Can.
12 F2 **Grand Banks of Newfoundland** sea feature Atlantic Ocean

100 B4 **Grand-Bassam** Côte d'Ivoire
23 G4 **Grand Bay** Can.
31 G4 **Grand Bend** Can.
60 D4 **Grand Canal** canal Rep. of Ireland
35 F3 **Grand Canyon** U.S.A.
35 F3 **Grand Canyon** gorge U.S.A.
35 F3 **Grand Canyon Nat. Park** nat. park U.S.A.
37 H5 **Grand Cayman** i. Cayman Is
21 G4 **Grand Centre** Can.
24 C2 **Grand Coulee** U.S.A.
47 C3 **Grande** r. Arg.
42 F7 **Grande** r. Bol.
43 J6 **Grande** r. Bahia Brazil
46 B2 **Grande** r. São Paulo Brazil
44 C8 **Grande, Bahía** b. Arg.
46 D3 **Grande, Ilha** i. Brazil
45 E4 **Grande, Serra** mt Brazil
20 F4 **Grande Cache** Can.
103 E5 **Grande Comore** i. Comoros
20 F3 **Grande Prairie** Can.
101 D3 **Grand Erg de Bilma** sand dunes Niger
100 B1 **Grand Erg Occidental** des. Alg.
100 C2 **Grand Erg Oriental** des. Alg.
23 H4 **Grande-Rivière** Can.
22 F3 **Grande Rivière de la Baleine** r. Can.
24 C2 **Grande Ronde** r. U.S.A.
44 C4 **Grandes, Salinas** salt flat Arg.
23 G4 **Grande-Vallée** Can.
23 G4 **Grand Falls** N.B. Can.
23 J4 **Grand Falls** Nfld Can.
20 F5 **Grand Forks** Can.
26 D2 **Grand Forks** U.S.A.
33 F3 **Grand Gorge** U.S.A.
30 D4 **Grand Harbour** Can.
30 D4 **Grand Haven** U.S.A.
20 F2 **Grandin, Lac** l. Can.
26 D3 **Grand Island** Can.
30 D2 **Grand Island** i. U.S.A.
27 F6 **Grand Isle** LA U.S.A.
33 J1 **Grand Isle** ME U.S.A.
35 H2 **Grand Junction** U.S.A.
100 B4 **Grand-Lahou** Côte d'Ivoire
23 G4 **Grand Lake** l. N.B. Can.
23 J4 **Grand Lake** l. Nfld Can.
23 H3 **Grand Lake** l. Nfld Can.
27 E6 **Grand Lake** l. LA U.S.A.
33 K2 **Grand Lake** l. ME U.S.A.
31 F3 **Grand Lake** l. MI U.S.A.
33 J1 **Grand Lake Matagamon** l. U.S.A.
33 J1 **Grand Lake Seboeis** l. U.S.A.
32 A4 **Grand Lake St Marys** l. U.S.A.
33 K2 **Grand Lake Stream** U.S.A.
30 E4 **Grand Ledge** U.S.A.
23 G5 **Grand Manan I.** i. Can.
30 E2 **Grand Marais** MI U.S.A.
30 B2 **Grand Marais** MN U.S.A.
23 H4 **Grand-Mère** Can.
65 B3 **Grândola** Port.
111 G3 **Grand Passage** chan. New Caledonia
30 C2 **Grand Portage** U.S.A.
21 K4 **Grand Rapids** Can.
30 E4 **Grand Rapids** MI U.S.A.
26 E2 **Grand Rapids** MN U.S.A.
111 G3 **Grand Récif de Cook** rf New Caledonia
111 G4 **Grand Récif du Sud** rf New Caledonia
24 E3 **Grand Teton** mt U.S.A.
24 E3 **Grand Teton Nat. Park** nat. park U.S.A.
30 E3 **Grand Traverse Bay** b. U.S.A.
37 K4 **Grand Turk** Turks and Caicos Is
24 C2 **Grandview** Can.
35 F3 **Grand Wash** r. U.S.A.
35 E4 **Grand Wash Cliffs** cliff U.S.A.
47 B2 **Graneros** Chile
60 D6 **Grange** Rep. of Ireland
24 E3 **Granger** U.S.A.
55 O6 **Grängesberg** Sweden
24 C2 **Grangeville** U.S.A.
20 D3 **Granisle** Can.
26 E2 **Granite Falls** U.S.A.
23 J4 **Granite Lake** l. Can.
35 E4 **Granite Mts** mts U.S.A.
24 E2 **Granite Peak** summit MT U.S.A.
35 F1 **Granite Peak** summit UT U.S.A.
66 E6 **Granitola, Capo** c. Italy
44 C6 **Gran Laguna Salada** l. Arg.
55 O7 **Gränna** Sweden
66 B2 **Gran Paradiso** mt Italy
62 E7 **Gran Pilastro** mt Austria/Italy
34 C2 **Grant, Mt** mt NV U.S.A.
34 D2 **Grant, Mt** mt NV U.S.A.
59 G5 **Grantham** U.K.
119 A4 **Grant I.** i. Antarctica
57 E3 **Grantown-on-Spey** U.K.
35 E2 **Grant Range** mts U.S.A.
25 F5 **Grants** U.S.A.
24 B3 **Grants Pass** U.S.A.
64 D2 **Granville** France

30 C5 **Granville** IL U.S.A.
33 G3 **Granville** NY U.S.A.
21 J3 **Granville Lake** l. Can.
46 D2 **Grão Mogol** Brazil
34 C4 **Grapevine** U.S.A.
34 C4 **Grapevine Mts** mts U.S.A.
33 G3 **Graphite** U.S.A.
21 G2 **Gras, Lac de** l. Can.
105 J2 **Graskop** S. Africa
33 F2 **Grass** r. U.S.A.
64 H5 **Grasse** France
58 F3 **Grassington** U.K.
21 H5 **Grasslands Nat. Park** nat. park Can.
24 E2 **Grassrange** U.S.A.
21 J4 **Grass River Prov. Park** res. Can.
34 B2 **Grass Valley** U.S.A.
115 F8 **Grassy** Austr.
29 C7 **Grassy Cr.** r. Bahamas
55 N7 **Grästorp** Sweden
30 B4 **Gratiot** U.S.A.
65 G1 **Graus** Spain
21 J2 **Gravel Hill Lake** l. Can.
105 J1 **Gravelotte** S. Africa
31 H3 **Gravenhurst** U.S.A.
115 J2 **Gravesend** Austr.
59 H6 **Gravesend** U.K.
66 G4 **Gravina in Puglia** Italy
30 E3 **Grawn** U.S.A.
64 G3 **Gray** France
33 H3 **Gray** U.S.A.
30 E3 **Grayling** U.S.A.
59 H6 **Grays** U.K.
24 A2 **Grays Harbor** in. U.S.A.
24 E3 **Grays L.** l. U.S.A.
32 B5 **Grayson** U.S.A.
23 H1 **Gray Strait** chan. Can.
28 B4 **Grayville** U.S.A.
62 G7 **Graz** Austria
29 E7 **Great Abaco** i. Bahamas
112 E6 **Great Australian Bight** g. Austr.
59 H6 **Great Baddow** U.K.
37 J3 **Great Bahama Bank** sea feature Bahamas
117 E2 **Great Barrier Island** i. N.Z.
113 J3 **Great Barrier Reef** rf Austr.
113 J3 **Great Barrier Reef Marine Park (Cairns Section)** nat. park Austr.
113 K4 **Great Barrier Reef Marine Park (Capricorn Section)** nat. park Austr.
113 J3 **Great Barrier Reef Marine Park (Central Section)** nat. park Austr.
113 H2 **Great Barrier Reef Marine Park (Far North Section)** nat. park Austr.
33 G3 **Great Barrington** U.S.A.
25 C4 **Great Basin** basin U.S.A.
35 E2 **Great Basin Nat. Park** nat. park U.S.A.
33 F5 **Great Bay** b. U.S.A.
20 E1 **Great Bear** r. Can.
20 E1 **Great Bear Lake** l. Can.
26 D4 **Great Bend** U.S.A.
57 B2 **Great Bernera** i. U.K.
60 A5 **Great Blasket I.** i. Rep. of Ireland
58 D3 **Great Clifton** U.K.
57 D5 **Great Cumbrae** i. U.K.
113 J4 **Great Dividing Range** mts Austr.
58 G3 **Great Driffield** U.K.
31 F3 **Great Duck I.** i. Can.
33 F5 **Great Egg Harbor Inlet** in. U.S.A.
37 H4 **Greater Antilles** is Caribbean Sea
37 J3 **Great Exuma** i. Bahamas
24 E2 **Great Falls** U.S.A.
105 G6 **Great Fish** r. S. Africa
105 G6 **Great Fish Point** pt S. Africa
85 F4 **Great Gandak** r. India
29 E7 **Great Guana Cay** i. Bahamas
29 E7 **Great Harbour Cay** i. Bahamas
37 K4 **Great Inagua** i. Bahamas
104 E6 **Great Karoo** plat. S. Africa
105 H6 **Great Kei** r. S. Africa
116 D4 **Great Keppel Island** i. Austr.
115 G8 **Great Lake** l. Austr.
59 E5 **Great Malvern** U.K.
32 A5 **Great Miami** r. U.S.A.
92 A5 **Great Nicobar** i. Andaman and Nicobar Is
59 D4 **Great Ormes Head** hd U.K.
59 H5 **Great Ouse** r. U.K.
115 H9 **Great Oyster Bay** b. Austr.
116 B2 **Great Palm Island** is Austr.
33 G4 **Great Peconic Bay** b. U.S.A.
33 H4 **Great Pt** pt U.S.A.
59 D5 **Great Rhos** h. U.K.
102 D3 **Great Rift Valley** v. Africa
102 D4 **Great Ruaha** r. Tanz.
33 F3 **Great Sacandaga L.** U.S.A.
29 E7 **Great Sale Cay** i. Bahamas
24 D3 **Great Salt Lake** l. U.S.A.

24 D3 **Great Salt Lake Desert** des. U.S.A.
101 E2 **Great Sand Sea** des. Egypt/Libya
112 D4 **Great Sandy Desert** des. Austr.
111 H3 **Great Sea Reef** rf Fiji
20 G2 **Great Slave Lake** l. Can.
29 D5 **Great Smoky Mts** mts U.S.A.
29 D5 **Great Smoky Mts Nat. Park** U.S.A.
20 E3 **Great Snow Mtn** mt Can.
33 G4 **Great South Bay** b. U.S.A.
66 B2 **Great St Bernard Pass** pass Italy/Switz.
59 H7 **Greatstone-on-Sea** U.K.
59 J6 **Great Stour** r. U.K.
59 C7 **Great Torrington** U.K.
112 E5 **Great Victoria Desert** des. Austr.
88 F1 **Great Wall** China
59 H6 **Great Waltham** U.K.
33 K2 **Great Wass I.** i. U.S.A.
115 G8 **Great Western Tiers** mts Austr.
58 F3 **Great Whernside** h. U.K.
59 J5 **Great Yarmouth** U.K.
66 E4 **Greco, Monte** mt Italy
65 D2 **Gredos, Sa de** mts Spain
49 **Greece** country Europe
24 F3 **Greeley** U.S.A.
76 H1 **Greem-Bell, Ostrov** i. Rus. Fed.
28 C4 **Green** r. KY U.S.A.
35 H2 **Green** r. UT/WY U.S.A.
31 H3 **Greenbank** Can.
30 C4 **Green Bay** U.S.A.
30 D3 **Green Bay** b. U.S.A.
115 J6 **Green C.** hd Austr.
60 E3 **Greencastle** U.K.
28 C4 **Greencastle** U.S.A.
29 E7 **Green Cay** i. Bahamas
29 D6 **Green Cove Springs** U.S.A.
30 A4 **Greene** IA U.S.A.
33 F3 **Greene** NY U.S.A.
29 D4 **Greeneville** U.S.A.
34 B3 **Greenfield** CA U.S.A.
30 E6 **Greenfield** IN U.S.A.
33 G3 **Greenfield** MA U.S.A.
32 B5 **Greenfield** OH U.S.A.
30 C4 **Greenfield** WV U.S.A.
116 B1 **Green I.** i. Austr.
94 A4 **Green Island Bay** b. Phil.
21 H4 **Green Lake** Can.
30 C4 **Green Lake** l. U.S.A.
16 **Greenland** country North America
12 J1 **Greenland Basin** sea feature Arctic Ocean
118 B4 **Greenland Sea** sea Greenland/Svalbard
57 F5 **Greenlaw** U.K.
114 A5 **Greenly Island** i. Austr.
33 G2 **Green Mountains** mts U.S.A.
57 D5 **Greenock** U.K.
60 E4 **Greenore** Rep. of Ireland
33 G4 **Greenport** U.S.A.
25 E4 **Green River** UT U.S.A.
24 E3 **Green River** WY U.S.A.
29 E4 **Greensboro** U.S.A.
28 C4 **Greensburg** IN U.S.A.
27 D4 **Greensburg** KS U.S.A.
32 D4 **Greensburg** PA U.S.A.
57 C3 **Greenstone Point** pt U.K.
32 B5 **Greenup** U.S.A.
30 C5 **Greenview** U.S.A.
100 B4 **Greenville** Liberia
29 C6 **Greenville** AL U.S.A.
34 B1 **Greenville** CA U.S.A.
29 D6 **Greenville** FL U.S.A.
30 E4 **Greenville** MI U.S.A.
27 F5 **Greenville** MS U.S.A.
29 E5 **Greenville** NC U.S.A.
33 H3 **Greenville** NH U.S.A.
32 A4 **Greenville** OH U.S.A.
32 C4 **Greenville** PA U.S.A.
29 D5 **Greenville** SC U.S.A.
27 D5 **Greenville** TX U.S.A.
115 J5 **Greenwell Point** Austr.
33 G4 **Greenwich** CT U.S.A.
33 G3 **Greenwich** NY U.S.A.
35 G2 **Greenwich** UT U.S.A.
27 F5 **Greenwood** MS U.S.A.
29 D5 **Greenwood** SC U.S.A.
27 E5 **Greers Ferry Lake** l. U.S.A.
26 D3 **Gregory** U.S.A.
114 C2 **Gregory, L.** salt flat Austr.
112 E4 **Gregory, Lake** salt flat Austr.
113 G3 **Gregory Downs** Austr.
112 F3 **Gregory National Park** nat. park Austr.
113 H3 **Gregory Range** h. Austr.
62 F2 **Greifswald** Ger.
80 C4 **Greko, Cape** c. Cyprus
55 M8 **Grenå** Denmark
16 **Grenada** country Caribbean Sea
27 F5 **Grenada** U.S.A.
64 D4 **Grenade** France
55 M8 **Grenen** spit Denmark
115 H4 **Grenfell** Austr.
21 J4 **Grenfell** Can.

64 G4 **Grenoble** France
45 E1 **Grenville** Grenada
113 H2 **Grenville, C.** hd Austr.
24 B2 **Gresham** U.S.A.
92 □ **Gresik** Indon.
58 F3 **Greta** r. U.K.
57 E6 **Gretna** U.K.
27 F6 **Gretna** U.S.A.
61 B3 **Grevelingen** chan. Neth.
61 D3 **Greven** Ger.
67 J4 **Grevena** Greece
61 D3 **Grevenbicht** Neth.
61 E3 **Grevenbroich** Ger.
62 E4 **Grevesmühlen** Ger.
117 C5 **Grey** r. N.Z.
24 E2 **Greybull** U.S.A.
20 B2 **Grey Hunter Pk** summit Can.
23 J3 **Grey Is** is Can.
117 C5 **Greymouth** N.Z.
114 F2 **Grey Range** h. Austr.
105 J4 **Greytown** S. Africa
61 C4 **Grez-Doiceau** Belgium
69 G5 **Gribanovskiy** Rus. Fed.
61 C3 **Grobbendonk** Belgium
105 H2 **Groblersdal** S. Africa
104 E4 **Groblershoop** S. Africa
116 B1 **Grodekovo** Rus. Fed.
Grodno see **Hrodna**
90 B2 **Grodekovo** Rus. Fed.
104 B5 **Groen** watercourse Northern Cape S. Africa
104 E5 **Groen** watercourse Northern Cape S. Africa
64 C3 **Groix, Île de** i. France
66 D6 **Grombalia** Tunisia
61 F2 **Gronau** Ger.
54 N4 **Grong** Norway
61 E1 **Groningen** Neth.
61 E1 **Groninger Wad** tidal flats Neth.
35 E3 **Groom L.** l. U.S.A.
104 D3 **Groot-Aar Pan** salt pan S. Africa
104 C6 **Groot Berg** r. S. Africa
104 E7 **Groot Brakrivier** S. Africa
105 H3 **Grootdraaidam** dam S. Africa
104 D4 **Grootdrink** S. Africa
104 C3 **Groot Karas Berg** plat. Namibia
105 J1 **Groot Letaba** r. S. Africa
105 G2 **Groot Marico** S. Africa
104 D6 **Groot Swartberge** mts S. Africa
104 D4 **Grootvloer** salt pan S. Africa
105 G6 **Groot Winterberg** mt S. Africa
30 E3 **Gros Cap** U.S.A.
23 J4 **Gros Morne Nat. Pk** nat. park Can.
62 G7 **Grosser Speikkogel** mt Austria
61 F1 **Großes Meer** l. Ger.
66 D3 **Grosseto** Italy
62 D5 **Groß-Gerau** Ger.
66 E1 **Großglockner** mt Austria
104 C1 **Gross Ums** Namibia
24 E3 **Gros Ventre Range** mts U.S.A.
23 J3 **Groswater Bay** b. Can.
33 E3 **Groton** U.S.A.
32 D5 **Grottoes** U.S.A.
20 F3 **Grouard** Can.
22 D4 **Groundhog** r. Can.
32 C4 **Grove City** U.S.A.
29 C6 **Grove Hill** U.S.A.
34 B3 **Groveland** U.S.A.
119 D5 **Grove Mts** mts Antarctica
34 A3 **Grover Beach** U.S.A.
33 H2 **Groveton** U.S.A.
35 F5 **Growler** U.S.A.
35 F5 **Growler Mts** mts U.S.A.
69 H7 **Groznyy** Rus. Fed.
63 J4 **Grudziądz** Pol.
58 E4 **Grundy Bay** b. U.K.
54 **Grundarfjörður** Iceland
32 B6 **Grundy** U.S.A.
69 F4 **Gryazi** Rus. Fed.
68 G3 **Gryazovets** Rus. Fed.
62 G4 **Gryfice** Pol.
62 G4 **Gryfino** Pol.
62 G5 **Gryfów Śląski** Pol.
54 P2 **Gryllefjord** Norway
44 □ **Grytviken** Atlantic Ocean

85 F5 **Gua** India
37 J4 **Guacanayabo, Golfo de** b. Cuba
45 D2 **Guacara** Venez.
45 C3 **Guacharía** r. Col.
65 C4 **Guadajoz** r. Spain
36 D4 **Guadalajara** Mex.
65 E2 **Guadalajara** Spain
65 F2 **Guadalaviar** r. Spain
111 G2 **Guadalcanal** i. Solomon Is
65 C4 **Guadalete** r. Spain
65 F2 **Guadalope** r. Spain
65 C4 **Guadalquivir** r. Spain
27 C7 **Guadalupe** Mex.
25 C6 **Guadalupe** i. Mex.
34 B4 **Guadalupe** U.S.A.
27 D6 **Guadalupe** r. U.S.A.
65 D3 **Guadalupe, Sierra de** mts Spain
27 B6 **Guadalupe Bravos** Mex.
27 B6 **Guadalupe Mts Nat. Park** nat. park U.S.A.
27 B6 **Guadalupe Pk** mt U.S.A.
65 D2 **Guadarrama, Sierra de** mts Spain
47 C2 **Guadel, Sa de** mts Arg.
37 M5 **Guadeloupe** terr. Caribbean
65 C4 **Guadiana** r. Port./Spain
65 E4 **Guadix** Spain
44 B6 **Guafo, I.** i. Chile
45 C4 **Guainía** r. Col./Venez.
45 E3 **Guaiquinima, Cerro** mt Venez.
46 A4 **Guaíra** Brazil
44 B6 **Guaitecas, Islas** is Chile
27 C7 **Guaje, Llano de** plain Mex.
45 C2 **Guajira, Península de la** pen. Col.
42 C4 **Gualaceo** Ecuador
34 A2 **Gualala** U.S.A.
47 E2 **Gualeguay** Arg.
47 E2 **Gualeguay** r. Arg.
47 E2 **Gualeguaychu** Arg.
47 C3 **Gualicho, Salina** salt flat Arg.
47 A4 **Gualjaina** Arg.
93 L4 **Guam** terr. Pac. Oc.
44 A4 **Guamblin, I.** i. Chile
47 D3 **Guamini** Arg.
45 A4 **Guamués** r. Col.
95 B4 **Gua Musang** Malaysia
47 D3 **Guanaco, Co** h. Arg.
36 D4 **Guanajuato** Mex.
46 D1 **Guanambi** Brazil
45 D4 **Guaname** r. Venez.
45 C2 **Guanare** Venez.
45 D2 **Guanare Viejo** r. Venez.
45 C2 **Guanarito** Venez.
45 C2 **Guanarito** r. Venez.
45 D3 **Guanay, Sierra** mts Venez.
88 D2 **Guandi Shan** mt China
37 H4 **Guane** Cuba
89 C4 **Guang'an** China
89 E5 **Guangchang** China
89 □ **Guangdong** prov. China
89 D4 **Guangfeng** China
89 D6 **Guanghai** China
88 B4 **Guanghan** China
88 D3 **Guanghe** China
88 E2 **Guangling** China
88 F2 **Guangming Ding** mt China
89 B5 **Guangnan** China
89 D6 **Guangning** China
88 F2 **Guangrao** China
88 E4 **Guangshan** China
88 D4 **Guangshui** China
89 C6 **Guangxi** div. China
88 D3 **Guangyuan** China
89 E5 **Guangze** China
89 D6 **Guangzhou** China
46 D2 **Guanhães** Brazil
46 D2 **Guanhães** r. Brazil
45 E2 **Guanipa** r. Venez.
89 B5 **Guanling** China
88 C4 **Guanmian Shan** mts China
88 D3 **Guanpo** China
45 D2 **Guanta** Venez.
37 J4 **Guantánamo** Cuba
88 E1 **Guanting Sk.** resr China
89 D5 **Guanyang** China
88 A4 **Guanyinqiao** China
88 F3 **Guanyun** China
45 A4 **Guapí** Col.
42 F6 **Guaporé** r. Bol./Brazil
42 E7 **Guaqui** Bol.
46 D1 **Guará** r. Brazil
43 L5 **Guarabira** Brazil
46 E3 **Guarapari** Brazil
46 B4 **Guarapuava** Brazil
46 D3 **Guaraqueçaba** Brazil
46 D3 **Guaratinguetá** Brazil
46 C4 **Guaratuba, Baía de** b. Brazil
65 C2 **Guarda** Port.
46 C2 **Guarda Mor** Brazil
65 D1 **Guardo** Spain
45 D2 **Guárico** r. Venez.
45 C3 **Guaviare** r. Col.
46 C4 **Guarujá** Brazil
45 C3 **Guasca** Col.
45 C4 **Guasacavi, Cerro** h. Col.
45 B2 **Guasare** r. Venez.
36 C3 **Guasave** Mex.
45 C3 **Guasdualito** Venez.
45 E3 **Guasipati** Venez.
46 B4 **Guassú** r. Brazil
16 **Guatemala** country Central America

36 F6 Guatemala Guatemala
45 D2 Guatope, Parque Nacional *nat. park* Venez.
47 D3 Guatrache Arg.
45 C4 Guaviare *r.* Col.
46 C3 Guaxupé Brazil
45 B4 Guayabero *r.* Col.
45 D3 Guayapo *r.* Venez.
42 C4 Guayaquil Ecuador
42 B4 Guayaquil, Golfo de *g.* Ecuador
42 E6 Guayaramerín Bol.
36 B3 Guaymas Mex.
102 D2 Guba Eth.
66 E3 Gubbio Italy
69 F5 Gubkin Rus. Fed.
88 D3 Gucheng China
69 G7 Gudaut'a Georgia
55 M6 Gudbrandsdalen *v.* Norway
84 B3 Guddu Barrage *barrage* Pak.
69 H7 Gudermes Rus. Fed.
83 F7 Gudivada India
90 A3 Gudong *r.* China
80 D1 Güdül Turkey
83 E8 Gudur India
55 K6 Gudvangen Norway
100 A4 Guéckédou Guinea
31 J1 Guéguen, Lac *l.* Can.
45 B4 Güejar *r.* Col.
100 C1 Guelma Alg.
100 A2 Guelmine Morocco
31 H3 Guelph Can.
45 D2 Güera *r.* Venez.
23 G2 Guérard, Lac *l.* Can.
64 E3 Guéret France
56 F7 Guernsey *i.* U.K.
24 F3 Guernsey U.S.A.
27 D7 Guerrero Mex.
36 B3 Guerrero Negro Mex.
12 F5 Guiana Basin *sea feature* Atlantic Ocean
114 C6 Guichen B. *b.* Austr.
89 E4 Guichi China
47 F2 Guichón Uru.
88 A3 Guide China
101 D4 Guider Cameroon
89 C5 Guiding China
66 E4 Guidonia-Montecelio Italy
89 C6 Guigang China
100 B4 Guiglo Côte d'Ivoire
105 K2 Guija Moz.
89 D6 Gui Jiang *r.* China
89 F4 Guiji Shan *mts* China
59 G6 Guildford U.K.
33 J2 Guilford U.S.A.
89 D5 Guilin China
22 E2 Guillaume-Delisle, Lac *l.* Can.
65 B2 Guimarães Port.
94 B4 Guimaras Str. *chan.* Phil.
88 E3 Guimeng Ding *mt* China
88 A3 Guinan China
34 A2 Guinda U.S.A.
94 C4 Guindulman Phil.
96 Guinea *country* Africa
98 Guinea, Gulf of *g.* Africa
12 J5 Guinea Basin *sea feature* Atlantic Ocean
96 Guinea-Bissau *country* Africa
37 H4 Güines Cuba
64 C2 Guingamp France
64 B2 Guipavas France
89 D6 Guiping China
46 B2 Guiratinga Brazil
45 E2 Güiria Venez.
61 B5 Guise France
94 C4 Guiuan Phil.
89 E4 Guixi China
89 C5 Guiyang *Guizhou* China
89 D5 Guiyang *Hunan* China
89 C5 Guizhou *div.* China
84 B5 Gujarat *div.* India
84 C2 Gujar Khan Pak.
84 C2 Gujranwala Pak.
84 C2 Gujrat Pak.
69 F5 Gukovo Rus. Fed.
81 K3 Gük Tappeh Iran
84 D2 Gulabgarh Jammu and Kashmir
79 H4 Gulabie Uzbek.
88 B2 Gulang China
115 H3 Gulargambone Austr.
83 E7 Gulbarga India
55 U8 Gulbene Latvia
79 L1 Gülchö Kyrgyzstan
80 E3 Gülek Turkey
118 A2 Gulf of Bothia *gulf* Can.
27 F6 Gulfport U.S.A.
115 H4 Gulgong Austr.
87 M1 Gulian China
89 B5 Gulin China
79 K1 Gulistan Uzbek.
30 E3 Gull I. *i.* U.S.A.
21 H4 Gull Lake Can.
54 R3 Gullträsk Sweden
80 D3 Gülnar Turkey
69 G7 Gulrip'shi Georgia
80 E2 Gülşehir Turkey
102 D3 Gulu Uganda
116 D6 Guluguba Austr.
84 B3 Gumal *r.* Pak.
103 C5 Gumare Botswana
79 G2 Gumdag Turkm.
85 F5 Gumia India
85 F5 Gumla India
61 F3 Gummersbach Ger.
80 E1 Gümüşhacıköy Turkey
81 G1 Gümüşhane Turkey
84 D1 Guna India
115 F5 Gunbar Austr.
115 H5 Gundagai Austr.

80 D3 Gündoğmuş Turkey
80 B2 Güney Turkey
102 B4 Gungu Dem. Rep. Congo
69 H7 Gunib Rus. Fed.
21 K4 Gunisao *r.* Can.
116 A1 Gunnawarra Austr.
115 J3 Gunnedah Austr.
115 H5 Gunning Austr.
25 F4 Gunnison *CO* U.S.A.
35 G2 Gunnison *UT* U.S.A.
25 E4 Gunnison *r.* U.S.A.
83 E7 Guntakal India
29 C5 Guntersville U.S.A.
29 C5 Guntersville L. *l.* U.S.A.
83 F7 Guntur India
113 G3 Gununa Austr.
92 B6 Gunungsitoli Indon.
95 A5 Gunungtua Indon.
62 E6 Günzburg Ger.
62 E6 Gunzenhausen Ger.
88 E1 Guojiatun China
88 E3 Guoyang China
88 A2 Gurban Hudag China
88 D1 Gurban Obo China
80 B2 Gürce Turkey
84 D3 Gurgaon India
43 K5 Gurgueia *r.* Brazil
84 B4 Gurha India
45 E3 Guri, Embalse de *resr* Venez.
112 F2 Gurig National Park *nat. park* Austr.
46 C2 Gurinhatã Brazil
69 H7 Gurjaani Georgia
81 J2 Gürpınar Turkey
85 G3 Guru China
103 D5 Gurué Moz.
80 F2 Gürün Turkey
43 J4 Gurupi *r.* Brazil
84 C4 Guru Sikhar *mt* India
68 B4 Gur'yevsk Rus. Fed.
100 C3 Gusau Nigeria
68 B4 Gusev Rus. Fed.
88 G2 Gushan China
35 H1 Gusher U.S.A.
79 J2 Gushgy Turkm.
88 E3 Gushi China
94 A5 Gusi Malaysia
77 M2 Gusikha Rus. Fed.
68 D4 Gusino Rus. Fed.
86 J1 Gusinoozersk Rus. Fed.
85 F5 Guskara India
68 G4 Gus'-Khrustal'nyy Rus. Fed.
66 C5 Guspini Italy
20 B3 Gustavus U.S.A.
34 B3 Gustine U.S.A.
62 F4 Güstrow Ger.
85 H3 Gutang China
62 D5 Gütersloh Ger.
35 H5 Guthrie *AZ* U.S.A.
28 C4 Guthrie *KY* U.S.A.
27 D5 Guthrie *OK* U.S.A.
27 C5 Guthrie *TX* U.S.A.
89 E5 Gutian *Fujian* China
89 E5 Gutian *Fujian* China
61 E5 Gutland *reg.* Ger./Lux.
85 F3 Gutsuo China
30 B4 Guttenberg U.S.A.
103 D5 Gutu Zimbabwe
85 G4 Guwahati India
81 J3 Guwēr Iraq
38 Guyana *country* S. America
88 D1 Guyang China
27 C4 Guymon U.S.A.
115 J3 Guyra Austr.
88 E1 Guyuan *Hebei* China
88 C3 Guyuan *Ningxia* China
79 K2 Guzar Uzbek.
89 C4 Guzhang China
88 E3 Guzhen China
25 F6 Guzmán Mex.
25 F6 Guzmán, Lago de *l.* Mex.
63 K3 Gvardeysk Rus. Fed.
115 H3 Gwabegar Austr.
79 J4 Gwadar Pak.
84 D4 Gwalior India
116 C5 Gwambegwine Austr.
103 C6 Gwanda Zimbabwe
60 C3 Gweebarra Bay *b.* Rep. of Ireland
60 C2 Gweedore Rep. of Ireland
103 C5 Gweru Zimbabwe
30 D2 Gwinn U.S.A.
101 D3 Gwoza Nigeria
115 H2 Gwydir *r.* Austr.
85 H3 Gyaca China
85 G3 Gyangrang China
85 G3 Gyangzê China
85 G3 Gyaring Co *l.* China
82 J4 Gyaring Hu *l.* China
67 L6 Gyaros *i.* Greece
85 G3 Gyarubtang China
76 J2 Gydanskiy Poluostrov *pen.* Rus. Fed.
85 H3 Gyimda China
85 F3 Gyirong *Xizang Zizhiqu* China
85 F3 Gyirong *Xizang Zizhiqu* China
85 H2 Gyiza China
116 E6 Gympie Austr.
63 J7 Gyöngyös Hungary
62 H7 Győr Hungary
21 K4 Gypsumville Can.
67 K6 Gytheio Greece
63 K7 Gyula Hungary
81 J1 Gyumri Armenia
79 H2 Gyzylarbat Turkm.

H

54 T5 Haapajärvi Fin.
54 T4 Haapavesi Fin.
55 S7 Haapsalu Estonia
61 C2 Haarlem Neth.
104 E6 Haarlem S. Africa
117 B5 Haast *r.* N.Z.
82 G1 Habahe China
102 D3 Habaswein Kenya
20 F3 Habay Can.
79 H6 Habban Yemen
81 J5 Habbānīyah, Hawr al *l.* Iraq
85 G4 Habiganj Bangl.
88 E1 Habirag China
84 B3 Habra India
45 B5 Hacha Col.
47 B3 Hachado, P. de *pass* Arg./Chile
91 F8 Hachijō-jima *i.* Japan
90 G4 Hachinohe Japan
91 F7 Hachiōji Japan
80 B2 Hacıbektaş Turkey
81 H2 Haciömer Turkey
114 C3 Hack, Mt *mt* Austr.
103 D6 Hacufera Moz.
79 H5 Ḥadd, Ra's al *pt* Oman
57 F5 Haddington U.K.
100 D3 Hadejia Nigeria
80 E5 Hadera Israel
55 L9 Haderslev Denmark
83 D10 Hadhdhunmathi Atoll *atoll* Maldives
80 D3 Hadım Turkey
59 H5 Hadleigh U.K.
80 F6 Ḥadraj, Wādī *watercourse* Saudi Arabia
78 F6 Ḥaḍramawt *reg.* Yemen
55 M8 Hadsund Denmark
69 E5 Hadyach Ukr.
47 F1 Haedo, Cuchilla de *h.* Uru.
87 N4 Haeju N. Korea
87 N4 Haeju-man *b.* N. Korea
105 H1 Haenertsburg S. Africa
21 H4 Hafford Can.
80 F2 Hafik Turkey
84 C2 Hafizabad Pak.
85 H4 Hāflong India
54 C4 Hafnarfjörður Iceland
54 B4 Hafursfjörður *b.* Iceland
31 G2 Hagar Can.
102 D2 Hagar Nish Plateau *plat.* Eritrea
61 C2 Hageland *reg.* Belgium
62 C5 Hagen Ger.
110 E2 Hagen, Mount *mt* P.N.G.
32 E5 Hagerstown U.S.A.
64 D5 Hagetmau France
55 N6 Hagfors Sweden
24 D2 Haggin, Mount *mt* U.S.A.
91 B7 Hagi Japan
89 B6 Ha Giang Vietnam
59 E5 Hagley U.K.
60 B5 Hag's Head *hd* Rep. of Ireland
21 H4 Hague Can.
64 H2 Haguenau France
88 E2 Hai *r.* China
102 D4 Hai Tanz.
88 F3 Hai'an China
104 B4 Haib *watercourse* Namibia
88 G1 Haicheng China
89 C6 Hai Dương Vietnam
80 E5 Haifa Israel
80 E5 Haifa, Bay of *b.* Israel
88 C3 Haifeng China
89 D6 Haikou China
78 C4 Hā'īl Saudi Arabia
87 L2 Hailar China
31 H2 Haileybury Can.
90 A2 Hailin China
59 H7 Hailsham U.K.
54 T4 Hailuoto Fin.
88 H4 Haimen China
89 C7 Hainan *div.* China
89 D7 Hainan *i.* China
20 B3 Haines U.S.A.
20 B2 Haines Junction Can.
89 C6 Hai Phong Vietnam
88 A2 Hairag China
88 B1 Hairhan Namag China
89 F5 Haitan Dao *i.* China
16 Haiti *country* Caribbean Sea
89 C7 Haitou China
35 G5 Haiwa Nakya U.S.A.
34 D3 Haiwee Reservoir U.S.A.
88 E3 Haixing China
101 F3 Haiya Sudan
88 A2 Haiyan *Qinghai* China
88 F4 Haiyan *Zhejiang* China
88 F2 Haiyang China
88 B2 Haiyuan China
88 F3 Haizhou Wan *b.* China
63 K7 Hajdúböszörmény Hungary
66 C7 Hajeb El Ayoun Tunisia
79 G2 Hajhir *mt* Yemen
90 F5 Hajiki-zaki *pt* Japan
85 F4 Hajipur India
85 H5 Hajo Myanmar
34 □2 Hakalau U.S.A.
47 C4 Hakelhuincul, Altiplanicie de *plat.* Arg.
Hakha *see* Haka
81 J3 Hakkâri Turkey
54 S4 Hakkas Sweden
91 D7 Hakken-zan *mt* Japan
90 G4 Hako-dake *mt* Japan
90 G4 Hakodate Japan
104 B1 Hakos Mts *mts* Namibia

104 D3 Hakseen Pan *salt pan* S. Africa
91 E6 Haku Japan
91 E6 Haku-san *vol.* Japan
91 E6 Haku-san National Park Japan
84 B4 Hala Pak.
Ḥalab *see* Aleppo
81 K4 Halabja Iraq
101 F2 Halaib Sudan
79 H6 Ḥalāniyāt, Juzur al *is* Oman
34 □1 Halawa U.S.A.
80 F4 Halba Lebanon
86 G2 Halban Mongolia
62 E5 Halberstadt Ger.
94 B3 Halcon, Mt *mt* Phil.
54 □ Haldarsvik Faroe Is
55 M7 Halden Norway
62 E4 Haldensleben Ger.
85 G5 Haldi *r.* India
85 G5 Haldia India
85 G4 Haldibari India
84 D3 Haldwani India
31 F3 Hale U.S.A.
34 □1 Haleiwa U.S.A.
59 E5 Halesowen U.K.
59 J5 Halesworth U.K.
80 F7 Halfeti Turkey
117 B7 Halfmoon Bay N.Z.
20 F3 Halfway *r.* Can.
60 C6 Halfway Rep. of Ireland
61 C2 Halfweg Neth.
85 G4 Halia India
81 G4 Ḥalībīyah Syria
31 H3 Haliburton Can.
114 E4 Halifax Austr.
23 H5 Halifax Can.
59 F4 Halifax U.K.
32 D6 Halifax U.S.A.
116 E2 Halifax, Mt *mt* Austr.
116 E2 Halifax Bay *b.* Austr.
57 E2 Halkirk U.K.
54 P5 Hälla Sweden
114 C4 Hall Bay *b.* Austr.
61 C4 Halle Belgium
62 E5 Halle Ger.
55 O7 Hällefors Sweden
62 F7 Hallein Austria
119 C3 Halley *U.K. Base* Antarctica
54 Q4 Hällnäs Sweden
26 D1 Hallock U.S.A.
55 O7 Hallsberg Sweden
112 E3 Halls Creek Austr.
31 H3 Halls Lake Can.
54 O5 Hallviken Sweden
93 H6 Halmahera *i.* Indon.
55 N8 Halmstad Sweden
84 C5 Halol India
55 M8 Hals Denmark
54 T5 Halsua Fin.
61 F3 Haltern Ger.
58 E3 Haltwhistle U.K.
116 D6 Haly, Mount *h.* Austr.
61 B5 Ham France
91 F7 Hamada Japan
100 B2 Hamâda El Ḥaricha *des.* Mali
81 M4 Hamadān Iran
100 B2 Hamada Tounassine *des.* Alg.
80 F4 Ḥamāh Syria
90 G3 Hamamasu Japan
91 F7 Hamamatsu Japan
55 M6 Hamar Norway
54 O2 Hamarøy Norway
78 C5 Ḥamâta, Gebel *mt* Egypt
90 H2 Hamatonbetsu Japan
83 F9 Hambantota Sri Lanka
58 F3 Hambleton Hills *h.* U.K.
62 D4 Hamburg Ger.
105 G6 Hamburg S. Africa
27 F5 Hamburg *AR* U.S.A.
32 D3 Hamburg *NY* U.S.A.
33 F4 Hamburg *PA* U.S.A.
33 G4 Hamden U.S.A.
55 T6 Hämeenlinna Fin.
62 D4 Hameln Ger.
112 C4 Hamersley Range *mts* Austr.
87 N4 Hamhŭng N. Korea
82 H1 Hami China
81 M6 Ḥamīd Iran
101 F2 Hamid Sudan
114 E6 Hamilton Austr.
37 M2 Hamilton Bermuda
31 H4 Hamilton Can.
117 E3 Hamilton N.Z.
57 D5 Hamilton U.K.
29 C5 Hamilton *AL* U.S.A.
30 B5 Hamilton *IL* U.S.A.
24 D2 Hamilton *MT* U.S.A.
33 F3 Hamilton *NY* U.S.A.
32 A5 Hamilton *OH* U.S.A.
34 B3 Hamilton, Mt *mt CA* U.S.A.
35 E2 Hamilton, Mt *mt NV* U.S.A.
34 A2 Hamilton City U.S.A.
55 U6 Hamina Fin.
81 H6 Ḥamīr, Wādī al *watercourse* Saudi Arabia
84 D3 Hamirpur India
23 J3 Hamiton Inlet *in.* Can.
114 C5 Hamley Bridge Austr.
30 D3 Hamlin Lake *l.* U.S.A.
62 C5 Hamm Ger.
100 B2 Hammada du Drâa *plat.* Alg.
81 J3 Ḥammām al 'Alīl Iraq
66 D6 Hammamet Tunisia
101 D1 Hammamet, Golfe de *b.* Tunisia

81 L6 Ḥammār, Hawr al *l.* Iraq
54 P5 Hammarstrand Sweden
54 O5 Hammerdal Sweden
54 S1 Hammerfest Norway
61 E3 Hamminkeln Ger.
114 C4 Hammond Austr.
30 D5 Hammond *IN* U.S.A.
27 F6 Hammond *LA* U.S.A.
24 E2 Hammond *MT* U.S.A.
31 E3 Hammond Bay *b.* U.S.A.
32 E3 Hammondsport U.S.A.
33 F5 Hammonton U.S.A.
117 C6 Hampden N.Z.
59 F6 Hampshire Downs *h.* U.K.
23 G4 Hampton Can.
27 E5 Hampton *AR* U.S.A.
33 H3 Hampton *NH* U.S.A.
33 E6 Hampton *VA* U.S.A.
81 K4 Hamrīn, Jabal *h.* Iraq
95 C3 Han Tân China
84 D2 Hamta Pass *pass* India
79 H4 Hāmūn-e Jaz Mūrīān *salt marsh* Iran
79 K4 Hamun-i-Lora *l.* Pak.
79 J4 Hamun-i-Mashkel *salt flat* Pak.
81 J2 Hamur Turkey
61 D4 Han, Grotte de *cave* Belgium
104 E1 Hanahai *watercourse* Botswana/Namibia
34 □2 Hanalei U.S.A.
90 G5 Hanamaki Japan
88 D3 Hancheng China
32 D5 Hancock *MD* U.S.A.
30 C2 Hancock *MI* U.S.A.
33 F4 Hancock *NY* U.S.A.
57 C2 Handa Island *i.* U.K.
88 E2 Handan China
102 D4 Handeni Tanz.
34 C3 Hanford U.S.A.
86 G2 Hangayn Nuruu *mts* Mongolia
Hanggin Houqi *see* Xamba
Hanggin Qi *see* Xin
88 E2 Hangu China
84 B2 Hangu Pak.
89 D5 Hanguang China
89 F4 Hangzhou China
89 F4 Hangzhou Wan *b.* China
81 H2 Hani Turkey
88 B2 Hanjiaoshui China
104 F6 Hankey S. Africa
55 S7 Hanko Fin.
35 H2 Hanksville U.S.A.
84 D2 Hanle Jammu and Kashmir
117 D5 Hanmer Springs N.Z.
21 G4 Hanna Can.
22 D3 Hanna Bay *b.* Can.
30 B6 Hannibal U.S.A.
62 D4 Hannover Ger.
55 O9 Hanöbukten *b.* Sweden
89 B6 Ha Nôi Vietnam
Hanoi *see* Ha Nôi
31 G3 Hanover Can.
104 F5 Hanover S. Africa
33 G3 Hanover *NH* U.S.A.
32 E5 Hanover *PA* U.S.A.
119 D4 Hansen Mts *mts* Antarctica
89 D4 Hanshou China
88 E4 Han Shui *r.* China
84 D3 Hansi India
54 Q2 Hansnes Norway
114 B3 Hanson, L. *salt flat* Austr.
32 B6 Hansonville U.S.A.
55 L8 Hanstholm Denmark
68 C4 Hantsavichy Belarus
84 C3 Hanumangarh India
115 G5 Hanwood Austr.
88 D3 Hanyin China
89 B4 Hanyuan China
88 C3 Hanzhong China
109 Hao *atoll* Pac. Oc.
85 G5 Hāora India
54 T4 Haparanda Sweden
85 H4 Hāpoli India
62 D4 Hapur India
54 Q2 Haora India
91 G6 Haramachi Japan
84 C2 Haramukh *mt* India
84 B3 Harappa Road Pak.
103 D5 Harare Zimbabwe
79 H6 Ḥarāsīs, Jiddat al *gravel area* Oman
87 J2 Har-Ayrag Mongolia
100 A4 Harbel Liberia
87 N2 Harbin China
31 F3 Harbor Beach U.S.A.
84 C3 Harbor Springs U.S.A.
23 J4 Harbour Breton Can.
44 E8 Harbours, B. of *b.* Falkland Is
35 H5 Harcuvar Mts *mts* U.S.A.
84 D5 Harda Khās India
55 K6 Hardangervidda *plat.* Norway
55 K6 Hardangervidda Nasjonalpark *nat. park* Norway
104 B3 Hardap *div.* Namibia
104 B2 Hardap Dam *dam* Namibia
61 D2 Hardenberg Neth.
61 D2 Harderwijk Neth.
104 C5 Hardeveld *mts* S. Africa
24 F2 Hardin U.S.A.
105 H5 Harding S. Africa

21 G4 Hardisty Can.
20 F2 Hardisty Lake *l.* Can.
84 E4 Hardoi India
33 G3 Hardwick U.S.A.
114 B5 Hardwicke B. *b.* Austr.
27 F4 Hardy U.S.A.
30 E4 Hardy Reservoir *resr* U.S.A.
80 D6 Hareidīn, W. *watercourse* Egypt
61 F2 Haren (Ems) Ger.
102 E3 Härer Eth.
33 H4 Harford U.S.A.
102 E3 Hargeysa Somalia
63 M7 Harghita-Mădăraş, Vârful *mt* Romania
81 H2 Harhal D. *mts* Turkey
88 C2 Harhatan China
82 J3 Har Hu *l.* China
84 D3 Haridwar India
117 C5 Harihari N.Z.
91 D7 Harima-nada *b.* Japan
85 G5 Haringhat *r.* Bangl.
61 C3 Haringvliet *est.* Neth.
79 L3 Haripur Pak.
55 S6 Harjavalta Fin.
26 E3 Harlan *IA* U.S.A.
32 B6 Harlan *KY* U.S.A.
59 C5 Harlech U.K.
24 E1 Harlem U.S.A.
59 J5 Harleston U.K.
61 D1 Harlingen Neth.
27 D7 Harlingen U.S.A.
59 H6 Harlow U.K.
23 G4 Harlowton U.S.A.
33 J2 Harmony *ME* U.S.A.
30 A4 Harmony *MN* U.S.A.
84 A3 Harnai Pak.
24 B3 Harney Basin *basin* U.S.A.
24 C3 Harney L. *l.* U.S.A.
55 P5 Härnösand Sweden
87 M2 Har Nur China
86 F2 Har Nuur *l.* Mongolia
57 □ Haroldswick U.K.
100 B4 Harper Liberia
34 D4 Harper Lake *l.* U.S.A.
32 E5 Harpers Ferry U.S.A.
23 H2 Harp Lake *l.* Can.
81 G2 Harput Turkey
Harqin Qi *see* Jinshan
35 F5 Harquahala Mts *mts* U.S.A.
81 G3 Harran Turkey
22 H3 Harricanaw *r.* Can.
29 C5 Harriman U.S.A.
33 G3 Harriman Reservoir *resr* U.S.A.
115 K3 Harrington Austr.
33 F5 Harrington U.S.A.
23 J3 Harrington Harbour Can.
57 B3 Harris U.K.
114 A3 Harris, Lake *salt flat* Austr.
57 A3 Harris, Sound of *chan.* U.K.
28 B4 Harrisburg *IL* U.S.A.
32 E4 Harrisburg *PA* U.S.A.
105 H4 Harrismith S. Africa
27 E4 Harrison *AR* U.S.A.
30 E3 Harrison *MI* U.S.A.
23 J3 Harrison, Cape *c.* Can.
32 D5 Harrisonburg U.S.A.
20 E5 Harrison L. *l.* Can.
26 E4 Harrisonville U.S.A.
31 F3 Harrisville *MI* U.S.A.
33 F2 Harrisville *NY* U.S.A.
32 C5 Harrisville *WV* U.S.A.
58 F4 Harrogate U.K.
81 L4 Harsīn Iran
81 G1 Harşit *r.* Turkey
67 M2 Hârşova Romania
54 P2 Harstad Norway
30 D4 Hart U.S.A.
114 B3 Hart, L. *salt flat* Austr.
88 G1 Hartao China
104 D4 Hartbees *watercourse* S. Africa
62 G7 Hartberg Austria
55 K6 Harteigan *mt* Norway
57 F4 Hart Fell *h.* U.K.
33 G4 Hartford *CT* U.S.A.
30 D4 Hartford *MI* U.S.A.
26 D3 Hartford *SD* U.S.A.
30 C4 Hartford *WV* U.S.A.
20 E3 Hart Highway Can.
23 G4 Hartland Can.
59 C7 Hartland U.K.
59 C6 Hartland Point *pt* U.K.
58 F3 Hartlepool U.K.
27 C5 Hartley U.K.
20 D4 Hartley Bay Can.
55 U6 Hartola Fin.
20 E4 Hart Ranges *mts* Can.
62 E5 Härtsfeld *h.* Ger.
104 F3 Hartswater S. Africa
29 D5 Hartwell Res. *resr* U.S.A.
86 F2 Har Us Nuur *l.* Mongolia
30 C4 Harvard U.S.A.
25 F4 Harvard, Mt *mt* U.S.A.
112 C6 Harvey Austr.
33 K2 Harvey Austr.
30 D5 Harvey *MI* U.S.A.
26 C2 Harvey *ND* U.S.A.
59 J6 Harwich U.K.
115 K2 Harwood Austr.
84 D3 Haryana *div.* India
80 F6 Ḥaşah, Wādī al *watercourse* Jordan
84 C2 Hasan Abdal Pak.
80 E2 Hasan Dağı *mts* Turkey
81 H3 Hasankeyf Turkey
81 L3 Ḥasan Sālārān Iran
80 E5 Hasbani *r.* Lebanon

80 E2 Hasbek Turkey
85 E5 Hasdo r. India
61 F2 Hase r. Ger.
61 F2 Haselünne Ger.
81 M3 Hashtpar Iran
81 L3 Hashtrud Iran
27 D5 Haskell U.S.A.
59 G6 Haslemere U.K.
63 M7 Hăşmaşul Mare mt
    Romania
83 E8 Hassan India
81 K4 Hassan Iraq
35 F5 Hassayampa r. U.S.A.
61 D4 Hasselt Belgium
100 C1 Hassi Messaoud Alg.
55 N8 Hässleholm Sweden
114 F7 Hastings Austr.
115 K3 Hastings r. Austr.
117 F3 Hastings N.Z.
59 H7 Hastings U.K.
30 E4 Hastings MI U.S.A.
30 A3 Hastings MN U.S.A.
26 D3 Hastings NE U.S.A.
    Hatay see Antakya
35 F3 Hatch U.S.A.
21 J3 Hatchet Lake l. Can.
29 B5 Hatchie r. U.S.A.
114 E4 Hatfield Austr.
58 G4 Hatfield U.K.
86 H1 Hatgal Mongolia
84 D4 Hathras India
85 F4 Hatia Nepal
95 C3 Ha Tiên Vietnam
95 C1 Ha Tinh Vietnam
114 E5 Hattah Austr.
29 F5 Hatteras, Cape c. U.S.A.
54 N4 Hattfjelldal Norway
85 E6 Hatti r. India
29 B6 Hattiesburg U.S.A.
95 B4 Hat Yai Thai.
102 E3 Haud reg. Eth.
55 K7 Hauge Norway
55 J7 Haugesund Norway
95 C3 Hâu Giang, Sông r.
    Vietnam
117 E3 Hauhungaroa mt N.Z.
55 K7 Haukeligrend Norway
54 T4 Haukipudas Fin.
55 V5 Haukivesi r. Fin.
21 H3 Haultain r. Can.
117 E2 Hauraki Gulf g. N.Z.
117 A7 Hauroko, L. l. N.Z.
33 J3 Haut, Isle au i. U.S.A.
100 B1 Haut Atlas mts Morocco
23 G4 Hauterive Can.
61 E4 Hautes Fagnes moorland
    Belgium
61 D5 Haut-Fourneau, Étang
    du l. France
100 B1 Hauts Plateaux plat. Alg.
34 □1 Hauula U.S.A.
30 B5 Havana U.S.A.
59 G7 Havant U.K.
35 F4 Havasu Lake l. U.S.A.
62 F4 Havel r. Ger.
31 J3 Havelock Can.
29 E5 Havelock U.S.A.
117 F3 Havelock North N.Z.
59 C6 Haverfordwest U.K.
33 H3 Haverhill U.S.A.
62 G6 Havlíčkův Brod
    Czech Rep.
54 T1 Havøysund Norway
67 M5 Havran Turkey
24 E1 Havre U.S.A.
23 H4 Havre Aubert, Île du
    i. Can.
33 G4 Havre de Grace U.S.A.
23 H3 Havre-St-Pierre Can.
67 M4 Havsa Turkey
80 E1 Havza Turkey
34 □2 Hawaii i. U.S.A.
14 H4 Hawaiian Islands is
    Pac. Oc.
14 Hawaiian Ridge
    sea feature Pac. Oc.
34 □2 Hawaii Volcanoes
    National Park nat. park
    U.S.A.
81 L7 Hawallī Kuwait
59 D4 Hawarden U.K.
117 B6 Hawea, L. l. N.Z.
117 E3 Hawera N.Z.
58 E3 Hawes U.K.
34 □2 Hawi U.S.A.
57 F5 Hawick U.K.
81 L6 Hawīzah, Hawr al l. Iraq
117 B6 Hawkdun Range mts N.Z.
117 F3 Hawke Bay b. N.Z.
23 J3 Hawke Island i. Can.
114 C3 Hawker Austr.
114 D2 Hawkers Gate Austr.
33 F2 Hawkesbury Can.
35 F3 Hawkins Peak summit
    U.S.A.
31 F3 Hawks U.S.A.
33 K2 Hawkshaw Can.
116 D5 Hawkwood Austr.
33 F4 Hawley U.S.A.
81 J5 Hawrān, Wādī
    watercourse Iraq
104 F7 Hawston S. Africa
34 C2 Hawthorne U.S.A.
58 F3 Haxby U.K.
114 F5 Hay Austr.
20 F2 Hay r. Can.
30 B3 Hay r. U.S.A.
88 B1 Haya China
90 G5 Hayachine-san mt Japan
61 E5 Hayange France
81 K3 Haydarābad Iran
35 G5 Hayden AZ U.S.A.
24 C2 Hayden ID U.S.A.
21 L3 Hayes r. Can.

59 B7 Hayle U.K.
79 H6 Haymā' Oman
80 D2 Haymana Turkey
116 C3 Hayman I. i. Austr.
32 E5 Haymarket U.S.A.
33 J2 Haynesville U.S.A.
59 D5 Hay-on-Wye U.K.
69 C7 Hayrabolu Turkey
20 F2 Hay River Can.
26 D4 Hays U.S.A.
69 D5 Haysyn Ukr.
34 A3 Hayward CA U.S.A.
30 C4 Hayward WV U.S.A.
59 G7 Haywards Heath U.K.
79 K3 Hazarajat reg. Afgh.
32 B6 Hazard U.S.A.
85 F5 Hazāribāg India
85 E5 Hazaribagh Range mts
    India
61 A4 Hazebrouck France
20 D3 Hazelton Can.
61 C2 Hazerswoude-Rijndijk
    Neth.
33 F4 Hazleton U.S.A.
81 G6 Hazm al Jalāmīd ridge
    Saudi Arabia
84 A1 Hazrat Sultan Afgh.
81 H2 Hazro Turkey
47 D2 H. Bouchard Arg.
60 B4 Headford Rep. of Ireland
112 F6 Head of Bight b. Austr.
34 A2 Headsburg U.S.A.
114 F6 Healesville Austr.
59 F4 Heanor U.K.
13 I7 Heard i. Indian Ocean
27 D6 Hearne U.S.A.
22 D4 Hearst Can.
59 H7 Heathfield U.K.
33 E6 Heathsville U.S.A.
27 D7 Hebbronville U.S.A.
88 E2 Hebei div. China
115 G2 Hebel Austr.
27 E5 Heber Springs U.S.A.
88 E3 Hebi China
23 H2 Hebron Can.
30 D5 Hebron IN U.S.A.
26 D3 Hebron NE U.S.A.
33 G3 Hebron NY U.S.A.
80 E6 Hebron West Bank
23 H2 Hebron Fiord in. Can.
20 C4 Hecate Strait chan. Can.
20 C3 Heceta I. i. U.S.A.
89 C5 Hechi China
89 C4 Hechuan China
55 N5 Hede Sweden
55 O6 Hedemora Sweden
89 D6 Hede Sk. resr China
24 C2 He Devil Mt. mt U.S.A.
30 A5 Hedrick U.S.A.
61 D2 Heerenveen Neth.
61 C2 Heerhugowaard Neth.
61 D4 Heerlen Neth.
    Hefa see Haifa
88 E3 Hefei China
88 D4 Hefeng China
90 B1 Hegang China
91 E6 Hegura-jima i. Japan
62 D3 Heide Ger.
103 B6 Heide Namibia
62 D6 Heidelberg Ger.
105 H3 Heidelberg Gauteng
    S. Africa
104 D7 Heidelberg Western Cape
    S. Africa
    Heihe see Heihe
87 N1 Heihe China
105 G3 Heilbron S. Africa
62 D6 Heilbronn Ger.
62 E3 Heiligenhafen Ger.
89 □ Hei Ling Chau i. China
87 N2 Heilongjiang div. China
87 P1 Heilong Jiang r.
    China/Rus. Fed.
54 M5 Heimdal Norway
55 U6 Heinola Fin.
95 A2 Heinze Is is Myanmar
88 G1 Heishan China
61 C3 Heist-op-den-Berg
    Belgium
88 E2 Hejian China
89 B4 Hejiang China
89 D6 He Jiang r. China
88 D3 Hejin China
80 F2 Hekimhan Turkey
54 D5 Hekla vol. Iceland
88 B2 Hekou Gansu China
89 B6 Hekou Yunnan China
54 N5 Helagsfjället mt Sweden
88 B2 Helan Shan mts China
85 H4 Helem India
34 D3 Helen, Mt mt U.S.A.
27 F5 Helena AR U.S.A.
24 E2 Helena MT U.S.A.
57 D4 Hensburgh U.K.
89 D7 Helen Shoal sand bank
    Paracel Is
80 E6 Helez Israel
62 C3 Helgoland i. Ger.
62 D3 Helgoländer Bucht
    b. Ger.
115 K1 Helidon Austr.
54 C5 Hella Iceland
54 P2 Helland Norway
61 C3 Hellevoetsluis Neth.
54 R2 Helligskogen Norway
65 F3 Hellín Spain
24 C2 Hells Canyon gorge U.S.A.
84 3 Helmand r. Afgh.
103 B6 Helmeringhausen
    Namibia
61 D3 Helmond Neth.
57 E2 Helmsdale U.K.
57 E2 Helmsdale r. U.K.
62 E4 Helmstedt Ger.

87 N3 Helong China
35 G2 Helper U.S.A.
55 N8 Helsingborg Sweden
55 N8 Helsingør Denmark
55 T6 Helsinki Fin.
59 B7 Helston U.K.
58 D3 Helvellyn mt U.K.
60 D5 Helvick Head hd China
    Rep. of Ireland
80 C7 Helwân Egypt
59 G6 Hemel Hempstead U.K.
34 D5 Hemet U.S.A.
32 E3 Hemlock Lake l. U.S.A.
33 G2 Hemmingford Can.
27 D6 Hempstead U.S.A.
59 J5 Hemsby U.K.
55 Q8 Hemse Sweden
88 A3 Henan China
88 D3 Henan div. China
28 E4 Henderson KY U.S.A.
29 E4 Henderson NC U.S.A.
35 E3 Henderson NV U.S.A.
33 E3 Henderson NY U.S.A.
27 E5 Henderson TX U.S.A.
29 D5 Hendersonville NC U.S.A.
29 C4 Hendersonville TN U.S.A.
59 G6 Hendon U.K.
82 J5 Hengduan Shan mts
    China
61 E2 Hengelo Neth.
89 D5 Hengshan Hunan China
88 C2 Hengshan Shaanxi China
90 B2 Hengshan China
88 D2 Heng Shan mt Shanxi
    China
89 D5 Heng Shan mt Hunan
    China
88 E2 Hengshui China
89 C6 Hengxian China
89 D5 Hengyang Hunan China
89 D5 Hengyang Hunan China
69 E6 Henicheskʹk Ukr.
117 C6 Henley N.Z.
59 G6 Henley-on-Thames U.K.
33 F5 Henlopen, Cape pt U.S.A.
61 F4 Hennef (Sieg) Ger.
105 G3 Hennenman S. Africa
33 H3 Henniker U.S.A.
27 D5 Henrietta U.S.A.
22 D2 Henrietta Maria, Cape
    c. Can.
35 G3 Henrieville U.S.A.
30 C5 Henry U.S.A.
119 B3 Henry Ice Rise
    ice feature Antarctica
35 G2 Henry Mts mts U.S.A.
31 G4 Hensall Can.
103 B6 Hentiesbaai Namibia
115 G5 Henty Austr.
83 J7 Henzada Myanmar
21 H4 Hepburn Can.
89 E5 Heping China
89 C6 Hepu China
59 G6 Hepworth U.K.
116 C1 Herald Cays atolls
    Coral Sea Is Terr.
79 J3 Herāt Afgh.
64 F5 Hérault r. France
116 A2 Herbert r. Austr.
21 H4 Herbert Can.
116 A1 Herberton Austr.
59 E5 Hereford U.K.
27 C5 Hereford U.S.A.
62 D4 Herford Ger.
26 D4 Herington U.S.A.
81 L2 Herīs Iran
62 D7 Herisau Switz.
61 E3 Herkenbosch Neth.
33 F3 Herkimer U.S.A.
27 C7 Hermanas Mex.
57 □ Herma Ness hd U.K.
104 C7 Hermanus S. Africa
105 H5 Hermes, Cape pt S. Africa
115 G3 Hermidale Austr.
24 C2 Hermiston U.S.A.
44 C9 Hermite, Is i. Chile
110 E2 Hermit Is is P.N.G.
80 E5 Hermon, Mount mt
    Lebanon/Syria
47 B2 Hermosa, P. de V. pass
    Chile
27 D7 Hermosa, Valle v. Arg.
36 B3 Hermosillo Mex.
44 F3 Hernandarias Para.
61 F3 Herne Ger.
59 J6 Herne Bay U.K.
55 L8 Herning Denmark
30 D1 Heron Bay Can.
116 D4 Heron I. i. Austr.
65 D3 Herrera del Duque Spain
27 B7 Herreras Mex.
115 G8 Herrick Austr.
32 E4 Hershey U.S.A.
59 G6 Hertford U.K.
61 E4 Hertogenwald forest
    Belgium
105 F4 Hertzogville S. Africa
116 E5 Hervey Bay Austr.
116 E5 Hervey Bay b. Austr.
116 B2 Hervey Ra. mts Austr.
81 M4 Heşar Iran
61 C4 Hesbaye reg. Belgium
89 C6 Heshan China
88 C3 Heshui China
88 D2 Heshun China
34 D4 Hesperia U.S.A.
20 C2 Hess r. Can.
89 B6 Het r. Laos
34 B3 Hetch Hetchy Aqueduct
    canal U.S.A.

61 D3 Heteren Neth.
26 C2 Hettinger U.S.A.
58 E3 Hetton U.K.
62 E5 Hettstedt Ger.
61 D3 Heusden Belgium
58 E3 Hexham U.K.
88 F4 Hexian Anhui China
89 D5 Hexian Guangxi China
    Hexigten Qi see Jingpeng
88 B2 Hexipu China
88 E3 Heyang China
58 E3 Heysham U.K.
89 E6 Heyuan China
114 D7 Heywood Austr.
58 E4 Heywood U.K.
30 C5 Heyworth U.S.A.
88 E3 Heze China
89 B5 Hezhang China
88 B3 Hezheng China
88 B3 Hezuozhen China
29 D7 Hialeah U.S.A.
26 E4 Hiawatha U.S.A.
30 A2 Hibbing U.S.A.
115 F9 Hibbs, Pt hd Austr.
29 D5 Hickory U.S.A.
117 G2 Hicks Bay N.Z.
21 K2 Hicks L. l. Can.
32 A4 Hicksville U.S.A.
27 D5 Hico U.S.A.
90 H3 Hidaka-sanmyaku mts
    Japan
27 D7 Hidalgo Mex.
36 C3 Hidalgo del Parral Mex.
46 C2 Hidrolândia Brazil
91 C7 Higashi-Hiroshima Japan
90 G5 Higashine Japan
91 D7 Higashi-ōsaka Japan
91 A8 Higashi-suidō chan.
    Japan
33 F4 Higgins Bay U.S.A.
30 E3 Higgins Lake l. U.S.A.
    High Atlas mts see
    Haut Atlas
24 B3 High Desert des. U.S.A.
30 C3 High Falls Reservoir
    resr U.S.A.
30 E3 High I. i. U.S.A.
89 □ High Island Reservoir
    resr China
30 D4 Highland Park U.S.A.
34 C2 Highland Peak summit
    CA U.S.A.
35 E3 Highland Peak summit
    NV U.S.A.
20 F3 High Level Can.
85 F5 High Level Canal canal
    India
29 E5 High Point U.S.A.
20 F3 High Prairie Can.
20 G4 High River Can.
29 E7 High Rock Bahamas
21 J3 Highrock Lake l. Can.
115 F9 High Rocky Pt hd Austr.
58 E3 High Seat h. U.K.
33 F4 Hightstown U.S.A.
59 G6 High Wycombe U.K.
45 D2 Higuerote Venez.
55 57 Hiiumaa i. Estonia
78 D4 Hijaz reg. Saudi Arabia
35 E3 Hiko U.S.A.
91 E7 Hikone Japan
117 G2 Hikurangi mt N.Z.
35 F3 Hildale U.S.A.
62 D4 Hildesheim Ger.
85 G4 Hili Bangl.
26 D4 Hill City U.S.A.
35 H2 Hill Creek r. U.S.A.
55 N9 Hillerød Denmark
116 A2 Hillgrove Austr.
26 D2 Hillsboro ND U.S.A.
33 H3 Hillsboro NH U.S.A.
32 B5 Hillsboro OH U.S.A.
27 D6 Hillsboro TX U.S.A.
32 C5 Hillsboro WV U.S.A.
30 B4 Hillsboro WV U.S.A.
116 C3 Hillsborough, C. pt Austr.
30 E5 Hillsdale MI U.S.A.
33 G3 Hillsdale NY U.S.A.
32 E4 Hillsgrove U.S.A.
57 F4 Hillside U.K.
35 F4 Hillside U.S.A.
115 F4 Hillston Austr.
32 C6 Hillsville U.S.A.
115 J5 Hilltop Austr.
34 □2 Hilo U.S.A.
105 J4 Hilton S. Africa
32 E3 Hilton U.S.A.
31 F2 Hilton Beach Can.
29 D5 Hilton Head Island U.S.A.
81 G3 Hilvan Turkey
61 D2 Hilversum Neth.
84 D3 Himachal Pradesh div.
    India
74 Himalaya mts Asia
85 F3 Himalchul mt Nepal
54 S4 Himanka Fin.
67 H4 Himarë Albania
84 C5 Himatnagar India
91 D7 Himeji Japan
90 G5 Himekami-dake mt Japan
105 H4 Himeville S. Africa
91 E6 Himi Japan
80 E7 Ḩimş Syria
94 C4 Hinatuan Phil.
116 B2 Hinchinbrook I. i. Austr.
59 F5 Hinckley U.K.
30 A2 Hinckley MN U.S.A.
35 F2 Hinckley UT U.S.A.
33 F3 Hinckley Reservoir
    resr U.S.A.
84 D3 Hindan r. India
84 D4 Hindaun India

58 G3 Hinderwell U.K.
58 E4 Hindley U.K.
32 B6 Hindman U.S.A.
114 D6 Hindmarsh, L. l. Austr.
85 F5 Hindola India
84 B2 Hindu Kush mts
    Afgh./Pak.
83 E8 Hindupur India
20 F3 Hines Creek Can.
29 D6 Hinesville U.S.A.
84 D5 Hinganghat India
84 D6 Hingoli India
81 H2 Hınıs Turkey
34 D4 Hinkley U.S.A.
54 O2 Hinnøya i. Norway
94 B4 Hinobaan Phil.
65 D3 Hinojosa del Duque Spain
91 C7 Hino-misaki pt Japan
33 G3 Hinsdale U.S.A.
20 F4 Hinton Can.
32 C6 Hinton U.S.A.
81 K2 Hirabit Dağ mt Turkey
91 A8 Hirado Japan
91 A8 Hirado-shima i. Japan
85 E5 Hirakud Reservoir resr
    India
90 H3 Hiroo Japan
90 G4 Hirosaki Japan
91 C7 Hiroshima Japan
62 E7 Hirschberg mt Ger.
64 G2 Hirson France
55 L8 Hirtshals Denmark
84 C3 Hisar India
81 M3 Hisar Iran
80 D1 Hisarönü Turkey
81 K6 Ḩisb, Shaʿīb watercourse
    Iraq
80 E6 Hisban Jordan
37 K4 Hispaniola i.
    Caribbean Sea
85 F4 Hisua India
81 J5 Ḩīt Iraq
91 G6 Hitachi Japan
91 G6 Hitachi-ōta Japan
91 B8 Hitoyoshi Japan
54 L5 Hitra i. Norway
91 C7 Hiuchi-nada b. Japan
20 E4 Hixon Can.
116 E4 Hixson Cay rf Austr.
81 J2 Hizan Turkey
55 O7 Hjälmaren l. Sweden
21 H2 Hjalmar Lake l. Can.
55 L5 Hjerkinn Norway
55 O7 Hjo Sweden
55 M8 Hjørring Denmark
105 J4 Hlabisa S. Africa
105 J3 Hlatikulu Swaziland
55 O7 Hlobyne Ukr.
105 G4 Hlohlowane S. Africa
105 H4 Hlotse Lesotho
105 K4 Hluhluwe S. Africa
69 E5 Hlukhiv Ukr.
68 O4 Hlusha Belarus
100 C4 Ho Ghana
103 B6 Hoachanas Namibia
115 G9 Hobart Austr.
27 D5 Hobart I.U.S.A.
27 C5 Hobbs U.S.A.
29 D7 Hobe Sound U.S.A.
88 D1 Hobor China
55 L8 Hobro Denmark
102 E3 Hobyo Somalia
95 C3 Hồ Chí Minh Vietnam
62 G7 Hochschwab mt Austria
32 B5 Hocking r. U.S.A.
84 D4 Hodal India
58 G3 Hodder r. U.K.
59 G6 Hoddesdon U.K.
    Hodeida see Al Ḩudaydah
33 K1 Hodgdon U.S.A.
63 K7 Hódmezővásárhely
    Hungary
65 J5 Hodna, Chott el
    salt l. Alg.
61 C3 Hoek van Holland Neth.
61 D3 Hoensbroek Neth.
90 A3 Hoeryŏng N. Korea
62 E6 Hof Ger.
105 F5 Hofmeyr S. Africa
54 F4 Höfn Iceland
55 P6 Hofors Sweden
54 D4 Hofsjökull ice cap
    Iceland
91 B7 Hōfu Japan
55 N8 Höganäs Sweden
115 G7 Hogan Group is Austr.
116 B3 Hoganthulla Cr. r. Austr.
100 C2 Hoggar plat. Alg.
33 F6 Hog I. i. U.S.A.
55 P8 Högsby Sweden
62 F7 Hohe Tauern mts Austria
61 E4 Hohe Venn moorland
    Belgium
85 G2 Hoh Xil Hu salt l. China
85 G2 Hoh Xil Shan mts China
95 D2 Hôi An Vietnam
102 D3 Hoima Uganda
89 B6 Hôi Xuân Vietnam
85 H4 Hojai India
91 C6 Hōjo Japan
117 D1 Hokianga Harbour
    in. N.Z.
117 C5 Hokitika N.Z.
90 H3 Hokkaidō i. Japan
81 K1 Hoktemberyan Armenia
55 L6 Hol Norway
55 N9 Holbæk Denmark
59 H5 Holbeach U.K.
116 C2 Holborne I. i. Austr.
35 G4 Holbrook U.S.A.
30 B3 Holcombe Flowage
    resr U.S.A.

21 G4 Holden Can.
35 F2 Holden U.S.A.
27 D5 Holdenville U.S.A.
26 D3 Holdrege U.S.A.
37 J4 Holguín Cuba
55 N6 Höljes Sweden
30 D4 Holland U.S.A.
119 B2 Hollick-Kenyon
    Peninsula pen. Antarctica
32 D4 Hollidaysburg U.S.A.
20 C3 Hollis AK U.S.A.
27 D5 Hollis OK U.S.A.
34 B3 Hollister U.S.A.
31 F4 Holly U.S.A.
27 F5 Holly Springs U.S.A.
29 D7 Hollywood U.S.A.
54 N4 Holm Norway
116 B1 Holmes Reef rf
    Coral Sea Is Terr.
55 M7 Holmestrand Norway
54 R5 Holmön i. Sweden
54 R5 Holmsund Sweden
104 B3 Holoog Namibia
55 L8 Holstebro Denmark
29 D4 Holston r. U.S.A.
32 C6 Holston Lake l. U.S.A.
59 C7 Holsworthy U.K.
59 J5 Holt U.K.
30 E4 Holt U.S.A.
26 E4 Holton U.S.A.
60 D5 Holycross Rep. of Ireland
59 C4 Holyhead U.K.
59 C4 Holyhead Bay b. U.K.
58 F2 Holy Island i. Eng. U.K.
59 C4 Holy Island i. Wales U.K.
33 G3 Holyoke CT U.S.A.
59 D4 Holywell U.K.
62 E7 Holzkirchen Ger.
100 B3 Hombori Mali
61 F5 Homburg Ger.
118 A3 Home Bay b. Can.
116 B2 Home Hill Austr.
27 E5 Homer U.S.A.
29 D6 Homerville U.S.A.
116 A3 Homestead Austr.
29 D7 Homestead U.S.A.
29 C5 Homewood U.S.A.
94 C4 Homonhon Island i. Phil.
    Homs see Ḩimş
69 D4 Homyel' Belarus
45 B3 Honda Col.
94 A4 Honda Bay b. Phil.
35 H4 Hon Dah U.S.A.
104 B5 Hondeklipbaai S. Africa
88 C1 Hondlon Ju China
27 D6 Hondo U.S.A.
61 E1 Hondsrug reg. Neth.
16 Honduras country
    Central America
55 M6 Hønefoss Norway
33 F4 Honesdale U.S.A.
34 B1 Honey Lake l. U.S.A.
33 E3 Honeyoye Lake l. U.S.A.
64 E2 Honfleur France
89 C6 Hong, Mouths of the
    est. Vietnam
89 C6 Hông, Sông r. Vietnam
88 E4 Hong'an China
89 C6 Hông Gai Vietnam
89 E6 Honghai Wan b. China
89 B6 Honghe China
88 E3 Hong He r. China
89 D4 Honghu China
89 C5 Hongjiang China
89 □ Hong Kong China
89 □ Hong Kong aut. reg.
    China
89 □ Hong Kong Island i.
    China
88 C2 Hongliu r. China
88 B2 Hongliuyuan China
95 C3 Hông Ngư Vietnam
88 B2 Hongshansi China
89 D6 Hongshui He r. China
88 D2 Hongtong China
23 G4 Honguedo, Détroit d'
    chan. Can.
88 B3 Hongyuan China
88 F3 Hongze China
88 F3 Hongze Hu l. China
111 F2 Honiara Solomon Is
59 D7 Honiton U.K.
90 G5 Honjō Japan
55 S6 Honkajoki Fin.
95 C3 Hon Khoai i. Vietnam
95 D2 Hon Lơn i. Vietnam
95 C1 Hon Mê i. Vietnam
54 T1 Honningsvåg Norway
34 □2 Honokaa U.S.A.
34 □2 Honolulu U.S.A.
95 C3 Hon Rai i. Vietnam
91 C7 Honshū i. Japan
24 B2 Hood, Mt vol. U.S.A.
112 C6 Hood Pt pt Austr.
61 E2 Hoogeveen Neth.
61 E1 Hoogezand-Sappemeer
    Neth.
27 C4 Hooker U.S.A.
60 E5 Hook Head hd
    Rep. of Ireland
116 C3 Hook Island i. Austr.
    Hook of Holland see
    Hoek van Holland
116 E5 Hook Point pt Austr.
116 C2 Hook Reef rf Austr.
20 B3 Hoonah U.S.A.
77 V3 Hooper Bay Alaska
33 E5 Hooper I. i. U.S.A.
30 D5 Hoopeston U.S.A.
105 F3 Hoopstad S. Africa
55 N9 Höör Sweden
61 D2 Hoorn Neth.
111 J3 Hoorn, Îles de is
    Wallis and Futuna Islands

33 G3 Hoosick U.S.A.
35 E3 Hoover Dam *dam* U.S.A.
32 B4 Hoover Memorial Reservoir *resr* U.S.A.
81 H1 Hopa Turkey
33 F4 Hop Bottom U.S.A.
20 E5 Hope Can.
117 D5 Hope *r.* N.Z.
27 C5 Hope AR U.S.A.
35 F5 Hope AZ U.S.A.
114 C2 Hope, L. *salt flat* Austr.
23 J2 Hopedale Can.
104 C6 Hopefield S. Africa
23 H3 Hope Mountains *mts* Can.
76 D2 Hopen *i.* Svalbard
117 D4 Hope Saddle *pass* N.Z.
23 G2 Hopes Advance, Baie *b.* Can.
114 E5 Hopetoun Austr.
104 F4 Hopetown S. Africa
32 E6 Hopewell U.S.A.
22 E2 Hopewell Islands *is* Can.
112 E4 Hopkins, L. *salt flat* Austr.
28 C4 Hopkinsville U.S.A.
34 A2 Hopland U.S.A.
24 B2 Hoquiam U.S.A.
88 A3 Hor China
81 L2 Horadiz Azer.
81 J1 Horasan Turkey
55 N9 Hörby Sweden
88 B1 Hörh Uul *mts* Mongolia
30 C4 Horicon U.S.A.
88 D1 Horinger China
111 J4 Horizon Deep *depth* Pac. Oc.
68 D4 Horki Belarus
119 B4 Horlick Mts *mts* Antarctica
69 F5 Horlivka Ukr.
79 H4 Hormuz, Strait of *str.* Iran/Oman
62 G6 Horn Austria
20 F2 Horn *r.* Can.
54 B3 Horn *c.* Iceland
44 C9 Horn, Cape *c.* Chile
54 B3 Hornavan *l.* Sweden
27 E6 Hornbeck U.S.A.
59 G4 Horncastle U.K.
55 P6 Horndal Sweden
54 Q5 Hörnefors Sweden
32 E3 Hornell U.S.A.
22 D4 Hornepayne Can.
29 B6 Horn I. *i.* U.S.A.
104 B1 Hornkranz Namibia
47 B4 Hornopiren, V. *vol.* Chile
Hornos, Cabo de *c.* see Horn, Cape
115 J4 Hornsby Austr.
58 G4 Hornsea U.K.
55 P6 Hornslandet *pen.* Sweden
63 M6 Horodenka Ukr.
69 D5 Horodnya Ukr.
69 C5 Horodok Khmel'nyts'kyy Ukr.
69 B5 Horodok L'viv Ukr.
90 H2 Horokanai Japan
63 M5 Horokhiv Ukr.
90 H3 Horoshiri-dake *mt* Japan
88 F1 Horqin Shadi *reg.* China
Horqin Youyi Qianqi see Ulanhot
Horqin Zuoyi Houqi see Ganjig
59 C7 Horrabridge U.K.
85 G3 Horru China
20 E4 Horsefly Can.
32 E3 Horseheads U.S.A.
23 J3 Horse Is *is* Can.
60 C4 Horseleap Rep. of Ireland
55 L9 Horsens Denmark
24 C3 Horseshoe Bend U.S.A.
114 E6 Horsham Austr.
59 G6 Horsham U.K.
55 M7 Horten Norway
31 F1 Horwood Lake *l.* Can.
63 N5 Horyn' *r.* Ukr.
85 H2 Ho Sai Hu *l.* China
102 D3 Hosa'ina Eth.
81 L4 Hoseynābād Iran
81 M6 Hoseynīyeh Iran
84 D5 Hoshangabad India
84 C3 Hoshiarpur India
83 E7 Hospet India
60 C5 Hospital Rep. of Ireland
47 F1 Hospital, Cuchilla del *h.* Uru.
44 C9 Hoste, I. *i.* Chile
54 O5 Hotagen *l.* Sweden
82 F3 Hotan China
104 E3 Hotazel S. Africa
35 G4 Hotevilla U.S.A.
115 G6 Hotham, Mt *mt* Austr.
54 P4 Hoting Sweden
27 E5 Hot Springs AR U.S.A.
26 C3 Hot Springs SD U.S.A.
20 F1 Hottah Lake *l.* Can.
61 D4 Houffalize Belgium
95 □ Hougang Sing.
116 B2 Houghton *r.* Austr.
30 C2 Houghton U.S.A.
30 D3 Houghton Lake U.S.A.
30 D3 Houghton Lake *l.* U.S.A.
58 F3 Houghton le Spring U.K.
33 K1 Houlton U.S.A.
88 D3 Houma China
27 F6 Houma U.S.A.
57 C2 Hourn, Loch *in.* U.K.
33 G3 Housatonic U.S.A.
35 F2 House Range *mts* U.S.A.

20 D4 Houston Can.
27 F4 Houston MO U.S.A.
27 F5 Houston MS U.S.A.
27 E6 Houston TX U.S.A.
105 H1 Hout *r.* S. Africa
112 B5 Houtman Abrolhos *is* Austr.
57 E2 Houton U.K.
104 E5 Houwater S. Africa
86 F2 Hovd Mongolia
59 G7 Hove U.K.
59 J5 Hoveton U.K.
81 M6 Hoveyzeh Iran
55 O8 Hovmantorp Sweden
88 C1 Hövsgöl Mongolia
86 H1 Hövsgöl Nuur *l.* Mongolia
86 H3 Höviiün Mongolia
101 E3 Howar, Wadi *watercourse* Sudan
116 B5 Howard Austr.
30 E4 Howard City U.S.A.
21 H2 Howard Lake *l.* Can.
58 G4 Howden U.K.
115 H6 Howe, C. *hd* Austr.
31 F4 Howell U.S.A.
26 C2 Howes U.S.A.
33 G2 Howick Can.
105 J4 Howick S. Africa
114 C1 Howitt, L. *salt flat* Austr.
115 G6 Howitt, Mt *mt* Austr.
33 J2 Howland U.S.A.
14 H5 Howland I. Pac. Oc.
115 H3 Howlong Austr.
60 E4 Howth Rep. of Ireland
62 D5 Höxter Ger.
57 E2 Hoy *i.* U.K.
55 K6 Høyanger Norway
62 G5 Hoyerswerda Ger.
54 N4 Høylandet Norway
54 V5 Höytiäinen *l.* Fin.
81 G2 Hozat Turkey
62 G5 Hradec Králové Czech Rep.
67 H3 Hrasnica Bos.-Herz.
81 K1 Hrazdan Armenia
69 E5 Hrebinka Ukr.
68 B4 Hrodna Belarus
89 F5 Hsinchu Taiwan
83 J6 Hsipaw Myanmar
89 F6 Hsiyüp'ing Yü *i.* Taiwan
89 F5 Hsüeh Shan *mt* Taiwan
89 E5 Hua'an China
45 D4 Huachamacari, Cerro *mt* Venez.
88 C2 Huachi China
42 C6 Huacho Peru
90 B1 Huachuan China
35 G6 Huachuca City U.S.A.
47 C1 Huaco Arg.
88 D1 Huade China
87 N3 Huadian China
89 D6 Huadu China
95 A2 Hua Hin Thai.
88 E1 Huai'an Hebei China
88 F3 Huai'an Jiangsu China
88 E3 Huaibei China
88 E3 Huaibin China
88 B3 Huai He *r.* China
89 C5 Huaihua China
89 D6 Huaiji China
88 E1 Huailai China
88 B7 Huai Luang *r.* Thai.
88 E3 Huainan China
89 E4 Huaining China
88 D2 Huairen China
88 E3 Huaiyang China
88 B3 Huaiyin Jiangsu China
88 F3 Huaiyin China
88 E3 Huaiyuan Anhui China
89 C5 Huaiyuan Guangxi China
88 B3 Huajialing China
93 H8 Huaki Indon.
35 F4 Hualapai Peak summit U.S.A.
89 F5 Hualien Taiwan
42 C5 Huallaga *r.* Peru
88 B2 Huancheng China
103 B5 Huambo Angola
90 B1 Huanan China
47 C4 Huancache, Sa *mts* Arg.
42 C6 Huancayo Peru
88 E2 Huangbizhuang Sk. *resr* China
88 A2 Huangcheng China
88 B3 Huangchuan China
89 E4 Huanggang China
Huang Hai sea see Yellow Sea
88 E2 Huanghe Kou *est.* China
85 H2 Huanghetan China
88 E2 Huanghua China
88 C3 Huangling China
89 C7 Huanglu China
89 E4 Huangmei China
89 E4 Huangpi China
89 C5 Huangping China
88 D1 Huangqi Hai *l.* China
89 H4 Huangshan China
89 E4 Huangshi China
88 B2 Huangtu Gaoyuan *plat.* China
88 F2 Huangxian China
89 F4 Huangyan China
88 A2 Huangyuan China
89 C5 Huanjiang China
88 C2 Huan Jiang *r.* China
88 F2 Huantai China
42 C6 Huánuco Peru
42 F7 Huanuni Bol.
88 C2 Huanxian China
89 G5 Huap'ing Yü *i.* China
42 C5 Huaráz Peru

42 C6 Huarmey Peru
89 D4 Huarong China
42 C5 Huascarán, Nevado de *mt* Peru
44 B3 Huasco Chile
44 B3 Huasco *r.* Chile
36 C3 Huatabampo Mex.
88 C3 Huating China
88 B3 Huaxian China
89 C4 Huayang China
Huayuan see Xiaochang
89 C4 Huayuan China
89 D6 Huazhou China
20 B2 Hubbard, Mt *mt* Can./U.S.A.
23 G2 Hubbard, Pointe *hd* Can.
31 F3 Hubbard Lake *l.* U.S.A.
88 D4 Hubei *div.* China
83 E7 Hubli India
61 E3 Hückelhoven Ger.
59 F4 Hucknall U.K.
58 F4 Huddersfield U.K.
32 B6 Huddy U.S.A.
55 P6 Hudiksvall Sweden
30 C5 Hudson MI U.S.A.
33 G3 Hudson NY U.S.A.
30 A3 Hudson WV U.S.A.
28 F3 Hudson *r.* U.S.A.
21 J4 Hudson Bay Can.
22 C2 Hudson Bay *sea* Can.
33 G3 Hudson Falls U.S.A.
119 A3 Hudson Mts *mts* Antarctica
20 E3 Hudson's Hope Can.
118 E2 Hudson Strait *str.* Can.
95 C1 Huê Vietnam
47 A4 Huechucuicui, Pta *pt* Chile
36 F5 Huehuetenango Guatemala
65 C4 Huelva Spain
81 B1 Huentelauquén Chile
47 B4 Huequi, Volcán *vol.* Chile
65 H4 Huércal-Overa Spain
65 F1 Huesca Spain
65 E3 Huéscar Spain
116 A3 Hughenden Austr.
32 E4 Hughesville U.S.A.
85 F5 Hugli *est.* India
85 G5 Hugli-Chunchura India
27 C5 Hugo U.S.A.
27 C4 Hugoton U.S.A.
88 D1 Huguan China
88 D1 Huhhot China
104 F3 Huhudi S. Africa
89 F5 Hui'an China
88 C2 Hui'anpu China
117 E3 Huiarau Range *mts* N.Z.
104 B3 Huib-Hoch Plateau *plat.* Namibia
89 E5 Huichang China
87 N3 Huich'ŏn N. Korea
89 C6 Huidong Guangdong China
89 B5 Huidong Sichuan China
61 C3 Huijbergen Neth.
89 B5 Huiji *r.* China
45 B4 Huila, Nevado de *mt* Col.
89 C5 Huilai China
89 B5 Huili China
88 E2 Huimin China
89 E4 Huinan China
44 C2 Huinahuaca Arg.
87 N3 Huinan China
47 D2 Huinca Renancó Arg.
88 B3 Huining China
89 C5 Huishui China
85 G2 Huiten Nur *l.* China
89 E5 Huitong China
55 S6 Huittinen Fin.
88 C3 Huixian Gansu China
88 D3 Huixian Henan China
36 F5 Huixtla Mex.
89 B5 Huize China
89 E6 Huizhou China
86 H2 Hujirt Mongolia
89 A4 Hukou China
104 D1 Hukuntsi Botswana
30 E2 Hulbert Lake *l.* U.S.A.
81 L5 Hulilan Iran
90 C2 Hulin China
31 K3 Hull Can.
55 O8 Hultsfred Sweden
88 F1 Huludao China
87 N2 Hulun Nur *l.* China
69 F6 Hulyaypole Ukr.
87 N1 Huma China
42 E5 Humaitá Brazil
104 F7 Humansdorp S. Africa
58 H4 Humber, Mouth of the *est.* U.K.
21 H4 Humboldt Can.
24 D3 Humboldt *r.* U.S.A.
24 A3 Humboldt Bay *b.* U.S.A.
34 C1 Humboldt Lake *l.* U.S.A.
34 C1 Humboldt Range *mts* U.S.A.
34 D2 Humbolt Salt Marsh *marsh* U.S.A.
115 F1 Humeburn Austr.
89 D6 Hu Men *chan.* China
63 K6 Humenné Slovakia
115 G6 Hume Reservoir *resr* Austr.
34 C4 Humphreys, Mt *mt* U.S.A.
35 G4 Humphreys Peak *summit* U.S.A.
88 G1 Hun *r.* China
54 C4 Húnaflói *b.* Iceland
89 D5 Hunan *div.* China
87 O3 Hunchun China
90 B1 Hunchun *r.* China
55 M9 Hundested Denmark
67 K2 Hunedoara Romania

48 Hungary *country* Europe
114 F2 Hungerford Austr.
89 □ Hung Fa Leng *h.* China
87 N4 Hŭngnam N. Korea
24 D1 Hungry Horse Res. *resr* U.S.A.
89 □ Hung Shui Kiu China
89 C6 Hung Yên Vietnam
57 B3 Hunish, Rubha *pt* U.K.
104 B3 Huns Mountains *mts* Namibia
61 F5 Hunsrück *reg.* Ger.
59 H5 Hunstanton U.K.
35 H4 Hunt U.S.A.
62 D4 Hunte *r.* Ger.
115 J4 Hunter *r.* Austr.
33 F3 Hunter U.S.A.
115 F8 Hunter I. *i.* Austr.
20 D4 Hunter I. *i.* Can.
111 H4 Hunter I. *i.* New Caledonia
115 F8 Hunter Is *is* Austr.
85 H6 Hunter's Bay *b.* Myanmar
33 F2 Huntingdon Can.
59 G5 Huntingdon U.K.
32 E4 Huntingdon U.S.A.
30 E5 Huntington IN U.S.A.
35 G2 Huntington UT U.S.A.
32 B5 Huntington WV U.S.A.
34 Huntington Beach U.S.A.
117 E2 Huntly N.Z.
57 F3 Huntly U.K.
114 B2 Hunt Pen. *ridge* Austr.
31 H3 Huntsville Can.
29 C5 Huntsville AL U.S.A.
27 E6 Huntsville TX U.S.A.
88 D2 Hunyuan China
84 C1 Hunza Pak.
84 C2 Hunza *r.* Pak.
95 C1 Hương Khê Vietnam
95 C1 Hương Thuy Vietnam
110 E2 Huon Peninsula *pen.* P.N.G.
115 G9 Huonville Austr.
88 E4 Huoqiu China
88 E4 Huoshan China
88 E4 Huo Shan *mt* China
88 D2 Huozhou China
31 G3 Hurd, Cape *hd* Can.
88 F1 Hure China
88 F1 Hure Jadgai China
78 C4 Hurghada Egypt
30 C1 Hurkett Can.
60 C5 Hurler's Cross Rep. of Ireland
30 B2 Hurley U.S.A.
26 D2 Huron U.S.A.
31 H3 Huron, Lake *l.* Can./U.S.A.
30 D2 Huron Bay *b.* U.S.A.
30 D2 Huron Mts *h.* U.S.A.
35 F3 Hurricane U.S.A.
59 F6 Hursley U.K.
59 H6 Hurst Green U.K.
117 D5 Hurunui *r.* N.Z.
54 E3 Húsavík Norðurland eystra Iceland
54 C4 Húsavík Vestfirðir Iceland
55 O7 Huşi Romania
55 O8 Huskvarna Sweden
55 J7 Husnes Norway
85 H4 Hussainabad India
62 D3 Husum Ger.
54 Q5 Husum Sweden
86 H2 Hutag Mongolia
26 D4 Hutchinson U.S.A.
35 G4 Hutch Mtn *mt* U.S.A.
95 A1 Huthi Myanmar
90 C2 Hutou China
21 N2 Hut Point *pt* Can.
116 C5 Hutton, Mt *h.* Austr.
32 D5 Huttonsville U.S.A.
88 D2 Hutuo *r.* China
83 D10 Huvadhu Atoll *atoll* Maldives
Hüvek see Bozova
88 C3 Huxian China
61 D4 Huy Belgium
88 F4 Huzhou China
88 A2 Huzhu China
54 E4 Hvannadalshnúkur *mt* Iceland
66 G3 Hvar *i.* Croatia
69 E6 Hvardiys'ke Ukr.
54 C4 Hveragerði Iceland
55 L8 Hvide Sande Denmark
54 C4 Hvíta *r.* Iceland
103 C5 Hwange Zimbabwe
103 C5 Hwange National Park *nat. park* Zimbabwe
103 D5 Hwedza Zimbabwe
33 H4 Hyannis MA U.S.A.
26 C3 Hyannis NE U.S.A.
86 F2 Hyargas Nuur *salt l.* Mongolia
20 D4 Hydaburg U.S.A.
117 C6 Hyde N.Z.
112 C6 Hyden Austr.
32 B6 Hyden U.S.A.
33 G4 Hyde Park U.S.A.
35 F5 Hyder U.S.A.
83 E7 Hyderabad India
84 B4 Hyderabad Pak.
64 H5 Hyères France
64 H5 Hyères, Îles d' *is* France
87 N3 Hyesan N. Korea
20 D2 Hyland *r.* Can.
115 K3 Hyland, Mount *mt* Austr.
55 J6 Hyllestad Norway
55 N8 Hyltebruk Sweden
114 D6 Hyland Austr.
91 D7 Hyōno-sen *mt* Japan
54 V4 Hyrynsalmi Fin.
20 F3 Hythe Can.

59 J6 Hythe U.K.
91 B8 Hyūga Japan
55 T6 Hyvinkää Fin.

I

42 E6 Iaco *r.* Brazil
43 K6 Iaçu Brazil
103 E6 Iakora Madag.
67 M2 Ialomiţa *r.* Romania
67 M2 Ianca Romania
63 N7 Iaşi Romania
94 A3 Iba Phil.
100 C4 Ibadan Nigeria
45 B3 Ibagué Col.
35 F1 Ibapah U.S.A.
42 C3 Ibarra Ecuador
78 E7 Ibb Yemen
44 E3 Iberá, Esteros de *marsh* Arg.
95 A4 Ibi Indon.
100 C4 Ibi Nigeria
46 C2 Ibiá Brazil
43 K4 Ibiapaba, Serra da *h.* Brazil
47 F1 Ibicuí da Cruz *r.* Brazil
46 E2 Ibiraçu Brazil
65 G3 Ibiza Spain
65 G3 Ibiza *i.* Spain
66 F6 Iblei, Monti *mts* Italy
43 K6 Ibotirama Brazil
79 H5 Ibrā' Oman
79 H5 Ibrī Oman
94 B1 Ibuhos *i.* Phil.
91 B9 Ibusuki Japan
42 C6 Ica Peru
42 C6 Ica *r.* Peru
45 D4 Içana Brazil
45 D4 Içana *r.* Brazil
35 E3 Iceberg Canyon U.S.A.
80 E3 İçel Turkey
48 Iceland *country* Europe
90 H3 Ichinoseki Japan
77 R4 Ichinskiy, Vulkan *mt* Rus. Fed.
69 E5 Ichnya Ukr.
20 B3 Icy Pt *pt* U.S.A.
20 B3 Icy Strait *chan.* U.S.A.
27 E5 Idabel U.S.A.
24 D2 Idaho *div.* U.S.A.
24 D3 Idaho City U.S.A.
24 D3 Idaho Falls U.S.A.
62 C6 Idar-Oberstein Ger.
61 F5 Idarwald *forest* Ger.
78 C5 Idfu Egypt
100 D3 Idhān Awbārī *des.* Libya
101 D2 Idhān Murzūq *des.* Libya
102 B4 Idiofa Dem. Rep. Congo
54 S2 Idivuoma Sweden
80 C6 Idku Egypt
80 F4 Idlib Syria
55 N6 Idre Sweden
105 H6 Idutywa S. Africa
55 T8 Iecava Latvia
46 B3 Iepê Brazil
61 A4 Ieper Belgium
67 L7 Ierapetra Greece
103 D4 Ifakara Tanz.
103 E6 Ifanadiana Madag.
100 C4 Ife Nigeria
54 U1 Ifjord Norway
100 C3 Ifôghas, Adrar des *reg.* Mali
92 E6 Igan Malaysia
46 C3 Igarapava Brazil
76 K3 Igarka Rus. Fed.
84 C6 Igatpuri India
81 K2 Iğdır Turkey
55 P6 Iggesund Sweden
66 C5 Iglesias Italy
22 B4 Ignace Can.
55 U9 Ignalina Lith.
69 C7 İğneada Turkey
67 N4 İğneada Burnu *pt* Turkey
63 Q3 Igorevskaya Rus. Fed.
67 J5 Igoumenitsa Greece
76 H3 Igrim Rus. Fed.
46 B4 Iguaçu *r.* Brazil
46 A4 Iguaçu Falls *waterfall* Arg./Brazil
46 E1 Iguaí Brazil
45 B4 Iguaje, Mesa de *h.* Col.
36 E5 Iguala Mex.
65 G2 Igualada Spain
46 C3 Iguape Brazil
46 B3 Iguaraçé Brazil
46 A3 Iguatemi Brazil
46 A3 Iguatemi *r.* Brazil
43 L5 Iguatu Brazil
Iguazú, Cataratas do *waterfall* see Iguaçu Falls
102 A4 Iguéla Gabon
102 D4 Igunga Tanz.
103 E6 Iharaña Madag.
86 J3 Ihbulag Mongolia
103 E6 Ihosy Madag.
88 G1 Ih Tal China
91 F6 Iide-san *mt* Japan
54 U2 Iijärvi *l.* Fin.
54 T4 Iijoki *r.* Fin.
54 U5 Iisalmi Fin.
91 B8 Iizuka Japan
100 C4 Ijebu-Ode Nigeria
81 K1 Ijevan Armenia
61 C2 IJmuiden Neth.
61 C2 IJssel *r.* Neth.
61 D2 IJsselmeer *l.* Neth.
55 S6 Ikaalinen Fin.
105 G2 Ikageleng S. Africa
105 G3 Ikageng S. Africa
67 M6 Ikaria *i.* Greece

55 L8 Ikast Denmark
90 H3 Ikeda Japan
102 C4 Ikela Dem. Rep. Congo
67 K3 Ikhtiman Bulg.
104 F4 Ikhutseng S. Africa
91 A8 Iki *i.* Japan
69 H6 Iki-Burul Rus. Fed.
100 C4 Ikom Nigeria
103 E6 Ikongo Madag.
69 H6 Ikryanoye Rus. Fed.
102 D4 Ikungu Tanz.
94 B2 Ilagan Phil.
102 D3 Ilaisamis Kenya
81 L5 Īlām Iran
85 F4 Ilam Nepal
100 C4 Ilaro Nigeria
63 J4 Iława Pol.
21 H3 Île-à-la-Crosse Can.
21 H3 Île-à-la-Crosse, Lac *l.* Can.
102 C4 Ilebo Dem. Rep. Congo
102 D3 Ileret Kenya
68 G2 Ileza Rus. Fed.
21 K3 Ilford Can.
59 H6 Ilford U.K.
116 A4 Ilfracombe Austr.
59 C6 Ilfracombe U.K.
80 D1 Ilgaz Turkey
80 D1 Ilgaz D. *mts* Turkey
80 C2 Ilgın Turkey
45 D5 Ilha Grande Brazil
46 D3 Ilha Grande, Baía da *b.* Brazil
46 B3 Ilha Grande, Represa *resr* Brazil
46 B3 Ilha Solteira, Represa *resr* Brazil
65 B2 Ílhavo Port.
46 E1 Ilhéus Brazil
118 A4 Iliamna Lake *l.* U.S.A.
80 C2 İliç Turkey
94 C4 Iligan Phil.
94 C4 Iligan Bay *b.* Phil.
68 H2 Il'insko-Podomskoye Rus. Fed.
33 F3 Ilion U.S.A.
59 F5 Ilkeston U.K.
58 F4 Ilkley U.K.
94 B5 Illana Bay *b.* Phil.
47 B1 Illapel Chile
47 B1 Illapel *r.* Chile
69 D6 Illichivs'k Ukr.
42 E7 Illimani, Nevado de *mt* Bol.
30 C5 Illinois *div.* U.S.A.
30 C5 Illinois *r.* U.S.A.
30 B5 Illinois and Mississippi Canal *canal* U.S.A.
69 D5 Illintsi Ukr.
100 C2 Illizi Alg.
54 S5 Ilmajoki Fin.
68 D3 Il'men', Ozero *l.* Rus. Fed.
59 E7 Ilminster U.K.
42 D7 Ilo Peru
94 A4 Iloc *i.* Phil.
94 B4 Iloilo Phil.
54 W5 Ilomantsi Fin.
100 C4 Ilorin Nigeria
69 F6 Ilovays'k Ukr.
69 G5 Ilovlya Rus. Fed.
69 H5 Ilovlya *r.* Rus. Fed.
115 K2 Iluka Austr.
91 C7 Imabari Japan
91 F6 Imaichi Japan
81 K6 Imām al Ḥamzah Iraq
80 E3 İmamOğlu Turkey
81 K5 Imām Ḥamīd Iraq
90 D2 Iman *r.* Rus. Fed.
91 A8 Imari Japan
45 E2 Imataca, Serranía de *mts* Venez.
55 V6 Imatra Fin.
91 E7 Imazu Japan
44 G3 Imbituba Brazil
46 B4 Imbituva Brazil
68 G3 imeni Babushkina Rus. Fed.
102 E3 Īmī Eth.
81 M2 İmişli Azer.
66 D2 Imola Italy
105 H4 Impendle S. Africa
43 J5 Imperatriz Brazil
66 C3 Imperia Italy
26 C3 Imperial U.S.A.
34 D5 Imperial Beach U.S.A.
35 E5 Imperial Valley *v.* U.S.A.
102 B3 Impfondo Congo
85 H4 Imphal India
67 L4 İmroz Turkey
80 F5 Imtān Syria
36 F5 Imuris Mex.
25 E6 Imuris Mex.
94 A4 Imuruan Bay *b.* Phil.
91 E7 Ina Japan
42 F6 Inambari *r.* Peru
100 C2 In Aménas Alg.
117 C6 Inangahua Junction N.Z.
93 J7 Inanwatan Indon.
54 U2 Inari Fin.
54 U2 Inarijärvi *l.* Fin.
54 T2 Inarijoki *r.* Fin./Norway
65 H3 Inca Spain
69 E7 İnce Burnu *pt* Turkey
69 C7 İnce Burnu *pt* Turkey
80 D3 İncekum Burnu *pt* Turkey
80 E2 İncesu Turkey
60 E5 Inch Rep. of Ireland
57 C2 Inchard, Loch *b.* U.K.
57 E4 Inchkeith *i.* U.K.
87 N4 Inch'ŏn S. Korea
105 K2 Incomati *r.* Moz.
57 B5 Indaal, Loch *in.* U.K.
46 D2 Indaiá *r.* Brazil
46 B2 Indaiá Grande *r.* Brazil

54 P5 Indalsälven r. Sweden
55 J6 Indalstø Norway
34 C3 Independence CA U.S.A.
30 B4 Independence IA U.S.A.
27 E4 Independence KS U.S.A.
30 A2 Independence MN U.S.A.
26 E4 Independence MO U.S.A.
32 C6 Independence VA U.S.A.
30 B3 Independence WV U.S.A.
24 C3 Independence Mts mts U.S.A.
76 G5 Inderborskiy Kazak.
70 India country Asia
30 D2 Indian r. U.S.A.
32 D4 Indiana U.S.A.
30 D5 Indiana div. U.S.A.
30 D5 Indiana Dunes National Lakeshore res. U.S.A.
13 O7 Indian-Antarctic Ridge sea feature Pac. Oc.
30 D6 Indianapolis U.S.A.
Indian Desert des. see Thar Desert
23 J3 Indian Harbour Can.
33 F3 Indian Lake U.S.A.
30 D3 Indian Lake l. MI U.S.A.
32 B4 Indian Lake l. OH U.S.A.
32 D4 Indian Lake l. PA U.S.A.
5 Indian Ocean
26 E3 Indianola IA U.S.A.
27 F5 Indianola MS U.S.A.
35 F2 Indian Peak summit U.S.A.
30 E3 Indian River U.S.A.
35 E3 Indian Springs U.S.A.
35 G4 Indian Wells U.S.A.
77 Q2 Indigirka r. Rus. Fed.
67 J2 Inđija Yugo.
20 F2 Indin Lake l. Can.
34 D5 Indio U.S.A.
111 G3 Indispensable Reefs rf Solomon Is
71 Indonesia country Asia
84 C5 Indore India
92 □ Indramayu, Tanjung pt Indon.
64 E3 Indre r. France
Indur see Nizamabad
84 B4 Indus r. Pak.
84 A5 Indus, Mouths of the est. Pak.
105 G5 Indwe S. Africa
69 E7 İnebolu Turkey
80 B1 İnegöl Turkey
32 B6 Inez U.S.A.
104 D7 Infanta, Cape hd S. Africa
36 D5 Infiernillo, Presa l. Mex.
95 B1 Ing, Mae Nam r. Thai.
30 C3 Ingalls U.S.A.
34 B2 Ingalls, Mt mt U.S.A.
21 J2 Ingalls Lake l. Can.
47 C4 Ingeniero Jacobacci Arg.
31 G4 Ingersoll Can.
116 B2 Ingham Austr.
58 E3 Ingleborough h. U.K.
58 E3 Ingleton U.K.
115 J2 Inglewood Qld. Austr.
114 E6 Inglewood Vic. Austr.
59 H4 Ingoldmells U.K.
62 E6 Ingolstadt Ger.
23 H4 Ingonish Can.
85 G4 Ingrāj Bāzār India
21 G2 Ingray Lake l. Can.
100 C3 I-n-Guezzam Alg.
69 H7 Ingushskaya Respublika div. Rus. Fed.
105 K3 Ingwavuma S. Africa
105 K2 Inhaca Moz.
105 K3 Inhaca, Península pen. Moz.
103 D6 Inhambane Moz.
105 K1 Inhambane div. Moz.
103 D5 Inhaminga Moz.
46 B3 Inhanduízinho r. Brazil
46 D1 Inhaúmas Brazil
45 C4 Inírida r. Col.
60 A4 Inishark i. Rep. of Ireland
60 A4 Inishbofin i. Rep. of Ireland
60 A3 Inishkea North i. Rep. of Ireland
60 A3 Inishkea South i. Rep. of Ireland
60 B4 Inishmaan i. Rep. of Ireland
60 B4 Inishmore i. Rep. of Ireland
60 C3 Inishmurray i. Rep. of Ireland
60 D2 Inishowen pen. Rep. of Ireland
60 E2 Inishowen Head hd Rep. of Ireland
60 D2 Inishtrahull i. Rep. of Ireland
60 D2 Inishtrahull Sound chan. Rep. of Ireland
60 A4 Inishturk i. Rep. of Ireland
116 C5 Injune Austr.
113 H3 Inkerman Austr.
117 D5 Inland Kaikoura Range mts N.Z.
114 D1 Innamincka Austr.
54 O3 Inndyr Norway
Inner Mongolian Aut. Region div. see Nei Mongol Zizhiqu
57 C3 Inner Sound chan. U.K.
116 B1 Innisfail Austr.
62 E7 Innsbruck Austria
60 D4 Inny r. Rep. of Ireland
102 B4 Inongo Dem. Rep. Congo
62 J4 Inowrocław Pol.
100 C2 In Salah Alg.
68 H4 Insar Rus. Fed.
57 F3 Insch U.K.
112 B5 Inscription, C. c. Austr.
76 H3 Inta Rus. Fed.
47 D2 Intendente Alvear Arg.
62 C7 Interlaken Switz.
26 E1 International Falls U.S.A.
91 G7 Inubō-zaki pt Japan
22 E2 Inukjuak Can.
118 C2 Inuvik Can.
57 C4 Inveraray U.K.
57 F4 Inverbervie U.K.
117 B7 Invercargill N.Z.
115 J2 Inverell Austr.
57 D3 Invergordon U.K.
57 E4 Inverkeithing U.K.
23 H4 Inverness Can.
57 D3 Inverness U.K.
29 D6 Inverness U.S.A.
57 F3 Inverurie U.K.
114 B5 Investigator Strait chan. Austr.
86 E1 Inya Rus. Fed.
25 C5 Inyokern U.S.A.
34 C3 Inyo Mts mts U.S.A.
102 D4 Inyonga Tanz.
68 H4 Inza Rus. Fed.
69 G4 Inzhavino Rus. Fed.
67 J5 Ioannina Greece
93 L2 Iō-jima i. Japan
27 E4 Iola U.S.A.
57 B4 Iona i. U.K.
24 C1 Ione U.S.A.
30 E4 Ionia U.S.A.
67 H5 Ionian Islands is Greece
66 G6 Ionian Sea sea Greece/Italy
Ionoi Nisoi is see Ionian Islands
81 L1 Iori r. Georgia
67 L6 Ios i. Greece
91 B9 Iō-shima i. Japan
30 A4 Iowa div. U.S.A.
30 B5 Iowa r. U.S.A.
30 B5 Iowa City U.S.A.
26 E3 Iowa Falls U.S.A.
46 C2 Ipameri Brazil
42 D5 Iparía Peru
46 D2 Ipatinga Brazil
69 G6 Ipatovo Rus. Fed.
105 F3 Ipelegeng S. Africa
45 A4 Ipiales Col.
46 E1 Ipiaú Brazil
46 B4 Ipiranga Brazil
92 C6 Ipoh Malaysia
43 L5 Ipojuca r. Brazil
46 B2 Iporá Brazil
102 C3 Ippy C.A.R.
67 M4 İpsala Turkey
115 K1 Ipswich Austr.
59 J5 Ipswich U.K.
44 B2 Iquique Chile
42 D4 Iquitos Peru
91 E7 Irago-misaki pt Japan
67 L6 Irakleia i. Greece
Irakleio see Iraklion
67 L7 Iraklion Greece
46 E1 Iramaia Brazil
70 Iran country Asia
81 L3 Īrānshāh Iran
79 J4 Īrānshahr Iran
36 D4 Irapuato Mex.
70 Iraq country Asia
33 G2 Irasville U.S.A.
46 B4 Irati Brazil
80 E5 Irbid Jordan
76 H4 Irbit Rus. Fed.
43 K6 Irecê Brazil
48 Ireland, Republic of country Europe
102 C4 Irema Dem. Rep. Congo
76 H5 Irgiz Kazak.
93 K8 Irian Jaya div. Indon.
110 D2 Irian Jaya reg. Indon.
81 L2 Īrī Dagh mt Iran
94 B3 Iriga Phil.
100 B3 Irîgui reg. Mali/Maur.
103 D4 Iringa Tanz.
43 H4 Iriri r. Brazil
56 D5 Irish Sea sea Rep. of Ireland
43 J4 Irituia Brazil
86 H1 Irkutsk Rus. Fed.
80 D2 Irmak Turkey
114 B4 Iron Baron Austr.
31 F2 Iron Bridge Can.
32 E3 Irondequoit U.S.A.
114 B4 Iron Knob Austr.
30 C3 Iron Mountain U.S.A.
35 F3 Iron Mountain mt U.S.A.
30 C2 Iron River U.S.A.
27 F4 Ironton MO U.S.A.
32 B5 Ironton OH U.S.A.
30 B2 Ironwood U.S.A.
33 F2 Iroquois Can.
30 D5 Iroquois r. U.S.A.
94 C3 Irosin Phil.
91 F7 Irō-zaki pt Japan
69 D5 Irpin' Ukr.
83 J7 Irrawaddy r. China/Myanmar
83 H7 Irrawaddy, Mouths of the est. Myanmar
68 J2 Irta Rus. Fed.
58 E3 Irthing r. U.K.
86 C1 Irtysh r. Kazak./Rus. Fed.
102 C3 Irumu Dem. Rep. Congo
65 F1 Irún Spain
57 D5 Irvine U.K.
34 D5 Irvine CA U.S.A.
32 B6 Irvine KY U.S.A.
116 A1 Irvinebank Austr.
27 D5 Irving U.S.A.
116 C4 Isaac r. Austr.
94 B5 Isabela Phil.
42 □ Isabela, Isla i. Ecuador
37 G6 Isabelia, Cordillera mts Nic.
30 B2 Isabella U.S.A.
34 C4 Isabella Lake l. U.S.A.
30 D2 Isabelle, Pt pt U.S.A.
54 B3 Ísafjarðardjúp est. Iceland
54 B3 Ísafjörður Iceland
91 B8 Isahaya Japan
84 B2 Isà Khel Pak.
68 G1 Isakogorka Rus. Fed.
45 C4 Isana r. Col.
57 □ Isbister U.K.
66 E4 Ischia, Isola d' i. Italy
45 A4 Iscuande r. Col.
91 E7 Ise Japan
102 C3 Isengi Dem. Rep. Congo
64 H4 Isère r. France
61 F3 Iserlohn Ger.
66 F4 Isernia Italy
91 F6 Isesaki Japan
91 E7 Ise-shima National Park Japan
91 E7 Ise-wan b. Japan
100 C4 Iseyin Nigeria
Isfahan see Eşfahān
79 L1 Isfara Tajik.
81 K5 Ishāq Iraq
68 J4 Isheyevka Rus. Fed.
90 G3 Ishikari-gawa r. Japan
90 G3 Ishikari-wan b. Japan
90 G5 Ishinomaki Japan
90 G5 Ishinomaki-wan b. Japan
91 G6 Ishioka Japan
91 C8 Ishizuchi-san mt Japan
84 C1 Ishkuman Pak.
30 D2 Ishpeming U.S.A.
85 G4 Ishurdi Bangl.
42 E7 Isiboro Sécure, Parque Nacional nat. park Bol.
80 B2 Işıklı Turkey
80 B2 Işıklı Barajı resr Turkey
76 J4 Isil'kul' Rus. Fed.
105 J4 Isipingo S. Africa
102 C3 Isiro Dem. Rep. Congo
116 A5 Isisford Austr.
80 F3 İskenderun Turkey
80 E1 İskilip Turkey
76 K4 Iskitim Rus. Fed.
67 L3 Iskŭr r. Bulg.
20 C3 Iskut Can.
20 C3 Iskut r. Can.
80 F3 İslahiye Turkey
84 C2 Islamabad Pak.
84 C3 Islam Barrage barrage Pak.
84 B4 Islamgarh Pak.
84 B4 Islamkot Pak.
29 D7 Islamorada U.S.A.
94 A4 Island Bay b. Phil.
33 J1 Island Falls U.S.A.
21 L4 Island L. l. Can.
114 B3 Island Lagoon salt flat Austr.
21 L4 Island Lake Can.
30 A2 Island Lake l. U.S.A.
60 F3 Island Magee pen. U.K.
34 A1 Island Mountain U.S.A.
24 E2 Island Park U.S.A.
33 H2 Island Pond U.S.A.
117 E1 Islands, Bay of b. N.Z.
57 B5 Islay i. U.K.
32 E6 Isle of Wight U.S.A.
30 C2 Isle Royale National Park nat. park U.S.A.
78 C3 Ismâ'ilîya Egypt
81 M1 İsmayıllı Azer.
55 R5 Isojoki Fin.
103 D5 Isoka Zambia
54 U3 Isokylä Fin.
66 G5 Isola di Capo Rizzuto Italy
80 C3 Isparta Turkey
67 M3 Isperikh Bulg.
81 H1 İspir Turkey
70 Israel country Asia
68 H4 Issa Rus. Fed.
100 B4 Issia Côte d'Ivoire
81 K6 Issin Iraq
64 F4 Issoire France
81 J4 Iştablāt Iraq
80 B1 İstanbul Turkey
İstanbul Boğazı str. see Bosporus
81 M5 Īstgāh-e Eznā Iran
67 K5 Istiaia Greece
45 A3 Istmina Col.
29 D7 Istokpoga, L. l. U.S.A.
66 E2 Istra pen. Croatia
64 G5 Istres France
Istria pen. see Istra
85 G5 Iswaripur Bangl.
43 L6 Itabaianinha Brazil
43 K6 Itaberaba Brazil
46 D2 Itabira Brazil
46 D3 Itabirito Brazil
46 E1 Itabuna Brazil
43 G4 Itacoatiara Brazil
46 B3 Itaguajé Brazil
46 C3 Itaí Brazil
46 A4 Itaimbey r. Para.
43 G4 Itaituba Brazil
44 G3 Itajaí Brazil
46 D3 Itajubá Brazil
85 F5 Itaki India
42 F6 Italia, Laguna l. Bol.
48 Italy country Europe
43 L7 Itamaraju Brazil
46 D2 Itamarandiba Brazil
46 E2 Itambacuri Brazil
46 E2 Itambacuri r. Brazil
46 D2 Itambé, Pico de mt Brazil
103 E6 Itampolo Madag.
85 H4 Itanagar India
46 D1 Itanguari r. Brazil
46 C4 Itanhaém Brazil
46 E2 Itanhém Brazil
46 E2 Itanhém r. Brazil
46 E2 Itaobím Brazil
46 C2 Itapajipe Brazil
46 E1 Itaparica, Ilha i. Brazil
46 E1 Itapebi Brazil
46 E3 Itapemirim Brazil
46 E3 Itaperuna Brazil
46 E1 Itapetinga Brazil
46 C3 Itapetininga Brazil
46 C3 Itapeva Brazil
43 L6 Itapicuru r. Bahia Brazil
43 K5 Itapicuru r. Maranhão Brazil
43 K4 Itapicuru Mirim Brazil
43 L4 Itapipoca Brazil
46 C4 Itararé Brazil
46 C3 Itararé r. Brazil
84 D5 Itarsi India
46 B2 Itarumã Brazil
94 B1 Itbayat i. Phil.
20 G1 Itchen Lake l. Can.
45 B3 Ité r. Col.
67 K5 Itea Greece
30 E4 Ithaca MI U.S.A.
32 E3 Ithaca NY U.S.A.
80 F6 Ithrah Saudi Arabia
91 B8 Itihusa-yama mt Japan
102 C3 Itimbiri r. Dem. Rep. Congo
46 E2 Itinga Brazil
46 A2 Itiquira Brazil
46 A2 Itiquira r. Brazil
91 F7 Itō Japan
91 E6 Itoigawa Japan
66 C4 Ittiri Italy
46 C3 Itu Brazil
45 B3 Ituango Col.
42 D5 Itui r. Brazil
46 C2 Ituiutaba Brazil
102 C4 Itula Dem. Rep. Congo
46 C2 Itumbiara Brazil
43 G2 Ituni Guyana
43 J5 Itupiranga Brazil
46 B2 Iturama Brazil
46 A4 Iturbe Para.
77 Q5 Iturup, Ostrov i. Rus. Fed.
42 E5 Ituxi r. Brazil
62 D4 Itzehoe Ger.
45 C4 Iuaretê Brazil
77 V3 Iul'tin Rus. Fed.
45 C4 Iutica Brazil
46 B3 Ivaí r. Brazil
54 U2 Ivalo Fin.
54 U2 Ivalojoki r. Fin.
69 C4 Ivanava Belarus
114 F4 Ivanhoe Austr.
31 F1 Ivanhoe r. Can.
21 H2 Ivanhoe Lake l. N.W.T. Can.
31 F1 Ivanhoe Lake l. Ont. Can.
63 O5 Ivankiv Ukr.
69 C5 Ivano-Frankivs'k Ukr.
68 G3 Ivanovo Rus. Fed.
68 G3 Ivanovskaya Oblast' div. Rus. Fed.
35 E4 Ivanpah Lake l. U.S.A.
68 J4 Ivanteyevka Rus. Fed.
68 C4 Ivatsevichy Belarus
67 M4 Ivaylovgrad Bulg.
76 H3 Ivdel' Rus. Fed.
46 B3 Ivinheima Brazil
46 B3 Ivinheima r. Brazil
103 E6 Ivohibe Madag.
66 B2 Ivrea Italy
67 M5 İvrindi Turkey
69 H7 Ivris Ugheltekhili pass Georgia
63 N4 Ivyanyets Belarus
90 G5 Iwaizumi Japan
91 G6 Iwaki Japan
90 G4 Iwaki-san vol. Japan
91 C7 Iwakuni Japan
90 G3 Iwamizawa Japan
90 G5 Iwate-san vol. Japan
100 C4 Iwo Nigeria
Iwo Jima i. see Iō-jima
68 C4 Iwye Belarus
36 E4 Ixmiquilpán Mex.
105 J5 Ixopo S. Africa
59 H5 Ixworth U.K.
86 H1 Iya r. Rus. Fed.
91 C8 Iyo Japan
91 C8 Iyo-nada b. Japan
36 G5 Izabal, L. de l. Guatemala
90 G3 Izari-dake mt Japan
102 D4 Izazi Tanz.
69 H7 Izberbash Rus. Fed.
63 Q3 Izdeshkovo Rus. Fed.
76 G4 Izhevsk Rus. Fed.
76 G3 Izhma Rus. Fed.
68 K1 Izhma r. Rus. Fed.
69 F4 Izmalkovo Rus. Fed.
69 D6 Izmayil Ukr.
67 M5 İzmir Turkey
67 M5 İzmir Körfezi g. Turkey
80 B1 İznik Gölü l. Turkey
69 G6 Izobil'nyy Rus. Fed.
91 F7 Izu-hantō pen. Japan
91 A7 Izuhara Japan
91 D7 Izumisano Japan
91 C7 Izumo Japan
91 F7 Izu-shotō is Japan
69 C5 Izyaslav Ukr.
69 F5 Izyum Ukr.

J

Jabal, Bahr el r. see White Nile
65 E3 Jabalón r. Spain
84 D5 Jabalpur India
80 F3 Jabbūl Syria
112 F2 Jabiru Austr.
80 E4 Jablah Syria
66 G3 Jablanica Bos.-Herz.
43 M5 Jaboatão Brazil
46 C3 Jaboticabal Brazil
65 F1 Jaca Spain
43 K6 Jacaré r. Brazil
43 G5 Jacareacanga Brazil
46 C3 Jacareí Brazil
47 C1 Jáchal r. Arg.
46 E2 Jacinto Brazil
42 F5 Jaciparaná r. Brazil
30 D1 Jackfish Can.
31 H3 Jack Lake l. Can.
33 H2 Jackman U.S.A.
27 D5 Jacksboro U.S.A.
116 C6 Jackson Austr.
27 G6 Jackson AL U.S.A.
34 B2 Jackson CA U.S.A.
32 B6 Jackson KY U.S.A.
30 E4 Jackson MI U.S.A.
26 E3 Jackson MN U.S.A.
27 F4 Jackson MO U.S.A.
27 F5 Jackson MS U.S.A.
32 B5 Jackson OH U.S.A.
29 B5 Jackson TN U.S.A.
24 E3 Jackson WY U.S.A.
117 B5 Jackson Head hd N.Z.
24 E2 Jackson L. l. U.S.A.
30 D3 Jacksonport U.S.A.
27 E5 Jacksonville AR U.S.A.
29 D6 Jacksonville FL U.S.A.
30 B6 Jacksonville IL U.S.A.
29 E5 Jacksonville NC U.S.A.
27 E6 Jacksonville TX U.S.A.
29 D6 Jacksonville Beach U.S.A.
37 K5 Jacmel Haiti
84 B3 Jacobabad Pak.
43 K6 Jacobina Brazil
35 F3 Jacob Lake U.S.A.
104 F4 Jacobsdal S. Africa
23 H4 Jacques-Cartier, Détroit de chan. Can.
23 G4 Jacques Cartier, Mt mt Can.
23 G4 Jacquet River Can.
47 G1 Jacuí r. Brazil
43 L6 Jacuípe r. Brazil
43 J4 Jacunda Brazil
46 C4 Jacupiranga Brazil
45 C2 Jacura Venez.
66 G3 Jadovnik mt Bos.-Herz.
101 D1 Jādū Libya
42 C5 Jaén Peru
94 B3 Jaen Phil.
65 E4 Jaén Spain
81 M4 Ja'farābād Iran
Jaffa see Tel Aviv-Yafo
114 C6 Jaffa, C. pt Austr.
83 E9 Jaffna Sri Lanka
33 G3 Jaffrey U.S.A.
84 D3 Jagadhri India
83 F7 Jagdalpur India
105 F4 Jagersfontein S. Africa
84 D2 Jaggang China
Jagok Tso salt l. see Urru Co
84 C3 Jagraon India
47 G2 Jaguarão Brazil
47 G2 Jaguarão r. Brazil/Uru.
46 C4 Jaguariaíva Brazil
85 F4 Jahanabad India
81 M3 Jahan Dagh mt Iran
84 C4 Jahazpur India
81 K7 Jahmah w. Iraq
79 G4 Jahrom Iran
88 B3 Jainca China
84 C4 Jaipur India
84 B4 Jaisalmer India
84 E5 Jaisinghnagar India
84 D5 Jaitgarh mt India
85 E3 Jajarkot Nepal
66 G2 Jajce Bos.-Herz.
85 G4 Jakar Bhutan
92 □ Jakarta Indon.
20 C2 Jakes Corner Can.
85 F4 Jakhan India
54 P3 Jäkkvik Sweden
54 S5 Jakobstad Fin.
27 C5 Jal U.S.A.
84 B2 Jalālābād Afgh.
79 L1 Jalal-Abad Kyrgyzstan
84 C3 Jalandhar India
36 E5 Jalapa Enríquez Mex.
55 S5 Jalasjärvi Fin.
81 K4 Jalawlā' Iraq
85 G4 Jaldhaka r. Bangl.
46 B3 Jales Brazil
85 F5 Jaleshwar India
84 C5 Jalgaon Maharashtra India
84 D5 Jalgaon Maharashtra India
81 L6 Jalībah Iraq
100 D4 Jalingo Nigeria
84 C6 Jalna India
65 F2 Jalón r. Spain
85 G4 Jalpaiguri India
101 E2 Jālū Libya
16 Jamaica country Caribbean Sea
37 J5 Jamaica Channel chan. Haiti/Jamaica
81 L3 Jamalabad Iran
81 M5 Jamālābād Iran
85 G4 Jamalpur Bangl.
85 F4 Jamalpur India
43 G5 Jamanxim r. Brazil
92 C7 Jambi Indon.
116 D5 Jambin Austr.
84 C4 Jambo India
95 A4 Jamboaye r. Indon.
94 A5 Jambongan i. Malaysia
95 A4 Jambuair, Tg pt Indon.
81 K4 Jambūr Iraq
26 D2 James r. ND U.S.A.
32 D6 James r. VA U.S.A.
84 B4 Jamesabad Pak.
22 D3 James Bay b. Can.
29 E7 James Cistern Bahamas
47 D2 James Craik Arg.
117 B6 James Pk mt N.Z.
119 B2 James Ross I. i. Antarctica
114 C4 Jamestown Austr.
105 G5 Jamestown S. Africa
26 D2 Jamestown ND U.S.A.
32 D3 Jamestown NY U.S.A.
81 M4 Jamīlābād Iran
84 C2 Jammu Jammu and Kashmir
84 C2 Jammu and Kashmir terr. Asia
84 B5 Jamnagar India
84 D4 Jamni r. India
84 B3 Jampur Pak.
55 T6 Jämsä Fin.
55 T6 Jämsänkoski Fin.
85 F5 Jamshedpur India
85 G5 Jamuna r. Bangl.
82 G5 Janakpur Nepal
46 D1 Janaúba Brazil
46 B2 Jandaia Brazil
79 G3 Jandaq Iran
84 B2 Jandola Pak.
116 D6 Jandowae Austr.
34 B1 Janesville CA U.S.A.
30 C4 Janesville WI U.S.A.
85 G4 Jangipur India
81 L2 Jānī Beyglū Iran
12 J1 Jan Mayen i. Arctic Ocean
81 L5 Jannah Iraq
25 E6 Janos Mex.
104 F6 Jansenville S. Africa
46 D1 Januária Brazil
84 C5 Jaora India
71 Japan country Asia
90 C5 Japan, Sea of sea Pac. Oc.
Japan Alps Nat. Park see Chibu-Sangaku Nat. Park
14 E4 Japan Tr. sea feature Pac. Oc.
42 E4 Japurá r. Brazil
85 H4 Jāpvo Mount mt India
45 A3 Jaqué Panama
80 G3 Jarābulus Syria
46 A3 Jaraguari Brazil
80 E5 Jarash Jordan
46 A3 Jardim Brazil
113 H2 Jardine River National Park nat. park Austr.
87 L2 Jargalant Mongolia
81 K4 Jarmo Iraq
55 P7 Järna Sweden
62 H5 Jarocin Pol.
63 L5 Jarosław Pol.
54 N5 Järpen Sweden
88 B2 Jartai China
42 F6 Jarú Brazil
55 T7 Järvakandi Estonia
55 T6 Järvenpää Fin.
84 B5 Jasdan India
79 H4 Jāsk Iran
63 K6 Jasło Pol.
44 D8 Jason Is is Falkland Is
119 B2 Jason Pen. pen. Antarctica
20 F4 Jasper Can.
29 C5 Jasper AL U.S.A.
27 E4 Jasper AR U.S.A.
29 D6 Jasper FL U.S.A.
28 C4 Jasper IN U.S.A.
32 E3 Jasper NY U.S.A.
32 B5 Jasper OH U.S.A.
27 E6 Jasper TX U.S.A.
20 F4 Jasper Nat. Park nat. park Can.
81 K5 Jaşşān Iraq
63 J6 Jastrzębie-Zdrój Pol.
84 C4 Jaswantpura India
63 J7 Jászberény Hungary
46 B2 Jataí Brazil
43 G4 Jatapu r. Brazil
84 B4 Jati Pak.
84 B3 Jatoi Pak.
46 C3 Jaú Brazil
42 F4 Jaú r. Brazil
42 F4 Jaú, Parque Nacional do nat. park Brazil
45 E5 Jauaperi r. Brazil
45 D3 Jaua Sarisariñama, Parque Nacional nat. park Venez.
55 S8 Jaunlutriņi Latvia
55 U8 Jaunpiebalga Latvia
85 E4 Jaunpur India
46 A2 Jauru Brazil
46 B2 Jauru r. Brazil
69 G7 Java Georgia
92 □ Java i. Indon.
13 M4 Java Ridge sea feature Indian Ocean
87 K2 Javarthushuu Mongolia
92 D7 Java Sea sea Indon.
13 M4 Java Trench sea feature Indian Ocean
Jawa i. see Java

92 □ Jawa Barat *div.* Indon.
84 C4 Jawai India
84 B4 Jawai *r.* India
92 □ Jawa Tengah *div.* Indon.
92 □ Jawa Timur *div.* Indon.
80 F3 Jawbān Bayk Syria
84 C6 Jawhar India
102 E3 Jawhar Somalia
62 H5 Jawor Pol.
93 K7 Jaya, Pk *mt* Indon.
93 L7 Jayapura Indon.
85 F4 Jaynagar India
80 F5 Jayrūd Syria
81 M3 Jazvān Iran
30 D5 J. C. Murphey Lake *l.* U.S.A.
35 E4 Jean U.S.A.
20 E2 Jean Marie River Can.
23 G2 Jeannin, Lac *l.* Can.
100 C4 Jebba Nigeria
101 E3 Jebel Abyad Plateau *plat.* Sudan
84 C3 Jech Doab *lowland* Pak.
57 F5 Jedburgh U.K.
78 D5 Jeddah Saudi Arabia
66 C6 Jedeida Tunisia
33 F3 Jefferson *NY* U.S.A.
30 C4 Jefferson *WV* U.S.A.
24 D2 Jefferson *r.* U.S.A.
34 D2 Jefferson, Mt *mt* U.S.A.
24 B2 Jefferson, Mt *vol.* U.S.A.
26 E4 Jefferson City U.S.A.
28 C4 Jeffersonville U.S.A.
104 F7 Jeffrey's Bay S. Africa
44 E2 Jejui Guazú *r.* Para.
55 T8 Jēkabpils Latvia
62 G5 Jelenia Góra Pol.
85 G4 Jelep La *pass* China
55 S8 Jelgava Latvia
32 A6 Jellico U.S.A.
95 C5 Jemaja *i.* Indon.
92 □ Jember Indon.
62 E5 Jena Ger.
100 C1 Jendouba Tunisia
80 E5 Jenīn West Bank
32 B6 Jenkins U.S.A.
34 A2 Jenner U.S.A.
27 E6 Jennings U.S.A.
21 K4 Jenpeg Can.
114 E6 Jeparit Austr.
46 E1 Jequié Brazil
46 D2 Jequitaí Brazil
46 D2 Jequitaí *r.* Brazil
46 E2 Jequitinhonha Brazil
46 E1 Jequitinhonha *r.* Brazil
95 B5 Jerantut Malaysia
101 F4 Jerbar Sudan
37 K5 Jérémie Haiti
65 C4 Jerez de la Frontera Spain
65 C3 Jerez de los Caballeros Spain
54 T2 Jerggul Norway
67 J5 Jergucat Albania
116 B4 Jericho Austr.
80 E6 Jericho West Bank
115 F5 Jerilderie Austr.
81 K2 Jermuk Armenia
24 D3 Jerome U.S.A.
112 C6 Jerramungup Austr.
56 E7 Jersey *i.* U.K.
33 F4 Jersey City U.S.A.
32 E4 Jersey Shore U.S.A.
28 B4 Jerseyville U.S.A.
43 K5 Jerumenha Brazil
80 E6 Jerusalem Israel/West Bank
115 J5 Jervis B. *b.* Austr.
115 J5 Jervis Bay Austr.
115 J5 Jervis Bay Territory *div.* Austr.
66 F1 Jesenice Slovenia
66 E3 Jesi Italy
55 M5 Jessheim Norway
85 G5 Jessore Bangl.
29 D6 Jesup U.S.A.
36 F5 Jesús Carranza Mex.
47 D1 Jesús María Arg.
84 B5 Jetalsar India
26 D4 Jetmore U.S.A.
85 F4 Jha Jha India
84 D3 Jhajjar India
84 D3 Jhajju India
84 A3 Jhal Pak.
85 G5 Jhalakati Bangl.
82 E6 Jhalawar India
84 C3 Jhang Pak.
84 D4 Jhansi India
85 F5 Jharia India
85 F5 Jharsuguda India
84 B3 Jhatpat Pak.
84 C2 Jhelum Pak.
84 C2 Jhelum *r.* Pak.
85 G5 Jhenida Bangl.
84 B4 Jhudo Pak.
85 F4 Jhumritilaiya India
84 C3 Jhunjhunūn India
88 C3 Jiachuan China
88 F4 Jiading China
89 D5 Jiahe China
89 B4 Jiajiang China
88 B3 Jialing Jiang *r.* China
90 B1 Jiamusi China
89 E5 Ji'an *Jiangxi* China
89 E5 Ji'an *Jiangxi* China
87 N3 Ji'an *Jilin* China
88 F1 Jianchang China
89 F4 Jiande China
89 B4 Jiang'an China
89 A6 Jiangcheng China
89 D5 Jiangchuan China
88 B4 Jiange China
89 C4 Jiangjin China
89 C5 Jiangkou China

89 E5 Jiangle China
88 B3 Jiangluozhen China
89 D6 Jiangmen China
89 F4 Jiangshan China
88 F3 Jiangsu *div.* China
89 E5 Jiangxi *div.* China
88 D3 Jiangxian China
88 B3 Jiangyan China
89 F4 Jiangyin China
89 D5 Jiangyong China
88 B4 Jiangyou China
88 F3 Jianhu China
89 D6 Jian Jiang *r.* China
89 D4 Jianli China
89 E5 Jianning China
89 F5 Jian'ou China
88 F1 Jianping *Liaoning* China
88 F1 Jianping *Liaoning* China
88 C4 Jianshi China
89 B6 Jianshui China
89 F5 Jianyang *Fujian* China
89 B4 Jianyang *Sichuan* China
88 D2 Jiaocheng China
88 E2 Jiaohe *Hebei* China
87 N3 Jiaohe *Jilin* China
Jiaojiang *see* Taizhou
88 F2 Jiaolai *r.* China
88 G1 Jiaolai *r.* China
89 E5 Jiaoling China
88 F3 Jiaonan China
88 F2 Jiaozhou China
88 F2 Jiaozhou Wan *b.* China
88 D3 Jiaozuo China
88 D2 Jiaxian China
88 F4 Jiaxing China
89 D4 Jiaya China
82 J3 Jiayuguan China
89 E6 Jiazi China
Jiddah *see* Jeddah
90 B2 Jidong China
88 B2 Jieheba China
54 Q2 Jiehkkevarri *mt* Norway
89 E6 Jieshi China
89 E6 Jieshi Wan *b.* China
88 E3 Jieshou China
54 T2 Jieš jávri *l.* Norway
89 E6 Jiexi China
88 D2 Jiexiu China
89 E6 Jieyang China
55 T9 Jieznas Lith.
88 A3 Jigzhi China
62 G6 Jihlava Czech Rep.
102 E3 Jijiga Eth.
89 A4 Jiju China
84 B2 Jilga *r.* Afgh.
102 E3 Jilib Somalia
87 N3 Jilin China
87 N3 Jilin *div.* China
88 A3 Jiling China
102 D3 Jīma Eth.
27 C6 Jiménez Mex.
36 D3 Jiménez *Chihuahua* Mex.
36 E4 Jiménez *Tamaulipas* Mex.
88 F2 Jimo China
82 G2 Jimsar China
33 F4 Jim Thorpe U.S.A.
88 E2 Jinan China
88 B2 Jinchang China
88 D3 Jincheng China
88 B4 Jinchuan China
84 D3 Jind India
115 H6 Jindabyne Austr.
115 G5 Jindera Austr.
62 G6 Jindřichův Hradec Czech Rep.
88 C3 Jing *r.* China
89 E4 Jing'an China
88 C2 Jingbian China
89 F4 Jingchuan China
89 E4 Jingde China
89 E4 Jingdezhen China
89 E5 Jinggangshan China
89 E4 Jinggongqiao China
88 E2 Jinghai China
83 K6 Jinghong China
89 F3 Jingjiang China
88 D2 Jingle China
89 D4 Jingmen China
88 B3 Jingning China
88 E1 Jingpeng China
90 A3 Jingpo China
90 A3 Jingpo Hu *resr* China
89 D4 Jingsha China
88 B2 Jingtai China
89 C6 Jingxi China
89 F4 Jingxian China
88 D2 Jingyuan China
89 C5 Jingzhou *Hunan* China
89 D4 Jingzhou China
88 F3 Jinhu China
89 F4 Jinhua China
88 D1 Jining *Nei Monggol Zizhiqu* China
88 E3 Jining *Shandong* China
102 D3 Jinja Uganda
89 F5 Jinjiang China
89 E4 Jin Jiang *r.* China
102 D3 Jinka Eth.
88 F1 Jinlingsi China
89 C7 Jinmu Jiao *pt* China
36 G6 Jinotepe Nic.
89 C5 Jinping *Guizhou* China
89 B6 Jinping *Yunnan* China
89 A5 Jinping Shan *mts* China
89 C5 Jinsha China
Jinsha Jiang *r. see* Yangtze
88 F1 Jinshan China
88 F4 Jinshan China
89 D4 Jinshi China
88 B4 Jintang China
94 B4 Jintotolo *i.* Phil.
94 B4 Jintotolo Channel *chan.* Phil.

84 D6 Jintur India
89 E3 Jinxi China
89 E4 Jinxian China
88 E3 Jinxiang *Shandong* China
89 F5 Jinxiang *Zhejiang* China
89 B5 Jinyang China
89 F4 Jinyun China
88 E4 Jinzhai China
88 F1 Jinzhou China
88 F2 Jinzhou China
42 F6 Ji-Paraná Brazil
42 F6 Jiparaná *r.* Brazil
42 C4 Jipijapa Ecuador
89 C4 Jishou China
89 E5 Jishui China
80 F4 Jisr ash Shughūr Syria
95 B4 Jitra Malaysia
88 C2 Jiudengkou China
88 B4 Jiuding Shan *mt* China
88 C3 Jiufoping China
89 E4 Jiujiang *Jiangxi* China
89 E4 Jiujiang *Jiangxi* China
89 B4 Jiuling Shan *mts* China
89 A4 Jiulong China
88 F1 Jiumiao China
82 J3 Jiuquan China
89 C5 Jiuxu China
79 J4 Jiwani Pak.
89 F4 Jixi *Anhui* China
91 O2 Jixi *Heilongjiang* China
90 B1 Jixian China
88 D3 Jiyuan China
78 E6 Jīzān Saudi Arabia
88 E2 Jizhou China
91 C7 Jizō-zaki *pt* Japan
43 M5 João Pessoa Brazil
46 C2 João Pinheiro Brazil
34 C2 Job Peak *summit* U.S.A.
85 F5 Joda India
84 C4 Jodhpur India
54 V5 Joensuu Fin.
91 F6 Jōetsu Japan
103 D6 Jofane Moz.
20 F4 Joffre, Mt *mt* Can.
55 U6 Jõgeva Estonia
55 U7 Jõgua Estonia
105 G3 Johannesburg S. Africa
34 D4 Johannesburg U.S.A.
84 E5 Johilla *r.* India
24 C2 John Day U.S.A.
24 B2 John Day *r.* U.S.A.
20 F3 John D'or Prairie Can.
33 G4 John F. Kennedy *airport* U.S.A.
32 D6 John H. Kerr Res. *resr* U.S.A.
57 E2 John o'Groats U.K.
29 D4 Johnson City U.S.A.
20 C2 Johnson's Crossing Can.
29 D5 Johnston U.S.A.
14 H4 Johnston Atoll Pac. Oc.
57 D5 Johnstone U.K.
60 D5 Johnstown Rep. of Ireland
33 F3 Johnstown *NY* U.S.A.
32 D4 Johnstown *PA* U.S.A.
31 F3 Johnswood U.S.A.
92 C6 Johor Bahru Malaysia
55 U7 Jõhvi Estonia
44 G3 Joinville Brazil
64 D2 Joinville France
119 B2 Joinville I. *i.* Antarctica
54 Q3 Jokkmokk Sweden
54 ⸠C4 Jökulsá á Dál *r.* Iceland
54 E3 Jökulsá á Fjöllum *r.* Iceland
54 F4 Jökulsá í Fljótsdal *r.* Iceland
81 K2 Jolfa Iran
30 D3 Joliet U.S.A.
22 F4 Joliette Can.
94 B5 Jolo Phil.
94 B5 Jolo *i.* Phil.
92 ⸠ Jomalig *i.* Phil.
92 ⸠ Jombang Indon.
82 J4 Jomda China
55 T9 Jonava Lith.
88 B3 Jonê China
27 F5 Jonesboro *AR* U.S.A.
33 K2 Jonesboro *ME* U.S.A.
33 K2 Jonesport U.S.A.
32 B6 Jonesville U.S.A.
101 F4 Jonglei Canal *canal* Sudan
85 E5 Jonk *r.* India
55 O8 Jönköping Sweden
23 F3 Jonquière Can.
27 E4 Joplin U.S.A.
33 F5 Joppatowne U.S.A.
84 D4 Jora India
70 Jordan *country* Asia
80 E6 Jordan *r.* Asia
24 F2 Jordan U.S.A.
24 E3 Jordan U.S.A.
116 B4 Jordan Cr. *watercourse* Austr.
24 C3 Jordan Valley U.S.A.
46 B4 Jordão *r.* Brazil
102 D3 Jorhat Eth.
88 F1 Jinlingsi China
85 H4 Jorhat India
54 R4 Jörn Sweden
55 U5 Joroinen Fin.
55 K7 Jørpeland Norway
100 C4 Jos Nigeria
94 C5 Jose Abad Santos Phil.
44 B4 José de San Martin Arg.
46 A2 Joselândia Brazil
47 F2 José Pedro Varela Uru.
23 ⸠ Joseph, Lac *l.* Can.
112 E2 Joseph Bonaparte Gulf *g.* Austr.
35 G4 Joseph City U.S.A.
34 ⸠¹ Kaala *mt* U.S.A.
102 E4 Kaambooni Kenya
55 S6 Kaarina Fin.

35 E5 Joshua Tree National Park *res.* U.S.A.
100 C4 Jos Plateau *plat.* Nigeria
55 K6 Jostedalsbreen Nasjonalpark *nat. park* Norway
55 L6 Jotunheimen Nasjonalpark *nat. park* Norway
104 E6 Joubertina S. Africa
105 G3 Jouberton S. Africa
55 U6 Joutsa Fin.
55 V6 Joutseno Fin.
85 H4 Jowai India
60 B4 Joyce's Country *reg.* Rep. of Ireland
24 A1 Juan de Fuca Strait *chan.* U.S.A.
103 E5 Juan de Nova *i.* Indian Ocean
15 O8 Juan Fernández, Islas *is* Chile
54 V5 Juankoski Fin.
27 C7 Juaréz Mex.
34 D5 Juárez, Sierra de *mts* Mex.
43 K5 Juàzeiro Brazil
43 L5 Juàzeiro do Norte Brazil
101 F4 Juba Sudan
102 E3 Jubba *r.* Somalia
34 D4 Jubilee Pass *pass* U.S.A.
65 F3 Júcar *r.* Spain
36 E5 Juchitán Mex.
46 E2 Jucuruçu *r.* Brazil
55 J7 Judaberg Norway
81 H6 Judaidat al Hamir Iraq
81 J4 Judaydah Syria
81 H6 Judayyidat 'Ar'ar *w.* Iraq
62 G7 Judenburg Austria
55 M9 Juelsminde Denmark
88 C2 Juh China
88 F1 Juhua Dao *i.* China
37 G6 Juigalpa Nic.
61 F1 Juist *i.* Ger.
46 D3 Juiz de Fora Brazil
42 E8 Julaca Bol.
26 C3 Julesburg U.S.A.
42 D7 Juliaca Peru
113 H4 Julia Creek Austr.
43 G3 Juliana Top *summit* Suriname
66 E1 Julijske Alpe *mts* Slovenia
47 E2 Julio, 9 de Arg.
42 C5 Jumbilla Peru
65 F3 Jumilla Spain
85 E3 Jumla Nepal
84 B5 Junagadh India
85 E6 Junagarh India
88 F3 Junan China
47 B2 Juncal *mt* Chile
47 D4 Juncal, L. *l.* Arg.
27 D6 Junction *TX* U.S.A.
25 D4 Junction *UT* U.S.A.
26 D4 Junction City U.S.A.
46 C3 Jundiaí Brazil
20 C3 Juneau U.S.A.
115 G5 Junee Austr.
62 C7 Jungfrau *mt* Switz.
86 E2 Junggar Pendi *basin* China
84 A4 Jungshahi Pak.
32 E4 Juniata *r.* U.S.A.
47 E2 Junín Arg.
47 B3 Junín de los Andes Arg.
33 K1 Juniper Can.
34 B3 Junipero Serro Peak *summit* U.S.A.
89 A4 Junlian China
54 P5 Junsele Sweden
24 C3 Juntura U.S.A.
55 T8 Juodupė Lith.
46 C4 Juquiá Brazil
101 E4 Jur *r.* Sudan
64 H3 Jura *mts* France/Switz.
57 C4 Jura *i.* U.K.
57 C5 Jura, Sound of *chan.* U.K.
46 E1 Juraci Brazil
45 A3 Juradó Col.
55 S9 Jurbarkas Lith.
80 E6 Jurf ad Darāwīsh Jordan
85 G2 Jurhen Ul Shan *mts* China
55 S8 Jūrmala Latvia
54 U4 Jurmu Fin.
88 F4 Jurong China
95 □ Jurong Sing.
42 E7 Juruá *r.* Brazil
43 G5 Juruena *r.* Brazil
54 R5 Jurva Fin.
47 D2 Justo Daract Arg.
42 E4 Jutaí *r.* Brazil
46 A3 Juti Brazil
36 G6 Jutiapa Guatemala
36 G6 Juticalpa Honduras
55 P3 Jutis Sweden
54 V5 Juuka Fin.
55 U6 Juva Fin.
88 F3 Juxian China
88 A3 Juyan China
88 E3 Juye China
103 C6 Jwaneng Botswana
55 T5 Jyväskylä Fin.

K

84 D2 K2 *mt* China/Jammu and Kashmir
34 ⸠¹ Kaala *mt* U.S.A.
102 E4 Kaambooni Kenya
55 S6 Kaarina Fin.

54 V5 Kaavi Fin.
93 G8 Kabaena *i.* Indon.
100 A4 Kabala Sierra Leone
102 C4 Kabale Uganda
102 C4 Kabalo Dem. Rep. Congo
102 C4 Kabambare Dem. Rep. Congo
103 C4 Kabangu Dem. Rep. Congo
95 A5 Kabanjahe Indon.
69 G7 Kabardino-Balkarskaya Respublika *div.* Rus. Fed.
102 C4 Kabinda Dem. Rep. Congo
81 L5 Kabīrkūh *mts* Iran
84 B3 Kabirwala Pak.
102 B3 Kabo C.A.R.
103 C5 Kabompo Zambia
102 C4 Kabongo Dem. Rep. Congo
81 M4 Kabūd Rāhang Iran
94 B2 Kabugao Phil.
84 B2 Kābul Afgh.
84 C2 Kabul *r.* Afgh.
94 C6 Kaburuang *i.* Indon.
103 C5 Kabwe Zambia
84 B4 Kadanai *r.* Afgh./Pak.
95 A2 Kadan Kyun *i.* Myanmar
111 H3 Kadavu *i.* Fiji
111 H3 Kadavu Passage *chan.* Fiji
100 B4 Kade Ghana
84 C5 Kadi India
80 B1 Kadıköy Turkey
114 B4 Kadina Austr.
80 D2 Kadınhanı Turkey
100 B3 Kadiolo Mali
80 F3 Kadirli Turkey
83 D8 Kadmat *i.* India
26 C3 Kadoka U.S.A.
103 C5 Kadoma Zimbabwe
101 E3 Kadugli Sudan
100 C3 Kaduna Nigeria
100 C4 Kaduna *r.* Nigeria
85 J3 Kadusam *mt* China
68 F3 Kaduy Rus. Fed.
68 G3 Kadyy Rus. Fed.
76 G3 Kadzherom Rus. Fed.
100 A3 Kaédi Maur.
101 D3 Kaélé Cameroon
34 ⸠¹ Kaena Pt *pt* U.S.A.
117 D1 Kaeo N.Z.
87 N4 Kaesŏng N. Korea
80 F6 Kāf Saudi Arabia
103 C4 Kafakumba Dem. Rep. Congo
100 A3 Kaffrine Senegal
67 L5 Kafireas, Akra *pt* Greece
80 C6 Kafr el Sheikh Egypt
103 C5 Kafue Zambia
103 C5 Kafue *r.* Zambia
103 C5 Kafue National Park *nat. park* Zambia
91 E6 Kaga Japan
102 B3 Kaga Bandoro C.A.R.
69 G6 Kagal'nitskaya Rus. Fed.
79 J2 Kagan Uzbek.
31 F3 Kagawong Can.
54 R4 Kåge Sweden
102 D4 Kagera, Parc National de la *nat. park* Rwanda
81 J1 Kağızman Turkey
91 B9 Kagoshima Japan
81 M3 Kahak Iran
34 ⸠¹ Kahaluu U.S.A.
102 D4 Kahama Tanz.
34 ⸠¹ Kahana U.S.A.
69 D5 Kharlyk Ukr.
92 E7 Kahayan *r.* Indon.
102 B4 Kahemba Dem. Rep. Congo
117 A6 Kaherekoau Mts *mts* N.Z.
30 B5 Kahoka U.S.A.
34 ⸠² Kahoolawe *i.* U.S.A.
80 F3 Kahramanmaraş Turkey
84 B3 Kahror Pak.
80 G3 Kahta Turkey
34 ⸠¹ Kahuku U.S.A.
34 ⸠¹ Kahului U.S.A.
117 D4 Kahurangi Point *pt* N.Z.
84 C2 Kahuta Pak.
102 C4 Kahuzi-Biega, Parc National du *nat. park* Dem. Rep. Congo
93 H7 Kai, Kepulauan *is* Indon.
100 C4 Kaiama Nigeria
117 D5 Kaiapoi N.Z.
35 F3 Kaibab U.S.A.
25 D4 Kaibab Plat. *plat.* U.S.A.
93 J8 Kai Besar *i.* Indon.
35 G3 Kaibito U.S.A.
35 G3 Kaibito Plateau *plat.* U.S.A.
88 E3 Kaifeng *Henan* China
88 E3 Kaifeng *Henan* China
89 F4 Kaihua China
104 D4 Kaiingveld *reg.* S. Africa
88 C4 Kaijiang China
93 J8 Kai Kecil *i.* Indon.
89 □ Kai Keung Leng China
117 D5 Kaikoura N.Z.
117 D5 Kaikoura Peninsula *pen.* N.Z.
100 A4 Kailahun Sierra Leone
Kailas *mt see* Kangrinboqê Feng
85 G4 Kailāshahar India

Kailas Range *mts see* Gangdisê Shan
89 C5 Kaili China
88 F1 Kailu China
34 ⸠¹ Kailua U.S.A.
34 ⸠² Kailua Kona U.S.A.
117 E2 Kaimai Range *h.* N.Z.
93 J7 Kaimana Indon.
117 E3 Kaimanawa Mountains *mts* N.Z.
85 H2 Kaimar China
84 E4 Kaimur Range *h.* India
55 S7 Käina Estonia
91 B8 Kainan Japan
91 D7 Kainan Japan
100 C3 Kainji Lake National Park *nat. park* Nigeria
100 C3 Kainji Reservoir *resr* Nigeria
117 E2 Kaipara Harbour *in.* N.Z.
35 G3 Kaiparowits Plateau *plat.* U.S.A.
89 D6 Kaiping China
23 J3 Kaipokok Bay *in.* Can.
84 D3 Kairana India
100 D1 Kairouan Tunisia
119 C5 Kaiser Wilhelm II Land *reg.* Antarctica
90 A3 Kaishantun China
117 D1 Kaitaia N.Z.
117 B7 Kaitangata N.Z.
117 F3 Kaitawa N.Z.
84 D3 Kaithal India
54 M3 Kaitum Sweden
93 H8 Kaiwatu Indon.
34 ⸠² Kaiwi Channel *chan.* U.S.A.
88 C4 Kaixian China
89 C5 Kaiyang China
88 G1 Kaiyuan *Liaoning* China
89 B6 Kaiyuan *Yunnan* China
54 U4 Kajaani Fin.
113 H4 Kajabbi Austr.
95 A5 Kajang Malaysia
84 B3 Kajanpur Pak.
81 L2 K'ajaran Armenia
81 L3 Kaju Iran
22 C4 Kakabeka Falls Can.
112 F2 Kakadu National Park *nat. park* Austr.
104 D4 Kakamas S. Africa
102 D3 Kakamega Kenya
117 C6 Kakanui Mts *mts* N.Z.
100 A4 Kakata Liberia
117 E3 Kakatahi N.Z.
85 H4 Kakching India
91 C7 Kake Japan
20 C3 Kake U.S.A.
102 C4 Kakenge Dem. Rep. Congo
69 E6 Kakhovka Ukr.
69 E6 Kakhovs'ke Vodoskhovyshche *resr* Ukr.
83 F7 Kākināda India
20 F2 Kakisa Can.
20 F2 Kakisa *r.* Can.
20 F2 Kakisa Lake *l.* Can.
91 D7 Kakogawa Japan
102 C4 Kakoswa Dem. Rep. Congo
84 D4 Kakrala India
91 G6 Kakuda Japan
20 F4 Kakwa *r.* Can.
84 B3 Kala Pak.
66 D7 Kalaâ Kebira Tunisia
84 B2 Kalabagh Pak.
93 G8 Kalabahi Indon.
94 A5 Kalabakan Malaysia
114 D3 Kalabity Austr.
103 C5 Kalabo Zambia
69 G5 Kalach Rus. Fed.
102 D3 Kalacha Dida Kenya
69 G5 Kalach-na-Donu Rus. Fed.
85 H5 Kaladan *r.* India/Myanmar
31 J3 Kaladar Can.
54 K Le *c.* U.S.A.
98 Kalahari Desert *des.* Africa
103 B6 Kalahari Gemsbok National Park *nat. park* S. Africa
54 S4 Kalajoki Fin.
54 T4 Kalajoki *r.* Fin.
84 B2 Kalam Pak.
105 G1 Kalamare Botswana
67 K4 Kalamata Greece
67 K6 Kalamata Greece
30 E4 Kalamazoo U.S.A.
30 D4 Kalamazoo *r.* U.S.A.
67 J5 Kalampaka Greece
114 C1 Kalamurra, Lake *salt flat* Austr.
84 C3 Kalanaur India
69 E6 Kalanchak Ukr.
114 D6 Kalangadoo Austr.
84 D3 Kalanwali India
94 C4 Kalaong Phil.
81 K4 Kalar Iraq
95 B1 Kalasin Thai.
54 R2 Kalaupapa U.S.A.
69 G6 Kalaus *r.* Rus. Fed.
81 L1 Kälbäcär Azer.
115 K1 Kalbar Austr.
112 B5 Kalbarri Austr.
112 B5 Kalbarri National Park *nat. park* Austr.
80 B3 Kale *Denizli* Turkey
81 G1 Kale Turkey
80 D1 Kalecik Turkey
81 M3 Kaleh Sarai Iran
102 C4 Kalema Dem. Rep. Congo
102 C4 Kalémié Dem. Rep. Congo
30 D3 Kaleva U.S.A.
54 W4 Kalevala Rus. Fed.
85 H5 Kalewa Myanmar
112 D6 Kalgoorlie Austr.

66 F2 **Kali** Croatia
84 E3 **Kali** r. India/Nepal
67 N3 **Kaliakra, Nos** pt Bulg.
94 B4 **Kalibo** Phil.
85 F4 **Kali Gandaki** r. Nepal
102 C4 **Kalima** Dem. Rep. Congo
92 E7 **Kalimantan** reg. Indon.
84 E4 **Kali Nadi** r. India
68 B4 **Kaliningrad** Rus. Fed.
68 B4 **Kaliningradskaya Oblast'** div. Rus. Fed.
68 G3 **Kalinino** Rus. Fed.
69 H5 **Kalininsk** Rus. Fed.
69 H6 **Kalininskaya** Rus. Fed.
69 D4 **Kalinkavichy** Belarus
84 D4 **Kali Sindh** r. India
24 D1 **Kalispell** U.S.A.
62 J5 **Kalisz** Pol.
69 G5 **Kalitva** r. Rus. Fed.
102 D4 **Kaliua** Tanz.
54 S4 **Kalix** Sweden
54 S3 **Kalixälven** r. Sweden
85 H4 **Kalkalighat** India
80 F2 **Kalkan** Turkey
112 F3 **Kalkaringi** Austr.
30 E3 **Kalkaska** U.S.A.
103 B6 **Kalkfeld** Namibia
105 F4 **Kalkfonteindam** dam S. Africa
95 □ **Kallang** Sing.
55 U7 **Kallaste** Estonia
54 U5 **Kallavesi** l. Fin.
54 N5 **Kallsedet** Sweden
54 N5 **Kallsjön** l. Sweden
55 P8 **Kalmar** Sweden
55 P8 **Kalmarsund** chan. Sweden
69 F6 **Kal'mius** r. Ukr.
83 F9 **Kalmunai** Sri Lanka
69 H6 **Kalmykiya – Khalm'g-Tangch, Respublika** div. Rus. Fed.
85 G4 **Kalni** r. Bangl.
63 N5 **Kalodnaye** Belarus
84 C5 **Kalol** India
94 C6 **Kaloma** i. Indon.
103 C5 **Kalomo** Zambia
20 D4 **Kalone Pk** summit Can.
81 L2 **Kalow** r. Iran
84 D3 **Kalpa** India
83 D8 **Kalpeni** i. India
84 D4 **Kalpi** India
81 L4 **Kal Safīd** Iran
84 C3 **Kalu** India
68 F4 **Kaluga** Rus. Fed.
55 M9 **Kalundborg** Denmark
84 B2 **Kalur Kot** Pak.
69 C5 **Kalush** Ukr.
68 E4 **Kaluzhskaya Oblast'** div. Rus. Fed.
54 S5 **Kälviä** Fin.
68 F3 **Kalyazin** Rus. Fed.
67 M6 **Kalymnos** i. Greece
102 C4 **Kama** Dem. Rep. Congo
90 G5 **Kamaishi** Japan
84 C3 **Kamalia** Pak.
80 D2 **Kaman** Turkey
103 B5 **Kamanjab** Namibia
112 D6 **Kambalda** Austr.
103 C5 **Kambove** Dem. Rep. Congo
77 S4 **Kamchatka** r. Rus. Fed.
67 M3 **Kamchiya** r. Bulg.
67 K4 **Kamenitsa** mt Bulg.
66 E2 **Kamenjak, Rt** pt Croatia
90 E2 **Kamenka** Rus. Fed.
68 H4 **Kamenka** Rus. Fed.
76 K4 **Kamen'-na-Obi** Rus. Fed.
68 F3 **Kamenniki** Rus. Fed.
68 D2 **Kamennogorsk** Rus. Fed.
69 G6 **Kamennomostskiy** Rus. Fed.
69 G6 **Kamenolomni** Rus. Fed.
90 C2 **Kamen'-Rybolov** Rus. Fed.
77 S3 **Kamenskoye** Rus. Fed.
69 G5 **Kamensk-Shakhtinskiy** Rus. Fed.
76 H4 **Kamensk-Ural'skiy** Rus. Fed.
68 G3 **Kameshkovo** Rus. Fed.
84 D3 **Kamet** mt China
104 C5 **Kamiesberge** mts S. Africa
104 B5 **Kamieskroon** S. Africa
21 J2 **Kamilukuak Lake** l. Can.
103 C4 **Kamina** Dem. Rep. Congo
21 L2 **Kaminak Lake** l. Can.
63 M5 **Kamin'-Kashyrs'kyy** Ukr.
90 H3 **Kamishihoro** Japan
85 H4 **Kamjong** India
85 F4 **Kamla** r. India
20 L4 **Kamloops** Can.
81 K1 **Kamo** Armenia
91 G2 **Kamogawa** Japan
84 C3 **Kamoke** Pak.
95 C2 **Kamon, Xé** r. Laos
102 C4 **Kamonia** Dem. Rep. Congo
102 D3 **Kampala** Uganda
94 A5 **Kampar** Malaysia
61 D2 **Kampen** Neth.
102 C4 **Kampene** Dem. Rep. Congo
95 A1 **Kamphaeng Phet** Thai.
95 C3 **Kâmpóng Cham** Cambodia
95 C2 **Kâmpóng Chhnǎng** Cambodia
95 C3 **Kâmpóng Khleǎng** Cambodia
95 C2 **Kâmpóng Spœ** Cambodia
95 C2 **Kâmpóng Thum** Cambodia
95 C3 **Kâmpôt** Cambodia
Kampuchea country see **Cambodia**

93 J7 **Kamrau, Teluk** b. Indon.
21 J4 **Kamsack** Can.
76 G4 **Kamskoye Vdkhr.** resr Rus. Fed.
102 E3 **Kamsuuma** Somalia
21 J3 **Kamuchawie Lake** l. Can.
102 D3 **Kamuli** Uganda
69 C5 **Kam''yane** Ukr.
69 C5 **Kam''yanets'-Podil's'kyy** Ukr.
69 C5 **Kam''yanka-Buz'ka** Ukr.
63 L4 **Kamyanyets** Belarus
81 L4 **Kāmyārān** Iran
69 F6 **Kamyshevatskaya** Rus. Fed.
69 H5 **Kamyshin** Rus. Fed.
69 J6 **Kamyzyak** Rus. Fed.
22 F3 **Kanaaupscow** r. Can.
35 F3 **Kanab** U.S.A.
35 F3 **Kanab Creek** r. U.S.A.
81 K5 **Kan'ān** Iraq
102 C4 **Kananga** Dem. Rep. Congo
115 J4 **Kanangra–Boyd National Park** nat. park Austr.
35 F3 **Kanarraville** U.S.A.
68 H4 **Kanash** Rus. Fed.
32 C5 **Kanawha** r. U.S.A.
91 E7 **Kanayama** Japan
91 E6 **Kanazawa** Japan
95 A2 **Kanchanaburi** Thai.
83 E8 **Kanchipuram** India
84 A3 **Kand** mt Pak.
79 K3 **Kandahār** Afgh.
54 X3 **Kandalaksha** Rus. Fed.
95 A5 **Kandang** Indon.
84 B2 **Kandhura** Pak.
100 C3 **Kandi** Benin
84 B4 **Kandiaro** Pak.
80 C1 **Kandıra** Turkey
115 H4 **Kandos** Austr.
103 E5 **Kandreho** Madag.
83 F9 **Kandy** Sri Lanka
76 G5 **Kandyagash** Kazak.
32 D4 **Kane** U.S.A.
34 □1 **Kaneohe** U.S.A.
34 □1 **Kaneohe Bay** b. U.S.A.
69 F6 **Kanevskaya** Rus. Fed.
103 C6 **Kang** Botswana
85 G5 **Kanga** r. Bangl.
100 B3 **Kangaba** Mali
80 F2 **Kangal** Turkey
79 G4 **Kangān** Iran
92 C5 **Kangar** Malaysia
114 B5 **Kangaroo I.** i. Austr.
54 V5 **Kangaslampi** Fin.
55 U6 **Kangasniemi** Fin.
81 L4 **Kangāvar** Iran
88 E1 **Kangbao** China
85 G4 **Kangchenjunga** mt Nepal
89 A4 **Kangding** China
92 F8 **Kangean, Kepulauan** is Indon.
87 N3 **Kanggye** N. Korea
23 G2 **Kangiqsualujjuaq** Can.
23 G1 **Kangirsuk** Can.
88 B3 **Kangle** China
85 F3 **Kangmar** Xizang Zizhiqu China
85 G3 **Kangmar** Xizang Zizhiqu China
87 N4 **Kangnŭng** S. Korea
102 B3 **Kango** Gabon
88 G1 **Kangping** China
85 J3 **Kangri Karpo Pass** pass India
84 E3 **Kangrinboqê Feng** mt China
85 H4 **Kangto** mt China
85 F2 **Kangtog** China
88 B3 **Kangxian** China
84 D5 **Kanhan** r. India
85 E4 **Kanhar** r. India
102 C4 **Kaniama** Dem. Rep. Congo
79 L1 **Kanibadam** Tajik.
117 C5 **Kaniere, L.** l. N.Z.
76 F3 **Kanin, Poluostrov** pen. Rus. Fed.
81 K3 **Kānī Rash** Iraq
69 D5 **Kaniv** Ukr.
114 D6 **Kaniva** Austr.
55 S6 **Kankaanpää** Fin.
30 D5 **Kankakee** U.S.A.
30 C5 **Kankakee** r. U.S.A.
100 B3 **Kankan** Guinea
85 E5 **Kanker** India
95 A3 **Kanmaw Kyun** i. Myanmar
29 D5 **Kannapolis** U.S.A.
84 D4 **Kannauj** India
84 D5 **Kannod** India
54 T5 **Kannonkoski** Fin.
Kannur see **Cannanore**
54 S5 **Kannus** Fin.
100 C3 **Kano** Nigeria
104 D7 **Kanonpunt** pt S. Africa
84 C4 **Kanor** India
91 B9 **Kanoya** Japan
84 E4 **Kanpur** India
84 B3 **Kanpur** Pak.
26 D4 **Kansas** div. U.S.A.
26 D4 **Kansas** r. U.S.A.
26 E4 **Kansas City** KS U.S.A.
26 E4 **Kansas City** MO U.S.A.
77 L4 **Kansk** Rus. Fed.
91 A5 **Kansŏng** S. Korea
85 G4 **Kantanagar** Bangl.
95 A4 **Kantang** Thai.
95 C2 **Kantaralak** Thai.
100 C3 **Kantchari** Burkina
69 F5 **Kantemirovka** Rus. Fed.
85 H4 **Kānthi** India
85 F4 **Kanti** India
84 C3 **Kantli** r. India
111 J2 **Kanton** i. Kiribati

60 C5 **Kanturk** Rep. of Ireland
104 C3 **Kanus** Namibia
105 J2 **KaNyamazane** S. Africa
103 C6 **Kanye** Botswana
89 H6 **Kaohsiung** Taiwan
95 A3 **Kaôh Smăch** i. Cambodia
103 B5 **Kaokoveld** plat. Namibia
100 A3 **Kaolack** Senegal
103 C5 **Kaoma** Zambia
84 B2 **Kaoshan Pass** pass Afgh.
34 □2 **Kapaa** U.S.A.
34 □2 **Kapaau** U.S.A.
81 L2 **Kapan** Armenia
103 C4 **Kapanga** Dem. Rep. Congo
82 E2 **Kapchagay** Kazak.
61 D3 **Kapellen** Belgium
67 K6 **Kapello, Akra** pt Greece
80 A1 **Kapıdağı Yarımadası** pen. Turkey
85 G4 **Kapili** r. India
14 F5 **Kapingamarangi Rise** sea feature Pac. Oc.
84 B3 **Kapip** Pak.
103 C5 **Kapiri Mposhi** Zambia
22 D3 **Kapiskau** Can.
22 D3 **Kapiskau** r. Can.
31 G2 **Kapiskong Lake** l. Can.
117 E4 **Kapiti I.** i. N.Z.
95 A3 **Kapoe** Thai.
101 F4 **Kapoeta** Sudan
62 F7 **Kaposvár** Hungary
62 D3 **Kappeln** Ger.
55 O7 **Kappelskär** Sweden
84 D4 **Kapran** India
102 D3 **Kapsabet** Kenya
90 A4 **Kapsan** N. Korea
92 E7 **Kapuas** r. Indon.
114 C5 **Kapunda** Austr.
84 C4 **Kapūriya** India
84 C3 **Kapurthala** India
22 D4 **Kapuskasing** Can.
22 D4 **Kapuskasing** r. Can.
69 H5 **Kapustin Yar** Rus. Fed.
115 J3 **Kaputar** mt Austr.
102 D3 **Kaputir** Kenya
62 H7 **Kapuvár** Hungary
68 C4 **Kapyl'** Belarus
100 C4 **Kara** Togo
81 H2 **Kara** r. Turkey
67 M5 **Kara Ada** i. Turkey
80 D2 **Karaali** Turkey
82 D2 **Kara–Balta** Kyrgyzstan
79 G1 **Kara–Bogaz Gol, Zaliv** b. Turkm.
80 D1 **Karabük** Turkey
76 H5 **Karabutak** Kazak.
80 B1 **Karacabey** Turkey
81 G3 **Karacadağ** Turkey
80 D3 **Karacadağ** mts Turkey
81 G3 **Karacaköy** Turkey
81 G3 **Karacalı Dağ** mt Turkey
80 B3 **Karacasu** Turkey
80 C3 **Karaca Yarımadası** pen. Turkey
69 G7 **Karachayevo-Cherkesskaya Respublika** div. Rus. Fed.
69 G7 **Karachayevsk** Rus. Fed.
68 E4 **Karachev** Rus. Fed.
79 K5 **Karachi** Pak.
81 J2 **Karaçoban** Turkey
83 D7 **Karad** India
80 D3 **Kara Dağ** mt Turkey
81 J3 **Kara Dağ** mt Turkey
Kara Deniz sea see **Black Sea**
86 B2 **Karaganda** Kazak.
82 E1 **Karagayly** Kazak.
77 S4 **Karaginskiy Zaliv** b. Rus. Fed.
80 B2 **Karahallı** Turkey
80 E2 **Karahasanlı** Turkey
83 E8 **Karaikal** India
80 E3 **Karaisalı** Turkey
79 G2 **Karaj** Iran
84 E1 **Karakax He** r. China
84 E2 **Karakax Shan** mts China
81 G3 **Karakeçi** Turkey
80 D2 **Karakeçili** Turkey
94 C5 **Karakelong** i. Indon.
81 H2 **Karakoçan** Turkey
82 D2 **Kara–Köl** Kyrgyzstan
82 E2 **Karakol** Kyrgyzstan
82 D3 **Karakoram** mts Asia
79 L2 **Karakoram** mts Asia
84 D2 **Karakoram Pass** pass China/Jammu and Kashmir
102 D2 **Kara K'orē** Eth.
76 G5 **Karakum Desert** des. Kazak.
79 H1 **Karakum Desert** des. Turkm.
Karakumy, Peski des. see **Karakum Desert**
81 J1 **Karakurt** Turkey
55 R7 **Karala** Estonia
80 D3 **Karaman** Turkey
80 B3 **Karamanlı** Turkey
82 F1 **Karamay** China
84 C1 **Karambar Pass** pass Afgh./Pak.
117 C4 **Karamea** N.Z.
117 C4 **Karamea Bight** b. N.Z.
85 F1 **Karamiran** China
85 F1 **Karamiran Shankou** pass China
80 B1 **Karamürsel** Turkey
68 D3 **Karamyshevo** Rus. Fed.
84 D5 **Karanja** India
85 F5 **Karanjia** India
84 C3 **Karanpura** India
80 D3 **Karapınar** Turkey
104 B3 **Karas** div. Namibia

104 B3 **Karas** watercourse Namibia
103 B6 **Karasburg** Namibia
76 J2 **Kara Sea** sea Rus. Fed.
54 T2 **Karasjok** Norway
80 C1 **Karasu** Turkey
81 J2 **Karasu** r. Turkey
76 J4 **Karasuk** Rus. Fed.
80 E3 **Karataş** Turkey
82 D2 **Karatau** Kazak.
82 C2 **Karatau, Khr.** mts Kazak.
95 A3 **Karathuri** Myanmar
91 A8 **Karatsu** Japan
94 C5 **Karatung** i. Indon.
84 D3 **Karauli** India
81 J1 **Karaurgan** Turkey
92 □ **Karawang** Indon.
81 K5 **Karbalā'** Iraq
63 K7 **Karcag** Hungary
67 J5 **Karditsa** Greece
55 S7 **Kärdla** Estonia
105 G4 **Karee** S. Africa
104 D5 **Kareeberge** mts S. Africa
101 F3 **Kareima** Sudan
69 G7 **K'areli** Georgia
85 G5 **Kareli** India
54 W4 **Kareliya, Respublika** div. Rus. Fed.
87 L1 **Karenga** r. Rus. Fed.
84 D4 **Karera** India
54 S2 **Karesuando** Sweden
69 H7 **Kargalinskaya** Rus. Fed.
81 H2 **Kargapazarı Dağları** mts Turkey
80 E1 **Kargı** Turkey
84 D2 **Kargil** Jammu and Kashmir
68 F2 **Kargopol'** Rus. Fed.
55 P6 **Karholmsbruk** Sweden
103 C5 **Kariba** Zimbabwe
103 C5 **Kariba, Lake** resr Zambia/Zimbabwe
90 F3 **Kariba-yama** vol. Japan
104 E6 **Kariega** r. S. Africa
54 T2 **Karigasniemi** Fin.
112 C4 **Karijini National Park** nat. park Austr.
55 R5 **Karijoki** Fin.
117 D1 **Karikari, Cape** c. N.Z.
92 D7 **Karimata, Pulau-pulau** is Indon.
92 D7 **Karimata, Selat** str. Indon.
83 E7 **Karimnagar** India
92 □ **Karimunjawa, Pulau-pulau** is Indon.
102 E2 **Karin** Somalia
85 F5 **Karkai** r. India
82 E1 **Karkaralinsk** Kazak.
94 C5 **Karkaralong, Kepulauan** is Indon.
110 E2 **Karkar I.** i. P.N.G.
81 M6 **Karkheh, Rūdkhāneh-ye** r. Iran
69 E6 **Karkinits'ka Zatoka** g. Ukr.
55 T6 **Kärkölä** Fin.
55 T7 **Karksi–Nuia** Estonia
81 H2 **Karlıova** Turkey
69 E5 **Karlivka** Ukr.
Karl–Marx–Stadt see **Chemnitz**
66 F2 **Karlovac** Croatia
67 L3 **Karlovo** Bulg.
62 F5 **Karlovy Vary** Czech Rep.
55 O7 **Karlsborg** Sweden
55 O8 **Karlshamn** Sweden
55 O7 **Karlskoga** Sweden
55 O8 **Karlskrona** Sweden
62 D6 **Karlsruhe** Ger.
55 N7 **Karlstad** Sweden
26 D1 **Karlstad** U.S.A.
68 D4 **Karma** Belarus
55 J7 **Karmøy** i. Norway
85 H5 **Karnafuli Reservoir** resr Bangl.
84 D3 **Karnal** India
85 E3 **Karnali** r. Nepal
83 D8 **Karnataka** div. India
67 M3 **Karnobat** Bulg.
103 C5 **Karoi** Zimbabwe
85 G3 **Karo La** pass China
85 H4 **Karong** India
103 C4 **Karonga** Malawi
104 E6 **Karoo National Park** nat. park S. Africa
114 C5 **Karoonda** Austr.
84 B3 **Karor** Pak.
102 D2 **Karora** Eritrea
67 M7 **Karpathos** i. Greece
67 M6 **Karpathou, Steno** chan. Greece
Karpaty mts see **Carpathian Mountains**
67 J5 **Karpenisi** Greece
68 H1 **Karpogory** Rus. Fed.
112 C4 **Karratha** Austr.
81 J1 **Kars** Turkey
54 T5 **Kärsämäki** Fin.
55 U8 **Kārsava** Latvia
79 K2 **Karshi** Uzbek.
85 G4 **Kārsiyāng** India
76 G3 **Karskiye Vorota, Proliv** str. Rus. Fed.
Karskoye More sea see **Kara Sea**
54 T5 **Karstula** Fin.
80 B1 **Kartal** Turkey
76 H4 **Kartaly** Rus. Fed.
54 U5 **Karttula** Fin.
114 A4 **Karumba** Austr.
81 M3 **Kārūn, Rūd-e** r. Iran

55 S5 **Karvia** Fin.
55 S6 **Karvianjoki** r. Fin.
83 D8 **Karwar** India
87 K1 **Karymskoye** Rus. Fed.
67 L5 **Karystos** Greece
80 B3 **Kaş** Turkey
22 C3 **Kasabonika** Can.
22 C3 **Kasabonika Lake** l. Can.
102 B4 **Kasai** r. Dem. Rep. Congo
103 C5 **Kasaji** Dem. Rep. Congo
103 D5 **Kasama** Zambia
103 C5 **Kasane** Botswana
102 B4 **Kasangulu** Dem. Rep. Congo
83 D8 **Kasaragod** India
21 J2 **Kasba Lake** l. Can.
100 B1 **Kasba Tadla** Morocco
91 B9 **Kaseda** Japan
81 L9 **Käseh Garän** Iran
103 C5 **Kasempa** Zambia
103 C5 **Kasenga** Dem. Rep. Congo
102 C4 **Kasese** Dem. Rep. Congo
102 D3 **Kasese** Uganda
84 D4 **Kasganj** India
79 G3 **Kāshān** Iran
22 D3 **Kashechewan** Can.
Kashgar see **Kashi**
82 E3 **Kashi** China
91 D7 **Kashihara** Japan
91 B8 **Kashima** Japan
91 G6 **Kashima-nada** b. Japan
68 F3 **Kashin** Rus. Fed.
84 D3 **Kashipur** India
91 F6 **Kashiwazaki** Japan
81 L5 **Kashkan** r. Iran
79 H2 **Kāshmar** Iran
84 C2 **Kashmir, Vale of** v. India
84 B3 **Kashmor** Pak.
84 B2 **Kashmund** reg. Afgh.
102 C4 **Kashyukulu** Dem. Rep. Congo
68 G4 **Kasimov** Rus. Fed.
28 B4 **Kaskaskia** r. U.S.A.
21 L3 **Kaskattama** r. Can.
55 R5 **Kaskinen** Fin.
102 C4 **Kasongo** Dem. Rep. Congo
102 B4 **Kasongo–Lunda** Dem. Rep. Congo
67 M7 **Kasos** i. Greece
67 M7 **Kasos, Steno** chan. Greece
69 H7 **Kaspi** Georgia
69 H7 **Kaspiysk** Rus. Fed.
63 P3 **Kaspiya** Rus. Fed.
101 F3 **Kassala** Sudan
84 D5 **Kassandra** pen. Greece
67 K4 **Kassandras, Kolpos** b. Greece
62 D5 **Kassel** Ger.
100 C1 **Kasserine** Tunisia
30 A3 **Kasson** U.S.A.
80 D1 **Kastamonu** Turkey
78 A2 **Kastelli** Greece
67 J4 **Kastoria** Greece
68 E4 **Kastsyukovichy** Belarus
91 E7 **Kasugai** Japan
102 B4 **Kasulu** Tanz.
91 D7 **Kasumi** Japan
91 G6 **Kasumiga-ura** l. Japan
69 J7 **Kasumkent** Rus. Fed.
103 D5 **Kasungu** Malawi
84 C3 **Kasur** Pak.
103 D5 **Katete** Zambia
85 E5 **Katghora** India
82 J6 **Katha** Myanmar
78 C4 **Katherina, Gebel** mt Egypt
112 F2 **Katherine** Austr.
112 F2 **Katherine** r. Austr.
84 B5 **Kathiawar** pen. India
80 D6 **Kathīb el Henu** sand dunes Egypt
105 H3 **Kathlehong** S. Africa
85 F4 **Kathmandu** Nepal
104 E3 **Kathu** S. Africa
84 C2 **Kathua** Jammu and Kashmir
100 B3 **Kati** Mali
85 F4 **Katihar** India
117 E2 **Katikati** N.Z.
105 G6 **Kati–Kati** S. Africa
103 C5 **Katima Mulilo** Namibia
100 B4 **Katiola** Côte d'Ivoire
104 D4 **Katkop Hills** reg. S. Africa
Katmandu see **Kathmandu**
67 J5 **Kato Achaïa** Greece
89 □ **Kat O Chau** i. China
84 D5 **Katol** India
95 □ **Katong** Sing.
115 J4 **Katoomba** Austr.
63 J5 **Katowice** Pol.
85 G5 **Katoya** India
57 D4 **Katrine, Loch** l. U.K.
55 P7 **Katrineholm** Sweden
100 C3 **Katsina** Nigeria
100 C4 **Katsina-Ala** Nigeria
91 G6 **Katsuta** Japan
91 G7 **Katsuura** Japan
91 E6 **Katsuyama** Japan
23 G2 **Kattaktoc, Cap** hd Can.

79 K2 **Kattakurgan** Uzbek.
84 B2 **Kattasang Hills** mts Afgh.
55 M8 **Kattegat** str. Denmark/Sweden
84 B3 **Katuri** Pak.
61 C2 **Katwijk aan Zee** Neth.
34 □2 **Kauai** i. U.S.A.
34 □2 **Kauai Channel** chan. U.S.A.
55 S5 **Kauhajoki** Fin.
55 S5 **Kauhava** Fin.
54 T3 **Kaukonen** Fin.
34 □2 **Kaula** i. U.S.A.
34 □2 **Kaulakahi Channel** chan. U.S.A.
23 H2 **Kaumajet Mts** mts Can.
34 □2 **Kaunakakai** U.S.A.
55 S9 **Kaunas** Lith.
55 U8 **Kaunata** Latvia
100 C3 **Kaura–Namoda** Nigeria
89 □ **Kau Sai Chau** i. China
54 S5 **Kaustinen** Fin.
54 S2 **Kautokeino** Norway
95 A3 **Kau-ye Kyun** i. Myanmar
67 K4 **Kavadarci** Macedonia
80 F1 **Kavak** Turkey
67 L4 **Kavala** Greece
90 D2 **Kavalerovo** Rus. Fed.
83 F8 **Kavali** India
83 D8 **Kavaratti** i. India
67 N3 **Kavarna** Bulg.
79 G3 **Kavīr, Dasht-e** des. Iran
79 H3 **Kavīr-i-Namak** salt flat Iran
91 F7 **Kawagoe** Japan
91 F7 **Kawaguchi** Japan
34 □2 **Kawaihae** U.S.A.
117 E1 **Kawakawa** N.Z.
103 C4 **Kawambwa** Zambia
22 E5 **Kawartha Lakes** lakes Can.
91 F7 **Kawasaki** Japan
117 E2 **Kawau I.** i. N.Z.
23 G2 **Kawawachikamach** Can.
117 F3 **Kawerau** N.Z.
117 E3 **Kawhia** N.Z.
117 E3 **Kawhia Harbour** in. N.Z.
34 D3 **Kawich Range** mts U.S.A.
95 A1 **Kawkareik** Myanmar
95 A1 **Kawludo** Myanmar
95 A3 **Kawthaung** Myanmar
100 B3 **Kaya** Burkina
80 F2 **Kayadibi** Turkey
102 C4 **Kayanaza** Burundi
24 J3 **Kaycee** U.S.A.
103 C4 **Kayembe–Mukulu** Dem. Rep. Congo
35 G3 **Kayenta** U.S.A.
100 A3 **Kayes** Mali
100 A4 **Kayima** Sierra Leone
80 F2 **Kaynar** Turkey
80 F2 **Kaypak** Turkey
69 H5 **Kaysatskoye** Rus. Fed.
80 E2 **Kayseri** Turkey
76 T3 **Kayyerkan** Rus. Fed.
77 P2 **Kazach'ye** Rus. Fed.
Kazakh see **Qazax**
86 B2 **Kazakhskiy Melkosopochnik** reg. Kazak.
70 **Kazakhstan** country Asia
21 K2 **Kazan** r. Can.
68 J4 **Kazan'** Rus. Fed.
80 D3 **Kazancı** Turkey
68 J4 **Kazanka** r. Rus. Fed.
67 L3 **Kazanlŭk** Bulg.
93 L1 **Kazan-rettō** is Japan
69 G5 **Kazanskaya** Rus. Fed.
69 H7 **Kazbek** mt Georgia/Rus. Fed.
67 M5 **Kaz Dağı** mts Turkey
79 G4 **Kāzerūn** Iran
68 J2 **Kazhim** Rus. Fed.
63 K6 **Kazincbarcika** Hungary
69 H7 **Kazret'i** Georgia
69 J5 **Kaztalovka** Kazak.
90 J2 **Kazuno** Japan
76 H3 **Kazymskiy Mys** Rus. Fed.
67 L6 **Kea** i. Greece
60 E3 **Keady** U.K.
34 □2 **Kealakekua Bay** b. U.S.A.
35 G4 **Keams Canyon** U.S.A.
26 D3 **Kearney** U.S.A.
35 G5 **Kearny** U.S.A.
80 G2 **Keban** Turkey
80 G2 **Keban Baraji** resr Turkey
100 A3 **Kébémèr** Senegal
80 F4 **Kebīr, Nahr al** r. Lebanon/Syria
101 E3 **Kebkabiya** Sudan
54 Q3 **Kebnekaise** mt Sweden
57 B2 **Kebock Head** hd U.K.
102 E3 **K'ebrī Dehar** Eth.
92 □ **Kebumen** Indon.
20 D3 **Kechika** r. Can.
80 C3 **Keçiborlu** Turkey
63 J7 **Kecskemét** Hungary
81 H1 **K'eda** Georgia
55 S9 **Kėdainiai** Lith.
84 D3 **Kedar Kanta** mt India
84 D3 **Kedarnath Peak** mt India
23 G4 **Kedgwick** Can.
92 □ **Kediri** Indon.
100 A3 **Kédougou** Senegal
20 D2 **Keele** r. Can.
20 C2 **Keele Pk** summit Can.
25 C4 **Keeler** U.S.A.
57 F4 **Keen, Mount** mt U.K.
94 A5 **Keenapusan** i. Phil.
33 G3 **Keene** U.S.A.
115 J3 **Keepit, Lake** resr Austr.
61 C3 **Keerbergen** Belgium
113 H2 **Keer-weer, C.** pt Austr.
103 B6 **Keetmanshoop** Namibia

21 L6 Keewatin Can.
21 L5 Keewatin U.S.A.
67 J5 Kefallonia i. Greece
93 G8 Kefamenanu Indon.
54 B4 Keflavik Iceland
82 E2 Kegen Kazak.
23 G2 Keglo, Baie de b. Can.
69 H6 Kegul'ta Rus. Fed.
55 T7 Kehra Estonia
83 J6 Kehsi Mansam Myanmar
58 F4 Keighley U.K.
55 T7 Keila Estonia
104 D6 Keimoes S. Africa
54 U5 Keitele Fin.
54 T5 Keitele l. Fin.
114 D6 Keith Austr.
57 F3 Keith U.K.
20 E1 Keith Arm b. Can.
23 G5 Kejimkujik National Park nat. park Can.
34 □² Kekaha U.S.A.
63 K7 Kékes mt Hungary
84 C4 Kekri India
83 D9 Kelai i. Maldives
88 D2 Kelan China
95 B5 Kelang Malaysia
95 B4 Kelantan r. Malaysia
62 E6 Kelheim Ger.
66 D6 Kelibia Tunisia
79 J2 Kelifskiy Uzboy marsh Turkm.
81 G1 Kelkit Turkey
80 F1 Kelkit r. Turkey
20 E2 Keller Lake l. Can.
32 B4 Kelleys I. i. U.S.A.
24 C2 Kellogg U.S.A.
54 V3 Kelloselkä Fin.
60 E4 Kells Rep. of Ireland
55 S9 Kelmė Lith.
101 D4 Kelo Chad
20 F5 Kelowna Can.
34 A2 Kelseyville U.S.A.
57 F5 Kelso U.K.
35 E4 Kelso CA U.S.A.
24 B2 Kelso WA U.S.A.
92 C6 Keluang Malaysia
21 J4 Kelvington Can.
68 L1 Kem' Rus. Fed.
68 E1 Kem' r. Rus. Fed.
81 G2 Kemah Turkey
80 G2 Kemaliye Turkey
67 M5 Kemalpaşa Turkey
20 D4 Kemano Can.
80 C3 Kemer Antalya Turkey
80 B3 Kemer Muğla Turkey
80 B3 Kemer Barajı resr Turkey
76 K4 Kemerovo Rus. Fed.
54 T4 Kemi Fin.
54 U3 Kemijärvi Fin.
54 U3 Kemijärvi l. Fin.
54 T3 Kemijoki r. Fin.
61 A4 Kemmelberg h. Belgium
24 E3 Kemmerer U.S.A.
57 F3 Kemnay U.K.
27 D5 Kemp, L. l. U.S.A.
54 T4 Kempele Fin.
61 C3 Kempen reg. Belgium
119 D4 Kemp Land reg. Antarctica
119 B2 Kemp Pen. pen. Antarctica
29 E7 Kemp's Bay Bahamas
115 K3 Kempsey Austr.
22 F4 Kempt, L. l. Can.
62 F2 Kempten Ger.
115 G9 Kempton Austr.
105 H4 Kempton Park S. Africa
31 K3 Kemptville Can.
92 □ Kemujan i. Indon.
84 E4 Ken r. India
58 E3 Kendal U.K.
115 K3 Kendall Austr.
21 M2 Kendall, Cape hd Can.
30 E5 Kendallville U.S.A.
93 G7 Kendari Indon.
92 E7 Kendawangan Indon.
101 D3 Kendégué Chad
85 F5 Kendrāparha India
24 C2 Kendrick U.S.A.
35 G4 Kendrick Peak summit U.S.A.
83 G6 Kendujhargarh India
115 H3 Kenebri Austr.
27 D6 Kenedy U.S.A.
100 A4 Kenema Sierra Leone
102 B4 Kenge Dem. Rep. Congo
83 J6 Kengtung Myanmar
104 D4 Kenhardt S. Africa
100 A3 Kéniéba Mali
100 B1 Kénitra Morocco
88 F2 Kenli China
60 B6 Kenmare Rep. of Ireland
26 C1 Kenmare U.S.A.
60 A6 Kenmare River in. Rep. of Ireland
25 G5 Kenna U.S.A.
33 J2 Kennebec r. U.S.A.
33 H3 Kennebunk U.S.A.
33 H3 Kennebunkport U.S.A.
116 A2 Kennedy Austr.
89 □ Kennedy Town China
27 F6 Kenner U.S.A.
59 F6 Kennet r. U.K.
27 F4 Kennett U.S.A.
24 C2 Kennewick U.S.A.
31 G1 Kenogami Lake Can.
31 G1 Kenogamissi Lake l. Can.
20 B2 Keno Hill Can.
21 L5 Kenora Can.
30 D4 Kenosha U.S.A.
68 F2 Kenozero, Ozero l. Rus. Fed.
58 E3 Kent r. U.K.
33 G4 Kent CT U.S.A.

27 B6 Kent TX U.S.A.
24 B2 Kent WA U.S.A.
105 H6 Kentani S. Africa
82 C2 Kentau Kazak.
115 G7 Kent Group is Austr.
30 D5 Kentland U.S.A.
32 B4 Kenton U.S.A.
32 A6 Kentucky div. U.S.A.
29 E4 Kentucky Lake l. U.S.A.
23 H4 Kentville Can.
27 F6 Kentwood LA U.S.A.
30 E4 Kentwood MI U.S.A.
96 Kenya country Africa
Kenya, Mount mt see Kirinyaga
30 A3 Kenyon U.S.A.
34 □² Keokea U.S.A.
30 B5 Keokuk U.S.A.
95 C1 Keo Neua, Col de pass Laos/Vietnam
30 B5 Keosauqua U.S.A.
116 D4 Keppel Bay b. Austr.
95 □ Keppel Harbour chan. Sing.
80 B2 Kepsut Turkey
83 E8 Kerala div. India
114 E5 Kerang Austr.
55 T6 Kerava Fin.
65 G4 Kerba Alg.
69 F6 Kerch Ukr.
110 E2 Kerema P.N.G.
20 F5 Keremeos Can.
69 F7 Kerempe Burun pt Turkey
102 D2 Keren Eritrea
81 L4 Kerend Iran
13 J7 Kerguelen Plateau sea feature Indian Ocean
102 D4 Kericho Kenya
117 D1 Kerikeri N.Z.
55 V6 Kerimäki Fin.
92 C7 Kerinci, G. vol. Indon.
85 E2 Keriya Shankou pass China
79 K2 Kerki Turkm.
67 K4 Kerkinitis, Limni l. Greece
67 H5 Kerkyra Greece
Kerkyra i. see Corfu
101 F3 Kerma Sudan
14 J5 Kermadec Islands is Pac. Oc.
14 H8 Kermadec Tr. sea feature Pac. Oc.
79 H3 Kerman Iran
34 B3 Kerman U.S.A.
81 L4 Kermānshāh Iran
27 C6 Kermit U.S.A.
25 C5 Kern r. U.S.A.
34 C4 Kern, South Fork r. U.S.A.
23 G2 Kernertut, Cap pt Can.
34 C4 Kernville U.S.A.
67 L6 Keros i. Greece
68 K2 Keros Rus. Fed.
100 B4 Kérouané Guinea
61 E4 Kerpen Ger.
119 B5 Kerr, C. c. Antarctica
21 H4 Kerrobert Can.
27 D6 Kerrville U.S.A.
60 B5 Kerry Head hd Rep. of Ireland
95 B4 Kerteh Malaysia
55 M9 Kerteminde Denmark
80 D4 Keryneia Cyprus
68 H3 Kerzhenets r. Rus. Fed.
22 D3 Kesagami Lake l. Can.
55 V6 Kesälahti Fin.
69 C7 Keşan Turkey
80 G1 Keşap Turkey
90 G5 Kesennuma Japan
84 B1 Keshem Afgh.
84 A1 Keshendeh-ye Bala Afgh.
84 B5 Keshod India
81 M5 Keshvar Iran
80 D2 Keskozero Rus. Fed.
61 E3 Kessel Neth.
105 H4 Kestell S. Africa
54 W4 Kesten'ga Rus. Fed.
54 U4 Kestilä Fin.
31 H3 Keswick Can.
58 D3 Keswick U.K.
62 H7 Keszthely Hungary
76 K4 Ket' r. Rus. Fed.
100 C4 Keta Ghana
95 □ Ketam, P. i. Sing.
92 E7 Ketapang Indon.
20 D3 Ketchikan U.S.A.
61 D2 Ketelmeer l. Neth.
86 D3 Ketmen', Khrebet mts China/Kazak.
59 G5 Kettering U.K.
32 A5 Kettering U.S.A.
20 F5 Kettle r. Can.
30 A2 Kettle U.S.A.
32 E4 Kettle Creek r. U.S.A.
34 C3 Kettleman City U.S.A.
24 C1 Kettle River Ra. mts U.S.A.
32 D3 Keuka Lake l. U.S.A.
55 T5 Keuruu Fin.
61 E3 Kevelaer Ger.
30 C5 Kewanee U.S.A.
30 D3 Kewaunee U.S.A.
30 C2 Keweenaw Bay b. U.S.A.
30 C2 Keweenaw Peninsula pen. U.S.A.
30 D2 Keweenaw Pt pt U.S.A.
45 E3 Keweigek Guyana
60 C3 Key, Lough l. Rep. of Ireland
22 D2 Keyano Can.
31 G3 Key Harbour Can.
29 D7 Key Largo U.S.A.
59 E6 Keynsham U.K.

32 D5 Keyser U.S.A.
32 D5 Keysers Ridge U.S.A.
35 G6 Keystone Peak summit U.S.A.
32 D5 Keysville U.S.A.
81 M4 Keytū Iran
29 D7 Key West FL U.S.A.
30 B7 Key West IA U.S.A.
33 H3 Kezar Falls U.S.A.
103 C6 Kezi Zimbabwe
63 K6 Kežmarok Slovakia
104 D2 Kgalagadi div. Botswana
105 G2 Kgatleng div. Botswana
104 D1 Kgomofatshe Pan salt pan Botswana
104 F2 Kgoro Pan salt pan Botswana
105 G3 Kgotsong S. Africa
87 P2 Khabarovsk Rus. Fed.
81 H4 Khābūr, Nahr al r. Syria
81 J7 Khadd, W. al watercourse Saudi Arabia
84 E4 Khaga India
85 G5 Khagrachari Bangl.
84 B3 Khairgarh Pak.
84 B4 Khairpur Pak.
84 D4 Khajurāho India
103 C6 Khakhea Botswana
81 M4 Khalajestan reg. Iran
84 D2 Khalatse Jammu and Kashmir
84 A3 Khalifat mt Pak.
81 M3 Khalkhāl Iran
85 F6 Khallikot India
68 D4 Khalopyenichy Belarus
86 H1 Khamar-Daban, Khrebet mts Rus. Fed.
84 C5 Khambhat India
84 B6 Khambhat, Gulf of g. India
84 D4 Khamgaon India
95 C1 Khamkkeut Laos
83 F7 Khammam India
77 N3 Khamra Rus. Fed.
81 M4 Khamseh reg. Iran
95 B1 Khan, Nam r. Laos
84 B1 Khānābād Afgh.
81 J5 Khān al Baghdādī Iraq
81 K5 Khān al Maḥāwīl Iraq
81 K5 Khān al Mashāhidah Iraq
81 K5 Khān al Muṣallá Iraq
81 J4 Khānaqāh Iran
81 L4 Khānaqīn Iraq
81 K6 Khān ar Raḥbah Iraq
81 K2 Khanasur Pass pass Iran/Turkey
80 F4 Khān az Zabīb Jordan
84 C2 Khanbari Pass pass Jammu and Kashmir
115 H4 Khancoban Austr.
84 B2 Khand Pass pass Afgh./Pak.
84 D5 Khandwa India
77 P3 Khandyga Rus. Fed.
84 B3 Khanewal Pak.
95 D2 Khanh Dương Vietnam
84 D4 Khaniadhana India
81 K5 Khān Jadwal Iraq
90 C2 Khanka, Lake l. China/Rus. Fed.
Khanka, Ozero l. see Khanka, Lake
84 C2 Khanki Weir barrage Pak.
84 D3 Khanna India
84 B3 Khanpur Pak.
80 F4 Khān Shaykhūn Syria
82 D2 Khantau Kazak.
76 L3 Khantayskoye, Ozero l. Rus. Fed.
76 H3 Khanty-Mansiysk Rus. Fed.
80 E6 Khān Yūnis Gaza
95 A3 Khao Chum Thong Thai.
34 D5 Khapa India
82 D5 Khapalu Pak.
87 K2 Khapcheranga Rus. Fed.
69 H6 Kharabali Rus. Fed.
85 F5 Kharagpur India
Kharari see Abu Road
84 C6 Khardi India
84 D2 Khardung La pass India
81 L6 Kharfiyah Iraq
84 C5 Khargon India
84 C4 Khari r. Rajasthan India
84 C4 Khari r. Rajasthan India
84 C2 Kharian Pak.
85 E5 Khariar India
69 F5 Kharkiv Ukr.
Khar'kov see Kharkiv
67 L4 Kharmanli Bulg.
68 G3 Kharovsk Rus. Fed.
81 M4 Khar Rūd r. Iran
85 E5 Kharsia India
101 F3 Khartoum Sudan
69 H7 Khasav'yurt Rus. Fed.
79 J4 Khāsh Iran
78 D7 Khashm el Girba Sudan
69 G7 Khashuri Georgia
85 H4 Khāsi Hills h. India
67 L4 Khaskovo Bulg.
77 M2 Khatanga Rus. Fed.
77 M2 Khatangskiy Zaliv b. Rus. Fed.
84 B1 Khatinza Pass pass Pak.
80 D6 Khatmia Pass pass Egypt
77 T3 Khatyrka Rus. Fed.
79 K1 Khavast Uzbek.
84 B5 Khavda India
84 D3 Khawak Pass pass Afgh.
95 A2 Khawsa Myanmar
105 F5 Khayamnandi S. Africa
79 L2 Khaydarken Kyrgyzstan
104 C7 Khayelitsha S. Africa
81 J3 Khāzir r. Iraq

95 C1 Khê Bo Vietnam
84 C4 Khedbrahma India
84 C4 Khela India
65 H4 Khemis Miliana Alg.
95 C1 Khemmarat Thai.
100 C1 Khenchela Alg.
100 B1 Khenifra Morocco
84 D4 Kherli India
69 E6 Kherson Ukr.
77 N3 Kheta r. Rus. Fed.
84 D4 Khilchipur India
87 K1 Khilok Rus. Fed.
80 F4 Khirbat Isrīyah Syria
84 D2 Khitai P. pass China/Jammu and Kashmir
81 L2 Khīyāv Iran
55 V6 Khiytola Rus. Fed.
95 B2 Khlong, Mae r. Thai.
69 C5 Khmel'nyts'kyy Ukr.
69 C5 Khmil'nyk Ukr.
81 K4 Khodā Āfarīn Iran
79 H1 Khodzheyli Uzbek.
104 D2 Khokhowe Pan salt pan Botswana
84 B4 Khokhropar Pak.
79 K2 Kholm Afgh.
68 C4 Kholmogory Rus. Fed.
87 Q2 Kholmsk Rus. Fed.
63 O2 Kholm-Zhirkovskiy Rus. Fed.
81 M3 Khoman Iran
104 B1 Khomas div. Namibia
104 A1 Khomas Highland reg. Namibia
81 M4 Khondāb Iran
69 G7 Khoni Georgia
95 B1 Khon Kaen Thai.
77 Q3 Khonuu Rus. Fed.
69 G5 Khoper r. Rus. Fed.
87 O2 Khor r. Rus. Fed.
84 B4 Khora Pak.
85 F5 Khordha India
87 J1 Khorinsk Rus. Fed.
103 B6 Khorixas Namibia
90 C2 Khorol Rus. Fed.
69 E5 Khorol Ukr.
81 L2 Khoroslū Dāgh h. Iran
81 M3 Khorramābād Iran
81 M3 Khorram Darreh Iran
81 M6 Khorramshahr Iran
79 L2 Khorugh Tajik.
77 H6 Khosheutovo Rus. Fed.
81 M6 Khosravī Iran
81 M6 Khosrowābād Iran
81 K4 Khosrowvī Iran
84 C1 Khotgaz Afgh.
84 B2 Khowst Afgh.
85 H5 Khreum Myanmar
85 A4 Khri r. India
68 H2 Khristoforovo Rus. Fed.
77 Q2 Khroma r. Rus. Fed.
76 B6 Khromtau Kazak.
90 D2 Khrustalnyy Rus. Fed.
63 O6 Khrystynivka Ukr.
104 F1 Khudumelapye Botswana
104 D3 Khuis Botswana
79 K1 Khŭjand Tajik.
95 C2 Khu Khan Thai.
84 A1 Khulm r. Afgh.
85 G5 Khulna Bangl.
69 J1 Khulo Georgia
105 G3 Khuma S. Africa
84 C2 Khunjerab Pass pass China/Jammu and Kashmir
79 G3 Khunsar Iran
84 E4 Khunti India
95 A1 Khun Yuam Thai.
84 D4 Khurai India
84 D3 Khurja India
81 J6 Khurr, Wādī al watercourse Saudi Arabia
84 C2 Khushab Pak.
81 M3 Khūshāvar Iran
69 B5 Khust Ukr.
105 G3 Khutsong S. Africa
68 J4 Khvalynsk Rus. Fed.
81 K4 Khvosh Maqām Iran
81 K2 Khvoy Iran
68 E3 Khvoynaya Rus. Fed.
95 A2 Khwae Noi r. Thai.
84 B2 Khwaja Kuram mt Afgh.
84 B1 Khwaja Muhammad Ra. mts Afgh.
84 B2 Khyber Pass pass Afgh./Pak.
115 J5 Kiama Austr.
94 C5 Kiamba Phil.
102 C5 Kiambi Dem. Rep. Congo
27 E5 Kiamichi r. U.S.A.
54 V4 Kiantajärvi l. Fin.
84 D2 Kibar India
94 C5 Kibawe Phil.
102 D4 Kibaya Tanz.
103 D4 Kibiti Tanz.
102 B4 Kibombo Dem. Rep. Congo
102 D4 Kibondo Tanz.
67 J4 Kičevo Macedonia
68 H3 Kichmengskiy Gorodok Rus. Fed.
100 C3 Kidal Mali
59 E5 Kidderminster U.K.
102 D3 Kidepo Valley National Park nat. park Uganda
100 A3 Kidira Senegal
84 D2 Kidmang Jammu and Kashmir
117 F3 Kidnappers, Cape c. N.Z.
59 E4 Kidsgrove U.K.
30 C4 Kiel Ger.
62 D3 Kiel Ger.
63 K5 Kielce Pol.
59 E3 Kielder Water resr U.K.
62 E3 Kieler Bucht b. Ger.

103 C5 Kienge Dem. Rep. Congo
61 F3 Kierspe Ger.
69 D5 Kiev Ukr.
100 A3 Kiffa Maur.
67 K5 Kifisia Greece
81 K4 Kifrī Iraq
102 D4 Kigali Rwanda
81 H2 Kiği Turkey
23 H2 Kiglapait Mts mts Can.
102 C4 Kigoma Tanz.
54 S3 Kihlanki Fin.
55 S5 Kihniö Fin.
54 T4 Kiiminki Fin.
91 D8 Kii-sanchi mts Japan
91 D8 Kii-suidō chan. Japan
67 J2 Kikinda Yugo.
68 H3 Kiknur Rus. Fed.
90 A4 Kikonai Japan
103 C4 Kikondja Dem. Rep. Congo
110 E2 Kikori P.N.G.
110 E2 Kikori r. P.N.G.
102 B4 Kikwit Dem. Rep. Congo
55 P6 Kilafors Sweden
84 D2 Kilar India
34 □¹ Kilauea U.S.A.
34 □² Kilauea Crater crater U.S.A.
57 C5 Kilbrannan Sound chan. U.K.
90 A4 Kilchu N. Korea
60 E4 Kilcoole Rep. of Ireland
60 D4 Kilcormac Rep. of Ireland
115 K1 Kilcoy Austr.
60 E4 Kildare Rep. of Ireland
54 X2 Kil'dinstroy Rus. Fed.
102 B4 Kilembe Dem. Rep. Congo
57 C5 Kilfinan U.K.
27 E5 Kilgore U.S.A.
58 E2 Kilham U.K.
102 D4 Kilifi Kenya
102 D4 Kilimanjaro mt Tanz.
111 F2 Kilinailau Is is P.N.G.
103 D4 Kilindoni Tanz.
55 T7 Kilingi-Nõmme Estonia
80 F1 Kilıs Turkey
69 D6 Kiliya Ukr.
60 B5 Kilkee Rep. of Ireland
60 F3 Kilkeel U.K.
60 D5 Kilkenny Rep. of Ireland
59 C7 Kilkhampton U.K.
67 K4 Kilkis Greece
116 E6 Kilkivan Austr.
60 B3 Killala Rep. of Ireland
60 B3 Killala Bay b. Rep. of Ireland
60 C5 Killaloe Rep. of Ireland
31 J3 Killaloe Station Can.
21 G4 Killam Can.
115 K2 Killarney Austr.
31 J3 Killarney Can.
60 B5 Killarney Rep. of Ireland
60 B6 Killarney National Park nat. park Rep. of Ireland
31 G2 Killarney Provincial Park nat. park Can.
60 B4 Killary Harbour b. Rep. of Ireland
27 D6 Killeen U.S.A.
60 D5 Killenaule Rep. of Ireland
60 C4 Killimor Rep. of Ireland
57 D4 Killin U.K.
60 F3 Killinchy U.K.
60 E5 Killinick Rep. of Ireland
23 H1 Killiniq Can.
23 H1 Killiniq Island i. Can.
60 B5 Killorglin Rep. of Ireland
60 E5 Killurin Rep. of Ireland
60 C3 Killybegs Rep. of Ireland
60 D2 Kilmacrenan Rep. of Ireland
60 B4 Kilmaine Rep. of Ireland
60 C5 Kilmallock Rep. of Ireland
57 D3 Kilmaluag U.K.
57 C4 Kilmelford U.K.
68 J3 Kil'mez' Rus. Fed.
68 J3 Kil'mez' r. Rus. Fed.
60 C6 Kilmona Rep. of Ireland
114 F6 Kilmore Austr.
60 E5 Kilmore Quay Rep. of Ireland
102 D4 Kilosa Tanz.
54 R2 Kilpisjärvi Fin.
54 X2 Kilp"yavr Rus. Fed.
60 E3 Kilrea U.K.
60 B5 Kilrush Rep. of Ireland
57 D5 Kilsyth U.K.
83 D8 Kilttān i. India
57 D5 Kilwinning U.K.
103 C4 Kilwa Dem. Rep. Congo
103 D4 Kilwa Masoko Tanz.
103 D4 Kimambi Tanz.
114 B4 Kimba Austr.
103 B4 Kimba Congo
26 C3 Kimball U.S.A.
110 F2 Kimbe P.N.G.
20 F5 Kimberley Can.
104 F4 Kimberley S. Africa
112 E3 Kimberley Plateau plat. Austr.
117 E2 Kimbolton N.Z.
87 N3 Kimch'aek N. Korea
55 S6 Kimito Fin.
67 L6 Kimolos i. Greece
68 F4 Kimovsk Rus. Fed.
102 B4 Kimpese Dem. Rep. Congo
91 F5 Kimpoku-san mt Japan
68 F3 Kimry Rus. Fed.
102 B4 Kimvula Dem. Rep. Congo
92 F5 Kinabalu, Gunung mt Malaysia
94 A5 Kinabatangan r. Malaysia

67 M6 Kinaros i. Greece
57 E2 Kinbrace U.K.
31 G3 Kincardine Can.
57 E4 Kincardine U.K.
114 E4 Kinchega National Park nat. park Austr.
20 D3 Kincolith Can.
103 C4 Kinda Dem. Rep. Congo
85 H5 Kindat Myanmar
27 E6 Kinder U.S.A.
59 F4 Kinder Scout h. U.K.
21 H4 Kindersley Can.
100 A3 Kindia Guinea
102 C4 Kindu Dem. Rep. Congo
68 G3 Kineshma Rus. Fed.
116 D6 Kingaroy Austr.
18 King Christian IX Land reg. Greenland
18 King Christian X Land reg. Greenland
119 C1 King Edward Point U.K. Base Antarctica
32 E3 King Ferry U.S.A.
33 H2 Kingfield U.S.A.
27 D5 Kingfisher U.S.A.
18 King Frederik VI Coast reg. Greenland
18 King Frederik VIII Land reg. Greenland
119 B1 King George I. i. Antarctica
22 E2 King George Islands is Can.
20 D4 King I. i. Can.
68 D3 Kingisepp Rus. Fed.
115 F8 King Island i. Austr.
31 H1 King Kirkland Can.
112 D3 King Leopold Ranges h. Austr.
35 E4 Kingman AZ U.S.A.
27 D4 Kingman KS U.S.A.
33 J2 Kingman ME U.S.A.
20 D3 King Mtn mt Can.
114 A3 Kingoonya Austr.
18 King Oscar Fjord fjord Greenland
60 C5 Kings r. Rep. of Ireland
34 C3 Kings r. U.S.A.
59 D7 Kingsbridge U.K.
34 C3 Kingsburg U.S.A.
33 J2 Kingsbury U.S.A.
34 C3 Kings Canyon National Park nat. park U.S.A.
115 K2 Kingscliff Austr.
114 B5 Kingscote Austr.
60 E4 Kingscourt Rep. of Ireland
119 B2 King Sejong Korea Base Antarctica
30 C3 Kingsford U.S.A.
29 D6 Kingsland GA U.S.A.
30 E5 Kingsland IN U.S.A.
59 H5 King's Lynn U.K.
111 H2 Kingsmill Group is Kiribati
59 H6 Kingsnorth U.K.
112 D3 King Sound b. Austr.
24 E3 Kings Peak summit U.S.A.
32 B6 Kingsport U.S.A.
31 J3 Kingston Can.
37 J5 Kingston Jamaica
117 B6 Kingston N.Z.
30 B6 Kingston IL U.S.A.
33 F4 Kingston NY U.S.A.
115 G9 Kingston
35 E4 Kingston Peak summit U.S.A.
114 C6 Kingston South East Austr.
58 G4 Kingston upon Hull U.K.
37 M6 Kingstown St Vincent
27 D7 Kingsville U.S.A.
59 E6 Kingswood U.K.
59 D5 Kington U.K.
57 D3 Kingussie U.K.
118 B2 King William I. i. Can.
105 G6 King William's Town S. Africa
27 E6 Kingwood TX U.S.A.
32 D5 Kingwood WV U.S.A.
21 J4 Kinistino Can.
90 C6 Kinka-san i. Japan
117 B6 Kinloch N.Z.
57 E3 Kinloss U.K.
31 H3 Kinmount Can.
55 N8 Kinna Sweden
60 D4 Kinnegad Rep. of Ireland
54 T5 Kinnula Fin.
21 J3 Kinoosao Can.
57 E4 Kinross U.K.
60 C6 Kinsale Rep. of Ireland
102 B4 Kinshasa Dem. Rep. Congo
26 D4 Kinsley U.S.A.
29 E5 Kinston U.S.A.
55 R9 Kintai Lith.
100 B4 Kintampo Ghana
57 E4 Kintore U.K.
57 C5 Kintyre pen. U.K.
20 F3 Kinuso Can.
101 F4 Kinyeti mt Sudan
31 H2 Kiosk Can.
22 E4 Kipawa, Lac l. Can.
33 F6 Kiptopeke U.S.A.
103 C5 Kipushi Dem. Rep. Congo
111 G3 Kirakira Solomon Is
68 D4 Kirawsk Belarus
77 M4 Kirensk Rus. Fed.
106 Kiribati country Pac. Oc.
81 H1 Kırık Turkey
80 F3 Kırıkhan Turkey
80 D2 Kırıkkale Turkey
68 F3 Kirillov Rus. Fed.
102 D3 Kirinyaga mt Kenya
68 E3 Kirishi Rus. Fed.

91 B9 **Kirishima-yama** *vol.* Japan
15 J5 **Kiritimati** *i.* Kiribati
80 A2 **Kırkağaç** Turkey
81 L3 **Kirk Bulāg D.** *mt* Iran
59 E4 **Kirkby** U.K.
59 F4 **Kirkby in Ashfield** U.K.
58 E3 **Kirkby Lonsdale** U.K.
58 E3 **Kirkby Stephen** U.K.
57 E4 **Kirkcaldy** U.K.
57 C6 **Kirkcolm** U.K.
60 F3 **Kirkcubbin** U.K.
57 D6 **Kirkcudbright** U.K.
55 N6 **Kirkenær** Norway
54 W2 **Kirkenes** Norway
31 H3 **Kirkfield** Can.
57 D5 **Kirkintilloch** U.K.
55 T6 **Kirkkonummi** Fin.
35 F4 **Kirkland** U.S.A.
35 F4 **Kirkland Junction** U.S.A.
31 G1 **Kirkland Lake** Can.
69 C7 **Kırklareli** Turkey
58 C3 **Kirk Michael** U.K.
58 E3 **Kirkoswald** U.K.
26 E3 **Kirksville** U.S.A.
81 K4 **Kirkūk** Iraq
57 F2 **Kirkwall** U.K.
105 F6 **Kirkwood** S. Africa
34 B2 **Kirkwood** *CA* U.S.A.
26 F4 **Kirkwood** *MO* U.S.A.
80 C1 **Kırmır** *r.* Turkey
62 E4 **Kirov** Rus. Fed.
Kirov *see* **Kirov**
68 J3 **Kirov** Rus. Fed.
Kirovabad *see* **Gäncä**
68 J3 **Kirovo-Chepetsk** Rus. Fed.
69 E5 **Kirovohrad** Ukr.
81 M2 **Kirovsk** Azer.
68 D3 **Kirovsk** *Leningrad.* Rus. Fed.
54 X3 **Kirovsk** *Murmansk.* Rus. Fed.
68 J3 **Kirovskaya Oblast'** *div.* Rus. Fed.
90 C2 **Kirovskiy** Rus. Fed.
119 B4 **Kirpatrick, Mt** *mt* Antarctica
57 E4 **Kirriemuir** U.K.
68 K3 **Kirs** Rus. Fed.
68 G4 **Kirsanov** Rus. Fed.
80 E2 **Kırşehir** Turkey
79 K4 **Kirthar Range** *mts* Pak.
54 R3 **Kiruna** Sweden
102 C4 **Kirundu** Dem. Rep. Congo
68 H4 **Kirya** Rus. Fed.
91 F6 **Kiryū** Japan
55 O8 **Kisa** Sweden
102 C3 **Kisangani** Dem. Rep. Congo
102 B4 **Kisantu** Dem. Rep. Congo
92 B6 **Kisaran** Indon.
85 F4 **Kishanganj** India
84 B4 **Kishangarh** *Rajasthan* India
84 C4 **Kishangarh** *Rajasthan* India
84 C2 **Kishen Ganga** *r.* India/Pak.
91 B9 **Kishika-zaki** *pt* Japan
Kishinev *see* **Chişinău**
91 D7 **Kishiwada** Japan
76 J4 **Kishkenekol'** Kazak.
85 G4 **Kishorganj** Bangl.
84 C2 **Kishtwar** Jammu and Kashmir
100 C4 **Kisi** Nigeria
102 D4 **Kisii** Kenya
21 K4 **Kiskittogisu L.** *l.* Can.
63 J7 **Kiskunfélegyháza** Hungary
63 J7 **Kiskunhalas** Hungary
69 G7 **Kislovodsk** Rus. Fed.
102 E4 **Kismaayo** Somalia
102 C4 **Kisoro** Uganda
91 E7 **Kiso-sanmyaku** *mts* Japan
100 A4 **Kissidougou** Guinea
29 D6 **Kissimmee** U.S.A.
29 D7 **Kissimmee, L.** *l.* U.S.A.
21 J3 **Kississing L.** *l.* Can.
102 D4 **Kisumu** Kenya
100 B3 **Kita** Mali
91 G6 **Kitaibaraki** Japan
90 G5 **Kitakami** Japan
90 G5 **Kitakami-gawa** *r.* Japan
91 F6 **Kitakata** Japan
91 B8 **Kita-Kyūshū** Japan
102 D3 **Kitale** Kenya
90 H3 **Kitami** Japan
25 G4 **Kit Carson** U.S.A.
31 G4 **Kitchener** Can.
54 W5 **Kitee** Fin.
102 D3 **Kitgum** Uganda
20 D4 **Kitimat** Can.
54 U3 **Kitinen** *r.* Fin.
102 B4 **Kitona** Dem. Rep. Congo
91 B8 **Kitsuki** Japan
114 C2 **Kittakittaooloo, L.** *salt flat* Austr.
32 D4 **Kittanning** U.S.A.
33 F4 **Kittatinny Mts** *h.* U.S.A.
33 H3 **Kittery** U.S.A.
54 T3 **Kittilä** Fin.
29 F4 **Kitty Hawk** U.S.A.
102 D4 **Kitunda** Tanz.
20 D3 **Kitwanga** Can.
103 C5 **Kitwe** Zambia
62 F7 **Kitzbüheler Alpen** *mts* Austria
54 U5 **Kiuruvesi** Fin.
54 T5 **Kivijärvi** Fin.
55 U7 **Kiviõli** Estonia
102 C4 **Kivu, Lake** *l.* Rwanda/Dem. Rep. Congo
90 C3 **Kiyevka** Rus. Fed.
67 N4 **Kıyıköy** Turkey
76 G4 **Kizel** Rus. Fed.
68 H2 **Kizema** Rus. Fed.
80 B3 **Kızılca D.** *mt* Turkey
80 D1 **Kızılcahamam** Turkey
80 G2 **Kızıl D.** *mt* Turkey
80 D1 **Kızılırmak** Turkey
80 D2 **Kızılırmak** *r.* Turkey
80 C3 **Kızılkaya** Turkey
80 D3 **Kızılören** Turkey
81 H3 **Kızıltepe** Turkey
69 H7 **Kizil"yurt** Rus. Fed.
69 H7 **Kizlyar** Rus. Fed.
54 U1 **Kjøllefjord** Norway
54 P2 **Kjøpsvik** Norway
62 G5 **Kladno** Czech Rep.
62 G7 **Klagenfurt** Austria
35 H4 **Klagetoh** U.S.A.
55 R9 **Klaipėda** Lith.
54 □ **Klaksvík** Faroe Is
24 B3 **Klamath** *r.* U.S.A.
24 B3 **Klamath Falls** U.S.A.
24 B3 **Klamath Mts** *mts* U.S.A.
55 N6 **Klarälven** *r.* Sweden
62 F6 **Klatovy** Czech Rep.
104 C5 **Klawer** S. Africa
20 C3 **Klawock** U.S.A.
61 E2 **Klazienaveen** Neth.
20 E4 **Kleena Kleene** Can.
104 D4 **Kleinbegin** S. Africa
104 C3 **Klein Karas** Namibia
104 D6 **Klein Roggeveldberge** *mts* S. Africa
104 B4 **Kleinsee** S. Africa
104 D6 **Klein Swartberg** *mts* S. Africa
20 D4 **Klemtu** Can.
105 G3 **Klerksdorp** S. Africa
68 E4 **Kletnya** Rus. Fed.
69 G5 **Kletskaya** Rus. Fed.
61 E3 **Kleve** Ger.
68 D4 **Klimavichy** Belarus
68 E4 **Klimovo** Rus. Fed.
68 F4 **Klimovsk** Rus. Fed.
68 F3 **Klin** Rus. Fed.
20 D4 **Klinaklini** *r.* Can.
62 F5 **Klínovec** *mt* Czech Rep.
55 Q8 **Klintehamn** Sweden
69 J5 **Klintsovka** Rus. Fed.
68 E4 **Klintsy** Rus. Fed.
104 C5 **Kliprand** S. Africa
66 G2 **Ključ** Bos.-Herz.
62 H5 **Kłodzko** Pol.
62 H6 **Klosterneuburg** Austria
22 F1 **Klotz, Lac** *l.* Can.
20 A2 **Kluane Game Sanctuary** *res.* Can.
20 B2 **Kluane Lake** *l.* Can.
20 B2 **Kluane National Park** *nat. park* Can.
62 J5 **Kluczbork** Pol.
84 B3 **Klupro** Pak.
68 C4 **Klyetsk** Belarus
77 S4 **Klyuchevskaya, Sopka** *vol.* Rus. Fed.
55 O6 **Knåda** Sweden
58 F3 **Knaresborough** U.K.
21 L3 **Knee Lake** *l.* Can.
30 B1 **Knife Lake** *l.* Can./U.S.A.
30 D4 **Knight In.** *in.* Can.
59 D5 **Knighton** U.K.
30 E6 **Knightstown** U.S.A.
66 G2 **Knin** Croatia
62 G7 **Knittelfeld** Austria
67 K3 **Knjaževac** Yugo.
60 C4 **Knock** Rep. of Ireland
60 B6 **Knockaboy** *h.* Rep. of Ireland
60 B5 **Knockacummer** *h.* Rep. of Ireland
60 C3 **Knockalongy** *h.* Rep. of Ireland
60 B5 **Knockalough** Rep. of Ireland
57 F3 **Knock Hill** *h.* U.K.
60 E2 **Knocklayd** *h.* U.K.
61 B3 **Knokke-Heist** Belgium
59 F5 **Knowle** U.K.
119 B2 **Knowles, C.** *c.* Antarctica
33 J1 **Knowles Corner** U.S.A.
33 G2 **Knowlton** Can.
30 D5 **Knox** U.S.A.
20 C4 **Knox, C.** *c.* Can.
34 A2 **Knoxville** *CA* U.S.A.
30 B5 **Knoxville** *IL* U.S.A.
29 D4 **Knoxville** *TN* U.S.A.
57 C3 **Knoydart** *reg.* U.K.
104 E7 **Knysna** S. Africa
91 B9 **Kobayashi** Japan
54 V2 **Kobbfoss** Norway
91 D7 **Kōbe** Japan
København *see* **Copenhagen**
100 B3 **Kobenni** Maur.
62 C5 **Koblenz** Ger.
68 J3 **Kobra** Rus. Fed.
93 J8 **Kobroör** *i.* Indon.
68 C4 **Kobryn** Belarus
69 G7 **K'obulet'i** Georgia
67 K4 **Kočani** Macedonia
80 B1 **Kocasu** *r.* Turkey
66 F2 **Kočevje** Slovenia
85 G4 **Koch Bihār** India
Kochi *see* **Cochin**
91 C8 **Kōchi** Japan
68 H4 **Kochkurovo** Rus. Fed.
69 H6 **Kochubey** Rus. Fed.
69 G6 **Kochubeyevskoye** Rus. Fed.
118 C1 **Kodiak Island** *i.* U.S.A.
105 G1 **Kodibeleng** Botswana
68 F2 **Kodino** Rus. Fed.
101 F4 **Kodok** Sudan
69 G7 **Kodori** *r.* Georgia
69 D5 **Kodyma** Ukr.
67 L4 **Kodzhaele** *mt* Bulg./Greece
104 D6 **Koedoesberg** *mts* S. Africa
104 D4 **Koegrabie** S. Africa
104 C5 **Koekenaap** S. Africa
85 E4 **Koel** *r.* India
103 B6 **Koës** Namibia
35 F5 **Kofa Mts** *mts* U.S.A.
104 F4 **Koffiefontein** S. Africa
100 B4 **Koforidua** Ghana
91 F7 **Kōfu** Japan
22 E2 **Kogaluc** *r.* Can.
22 E2 **Kogaluc, Baie de** *b.* Can.
23 H2 **Kogaluk** *r.* Can.
115 J1 **Kogan** Austr.
55 N9 **Køge** Denmark
84 B2 **Kohat** Pak.
55 T7 **Kohila** Estonia
85 H4 **Kohima** India
84 B3 **Kohlu** Pak.
55 U7 **Kohtla-Järve** Estonia
117 E2 **Kohukohunui** *h.* N.Z.
91 F6 **Koide** Japan
20 A2 **Koidern** Can.
81 K3 **Koi Sanjaq** Iraq
90 F4 **Ko-jima** *i.* Japan
91 F8 **Ko-jima** *i.* Japan
112 C6 **Kojonup** Austr.
95 A1 **Kok** *r.* Thai.
33 J2 **Kokadjo** U.S.A.
79 L1 **Kokand** Uzbek.
55 R7 **Kökar** Fin.
84 B1 **Kokcha** *r.* Afgh.
55 R6 **Kokemäenjoki** *r.* Fin.
104 C4 **Kokerboom** Namibia
63 O3 **Kokhanava** Belarus
68 G3 **Kokhma** Rus. Fed.
54 S5 **Kokkola** Fin.
34 □1 **Koko Hd** *hd* U.S.A.
30 D5 **Kokomo** U.S.A.
104 E2 **Kokong** Botswana
105 G3 **Kokosi** S. Africa
82 F1 **Kokpekti** Kazak.
68 H3 **Koksharka** Rus. Fed.
76 H4 **Kokshetau** Kazak.
23 G2 **Koksoak** *r.* Can.
105 H5 **Kokstad** S. Africa
54 X2 **Kola** Rus. Fed.
84 C2 **Kolahoi** *mt* India
93 G7 **Kolaka** Indon.
95 A4 **Ko Lanta** Thai.
76 E3 **Kola Peninsula** *pen.* Rus. Fed.
84 E6 **Kolar** India
84 D4 **Kolaras** India
83 E8 **Kolar Gold Fields** India
54 S3 **Kolari** Fin.
84 C4 **Kolayat** India
68 F3 **Kol'chugino** Rus. Fed.
100 A3 **Kolda** Senegal
55 L9 **Kolding** Denmark
102 C3 **Kole** *Haute-Zaïre* Dem. Rep. Congo
102 C4 **Kole** *Kasai-Oriental* Dem. Rep. Congo
65 H4 **Koléa** Alg.
54 R4 **Koler** Sweden
76 G3 **Kolguyev, O.** *i.* Rus. Fed.
85 F5 **Kolhan** *reg.* India
83 D7 **Kolhapur** India
83 D10 **Kolhumadulu Atoll** *atoll* Maldives
55 S7 **Kõljala** Estonia
55 S8 **Kolkasrags** *pt* Latvia
Kollam *see* **Quilon**
Köln *see* **Cologne**
62 G3 **Kołobrzeg** Pol.
68 H3 **Kologriv** Rus. Fed.
100 B3 **Kolokani** Mali
111 F2 **Kolombangara** *i.* Solomon Is
68 F4 **Kolomna** Rus. Fed.
69 C5 **Kolomyya** Ukr.
100 B3 **Kolondiéba** Mali
93 G7 **Kolonedale** Indon.
104 D3 **Kolonkwane** Botswana
76 K4 **Kolpashevo** Rus. Fed.
69 F4 **Kolpny** Rus. Fed.
Kol'skiy Poluostrov *pen.* *see* **Kola Peninsula**
78 E7 **Koluli** Eritrea
54 M4 **Kolvereid** Norway
54 T1 **Kolvik** Norway
103 C5 **Kolwezi** Dem. Rep. Congo
77 R3 **Kolyma** *r.* Rus. Fed.
77 R3 **Kolymskaya Nizmennost'** *lowland* Rus. Fed.
77 R3 **Kolymskiy, Khrebet** *mts* Rus. Fed.
68 H4 **Kolyshley** Rus. Fed.
67 K3 **Kom** *mt* Bulg.
90 G3 **Komaga-take** *vol.* Japan
104 B4 **Komaggas** S. Africa
104 B4 **Komaggas Mts** *mts* S. Africa
77 S4 **Komandorskiye Ostrova** *is* Rus. Fed.
62 J7 **Komárno** Slovakia
105 J2 **Komatipoort** S. Africa
91 E6 **Komatsu** Japan
91 D7 **Komatsushima** Japan
102 C4 **Kombe** Dem. Rep. Congo
100 B3 **Kombissiri** Burkina
105 G6 **Komga** S. Africa
68 J2 **Komi, Respublika** *div.* Rus. Fed.
69 D6 **Kominternivs'ke** Ukr.
66 G3 **Komiža** Croatia
67 H1 **Komló** Hungary
102 B4 **Komono** Congo
91 F6 **Komoro** Japan
67 L4 **Komotini** Greece
104 D6 **Komsberg** *mts* S. Africa
77 L1 **Komsomolets, O.** *i.* Rus. Fed.
68 G3 **Komsomol'sk** Rus. Fed.
69 E5 **Komsomol's'k** Ukr.
69 H6 **Komsomol'skiy** *Kalmyk.* Rus. Fed.
68 H4 **Komsomol'skiy** *Mordov.* Rus. Fed.
87 P1 **Komsomol'sk-na-Amure** Rus. Fed.
81 J1 **Kömürlü** Turkey
35 F6 **Kom Vo** U.S.A.
68 F3 **Konakovo** Rus. Fed.
85 F5 **Konar Res.** *resr* India
84 D4 **Konch** India
85 E6 **Kondagaon** India
31 J2 **Kondiaronk, Lac** *l.* Can.
102 D4 **Kondoa** Tanz.
68 E2 **Kondopoga** Rus. Fed.
68 E4 **Kondrovo** Rus. Fed.
84 B1 **Kondūz** Afgh.
95 B3 **Kông, Kaôh** *i.* Cambodia
95 C2 **Kông, T.** *r.* Cambodia
95 C2 **Kong, Xé** *r.* Laos
76 D2 **Kong Karls Land** *is* Svalbard
102 C4 **Kongolo** Dem. Rep. Congo
100 B3 **Kongoussi** Burkina
55 L7 **Kongsberg** Norway
55 N6 **Kongsvinger** Norway
102 D4 **Kongwa** Tanz.
61 F4 **Königswinter** Ger.
62 J4 **Konin** Pol.
67 G3 **Konjic** Bos.-Herz.
104 B4 **Konkiep** *watercourse* Namibia
100 B3 **Konna** Mali
54 U5 **Konnevesi** Fin.
68 G2 **Konosha** Rus. Fed.
91 F6 **Kōnosu** Japan
69 E5 **Konotop** Ukr.
95 D2 **Kon Plong** Vietnam
62 D7 **Konstanz** Ger.
100 C3 **Kontagora** Nigeria
54 V5 **Kontiolahti** Fin.
54 U4 **Konttila** Fin.
95 C2 **Kon Tum** Vietnam
95 D2 **Kontum, Plateau du** *plat.* Vietnam
80 D3 **Konya** Turkey
112 D5 **Kookynie** Austr.
34 □1 **Koolau Range** *mts* U.S.A.
114 F5 **Koondrook** Austr.
32 D5 **Koon Lake** *l.* U.S.A.
115 H5 **Koorawatha** Austr.
24 C2 **Kooskia** U.S.A.
20 F5 **Kootenay** *r.* Can./U.S.A.
20 F5 **Kootenay L.** *l.* Can.
20 F4 **Kootenay Nat. Park** *nat. park* Can.
104 D5 **Kootjieskolk** S. Africa
69 H6 **Kopanovka** Rus. Fed.
84 C6 **Kopargaon** India
54 E3 **Kópasker** Iceland
66 E2 **Koper** Slovenia
55 P7 **Köping** Sweden
55 Q5 **Köpmanholmen** Sweden
105 F2 **Kopong** Botswana
55 M6 **Koppang** Norway
55 O7 **Kopparberg** Sweden
105 G3 **Koppies** S. Africa
104 D3 **Koppieskraal Pan** *salt pan* S. Africa
66 G1 **Koprivnica** Croatia
80 C3 **Köprü** *r.* Turkey
68 G4 **Korablino** Rus. Fed.
22 E1 **Korak, Baie** *b.* Can.
83 F7 **Koraput** India
Korat *see* **Nakhon Ratchasima**
85 E5 **Korba** India
66 D6 **Korba** Tunisia
95 B4 **Korbu, Gunung** *mt* Malaysia
67 J4 **Korçë** Albania
66 G3 **Korčula** Croatia
66 G3 **Korčula** *i.* Croatia
66 G3 **Korčulanski Kanal** *chan.* Croatia
81 M4 **Kord Khvord** Iran
88 G2 **Korea Bay** *g.* China/N. Korea
91 A7 **Korea Strait** *str.* Japan/S. Korea
69 F6 **Korenovsk** Rus. Fed.
69 C5 **Korets'** Ukr.
80 B1 **Körfez** Turkey
119 B3 **Korff Ice Rise** *ice feature* Antarctica
54 N3 **Korgen** Norway
100 B4 **Korhogo** Côte d'Ivoire
84 B5 **Kori Creek** *in.* India
67 K5 **Korinthiakos Kolpos** *chan.* Greece
67 K6 **Korinthos** Greece
62 H7 **Kőris-hegy** *mt* Hungary
67 J3 **Koritnik** *mt* Albania
91 G6 **Kōriyama** Japan
80 C3 **Korkuteli** Turkey
80 D4 **Kormakitis, Cape** *c.* Cyprus
62 H7 **Körmend** Hungary
100 B4 **Koro** Côte d'Ivoire
111 H3 **Koro** *i.* Fiji
100 B3 **Koro** Mali
69 F5 **Korocha** Rus. Fed.
80 D1 **Köroğlu Dağları** *mts* Turkey
80 D1 **Köroğlu Tepesi** *mt* Turkey
102 D4 **Korogwe** Tanz.
114 E7 **Koroit** Austr.
114 E6 **Korong Vale** Austr.
67 K4 **Koronia, L.** *l.* Greece
93 J5 **Koror** Palau
111 H3 **Koro Sea** *b.* Fiji
69 D5 **Korosten'** Ukr.
69 D5 **Korostyshiv** Ukr.
101 D3 **Koro Toro** Chad
55 T5 **Korpilahti** Fin.
55 R6 **Korpo** Fin.
87 Q2 **Korsakov** Rus. Fed.
68 J3 **Korshik** Rus. Fed.
54 R5 **Korsnäs** Fin.
55 M9 **Korsør** Denmark
69 D5 **Korsun'-Shevchenkivs'kyy** Ukr.
63 K3 **Korsze** Pol.
54 S5 **Kortesjärvi** Fin.
68 J2 **Kortkeros** Rus. Fed.
61 B4 **Kortrijk** Belgium
68 G3 **Kortsovo** Rus. Fed.
115 F7 **Korumburra** Austr.
100 D4 **Korup, Parc National de** *nat. park* Cameroon
54 U3 **Korvala** Fin.
84 D4 **Korwai** India
77 R4 **Koryakskaya, Sopka** *vol.* Rus. Fed.
77 S3 **Koryakskiy Khrebet** *mts* Rus. Fed.
68 H2 **Koryazhma** Rus. Fed.
69 E5 **Koryukivka** Ukr.
67 M6 **Kos** *i.* Greece
62 H4 **Kościan** Pol.
27 F5 **Kosciusko** U.S.A.
20 C3 **Kosciusko I.** *i.* U.S.A.
115 H6 **Kosciuszko, Mount** *mt* Austr.
115 H6 **Kosciuszko National Park** *nat. park* Austr.
81 G1 **Köse** Turkey
80 F1 **Köse Dağı** *mt* Turkey
86 E2 **Kosh-Agach** Rus. Fed.
91 A9 **Koshikijima-rettō** *is* Japan
30 C4 **Koshkoning, Lake** *l.* U.S.A.
84 D4 **Kosi** India
84 D3 **Kosi** *r.* India
105 K3 **Kosi Bay** *b.* S. Africa
63 K6 **Košice** Slovakia
54 R3 **Koskullskulle** Sweden
68 J2 **Koslan** Rus. Fed.
90 A5 **Kosŏng** N. Korea
90 A4 **Kosŏng-ni** N. Korea
67 J3 **Kosovo** *div.* Yugo.
67 J3 **Kosovska Mitrovica** Yugo.
100 B4 **Kossou, Lac de** *l.* Côte d'Ivoire
76 H4 **Kostanay** Kazak.
67 K3 **Kostenets** Bulg.
105 G2 **Koster** S. Africa
101 F3 **Kosti** Sudan
67 K3 **Kostinbrod** Bulg.
76 K3 **Kostino** Rus. Fed.
68 D1 **Kostomuksha** Rus. Fed.
69 C5 **Kostopil'** Ukr.
68 G3 **Kostroma** Rus. Fed.
68 G3 **Kostroma** *r.* Rus. Fed.
68 G3 **Kostromskaya Oblast'** *div.* Rus. Fed.
62 G4 **Kostrzyn** Pol.
69 F5 **Kostyantynivka** Ukr.
62 H3 **Koszalin** Pol.
62 H7 **Kőszeg** Hungary
85 E5 **Kota** *Madhya Pradesh* India
84 C4 **Kota** *Rajasthan* India
92 C8 **Kotaagung** Indon.
92 F7 **Kotabaru** Indon.
92 C5 **Kota Bharu** Malaysia
92 C7 **Kotabumi** Indon.
92 F5 **Kota Kinabalu** Malaysia
83 F7 **Kotapārh** India
95 B5 **Kotapinang** Indon.
84 C4 **Kotari** *r.* India
95 B5 **Kota Tinggi** Malaysia
68 J3 **Kotel'nich** Rus. Fed.
69 G6 **Kotel'nikovo** Rus. Fed.
77 P2 **Kotel'nyy, O.** *i.* Rus. Fed.
84 D3 **Kotgarh** India
84 E4 **Kothi** India
55 U6 **Kotka** Fin.
84 C3 **Kot Kapura** India
68 H2 **Kotlas** Rus. Fed.
84 C2 **Kotli** Pak.
77 V3 **Kotlik** Alaska
54 D5 **Kötlutangi** *pt* Iceland
55 V7 **Kotly** Rus. Fed.
66 G2 **Kotor Varoš** Bos.-Herz.
100 B4 **Kotouba** Côte d'Ivoire
69 H5 **Kotovo** Rus. Fed.
69 G4 **Kotovsk** Rus. Fed.
69 D6 **Kotovs'k** Ukr.
84 C4 **Kotra** India
84 E6 **Kotri** *r.* India
84 B4 **Kotri** Pak.
84 A5 **Kot Sarae** Pak.
83 F7 **Kottagudem** India
83 E9 **Kottayam** India
77 M2 **Kotuy** *r.* Rus. Fed.
77 V3 **Kotzebue Sound** *b.* Alaska
100 A3 **Koubia** Guinea
100 B3 **Koudougou** Burkina
104 E6 **Koueveldberge** *mts* S. Africa
101 D3 **Koufey** Niger
67 M7 **Koufonisi** *i.* Greece
104 E6 **Kougaberge** *mts* S. Africa
80 D4 **Kouklia** Cyprus
102 B4 **Koulamoutou** Gabon
100 B3 **Koulikoro** Mali
111 G4 **Koumac** New Caledonia
116 C3 **Koumala** Austr.
100 A3 **Koundâra** Guinea
100 B3 **Koupéla** Burkina
43 H2 **Kourou** Fr. Guiana
100 B3 **Kouroussa** Guinea
101 D3 **Kousséri** Cameroon
100 B3 **Koutiala** Mali
55 U6 **Kouvola** Fin.
54 W3 **Kovdor** Rus. Fed.
54 W3 **Kovdozero, Oz.** *l.* Rus. Fed.
69 C5 **Kovel'** Ukr.
68 G3 **Kovernino** Rus. Fed.
68 G3 **Kovrov** Rus. Fed.
68 G4 **Kovylkino** Rus. Fed.
68 F2 **Kovzhskoye, Ozero** *l.* Rus. Fed.
117 C5 **Kowhitirangi** N.Z.
89 □ **Kowloon** China
91 B7 **Kōyama-misaki** *pt* Japan
80 B3 **Köyceğiz** Turkey
68 J2 **Koygorodok** Rus. Fed.
68 H1 **Koynas** Rus. Fed.
80 F1 **Koyulhisar** Turkey
68 F3 **Koza** Rus. Fed.
91 A7 **Kō-zaki** *pt* Japan
80 E3 **Kozan** Turkey
67 J4 **Kozani** Greece
66 G2 **Kozara** *mts* Bos.-Herz.
69 D5 **Kozelets'** Ukr.
68 E4 **Kozel'sk** Rus. Fed.
Kozhikode *see* **Calicut**
80 C1 **Kozlu** Turkey
68 H3 **Koz'modem'yansk** Rus. Fed.
67 K4 **Kožuf** *mts* Greece/Macedonia
91 F7 **Kōzu-shima** *i.* Japan
69 D5 **Kozyatyn** Ukr.
100 C4 **Kpalimé** Togo
95 A3 **Kra, Isthmus of** *isth.* Thai.
95 A3 **Krabi** Thai.
95 A3 **Kra Buri** Thai.
95 C2 **Krâchéh** Cambodia
54 P4 **Kraddsele** Sweden
55 L7 **Kragerø** Norway
67 J2 **Kragujevac** Yugo.
92 □ **Krakatau** *i.* Indon.
95 C2 **Krâkôr** Cambodia
63 J5 **Kraków** Pol.
95 B2 **Krâlănh** Cambodia
45 C1 **Kralendijk** Neth. Ant.
69 F5 **Kramators'k** Ukr.
54 P5 **Kramfors** Sweden
61 C3 **Krammer** *est.* Neth.
67 K6 **Kranidi** Greece
66 F1 **Kranj** Slovenia
95 □ **Kranji Res.** *resr* Sing.
105 J4 **Kranskop** S. Africa
68 H2 **Krasavino** Rus. Fed.
76 G2 **Krasino** Rus. Fed.
90 B3 **Kraskino** Rus. Fed.
55 U9 **Krāslava** Latvia
63 P4 **Krasnapollye** Belarus
68 D4 **Krasnaya Gora** Rus. Fed.
69 H5 **Krasnoarmeysk** Rus. Fed.
69 F5 **Krasnoarmiys'k** Ukr.
68 H2 **Krasnoborsk** Rus. Fed.
69 F6 **Krasnodar** Rus. Fed.
69 F6 **Krasnodarskiy Kray** *div.* Rus. Fed.
69 F5 **Krasnodon** Ukr.
68 D3 **Krasnogorodskoye** Rus. Fed.
87 Q2 **Krasnogorsk** Rus. Fed.
69 G6 **Krasnogvardeyskoye** Rus. Fed.
69 E5 **Krasnohrad** Ukr.
69 E6 **Krasnohvardiys'ke** Ukr.
63 R2 **Krasnomayskiy** Rus. Fed.
69 E6 **Krasnoperekops'k** Ukr.
90 D2 **Krasnorechenskiy** Rus. Fed.
55 V6 **Krasnosel'skoye** Rus. Fed.
68 G4 **Krasnoslobodsk** Rus. Fed.
Krasnovodsk *see* **Turkmenbashi**
76 L4 **Krasnoyarsk** Rus. Fed.
63 P3 **Krasnyy** Rus. Fed.
68 H3 **Krasnyye Baki** Rus. Fed.
69 H6 **Krasnyye Barrikady** Rus. Fed.
68 F3 **Krasnyy Kholm** Rus. Fed.
69 H5 **Krasnyy Kut** Rus. Fed.
68 D3 **Krasnyy Luch** Rus. Fed.
69 F5 **Krasnyy Lyman** Ukr.
69 J6 **Krasnyy Yar** *Astrak.* Rus. Fed.
69 H5 **Krasnyy Yar** *Volgograd.* Rus. Fed.
69 C5 **Krasyliv** Ukr.
95 B2 **Krâvanh, Chuŏr Phnum** *mts* Cambodia
69 H7 **Kraynovka** Rus. Fed.
62 C5 **Krefeld** Ger.
69 E5 **Kremenchuk** Ukr.
69 E5 **Kremenchuts'ka Vodoskhovyshche** *resr* Ukr.
69 G5 **Kremenskaya** Rus. Fed.
62 G6 **Křemešník** *h.* Czech Rep.
24 F3 **Kremmling** U.S.A.
62 G6 **Krems an der Donau** Austria
77 U3 **Kresta, Zaliv** *b.* Rus. Fed.
68 E3 **Kresttsy** Rus. Fed.
55 R9 **Kretinga** Lith.
63 N3 **Kreva** Belarus
100 C4 **Kribi** Cameroon
105 H3 **Kriel** S. Africa
67 J5 **Krikellos** Greece
90 H2 **Kril'on, Mys** *c.* Rus. Fed.

83 F7 Krishna r. India
83 F7 Krishna, Mouths of the est. India
83 E8 Krishnagiri India
85 G5 Krishnanagar India
55 K7 Kristiansand Norway
55 O8 Kristianstad Sweden
54 K5 Kristiansund Norway
55 O7 Kristinehamn Sweden
55 R5 Kristinestad Fin.
Kriti i. see Crete
Krivoy Rog see Kryvyy Rih
66 G1 Križevci Croatia
66 F2 Krk i. Croatia
54 O5 Krokom Sweden
54 L5 Krokstadøra Norway
54 O3 Krokstranda Norway
69 E5 Krolevets' Ukr.
95 B3 Krŏng Kaôh Kŏng Cambodia
54 S5 Kronoby Fin.
95 A2 Kronwa Myanmar
105 G3 Kroonstad S. Africa
69 G6 Kropotkin Rus. Fed.
63 K6 Krosno Pol.
62 H5 Krotoszyn Pol.
105 J2 Kruger National Park nat. park S. Africa
63 O3 Kruhlaye Belarus
92 C8 Krui Indon.
104 F7 Kruisfontein S. Africa
67 H4 Krujë Albania
67 L4 Krumovgrad Bulg.
Krungkao see Ayutthaya
Krung Thep see Bangkok
63 O3 Krupki Belarus
67 J3 Kruševac Yugo.
20 B3 Kruzof I. i. U.S.A.
68 D4 Krychaw Belarus
69 F6 Krymsk Rus. Fed.
67 L6 Krytiko Pelagos sea Greece
69 E6 Kryvyy Rih Ukr.
100 B2 Ksabi Alg.
100 C1 Ksar el Boukhari Alg.
100 B1 Ksar el Kebir Morocco
69 F5 Kshenskiy Rus. Fed.
66 D7 Ksour Essaf Tunisia
68 H3 Kstovo Rus. Fed.
95 A4 Kuah Malaysia
95 B4 Kuala Kangsar Malaysia
95 B4 Kuala Kerai Malaysia
95 B5 Kuala Kubu Baharu Malaysia
92 C6 Kuala Lipis Malaysia
92 C6 Kuala Lumpur Malaysia
95 B4 Kuala Nerang Malaysia
95 B5 Kuala Pilah Malaysia
95 B5 Kuala Rompin Malaysia
95 A4 Kualasimpang Indon.
92 C5 Kuala Terengganu Malaysia
94 A5 Kuamut Malaysia
89 F6 Kuanshan Taiwan
92 C6 Kuantan Malaysia
69 G6 Kuban' r. Rus. Fed.
81 G4 Kubār Syria
81 J5 Kubaysah Iraq
68 F3 Kubenskoye, Ozero l. Rus. Fed.
68 H4 Kubnya r. Rus. Fed.
67 M3 Kubrat Bulg.
84 C4 Kuchāman India
84 C4 Kuchera India
92 D6 Kuching Malaysia
91 A10 Kuchino-shima i. Japan
Kucing see Kuching
67 H4 Kuçovë Albania
92 □ Kudus Indon.
62 F7 Kufstein Austria
68 H3 Kugesi Rus. Fed.
81 L5 Kūhdasht Iran
81 M3 Kūhīn Iran
54 V4 Kuhmo Fin.
55 T6 Kuhmoinen Fin.
95 A2 Kui Buri Thai.
104 B2 Kuis Namibia
104 A1 Kuiseb Pass pass Namibia
103 B5 Kuito Angola
20 C3 Kuiu Island i. U.S.A.
54 T4 Kuivaniemi Fin.
85 F5 Kujang India
90 G4 Kuji Japan
91 B8 Kujū-san vol. Japan
31 F1 Kukatush Can.
67 J3 Kukës Albania
68 J3 Kukmor Rus. Fed.
95 B5 Kukup Malaysia
80 B2 Kula Turkey
85 G3 Kula Kangri mt Bhutan
82 A1 Kulandy Kazak.
77 P2 Kular Rus. Fed.
94 B5 Kulassein i. Phil.
85 H4 Kulaura Bangl.
55 R8 Kuldīga Latvia
104 D1 Kule Botswana
68 G4 Kulebaki Rus. Fed.
95 C2 Kulen Cambodia
113 F5 Kulgera Austr.
68 H2 Kulikovo Rus. Fed.
95 B4 Kulim Malaysia
114 F3 Kulkyne watercourse Austr.
84 D3 Kullu India
62 E5 Kulmbach Ger.
79 K2 Kŭlob Tajik.
81 H2 Kulp Turkey
84 D4 Kulpahar India
33 F4 Kulpsville U.S.A.
76 G5 Kul'sary Kazak.
80 D2 Kulu Turkey
80 C3 Kulübe Tepe mt Turkey
76 J4 Kulunda Rus. Fed.
76 J4 Kulundinskoye, Ozero salt l. Rus. Fed.
114 E5 Kulwin Austr.
69 H6 Kuma r. Rus. Fed.
91 F6 Kumagaya Japan
90 F3 Kumaishi Japan
91 B8 Kumamoto Japan
91 E8 Kumano Japan
67 J3 Kumanovo Macedonia
100 B4 Kumasi Ghana
Kumayri see Gyumri
100 C4 Kumba Cameroon
83 E8 Kumbakonam India
80 C2 Kümbet Turkey
104 E1 Kumchuru Botswana
76 G4 Kumertau Rus. Fed.
91 A7 Kŭmho-gang r. S. Korea
55 O7 Kumla Sweden
100 D3 Kumo Nigeria
95 B1 Kumphawapi Thai.
104 C4 Kums Namibia
69 H7 Kumukh Rus. Fed.
84 B2 Kunar r. Afgh.
87 R3 Kunashir, Ostrov i. Rus. Fed.
85 E2 Kunchuk Tso salt l. China
55 U7 Kunda Estonia
85 E4 Kunda India
84 B2 Kundar r. Afgh./Pak.
92 F5 Kundat Malaysia
55 M8 Kungälv Sweden
82 E2 Kungei Alatau mts Kazak./Kyrg.
20 C4 Kunghit I. i. Can.
55 N8 Kungsbacka Sweden
55 M7 Kungshamn Sweden
102 B3 Kungu Dem. Rep. Congo
84 D6 Kuni r. India
91 B8 Kunimi-dake mt Japan
85 F5 Kunjabar India
85 G4 Kunlui r. India/Nepal
74 Kunlun Shan mts China
85 H2 Kunlun Shankou pass China
89 B5 Kunming China
84 D4 Kuno r. India
87 N4 Kunsan S. Korea
88 F4 Kunshan China
112 E3 Kununurra Austr.
84 D4 Kunwari r. India
68 D3 Kun'ya Rus. Fed.
88 F2 Kunyu Shan h. China
89 F4 Kuocang Shan mts China
55 T6 Kuohijärvi l. Fin.
54 V3 Kuolayarvi Rus. Fed.
54 U5 Kuopio Fin.
54 S5 Kuortane Fin.
66 2 Kupa r. Croatia/Slovenia
93 G9 Kupang Indon.
55 T9 Kupiškis Lith.
20 C3 Kupreanof Island i. U.S.A.
69 F5 Kup"yans'k Ukr.
82 F2 Kuqa China
81 M2 Kür r. Azer.
81 K1 Kura r. Azer./Georgia
69 G7 Kura r. Georgia/Rus. Fed.
69 H7 Kurakh Rus. Fed.
116 A1 Kuranda Austr.
91 C7 Kurashiki Japan
85 E5 Kurasia India
91 C7 Kurayoshi Japan
80 D2 Kurban Dağı mt Turkey
69 E5 Kurchatov Rus. Fed.
81 M1 Kürdämir Azer.
81 M2 Kür Dili pt Azer.
67 L4 Kŭrdzhali Bulg.
91 C7 Kure Japan
80 D1 Küre Turkey
55 S7 Kuressaare Estonia
76 H4 Kurgan Rus. Fed.
69 G6 Kurganinsk Rus. Fed.
84 B1 Kuri Afgh.
84 B4 Kuri India
Kuria Muria Islands is see Ḥalāniyāt, Juzur al
85 G4 Kuri Chhu r. Bhutan
54 S5 Kurikka Fin.
90 G5 Kurikoma-yama vol. Japan
77 Q5 Kuril Islands is Rus. Fed.
77 Q5 Kuril'sk Japan
Kuril'skiye Ostrova is see Kuril Islands
101 F3 Kurmuk Sudan
83 E7 Kurnool India
80 E6 Kurnub Israel
91 E6 Kurobe Japan
90 G4 Kuroishi Japan
91 G6 Kuroiso Japan
91 A9 Kuro-shima i. Japan
68 F4 Kurovskoye Rus. Fed.
117 C6 Kurow N.Z.
84 B2 Kurram r. Afgh./Pak.
84 B2 Kurramgarhi Dam dam Pak.
115 J4 Kurri Kurri Austr.
Kuršių Marios lag. see Courland Lagoon
69 F5 Kursk Rus. Fed.
69 H6 Kurskaya Rus. Fed.
69 F5 Kurskaya Oblast' div. Rus. Fed.
Kurskiy Zaliv lag. see Courland Lagoon
80 D1 Kurşunlu Turkey
81 H3 Kurtalan Turkey
80 G2 Kuruçay Turkey
84 D3 Kurukshetra India
82 G2 Kuruktag mts China
104 E3 Kuruman S. Africa
104 D3 Kuruman watercourse S. Africa
91 B8 Kurume Japan
87 K1 Kurumkan Rus. Fed.
83 F9 Kurunegala Sri Lanka
101 F2 Kurush, Jebel reg. Sudan
67 M6 Kuşadası Turkey
67 M6 Kuşadası Körfezi b. Turkey
20 B2 Kusawa Lake l. Can.
80 A1 Kuş Gölü l. Turkey
69 F6 Kushchevskaya Rus. Fed.
91 B9 Kushikino Japan
91 D8 Kushimoto Japan
90 J3 Kushiro Japan
90 J3 Kushiro-Shitsugen National Park Japan
81 M5 Kūshkak Iran
76 H4 Kushmurun Kazak.
85 G5 Kushtia Bangl.
88 C2 Kushui r. China
77 V4 Kuskokwim Bay b. Alaska
90 J3 Kussharo-ko l. Japan
81 M6 Kut Iran
95 B3 Kut, Ko i. Thai.
81 M6 Kūt 'Abdollāh Iran
95 A5 Kutacane Indon.
80 B2 Kütahya Turkey
69 G7 K'ut'aisi Georgia
Kut-al-Imara see Al Kūt
69 H6 Kutan Rus. Fed.
90 G3 Kutchan Japan
81 M5 Kūt-e Gapu Iran
66 G2 Kutina Croatia
66 G2 Kutjevo Croatia
63 J4 Kutno Pol.
102 B4 Kutu Dem. Rep. Congo
85 G5 Kutubdia I. i. Bangl.
23 G2 Kuujjuaq Can.
Kuujjuarapik see Poste-de-la-Baleine
54 V4 Kuusamo Fin.
55 U6 Kuusankoski Fin.
103 B5 Kuvango Angola
68 E3 Kuvshinovo Rus. Fed.
70 Kuwait country Asia
81 L7 Kuwait Kuwait
81 L7 Kuwait Jun b. Kuwait
91 E7 Kuwana Japan
68 G1 Kuya Rus. Fed.
76 J4 Kuybyshev Rus. Fed.
Kuybyshev see Samara
68 J4 Kuybyshevskoye Vdkhr. resr Rus. Fed.
88 D2 Kuye r. China
82 F2 Kuytun China
67 N6 Kuyucak Turkey
55 V6 Kuznechnoye Rus. Fed.
68 H4 Kuznetsk Rus. Fed.
90 F1 Kuznetsovo Rus. Fed.
69 C5 Kuznetsovs'k Ukr.
54 R1 Kvænangen chan. Norway
54 Q2 Kvaløya i. Norway
54 S1 Kvalsund Norway
Kvareli see Qvareli
66 F2 Kvarnerić chan. Croatia
20 D3 Kwadacha Wilderness Prov. Park res. Can.
95 A5 Kwala Indon.
105 J4 KwaMashu S. Africa
105 H2 KwaMhlanga S. Africa
87 N4 Kwangju S. Korea
102 B4 Kwango r. Dem. Rep. Congo
102 D4 Kwangwazi Tanz.
90 A4 Kwanmo-bong mt N. Korea
105 F6 Kwanobuhle S. Africa
105 F6 KwaNojoli S. Africa
105 G6 Kwanonqubela S. Africa
104 F5 Kwanonzame S. Africa
105 G6 Kwatinidubu S. Africa
105 H3 KwaZamokhule S. Africa
104 F6 Kwazamukucinga S. Africa
104 F5 Kwazamuxolo S. Africa
105 H3 KwaZanele S. Africa
105 J4 Kwazulu-Natal div. S. Africa
103 C5 Kwekwe Zimbabwe
104 F1 Kweneng div. Botswana
102 B4 Kwenge r. Dem. Rep. Congo
105 G5 Kwezi-Naledi S. Africa
63 J4 Kwidzyn Pol.
77 V4 Kwigillingok Alaska
110 E2 Kwikila P.N.G.
102 B4 Kwilu r. Angola/Dem. Rep. Congo
89 □ Kwo Chau Kwan To is China
93 J7 Kwoka mt Indon.
89 □ Kwun Tong China
101 D4 Kyabé Chad
114 F6 Kyabram Austr.
95 A1 Kyaikto Myanmar
95 A1 Kya-in Seikkyi Myanmar
86 J1 Kyakhta Rus. Fed.
114 E5 Kyalite Austr.
114 A4 Kyancutta Austr.
68 F1 Kyanda Rus. Fed.
95 A1 Kyaukhnyat Myanmar
83 H7 Kyaukpyu Myanmar
85 H5 Kyauktaw Myanmar
55 S9 Kybartai Lith.
114 D6 Kybybolite Austr.
89 C6 Ky Cung, Sông r. Vietnam
85 G2 Kyêbxang l. China
84 D2 Kyelang India
88 A2 Kyikug China
Kyiv see Kiev
Kyklades is see Cyclades
21 H4 Kyle Can.
57 C3 Kyle of Lochalsh U.K.
61 E5 Kyll r. Ger.
67 K6 Kyllini mt Greece
114 F6 Kyneton Austr.
102 D3 Kyoga, Lake l. Uganda
91 D7 Kyōga-misaki pt Japan
115 K2 Kyogle Austr.
95 A1 Kyondo Myanmar
116 A3 Kyong Austr.
87 A7 Kyŏngju S. Korea
91 D7 Kyōto Japan
67 J6 Kyparissia Greece
67 J6 Kyparissiakos Kolpos b. Greece
76 H4 Kypshak, Ozero salt l. Kazak.
67 L5 Kyra Panagia i. Greece
70 Kyrgyzstan country Asia
54 L5 Kyrksæterøra Norway
76 G3 Kyrta Rus. Fed.
68 H1 Kyssa Rus. Fed.
77 P3 Kytalyktakh Rus. Fed.
67 K6 Kythira i. Greece
67 L6 Kythnos i. Greece
95 A2 Kyungyaung Myanmar
91 B8 Kyūshū i. Japan
14 D5 Kyushu-Palau Ridge sea feature Pac. Oc.
67 K3 Kyustendil Bulg.
115 G5 Kywong Austr.
69 D5 Kyyivs'ke Vdskh. resr Ukr.
54 T5 Kyyjärvi Fin.
86 F1 Kyzyl Rus. Fed.
82 B2 Kyzylkum Desert des. Uzbek.
79 L1 Kyzyl-Kyya Kyrgyzstan
86 F1 Kyzyl-Mazhalyk Rus. Fed.
82 C2 Kyzylorda Kazak.
82 C1 Kyzylzhar Kazak.

L

61 F4 Laacher See l. Ger.
55 T7 Laagri Estonia
25 E6 La Angostura, Presa de resr Mex.
54 U2 Laanila Fin.
47 B3 La Araucania div. Chile
102 E3 Laascaanood Somalia
36 G5 La Ascensión, Bahía de b. Mex.
102 E2 Laasgoray Somalia
45 E2 La Asunción Venez.
100 A2 Laâyoune Western Sahara
69 G6 Laba r. Rus. Fed.
27 C6 La Babia Mex.
36 G5 La Bahía, Islas de is Honduras
23 G2 La Baleine, Rivière à r. Can.
44 D3 La Banda Arg.
24 E3 La Barge U.S.A.
111 H3 Labasa Fiji
57 C5 La Baule-Escoublac France
100 A3 Labé Guinea
22 F4 Labelle Can.
30 B5 La Belle U.S.A.
101 D4 La Bénoué, Parc National de nat. park Cameroon
20 B2 Laberge, Lake l. Can.
94 A5 Labian, Tg pt Malaysia
20 E2 La Biche r. Can.
21 G4 La Biche, Lac l. Can.
69 G6 Labinsk Rus. Fed.
95 B5 Labis Malaysia
94 B3 Labo Phil.
27 B7 La Boquilla Mex.
27 B7 La Boquilla, Presa de resr Mex.
100 B3 La Boucle du Baoulé, Parc National de nat. park Mali
80 F4 Laboué Lebanon
64 D4 Labouheyre France
47 D2 Laboulaye Arg.
23 H3 Labrador Can.
23 G3 Labrador City Can.
47 F5 Lábrea Brazil
92 F5 Labuan Malaysia
92 C6 Labuhanbilik Indon.
95 A5 Labuhanruku Indon.
94 A5 Labuk r. Malaysia
94 A5 Labuk, Telukan b. Malaysia
93 H7 Labuna Indon.
114 A3 Labyrinth, L. salt flat Austr.
76 H3 Labytnangi Rus. Fed.
67 H4 Laç Albania
65 C1 La Cabrera, Sierra de mts Spain
47 D1 La Calera Arg.
47 B2 La Calera Chile
64 F2 La Capelle France
47 B4 Lacar, L. l. Arg.
47 D2 La Carlota Arg.
65 E3 La Carolina Spain
67 M2 Lăcăuți, Vârful mt Romania
33 J1 Lac-Baker Can.
83 D8 Laccadive Islands is India
21 K4 Lac du Bonnet Can.
36 G5 La Ceiba Honduras
45 C2 La Ceiba Venez.
114 C6 Lacepede B. b. Austr.
45 D3 La Cerbatana, Sierra de mt Venez.
33 E4 Laceyville U.S.A.
33 H1 Lac Frontière Can.
68 F2 Lacha, Ozero l. Rus. Fed.
61 D5 Lachaussée, Étang de l. France
31 F3 Lachine U.S.A.
114 F5 Lachlan r. Austr.
37 J7 La Chorrera Panama
22 F4 Lachute Can.
81 L2 Laçın Azer.
64 G5 La Ciotat France
32 D3 Lackawanna U.S.A.
21 G4 Lac La Biche Can.
20 E4 Lac La Hache Can.
Lac la Martre see Wha Ti
21 H3 Lac La Ronge Provincial Park res. Can.
23 F4 Lac-Mégantic Can.
33 G2 Lacolle Can.
25 E6 La Colorada Mex.
20 G4 Lacombe Can.
100 B4 La Comoé, Parc National de nat. park Côte d'Ivoire
66 C5 Laconi Italy
33 H3 Laconia U.S.A.
31 J1 La Corne Can.
30 B4 La Crescent U.S.A.
30 B4 La Crosse U.S.A.
45 B4 La Cruces, Paso de mt Col.
45 A4 La Cruz Col.
27 C6 La Cuesta Mex.
65 C2 La Culebra, Sierra de mts Spain
26 E4 La Cygne U.S.A.
84 D2 Ladakh Range mts India
95 A4 Ladang i. Thai.
65 E1 La Demanda, Sierra de mts Spain
80 E1 Ladik Turkey
104 D6 Ladismith S. Africa
79 J4 Lādīz Iran
84 C4 Ladnun India
68 D2 Ladoga, Lake l. Rus. Fed.
45 B3 La Dorada Col.
Ladozhskoye Ozero l. see Ladoga, Lake
85 H4 Ladu mt India
68 E2 Ladva Rus. Fed.
68 E2 Ladva-Vetka Rus. Fed.
57 E4 Ladybank U.K.
105 G4 Ladybrand S. Africa
31 G2 Lady Evelyn Lake l. Can.
105 G5 Lady Frere S. Africa
105 G5 Lady Grey S. Africa
20 E5 Ladysmith Can.
105 H4 Ladysmith S. Africa
30 B3 Ladysmith U.S.A.
110 E2 Lae P.N.G.
95 B2 Laem Ngop Thai.
55 K6 Lærdalsøyri Norway
42 F8 La Esmeralda Bol.
45 D4 La Esmeralda Venez.
55 M8 Læsø i. Denmark
47 D1 La Falda Arg.
24 F4 Lafayette CO U.S.A.
30 D5 Lafayette IN U.S.A.
27 E6 Lafayette LA U.S.A.
29 C5 La Fayette U.S.A.
100 C4 Lafia Nigeria
64 D3 La Flèche France
32 A6 La Follette U.S.A.
31 H2 Laforce Can.
31 G2 Laforest Can.
23 F3 Laforge Can.
45 B2 La Fría Venez.
66 C6 La Galite i. Tunisia
66 C6 La Galite, Canal de chan. Tunisia
69 H6 Lagan' Rus. Fed.
60 E3 Lagan r. U.K.
102 C3 La Garamba, Parc National de nat. park Dem. Rep. Congo
43 L6 Lagarto Brazil
55 L7 Lågen r. Norway
57 C5 Lagg U.K.
57 D3 Laggan U.K.
57 D4 Laggan, Loch l. U.K.
100 C1 Laghouat Alg.
85 F2 Lagkor Co salt l. China
45 B2 La Gloria Col.
46 D2 Lagoa Santa Brazil
81 L1 Lagodekhi Georgia
100 A2 La Gomera i. Canary Is
37 K5 La Gonâve, Île de i. Haiti
95 D5 Lagong i. Indon.
94 B3 Lagonoy Gulf b. Phil.
44 B7 Lago Posadas Arg.
47 B4 Lago Ranco Chile
100 C4 Lagos Nigeria
65 B4 Lagos Port.
36 D4 Lagos de Moreno Mex.
22 E3 La Grande r. Can.
24 C2 La Grande U.S.A.
22 F3 La Grande 4, Réservoir resr Can.
22 E3 La Grande 2, Réservoir resr Can.
22 E3 La Grande 3, Réservoir resr Can.
64 H4 La Grande Casse, Pointe de mt France
112 D3 Lagrange Austr.
29 C5 La Grange GA U.S.A.
33 J2 La Grange ME U.S.A.
30 D5 La Grange MI U.S.A.
30 B5 La Grange MO U.S.A.
27 D6 La Grange TX U.S.A.
30 E5 Lagrange U.S.A.
45 E3 La Gran Sabana plat. Venez.
44 G3 Laguna Brazil
34 D5 Laguna Beach U.S.A.
47 B3 Laguna de Laja, Parque Nacional nat. park Chile
34 D5 Laguna Mts mts U.S.A.
42 C5 Lagunas Peru
44 A7 Laguna San Rafael, Parque Nacional nat. park Chile
45 C2 Lagunillas Venez.
37 H4 La Habana Cuba
La Habana see La Habana
93 F5 Lahad Datu Malaysia
94 A5 Lahad Datu, Telukan b. Malaysia
64 D2 La Hague, Cap de pt France
34 □2 Lahaina U.S.A.
92 C7 Lahat Indon.
95 A5 Lahewa Indon.
78 E7 Laḥij Yemen
81 M3 Lāhījān Iran
34 □1 Lahilahi Pt pt U.S.A.
55 N8 Laholm Sweden
34 C2 Lahontan Res. resr U.S.A.
84 C3 Lahore Pak.
45 E3 La Horqueta Venez.
37 K5 La Hotte, Massif de mts Haiti
84 B3 Lahri Pak.
55 T6 Lahti Fin.
101 D4 Laï Chad
88 F3 Lai'an China
89 C6 Laibin China
115 K1 Laidley Austr.
34 □1 Laie U.S.A.
34 □1 Laie Pt pt U.S.A.
89 C4 Laifeng China
64 E2 L'Aigle France
54 S5 Laihia Fin.
85 H4 Laimakuri India
104 D6 Laingsburg S. Africa
54 S3 Lainioälven r. Sweden
100 C3 L'Aïr, Massif de mts Niger
57 D2 Lairg U.K.
94 C5 Lais Phil.
55 R6 Laitila Fin.
66 D1 Laives Italy
88 E2 Laiwu China
88 F2 Laiyang China
88 E2 Laiyuan China
88 F2 Laizhou China
88 F2 Laizhou Wan b. China
47 B3 Laja r. Chile
47 B3 Laja, Laguna de l. Chile
112 F3 Lajamanu Austr.
43 L5 Lajes Rio Grande do Norte Brazil
44 F3 Lajes Santa Catarina Brazil
25 F7 La Joya Mex.
25 G4 La Junta U.S.A.
37 H4 La Juventud, Isla de i. Cuba
24 E2 Lake U.S.A.
26 D3 Lake Andes U.S.A.
111 J3 Lakeba i. Fiji
80 D6 Lake Bardawîl Reserve res. Egypt
114 E6 Lake Bolac Austr.
115 G4 Lake Cargelligo Austr.
115 K3 Lake Cathie Austr.
27 E6 Lake Charles U.S.A.
24 B1 Lake Chelan Nat. Recreation Area res. U.S.A.
29 D6 Lake City FL U.S.A.
30 E3 Lake City MI U.S.A.
30 A3 Lake City MN U.S.A.
29 E5 Lake City SC U.S.A.
58 D3 Lake District National Park nat. park U.K.
114 B2 Lake Eyre Nat. Park nat. park Austr.
31 H3 Lakefield Can.
113 H2 Lakefield National Park nat. park Austr.
30 C4 Lake Geneva U.S.A.
35 E4 Lake Havasu City U.S.A.
34 C4 Lake Isabella U.S.A.
27 E6 Lake Jackson U.S.A.
112 C6 Lake King Austr.
29 D6 Lakeland U.S.A.
30 C2 Lake Linden U.S.A.
20 F4 Lake Louise Can.
35 E4 Lake Mead National Recreation Area res. U.S.A.
33 J2 Lake Moxie U.S.A.
24 B2 Lake Oswego U.S.A.
117 B5 Lake Paringa N.Z.
33 G2 Lake Placid U.S.A.
34 A2 Lakeport U.S.A.
27 F5 Lake Providence U.S.A.
117 C6 Lake Pukaki N.Z.
100 C4 La Kéran, Parc National de nat. park Togo
22 D3 Lake River Can.
115 H6 Lakes Entrance Austr.
81 K1 Lake Sevan l. Armenia
31 H3 Lake St Peter Can.
30 E2 Lake Superior Provincial Park nat. park Can.
115 J5 Lake Tabourie Austr.
117 C6 Lake Tekapo N.Z.
22 E4 Lake Traverse Can.
24 B3 Lakeview U.S.A.
27 F5 Lake Village U.S.A.
24 F4 Lakewood CO U.S.A.
33 F4 Lakewood NJ U.S.A.
32 C4 Lakewood OH U.S.A.
29 D7 Lake Worth U.S.A.
68 D2 Lakhdenpokh'ya Rus. Fed.
84 E4 Lakhimpur India
84 D5 Lakhnadon India

84 B5 Lakhpat India
79 L3 Lakki Pak.
67 K6 Lakonikos Kolpos *b.* Greece
100 B4 Lakota Côte d'Ivoire
54 U1 Laksefjorden *chan.* Norway
54 T1 Lakselv Norway
83 D8 Lakshadweep *div.* India
85 G5 Laksham Bangl.
85 G5 Lakshmikantapur India
94 B5 Lala Phil.
47 D2 La Laguna Arg.
47 B3 La Laja Chile
102 B3 Lalara Gabon
116 C4 Laleham Austr.
81 M5 Lālī Iran
47 B2 La Ligua Chile
65 B1 Lalín Spain
65 D4 La Línea de la Concepción Spain
84 D4 Lalitpur India
94 B2 Lal-Lo Phil.
21 H3 La Loche Can.
21 H3 La Loche, Lac *l.* Can.
47 D3 La Loma Negra, Planicie de *plain* Arg.
61 C4 La Louvière Belgium
68 H2 Lal'sk Rus. Fed.
85 H5 Lama Bangl.
45 B4 La Macarena, Parque Nacional *nat. park* Col.
66 C4 La Maddalena Italy
23 H4 La Madeleine, Îles de *is* Can.
94 A5 Lamag Malaysia
102 C4 La Maiko, Parc National de *nat. park* Dem. Rep. Congo
95 A2 Lamaing Myanmar
La Manche *str. see* English Channel
26 C4 Lamar *CO* U.S.A.
27 E4 Lamar *MO* U.S.A.
79 G4 Lamard Iran
66 C5 La Marmora, Punta *mt* Italy
47 D3 Lamarque Arg.
27 E6 La Marque U.S.A.
20 F2 La Martre, Lac *l.* Can.
102 B4 Lambaréné Gabon
42 C5 Lambayeque Peru
60 F4 Lambay Island *i.* Rep. of Ireland
119 D4 Lambert Gl. *gl.* Antarctica
104 C6 Lambert's Bay S. Africa
84 C3 Lambi India
61 D4 L'Amblève, Vallée de *v.* Belgium
59 F6 Lambourn Downs *h.* U.K.
95 C2 Lam Chi *r.* Thai.
66 B6 La Medjerda, Monts de *mts* Alg.
65 C2 Lamego Port.
23 H4 Lamèque, Île *i.* Can.
42 C6 La Merced Peru
114 D5 Lameroo Austr.
34 D5 La Mesa U.S.A.
27 C5 Lamesa U.S.A.
67 K5 Lamia Greece
115 K2 Lamington Nat. Park *nat. park* Austr.
25 E6 La Misa Mex.
34 D5 La Misión Mex.
94 B5 Lamitan Phil.
89 □ Lamma Island *i.* China
117 B6 Lammerlaw Ra. *mts* N.Z.
57 F5 Lammermuir Hills *h.* U.K.
55 O8 Lammhult Sweden
55 T6 Lammi Fin.
30 C5 La Moille U.S.A.
33 G2 Lamoille *r.* U.S.A.
30 B5 La Moine *r.* U.S.A.
94 B3 Lamon Bay *b.* Phil.
26 E3 Lamoni U.S.A.
24 F3 Lamont U.S.A.
103 E5 La Montagne d'Ambre, Parc National de *nat. park* Madag.
27 B6 La Morita Mex.
31 H1 La Motte Can.
95 A1 Lampang Thai.
95 B1 Lam Pao Res. *resr* Thai.
27 D6 Lampasas U.S.A.
27 C7 Lampazos Mex.
66 E7 Lampedusa, Isola di *i.* Italy
59 C5 Lampeter U.K.
95 A1 Lamphun Thai.
95 B2 Lam Plai Mat *r.* Thai.
68 F4 Lamskoye Rus. Fed.
102 E4 Lamu Kenya
85 H6 Lamu Myanmar
34 □2 Lanai *i.* U.S.A.
34 □2 Lanai City U.S.A.
65 G3 La Nao, Cabo de *hd* Spain
94 C5 Lanao, Lake *l.* Phil.
31 J3 Lanark Can.
57 E5 Lanark U.K.
30 C4 Lanark U.S.A.
94 A5 Lanas Malaysia
95 A3 Lanbi Kyun *i.* Myanmar
Lancang Jiang *r. see* Mekong
33 F2 Lancaster Can.
58 E3 Lancaster U.K.
34 C4 Lancaster *CA* U.S.A.
30 A5 Lancaster *MO* U.S.A.
33 H2 Lancaster *NH* U.S.A.
32 B5 Lancaster *OH* U.S.A.
33 E4 Lancaster *PA* U.S.A.
29 D5 Lancaster *SC* U.S.A.
30 B4 Lancaster *WV* U.S.A.
58 E4 Lancaster Canal *canal* U.K.
66 F3 Lanciano Italy
47 B3 Lanco Chile
88 F2 Lancun China
62 F6 Landau an der Isar Ger.
62 E7 Landeck Austria
24 E3 Lander U.S.A.
21 H4 Landis Can.
62 E6 Landsberg am Lech Ger.
116 A4 Landsborough Cr. *watercourse* Austr.
59 B7 Land's End *pt* U.K.
62 F6 Landshut Ger.
55 N9 Landskrona Sweden
60 D4 Lanesborough Rep. of Ireland
95 C3 La Nga *r.* Vietnam
84 E3 Lan'ga Co *l.* China
88 C3 Langao China
57 B2 Langavat, Loch *l.* U.K.
104 E4 Langberg *mts* S. Africa
26 D1 Langdon U.S.A.
104 C6 Langeberg *mts* S. Africa
55 M9 Langeland *i.* Denmark
55 T6 Längelmäki Fin.
55 T6 Längelmävesi *l.* Fin.
62 C7 Langenthal Switz.
61 F1 Langeoog *i.* Ger.
55 L7 Langesund Norway
95 B5 Langgapayung Indon.
21 H4 Langham Can.
54 C4 Langjökull *ice cap* Iceland
95 A4 Langkawi *i.* Malaysia
95 A3 Lang Kha Toek, Khao *mt* Thai.
104 D4 Langklip S. Africa
94 A5 Langkon Malaysia
31 K1 Langlade Can.
30 C3 Langlade U.S.A.
116 A5 Langlo *watercourse* Austr.
116 A6 Langlo Crossing Austr.
64 F4 Langogne France
54 O2 Langøya *i.* Norway
59 E6 Langport U.K.
89 F5 Langqi China
64 G3 Langres France
84 D1 Langru China
92 B6 Langsa Indon.
95 A4 Langsa, Teluk *b.* Indon.
54 P5 Långsele Sweden
88 C1 Langshan China
88 C1 Lang Shan *mts* China
95 C6 Lang Sơn Vietnam
58 G3 Langtoft U.K.
27 C6 Langtry U.S.A.
64 F5 Languedoc *reg.* France
54 R4 Långvattnet Sweden
88 F4 Langxi China
88 C4 Langzhong China
31 H2 Laniel Can.
21 H4 Lanigan Can.
34 □1 Lanikai U.S.A.
47 B3 Lanín, Parque Nacional *nat. park* Arg.
47 B3 Lanín, Volcán *vol.* Arg.
88 E3 Lankao China
81 M2 Länkäran Azer.
89 □ Lan Kok Tsui *pt* China
64 C2 Lannion France
54 S3 Lansån Sweden
30 C2 L'Anse U.S.A.
20 C2 Lansing *r.* Can.
30 B4 Lansing *IA* U.S.A.
30 E4 Lansing *MI* U.S.A.
95 A4 Lanta, Ko *i.* Thai.
89 □ Lantau Island *i.* China
94 C4 Lanuza Bay *b.* Phil.
84 F4 Lanxi China
89 F4 Lanxi China
101 F4 Lanya Sudan
89 F6 Lan Yü *i.* Taiwan
100 A2 Lanzarote *i.* Canary Is
88 B2 Lanzhou China
95 A1 Lao, Mae *r.* Thai.
94 B2 Laoag Phil.
94 C3 Laoang Phil.
89 B6 Lao Cai Vietnam
88 F1 Laoha *r.* China
88 D3 Laohekou China
88 F2 Laohutun China
102 C3 La Okapi, Parc National de *nat. park* Dem. Rep. Congo
64 F2 Laon France
30 C3 Laona U.S.A.
70 Laos *country* Asia
88 F2 Lao Shan *mt* China
90 A3 Laotougou China
Laowohi *pass see* Khardung La
88 A1 Laoximiao China
90 A3 Laoye Ling *mts* China
46 C4 Lapa Brazil
94 B5 Lapac *i.* Phil.
100 A2 La Palma *i.* Canary Is
37 J7 La Palma Panama
65 C4 La Palma del Condado Spain
47 F2 La Paloma Uru.
47 D3 La Pampa *div.* Arg.
34 B4 La Panza Range *mts* U.S.A.
45 E3 La Paragua Venez.
94 A5 Laparan *i.* Phil.
45 B4 La Paya, Parque Nacional *nat. park* Col.
47 E1 La Paz *Entre Ríos* Arg.
47 C2 La Paz *Mendoza* Arg.
42 E7 La Paz Bol.
36 B4 La Paz Mex.
30 D5 Lapaz U.S.A.
42 E4 La Pedrera Col.
31 F4 Lapeer U.S.A.
100 C3 La Pendjari, Parc National de *nat. park* Benin
27 B6 La Perla Mex.
90 G2 La Pérouse Strait *str.* Japan/Rus. Fed.
45 E3 La Piña *r.* Venez.
24 B3 La Pine U.S.A.
94 C3 Lapinig Phil.
94 C4 Lapinin *i.* Phil.
54 U5 Lapinlahti Fin.
80 D4 Lapithos Cyprus
27 F6 Laplace U.S.A.
26 C2 La Plant U.S.A.
47 F2 La Plata Arg.
45 B4 La Plata Col.
42 B4 La Plata, Isla *i.* Ecuador
47 F2 La Plata, Río de *chan.* Arg./Uru.
21 H3 La Plonge, Lac *l.* Can.
68 G1 Lapominka Rus. Fed.
30 D5 La Porte U.S.A.
30 A4 La Porte City U.S.A.
22 F2 La Potherie, Lac *l.* Can.
54 S5 Lappajärvi Fin.
54 S5 Lappajärvi *l.* Fin.
55 V6 Lappeenranta Fin.
54 S2 Lappland *reg.* Europe
33 G2 La Prairie Can.
27 D6 La Pryor U.S.A.
67 M4 Lâpseki Turkey
54 S5 Lapua Fin.
77 N2 Laptev Sea *sea* Rus. Fed.
94 B4 Lapu-Lapu Phil.
45 C2 La Quebrada del Toro, Parque Nacional de *nat. park* Venez.
44 C2 La Quiaca Arg.
66 E3 L'Aquila Italy
34 D5 La Quinta U.S.A.
100 B1 Larache Morocco
24 F3 Laramie U.S.A.
24 F3 Laramie Mts *mts* U.S.A.
Laranda *see* Karaman
46 B4 Laranjeiras do Sul Brazil
46 B3 Laranjinha *r.* Brazil
93 G8 Larantuka Indon.
93 J8 Larat *i.* Indon.
65 H4 Larba Alg.
55 Q8 Lärbro Sweden
31 G2 Larchwood Can.
61 C5 L'Ardenne, Plateau de *plat.* Belgium
31 H1 Larder Lake Can.
65 E1 Laredo Spain
27 D7 Laredo U.S.A.
44 B8 La Reina Adelaida, Archipiélago de *is* Chile
29 D7 Largo U.S.A.
57 D5 Largs U.K.
81 L2 Lārī Iran
66 D6 L'Ariana Tunisia
21 K5 Larimore U.S.A.
44 C3 La Rioja Arg.
47 C1 La Rioja *div.* Arg.
65 E1 La Rioja *div.* Spain
67 K5 Larisa Greece
84 B4 Larkana Pak.
62 C7 Larmont *mt* France/Switz.
80 D4 Larnaka Cyprus
60 F3 Larne U.K.
26 D4 Larned U.S.A.
57 C6 Larne Lough *in.* U.K.
65 D1 La Robla Spain
61 D4 La Roche-en-Ardenne Belgium
64 D3 La Rochelle France
64 D3 La Roche-sur-Yon France
65 E3 La Roda Spain
37 L5 La Romana Dom. Rep.
21 H3 La Ronge Can.
21 H3 La Ronge, Lac *l.* Can.
27 C7 La Rosa Mex.
27 C6 La Rosita Mex.
112 F3 Larrimah Austr.
119 B2 Larsen Ice Shelf *ice feature* Antarctica
61 A4 L'Artois, Collines de *h.* France
55 M7 Larvik Norway
35 H2 La Sal Junction U.S.A.
33 G2 La Salle Can.
30 C5 La Salle U.S.A.
102 C4 La Salonga Nord, Parc National de *nat. park* Dem. Rep. Congo
22 E4 La Sarre Can.
45 D2 Las Aves, Islas *is* Venez.
47 B2 Las Cabras Chile
23 J4 La Scie Can.
25 F5 Las Cruces U.S.A.
37 K5 La Selle *mt* Haiti
47 B1 La Serena Chile
27 C7 Las Esperanças Mex.
47 E3 Las Flores Arg.
21 H4 Lashburn Can.
47 C2 Las Heras Arg.
45 B4 Las Hermosas, Parque Nacional *nat. park* Col.
83 J6 Lashio Myanmar
47 B3 Las Lajas Arg.
45 D3 Las Lajitas Venez.
44 D2 Las Lomitas Arg.
65 C4 Las Marismas *marsh* Spain
44 C7 Las Martinetas Arg.
45 D2 Las Mercedes Venez.
27 B7 Las Nieves Mex.
34 D5 Las Palmas *r.* Mex.
100 A2 Las Palmas de Gran Canaria Canary Is
66 C2 La Spezia Italy
47 F2 Las Piedras Uru.
42 D6 Las Piedras, Río de *r.* Peru
44 C6 Las Plumas Arg.
47 E2 Las Rosas Arg.
47 C2 Las Salinas, Pampa de *salt pan* Arg.
24 B3 Lassen Pk *vol.* U.S.A.
24 B3 Lassen Volcanic Nat. Park *nat. park* U.S.A.
37 H7 Las Tablas Panama
44 D3 Las Termas Arg.
21 H4 Last Mountain L. *l.* Can.
47 C1 Las Tórtolas, Cerro *mt* Chile
102 B4 Lastoursville Gabon
66 G3 Lastovo *i.* Croatia
45 D3 Las Trincheras Venez.
37 J4 Las Tunas Cuba
25 F6 Las Varas Mex.
47 D1 Las Varillas Arg.
25 F5 Las Vegas *NM* U.S.A.
35 E3 Las Vegas *NV* U.S.A.
42 C6 Las Viajas, Isla de *i.* Peru
65 D3 Las Villuercas *mt* Spain
23 J3 La Tabatière Can.
42 C4 Latacunga Ecuador
45 B5 La Tagua Col.
80 E4 Latakia Syria
31 H2 Latchford Can.
85 F5 Latehar India
64 D4 La Teste France
52 E2 Latheron U.K.
66 E4 Latina Italy
47 D2 La Toma Arg.
45 D2 La Tortuga, Isla *i.* Venez.
115 G8 Latrobe Austr.
32 D4 Latrobe U.S.A.
31 H2 Latulipe Can.
22 F4 La Tuque Can.
83 E7 Latur India
49 Latvia *country* Europe
44 C1 Lauca, Parque Nacional *nat. park* Chile
62 F5 Lauchhammer Ger.
57 F5 Lauder U.K.
62 C7 Laufen Switz.
30 D2 Laughing Fish Pt *pt* U.S.A.
55 S7 Lauka Estonia
54 V1 Laukvik Norway
90 D2 Laulyu Rus. Fed.
95 A3 Laun Thai.
115 G8 Launceston Austr.
59 C7 Launceston U.K.
60 B5 Laune *r.* Rep. of Ireland
95 A2 Launglon Bok Is *is* Myanmar
47 B4 La Unión Chile
45 A4 La Unión Col.
36 G6 La Unión El Salvador
94 B3 Laur Phil.
113 H3 Laura *Qld.* Austr.
114 C4 Laura *S.A.* Austr.
45 D3 La Urbana Venez.
33 F5 Laurel *DE* U.S.A.
27 F6 Laurel *MS* U.S.A.
24 E2 Laurel *MT* U.S.A.
32 D4 Laurel Hill *h.* U.S.A.
32 A6 Laurel River Lake *l.* U.S.A.
57 F4 Laurencekirk U.K.
23 F4 Laurentides, Réserve Faunique des *res.* Can.
66 F4 Lauria Italy
115 K3 Laurieton Austr.
29 E5 Laurinburg U.S.A.
30 C2 Laurium U.S.A.
62 C7 Lausanne Switz.
92 F7 Laut *i.* Indon.
47 B3 Lautaro Chile
92 F8 Laut Kecil, Kepulauan *is* Indon.
111 H3 Lautoka Fiji
54 V5 Lauvuskylä Fin.
61 E1 Lauwersmeer *l.* Neth.
22 F4 Laval Can.
64 D2 Laval France
66 F1 Lavant *r.* Austria/Slovenia
44 B5 Lavapié, Pta *pt* Chile
45 B1 La Vela, Cabo de *pt* Col.
47 D3 La Ventana, Serra de *h.* Arg.
31 J2 La Vérendrye, Réserve Faunique de *res.* Can.
114 E7 Lavers Hill Austr.
112 D5 Laverton Austr.
27 C7 La Víbora Mex.
45 D2 La Victoria Venez.
31 G2 Lavigne Can.
24 E2 Lavina U.S.A.
46 D3 Lavras Brazil
47 G1 Lavras do Sul Brazil
105 J3 Lavumisa Swaziland
84 B2 Lawa Pak.
95 B4 Lawit, Gunung *mt* Malaysia
61 D5 La Woëvre, Plaine de *plain* France
81 J7 Lawqah *waterhole* Saudi Arabia
100 B3 Lawra Ghana
26 E4 Lawrence *KS* U.S.A.
33 H3 Lawrence *MA* U.S.A.
29 C5 Lawrenceburg U.S.A.
33 K2 Lawrence Station Can.
32 E6 Lawrenceville U.S.A.
27 D5 Lawton U.S.A.
78 D4 Lawz, J. al *mt* Saudi Arabia
55 O7 Laxå Sweden
104 E3 Laxey S. Africa
58 C3 Laxey U.K.
57 C2 Laxford, Loch *in.* U.K.
57 □ Laxo U.K.
81 K4 Laylān Iraq
34 A2 Laytonville U.S.A.
67 J2 Lazarevac Yugo.
69 F7 Lazarevskoye Rus. Fed.
25 D6 Lázaro Cárdenas *Baja California* Mex.
36 D5 Lázaro Cárdenas *Michoacán* Mex.
36 A2 Lázaro Cárdenas Mex.
27 B7 Lázaro Cárdenas, Presa *resr* Mex.
47 F2 Lazcano Uru.
55 S9 Lazdijai Lith.
90 C3 Lazo Rus. Fed.
77 P3 Lazo Rus. Fed.
95 B2 Leach Cambodia
30 E2 Leach I. *i.* Can.
26 C2 Lead U.S.A.
21 H4 Leader Can.
115 H4 Leadville Austr.
25 F4 Leadville U.S.A.
27 F6 Leaf *r.* U.S.A.
21 J3 Leaf Rapids Can.
27 D6 Leakey U.S.A.
31 F4 Leamington Can.
35 F2 Leamington U.S.A.
59 F5 Leamington Spa, Royal U.K.
89 E5 Le'an China
60 B5 Leane, Lough *l.* Rep. of Ireland
60 B6 Leap Rep. of Ireland
21 H4 Leask Can.
59 G6 Leatherhead U.K.
22 F2 L'Eau Claire, Lac à *l.* Can.
61 C4 L'Eau d'Heure *l.* Belgium
26 E4 Leavenworth *KS* U.S.A.
24 B2 Leavenworth *WA* U.S.A.
34 C2 Leavitt Peak *summit* U.S.A.
61 E5 Lebach Ger.
94 C5 Lebak Phil.
70 Lebanon *country* Asia
30 D5 Lebanon *IN* U.S.A.
26 D4 Lebanon *KS* U.S.A.
27 E4 Lebanon *MO* U.S.A.
33 G3 Lebanon *NH* U.S.A.
33 F4 Lebanon *NJ* U.S.A.
32 A5 Lebanon *OH* U.S.A.
24 B2 Lebanon *OR* U.S.A.
33 E4 Lebanon *PA* U.S.A.
29 C4 Lebanon *TN* U.S.A.
61 C3 Lebbeke Belgium
68 F4 Lebedyan' Rus. Fed.
69 E5 Lebedyn Ukr.
64 E3 Le Blanc France
62 H3 Lębork Pol.
105 H2 Lebowakgomo S. Africa
65 C4 Lebrija Spain
62 H3 Łebsko, Jezioro *lag.* Pol.
47 B3 Lebu Chile
61 B4 Le Cateau-Cambrésis France
67 H4 Lecce Italy
66 C2 Lecco Italy
62 E7 Lech *r.* Austria/Ger.
67 J6 Lechaina Greece
89 D5 Lechang China
62 E7 Lechtaler Alpen *mts* Austria
62 D3 Leck Ger.
64 G3 Le Creusot France
64 E5 Lectoure France
95 B5 Ledang, Gunung *mt* Malaysia
59 E5 Ledbury U.K.
65 D2 Ledesma Spain
57 D2 Ledmore U.K.
68 E1 Ledmozero Rus. Fed.
89 C7 Ledong China
88 B2 Ledu China
20 G4 Leduc Can.
33 G3 Lee U.S.A.
26 E2 Leech L. *l.* U.S.A.
58 F4 Leeds U.K.
33 H2 Leeds Junction U.S.A.
59 B7 Leedstown U.K.
59 E4 Leek U.K.
61 D3 Leende Neth.
32 D4 Leeper U.S.A.
61 F1 Leer (Ostfriesland) Ger.
29 D6 Leesburg *FL* U.S.A.
32 E5 Leesburg *VA* U.S.A.
27 E6 Leesville U.S.A.
32 C4 Leesville Lake *l.* U.S.A.
115 G5 Leeton Austr.
104 D6 Leeu-Gamka S. Africa
61 D1 Leeuwarden Neth.
112 C6 Leeuwin, C. *c.* Austr.
34 C3 Lee Vining U.S.A.
37 M5 Leeward Islands *is* Caribbean Sea
80 D4 Lefka Cyprus
67 J5 Lefkada Greece
67 J5 Lefkada *i.* Greece
80 D4 Lefkara Cyprus
67 J5 Lefkimmi Greece
Lefkosia *see* Nicosia
94 B3 Legaspi Phil.
115 G8 Legges Tor *mt* Austr.
34 A2 Leggett U.S.A.
66 D2 Legnago Italy
62 H5 Legnica Pol.
84 D2 Leh Jammu and Kashmir
64 E2 Le Havre France
33 F4 Lehighton U.S.A.
54 V5 Lehmo Fin.
54 S5 Lehtimäki Fin.
104 D1 Lehututu Botswana
84 B3 Leiah Pak.
62 G7 Leibnitz Austria
59 F5 Leicester U.K.
113 G3 Leichhardt *r.* Austr.
116 B3 Leichhardt Range *mts* Austr.
61 C2 Leiden Neth.
114 C3 Leigh *watercourse* Austr.
117 E2 Leigh N.Z.
58 E4 Leigh U.K.
114 C3 Leigh Creek Austr.
59 G6 Leighton Buzzard U.K.
60 E5 Leinster, Mount *h.* Rep. of Ireland
67 M6 Leipsoi *i.* Greece
62 F5 Leipzig Ger.
54 O3 Leiranger Norway
65 B3 Leiria Port.
55 J7 Leirvik Norway
89 C5 Leishan China
89 D5 Lei Shui *r.* China
28 C4 Leitchfield U.S.A.
45 B4 Leiva, Co *mt* Col.
60 E4 Leixlip Rep. of Ireland
89 D5 Leiyang China
89 D6 Leizhou China
89 C6 Leizhou Bandao *pen.* China
89 D6 Leizhou Wan *b.* China
54 M4 Leka Norway
102 B4 Lékana Congo
66 C6 Le Kef Tunisia
104 B4 Lekkersing S. Africa
102 B4 Lékoni Gabon
55 O6 Leksand Sweden
54 W5 Leksozero, Oz. *l.* Rus. Fed.
30 E3 Leland *MI* U.S.A.
27 F5 Leland *MS* U.S.A.
100 A3 Lélouma Guinea
61 D2 Lelystad Neth.
44 C9 Le Maire, Estrecho de *chan.* Arg.
64 H3 Léman, Lac *l.* France/Switz.
64 E2 Le Mans France
26 D3 Le Mars U.S.A.
46 C3 Leme Brazil
94 B3 Lemery Phil.
Lemesos *see* Limassol
55 U6 Lemi Fin.
54 T2 Lemmenjoen Kansallispuisto *nat. park* Fin.
26 C2 Lemmon U.S.A.
35 G5 Lemmon, Mt *mt* U.S.A.
34 C3 Lemoore U.S.A.
23 G2 Le Moyne, Lac *l.* Can.
85 H5 Lemro *r.* Myanmar
95 A3 Lem Tom Chob *pt* Thai.
66 G4 Le Murge *reg.* Italy
55 L8 Lemvig Denmark
86 J1 Lena *r.* Rus. Fed.
30 C4 Lena U.S.A.
85 E2 Lenchung Tso *salt l.* China
43 K4 Lençóis Maranhenses, Parque Nacional dos *nat. park* Brazil
88 A2 Lenglong Ling *mts* China
89 D5 Lengshuijiang China
89 D5 Lengshuitan China
47 B1 Lengua de Vaca, Pta *hd* Chile
59 H6 Lenham U.K.
55 O8 Lenhovda Sweden
69 H7 Lenina, Kanal *canal* Rus. Fed.
Leningrad *see* St Petersburg
69 F6 Leningradskaya Rus. Fed.
68 E3 Leningradskaya Oblast' *div.* Rus. Fed.
77 T3 Leningradskiy Rus. Fed.
90 D2 Lenino Rus. Fed.
69 H5 Leninsk Rus. Fed.
68 F4 Leninskiy Rus. Fed.
76 K4 Leninsk-Kuznetskiy Rus. Fed.
68 H3 Leninskoye Rus. Fed.
115 K2 Lennox Head Austr.
29 D5 Lenoir U.S.A.
33 G3 Lenox U.S.A.
64 F1 Lens France
77 N3 Lensk Rus. Fed.
69 G7 Lentekhi Georgia
62 H7 Lenti Hungary
66 F6 Lentini Italy
100 B3 Léo Burkina
62 G7 Leoben Austria
59 E5 Leominster U.K.
33 H3 Leominster U.S.A.
45 A3 León *r.* Col.
36 D4 León Mex.
36 G6 León Nic.
65 D1 León Spain
103 B6 Leonardville Namibia
80 E4 Leonarisson Cyprus
115 F7 Leongatha Austr.
112 D5 Leonora Austr.
46 D3 Leopoldina Brazil
21 H4 Leoville Can.
105 G1 Lephalala *r.* S. Africa
103 C6 Lephepe Botswana
105 F5 Lephoi S. Africa
89 E4 Leping China
64 G4 Le Pont-de-Claix France
54 U5 Leppävirta Fin.
82 E1 Lepsy Kazak.
64 F4 Le-Puy-en-Velay France
61 B4 Le Quesnoy France
105 G1 Lerala Botswana
105 G4 Leratswana S. Africa
101 D4 Léré Chad
45 C5 Lérida Col.
Lérida *see* Lleida
81 M2 Lerik Azer.

65 E1 **Lerma** Spain
69 G6 **Lermontov** Rus. Fed.
90 D1 **Lermontovka** Rus. Fed.
67 M6 **Leros** *i.* Greece
30 C5 **Le Roy** U.S.A.
22 E2 **Le Roy, Lac** *l.* Can.
55 N8 **Lerum** Sweden
57 □ **Lerwick** U.K.
67 L5 **Lesbos** *i.* Greece
37 K5 **Les Cayes** Haiti
23 G4 **Les Escoumins** Can.
33 J1 **Les Étroits** Can.
65 G1 **Le Seu d'Urgell** Spain
89 B4 **Leshan** China
67 J3 **Leskovac** Yugo.
57 E4 **Leslie** U.K.
64 B2 **Lesneven** France
68 K3 **Lesnoy** Rus. Fed.
90 D1 **Lesopil'noye** Rus. Fed.
76 L4 **Lesosibirsk** Rus. Fed.
96 **Lesotho** *country* Africa
90 C2 **Lesozavodsk** Rus. Fed.
64 D3 **Les Sables-d'Olonne** France
37 L6 **Lesser Antilles** *is* Caribbean Sea
Lesser Caucasus *mts see* Malyy Kavkaz
20 G3 **Lesser Slave Lake** *l.* Can.
20 G3 **Lesser Slave Lake Provincial Park** *res.* Can.
23 H4 **L'Est, Île de** *i.* Can.
33 J1 **L'Est, Lac de** *l.* Can.
54 T5 **Lestijärvi** Fin.
54 T5 **Lestijärvi** *l.* Fin.
Lesvos *i. see* Lesbos
62 H5 **Leszno** Pol.
105 J1 **Letaba** S. Africa
59 G6 **Letchworth** U.K.
64 G3 **Le Télégraphe** *h.* France
84 D4 **Leteri** India
85 H5 **Letha Range** *mts* Myanmar
20 G5 **Lethbridge** Can.
42 G3 **Lethem** Guyana
93 H8 **Leti, Kepulauan** *is* Indon.
42 E4 **Leticia** Col.
88 F2 **Leting** China
105 F2 **Letlhakeng** Botswana
59 J7 **Le Touquet-Paris-Plage** France
64 E1 **Le Tréport** France
105 J1 **Letsitele** S. Africa
95 A3 **Letsok-aw Kyun** *i.* Myanmar
105 F3 **Letsopa** S. Africa
60 D3 **Letterkenny** Rep. of Ireland
95 C5 **Letung** Indon.
57 F4 **Leuchars** U.K.
68 G1 **Leunovo** Rus. Fed.
35 G4 **Leupp Corner** U.S.A.
116 C4 **Leura** Austr.
95 A5 **Leuser, G.** *mt* Indon.
61 C4 **Leuven** Belgium
67 K5 **Levadeia** Greece
35 G2 **Levan** U.S.A.
54 M5 **Levanger** Norway
66 C2 **Levanto** Italy
66 E5 **Levanzo, Isola di** *i.* Italy
69 H7 **Levashi** Rus. Fed.
27 C5 **Levelland** U.S.A.
58 G4 **Leven** *Eng.* U.K.
57 F4 **Leven** *Scot.* U.K.
57 C4 **Leven, Loch** *in.* U.K.
57 E4 **Leven, Loch** *l.* U.K.
112 D3 **Lévêque, C.** *c.* Austr.
30 E4 **Levering** U.S.A.
62 C5 **Leverkusen** Ger.
63 J6 **Levice** Slovakia
117 E4 **Levin** N.Z.
23 F4 **Lévis** Can.
67 M6 **Levitha** *i.* Greece
33 G4 **Levittown** *NY* U.S.A.
33 F4 **Levittown** *PA* U.S.A.
67 L3 **Levski** Bulg.
59 H7 **Lewes** U.K.
33 F5 **Lewes** U.S.A.
57 B2 **Lewis, Isle of** *i.* U.K.
32 E4 **Lewisburg** *PA* U.S.A.
32 C6 **Lewisburg** *WV* U.S.A.
117 D5 **Lewis Pass** *pass* N.Z.
24 D1 **Lewis Range** *mts* U.S.A.
29 C4 **Lewis Smith, L.** *l.* U.S.A.
35 G6 **Lewis Springs** U.S.A.
24 C2 **Lewiston** *ID* U.S.A.
33 H2 **Lewiston** *ME* U.S.A.
30 B4 **Lewiston** *MN* U.S.A.
30 B5 **Lewiston** *IL* U.S.A.
24 E2 **Lewistown** *MT* U.S.A.
32 E4 **Lewistown** *PA* U.S.A.
27 E5 **Lewisville** U.S.A.
27 D5 **Lewisville, Lake** *l.* U.S.A.
30 C5 **Lexington** *IL* U.S.A.
28 C4 **Lexington** *KY* U.S.A.
26 E4 **Lexington** *MO* U.S.A.
29 D5 **Lexington** *NC* U.S.A.
26 D3 **Lexington** *NE* U.S.A.
29 B5 **Lexington** *TN* U.S.A.
32 D6 **Lexington** *VA* U.S.A.
32 E5 **Lexington Park** U.S.A.
105 J1 **Leydsdorp** S. Africa
89 C5 **Leye** China
81 L3 **Leyla D.** *h.* Iran
94 C4 **Leyte** *i.* Phil.
94 C4 **Leyte Gulf** *g.* Phil.
67 H4 **Lezhë** Albania
89 B4 **Lezhi** China
69 E5 **L'gov** Rus. Fed.
85 F3 **Lhagoi Kangri** *mt* China
85 H3 **Lhari** China
85 G3 **Lhasa** China
85 G3 **Lhasa He** *r.* China
85 F3 **Lhazê** China

85 F3 **Lhazhong** China
92 B5 **Lhokseumawe** Indon.
95 A4 **Lhoksukon** Indon.
85 H3 **Lhorong** China
85 H3 **Lhünzê** China
85 G3 **Lhünzhub** China
95 A1 **Li, Mae** *r.* Thai.
89 C1 **Liancheng** China
91 B6 **Liancourt Rocks** *i.* Japan
Liancourt Rocks *i. see* Liancourt Rocks
94 C4 **Lianga** Phil.
94 C4 **Lianga Bay** *b.* Phil.
89 C4 **Liangaz Hu** *l.* China
88 D1 **Liangcheng** China
88 C3 **Liangdang** China
88 B3 **Lianghekou** China
89 C4 **Liangping** China
89 B5 **Liangwang Shan** *mts* China
88 C2 **Liangzhen** China
89 D5 **Lianhua** China
89 E6 **Lianhua Shan** *mts* China
89 F5 **Lianjiang** *Fujian* China
89 D6 **Lianjiang** *Guangdong* China
89 D5 **Liannan** China
89 E5 **Lianping** China
88 F1 **Lianshan** *Liaoning* China
89 D5 **Lianshan** China
88 F3 **Lianshui** China
89 D5 **Lianyuan** China
88 F3 **Lianyungang** *Jiangsu* China
88 F3 **Lianyungang** *Jiangsu* China
89 D5 **Lianzhou** China
90 B2 **Lianzhushan** China
88 G1 **Liao** *r.* China
88 E2 **Liaocheng** China
88 G1 **Liaodong Bandao** *pen.* China
88 F1 **Liaodong Wan** *b.* China
88 F1 **Liaoning** *div.* China
88 G1 **Liaoyang** China
87 N3 **Liaoyuan** China
88 G1 **Liaozhong** China
67 H5 **Liapades** Greece
84 B2 **Liaqatabad** Pak.
20 E2 **Liard** *r.* Can.
20 D3 **Liard River** Can.
57 C3 **Liathach** *mt* U.K.
80 F4 **Liban, Jebel** *mts* Lebanon
45 B3 **Libano** Col.
24 D1 **Libby** U.S.A.
102 B3 **Libenge** Dem. Rep. Congo
27 C4 **Liberal** U.S.A.
62 G5 **Liberec** Czech Rep.
96 **Liberia** *country* Africa
37 G6 **Liberia** Costa Rica
45 C2 **Libertad** Venez.
45 C2 **Libertad** Venez.
30 B6 **Liberty** *IL* U.S.A.
33 J2 **Liberty** *ME* U.S.A.
26 E4 **Liberty** *MO* U.S.A.
33 F4 **Liberty** *NY* U.S.A.
27 E6 **Liberty** *TX* U.S.A.
61 D5 **Libin** Belgium
94 B3 **Libmanan** Phil.
89 C5 **Libo** China
105 H5 **Libode** S. Africa
95 A4 **Libong, Ko** *i.* Thai.
64 D4 **Libourne** France
102 A3 **Libreville** Gabon
94 C5 **Libuganon** *r.* Phil.
96 **Libya** *country* Africa
101 E2 **Libyan Desert** *des.* Egypt/Libya
78 B3 **Libyan Plateau** *plat.* Egypt
47 B2 **Licantén** Chile
66 E6 **Licata** Italy
81 H2 **Lice** Turkey
59 F5 **Lichfield** U.K.
103 D5 **Lichinga** Moz.
105 G3 **Lichtenburg** S. Africa
89 C4 **Lichuan** *Hubei* China
89 E5 **Lichuan** *Jiangxi* China
32 B5 **Licking** *r.* U.S.A.
68 C4 **Lida** Belarus
34 D3 **Lida** U.S.A.
29 C5 **Linden** Guyana
30 A2 **Linden** *AL* U.S.A.
24 D1 **Lidfontein** Namibia
55 N7 **Lidköping** Sweden
54 O4 **Lidsjöberg** Sweden
112 F4 **Liebig, Mt** *mt* Austr.
48 **Liechtenstein** *country* Europe
61 D4 **Liège** Belgium
54 W5 **Lieksa** Fin.
63 N2 **Lielupe** *r.* Latvia
55 T8 **Lielvärde** Latvia
54 P5 **Lien** Sweden
102 C3 **Lienart** Dem. Rep. Congo
62 F7 **Lienz** Austria
55 R8 **Liepāja** Latvia
61 D3 **Lieshout** Neth.
61 A4 **Liévin** France
31 K2 **Lièvre** *r.* Can.
62 G2 **Liezen** Austria
60 E4 **Liffey** *r.* Rep. of Ireland
60 D3 **Lifford** Rep. of Ireland
47 C4 **Lifi Mahuida** *mt* Arg.
111 G4 **Lifou** *i.* New Caledonia
62 C4 **Ligen (Ems)** Ger.
94 B3 **Ligao** China
55 T8 **Līgatne** Latvia
115 G2 **Lightning Ridge** Austr.
103 D5 **Ligonha** *r.* Moz.
30 D5 **Ligonier** U.S.A.
Ligure, Mar *sea see* Ligurian Sea
64 J5 **Ligurian Sea** *sea* France/Italy
110 F2 **Lihir Group** *is* P.N.G.

116 D1 **Lihou Reef and Cays** *rf* Coral Sea Is Terr.
34 □² **Lihue** U.S.A.
89 D5 **Li Jiang** *r.* China
88 F2 **Lijin** China
95 B1 **Lik, Nam** *r.* Laos
103 C5 **Likasi** Dem. Rep. Congo
20 E4 **Likely** U.S.A.
68 E3 **Likhoslavl'** Rus. Fed.
92 D6 **Liku** Indon.
68 G3 **Likurga** Rus. Fed.
66 C2 **L'Île-Rousse** France
89 D5 **Liling** China
84 C2 **Lilla** Pak.
55 N7 **Lilla Edet** Sweden
61 C3 **Lille** Belgium
64 F1 **Lille** France
L9 **Lille Bælt** *chan.* Denmark
55 M6 **Lillehammer** Norway
55 L7 **Lillesand** Norway
55 M7 **Lillestrøm** Norway
30 D4 **Lilley** U.S.A.
54 O5 **Lillholmsjö** Sweden
20 E4 **Lillooet** Can.
20 E4 **Lillooet** *r.* Can.
85 H4 **Lilong** India
103 D5 **Lilongwe** Malawi
94 B4 **Liloy** Phil.
114 C4 **Lilydale** *S.A.* Austr.
115 G8 **Lilydale** *Tas.* Austr.
42 C6 **Lima** Peru
24 D2 **Lima** *MT* U.S.A.
32 A4 **Lima** *OH* U.S.A.
69 H6 **Liman** Rus. Fed.
47 B1 **Limarí** *r.* Chile
85 E2 **Lima Ringma Tso** *salt l.* China
80 D4 **Limassol** Cyprus
60 D2 **Limavady** U.K.
47 C3 **Limay** *r.* Arg.
47 C3 **Limay Mahuida** Arg.
55 T8 **Limbaži** Latvia
100 C4 **Limbe** Cameroon
95 □ **Lim Chu Kang** Sing.
95 □ **Lim Chu Kang** *r.* Sing.
104 E4 **Lime Acres** S. Africa
46 C3 **Limeira** Brazil
60 C5 **Limerick** Rep. of Ireland
30 A4 **Lime Springs** U.S.A.
33 K1 **Limestone** U.S.A.
54 N4 **Limingen** Norway
54 N4 **Limingen** *l.* Norway
33 H3 **Liminka** Fin.
54 T4 **Liminka** Fin.
113 G3 **Limmen Bight** *b.* Austr.
67 L5 **Limnos** *i.* Greece
33 F2 **Limoges** Can.
64 E4 **Limoges** France
37 H6 **Limón** Costa Rica
25 G4 **Limon** U.S.A.
80 E3 **Limonlu** Turkey
64 E4 **Limousin** *reg.* France
64 E5 **Limoux** France
105 K2 **Limpopo** *r.* Africa
54 W2 **Linakhamari** Rus. Fed.
89 C4 **Lin'an** China
94 A4 **Linapacan** *i.* Phil.
94 A4 **Linapacan Strait** *chan.* Phil.
47 B2 **Linares** Chile
36 E4 **Linares** Mex.
65 E3 **Linares** Spain
88 E2 **Lincheng** China
89 E5 **Linchuan** China
47 E2 **Lincoln** Arg.
59 G4 **Lincoln** U.K.
34 B2 **Lincoln** *CA* U.S.A.
30 C5 **Lincoln** *IL* U.S.A.
33 J2 **Lincoln** *ME* U.S.A.
31 F1 **Lincoln** *MI* U.S.A.
26 D3 **Lincoln** *NE* U.S.A.
33 H2 **Lincoln** *NH* U.S.A.
24 A2 **Lincoln City** U.S.A.
31 F4 **Lincoln Park** U.S.A.
59 G4 **Lincolnshire Wolds** *reg.* U.K.
33 J2 **Lincolnville** U.S.A.
46 E1 **Linda, Sa** *h.* Brazil
62 D7 **Lindau (Bodensee)** Ger.
116 D1 **Lindeman Gr.** *is* Austr.
43 G2 **Linden** Guyana
29 C5 **Linden** *AL* U.S.A.
29 C5 **Linden** *TN* U.S.A.
30 A2 **Linden Grove** U.S.A.
55 K7 **Lindesnes** *c.* Norway
102 C3 **Lindi** *r.* Dem. Rep. Congo
103 D4 **Lindi** Tanz.
Lindisfarne *i. see* Holy Island
105 G3 **Lindley** S. Africa
88 F1 **Lindong** China
67 N6 **Lindos, Akra** *pt* Greece
33 K1 **Lindsay** *N.B.* Can.
31 H3 **Lindsay** *Ont.* Can.
34 C3 **Lindsay** U.S.A.
88 D2 **Linfen** China
94 B2 **Lingayen** Phil.
94 B2 **Lingayen Gulf** *b.* Phil.
88 D3 **Lingbao** China
88 D3 **Lingbi** China
89 D5 **Lingchuan** *Guangxi* China
88 D3 **Lingchuan** *Shanxi* China
105 G6 **Lingelethu** S. Africa
105 F6 **Lingelihle** S. Africa
62 C4 **Lingen (Ems)** Ger.
92 D7 **Lingga, Kepulauan** *is* Indon.
94 C5 **Lingig** Phil.
24 F3 **Lingle** U.S.A.
102 C3 **Lingomo** Dem. Rep. Congo
88 E2 **Lingqiu** China
89 C6 **Lingshan** China
89 C7 **Lingshui** China
88 C3 **Lingtai** China

89 C7 **Lingtou** China
100 A3 **Linguère** Senegal
89 D5 **Lingui** China
88 C2 **Lingwu** China
88 F1 **Lingyuan** China
89 C5 **Lingyun** China
89 F4 **Linhai** China
46 E2 **Linhares** Brazil
95 C1 **Linh Cam** Vietnam
88 C1 **Linhe** China
33 H1 **Linière** Can.
81 J3 **Līnik, Chiyā-ē** *h.* Iraq
55 O7 **Linköping** Sweden
87 O2 **Linkou** China
88 E2 **Linli** China
57 E5 **Linlithgow** U.K.
88 D2 **Linlü Shan** *mt* China
34 A1 **Linn, Mt** *mt* U.S.A.
57 C4 **Linnhe, Loch** *in.* U.K.
88 E2 **Linqing** China
88 F2 **Linqu** China
88 E2 **Linquan** China
46 C3 **Lins** Brazil
89 F3 **Linshu** China
89 C4 **Linshui** China
88 B3 **Lintan** China
88 B3 **Lintao** China
26 C3 **Linton** U.S.A.
88 C3 **Lintong** China
88 F1 **Linxi** China
88 B3 **Linxia** China
88 F3 **Linxian** China
89 D4 **Linxiang** China
88 F3 **Linyi** *Shandong* China
88 F3 **Linyi** *Shandong* China
88 D3 **Linyi** *Shanxi* China
88 E3 **Linying** China
62 G6 **Linz** Austria
88 A2 **Linze** China
64 C3 **Lion, Golfe du** *g.* France
31 G3 **Lion's Head** Can.
33 F4 **Lionville** U.S.A.
102 B3 **Liouesso** Congo
94 B3 **Lipa** Phil.
66 F5 **Lipari** Italy
66 F5 **Lipari, Isola** *i.* Italy
66 F5 **Lipari, Isole** *is* Italy
69 F5 **Lipetsk** Rus. Fed.
69 F4 **Lipetskaya Oblast'** *div.* Rus. Fed.
68 F2 **Lipin Bor** Rus. Fed.
89 C5 **Liping** China
67 J1 **Lipova** Romania
90 B2 **Lipovtsy** Rus. Fed.
61 E3 **Lippe** *r.* Ger.
84 E3 **Lipti Lekh** *pass* Nepal
115 F7 **Liptrap, C.** *hd* Austr.
89 D5 **Lipu** China
102 D3 **Lira** Uganda
102 B4 **Liranga** Congo
94 C4 **Lirung** Indon.
102 C3 **Lisala** Dem. Rep. Congo
103 E6 **L'Isalo, Massif de** *mts* Madag.
103 E6 **L'Isalo, Parc National de** *nat. park* Madag.
60 D3 **Lisbellaw** U.K.
Lisboa *see* Lisbon
65 B3 **Lisbon** Port.
30 C5 **Lisbon** *IL* U.S.A.
33 H2 **Lisbon** *ME* U.S.A.
26 D2 **Lisbon** *ND* U.S.A.
33 H2 **Lisbon** *NH* U.S.A.
32 C4 **Lisbon** *OH* U.S.A.
60 E3 **Lisburn** U.K.
60 B5 **Liscannor Bay** *b.* Rep. of Ireland
60 B4 **Lisdoonvarna** Rep. of Ireland
89 D5 **Lishan** Taiwan
88 D2 **Lishi** China
88 F4 **Lishui** *Jiangsu* China
89 E5 **Lishui** *Zhejiang* China
89 D4 **Li Shui** *r.* China
64 E2 **Lisieux** France
57 C7 **Liskeard** U.K.
69 F5 **Liski** Rus. Fed.
64 G5 **L'Isle-sur-la-Sorgue** France
115 K2 **Lismore** Austr.
60 D5 **Lismore** Rep. of Ireland
57 C4 **Lismore** *i.* U.K.
60 D3 **Lisnarrick** U.K.
60 D3 **Lisnaskea** U.K.
31 G4 **Listowel** Can.
60 B5 **Listowel** Rep. of Ireland
116 A5 **Listowel Downs** Austr.
54 O5 **Lit** Sweden
89 C6 **Litang** *Guangxi* China
82 K4 **Litang** *Sichuan* China
43 H3 **Litani** *r.* Fr. Guiana/Suriname
80 E5 **Lītāni** *r.* Lebanon
34 B1 **Litchfield** *CA* U.S.A.
28 B4 **Litchfield** *IL* U.S.A.
64 D4 **Lit-et-Mixe** France
49 **Lithuania** *country* Europe
33 E4 **Lititz** U.S.A.
62 G5 **Litoměřice** Czech Rep.
29 E7 **Little Abaco** *i.* Bahamas
92 A4 **Little Andaman** *i.* Andaman and Nicobar Is
29 E7 **Little Bahama Bank** *sand bank* Bahamas
117 E2 **Little Barrier** *i.* N.Z.
30 D3 **Little Bay de Noc** *b.* U.S.A.
24 E2 **Little Belt Mts** *mts* U.S.A.
37 H5 **Little Cayman** *i.* Cayman Is

89 C7 **Lingtou** China
100 A3 **Linguère** Senegal
89 D5 **Lingui** China
88 C2 **Lingwu** China
88 F1 **Lingyuan** China
89 C5 **Lingyun** China
89 F4 **Linhai** China
46 E2 **Linhares** Brazil
35 H4 **Little Colorado** *r.* U.S.A.
35 F3 **Little Creek Peak** *summit* U.S.A.
31 G3 **Little Current** Can.
22 C3 **Little Current** *r.* Can.
59 D7 **Little Dart** *r.* U.K.
114 D6 **Little Desert Nat. Park** *nat. park* Austr.
33 F5 **Little Egg Harbor** *in.* U.S.A.
29 F7 **Little Exuma** *i.* Bahamas
26 E2 **Little Falls** *MN* U.S.A.
33 F3 **Little Falls** *NY* U.S.A.
35 F3 **Littlefield** *AZ* U.S.A.
27 C5 **Littlefield** *TX* U.S.A.
26 E1 **Little Fork** U.S.A.
30 A1 **Little Fork** *r.* U.S.A.
85 F4 **Little Gandak** *r.* India
21 K4 **Little Grand Rapids** Can.
59 G7 **Littlehampton** U.K.
32 C5 **Little Kanawha** *r.* U.S.A.
104 C3 **Little Karas Berg** *plat.* Namibia
104 D6 **Little Karoo** *plat.* S. Africa
30 D2 **Little Lake** U.S.A.
23 H3 **Little Mecatina** *r.* Can.
32 A5 **Little Miami** *r.* U.S.A.
57 B3 **Little Minch** *str.* U.K.
26 C3 **Little Missouri** *r.* U.S.A.
59 H5 **Little Ouse** *r.* U.K.
30 D1 **Little Pic** *r.* Can.
20 D2 **Little Rancheria** *r.* Can.
84 B5 **Little Rann** *marsh* India
27 E5 **Little Rock** U.S.A.
30 C4 **Little Sable Pt** *pt* U.S.A.
29 F7 **Little San Salvador** *i.* Bahamas
20 H4 **Little Smoky** *r.* Can.
25 F4 **Littleton** *CO* U.S.A.
33 H2 **Littleton** *NH* U.S.A.
32 C5 **Littleton** *WV* U.S.A.
30 E3 **Little Traverse Bay** *b.* U.S.A.
103 D5 **Litunde** Moz.
20 B3 **Lituya Bay** *b.* U.S.A.
88 F1 **Liu** *r.* China
88 G1 **Liu** *r.* China
88 D3 **Liuba** China
89 C5 **Liuchong He** *r.* China
89 F1 **Liugu** *r.* China
89 D4 **Liujiachang** China
89 C5 **Liujiang** China
88 B3 **Liujiaxia Sk.** *resr* China
88 B3 **Liupan Shan** *mts* China
89 D4 **Liuyang** China
89 C5 **Liuzhou** China
90 D3 **Livadiya** Rus. Fed.
55 U8 **Līvāni** Latvia
34 B2 **Live Oak** *CA* U.S.A.
29 D6 **Live Oak** *FL* U.S.A.
34 B3 **Livermore** U.S.A.
27 B6 **Livermore, Mt** *mt* U.S.A.
33 H2 **Livermore Falls** U.S.A.
115 J4 **Liverpool** Austr.
23 H5 **Liverpool** Can.
59 D4 **Liverpool** U.K.
115 J3 **Liverpool Bay** U.K.
115 J3 **Liverpool Plains** *plain* Austr.
115 J3 **Liverpool Ra.** *mts* Austr.
57 E5 **Livingston** U.K.
34 B3 **Livingston** *CA* U.S.A.
24 E2 **Livingston** *MT* U.S.A.
29 C4 **Livingston** *TN* U.S.A.
27 E6 **Livingston** *TX* U.S.A.
27 E6 **Livingston, L.** *l.* U.S.A.
103 C5 **Livingstone** Zambia
119 B2 **Livingstone I.** *i.* Antarctica
66 G3 **Livno** Bos.-Herz.
69 F4 **Livny** Rus. Fed.
54 U4 **Livojoki** *r.* Fin.
31 F4 **Livonia** U.S.A.
66 D3 **Livorno** Italy
46 E1 **Livramento do Brumado** Brazil
103 D4 **Liwale** Tanz.
88 B3 **Lixian** *Gansu* China
89 D4 **Lixian** *Hunan* China
88 B4 **Lixian** *Sichuan* China
88 E3 **Lixin** China
88 F4 **Liyang** China
59 B8 **Lizard** U.K.
59 B8 **Lizard Point** *pt* U.K.
66 F1 **Ljubljana** Slovenia
55 Q8 **Ljugarn** Sweden
55 P5 **Ljungan** *r.* Sweden
55 N8 **Ljungby** Sweden
55 P6 **Ljusdal** Sweden
55 O6 **Ljusnan** *r.* Sweden
55 P6 **Ljusne** Sweden
44 B5 **Llaima, Volcán** *vol.* Chile
59 D5 **Llanbadarn Fawr** U.K.
59 D5 **Llanbister** U.K.
59 C6 **Llancanelo, Salina** *salt flat* Arg.
59 D6 **Llandeilo** U.K.
59 C6 **Llandissilio** U.K.
59 D5 **Llandovery** U.K.
59 D5 **Llandrindod Wells** U.K.
59 D4 **Llandudno** U.K.
59 C5 **Llanegwad** U.K.
59 C5 **Llanelli** U.K.
59 C5 **Llanerchymedd** U.K.
59 D5 **Llanfair Caereinion** U.K.
59 C5 **Llangefni** U.K.
59 D5 **Llangollen** U.K.
59 D6 **Llangurig** U.K.
59 C5 **Llanllyfni** U.K.
59 C5 **Llannor** U.K.

27 D6 **Llano** *r.* U.S.A.
27 C5 **Llano Estacado** *plain* U.S.A.
45 C3 **Llanos** *reg.* Col./Venez.
47 B4 **Llanquihue, L.** *l.* Chile
59 C5 **Llanrhystud** U.K.
59 D6 **Llantrisant** U.K.
59 C5 **Llanuwchllyn** U.K.
59 D5 **Llanwnog** U.K.
59 D4 **Llay** U.K.
65 G2 **Lleida** Spain
65 C3 **Llerena** Spain
65 F3 **Lliria** Spain
65 E1 **Llodio** Spain
21 G4 **Lloyd Lake** *l.* Can.
21 G4 **Lloydminster** Can.
65 H3 **Llucmajor** Spain
44 C2 **Llullaillaco, Vol.** *vol.* Chile
89 B6 **Lô** *r.* China/Vietnam
44 C2 **Loa** *r.* Chile
35 G2 **Loa** U.S.A.
68 J3 **Loban'** *r.* Rus. Fed.
65 D4 **Lobatejo** *mt* Spain
103 C6 **Lobatse** Botswana
47 E3 **Loberia** Arg.
61 E3 **Lobith** Neth.
103 B5 **Lobito** Angola
47 E2 **Lobos** Arg.
57 C3 **Lochaber** *reg.* U.K.
57 C4 **Lochaline** U.K.
31 E1 **Lochalsh** Can.
57 A3 **Lochboisdale** U.K.
57 C4 **Lochcarron** U.K.
58 C1 **Lochearnhead** U.K.
64 E3 **Loches** France
57 E4 **Lochgelly** U.K.
57 C4 **Lochgilphead** U.K.
57 C4 **Lochinver** U.K.
57 A3 **Lochmaddy** U.K.
57 E4 **Lochnagar** *mt* U.K.
32 E5 **Loch Raven Reservoir** *resr* U.S.A.
57 C4 **Lochy, Loch** *l.* U.K.
114 A4 **Lock** Austr.
57 E5 **Lockerbie** U.K.
115 G5 **Lockhart** Austr.
27 D6 **Lockhart** U.S.A.
32 E4 **Lock Haven** U.S.A.
32 D3 **Lockport** U.S.A.
95 B4 **Lôc Ninh** Vietnam
32 B5 **Locust Grove** U.S.A.
80 E6 **Lod** Israel
114 E5 **Loddon** *r.* Austr.
64 F5 **Lodève** France
68 E2 **Lodeynoye Pole** Rus. Fed.
24 F2 **Lodge Grass** U.S.A.
84 B3 **Lodhran** Pak.
66 C2 **Lodi** Italy
34 B2 **Lodi** *CA* U.S.A.
32 B4 **Lodi** *OH* U.S.A.
54 O2 **Lødingen** Norway
102 D3 **Lodwar** Kenya
63 J5 **Łódź** Pol.
84 B2 **Loe Dakka** Afgh.
95 B1 **Loei** Thai.
104 C5 **Loeriesfontein** S. Africa
54 N2 **Lofoten** *is* Norway
69 G5 **Log** Rus. Fed.
115 K1 **Logan** *r.* Austr.
25 G5 **Logan** *NM* U.S.A.
32 B5 **Logan** *OH* U.S.A.
24 E3 **Logan** *UT* U.S.A.
32 C6 **Logan** *WV* U.S.A.
20 A2 **Logan, Mt** *mt* Can.
116 B4 **Logan Cr.** *r.* Austr.
20 D2 **Logan Mountains** *mts* Can.
30 D5 **Logansport** U.S.A.
66 F2 **Logatec** Slovenia
65 E1 **Logroño** Spain
85 H3 **Logtak L.** *l.* India
104 E3 **Lohatlha** S. Africa
54 T3 **Lohiniva** Fin.
54 S6 **Lohjanjärvi** *l.* Fin.
54 S4 **Lohtaja** Fin.
95 A1 **Loikaw** Myanmar
95 A1 **Loi Lan** *mt* Myanmar/Thai.
54 S6 **Loimaa** Fin.
64 C3 **Loire** *r.* France
61 B5 **L'Oise à l'Aisne, Canal de** *canal* France
42 C4 **Loja** Ecuador
65 D4 **Loja** Spain
94 A5 **Lokan** *r.* Malaysia
54 U3 **Lokan tekojärvi** *l.* Fin.
61 C3 **Lokeren** Belgium
104 D2 **Lokgwabe** Botswana
102 D3 **Lokichar** Kenya
102 D3 **Lokichokio** Kenya
55 L8 **Løkken** Denmark
54 L5 **Løkken** Norway
63 P2 **Loknya** Rus. Fed.
100 C3 **Lokoja** Nigeria
100 C4 **Lokossa** Benin
69 E4 **Lokot'** Rus. Fed.
55 T7 **Loksa** Estonia
100 B4 **Lola** Guinea
34 B2 **Lola, Mt** *mt* U.S.A.
55 M9 **Lolland** *i.* Denmark
102 D4 **Lolindo** Tanz.
24 D2 **Lolo** U.S.A.
104 E3 **Lolwane** S. Africa
67 K3 **Lom** Bulg.
55 L6 **Lom** Norway
102 C3 **Lomami** *r.* Dem. Rep. Congo
84 A2 **Lomar P.** *pass* Afgh.
47 D3 **Lomas de Zamora** Arg.
112 D3 **Lombardina** Austr.
93 G8 **Lomblen** *i.* Indon.
92 F8 **Lombok** *i.* Indon.
92 F8 **Lombok, Selat** *chan.* Indon.

00 C4 Lomé Togo
02 C4 Lomela Dem. Rep. Congo
02 C4 Lomela r. Dem. Rep. Congo
61 D3 Lommel Belgium
47 D4 Lomond, Loch l. U.K.
48 G1 Lomovoye Rus. Fed.
83 F8 Lompobattang, Gunung mt Indon.
84 B4 Lompoc U.S.A.
95 B1 Lom Sak Thai.
43 L4 Łomża Pol.
84 D6 Lonar India
47 B3 Loncoche Chile
47 B3 Loncopue Arg.
41 G4 London Can.
59 G6 London U.K.
32 A6 London KY U.S.A.
32 B5 London OH U.S.A.
60 D3 Londonderry U.K.
33 G3 Londonderry U.S.A.
12 E2 Londonderry, I. i. Chile
84 B9 Londonderry, I. i. Chile
84 C3 Lone Pine U.S.A.
95 A1 Long Thai.
47 D4 Long, Loch in. U.K.
67 T2 Longa, Proliv chan. Rus. Fed.
89 C6 Long'an China
59 C9 Long Ashton U.K.
47 B3 Longavi, Nev. de mt Chile
9 E5 Long Bay b. U.S.A.
87 C6 Longbeach N.Z.
84 C5 Long Beach CA U.S.A.
33 G4 Long Beach NY U.S.A.
33 F4 Long Branch U.S.A.
30 A6 Long Branch Lake l. U.S.A.
9 B4 Longchang China
9 C5 Longchuan China
5 H3 Longju China
9 F5 Long Eaton U.K.
60 D4 Longford Rep. of Ireland
9 E5 Longhai China
8 F2 Longhoughton U.K.
6 C4 Long Island i. Austr.
2 E3 Long Island i. Can.
10 E2 Long Island i. P.N.G.
7 J4 Long Island i. Bahamas
3 G4 Long Island i. U.S.A.
3 G4 Long Island Sound chan. U.S.A.
7 M2 Longjiang China
9 C5 Long Jiang r. China
5 H3 Longju China
9 F2 Longkou Wan b. China
2 C4 Longlac Can.
3 F4 Long Lake l. Can.
3 F3 Long Lake U.S.A.
1 J4 Long Lake l. ME U.S.A.
0 E3 Long Lake l. MI U.S.A.
1 F3 Long Lake l. MI U.S.A.
1 F3 Long Lake l. ND U.S.A.
3 F2 Long Lake l. NY U.S.A.
9 C5 Longli China
9 B5 Longlin China
9 H5 Long Melford U.K.
9 E6 Longmen China
8 B3 Longmen Shan mts China
4 F3 Longmont U.S.A.
9 E5 Longnan China
1 G4 Long Point pt Can.
7 B7 Long Point pt N.Z.
1 G4 Long Point Bay b. Can.
9 F5 Long Preston U.K.
9 F4 Longquan China
3 J4 Long Range Mts h. Can.
3 J4 Long Range Mts h. Can.
6 A4 Longreach Austr.
8 B3 Longriba China
9 C4 Longshan China
9 D5 Longsheng China
4 F3 Longs Peak summit U.S.A.
9 J5 Long Stratton U.K.
9 D4 Longtian China
6 A3 Longtou Austr.
8 E2 Longtown U.K.
2 F4 Longueuil Can.
1 D5 Longuyon France
5 F3 Long Valley Junction U.S.A.
7 E5 Longview TX U.S.A.
4 B2 Longview WA U.S.A.
0 C2 Longwangmiao Rus. Fed.
1 D5 Longwy France
8 B3 Longxi China
8 B3 Longxian China
9 E5 Longxi Shan mt China
5 C3 Long Xuyên Vietnam
9 E5 Longyan China
9 C6 Longzhou China
4 E6 Lonsdale, Lake l. Austr.
4 G3 Lons-le-Saunier France
4 B3 Lontra r. Brazil
4 B3 Looc Phil.
3 F4 Lookout U.S.A.
2 D2 Lookout, Cape c. U.S.A.
2 E5 Lookout, Cape c. Can.
5 K1 Lookout, Point pt Austr.
4 C3 Lookout, Pt pt U.S.A.
4 C3 Lookout Mt mt U.S.A.
0 C1 Loon r. Can.
0 C1 Loon r. Can.
1 H4 Loon Lake Can.
2 C4 Loon Lake l. U.S.A.
0 B5 Loop Head hd Rep. of Ireland
4 E1 Lop China

87 Q1 Lopatina, Gora mt Rus. Fed.
68 H4 Lopatino Rus. Fed.
95 B2 Lop Buri Thai.
94 B3 Lopez Phil.
33 E4 Lopez U.S.A.
82 H2 Lop Nur salt l. China
102 B3 Lopori r. Dem. Rep. Congo
54 R1 Lopphavet b. Norway
68 J2 Loptyuga Rus. Fed.
84 A3 Lora r. Afgh.
114 A2 Lora watercourse Austr.
45 B2 Lora r. Venez.
65 D3 Lora del Río Spain
32 B4 Lorain U.S.A.
84 B3 Loralai Pak.
84 B3 Loralai r. Pak.
32 A4 Loramie, Lake l. U.S.A.
65 F4 Lorca Spain
94 A4 Lord Auckland sand bank Phil.
111 F5 Lord Howe Island i. Pac. Oc.
14 F8 Lord Howe Rise sea feature Pac. Oc.
35 H5 Lordsburg U.S.A.
46 D3 Lorena Brazil
93 K8 Lorentz r. Indon.
42 F7 Loreto Bol.
43 J5 Loreto Brazil
36 B3 Loreto Mex.
94 C4 Loreto Phil.
45 B2 Lorica Col.
64 C3 Lorient France
21 L1 Lorillard r. Can.
57 C4 Lorn, Firth of est. U.K.
116 A5 Lorne Qld. Austr.
114 E7 Lorne Vic. Austr.
85 H3 Loro r. China
64 G2 Lorraine reg. France
84 C4 Losal India
27 C7 Los Alamitos, Sierra de mt Mex.
25 F5 Los Alamos U.S.A.
47 B2 Los Andes Chile
47 B3 Los Angeles Chile
34 C5 Los Angeles U.S.A.
34 C4 Los Angeles Aqueduct canal U.S.A.
34 B3 Los Banos U.S.A.
44 D2 Los Blancos Arg.
27 B6 Los Caballos Mesteños, Llano de plain Mex.
44 B7 Los Chonos, Archipiélago de is Chile
47 B4 Los Coronados, Golfo de b. Chile
34 D5 Los Coronados, Islas is Mex.
44 D8 Los Estados, Isla de i. Arg.
34 B3 Los Gatos U.S.A.
27 B7 Los Gigantes, Llanos de plain Mex.
44 B3 Los Glaciares, Parque Nacional nat. park Arg.
66 F2 Lošinj i. Croatia
37 J4 Los Jardines de la Reina, Archipiélago de is Cuba
105 H2 Loskop Dam dam S. Africa
47 B4 Los Lagos div. Chile
25 F5 Los Lunas U.S.A.
47 C4 Los Menucos Arg.
25 F6 Los Mexicanos, Lago de l. Mex.
36 C3 Los Mochis Mex.
34 A1 Los Molinos U.S.A.
37 H7 Los Mosquitos, Golfo de b. Panama
102 B3 Losombo Dem. Rep. Congo
47 D4 Los Riachos, Islas de i. Arg.
45 D2 Los Roques, Islas is Venez.
57 E3 Lossie r. U.K.
57 E3 Lossiemouth U.K.
45 C2 Los Taques Venez.
45 D2 Los Teques Venez.
45 E2 Los Testigos is Venez.
34 C4 Lost Hills U.S.A.
24 D2 Lost Trail Pass pass U.S.A.
59 C7 Lostwithiel U.K.
44 C3 Los Vientos Chile
47 B3 Los Vilos Chile
47 B3 Lota Chile
105 J3 Lothair S. Africa
102 D3 Lotikipi Plain plain Kenya
102 C4 Loto Dem. Rep. Congo
68 E3 Lotoshino Rus. Fed.
105 G1 Lotsane r. Botswana
54 V2 Lotta r. Fin./Rus. Fed.
86 H7 Louang Namtha Laos
92 Louangphrabang Laos
102 B4 Loubomo Congo
64 C2 Loudéac France
89 D5 Loudi China
102 B4 Loudima Congo
32 B4 Loudonville U.S.A.
100 A3 Louga Senegal
59 F5 Loughborough U.K.
59 C6 Loughor r. U.K.
60 C4 Loughrea Rep. of Ireland
59 H6 Loughton U.K.
32 B3 Louisa KY U.S.A.
32 C5 Louisa VA U.S.A.
60 B4 Louisburgh Rep. of Ireland
20 C4 Louise I. i. Can.
111 F3 Louisiade Archipelago is P.N.G.
27 E6 Louisiana div. U.S.A.
105 H1 Louis Trichardt S. Africa

29 D5 Louisville GA U.S.A.
28 C4 Louisville KY U.S.A.
27 F5 Louisville MS U.S.A.
22 E3 Louis-XIV, Pointe c. Can.
76 E3 Loukh Rus. Fed.
65 B4 Loulé Port.
21 L4 Lount L. l. Can.
62 F3 Louny Czech Rep.
26 D3 Loup r. U.S.A.
22 F2 Loups-Marins, Lacs des l. Can.
23 J4 Lourdes Can.
64 D5 Lourdes France
65 B4 Lousã Port.
90 A2 Loushan China
115 F3 Louth Austr.
59 G4 Louth U.K.
67 K5 Loutra Aidipsou Greece
Louvain see Leuven
104 B1 Louwater-Suid Namibia
105 J3 Louwsburg S. Africa
54 R4 Lövånger Sweden
68 D3 Lovat' r. Rus. Fed.
67 L3 Lovech Bulg.
24 F3 Loveland U.S.A.
24 E3 Lovell U.S.A.
34 C1 Lovelock U.S.A.
61 B3 Lovendegem Belgium
55 U6 Loviisa Fin.
32 D6 Lovington U.S.A.
30 C6 Lovington IL U.S.A.
27 C5 Lovington NM U.S.A.
31 K3 Low Can.
21 M2 Low, Cape c. Can.
22 E3 Low, Lac l. Can.
102 C4 Lowa Dem. Rep. Congo
84 B2 Lowarai Pass pass Pak.
33 H3 Lowell MA U.S.A.
30 E4 Lowell MI U.S.A.
33 G2 Lowell VT U.S.A.
20 F5 Lower Arrow L. l. Can.
35 F4 Lower Granite Gorge gorge U.S.A.
117 E4 Lower Hutt N.Z.
34 A2 Lower Lake U.S.A.
60 D3 Lower Lough Erne l. U.K.
95 Lower Peirce Res. resr Sing.
20 D3 Lower Post Can.
23 H5 Lower Sackville Can.
59 J5 Lowestoft U.K.
63 J4 Łowicz Pol.
115 F9 Low Rocky Pt hd Austr.
57 E5 Lowther Hills h. U.K.
33 F3 Lowville U.S.A.
114 D5 Loxton Austr.
32 E4 Loyalsock Creek r. U.S.A.
34 B2 Loyalton U.S.A.
Loyalty Is is see Loyauté, Îs
111 G4 Loyauté, Îs is New Caledonia
69 D5 Loyew Belarus
67 H2 Loznica Yugo.
69 F5 Lozova Ukr.
103 C5 Luacano Angola
88 E4 Lu'an China
88 D3 Luanchuan China
103 B4 Luanda Angola
95 A3 Luang, Khao mt Thai.
103 D5 Luangwa r. Zambia
85 H2 Luanhaizi China
88 F1 Luan He r. China
88 F2 Luannan China
88 E1 Luanping China
103 C5 Luanshya Zambia
88 F2 Luanxian China
103 C4 Luanza Dem. Rep. Congo
65 C1 Luarca Spain
103 C5 Luau Angola
63 L5 Lubaczów Pol.
55 U8 Lubānas ezers l. Latvia
94 B3 Lubang Phil.
94 A3 Lubang Islands is Phil.
103 B5 Lubango Angola
102 C4 Lubao Dem. Rep. Congo
63 L5 Lubartów Pol.
104 C3 Lubbeskolk salt pan S. Africa
27 C5 Lubbock U.S.A.
62 E4 Lübeck Ger.
87 M3 Lubei China
63 L5 Lubelska, Wyżyna reg. Pol.
102 C4 Lubero Dem. Rep. Congo
62 H5 Lubin Pol.
63 L5 Lublin Pol.
69 E5 Lubny Ukr.
92 E6 Lubok Antu Malaysia
94 B2 Lubuagan Phil.
103 C4 Lubudi Dem. Rep. Congo
92 C7 Lubuklinggau Indon.
95 A5 Lubukpakam Indon.
103 C5 Lubumbashi Dem. Rep. Congo
103 C5 Lubungu Zambia
102 C4 Lubutu Dem. Rep. Congo
103 B4 Lucala Angola
60 C4 Lucan Rep. of Ireland
20 A2 Lucania, Mt mt Can.
103 C4 Lucapa Angola
29 E7 Lucaya Bahamas
66 D3 Lucca Italy
57 D6 Luce Bay b. U.K.
46 B3 Lucélia Brazil
94 B3 Lucena Phil.
65 D4 Lucena Spain
63 J6 Lučenec Slovakia
66 F4 Lucera Italy
Lucerne see Luzern
90 D1 Luchegorsk Rus. Fed.
89 D6 Luchuan China
89 B6 Lüchun China

116 B2 Lucinda Austr.
114 D1 Lucindale Austr.
103 B5 Lucira Angola
85 F4 Luckeesarai India
62 F3 Luckenwalde Ger.
104 F4 Luckhoff S. Africa
31 G4 Lucknow Can.
84 E4 Lucknow India
103 C5 Lucusse Angola
67 F1 Luda Rus. Fed.
103 B6 Lüderitz Namibia
84 C3 Ludhiana India
89 B5 Ludian China
30 D2 Ludington U.S.A.
59 E5 Ludlow U.K.
34 C4 Ludlow CA U.S.A.
33 J1 Ludlow ME U.S.A.
33 G3 Ludlow VT U.S.A.
67 M3 Ludogorie reg. Bulg.
55 O6 Ludvika Sweden
62 F6 Ludwigsburg Ger.
62 D6 Ludwigshafen am Rhein Ger.
62 E4 Ludwigslust Ger.
55 U8 Ludza Latvia
102 C4 Luebo Dem. Rep. Congo
103 C4 Luena Angola
45 E3 Luepa Venez.
88 E3 Lüeyang China
89 E6 Lufeng China
27 E6 Lufkin U.S.A.
68 D3 Luga Rus. Fed.
68 D3 Luga r. Rus. Fed.
66 D1 Lugano Switz.
103 D5 Lugenda r. Moz.
59 D5 Lugg r. U.K.
66 D2 Lugo Italy
65 C1 Lugo Spain
67 J2 Lugoj Romania
82 D2 Lugovoy Kazak.
94 B3 Lugus i. Phil.
69 F5 Luhans'k Ukr.
88 E3 Luhe China
85 H4 Luhit r. India
103 D4 Luhombero Tanz.
69 D5 Luhyny Ukr.
103 C5 Luiana Angola
Luik see Liège
102 C4 Luilaka r. Dem. Rep. Congo
57 C4 Luing i. U.K.
66 C2 Luino Italy
54 U3 Luiro r. Fin.
102 C4 Luiza Dem. Rep. Congo
47 E2 Luján r. Arg.
47 E2 Luján de Cuyo Arg.
88 E4 Lujiang China
67 H2 Lukavac Bos.-Herz.
102 B4 Lukenie r. Dem. Rep. Congo
35 F6 Lukeville U.S.A.
68 G3 Lukh r. Rus. Fed.
68 F4 Lukhovitsy Rus. Fed.
89 Luk Keng China
67 L3 Lukovit Bulg.
63 L5 Łuków Pol.
68 H4 Lukoyanov Rus. Fed.
103 C5 Lukulu Zambia
54 S4 Luleå Sweden
54 R4 Luleälven r. Sweden
80 A1 Lüleburgaz Turkey
89 B5 Luliang China
88 D2 Lüliang Shan mts China
27 D6 Luling U.S.A.
85 F2 Lulong China
85 F3 Lülung China
89 D5 Lumachomo China
92 Lumajang Indon.
85 E2 Lumajangdong Co salt l. China
103 C5 Lumbala Kaquengue Angola
103 C5 Lumbala N'guimbo Angola
29 E5 Lumberton U.S.A.
65 C2 Lumbrales Spain
85 H4 Lumding India
54 T4 Lumijoki Fin.
95 C2 Lumphăt Cambodia
117 B6 Lumsden N.Z.
94 B2 Luna Phil.
35 H5 Luna U.S.A.
57 F4 Lunan Bay b. U.K.
21 L2 Lunan Lake l. Can.
31 F5 Luna Pier U.S.A.
84 B4 Lunavada India
58 E3 Lune r. U.K.
62 E4 Lüneburg Ger.
61 F3 Lünen Ger.
64 H2 Lunéville France
103 C5 Lunga r. Zambia
103 C5 Lungdo China
85 G3 Lunggar China
100 A4 Lungi Sierra Leone
89 Lung Kwu Chau i. China
85 H5 Lunglei India
60 E5 Lungnaquilla Mountain mt Rep. of Ireland
103 C5 Lungwebungu r. Zambia
85 F3 Lunh Nepal
84 C4 Luni India
84 B3 Luni r. India
84 B3 Luni r. Pak.
34 C2 Luning U.S.A.
68 H4 Lunino Rus. Fed.

69 C4 Luninyets Belarus
84 C1 Lunkho mt Afgh./Pak.
100 A4 Lunsar Sierra Leone
105 H2 Lunsklip S. Africa
82 F2 Luntai China
88 D3 Luo r. Henan China
88 D3 Luo r. Shaanxi China
89 C5 Luocheng China
88 C3 Luochuan China
89 C5 Luodian China
89 D6 Luoding China
89 D6 Luodou Sha i. China
88 E3 Luohe China
88 D3 Luoning China
89 B5 Luoping China
88 E3 Luoshan China
89 E4 Luotian China
54 S5 Luoto Fin.
88 D3 Luoyang China
89 F5 Luoyuan China
90 B3 Luozigou China
103 C5 Lupane Zimbabwe
89 B5 Lupanshui China
103 C4 L'Upemba, Parc National de nat. park Dem. Rep. Congo
67 K2 Lupeni Romania
103 D5 Lupilichi Moz.
94 C5 Lupon Phil.
35 H4 Lupton U.S.A.
88 B3 Luqu China
89 B5 Luquan China
88 E2 Luquan China
81 K3 Lūrā Shīrīn Iran
103 B4 Luremo Angola
57 C2 Lurgainn, Loch l. U.K.
60 E3 Lurgan U.K.
103 E5 Lúrio Moz.
103 D5 Lurio r. Moz.
103 C5 Lusaka Zambia
102 C4 Lusambo Dem. Rep. Congo
110 F2 Lusancay Islands and Reefs is P.N.G.
20 F4 Luscar Can.
21 H4 Luseland Can.
88 D3 Lushi China
67 H4 Lushnjë Albania
88 F2 Lushunkou China
105 H5 Lusikisiki S. Africa
24 F3 Lusk U.S.A.
116 B6 Lussvale Austr.
79 H3 Lut, Dasht-e des. Iran
89 F6 Lü Tao i. Taiwan
31 G4 Luther Lake l. Can.
62 F5 Lutherstadt Wittenberg Ger.
59 G6 Luton U.K.
92 Lutong Malaysia
21 G2 Łutselk'e Can.
69 C5 Luts'k Ukr.
104 D4 Lutzputs S. Africa
104 C5 Lutzville S. Africa
94 B5 Luuk Phil.
55 U6 Luumäki Fin.
102 E3 Luuq Somalia
26 D3 Luverne U.S.A.
102 C4 Luvua r. Dem. Rep. Congo
105 J1 Luvuvhu r. S. Africa
102 D3 Luwero Uganda
93 Luwuk Indon.
48 Luxembourg country Europe
61 E5 Luxembourg Lux.
64 H3 Luxeuil-les-Bains France
89 Luxi Hunan China
89 B5 Luxi Yunnan China
105 Luxolweni S. Africa
78 C4 Luxor Egypt
88 E3 Luyi China
61 Luyksgestel Neth.
68 H2 Luza Rus. Fed.
68 J2 Luza r. Rus. Fed.
62 D7 Luzern Switz.
89 C5 Luzhai China
89 B5 Luzhi China
89 B4 Luzhou China
46 C2 Luziânia Brazil
43 K4 Luzilândia Brazil
94 B3 Luzon i. Phil.
94 B1 Luzon Strait str. Phil.
64 F3 Luzy France
69 Lviv Ukr.
L'vov see L'viv
68 D3 Lyady Rus. Fed.
69 Lyakhavichy Belarus
20 G5 Lyall, Mt mt Can.
Lyallpur see Faisalabad
54 Q4 Lycksele Sweden
59 H7 Lydd U.K.
119 Lyddan I. i. Antarctica
105 J2 Lydenburg S. Africa
59 E6 Lydney U.K.
69 Lyel'chytsy Belarus
34 C3 Lyell, Mt mt U.S.A.
20 C4 Lyell I. i. Can.
68 D7 Lyepyel' Belarus
32 E4 Lykens U.S.A.
24 E3 Lyman U.S.A.
59 E7 Lyme Bay b. U.K.
59 E7 Lyme Regis U.K.
59 F7 Lymington U.K.
32 D6 Lynchburg U.S.A.
33 H2 Lynchville U.S.A.
116 A1 Lynd r. Austr.
115 H4 Lyndhurst N.S.W. Austr.
116 A2 Lyndhurst Qld. Austr.
114 C1 Lyndhurst S.A. Austr.
33 G3 Lyndonville U.S.A.
57 G2 Lyness U.K.
55 K7 Lyngdal Norway
33 H2 Lynn U.S.A.
20 B3 Lynn Canal chan. U.S.A.
35 F2 Lynndyl U.S.A.
21 J3 Lynn Lake Can.

59 D6 Lynton U.K.
21 H2 Lynx Lake l. Can.
64 G4 Lyon France
33 G2 Lyon Mountain U.S.A.
29 D5 Lyons GA U.S.A.
32 E3 Lyons NY U.S.A.
33 F3 Lyons Falls U.S.A.
68 D4 Lyozna Belarus
111 F2 Lyra Reef rf P.N.G.
55 M7 Lysekil Sweden
68 H3 Lyskovo Rus. Fed.
76 G4 Lys'va Rus. Fed.
69 F5 Lysychans'k Ukr.
58 D4 Lytham St Anne's U.K.
20 E4 Lytton Can.
68 D4 Lyuban' Belarus
69 C5 Lyubeshiv Ukr.
68 E4 Lyudinovo Rus. Fed.
68 H3 Lyunda r. Rus. Fed.

M

89 B6 Ma, Sông r. Laos/Vietnam
83 D9 Maalhosmadulu Atoll atoll Maldives
103 C5 Maamba Zambia
80 E6 Ma'an Jordan
54 U5 Maaninka Fin.
54 V3 Maaninkavaara Fin.
88 F4 Ma'anshan China
55 T7 Maardu Estonia
80 F4 Ma'arrat an Nu'mān Syria
61 E3 Maas r. Neth.
61 D3 Maaseik Belgium
94 C4 Maasin Phil.
61 D3 Maas-Schwalm-Nette nat. park Neth.
105 H1 Maasstroom S. Africa
61 D4 Maastricht Neth.
115 G9 Maatsuyker Group is Austr.
94 B3 Mabalacat Phil.
103 D6 Mabalane Moz.
42 G2 Mabaruma Guyana
31 J3 Maberly Can.
89 B4 Mabian China
59 H4 Mablethorpe U.K.
105 H2 Mabopane S. Africa
103 D6 Mabote Moz.
94 B1 Mabudis i. Phil.
104 F2 Mabule Botswana
104 E2 Mabutsane Botswana
44 B7 Maca, Mt mt Chile
47 D3 Macachín Arg.
46 E3 Macaé Brazil
94 C4 Macajalar Bay b. Phil.
115 G6 Macalister r. Austr.
103 D5 Macaloge Moz.
105 K1 Macandze Moz.
43 H3 Macapá Brazil
42 C4 Macará Ecuador
46 E1 Macarani Brazil
45 B4 Macarena, Cordillera mts Col.
114 E7 Macarthur Austr.
42 C4 Macas Ecuador
93 F7 Macassar Strait str. Indon.
43 G4 Macau Brazil
89 D6 Macau Macau
43 H6 Macaúba Brazil
46 D1 Macaúbas Brazil
45 A4 Macaya r. Col.
45 B4 Macayari Col.
105 K2 Maccaretane Moz.
59 F4 Macclesfield U.K.
112 F4 Macdonald, L. salt flat Austr.
112 F4 Macdonnell Ranges mts Austr.
22 C3 MacDowell L. l. Can.
57 F3 Macduff U.K.
65 C2 Macedo de Cavaleiros Port.
114 F6 Macedon mt Austr.
49 Macedonia country Europe
43 L5 Maceió Brazil
100 B4 Macenta Guinea
66 E3 Macerata Italy
114 B4 Macfarlane, L. salt flat Austr.
60 B6 Macgillycuddy's Reeks mts Rep. of Ireland
84 A3 Mach Pak.
42 C4 Machachi Ecuador
46 D3 Machado Brazil
103 D6 Machaila Moz.
102 D4 Machakos Kenya
42 C4 Machala Ecuador
103 D6 Machanga Moz.
105 K2 Machatuine Moz.
88 E4 Macheng China
33 K2 Machias ME U.S.A.
32 D3 Machias NY U.S.A.
33 J1 Machias r. U.S.A.
84 E5 Machilipatnam India
45 B2 Machiques Venez.
57 C5 Machrihanish U.K.
42 D6 Machupicchu tourist site Peru
59 D5 Machynlleth U.K.
105 K2 Macia Moz.
67 N2 Măcin Romania
Macintyre r. see Barwon
115 J2 Macintyre r. Austr.
115 J2 Macintyre Brook r. Austr.
35 H2 Mack U.S.A.
81 G1 Maçka Turkey
116 C3 Mackay Austr.

24 D2 Mackay U.S.A.
112 E4 Mackay, Lake salt flat Austr.
21 D2 MacKay Lake l. Can.
116 C4 Mackenzie r. Austr.
20 E3 Mackenzie B.C. Can.
30 C1 Mackenzie Ont. Can.
20 E2 Mackenzie r. Can.
119 D5 Mackenzie Bay b. Antarctica
20 F2 Mackenzie Bison Sanctuary res. Can.
20 C2 Mackenzie Mountains mts Can.
30 E3 Mackinac, Straits of chan. U.S.A.
30 E3 Mackinac I. i. U.S.A.
30 C5 Mackinaw r. U.S.A.
30 C5 Mackinaw City U.S.A.
21 H4 Macklin Can.
115 K3 Macksville Austr.
115 K2 Maclean Austr.
105 H5 Maclear S. Africa
115 K3 Macleay r. Austr.
112 B4 MacLeod, Lake l. Austr.
20 C2 Macmillan r. Can.
30 B5 Macomb U.S.A.
66 C4 Macomer Italy
64 G3 Mâcon France
29 D5 Macon GA U.S.A.
26 E4 Macon MO U.S.A.
103 C5 Macondo Angola
115 G3 Macquarie r. N.S.W. Austr.
115 G8 Macquarie r. Tas. Austr.
115 J4 Macquarie, L. b. Austr.
115 F9 Macquarie Harbour in. Austr.
115 G3 Macquarie Marshes marsh Austr.
115 H4 Macquarie Mt mt Austr.
14 F9 Macquarie Ridge sea feature Pac. Oc.
95 □ MacRitchie Res. resr Sing.
119 D4 Mac. Robertson Land reg. Antarctica
60 C6 Macroom Rep. of Ireland
45 C1 Macuira, Parque Nacional nat. park Col.
45 B4 Macuje Col.
113 G5 Macumba watercourse Austr.
42 D6 Macusani Peru
33 J2 Macwahoc U.S.A.
80 E6 Mādabā Jordan
105 J3 Madadeni S. Africa
96 Madagascar country Africa
13 H5 Madagascar Basin sea feature Indian Ocean
13 G6 Madagascar Ridge sea feature Indian Ocean
101 D2 Madama Niger
67 L4 Madan Bulg.
110 E2 Madang P.N.G.
100 C3 Madaoua Niger
85 G5 Madaripur Bangl.
31 J3 Madawaska r.
31 J3 Madawaska r. Can.
33 J1 Madawaska U.S.A.
42 F5 Madeira r. Brazil
30 B2 Madeline I. i. U.S.A.
81 G2 Maden Turkey
36 C3 Madera Mex.
34 B3 Madera U.S.A.
83 D7 Madgaon India
85 F4 Madhepura India
85 F4 Madhubani India
84 D5 Madhya Pradesh div. India
105 F3 Madibogo S. Africa
114 B2 Madigan Gulf salt flat Austr.
83 E8 Madikeri India
102 B4 Madingou Congo
42 E6 Madini r. Bol.
103 E5 Madirovalo Madag.
28 C4 Madison IN U.S.A.
33 J2 Madison ME U.S.A.
26 D2 Madison MN U.S.A.
26 D3 Madison NE U.S.A.
26 D2 Madison SD U.S.A.
32 C5 Madison WV U.S.A.
30 C4 Madison WV U.S.A.
28 C4 Madisonville KY U.S.A.
27 E6 Madisonville TX U.S.A.
92 □ Madiun Indon.
31 J3 Madoc Can.
102 D3 Mado Gashi Kenya
82 J4 Madoi China
55 U8 Madona Latvia
84 B4 Madpura India
67 M5 Madra Dağı mts Turkey
24 E3 Madras India
36 E3 Madre, Laguna lag. Mex.
27 D7 Madre, Laguna l. U.S.A.
94 B2 Madre, Sierra mt Phil.
42 D6 Madre de Dios r. Peru
44 A8 Madre de Dios, I. i. Chile
36 D5 Madre del Sur, Sierra mts Mex.
36 C3 Madre Occidental, Sierra mts Mex.
36 D3 Madre Oriental, Sierra mts Mex.
94 C4 Madrid Phil.
65 E2 Madrid Spain
94 B4 Madridejos Phil.
65 E3 Madridejos Spain
92 □ Madura i. Indon.
92 □ Madura, Selat chan. Indon.

83 E9 Madurai India
85 E4 Madwas India
84 C2 Maebashi Pak.
69 H7 Madzhalis Rus. Fed.
91 F6 Maebashi Japan
95 A1 Mae Hong Son Thai.
95 A1 Mae Sariang Thai.
95 A1 Mae Sot Thai.
59 D6 Maesteg U.K.
37 J5 Maestra, Sierra mts Cuba
103 E5 Maevatanana Madag.
111 G3 Maéwo i. Vanuatu
21 J4 Mafeking Can.
105 G4 Mafeteng Lesotho
115 G6 Maffra Austr.
103 D4 Mafia I. i. Tanz.
105 F2 Mafikeng S. Africa
103 D4 Mafinga Tanz.
46 C4 Mafra Brazil
105 J5 Magabeni S. Africa
77 R4 Magadan Rus. Fed.
102 D4 Magadi Kenya
105 K2 Magaiza Moz.
94 B3 Magallanes Phil.
44 B8 Magallanes, Estrecho de chan. Chile
45 B2 Magangue Col.
80 D3 Mağara Turkey
94 B2 Magat r. Phil.
87 N1 Magdagachi Rus. Fed.
47 F2 Magdalena Arg.
42 F6 Magdalena Bol.
42 B3 Magdalena r. Col.
36 B2 Magdalena Mex.
25 E6 Magdalena r. Mex.
25 F5 Magdalena U.S.A.
44 B6 Magdalena, Isla i. Chile
94 A5 Magdalene, Gunung mt Malaysia
62 E4 Magdeburg Ger.
116 D1 Magdelaine Cays atoll Coral Sea Is Terr.
92 □ Magelang Indon.
14 F4 Magellan Seamounts sea feature Pac. Oc.
54 T1 Magerøya i. Norway
91 B9 Mage-shima i. Japan
66 C2 Maggiorasca, Monte mt Italy
66 C2 Maggiore, Lago l. Italy
100 A3 Maghama Maur.
60 E3 Maghera U.K.
60 E3 Magherafelt U.K.
58 E4 Maghull U.K.
24 D3 Magna U.S.A.
66 F6 Magna Grande mt Italy
119 D4 Magnet Bay b. Antarctica
116 B2 Magnetic I. i. Austr.
116 B2 Magnetic Passage chan. Austr.
54 X2 Magnetity Rus. Fed.
76 G4 Magnitogorsk Rus. Fed.
27 E5 Magnolia U.S.A.
23 F4 Magog Can.
23 H3 Magpie Can.
30 E1 Magpie r. Can.
23 H3 Magpie L. l. Can.
20 G5 Magrath Can.
34 D3 Magruder Mt mt U.S.A.
100 A3 Magta' Lahjar Maur.
102 D4 Magu Tanz.
89 B6 Maguan China
43 J4 Maguarinho, Cabo pt Brazil
105 K2 Magude Moz.
33 K2 Magundy Can.
21 K2 Maguse Lake l. Can.
83 H6 Magwe Myanmar
85 H5 Magyichaung Myanmar
81 K3 Mahābād Iran
85 F4 Mahabharat Range mts Nepal
103 E6 Mahabo Madag.
84 D5 Mahadeo Hills h. India
102 D3 Mahagi Dem. Rep. Congo
84 C3 Mahajan India
103 E5 Mahajanga Madag.
103 C6 Mahalapye Botswana
103 E5 Mahalevona Madag.
84 D3 Maham India
92 □ Mahameru, Gunung vol. Indon.
85 F5 Mahanadi r. India
103 E6 Mahanoro Madag.
84 C6 Maharashtra div. India
85 E5 Mahasamund India
95 B1 Maha Sarakham Thai.
103 E6 Mahatalaky Madag.
80 E6 Maḥaṭṭat Ḍab'ah Jordan
103 E5 Mahavanona Madag.
103 E5 Mahavavy r. Madag.
95 C1 Mahaxai Laos
83 E7 Mahbubnagar India
43 G2 Mahdia Guyana
66 D7 Mahdia Tunisia
84 C5 Mahesana India
84 C5 Maheshwar India
84 C5 Mahi r. India
117 H7 Mahia Peninsula pen. N.Z.
68 D4 Mahilyow Belarus
105 J4 Mahlabatini S. Africa
84 B2 Maḥmūd-e 'Erāqī Afgh.
81 M4 Mahnīān Iran
26 D2 Mahnomen U.S.A.
84 D4 Mahoba India
65 J3 Mahón Spain
32 D4 Mahoning Creek Lake l. U.S.A.
85 H5 Mahudaung mts Myanmar
84 B5 Mahuva India
67 M4 Mahya Dağı mt Turkey

85 H4 Maibang India
45 B2 Maicao Col.
22 E4 Maicasagi, Lac l. Can.
89 C6 Maichen China
59 G6 Maidenhead U.K.
21 H4 Maidstone Can.
59 H6 Maidstone U.K.
101 D3 Maiduguri Nigeria
45 D3 Maigualida, Sierra mts Venez.
84 E4 Maihar India
88 C3 Maiji Shan mt China
84 E5 Maikala Range h. India
84 E3 Mailani India
60 E3 Main r. U.K.
23 J3 Main Brook Can.
31 F3 Main Channel chan. Can.
102 B4 Mai-Ndombe, Lac l. Dem. Rep. Congo
31 J4 Main Duck I. i. Can.
33 J2 Maine div. U.S.A.
100 D3 Maïné-Soroa Niger
95 A2 Maingy I. i. Myanmar
94 C4 Mainit Phil.
94 C4 Mainit, Lake l. Phil.
57 E1 Mainland i. Orkney U.K.
57 □ Mainland i. Shetland U.K.
85 E5 Mainpat reg. India
84 D4 Mainpuri India
103 E5 Maintirano Madag.
62 D5 Mainz Ger.
100 □ Maio i. Cape Verde
47 C2 Maipó, Vol. vol. Chile
47 F3 Maipú Buenos Aires Arg.
47 C2 Maipú Mendoza Arg.
57 D2 Maiquetía Venez.
85 G5 Maiskhal I. i. Bangl.
103 C6 Maitengwe Botswana
115 J4 Maitland N.S.W. Austr.
114 B5 Maitland S.A. Austr.
119 D3 Maitri India Base Antarctica
37 H4 Maíz, Islas del is Nic.
85 G3 Maizhokunggar China
91 D7 Maizuru Japan
67 H3 Maja Jezercë mt Albania
45 E4 Majari r. Brazil
93 F7 Majene Indon.
102 D3 Maji Eth.
88 E2 Majia r. China
89 D6 Majiang China
Majorca i. see Mallorca
85 H4 Majuli I. i. India
105 G4 Majwemasweu S. Africa
102 B4 Makabana Congo
34 □1 Makaha U.S.A.
93 F7 Makale Indon.
85 H4 Makalu mt China
102 C4 Makamba Burundi
82 F1 Makanchi Kazak.
34 □1 Makapuu Hd hd U.S.A.
68 J2 Makar-Ib Rus. Fed.
87 Q2 Makarov Rus. Fed.
66 G3 Makarska Croatia
76 G3 Makat Kazak.
105 K3 Makatini Flats lowland S. Africa
100 A4 Makeni Sierra Leone
103 C6 Makgadikgadi salt pan Botswana
69 H7 Makhachkala Rus. Fed.
80 G4 Makhfar al Ḥammām Syria
81 J4 Makhmūr Iraq
102 D4 Makindu Kenya
76 J4 Makinsk Kazak.
69 F5 Makiyivka Ukr.
Makkah see Mecca
23 J2 Makkovik Can.
23 J2 Makkovik, Cape c. Can.
67 J1 Makó Hungary
102 B3 Makokou Gabon
103 D4 Makongolosi Tanz.
104 D2 Makopong Botswana
102 B4 Makotipoko Congo
79 J4 Makran reg. Iran/Pak.
84 C4 Makrana India
85 E6 Makri India
67 L6 Makronisi i. Greece
68 E3 Maksatikha Rus. Fed.
90 E1 Maksimovka Rus. Fed.
81 K2 Mākū Iran
85 H4 Makum India
103 D4 Makumbako Tanz.
103 D5 Makunguwiro Tanz.
91 B9 Makurazaki Japan
100 C4 Makurdi Nigeria
95 F3 Makwassie S. Africa
54 M3 Malå Sweden
37 H7 Mala, Pta pt Panama
94 C5 Malabang Phil.
83 D8 Malabar Coast coastal area India
100 C4 Malabo Equatorial Guinea
94 A4 Malabuñgan Phil.
Malacca see Melaka
92 C6 Malacca, Strait of str. Indon./Malaysia
24 D3 Malad City U.S.A.
68 D4 Maladzyechna Belarus
65 D4 Málaga Spain
33 F5 Malaga NJ U.S.A.
25 F5 Malaga NM U.S.A.
111 G2 Malaita i. Solomon Is
101 F4 Malakal Sudan
111 G3 Malakula i. Vanuatu
84 C2 Malakwal Pak.
93 F7 Malamala Indon.
116 A1 Malanda Austr.
92 □ Malang Indon.
103 B4 Malanje Angola
47 C1 Malanzán, Sa de mts Arg.
55 P7 Mälaren l. Sweden

47 C2 Malargüe Arg.
31 H1 Malartic Can.
31 H1 Malartic, Lac l. Can.
20 A3 Malaspina Glacier gl. U.S.A.
80 G2 Malatya Turkey
84 C3 Malaut India
81 L5 Malāvī Iran
94 A5 Malawali i. Malaysia
96 Malawi country Africa
Malawi, Lake l. see Nyasa, Lake
92 C6 Malaya reg. Malaysia
68 E3 Malaya Vishera Rus. Fed.
94 C4 Malaybalay Phil.
81 M4 Malāyer Iran
116 C1 Malay Reef rf Coral Sea Is Terr.
70 Malaysia country Asia
81 J2 Malazgirt Turkey
63 J3 Malbork Pol.
62 F4 Malchin Ger.
85 G4 Māldah India
61 B3 Maldegem Belgium
27 F4 Malden U.S.A.
70 Maldives country Indian Ocean
59 H6 Maldon U.K.
47 F2 Maldonado Uru.
83 D10 Male Maldives
67 K6 Maleas, Akra i. Greece
83 D10 Male Atoll atoll Maldives
105 F4 Malebogo S. Africa
84 C5 Malegaon India
62 H6 Malé Karpaty h. Slovakia
102 B4 Malele Dem. Rep. Congo
103 D5 Malema Moz.
84 C3 Maler Kotla India
69 H7 Malgobek Rus. Fed.
54 P4 Malgomaj l. Sweden
24 C3 Malheur L. l. U.S.A.
96 Mali country Africa
102 C4 Mali Dem. Rep. Congo
100 A3 Mali Guinea
88 C3 Malian r. China
84 E4 Malihabad India
95 A2 Mali Kyun i. Myanmar
93 G7 Malili Indon.
102 E4 Malindi Kenya
Malines see Mechelen
60 D2 Malin Head hd Rep. of Ireland
60 C3 Malin More Rep. of Ireland
90 C2 Malinovka r. Rus. Fed.
89 B6 Malipo China
66 F7 Mali Raginac mt Croatia
94 C5 Malita Phil.
95 A3 Maliwun Myanmar
84 B5 Maliya India
81 L5 Malkaili Iran
84 D5 Malkapur India
69 C7 Malkara Turkey
63 N4 Mal'kavichy Belarus
67 M4 Malko Tŭrnovo Bulg.
115 H6 Mallacoota Austr.
115 H6 Mallacoota Inlet b. Austr.
57 C4 Mallaig U.K.
114 C5 Mallala Austr.
114 E5 Mallee Cliffs Nat. Park nat. park Austr.
21 K2 Mallery Lake l. Can.
65 H3 Mallorca i. Spain
60 C5 Mallow Rep. of Ireland
59 D5 Mallwyd U.K.
54 M4 Malm Norway
54 R3 Malmberget Sweden
61 E4 Malmédy Belgium
104 C6 Malmesbury S. Africa
59 E6 Malmesbury U.K.
55 N9 Malmö Sweden
68 J3 Malmyzh Rus. Fed.
111 G3 Malo i. Vanuatu
33 F2 Malone U.S.A.
89 B5 Malong China
103 C5 Malonga Dem. Rep. Congo
62 F2 Maloshuyka Rus. Fed.
55 J6 Måløy Norway
68 F4 Maloyaroslavets Rus. Fed.
42 B3 Malpelo, Isla de i. Col.
48 Malta country Europe
55 U8 Malta Latvia
24 F1 Malta U.S.A.
66 F6 Malta Channel chan. Italy/Malta
103 B6 Maltahöhe Namibia
59 F4 Maltby U.K.
59 H4 Maltby le Marsh U.K.
58 F3 Malton U.K.
Maluku is see Moluccas
56 N6 Malung Sweden
105 H4 Maluti Mountains mts Lesotho
111 Malu'u Solomon Is
27 E5 Malvern U.S.A.
Malvinas, Islas terr. see Falkland Islands
69 D5 Malyn Ukr.
77 S3 Malyy Anyuy r. Rus. Fed.
69 H6 Malyye Derbety Rus. Fed.
69 G7 Malyy Kavkaz mts Asia
77 Q2 Malyy Lyakhovskiy, Ostrov i. Rus. Fed.
69 H5 Malyy Uzen' r. Kazak./Rus. Fed.
77 Q3 Mama r. Rus. Fed.
105 H3 Mamafubedu S. Africa
94 A5 Mambahenauhan i. Phil.
94 C5 Mambajao Phil.
102 C3 Mambasa Dem. Rep. Congo

102 B3 Mambéré r. C.A.R.
94 B3 Mamburao Phil.
105 H2 Mamelodi S. Africa
100 C4 Mamfé Cameroon
35 G5 Mammoth U.S.A.
28 C4 Mammoth Cave Nat. Park nat. park U.S.A.
34 C3 Mammoth Lakes U.S.A.
42 E6 Mamoré r. Bol./Brazil
100 A3 Mamou Guinea
103 E5 Mampikony Madag.
100 B4 Mampong Ghana
47 B3 Mamuil Malal, P. pass Arg./Chile
93 F7 Mamuju Indon.
104 D1 Mamuno Botswana
100 B4 Man Côte d'Ivoire
56 C4 Man, Isle of terr. Europe
116 C1 Man Reef rf Coral Sea Is Terr.
45 B3 Manacacias r. Col.
42 F4 Manacapuru Brazil
65 H3 Manacor Spain
93 G6 Manado Indon.
36 G6 Managua Nic.
36 G6 Managua, L. de l. Nic.
103 E6 Manakara Madag.
117 D5 Manakau mt N.Z.
110 E2 Manam I. i. P.N.G.
34 □1 Manana i. U.S.A.
103 E6 Mananara r. Madag.
103 E5 Mananara, Parc National de nat. park Madag.
103 E5 Mananara Avaratra Madag.
114 C5 Manangatang Austr.
103 E6 Mananjary Madag.
84 D3 Mana Pass pass India
45 D2 Manapire r. Venez.
117 A6 Manapouri, L. l. N.Z.
103 E5 Manarantsandry Madag.
85 A5 Manas r. Bhutan
82 G1 Manas Hu l. China
85 F3 Manaslu mt Nepal
32 G5 Manassas U.S.A.
42 F4 Manaus Brazil
80 C3 Manavgat Turkey
117 E4 Manawatu r. N.Z.
94 C5 Manay Phil.
80 F3 Manbij Syria
59 H4 Manby U.K.
30 E3 Mancelona U.S.A.
59 E4 Manchester U.K.
34 A2 Manchester CA U.S.A.
33 G4 Manchester CT U.S.A.
30 B4 Manchester IA U.S.A.
32 B6 Manchester KY U.S.A.
31 H3 Manchester MI U.S.A.
33 H3 Manchester NH U.S.A.
32 B5 Manchester OH U.S.A.
29 C5 Manchester TN U.S.A.
33 G3 Manchester VT U.S.A.
84 A4 Manchhar L. l. Pak.
80 F2 Mancılık Turkey
35 H4 Mancos U.S.A.
35 H3 Mancos r. U.S.A.
101 D4 Manda, Parc National de nat. park Chad
103 E6 Mandabe Madag.
95 □ Mandai Sing.
84 C4 Mandal India
55 K7 Mandal Norway
93 L7 Mandala, Pk mt Indon.
83 J6 Mandalay Myanmar
82 J2 Mandalgovĭ Mongolia
81 K5 Mandalī Iraq
88 D1 Mandalt China
88 D1 Mandalt Sum China
26 C2 Mandan U.S.A.
94 B3 Mandaon Phil.
101 D3 Mandara Mountains mts Cameroon/Nigeria
66 C5 Mandas Italy
102 E3 Mandera Kenya
35 F2 Manderfield U.S.A.
37 J5 Mandeville Jamaica
117 B6 Mandeville N.Z.
84 B4 Mandha India
82 E4 Mandi India
100 B3 Mandiana Guinea
84 C3 Mandi Burewala Pak.
103 D5 Mandié Moz.
103 D5 Mandimba Moz.
105 J4 Mandini S. Africa
84 E5 Mandla India
103 E5 Mandritsara Madag.
84 C4 Mandsaur India
112 A6 Mandurah Austr.
66 G4 Manduria Italy
84 B5 Mandvi Gujarat India
84 C5 Mandvi Gujarat India
83 E8 Mandya India
66 D2 Manerbio Italy
81 L5 Manesht Kūh mt Iran
69 F6 Manevychi Ukr.
66 F4 Manfredonia Italy
66 G4 Manfredonia, Golfo di g. Italy
100 D1 Manga Brazil
100 B3 Manga Burkina
102 B4 Manga Dem. Rep. Congo
15 J7 Mangaia i. Pac. Oc.
117 E3 Mangakino N.Z.
85 H4 Mangaldai India
67 N3 Mangalia Romania
83 D8 Mangalore India
85 G4 Mangan India
94 C6 Mangarang Indon.
105 G4 Manguang S. Africa
117 E3 Mangaweka N.Z.
85 G4 Mangde Chhu r. Bhutan
60 B6 Mangerton Mt h. Rep. of Ireland
92 D7 Manggar Indon.

82 H3 Mangnai China
103 D5 Mangochi Malawi
93 H7 Mangole i. Indon.
59 E6 Mangotsfield U.K.
84 B5 Mângral India
65 B5 Mangualde Port.
47 G2 Mangueira, L. l. Brazil
46 B4 Mangueirinha Brazil
101 D2 Manguéni, Plateau du plat. Niger
87 M1 Mangui China
94 C5 Mangupung i. Indon.
26 C5 Manhattan KS U.S.A.
34 D2 Manhattan NV U.S.A.
103 D6 Manhica Moz.
105 K2 Manhoca Moz.
46 D3 Manhuaçu Brazil
46 D3 Manhuaçu r. Brazil
61 D5 Manhuelles France
45 B3 Mani Col.
103 E5 Mania r. Madag.
66 F1 Maniago Italy
42 F5 Manicoré Brazil
23 G3 Manicouagan Can.
23 G3 Manicouagan r. Can.
23 G3 Manicougan, Réservoir resr Can.
116 D4 Manifold, Cape c. Austr.
84 E4 Manikpur India
94 B3 Manila Phil.
24 E3 Manila U.S.A.
115 H4 Manildra Austr.
115 J3 Manilla Austr.
113 F2 Maningrida Austr.
Manipur see Imphal
85 H4 Manipur div. India
67 M5 Manisa Turkey
30 D3 Manistee U.S.A.
30 E3 Manistee r. U.S.A.
30 D3 Manistique U.S.A.
30 E2 Manistique Lake l. U.S.A.
21 K4 Manitoba div. Can.
21 H4 Manitoba, Lake l. Can.
21 K5 Manito L. l. Can.
21 K5 Manitou Can.
31 G3 Manitou, Lake l. Can.
32 E3 Manitou Beach U.S.A.
22 B3 Manitou Falls Can.
30 D2 Manitou Islands is U.S.A.
31 F3 Manitoulin I. i. Can.
31 G3 Manitowaning Can.
22 D4 Manitowik Lake l. Can.
30 D3 Manitowoc U.S.A.
31 K2 Maniwaki Can.
45 B3 Manizales Col.
103 E6 Manja Madag.
105 K2 Manjacaze Moz.
81 M3 Manjil Iran
112 C6 Manjimup Austr.
26 E2 Mankato U.S.A.
105 J3 Mankayane Swaziland
100 B4 Mankono Côte d'Ivoire
115 J4 Manly Austr.
84 C5 Manmad India
114 C4 Mannahill Austr.
83 E9 Mannar Sri Lanka
83 E9 Mannar, Gulf of g. India/Sri Lanka
62 D6 Mannheim Ger.
60 A4 Mannin Bay b. Rep. of Ireland
20 F3 Manning Can.
29 D5 Manning U.S.A.
59 J6 Manningtree U.K.
66 C5 Mannu, Capo pt Italy
114 C5 Mannum Austr.
93 J7 Manokwari Indon.
102 C4 Manono Dem. Rep. Congo
95 A3 Manoron Myanmar
64 G5 Manosque France
111 J2 Manra i. Kiribati
65 G2 Manresa Spain
84 C3 Mānsa India
103 C5 Mansa Zambia
100 A3 Mansa Konko The Gambia
84 C1 Mansehra Pak.
118 A2 Mansel I. i. Can.
115 G6 Mansfield Austr.
59 F4 Mansfield U.K.
27 E5 Mansfield LA U.S.A.
32 B4 Mansfield OH U.S.A.
32 E4 Mansfield PA U.S.A.
20 D3 Manson Creek Can.
81 M6 Manṣūrī Iran
80 E3 Mansurlu Turkey
42 B4 Manta Ecuador
42 B4 Manta, B. de b. Ecuador
94 A4 Mantalingajan, Mount mt Phil.
34 B3 Manteca U.S.A.
45 D1 Mantecal Venez.
29 F5 Manteo U.S.A.
64 E2 Mantes-la-Jolie France
35 G2 Manti U.S.A.
46 D3 Mantiqueira, Serra da mts Brazil
30 E3 Manton U.S.A.
66 D2 Mantova Italy
55 T6 Mäntsälä Fin.
55 T5 Mänttä Fin.
Mantua see Mantova
116 B5 Mantuan Downs Austr.
68 H4 Manturovo Rus. Fed.
55 U6 Mäntyharju Fin.
55 T5 Mäntyjärvi Fin.
42 D6 Manu, Parque Nacional nat. park Peru
35 H4 Manuelito U.S.A.
47 F2 Manuel J. Cobo Arg.
46 E1 Manuel Vitorino Brazil
43 H5 Manuelzinho Brazil
93 G7 Manui i. Indon.
94 B4 Manukan Phil.

17 E2 **Manukau** N.Z.
17 E2 **Manukau Harbour** *in.* N.Z.
94 A5 **Manuk Manka** *i.* Phil.
14 C4 **Manunda** *watercourse* Austr.
10 E2 **Manus I.** *i.* P.N.G.
05 F2 **Manyana** Botswana
G6 **Manych-Gudilo, Ozero** *l.* Rus. Fed.
35 H3 **Many Farms** U.S.A.
02 D4 **Manyoni** Tanz.
16 D5 **Many Peaks** Austr.
80 D6 **Manzala, Bahra el** *l.* Egypt
65 E3 **Manzanares** Spain
37 J4 **Manzanillo** Cuba
36 D5 **Manzanillo** Mex.
87 L2 **Manzhouli** China
05 J3 **Manzini** Swaziland
01 D3 **Mao** Chad
Maó *see* Mahón
88 D4 **Maocifan** China
88 C2 **Maojiachuan** China
93 K7 **Maoke, Pegunungan** *mts* Indon.
05 G3 **Maokeng** S. Africa
88 B2 **Maomao Shan** *mt* China
89 D6 **Maoming** China
89 □ **Ma On Shan** *h.* China
03 D6 **Mapai** Moz.
84 E3 **Mapam Yumco** *l.* China
95 **Mapane** Indon.
05 F5 **Maphodi** S. Africa
27 C7 **Mapimí** Mex.
36 D3 **Mapimí, Bolsón de** *des.* Mex.
94 A5 **Mapin** *i.* Phil.
03 D6 **Mapinhane** Moz.
45 D3 **Mapire** Venez.
30 E4 **Maple** *r.* U.S.A.
21 H5 **Maple Creek** Can.
05 H4 **Mapoteng** Lesotho
93 L7 **Maprik** P.N.G.
43 G4 **Mapuera** *r.* Brazil
05 K2 **Mapulanguene** Moz.
03 D6 **Maputo** Moz.
05 J4 **Maputo** *div.* Moz.
05 K3 **Maputo** *r.* Moz.
05 J4 **Maputsoe** Lesotho
81 H6 **Maqar an Na'am** *w.* Iraq
88 B3 **Maqu** China
85 D2 **Maquan He** *r.* China
02 B4 **Maquela do Zombo** Angola
47 C4 **Maquinchao** Arg.
47 C4 **Maquinchao** *r.* Arg.
30 B4 **Maquoketa** U.S.A.
30 B4 **Maquoketa** *r.* U.S.A.
46 D3 **Mar, Serra do** *mts* Brazil
21 H1 **Mara** *r.* Can.
85 E3 **Mara** India
05 H1 **Mara** S. Africa
45 C2 **Mara** Venez.
42 E4 **Maraã** Brazil
43 J5 **Maraba** Brazil
16 C4 **Maraboon, L.** *resr* Austr.
43 H3 **Maracá, Ilha de** *i.* Brazil
45 C2 **Maracaibo** Venez.
45 C2 **Maracaibo, Lago de** *l.* Venez.
46 A3 **Maracaju** Brazil
46 A3 **Maracaju, Serra de** *h.* Brazil
46 E1 **Maracás, Chapada de** *reg.* Brazil
45 D2 **Maracay** Venez.
01 D2 **Marādah** Libya
00 C3 **Maradi** Niger
81 L3 **Marāgheh** Iran
46 E1 **Maragogipe** Brazil
94 B3 **Maragondon** Phil.
45 D4 **Marahuaca, Co** *mt* Venez.
43 J4 **Marajó, Baía de** *est.* Brazil
43 J3 **Marajó, Ilha de** *i.* Brazil
02 D3 **Maralal** Kenya
84 C2 **Marala Weir** *barrage* Pak.
81 J1 **Maralik** Armenia
11 G2 **Maramasike** *i.* Solomon Is
94 C5 **Marampit** *i.* Indon.
81 K4 **Marāna** Iraq
35 G5 **Marana** U.S.A.
81 K2 **Marand** Iran
95 A3 **Marang** Malaysia
95 A3 **Marang** Myanmar
46 C1 **Maranhão** *r.* Brazil
16 C6 **Maranoa** *r.* Austr.
42 D4 **Marañón** *r.* Peru
05 L2 **Marão** Moz.
65 C2 **Marão** *mt* Port.
84 E1 **Marari** *r.* Brazil
17 A6 **Mararoa** *r.* N.Z.
30 D1 **Marathon** Can.
29 D7 **Marathon** FL U.S.A.
27 C6 **Marathon** TX U.S.A.
46 E1 **Maraú** Brazil
43 H2 **Marauiá** *r.* Brazil
94 C4 **Marawi** Phil.
81 M1 **Marāwah** Libya
65 D4 **Marbella** Spain
12 C4 **Marble Bar** Austr.
35 G3 **Marble Canyon** U.S.A.
35 G3 **Marble Canyon** *gorge* U.S.A.
05 H2 **Marble Hall** S. Africa
33 H3 **Marblehead** U.S.A.
21 L2 **Marble I.** *i.* Can.
05 J5 **Marburg** S. Africa
32 E5 **Marburg, Lake** *l.* U.S.A.
62 D5 **Marburg an der Lahn** Ger.
62 H7 **Marcali** Hungary

59 H5 **March** U.K.
14 C4 **Marchant Hill** *h.* Austr.
61 D4 **Marche-en-Famenne** Belgium
65 D4 **Marchena** Spain
42 □ **Marchena, Isla** *i.* Ecuador
47 D1 **Mar Chiquita, L.** *l.* Arg.
62 G6 **Marchtrenk** Austria
29 D7 **Marco** U.S.A.
22 E2 **Marcopeet Islands** *is* Can.
47 D2 **Marcos Juárez** Arg.
33 D2 **Marcy, Mt** *mt* U.S.A.
84 C2 **Mardan** Pak.
47 E3 **Mar del Plata** Arg.
81 H3 **Mardın** Turkey
111 G4 **Maré** *i.* New Caledonia
57 C3 **Maree, Loch** *l.* U.K.
116 A1 **Mareeba** Austr.
30 A5 **Marengo** IA U.S.A.
30 C4 **Marengo** U.S.A.
66 E6 **Marettimo, Isola** *i.* Italy
68 E3 **Marevo** Rus. Fed.
27 B6 **Marfa** U.S.A.
114 B2 **Margaret** *watercourse* Austr.
112 C6 **Margaret River** Austr.
45 E2 **Margarita, Isla de** *i.* Venez.
90 D3 **Margaritovo** Rus. Fed.
115 G9 **Margate** Austr.
105 J5 **Margate** S. Africa
59 J6 **Margate** U.K.
79 L1 **Margilan** Uzbek.
79 J3 **Margo, Dasht-i** *des.* Afgh.
94 B5 **Margosatubig** Phil.
61 D4 **Margraten** Neth.
30 E3 **Margrethe, Lake** *l.* U.S.A.
20 E4 **Marguerite** Can.
119 B2 **Marguerite Bay** *b.* Antarctica
85 G3 **Margyang** China
81 L5 **Marhaj Khalīl** Iraq
81 J3 **Marhan D.** *h.* Iraq
69 E6 **Marhanets'** Ukr.
15 J7 **Maria** *is* Pac. Oc.
44 C2 **María Elena** Chile
113 G2 **Maria I.** *i. N.T.* Austr.
115 H9 **Maria I.** *i. Tas.* Austr.
47 E3 **Maria Ignacia** Arg.
116 C3 **Marian** Austr.
14 E4 **Mariana Ridge** *sea feature* Pac. Oc.
14 E5 **Mariana Trench** *sea feature* Pac. Oc.
85 H4 **Mariani** India
20 F2 **Marian Lake** *l.* Can.
27 F5 **Marianna** AR U.S.A.
29 C6 **Marianna** FL U.S.A.
62 F6 **Mariánské Lázně** Czech Rep.
36 C4 **Marías, Islas** *is* Mex.
37 H7 **Mariato, Pta** *pt* Panama
117 D1 **Maria van Diemen, Cape** *c.* N.Z.
66 F1 **Maribor** Slovenia
35 F5 **Maricopa** AZ U.S.A.
34 C4 **Maricopa** CA U.S.A.
35 F5 **Maricopa Mts** *mts* U.S.A.
101 E4 **Maridi** *watercourse* Sudan
119 A4 **Marie Byrd Land** *reg.* Antarctica
37 M5 **Marie-Galante** *i.* Guadeloupe
55 Q6 **Mariehamn** Fin.
46 B1 **Mariembero** *r.* Brazil
103 B6 **Mariental** Namibia
55 N7 **Mariestad** Sweden
29 C5 **Marietta** GA U.S.A.
32 C5 **Marietta** OH U.S.A.
64 G5 **Marignane** France
76 K4 **Mariinsk** Rus. Fed.
55 S9 **Marijampolė** Lith.
46 C3 **Marília** Brazil
27 C7 **Marín** Mex.
65 B1 **Marín** Spain
66 G5 **Marina di Gioiosa Ionica** Italy
68 D4 **Mar''ina Horka** Belarus
94 B3 **Marinduque** *i.* Phil.
30 D3 **Marinette** U.S.A.
46 B3 **Maringá** Brazil
65 B3 **Marinha Grande** Port.
28 B4 **Marion** IL U.S.A.
30 E5 **Marion** IN U.S.A.
33 K2 **Marion** ME U.S.A.
32 B4 **Marion** OH U.S.A.
29 E5 **Marion** SC U.S.A.
32 C6 **Marion** VA U.S.A.
29 D5 **Marion, L.** *l.* U.S.A.
114 B5 **Marion Bay** Austr.
116 E2 **Marion Reef** *rf* Coral Sea Is Terr.
45 D3 **Maripa** Venez.
43 H3 **Maripasoula** Fr. Guiana
44 D2 **Mariscal Estigarribia** Para.
64 H4 **Maritime Alps** *mts* France/Italy
67 L3 **Maritsa** *r.* Bulg.
68 J3 **Mari-Turek** Rus. Fed.
69 F6 **Mariupol'** Ukr.
81 L4 **Marīvān** Iran
68 J3 **Mariy El, Respublika** *div.* Rus. Fed.
102 E3 **Marka** Somalia
81 K2 **Mārkān** Iran
55 N8 **Markaryd** Sweden
31 G3 **Markdale** Can.
61 D2 **Marken** *i.* Neth.
105 H1 **Markermeer** *l.* Neth.
61 D2 **Markermeer** *l.* Neth.

59 G5 **Market Deeping** U.K.
59 E5 **Market Drayton** U.K.
59 G5 **Market Harborough** U.K.
60 E3 **Markethill** U.K.
58 G4 **Market Weighton** U.K.
77 N3 **Markha** *r.* Rus. Fed.
31 H4 **Markham** Can.
69 F5 **Markivka** Ukr.
77 T3 **Markovo** Rus. Fed.
69 H5 **Marks** Rus. Fed.
62 D6 **Marktheidenfeld** Ger.
62 E7 **Marktoberdorf** Ger.
30 B6 **Mark Twain Lake** *l.* U.S.A.
61 F3 **Marl** Ger.
113 F5 **Marla** Austr.
116 C4 **Marlborough** Austr.
33 H3 **Marlborough** U.S.A.
59 F6 **Marlborough Downs** *h.* U.K.
27 D6 **Marlin** U.S.A.
32 C5 **Marlinton** U.S.A.
115 H6 **Marlo** Austr.
64 E4 **Marmande** France
80 B1 **Marmara, Sea of** *g.* Turkey
Marmara Denizi *see* **Marmara, Sea of**
80 B2 **Marmara Gölü** *l.* Turkey
80 B3 **Marmaris** Turkey
26 C2 **Marmarth** U.S.A.
32 C5 **Marmet** U.S.A.
22 B4 **Marmion L.** *l.* Can.
66 D1 **Marmolada** *mt* Italy
64 F2 **Marne-la-Vallée** France
81 K1 **Marneuli** Georgia
114 E6 **Marnoo** Austr.
103 E5 **Maroantsetra** Madag.
103 E5 **Maromokotro** *mt* Madag.
103 D5 **Marondera** Zimbabwe
43 H2 **Maroni** *r.* Fr. Guiana
115 K1 **Maroochydore** Austr.
109 **Marotiri** *is* Pac. Oc.
101 D3 **Maroua** Cameroon
103 E5 **Marovoay** Madag.
81 H4 **Marqādah** Syria
88 A3 **Mar Qu** *r.* China
105 G4 **Marquard** S. Africa
29 D7 **Marquesas Keys** *is* U.S.A.
30 D2 **Marquette** U.S.A.
109 **Marquises, Îles** *is* Pac. Oc.
114 E3 **Marra** Austr.
115 G3 **Marra** *r.* Austr.
105 K2 **Marracuene** Moz.
100 B1 **Marrakech** Morocco
Marrakesh *see* **Marrakech**
105 L2 **Marrangua, Lagoa** *l.* Moz.
101 E3 **Marra Plateau** *plat.* Sudan
115 G5 **Marrar** Austr.
115 F8 **Marrawah** Austr.
114 C2 **Marree** Austr.
27 F6 **Marrero** U.S.A.
103 D5 **Marromeu** Moz.
103 D5 **Marrupa** Moz.
78 C4 **Marsa Alam** Egypt
101 D1 **Marsa al Burayqah** Libya
102 D1 **Marsabit** Kenya
66 E6 **Marsala** Italy
78 B3 **Marsa Matrûh** Egypt
66 E3 **Marsciano** Italy
115 G4 **Marsden** Austr.
61 C2 **Marsdiep** *chan.* Neth.
64 G5 **Marseille** France
30 C5 **Marseilles** U.S.A.
54 O4 **Marsfjället** *mt* Sweden
21 H4 **Marshall** Can.
27 E5 **Marshall** AR U.S.A.
28 C4 **Marshall** IL U.S.A.
30 E4 **Marshall** MI U.S.A.
26 E2 **Marshall** MN U.S.A.
26 E4 **Marshall** MO U.S.A.
27 E5 **Marshall** TX U.S.A.
115 G7 **Marshall B.** *b.* Austr.
106 **Marshall Islands** *is* Pac. Oc.
26 E3 **Marshalltown** U.S.A.
30 B3 **Marshfield** U.S.A.
29 F7 **Marsh Harbour** Bahamas
33 K1 **Mars Hill** U.S.A.
27 F6 **Marsh Island** *i.* U.S.A.
20 C2 **Marsh Lake** *l.* Can.
81 M3 **Marshūn** Iran
24 C3 **Marsing** U.S.A.
55 P7 **Märsta** Sweden
85 F4 **Marsyangdi** *r.* Nepal
95 A1 **Martaban** Myanmar
83 J7 **Martaban, Gulf of** *g.* Myanmar
92 E7 **Martapura** Indon.
92 C7 **Martapura** Indon.
31 H2 **Marten River** Can.
21 H4 **Martensville** Can.
27 D7 **Marte R. Gómez, Presa** *resr* Mex.
27 D7 **Marte R. Gómez, Presa** *resr* Mex.
33 H4 **Martha's Vineyard** *i.* U.S.A.
62 C7 **Martigny** Switz.
63 J6 **Martin** Slovakia
26 C3 **Martin** SD U.S.A.
29 B4 **Martin** TN U.S.A.
29 C5 **Martin, L.** *l.* U.S.A.
35 E5 **Martinez Lake** U.S.A.
37 M6 **Martinique** *terr.* Caribbean
119 A3 **Martin Pen.** *pen.* Antarctica
32 E4 **Martinsburg** PA U.S.A.
32 C5 **Martinsburg** WV U.S.A.
32 C4 **Martins Ferry** U.S.A.
32 D6 **Martinsville** U.S.A.
12 H7 **Martin Vas, Ilhas** *is* Atlantic Ocean

117 E4 **Marton** N.Z.
65 G2 **Martorell** Spain
65 E2 **Martos** Spain
76 G4 **Martuk** Kazak.
81 K1 **Martuni** Armenia
91 C7 **Marugame** Japan
117 D5 **Maruia** *r.* N.Z.
43 L6 **Maruim** Brazil
69 G7 **Marukhis Ugheltekhili** *pass* Georgia/Rus. Fed.
115 H5 **Marulan** Austr.
64 F4 **Marvejols** France
35 F2 **Marvine, Mt** *mt* U.S.A.
21 G4 **Marwayne** Can.
116 E6 **Mary** *r.* Austr.
79 J2 **Mary** Turkm.
116 E5 **Maryborough** *Qld.* Austr.
114 E6 **Maryborough** *Vic.* Austr.
104 E4 **Marydale** S. Africa
68 J4 **Mar'yevka** Rus. Fed.
21 H2 **Mary Frances Lake** *l.* Can.
33 E5 **Maryland** *div.* U.S.A.
58 D3 **Maryport** U.K.
23 J3 **Mary's Harbour** Can.
23 K4 **Marystown** Can.
35 F2 **Marysvale** U.S.A.
34 B2 **Marysville** Can.
23 G4 **Marysville** CA U.S.A.
26 D2 **Marysville** KS U.S.A.
32 B4 **Marysville** OH U.S.A.
116 A2 **Maryvale** Austr.
37 H1 **Maryville** Tennessee
26 E3 **Maryville** U.S.A.
102 D4 **Masai Steppe** *plain* Tanz.
102 D4 **Masaka** Uganda
105 G5 **Masakhane** S. Africa
81 M2 **Masallı** Azer.
93 M2 **Masamba** Indon.
87 N4 **Masan** S. Korea
33 J1 **Masardis** U.S.A.
103 D5 **Masasi** Tanz.
42 F7 **Masavi** Bol.
94 B3 **Masbate** Phil.
94 B4 **Masbate** *i.* Phil.
100 C1 **Mascara** Alg.
13 H4 **Mascarene Basin** *sea feature* Indian Ocean
13 J4 **Mascarene Ridge** *sea feature* Indian Ocean
33 G2 **Mascouche** Can.
105 G4 **Maseru** Lesotho
105 H4 **Mashai** Lesotho
89 C6 **Mashan** China
84 D2 **Masherbrum** *mt* Pak.
79 H2 **Mashhad** Iran
84 A4 **Mashi** *r.* India
81 L2 **Mashīrān** Iran
54 S2 **Masi** Norway
105 J5 **Masibambane** S. Africa
105 G4 **Masilo** S. Africa
102 D3 **Masindi** Uganda
94 A3 **Masinloc** Phil.
104 E5 **Masinyusane** S. Africa
79 H6 **Maşīrah, Gulf of** *b.* Oman
79 H5 **Maşīrah, Jazīrat** *i.* Oman
81 K1 **Masis** Armenia
81 M6 **Masjed Soleymān** Iran
60 B4 **Mask, Lough** *l.* Rep. of Ireland
80 G3 **Maskanah** Syria
103 F5 **Masoala, Tanjona** *c.* Madag.
30 E4 **Mason** MI U.S.A.
34 C4 **Mason** NV U.S.A.
27 D6 **Mason** TX U.S.A.
117 A7 **Mason Bay** *b.* N.Z.
26 E3 **Mason City** IA U.S.A.
30 C5 **Mason City** IL U.S.A.
32 D5 **Masontown** U.S.A.
Masqaṭ *see* **Muscat**
66 D2 **Massa** Italy
33 G3 **Massachusetts** *div.* U.S.A.
33 H3 **Massachusetts Bay** *b.* U.S.A.
35 H1 **Massadona** U.S.A.
66 E4 **Massafra** Italy
101 D3 **Massakory** Chad
66 D3 **Massa Marittima** Italy
103 D6 **Massangena** Moz.
103 B4 **Massango** Angola
102 D2 **Massawa** Eritrea
33 G2 **Massawippi, Lac** *l.* Can.
33 F2 **Massena** U.S.A.
20 C4 **Masset** Can.
31 F2 **Massey** Can.
64 F4 **Massif Central** *mts* France
32 C4 **Massillon** U.S.A.
100 B3 **Massina** Mali
103 D6 **Massinga** Moz.
103 D6 **Massingir** Moz.
105 K1 **Massingir, Barragem de** *resr* Moz.
105 K2 **Massintonto** *r.* Moz./S. Africa
31 K3 **Masson** Can.
81 M1 **Maştağa** Azer.
117 E4 **Masterton** N.Z.
67 M5 **Masticho, Akra** *pt* Greece
29 F7 **Mastic Point** Bahamas
84 C1 **Mastuj** Pak.
79 K4 **Mastung** Pak.
68 C4 **Masty** Belarus
91 B7 **Masuda** Japan
81 M3 **Masuleh** Iran
103 D6 **Masvingo** Zimbabwe
80 F4 **Maşyāf** Syria
31 G2 **Matachewan** Can.
25 F6 **Matachic** Mex.
45 D4 **Matacuni** *r.* Venez.
102 B4 **Matadi** Dem. Rep. Congo
37 G6 **Matagalpa** Nic.
22 E4 **Matagami** Can.

22 E4 **Matagami, Lac** *l.* Can.
27 D6 **Matagorda I.** *i.* U.S.A.
95 **Matak** *i.* Indon.
117 F2 **Matakana Island** *i.* N.Z.
103 B5 **Matala** Angola
100 A3 **Matam** Senegal
36 D3 **Matamoros** *Coahuila* Mex.
36 E3 **Matamoros** *Tamaulipas* Mex.
94 B5 **Matanal Point** *pt* Phil.
103 D4 **Matandu** *r.* Tanz.
23 G4 **Matane** Can.
84 B2 **Matanui** Pak.
37 H4 **Matanzas** Cuba
Matapan, Cape *pt see* **Tainaro, Akra**
23 G4 **Matapédia** *r.* Can.
47 B4 **Mataquito** *r.* Chile
83 F9 **Matara** Sri Lanka
92 F3 **Mataram** Indon.
42 D7 **Matarani** Peru
112 F2 **Mataranka** Austr.
65 H2 **Mataró** Spain
105 H5 **Matatiele** S. Africa
117 B7 **Mataura** N.Z.
117 B7 **Mataura** *r.* N.Z.
45 D3 **Mataveni** *r.* Col.
117 F3 **Matawai** N.Z.
42 F6 **Mategua** Bol.
36 D4 **Matehuala** Mex.
103 D5 **Matemanga** Tanz.
66 F4 **Matera** Italy
66 C6 **Mateur** Tunisia
22 D4 **Matheson** Can.
27 D6 **Mathis** U.S.A.
114 F5 **Mathoura** Austr.
84 D4 **Mathura** India
94 C5 **Mati** Phil.
85 E4 **Matiali** India
89 D5 **Matianxu** China
84 B4 **Matiari** Pak.
36 E5 **Matías Romero** Mex.
23 G3 **Matimekosh** Can.
31 F2 **Matinenda Lake** *l.* Can.
33 J3 **Matinicus I.** *i.* U.S.A.
85 G3 **Matla** *r.* India
105 G1 **Matlabas** *r.* S. Africa
84 B4 **Matli** Pak.
59 F4 **Matlock** U.K.
45 D3 **Mato** *r.* Venez.
45 D3 **Mato, Co** *mt* Venez.
42 G7 **Mato Grosso** Brazil
46 A1 **Mato Grosso** *div.* Brazil
40 **Mato Grosso, Planalto do** *plat.* Brazil
46 B3 **Mato Grosso do Sul** *div.* Brazil
105 K2 **Matola** Moz.
65 B2 **Matosinhos** Port.
79 H5 **Maţraḥ** Oman
104 C6 **Matroosberg** *mt* S. Africa
91 G4 **Matsue** Japan
90 G4 **Matsumae** Japan
91 E6 **Matsumoto** Japan
91 F5 **Matsusaka** Japan
91 F5 **Matsu Tao** *i.* Taiwan
91 F7 **Matsuyama** Japan
22 D4 **Mattagami** *r.* Can.
31 H2 **Mattawa** Can.
33 J2 **Mattawamkeag** U.S.A.
62 C7 **Matterhorn** *mt* Italy/Switz.
24 D3 **Matterhorn** *mt* U.S.A.
111 H4 **Matthew Island** *i.* New Caledonia
45 E3 **Matthews Ridge** Guyana
37 K4 **Matthew Town** Bahamas
28 B4 **Mattoon** U.S.A.
111 H3 **Matuku** *i.* Fiji
45 E2 **Maturín** Venez.
94 C5 **Matutuang** *i.* Indon.
105 G4 **Matwabeng** S. Africa
85 E3 **Mau** *Uttar Pradesh* India
85 E4 **Mau** *Uttar Pradesh* India
85 E4 **Mau Aimma** India
61 B4 **Maubeuge** France
64 E5 **Maubourguet** France
57 D5 **Mauchline** U.K.
43 G4 **Maués** Brazil
85 E4 **Mauganj** India
93 L2 **Maug Islands** *is* N. Mariana Is
34 □² **Maui** *i.* U.S.A.
47 B2 **Maule** *div.* Chile
47 B2 **Maule** *r.* Chile
47 B3 **Maullín** Chile
60 B3 **Maumakeogh** *h.* Rep. of Ireland
32 B4 **Maumee** U.S.A.
32 B4 **Maumee** *r.* U.S.A.
31 F5 **Maumee Bay** *b.* U.S.A.
93 G8 **Maumere** Indon.
60 B4 **Maumturk Mts** *h.* Rep. of Ireland
103 C5 **Maun** Botswana
34 □¹ **Mauna Kea** *vol.* U.S.A.
34 □¹ **Mauna Loa** *vol.* U.S.A.
34 □¹ **Maunalua B.** *b.* U.S.A.
105 G1 **Maunatlala** Botswana
117 E2 **Maungaturoto** N.Z.
85 H5 **Maungdaw** Myanmar
95 A2 **Maungmagan Is** *is* Myanmar
114 B5 **Maupertuis B.** *b.* Austr.
112 F5 **Maurice, L.** *salt flat* Austr.
61 D3 **Maurik** Neth.
96 **Mauritania** *country* Africa
96 **Mauritius** *country* Africa
30 B4 **Mauston** U.S.A.
45 D4 **Mavaca** *r.* Venez.
103 C5 **Mavinga** Angola

105 G5 **Mavuya** S. Africa
84 D3 **Mawana** India
102 B4 **Mawanga** Dem. Rep. Congo
89 D4 **Ma Wang Dui** China
95 A3 **Mawdaung Pass** *pass* Myanmar/Thai.
117 D3 **Mawhai Point** *pt* N.Z.
83 H6 **Mawlaik** Myanmar
119 D4 **Mawson** *Austr. Base* Antarctica
119 D4 **Mawson Escarpment** *escarpment* Antarctica
119 B6 **Mawson Pen.** *pen.* Antarctica
95 A1 **Maw Taung** *mt* Myanmar
26 C2 **Max** U.S.A.
66 C5 **Maxia, Punta** *mt* Italy
30 D5 **Maxinkuckee, Lake** *l.* U.S.A.
54 S5 **Maxmo** Fin.
31 F4 **Maxton** U.S.A.
34 A2 **Maxwell** U.S.A.
57 F4 **May, Isle of** *i.* U.K.
77 P3 **Maya** *r.* Rus. Fed.
37 K4 **Mayaguana** *i.* Bahamas
37 L5 **Mayagüez** Puerto Rico
100 C3 **Mayahi** Niger
102 B4 **Mayama** Congo
79 H2 **Mayamey** Iran
36 G5 **Maya Mountains** *mts* Belize/Guatemala
89 C5 **Mayang** China
88 B3 **Mayanhe** China
90 F5 **Maya-san** *mt* Japan
57 D5 **Maybole** U.K.
81 K4 **Maydān Sarāy** Iraq
84 B2 **Maydā Shahr** Afgh.
115 G9 **Maydena** Austr.
61 F4 **Mayen** Ger.
64 D2 **Mayenne** France
64 D2 **Mayenne** *r.* France
35 F4 **Mayer** U.S.A.
20 F4 **Mayerthorpe** Can.
117 C5 **Mayfield** N.Z.
28 B4 **Mayfield** U.S.A.
25 F5 **Mayhill** U.S.A.
90 A2 **Mayi** *r.* China
69 G6 **Maykop** Rus. Fed.
83 J6 **Maymyo** Myanmar
86 F1 **Mayna** Rus. Fed.
31 J3 **Maynooth** Can.
20 B2 **Mayo** Can.
47 E2 **Mayo, 25 de** *Buenos Aires* Arg.
47 C4 **Mayo, 25 de** *La Pampa* Arg.
94 B5 **Mayo Bay** *b.* Phil.
102 B4 **Mayoko** Congo
20 B2 **Mayo Lake** *l.* Can.
94 B3 **Mayon** *vol.* Phil.
47 D3 **Mayor Buratovich** Arg.
117 F2 **Mayor I.** *i.* N.Z.
44 D1 **Mayor Pablo Lagerenza** Para.
103 E5 **Mayotte** *terr.* Africa
94 B2 **Mayraira Point** *pt* Phil.
87 N1 **Mayskiy** Rus. Fed.
32 B5 **Maysville** U.S.A.
102 B4 **Mayumba** Gabon
85 E3 **Mayum La** *pass* China
31 F4 **Mayville** MI U.S.A.
26 D2 **Mayville** ND U.S.A.
32 D3 **Mayville** NY U.S.A.
30 C4 **Mayville** WV U.S.A.
23 C3 **Maywood** U.S.A.
47 D3 **Maza** Arg.
68 F3 **Maza** Rus. Fed.
103 C5 **Mazabuka** Zambia
43 H4 **Mazagão** Brazil
61 C5 **Mazagran** France
64 F5 **Mazamet** France
84 D1 **Mazar** China
66 E6 **Mazara del Vallo** Italy
79 K2 **Mazār-e Sharīf** Afgh.
45 E3 **Mazaruni** *r.* Guyana
25 E6 **Mazatán** Mex.
36 F6 **Mazatenango** Guatemala
36 C4 **Mazatlán** Mex.
35 G4 **Mazatzal Peak** *summit* U.S.A.
55 S8 **Mažeikiai** Lith.
81 G2 **Mazgirt** Turkey
55 S8 **Mazirbe** Latvia
25 E6 **Mazocahui** Mex.
102 D4 **Mazomora** Tanz.
81 M3 **Mazr'eh** Iran
81 M5 **Māzū** Iran
103 C6 **Mazunga** Zimbabwe
69 D4 **Mazyr** Belarus
105 J3 **Mbabane** Swaziland
100 B4 **Mbahiakro** Côte d'Ivoire
102 B3 **Mbaïki** C.A.R.
103 D4 **Mbala** Zambia
102 D3 **Mbale** Uganda
100 D4 **Mbalmayo** Cameroon
102 B4 **Mbandaka** Dem. Rep. Congo
100 B4 **Mbanga** Cameroon
102 B4 **M'banza Congo** Angola
102 C3 **Mbarara** Uganda
102 B3 **Mbari** *r.* C.A.R.
100 D4 **Mbengwi** Cameroon
103 C5 **Mbeya** Tanz.
103 D6 **Mbizi** Zimbabwe
102 B3 **Mbomo** Congo
100 D4 **Mbouda** Cameroon
100 A3 **Mbour** Senegal
100 A3 **Mbout** Maur.
103 D3 **Mbozi** Tanz.
102 C4 **Mbuji-Mayi** Dem. Rep. Congo
102 D4 **Mbulu** Tanz.

102 D4 Mbuyuni Tanz.
33 K2 McAdam Can.
27 E5 McAlester U.S.A.
32 E4 McAlevys Fort U.S.A.
115 H5 McAlister mt Austr.
27 D7 McAllen U.S.A.
32 B5 McArthur U.S.A.
31 J3 McArthur Mills Can.
20 B2 McArthur Wildlife
   Sanctuary res. Can.
20 E4 McBride Can.
24 C2 McCall U.S.A.
27 C6 McCamey U.S.A.
24 D3 McCammon U.S.A.
20 C4 McCaulay I. i. Can.
34 B3 McClure, L. l. U.S.A.
27 F6 McComb U.S.A.
26 C3 McConaughy, L. l. U.S.A.
32 E5 McConnellsburg U.S.A.
32 C5 McConnelsville U.S.A.
26 C3 McCook U.S.A.
21 K4 McCreary Can.
35 E4 McCullough Range
   mts U.S.A.
20 D3 McDame Can.
24 C3 McDermitt U.S.A.
24 D2 McDonald Peak summit
   U.S.A.
114 C2 McDonnell Creek
   watercourse Austr.
104 B4 McDougall's Bay b.
   S. Africa
35 G5 McDowell Peak summit
   U.S.A.
34 C4 McFarland U.S.A.
21 H3 McFarlane r. Can.
35 E2 McGill U.S.A.
20 E4 McGregor r. Can.
104 C6 McGregor S. Africa
30 A2 McGregor U.S.A.
31 G2 McGregor Bay Can.
24 D2 McGuire, Mt mt U.S.A.
103 D4 Mchinga Tanz.
33 G2 McIndoe Falls U.S.A.
26 C2 McIntosh U.S.A.
111 J2 McKean i. Kiribati
32 A6 McKee U.S.A.
32 D4 McKeesport U.S.A.
33 F3 McKeever U.S.A.
29 B4 McKenzie U.S.A.
18 McKinley, Mt mt U.S.A.
27 D5 McKinney U.S.A.
34 C4 McKittrick U.S.A.
26 C2 McLaughlin U.S.A.
20 F3 McLennan Can.
20 F4 McLeod r. Can.
20 E3 McLeod Lake Can.
24 B3 McLoughlin, Mt mt U.S.A.
30 E2 McMillan U.S.A.
24 B2 McMinnville OR U.S.A.
29 C5 McMinnville TN U.S.A.
119 B5 McMurdo U.S.A. Base
   Antarctica
35 H4 McNary U.S.A.
20 F4 McNaughton Lake l. Can.
35 H6 McNeal U.S.A.
26 D4 McPherson U.S.A.
115 K2 McPherson Ra. mts Austr.
20 B2 McQuesten r. Can.
29 D5 McRae U.S.A.
20 E1 McVicar Arm b. Can.
105 G6 Mdantsane S. Africa
66 B6 M'Daourouch Alg.
35 E3 Mead, Lake l. U.S.A.
27 C4 Meade U.S.A.
21 H4 Meadow Lake Can.
21 H4 Meadow Lake Provincial
   Park res. Can.
35 E3 Meadow Valley Wash r.
   U.S.A.
32 C4 Meadville U.S.A.
31 G3 Meaford Can.
90 J3 Meaken-dake vol. Japan
57 A2 Mealasta Island i. U.K.
65 B2 Mealhada Port.
57 D4 Meall a'Bhuiridh mt U.K.
23 J3 Mealy Mountains mts
   Can.
115 H1 Meandarra Austr.
20 F3 Meander River Can.
94 C5 Meares i. Indon.
64 F2 Meaux France
102 B4 Mebridege r. Angola
78 D5 Mecca Saudi Arabia
33 H2 Mechanic Falls U.S.A.
32 B4 Mechanicsburg U.S.A.
30 B5 Mechanicsville U.S.A.
61 C3 Mechelen Belgium
61 D4 Mechelen Neth.
100 B1 Mecheria Alg.
61 E4 Mechernich Ger.
80 E1 Mecitözü Turkey
61 F4 Meckenheim Ger.
62 E2 Mecklenburger Bucht
   b. Ger.
103 D5 Mecula Moz.
65 C2 Meda Port.
92 B6 Medan Indon.
47 D3 Médanos Arg.
44 C7 Medanosa, Pta pt Arg.
33 K2 Meddybemps L. l. U.S.A.
65 H4 Médéa Alg.
45 B3 Medellín Col.
59 F4 Meden r. U.K.
100 D1 Medenine Tunisia
100 A3 Mederdra Maur.
24 B3 Medford OR U.S.A.
30 B3 Medford WI U.S.A.
33 F5 Medford Farms U.S.A.
67 N2 Medgidia Romania
30 B5 Media U.S.A.
47 D2 Media Luna Arg.
63 M7 Mediaş Romania
24 C2 Medical Lake U.S.A.

24 F3 Medicine Bow U.S.A.
24 F3 Medicine Bow Mts mts
   U.S.A.
24 F3 Medicine Bow Peak
   summit U.S.A.
21 G4 Medicine Hat Can.
27 D4 Medicine Lodge U.S.A.
46 E2 Medina Brazil
78 D5 Medina Saudi Arabia
32 D3 Medina NY U.S.A.
32 C4 Medina OH U.S.A.
65 E2 Medinaceli Spain
65 D2 Medina del Campo Spain
65 D2 Medina de Rioseco Spain
85 F5 Medinīpur India
52 Mediterranean Sea sea
   Africa/Europe
76 G4 Mednogorsk Rus. Fed.
64 D4 Médoc reg. France
68 H3 Medvedevo Rus. Fed.
69 H5 Medveditsa r. Rus. Fed.
66 F2 Medvednica mts Croatia
77 S2 Medvezh'i, O-va is
   Rus. Fed.
87 P2 Medvezh'ya, Gora mt
   China/Rus. Fed.
68 E2 Medvezh'yegorsk
   Rus. Fed.
59 H6 Medway r. U.K.
112 C5 Meekatharra Austr.
35 H1 Meeker U.S.A.
34 B2 Meeks Bay U.S.A.
23 J4 Meelpaeg Res. resr Can.
61 E3 Meerlo Neth.
84 D3 Meerut India
24 E2 Meeteetse U.S.A.
102 D3 Mēga Eth.
85 G4 Meghalaya div. India
85 F5 Meghāsani mt India
85 G5 Meghna r. Bangl.
81 L2 Meghri Armenia
80 B3 Megisti i. Greece
54 U1 Mehamn Norway
112 C4 Meharry, Mt mt
   Austr.
81 L4 Mehdīkhān Iran
84 D5 Mehekar India
85 G5 Meherpur Bangl.
32 E6 Meherrin r. U.S.A.
81 L2 Mehrābān Iran
81 L5 Mehrān Iraq
84 B2 Mehtar Lām Afgh.
46 C2 Meia Ponte r. Brazil
101 D4 Meiganga Cameroon
89 B4 Meigu China
87 N3 Meihekou China
89 E5 Mei Jiang r. China
57 D5 Meikle Millyea h. U.K.
83 J6 Meiktila Myanmar
62 E5 Meiningen Ger.
104 E6 Meiringspoort pass
   S. Africa
89 B4 Meishan China
62 F5 Meißen Ger.
89 C5 Meitan China
88 C3 Meixian China
89 E5 Meizhou China
84 D4 Mej r. India
44 C3 Mejicana mt Arg.
44 B2 Mejillones Chile
102 D2 Mek'elē Eth.
100 A3 Mékhé Senegal
84 B4 Mekhtar Pak.
66 C7 Meknassy Tunisia
100 B1 Meknès Morocco
95 C3 Mekong r. Asia
82 K6 Mekong r. China
95 C3 Mekong, Mouths of the
   est. Vietnam
92 C6 Melaka Malaysia
14 G6 Melanesia is Pac. Oc.
94 A5 Melaut r. Malaysia
114 F6 Melbourne Austr.
29 D6 Melbourne U.S.A.
57 □ Melby U.K.
62 D3 Meldorf Ger.
31 F1 Meldrum Bay Can.
80 E2 Melendiz Dağı mt Turkey
68 G4 Melenki Rus. Fed.
23 F2 Mélèzes, Rivière aux
   r. Can.
101 D3 Mélfi Chad
66 F4 Melfi Italy
21 J4 Melfort Can.
54 M5 Melhus Norway
94 A5 Meliau, Gunung mt
   Malaysia
65 C1 Melide Spain
100 B1 Melilla Spain
47 E2 Melincué Arg.
47 B2 Melipilla Chile
61 B3 Meliskerke Neth.
21 J5 Melita Can.
69 E6 Melitopol' Ukr.
62 G6 Melk Austria
105 H1 Melkrivier S. Africa
59 E6 Melksham U.K.
54 T3 Mellakoski Fin.
54 Q5 Mellansel Sweden
62 D4 Mellen U.S.A.
55 N7 Mellerud Sweden
105 J4 Melmoth S. Africa
47 F2 Melo Uru.
114 C4 Melrose Austr.
57 F5 Melrose U.K.
59 G5 Melton Mowbray U.K.
64 F2 Melun France
21 J4 Melville Can.
113 H2 Melville, C. c. Austr.
94 A5 Melville, C. c. Phil.
23 J3 Melville, Lake l. Can.
113 G2 Melville Bay b. Austr.
118 B2 Melville I. i. Can.
112 F2 Melville Island i. Austr.

118 A2 Melville Peninsula pen.
   Can.
60 C3 Melvin, Lough l.
   Rep. of Ireland/U.K.
77 T3 Melyuveyem Rus. Fed.
85 E2 Mêmar Co salt l. China
93 K7 Memberamo r. Indon.
93 K8 Memboro Indon.
105 H3 Memel S. Africa
62 F7 Memmingen Ger.
61 C5 Mémorial Américain h.
   France
92 D6 Mempawah Indon.
80 C7 Memphis Egypt
30 A5 Memphis MO U.S.A.
29 B5 Memphis TN U.S.A.
27 C5 Memphis TX U.S.A.
33 G2 Memphrémagog, Lac
   l. Can.
90 H3 Memuro-dake mt Japan
69 E5 Mena Ukr.
27 E5 Mena U.S.A.
100 C3 Ménaka Mali
   Mènam Khong r. see
   Mekong
27 D6 Menard U.S.A.
30 C3 Menasha U.S.A.
64 F4 Mende France
102 D2 Mendefera Eritrea
81 M3 Mendejīn Iran
20 C3 Mendenhall Glacier gl.
   U.S.A.
102 D3 Mendī Eth.
110 E2 Mendi P.N.G.
59 E6 Mendip Hills h. U.K.
34 A2 Mendocino U.S.A.
24 A3 Mendocino, C. c. U.S.A.
30 E4 Mendon U.S.A.
115 H3 Mendooran Austr.
34 B3 Mendota CA U.S.A.
30 C5 Mendota IL U.S.A.
30 C4 Mendota, Lake l. U.S.A.
47 C2 Mendoza Arg.
47 C2 Mendoza div. Arg.
47 C2 Mendoza r. Arg.
45 C2 Mene de Mauroa Venez.
45 C2 Mene Grande Venez.
67 M5 Menemen Turkey
88 E3 Mengcheng China
80 D1 Mengen Turkey
92 D7 Menggala Indon.
89 D5 Mengshan China
88 F3 Meng Shan mts China
88 E3 Mengyin China
89 B6 Mengzi China
23 G3 Menihek Can.
23 G3 Menihek Lakes lakes
   Can.
114 E4 Menindee Austr.
114 E4 Menindee Lake l. Austr.
114 C5 Meningie Austr.
81 M4 Menjan Iran
77 O3 Menkere Rus. Fed.
64 F3 Mennecy France
30 D3 Menominee U.S.A.
30 D3 Menominee r. U.S.A.
30 C4 Menomonee Falls U.S.A.
30 B3 Menomonie U.S.A.
103 B5 Menongue Angola
65 J2 Menorca i. Spain
94 A6 Mensalong Indon.
92 B7 Mentawai, Kepulauan is
   Indon.
   Mentawai Islands is see
   Mentawai, Kepulauan
95 B5 Mentekab Malaysia
35 H4 Mentmore U.S.A.
92 D7 Mentok Indon.
64 H5 Menton France
32 C4 Mentor U.S.A.
61 D5 Menuchenet Belgium
100 C1 Menzel Bourguiba Tunisia
66 D2 Menzel Temime Tunisia
112 D5 Menzies Austr.
119 D4 Menzies, Mt mt
   Antarctica
27 B6 Meoqui Mex.
61 E2 Meppel Neth.
62 C4 Meppen Ger.
105 K1 Mepuze Moz.
105 G4 Meqheleng S. Africa
68 G3 Mera r. Rus. Fed.
54 M5 Meråker Norway
26 F4 Meramec r. U.S.A.
66 D1 Merano Italy
45 E3 Merari, Sa. mt Brazil
104 F1 Meratswe r. Botswana
93 L8 Merauke Indon.
114 E5 Merbein Austr.
34 B3 Merced U.S.A.
47 B1 Mercedario, Cerro
   mt Arg.
47 E2 Mercedes Buenos Aires
   Arg.
44 E3 Mercedes Corrientes Arg.
47 D2 Mercedes San Luis Arg.
47 E2 Mercedes Uru.
32 A4 Mercer OH U.S.A.
30 B2 Mercer WV U.S.A.
20 F4 Mercoal Can.
117 E2 Mercury Islands is N.Z.
59 E6 Mere U.K.
33 H3 Meredith U.S.A.
27 C5 Meredith, Lake l. U.S.A.
27 C5 Meredith Nat.
   Recreation Area, Lake
   res. U.S.A.
30 B6 Meredosia U.S.A.
69 E5 Merefa Ukr.
101 E3 Merga Oasis oasis Sudan
95 A2 Mergui Myanmar
95 A3 Mergui Archipelago is
   Myanmar
114 D5 Meribah Austr.

67 M4 Meriç r. Greece/Turkey
36 G4 Mérida Mex.
65 C2 Mérida Spain
45 C2 Mérida Venez.
45 C2 Mérida, Cordillera de
   mts Venez.
33 G4 Meriden U.S.A.
34 B2 Meriden CA U.S.A.
27 F5 Meridian MS U.S.A.
64 D4 Mérignac France
54 T4 Merijärvi Fin.
55 R6 Merikarvia Fin.
115 H6 Merimbula Austr.
116 C3 Merinda Austr.
114 D5 Meringur Austr.
114 D6 Merino Austr.
116 B5 Merivale r. Austr.
27 C5 Merkel U.S.A.
95 □ Merlimau, P. i. Sing.
101 F3 Merowe Sudan
85 F3 Mêrqung Co salt l. China
112 C6 Merredin Austr.
57 D5 Merrick h. U.K.
31 K3 Merrickville Can.
30 C2 Merrill U.S.A.
30 D5 Merrillville U.S.A.
26 C2 Merriman U.S.A.
20 E4 Merritt Can.
29 D6 Merritt Island U.S.A.
115 J4 Merriwa Austr.
115 H3 Merrygoen Austr.
102 E2 Mersa Fatma Eritrea
61 E5 Mersch Lux.
59 E4 Mersey est. U.K.
   Mersin see İçel
92 C6 Mersing Malaysia
55 S8 Mērsrags Latvia
84 C4 Merta India
59 D6 Merthyr Tydfil U.K.
102 D3 Merti Kenya
65 C4 Mértola Port.
102 D4 Meru vol. Tanz.
104 D6 Merweville S. Africa
80 E1 Merzifon Turkey
62 C6 Merzig Ger.
119 B2 Merz Pen. pen. Antarctica
35 G5 Mesa U.S.A.
30 A2 Mesabi Range h. U.S.A.
66 G4 Mesagne Italy
67 L7 Mesara, Ormos b. Greece
35 H3 Mesa Verde Nat. Park
   nat. park U.S.A.
45 B4 Meta r. Col.
54 P4 Meselefors Sweden
22 F3 Mesgouez L. l. Can.
68 J2 Meshchura Rus. Fed.
   Meshed see Mashhad
69 G5 Meshkovskaya Rus. Fed.
30 E3 Mesick U.S.A.
67 K4 Mesimeri Greece
67 J5 Mesolongi Greece
81 J4 Mesopotamia reg. Iraq
35 E3 Mesquite NV U.S.A.
27 D5 Mesquite TX U.S.A.
35 E4 Mesquite Lake l. U.S.A.
103 D5 Messalo r. Moz.
66 F5 Messina Italy
105 J1 Messina S. Africa
66 F5 Messina, Stretta di str.
   Italy
31 J2 Messines Can.
67 K6 Messisini Greece
67 K6 Messiniakos Kolpos b.
   Greece
67 L5 Meston, Akra pt Greece
66 E2 Mestre Italy
80 F1 Mesudiye Turkey
45 C2 Meta r. Col./Venez.
31 G2 Metagama Can.
27 F6 Metairie U.S.A.
30 C5 Metamora U.S.A.
44 C2 Metán Arg.
116 C5 Meteor Creek r. Austr.
12 H9 Meteor Depth depth
   Atlantic Ocean
67 J6 Methoni Greece
33 H4 Methuen U.S.A.
57 E4 Methven U.K.
66 G3 Metković Croatia
20 C3 Metlakatla U.S.A.
103 D5 Metoro Moz.
92 D8 Metro Indon.
28 B4 Metropolis U.S.A.
34 C4 Mettler U.S.A.
102 D3 Metu Eth.
64 H2 Metz France
64 D4 Meuse r. Belgium/France
59 C7 Mevagissey U.K.
88 B3 Mêwa China
27 D6 Mexia U.S.A.
36 A2 Mexicali Mex.
35 H4 Mexican Hat U.S.A.
35 H3 Mexican Water U.S.A.
16 Mexico country
   Central America
36 E5 México Mex.
36 E5 México div. Mex.
26 F4 Mexico MO U.S.A.
33 H3 Mexico NY U.S.A.
18 Mexico, Gulf of g.
   Mex./U.S.A.
79 J2 Meymaneh Afgh.
81 L5 Meymeh, Rūdkhāneh-ye
   r. Iran
67 K3 Mezdra Bulg.
76 F3 Mezen' Rus. Fed.
64 G4 Mézenc, Mont mt France
68 J2 Mezhdurechensk
   Rus. Fed.
86 E1 Mezhdurechensk
   Rus. Fed.
76 G2 Mezhdusharskiy, O. i.
   Rus. Fed.
63 K7 Mezőtúr Hungary

36 C4 Mezquital r. Mex.
55 U8 Mežvidi Latvia
103 D5 Mfuwe Zambia
105 J3 Mhlume Swaziland
84 C5 Mhow India
85 H5 Mi r. Myanmar
36 E5 Miahuatlán Mex.
65 D3 Miajadas Spain
35 G5 Miami AZ U.S.A.
29 D7 Miami FL U.S.A.
27 E4 Miami OK U.S.A.
29 D7 Miami Beach U.S.A.
81 M6 Mīān Āb Iran
81 L3 Miandowāb Iran
103 E5 Miandrivazo Madag.
81 L3 Mīāneh Iran
94 C5 Miangas i. Phil.
89 C5 Mianning China
84 B2 Mianwali Pak.
88 C3 Mianxian China
88 B4 Mianyang China
88 B4 Mianzhu China
88 F2 Miao Dao i. China
88 F2 Miaodao Qundao is
   China
89 F5 Miaoli Taiwan
103 E5 Miarinarivo Madag.
76 H4 Miass Rus. Fed.
35 G5 Mica Mt mt U.S.A.
88 C3 Micang Shan mts China
63 K6 Michalovce Slovakia
21 H3 Michel Can.
30 C2 Michigamme Lake l.
   U.S.A.
30 C2 Michigamme Reservoir
   resr U.S.A.
30 D2 Michigan div. U.S.A.
30 D4 Michigan, Lake l. U.S.A.
30 D5 Michigan City U.S.A.
30 E2 Michipicoten Bay b. Can.
30 E2 Michipicoten i. i. Can.
30 E1 Michipicoten River Can.
68 G4 Michurinsk Rus. Fed.
37 H6 Mico r. Nic.
14 E5 Micronesia is Pac. Oc.
95 C5 Midai i. Indon.
12 F4 Mid-Atlantic Ridge
   sea feature Atlantic Ocean
104 C7 Middelberg Pass pass
   S. Africa
61 B3 Middelburg Neth.
104 F5 Middelburg Eastern Cape
   S. Africa
105 H2 Middelburg Mpumalanga
   S. Africa
55 L9 Middelfart Denmark
61 C3 Middelharnis Neth.
104 D5 Middelpos S. Africa
105 G2 Middelwit S. Africa
24 C3 Middle Alkali Lake l.
   U.S.A.
14 N5 Middle America Trench
   sea feature Pac. Oc.
92 A4 Middle Andaman i.
   Andaman and Nicobar Is
33 H3 Middleboro U.S.A.
32 E4 Middleburg U.S.A.
33 F3 Middleburgh U.S.A.
33 G2 Middlebury U.S.A.
117 C6 Middlemarch N.Z.
116 C3 Middlemount Austr.
32 B6 Middlesboro U.S.A.
58 F3 Middlesbrough U.K.
34 A2 Middletown CA U.S.A.
33 G4 Middletown CT U.S.A.
33 F5 Middletown DE U.S.A.
33 H4 Middletown NY U.S.A.
32 A5 Middletown OH U.S.A.
30 E4 Middleville U.S.A.
59 G7 Midhurst U.K.
13 K4 Mid-Indian Basin
   sea feature Indian Ocean
13 K6 Mid-Indian Ridge
   sea feature Indian Ocean
31 H3 Midland Can.
31 E4 Midland MI U.S.A.
27 C5 Midland TX U.S.A.
60 C6 Midleton Rep. of Ireland
14 F4 Mid-Pacific Mountains
   sea feature Pac. Oc.
54 □ Miðvágur Faroe Is
   Midway see Thamarīt
14 H4 Midway Islands is
   Pac. Oc.
24 F3 Midwest U.S.A.
27 D5 Midwest City U.S.A.
61 D2 Midwoud Neth.
81 H3 Midyat Turkey
57 □ Mid Yell U.K.
67 K7 Midzhur mt Bulg./Yugo.
55 U6 Miehikkälä Fin.
54 T3 Miekojärvi l. Fin.
63 K5 Mielec Pol.
65 D1 Mieres Spain
102 E3 Mī'ēso Eth.
32 E4 Mifflinburg U.S.A.
32 E4 Mifflintown U.S.A.
88 C3 Migang Shan mt China
105 F3 Migdol S. Africa
85 H3 Miging India
36 E5 Miguel Alemán, Presa
   resr Mex.
36 D4 Miguel Hidalgo, Presa
   resr Mex.
80 D2 Mihaliçcik Turkey
91 C7 Mihara Japan
91 F7 Mihara-yama vol. Japan
65 F2 Mijares r. Spain
61 C2 Mijdrecht Neth.

63 N4 Mikashevichy Belarus
68 F4 Mikhaylov Rus. Fed.
90 C3 Mikhaylovka Rus. Fed.
69 G5 Mikhaylovka Rus. Fed.
86 C1 Mikhaylovskiy Rus. Fed.
85 H4 Mikīr Hills mts India
55 U6 Mikkeli Fin.
55 U6 Mikkelin mlk Fin.
20 G3 Mikkwa r. Can.
102 D4 Mikumi Tanz.
68 J2 Mikun' Rus. Fed.
91 F6 Mikuni-sanmyaku mts
   Japan
91 H8 Mikura-jima i. Japan
26 E2 Milaca U.S.A.
83 D9 Miladhunmadulu Atoll
   atoll Maldives
66 C2 Milan Italy
29 B5 Milan U.S.A.
114 C5 Milang Austr.
103 D5 Milange Moz.
   Milano see Milan
80 A3 Milas Turkey
66 F5 Milazzo Italy
26 D2 Milbank U.S.A.
59 H5 Mildenhall U.K.
114 E5 Mildura Austr.
89 B5 Mile China
116 D6 Miles Austr.
24 F2 Miles City U.S.A.
60 C5 Milestone Rep. of Ireland
66 F4 Miletto, Monte mt
   Italy
60 D2 Milford Rep. of Ireland
34 B1 Milford CA U.S.A.
33 G4 Milford CT U.S.A.
33 F5 Milford DE U.S.A.
30 D5 Milford IL U.S.A.
35 F3 Milford MA U.S.A.
33 J2 Milford ME U.S.A.
33 F3 Milford NH U.S.A.
33 F3 Milford NY U.S.A.
35 F2 Milford UT U.S.A.
59 B6 Milford Haven U.K.
117 A6 Milford Sound N.Z.
117 A6 Milford Sound in. N.Z.
65 H3 Miliana Alg.
14 M1 Milk r. Can./U.S.A.
101 F3 Milk, Wadi el
   watercourse Sudan
77 R4 Mil'kovo Rus. Fed.
116 A1 Millaa Millaa Austr.
65 F2 Millárs r. Spain
64 F4 Millau France
34 B1 Mill Creek r. U.S.A.
29 D5 Milledgeville GA U.S.A.
30 C5 Milledgeville IL U.S.A.
26 E2 Mille Lacs l. U.S.A.
22 B4 Mille Lacs, Lac des
   l. Can.
   Millennium I. i. see
   Caroline Island
114 A2 Miller watercourse Austr.
26 D2 Miller U.S.A.
30 B3 Miller Dam Flowage res
   U.S.A.
31 G3 Miller Lake Can.
69 G5 Millerovo Rus. Fed.
35 G6 Miller Peak summit
   U.S.A.
32 C4 Millersburg OH U.S.A.
32 E4 Millersburg PA U.S.A.
114 B3 Millers Creek Austr.
32 E6 Millers Tavern U.S.A.
34 C3 Millerton Lake l. U.S.A.
57 C3 Milleur Point pt U.K.
119 D6 Mill I. i. Antarctica
114 D6 Millicent Austr.
31 H4 Millington MI U.S.A.
29 B5 Millington TN U.S.A.
33 J2 Millinocket U.S.A.
115 J1 Millmerran Austr.
58 D3 Millom U.K.
57 D5 Millport U.K.
33 F5 Millsboro U.S.A.
20 F2 Mills Lake l. Can.
32 C5 Millstone U.S.A.
112 C4 Millstream-Chichester
   National Park nat. park
   Austr.
23 A2 Milltown Can.
60 B5 Milltown Malbay
   Rep. of Ireland
33 K1 Millville Can.
33 F5 Millville U.S.A.
33 J2 Milo U.S.A.
90 D3 Milogradovo Rus. Fed.
67 L6 Milos i. Greece
68 D4 Miloslavskoye Rus. Fed.
114 D2 Milparinka Austr.
32 E4 Milroy U.S.A.
31 H4 Milton Can.
117 B7 Milton N.Z.
29 C6 Milton FL U.S.A.
30 A5 Milton IA U.S.A.
33 H2 Milton PA U.S.A.
33 G2 Milton VT U.S.A.
35 E2 Milton, Lake l. U.S.A.
24 C2 Milton-Freewater U.S.A.
59 G5 Milton Keynes U.K.
89 B5 Miluo China
30 D4 Milwaukee U.S.A.
69 G6 Milyutinskaya Rus. Fed.
64 D4 Mimizan France
102 B4 Mimongo Gabon
27 C7 Mina Mex.
34 C2 Mina U.S.A.
79 H4 Mīnāb Iran
93 G6 Minahassa Peninsula
   pen. Indon.
21 L4 Minaki Can.
91 B8 Minamata Japan
91 E7 Minami Alps National
   Park Japan

92 C6 **Minas** Indon.
47 F2 **Minas** Uru.
81 M7 **Mīnā' Sa'ūd** Kuwait
23 H4 **Minas Basin** *b.* Can.
47 F1 **Minas de Corrales** Uru.
46 D2 **Minas Gerais** *div.* Brazil
46 D2 **Minas Novas** Brazil
36 F5 **Minatitlán** Mex.
85 H5 **Minbu** Myanmar
85 H5 **Minbya** Myanmar
44 B6 **Minchinmávida** *vol.*
Chile
66 D2 **Mincio** *r.* Italy
81 L2 **Mincivan** Azer.
94 C5 **Mindanao** *i.* Phil.
114 D5 **Mindarie** Austr.
100 □ **Mindelo** Cape Verde
31 H3 **Minden** Ger.
62 D4 **Minden** Ger.
27 E5 **Minden** *LA* U.S.A.
34 C2 **Minden** *NV* U.S.A.
85 H6 **Mindon** Myanmar
114 E4 **Mindona L.** *l.* Austr.
94 B3 **Mindoro** *i.* Phil.
94 A3 **Mindoro Strait** *str.* Phil.
102 B4 **Mindouli** Congo
60 D6 **Mine Head** *hd*
Rep. of Ireland
59 D6 **Minehead** U.K.
46 B2 **Mineiros** Brazil
27 E5 **Mineola** U.S.A.
34 C3 **Mineral** U.S.A.
34 C3 **Mineral King** U.S.A.
69 G6 **Mineral'nyye Vody**
Rus. Fed.
30 B4 **Mineral Point** U.S.A.
27 D5 **Mineral Wells** U.S.A.
33 F2 **Minersville** U.S.A.
66 G4 **Minervino Murge** Italy
85 E1 **Minfeng** China
103 C5 **Minga** Dem. Rep. Congo
81 L1 **Mingäçevir** Azer.
81 L1 **Mingäçevir Su Anbarı**
resr Azer.
23 H3 **Mingan** Can.
114 D4 **Mingary** Austr.
116 B2 **Mingela** Austr.
112 C5 **Mingenew** Austr.
88 E3 **Minggang** China
88 F3 **Mingguang** China
65 F3 **Minglanilla** Spain
103 D5 **Mingoyo** Tanz.
89 B4 **Mingshan** China
87 N2 **Mingshui** China
57 A4 **Mingulay** *i.* U.K.
89 E5 **Mingxi** China
88 B2 **Minhe** China
89 F5 **Minhou** China
83 D9 **Minicoy** *i.* India
112 B4 **Minilya** Austr.
23 H3 **Minipi Lake** *l.* Can.
21 J4 **Minitonas** Can.
89 F5 **Min Jiang** *r.* China
88 B4 **Min Jiang** *r.* China
88 A2 **Minle** China
100 C4 **Minna** Nigeria
55 O5 **Minne** Sweden
26 E2 **Minneapolis** U.S.A.
21 K4 **Minnedosa** Can.
30 A2 **Minnesota** *div.* U.S.A.
114 A4 **Minnipa** Austr.
22 B4 **Minnitaki L.** *l.* Can.
65 B2 **Miño** *r.* Port./Spain
30 C3 **Minocqua** U.S.A.
30 B2 **Minong** U.S.A.
30 C5 **Minonk** U.S.A.
Minorca *i. see* **Menorca**
26 C1 **Minot** U.S.A.
88 B2 **Minqin** China
89 F5 **Minqing** China
88 B3 **Min Shan** *mts* China
85 H4 **Minsin** Myanmar
68 C4 **Minsk** Belarus
63 K4 **Mińsk Mazowiecki** Pol.
59 E5 **Minsterley** U.K.
84 C1 **Mintaka Pass** *pass*
China/Jammu and Kashmir
88 A3 **Mintang** China
23 G4 **Minto** Can.
22 F2 **Minto, Lac** *l.* Can.
25 F4 **Minturn** U.S.A.
80 C6 **Minûf** Egypt
86 F1 **Minusinsk** Rus. Fed.
85 J3 **Minutang** India
88 B3 **Minxian** China
114 E6 **Minyip** Austr.
31 E3 **Mio** U.S.A.
22 K4 **Miquelon** Can.
23 J4 **Miquelon** *i.* N. America
45 A4 **Mira** *r.* Col.
33 F2 **Mirabel** Can.
46 D2 **Mirabela** Brazil
43 J5 **Miracema do Norte**
Brazil
43 J5 **Mirador, Parque**
Nacional de *nat. park*
Brazil
45 B4 **Miraflores** Col.
81 H5 **Mīrah, Wādī al**
watercourse Iraq/S. Arabia
46 D2 **Miralta** Brazil
47 F3 **Miramar** Arg.
64 G5 **Miramas** France
23 G4 **Miramichi** *r.* Can.
67 L7 **Mirampélou, Kolpos** *b.*
Greece
46 A3 **Miranda** Brazil
46 A3 **Miranda** *r.* Brazil
34 A1 **Miranda** U.S.A.
65 E1 **Miranda de Ebro** Spain
65 B3 **Mirandela** Port.
66 D2 **Mirandola** Italy
46 B3 **Mirandópolis** Brazil
79 G6 **Mirbāṭ** Oman

64 E5 **Mirepoix** France
92 E6 **Miri** Malaysia
47 G2 **Mirim, Lagoa** *l.* Brazil
119 D5 **Mirnyy** *Rus. Fed. Base*
Antarctica
77 N3 **Mirnyy** Rus. Fed.
68 G2 **Mirnyy** Rus. Fed.
21 J3 **Mirond L.** *l.* Can.
84 C2 **Mirpur** Pak.
84 B4 **Mirpur Batoro** Pak.
84 B4 **Mirpur Khas** Pak.
84 A4 **Mirpur Sakro** Pak.
20 G4 **Mirror** Can.
116 B3 **Mirtna** Austr.
67 K6 **Mirtoö Pelagos** *sea*
Greece
91 A7 **Miryang** S. Korea
85 E4 **Mirzapur** India
91 C8 **Misaki** Japan
90 B3 **Misawa** Japan
23 H4 **Miscou I.** *i.* Can.
84 C1 **Misgar** Pak.
90 B2 **Mishan** China
30 D3 **Mishawaka** U.S.A.
30 E1 **Mishibishu Lake** *l.* Can.
91 B7 **Mi-shima** *i.* Japan
85 H3 **Mishmi** *mts* India
110 F3 **Misima I.** *i.* P.N.G.
37 H6 **Miskitos, Cayos**
atolls Nic.
63 K6 **Miskolc** Hungary
93 H7 **Misoöl** *i.* Indon.
30 B2 **Misquah Hills** *h.* U.S.A.
101 D1 **Miṣrātah** Libya
84 E4 **Misrikh** India
31 E1 **Missanabie** Can.
22 D3 **Missinaibi** *r.* Can.
31 F1 **Missinaibi Lake** *l.* Can.
21 J3 **Missinipe** Can.
20 E5 **Mission** Can.
26 C3 **Mission** U.S.A.
116 B1 **Mission Beach** Austr.
22 D3 **Missisa L.** *l.* Can.
31 F2 **Mississagi** *r.* Can.
31 H4 **Mississauga** Can.
30 E5 **Mississinewa Lake** *l.*
U.S.A.
31 J3 **Mississippi** *r.* Can.
27 F6 **Mississippi** *div.* U.S.A.
27 F6 **Mississippi** *r.* U.S.A.
27 F6 **Mississippi Delta** *delta*
U.S.A.
24 D2 **Missoula** U.S.A.
30 A6 **Missouri** *div.* U.S.A.
26 C2 **Missouri** *r.* U.S.A.
26 E3 **Missouri Valley** U.S.A.
116 B4 **Mistake Cr.** *r.* Austr.
23 H4 **Mistassini** Can.
23 H4 **Mistassini** *r.* Can.
22 F3 **Mistassini, L.** *l.* Can.
23 H2 **Mistastin Lake** *l.* Can.
62 H6 **Mistelbach** Austria
23 H2 **Mistinibi, Lac** *l.* Can.
22 F3 **Mistissini** Can.
20 C3 **Misty Fiords National**
Monument Wilderness
res. U.S.A.
116 B6 **Mitchell** Austr.
115 K2 **Mitchell** *r. N.S.W.* Austr.
113 H1 **Mitchell** *r. Qld.* Austr.
115 G6 **Mitchell** *r. Vic.* Austr.
31 G4 **Mitchell** Can.
26 D3 **Mitchell** U.S.A.
30 E3 **Mitchell, Lake** *l.* U.S.A.
29 D5 **Mitchell, Mt** *mt* U.S.A.
60 C5 **Mitchelstown**
Rep. of Ireland
80 C6 **Mît Ghamr** Egypt
84 B3 **Mithankot** Pak.
84 B4 **Mithi** Pak.
84 B4 **Mithrani Canal**
canal Pak.
67 M5 **Mithymna** Greece
20 C3 **Mitkof I.** *i.* U.S.A.
91 G6 **Mito** Japan
103 D4 **Mitole** Tanz.
117 E4 **Mitre** *mt* N.Z.
111 H3 **Mitre Island** *i.*
Solomon Is
115 J5 **Mittagong** Austr.
115 G6 **Mitta Mitta** Austr.
62 D4 **Mittellandkanal**
canal Ger.
45 C4 **Mitú** Col.
45 C4 **Mituas** Col.
103 C5 **Mitumba, Chaîne des**
mts Dem. Rep. Congo
102 C4 **Mitumba, Monts** *mts*
Dem. Rep. Congo
102 B3 **Mitzic** Gabon
91 F7 **Miura** Japan
81 F2 **Miyāh, Wādī al**
watercourse Syria
91 F7 **Miyake-jima** *i.* Japan
90 G5 **Miyako** Japan
91 B9 **Miyakonojō** Japan
88 B4 **Miyaluo** China
84 B5 **Miyāni** India
91 B9 **Miyazaki** Japan
91 D7 **Miyazu** Japan
89 B5 **Miyi** China
91 C7 **Miyoshi** Japan
88 E1 **Miyun** China
88 E1 **Miyun Sk.** *resr* China
102 D3 **Mīzan Teferī** Eth.
101 D1 **Mizdah** Libya
60 B6 **Mizen Head** *hd*
Rep. of Ireland
69 B5 **Mizhhir''ya** Ukr.
88 E2 **Mizhi** China
85 H5 **Mizoram** *div.* India
90 G5 **Mizusawa** Japan
55 O7 **Mjölby** Sweden
102 D4 **Mkata** Tanz.

102 D4 **Mkomazi** Tanz.
103 C5 **Mkushi** Zambia
62 G5 **Mladá Boleslav**
Czech Rep.
67 J2 **Mladenovac** Yugo.
63 K4 **Mława** Pol.
66 G3 **Mljet** *i.* Croatia
105 G5 **Mlungisi** S. Africa
63 M5 **Mlyniv** Ukr.
105 F2 **Mmabatho** S. Africa
105 G1 **Mmamabula** Botswana
105 F2 **Mmathethe** Botswana
55 J6 **Mo** Norway
35 H2 **Moab** U.S.A.
113 H4 **Moa I.** *i.* Austr.
111 H3 **Moala** *i.* Fiji
105 K2 **Moamba** Moz.
114 D2 **Moanba, Lake** *salt flat*
Austr.
35 E3 **Moapa** U.S.A.
60 D4 **Moate** Rep. of Ireland
102 C4 **Moba** Dem. Rep. Congo
91 G7 **Mobara** Japan
102 C3 **Mobayi-Mbongo**
Dem. Rep. Congo
26 E4 **Moberly** U.S.A.
29 B6 **Mobile** *AL* U.S.A.
35 H5 **Mobile** *AZ* U.S.A.
29 B6 **Mobile Bay** *b.* U.S.A.
26 C2 **Mobridge** U.S.A.
Mobutu, Lake *l. see*
Albert, Lake
43 J4 **Mocajuba** Brazil
103 E5 **Moçambique** Moz.
45 D2 **Mocapra** *r.* Venez.
89 B6 **Môc Châu** Vietnam
45 D2 **Mochirma, Parque**
Nacional *nat. park*
Venez.
103 E5 **Mochudi** Botswana
103 E5 **Mocimboa da Praia**
Moz.
54 R4 **Mockträsk** Sweden
45 A4 **Mocoa** Col.
46 C3 **Mococa** Brazil
25 F6 **Moctezuma** *Chihuahua*
Mex.
25 E6 **Moctezuma** *Sonora* Mex.
103 D5 **Mocuba** Moz.
64 H4 **Modane** France
84 C5 **Modasa** India
104 F4 **Modder** *r.* S. Africa
66 D2 **Modena** Italy
35 F3 **Modena** U.S.A.
34 B3 **Modesto** U.S.A.
115 G7 **Moe** Austr.
59 D5 **Moel Sych** *h.* U.K.
55 M6 **Moelv** Norway
54 Q2 **Moen** Norway
35 G3 **Moenkopi** U.S.A.
117 C6 **Moeraki Pt** *pt* N.Z.
57 E5 **Moffat** U.K.
84 D3 **Moga** India
Mogadishu *see* **Muqdisho**
32 C4 **Mogadore Reservoir** *resr*
U.S.A.
105 H1 **Mogalakwena** *r.* S. Africa
105 H2 **Moganyaka** S. Africa
46 C3 **Mogi-Mirim** Brazil
87 L1 **Mogocha** Rus. Fed.
66 C6 **Mogod** *mts* Tunisia
105 F2 **Mogoditshane** Botswana
83 J6 **Mogok** Myanmar
35 H5 **Mogollon Mts** *mts* U.S.A.
35 G4 **Mogollon Plateau** *plat.*
U.S.A.
105 G2 **Mogwase** S. Africa
67 H2 **Mohács** Hungary
117 F3 **Mohaka** *r.* N.Z.
105 G5 **Mohale's Hoek** Lesotho
21 J5 **Mohall** U.S.A.
65 G5 **Mohammadia** Alg.
84 E3 **Mohan** *r.* India/Nepal
35 E4 **Mohave, L.** *l.* U.S.A.
35 F5 **Mohawk** U.S.A.
33 F3 **Mohawk** *r.* U.S.A.
35 F5 **Mohawk Mts** *mts* U.S.A.
103 E5 **Moheli** *i.* Comoros
60 D4 **Mohill** Rep. of Ireland
35 H4 **Mohon Peak** *summit*
U.S.A.
103 D4 **Mohoro** Tanz.
81 M5 **Moh Reza Shah Pahlavi**
resr Iran
69 C5 **Mohyliv Podil's'kyy** Ukr.
55 K7 **Moi** Norway
105 G1 **Moijabana** Botswana
105 K2 **Moine** Moz.
63 N7 **Moineşti** Romania
33 F2 **Moira** U.S.A.
54 O3 **Mo i Rana** Norway
85 H4 **Moirang** India
55 T7 **Mõisaküla** Estonia
47 E5 **Moisés Ville** Arg.
23 G3 **Moisie** Can.
23 G3 **Moisie** *r.* Can.
64 E4 **Moissac** France
34 C4 **Mojave** U.S.A.
34 C4 **Mojave** *r.* U.S.A.
34 D4 **Mojave Desert** *des.* U.S.A.
46 C3 **Moji das Cruzes** Brazil
46 C3 **Moji-Guaçu** *r.* Brazil
91 B8 **Mojikō** Japan
85 F4 **Mokāma** India
34 □¹ **Mokapu Pen.** *pen.* U.S.A.
117 E3 **Mokau** N.Z.
117 E3 **Mokau** *r.* N.Z.
34 B2 **Mokelumne** *r.* U.S.A.
105 H4 **Mokhoabong Pass** *pass*
Lesotho
105 H4 **Mokhotlong** Lesotho
66 D7 **Moknine** Tunisia
117 E1 **Mokohinau Is** *i.* N.Z.
101 D3 **Mokolo** Cameroon

105 G1 **Mokolo** *r.* S. Africa
87 N5 **Mokp'o** S. Korea
68 G4 **Moksha** *r.* Rus. Fed.
68 H4 **Mokshan** Rus. Fed.
34 □¹ **Mokuauia I.** *i.* U.S.A.
34 □¹ **Mokulua** *is* U.S.A.
65 F3 **Molatón** *mt* Spain
54 K5 **Molde** Norway
54 O3 **Moldjord** Norway
48 **Moldova** *country* Europe
67 L2 **Moldoveanu, Vârful** *mt*
Romania
59 D7 **Mole** *r.* U.K.
100 B4 **Mole National Park**
nat. park Ghana
103 C6 **Molepolole** Botswana
55 T9 **Molėtai** Lith.
66 G4 **Molfetta** Italy
65 F2 **Molina de Aragón** Spain
30 B5 **Moline** U.S.A.
55 N7 **Molkom** Sweden
81 M4 **Mollā Bodāgh** Iran
85 E4 **Mol Len** *mt* India
42 D7 **Mollendo** Peru
55 N8 **Mölnlycke** Sweden
68 F3 **Molochnoye** Rus. Fed.
54 X2 **Molochnyy** Rus. Fed.
119 D3 **Molodezhnaya**
Rus. Fed. Base Antarctica
68 D3 **Molodoy Tud** Rus. Fed.
34 □² **Molokai** *i.* U.S.A.
15 K4 **Molokai Fracture Zone**
sea feature Pac. Oc.
68 J3 **Moloma** *r.* Rus. Fed.
115 H4 **Molong** Austr.
104 F2 **Molopo** *watercourse*
Botswana/S. Africa
101 D4 **Moloundou** Cameroon
21 K4 **Molson L.** *l.* Can.
93 H7 **Moluccas** *is* Indon.
93 H6 **Molucca Sea** *g.* Indon.
103 D5 **Moma** Moz.
114 E3 **Momba** Austr.
102 D4 **Mombasa** Kenya
85 H4 **Mombi New** India
46 B2 **Mombuca, Serra da** *h.*
Brazil
69 C7 **Momchilgrad** Bulg.
30 C5 **Momence** U.S.A.
45 B2 **Mompós** Col.
55 N9 **Møn** *i.* Denmark
35 G2 **Mona** U.S.A.
37 L5 **Mona, I.** *i.* Puerto Rico
57 A3 **Monach, Sound of** *chan.*
U.K.
57 A3 **Monach Islands** *is* U.K.
48 **Monaco** *country* Europe
57 D3 **Monadhliath Mountains**
mts U.K.
60 E3 **Monaghan** Rep. of Ireland
27 C6 **Monahans** U.S.A.
37 L5 **Mona Passage** *chan.*
Dom. Rep./Puerto Rico
103 E5 **Monapo** Moz.
57 C2 **Monar, Loch** *l.* U.K.
20 G4 **Monarch Mt.** *mt* Can.
25 F4 **Monarch Pass** *pass* U.S.A.
20 F4 **Monashee Mts** *mts* Can.
66 D7 **Monastir** Tunisia
63 P3 **Monastyrshchina**
Rus. Fed.
69 D5 **Monastyryshche** Ukr.
90 H2 **Monbetsu** Japan
90 H3 **Monbetsu** Japan
66 B2 **Moncalieri** Italy
54 X3 **Monchegorsk** Rus. Fed.
62 C5 **Mönchengladbach** Ger.
65 B4 **Monchique** Port.
29 E5 **Moncks Corner** U.S.A.
36 D3 **Monclova** Mex.
23 H4 **Moncton** Can.
65 C2 **Mondego** *r.* Port.
66 B2 **Mondovì** Italy
66 E4 **Mondragone** Italy
67 K6 **Monemvasia** Greece
90 G1 **Moneron, Ostrov** *i.*
Rus. Fed.
32 D4 **Monessen** U.S.A.
31 K1 **Monet** Can.
60 D5 **Moneygall** Rep. of Ireland
66 E2 **Moneymore** U.K.
65 C1 **Monforte** Spain
102 C3 **Monga** Dem. Rep. Congo
89 C6 **Mông Cai** Vietnam
95 C6 **Mong Mau** Myanmar
70 **Mongolia** *country* Asia
84 C2 **Mongora** Pak.
103 C5 **Mongu** Zambia
33 J3 **Monhegan I.** *i.* U.S.A.
57 E5 **Moniaive** U.K.
34 D2 **Monitor Mt** *mt* U.S.A.
34 D2 **Monitor Range** *mts*
U.S.A.
60 C4 **Monivea** Rep. of Ireland
31 G4 **Monkton** Can.
85 F3 **Mon La** *pass* China
59 E6 **Monmouth** U.K.
30 B5 **Monmouth** *IL* U.S.A.
33 H2 **Monmouth** *ME* U.S.A.
20 E5 **Monmouth Mt.** *mt* Can.
47 E1 **Mono** *r.* Togo
34 C3 **Mono Lake** *l.* U.S.A.
33 H4 **Monomoy Pt** *pt* U.S.A.
30 C5 **Monon** U.S.A.
30 B4 **Monona** U.S.A.
66 G4 **Monopoli** Italy
32 C4 **Monongahela** *r.* U.S.A.
65 F2 **Monreal del Campo**
Spain
66 E5 **Monreale** Italy

27 E5 **Monroe** *LA* U.S.A.
31 F5 **Monroe** *MI* U.S.A.
29 D5 **Monroe** *NC* U.S.A.
33 F4 **Monroe** *NY* U.S.A.
35 F2 **Monroe** *UT* U.S.A.
30 C4 **Monroe** *WV* U.S.A.
30 B6 **Monroe City** U.S.A.
29 C6 **Monroeville** U.S.A.
100 A4 **Monrovia** Liberia
61 B4 **Mons** Belgium
66 D2 **Monselice** Italy
104 D6 **Montagu** S. Africa
30 D4 **Montague** U.S.A.
119 C1 **Montagu I.** *i.*
Atlantic Ocean
66 F5 **Montalto** *mt* Italy
66 G5 **Montalto Uffugo** Italy
67 K3 **Montana** Bulg.
24 F3 **Montana** *div.* U.S.A.
64 F3 **Montargis** France
64 E4 **Montauban** France
33 H4 **Montauk** U.S.A.
33 H4 **Montauk Pt** *pt* U.S.A.
64 G3 **Montbard** France
64 H4 **Mont Blanc** *mt*
France/Italy
65 G2 **Montblanc** Spain
64 G3 **Montbrison** France
64 G3 **Montceau-les-Mines**
France
64 D5 **Mont-de-Marsan** France
64 F2 **Montdidier** France
43 H4 **Monte Alegre** Brazil
46 C1 **Monte Alegre de Goiás**
Brazil
46 D1 **Monte Azul** Brazil
22 D1 **Montebello** Can.
66 F6 **Montebello Ionico** Italy
66 E2 **Montebelluna** Italy
47 D2 **Monte Buey** Arg.
64 H5 **Monte-Carlo** Monaco
47 C5 **Monte Caseros** Arg.
105 G1 **Monte Christo** S. Africa
47 C2 **Monte Comán** Arg.
37 K5 **Monte Cristi** Dom. Rep.
66 D3 **Montecristo, Isola di** *i.*
Italy
37 J5 **Montego Bay** Jamaica
64 G4 **Montélimar** France
44 E2 **Monte Lindo** *r.* Para.
66 F4 **Montella** Italy
30 C4 **Montello** U.S.A.
36 E3 **Montemorelos** Mex.
65 B3 **Montemor-o-Novo** Port.
67 H3 **Montenegro** *div.* Yugo.
103 D5 **Montepuez** Moz.
66 D3 **Montepulciano** Italy
64 F2 **Montereau-faut-Yonne**
France
34 B3 **Monterey** *CA* U.S.A.
32 D5 **Monterey** *VA* U.S.A.
34 B3 **Monterey Bay** *b.* U.S.A.
45 B2 **Montería** Col.
42 F7 **Montero** Bol.
36 D3 **Monterrey** Mex.
66 F4 **Montesano sulla**
Marcellana Italy
43 L6 **Monte Santo** Brazil
46 D2 **Montes Claros** Brazil
66 F3 **Montesilvano** Italy
66 D3 **Montevarchi** Italy
47 F2 **Montevideo** Uru.
26 E2 **Montevideo** U.S.A.
25 F4 **Monte Vista** U.S.A.
30 A5 **Montezuma** U.S.A.
35 H3 **Montezuma Castle**
National Monument *res.*
U.S.A.
35 H3 **Montezuma Creek** U.S.A.
34 D3 **Montezuma Peak**
summit U.S.A.
59 D5 **Montgomery** U.K.
29 C5 **Montgomery** U.S.A.
62 C7 **Monthey** Switz.
27 C7 **Monticello** *AR* U.S.A.
29 D6 **Monticello** *FL* U.S.A.
30 B4 **Monticello** *IA* U.S.A.
30 D5 **Monticello** *IN* U.S.A.
33 K1 **Monticello** *ME* U.S.A.
30 B6 **Monticello** *MO* U.S.A.
33 F4 **Monticello** *NY* U.S.A.
35 H2 **Monticello** *UT* U.S.A.
30 C4 **Monticello** *WV* U.S.A.
47 E1 **Montiel, Cuchilla de**
h. Arg.
64 E4 **Montignac** France
65 D4 **Montilla** Spain
23 G4 **Mont-Joli** Can.
31 K2 **Mont-Laurier** Can.
23 G4 **Mont Louis** Can.
64 F3 **Montluçon** France
61 D5 **Montmédy** France
23 G4 **Montmagny** Can.
31 K2 **Montmorenci** U.S.A.
23 H4 **Montmorency** Can.
64 F3 **Montmorillon** France
116 D5 **Monto** Austr.
24 E3 **Montpelier** *ID* U.S.A.
30 D5 **Montpelier** *IN* U.S.A.
32 A4 **Montpelier** *OH* U.S.A.
33 G2 **Montpelier** *VT* U.S.A.
64 F5 **Montpellier** France
22 F4 **Montréal** Can.
31 G2 **Montreal** *r.* Can.
31 F2 **Montreal** Can.
21 H4 **Montreal L.** *l.* Can.
21 H4 **Montreal Lake** Can.
30 D2 **Montréal-Mirabel** Can.
31 F2 **Montreal River** Can.
62 C7 **Montreux** Switz.
104 D3 **Montrose** *w.* S. Africa
57 F4 **Montrose** U.K.
25 F4 **Montrose** *CO* U.S.A.

31 F4 **Montrose** *MI* U.S.A.
33 F4 **Montrose** *PA* U.S.A.
23 G4 **Monts, Pte des** *pt* Can.
37 M5 **Montserrat** *terr.*
Caribbean
35 G3 **Monument Valley** *reg.*
U.S.A.
83 J6 **Monywa** Myanmar
66 C2 **Monza** Italy
103 C5 **Monze** Zambia
65 G2 **Monzón** Spain
105 J4 **Mooi** *r.* S. Africa
104 B3 **Mooifontein** Namibia
105 J4 **Mooirivier** S. Africa
105 G5 **Mookane** Botswana
114 C2 **Moolawatana** Austr.
115 H2 **Moomin Cr.** *r.* Austr.
114 A3 **Moonaree** Austr.
115 J3 **Moonbi Ra.** *mts* Austr.
115 J1 **Moonie** Austr.
115 H2 **Moonie** *r.* Austr.
114 B5 **Moonta** Austr.
112 C6 **Moora** Austr.
24 F2 **Moorcroft** U.S.A.
112 C5 **Moore, Lake** *salt flat*
Austr.
32 D5 **Moorefield** U.S.A.
29 E7 **Moores I.** *i.* Bahamas
33 K2 **Moores Mills** Can.
57 D5 **Moorfoot Hills** *h.* U.K.
26 D2 **Moorhead** U.S.A.
114 C2 **Moornanyah Lake** *l.*
Austr.
114 D5 **Moonok** Austr.
114 F6 **Mooroopna** Austr.
104 C6 **Mooreesburg** S. Africa
22 C3 **Moose** *r.* Can.
22 D3 **Moose Factory** Can.
33 J2 **Moosehead Lake** *l.* U.S.A.
21 H4 **Moose Jaw** Can.
21 J4 **Moose Lake** *l.* Can.
30 A2 **Moose Lake** U.S.A.
33 H2 **Mooselookmeguntic**
Lake *l.* U.S.A.
22 C3 **Moose River** Can.
21 J4 **Moosomin** Can.
22 D3 **Moosonee** Can.
114 E3 **Mootwingee** Austr.
105 H1 **Mopane** S. Africa
100 B3 **Mopti** Mali
84 A2 **Moqor** Afgh.
42 D7 **Moquegua** Peru
101 D3 **Mora** Cameroon
65 E3 **Mora** Spain
55 O6 **Mora** Sweden
47 B2 **Mora, Cerro** *mt* Arg./Chile
84 A3 **Morad** *r.* Pak.
84 D3 **Moradabad** India
103 E5 **Morafenobe** Madag.
103 E5 **Moramanga** Madag.
30 E3 **Moran** *MI* U.S.A.
24 E3 **Moran** *WY* U.S.A.
116 C3 **Moranbah** Austr.
57 C4 **Morar, Loch** *l.* U.K.
83 F9 **Moratuwa** Sri Lanka
62 H6 **Morava** *r.*
Austria/Slovakia
33 E3 **Moravia** U.S.A.
116 B3 **Moray Downs** Austr.
57 E3 **Moray Firth** *est.* U.K.
61 B1 **Morbach** Ger.
66 C1 **Morbegno** Italy
84 B5 **Morbi** India
64 D4 **Morcenx** France
87 M1 **Mordaga** China
81 K3 **Mor Daği** *mt* Turkey
21 K5 **Morden** Can.
114 F7 **Mordialloc** Austr.
68 H4 **Mordoviya, Respublika**
div. Rus. Fed.
69 G4 **Mordovo** Rus. Fed.
57 D2 **More, Loch** *l.* U.K.
26 C2 **Moreau** *r.* U.S.A.
58 E3 **Morecambe** U.K.
58 D3 **Morecambe Bay** *b.* U.K.
115 H2 **Moree** Austr.
110 F2 **Morehead** P.N.G.
32 B5 **Morehead** U.S.A.
29 E5 **Morehead City** U.S.A.
84 D4 **Morel** *r.* India
36 D5 **Morelia** Mex.
65 F2 **Morella** Spain
84 D4 **Morena** India
65 D3 **Morena, Sierra** *mts* Spain
35 H5 **Morenci** *AZ* U.S.A.
31 E5 **Morenci** *MI* U.S.A.
67 L2 **Moreni** Romania
47 E2 **Moreno** Arg.
25 E6 **Moreno** Mex.
34 D5 **Moreno Valley** U.S.A.
20 C4 **Moresby Island** *i.* Can.
104 F1 **Moreswe Pan** *salt pan*
Botswana
115 K1 **Moreton B.** *b.* Austr.
115 K1 **Moreton I.** *i.* Austr.
59 F6 **Moreton-in-Marsh** U.K.
80 D4 **Morfou** Cyprus
80 D4 **Morfou Bay** *b.* Cyprus
114 C5 **Morgan** Austr.
34 C4 **Morgan, Mt** *mt* U.S.A.
27 F6 **Morgan City** U.S.A.
34 B3 **Morgan Hill** U.S.A.
33 F4 **Morgantown** *PA* U.S.A.
32 D5 **Morgantown** *WV* U.S.A.
105 H3 **Morgenzon** S. Africa
62 C7 **Morges** Switz.
85 F4 **Morhar** *r.* India
82 H2 **Mori** China
90 G3 **Mori** Japan
35 E2 **Moriah, Mt** *mt* U.S.A.
25 F5 **Moriarty** U.S.A.
115 F2 **Moriarty's Ra.** *h.* Austr.
45 C4 **Morichal** Col.
45 E2 **Morichal Largo** *r.* Venez.

105 G4 Morija Lesotho
68 D3 Morino Rus. Fed.
90 G5 Morioka Japan
115 J4 Morisset Austr.
90 G5 Moriyoshi-zan *vol.* Japan
54 S3 Morjärv Sweden
68 J3 Morki Rus. Fed.
64 C2 Morlaix France
58 F4 Morley U.K.
35 G4 Mormon Lake *l.* U.S.A.
44 A7 Mornington, I. *i.* Chile
113 G3 Mornington I. *i.* Austr.
84 A4 Moro Pak.
110 E2 Morobe P.N.G.
96 Morocco *country* Africa
30 D5 Morocco U.S.A.
102 D4 Morogoro Tanz.
94 B5 Moro Gulf *g.* Phil.
105 G4 Morojaneng S. Africa
104 E3 Morokweng S. Africa
103 E6 Morombe Madag.
37 J4 Morón Cuba
86 H2 Mörön Mongolia
103 E6 Morondava Madag.
65 D4 Morón de la Frontera
Spain
103 E5 Moroni Comoros
93 H6 Morotai *i.* Indon.
102 D3 Moroto Uganda
69 G5 Morozovsk Rus. Fed.
31 G4 Morpeth Can.
58 F2 Morpeth U.K.
46 C2 Morrinhos Brazil
21 K5 Morris Can.
30 C5 Morris *IL* U.S.A.
26 E2 Morris *MN* U.S.A.
33 F2 Morrisburg Can.
30 C5 Morrison U.S.A.
35 F5 Morristown *AZ* U.S.A.
33 F4 Morristown *NJ* U.S.A.
33 H2 Morristown *NY* U.S.A.
29 D4 Morristown *TN* U.S.A.
33 H4 Morrisville *PA* U.S.A.
33 G2 Morrisville *VT* U.S.A.
44 B3 Morro, Pta *pt* Chile
34 B4 Morro Bay U.S.A.
45 C2 Morrocoy, Parque
Nacional *nat. park*
Venez.
43 H4 Morro Grande *h.* Brazil
45 B2 Morrosquillo, Golfo de
b. Col.
119 B6 Morse, C. *c.* Antarctica
30 D5 Morse Reservoir *resr*
U.S.A.
68 G4 Morshanka Rus. Fed.
68 E2 Morskaya Masel'ga
Rus. Fed.
66 C7 Morsott Alg.
64 E2 Mortagne-au-Perche
France
64 D3 Mortagne-sur-Sèvre
France
59 C6 Mortehoe U.K.
47 E1 Morteros Arg.
Mortes *r. see* Mortes,
Rio das
43 H6 Mortes, Rio das *r.* Brazil
29 F7 Mortimer's Bahamas
114 E7 Mortlake Austr.
Mortlock Is *is see*
Tauu Islands
59 G5 Morton U.K.
30 C5 Morton *IL* U.S.A.
24 B2 Morton *WA* U.S.A.
115 J5 Morton Nat. Park
nat. park Austr.
115 G5 Morundah Austr.
105 G1 Morupule Botswana
115 J5 Moruya Austr.
116 B6 Morven Austr.
57 C4 Morvern *reg.* U.K.
Morvi *see* Morbi
115 G7 Morwell Austr.
62 D6 Mosbach Ger.
59 F4 Mosborough U.K.
68 F4 Moscow Rus. Fed.
24 C2 Moscow U.S.A.
61 F4 Mosel *r.* Ger.
104 E2 Moselebe *watercourse*
Botswana
64 H2 Moselle *r.* France
34 D1 Moses, Mt *mt* U.S.A.
24 C2 Moses Lake U.S.A.
117 C6 Mosgiel N.Z.
104 E3 Moshaweng *watercourse*
S. Africa
102 D4 Moshi Tanz.
30 C3 Mosinee U.S.A.
54 N4 Mosjøen Norway
54 N3 Moskenesøy *i.* Norway
68 F4 Moskovskaya Oblast'
div. Rus. Fed.
Moskva *see* Moscow
62 H7 Mosonmagyaróvár
Hungary
45 A4 Mosquera Col.
25 F5 Mosquero U.S.A.
37 H5 Mosquitia *reg.* Honduras
46 E1 Mosquito *r.* Brazil
32 C4 Mosquito Creek Lake *l.*
U.S.A.
21 J2 Mosquito Lake *l.* Can.
55 M7 Moss Norway
57 F3 Mossat U.K.
117 B6 Mossburn N.Z.
104 E7 Mossel Bay S. Africa
104 E7 Mossel Bay *b.* S. Africa
102 B4 Mossendjo Congo
114 F4 Mossgiel Austr.
116 A1 Mossman Austr.
43 L5 Mossoró Brazil
115 J5 Moss Vale Austr.
62 F5 Most Czech Rep.

100 C1 Mostaganem Alg.
66 G3 Mostar Bos.-Herz.
44 F4 Mostardas Brazil
21 G3 Mostoos Hills *h.* Can.
69 G6 Mostovskoy Rus. Fed.
94 A5 Mostyn Malaysia
55 L7 Møsvatnet *l.* Norway
55 O7 Motala Sweden
45 C2 Motatán *r.* Venez.
105 K2 Motaze Moz.
105 H2 Motetema S. Africa
84 D4 Moth India
57 E5 Motherwell U.K.
85 F4 Motihari India
65 F3 Motilla del Palancar
Spain
117 F2 Motiti I. *i.* N.Z.
104 E2 Motokwe Botswana
65 E4 Motril Spain
67 K2 Motru Romania
36 G4 Motul Mex.
89 A5 Mouding China
100 A3 Moudjéria Maur.
67 L5 Moudros Greece
55 S6 Mouhijärvi Fin.
102 B4 Mouila Gabon
114 F5 Moulamein Austr.
114 F5 Moulamein Creek *r.*
Austr.
102 B4 Moulèngui Binza Gabon
64 F3 Moulins France
95 A1 Moulmein Myanmar
29 D6 Moultrie U.S.A.
28 B4 Mound City *IL* U.S.A.
26 E3 Mound City *MO* U.S.A.
101 D4 Moundou Chad
32 C5 Moundsville U.S.A.
84 C4 Mount Abu India
29 C5 Mountain Brook U.S.A.
32 C6 Mountain City U.S.A.
27 E4 Mountain Grove U.S.A.
27 E4 Mountain Home *AR* U.S.A.
24 D3 Mountain Home *ID* U.S.A.
105 F6 Mountain Zebra
National Park *nat. park*
S. Africa
32 C6 Mount Airy U.S.A.
117 B6 Mount Aspiring National
Park *nat. park* N.Z.
105 H5 Mount Ayliff S. Africa
26 E3 Mount Ayr U.S.A.
114 C5 Mount Barker *S.A.* Austr.
112 C6 Mount Barker *W.A.* Austr.
115 G6 Mount Beauty Austr.
60 C4 Mount Bellew
Rep. of Ireland
113 J7 Mount Bogong National
Park *nat. park* Austr.
115 G6 Mount Buffalo National
Park *nat. park* Austr.
116 A1 Mount Carbine Austr.
33 K1 Mount Carleton
Provincial Park *res.* Can.
35 F3 Mount Carmel Junction
U.S.A.
30 C4 Mount Carroll U.S.A.
117 C5 Mount Cook N.Z.
Mt Cook *nat see* Aoraki
117 C5 Mount Cook National
Park *nat. park* N.Z.
116 B3 Mount Coolon Austr.
103 D5 Mount Darwin Zimbabwe
33 J2 Mount Desert Island *i.*
U.S.A.
114 A1 Mount Dutton Austr.
114 A3 Mount Eba Austr.
115 G9 Mount Field Nat. Park
nat. park Austr.
105 H5 Mount Fletcher S. Africa
31 G4 Mount Forest Can.
105 H5 Mount Frere S. Africa
Mount Fuji *vol. see*
Fuji-san
114 D6 Mount Gambier Austr.
116 A1 Mount Garnet Austr.
32 B4 Mount Gilead U.S.A.
110 E2 Mount Hagen P.N.G.
115 F4 Mount Hope *N.S.W.* Austr.
114 A5 Mount Hope *S.A.* Austr.
32 C6 Mount Hope U.S.A.
30 C4 Mount Horeb U.S.A.
113 G4 Mount Isa Austr.
33 G4 Mount Kisco U.S.A.
116 D4 Mount Larcom Austr.
114 C5 Mount Lofty Range *mts*
Austr.
31 G2 Mount MacDonald Can.
112 C5 Mount Magnet Austr.
114 E4 Mount Manara Austr.
34 B1 Mount Meadows
Reservoir *resr* U.S.A.
60 C4 Mountmellick
Rep. of Ireland
116 A1 Mount Molloy Austr.
105 G5 Mount Moorosi Lesotho
116 D4 Mount Morgan Austr.
114 E3 Mount Murchison Austr.
116 D5 Mount Perry Austr.
30 D5 Mount Pleasant *IA* U.S.A.
30 E4 Mount Pleasant *MI* U.S.A.
28 B3 Mount Pleasant *MI* U.S.A.
32 D4 Mount Pleasant *PA* U.S.A.
29 E5 Mount Pleasant *SC* U.S.A.
27 E5 Mount Pleasant *TX* U.S.A.
35 G2 Mount Pleasant *UT* U.S.A.
30 C5 Mount Pulaski U.S.A.
24 B2 Mount Rainier Nat. Park
nat. park U.S.A.
20 D3 Mount Robson Prov.
Park *res.* Can.
32 C6 Mount Rogers National
Recreation Area *res.*
U.S.A.
59 B7 Mount's Bay *b.* U.K.

59 F5 Mountsorrel U.K.
30 B6 Mount Sterling *IL* U.S.A.
32 B5 Mount Sterling *KY* U.S.A.
32 D5 Mount Storm U.S.A.
116 A2 Mount Surprise Austr.
32 E4 Mount Union U.S.A.
29 B6 Mount Vernon *AL* U.S.A.
30 B5 Mount Vernon *IA* U.S.A.
28 B4 Mount Vernon *IL* U.S.A.
32 A6 Mount Vernon *KY* U.S.A.
32 B4 Mount Vernon *OH* U.S.A.
24 B1 Mount Vernon *WA* U.S.A.
114 A4 Mount Wedge Austr.
115 H8 Mount William National
Park *nat. park* Austr.
116 C5 Moura Austr.
42 F4 Moura Brazil
101 E3 Mourdi, Dépression du
depression Chad
116 B1 Mourilyan Harbour Austr.
60 D3 Mourne *r.* U.K.
60 E3 Mourne Mountains *h.*
U.K.
61 B3 Mouscron Belgium
101 D3 Moussoro Chad
93 G6 Moutong Indon.
100 C2 Mouydir, Mts de
61 D5 Mouzon France
115 J1 Mowbullan, Mt *mt* Austr.
29 E7 Moxey Town Bahamas
60 C4 Moy *r.* Rep. of Ireland
102 D3 Moyale Eth.
100 A4 Moyamba Sierra Leone
100 D1 Moyen Atlas *mts* Morocco
105 G5 Moyeni Lesotho
60 C4 Moyer *h.* Rep. of Ireland
82 D1 Moyynty Kazak.
96 Mozambique *country*
Africa
103 E5 Mozambique Channel
str. Africa
13 G5 Mozambique Ridge
sea feature Indian Ocean
69 H7 Mozdok Rus. Fed.
68 F4 Mozhaysk Rus. Fed.
85 H6 Mozo Myanmar
102 C4 Mpala Dem. Rep. Congo
102 D4 Mpanda Tanz.
103 D5 Mpika Zambia
105 J4 Mpolweni S. Africa
103 D4 Mporokoso Zambia
105 H2 Mpumalanga *div.*
S. Africa
105 H5 Mqanduli S. Africa
66 G2 Mrkonjić-Grad Bos.-Herz.
100 D1 M'Saken Tunisia
68 D3 Mshinskaya Rus. Fed.
68 J5 M'Sila Alg.
68 E4 Msta *r.* Rus. Fed.
68 D4 Mstsislaw Belarus
105 H4 Mt-aux-Sources *mt*
Lesotho
68 F4 Mtsensk Rus. Fed.
105 K4 Mtubatuba S. Africa
105 J4 Mtunzini S. Africa
103 E5 Mtwara Tanz.
102 B4 Muanda Dem. Rep. Congo
89 B6 Muang Hiam Laos
95 B1 Muang Hôngsa Laos
95 C1 Muang Khammouan Laos
95 C2 Muang Khôngxédôn Laos
89 B6 Muang Khoua Laos
95 A3 Muang Kirirath *r.* Thai.
95 A3 Muang Luang *r.* Thai.
95 C1 Muang Mok Laos
89 B6 Muang Ngoy Laos
95 C1 Muang Nong Laos
89 A6 Muang Ou Nua Laos
95 B1 Muang Pakxan Laos
95 C1 Muang Phalan Laos
95 B1 Muang Phiang Laos
95 C1 Muang Phin Laos
95 B1 Muang Phôn-Hông Laos
95 B1 Muang Souy Laos
95 B1 Muang Vangviang Laos
95 B1 Muang Xaignabouri Laos
89 B6 Muang Xay Laos
89 B6 Muang Xon Laos
92 C6 Muar Malaysia
95 B4 Muar *r.* Malaysia
92 C7 Muarabungo Indon.
92 C7 Muaradua Indon.
92 B7 Muarasiberut Indon.
92 C7 Muaratembesi Indon.
85 E4 Mubarakpur India
81 H7 Mubarraz *w.* Saudi Arabia
102 D3 Mubende Uganda
101 D3 Mubi Nigeria
45 A4 Mucajaí *r.* Brazil
45 A5 Mucajaí, Serra do *mts*
Brazil
103 D5 Muchinga Escarpment
escarpment Zambia
89 B4 Muchuan China
57 B4 Muck *i.* U.K.
116 C6 Muckadilla Austr.
57 □ Muckle Roe *i.* U.K.
45 B4 Muco *r.* Col.
103 C5 Muconda Angola
45 E4 Mucucuaú *r.* Brazil
80 E2 Mucur Turkey
46 E2 Mucuri Brazil
46 E2 Mucuri *r.* Brazil
103 C5 Mucussueje Angola
95 B4 Muda *r.* Malaysia
87 N3 Mudanjiang China
90 A2 Mudan Jiang *r.* China
80 B1 Mudanya Turkey
81 L7 Mudayrah Kuwait
32 C5 Muddlety U.S.A.
54 R3 Muddus Nationalpark
nat. park Sweden

35 G2 Muddy Creek *r.* U.S.A.
35 E3 Muddy Peak *summit*
U.S.A.
115 H4 Mudgee Austr.
84 C3 Mudki India
34 C3 Mud Lake *l.* U.S.A.
95 A1 Mudon Myanmar
80 C1 Mudurnu Turkey
68 F2 Mud'yuga Rus. Fed.
103 D5 Mueda Moz.
68 H1 Muftyuga Rus. Fed.
103 C5 Mufulira Zambia
103 C5 Mufumbwe Zambia
89 A6 Mufu Shan *mts* China
33 K2 Mugaguadavic Lake
l. Can.
81 M2 Muğan Düzü *lowland*
Azer.
85 F2 Mugarripug China
Mughalbhin *see* Jati
85 E4 Mughal Sarai India
80 F7 Mughayra' Saudi Arabia
80 B3 Muğla Turkey
85 H2 Mug Qu *r.* China
85 H2 Mugu Karnali *r.* Nepal
84 B4 Muhammad Ashraf Pak.
101 F2 Muhammad Qol Sudan
119 C3 Mühlig-Hofman
Mountains *mts* Antarctica
54 T4 Muhos Fin.
102 C4 Muhulu Dem. Rep. Congo
95 C3 Mui Ca Mau *c.* Vietnam
95 C3 Mui Dinh *hd* Vietnam
95 D2 Mui Nây *pt* Vietnam
60 E5 Muine Bheag
Rep. of Ireland
57 D5 Muirkirk U.K.
57 H2 Muirneag *h.* U.K.
57 D3 Muir of Ord U.K.
34 A3 Muir Woods National
Monument *res.* U.S.A.
105 D5 Muite Moz.
69 B5 Mukacheve Ukr.
92 E6 Mukah Malaysia
85 F3 Mükangsar China
95 C1 Mukdahan Thai.
112 C6 Mukinbudin Austr.
92 C7 Mukomuko Indon.
84 C3 Muktsar India
21 K4 Mukutawa *r.* Can.
30 C4 Mukwonago U.S.A.
84 D5 Mul India
84 A3 Mula *r.* Pak.
83 D10 Mulakatholhu Atoll *atoll*
Maldives
90 A2 Mulan China
94 B3 Mulanay Phil.
103 D5 Mulanje, Mt *mt* Malawi
27 E5 Mulberry U.S.A.
47 B3 Mulchén Chile
62 F5 Mulde *r.* Ger.
102 D4 Muleba Tanz.
35 H5 Mule Creek *NM* U.S.A.
24 F3 Mule Creek *WY* U.S.A.
27 C5 Muleshoe U.S.A.
65 E4 Mulhacén *mt* Spain
61 E3 Mülheim an der Ruhr
Ger.
64 H3 Mulhouse France
89 B4 Muli China
90 B2 Muling China
90 B2 Muling China
90 B2 Muling *r.* China
57 C4 Mull *i.* U.K.
57 B4 Mull, Sound of *chan.*
U.K.
81 M3 Mulla Ali Iran
60 B5 Mullaghareirk Mts *h.*
Rep. of Ireland
115 H3 Mullaley Austr.
115 G3 Mullengudgery Austr.
30 E3 Mullett Lake *l.* U.S.A.
112 C5 Mullewa Austr.
57 F1 Mull Head *hd* U.K.
33 F5 Mullica *r.* U.S.A.
60 D4 Mullingar Rep. of Ireland
115 H4 Mullion Cr. Austr.
57 D6 Mull of Galloway *c.* U.K.
57 C5 Mull of Kintyre *hd* U.K.
57 B5 Mull of Oa *hd* U.K.
103 C5 Mulobezi Zambia
84 D5 Multai India
84 B3 Multan Pak.
55 T5 Multia Fin.
61 A5 Multien *reg.* France
83 D7 Mumbai India
115 H4 Mumbil Austr.
103 C5 Mumbwa Zambia
69 H6 Mumra Rus. Fed.
95 C2 Mun, Mae Nam *r.* Thai.
93 G8 Muna *i.* Indon.
36 G4 Muna Mex.
77 N3 Muna *r.* Rus. Fed.
54 Munaðarnes Iceland
München *see* Munich
45 A4 Munchique, Co *mt* Col.
20 D3 Muncho Lake Can.
20 D3 Muncho Lake Provincial
Park *res.* Can.
30 E5 Muncie U.S.A.
32 E4 Muncy U.S.A.
59 J5 Mundesley U.K.
59 H5 Mundford U.K.
112 E6 Mundrabilla Austr.
116 D5 Mundubbera Austr.
84 C4 Mundwa India
116 B6 Mungallala Austr.
115 G2 Mungallala Cr. *r.* Austr.
116 A1 Mungana Austr.
84 D4 Mungaoli India
102 C3 Mungbere
Dem. Rep. Congo
85 E5 Mungeli India

85 F4 Munger India
114 C2 Mungeranie Austr.
95 D5 Mungguresak, Tanjung
pt Indon.
115 H2 Mungindi Austr.
62 E6 Munich Ger.
43 K4 Munim *r.* Brazil
30 D2 Munising U.S.A.
55 M7 Munkedal Sweden
54 V2 Munkelva Norway
55 N7 Munkfors Sweden
105 H1 Munnik S. Africa
115 H8 Munro, Mt *mt* Austr.
62 C7 Münsingen Switz.
62 C5 Münster Ger.
62 E4 Münster Ger.
61 F3 Münsterland *reg.* Ger.
23 H3 Muntviel, Lac *l.* Can.
54 V4 Muojärvi *l.* Fin.
95 C1 Mường Lam Vietnam
89 B6 Mường Nhie Vietnam
54 S3 Muonio Fin.
54 S2 Muonioälven *r.*
Fin./Sweden
88 F2 Muping China
102 E3 Muqdisho Somalia
81 M1 Müqtädir Azer.
81 J2 Muradiye Turkey
90 F5 Murakami Japan
114 F6 Murchison Austr.
112 C5 Murchison *watercourse*
Austr.
102 D3 Murchison Falls National
Park *nat. park* Uganda
65 F4 Murcia Spain
65 F4 Murcia *div.* Spain
26 C3 Murdo U.S.A.
23 G4 Murdochville Can.
103 D5 Murehwa Zimbabwe
63 M7 Mureş *r.* Romania
64 E5 Muret France
29 E4 Murfreesboro *NC* U.S.A.
29 C5 Murfreesboro *TN* U.S.A.
84 B3 Murgha Kibzai Pak.
79 L2 Murghob Tajik.
84 B2 Murgh Pass *pass* Afgh.
116 D6 Murgon Austr.
88 A2 Muri China
85 F5 Muri India
46 D3 Muriaé Brazil
103 C4 Muriege Angola
62 F4 Müritz *l.* Ger.
54 X2 Murmansk Rus. Fed.
54 W2 Murmanskaya Oblast'
admin. div. Rus. Fed.
66 G6 Muro, Capo di *pt* France
68 G4 Murom Rus. Fed.
90 G3 Muroran Japan
65 B1 Muros Spain
91 D8 Muroto Japan
91 D8 Muroto-zaki *pt* Japan
24 C3 Murphy *ID* U.S.A.
29 D5 Murphy *NC* U.S.A.
34 B2 Murphys U.S.A.
115 G2 Murra Murra Austr.
114 D5 Murray Austr.
20 E3 Murray *r.* Can.
28 B4 Murray *KY* U.S.A.
24 E3 Murray *UT* U.S.A.
29 D5 Murray, L. *l.* U.S.A.
110 E2 Murray, Lake *l.* P.N.G.
114 C5 Murray Bridge Austr.
104 E5 Murraysburg S. Africa
L3 Murray Seascarp
sea feature Pac. Oc.
114 D5 Murrayville Austr.
115 H5 Murrumbidgee *r.* Austr.
60 B4 Murrisk *reg.*
Rep. of Ireland
60 B4 Murroogh Rep. of Ireland
115 H5 Murrumbateman Austr.
114 F5 Murrumbidgee *r.*
Austr.
103 D5 Murrupula Moz.
115 J3 Murrurundi Austr.
66 G1 Murska Sobota Slovenia
114 D2 Murteree, Lake *salt flat*
Austr.
114 E6 Murtoa Austr.
83 D7 Murud India
117 F3 Murupara N.Z.
109 Mururoa *atoll* Pac. Oc.
84 E5 Murwara India
115 K2 Murwillumbah Austr.
101 E2 Murzūq Libya
62 G7 Mürzzuschlag Austria
81 H2 Muş Turkey
84 B3 Musa Khel Bazar Pak.
67 K3 Musala *mt* Bulg.
95 A5 Musala *i.* Indon.
90 A3 Musan N. Korea
79 H5 Muscat Oman
30 B5 Muscatine U.S.A.
30 A4 Muscoda U.S.A.
33 J3 Muscongus Bay
b. U.S.A.
113 H3 Musgrave Austr.
112 F5 Musgrave Ranges *mts*
Austr.
60 C5 Musheramore *h.*
Rep. of Ireland
102 B3 Mushie Dem. Rep. Congo
92 D7 Musi *r.* Indon.
35 F4 Music Mt *mt* U.S.A.

35 G2 Musinia Peak *summit*
U.S.A.
20 E2 Muskeg *r.* Can.
33 H4 Muskeget Channel *chan.*
U.S.A.
30 D4 Muskegon U.S.A.
30 D4 Muskegon *r.* U.S.A.
32 C5 Muskingum *r.* U.S.A.
27 E5 Muskogee U.S.A.
31 H3 Muskoka Can.
31 H3 Muskoka, Lake
l. Can.
20 E2 Muskwa *r.* Can.
79 K3 Muslimbagh Pak.
80 F3 Muslimīyah Syria
101 F3 Musmar Sudan
102 D4 Musoma Tanz.
110 E2 Mussau I. *i.* P.N.G.
57 E5 Musselburgh U.K.
24 E2 Musselshell *r.* U.S.A.
80 B1 Mustafakemalpaşa
Turkey
55 S7 Mustjala Estonia
90 A4 Musu-dan *pt* N. Korea
115 J4 Muswellbrook Austr.
78 B4 Mut Egypt
80 D3 Mut Turkey
46 E1 Mutá, Pta do *pt* Brazil
103 D5 Mutare Zimbabwe
93 G8 Mutis, G. *mt* Indon.
114 D4 Mutooroo Austr.
103 D5 Mutorashanga
Zimbabwe
90 G4 Mutsu Japan
90 G4 Mutsu-wan *b.* Japan
116 A4 Muttaburra Austr.
117 A7 Muttonbird Islands *is*
N.Z.
60 B5 Mutton Island *i.*
Rep. of Ireland
103 D5 Mutuali Moz.
46 C1 Mutunópolis Brazil
54 U2 Mutusjärvi *r.* Fin.
54 T3 Muurola Fin.
88 C2 Mu Us Shamo *des.*
China
103 B4 Muxaluando Angola
68 E2 Muyezerskiy Rus. Fed.
102 D4 Muyinga Burundi
102 C4 Muyumba
Dem. Rep. Congo
82 C2 Muyunkum, Peski *des.*
Kazak.
88 D4 Muyuping China
84 C2 Muzaffarabad Pak.
84 C3 Muzaffargarh Pak.
84 D3 Muzaffarnagar India
85 F4 Muzaffarpur India
105 K1 Muzamane Moz.
20 C4 Muzon, C. *c.* U.S.A.
27 C6 Múzquiz Mex.
84 E2 Muztag *mt* China
85 F1 Muztag *mt* China
101 E4 Mvolo Sudan
102 D4 Mvomero Tanz.
103 D5 Mvuma Zimbabwe
Mwali *i. see* Moheli
103 C4 Mwanza Dem. Rep. Congo
102 D4 Mwanza Tanz.
60 B4 Mweelrea *h.*
Rep. of Ireland
102 C4 Mweka Dem. Rep. Congo
103 C5 Mwenda Zambia
102 C4 Mwene-Ditu
Dem. Rep. Congo
103 D6 Mwenezi Zimbabwe
103 C4 Mweru, Lake *l.*
Dem. Rep. Congo/Zambia
103 C4 Mwimba Dem. Rep. Congo
103 C5 Mwinilunga Zambia
68 C4 Myadzyel Belarus
85 H5 Myaing Myanmar
84 B4 Myājlār India
115 K4 Myall L. *l.* Austr.
83 J7 Myanaung Myanmar
70 Myanmar *country* Asia
91 B9 Myanoura-dake *mt*
Japan
57 E2 Mybster U.K.
85 H5 Myebon Myanmar
83 J6 Myingyan Myanmar
95 A2 Myinmoletkat *mt*
Myanmar
82 J5 Myitkyina Myanmar
95 A2 Myitta Myanmar
85 H5 Myittha *r.* Myanmar
69 K6 Mykolayiv Ukr.
67 L6 Mykonos Greece
67 L6 Mykonos *i.* Greece
76 S3 Myla Rus. Fed.
85 G4 Mymensingh Bangl.
55 S5 Mynämäki Fin.
85 H5 Myohaung Myanmar
90 A4 Myŏnggan N. Korea
68 A4 Myory Belarus
54 D5 Mýrdalsjökull *ice cap*
Iceland
54 O2 Myre Norway
54 R4 Myrheden Sweden
69 D5 Myrhorod Ukr.
69 D5 Myronivka Ukr.
29 E5 Myrtle Beach U.S.A.
115 G6 Myrtleford Austr.
24 A3 Myrtle Point U.S.A.
62 G4 Myślibórz Pol.
83 E8 Mysore India
77 U3 Mys Shmidta Rus. Fed.
33 F5 Mystic Island U.S.A.
95 C5 My Tho Vietnam
67 M5 Mytilini Greece
67 F4 Mytishchi Rus. Fed.
105 G5 Mzamomhle S. Africa
103 D5 Mzimba Malawi
103 D5 Mzuzu Malawi

N

89 B6 Na, Nam r. China/Vietnam
34 □² Naalehu U.S.A.
55 S6 Naantali Fin.
60 E4 Naas Rep. of Ireland
104 B4 Nababeep S. Africa
91 E7 Nabari Japan
94 B4 Nabas Phil.
80 E5 Nabatiyet et Tahta Lebanon
102 D4 Naberera Tanz.
76 G4 Naberezhnyye Chelny Rus. Fed.
101 D1 Nabeul Tunisia
84 D3 Nabha India
115 K4 Nabiac Austr.
93 K7 Nabire Indon.
80 E5 Näblus West Bank
105 H2 Naboomspruit S. Africa
95 A2 Nabule Myanmar
103 E5 Nacala Moz.
24 B2 Naches U.S.A.
84 B4 Nachna India
34 B4 Nacimiento Reservoir resr U.S.A.
27 E6 Nacogdoches U.S.A.
36 C2 Nacozari de García Mex.
84 C5 Nadiad India
100 B1 Nador Morocco
69 C5 Nadvirna Ukr.
76 E3 Nadvoitsy Rus. Fed.
76 J3 Nadym Rus. Fed.
55 M9 Næstved Denmark
67 J5 Nafpaktos Greece
67 K6 Nafplio Greece
81 K5 Naft Khāneh Iraq
81 K4 Naft Shahr Iran
85 G2 Nag, Co l. China
94 B3 Naga Phil.
22 D4 Nagagami r. Can.
91 C8 Nagahama Japan
85 H4 Naga Hills mts India
91 G5 Nagai Japan
85 H4 Nagaland div. India
114 F6 Nagambie Austr.
91 F6 Nagano Japan
91 F6 Nagaoka Japan
85 H4 Nagaon India
84 D2 Nagar India
84 Nagar Parkar Pak.
85 G3 Nagarzê China
91 A8 Nagasaki Japan
91 B7 Nagato Japan
84 C4 Nagaur India
84 C5 Nagda India
83 E9 Nagercoil India
79 K4 Nagha Kalat Pak.
84 D3 Nagina India
85 E3 Nagma Nepal
68 J3 Nagorsk Rus. Fed.
91 E7 Nagoya Japan
84 D5 Nagpur India
85 H3 Nagqu China
94 C3 Nagumbuaya Point pt Phil.
76 F1 Nagurskoye Rus. Fed.
66 L2 Nagyatád Hungary
62 H7 Nagykanizsa Hungary
87 N6 Naha Japan
84 D3 Nahan India
20 E2 Nahanni Butte Can.
20 D2 Nahanni National Park nat. park Can.
80 E5 Nahariyya Israel
81 M4 Nahāvand Iran
81 L6 Nahr 'Umr Iraq
47 B3 Nahuelbuta, Parque Nacional nat. park Chile
47 B4 Nahuel Huapí, L. Arg.
47 C5 Nahuel Huapí, Parque Nacional nat. park Arg.
29 D6 Nahunta U.S.A.
27 B7 Naica Mex.
85 H2 Naij Tal China
23 H2 Nain Can.
79 G3 Nā'īn Iran
84 D3 Naini Tal India
84 E5 Nainpur India
57 E3 Nairn U.K.
31 G2 Nairn Centre Can.
102 D4 Nairobi Kenya
102 D4 Naivasha Kenya
78 E4 Najd reg. Saudi Arabia
65 E1 Nájera Spain
84 D3 Najibabad India
87 O3 Najin N. Korea
78 E6 Najrān Saudi Arabia
91 A8 Nakadōri-shima i. Japan
95 C1 Na Kae Thai.
91 B8 Nakama Japan
91 C8 Nakamura Japan
77 M3 Nakanno Rus. Fed.
91 F6 Nakano Japan
91 A10 Nakano-shima i. Japan
91 C6 Nakano-shima i. Japan
84 B2 Naka Pass Afgh.
91 B8 Nakatsu Japan
91 E7 Nakatsugawa Japan
102 D2 Nakfa Eritrea
80 D7 Nakhl Egypt
87 O3 Nakhodka Rus. Fed.
95 B2 Nakhon Nayok Thai.
95 B2 Nakhon Pathom Thai.
95 C1 Nakhon Phanom Thai.
95 B2 Nakhon Ratchasima Thai.
95 B2 Nakhon Sawan Thai.
95 A3 Nakhon Si Thammarat Thai.
84 B5 Nakhtarana India
20 C3 Nakina B.C. Can.
22 C3 Nakina Ont. Can.

103 D4 Nakonde Zambia
55 M9 Nakskov Denmark
102 D4 Nakuru Kenya
20 F4 Nakusp Can.
105 K2 Nalázi Moz.
85 G4 Nalbari India
69 G7 Nal'chik Rus. Fed.
80 C1 Nallıhan Turkey
100 D1 Nālūt Libya
105 K2 Namaacha Moz.
105 H3 Namahadi S. Africa
79 H3 Namakzar-e Shadad salt flat Iran
102 D4 Namanga Kenya
79 L1 Namangan Uzbek.
103 D5 Namapa Moz.
104 B3 Namaqualand reg. Namibia
104 B4 Namaqualand reg. S. Africa
81 K3 Namashīr Iran
110 F2 Namatanai P.N.G.
115 K1 Nambour Austr.
115 K3 Nambucca Heads Austr.
95 C3 Năm Căn Vietnam
86 F5 Nam Co salt l. China
54 N4 Namdalen v. Norway
54 M4 Namdalseid Norway
89 C6 Nam Đinh Vietnam
30 B3 Namekagon r. U.S.A.
21 J4 Namew Lake l. Can.
103 B6 Namib Desert des. Namibia
103 B5 Namibe Angola
96 Namibia country Africa
91 G6 Namie Japan
85 H3 Namjagbarwa Feng mt China
93 H7 Namlea Indon.
95 A1 Nammekon Myanmar
115 H3 Namoi r. Austr.
20 F3 Nampa Can.
84 E3 Nampa mt Nepal
24 C3 Nampa U.S.A.
100 B3 Nampala Mali
95 B1 Nam Pat Thai.
95 B1 Nam Phong Thai.
87 N4 Namp'o N. Korea
103 D5 Nampula Moz.
86 G6 Namrup India
85 E3 Namsê La pass Nepal
54 N4 Namsen r. Norway
85 H4 Namsi India
85 G3 Namsi La pass Bhutan
54 M4 Namsos Norway
92 B4 Nam Tok Thai.
77 O3 Namtsy Rus. Fed.
83 J6 Namtu Myanmar
61 C4 Namur Belgium
103 C5 Namwala Zambia
95 B1 Nan Thai.
95 B2 Nan, Mae Nam r. Thai.
102 B3 Nana Bakassa C.A.R.
20 E5 Nanaimo Can.
34 □¹ Nanakuli U.S.A.
90 A4 Nanam N. Korea
89 F5 Nan'an China
116 E6 Nanango Austr.
104 B2 Nananib Plateau plat. Namibia
89 E6 Nan'ao China
91 E6 Nanao Japan
91 E6 Nanatsu-shima i. Japan
88 C4 Nanbu China
90 A1 Nancha China
89 E4 Nanchang Jiangxi China
89 F4 Nanchang Jiangxi China
89 E5 Nancheng China
88 C4 Nanchong China
89 C4 Nanchuan China
64 H2 Nancy France
84 E3 Nanda Devi mt India
84 E3 Nanda Kot mt India
89 C5 Nandan China
83 E7 Nänded India
115 J3 Nandewar Range mts Austr.
84 C5 Nandgaon India
89 D6 Nandu Jiang r. China
84 C5 Nandurbar India
83 E7 Nandyal India
89 D6 Nanfeng Guangdong China
89 E5 Nanfeng Jiangxi China
85 H3 Nang China
101 D4 Nanga Eboko Cameroon
90 A3 Nangang Shan mts China/N. Korea
84 C2 Nanga Parbat mt Jammu and Kashmir
95 A3 Nangin Myanmar
88 E2 Nangong China
103 D4 Nangulangwa Tanz.
88 A2 Nanhua China
88 D4 Nanhui China
88 C3 Nanjiang China
89 E5 Nanjing Fujian China
88 F3 Nanjing Jiangsu China
89 E5 Nanjing Jiangsu China
Nanking see Nanjing
91 C8 Nankoku Japan
103 B5 Nankova Angola
88 C5 Nanle China
88 F4 Nanling China
89 D5 Nan Ling mts China
89 C6 Nanliu Jiang r. China
89 D6 Nanning China
89 E6 Nan'oa Dao i. China
95 B1 Na Noi Thai.
89 C5 Nanpan Jiang r. China
88 D6 Nanpara India
88 F3 Nanpiao China
89 F5 Nanping Fujian China
88 B3 Nanping Sichuan China

89 F5 Nanri Dao i. China
87 N7 Nansei-shotō is Japan
64 D3 Nantes France
31 G4 Nanticoke Can.
33 F5 Nanticoke r. U.S.A.
20 G4 Nanton Can.
88 F4 Nantong Jiangsu China
88 F3 Nantong Jiangsu China
89 F6 Nant'ou Taiwan
33 H4 Nantucket U.S.A.
33 H4 Nantucket I. i. U.S.A.
33 H4 Nantucket Sound g. U.S.A.
59 E4 Nantwich U.K.
111 H2 Nanumanga i. Tuvalu
111 H2 Nanumea i. Tuvalu
46 E2 Nanuque Brazil
94 C5 Nanusa, Kepulauan is Indon.
112 C4 Nanutarra Roadhouse Austr.
89 B4 Nanxi China
89 D4 Nanxian China
89 E5 Nanxiong China
88 D3 Nanyang China
88 D4 Nanzhang China
88 D3 Nanzhao China
23 J3 Naococane, Lac l. Can.
85 G4 Naogaon Bangl.
84 B4 Naokot Pak.
90 C1 Naoli r. China
84 C2 Naoshera Jammu and Kashmir
89 D6 Naozhou Dao i. China
34 A2 Napa U.S.A.
33 K1 Napadogan Can.
31 J3 Napanee Can.
84 C4 Napasar India
30 C5 Naperville U.S.A.
117 F3 Napier N.Z.
33 G2 Napierville Can.
66 F4 Naples Italy
29 D7 Naples FL U.S.A.
33 H3 Naples ME U.S.A.
89 B6 Napo China
42 D4 Napo r. Ecuador/Peru
32 A4 Napoleon U.S.A.
Napoli see Naples
47 D3 Naposta Arg.
47 D3 Naposta r. Arg.
30 E5 Nappanee U.S.A.
81 K3 Naqadeh Iran
81 M4 Naqqash Iran
91 D7 Nara Japan
100 B3 Nara Mali
63 N3 Narach Belarus
114 D6 Naracoorte Austr.
115 G4 Naradhan Austr.
84 C4 Naraina India
84 E6 Narainpur India
86 B2 Narasapur India
85 F5 Narasinghapur India
95 A3 Narathiwat Thai.
Narbada r. see Narmada
59 C6 Narberth U.K.
64 F5 Narbonne France
65 C1 Narcea r. Spain
66 H4 Nardò Italy
47 E1 Nare Arg.
84 B3 Narechi r. Pak.
12 E4 Nares Deep sea feature Atlantic Ocean
63 K4 Narew r. Pol.
84 A3 Nari r. Pak.
103 B6 Narib Namibia
104 B5 Nariep S. Africa
69 H6 Narimanov Rus. Fed.
84 B1 Narin Afgh.
84 B1 Narin reg. Afgh.
80 D3 Narince Turkey
85 H1 Narin Gol watercourse China
91 F7 Narita Japan
25 E7 Narizon, Punta pt Mex.
84 C5 Narmada r. India
81 H1 Narman Turkey
84 D3 Naraul India
66 E3 Narni Italy
63 O5 Narodychi Ukr.
68 F4 Naro-Fominsk Rus. Fed.
115 J6 Narooma Austr.
68 G4 Narovchat Rus. Fed.
69 D5 Narowlya Belarus
55 N5 Närpes Fin.
115 H3 Narrabri Austr.
33 H4 Narragansett Bay b. U.S.A.
115 G5 Narran r. Austr.
115 G5 Narrandera Austr.
115 G2 Narran L. l. Austr.
112 C6 Narrogin Austr.
115 H4 Narromine Austr.
21 J4 Narrow Hills Provincial Park res. Can.
32 C6 Narrows U.S.A.
33 F4 Narrowsburg U.S.A.
84 D5 Narsimhapur India
85 G5 Narsingdi Bangl.
84 D5 Narsinghgarh India
88 E1 Nart China
91 D7 Naruto Japan
55 V7 Narva Estonia
55 U7 Narva Bay b. Estonia/Rus. Fed.
94 B3 Narvacan Phil.
54 P2 Narvik Norway
55 V7 Narvskoye Vdkhr. resr Estonia/Rus. Fed.
84 D3 Narwana India
84 D4 Narwar India
76 G3 Nar'yan-Mar Rus. Fed.
82 E2 Naryn Kyrgyzstan
54 P5 Näsåker Sweden
35 H3 Naschitti U.S.A.

117 C6 Naseby N.Z.
84 C5 Nashik India
30 A4 Nashua IA U.S.A.
33 H3 Nashua NH U.S.A.
29 C4 Nashville U.S.A.
80 F5 Nasib Syria
55 S6 Näsijärvi l. Fin.
101 F4 Nasir Sudan
Nasirabad see Mymensingh
84 B3 Nasirabad Pak.
103 C5 Nasondoye Dem. Rep. Congo
80 C6 Nasr Egypt
Nasratabad see Zābol
81 L5 Naşrīan-e-Pā'īn Iran
20 D3 Nass r. Can.
29 E7 Nassau Bahamas
37 J3 Nassau Bahamas
78 C5 Nasser, Lake resr Egypt
55 O8 Nässjö Sweden
22 E2 Nastapoca r. Can.
22 E2 Nastapoka Islands is Can.
91 F6 Nasu-dake vol. Japan
94 B3 Nasugbu Phil.
63 P2 Nasva Rus. Fed.
103 C6 Nata Botswana
102 D4 Nata Tanz.
45 B4 Natagaima Col.
43 L5 Natal Brazil
Natal div. see Kwazulu-Natal
13 G6 Natal Basin sea feature Indian Ocean
23 H3 Natashquan Can.
23 H3 Natashquan r. Can.
27 E6 Natchez U.S.A.
27 E6 Natchitoches U.S.A.
114 F6 Nathalia Austr.
84 C4 Nathdwara India
34 D5 National City U.S.A.
100 C3 Natitingou Benin
116 B4 Native Companion Cr. r. Austr.
43 J6 Natividade Brazil
25 E6 Nátora Mex.
90 G5 Natori Japan
102 D4 Natron, Lake salt l. Tanz.
95 A1 Nattaung mt Myanmar
92 D6 Natuna, Kepulauan is Indon.
92 D6 Natuna Besar i. Indon.
33 F2 Natural Bridge U.S.A.
35 G3 Natural Bridges National Monument res. U.S.A.
13 M6 Naturaliste Plateau sea feature Indian Ocean
35 H2 Naturita U.S.A.
30 E2 Naubinway U.S.A.
103 B6 Nauchas Namibia
33 G4 Naugatuck U.S.A.
94 B3 Naujan Phil.
94 B3 Naujan, L. l. Phil.
55 S8 Naujoji Akmenė Lith.
84 C4 Naukh India
95 A1 Naungpale Myanmar
80 E6 Na'ūr Jordan
106 Nauru country Pac. Oc.
84 B4 Naushara Pak.
55 J6 Naustdal Norway
42 D4 Nauta Peru
104 B3 Naute Dam dam Namibia
36 E4 Nautla Mex.
85 G5 Navadwip India
68 C4 Navahrudak Belarus
35 H4 Navajo U.S.A.
25 F4 Navajo Lake l. U.S.A.
35 G3 Navajo Mt mt U.S.A.
94 C4 Naval Phil.
65 D3 Navalmoral de la Mata Spain
65 D3 Navalvillar de Pela Spain
60 E4 Navan Rep. of Ireland
68 D4 Navapolatsk Belarus
77 T3 Navarin, Mys c. Rus. Fed.
44 C9 Navarino, I. i. Chile
65 F1 Navarra div. Spain
114 E6 Navarre Austr.
34 A2 Navarro U.S.A.
68 G4 Navashino Rus. Fed.
27 D6 Navasota U.S.A.
57 D2 Naver, Loch l. U.K.
54 O5 Näverede Sweden
47 B2 Navidad Chile
68 E4 Navlya Rus. Fed.
67 N2 Năvodari Romania
79 K1 Navoi Uzbek.
36 C3 Navojoa Mex.
68 G3 Navoloki Rus. Fed.
84 C5 Navsari India
84 C4 Nawa India
80 F5 Nawá Syria
85 G4 Nawabganj Bangl.
84 B4 Nawabshah Pak.
85 F4 Nawada India
84 B3 Nawah Afgh.
84 C4 Nawalgarh India
81 K2 Naxçıvan Azer.
89 C4 Naxi China
67 L6 Naxos Greece
67 L6 Naxos i. Greece
45 A4 Naya Col.
85 F5 Nayagarh India
90 H2 Nayoro Japan
46 E1 Nazaré Brazil
80 E5 Nazareth Israel
36 C3 Nazas Mex.
36 D3 Nazas r. Mex.
42 D6 Nazca Peru
15 O7 Nazca Ridge sea feature Pac. Oc.
81 M5 Nazian Iran

81 K2 Nāzīk Iran
81 J2 Nazik Gölü l. Turkey
80 B3 Nazilli Turkey
81 G2 Nazımiye Turkey
85 H4 Nazira India
20 E4 Nazko Can.
20 E4 Nazko r. Can.
81 K3 Näzlü r. Iran
69 H7 Nazran' Rus. Fed.
102 D3 Nazrēt Eth.
79 H5 Nazwá Oman
103 C4 Nchelenge Zambia
103 C6 Ncojane Botswana
103 B4 N'dalatando Angola
102 C3 Ndélé C.A.R.
102 B4 Ndendé Gabon
111 G3 Ndeni i. Solomon Is
101 D3 Ndjamena Chad
103 C5 Ndola Zambia
105 J4 Ndwedwe S. Africa
115 G1 Neabul Cr. r. Austr.
60 E3 Neagh, Lough l. U.K.
24 A1 Neah Bay U.S.A.
112 F4 Neale, L. salt flat Austr.
114 B2 Neales watercourse Austr.
67 K5 Nea Liosia Greece
67 K6 Neapoli Greece
59 D6 Neath U.K.
59 D6 Neath r. U.K.
115 G1 Nebine Cr. r. Austr.
79 G2 Nebitdag Turkm.
45 D4 Neblina, Pico da mt Brazil
116 C3 Nebo Austr.
35 G2 Nebo, Mount mt U.S.A.
68 E3 Nebolchi Rus. Fed.
26 E3 Nebraska div. U.S.A.
26 E3 Nebraska City U.S.A.
66 F6 Nebrodi, Monti mts Italy
27 E6 Neches r. U.S.A.
45 B3 Nechí r. Col.
102 D3 Nechisar National Park nat. park Eth.
14 J4 Necker I. U.S.A.
47 E3 Necochea Arg.
22 F2 Nedlouc, Lac l. Can.
54 R2 Nedre Soppero Sweden
35 E4 Needles U.S.A.
30 C3 Neenah U.S.A.
21 K4 Neepawa Can.
61 D3 Neerijnen Neth.
81 M2 Neftçala Azer.
76 G4 Neftekamsk Rus. Fed.
69 H6 Neftekumsk Rus. Fed.
76 J3 Nefteyugansk Rus. Fed.
55 C5 Nefyn U.K.
66 C6 Nefza Tunisia
102 B4 Negage Angola
102 D3 Negēlē Eth.
46 A3 Negla r. Para.
103 D5 Negomane Moz.
83 E9 Negombo Sri Lanka
67 K4 Negotino Macedonia
42 C5 Negra, Cordillera mts Peru
42 D3 Negra, Pta pt Peru
66 B7 Négrine Alg.
42 B6 Negritos Peru
47 D4 Negro r. Arg.
46 A2 Negro r. Brazil
42 F4 Negro r. S. America
94 B3 Negros i. Phil.
67 N3 Negru Vodă Romania
81 M4 Nehavand Iran
87 M2 Nehe China
89 B4 Neijiang China
21 H4 Neilburg Can.
87 J3 Nei Mongol Zizhiqu div. China
62 G5 Neiße r. Ger./Pol.
45 B4 Neiva Col.
88 D3 Neixiang China
21 K3 Nejanilini Lake l. Can.
102 D3 Nek'emtē Eth.
90 E2 Nekrasovka Rus. Fed.
55 O9 Neksø Denmark
68 E3 Nelidovo Rus. Fed.
26 D3 Neligh U.S.A.
77 Q3 Nel'kan Rus. Fed.
77 P4 Nel'kan Rus. Fed.
83 E8 Nellore India
20 F5 Nelson Can.
21 L3 Nelson r. Can.
117 D4 Nelson N.Z.
58 E4 Nelson U.K.
35 E4 Nelson U.S.A.
114 D7 Nelson, C. c. Austr.
44 B8 Nelson, Estrecho chan. Chile
115 K4 Nelson Bay Austr.
20 E3 Nelson Forks Can.
21 K3 Nelson House Can.
105 J2 Nelspruit S. Africa
100 B3 Néma Mauritania
68 J3 Nema Rus. Fed.
30 A2 Nemadji r. U.S.A.
84 B2 Neman Rus. Fed.
68 G3 Nemda r. Rus. Fed.
68 K2 Nemed Rus. Fed.
31 F2 Nemegos Can.
54 W2 Nemetskiy, Mys c. Rus. Fed.
64 F2 Nemours France
81 J2 Nemrut Dağı h. Turkey
90 J3 Nemuro Japan
90 J3 Nemuro-kaikyō chan. Japan
69 D5 Nemyriv Ukr.
60 C5 Nenagh Rep. of Ireland
59 H5 Nene r. U.K.
87 M2 Nenjiang China
61 E5 Nennig Ger.
68 F1 Nenoksa Rus. Fed.
27 E4 Neosho U.S.A.

26 E4 Neosho r. U.S.A.
70 Nepal country Asia
31 K3 Nepean Can.
35 G2 Nephi U.S.A.
60 B3 Nephin h. Rep. of Ireland
60 B3 Nephin Beg Range h. Rep. of Ireland
102 C3 Nepoko r. Dem. Rep. Congo
33 F4 Neptune U.S.A.
64 F4 Nérac France
115 K1 Nerang Austr.
87 L1 Nerchinsk Rus. Fed.
68 G3 Nerekhta Rus. Fed.
66 G3 Neretva r. Bos.-Herz./Croatia
103 C5 Neriquinha Angola
55 T9 Neris r. Lith.
68 F3 Nerl' r. Rus. Fed.
46 C2 Nerópolis Brazil
77 O4 Neryungri Rus. Fed.
55 L6 Nes Norway
55 L6 Nesbyen Norway
54 G4 Neskaupstaður Iceland
54 N3 Nesna Norway
57 D3 Ness, Loch l. U.K.
26 D4 Ness City U.S.A.
20 C3 Nesselrode, Mt mt Can./U.S.A.
67 L4 Nestos r. Greece
80 E5 Netanya Israel
21 N2 Netchek, Cape c. Can.
48 Netherlands country Europe
37 L6 Netherlands Antilles terr. Caribbean
85 G4 Netrakona Bangl.
84 C5 Netrang India
118 A3 Nettilling L. l. Can.
30 A1 Nett Lake U.S.A.
30 A1 Nett Lake l. U.S.A.
62 F4 Neubrandenburg Ger.
62 C7 Neuchâtel Switz.
62 C7 Neuchâtel, Lac de l. Switz.
61 F4 Neuenkirchen-Seelscheid Ger.
61 D5 Neufchâteau Belgium
64 G2 Neufchâteau France
64 E2 Neufchâtel-en-Bray France
21 K2 Neultin Lake l. Can.
119 C2 Neumayer Ger. Base Antarctica
62 D3 Neumünster Ger.
62 H7 Neunkirchen Austria
62 C5 Neunkirchen Ger.
47 C5 Neuquén Arg.
47 C5 Neuquén div. Arg.
47 C5 Neuquén r. Arg.
62 F4 Neuruppin Ger.
29 E5 Neuse r. U.S.A.
62 H7 Neusiedler See l. Austria/Hungary
61 E3 Neuss Ger.
61 F4 Neustadt (Wied) Ger.
62 F4 Neustrelitz Ger.
62 C5 Neuwied Ger.
27 C4 Nevada U.S.A.
34 D2 Nevada div. U.S.A.
65 E4 Nevada, Sierra mts Spain
34 B1 Nevada, Sierra mts U.S.A.
47 C2 Nevado, Cerro mt Arg.
47 C3 Nevado, Sierra del mts Arg.
68 D3 Nevel' Rus. Fed.
64 F3 Nevers France
115 G3 Nevertire Austr.
67 H3 Nevesinje Bos.-Herz.
69 G6 Nevinnomyssk Rus. Fed.
57 C3 Nevis, Loch in. U.K.
80 E2 Nevşehir Turkey
90 F2 Nevskoye Rus. Fed.
35 E4 New r. CA U.S.A.
32 C6 New r. WV U.S.A.
20 D3 New Aiyansh Can.
28 C4 New Albany IN U.S.A.
27 F5 New Albany MS U.S.A.
33 F4 New Albany PA U.S.A.
43 G2 New Amsterdam Guyana
115 G2 New Angledool Austr.
33 F5 Newark DE U.S.A.
33 F5 Newark MD U.S.A.
33 F4 Newark NJ U.S.A.
32 E4 Newark NY U.S.A.
32 B4 Newark OH U.S.A.
33 F4 Newark airport U.S.A.
35 E2 Newark Lake l. U.S.A.
59 G4 Newark-on-Trent U.K.
33 H4 New Bedford U.S.A.
24 B3 Newberg U.S.A.
33 F3 New Berlin U.S.A.
29 E5 New Bern U.S.A.
30 E2 Newberry MI U.S.A.
29 D5 Newberry SC U.S.A.
34 D4 Newberry Springs U.S.A.
58 F2 Newbiggin-by-the-Sea U.K.
29 F6 New Bight Bahamas
31 J3 Newboro Can.
33 G3 New Boston MA U.S.A.
32 B5 New Boston OH U.S.A.
27 D6 New Braunfels U.S.A.
60 E4 Newbridge Rep. of Ireland
110 F2 New Britain i. P.N.G.
33 G3 New Britain U.S.A.
23 G4 New Brunswick div. Can.
33 F4 New Brunswick U.S.A.
30 D5 New Buffalo U.S.A.
57 F3 Newburgh U.K.
33 F4 Newburgh U.S.A.
59 F6 Newbury U.K.
33 H3 Newburyport U.S.A.

58 E3 Newby Bridge U.K.
106 New Caledonia terr. Pac. Oc.
14 F7 New Caledonia Trough sea feature Pac. Oc.
23 G4 New Carlisle Can.
115 J4 Newcastle Austr.
23 G4 Newcastle N.B. Can.
31 H4 Newcastle Ont. Can.
60 E4 Newcastle Rep. of Ireland
105 H3 Newcastle S. Africa
60 F3 Newcastle U.K.
34 B2 Newcastle CA U.S.A.
30 E6 New Castle IN U.S.A.
32 B4 New Castle OH U.S.A.
32 C4 New Castle PA U.S.A.
35 F3 Newcastle UT U.S.A.
32 C6 New Castle VA U.S.A.
24 H3 Newcastle WY U.S.A.
59 C5 Newcastle Emlyn U.K.
59 E4 Newcastle-under-Lyme U.K.
58 F3 Newcastle upon Tyne U.K.
113 F3 Newcastle Waters Austr.
60 B5 Newcastle West Rep. of Ireland
33 F6 New Church U.S.A.
35 H3 Newcomb U.S.A.
57 D5 New Cumnock U.K.
57 F3 New Deer U.K.
84 D3 New Delhi India
33 K1 New Denmark Can.
34 B3 New Don Pedro Reservoir resr U.S.A.
115 J3 New England Range mts Austr.
59 E6 Newent U.K.
23 H4 Newfoundland div. Can.
12 G2 Newfoundland Basin sea feature Atlantic Ocean
24 D3 Newfoundland Evaporation Basin salt l. U.S.A.
57 D5 New Galloway U.K.
111 F2 New Georgia i. Solomon Is
111 F2 New Georgia Islands is Solomon Is
23 H4 New Glasgow Can.
93 L7 New Guinea i. Asia
32 B4 New Hampshire i.
33 G3 New Hampshire div. U.S.A.
30 A4 New Hampton U.S.A.
110 F2 New Hanover i. P.N.G.
105 J4 New Hanover S. Africa
33 G4 New Haven U.S.A.
20 D3 New Hazelton Can.
34 B2 New Hogan Reservoir resr U.S.A.
30 C4 New Holstein U.S.A.
27 F6 New Iberia U.S.A.
105 J2 Newington S. Africa
60 D5 Newinn Rep. of Ireland
110 F2 New Ireland i. P.N.G.
33 F5 New Jersey div. U.S.A.
32 E6 New Kent U.S.A.
32 B5 New Lexington U.S.A.
30 B4 New Lisbon U.S.A.
31 H2 New Liskeard Can.
33 G4 New London CT U.S.A.
30 B5 New London IA U.S.A.
30 B6 New London MO U.S.A.
30 C3 New London WI U.S.A.
112 C4 Newman Austr.
30 D6 Newman U.S.A.
31 H3 Newmarket Can.
60 B5 Newmarket Rep. of Ireland
59 H5 Newmarket U.K.
32 D5 New Market U.S.A.
60 C5 Newmarket on-Fergus Rep. of Ireland
32 C5 New Martinsville U.S.A.
24 C2 New Meadows U.S.A.
34 B3 New Melanes L. l. U.S.A.
25 F5 New Mexico div. U.S.A.
29 C5 Newnan U.S.A.
115 G9 New Norfolk Austr.
27 F6 New Orleans U.S.A.
33 F4 New Paltz U.S.A.
32 C4 New Philadelphia U.S.A.
57 F3 New Pitsligo U.K.
117 E3 New Plymouth N.Z.
60 B4 Newport Mayo Rep. of Ireland
60 C5 Newport Tipperary Rep. of Ireland
59 E5 Newport Eng. U.K.
59 F7 Newport Eng. U.K.
59 D6 Newport Wales U.K.
27 F5 Newport AR U.S.A.
32 A5 Newport KY U.S.A.
33 J2 Newport ME U.S.A.
31 F5 Newport MI U.S.A.
33 G3 Newport NH U.S.A.
24 A2 Newport OR U.S.A.
33 H4 Newport RI U.S.A.
33 G2 Newport VT U.S.A.
24 C1 Newport WA U.S.A.
34 D5 Newport Beach U.S.A.
32 E6 Newport News U.S.A.
59 G5 Newport Pagnell U.K.
29 E7 New Providence i. Bahamas
59 B7 Newquay U.K.
23 G4 New Richmond Can.
30 A3 New Richmond U.S.A.
35 F5 New River U.S.A.
57 F6 New Romney U.K.
59 H7 New Romney U.K.
60 E5 New Ross Rep. of Ireland
60 E3 Newry U.K.

57 E4 New Scone U.K.
30 A5 New Sharon U.S.A.
New Siberia Islands is see Novosibirskiye Ostrova
29 D6 New Smyrna Beach U.S.A.
115 G4 New South Wales div. Austr.
58 E4 Newton U.K.
26 E3 Newton IA U.S.A.
26 D4 Newton KS U.S.A.
33 H3 Newton MA U.S.A.
27 F5 Newton MS U.S.A.
33 F4 Newton NJ U.S.A.
59 D7 Newton Abbot U.K.
57 F3 Newtonhill U.K.
57 D5 Newton Mearns U.K.
57 D6 Newton Stewart U.K.
60 C5 Newtown Rep. of Ireland
59 E5 Newtown U.K.
59 D5 Newtown Wales U.K.
26 C1 New Town U.S.A.
60 F3 Newtownabbey U.K.
60 F3 Newtownards U.K.
60 D3 Newtownbutler U.K.
60 E4 Newtownmountkennedy Rep. of Ireland
57 E5 Newtown St Boswells U.K.
60 D3 Newtownstewart U.K.
26 E2 New Ulm U.S.A.
34 A2 Newville U.S.A.
20 E5 New Westminster Can.
33 G4 New York U.S.A.
33 F4 New York div. U.S.A.
106 N.Z. country Australasia
68 G3 Neya Rus. Fed.
79 G4 Neyriz Iran
79 H2 Neyshābūr Iran
36 F5 Nezahualcóyotl, Presa resr Mex.
102 B4 Ngabé Congo
95 A2 Nga Chong, Khao mt Myanmar/Thai.
94 C6 Ngalipaëng Indon.
103 C6 Ngami, Lake l. Botswana
85 F3 Ngamring China
85 E3 Ngangla Ringco salt l. China
84 E2 Nganglong Kangri mt China
84 E2 Nganglong Kangri mts China
85 F3 Ngangzê Co salt l. China
95 C1 Ngan Sau, Sông r. Vietnam
95 A1 Ngao Thai.
101 D4 Ngaoundéré Cameroon
117 E2 Ngaruawahia N.Z.
117 F3 Ngaruroro r. N.Z.
117 E2 Ngauruhoe vol. N.Z.
92 □ Ngawi Indon.
95 B1 Ngiap r. Laos
102 B4 Ngo Congo
95 C2 Ngoc Linh mt Vietnam
85 F3 Ngoin, Co salt l. China
100 D4 Ngol Bembo Nigeria
85 H2 Ngom Qu r. China
85 F2 Ngoqumaima China
82 J4 Ngoring Hu l. China
101 D3 Ngourti Niger
101 D3 Nguigmi Niger
93 K5 Ngulu i. Micronesia
95 B1 Ngum, Nam r. Laos
92 □ Ngunut Indon.
100 D3 Nguru Nigeria
89 B6 Nguyên Binh Vietnam
104 E2 Ngwaketse div. Botswana
105 G3 Ngwathe S. Africa
105 K3 Ngwavuma r. Swaziland
105 J4 Ngwelezana S. Africa
103 D5 Nhamalabué Moz.
95 D2 Nha Trang Vietnam
114 D6 Nhill Austr.
105 J3 Nhlangano Swaziland
89 B6 Nho Quan Vietnam
113 G2 Nhulunbuy Austr.
21 J4 Niacam Can.
100 B3 Niafounké Mali
30 D3 Niagara U.S.A.
31 H4 Niagara Falls Can.
32 D3 Niagara Falls U.S.A.
31 H4 Niagara River r. Can./U.S.A.
100 C3 Niamey Niger
94 C5 Niampak Indon.
103 D4 Niangandu Tanz.
102 C3 Niangara Dem. Rep. Congo
92 B6 Nias i. Indon.
Niassa, Lago l. see Nyasa, Lake
55 R8 Nica Latvia
16 Nicaragua country Central America
37 G6 Nicaragua, Lago de l. Nic.
66 G5 Nicastro Italy
64 H5 Nice France
23 F3 Nichicun, Lac l. Can.
85 E4 Nichlaul India
29 E7 Nicholl's Town Bahamas
31 F2 Nicholson Can.
83 H9 Nicobar Islands is Andaman and Nicobar Is
80 E4 Nicosia Cyprus
37 H7 Nicoya, G. de b. Costa Rica
37 G7 Nicoya, Pen. de pen. Costa Rica
33 K1 Nictau Can.
55 R9 Nida Lith.
58 F4 Nidd r. U.K.

63 K4 Nidzica Pol.
62 D3 Niebüll Ger.
62 F7 Niedere Tauern mts Austria
61 F2 Niedersachsen div. Ger.
100 D4 Niefang Equatorial Guinea
100 B3 Niellé Côte d'Ivoire
62 D4 Nienburg (Weser) Ger.
61 E3 Niers r. Ger.
43 G2 Nieuw Amsterdam Suriname
61 C2 Nieuwe-Niedorp Neth.
61 C2 Nieuwerkerk aan de IJssel Neth.
43 G2 Nieuw Nickerie Suriname
104 C5 Nieuwoudtville S. Africa
61 A3 Nieuwpoort Belgium
61 C4 Nieuw-Vossemeer Neth.
80 E3 Niğde Turkey
96 Niger country Africa
100 C4 Niger r. Africa
100 C4 Niger, Mouths of the est. Nigeria
96 Nigeria country Africa
31 G1 Nighthawk Lake l. Can.
67 K4 Nigrita Greece
91 G6 Nihonmatsu Japan
91 F6 Niigata Japan
91 F6 Niigata-yake-yama vol. Japan
91 C8 Niihama Japan
34 □2 Niihau i. U.S.A.
91 E7 Nii-jima i. Japan
91 H3 Niikappu Japan
91 C7 Niimi Japan
91 F6 Niitsu Japan
61 D2 Nijkerk Neth.
61 D3 Nijmegen Neth.
61 E2 Nijverdal Neth.
54 W2 Nikel' Rus. Fed.
100 C4 Nikki Benin
91 F6 Nikkō Nat. Park Japan
68 H4 Nikolayevka Rus. Fed.
69 H5 Nikolayevsk Rus. Fed.
68 H4 Nikol'sk Penzen. Rus. Fed.
68 H3 Nikol'sk Vologod. Rus. Fed.
77 S4 Nikol'skoye Rus. Fed.
69 E6 Nikopol' Ukr.
81 M3 Nīk Pey Iran
80 F1 Niksar Turkey
67 H4 Nikšić Yugo.
111 J2 Nikumaroro i. Kiribati
111 H2 Nikunau i. Kiribati
84 C2 Nila Pak.
85 F5 Nilagiri India
35 H3 Niland U.S.A.
83 D10 Nilandhoo Atoll atoll Maldives
84 D3 Nilang India
78 C4 Nile r. Africa
30 D5 Niles U.S.A.
54 V5 Nilsiä Fin.
84 C4 Nimach India
115 K2 Nimbin Austr.
64 G5 Nîmes France
115 H6 Nimmitabel Austr.
101 F4 Nimule Sudan
81 J4 Nīnawá Iraq
115 H2 Nindigully Austr.
83 D9 Nine Degree Channel chan. India
114 E3 Nine Mile Lake salt flat Austr.
34 D2 Ninemile Peak summit U.S.A.
13 K5 Ninetyeast Ridge sea feature Indian Ocean
115 G7 Ninety Mile Beach beach Austr.
117 D1 Ninety Mile Beach beach N.Z.
33 F3 Nineveh U.S.A.
90 A2 Ning'an China
89 F4 Ningbo China
88 F3 Ningcheng China
89 F5 Ningde China
89 E5 Ningdu China
89 D5 Ninggang China
89 F4 Ningguo China
89 F4 Ninghai China
88 E2 Ninghe China
89 E5 Ninghua China
82 J4 Ningjing Shan mts China
88 E3 Ningling China
89 C6 Ningming China
89 B5 Ningnan China
88 D3 Ningqiang China
88 D2 Ningshan China
88 D3 Ningwu China
88 B2 Ningxia div. China
89 D4 Ningxian China
88 D4 Ningxiang China
89 F4 Ningyang China
89 D5 Ningyuan China
89 C6 Ninh Binh Vietnam
95 D2 Ninh Hoa Vietnam
90 G4 Ninohe Japan
46 A3 Nioaque Brazil
26 C3 Niobrara r. U.S.A.
85 H4 Niolo India
100 A3 Niokolo Koba, Parc National du nat. park Senegal
100 B3 Niono Mali
100 B3 Nioro Mali
64 D3 Niort France
21 J4 Nipawin Can.
22 C4 Nipigon Can.
22 C4 Nipigon, Lake l. Can.
30 C1 Nipigon Bay b. Can.
23 H3 Nipishish Lake l. Can.
31 H2 Nipissing Can.
31 G2 Nipissing, L. l. Can.

34 B4 Nipomo U.S.A.
81 K5 Nippur Iraq
35 E4 Nipton U.S.A.
46 C1 Niquelândia Brazil
81 L2 Nīr Iran
83 E7 Nirmal India
67 J3 Niš Yugo.
65 C3 Nisa Port.
66 F6 Niscemi Italy
Nishāpūr see Neyshābūr
91 B9 Nishino-'omote Japan
91 C6 Nishino-shima i. Japan
91 A8 Nishi-Sonogi-hantō pen. Japan
91 D7 Nishiwaki Japan
20 B2 Nisling r. Can.
61 C4 Nismes, Forêt de forest Belgium
61 C3 Nispen Neth.
55 N8 Nissan r. Sweden
63 O7 Nistrului Inferior, Câmpia lowland Moldova
20 C2 Nisutlin r. Can.
67 M6 Nisyros i. Greece
23 F3 Nitchequon Can.
46 D3 Niterói Brazil
57 E5 Nith r. U.K.
57 E5 Nithsdale v. U.K.
84 D3 Niti Pass China
112 F2 Nitmiluk National Park nat. park Austr.
62 J6 Nitra Slovakia
32 C5 Nitro U.S.A.
111 J3 Niuatoputopu i. Tonga
106 Niue terr. Pac. Oc.
111 H3 Niulakita i. Tuvalu
89 B5 Niulan Jiang r. China
111 H2 Niutao i. Tuvalu
88 G1 Niuzhuang China
54 T5 Nivala Fin.
116 B5 Nive watercourse Austr.
116 B5 Nive Downs Austr.
61 C4 Nivelles Belgium
62 K2 Nivshera Rus. Fed.
84 C4 Niwāi India
34 C2 Nixon U.S.A.
85 E1 Niya He r. China
81 M1 Niyazoba Azer.
83 E7 Nizamabad India
68 H3 Nizhegorodskaya Oblast' div. Rus. Fed.
77 S3 Nizhnekolymsk Rus. Fed.
77 L4 Nizhneudinsk Rus. Fed.
76 J3 Nizhnevartovsk Rus. Fed.
77 P2 Nizhneyansk Rus. Fed.
64 G4 Nizhniy Lomov Rus. Fed.
68 G3 Nizhniy Novgorod Rus. Fed.
68 K2 Nizhniy Odes Rus. Fed.
68 H3 Nizhniy Yenangsk Rus. Fed.
54 W3 Nizhnyaya Pirenga, Ozero l. Rus. Fed.
77 K3 Nizhnyaya Tunguska r. Rus. Fed.
69 D5 Nizhyn Ukr.
63 K4 Nizina reg. Pol.
80 F3 Nizip Turkey
90 D3 Nizmennyy, Mys pt Rus. Fed.
54 R2 Njallavarri mt Norway
54 Q3 Njavve Sweden
Njazidja i. see Grande Comore
103 D3 Njinjo Tanz.
103 D4 Njombe Tanz.
55 P5 Njurundabommen Sweden
100 D4 Nkambe Cameroon
105 J4 Nkandla S. Africa
100 B4 Nkawkaw Ghana
103 C5 Nkayi Zimbabwe
103 D5 Nkhata Bay Malawi
103 D5 Nkhotakota Malawi
100 C4 Nkongsamba Cameroon
105 G5 Nkululeko S. Africa
103 B5 Nkurenkuru Namibia
105 G6 Nkwenkwezi S. Africa
85 J4 Noa Dihing r. India
85 J5 Noakhali Bangl.
85 F5 Noamundi India
60 E4 Nobber Rep. of Ireland
91 B8 Nobeoka Japan
90 G3 Noboribetsu Japan
46 A1 Nobres Brazil
114 E1 Noccundra Austr.
114 E1 Nockatunga Austr.
31 G2 Noelville Can.
36 B2 Nogales Arizona
36 B2 Nogales Mex.
91 B8 Nōgata Japan
64 E2 Nogent-le-Rotrou France
61 A5 Nogent-sur-Oise France
68 F4 Noginsk Rus. Fed.
116 D5 Nogo r. Austr.
116 B5 Nogoa r. Austr.
91 A8 Nogōhaku-san mt Japan
47 E2 Nogoyá Arg.
47 E2 Nogoyá r. Arg.
84 C3 Nohar India
90 G4 Noheji Japan
61 D2 Nohfelden Ger.
64 C3 Noirmoutier, Île de i. France
64 C3 Noirmoutier-en-l'Île France
91 F7 Nojima-zaki c. Japan
84 C4 Nokha India
79 H4 Nok Kundi Pak.
21 J3 Nokomis Lake l. Can.
102 B3 Nola C.A.R.
68 J3 Nolinsk Rus. Fed.
33 H4 No Mans Land i. U.S.A.
77 V3 Nome Alaska

88 B1 Nomgon Mongolia
85 J1 Nomhon China
105 G5 Nomonde S. Africa
91 A8 Nomo-zaki pt Japan
68 G3 Nomzha Rus. Fed.
21 H2 Nonacho Lake l. Can.
105 J4 Nondweni S. Africa
95 C1 Nông Hèt Laos
95 B5 Nong Hong Thai.
95 B1 Nong Khai Thai.
105 J3 Nongoma S. Africa
114 B4 Nonning Austr.
25 F7 Nonoava Mex.
111 H2 Nonouti i. Kiribati
95 B5 Nonthaburi Thai.
104 F5 Nonzwakazi S. Africa
115 G2 Noorama Cr. watercourse Austr.
61 B3 Noordbeveland i. Neth.
61 C2 Noorderhaaks i. Neth.
61 D2 Noordoost Polder reclaimed land Neth.
116 E6 Noosa Heads Austr.
20 D5 Nootka I. i. Can.
79 K2 Norak Tajik.
94 C5 Norala Phil.
31 H1 Noranda Can.
55 O6 Norberg Sweden
76 D2 Nordaustlandet i. Svalbard
20 F4 Nordegg Can.
62 G4 Norden Ger.
76 L2 Nordenshel'da, Arkhipelag is Rus. Fed.
61 B3 Norderland reg. Ger.
61 F1 Norderney Ger.
61 F1 Norderney i. Ger.
62 E4 Norderstedt Ger.
55 M2 Nordfjordeid Norway
54 O3 Nordfold Norway
Nordfriesische Inseln is see North Frisian Islands
62 E5 Nordhausen Ger.
61 F2 Nordhorn Ger.
54 T1 Nordkapp c. Norway
54 Q2 Nordkjosbotn Norway
54 N4 Nordli Norway
62 E6 Nördlingen Ger.
55 P6 Nordmaling Sweden
62 D3 Nord-Ostsee-Kanal canal Ger.
61 E3 Nordrhein-Westfalen div. Ger.
60 B5 Nore r. Rep. of Ireland
64 F5 Nore, Pic de mt France
26 D3 Norfolk NE U.S.A.
33 F2 Norfolk NY U.S.A.
111 G4 Norfolk Island terr. Pac. Oc.
14 G7 Norfolk Island Ridge sea feature Pac. Oc.
91 E6 Norikura-dake vol. Japan
76 K3 Noril'sk Rus. Fed.
81 K1 Nor Kharberd Armenia
31 H3 Norland Can.
30 C5 Normal U.S.A.
27 D5 Norman U.S.A.
29 D5 Norman r. U.S.A.
110 F2 Normanby I. i. P.N.G.
116 D4 Normanby Ra. h. Austr.
Normandes, Îles is see Channel Islands
56 F7 Normandie reg. France
Normandy reg. see Normandie
113 H3 Normanton Austr.
114 C5 Normanville Austr.
20 D1 Norman Wells Can.
47 B4 Ñorquinco Arg.
54 R5 Norra Kvarken str. Fin./Sweden
54 O4 Norra Storfjället mts Sweden
32 B6 Norris Lake l. U.S.A.
33 F4 Norristown U.S.A.
55 P7 Norrköping Sweden
55 Q7 Norrtälje Sweden
112 D6 Norseman Austr.
54 Q4 Norsjö Sweden
111 G3 Norsup Vanuatu
47 F5 Norte, Pta pt Buenos Aires Arg.
44 D6 Norte, Pta pt Chubut Arg.
119 A5 North, C. c. Antarctica
114 C1 North, C. c. Antarctica
33 H4 North Adams U.S.A.
58 F3 Northallerton U.K.
112 C6 Northam Austr.
112 B5 Northampton Austr.
59 G5 Northampton U.K.
33 G3 Northampton U.S.A.
116 A5 Northampton Downs Austr.
92 A4 North Andaman i. Andaman and Nicobar Is
32 E5 North Anna r. U.S.A.
33 J2 North Anson U.S.A.
20 G2 North Arm b. Can.
29 D5 North Augusta U.S.A.
23 H2 North Aulatsivik Island i. Can.
21 H4 North Battleford Can.
31 H2 North Bay Can.
22 F2 North Belcher Islands is Can.
24 A3 North Bend U.S.A.
57 F4 North Berwick U.K.
33 J2 North Berwick U.S.A.
115 F3 North Bourke Austr.
30 A3 North Branch U.S.A.
23 H4 North Cape pt Can.

North Cape c. see Nordkapp
117 D1 North Cape c. N.Z.
22 B3 North Caribou Lake l. Can.
29 D5 North Carolina div. U.S.A.
24 B1 North Cascades Nat. Park nat. park U.S.A.
31 F2 North Channel chan. Can.
60 E2 North Channel str. U.K.
33 H2 North Conway U.S.A.
26 C2 North Dakota div. U.S.A.
59 H6 North Downs h. U.K.
32 D3 North East U.S.A.
12 H2 North-Eastern Atlantic Basin sea feature Atlantic Ocean
29 E7 Northeast Providence Chan. chan. Bahamas
29 F7 North End Pt pt Bahamas
105 H1 Northern div. S. Africa
84 C1 Northern Areas div. Pak.
104 D4 Northern Cape div. S. Africa
21 K3 Northern Indian Lake l. Can.
56 C4 Northern Ireland div. U.K.
22 B4 Northern Light L. l. Can.
106 Northern Mariana Islands terr. Pac. Oc.
113 F3 Northern Territory div. Austr.
57 F4 North Esk r. U.K.
33 G3 Northfield MA U.S.A.
26 E2 Northfield MN U.S.A.
33 G2 Northfield VT U.S.A.
59 J6 North Foreland c. U.K.
34 C3 North Fork U.S.A.
30 E3 North Fox I. i. U.S.A.
22 D3 North French r. Can.
62 C3 North Frisian Islands is Ger.
118 B3 North Geomagnetic Pole Can.
58 G3 North Grimston U.K.
33 K2 North Head Can.
117 E2 North Head hd N.Z.
21 K3 North Henik Lake l. Can.
33 G3 North Hudson U.S.A.
117 E3 North Island i. N.Z.
94 B1 North Island i. Phil.
94 B4 North Islet rf Phil.
35 G4 North Jadito Canyon U.S.A.
30 D5 North Judson U.S.A.
21 K3 North Knife r. Can.
85 E4 North Koel r. India
35 G5 North Komelik U.S.A.
71 North Korea country Asia
85 H4 North Lakhimpur India
35 E3 North Las Vegas U.S.A.
27 E5 North Little Rock U.S.A.
103 D5 North Luangwa National Park nat. park Zambia
118 B3 North Magnetic Pole Can.
30 E5 North Manchester U.S.A.
30 D3 North Manitou I. i. U.S.A.
20 D2 North Nahanni r. Can.
21 L5 Northome U.S.A.
34 C3 North Palisade summit U.S.A.
26 C3 North Platte U.S.A.
26 C3 North Platte r. U.S.A.
115 G7 North Point pt Austr.
89 □ North Point pt China
28 D2 North Point pt U.S.A.
30 E3 Northport U.S.A.
35 F3 North Rim U.S.A.
57 F1 North Ronaldsay i. U.K.
57 F1 North Ronaldsay Firth chan. U.K.
34 B2 North San Juan U.S.A.
21 G4 North Saskatchewan r. Can.
52 North Sea sea Europe
21 J3 North Seal r. Can.
58 F2 North Shields U.K.
34 D2 North Shoshone Peak summit U.S.A.
59 H4 North Somercotes U.K.
115 K1 North Stradbroke I. i. Austr.
33 H2 North Stratford U.S.A.
58 F2 North Sunderland U.K.
117 E3 North Taranaki Bight b. N.Z.
20 F4 North Thompson r. Can.
57 A3 Northton U.K.
32 D3 North Tonawanda U.S.A.
117 A7 North Trap rf N.Z.
33 G2 North Troy U.S.A.
22 D3 North Twin I. i. Can.
58 F2 North Tyne r. U.K.
57 A3 North Uist i. U.K.
116 D3 Northumberland Is is Austr.
58 E2 Northumberland National Park nat. park U.K.
23 H4 Northumberland Strait chan. Can.
20 E5 North Vancouver Can.
33 F3 Northville U.S.A.
59 J5 North Walsham U.K.
104 F3 North West div. S. Africa
112 B4 North West C. c. Austr.
84 C2 North West Frontier div. Pak.
29 E7 Northwest Providence Chan. chan. Bahamas
23 J3 North West River Can.

21 G2 Northwest Territories div. Can.
59 E4 Northwich U.K.
33 F5 North Wildwood U.S.A.
33 H2 North Woodstock U.S.A.
58 G3 North York Moors reg. U.K.
58 G3 North York Moors National Park U.K.
23 G4 Norton Can.
58 G3 Norton U.K.
26 D4 Norton KS U.S.A.
32 B6 Norton VA U.S.A.
33 H2 Norton VT U.S.A.
103 D5 Norton Zimbabwe
77 V3 Norton Sound b. Alaska
119 C2 Norvegia, Kap c. Antarctica
33 G4 Norwalk CT U.S.A.
32 B4 Norwalk OH U.S.A.
48 Norway country Europe
33 H2 Norway U.S.A.
31 J3 Norway Bay Can.
21 K4 Norway House Can.
12 J1 Norwegian Basin sea feature Atlantic Ocean
52 Norwegian Sea sea Atlantic Ocean
31 G4 Norwich Can.
59 J5 Norwich U.K.
33 G4 Norwich CT U.S.A.
33 F3 Norwich NY U.S.A.
33 H3 Norwood MA U.S.A.
33 F2 Norwood NY U.S.A.
32 A5 Norwood OH U.S.A.
21 H1 Nose Lake l. Can.
90 G2 Noshappu–misaki hd Japan
90 G4 Noshiro Japan
69 D5 Nosivka Ukr.
68 H3 Noskovo Rus. Fed.
104 D2 Nosop r. Botswana/S. Africa
76 G3 Novaya Rus. Fed.
57 □ Noss, Isle of i. U.K.
46 A1 Nossa Senhora do Livramento Brazil
55 N7 Nossebro Sweden
104 C2 Nossob r. Namibia
103 E5 Nosy Bé i. Madag.
103 F5 Nosy Boraha i. Madag.
103 E6 Nosy Varika Madag.
35 F2 Notch Peak summit U.S.A.
62 H4 Noteć r. Pol.
66 F6 Noto, Golfo di g. Italy
55 L7 Notodden Norway
91 E6 Noto–hantō pen. Japan
23 G4 Notre Dame, Monts mts Can.
23 K4 Notre Dame Bay b. Can.
31 K3 Notre-Dame-de-la-Salette Can.
33 H2 Notre-Dame-des-Bois Can.
31 K2 Notre-Dame-du-Laus Can.
31 H2 Notre-Dame-du-Nord Can.
31 G3 Nottawasaga Bay b. Can.
22 E3 Nottaway r. Can.
59 F5 Nottingham U.K.
32 E6 Nottoway r. U.S.A.
21 H5 Notukeu Cr. r. Can.
100 A2 Nouâdhibou Maur.
100 A3 Nouakchott Maur.
100 A3 Nouâmghâr Maur.
95 C2 Nouei Vietnam
111 G4 Nouméa New Caledonia
100 B3 Nouna Burkina
104 F5 Noupoort S. Africa
54 V3 Nousu Fin.
Nouveau-Comptoir see Wemindji
Nouvelle Calédonie is see New Caledonia
46 C1 Nova América Brazil
46 B3 Nova Esperança Brazil
46 D3 Nova Friburgo Brazil
66 G2 Nova Gradiška Croatia
46 C3 Nova Granada Brazil
46 D3 Nova Iguaçu Brazil
69 E6 Nova Kakhovka Ukr.
46 D2 Nova Lima Brazil
68 D4 Novalukoml' Belarus
69 D6 Nova Odesa Ukr.
66 C2 Novara Italy
46 C1 Nova Roma Brazil
23 H5 Nova Scotia div. Can.
34 A2 Novato U.S.A.
46 E2 Nova Venécia Brazil
46 B1 Nova Xavantino Brazil
77 R2 Novaya Sibir', Ostrov i. Rus. Fed.
76 G2 Novaya Zemlya is Rus. Fed.
67 M3 Nova Zagora Bulg.
65 F3 Novelda Spain
62 J7 Nové Zámky Slovakia
68 E3 Novgorodskaya Oblast' div. Rus. Fed.
69 E5 Novhorod-Sivers'kyy Ukr.
67 K3 Novi Iskür Bulg.
66 C2 Novi Ligure Italy
67 M3 Novi Pazar Bulg.
67 J3 Novi Pazar Yugo.
67 H2 Novi Sad Yugo.
69 G6 Novoaleksandrovsk Rus. Fed.
69 G5 Novoanninskiy Rus. Fed.
42 F5 Novo Aripuanã Brazil
69 E5 Novoazovs'k Ukr.
68 H3 Novocheboksarsk Rus. Fed.
69 G6 Novocherkassk Rus. Fed.
68 G1 Novodvinsk Rus. Fed.
44 F3 Novo Hamburgo Brazil
46 C3 Novo Horizonte Brazil
62 G6 Novohradské Hory mts Czech Rep.
69 C5 Novohrad-Volyns'kyy Ukr.
69 G6 Novokubansk Rus. Fed.
76 K4 Novokuznetsk Rus. Fed.
119 D3 Novolazarevskaya Rus. Fed. Base Antarctica
77 M2 Novoletov'ye Rus. Fed.
66 F2 Novo Mesto Slovenia
68 F4 Novomichurinsk Rus. Fed.
69 F6 Novomikhaylovskiy Rus. Fed.
68 F4 Novomoskovsk Rus. Fed.
69 E5 Novomoskovs'k Ukr.
69 D5 Novomyrhorod Ukr.
69 G5 Novonikolayevskiy Rus. Fed.
69 E6 Novooleksiyivka Ukr.
90 D2 Novopokrovka Rus. Fed.
69 G6 Novopokrovskaya Rus. Fed.
69 J5 Novorepnoye Rus. Fed.
69 F6 Novorossiysk Rus. Fed.
77 M2 Novorybnaya Rus. Fed.
63 O2 Novorzhev Rus. Fed.
69 E6 Novoselivs'ke Ukr.
63 O1 Novosel'ye Rus. Fed.
69 F6 Novoshakhtinsk Rus. Fed.
90 C2 Novoshakhtinskiy Rus. Fed.
76 K4 Novosibirsk Rus. Fed.
77 Q2 Novosibirskiye Ostrova is Rus. Fed.
68 D3 Novosokol'niki Rus. Fed.
68 H4 Novospasskoye Rus. Fed.
69 E6 Novotroyits'ke Ukr.
69 D5 Novoukrayinka Ukr.
69 J5 Novouzensk Rus. Fed.
69 C5 Novovolyns'k Ukr.
69 F5 Novovoronezh Rus. Fed.
69 D4 Novozybkov Rus. Fed.
62 H6 Nový Jičín Czech Rep.
77 M2 Novyy Rus. Fed.
69 F5 Novyy Oskol Rus. Fed.
76 J3 Novyy Port Rus. Fed.
68 J3 Novyy Tor'yal Rus. Fed.
76 J3 Novyy Urengoy Rus. Fed.
77 P4 Novyy Urgal Rus. Fed.
27 E4 Nowata U.S.A.
81 M4 Nowbarān Iran
81 M3 Nowdī Iran
Nowgong see Nagaon
84 D4 Nowgong India
21 J2 Nowleye Lake l. Can.
62 G4 Nowogard Pol.
115 J5 Nowra Austr.
81 M2 Nowshahr Iran
79 G2 Now Shahr Iran
84 C2 Nowshera Pak.
63 K6 Nowy Sącz Pol.
63 K6 Nowy Targ Pol.
33 E4 Noxen U.S.A.
95 C1 Noy, Xé r. Laos
95 C1 Noy, Xé r. Laos
76 J3 Noyabr'sk r. Rus. Fed.
20 C3 Noyes I. i. U.S.A.
64 F2 Noyon France
105 F5 Nozizwe S. Africa
105 G6 Nqamakwe S. Africa
105 J4 Nqutu S. Africa
103 D5 Nsanje Malawi
102 B4 Ntandembele Dem. Rep. Congo
105 G3 Ntha S. Africa
102 D4 Ntungamo Uganda
101 F3 Nuba Mountains mts Sudan
81 K1 Nubarashen Armenia
101 F2 Nubian Desert des. Sudan
47 B3 Ñuble r. Chile
88 D1 Nüden Mongolia
42 D7 Nudo Coropuna mt Peru
27 D6 Nueces r. U.S.A.
45 C2 Nueva Florida Venez.
47 F2 Nueva Helvecia Uru.
47 B3 Nueva Imperial Chile
45 A4 Nueva Loja Ecuador
44 B6 Nueva Lubecka Arg.
36 D3 Nueva Rosita Mex.
37 J4 Nuevitas Cuba
47 D4 Nuevo, Golfo g. Arg.
36 C2 Nuevo Casas Grandes Mex.
36 E3 Nuevo Laredo Mex.
27 D6 Nuevo León div. Mex.
102 E3 Nugaal watercourse Somalia
116 C5 Nuga Nuga, L. l. Austr.
117 B7 Nugget Pt pt N.Z.
111 F2 Nuguria Is is P.N.G.
117 H3 Nuhaka N.Z.
111 H2 Nui i. Tuvalu
95 C2 Nui Ti On mt Vietnam
82 J5 Nu Jiang r. China
114 A4 Nukey Bluff h. Austr.
111 H2 Nuku'alofa Tonga
111 H2 Nukufetau i. Tuvalu
111 H2 Nukulaelae i. Tuvalu
111 F2 Nukumanu Is is P.N.G.
111 J2 Nukunonu i. Pac. Oc.
79 H1 Nukus Uzbek.
112 D4 Nullagine Austr.
112 F6 Nullarbor Austr.
114 D4 Nullarbor National Park nat. park Austr.
112 E6 Nullarbor Plain plain Austr.
88 F1 Nulu'erhu Shan mts China

114 F2 Numalla, Lake salt flat Austr.
100 D4 Numan Nigeria
91 F6 Numata Japan
91 F7 Numazu Japan
113 G2 Numbulwar Austr.
55 L6 Numedal v. Norway
93 J7 Numfoor i. Indon.
115 F6 Numurkah Austr.
23 H2 Nunaksaluk Island i. Can.
16 Nunavut reg. Can.
32 E3 Nunda U.S.A.
115 J3 Nundle Austr.
59 F5 Nuneaton U.K.
22 B3 Nungesser L. l. Can.
77 V4 Nunivak I. i. Alaska
84 D2 Nunkun mt India
77 U3 Nunligran Rus. Fed.
65 C2 Nuñomoral Spain
66 C4 Nuoro Italy
111 G3 Nupani i. Solomon Is
78 A4 Nuqrah Saudi Arabia
45 A3 Nuquí Col.
84 L1 Nur Turkey
81 J2 Nurettin Turkey
25 E6 Nuri Mex.
114 C5 Nurioorpa Austr.
84 B2 Nuristan reg. Afgh.
68 J4 Nurlaty Rus. Fed.
54 V5 Nurmes Fin.
54 S5 Nurmo Fin.
62 E6 Nürnberg Ger.
Nürnberg see Nürnberg
115 G3 Nurri, Mt h. Austr.
85 H1 Nur Turu China
81 H3 Nusaybin Turkey
80 F4 Nuşayrīyah, Jabal an mts Syria
79 K4 Nushki Pak.
23 H2 Nutak Can.
35 H5 Nutrioso U.S.A.
84 B3 Nuttal Pak.
16 Nuuk Greenland
54 U3 Nuupas Fin.
104 C5 Nuwerus S. Africa
104 D6 Nuweveldberge mts S. Africa
81 K4 Nuzi Iraq
105 J1 Nwanedi National Park nat. park S. Africa
76 H3 Nyagan' Rus. Fed.
114 E2 Nyah West Austr.
85 G3 Nyainqêntanglha Feng mt China
85 G3 Nyainqêntanglha Shan mts China
85 H3 Nyainrong China
54 Q5 Nyåker Sweden
101 E3 Nyala Sudan
85 F3 Nyalam China
103 C5 Nyamandhlovu Zimbabwe
68 G2 Nyandoma Rus. Fed.
68 F2 Nyandomskiy Vozvyshennost' reg. Rus. Fed.
102 B4 Nyanga r. Gabon
103 D5 Nyanga Zimbabwe
85 H3 Nyang Qu r. Tibet China
85 G3 Nyang Qu r. Tibet China
84 D3 Nyar r. India
103 D5 Nyasa, Lake l. Africa
68 C4 Nyasvizh Belarus
55 M9 Nyborg Denmark
54 V1 Nyborg Norway
55 O8 Nybro Sweden
85 G3 Nyêmo China
102 D4 Nyeri Kenya
85 F3 Nyima China
86 F6 Nyingchi China
63 K7 Nyíregyháza Hungary
54 S5 Nykarleby Fin.
55 M9 Nykøbing Denmark
55 M9 Nykøbing Sjælland Denmark
55 P7 Nyköping Sweden
54 P5 Nyland Sweden
105 H2 Nylstroom S. Africa
115 G4 Nymagee Austr.
115 K2 Nymboida Austr.
115 K2 Nymboida r. Austr.
55 P7 Nynäshamn Sweden
115 G3 Nyngan Austr.
63 L4 Nyoman r. Belarus/Lith.
62 C7 Nyon Switz.
64 G4 Nyons France
76 G3 Nyrob Rus. Fed.
62 H5 Nysa Pol.
Nysa Łużycka r. see Neiße
68 J2 Nyuchpas Rus. Fed.
90 F5 Nyūdō–zaki pt Japan
102 C4 Nyunzu Dem. Rep. Congo
77 N3 Nyurba Rus. Fed.
68 J2 Nyuvchim Rus. Fed.
69 D5 Nyzh'ohirs'kyy Ukr.
102 D4 Nzega Tanz.
100 B4 Nzérékoré Guinea
102 B4 N'zeto Angola
105 J1 Nzhelele Dam dam S. Africa
Nzwani i. see Anjouan

O

26 C2 Oahe, Lake l. U.S.A.
34 □¹ Oahu i. U.S.A.
114 D4 Oakbank Austr.
35 F2 Oak City U.S.A.
27 E6 Oakdale U.S.A.
26 D2 Oakes U.S.A.
115 J1 Oakey Austr.
59 G5 Oakham U.K.

24 B1 Oak Harbor U.S.A.
32 C6 Oak Hill U.S.A.
34 C3 Oakhurst U.S.A.
30 B2 Oak I. i. U.S.A.
34 A3 Oakland CA U.S.A.
32 D5 Oakland MD U.S.A.
26 D3 Oakland NE U.S.A.
24 B3 Oakland OR U.S.A.
115 G5 Oaklands Austr.
30 C5 Oak Lawn U.S.A.
26 C4 Oakley U.S.A.
112 D4 Oakover r. Austr.
24 B3 Oakridge U.S.A.
29 C4 Oak Ridge U.S.A.
114 D4 Oakvale Austr.
31 H4 Oakville Can.
117 C6 Oamaru N.Z.
117 D5 Oaro N.Z.
94 B3 Oas Phil.
24 D3 Oasis U.S.A.
119 B5 Oates Land reg. Antarctica
115 G9 Oatlands Austr.
35 E4 Oatman U.S.A.
36 E5 Oaxaca Mex.
76 H3 Ob' r. Rus. Fed.
43 H3 Óbidos Brazil
79 K2 Obigarm Tajik.
90 H3 Obihiro Japan
69 H6 Obil'noye Rus. Fed.
45 C2 Obispos Venez.
87 O2 Obluch'ye Rus. Fed.
68 F3 Obninsk Rus. Fed.
102 C3 Obo C.A.R.
88 A2 Obo China
102 E2 Obock Djibouti
90 D4 Obok N. Korea
102 C4 Obokote Dem. Rep. Congo
102 B4 Obouya Congo
69 F5 Oboyan' Rus. Fed.
68 G2 Obozerskiy Rus. Fed.
85 E4 Obra India
25 E7 Obregón, Presa resr Mex.
67 J2 Obrenovac Yugo.
80 D2 Obruk Turkey
76 J2 Obskaya Guba chan. Rus. Fed.
100 B4 Obuasi Ghana
69 D5 Obukhiv Ukr.
68 J2 Ob''yachevo Rus. Fed.
29 C6 Ocala U.S.A.
45 D4 Ocamo r. Venez.
27 C7 Ocampo Mex.
45 B2 Ocaña Col.
65 E3 Ocaña Spain
42 E7 Occidental, Cordillera mts Chile
45 A4 Occidental, Cordillera mts Col.
42 C6 Occidental, Cordillera mts Peru
20 B3 Ocean Cape pt U.S.A.
33 F5 Ocean City MD U.S.A.
33 F5 Ocean City NJ U.S.A.
20 D3 Ocean Falls Can.
12 G3 Oceanographer Fracture sea feature Atlantic Ocean
34 D5 Oceanside U.S.A.
27 F6 Ocean Springs U.S.A.
69 D6 Ochakiv Ukr.
69 G7 Och'amch'ire Georgia
57 E4 Ochil Hills h. U.K.
84 C1 Ochili Pass pass Afgh.
62 E6 Ochsenfurt Ger.
55 P6 Ockelbo Sweden
63 M7 Ocolaşul Mare, Vârful mt Romania
30 C4 Oconomowoc U.S.A.
30 D3 Oconto U.S.A.
34 D5 Ocotillo Wells U.S.A.
100 B4 Oda Ghana
91 C7 Ōda Japan
78 D5 Oda, Jebel mt Sudan
54 E4 Ódáðahraun lava field Iceland
90 A4 Ödaejin N. Korea
90 G4 Ödate Japan
91 F7 Odawara Japan
55 K6 Odda Norway
21 K3 Odei r. Can.
35 C5 Odell U.S.A.
65 B3 Odemira Port.
80 A2 Ödemiş Turkey
105 G3 Odendaalsrus S. Africa
55 M9 Odense Denmark
62 D6 Odenwald reg. Ger.
64 G4 Oder r. Ger.
62 G3 Oderbucht b. Ger.
69 D6 Odesa Ukr.
55 O7 Ödeshog Sweden
27 C6 Odessa U.S.A.
54 O5 Ödiel r. Spain
100 B4 Odienné Côte d'Ivoire
68 F4 Odintsovo Rus. Fed.
95 C3 Ôdôngk Cambodia
62 J6 Odra r. Ger./Pol.
43 K5 Oeiras Brazil
26 C3 Oelrichs U.S.A.
30 B4 Oelwein U.S.A.
61 D5 Oesling h. Lux.

81 H1 Of Turkey
66 C4 Ofanto r. Italy
62 D5 Offenbach am Main Ger.
62 C6 Offenburg Ger.
67 M6 Ofidoussa i. Greece
90 G5 Ōfunato Japan
90 F5 Oga Japan
102 E3 Ogadēn reg. Eth.
90 F5 Oga-hantō pen. Japan
91 E7 Ōgaki Japan
26 C3 Ogallala U.S.A.
31 H2 Ogascanane, Lac l. Can.
100 C4 Ogbomoso Nigeria
26 D3 Ogden IA U.S.A.
24 E3 Ogden UT U.S.A.
20 C3 Ogden, Mt mt Can.
33 F2 Ogdensburg U.S.A.
29 C5 Oglethorpe, Mt mt U.S.A.
66 D1 Oglio r. Italy
116 C4 Ogmore Austr.
100 C4 Ogoja Nigeria
22 C3 Ogoki r. Can.
22 C3 Ogoki Res. resr Can.
67 K3 Ogosta r. Bulg.
55 T8 Ogre Latvia
66 F2 Ogulin Croatia
81 L1 Oğuz Azer.
117 A6 Ohai N.Z.
117 E3 Ohakune N.Z.
90 G4 Ōhata Japan
117 B6 Ohau, L. l. N.Z.
47 B2 O'Higgins div. Chile
44 B7 O'Higgins, Lago l. Chile
32 B4 Ohio div. U.S.A.
28 C4 Ohio r. U.S.A.
67 J4 Ohrid Macedonia
67 J4 Ohrid, Lake l. Albania/Macedonia
105 J2 Ohrigstad S. Africa
117 E3 Ohura N.Z.
43 H3 Oiapoque Brazil
57 D3 Oich, Loch l. U.K.
85 H3 Oiga China
32 D4 Oil City U.S.A.
34 C4 Oildale U.S.A.
64 F2 Oise r. France
91 B8 Ōita Japan
67 K5 Oiti mt Greece
34 C4 Ojai U.S.A.
30 B3 Ojeda Arg.
30 B3 Ojibwa U.S.A.
27 B6 Ojinaga Mex.
91 F6 Ojiya Japan
25 F6 Ojo de Laguna Mex.
25 D7 Ojo de Liebre, Lago b. Mex.
44 C3 Ojos del Salado, Nevado mt Arg.
68 G4 Oka r. Rus. Fed.
103 B6 Okahandja Namibia
117 E3 Okahukura N.Z.
103 B6 Okakarara Namibia
23 H2 Okak Islands is Can.
20 F5 Okanagan Falls Can.
20 F4 Okanagan Lake l. Can.
24 C1 Okanagan r. Can./U.S.A.
20 F5 Okanogan U.S.A.
24 B1 Okanogan Range mts U.S.A.
84 C3 Okara Pak.
103 B5 Okaukuejo Namibia
103 C5 Okavango r. Botswana/Namibia
103 C5 Okavango Delta swamp Botswana
91 F6 Okaya Japan
91 C7 Okayama Japan
91 E7 Okazaki Japan
29 D7 Okeechobee U.S.A.
29 D7 Okeechobee, L. l. U.S.A.
29 D6 Okefenokee Swamp swamp U.S.A.
59 C7 Okehampton U.K.
100 C4 Okene Nigeria
84 B5 Okha India
77 Q4 Okha Rus. Fed.
85 F4 Okhaldhunga Nepal
84 B5 Okha Rann marsh India
77 Q3 Okhotka r. Rus. Fed.
77 Q4 Okhotsk Rus. Fed.
77 Q4 Okhotsk, Sea of g. Rus. Fed.
Okhotskoye More g. see Okhotsk, Sea of
69 E5 Okhtyrka Ukr.
87 N6 Okinawa i. Japan
87 N6 Okinawa-shotō is Japan
91 B7 Okino-shima i. Japan
91 P6 Oki-shotō i. Japan
91 C6 Oki-shotō is Japan
27 D5 Oklahoma div. U.S.A.
27 D5 Oklahoma City U.S.A.
27 D5 Okmulgee U.S.A.
102 B4 Okondja Gabon
20 G4 Okotoks Can.
68 E4 Okovskiy Les forest Rus. Fed.
102 B4 Okoyo Congo
54 S1 Øksfjord Norway
68 F2 Oksovskiy Rus. Fed.
68 G2 Oktyabr'sk Rus. Fed.
68 G2 Oktyabr'skiy Archangel. Rus. Fed.
69 G6 Oktyabr'skiy Volgograd. Rus. Fed.
77 R4 Oktyabr'skiy Rus. Fed.
76 J4 Oktyabr'skiy Rus. Fed.
77 H3 Oktyabr'skoye Rus. Fed.
77 L2 Oktyabr'skoy Revolyutsii, Ostrov i. Rus. Fed.
68 J3 Okulovka Rus. Fed.
90 F3 Okushiri-tō i. Japan
104 E1 Okwa watercourse Botswana

54 B4 Ólafsvík Iceland
34 C3 Olancha U.S.A.
34 C3 Olancha Peak summit U.S.A.
55 P8 Öland i. Sweden
54 W3 Olanga Rus. Fed.
114 D4 Olary Austr.
114 D4 Olary watercourse Austr.
26 E4 Olathe U.S.A.
47 E3 Olavarría Arg.
62 H5 Oława Pol.
35 G5 Olberg U.S.A.
66 C4 Olbia Italy
32 D3 Olcott U.S.A.
115 K3 Old Bar Austr.
60 D4 Oldcastle Rep. of Ireland
62 D4 Oldenburg Ger.
62 E3 Oldenburg in Holstein Ger.
61 E2 Oldenzaal Neth.
54 R2 Olderdalen Norway
33 F3 Old Forge NY U.S.A.
33 F4 Old Forge PA U.S.A.
58 E4 Oldham U.K.
60 C6 Old Head of Kinsale hd Rep. of Ireland
20 G4 Oldman r. Can.
57 F3 Oldmeldrum U.K.
33 H3 Old Orchard Beach U.S.A.
23 K4 Old Perlican Can.
20 G4 Olds Can.
33 J2 Old Town U.S.A.
21 H4 Old Wives L. l. Can.
35 E4 Old Woman Mts mts U.S.A.
32 D3 Olean U.S.A.
63 L3 Olecko Pol.
77 O4 Olekma r. Rus. Fed.
77 O3 Olekminsk Rus. Fed.
69 E5 Oleksandriya Ukr.
68 H1 Olema Rus. Fed.
55 J7 Ølen Norway
54 X2 Olenegorsk Rus. Fed.
77 N3 Olenek Rus. Fed.
77 O2 Olenek r. Rus. Fed.
77 O2 Olenekskiy Zaliv b. Rus. Fed.
68 E3 Olenino Rus. Fed.
69 C5 Olevs'k Ukr.
90 D3 Ol'ga Rus. Fed.
65 C4 Olhão Port.
104 C2 Olifants watercourse Namibia
105 J1 Olifants S. Africa
104 C6 Olifants r. S. Africa
104 D6 Olifants r. S. Africa
104 C6 Olifants r. S. Africa
104 E3 Olifantshoek S. Africa
104 C6 Olifantsrivierberge mts S. Africa
47 G2 Olimar Grande r. Uru.
46 C3 Olímpia Brazil
43 M5 Olinda Brazil
103 D5 Olinga Moz.
105 G2 Oliphants Drift Botswana
47 D2 Oliva Arg.
65 F3 Oliva Spain
44 C3 Oliva, Cordillera de mts Arg./Chile
47 C1 Olivares, Co del mt Chile
32 B5 Olive Hill U.S.A.
46 D3 Oliveira Brazil
65 C3 Olivenza Spain
26 E2 Olivia U.S.A.
68 G4 Ol'khi Rus. Fed.
44 C2 Ollagüe Chile
47 B1 Ollita, Cordillera de mts Arg./Chile
47 B1 Ollitas mt Arg.
42 C5 Olmos Peru
33 G3 Olmstedville U.S.A.
59 G5 Olney U.K.
28 C4 Olney U.S.A.
55 O8 Olofström Sweden
62 H6 Olomouc Czech Rep.
68 E2 Olonets Rus. Fed.
94 B3 Olongapo Phil.
64 D5 Oloron-Ste-Marie France
65 H1 Olot Spain
87 L1 Olovyannaya Rus. Fed.
84 C3 Olpad India
63 K4 Olsztyn Pol.
62 C7 Olten Switz.
67 M2 Olteniţa Romania
81 H1 Oltu Turkey
94 B5 Olutanga i. Phil.
24 B2 Olympia U.S.A.
24 A2 Olympic Nat. Park U.S.A.
24 A2 Olympic Nat. Park nat. park U.S.A.
Olympus mt see Troödos, Mount
67 K4 Olympus mt Greece
24 B2 Olympus, Mt mt U.S.A.
77 S3 Olyutorskiy Rus. Fed.
77 T4 Olyutorskiy, Mys c. Rus. Fed.
77 S4 Olyutorskiy Zaliv b. Rus. Fed.
85 E3 Oma China
90 G4 Ōma Japan
91 E6 Ōmachi Japan
91 F7 Omae-zaki pt Japan
60 D3 Omagh U.K.
26 E3 Omaha U.S.A.
104 C1 Omaheke div. Namibia
24 C1 Omak U.S.A.
70 Oman country Asia
79 H4 Oman, Gulf of g. Asia
117 B6 Omarama N.Z.
103 B6 Omaruru Namibia
103 B5 Omatako watercourse Namibia
42 D7 Omate Peru

162

104 E2 Omaweneno Botswana
90 G4 Ōma-zaki c. Japan
102 A4 Omboué Gabon
66 D3 Ombrone r. Italy
85 F3 Ombu China
104 E5 Omdraaisvlei S. Africa
101 F3 Omdurman Sudan
66 C2 Omegna Italy
115 G6 Omeo Austr.
102 D2 Om Hajēr Eritrea
20 D3 Omineca Mountains mts Can.
104 B1 Omitara Namibia
91 F7 Ōmiya Japan
20 C3 Ommaney, Cape hd U.S.A.
61 C2 Ommen Neth.
88 B1 Ömnögovĭ div. Mongolia
77 S3 Omolon Rus. Fed.
77 R3 Omolon r. Rus. Fed.
102 D3 Omo National Park nat. park Eth.
90 G5 Omono-gawa r. Japan
76 J4 Omsk Rus. Fed.
77 R3 Omsukchan Rus. Fed.
90 H2 Ōmū Japan
67 L2 Omu, Vârful mt Romania
91 A8 Ōmura Japan
30 B4 Onalaska U.S.A.
33 F6 Onancock U.S.A.
22 C2 Onaping Lake l. Can.
25 E6 Onavas Mex.
31 E3 Onaway U.S.A.
95 A2 Onbingwin Myanmar
47 D1 Oncativo Arg.
58 C3 Onchan U.K.
103 B5 Oncócua Angola
103 B5 Ondangwa Namibia
104 B1 Ondekaremba Namibia
104 D5 Onderstedorings S. Africa
103 B5 Ondjiva Angola
100 C4 Ondo Nigeria
87 K2 Öndörhaan Mongolia
88 B1 Ondor Mod China
88 D1 Ondor Sum China
68 E2 Ondozero Rus. Fed.
104 D1 One Botswana
83 D10 One and a Half Degree Channel chan. Maldives
68 F2 Onega r. Rus. Fed.
68 F2 Onega r. Rus. Fed.
76 E3 Onega, Lake chan. Rus. Fed.
68 E2 Onega, Lake l. Rus. Fed.
20 E4 One Hundred Mile House Can.
33 F3 Oneida U.S.A.
33 F3 Oneida Lake l. U.S.A.
26 D3 O'Neill U.S.A.
77 R5 Onekotan, O. i. Rus. Fed.
33 F3 Oneonta U.S.A.
117 E2 Oneroa N.Z.
63 N7 Onești Romania
68 E1 Onezhskaya Guba g. Rus. Fed.
Onezhskove Ozero chan. see Onega, Lake
Onezhskoye Ozero l. see Onega, Lake
85 E5 Ong r. India
102 B4 Onga Gabon
117 F3 Ongaonga N.Z.
104 E4 Ongers watercourse S. Africa
Ongniud Qi see Wudan
83 F7 Ongole India
69 G7 Oni Georgia
103 E6 Onilahy r. Madag.
100 C4 Onitsha Nigeria
104 B1 Onjati Mountain mt Namibia
91 E7 Ōno Japan
111 J4 Ono-i-Lau i. Fiji
91 C7 Onomichi Japan
111 H2 Onotoa i. Kiribati
20 G4 Onoway Can.
104 C4 Onseepkans S. Africa
112 C4 Onslow Austr.
29 E5 Onslow Bay b. U.S.A.
90 B3 Onsong N. Korea
91 E7 Ontake-san vol. Japan
22 B3 Ontario div. Can.
24 C2 Ontario U.S.A.
31 H4 Ontario, Lake l. Can./U.S.A.
30 C2 Ontonagon U.S.A.
111 F2 Ontong Java Atoll atoll Solomon Is
113 G5 Oodnadatta Austr.
112 F6 Ooldea Austr.
27 E4 Oologah L. resr U.S.A.
61 B3 Oostakker Belgium
Oostende see Ostend
61 D2 Oostendorp Neth.
61 C3 Oosterhout Neth.
61 B3 Oosterschelde est. Neth.
61 B3 Oosterscheldekering barrage Neth.
61 A4 Oostvleteren Belgium
Ootacamund see Udagamandalam
20 D4 Ootsa Lake Can.
20 D4 Ootsa Lake l. Can.
32 E5 Opal U.S.A.
102 C4 Opala Dem. Rep. Congo
68 J3 Oparino Rus. Fed.
22 B3 Opasquia Can.
22 B3 Opasquia Provincial Park res. Can.
22 F3 Opataca L. l. Can.
62 H6 Opava Czech Rep.
29 C5 Opelika U.S.A.
27 E6 Opelousas U.S.A.
24 F1 Opheim U.S.A.
31 F2 Ophir Can.

117 C6 Opihi r. N.Z.
22 E3 Opinaca r. Can.
22 E3 Opinaca, Réservoir resr Can.
22 D3 Opinnagau r. Can.
81 K5 Opis Iraq
23 G3 Opiscotéo, Lac l. Can.
68 D3 Opochka Rus. Fed.
62 H5 Opole Pol.
65 B2 Oporto Port.
117 F3 Opotiki N.Z.
29 C6 Opp U.S.A.
54 L5 Oppdal Norway
117 D3 Opunake N.Z.
103 B5 Opuwo Namibia
30 B5 Oquawka U.S.A.
33 H2 Oquossoc U.S.A.
35 G5 Oracle U.S.A.
35 G5 Oracle Junction U.S.A.
63 K7 Oradea Romania
54 E4 Öræfajökull gl. Iceland
67 J3 Orahovac Yugo.
84 D4 Orai India
100 B1 Oran Alg.
44 D2 Orán Arg.
95 C2 O Rang Cambodia
90 A4 Orang N. Korea
115 H4 Orange Austr.
64 G4 Orange France
103 B6 Orange r. Namibia/S. Africa
33 G3 Orange MA U.S.A.
27 E6 Orange TX U.S.A.
32 D5 Orange VA U.S.A.
43 H3 Orange, Cabo c. Brazil
29 D5 Orangeburg U.S.A.
Orange Free State div. see Free State
31 G3 Orangeville Can.
35 G2 Orangeville U.S.A.
36 G5 Orange Walk Belize
94 B3 Orani Phil.
103 B6 Oranjemund Namibia
45 C1 Oranjestad Aruba
60 C4 Oranmore Rep. of Ireland
103 C6 Orapa Botswana
94 C3 Oras Phil.
67 K2 Orăștie Romania
54 S5 Oravais Fin.
67 J2 Oravița Romania
84 E2 Orba Co l. Can.
66 D3 Orbetello Italy
65 D1 Orbigo r. Spain
115 H6 Orbost Austr.
119 B1 Orcadas Arg. Base Antarctica
35 H2 Orchard Mesa U.S.A.
45 D2 Orchila, Isla i. Venez.
34 B4 Orcutt U.S.A.
112 E3 Ord r. Austr.
112 E3 Ord, Mt h. Austr.
25 D4 Orderville U.S.A.
65 B1 Ordes Spain
34 D4 Ord Mt mt U.S.A.
80 F1 Ordu Turkey
81 L2 Ordubad Azer.
25 G4 Ordway U.S.A.
Ordzhonikidze see Vladikavkaz
69 E6 Ordzhonikidze Ukr.
34 C1 Oreana U.S.A.
55 O7 Örebro Sweden
30 C4 Oregon IL U.S.A.
32 B4 Oregon OH U.S.A.
30 C4 Oregon WV U.S.A.
24 B3 Oregon div. U.S.A.
24 B2 Oregon City U.S.A.
68 F4 Orekhovo-Zuyevo Rus. Fed.
68 F4 Orel Rus. Fed.
35 G1 Orem U.S.A.
80 A2 Ören Turkey
67 M6 Ören Turkey
76 H4 Orenburg Rus. Fed.
47 E3 Orense Arg.
117 A7 Orepuki N.Z.
55 N9 Öresund str. Denmark
117 E2 Orewa N.Z.
67 K4 Orfanou, Kolpos b. Greece
115 G9 Orford Austr.
59 J5 Orford U.K.
59 J5 Orford Ness spit U.K.
35 F5 Organ Pipe Cactus National Monument res. U.S.A.
84 B2 Orgün Afgh.
80 B2 Orhaneli Turkey
69 D7 Orhangazi Turkey
68 J3 Orichi Rus. Fed.
33 K2 Orient U.S.A.
42 E7 Oriental, Cordillera mts Bol.
45 B3 Oriental, Cordillera mts Col.
42 D6 Oriental, Cordillera mts Peru
47 E3 Oriente Arg.
65 F3 Orihuela Spain
69 E6 Orikhiv Ukr.
31 H3 Orillia Can.
55 T6 Orimattila Fin.
45 E2 Orinoco r. Col./Venez.
45 E2 Orinoco Delta delta Venez.
85 E5 Orissa div. India
55 S7 Orissaare Estonia
66 C5 Oristano Italy
55 T6 Orivesi Fin.
54 V5 Orivesi l. Fin.
43 G4 Oriximiná Brazil
36 E4 Orizaba Mex.
36 E5 Orizaba, Pico de vol. Mex.

54 L5 Orkanger Norway
55 N8 Örkelljunga Sweden
54 L5 Orkla r. Norway
105 G3 Orkney S. Africa
56 E2 Orkney is U.K.
27 C6 Orla U.S.A.
34 A2 Orland U.S.A.
46 C3 Orlândia Brazil
29 D6 Orlando U.S.A.
64 E3 Orléans France
33 J4 Orleans MA U.S.A.
33 G2 Orleans VT U.S.A.
68 J3 Orlov Rus. Fed.
68 F4 Orlovskaya Oblast' div. Rus. Fed.
69 G6 Orlovskiy Rus. Fed.
94 C4 Ormoc Phil.
29 D6 Ormond Beach U.S.A.
58 E4 Ormskirk U.K.
33 G2 Ormstown Can.
64 D2 Orne r. France
54 N3 Ørnes Norway
54 Q5 Örnsköldsvik Sweden
45 C3 Orocué Col.
100 B3 Orodara Burkina
24 C2 Orofino U.S.A.
25 F5 Orogrande U.S.A.
23 G4 Oromocto Can.
80 E6 Oron Israel
111 J2 Orona i. Kiribati
33 J2 Orono U.S.A.
57 B4 Oronsay i. U.K.
Orontes r. see 'Āṣī, Nahr al
Oroqen Zizhiqi see Alihe
94 B4 Oroquieta Phil.
43 L5 Orós, Açude resr Brazil
66 C4 Orosei Italy
66 C4 Orosei, Golfo di b. Italy
63 K7 Orosháza Hungary
35 G5 Oro Valley U.S.A.
34 B2 Oroville CA U.S.A.
24 C1 Oroville WA U.S.A.
34 B2 Oroville, Lake l. U.S.A.
116 B2 Orpheus I. i. Austr.
114 C4 Orroroo Austr.
55 O6 Orsa Sweden
68 D4 Orsha Belarus
76 G4 Orsk Rus. Fed.
55 K5 Ørsta Norway
55 C1 Ortegal, Cabo c. Spain
64 D5 Orthez France
65 C1 Ortigueira Spain
25 E6 Ortiz Mex.
45 D2 Ortíz Venez.
66 D1 Ortles mt Italy
58 E3 Orton U.K.
66 F1 Ortona Italy
26 D2 Ortonville U.S.A.
77 O3 Orulgan, Khrebet mts Rus. Fed.
104 B1 Orumbo Namibia
81 K3 Orūmīyeh Iran
81 K3 Orūmīyeh, Daryācheh-ye salt l. Iran
42 E7 Oruro Bol.
66 E3 Orvieto Italy
32 C4 Orwell OH U.S.A.
33 G3 Orwell VT U.S.A.
55 M5 Os Norway
37 H7 Osa, Pen. de pen. Costa Rica
30 A4 Osage U.S.A.
26 E4 Osage r. U.S.A.
91 D7 Ōsaka Japan
61 E5 Osburger Hochwald forest Ger.
55 N8 Osby Sweden
27 F5 Osceola AR U.S.A.
26 E3 Osceola IA U.S.A.
66 C4 Oschiri Italy
31 F3 Oscoda U.S.A.
68 F4 Osetr r. Rus. Fed.
91 A8 Ōse-zaki pt Japan
31 K3 Osgoode Can.
79 L1 Osh Kyrgyzstan
103 B5 Oshakati Namibia
90 D3 Oshamambe Japan
31 H4 Oshawa Can.
90 G5 Oshika-hantō pen. Japan
90 F4 Ō-shima i. Japan
91 F7 Ō-shima i. Japan
26 C3 Oshkosh NE U.S.A.
30 C3 Oshkosh WV U.S.A.
81 K3 Oshnovīyeh Iran
100 C4 Oshogbo Nigeria
81 M5 Oshtorān Kūh mt Iran
81 M5 Oshtorīnān Iran
102 B4 Oshwe Dem. Rep. Congo
67 H2 Osijek Croatia
66 E3 Osimo Italy
84 C4 Osiyan India
105 J3 Osizweni S. Africa
62 G5 Osječenica mt Bos.-Herz.
54 L5 Ösjön l. Sweden
26 E3 Oskaloosa U.S.A.
55 P8 Oskarshamn Sweden
31 K1 Oskélanéo Can.
69 F5 Oskol r. Rus. Fed.
55 M7 Oslo Norway
94 B4 Oslob Phil.
55 M7 Oslofjorden chan. Norway
80 E1 Osmancık Turkey
80 B1 Osmaneli Turkey
80 F3 Osmaniye Turkey
55 V7 Os'mino Rus. Fed.
62 D4 Osnabrück Ger.
67 K3 Osogovske Planine mts Bulg./Macedonia
46 B4 Osorno Chile
65 D1 Osorno Spain
47 B4 Osorno, Vol. vol. Chile
20 F5 Osoyoos Can.

55 J6 Osøyri Norway
113 J2 Osprey Reef rf Coral Sea Is Terr.
61 D3 Oss Neth.
115 G8 Ossa, Mt mt Austr.
30 B3 Osseo U.S.A.
31 F3 Ossineke U.S.A.
33 H3 Ossipee Lake l. U.S.A.
23 H3 Ossokmanuan Lake l. Can.
68 E3 Ostashkov Rus. Fed.
61 A3 Ostend Belgium
63 P5 Oster Ukr.
55 O8 Österbymo Sweden
55 N6 Österdalälven l. Sweden
55 M5 Österdalen v. Norway
55 O5 Östersund Sweden
55 Q6 Östhammar Sweden
62 J6 Ostrava Czech Rep.
63 J4 Ostróda Pol.
69 F5 Ostrogozhsk Rus. Fed.
68 D3 Ostrov Rus. Fed.
63 K5 Ostrowiec Świętokrzyski Pol.
63 K4 Ostrów Mazowiecka Pol.
62 H5 Ostrów Wielkopolski Pol.
67 L3 Osům r. Bulg.
91 B9 Ōsumi-Kaikyō chan. Japan
91 B9 Ōsumi-shotō is Japan
65 D4 Osuna Spain
33 F2 Oswegatchie U.S.A.
30 C5 Oswego IL U.S.A.
32 E3 Oswego NY U.S.A.
33 E3 Oswego r. U.S.A.
59 D5 Oswestry U.K.
91 F6 Ōta Japan
117 C6 Otago Peninsula pen. N.Z.
117 E4 Otaki N.Z.
54 U4 Otanmäki Fin.
45 E4 Otare, Co h. Col.
90 D3 Otaru Japan
117 B7 Otatara N.Z.
42 C3 Otavalo Ecuador
103 B5 Otavi Namibia
91 G6 Otawara Japan
117 C6 Otematata N.Z.
55 U7 Otepää Estonia
24 C2 Othello U.S.A.
117 C5 Otira N.Z.
33 E3 Otisco Lake l. U.S.A.
23 H3 Otish, Monts mts Can.
103 B6 Otjiwarongo Namibia
58 F4 Otley U.K.
Otog Qi see Ulan
90 H2 Otoineppu Japan
117 E3 Otorohanga N.Z.
22 C3 Otoskwin r. Can.
67 H4 Otranto Italy
67 H4 Otranto, Strait of str. Albania/Italy
77 T3 Otrozhnyy Rus. Fed.
30 E4 Otsego U.S.A.
30 E3 Otsego Lake l. MI U.S.A.
33 F3 Otsego Lake l. NY U.S.A.
33 F3 Otselic U.S.A.
91 D7 Ōtsu Japan
55 L6 Otta Norway
31 K3 Ottawa Can.
31 H2 Ottawa r. Can.
30 C5 Ottawa IL U.S.A.
26 E4 Ottawa KS U.S.A.
32 A4 Ottawa OH U.S.A.
22 D2 Ottawa Islands is Can.
58 E2 Otterburn U.K.
35 G2 Otter Creek Reservoir resr U.S.A.
30 D1 Otter I. i. Can.
22 D1 Otter Rapids Can.
59 C7 Ottery r. U.K.
61 C4 Ottignies Belgium
30 A5 Ottumwa U.S.A.
100 C4 Otukpo Nigeria
44 D3 Otumpa Arg.
42 C5 Otuzco Peru
114 E7 Otway, C. c. Austr.
89 B6 Ou, Nam r. Laos
27 E5 Ouachita, L. l. U.S.A.
27 E5 Ouachita Mts mts U.S.A.
102 C3 Ouadda C.A.R.
101 E3 Ouaddaï reg. Chad
100 B3 Ouagadougou Burkina
100 B3 Ouahigouya Burkina
100 B3 Oualâta Maur.
102 C3 Ouanda-Djalié C.A.R.
100 B2 Ouarâne reg. Maur.
100 C1 Ouargla Alg.
100 B1 Ouarzazate Morocco
104 F6 Oubergpas pass S. Africa
61 B4 Oudenaarde Belgium
104 E6 Oudtshoorn S. Africa
64 B2 Oued Tlélat Alg.
100 B1 Oued Zem Morocco
64 B2 Oued Zénati Alg.
64 B2 Ouessant, Île d' i. France
102 B3 Ouésso Congo
100 C4 Ouidah Benin
25 F2 Ouiriego Mex.
100 B1 Oujda Morocco
54 T4 Oulainen Fin.
65 G4 Ouled Farès Alg.
54 T4 Oulu Fin.
54 U4 Oulujärvi l. Fin.
54 U4 Oulujoki r. Fin.
54 U4 Oulunsalo Fin.
64 H4 Oulx Italy
101 E3 Oum-Chalouba Chad
100 B4 Oumé Côte d'Ivoire
101 D3 Oum-Hadjer Chad
54 T3 Ounasjoki r. Fin.
66 C4 Ouzeri Italy
59 G5 Oundle U.K.

101 E3 Ounianga Kébir Chad
61 D4 Oupeye Belgium
61 E5 Our r. Lux.
62 C6 Our, Vallée de l' v. Ger./Lux.
25 F4 Ouray CO U.S.A.
35 H1 Ouray UT U.S.A.
65 C1 Ourense Spain
43 K5 Ouricurí Brazil
46 C3 Ourinhos Brazil
46 C1 Ouro r. Brazil
46 D3 Ouro Preto Brazil
61 D4 Ourthe r. Belgium
58 G4 Ouse r. Eng. U.K.
59 H7 Ouse r. Eng. U.K.
23 G3 Outardes r. Can.
104 E6 Outeniekpas pass S. Africa
57 A2 Outer Hebrides is U.K.
30 D1 Outer I. i. U.S.A.
34 C5 Outer Santa Barbara Channel chan. U.S.A.
103 B6 Outjo Namibia
54 V5 Outokumpu Fin.
57 □ Out Skerries is U.K.
111 G4 Ouvéa i. New Caledonia
89 D5 Ouyanghai Skuiku resr China
114 E5 Ouyen Austr.
59 G5 Ouzel r. U.K.
66 C4 Ovace, Pte d' mt France
81 K5 Ovacık Turkey
66 C2 Ovada Italy
111 H3 Ovalau i. Fiji
47 B1 Ovalle Chile
65 B2 Ovar Port.
47 D2 Oveja mt Arg.
115 G6 Ovens r. Austr.
54 S3 Överkalix Sweden
54 S3 Övertorneå Sweden
55 P8 Överum Sweden
61 C2 Overveen Neth.
30 E4 Ovid U.S.A.
65 D1 Oviedo Spain
54 T2 Øvre Anarjokka Nasjonalpark nat. park Norway
54 Q2 Øvre Dividal Nasjonalpark nat. park Norway
55 M6 Øvre Rendal Norway
69 D5 Ovruch Ukr.
117 B7 Owaka N.Z.
102 B4 Owando Congo
91 E7 Owase Japan
26 E2 Owatonna U.S.A.
33 E3 Owego U.S.A.
13 H3 Owen Fracture sea feature Indian Ocean
60 B3 Owenmore r. Rep. of Ireland
117 D4 Owen River N.Z.
34 C3 Owens r. U.S.A.
28 C4 Owensboro U.S.A.
34 D3 Owens Lake l. U.S.A.
31 G3 Owen Sound Can.
31 G3 Owen Sound in. Can.
110 E2 Owen Stanley Range mts P.N.G.
100 C4 Owerri Nigeria
20 D4 Owikeno L. l. Can.
32 B5 Owingsville U.S.A.
33 J2 Owls Head U.S.A.
100 C4 Owo Nigeria
31 E4 Owosso U.S.A.
81 L4 Owrāmān, Kūh-e mts Iran/Iraq
24 C3 Owyhee U.S.A.
24 C3 Owyhee r. U.S.A.
24 C3 Owyhee Mts mts U.S.A.
42 C6 Oxapampa Peru
54 □ Öxarfjörður b. Iceland
21 J5 Oxbow Can.
33 J1 Oxbow U.S.A.
55 P7 Oxelösund Sweden
117 D5 Oxford N.Z.
59 F6 Oxford U.K.
31 F4 Oxford MI U.S.A.
27 F5 Oxford MS U.S.A.
33 F3 Oxford NY U.S.A.
33 F5 Oxford PA U.S.A.
116 C3 Oxford Downs Austr.
21 K4 Oxford House Can.
21 K4 Oxford L. l. Can.
114 F5 Oxley Austr.
115 J3 Oxleys Pk mt Austr.
34 C4 Oxnard U.S.A.
31 H3 Oxtongue Lake Can.
54 N3 Øya Norway
91 F6 Oyama Japan
43 H3 Oyapock r. Brazil/Fr. Guiana
102 B3 Oyem Gabon
57 D3 Oykel r. U.K.
100 C4 Oyo Nigeria
64 G3 Oyonnax France
85 H5 Oyster I. i. Myanmar
81 J2 Ozalp Turkey
94 B4 Ozamiz Phil.
29 C6 Ozark AL U.S.A.
30 E2 Ozark MI U.S.A.
27 E4 Ozark Plateau plat. U.S.A.
26 E4 Ozarks, Lake of the l. U.S.A.
77 R4 Ozernovskiy Rus. Fed.
68 J4 Ozernyy Rus. Fed.
63 L3 Ozersk Rus. Fed.
68 F4 Ozery Rus. Fed.
77 Q3 Ozhogino Rus. Fed.
66 C4 Ozieri Italy
27 C6 Ozona U.S.A.

91 B7 Ozuki Japan
69 G7 Ozurget'i Georgia

P

95 A1 Pa-an Myanmar
104 C6 Paarl S. Africa
104 D4 Paballelo S. Africa
90 A4 P'abal-li N. Korea
57 A3 Pabbay i. Scot. U.K.
57 A3 Pabbay i. Scot. U.K.
63 J5 Pabianice Pol.
85 G4 Pabna Bangl.
59 T9 Pabradė Lith.
79 K4 Pab Range mts Pak.
42 F6 Pacaás Novos, Parque Nacional nat. park Brazil
45 E4 Pacaraima, Serra mts Brazil
42 C5 Pacasmayo Peru
25 E6 Pacheco Mex.
68 H2 Pachikha Rus. Fed.
66 F6 Pachino Italy
84 D5 Pachor India
36 E4 Pachuca Mex.
34 B2 Pacific U.S.A.
91 F8 Pacific Ocean
94 C4 Pacijan i. Phil.
43 H4 Pacoval Brazil
46 D2 Pacuí r. Brazil
62 E5 Paczków Pol.
94 C5 Padada Phil.
45 D4 Padamo r. Venez.
92 C7 Padang Indon.
92 C7 Padangpanjang Indon.
95 A5 Padangsidimpuan Indon.
68 E2 Padany Rus. Fed.
81 M5 Padatha, Kūh-e mt Iran
45 D4 Padauiri r. Brazil
42 F8 Padcaya Bol.
20 F3 Paddle Prairie Can.
32 C5 Paden City U.S.A.
62 D5 Paderborn Ger.
67 K2 Padeşu, Vârful mt Romania
42 F7 Padilla Bol.
54 P3 Padjelanta Nationalpark nat. park Sweden
85 G5 Padma r. Bangl.
Padova see Padua
27 D7 Padre Island i. U.S.A.
66 C3 Padro, Monte mt France
59 C7 Padstow U.K.
63 N3 Padsvillye Belarus
114 D6 Paddthaway Austr.
66 D2 Padua Italy
28 B4 Paducah KY U.S.A.
27 C5 Paducah TX U.S.A.
84 D2 Padum Jammu and Kashmir
90 A4 Paegam N. Korea
117 E2 Paeroa N.Z.
94 B3 Paete Phil.
80 D4 Pafos Cyprus
105 J1 Pafúri Moz.
66 F2 Pag Croatia
66 F2 Pag i. Croatia
94 B5 Pagadian Phil.
92 C7 Pagai Selatan i. Indon.
92 C7 Pagai Utara i. Indon.
93 L3 Pagan i. N. Mariana Is
92 F7 Pagatan Indon.
35 G3 Page U.S.A.
55 R9 Pagėgiai Lith.
44 □ Paget, Mt mt Atlantic Ocean
116 E2 Paget Cay rf Coral Sea Is Terr.
25 F4 Pagosa Springs U.S.A.
85 G4 Pagri China
22 C3 Pagwa River Can.
34 □2 Pahala U.S.A.
95 B5 Pahang r. Malaysia
84 B2 Paharpur Pak.
117 A7 Pahia Pt pt N.Z.
34 □ Pahoa U.S.A.
29 D7 Pahokee U.S.A.
35 E3 Pahranagat Range mts U.S.A.
84 D4 Pahuj r. India
34 D3 Pahute Mesa plat. U.S.A.
95 A1 Pai Thai.
55 T7 Paide Estonia
59 E4 Paignton U.K.
55 T6 Päijänne l. Fin.
85 F1 Paikü Co l. China
95 B2 Pailin Cambodia
47 B4 Paillaco Chile
55 □2 Pailolo Chan. chan. U.S.A.
55 S6 Paimio Fin.
47 B2 Paine Chile
32 C4 Painesville U.S.A.
35 G3 Painted Desert des. U.S.A.
35 F5 Painted Rock Reservoir resr U.S.A.
114 C3 Painter, Mount mt Austr.
21 K3 Paint Lake Provincial Recr. Park res. Can.
32 B6 Paintsville U.S.A.
31 G3 Paisley Can.
57 D5 Paisley U.K.
42 B5 Paita Peru
89 D4 Paitan, Teluk b. Malaysia
89 D4 Paizhou China
54 S3 Pajala Sweden
43 L5 Pajeú r. Brazil
95 B4 Paka Malaysia
42 F2 Pakaraima Mountains mts Guyana
31 G3 Pakesley Can.
77 S3 Pakhachi Rus. Fed.

70 Pakistan *country* Asia
89 ☐ Pak Ka Shan *h.* China
Paknampho *see*
Nakhon Sawan
83 J6 Pakokku Myanmar
117 D1 Pakotai N.Z.
84 C3 Pakpattan Pak.
95 B3 Pak Phanang Thai.
95 B4 Pak Phayun Thai.
55 S9 Pakruojis Lith.
63 J7 Paks Hungary
89 ☐ Pak Tam Chung China
95 B2 Pak Thong Chai Thai.
84 B2 Paktīkā Afgh.
95 C2 Pakxé Laos
101 D4 Pala Chad
95 A4 Pala Myanmar
66 G3 Palagruža *i.* Croatia
67 K7 Palaiochora Greece
64 F2 Palaiseau France
Palakkat *see* Palghat
104 E1 Palamakoloi Botswana
65 H2 Palamós Spain
84 C4 Palana India
77 R4 Palana Rus. Fed.
94 B2 Palanan Phil.
94 B2 Palanan Point *pt* Phil.
81 L4 Palangān Iran
84 C4 Palanpur India
94 C3 Palapag Phil.
103 C6 Palapye Botswana
85 G4 Palasbari India
77 R3 Palatka Rus. Fed.
71 Palau *country* Pac. Oc.
94 A3 Palaui *i.* Phil.
94 A3 Palauig Phil.
95 A2 Palauk Myanmar
14 E5 Palau Tr. *sea feature*
Pac. Oc.
95 A2 Palaw Myanmar
94 A4 Palawan *i.* Phil.
94 B3 Palayan Phil.
55 T7 Paldiski Estonia
85 H5 Pale Myanmar
61 D2 Paleis Het Loo Neth.
92 C7 Palembang Indon.
44 B6 Palena Chile
65 D1 Palencia Spain
36 F5 Palenque Mex.
66 E5 Palermo Italy
27 E6 Palestine U.S.A.
85 H5 Paletwa Myanmar
83 E8 Palghat India
84 C4 Pali India
94 C5 Palimbang Phil.
66 F4 Palinuro, Capo *c.* Italy
35 H2 Palisade U.S.A.
61 D5 Paliseul Belgium
84 B5 Palitana India
55 T7 Palivere Estonia
68 D3 Palkino Rus. Fed.
83 E9 Palk Strait *str.*
India/Sri Lanka
115 H6 Pallamallawa Austr.
60 C5 Pallas Green
Rep. of Ireland
54 S2 Pallas ja Ounastunturin
Kansallispuisto
nat. park Fin.
69 H5 Pallasovka Rus. Fed.
117 E4 Palliser, Cape *c.* N.Z.
117 E4 Palliser Bay *b.* N.Z.
84 C3 Pallu India
65 D4 Palma del Río Spain
65 H3 Palma de Mallorca Spain
45 C2 Palmar *r.* Venez.
45 C3 Palmarito Venez.
100 B4 Palmas, Cape *c.* Liberia
46 D1 Palmas de Monte Alto
Brazil
29 D7 Palm Bay U.S.A.
29 D7 Palm Beach U.S.A.
34 C4 Palmdale U.S.A.
46 B4 Palmeira Brazil
43 L5 Palmeira dos Índios Brazil
43 K5 Palmeirais Brazil
119 B2 Palmer *U.S.A. Base*
Antarctica
117 C6 Palmerston N.Z.
108 Palmerston *i.* Pac. Oc.
116 C3 Palmerston, C. *pt* Austr.
117 E4 Palmerston North N.Z.
33 F4 Palmerton U.S.A.
29 E7 Palmetto Pt *pt* Bahamas
66 F5 Palmi Italy
45 A4 Palmira Col.
34 D5 Palm Springs U.S.A.
116 C5 Palm Tree Cr. *r.* Austr.
Palmyra *see* Tadmur
30 B6 Palmyra *MO* U.S.A.
32 E3 Palmyra *NY* U.S.A.
30 C4 Palmyra *WV* U.S.A.
109 Palmyra Atoll *i.* Pac. Oc.
85 Palmyras Point *pt* India
34 A3 Palo Alto U.S.A.
45 A3 Palo de las Letras Col.
101 F3 Paloich Sudan
54 S2 Palojärvi Fin.
54 U2 Palojoensuu Fin.
34 D5 Palomar Mt *mt* U.S.A.
35 G6 Palominas U.S.A.
93 G7 Palopo Indon.
65 F4 Palos, Cabo de *c.* Spain
35 F5 Palo Verde *AZ* U.S.A.
35 E5 Palo Verde *CA* U.S.A.
54 U4 Paltamo Fin.
93 F7 Palu Indon.
81 G2 Palu Turkey
94 B3 Paluan Phil.
84 D3 Palwal India
77 T3 Palyavaam *r.* Rus. Fed.
115 H6 Pambula Austr.
92 ☐ Pamekasan Indon.
92 ☐ Pameungpeuk Indon.

64 E5 Pamiers France
82 D3 Pamir *mts* Asia
29 E5 Pamlico Sound *chan.*
U.S.A.
27 C5 Pampa U.S.A.
42 F7 Pampa Grande Bol.
40 Pampas *reg.* Arg.
45 B3 Pamplona Col.
94 B3 Pamplona Phil.
65 F1 Pamplona Spain
80 C1 Pamukova Turkey
32 E6 Pamunkey *r.* U.S.A.
84 D2 Pamzal
Jammu and Kashmir
28 B4 Pana U.S.A.
94 C5 Panabo Phil.
35 E3 Panaca U.S.A.
94 A4 Panagtaran Point *pt* Phil.
92 ☐ Panaitan *i.* Indon.
83 D7 Panaji India
16 Panama *country* Central
America
37 J7 Panamá Panama
37 J7 Panamá, Golfo de *b.*
Panama
37 J7 Panama Canal *canal*
Panama
29 C6 Panama City U.S.A.
34 D3 Panamint Range *mts*
U.S.A.
34 D3 Panamint Springs U.S.A.
34 D3 Panamint Valley U.S.A.
94 C4 Panaon *i.* Phil.
85 G4 Panar *r.* India
66 F5 Panarea, Isola *i.* Italy
95 D5 Panarik Indon.
94 B4 Panay *i.* Phil.
94 C3 Panay *i.* Phil.
94 B4 Panay Gulf *b.* Phil.
35 E2 Pancake Range *mts* U.S.A.
67 J2 Pančevo Yugo.
94 B4 Pandan Phil.
94 C3 Pandan Phil.
94 B4 Pandan B. *b.* Phil.
95 ☐ Pandan Res. *resr* Sing.
84 E5 Pandaria India
46 D1 Pandeiros *r.* Brazil
83 E7 Pandharpur India
84 D3 Pandhurna India
47 F2 Pando Uru.
59 E6 Pandy U.K.
55 T9 Panevėžys Lith.
92 ☐ Pangandaran Indon.
84 C2 Pangi Range *mts* Pak.
92 E7 Pangkalanbuun Indon.
92 B6 Pangkalansusu Indon.
92 D7 Pangkalpinang Indon.
93 G7 Pangkalsiang, Tanjung *pt*
Indon.
94 B4 Panglao *i.* Phil.
76 J3 Pangody Rus. Fed.
84 D2 Pangong Tso *l.* India
92 ☐ Pangrango *vol.* Indon.
47 B3 Panguipulli Chile
47 B3 Panguipulli, L. *l.* Chile
35 F3 Panguitch U.S.A.
95 A5 Pangururan Indon.
94 B5 Pangutaran *i.* Phil.
94 B5 Pangutaran Group *is* Phil.
27 C5 Panhandle U.S.A.
102 C4 Pania-Mwanga
Dem. Rep. Congo
84 B5 Pānikoita *i.* India
69 G5 Panino Rus. Fed.
94 A4 Panitan Phil.
95 D5 Panjang *i.* Indon.
81 L5 Panjbarār Iran
79 J4 Panjgur Pak.
84 C5 Panjhra *r.* India
Panjim *see* Panaji
88 G1 Panjin China
84 B2 Panjkora *r.* Pak.
84 B3 Panjnad *r.* Pak.
54 W5 Pankakoski Fin.
100 C4 Pankshin Nigeria
90 B3 Pan Ling *mts* China
82 F6 Panna India
84 D4 Panna *reg.* India
112 C4 Pannawonica Austr.
46 B3 Panorama Brazil
Panshan *see* Panjin
87 N3 Panshi China
46 A2 Pantanal de São
Lourenço *marsh* Brazil
46 A2 Pantanal do Taquari
marsh Brazil
43 G7 Pantanal Matogrossense,
Parque Nacional do
nat. park Brazil
66 D6 Pantelleria Italy
66 E6 Pantelleria, Isola di *i.*
Italy
93 G8 Pantemakassar Indon.
94 C5 Pantukan Phil.
36 F4 Pánuco Mex.
89 B5 Panxian China
89 D6 Panyu China
89 A5 Panzhihua China
102 B4 Panzi Dem. Rep. Congo
66 G5 Paola Italy
28 C4 Paoli U.S.A.
102 B3 Paoua C.A.R.
62 H7 Pápa Hungary
66 F4 Papa, Monte del *mt* Italy
117 E2 Papakura N.Z.
36 E4 Papantla Mex.
117 E2 Paparoa Range *mts* N.Z.
57 ☐ Papa Stour *i.* U.K.
117 B7 Papatoetoe N.Z.
117 B7 Papatowai N.Z.
57 F1 Papa Westray *i.* U.K.
62 C4 Papenburg Ger.

31 K2 Papineau-Labelle,
Réserve Faunique de
res. Can.
35 E3 Papoose L. *l.* U.S.A.
57 B5 Paps of Jura *h.* U.K.
110 E2 Papua, Gulf of *g.* P.N.G.
106 Papua New Guinea
country Australasia
95 A1 Papun Myanmar
59 C7 Par U.K.
46 D2 Pará *r.* Brazil
43 J4 Pará *r.* Brazil
68 G4 Para *r.* Rus. Fed.
112 C4 Paraburdoo Austr.
94 B3 Paracale Phil.
46 C2 Paracatu Brazil
46 C2 Paracatu *r.* Brazil
114 C3 Parachilna Austr.
67 J3 Paraćin Yugo.
46 D2 Pará de Minas Brazil
31 J1 Paradis Can.
34 B2 Paradise *CA* U.S.A.
30 E2 Paradise *MI* U.S.A.
21 H4 Paradise Hill Can.
34 D2 Paradise Peak *summit*
U.S.A.
23 J3 Paradise River Can.
27 F4 Paragould U.S.A.
42 F6 Paragua *r.* Bol.
45 E3 Paragua *r.* Venez.
43 G7 Paraguaçu *r.* Brazil
45 C2 Paraguáipoa Venez.
45 C1 Paraguaná, Pen. de *pen.*
Venez.
44 E3 Paraguay *r.* Arg./Para.
38 Paraguay *country*
S. America
43 L5 Paraíba *r.* Brazil
46 D3 Paraíba do Sul *r.* Brazil
100 C4 Parakou Benin
114 B3 Parakylia Austr.
84 E6 Paralkot India
43 G2 Paramaribo Suriname
45 B3 Paramillo *mt* Col.
45 A3 Paramillo, Parque
Nacional *nat. park* Col.
46 D1 Paramirim Brazil
45 A3 Paramo Frontino *mt* Col.
33 F4 Paramus U.S.A.
77 R4 Paramushir, O. *i.*
Rus. Fed.
47 E1 Paraná Arg.
43 J6 Paraná Brazil
46 B3 Paraná *div.* Brazil
46 C1 Paraná *r.* Brazil
47 E2 Paraná *r.* S. America
46 C1 Paranã, Sa do *h.* Brazil
46 B2 Paranaíba Brazil
46 B2 Paranaíba *r.* Brazil
47 E2 Paraná Ibicuy *r.* Arg.
46 B3 Paranapanema *r.* Brazil
46 C4 Paranapiacaba, Serra
mts Brazil
46 B3 Paranavaí Brazil
84 B2 Parandev Pass *pass* Afgh.
94 B5 Parang Phil.
67 K2 Parângul Mare, Vârful
mt Romania
84 C5 Parantij India
46 D2 Paraopeba *r.* Brazil
81 K4 Pārapāra Iraq
117 E4 Paraparaumu N.Z.
45 D3 Paraque, Co *mt* Venez.
27 D7 Paras Mex.
84 D5 Paratwada India
81 L4 Parāū, Kūh-e *mt* Iraq
46 B2 Paraúna Brazil
64 G4 Paray-le-Monial France
84 D4 Parbati *r.* India
83 E7 Parbhani India
62 F4 Parchim Ger.
30 C4 Pardeeville U.S.A.
85 G2 Parding China
46 E1 Pardo *r.*
Bahia/Minas Gerais Brazil
46 B3 Pardo *r.*
Mato Grosso do Sul Brazil
46 D1 Pardo *r. Minas Gerais*
Brazil
46 C3 Pardo *r. São Paulo* Brazil
62 G5 Pardubice Czech Rep.
92 ☐ Pare Indon.
84 D2 Pare Chu *r.* China
42 F6 Parecis, Serra dos *h.*
Brazil
27 C7 Paredón Mex.
81 K2 Pareh Iran
117 D1 Parengarenga Harbour
in. N.Z.
22 H4 Parent, Lac *l.* Can.
117 C6 Pareora N.Z.
93 F7 Parepare Indon.
47 D2 Parera Arg.
68 G3 Parfen'yevo Rus. Fed.
63 P7 Parfino Rus. Fed.
67 J5 Parga Greece
55 S6 Pargas Fin.
45 C2 Paria, Gulf of *g.*
Trinidad/Venez.
45 E2 Paria, Península de *pen.*
Venez.
45 D2 Pariaguán Venez.
35 F3 Paria Plateau *plat.* U.S.A.
55 V6 Parikkala Fin.
Parima *see* Uatatás
45 D3 Parima, Serra *mts* Brazil
45 D4 Parima-Tapirapecó,
Parque Nacional
nat. park Venez.
42 B4 Pariñas, Pta *pt* Peru
114 D5 Paringa Austr.
43 G4 Parintins Brazil
31 G4 Paris Can.

64 F2 Paris France
32 A5 Paris *KY* U.S.A.
29 B4 Paris *TN* U.S.A.
27 E5 Paris *TX* U.S.A.
30 D3 Park U.K.
35 S5 Parkano Fin.
23 J4 Parke Lake *l.* Can.
35 E4 Parker U.S.A.
35 E4 Parker Dam *dam* U.S.A.
21 K2 Parker Lake *l.* Can.
30 A4 Parkersburg *IA* U.S.A.
32 C5 Parkersburg *WV* U.S.A.
115 H4 Parkes Austr.
30 B3 Park Falls U.S.A.
30 D5 Park Forest U.S.A.
31 F2 Parkinson U.S.A.
26 E2 Park Rapids U.S.A.
20 E5 Parksville Can.
33 C4 Parksville U.S.A.
66 D2 Parma Italy
24 C3 Parma *ID* U.S.A.
32 A5 Parma *OH* U.S.A.
45 D3 Parmana Venez.
43 K4 Parnaíba Brazil
43 K4 Parnaíba *r.* Brazil
67 K5 Parnassos *mt* Greece
117 D5 Parnassus N.Z.
114 B5 Parndana Austr.
30 A5 Parnell U.S.A.
67 K6 Parnon *mts* Greece
55 T7 Pärnu Estonia
55 T7 Pärnu-Jaagupi Estonia
54 T4 Pattijoki Fin.
54 R2 Pättikkä Fin.
20 D3 Pattullo, Mt *mt* Can.
85 G5 Patuakhali Bangl.
21 H3 Patuanak Can.
32 E5 Patuxent *r.* U.S.A.
36 D5 Pátzcuaro Mex.
64 D5 Pau France
64 D4 Pauillac France
85 H5 Pauktaw Myanmar
35 F4 Paulden U.S.A.
32 A4 Paulding U.S.A.
23 H2 Paul Island *i.* Can.
43 K5 Paulistana Brazil
43 L5 Paulo Afonso Brazil
105 J3 Paulpietersburg S. Africa
105 G4 Paul Roux S. Africa
33 G4 Paul Smiths U.S.A.
27 D5 Pauls Valley U.S.A.
83 J7 Paungde Myanmar
45 C3 Pauto *r.* Col.
46 E2 Pavão Brazil
81 L4 Pāveh Iran
66 C2 Pavia Italy
55 R8 Pāvilosta Latvia
68 H3 Pavino Rus. Fed.
67 L3 Pavlikeni Bulg.
76 J4 Pavlodar Kazak.
69 E5 Pavlohrad Ukr.
68 H4 Pavlovka Rus. Fed.
68 G4 Pavlovo Rus. Fed.
69 G5 Pavlovsk Rus. Fed.
69 F6 Pavlovskaya Rus. Fed.
45 B4 Pavon Col.
84 E3 Pawayan India
30 E4 Paw Paw U.S.A.
33 H4 Pawtucket U.S.A.
95 A2 Pawut Myanmar
30 C5 Paxton U.S.A.
92 C7 Payakumbuh Indon.
95 ☐ Paya Lebar Sing.
24 C2 Payette U.S.A.
76 H3 Pay-Khoy, Khrebet *h.*
Rus. Fed.
22 F2 Payne, Lac *l.* Can.
34 B1 Paynes Creek U.S.A.
112 C4 Payne's Find Austr.
47 E2 Paysandú Uru.
35 G4 Payson *AZ* U.S.A.
35 G1 Payson *UT* U.S.A.
47 C3 Payún, Cerro *vol.* Arg.
80 D1 Pazar Turkey
81 H1 Pazar Turkey
80 D2 Pazarcık Turkey
80 F2 Pazardzhik Bulg.
45 C3 Paz de Ariporo Col.
45 B3 Paz de Rio Col.
66 E2 Pazin Croatia
20 F3 Peace *r.* Can.
20 F3 Peace River Can.
35 H3 Peach Springs U.S.A.
59 F4 Peak District National
Park U.K.
114 A2 Peake *watercourse* Austr.
23 G4 Peaked Mt. *h.* U.S.A.
94 A4 Peaked Point *pt* Phil.
115 H4 Peak Hill Austr.
116 C4 Peak Ra. *h.* Austr.
35 H2 Peale, Mt *mt* U.S.A.
35 H6 Pearce U.S.A.
30 C4 Pearl Can.
27 F6 Pearl *r.* U.S.A.
34 C2 Pearl City U.S.A.
34 ☐1 Pearl Harbor *in.* U.S.A.
27 D6 Pearsall U.S.A.
29 D5 Pearson U.S.A.
18 Peary Land *reg.*
Greenland
22 C2 Peawanuck Can.
103 D5 Pebane Moz.
67 J4 Peć Yugo.
54 W2 Pechenga Rus. Fed.
76 G3 Pechora Rus. Fed.
68 C2 Pechory Rus. Fed.
31 F4 Peck U.S.A.
21 C6 Pecos U.S.A.
27 C5 Pecos *r.* U.S.A.
33 F4 Peconic U.S.A.
62 H7 Pécs Hungary
115 G9 Pedder, L. *l.* Austr.
105 G6 Peddie S. Africa
25 F6 Pedernales Mex.
45 D2 Pedernales Venez.

85 E3 Pêdo La *pass* China
46 F1 Pedra Azul Brazil
45 C3 Pedraza la Vieja Venez.
45 C2 Pedregal Venez.
46 C2 Pedregulho Brazil
43 K4 Pedreiras Brazil
43 J5 Pedro Afonso Brazil
45 C3 Pedro Chico Col.
44 C2 Pedro de Valdivia Chile
46 A2 Pedro Gomes Brazil
45 D4 Pedro II, Ilha *i.* Brazil
44 E2 Pedro Juan Caballero Para.
43 K4 Pedroll Brazil
47 G1 Pedro Osório Brazil
57 E5 Peebles U.K.
29 E5 Pee Dee *r.* U.S.A.
33 G4 Peekskill U.S.A.
115 J3 Peel *r.* Austr.
58 C3 Peel U.K.
20 F4 Peers U.S.A.
114 E3 Peery L. *salt flat* Austr.
117 D5 Pegasus Bay *b.* N.Z.
83 J7 Pegu Myanmar
68 J2 Pegysh Rus. Fed.
47 E2 Pehuajó Arg.
89 F6 Peikang Taiwan
Peipsi Järve *l. see*
Peipus, Lake
55 U7 Peipus, Lake *l.*
Estonia/Rus. Fed.
67 K6 Peiraias Greece
88 B1 Peitun China
43 J6 Peixe Brazil
46 B1 Peixe *r. Goiás* Brazil
46 B3 Peixe *r. São Paulo* Brazil
88 E3 Peixian China
46 A2 Peixo de Couro *r.* Brazil
105 G4 Peka Lesotho
92 ☐ Pekalongan Indon.
95 B5 Pekan Malaysia
30 C5 Pekin U.S.A.
95 B5 Pelabuhan Kelang
Malaysia
31 F5 Pelee I. *i.* Can.
31 F5 Pelee Pt *pt* Can.
93 G7 Peleng *i.* Indon.
68 J2 Peles Rus. Fed.
30 A1 Pelican Lake *l. MN* U.S.A.
30 C3 Pelican Lake *l. WV* U.S.A.
21 J3 Pelican Narrows Can.
54 U3 Pelkosenniemi Fin.
104 C4 Pella S. Africa
21 H1 Pellat Lake *l.* Can.
110 E2 Pelleluhu Is *is* P.N.G.
30 C4 Pell Lake U.S.A.
54 S3 Pello Fin.
20 B2 Pelly *r.* Can.
20 B2 Pelly Crossing Can.
21 J1 Pelly Lake *l.* Can.
20 C2 Pelly Mountains *mts* Can.
47 G1 Pelotas Brazil
44 F3 Pelotas, R. das *r.* Brazil
80 D6 Pelusium Egypt
64 H4 Pelvoux, Massif du *mts*
France
33 J2 Pemadumcook Lake *l.*
U.S.A.
92 ☐ Pemalang Indon.
92 D6 Pemangkat Indon.
95 A5 Pematangsiantar Indon.
103 E5 Pemba Moz.
103 C5 Pemba Zambia
102 D4 Pemba I. *i.* Tanz.
20 F4 Pembina *r.* Can.
26 D1 Pembina U.S.A.
31 J3 Pembroke Can.
59 C6 Pembroke U.K.
33 K2 Pembroke U.S.A.
59 B6 Pembrokeshire Coast
National Park U.K.
85 H6 Pen *r.* Myanmar
65 D1 Peña Cerredo *mt* Spain
65 E2 Peñalara *mt* Spain
36 E4 Peña Nevada, Co *mt* Mex.
46 B3 Penápolis Brazil
65 D1 Peña Prieta *mt* Spain
65 D2 Peñaranda de
Bracamonte Spain
114 E5 Penarie Austr.
65 F2 Peñarroya *mt* Spain
65 D3 Peñarroya-Pueblonuevo
Spain
59 D6 Penarth U.K.
65 D1 Peñas, Cabo de *c.* Spain
44 A7 Penas, Golfo de *b.* Chile
45 E2 Peñas, Pta *pt* Venez.
65 D1 Peña Ubiña *mt* Spain
84 D5 Pench *r.* India
119 D5 Penck, C. *c.* Antarctica
58 E4 Pendle Hill *h.* U.K.
24 C2 Pendleton U.S.A.
20 D4 Pendleton Bay Can.
24 C1 Pend Oreille *r.* U.S.A.
24 C1 Pend Oreille L. *l.* U.S.A.
85 E5 Pendra India
31 H3 Penetanguishene Can.
84 D6 Penganga *r.* India
89 ☐ Peng Chau *i.* China
89 G5 P'engchia Yü *i.* Taiwan
102 C4 Penge Dem. Rep. Congo
105 J2 Penge S. Africa
89 F6 P'enghu Ch'üntao *is*
Taiwan
89 F6 P'enghu Tao *i.* Taiwan
95 ☐ Peng Kang *h.* Sing.
88 F2 Penglai China
89 B4 Pengshan China
89 D4 Pengshui China
89 E1 Pengxi China
89 E4 Pengze China
105 G5 Penhoek Pass *pass*
S. Africa
65 B3 Peniche Port.

57 E5 Penicuik U.K.
68 E2 Peninga Rus. Fed.
92 C6 Peninsular Malaysia *pen.* Malaysia
81 K4 Pênjwîn Iraq
66 E3 Penne Italy
114 B5 Penneshaw Austr.
58 E3 Pennines *h.* U.K.
105 J5 Pennington S. Africa
33 F5 Pennsville U.S.A.
32 D4 Pennsylvania *div.* U.S.A.
32 E3 Penn Yan U.S.A.
21 H2 Pennylan Lake *l.* Can.
33 J2 Penobscot *r.* U.S.A.
33 J2 Penobscot Bay *b.* U.S.A.
114 D6 Penola Austr.
113 F6 Penong Austr.
58 E4 Penrith U.K.
29 C6 Pensacola U.S.A.
119 B3 Pensacola Mts *mts* Antarctica
81 M2 Pensär Azer.
114 E6 Penshurst Austr.
111 Pentecost I. *i.* Vanuatu
20 F5 Penticton Can.
59 B7 Pentire Point *pt* U.K.
116 A3 Pentland Austr.
57 E2 Pentland Firth *chan.* U.K.
57 E5 Pentland Hills *h.* U.K.
30 D4 Pentwater U.S.A.
59 D5 Penygadair *h.* U.K.
58 E3 Pen-y-Ghent *h.* U.K.
68 H4 Penza Rus. Fed.
59 B7 Penzance U.K.
68 H4 Penzenskaya Oblast' *div.* Rus. Fed.
77 S3 Penzhino Rus. Fed.
77 S3 Penzhinskaya Guba *b.* Rus. Fed.
35 F5 Peoria *AZ* U.S.A.
30 C5 Peoria *IL* U.S.A.
95 A4 Perai Malaysia
95 A4 Perak *i.* Malaysia
95 A4 Perak *r.* Malaysia
65 F2 Perales del Alfambra Spain
23 H4 Percé Can.
33 H2 Percy U.S.A.
116 D3 Percy Is *is* Austr.
31 J3 Percy Reach *l.* Can.
65 G1 Perdido, Monte *mt* Spain
76 H3 Peregrebnoye Rus. Fed.
45 B3 Pereira Col.
46 B3 Pereira Barreto Brazil
68 D3 Perekhoda *r.* Rus. Fed.
69 G5 Perelazovskiy Rus. Fed.
30 D4 Pere Marquette *r.* U.S.A.
63 M6 Peremyshlyany Ukr.
68 F3 Pereslavl'-Zalesskiy Rus. Fed.
Pereval Torugart *pass* see Turugart Pass
68 H4 Perevoz Rus. Fed.
69 D5 Pereyaslav-Khmel'nyts'kyy Ukr.
47 E2 Pergamino Arg.
95 B4 Perhentian Besar *i.* Malaysia
54 T5 Perho Fin.
23 F3 Péribonca, Lac *l.* Can.
44 C2 Perico Arg.
64 E4 Périgueux France
45 B2 Perijá, Parque Nacional *nat. park* Venez.
45 B2 Perija, Sierra de *mts* Venez.
44 B7 Perito Moreno Arg.
30 D3 Perkins U.S.A.
37 H6 Perlas, Pta de *pt* Nic.
62 E4 Perleberg Ger.
76 G4 Perm' Rus. Fed.
68 H3 Permas Rus. Fed.
114 B3 Pernatty Lagoon *salt flat* Austr.
67 K3 Pernik Bulg.
64 F2 Péronne France
64 F5 Perpignan France
59 B7 Perranporth U.K.
34 D5 Perris U.S.A.
64 C2 Perros-Guirec France
29 D6 Perry *FL* U.S.A.
29 D5 Perry *GA* U.S.A.
26 E3 Perry *IA* U.S.A.
27 D4 Perry *OK* U.S.A.
32 B4 Perrysburg U.S.A.
27 C4 Perryton U.S.A.
27 F4 Perryville U.S.A.
59 E5 Pershore U.K.
Persia *country* see Iran
Persian Gulf *g.* see The Gulf
81 G2 Pertek Turkey
112 C6 Perth Austr.
31 J3 Perth Can.
57 F4 Perth U.K.
33 F4 Perth Amboy U.S.A.
33 K1 Perth-Andover Can.
68 F1 Pertominsk Rus. Fed.
64 G5 Pertuis France
55 U6 Pertunmaa Fin.
66 C4 Pertusato, Capo *pt* France
38 Peru *country* S. America
30 C5 Peru U.S.A.
15 N7 Peru Basin *sea feature* Pac. Oc.
15 P7 Peru-Chile Trench *sea feature* Pac. Oc.
66 E3 Perugia Italy
46 C4 Peruíbe Brazil
61 B4 Péruwelz Belgium
68 G4 Pervomaysk Rus. Fed.
69 D5 Pervomays'k Ukr.

68 K2 Pervomayskaya Rus. Fed.
69 E6 Pervomays'ke Ukr.
68 G4 Pervomayskiy Rus. Fed.
69 F5 Pervomays'kyy Ukr.
77 S3 Pervorechenskiy Rus. Fed.
66 E3 Pesaro Italy
34 A3 Pescadero U.S.A.
35 H4 Pescado U.S.A.
66 F3 Pescara Italy
66 F3 Pescara *r.* Italy
69 G6 Peschanokopskoye Rus. Fed.
95 □ Pesek, P. *i.* Sing.
84 B2 Peshawar Pak.
67 J4 Peshkopi Albania
67 L3 Peshtera Bulg.
30 D3 Peshtigo U.S.A.
30 D3 Peshtigo *r.* U.S.A.
66 F1 Pesnica Slovenia
64 D4 Pessac France
68 E3 Pestovo Rus. Fed.
68 F1 Pet *r.* Rus. Fed.
80 E5 Petah Tiqwa Israel
67 L5 Petalioi *i.* Greece
34 A2 Petaluma U.S.A.
61 D5 Pétange Lux.
45 D2 Petare Venez.
36 D5 Petatlán Mex.
103 D5 Petauke Zambia
31 J3 Petawawa Can.
30 C3 Petenwell Lake *l.* U.S.A.
114 C4 Peterborough *S.A.* Austr.
114 E7 Peterborough *Vic.* Austr.
31 H3 Peterborough Can.
59 G5 Peterborough U.K.
57 F3 Peterculter U.K.
57 G3 Peterhead U.K.
119 A3 Peter I Island *i.* Antarctica
21 L2 Peter Lake *l.* Can.
58 F3 Peterlee U.K.
112 E5 Petermann Ranges *mts* Austr.
47 B2 Peteroa, Vol. *vol.* Chile
21 H3 Peter Pond L. *l.* Can.
23 F2 Peters, Lac *l.* Can.
20 C3 Petersburg *AK* U.S.A.
30 C6 Petersburg *IL* U.S.A.
32 E6 Petersburg *VA* U.S.A.
32 D5 Petersburg *WV* U.S.A.
59 G6 Petersfield U.K.
66 G5 Petilia Policastro Italy
22 E2 Petite Rivière de la Baleine *r.* Can.
23 G3 Petit Lac Manicouagan *l.* Can.
33 K2 Petit Manan Pt *pt* U.S.A.
22 J3 Petit Mécatina *r.* Can.
20 C3 Petitot *r.* Can.
36 G4 Peto Mex.
30 E3 Petoskey U.S.A.
80 E6 Petra Jordan
87 O3 Petra Velikogo, Zaliv *b.* Rus. Fed.
31 J4 Petre, Pt *pt* Can.
67 K4 Petrich Bulg.
35 H4 Pergamino Forest Nat. Park *nat. park* U.S.A.
66 G2 Petrinja Croatia
67 K3 Petrokhanski Prokhod *pass* Bulg.
31 F4 Petrolia Can.
43 F4 Petrolina Brazil
69 G5 Petropavlovka Rus. Fed.
76 H4 Petropavlovsk Kazak.
77 R4 Petropavlovsk-Kamchatskiy Rus. Fed.
67 K2 Petroşani Romania
69 H4 Petrovsk Rus. Fed.
87 J1 Petrovsk-Zabaykal'skiy Rus. Fed.
69 H5 Petrov Val Rus. Fed.
68 E2 Petrozavodsk Rus. Fed.
105 F4 Petrusburg S. Africa
105 H3 Petrus Steyn S. Africa
104 F5 Petrusville S. Africa
60 F3 Pettigo U.K.
76 H4 Petukhovo Rus. Fed.
95 A4 Peureula Indon.
77 T3 Pevek Rus. Fed.
62 H6 Pezinok Slovakia
62 D6 Pforzheim Ger.
62 D7 Pfullendorf Ger.
84 C3 Phagwara India
105 G4 Phahameng *Free State* S. Africa
105 H2 Phahameng *Northern Province* S. Africa
105 J1 Phalaborwa S. Africa
84 C4 Phalodi India
84 B4 Phalsund India
95 B2 Phan Thai.
95 B2 Phanat Nikhom Thai.
95 B3 Phangan, Ko *i.* Thai.
95 A3 Phangnga Thai.
95 D3 Phan Rang Vietnam
95 D3 Phan Ri Vietnam
95 D3 Phan Thiêt Vietnam
27 D7 Pharr U.S.A.
89 C6 Phat Diêm Vietnam
95 B3 Phatthalung Thai.
95 A1 Phayao Thai.
84 H4 Phek India
21 J3 Phelps Lake *l.* Can.
95 B1 Phen Thai.
29 C5 Phenix City U.S.A.
95 A2 Phet Buri Thai.
95 B1 Phetchabun Thai.
95 B2 Phiafai Laos
95 B1 Phichai Thai.
95 B1 Phichit Thai.
27 F5 Philadelphia *MS* U.S.A.
33 F2 Philadelphia *NY* U.S.A.
33 F5 Philadelphia *PA* U.S.A.

26 C2 Philip U.S.A.
61 C4 Philippeville Belgium
32 C5 Philippi U.S.A.
71 Philippines *country* Asia
94 C2 Philippine Sea *sea* Phil.
13 N3 Philippine Trench *sea feature* Pac. Oc.
105 F5 Philippolis S. Africa
32 D4 Philipsburg U.S.A.
61 C3 Philipsdam *barrage* Neth.
104 F5 Philipstown S. Africa
114 F7 Phillip I. *i.* Austr.
33 H2 Phillips *ME* U.S.A.
30 B3 Phillips *WI* U.S.A.
26 D4 Phillipsburg *KS* U.S.A.
33 F4 Phillipsburg *NJ* U.S.A.
32 D4 Phillipston U.S.A.
33 G3 Philmont U.S.A.
21 G3 Philomena Can.
32 C6 Philpott Reservoir *resr* U.S.A.
95 B2 Phimae Thai.
95 C2 Phimun Mangsahan Thai.
105 G3 Phiritona S. Africa
95 B1 Phitsanulok Thai.
95 C3 Phnum Pénh Cambodia
95 B4 Pho, Laem *pt* Thai.
35 F5 Phoenix U.S.A.
14 H6 Phoenix Islands *is* Pac. Oc.
105 G3 Phomolong S. Africa
95 B2 Phon Thai.
92 C2 Phôngsali Laos
89 B6 Phong Thô Vietnam
95 B1 Phon Phisai Thai.
95 B1 Phon Thong Thai.
114 E7 Phoques Bay *b.* Austr.
95 B1 Phou San *mt* Laos
95 B1 Phrae Thai.
95 A1 Phrao Thai.
95 B2 Phra Phutthabat Thai.
95 A3 Phra Thong, Ko *i.* Thai.
89 B6 Phuc Yên Vietnam
95 D2 Phu Hôi Vietnam
95 A3 Phuket Thai.
95 A3 Phuket, Ko *i.* Thai.
84 C4 Phulera India
85 G5 Phultala Bangl.
89 B6 Phu Ly Vietnam
95 B2 Phumĭ Bânhchok Kon Cambodia
95 C3 Phumĭ Chhuk Cambodia
95 C2 Phumĭ Kâmpóng Trâlach Cambodia
95 B2 Phumĭ Kaôh Kŏng Cambodia
95 B2 Phumĭ Kiliĕk Cambodia
95 C2 Phumĭ Mlu Prey Cambodia
95 C2 Phumĭ Moŭng Cambodia
95 B2 Phumĭ Prâmaôy Cambodia
95 B2 Phumĭ Sâmraông Cambodia
95 C2 Phumĭ Toêng Cambodia
95 D2 Phu My Vietnam
95 B1 Phu Nhon Vietnam
95 C3 Phuoc Long Vietnam
95 C3 Phu Quôc Vietnam
95 B3 Phu Quôc, Dao *i.* Vietnam
105 H4 Phuthaditjhaba S. Africa
89 B6 Phu Tho Vietnam
95 B1 Phu Wiang Thai.
43 J5 Piaca Brazil
66 C2 Piacenza Italy
115 H3 Pian *r.* Austr.
88 D2 Pianguan China
66 D3 Pianosa, Isola *i.* Italy
63 N7 Piatra Neamţ Romania
43 K5 Piauí *r.* Brazil
66 E1 Piave *r.* Italy
101 F4 Pibor *r.* Sudan
101 F4 Pibor Post Sudan
30 D1 Pic *r.* Can.
30 D1 Pic, I. *i.* Can.
35 F4 Pica U.S.A.
35 G5 Picacho *AZ* U.S.A.
35 E5 Picacho *CA* U.S.A.
25 D6 Picachos, Cerro dos *mt* Mex.
64 F2 Picardie *reg.* France
Picardy *reg.* see Picardie
29 B6 Picayune U.S.A.
25 F6 Picháchic Mex.
44 D2 Pichanal Arg.
47 C2 Pichi Ciego Arg.
44 B3 Pichilemu Chile
47 D3 Pichi Mahuida Arg.
84 D4 Pichor India
58 G3 Pickering U.K.
58 G3 Pickering, Vale of *v.* U.K.
30 E2 Pickford U.S.A.
22 B3 Pickle Lake Can.
45 D4 Pico da Neblina, Parque Nacional do *nat. park* Brazil
37 K5 Pico Duarte *mt* Dom. Rep.
45 E4 Pico Redondo *summit* Brazil
45 E4 Pico Rondon *summit* Brazil
43 K5 Picos Brazil
44 C7 Pico Truncado Arg.
30 D1 Pic River Can.
115 J5 Picton Austr.
31 J4 Picton Can.
115 G5 Piton, Mt *mt* Austr.
23 H4 Pictou Can.
30 D2 Pictured Rocks National Lakeshore *res.* U.S.A.
47 C3 Picún Leufú *r.* Arg.
45 B3 Piedecuesta Col.
47 C1 Pie de Palo, Sa *mts* Arg.

29 C5 Piedmont U.S.A.
32 C4 Piedmont Lake *l.* U.S.A.
47 F2 Piedras, Punta *pt* Arg.
36 D3 Piedras Negras Mex.
30 C1 Pie Island *i.* Can.
54 U5 Pieksämäki Fin.
54 U5 Pielavesi Fin.
54 V5 Pielinen *l.* Fin.
105 H2 Pietermaritzburg S. Africa
30 A2 Pierceton U.S.A.
34 A2 Piercy U.S.A.
67 K4 Pieria *mts* Greece
57 F1 Pierowall U.K.
26 C2 Pierre U.S.A.
64 G4 Pierrelatte France
105 J4 Pietermaritzburg S. Africa
105 H1 Pietersburg S. Africa
66 G5 Pietra Spada, Passo di *pass* Italy
105 J3 Piet Retief S. Africa
63 M7 Pietrosa *mt* Romania
31 H4 Pigeon U.S.A.
31 F5 Pigeon Bay *b.* Can.
32 D6 Pigg *r.* U.S.A.
27 F4 Piggott U.S.A.
105 J2 Pigg's Peak Swaziland
47 D3 Pigüé Arg.
84 E4 Pihani India
88 E1 Pi He *r.* China
55 V6 Pihlajavesi *l.* Fin.
55 R6 Pihlava Fin.
54 T5 Pihtipudas Fin.
54 T4 Piippola Fin.
54 V4 Piispajärvi Fin.
36 F5 Pijijiapan Mex.
68 E3 Pikalevo Rus. Fed.
32 D3 Pike U.S.A.
31 G3 Pike Bay Can.
104 C6 Piketberg S. Africa
32 B6 Pikeville U.S.A.
88 G2 Pikou China
47 D3 Pila Arg.
62 H4 Piła Pol.
105 G2 Pilanesberg National Park *nat. park* S. Africa
47 E2 Pilar Arg.
44 E3 Pilar Para.
94 B5 Pilas *i.* Phil.
47 B4 Pilcaniyeu Arg.
44 E3 Pilcomayo *r.* Bol./Para.
94 B3 Pili Phil.
84 D3 Pilibhit India
115 H9 Pillar, C. *c.* Austr.
115 K9 Pilliga Austr.
47 E2 Pillo, Isla del *i.* Arg.
46 C2 Pilões, Serra dos *mts* Brazil
34 D2 Pilot Peak *summit* U.S.A.
27 F6 Pilottown U.S.A.
35 F6 Pinacate, Cerro del *summit* Mex.
84 D4 Pinahat India
35 G5 Pinaleno Mts *mts* U.S.A.
94 B3 Pinamalayan Phil.
47 F3 Pinamar Arg.
95 B4 Pinang *i.* Malaysia
80 F2 Pınarbaşı Turkey
37 H4 Pinar del Río Cuba
67 J7 Pınarhisar Turkey
94 B3 Pinatubo, Mount *vol.* Phil.
63 K5 Pińczów Pol.
84 D3 Pindar *r.* India
84 J4 Pindar Arg.
84 C2 Pindi Gheb Pak.
67 J5 Pindos *mts* Greece
Pindu Pass *pass* see Pêdo La
Pindus Mts *mts* see Pindos
35 G4 Pine *r.* MI U.S.A.
30 E3 Pine *r.* MI U.S.A.
30 C3 Pine *r.* WV U.S.A.
23 K4 Pine, C. *c.* Can.
27 E5 Pine Bluff U.S.A.
24 F3 Pine Bluffs U.S.A.
30 A3 Pine City U.S.A.
112 E4 Pine Creek Austr.
32 E4 Pine Creek *r.* U.S.A.
34 B2 Pinecrest U.S.A.
34 C3 Pinedale *CA* U.S.A.
24 E3 Pinedale *WY* U.S.A.
21 K4 Pine Falls Can.
34 C3 Pine Flat Lake *l.* U.S.A.
68 G1 Pinega Rus. Fed.
68 G1 Pinega *r.* Rus. Fed.
33 H4 Pine Grove U.S.A.
29 D6 Pine Hills U.S.A.
21 H3 Pinehouse Lake Can.
30 A3 Pine Island Can.
119 A3 Pine Island Bay *b.* Antarctica
33 F4 Pine Lake U.S.A.
27 E6 Pineland U.S.A.
34 B4 Pine Mt *mt* U.S.A.
35 F4 Pine Peak *summit* U.S.A.
26 C2 Pine Point U.S.A.
26 C2 Pine Ridge U.S.A.
34 C3 Pineridge U.S.A.
66 B2 Pinerolo Italy
42 C6 Pinar de Río Cuba
33 F3 Pinestone U.S.A.
62 G6 Písek Czech Rep.
42 C6 Pisco, B. de *b.* Peru
42 C6 Pisco Peru
33 F3 Piseco Lake *l.* U.S.A.
105 J4 Pinetown S. Africa
32 B6 Pineville *KY* U.S.A.
27 E6 Pineville *LA* U.S.A.
32 C6 Pineville *WV* U.S.A.
95 B2 Ping, Mae Nam *r.* Thai.
88 B2 Ping'an China

89 B6 Pingbian China
88 F3 Ping Dao *i.* China
88 D2 Pingding China
88 D3 Pingdingshan China
88 F2 Pingdu China
89 E5 Pingguo China
88 E5 Pinghe China
89 D5 Pingjiang China
88 D5 Pingle China
88 C3 Pingli China
88 D2 Pingliang China
88 D2 Pinglu China
88 C2 Pingluo China
89 F5 Pingnan *Fujian* China
89 D6 Pingnan *Guangxi* China
88 F1 Pingquan China
88 E2 Pingshan China
89 F5 Pingshi China
89 F5 Pingtan China
89 F6 P'ingtung Taiwan
88 C3 Pingwu China
89 C6 Pingxiang *Guangxi* China
89 D5 Pingxiang *Jiangxi* China
89 E5 Pingyang China
88 D2 Pingyao China
88 E2 Pingyin China
88 E2 Pingyu China
89 E5 Pingyuan China
89 B6 Pingyuanjie China
89 C5 Pingzhai China
43 J4 Pinheiro Brazil
46 C3 Pinheiro Machado Brazil
59 D7 Pinhoe U.K.
112 C6 Pinjarra Austr.
20 E3 Pink Mountain Can.
117 D4 Pinnacle *mt* N.Z.
114 D5 Pinnaroo Austr.
34 C4 Pinos, Mt *mt* U.S.A.
36 E5 Pinotepa Nacional Mex.
111 G4 Pins, Î. des *i.* New Caledonia
31 G4 Pins, Pointe aux *pt* Can.
69 C4 Pinsk Belarus
42 Pinta, Isla *i.* Ecuador
35 Pinta, Sierra *summit* U.S.A.
35 F3 Pintura U.S.A.
35 F3 Pioche U.S.A.
103 Piodi Dem. Rep. Congo
76 K1 Pioner, O. *i.* Rus. Fed.
63 Pionerskiy Rus. Fed.
63 K5 Pionki Pol.
117 E3 Piopio N.Z.
42 F4 Piorini, Lago *l.* Brazil
63 J5 Piotrków Trybunalski Pol.
90 A3 Pipa Dingzi *mt* China
84 C4 Pipar India
23 F4 Pipmuacan, Réservoir *resr* Can.
32 A4 Piqua U.S.A.
46 A2 Piquiri *r.* Mato Grosso do Sul Brazil
46 A2 Piquiri *r.* Paraná Brazil
46 C3 Piracanjuba Brazil
46 C3 Piracicaba Brazil
46 D2 Piracicaba *r.* Minas Gerais Brazil
46 C3 Piracicaba *r.* São Paulo Brazil
46 D2 Piraçununga Brazil
43 K4 Piracuruca Brazil
Piraeus see Peiraias
46 C3 Piraí do Sul Brazil
46 C3 Pirajuí Brazil
84 C2 Piram I. *i.* India
46 B2 Piranhas Brazil
46 B2 Piranhas *r.* Goiás Brazil
43 L5 Piranhas *r.* Paraíba/Rio Grande do Norte Brazil
45 B3 Piraparaná *r.* Col.
46 B3 Pirapó *r.* Brazil
46 D2 Pirapora Brazil
47 G1 Piratini Brazil
47 G1 Piratini *r.* Brazil
84 C4 Pirawa India
46 C3 Pires do Rio Brazil
85 G4 Pirganj Bangl.
43 K4 Piripiri Brazil
45 C2 Piritu Venez.
46 A2 Pirizal Brazil
67 K3 Pirot Yugo.
84 C2 Pir Panjal Pass *pass* India
84 C2 Pir Panjal Range *mts* India/Pak.
45 A3 Pirre, Co *mt* Panama
81 M2 Pirsaat Azer.
81 M1 Pirsaatçay *r.* Azer.
93 H7 Piru Indon.
66 D3 Pisa Italy
117 B6 Pisa, Mt *mt* N.Z.
44 B1 Pisagua Chile
35 F4 Piscataway U.S.A.

100 A3 Pita Guinea
23 G3 Pitaga Can.
45 A4 Pitalito Col.
46 B4 Pitanga Brazil
46 D2 Pitangui Brazil
114 E5 Pitarpunga L. *l.* Austr.
54 R4 Piteå Sweden
54 R4 Piteälven *r.* Sweden
69 H5 Piterka Rus. Fed.
67 L2 Piteşti Romania
112 C6 Pithara Austr.
57 F4 Pitlochry U.K.
20 D4 Pitt I. *i.* Can.
111 J6 Pitt Island *i.* Pac. Oc.
32 D4 Pittsburg U.S.A.
30 B6 Pittsfield *IL* U.S.A.
33 G3 Pittsfield *MA* U.S.A.
33 J2 Pittsfield *ME* U.S.A.
33 H3 Pittsfield *NH* U.S.A.
33 G3 Pittsfield *VT* U.S.A.
115 J1 Pittsworth Austr.
21 K2 Pitz Lake *l.* Can.
46 D3 Piumhi Brazil
42 B5 Piura Peru
34 C4 Piute Peak *summit* U.S.A.
85 E3 Piuthan Nepal
63 O6 Pivdennyy Buh *r.* Ukr.
66 F2 Pivka Slovenia
84 D1 Pixa China
62 E7 Piz Buin *mt* Austria/Switz.
68 H3 Pizhma Rus. Fed.
68 H3 Pizhma *r.* Rus. Fed.
88 F3 Pizhou China
23 K4 Placentia Can.
23 K4 Placentia B. *b.* Can.
94 C4 Placer Phil.
94 B4 Placer Phil.
34 B2 Placerville U.S.A.
37 J4 Placetas Cuba
33 H4 Plainfield *CT* U.S.A.
30 C5 Plainfield *IL* U.S.A.
30 A3 Plainview *MN* U.S.A.
26 D3 Plainview *NE* U.S.A.
27 C5 Plainview *TX* U.S.A.
33 J1 Plaisted U.S.A.
77 T3 Plamennyy Rus. Fed.
20 G4 Plamondon Can.
34 B3 Planada U.S.A.
46 C1 Planaltina Brazil
47 B2 Planchón, Paso del *pass* Arg.
45 B2 Planeta Rica Col.
26 D3 Plankinton U.S.A.
30 C5 Plano *IL* U.S.A.
27 D5 Plano *TX* U.S.A.
29 D7 Plantation U.S.A.
27 F6 Plaquemine U.S.A.
65 C2 Plasencia Spain
33 K1 Plaster Rock Can.
90 D2 Plastun Rus. Fed.
66 E6 Platani *r.* Italy
45 B2 Plato Col.
26 C3 Platte U.S.A.
30 C5 Platteville U.S.A.
33 G2 Plattsburgh U.S.A.
26 E3 Plattsmouth U.S.A.
62 F5 Plauen Ger.
68 F4 Plavsk Rus. Fed.
25 E6 Playa Noriega, L. *l.* Mex.
42 B4 Playas Ecuador
95 D2 Plây Cu Vietnam
21 K4 Playgreen L. *l.* Can.
47 C3 Plaza Huincul Arg.
35 F5 Pleasant, Lake *l.* U.S.A.
35 G1 Pleasant Grove U.S.A.
35 H5 Pleasanton *NM* U.S.A.
27 D6 Pleasanton *TX* U.S.A.
117 C6 Pleasant Point N.Z.
35 H3 Pleasant View U.S.A.
28 C4 Pleasure Ridge Park U.S.A.
64 F4 Pleaux France
95 C2 Plei Doch Vietnam
117 F2 Plenty, Bay of *b.* N.Z.
24 F1 Plentywood U.S.A.
68 G2 Plesetsk Rus. Fed.
23 F3 Pletipi, Lac *l.* Can.
104 E7 Plettenberg Bay S. Africa
67 L3 Pleven Bulg.
67 H3 Pljevlja Yugo.
63 J4 Płock Pol.
66 G3 Plo<no *mt* Bos.-Herz.
68 D2 Plodovoye Rus. Fed.
64 C3 Ploemeur France
67 M2 Ploiești Romania
63 P2 Ploskosh' Rus. Fed.
68 E3 Ploskoye Rus. Fed.
62 G4 Ploty Pol.
64 B2 Ploudalmézeau France
64 B2 Plouzané France
67 L3 Plovdiv Bulg.
30 C3 Plover U.S.A.
30 C3 Plover *r.* U.S.A.
89 □ Plover Cove Reservoir *resr* China
33 G4 Plum I. *i.* U.S.A.
24 C3 Plummer U.S.A.
55 R9 Plungė Lith.
63 N3 Plyeshchanitsy Belarus
95 A1 Ply Huey Wati, Khao *mt* Myanmar/Thai.
37 M5 Plymouth Montserrat

59	C7	Plymouth U.K.
34	B2	Plymouth CA U.S.A.
30	D5	Plymouth IN U.S.A.
33	H4	Plymouth MA U.S.A.
33	H3	Plymouth NH U.S.A.
28	F3	Plymouth PA U.S.A.
33	H4	Plymouth WV U.S.A.
33	H4	Plymouth Bay b. U.S.A.
59	D5	Plynlimon h. U.K.
62	F6	Plzeň Czech Rep.
100	B3	Pô Burkina
100	B3	Pô, Parc National de nat. park Burkina
76	K5	Pobedy, Pik mt China/Kyrgyzstan
27	F4	Pocahontas U.S.A.
32	C5	Pocatalico r. U.S.A.
24	D3	Pocatello U.S.A.
69	C5	Pochayiv Ukr.
68	E4	Pochep Rus. Fed.
68	H4	Pochinki Rus. Fed.
68	E4	Pochinok Rus. Fed.
62	F6	Pocking Ger.
58	G4	Pocklington U.K.
46	E1	Poções Brazil
33	F5	Pocomoke City U.S.A.
33	F6	Pocomoke Sound b. U.S.A.
46	A2	Poconé Brazil
33	H4	Pocono Mountains h. U.S.A.
33	F4	Pocono Summit U.S.A.
46	C3	Poços de Caldas Brazil
68	D3	Poddor'ye Rus. Fed.
69	F5	Podgorenskiy Rus. Fed.
67	H3	Podgorica Yugo.
76	K4	Podgornoye Rus. Fed.
77	L3	Podkamennaya Tunguska r. Rus. Fed.
42	C6	Podocarpus, Parque Nacional nat. park Ecuador
68	F4	Podol'sk Rus. Fed.
69	F5	Podporozh'ye Rus. Fed.
66	G1	Podravina reg. Hungary
67	J3	Podujevo Yugo.
69	H2	Podvoloch'ye Rus. Fed.
68	J2	Podz' Rus. Fed.
104	C4	Pofadder S. Africa
31	G2	Pogamasing Can.
69	E4	Pogar Rus. Fed.
66	D3	Poggibonsi Italy
67	J4	Pogradec Albania
69	A2	Poguba r. Brazil
87	N4	P'ohang S. Korea
69	D5	Pohrebyshche Ukr.
84	D4	Pohri India
67	K3	Poiana Mare Romania
102	C4	Poie Dem. Rep. Congo
119	C6	Poinsett, C. c. Antarctica
20	G4	Point Arena U.S.A.
118	C2	Point Barrow pt U.S.A.
31	K2	Point-Comfort Can.
37	M5	Pointe-à-Pitre Guadeloupe
31	J3	Pointe au Baril Sta. Can.
102	B4	Pointe-Noire Congo
114	A4	Point Kenny Austr.
20	G1	Point Lake l. Can.
115	K3	Point Lookout mt Austr.
31	F5	Point Pelee National Park nat. park Can.
33	F4	Point Pleasant NJ U.S.A.
32	B5	Point Pleasant WV U.S.A.
31	K3	Poisson Blanc, Lac du l. Can.
112	C3	Poissonnier Pt pt Austr.
64	E3	Poitiers France
64	D3	Poitou reg. France
46	E1	Pojuca Brazil
84	B4	Pokaran India
115	H2	Pokataroo Austr.
85	E3	Pokhara Nepal
102	C3	Poko Dem. Rep. Congo
84	A4	Pokran U.K.
90	C2	Pokrovka Rus. Fed.
90	B3	Pokrovka Rus. Fed.
77	O3	Pokrovsk Rus. Fed.
69	F6	Pokrovskoye Rus. Fed.
68	H2	Pokshen'ga r. Rus. Fed.
94	B3	Pola Phil.
35	G4	Polacca U.S.A.
35	G4	Polacca Wash r. U.S.A.
65	D1	Pola de Lena Spain
65	D1	Pola de Siero Spain
48		Poland country Europe
33	F3	Poland U.S.A.
22	D3	Polar Bear Provincial Park res. Can.
80	D2	Polatlı Turkey
68	D4	Polatsk Belarus
63	N3	Polatskaya Nizina lowland Belarus
54	N3	Polcirkeln Sweden
68	H2	Poldarsa Rus. Fed.
81	K2	Pol Dasht Iran
84	B2	Pol-e Khomrī Afgh.
68	G4	Polessk Rus. Fed.
93	H7	Polewali Indon.
101	D4	Poli Cameroon
62	G4	Police Pol.
66	G4	Policoro Italy
64	G3	Poligny France
94	B3	Polillo i. Phil.
94	B3	Polillo Islands is Phil.
94	B3	Polillo Strait chan. Phil.
80	D4	Polis Cyprus
69	D5	Polis'ke Ukr.
62	H5	Polkowice Pol.
65	H3	Pollença Spain
66	F4	Pollino, Monte mt Italy
54	U1	Polmak Norway
54	V4	Polo Fin.
30	C5	Polo U.S.A.
89	□	Polo Channel sea chan. China
69	F6	Polohy Ukr.
68	J3	Polom Rus. Fed.
94	C5	Polomoloc Phil.
69	C5	Polonne Ukr.
59	C7	Polperro U.K.
24	D2	Polson U.S.A.
68	U1	Polta r. Rus. Fed.
69	E5	Poltava Ukr.
90	B2	Poltavka Rus. Fed.
69	F6	Poltavskaya Rus. Fed.
55	T7	Põltsamaa Estonia
55	U7	Põlva Estonia
54	V5	Polvijärvi Fin.
54	X2	Polyarnyy Rus. Fed.
77	T3	Polyarnyy Rus. Fed.
54	X3	Polyarnyye Zori Rus. Fed.
67	K4	Polygyros Greece
67	K4	Polykastro Greece
14	H6	Polynesia is Pac. Oc.
55	S6	Pomarkku Fin.
46	D3	Pomba r. Brazil
65	B3	Pombal Port.
46	B3	Pombo r. Brazil
105	J4	Pomeroy S. Africa
60	E3	Pomeroy U.K.
32	B5	Pomeroy U.S.A.
66	E4	Pomezia Italy
104	E2	Pomfret S. Africa
110	F2	Pomio P.N.G.
116	E6	Pomona U.S.A.
34	D4	Pomona U.S.A.
67	M3	Pomorie Bulg.
62	G3	Pomorska, Zatoka b. Pol.
68	E1	Pomorskiy Bereg coastal area Rus. Fed. Pomo Tso l. see Puma Yumco
29	D7	Pompano Beach U.S.A.
46	D2	Pompéu Brazil
68	H3	Ponazyrevo Rus. Fed.
27	D4	Ponca City U.S.A.
37	L5	Ponce Puerto Rico
25	F4	Poncha Springs U.S.A.
22	E3	Poncheville, Lac l. Can.
83	E8	Pondicherry India
23	J3	Ponds, Island of i. Can.
65	C1	Ponferrada Spain
117	F4	Pongaroa N.Z.
101	E4	Pongo watercourse Sudan
105	K3	Pongola r. S. Africa
105	J3	Pongolapoort Dam resr S. Africa
63	P3	Ponizov'ye Rus. Fed.
85	H5	Ponnyadaung Range mts Myanmar
20	G4	Ponoka Can.
100	□	Ponta do Sol Cape Verde
46	B4	Ponta Grossa Brazil
46	C2	Pontalina Brazil
64	H2	Pont-à-Mousson France
46	A3	Ponta Porã Brazil
64	H3	Pontarlier France
27	F6	Pontchartrain, L. l. U.S.A.
65	B3	Ponte de Sor Port.
58	F4	Pontefract U.K.
58	F2	Ponteland U.K.
43	G7	Pontes-e-Lacerda Brazil
65	B1	Pontevedra Spain
30	C5	Pontiac IL U.S.A.
31	F4	Pontiac MI U.S.A.
64	C2	Pontivy France
64	B3	Pont-l'Abbé France
64	F2	Pontoise France
21	K4	Ponton Can.
27	F5	Pontotoc U.S.A.
66	C2	Pontremoli Italy
61	A5	Pont-Ste-Maxence France
115	G9	Pontville Austr.
31	H3	Pontypool Can.
59	D6	Pontypool U.K.
59	D6	Pontypridd U.K.
66	E4	Ponza, Isola di i. Italy
66	E4	Ponziane, Isole is Italy
114	A4	Poochera Austr.
59	F7	Poole U.K.
114	E4	Pooncarie Austr.
114	F3	Poopelloe, L. salt l. Austr.
42	E7	Poopó, Lago de l. Bol.
117	E1	Poor Knights Is is N.Z.
45	A4	Popayán Col.
77	M2	Popigay r. Rus. Fed.
114	D4	Popiltah Austr.
114	D4	Popilta L. l. Austr.
21	K4	Poplar r. Can.
24	F1	Poplar U.S.A.
27	F4	Poplar Bluff U.S.A.
32	C6	Poplar Camp U.S.A.
27	F6	Poplarville U.S.A.
36	E5	Popocatépetl, Volcán vol. Mex.
92	□	Popoh Indon.
102	B4	Popokabaka Dem. Rep. Congo
67	M3	Popovo Bulg.
63	K6	Poprad Slovakia
117	F4	Porangahau N.Z.
46	C1	Porangatu Brazil
84	B5	Porbandar India
45	B3	Porce r. Col.
20	C4	Porcher I. i. Can.
18		Porcupine r. Can./U.S.A.
23	J3	Porcupine, Cape c. Can.
116	A3	Porcupine Cr. r. Austr.
21	J4	Porcupine Hills h. Can.
30	C2	Porcupine Mts mts U.S.A.
21	J4	Porcupine Plain Can.
21	J4	Porcupine Prov. Forest res. Can.
45	C3	Pore Col.
66	E2	Poreč Croatia
68	H4	Poretskoye Rus. Fed.
55	R6	Pori Fin.
117	R6	Porirua N.Z.
68	D3	Porkhov Rus. Fed.
45	D2	Porlamar Venez.
64	C3	Pornic France
94	C4	Poro i. Phil.
77	Q5	Poronaysk Rus. Fed.
67	K6	Poros Greece
68	F2	Porosozero Rus. Fed.
119	C6	Porpoise Bay b. Antarctica
54	T1	Porsangen chan. Norway
55	L7	Porsgrunn Norway
80	C2	Porsuk r. Turkey
114	C5	Port Adelaide Austr.
60	E3	Portadown U.K.
60	F3	Portaferry U.K.
33	J1	Portage ME U.S.A.
30	E4	Portage MI U.S.A.
30	C4	Portage WI U.S.A.
21	K5	Portage la Prairie Can.
26	C1	Portal U.S.A.
20	E5	Port Alberni Can.
115	G7	Port Albert Austr.
65	C3	Portalegre Port.
27	C5	Portales U.S.A.
20	C3	Port Alexander U.S.A.
105	G6	Port Alfred S. Africa
20	D4	Port Alice Can.
32	D4	Port Allegany U.S.A.
27	F6	Port Allen U.S.A.
116	D4	Port Alma Austr.
24	B1	Port Angeles U.S.A.
60	D4	Portarlington Rep. of Ireland
115	G9	Port Arthur Austr.
27	E6	Port Arthur U.S.A.
57	B5	Port Askaig U.K.
114	B4	Port Augusta Austr.
37	K5	Port-au-Prince Haiti
31	F3	Port Austin U.S.A.
23	J3	Port aux Choix Can.
60	F3	Portavogie U.K.
104	D7	Port Beaufort S. Africa
92	A4	Port Blair Andaman and Nicobar Is
31	H3	Port Burwell Can.
65	H1	Portbou Spain
31	G4	Port Burwell Can.
114	E7	Port Campbell Austr.
31	H3	Port Carling Can.
117	C6	Port Chalmers N.Z.
29	D7	Port Charlotte U.S.A.
33	G4	Port Chester U.S.A.
20	C4	Port Clements Can.
32	B4	Port Clinton U.S.A.
33	J3	Port Clyde U.S.A.
31	H4	Port Colborne Can.
20	E5	Port Coquitlam Can.
31	H4	Port Credit Can.
115	F9	Port Davey b. Austr.
37	K5	Port-de-Paix Haiti
95	B5	Port Dickson Malaysia
116	A1	Port Douglas Austr.
32	C3	Port Dover Can.
30	D3	Porte des Morts chan. U.S.A.
20	C4	Port Edward Can.
105	J5	Port Edward S. Africa
30	C3	Port Edwards U.S.A.
46	D1	Porteirinha Brazil
43	H4	Portel Brazil
31	G3	Port Elgin Can.
105	F6	Port Elizabeth S. Africa
57	B5	Port Ellen U.K.
114	C5	Port Elliot Austr.
58	C3	Port Erin U.K.
21	H2	Porter Lake l. Can.
20	C3	Porter Landing Can.
104	C6	Porterville S. Africa
34	C3	Porterville U.S.A.
114	E7	Port Fairy Austr.
117	E2	Port Fitzroy N.Z.
102	A4	Port-Gentil Gabon
114	C4	Port Germein Austr.
27	C6	Port Gibson U.S.A.
57	D5	Port Glasgow U.K.
100	C4	Port Harcourt Nigeria
20	D4	Port Hardy Can. Port Harrison see Inukjuak
23	H4	Port Hawkesbury Can.
59	D6	Porthcawl U.K.
112	C4	Port Hedland Austr.
33	G2	Port Henry U.S.A.
59	B7	Porthleven U.K.
59	C5	Porthmadog U.K.
31	H4	Port Huron U.S.A.
23	J3	Port Hope Simpson Can.
31	F4	Port Huron U.S.A.
81	M2	Port-Iliç Azer.
65	B4	Portimão Port.
115	J4	Port Jackson in. Austr.
33	G4	Port Jefferson U.S.A.
33	F4	Port Jervis U.S.A.
42	G2	Port Kaituma Guyana
115	J5	Port Kembla Austr.
115	H4	Portland N.S.W. Austr.
114	D7	Portland Vic. Austr.
30	E5	Portland IN U.S.A.
33	H3	Portland ME U.S.A.
24	B2	Portland OR U.S.A.
59	E7	Portland, Isle of pen. U.K.
20	C3	Portland Canal in. Can.
117	F3	Portland I. i. N.Z.
60	D4	Portlaoise Rep. of Ireland
27	D6	Port Lavaca U.S.A.
60	D5	Portlaw Rep. of Ireland
57	F3	Portlethen U.K.
114	A5	Port Lincoln Austr.
100	A4	Port Loko Sierra Leone
114	D7	Port MacDonnell Austr.
115	K3	Port Macquarie Austr.
23	H2	Port Manvers in. Can.
20	D4	Port McNeill Can.
23	H4	Port-Menier Can.
24	B1	Port Moody Can.
110	E2	Port Moresby P.N.G.
57	B2	Portnaguran U.K.
57	B5	Portnahaven U.K.
114	B5	Port Neill Austr.
29	F7	Port Nelson Bahamas
57	B2	Port Nis U.K.
104	B4	Port Nolloth S. Africa Port-Nouveau-Québec see Kangiqsualujjuaq Porto see Oporto
42	E5	Porto Acre Brazil
46	B3	Porto Alegre Mato Grosso do Sul Brazil
44	F4	Porto Alegre Rio Grande do Sul Brazil
43	G6	Porto Artur Brazil
43	G6	Porto dos Gaúchos Óbidos Brazil
43	G7	Porto Esperidião Brazil
66	D3	Portoferraio Italy
43	J5	Porto Franco Brazil
45	E2	Port of Spain Trinidad and Tobago
66	E2	Portogruaro Italy
100	□	Porto Inglês Cape Verde
46	A2	Porto Jofre Brazil
34	B2	Portola U.S.A.
66	D2	Portomaggiore Italy
43	G8	Porto Murtinho Brazil
43	J6	Porto Nacional Brazil
100	C4	Porto-Novo Benin
46	B3	Porto Primavera, Represa resr Brazil
24	A3	Port Orford U.S.A.
43	H4	Porto Santana Brazil
46	E2	Porto Seguro Brazil
66	E2	Porto Tolle Italy
66	C4	Porto-Vecchio France
42	F5	Porto Velho Brazil
42	B4	Portoviejo Ecuador
57	C6	Portpatrick U.K.
31	H3	Port Perry Can.
114	F7	Port Phillip Bay b. Austr.
114	C4	Port Pirie Austr.
59	B7	Portreath U.K.
57	B3	Portree U.K.
20	E5	Port Renfrew Can.
31	G4	Port Rowan Can.
32	E5	Port Royal U.S.A.
60	E2	Portrush U.K.
78	C3	Port Said Egypt
60	D2	Portsalon Rep. of Ireland
31	F4	Port Sanilac U.S.A.
31	H3	Port Severn Can.
89	□	Port Shelter b. China
105	J5	Port Shepstone S. Africa
20	C4	Port Simpson Can.
59	F7	Portsmouth U.K.
33	H3	Portsmouth NH U.S.A.
32	B5	Portsmouth OH U.S.A.
33	E6	Portsmouth VA U.S.A.
57	F3	Portsoy U.K.
115	K4	Port Stephens b. Austr.
60	E2	Portstewart U.K.
29	C7	Port St Joe U.S.A.
105	H5	Port St Johns S. Africa
58	C4	Port St Mary U.K.
101	F3	Port Sudan Sudan
29	B6	Port Sulphur U.S.A.
59	D6	Port Talbot U.K.
54	U2	Porttipahdan tekojärvi l. Fin.
48		Portugal country Europe
45	C2	Portuguesa r. Venez.
60	C4	Portumna Rep. of Ireland
114	B5	Port Victoria Austr.
111	G3	Port-Vila Vanuatu
54	X2	Port Vladimir Rus. Fed.
117	E2	Port Waikato N.Z.
114	C5	Port Wakefield Austr.
30	D4	Port Washington U.S.A.
57	D6	Port William U.K.
30	B2	Port Wing U.S.A.
47	D2	Porvenir Arg.
55	T6	Porvoo Fin.
65	D1	Posada de Llanera Spain
44	E3	Posadas Arg.
67	H2	Posavina reg. Bos.-Herz./Croatia
31	F3	Posen U.S.A.
81	L5	Posht-e Küh mts Iran
81	M3	Posht Küh h. Iran
54	V3	Posio Fin.
93	G7	Poso Indon.
81	J5	Posof Turkey
46	C1	Posse Brazil
119	A5	Possession Is is Antarctica
27	C5	Post U.S.A.
22	E2	Poste-de-la-Baleine Can.
104	E4	Postmasburg S. Africa
30	B4	Postville U.S.A.
66	G3	Posušje Bos.-Herz.
90	D3	Pos'yet Rus. Fed.
105	G3	Potchefstroom S. Africa
27	E5	Poteau U.S.A.
43	L5	Potengi r. Brazil
66	F4	Potenza Italy
114	A7	Poteriteri, Lake l. N.Z.
105	H2	Potgietersrus S. Africa
43	K5	Poti r. Brazil
81	J1	Poti r. Georgia
100	D3	Potiskum Nigeria
24	D2	Pot Mt. mt U.S.A.
89	□	Po Toi i. China
32	E5	Potomac r. U.S.A.
32	D5	Potomac, South Branch r. U.S.A.
32	D5	Potomac, South Fork South Branch r. U.S.A.
42	E7	Potosí Bol.
26	F4	Potosi U.S.A.
35	E4	Potosi Mt mt U.S.A.
94	B4	Pototan Phil.
62	F4	Potsdam Ger.
33	F2	Potsdam U.S.A.
59	E6	Potterne U.K.
59	G6	Potters Bar U.K.
33	F4	Pottstown U.S.A.
33	E4	Pottsville U.S.A.
20	E3	Pouce Coupe Can.
23	K4	Pouch Cove Can.
33	G4	Poughkeepsie U.S.A.
33	G3	Poultney U.S.A.
58	E4	Poulton-le-Fylde U.K.
46	D3	Pouso Alegre Brazil
95	B2	Poŭthĭsăt Cambodia
63	J6	Považská Bystrica Slovakia
68	E2	Povenets Rus. Fed.
117	F3	Poverty Bay b. N.Z.
67	H2	Povlen mt Yugo.
65	B2	Póvoa de Varzim Port.
69	G5	Povorino Rus. Fed.
90	C3	Povorotnyy, Mys hd Rus. Fed.
34	D5	Poway U.S.A.
24	F2	Powder r. U.S.A.
24	F3	Powder River U.S.A.
24	E2	Powell U.S.A.
32	B6	Powell r. U.S.A.
35	G3	Powell, Lake resr U.S.A.
34	C2	Powell Mt mt U.S.A.
29	F7	Powell Pt pt Bahamas
20	E5	Powell River Can.
30	D3	Powers U.S.A.
32	C6	Powhatan U.S.A.
46	A1	Poxoréu Brazil
89	E4	Poyang Hu l. China
95	□	Poyan Res. resr Sing.
30	C3	Poygan, Lake l. U.S.A.
80	E3	Pozantı Turkey
67	J2	Požarevac Yugo.
36	E4	Poza Rica Mex.
66	G2	Požega Croatia
67	J3	Požega Yugo.
90	D1	Pozharskoye Rus. Fed.
62	H4	Poznań Pol.
65	D3	Pozoblanco Spain
25	E6	Pozo Nuevo Mex.
66	F4	Pozzuoli Italy
92	C7	Prabumulih Indon.
62	G6	Prachatice Czech Rep.
85	F6	Prachi r. India
95	B2	Prachin Buri Thai.
95	A3	Prachuap Khiri Khan Thai.
64	F5	Prades France
46	E2	Prado Brazil
62	G5	Prague Czech Rep. Praha see Prague
100	□	Praia Cape Verde
105	K2	Praia do Bilene Moz.
46	A1	Praia Rica Brazil
116	A3	Prairie Austr.
30	E5	Prairie Creek Reservoir resr U.S.A.
27	C5	Prairie Dog Town Fork r. U.S.A.
30	B4	Prairie du Chien U.S.A.
95	B2	Prakhon Chai Thai.
95	B2	Pran r. Thai.
92	B6	Prapat Indon.
67	M7	Prasonisi, Akra pt Greece
46	C2	Prata Brazil
46	C2	Prata r. Brazil
66	D3	Prato Italy
27	D4	Pratt U.S.A.
27	G5	Prattville U.S.A.
63	K3	Pravdinsk Rus. Fed.
65	C1	Pravia Spain
92	F8	Praya Indon.
95	C2	Preăh Vihéar Cambodia
63	Q3	Prechistoye Rus. Fed.
21	J4	Preeceville Can.
68	B4	Pregolya r. Rus. Fed.
55	U8	Preiļi Latvia
31	H1	Preissac, Lac l. Can.
95	C3	Prêk Tnaôt l. Cambodia
115	H3	Premer Austr.
64	F3	Prémery France
30	B3	Prentice U.S.A.
62	F4	Prenzlau Ger.
90	C3	Preobrazheniye Rus. Fed.
62	H6	Přerov Czech Rep.
33	F2	Prescott Can.
35	F4	Prescott U.S.A.
35	F4	Prescott Valley U.S.A.
59	C6	Preseli, Mynydd h. U.K.
67	J3	Preševo Yugo.
26	C3	Presho U.S.A.
44	D3	Presidencia Roque Sáenz Peña Arg.
43	K5	Presidente Dutra Brazil
119	B2	Presidente Eduardo Frei Chile Base Antarctica
46	B3	Presidente Epitácio Brazil
42	F6	Presidente Hermes Brazil
46	B3	Presidente Prudente Brazil
46	B3	Presidente Venceslau Brazil
27	B6	Presidio U.S.A.
63	K6	Prešov Slovakia
67	J4	Prespa, Lake l. Europe
33	K1	Presque Isle U.S.A.
30	D2	Presque Isle Pt pt U.S.A.
59	D5	Presteigne U.K.
58	E4	Preston U.K.
24	E3	Preston ID U.S.A.
30	A4	Preston MN U.S.A.
27	E4	Preston MO U.S.A.
35	E2	Preston NV U.S.A.
57	F5	Prestonpans U.K.
32	B6	Prestonsburg U.S.A.
57	D5	Prestwick U.K.
46	E1	Preto r. Bahia Brazil
46	C2	Preto r. Minas Gerais Brazil
105	H2	Pretoria S. Africa
32	E5	Prettyboy Lake l. U.S.A.
67	J5	Preveza Greece
95	C3	Prey Vêng Cambodia
87	L1	Priazovs'ke Ukr.
77	V4	Pribilof Islands is Alaska
67	H3	Priboj Yugo.
23	G4	Price Can.
35	G2	Price U.S.A.
20	D4	Price I. i. Can.
29	B6	Prichard U.S.A.
55	R8	Priekule Latvia
55	T8	Priekuli Latvia
55	S9	Prienai Lith.
104	E4	Prieska S. Africa
24	C1	Priest L. l. U.S.A.
24	C1	Priest River U.S.A.
63	J6	Prievidza Slovakia
66	G2	Prijedor Bos.-Herz.
67	H3	Prijepolje Yugo.
76	F5	Prikaspiyskaya Nizmennost' lowland Kazak./Rus. Fed.
67	J4	Prilep Macedonia
47	J4	Primero r. Arg.
115	G8	Prime Seal I. i. Austr.
55	V6	Primorsk Rus. Fed.
90	C2	Primorskiy Kray div. Rus. Fed.
69	F6	Primorsko-Akhtarsk Rus. Fed.
34	D5	Primo Tapia Mex.
21	H4	Primrose Lake l. Can.
21	H4	Prince Albert Can.
104	E6	Prince Albert S. Africa
21	H4	Prince Albert National Park nat. park Can.
104	D6	Prince Albert Road S. Africa
118	A3	Prince Charles I. i. Can.
119	D4	Prince Charles Mts mts Antarctica
23	H4	Prince Edward Island div. Can.
13	G7	Prince Edward Islands is Indian Ocean
31	J4	Prince Edward Pt pt Can.
32	C5	Prince Frederick U.S.A.
20	E4	Prince George Can.
113	H2	Prince of Wales I. i. Austr.
118	B2	Prince of Wales I. i. Can.
20	C3	Prince of Wales Island i. U.S.A.
118	B2	Prince Patrick I. i. Can.
20	C4	Prince Rupert Can.
21	K2	Princes Mary Lake l. Can.
33	F5	Princess Anne U.S.A.
113	H2	Princess Charlotte Bay b. Austr.
119	D5	Princess Elizabeth Land reg. Antarctica
20	D4	Princess Royal I. i. Can.
20	E5	Princeton Can.
34	A2	Princeton CA U.S.A.
30	C5	Princeton IL U.S.A.
28	C4	Princeton IN U.S.A.
28	C4	Princeton KY U.S.A.
33	K2	Princeton ME U.S.A.
26	E3	Princeton MO U.S.A.
33	F4	Princeton NJ U.S.A.
32	C6	Princeton WV U.S.A.
30	C4	Princeton WV U.S.A.
33	K2	Prince William Can.
100	C4	Príncipe i. Sao Tome and Principe
24	C2	Prineville U.S.A.
76	C2	Prins Karls Forland i. Svalbard
37	H6	Prinzapolca Nic.
68	D2	Priozersk Rus. Fed. Pripet r. see Pryp"yat Pripet r. see Prypyats'
54	W2	Prirechnyy Rus. Fed.
67	J3	Priština Yugo.
62	F4	Pritzwalk Ger.
64	G4	Privas France
66	F2	Privlaka Croatia
68	G3	Privolzhsk Rus. Fed.
68	H4	Privolzhskaya Vozvyshennost' reg. Rus. Fed.
69	G6	Priyutnoye Rus. Fed.
67	J3	Prizren Yugo.
92	□	Probolinggo Indon.
59	C7	Probus U.K.
30	A2	Proctor MN U.S.A.
33	G3	Proctor VT U.S.A.
43	G3	Professor van Blommestein Meer resr Suriname
36	G5	Progreso Honduras
27	C7	Progreso Coahuila Mex.
36	G4	Progreso Yucatan Mex.
69	H7	Prokhladnyy Rus. Fed.
76	K4	Prokop'yevsk Rus. Fed.
67	J3	Prokuplje Yugo.
68	D3	Proletariy Rus. Fed.
69	G6	Proletarsk Rus. Fed. Prome see Pyè
46	A2	Promissão Brazil
20	F3	Prophet River Can.
30	C5	Prophetstown U.S.A.
116	C3	Proserpine Austr.
33	F3	Prospect U.S.A.

94 C4 Prosperidad Phil.
116 D6 Proston Austr.
104 D7 Protem S. Africa
30 A4 Protivin U.S.A.
67 M3 Provadiya Bulg.
64 H5 Provence *reg.* France
33 H4 Providence U.S.A.
117 A7 Providence, Cape *c.* N.Z.
31 F3 Providence Bay Can.
42 B1 Providencia, Isla de *i.* Col.
33 H3 Provincetown U.S.A.
35 G1 Provo U.S.A.
21 G4 Provost Can.
46 B4 Prudentópolis Brazil
116 C3 Prudhoe I. *i.* Austr.
61 E4 Prüm Ger.
61 E4 Prüm *r.* Ger.
66 C3 Prunelli-di-Fiumorbo France
63 K4 Pruszków Pol.
69 D6 Prut *r.* Moldova/Romania
119 D5 Prydz Bay *b.* Antarctica
69 E5 Pryluky Ukr.
69 F6 Prymors'k Ukr.
63 M5 Pryp"yat *r.* Ukr.
63 N4 Prypyats' *r.* Belarus
63 L6 Przemyśl Pol.
Przheval'sk *see* Karakol
67 L5 Psara *i.* Greece
69 G6 Psebay Rus. Fed.
69 F6 Pshish *r.* Rus. Fed.
68 D3 Pskov Rus. Fed.
55 U7 Pskov, Lake *l.* Estonia/Rus. Fed.
68 D3 Pskovskaya Oblast' *div.* Rus. Fed.
67 J4 Ptolemaïda Greece
66 F1 Ptuj Slovenia
88 C3 Pu *r.* China
95 B1 Pua Thai.
47 D3 Puán Arg.
89 B5 Pu'an China
89 C6 Pubei China
42 D5 Pucallpa Peru
89 F5 Pucheng *Fujian* China
88 C3 Pucheng *Shaanxi* China
68 G3 Puchezh Rus. Fed.
94 B4 Pucio Pt *pt* Phil.
62 J3 Puck Pol.
30 C4 Puckaway Lake *l.* U.S.A.
47 B3 Pucón Chile
54 U4 Pudasjärvi Fin.
104 F3 Pudimoe S. Africa
68 F2 Pudozh Rus. Fed.
58 F4 Pudsey U.K.
36 E5 Puebla Mex.
65 C1 Puebla de Sanabria Spain
25 F4 Pueblo U.S.A.
45 C2 Pueblo Nuevo Venez.
47 D3 Puelches Arg.
47 C3 Puelén Arg.
47 B2 Puente Alto Chile
65 D4 Puente-Genil Spain
45 C2 Puente Torres Venez.
44 B7 Puerto Aisén Chile
42 F6 Puerto Alegre Bol.
36 E5 Puerto Ángel Mex.
37 H7 Puerto Armuelles Panama
45 A4 Puerto Asís Col.
45 D3 Puerto Ayacucho Venez.
42 □ Puerto Baquerizo Moreno Ecuador
36 G5 Puerto Barrios Guatemala
45 B3 Puerto Berrío Col.
45 C2 Puerto Cabello Venez.
37 H6 Puerto Cabezas Nic.
45 D3 Puerto Carreño Col.
44 E2 Puerto Casado Para.
44 B6 Puerto Cisnes Chile
44 C8 Puerto Coig Arg.
37 H7 Puerto Cortés Costa Rica
45 C2 Puerto Cumarebo Venez.
25 D6 Puerto de Lobos Mex.
36 E5 Puerto Escondido Mex.
45 C1 Puerto Estrella Col.
42 F6 Puerto Frey Bol.
44 E2 Puerto Guarani Para.
42 E6 Puerto Heath Bol.
45 D4 Puerto Inírida Col.
43 G7 Puerto Isabel Bol.
45 D2 Puerto La Cruz Venez.
42 D4 Puerto Leguizamo Col.
25 D6 Puerto Libertad Mex.
65 D3 Puertollano Spain
47 D4 Puerto Lobos Arg.
45 B3 Puerto Lopéz Col.
47 D4 Puerto Madryn Arg.
42 E6 Puerto Maldonado Peru
42 B4 Puerto Máncora Peru
45 D3 Puerto Miranda Venez.
47 B4 Puerto Montt Chile
44 B8 Puerto Natáles Chile
45 C3 Puerto Nuevo Col.
45 A2 Puerto Obaldia Panama
45 E2 Puerto Ordaz Venez.
45 D3 Puerto Páez Venez.
36 B2 Puerto Peñasco Mex.
44 E2 Puerto Pinasco Para.
47 D4 Puerto Pirámides Arg.
37 K5 Puerto Plata Dom. Rep.
42 D5 Puerto Portillo Peru
94 A4 Puerto Princesa Phil.
45 A2 Puerto Rey Col.
37 L5 Puerto Rico *terr.* Caribbean
44 E2 Puerto Sastre Para.
45 A4 Puerto Tejado Col.
36 C4 Puerto Vallarta Mex.
47 B4 Puerto Varas Chile
69 J4 Pugachev Rus. Fed.
84 C3 Pugal India
89 B5 Puge China
65 H3 Puig Major *mt* Spain
65 H1 Puigmal *mt* France/Spain
89 □ Pui O Wan *b.* China
89 F4 Pujiang China
90 A4 Pujonryong Sanmaek *mts* N. Korea
111 H6 Pukaki, Lake *l.* N.Z.
117 C6 Pukaki, Lake *l.* N.Z.
30 E1 Pukaskwa *r.* Can.
30 E1 Pukaskwa National Park *nat. park* Can.
21 J3 Pukatawagan Can.
87 N3 Pukch'ŏng N. Korea
117 E2 Pukekohe N.Z.
117 D5 Puketeraki Ra. *mts* N.Z.
117 F4 Puketoi Range *h.* N.Z.
117 C6 Pukeuri Junction N.Z.
63 P3 Pukhnovo Rus. Fed.
68 G2 Puksoozero Rus. Fed.
66 E2 Pula Croatia
42 E8 Pulacayo Bol.
88 G2 Pulandian China
88 F2 Pulandian Wan *b.* China
94 C5 Pulangi *r.* Phil.
33 E3 Pulaski *NY* U.S.A.
29 C5 Pulaski *TN* U.S.A.
32 C6 Pulaski *VA* U.S.A.
30 C3 Pulaski *WV* U.S.A.
63 K5 Puławy Pol.
54 T4 Pulkkila Fin.
24 C2 Pullman U.S.A.
54 X2 Pulozero Rus. Fed.
84 E1 Pulu China
81 G2 Pülümür Turkey
94 C5 Pulutan Indon.
85 G3 Puma Yumco *l.* China
42 B4 Puná, Isla *i.* Ecuador
85 G4 Punakha Bhutan
84 C2 Punch Jammu and Kashmir
20 E4 Punchaw Can.
85 G3 Püncogling China
105 J1 Punda Maria S. Africa
84 D3 Pundri India
95 □ Punggol Sing.
90 A4 P'ungsan N. Korea
103 D5 Púnguè *r.* Moz.
102 C4 Punia Dem. Rep. Congo
47 B1 Punitaqui Chile
84 C3 Punjab *div.* India
83 J4 Punjab *div.* Pak.
84 D2 Punmah Gl. *gl.* China/Jammu and Kashmir
85 F4 Punpun *r.* India
37 L5 Punta, Cerro de *mt* Puerto Rico
47 D3 Punta Alta Arg.
44 B8 Punta Arenas Chile
66 C4 Punta Balestrieri *mt* Italy
47 D4 Punta Delgada Arg.
36 G5 Punta Gorda Belize
29 D7 Punta Gorda U.S.A.
47 D4 Punta Norte Arg.
25 D6 Punta Prieta Mex.
37 H6 Puntarenas Costa Rica
45 C2 Punto Fijo Venez.
32 D4 Punxsutawney U.S.A.
54 U4 Puokio Fin.
54 U4 Puolanka Fin.
89 D4 Puqi China
76 J3 Pur *r.* Rus. Fed.
45 A4 Puracé, Parque Nacional *nat. park* Col.
45 A4 Puracé, Volcán de *vol.* Col.
27 D5 Purcell U.S.A.
20 F4 Purcell Mts *mts* Can.
47 B3 Purén Chile
25 G4 Purgatoire *r.* U.S.A.
85 F6 Puri India
61 C2 Purmerend Neth.
84 D6 Purna *r. Maharashtra* India
84 D5 Purna *r. Maharashtra* India
85 G4 Purnabhaba *r.* India
85 F4 Pūrnia India
112 E3 Purnululu National Park *nat. park* Austr.
47 B4 Purranque Chile
85 F5 Puruliya India
42 F4 Purus *r.* Brazil
55 V6 Puruvesi *l.* Fin.
92 □ Purwakarta Indon.
92 □ Purwodadi Indon.
92 □ Purwokerto Indon.
90 A3 Puryŏng N. Korea
84 D6 Pus *r.* India
84 D6 Pusad India
87 N4 Pusan S. Korea
33 J2 Pushaw Lake *l.* U.S.A.
68 H2 Pushemskiy Rus. Fed.
84 C4 Pushkar India
68 D3 Pushkin Rus. Fed.
69 H5 Pushkino Rus. Fed.
68 D3 Pushkinskiye Gory Rus. Fed.
63 O2 Pustoshka Rus. Fed.
63 L4 Puszcza Augustowska *forest* Pol.
62 G4 Puszcza Natecka *forest* Pol.
82 J5 Putao Myanmar
89 F5 Putian China
92 E7 Puting, Tanjung *pt* Indon.
67 M2 Putna *r.* Romania
33 H4 Putnam U.S.A.
33 G3 Putney U.S.A.
85 H3 Putrang La *pass* China
104 D4 Putsonderwater S. Africa
83 E9 Puttalam Sri Lanka
61 D2 Putten Neth.
61 C3 Puttershoek Neth.
62 E3 Puttgarden Ger.
42 D4 Putumayo *r.* Col.
80 G2 Pütürge Turkey
68 G4 Putyatino Rus. Fed.
69 E5 Putyvl' Ukr.
55 V6 Puumala Fin.
34 □2 Puuwai U.S.A.
22 E1 Puvurnituq Can.
24 B2 Puyallup U.S.A.
88 E3 Puyang China
47 B4 Puyehue Chile
47 B4 Puyehue, Parque Nacional *nat. park* Chile
64 F5 Puylaurens France
117 A7 Puysegur Pt *pt* N.Z.
103 C4 Pweto Dem. Rep. Congo
59 C5 Pwllheli U.K.
68 E2 Pyal'ma Rus. Fed.
68 H4 P'yana *r.* Rus. Fed.
84 B1 Pyandzh *r.* Afgh./Tajik.
54 W3 Pyaozero, Ozero *l.* Rus. Fed.
54 W4 Pyaozerskiy Rus. Fed.
83 J7 Pyapon Myanmar
76 K2 Pyasina *r.* Rus. Fed.
69 G6 Pyatigorsk Rus. Fed.
69 E5 P"yatykhatky Ukr.
83 J7 Pyè Myanmar
117 B7 Pye, Mt *h.* N.Z.
69 D4 Pyetrykaw Belarus
54 T4 Pyhäjoki Fin.
54 T4 Pyhäjoki *r.* Fin.
54 U4 Pyhäntä Fin.
54 T5 Pyhäsalmi Fin.
54 V5 Pyhäselkä *l.* Fin.
85 H5 Pyingaing Myanmar
83 J7 Pyinmana Myanmar
59 D6 Pyle U.K.
76 K3 Pyl'karamo Rus. Fed.
67 J6 Pylos Greece
32 C4 Pymatuning Reservoir *resr* U.S.A.
91 A6 P'yŏnghae S. Korea
87 N4 P'yŏngyang N. Korea
114 F6 Pyramid Hill Austr.
34 C1 Pyramid Lake *l.* U.S.A.
30 E3 Pyramid Pt *pt* U.S.A.
34 C2 Pyramid Range *mts* U.S.A.
64 F5 Pyrenees *mts* France/Spain
67 J6 Pyrgos Greece
69 E5 Pyryatyn Ukr.
62 G4 Pyrzyce Pol.
68 H3 Pyshchug Rus. Fed.
63 N2 Pytalovo Rus. Fed.
67 K5 Pyxaria *mt* Greece

Q

81 J6 Qabr Bandar Iraq
105 H5 Qacha's Nek Lesotho
81 K4 Qādir Karam Iraq
81 J4 Qādisīyah, Buḩayrat al *resr* Iraq
88 C1 Qagan Ders China
88 D1 Qagan Nur China
88 C2 Qagan Nur China
88 E1 Qagan Nur China
88 E1 Qagan Nur *l.* China
88 E1 Qagan Nur *resr* China
88 D1 Qagan Obo Mongolia
88 D1 Qagan Teg China
88 E1 Qagan Us China
85 H3 Qagbasêrag China
85 E2 Qagcaka China
Qahar Youyi Qianqi *see* Togrog Ul
Qahar Youyi Zhongqi *see* Hobor
82 H3 Qaidam Pendi *basin* China
81 K3 Qalā Diza Iraq
84 A2 Qalāt Afgh.
80 E6 Qal'at el Hasal Jordan
81 L6 Qal'at Şāliḩ Iraq
81 L6 Qal'at Şukkar Iraq
81 K2 Qal'eh D. *mt* Iran
81 M5 Qal'eh-ye-Now Iran
81 K7 Qalīb Bāqūr *w.* Iraq
80 C6 Qalyûb Egypt
105 G5 Qamata S. Africa
84 B4 Qambar Pak.
81 L4 Qāmchīān Iran
82 J4 Qamdo China
84 B3 Qamruddin Karez Pak.
81 L2 Qandaranbashi *mt* Iran
88 E1 Qangdin Sum China
81 M2 Qaraçala Azer.
81 J4 Qarachōq, J. *mts* Iraq
81 K4 Qara D. *r.* Iraq
81 H7 Qārah Saudi Arabia
84 B2 Qarah Bāgh Afgh.
81 L3 Qaranqu *r.* Iran
102 E3 Qardho Somalia
81 L3 Qar'eh Aqāj Iran
81 L2 Qareh D. *mts* Iran
81 L3 Qareh Dāsh, Kūh-e *mt* Iran
81 M2 Qareh Sū *r.* Iran
81 L3 Qareh Urgān, Kūh-e *mt* Iran
85 H1 Qarhan China
81 K6 Qaryat al Gharab Iraq
88 D1 Qasq China
80 F6 Qaşr al Azraq Jordan
81 J5 Qasr al Khubbāz Iraq
81 M7 Qaşr aş Şabīyah Kuwait
81 K4 Qaşr-e Shīrīn Iran
81 L6 Qaşr Shaqrah Iraq
80 F5 Qaţanā Syria
70 Qatar *country* Asia
80 C7 Qaţrâni, Gebel *escarpment* Egypt
78 B4 Qattâra Depression *depression* Egypt
80 F4 Qaţţīnah, Buḩayrat *resr* Syria
81 L1 Qax Azer.
79 H3 Qāyen Iran
85 H3 Qayü China
81 J4 Qayyārah Iraq
81 L2 Qazangödağ *mt* Azer.
81 K1 Qazax Azer.
84 B4 Qazi Ahmad Pak.
81 M1 Qazımämmäd Azer.
81 M3 Qazvīn Iran
88 A1 Qeh China
78 C4 Qena Egypt
118 A3 Qeqertarsuaq *i.* Greenland
81 L4 Qeshlāq Iran
81 K4 Qeshlāq, Rūdkhāneh-ye *r.* Iran
79 H4 Qeshm Iran
81 M3 Qeydār Iran
81 M3 Qezel Owzan, Rūdkhāneh-ye *r.* Iran
80 E6 Qeẕi'ot Israel
88 C3 Qian *r.* China
88 F2 Qian'an China
89 C5 Qiancheng China
88 F3 Qiang *r.* China
89 D4 Qianjiang *Hubei* China
89 C4 Qianjiang *Sichuan* China
90 A2 Qianjin China
88 A4 Qianning China
88 G1 Qian Shan *mts* China
89 C5 Qianxi China
88 C3 Qianxian China
89 D5 Qianyang *Hunan* China
88 C3 Qianyang *Shaanxi* China
89 F4 Qianyang *Zhejiang* China
88 D2 Qiaocun China
89 B5 Qiaojia China
81 K2 Qīās Iran
105 G4 Qibing S. Africa
89 D5 Qidong *Hunan* China
88 F4 Qidong *Jiangsu* China
85 H2 Qidukou China
82 G3 Qiemo China
82 E2 Qihe China
89 C4 Qijiang China
82 H2 Qijiaojing China
88 E1 Qilaotu Shan *mts* China
84 B3 Qila Saifullah Pak.
82 J3 Qilian Shan *mts* China
85 G1 Qimantag *mts* China
89 E4 Qimen China
88 D3 Qin *r.* China
88 B3 Qin'an China
88 G1 Qingchengzi China
88 F2 Qingdao China
88 A2 Qinghai *div.* China
88 A2 Qinghai Hu *salt l.* China
82 J3 Qinghai Nanshan *mts* China
90 A1 Qinghe China
88 D2 Qingjian China
89 D4 Qing Jiang *r.* China
89 C5 Qingliu China
89 B5 Qinglong *Guizhou* China
89 F1 Qinglong *Hebei* China
88 F2 Qinglong *r.* China
89 C6 Qingping China
89 F4 Qingpu China
88 C3 Qingshui China
88 D2 Qingshuihe China
89 F4 Qingtian China
88 C2 Qingtongxia China
88 E2 Qingxian China
88 D2 Qingxu China
89 E4 Qingyang *Anhui* China
88 C2 Qingyang *Gansu* China
89 D6 Qingyuan *Guangdong* China
89 F5 Qingyuan *Zhejiang* China
82 F4 Qing Zang Gaoyuan *plat.* China
89 C5 Qingzhen China
89 D4 Qingzhou *Hubei* China
88 F2 Qingzhou *Shandong* China
88 F2 Qinhuangdao China
88 C3 Qin Ling *mts* China
88 D2 Qinxian China
88 D3 Qinyang China
88 D2 Qinyuan China
89 C6 Qinzhou China
89 C6 Qinzhou Wan *b.* China
89 D7 Qionghai China
89 B4 Qionglai China
88 B4 Qionglai Shan *mts* China
89 D7 Qiongshan China
89 C6 Qiongzhou Haixia *str.* China
87 M2 Qiqihar China
81 M5 Qīr Iran
84 E1 Qira China
80 E6 Qiryat Gat Israel
80 F6 Qitab ash Shāmah *crater* Saudi Arabia
90 B2 Qitaihe China
89 B5 Qiubei China
88 F2 Qixia China
88 E3 Qixian *Henan* China
88 D2 Qixian *Shanxi* China
90 C1 Qixing *r.* China
89 D5 Qiyang China
88 C2 Qiying China
89 D7 Qizhou Liedao *i.* China
81 M2 Qızılağac Körfäzi *b.* Azer.
Qogir Feng *mt see* K2
88 C1 Qog Qi China
81 L3 Qojūr Iran
79 G3 Qom Iran
79 G3 Qomishēh Iran
Qomolangma Feng *mt see* Everest, Mt
81 M1 Qonaqkänd Azer.
85 G3 Qonggyai China
88 C1 Qongj China
80 F4 Qornet es Saouda *mt* Lebanon
81 L4 Qorveh Iran
81 K2 Qoţūr Iran
33 G3 Quabbin Reservoir *resr* U.S.A.
34 D4 Quail Mts *mts* U.S.A.
33 F4 Quakertown U.S.A.
21 K2 Quamarirjung Lake *l.* Can.
114 E5 Quambatook Austr.
115 G3 Quambone Austr.
27 D5 Quanah U.S.A.
88 D3 Quanbao Shan *mt* China
95 D2 Quang Ngai Vietnam
95 C1 Quang Tri Vietnam
89 C6 Quang Yen Vietnam
89 E5 Quannan China
89 F5 Quanzhou *Fujian* China
89 D5 Quanzhou *Guangxi* China
21 J4 Qu'Appelle Can.
21 J4 Qu'Appelle *r.* Can.
47 F1 Quaraí Brazil
47 F1 Quaraí *r.* Brazil
89 □ Quarry Bay China
66 C5 Quartu Sant'Elena Italy
34 D3 Quartzite Mt *mt* U.S.A.
35 E5 Quartzsite U.S.A.
20 D4 Quatsino Sound *in.* Can.
81 M1 Quba Azer.
115 H5 Queanbeyan Austr.
23 F4 Québec Can.
31 H2 Québec *div.* Can.
46 C2 Quebra Anzol *r.* Brazil
47 B4 Quedal, C. *hd* Chile
20 E4 Queen Bess, Mt *mt* Can.
20 C4 Queen Charlotte Can.
20 C4 Queen Charlotte Islands *is* Can.
20 D4 Queen Charlotte Sound *chan.* Can.
20 D4 Queen Charlotte Str. *chan.* Can.
118 B3 Queen Elizabeth Islands *is* Can.
102 D4 Queen Elizabeth National Park *nat. park* Uganda
119 C5 Queen Mary Land *reg.* Antarctica
118 B2 Queen Maud Gulf *g.* Can.
119 B4 Queen Maud Mts *mts* Antarctica
113 H4 Queensland *div.* Austr.
115 F9 Queenstown Austr.
117 B6 Queenstown N.Z.
95 □ Queenstown Sing.
105 G5 Queenstown S. Africa
33 E5 Queenstown U.S.A.
24 A2 Queets U.S.A.
47 F2 Queguay Grande *r.* Uru.
47 D3 Quehué Arg.
103 D5 Quelimane Moz.
44 B6 Quellón Chile
Quelpart I. *i. see* Cheju-do
35 H4 Quemado U.S.A.
47 B4 Quemchi Chile
47 D3 Quemú-Quemú Arg.
47 E3 Quequén Grande *r.* Arg.
46 B3 Querência do Norte Brazil
36 D4 Querétaro Mex.
25 E6 Querobabi Mex.
88 E3 Queshan China
20 E4 Quesnel Can.
20 E4 Quesnel *r.* Can.
20 E4 Quesnel L. *l.* Can.
30 B1 Quetico Provincial Park *res.* Can.
84 A3 Quetta Pak.
47 B3 Queuco Chile
47 B3 Queule Chile
36 F6 Quezaltenango Guatemala
94 A4 Quezon Phil.
94 B3 Quezon City Phil.
88 E3 Qufu China
103 B5 Quibala Angola
103 B4 Quibaxe Angola
45 A3 Quibdó Col.
64 C3 Quiberon France
103 B4 Quiçama, Parque Nacional do *nat. park* Angola
95 C1 Qui Châu Vietnam
35 F5 Quijotoa U.S.A.
47 D1 Quilino Arg.
64 F5 Quillan France
21 J4 Quill Lakes *lakes* Can.
47 B2 Quillota Chile
47 E2 Quilmes Arg.
83 E9 Quilon India
113 H5 Quilpie Austr.
47 B2 Quilpué Chile
102 B4 Quimbele Angola
44 D3 Quimilí Arg.
64 B3 Quimper France
64 C3 Quimperlé France
42 D6 Quince Mil Peru
34 B2 Quincy *CA* U.S.A.
29 C6 Quincy *FL* U.S.A.
30 B6 Quincy *IL* U.S.A.
33 H3 Quincy *MA* U.S.A.
47 D2 Quines Arg.
95 D2 Qui Nhơn Vietnam
35 E3 Quinn Canyon Range *mts* U.S.A.
65 E3 Quintanar de la Orden Spain
47 B2 Quintero Chile
47 D2 Quinto *r.* Arg.
65 F2 Quinto Spain
103 E5 Quionga Moz.
103 B4 Quipungo Angola
47 B3 Quirihue Chile
103 B5 Quirima Angola
115 J3 Quirindi Austr.
47 E2 Quiroga Arg.
103 D6 Quissico Moz.
103 B5 Quitapa Angola
46 B2 Quitéria *r.* Brazil
29 D6 Quitman *GA* U.S.A.
29 B5 Quitman *MS* U.S.A.
42 C4 Quito Ecuador
25 D6 Quitovac Mex.
35 F4 Quivero U.S.A.
43 L4 Quixadá Brazil
89 D5 Qujiang China
89 C4 Qu Jiang *r.* China
89 D6 Qujie China
89 B5 Qujing China
81 L7 Qulbān Layyah *w.* Iraq
85 H2 Qumar He *r.* China
85 H2 Qumarheyan China
85 H2 Qumarlêb China
85 H2 Qumarrabdün China
105 H5 Qumbu S. Africa
85 H3 Qumdo China
105 G6 Qumrha S. Africa
21 L2 Quoich *r.* Can.
57 C3 Quoich, Loch *l.* U.K.
60 F3 Quoile *r.* U.K.
104 C7 Quoin Pt *pt* S. Africa
85 E2 Quong Muztag *mt* China
113 G6 Quorn Austr.
104 F1 Quoxo *r.* Botswana
79 K2 Qŭrghonteppa Tajik.
23 G2 Qurlutu *r.* Can.
81 K2 Qūrū Gol *pass* Iran
81 M1 Qusar Azer.
78 C4 Quseir Egypt
81 K3 Qūshchī Iran
81 L2 Qūsheh D. *mts* Iran
81 M4 Qūtīābād Iran
88 B2 Quwu Shan *mts* China
88 C4 Quxian China
85 G3 Qüxü China
95 C1 Quynh Lưu Vietnam
89 B6 Quynh Nhai Vietnam
31 J3 Quyon Can.
88 E3 Quzhou *Hebei* China
89 F4 Quzhou *Zhejiang* China
69 H7 Qvareli Georgia
Qyteti Stalin *see* Kuçovë

R

62 H7 Raab *r.* Austria
54 T4 Raahe Fin.
54 V5 Rääkkylä Fin.
61 E2 Raalte Neth.
54 T3 Raanujärvi Fin.
92 □ Raas *i.* Indon.
57 B3 Raasay *i.* U.K.
57 B3 Raasay, Sound of *chan.* U.K.
93 F8 Raba Indon.
84 E2 Rabang China
66 F7 Rabat Malta
100 B1 Rabat Morocco
110 F2 Rabaul P.N.G.
20 D3 Rabbit *r.* Can.
78 D5 Rābigh Saudi Arabia
85 G5 Rabnabad Islands *is* Bangl.
69 D6 Râbniţa Moldova
32 B5 Raccoon Creek *r.* U.S.A.
23 K4 Race, C. *c.* Can.
33 H3 Race Pt *pt* U.S.A.
80 E5 Rachaïya Lebanon
27 D7 Rachal U.S.A.
35 E3 Rachel U.S.A.
95 C3 Rach Gia Vietnam
95 C3 Rach Gia, Vinh *b.* Vietnam
62 J5 Racibórz Pol.
30 D4 Racine U.S.A.
31 F1 Racine Lake *l.* Can.
30 E2 Raco U.S.A.
63 M7 Rădăuţi Romania
28 C4 Radcliff U.S.A.
32 C6 Radford U.S.A.
84 B5 Radhanpur India
22 E3 Radisson Can.
20 F4 Radium Hot Springs Can.
67 L3 Radnevo Bulg.
63 K5 Radom Pol.
67 K3 Radomir Bulg.
101 E4 Radom National Park *nat. park* Sudan
63 J5 Radomsko Pol.
69 D5 Radomyshl' Ukr.
67 K4 Radoviš Macedonia
59 E6 Radstock U.K.
68 C4 Radun' Belarus
55 S9 Radviliškis Lith.
63 M5 Radyvyliv Ukr.
84 E4 Rae Bareli India
20 F2 Rae-Edzo Can.
20 F2 Rae Lakes Can.
61 E4 Raeren Belgium
117 E3 Raetihi N.Z.
47 E1 Rafaela Arg.
80 E6 Rafaḩ Gaza
102 C3 Rafaï C.A.R.
78 E4 Rafḩā' Saudi Arabia
79 H3 Rafsanjān Iran
94 C5 Ragang, Mt *vol.* Phil.
94 B3 Ragay Gulf *b.* Phil.
33 J3 Ragged I. *i.* U.S.A.
66 F6 Ragusa Italy

88 A3 Ra'gyagoinba China
93 G7 Raha Indon.
68 D4 Rahachow Belarus
102 D2 Rahad r. Sudan
Rahaeng see Tak
84 B3 Rahimyar Khan Pak.
47 B3 Rahue mt Chile
83 E7 Raichur India
85 G4 Raiganj India
85 E5 Raigarh India
35 E2 Railroad Valley v. U.S.A.
23 G3 Raimbault, Lac l. Can.
114 E5 Rainbow Austr.
116 E5 Rainbow Beach Austr.
35 G3 Rainbow Bridge Nat. Mon. res. U.S.A.
20 F3 Rainbow Lake Can.
32 C6 Rainelle U.S.A.
84 B3 Raini r. Pak.
24 B2 Rainier, Mt vol. U.S.A.
22 B4 Rainy r. U.S.A.
21 L5 Rainy River Can.
85 E5 Raipur Madhya Pradesh India
84 C4 Raipur Rajasthan India
55 S6 Raisio Fin.
84 D5 Raitalai India
109 Raivavae i. Pac. Oc.
83 F7 Rajahmundry India
54 V2 Raja-Jooseppi Fin.
79 L4 Rajanpur Pak.
83 E9 Rajapalaiyam India
84 C4 Rajasthan div. India
84 C3 Rajasthan Canal canal India
85 F4 Rajauli India
85 G5 Rajbari Bangl.
84 D4 Rajgarh Rajasthan India
84 C3 Rajgarh Rajasthan India
80 F6 Rajil, W. watercourse Jordan
85 E5 Rajim India
84 B5 Rajkot India
85 F4 Rajmahal India
85 F4 Rajmahal Hills h. India
84 E5 Raj Nandgaon India
84 D3 Rajpura India
85 G4 Rajshahi Bangl.
85 F3 Raka China
117 C5 Rakaia r. N.Z.
84 C1 Rakaposhi mt Pak.
69 C5 Rakhiv Ukr.
84 B3 Rakhni Pak.
92 □ Rakit i. Indon.
90 D2 Rakitnoye Rus. Fed.
69 E5 Rakitnoye Rus. Fed.
55 U7 Rakke Estonia
55 M7 Rakkestad Norway
84 B3 Rakni r. Pak.
55 U7 Rakvere Estonia
29 E5 Raleigh U.S.A.
30 D2 Ralph U.S.A.
20 E2 Ram r. Can.
23 H2 Ramah Can.
35 H4 Ramah U.S.A.
46 D1 Ramalho, Serra do h. Brazil
80 E6 Ramallah West Bank
14 E3 Ramapo Deep sea feature N. Pacific Ocean
105 F2 Ramatlabama S. Africa
110 E2 Rambutyo I. i. P.N.G.
59 C7 Rame Head hd U.K.
103 E5 Ramena Madag.
68 F3 Rameshki Rus. Fed.
83 E9 Rameswaram India
84 D4 Ramganga r. India
85 G5 Ramgarh Bangl.
85 F5 Ramgarh Bihar India
84 B4 Ramgarh Rajasthan India
78 F3 Rāmhormoz Iran
80 E6 Ramla Israel
Ramlat Rabyānah des. see Rebiana Sand Sea
80 E7 Ramm, Jabal mt Jordan
84 D3 Ramnagar India
67 M2 Râmnicu Sărat Romania
67 L2 Râmnicu Vâlcea Romania
34 D5 Ramona U.S.A.
31 G1 Ramore Can.
103 C6 Ramotswa Botswana
84 D3 Rampur India
84 C4 Rampura India
Rampur Boalia see Rajshahi
85 F4 Rampur Hat India
85 H6 Ramree I. i. Myanmar
54 P5 Ramsele Sweden
31 F2 Ramsey Can.
58 C3 Ramsey Isle of Man
59 G5 Ramsey U.K.
59 B6 Ramsey Island i. U.K.
31 F2 Ramsey Lake l. Can.
59 J6 Ramsgate U.K.
84 D5 Ramtek India
55 T9 Ramygala Lith.
45 C4 Rana, Co h. Col.
85 G5 Ranaghat India
84 C5 Ranapur India
92 F5 Ranau Malaysia
47 B2 Rancagua Chile
85 F5 Ranchi India
47 B4 Ranco, Lago l. Chile
115 G5 Rand Austr.
60 E3 Randalstown U.K.
66 F6 Randazzo Italy
55 M8 Randers Denmark
33 H3 Randolph MA U.S.A.
33 G3 Randolph VT U.S.A.
55 N5 Randsjö Sweden
54 S4 Råneå Sweden
117 C6 Ranfurly N.Z.
95 B4 Rangae Thai.
85 H5 Rangamati Bangl.
117 D1 Rangaunu Bay b. N.Z.
33 H2 Rangeley U.S.A.
33 H2 Rangeley Lake l. U.S.A.
35 H1 Rangely U.S.A.
31 F2 Ranger Lake Can.
117 D5 Rangiora N.Z.
117 C5 Rangitata r. N.Z.
117 E4 Rangitikei r. N.Z.
92 □ Rangkasbitung Indon.
Rangoon see Yangôn
85 G4 Rangpur Bangl.
83 E8 Ranibennur India
85 F5 Raniganj India
85 E5 Ranijula Peak mt India
84 B4 Ranipur Pak.
27 C6 Rankin U.S.A.
21 L2 Rankin Inlet Can.
21 L2 Rankin Inlet in. Can.
115 G4 Rankin's Springs Austr.
55 U7 Ranna Estonia
116 D5 Rannes Austr.
57 D4 Rannoch, L. l. U.K.
57 D4 Rannoch Moor moorland U.K.
84 B4 Rann of Kachchh marsh India
95 A3 Ranong Thai.
95 B4 Ranot Thai.
68 G4 Ranova r. Rus. Fed.
81 M5 Rānsa Iran
55 N6 Ransby Sweden
93 J7 Ransiki Indon.
55 V5 Rantasalmi Fin.
92 B6 Rantauprapat Indon.
93 F7 Rantepao Indon.
30 C5 Rantoul U.S.A.
63 R2 Rantsevo Rus. Fed.
54 T4 Rantsila Fin.
54 U4 Ranua Fin.
81 K3 Rānya Iraq
90 C1 Raohe China
89 E6 Raoping China
109 Rapa i. Pac. Oc.
66 C2 Rapallo Italy
84 B5 Rapar India
47 B2 Rapel r. Chile
60 D3 Raphoe Rep. of Ireland
32 E5 Rapidan r. U.S.A.
114 C5 Rapid Bay Austr.
26 C2 Rapid City U.S.A.
31 H2 Rapide-Deux Can.
31 H2 Rapide-Sept Can.
30 D3 Rapid River U.S.A.
55 T7 Rapla Estonia
32 E5 Rappahannock r. U.S.A.
85 E4 Rapti r. India
84 B5 Rapur India
94 C3 Rapurapu i. Phil.
33 F2 Raquette r. U.S.A.
33 F3 Raquette Lake U.S.A.
33 F3 Raquette Lake l. U.S.A.
33 F4 Raritan Bay b. U.S.A.
15 J7 Rarotonga i. Pac. Oc.
94 A4 Rasa i. Phil.
47 D4 Rasa, Pta pt Arg.
80 E6 Ra's an Naqb Jordan
102 D2 Ras Dashen mt Eth.
55 S9 Raseiniai Lith.
80 C6 Rashîd Egypt
84 A3 Rashid Qala Afgh.
81 M3 Rasht Iran
84 C1 Raskam mts China
79 K4 Raskoh mts Pak.
101 F2 Ras Muhammad c. Egypt
44 C6 Raso, C. pt Arg.
68 D4 Rasony Belarus
85 E4 Rasra India
66 D6 Rass Jebel Tunisia
68 G4 Rasskazovo Rus. Fed.
79 G4 Ras Tannūrah Saudi Arabia
55 O5 Rätan Sweden
105 H3 Ratanda S. Africa
84 C3 Ratangarh India
85 E5 Ratanpur India
55 O5 Rätansbyn Sweden
95 A2 Rat Buri Thai.
84 D4 Rath India
60 E4 Rathangan Rep. of Ireland
60 D5 Rathdowney Rep. of Ireland
60 E5 Rathdrum Rep. of Ireland
85 H5 Rathedaung Myanmar
62 F4 Rathenow Ger.
60 E3 Rathfriland U.K.
60 C5 Rathkeale Rep. of Ireland
60 E2 Rathlin Island i. U.K.
60 C5 Rathluirc Rep. of Ireland
85 E5 Ratiya India
84 C5 Ratlam India
83 D7 Ratnagiri India
83 F9 Ratnapura Sri Lanka
69 C5 Ratne Ukr.
84 B4 Rato Dero Pak.
25 F4 Raton U.S.A.
57 G3 Rattray Head hd U.K.
55 O6 Rättvik Sweden
20 E5 Ratz, Mt mt Can.
95 B5 Raub Malaysia
47 E3 Rauch Arg.
81 L7 Raudhatain Kuwait
54 F3 Raufarhöfn Iceland
117 G2 Raukumara mt N.Z.
117 F3 Raukumara Range mts N.Z.
55 R6 Rauma Fin.
92 E8 Raung, G. vol. Indon.
85 F5 Raurkela India
90 J2 Rausu Japan
54 V5 Rautavaara Fin.
55 V6 Rautjärvi Fin.
24 D2 Ravalli U.S.A.
81 L4 Ravānsar Iran
33 G3 Ravena U.S.A.
58 D3 Ravenglass U.K.
66 E2 Ravenna Italy
116 A5 Ravensbourne Cr. watercourse Austr.
62 D7 Ravensburg Ger.
116 A1 Ravenshoe Austr.
112 D6 Ravensthorpe Austr.
116 B3 Ravenswood Austr.
32 C5 Ravenswood U.S.A.
84 C3 Ravi r. Pak.
81 H4 Rāwah Iraq
82 C2 Rawalpindi Pak.
81 K3 Rawāndiz Iraq
84 C3 Rawatsar India
62 H5 Rawicz Pol.
32 D5 Rawley Springs U.S.A.
112 E6 Rawlinna Austr.
24 F3 Rawlins U.S.A.
44 C6 Rawson Arg.
85 F4 Raxaul India
23 J4 Ray, C. hd Can.
83 F7 Rāyagarha India
80 F5 Rayak Lebanon
87 N2 Raychikhinsk Rus. Fed.
59 H6 Rayleigh U.K.
20 G5 Raymond Can.
33 H3 Raymond NH U.S.A.
24 B2 Raymond WA U.S.A.
115 J4 Raymond Terrace Austr.
27 D7 Raymondville U.S.A.
95 B2 Rayong Thai.
32 D4 Raystown Lake l. U.S.A.
64 B2 Raz, Pte du pt France
81 M4 Razan Iran
81 M5 Rāzān Iran
81 J5 Razāzah, Buḥayrat ar l. Iraq
Razdan see Hrazdan
90 B3 Razdol'noye Rus. Fed.
81 M5 Razeh Iran
67 M3 Razgrad Bulg.
67 N2 Razim, Lacul lag. Romania
67 K4 Razlog Bulg.
64 D3 Ré, Île de i. France
59 G6 Reading U.K.
33 F4 Reading U.S.A.
30 B4 Readstown U.S.A.
105 G2 Reagile S. Africa
47 D2 Realicó Arg.
64 F5 Réalmont France
95 B2 Reăng Kesei Cambodia
27 C7 Reata Mex.
101 E2 Rebiana Sand Sea des. Libya
68 D2 Reboly Rus. Fed.
90 G2 Rebun-tō i. Japan
112 D6 Recherche, Archipelago of the is Austr.
84 C3 Rechna Doab lowland Pak.
69 D4 Rechytsa Belarus
43 M5 Recife Brazil
105 F7 Recife, Cape c. S. Africa
62 C5 Recklinghausen Ger.
44 E3 Reconquista Arg.
44 C3 Recreo Arg.
21 K5 Red r. Can./U.S.A.
27 E6 Red r. U.S.A.
95 B4 Redang i. Malaysia
33 F4 Red Bank NJ U.S.A.
29 C5 Red Bank TN U.S.A.
23 J3 Red Bay Can.
34 A1 Red Bluff U.S.A.
35 F4 Red Butte summit U.S.A.
58 F3 Redcar U.K.
21 G4 Redcliff Can.
114 E5 Red Cliffs Austr.
26 D3 Red Cloud U.S.A.
20 G4 Red Deer Can.
21 G4 Red Deer r. Alta. Can.
21 J4 Red Deer r. Sask. Can.
21 J4 Red Deer L. l. Can.
33 F5 Redden U.S.A.
105 G4 Reddersburg S. Africa
24 B3 Redding U.S.A.
59 F5 Redditch U.K.
33 F3 Redfield NY U.S.A.
26 D2 Redfield SD U.S.A.
114 C4 Redhill Austr.
35 H4 Red Hill U.S.A.
27 D4 Red Hills h. U.S.A.
23 J4 Red Indian L. l. Can.
30 E5 Redkey U.S.A.
21 L4 Red L. l. Can.
35 E4 Red L. U.S.A.
21 L4 Red Lake Can.
26 E1 Red Lakes lakes U.S.A.
24 E2 Red Lodge U.S.A.
24 B2 Redmond U.S.A.
26 E3 Red Oak U.S.A.
65 C3 Redondo Port.
30 C1 Red Rock Can.
33 E4 Red Rock U.S.A.
98 Red Sea sea Africa/Asia
20 E4 Redstone Can.
20 D2 Redstone r. Can.
21 L4 Red Sucker L. l. Can.
20 G4 Redwater Can.
23 H3 Red Wine r. Can.
30 A3 Red Wing U.S.A.
34 A3 Redwood City U.S.A.
26 E2 Redwood Falls U.S.A.
24 B3 Redwood Nat. Park U.S.A.
34 A2 Redwood Valley U.S.A.
60 D4 Ree, Lough l. Rep. of Ireland
30 E4 Reed City U.S.A.
34 C3 Reedley U.S.A.
30 C4 Reedsburg U.S.A.
24 A3 Reedsport U.S.A.
33 E6 Reedville U.S.A.
116 A4 Reedy Cr. watercourse Austr.
117 C5 Reefton N.Z.
80 G2 Refahiye Turkey
27 D6 Refugio U.S.A.
62 F6 Regen Ger.
62 F6 Regensburg Ger.
100 C2 Reggane Alg.
66 F5 Reggio di Calabria Italy
66 D2 Reggio nell'Emilia Italy
63 M7 Reghin Romania
21 J4 Regina Can.
54 W4 Regozero Rus. Fed.
84 D5 Rehli India
103 B6 Rehoboth Namibia
35 H4 Rehoboth U.S.A.
33 F5 Rehoboth Bay b. U.S.A.
33 F5 Rehoboth Beach U.S.A.
80 E6 Rehovot Israel
57 C3 Reidh, Rubha pt U.K.
27 E4 Reidsville U.S.A.
59 G6 Reigate U.K.
35 G5 Reiley Peak summit U.S.A.
64 G2 Reims France
30 A4 Reinbeck U.S.A.
62 E4 Reinbek Ger.
21 J3 Reindeer r. Can.
21 K4 Reindeer I. i. Can.
21 J3 Reindeer Lake l. Can.
54 N3 Reine Norway
117 D1 Reinga, Cape c. N.Z.
65 D1 Reinosa Spain
54 B4 Reiphólsfjöll mt Iceland
54 R2 Reisaelva r. Norway
54 S2 Reisa Nasjonalpark nat. park Norway
54 T5 Reisjärvi Fin.
105 H3 Reitz S. Africa
104 F3 Reivilo S. Africa
45 D3 Rejunya Venez.
21 H2 Reliance Can.
100 C1 Relizane Alg.
114 C4 Remarkable, Mt mt Austr.
104 B1 Remhoogte Pass pass Namibia
62 C6 Remiremont France
84 D2 Remo Gl. gl. India
68 G6 Remontnoye Rus. Fed.
62 C5 Remscheid Ger.
30 E4 Remus U.S.A.
55 M6 Rena Norway
28 B4 Rend L. l. U.S.A.
111 F2 Rendova i. Solomon Is
62 D3 Rendsburg Ger.
31 J3 Renfrew Can.
57 D5 Renfrew U.K.
47 B2 Rengo Chile
88 C3 Ren He r. China
88 E4 Renheji China
89 D5 Renhua China
89 C5 Renhuai China
69 D6 Reni Ukr.
114 D5 Renmark Austr.
111 G3 Rennell i. Solomon Is
64 D2 Rennes France
119 B5 Rennick Gl. gl. Antarctica
21 H2 Rennie Lake l. Can.
66 D2 Reno r. Italy
34 C2 Reno U.S.A.
32 E4 Renovo U.S.A.
88 E2 Renqiu China
89 B4 Renshou China
30 D5 Rensselaer IN U.S.A.
33 G3 Rensselaer NY U.S.A.
61 D2 Renswoude Neth.
24 B2 Renton U.S.A.
85 E4 Renukut India
117 D4 Renwick N.Z.
83 B3 Réo Burkina
93 G8 Reo Indon.
24 C1 Republic U.S.A.
26 D3 Republican r. U.S.A.
116 C3 Repulse B. b. Austr.
42 D5 Requena Peru
65 F3 Requena Spain
80 F1 Reşadiye Turkey
81 J2 Reşadıye Turkey
46 B4 Reserva Brazil
44 E3 Resistencia Arg.
67 J2 Reşiţa Romania
118 B2 Resolute Bay Can.
117 A6 Resolution Island i. N.Z.
95 □ Retan Laut, P. i. Sing.
59 G4 Retford U.K.
64 G2 Rethel France
67 L7 Rethymno Greece
90 C2 Rettikhovka Rus. Fed.
98 Réunion i. Indian Ocean
65 G2 Reus Spain
62 D6 Reutlingen Ger.
34 D3 Reveille Peak summit U.S.A.
64 F5 Revel France
20 F4 Revelstoke Can.
36 B5 Revillagigedo, Islas is Mex.
20 C3 Revillagigedo I. i. U.S.A.
61 C5 Revin France
80 E6 Revivim Israel
84 E4 Rewa India
84 D3 Rewari India
24 E3 Rexburg U.S.A.
23 H4 Rexton Can.
34 A2 Reyes, Point pt U.S.A.
34 C4 Reyes Peak summit U.S.A.
80 F3 Reyhanlı Turkey
54 C4 Reykir Iceland
12 G2 Reykjanes Ridge sea feature Atlantic Ocean
54 B5 Reykjanestá pt Iceland
54 C4 Reykjavík Iceland
36 E3 Reynosa Mex.
55 U8 Rēzekne Latvia
81 M3 Rezvānshahr Iran
80 F5 Rharaz, W. watercourse Syria
59 D5 Rhayader U.K.
Rhein r. see Rhine
62 C4 Rheine Ger.
61 E4 Rheinisches Schiefergebirge h. Ger.
61 F5 Rheinland-Pfalz div. Ger.
Rhin r. see Rhine
62 C5 Rhine r. Europe
33 G4 Rhinebeck U.S.A.
30 C3 Rhinelander U.S.A.
66 C2 Rho Italy
33 H4 Rhode Island div. U.S.A.
67 N6 Rhodes Greece
67 N6 Rhodes i. Greece
24 D2 Rhodes Pk summit U.S.A.
67 L4 Rhodope Mountains mts Bulg./Greece
64 G4 Rhône r. France/Switz.
Rhum i. see Rum
59 D4 Rhyl U.K.
46 E2 Riacho Brazil
46 D1 Riacho de Santana Brazil
46 C1 Rialma Brazil
46 C1 Rianópolis Brazil
84 C2 Riasi Jammu and Kashmir
92 C6 Riau, Kepulauan is Indon.
65 C1 Ribadeo Spain
65 D1 Ribadesella Spain
46 B3 Ribas do Rio Pardo Brazil
103 D5 Ribáuè Moz.
58 E4 Ribble r. U.K.
55 L9 Ribe Denmark
46 C4 Ribeira r. Brazil
46 C3 Ribeirão Preto Brazil
64 E4 Ribérac France
42 E6 Riberalta Bol.
62 F3 Ribnitz-Damgarten Ger.
62 G6 Říčany Czech Rep.
25 F6 Ricardo Flores Magón Mex.
35 E4 Rice U.S.A.
31 F2 Rice Lake l. Can.
30 B3 Rice Lake U.S.A.
30 A4 Riceville IA U.S.A.
32 D4 Riceville PA U.S.A.
105 K4 Richards Bay S. Africa
21 G3 Richardson r. Can.
27 D5 Richardson U.S.A.
33 H2 Richardson Lakes l. U.S.A.
117 B6 Richardson Mts mts N.Z.
61 D1 Richel i. Neth.
35 F2 Richfield U.S.A.
33 F3 Richfield Springs U.S.A.
33 E3 Richford NY U.S.A.
33 G2 Richford VT U.S.A.
30 B5 Richland U.S.A.
30 B4 Richland Center U.S.A.
32 C6 Richlands U.S.A.
115 J4 Richmond N.S.W. Austr.
113 H4 Richmond Qld. Austr.
31 K3 Richmond Can.
117 D4 Richmond N.Z.
105 J4 Richmond Kwazulu-Natal S. Africa
104 E5 Richmond Northern Cape S. Africa
58 F3 Richmond U.K.
30 E6 Richmond IN U.S.A.
32 A6 Richmond KY U.S.A.
33 J2 Richmond ME U.S.A.
31 F4 Richmond MI U.S.A.
32 E6 Richmond VA U.S.A.
33 G2 Richmond VT U.S.A.
117 D4 Richmond, Mt mt N.Z.
31 H4 Richmond Hill Can.
115 K2 Richmond Ra. h. Austr.
104 B4 Richtersveld National Park nat. park S. Africa
32 B4 Richwood OH U.S.A.
32 C5 Richwood WV U.S.A.
31 K3 Rideau r. Can.
31 J3 Rideau Lakes l. Can.
34 D4 Ridgecrest U.S.A.
32 D4 Ridgway U.S.A.
21 J4 Riding Mountain Nat. Park nat. park Can.
62 D6 Riedlingen Ger.
62 F5 Riesa Ger.
44 B8 Riesco, Isla i. Chile
104 D5 Riet r. S. Africa
55 R9 Rietavas Lith.
104 D3 Rietfontein S. Africa
61 D3 Rietheven Neth.
66 E3 Rieti Italy
25 F4 Rifle U.S.A.
54 E3 Rifstangi pt Iceland
85 H3 Riga India
55 T8 Rīga Latvia
55 S8 Riga, Gulf of g. Estonia/Latvia
Rīgas Jūras Līcis g. see Riga, Gulf of
33 F2 Rigaud Can.
24 C2 Riggins U.S.A.
23 J3 Rigolet Can.
57 E5 Rigside U.K.
85 E4 Rihand r. India
85 E4 Rihand Dam dam India
Riia Laht g. see Riga, Gulf of
55 T6 Riihimäki Fin.
25 D5 Riito Mex.
66 F2 Rijeka Croatia
90 G5 Rikuzen-takata Japan
67 K3 Rila mts Bulg.
24 C3 Riley U.S.A.
64 G4 Rillieux-la-Pape France
63 K6 Rimavská Sobota Slovakia
20 G4 Rimbey Can.
66 E2 Rimini Italy
23 G4 Rimouski Can.
57 D2 Rimsdale, Loch l. U.K.
85 G3 Rinbung China
84 E4 Rind r. India
54 L5 Rindal Norway
115 G8 Ringarooma B. b. Austr.
84 C4 Rīngas India
85 G2 Ring Co salt l. China
55 M6 Ringebu Norway
55 L8 Ringkøbing Denmark
60 E2 Ringsend U.K.
55 M9 Ringsted Denmark
54 Q2 Ringvassøy i. Norway
59 F7 Ringwood U.K.
47 B3 Riñihue Chile
47 B3 Riñihue, L. l. Chile
30 C4 Rio U.S.A.
46 A2 Rio Alegre Brazil
42 C4 Riobamba Ecuador
35 H2 Rio Blanco U.S.A.
42 E6 Rio Branco Brazil
45 E4 Rio Branco, Parque Nacional do nat. park Brazil
46 C4 Rio Branco do Sul Brazil
46 A3 Rio Brilhante Brazil
47 B4 Río Bueno Chile
45 E2 Río Caribe Venez.
47 D1 Río Ceballos Arg.
46 C3 Rio Claro Brazil
45 E2 Rio Claro Trinidad and Tobago
47 D3 Río Colorado Arg.
47 D2 Río Cuarto Arg.
46 D3 Rio de Janeiro Brazil
46 D3 Rio de Janeiro div. Brazil
44 G3 Rio do Sul Brazil
44 C8 Río Gallegos Arg.
44 C8 Río Grande Arg.
47 G2 Rio Grande Brazil
36 D4 Río Grande Mex.
36 C2 Rio Grande r. Mex./U.S.A.
37 H6 Rio Grande r. Mex./U.S.A.
27 D7 Rio Grande City U.S.A.
12 G7 Rio Grande Rise sea feature Atlantic Ocean
45 B2 Riohacha Col.
42 C5 Rioja Peru
43 L5 Rio Largo Brazil
64 F4 Riom France
42 E7 Río Mulatos Bol.
47 C4 Río Negro div. Arg.
46 C4 Rio Negro Brazil
69 G7 Rioni r. Georgia
47 G1 Rio Pardo Brazil
46 D1 Rio Pardo de Minas Brazil
47 D1 Río Primero Arg.
25 F5 Rio Rancho U.S.A.
35 G6 Rio Rico U.S.A.
47 D1 Río Segundo Arg.
45 A3 Ríosucio Col.
47 D2 Río Tercero Arg.
42 C4 Río Tigre Ecuador
94 A4 Rio Tuba Phil.
46 B2 Rio Verde Brazil
36 E4 Río Verde Mex.
46 A2 Rio Verde de Mato Grosso Brazil
34 B2 Rio Vista U.S.A.
46 A2 Riozinho r. Brazil
63 P5 Ripky Ukr.
58 F3 Ripley Eng. U.K.
59 F4 Ripley Eng. U.K.
32 B5 Ripley OH U.S.A.
29 B5 Ripley TN U.S.A.
32 C5 Ripley WV U.S.A.
65 H1 Ripoll Spain
58 F3 Ripon U.K.
34 B3 Ripon CA U.S.A.
30 C4 Ripon WV U.S.A.
59 D6 Risca U.K.
90 G2 Rishiri-tō i. Japan
80 E6 Rishon Le Ẕiyyon Israel
55 L7 Risør Norway
54 L5 Rissa Norway
55 U6 Ristiina Fin.
54 V4 Ristijärvi Fin.
54 W2 Ristikent Rus. Fed.
104 F4 Ritchie S. Africa
119 C3 Ritscher Upland mts Antarctica
54 P3 Ritsem Sweden
25 C4 Ritter, Mt mt U.S.A.
65 E2 Rituerto r. Spain
24 C2 Ritzville U.S.A.
47 C2 Rivadavia Mendoza Arg.
47 D2 Rivadavia Pampas Arg.
44 D2 Rivadavia Salta Arg.
47 B1 Rivadavia Chile
66 D2 Riva del Garda Italy
25 F6 Riva Palacio Mex.
37 G6 Rivas Nic.
47 D3 Rivera Arg.
47 F1 Rivera Uru.
100 B4 River Cess Liberia
33 G4 Riverhead U.S.A.
115 F5 Riverina reg. Austr.
104 D7 Riversdale S. Africa
105 H5 Riverside S. Africa
34 D5 Riverside U.S.A.
114 C5 Riverton Austr.
21 K4 Riverton Can.
117 B7 Riverton N.Z.
24 E3 Riverton U.S.A.
23 H4 Riverview Can.
64 F5 Rivesaltes France
29 D7 Riviera Beach U.S.A.
33 J1 Rivière Bleue Can.
23 G4 Rivière-du-Loup Can.
69 C5 Rivne Ukr.
117 D4 Riwaka N.Z.
82 J4 Riwoqê China
78 F5 Riyadh Saudi Arabia
88 A2 Riyue Shankou pass China
81 H1 Rize Turkey

88 F3 Rizhao China
80 E4 Rizokarpason Cyprus
55 L7 Rjukan Norway
55 K7 Rjuvbrokkene mt Norway
100 A3 Rkîz Maur.
55 M6 Roa Norway
59 G5 Roade U.K.
54 M4 Roan Norway
35 H2 Roan Cliffs cliff U.S.A.
64 C3 Roanne France
29 C5 Roanoke AL U.S.A.
30 C5 Roanoke IL U.S.A.
32 D6 Roanoke VA U.S.A.
28 E4 Roanoke r. U.S.A.
29 E4 Roanoke Rapids U.S.A.
35 H2 Roan Plateau plat. U.S.A.
60 B6 Roaringwater Bay b. Rep. of Ireland
54 R5 Röbäck Sweden
115 F8 Robbins I. i. Austr.
114 C6 Robe Austr.
60 B4 Robe r. Rep. of Ireland
114 D3 Robe, Mt h. Austr.
27 C4 Robert Lee U.S.A.
24 D3 Roberts U.S.A.
115 K2 Roberts, Mt mt Austr.
34 D2 Roberts Creek Mt mt U.S.A.
54 R4 Robertsfors Sweden
85 E4 Robertsganj India
27 E5 Robert S. Kerr Res. resr U.S.A.
104 C6 Robertson S. Africa
100 A4 Robertsport Liberia
114 C4 Robertstown Austr.
23 F4 Roberval Can.
58 G3 Robin Hood's Bay U.K.
28 C4 Robinson U.S.A.
116 C5 Robinson Cr. r. Austr.
112 C5 Robinson Range h. Austr.
114 E5 Robinvale Austr.
35 G5 Robles Junction U.S.A.
35 G5 Robles Pass pass U.S.A.
21 J4 Roblin Can.
20 F4 Robson, Mt mt Can.
27 D7 Robstown U.S.A.
66 K6 Rocca Busambra mt Italy
47 F2 Rocha Uru.
58 E4 Rochdale U.K.
46 A2 Rochedo Brazil
61 D4 Rochefort Belgium
64 D4 Rochefort France
22 F2 Rochefort, Lac l. Can.
68 G2 Rochegda Rus. Fed.
30 C4 Rochelle U.S.A.
114 F6 Rochester Austr.
59 H6 Rochester U.K.
30 D5 Rochester IN U.S.A.
30 A3 Rochester MN U.S.A.
33 H3 Rochester NH U.S.A.
32 E3 Rochester NY U.S.A.
59 H6 Rochford U.K.
64 C2 Roc'h Trévezel h. France
20 D2 Rock r. Can.
30 B5 Rock r. U.S.A.
12 H2 Rockall Bank sea feature Atlantic Ocean
119 B4 Rockefeller Plateau plat. Antarctica
30 C4 Rockford U.S.A.
21 H5 Rockglen Can.
116 E4 Rockhampton Austr.
30 C1 Rock Harbor U.S.A.
29 C5 Rock Hill U.S.A.
112 C6 Rockingham Austr.
29 E5 Rockingham U.S.A.
116 B2 Rockingham B. b. Austr.
33 G2 Rock Island Can.
30 B5 Rock Island U.S.A.
26 D1 Rocklake U.S.A.
33 F2 Rockland Can.
33 H3 Rockland MA U.S.A.
33 J2 Rockland ME U.S.A.
30 C2 Rockland MI U.S.A.
114 E6 Rocklands Reservoir resr Austr.
35 H3 Rock Point U.S.A.
33 H3 Rockport U.S.A.
26 D3 Rock Rapids U.S.A.
24 F2 Rock Springs MT U.S.A.
24 E3 Rock Springs WY U.S.A.
27 C6 Rocksprings U.S.A.
32 D3 Rockton Can.
30 D6 Rockville IN U.S.A.
32 E5 Rockville MD U.S.A.
33 J2 Rockwood U.S.A.
25 G4 Rocky Ford U.S.A.
32 B5 Rocky Fork Lake l. U.S.A.
31 F2 Rocky Island Lake l. Can.
29 E5 Rocky Mount NC U.S.A.
32 D6 Rocky Mount VA U.S.A.
20 G4 Rocky Mountain House Can.
24 F3 Rocky Mountain Nat. Park nat. park Can./U.S.A.
18 Rocky Mountains mts Can./U.S.A.
20 F4 Rocky Mountains Forest Reserve res. Can.
61 C5 Rocroi France
55 L6 Rødberg Norway
55 M9 Rødbyhavn Denmark
23 J3 Roddickton Can.
57 B3 Rodel U.K.
47 C1 Rodeo Arg.
27 B7 Rodeo Mex.
35 H6 Rodeo U.S.A.
64 F4 Rodez France
68 G3 Rodniki Rus. Fed.
Rodos see Rhodes
Rodos i. see Rhodes
13 J5 Rodrigues Fracture sea feature Indian Ocean
112 C4 Roebourne Austr.

112 D3 Roebuck Bay b. Austr.
105 H2 Roedtan S. Africa
61 D3 Roermond Neth.
61 B4 Roeselare Belgium
27 E4 Rogers U.S.A.
31 F3 Rogers City U.S.A.
34 D4 Rogers Lake l. U.S.A.
24 D3 Rogerson U.S.A.
32 B6 Rogersville U.S.A.
22 E3 Roggan r. Can.
104 D6 Roggeveld plat. S. Africa
104 D6 Roggeveldberge escarpment S. Africa
54 O3 Rognan Norway
24 A3 Rogue r. U.S.A.
34 A2 Rohnert Park U.S.A.
62 F6 Rohrbach in Oberösterreich Austria
84 B4 Rohri Pak.
84 D3 Rohtak India
95 B1 Roi Et Thai.
15 K6 Roi Georges, Îles du is Pac. Oc.
55 S8 Roja Latvia
47 E2 Rojas Arg.
84 B3 Rojhan Pak.
95 B5 Rokan r. Indon.
113 H2 Rokeby National Park nat. park Austr.
55 T9 Rokiškis Lith.
54 R4 Roknäs Sweden
69 C5 Rokytne Ukr.
46 B3 Rolândia Brazil
26 F4 Rolla U.S.A.
55 L6 Rollag Norway
116 C5 Rolleston Austr.
117 D5 Rolleston N.Z.
31 H2 Rollet Can.
29 F7 Rolleville Bahamas
31 J2 Rolphton Can.
116 C6 Roma Austr.
93 H8 Roma r. Indon.
Roma see Rome
105 G4 Roma Lesotho
55 Q8 Roma Sweden
29 E5 Romain, Cape c. U.S.A.
23 H3 Romaine r. Can.
63 N7 Roman Romania
12 H6 Romanche Gap sea feature Atlantic Ocean
80 D6 Români Egypt
49 Romania country Europe
69 G5 Romanovka Rus. Fed.
87 K1 Romanovka Rus. Fed.
64 G4 Romans-sur-Isère France
118 D1 Romanzof, Cape c. U.S.A.
64 H2 Rombas France
94 B3 Romblon Phil.
94 B3 Romblon i. Phil.
66 E4 Rome Italy
29 C5 Rome GA U.S.A.
33 J2 Rome ME U.S.A.
33 F3 Rome NY U.S.A.
31 H4 Rome U.S.A.
59 H6 Romford U.K.
64 F2 Romilly-sur-Seine France
32 D5 Romney U.S.A.
59 H6 Romney Marsh reg. U.K.
69 E5 Romny Ukr.
55 L9 Rømø i. Denmark
64 E3 Romorantin-Lanthenay France
95 B5 Rompin r. Malaysia
59 F7 Romsey U.K.
95 C1 Ron Vietnam
57 C3 Rona i. Scot. U.K.
57 C1 Rona i. Scot. U.K.
57 □ Ronas Hill h. U.K.
43 H6 Roncador, Serra do h. Brazil
111 F2 Roncador Reef rf Solomon Is
65 D4 Ronda Spain
55 L6 Rondane Nasjonalpark nat. park Norway
45 C3 Rondón Col.
46 A2 Rondonópolis Brazil
82 E3 Rondu Jammu and Kashmir
47 F2 Río Negro, Embalse del resr Uru.
89 C5 Rong'an China
89 B4 Rongchang China
88 G2 Rongcheng Wan b. China
85 G3 Rong Chu r. China
89 C5 Rongjiang China
89 C6 Rong Jiang r. China
85 H5 Rongklang Range mts Myanmar
117 E4 Rongotea N.Z.
89 C5 Rongshui China
89 D6 Rongxian Guangxi China
89 B4 Rongxian Sichuan China
55 O9 Rønne Denmark
55 O8 Ronneby Sweden
119 B3 Ronne Entrance str. Antarctica
119 B3 Ronne Ice Shelf ice feature Antarctica
61 B4 Ronse Belgium
84 D3 Roorkee India
61 C3 Roosendaal Neth.
35 G5 Roosevelt AZ U.S.A.
35 G1 Roosevelt UT U.S.A.
20 D3 Roosevelt, Mt mt Can.
35 G5 Roosevelt Dam dam U.S.A.
119 A4 Roosevelt I. i. Antarctica
20 E2 Root r. Can.
30 B4 Root r. U.S.A.
68 K2 Ropcha Rus. Fed.
116 C4 Roper r. Austr.
64 D4 Roquefort France
45 E4 Roraima div. Brazil

42 F2 Roraima, Mt mt Guyana
54 M5 Røros Norway
54 M4 Rørvik Norway
63 P6 Ros' r. Ukr.
42 □ Rosa, C. pt Ecuador
37 K4 Rosa, Lake l. Bahamas
34 C4 Rosamond U.S.A.
34 C4 Rosamond Lake l. U.S.A.
47 E2 Rosario Arg.
25 E7 Rosario Mex.
36 A2 Rosario Baja California Mex.
27 C7 Rosario Coahuila Mex.
94 B3 Rosario Phil.
94 B2 Rosario Phil.
45 B2 Rosario Venez.
47 E2 Rosario del Tala Arg.
47 F1 Rosario del Sul Brazil
46 A1 Rosário Oeste Brazil
34 D5 Rosarito Mex.
66 F5 Rosarno Italy
33 F4 Roscoe U.S.A.
64 C2 Roscoff France
60 C4 Roscommon Rep. of Ireland
60 D5 Roscommon U.S.A.
60 D5 Roscrea Rep. of Ireland
34 C2 Rose, Mt mt U.S.A.
37 M5 Roseau Dominica
21 K5 Roseau U.S.A.
115 F8 Rosebery Austr.
23 J4 Rose Blanche Can.
24 B3 Roseburg U.S.A.
31 E3 Rose City U.S.A.
116 D5 Rosedale Austr.
58 G3 Rosedale Abbey U.K.
101 F3 Roseires Reservoir resr Sudan
27 E6 Rosenberg U.S.A.
55 K7 Rosendal Norway
105 G4 Rosendal S. Africa
62 F7 Rosenheim Ger.
20 C4 Rose Pt pt Can.
66 F3 Roseto degli Abruzzi Italy
21 H4 Rosetown Can.
Rosetta see Rashid
116 B3 Rosetta Cr. r. Austr.
21 J4 Rose Valley Can.
34 B2 Roseville CA U.S.A.
30 B5 Roseville IL U.S.A.
115 K1 Rosewood Austr.
90 D2 Roshchino Rus. Fed.
68 D2 Roshchino Rus. Fed.
104 B3 Rosh Pinah Namibia
66 D2 Rosignano Marittimo Italy
67 L2 Roşiori de Vede Romania
55 N9 Roskilde Denmark
68 E4 Roslavl' Rus. Fed.
54 X2 Roslyakovo Rus. Fed.
115 G9 Ross Austr.
20 C2 Ross r. Can.
117 C5 Ross N.Z.
117 E4 Ross, Mt mt N.Z.
66 E4 Rossano Italy
60 C3 Rossan Point pt Rep. of Ireland
27 F5 Ross Barnett Res. l. U.S.A.
23 G3 Ross Bay Junction Can.
60 B6 Ross Carbery Rep. of Ireland
111 F3 Rossel Island i. P.N.G.
119 B4 Ross Ice Shelf ice feature Antarctica
23 H5 Rossignol, L. l. Can.
119 B3 Ross Island i. Antarctica
60 E5 Rosslare Rep. of Ireland
59 A5 Rosslare Harbour Rep. of Ireland
31 J3 Rossmore Can.
100 A3 Rosso Maur.
66 C3 Rosso, Capo pt France
59 E6 Ross-on-Wye U.K.
69 F5 Rossosh' Rus. Fed.
30 D5 Rossport Can.
20 C2 Ross River Can.
119 A5 Ross Sea sea Antarctica
54 O4 Røssvatnet l. Norway
30 D5 Rosswille U.S.A.
20 D3 Rosswood Can.
81 K3 Röst Iraq
21 H4 Rosthern Can.
62 F3 Rostock Ger.
68 F3 Rostov Rus. Fed.
69 F6 Rostov-na-Donu Rus. Fed.
69 G6 Rostovskaya Oblast' div. Rus. Fed.
54 R4 Rosvik Sweden
29 C5 Roswell GA U.S.A.
25 F5 Roswell NM U.S.A.
93 L4 Rota i. N. Mariana Is
93 G9 Rote i. Indon.
62 E6 Roth Ger.
58 F2 Rothbury U.K.
58 F2 Rothbury Forest forest U.K.
62 E6 Rothenburg ob der Tauber Ger.
59 G7 Rother r. U.K.
119 B2 Rothera U.K. Base Antarctica
117 D5 Rotherham N.Z.
59 F4 Rotherham U.K.
57 E3 Rothes U.K.
57 C5 Rothesay U.K.
30 C3 Rothschild U.S.A.
59 G5 Rothwell U.K.
115 F4 Roto U.S.A.
117 C5 Rotomanu N.Z.
66 C3 Rotondo, Monte mt France
117 D4 Rotoroa, L. l. N.Z.

117 F3 Rotorua N.Z.
117 F3 Rotorua, L. l. N.Z.
62 F6 Rott r. Ger.
62 G7 Rottenmann Austria
61 C5 Rotterdam Neth.
61 E1 Rottumeroog i. Neth.
61 E1 Rottumerplaat i. Neth.
62 D6 Rottweil Ger.
111 H3 Rotuma i. Fiji
54 O5 Rötviken Sweden
64 F1 Roubaix France
64 F2 Rouen France
117 B6 Rough Ridge ridge N.Z.
Roulers see Roeselare
23 F3 Roundeyed, Lac l. Can.
58 F3 Round Hill h. U.K.
116 F3 Round Hill Hd hd Austr.
34 D2 Round Mountain U.S.A.
115 K3 Round Mt mt Austr.
35 H3 Round Rock U.S.A.
24 E2 Roundup U.S.A.
57 E1 Rousay i. U.K.
33 G2 Rouses Point U.S.A.
64 F5 Roussillon reg. France
Routh Bank sand bank see Seahorse Bank
105 G5 Rouxville S. Africa
31 H1 Rouyn Can.
54 T3 Rovaniemi Fin.
69 F5 Roven'ki Rus. Fed.
66 D2 Rovereto Italy
66 D2 Rovigo Italy
66 F2 Rovinj Croatia
69 H5 Rovnoye Rus. Fed.
115 H3 Rowena Austr.
94 B2 Roxas Phil.
94 A4 Roxas Phil.
94 B3 Roxas Phil.
94 B4 Roxas Phil.
94 B4 Roxas Phil.
29 E4 Roxboro U.S.A.
117 B6 Roxburgh N.Z.
114 B3 Roxby Downs Austr.
25 F4 Roy U.S.A.
60 E4 Royal Canal canal Rep. of Ireland
30 C1 Royale, Isle i. U.S.A.
105 H4 Royal Natal National Park nat. park S. Africa
31 F4 Royal Oak U.S.A.
64 D4 Royan France
61 A5 Roye France
59 G6 Royston U.K.
69 D6 Rozdil'na Ukr.
69 E6 Rozdol'ne Ukr.
69 G4 Rtishchevo Rus. Fed.
69 E6 Rozivka Ukr.
59 D6 Ruabon U.K.
103 B5 Ruacana Namibia
102 D4 Ruaha National Park nat. park Tanz.
117 F3 Ruahine Range mts N.Z.
117 E3 Ruapehu, Mt vol. N.Z.
117 B7 Ruapuke I. i. N.Z.
117 G2 Ruatoria N.Z.
68 D4 Ruba Belarus
78 F6 Rub' al Khālī des. Saudi Arabia
90 A3 Rubeshibe Japan
34 B2 Rubicon r. U.S.A.
69 F5 Rubizhne Ukr.
86 D1 Rubtsovsk Rus. Fed.
35 E1 Ruby Lake l. U.S.A.
35 E1 Ruby Mountains mts U.S.A.
116 B4 Rubyvale Austr.
89 D5 Rucheng China
32 D5 Ruckersville U.S.A.
112 D4 Rudall River National Park nat. park Austr.
85 E4 Rudauli India
81 M3 Rūdbār Iran
55 M9 Rudkøbing Denmark
87 P3 Rudnaya Pristan' China
77 P5 Rudnaya Pristan' Rus. Fed.
68 K3 Rudnichnyy Rus. Fed.
68 D4 Rudnya Rus. Fed.
76 H4 Rudnyy Kazak.
90 D2 Rudnyy Rus. Fed.
76 G1 Rudol'fa, Ostrov i. Rus. Fed.
88 F3 Rudong China
30 E2 Rudyard U.S.A.
103 D4 Rufiji r. Tanz.
47 D2 Rufino Arg.
100 A3 Rufisque Senegal
103 C5 Rufunsa Zambia
88 F3 Rugao China
59 F5 Rugby U.K.
26 C1 Rugby U.S.A.
59 F5 Rugeley U.K.
62 F3 Rügen i. Ger.
102 C4 Ruhengeri Rwanda
55 S8 Ruhnu i. Estonia
61 E3 Ruhr r. Ger.
89 F5 Rui'an China
25 F5 Ruidoso U.S.A.
89 E5 Ruijin China
21 N0 Ruin Point pt Can.
103 D4 Ruipa Tanz.
45 B3 Ruiz, Nevado del vol. Col.
80 F5 Rujaylah, Ḥarrat ar lava Jordan
55 T8 Rüjiena Latvia
85 E3 Rukumkot Nepal
102 D4 Rukwa, Lake l. Tanz.
56 C3 Rum i. U.K.
67 H2 Ruma Yugo.
101 F4 Rumbek Sudan
37 J4 Rum Cay i. Bahamas
33 H2 Rumford U.S.A.

64 G4 Rumilly France
112 F2 Rum Jungle Austr.
90 G3 Rumoi Japan
88 E3 Runan China
117 C5 Runanga N.Z.
117 F2 Runaway, Cape c. N.Z.
59 E4 Runcorn U.K.
103 B5 Rundu Namibia
54 Q5 Rundvik Sweden
95 B3 Rŭng, Kaôh i. Cambodia
95 B3 Rŭng Sânlœm, Kaôh i. Cambodia
88 E3 Runheji China
55 V6 Ruokolahti Fin.
82 G3 Ruoqiang China
85 H4 Rupa India
47 B5 Rupanco, L. l. Chile
114 E6 Rupanyup Austr.
95 B5 Rupat i. Indon.
22 F3 Rupert r. Can.
24 D3 Rupert U.S.A.
22 E3 Rupert Bay b. Can.
61 E4 Rurstausee resr Ger.
103 D5 Rusape Zimbabwe
67 L3 Ruse Bulg.
59 G5 Rushden U.K.
30 B4 Rushford U.S.A.
30 C4 Rush Lake l. U.S.A.
85 H3 Rushon India
79 L2 Rushon Tajik.
30 B5 Rushville IL U.S.A.
26 C3 Rushville NE U.S.A.
114 F6 Rushworth Austr.
27 E6 Rusk U.S.A.
29 D7 Ruskin U.S.A.
21 J4 Russell Man. Can.
33 F2 Russell Ont. Can.
117 E1 Russell N.Z.
26 D4 Russell U.S.A.
20 F2 Russel Lake l. Can.
111 F2 Russell Is Solomon Is
29 C4 Russellville AL U.S.A.
27 E5 Russellville AR U.S.A.
28 C4 Russellville KY U.S.A.
62 D5 Rüsselsheim Ger.
70 Russian Federation country Asia/Europe
90 C3 Russkiy, Ostrov i. Rus. Fed.
81 K1 Rust'avi Georgia
105 G2 Rustenburg S. Africa
27 E5 Ruston U.S.A.
93 G8 Ruteng Indon.
35 E2 Ruth U.S.A.
31 H2 Rutherglen Can.
59 D4 Ruthin U.K.
68 H3 Rutka r. Rus. Fed.
33 G3 Rutland U.S.A.
59 G5 Rutland Water resr U.K.
21 G2 Rutledge Lake l. Can.
84 D2 Rutog China
31 H2 Rutter Can.
54 T4 Ruukki Fin.
103 D5 Ruvuma r. Moz./Tanz.
80 F5 Ruwayshid, Wādī watercourse Jordan
89 D5 Ruyuan China
76 H4 Ruzayevka Kazak.
68 H4 Ruzayevka Rus. Fed.
88 D3 Ruzhou China
63 J6 Ružomberok Slovakia
102 C4 Rwanda country Africa
68 H2 Ryadovo Rus. Fed.
57 F5 Ryan, Loch b. U.K.
68 F4 Ryazan' Rus. Fed.
68 G4 Ryazanskaya Oblast' div. Rus. Fed.
68 G4 Ryazhsk Rus. Fed.
76 E2 Rybachiy, Poluostrov pen. Rus. Fed.
Rybach'ye see Balykchy
68 F3 Rybinsk Rus. Fed.
68 F3 Rybinskoye Vdkhr. resr Rus. Fed.
68 J4 Rybnaya Sloboda Rus. Fed.
63 J5 Rybnik Pol.
68 F4 Rybnoye Rus. Fed.
20 F3 Rycroft Can.
55 O8 Ryd Sweden
119 B3 Rydberg Pen. pen. Antarctica
59 F7 Ryde U.K.
59 H7 Rye U.K.
58 G3 Rye r. U.K.
69 E5 Ryl'sk Rus. Fed.
115 H4 Rylstone Austr.
91 F7 Ryōtsu Japan
Ryuku Islands is see Nansei-shotō
63 L5 Rzeszów Pol.
69 G4 Rzhaksa Rus. Fed.
68 E3 Rzhev Rus. Fed.

S

80 F5 Sab' Ābār Syria
67 H2 Šabac Yugo.
65 H2 Sabadell Spain
91 E2 Sabae Japan
93 F5 Sabah div. Malaysia
95 B5 Sabak Malaysia
81 L2 Sabalan, Kūhhā-ye mts Iran
84 D4 Sabalgarh India
37 H4 Sabana, Arch. de is Cuba
45 B2 Sabanalarga Col.
80 D1 Sabanözü Turkey
46 D2 Šabará Brazil
84 C5 Sabarmati r. India
66 E4 Sabaudia Italy
104 E5 Sabelo S. Africa
101 D2 Sabhā Libya
84 D3 Sabi r. India
105 K2 Sabie Moz.
105 K2 Sabie r. Moz./S. Africa
105 J2 Sabie S. Africa
25 F6 Sabinal Mex.
36 D3 Sabinas Mex.
27 C7 Sabinas Hidalgo Mex.
27 E6 Sabine L. l. U.S.A.
81 M1 Sabirabad Azer.
94 B3 Sablayan Phil.
29 C5 Sable, Cape c. U.S.A.
111 F3 Sable, Île de i. New Caledonia
31 F2 Sables, River aux r. Can.
94 B1 Sabtang i. Phil.
65 C2 Sabugal Port.
30 B4 Sabula U.S.A.
78 E6 Şabyā Saudi Arabia
Sabzanar see Shīndand
79 N2 Sabzevār Iran
67 L2 Săcele Romania
103 B5 Sachanga Angola
22 B3 Sachigo r. Can.
22 B3 Sachigo L. l. Can.
84 C5 Sachin India
84 D4 Sach Pass pass India
33 E3 Sackets Harbor U.S.A.
23 H3 Sackville Can.
33 H3 Saco ME U.S.A.
24 F1 Saco MT U.S.A.
94 B5 Sacol i. Phil.
34 B2 Sacramento U.S.A.
34 B2 Sacramento r. U.S.A.
25 F5 Sacramento Mts mts U.S.A.
24 B3 Sacramento Valley v. U.S.A.
105 G6 Sada S. Africa
65 F1 Sádaba Spain
80 F4 Şadad Syria
95 B4 Sadao Thai.
81 K5 Saddat al Hindīyah Iraq
105 J2 Saddleback pass S. Africa
95 C3 Sa Dec Vietnam
85 H3 Sadêng China
84 B3 Sadiqabad Pak.
84 C1 Sad Istragh mt Afgh./Pak.
82 J5 Sadiya India
81 L5 Sa'dīyah, Hawr as l. Iraq
65 B3 Sado r. Port.
91 F6 Sadoga-shima i. Japan
63 H3 Sa Dragonera i. Spain
55 M8 Sæby Denmark
Safad see Zefat
81 L6 Safayal Maqūf w. Iraq
55 N7 Säffle Sweden
33 H5 Safford U.S.A.
59 H5 Saffron Walden U.K.
100 B1 Safi Morocco
81 M3 Safīd r. Iran
81 M5 Safīd Dasht Iran
80 F3 Şāfītā Syria
54 X2 Safonovo Murmansk. Rus. Fed.
68 E4 Safonovo Smolensk. Rus. Fed.
76 F3 Safonovo Rus. Fed.
80 D1 Safranbolu Turkey
81 K5 Safwān Iraq
85 F3 Saga China
91 B8 Saga Japan
91 F7 Sagamihara Japan
91 F7 Sagami-nada g. Japan
91 F7 Sagami-wan b. Japan
45 B3 Sagamoso r. Col.
95 A2 Saganthit Kyun i. Myanmar
84 D3 Sagar India
69 H7 Sagarejo Georgia
85 G2 Sagar I. i. India
77 O2 Sagastyr Rus. Fed.
31 F4 Saginaw U.S.A.
31 F4 Saginaw Bay b. U.S.A.
23 H2 Saglek Bay b. Can.
66 C3 Sagone, Golfe de b. France
65 B4 Sagres Port.
85 H5 Sagu Myanmar
25 F4 Saguache U.S.A.
37 H4 Sagua la Grande Cuba
35 G5 Saguaro National Monument res. U.S.A.
23 F4 Saguenay r. Can.
65 F3 Sagunto Spain
84 C5 Sagwara India
45 B2 Sahagún Col.
65 D2 Sahagún Spain
81 L3 Sahand, Küh-e mt Iran
98 Sahara des. Africa
Saharan Atlas mts see Atlas Saharien
84 D3 Saharanpur India
85 F4 Saharsa India
84 D3 Sahaswan India

84 C3 Sahiwal Pak.
81 L4 Saḩneh Iran
81 K6 Ṣaḩrā al Ḩijārah reg. Iraq
25 E6 Sahuaripa Mex.
35 G6 Sahuarita U.S.A.
95 D2 Sa Huynh Vietnam
Sahyadri mts see Western Ghats
84 C5 Sahyadriparvat Range h. India
84 E4 Sai r. India
95 B4 Sai Buri Thai.
95 B4 Sai Buri r. Thai.
Saïda see Sidon
95 B2 Sai Dao Tai, Khao mt Thai.
85 G4 Saidpur Bangl.
84 C2 Saidu Pak.
91 C6 Saigō Japan
Saigon see Hô Chi Minh
95 C3 Saigon, Sông r. Vietnam
85 H5 Saiha India
88 D1 Saihan Tal China
88 A1 Saihan Toroi China
91 C8 Saijō Japan
91 B8 Saiki Japan
89 □ Sai Kung China
55 V6 Saimaa l. Fin.
80 F2 Saimbeyli Turkey
81 L3 Sa'īndezh Iran
57 F5 St Abb's Head hd U.K.
59 B7 St Agnes U.K.
59 A8 St Agnes i. U.K.
23 J4 St Alban's Can.
59 G6 St Albans U.K.
33 G2 St Albans VT U.S.A.
32 C5 St Albans WV U.S.A.
59 E7 St Aldhelm's Head hd U.K.
20 G4 St Albert Can.
61 B4 St-Amand-les-Eaux France
64 F3 St-Amand-Montrond France
64 G3 St-Amour France
33 K2 St Andrews Can.
57 F4 St Andrews U.K.
37 J5 St Ann's Bay Jamaica
60 F6 St Ann's Head hd Wales
23 J3 St Anthony Can.
24 E3 St Anthony U.S.A.
114 E6 St Arnaud Austr.
117 D5 St Arnaud Range mts N.Z.
23 J3 St-Augustin Can.
29 D6 St Augustine U.S.A.
59 C7 St Austell U.K.
64 E3 St-Avertin France
61 E5 St-Avold France
37 M5 St Barthélemy i. Guadeloupe
58 D3 St Bees U.K.
58 D3 St Bees Head hd U.K.
59 B6 St Bride's Bay b. U.K.
64 C2 St-Brieuc France
35 G5 St Carlos Lake l. U.S.A.
31 H4 St Catharines Can.
24 D6 St Catherines I. i. U.S.A.
59 F7 St Catherine's Point pt U.K.
64 E4 St-Céré France
33 G2 St-Césaire Can.
64 G4 St-Chamond France
24 E3 St Charles ID U.S.A.
32 E5 St Charles MD U.S.A.
30 A4 St Charles MN U.S.A.
26 F4 St Charles MO U.S.A.
31 F4 St Clair U.S.A.
31 F4 St Clair Shores U.S.A.
64 G3 St-Claude France
59 C6 St Clears U.K.
26 E2 St Cloud U.S.A.
23 G4 St Croix r. Can.
30 A2 St Croix r. U.S.A.
37 M5 St Croix i. Virgin Is
30 A3 St Croix Falls U.S.A.
36 G5 St David U.S.A.
59 B6 St David's Wales
59 B6 St David's Head hd U.K.
64 H2 St-Dié France
64 G2 St-Dizier France
21 K5 Ste Anne Can.
23 G3 Ste Anne, L. l. Can.
23 F4 Ste-Anne-de-Beaupré Can.
33 J1 Sainte-Anne-de-Madawaska Can.
31 K2 Sainte-Anne-du-Lac Can.
33 H1 Ste-Camille-de-Lellis Can.
64 G4 St-Égrève France
33 H1 Sainte-Justine Can.
33 J1 St-Éleuthère Can.
20 B2 St Elias Mountains mts Can.
23 G3 Ste Marguerite r. Can.
64 H5 Ste-Maxime France
64 D4 Saintes France
33 G2 Ste-Thérèse Can.
64 G4 St-Étienne France
33 F2 St Eugene Can.
33 G2 St-Eustache Can.
37 M5 St Eustatius i. Neth. Ant.
23 F4 St-Félicien Can.
60 F3 Saintfield U.K.
66 C3 St-Florent France
64 F3 St-Florent-sur-Cher France
102 C3 St Floris, Parc National nat. park C.A.R.
33 J1 St-Francis r. Can./U.S.A.
26 C4 St Francis KS U.S.A.
33 J1 St Francis ME U.S.A.
27 F4 St Francis r. U.S.A.

23 K4 St Francis, C. c. Can.
33 J1 St Froid Lake l. U.S.A.
62 D7 St Gallen Switz.
64 C5 St-Gaudens France
33 H2 St-Gédéon Can.
115 H2 St George Austr.
33 K2 St George Can.
29 D5 St George SC U.S.A.
35 F3 St George UT U.S.A.
111 F2 St George, C. pt P.N.G.
24 A3 St George, Pt pt U.S.A.
29 C6 St George I. i. U.S.A.
23 F4 St-Georges Can.
37 M6 St George's Grenada
23 J4 St George's B. b. Can.
110 F2 St George's Channel chan. P.N.G.
56 C6 St George's Channel chan. Rep. of Ireland/U.K.
59 C6 St Govan's Head hd U.K.
30 E3 St Helen U.K.
12 J7 St Helena i. Atlantic Ocean
34 A2 St Helena U.S.A.
104 C6 St Helena Bay S. Africa
104 C6 St Helena Bay b. S. Africa
12 J7 St Helena Fracture sea feature Atlantic Ocean
115 H8 St Helens Austr.
59 E4 St Helens U.K.
24 B2 St Helens U.S.A.
24 B2 St Helens, Mt vol. U.S.A.
115 H8 St Helens Pt pt Austr.
56 E7 St Helier U.K.
61 D4 St-Hubert Belgium
22 F4 St-Hyacinthe Can.
30 E3 St Ignace U.S.A.
30 C1 St Ignace I. i. Can.
59 C6 St Ishmael U.K.
59 G5 St Ives Eng. U.K.
59 B7 St Ives Eng. U.K.
33 J1 St-Jacques Can.
30 E3 St James U.S.A.
20 C4 St James, Cape pt Can.
23 F4 St-Jean, Lac l. Can.
64 D4 St-Jean-d'Angély France
64 C3 St-Jean-de-Monts France
22 F4 St-Jean-sur-Richelieu Can.
22 F4 St-Jérôme Can.
24 C2 St Joe r. U.S.A.
23 G4 St John Can.
33 K2 St John r. Can./U.S.A.
35 F1 St John U.S.A.
37 M5 St John i. Virgin Is
37 M5 St John's Antigua
23 K4 St John's Can.
35 H4 St Johns AZ U.S.A.
30 E4 St Johns MI U.S.A.
29 D6 St Johns r. U.S.A.
33 H2 St Johnsbury U.S.A.
58 E3 St John's Chapel U.K.
30 D4 St Joseph MI U.S.A.
26 E4 St Joseph MO U.S.A.
30 E5 St Joseph r. U.S.A.
22 B3 St Joseph, Lac l. Can.
23 F4 St-Joseph-de-Beauce Can.
31 F2 St Joseph I. i. Can.
27 D7 St Joseph I. i. U.S.A.
22 F4 St Jovité Can.
64 E4 St-Junien France
59 B7 St Just U.K.
59 B7 St Keverne U.K.
56 B3 St Kilda is U.K.
16 St Kitts and Nevis country Caribbean Sea
61 B3 St-Laureins Belgium
St-Laurent, Golfe du g. see St Lawrence, Gulf of
43 H2 St-Laurent-du-Maroni Fr. Guiana
116 C4 St Lawrence Austr.
23 K4 St Lawrence Can.
23 G4 St Lawrence in. Can.
23 H4 St Lawrence, Gulf of g. Can./U.S.A.
77 V3 St Lawrence I. i. Alaska
31 K3 St Lawrence Islands National Park nat. park Can.
33 F2 St Lawrence Seaway chan. Can./U.S.A.
23 G4 St-Léonard Can.
23 J3 St Lewis Can.
23 J3 Saint Lewis r. Can.
64 D2 St-Lô France
100 A3 St Louis Senegal
30 E4 St Louis MI U.S.A.
26 F4 St Louis MO U.S.A.
30 A2 St Louis r. U.S.A.
16 St Lucia country Caribbean Sea
105 K3 St Lucia, Lake l. S. Africa
105 K4 St Lucia Estuary S. Africa
37 M5 St Maarten i. Neth. Ant.
57 □ St Magnus Bay b. U.K.
64 D3 St-Maixent-l'École France
64 C2 St-Malo France
64 C2 St-Malo, Golfe de g. France
105 G6 St Marks S. Africa
37 M5 Saint Martin i. Guadeloupe
104 B6 St Martin, Cape hd S. Africa
21 K4 St Martin, L. l. Can.
30 D3 St Martin's I. i. U.S.A.
59 A8 St Martin's U.K.
85 H5 St Martin's I. i. Bangl.
114 C3 St Mary Pk mt Austr.
115 H8 St Marys Austr.

31 G4 St Mary's Can.
57 F2 St Mary's U.K.
59 A8 St Mary's i. U.K.
32 A4 St Marys OH U.S.A.
32 D4 St Marys PA U.S.A.
32 C5 Saint Marys U.S.A.
32 A4 St Marys r. U.S.A.
23 K4 St Mary's, C. hd Can.
77 V3 St Matthew I. i. Alaska
110 E2 St Matthias Group is P.N.G.
22 F4 St Maurice r. Can.
59 B7 St Mawes U.K.
64 D4 St-Médard-en-Jalles France
23 J3 St Michaels Bay b. Can.
62 D7 St Moritz Switz.
64 C3 St-Nazaire France
59 G5 St Neots U.K.
64 H2 St-Nicolas-de-Port France
61 C3 St-Niklaas Belgium
64 F1 St-Omer France
33 J1 St-Pamphile Can.
23 G4 St Pascal Can.
23 G4 St Paul Can.
13 K6 St Paul i. Indian Ocean
30 A3 St Paul MN U.S.A.
26 D3 St Paul NE U.S.A.
32 B6 St Paul VA U.S.A.
56 E7 St Peter Port U.K.
68 D3 St Petersburg Rus. Fed.
29 D7 St Petersburg U.S.A.
64 G5 St-Pierre mt France
23 J4 St-Pierre N. America
23 F4 St-Pierre, Lake l. Can.
64 D4 St-Pierre-d'Oléron France
64 F3 St-Pierre-le-Moûtier France
61 A4 St-Pol-sur-Ternoise France
62 G6 St Pölten Austria
64 F3 St-Pourçain-sur-Sioule France
33 H1 Saint-Prosper Can.
64 F2 St-Quentin France
64 H5 St-Raphaël France
33 F2 St Regis r. U.S.A.
33 F2 St Regis Falls U.S.A.
33 G2 St-Rémi Can.
33 H2 St-Sébastien Can.
23 G4 St Siméon Can.
29 D6 St Simons I. i. U.S.A.
33 K2 St Stephen Can.
29 E5 St Stephen U.S.A.
33 H2 St-Théophile Can.
21 L4 St Theresa Point Can.
31 G4 St Thomas Can.
64 H5 St-Tropez France
21 K5 St Vincent U.S.A.
115 F9 St Vincent, C. hd Austr.
St Vincent, Cape c. see São Vicente, Cabo de
114 B5 St Vincent, Gulf b. Austr.
16 St Vincent and the Grenadines country Caribbean Sea
61 E4 St-Vith Belgium
21 H4 St Walburg Can.
61 F5 St Wendel Ger.
31 G4 St Williams Can.
64 E4 St-Yrieix-la-Perche France
84 E3 Saipal mt Nepal
93 L3 Saipan i. N. Mariana Is
85 H5 Saitlai Myanmar
54 T3 Saittanulkki h. Fin.
62 F7 Sajama, Nevado mt Bol.
104 D5 Sak watercourse S. Africa
91 D7 Sakai Japan
91 C7 Sakaide Japan
91 G7 Sakaiminato Japan
81 H7 Sakākah Saudi Arabia
26 C2 Sakakawea, Lake l. U.S.A.
22 F3 Sakami Can.
22 F3 Sakami r. Can.
22 F3 Sakami, Lac l. Can.
67 M4 Sakar mts Bulg.
80 C1 Sakarya Turkey
80 C1 Sakarya r. Turkey
90 F5 Sakata Japan
95 B2 Sa Keo r. Thai.
100 B3 Sakété Benin
87 Q1 Sakhalin i. Rus. Fed.
77 Q4 Sakhalinskiy Zaliv b. Rus. Fed.
84 C3 Sakhi India
105 H3 Sakhile S. Africa
81 L1 Şäki Azer.
55 S9 Šakiai Lith.
84 A3 Sakir mt Pak.
87 M7 Sakishima-shotō is Japan
95 □ Sakon Nakhon Thai.
95 □ Sakra, P. i. Sing.
84 B4 Sakrand Pak.
104 D5 Sakrivier S. Africa
91 B9 Sakura-jima vol. Japan
69 G6 Saky Ukr.
55 S6 Säkylä Fin.
100 □ Sal i. Cape Verde
69 G6 Sal r. Rus. Fed.
55 S8 Sala Latvia
55 P7 Sala Sweden
22 F4 Salaberry-de-Valleyfield Can.
55 T8 Salacgrīva Latvia
66 F4 Sala Consilina Italy
35 E5 Salada, Laguna salt l. Mex.
47 E2 Saladillo Arg.
47 D2 Saladillo r. Arg.
47 E1 Salado r. Buenos Aires Arg.

47 C3 Salado r. Mendoza/San Luis Arg.
47 D4 Salado r. Rio Negro Arg.
47 E2 Salado r. Santa Fé Arg.
36 E3 Salado r. Mex.
44 B3 Salado, Quebrada de r. Chile
100 B4 Salaga Ghana
104 F1 Salajwe Botswana
101 D3 Salal Chad
79 G6 Şalālah Oman
47 B1 Salamanca Chile
36 D4 Salamanca Mex.
65 D2 Salamanca Spain
32 D3 Salamanca U.S.A.
105 K3 Salamanga Moz.
81 L4 Salāmatābād Iran
45 B3 Salamina Col.
80 F4 Salamīyah Syria
30 E5 Salamonie r. U.S.A.
30 E5 Salamonie Lake l. U.S.A.
85 F5 Salandi r. India
55 R8 Salantai Lith.
88 D1 Salaqi China
65 C1 Salas Spain
55 T8 Salaspils Latvia
92 □ Salatiga Indon.
93 □ Salawati i. Indon.
84 B5 Salaya India
93 G8 Salayar i. Indon.
15 N7 Sala y Gómez, Isla i. Chile
47 D3 Salazar Arg.
55 T9 Šalčininkai Lith.
59 D7 Salcombe U.K.
45 B4 Saldaña r. Col.
65 D1 Saldaña Spain
104 B6 Saldanha S. Africa
104 B6 Saldanha Bay b. S. Africa
47 E3 Saldungaray Arg.
55 S8 Saldus Latvia
115 G7 Sale Austr.
81 L5 Şāleḩābād Iran
81 M4 Şāleḩābād Iran
76 H3 Salekhard Rus. Fed.
83 E8 Salem India
33 H3 Salem MA U.S.A.
27 F4 Salem MO U.S.A.
28 F4 Salem NJ U.S.A.
33 G3 Salem NY U.S.A.
32 C4 Salem OH U.S.A.
24 B2 Salem OR U.S.A.
28 D4 Salem VA U.S.A.
57 C4 Salen U.K.
57 C4 Salen 187351
66 F4 Salerno Italy
66 F4 Salerno, Golfo di g. Italy
59 E4 Salford U.K.
43 L5 Salgado r. Brazil
63 J6 Salgótarján Hungary
43 L5 Salgueiro Brazil
80 C1 Salihli Turkey
94 C4 Salibabu i. Indon.
64 D5 Salies-de-Béarn France
80 B2 Salihli Turkey
68 C4 Salihorsk Belarus
103 D5 Salima Malawi
103 D5 Salimo Moz.
26 D4 Salina KS U.S.A.
35 G2 Salina UT U.S.A.
66 F5 Salina, Isola i. Italy
36 E5 Salina Cruz Mex.
46 D2 Salinas Brazil
42 B4 Salinas Ecuador
34 B3 Salinas U.S.A.
34 B3 Salinas r. U.S.A.
25 F5 Salinas Peak summit U.S.A.
27 B5 Saline r. AR U.S.A.
26 C4 Saline r. KS U.S.A.
34 D3 Saline Valley v. U.S.A.
43 J4 Salinópolis Brazil
42 C6 Salinosó Lachay, Pta pt Peru
59 F6 Salisbury U.K.
33 F5 Salisbury MD U.S.A.
29 D5 Salisbury NC U.S.A.
59 E6 Salisbury Plain plain U.K.
43 K6 Salitre r. Brazil
80 F5 Şalkhad Syria
85 F5 Salki r. India
54 V3 Salla Fin.
47 D3 Salliqueló Arg.
27 E5 Sallisaw U.S.A.
85 E3 Sallyana Nepal
64 G5 Salon-de-Provence France
102 C4 Salonga Sud, Parc National de la nat. park Dem. Rep. Congo
63 K7 Salonta Romania
47 D1 Salsacate Arg.
69 G6 Sal'sk Rus. Fed.
66 C2 Salsomaggiore Terme Italy
104 E5 Salt watercourse S. Africa
35 G5 Salt r. AZ U.S.A.
30 B6 Salt r. MO U.S.A.
44 C2 Salta Arg.
59 C7 Saltash U.K.
57 D5 Saltcoats U.K.
32 B5 Salt Creek r. U.S.A.
47 B2 San Antonio Chile

60 E5 Saltee Islands is Rep. of Ireland
54 O3 Saltfjellet Svartisen Nasjonalpark nat. park Norway
27 B6 Salt Flat U.S.A.
32 C4 Salt Fork Lake l. U.S.A.
36 D3 Saltillo Mex.
24 E3 Salt Lake City U.S.A.
47 C2 Salto Arg.
46 C3 Salto Brazil
47 C3 Salto Uru.
46 E2 Salto da Divisa Brazil
44 E4 Salto Grande, Embalse de resr Uru.
35 E5 Salton Sea salt l. U.S.A.
84 C2 Salt Ra. h. Pak.
21 G2 Salt River Can.
32 B5 Salt Rock U.S.A.
29 C3 Saluda SC U.S.A.
32 C6 Saluda VA U.S.A.
84 C4 Salumbar India
66 B2 Saluzzo Italy
47 D2 Salvador Arg.
46 E1 Salvador Brazil
27 F6 Salvador, L. l. U.S.A.
35 G2 Salvation Creek r. U.S.A.
Salween r. see Nu Jiang
95 A1 Salween r. Myanmar
81 M2 Salyan Azer.
32 B6 Salyersville U.S.A.
104 B2 Salzbrunn Namibia
62 F7 Salzburg Austria
62 E4 Salzgitter Ger.
84 B4 Sam India
89 B7 Sam, Nam r. Laos/Vietnam
95 B2 Samae San, Laem pt Thai.
94 C5 Samal i. Phil.
25 C6 Samalayuca Mex.
94 B5 Samales Group is Phil.
80 E3 Samandağı Turkey
90 H3 Samani Japan
80 C6 Samannūd Egypt
94 C4 Samar i. Phil.
76 H4 Samara Rus. Fed.
113 K2 Samarai P.N.G.
45 D3 Samariapo Venez.
92 F7 Samarinda Indon.
90 D4 Samarka Rus. Fed.
79 K2 Samarkand Uzbek.
81 J4 Sāmarrā' Iraq
94 C4 Samar Sea g. Phil.
68 J4 Samarskaya Oblast' div. Rus. Fed.
81 M1 Şamaxı Azer.
102 C4 Samba Dem. Rep. Congo
93 F6 Sambaliung mts Indon.
85 F5 Sambalpur India
92 E7 Sambar, Tanjung pt Indon.
92 D6 Sambas Indon.
103 F5 Sambava Madag.
85 G4 Sambha India
84 D3 Sambhal India
84 D4 Sambhar L. l. India
69 B5 Sambir Ukr.
43 K5 Sambito r. Brazil
47 E2 Samborombón, Bahía b. Arg.
61 B4 Sambre r. Belgium/France
45 A2 Sambú r. Panama
91 A6 Samch'ŏk S. Korea
81 K3 Samdi Dag mt Turkey
102 D4 Same Tanz.
90 A4 Samjiyŏn N. Korea
81 L1 Sämkir Azer.
91 A7 Samnangjin S. Korea
106 Samoa country Pac. Oc.
66 F2 Samobor Croatia
68 G2 Samoded Rus. Fed.
67 K3 Samokov Bulg.
62 H6 Šamorín Slovakia
67 M6 Samos i. Greece
95 A5 Samosir i. Indon.
67 L4 Samothraki Greece
67 L4 Samothraki i. Greece
94 B3 Sampaloc Point pt Phil.
92 E7 Sampit Indon.
103 C4 Sampwe Dem. Rep. Congo
27 E6 Sam Rayburn Res. resr U.S.A.
85 E3 Samsang China
89 B6 Sam Sao, Phou mts Laos/Vietnam
95 C1 Sâm Sơn Vietnam
80 F1 Samsun Turkey
69 G7 Samtredia Georgia
95 B3 Samui, Ko i. Thai.
69 J7 Samur r. Azer./Rus. Fed.
95 B2 Samut Prakan Thai.
95 B2 Samut Sakhon Thai.
95 B2 Samut Songkhram Thai.
95 C2 Samyai China
55 S6 Salo Fin.
85 E4 Salon India
95 C2 San, T. r. Cambodia
78 E6 Şan'ä' Yemen
119 D2 Sanae S. Africa Base Antarctica
101 D4 Sanaga r. Cameroon
45 A4 San Agustín Col.
94 C5 San Agustín, Cape c. Phil.
81 L4 Sanandaj Iran
34 B2 San Andreas U.S.A.
94 C3 San Andres Phil.
42 B1 San Andrés, Isla de i. Col.
25 F5 San Andres Mts mts U.S.A.
36 E5 San Andrés Tuxtla Mex.
27 C6 San Angelo U.S.A.
47 B2 San Antonio Chile

94 B3 San Antonio Phil.
27 D6 San Antonio U.S.A.
34 C3 San Antonio r. U.S.A.
37 H4 San Antonio, C. pt Cuba
47 C3 San Antonio, Cabo pt Arg.
34 D4 San Antonio, Mt mt U.S.A.
65 G3 San Antonio Abad Spain
44 C2 San Antonio de los Cobres Arg.
45 D2 San Antonio de Tamanaco Venez.
47 C1 San Antonio Oeste Arg.
34 B4 San Antonio Reservoir resr U.S.A.
34 B3 San Ardo U.S.A.
47 B3 San Augustín Arg.
47 C1 San Augustín de Valle Fértil Arg.
84 D5 Sanawad India
66 D3 San Benedetto del Tronto Italy
36 B3 San Benedicto, I. i. Mex.
27 D7 San Benito U.S.A.
34 B3 San Benito r. U.S.A.
34 B3 San Benito Mt mt U.S.A.
25 C4 San Bernardino Mts mts U.S.A.
47 B2 San Bernardo Chile
27 B7 San Bernardo Mex.
91 C7 Sanbe-san vol. Japan
29 C6 San Blas, C. c. U.S.A.
42 E6 San Borja Bol.
33 H3 Sanbornville U.S.A.
27 C7 San Buenaventura Mex.
47 C2 San Carlos Chile
47 B3 San Carlos Chile
27 C6 San Carlos Mex.
94 B3 San Carlos Luzon Phil.
94 B4 San Carlos Negros Phil.
47 F2 San Carlos Uru.
35 G5 San Carlos U.S.A.
45 D4 San Carlos Amazonas Venez.
45 C2 San Carlos Cojedes Venez.
25 D6 San Carlos, Mesa de h. Mex.
47 C1 San Carlos Centro Arg.
47 B4 San Carlos de Bariloche Arg.
47 C3 San Carlos de Bolívar Arg.
45 C2 San Carlos del Zulia Venez.
88 C2 Sancha Gansu China
88 D2 Sancha Shanxi China
89 C5 Sancha He r. China
89 B6 San Chien Pau mt Laos
84 B4 Sanchor India
88 D2 Sanchuan r. China
68 H3 Sanchursk Rus. Fed.
47 B2 San Clemente Chile
34 C5 San Clemente U.S.A.
34 C5 San Clemente I. i. U.S.A.
64 F3 Sancoins France
47 E1 San Cristóbal Arg.
111 G3 San Cristóbal i. Solomon Is
45 B3 San Cristóbal Venez.
42 □ San Cristóbal, Isla i. Ecuador
36 F5 San Cristóbal de las Casas Mex.
35 F5 San Cristobal Wash r. U.S.A.
37 J4 Sancti Spíritus Cuba
105 H1 Sand r. S. Africa
90 D3 Sandagou Rus. Fed.
57 C5 Sanda Island i. U.K.
93 F5 Sandakan Malaysia
55 K6 Sandane Norway
67 K4 Sandanski Bulg.
57 F1 Sanday i. U.K.
57 F1 Sanday Sound chan. U.K.
59 E4 Sandbach U.K.
55 M7 Sandefjord Norway
119 D4 Sandercock Nunataks nunatak Antarctica
35 H4 Sanders U.S.A.
27 C6 Sanderson U.S.A.
112 D3 Sandfire Roadhouse Austr.
115 K1 Sandgate Austr.
57 D6 Sandhead U.K.
30 B2 Sand I. i. U.S.A.
42 E6 Sandia Peru
25 E6 San Diego Mex.
34 D5 San Diego U.S.A.
44 C8 San Diego, C. c. Arg.
80 C2 Sandıklı Turkey
84 E4 Sandila India
30 E2 Sand Lake Can.
55 J7 Sandnes Norway
54 N3 Sandnessjøen Norway
103 C4 Sandoa Dem. Rep. Congo
63 K5 Sandomierz Pol.
45 A4 Sandoná Col.
66 E2 San Donà di Piave Italy
83 H7 Sandoway Myanmar
59 F7 Sandown U.K.
104 C7 Sandown Bay b. S. Africa
54 □ Sandoy i. Faroe Is
24 C1 Sandpoint U.S.A.
57 A4 Sandray i. U.K.
63 N7 Şandrul Mare, Vârful mt Romania
55 O6 Sandsjö Sweden
20 C4 Sandspit Can.
27 D4 Sand Springs U.S.A.
34 C2 Sand Springs Salt Flat salt flat U.S.A.
30 A2 Sandstone U.S.A.

35 F5 **Sand Tank Mts** mts U.S.A.
89 C5 **Sandu** Guizhou China
89 D5 **Sandu** Hunan China
31 F4 **Sandusky** MI U.S.A.
32 B4 **Sandusky** OH U.S.A.
32 B4 **Sandusky Bay** b. U.S.A.
104 C5 **Sandveld** mts S. Africa
104 B3 **Sandverhaar** Namibia
55 M7 **Sandvika** Norway
54 N5 **Sandvika** Sweden
55 P6 **Sandviken** Sweden
23 J3 **Sandwich Bay** b. Can.
57 □ **Sandwick** U.K.
85 G5 **Sandwip Ch.** chan. Bangl.
33 H2 **Sandy** r. U.S.A.
21 J3 **Sandy Bay** Can.
115 F4 **Sandy C.** hd Austr.
116 E5 **Sandy Cape** c. Austr.
32 B5 **Sandy Hook** U.S.A.
33 F4 **Sandy Hook** pt U.S.A.
22 B3 **Sandy L.** l. Can.
22 B3 **Sandy Lake** Can.
33 E3 **Sandy Pond** U.S.A.
46 A4 **San Estanislao** Para.
94 B3 **San Fabian** Phil.
47 B2 **San Felipe** Chile
25 F7 **San Felipe** Mex.
36 B2 **San Felipe** Mex.
45 C2 **San Felipe** Venez.
47 E2 **San Fernando** Arg.
47 B2 **San Fernando** Chile
25 D6 **San Fernando** Mex.
36 E4 **San Fernando** Mex.
94 B2 **San Fernando** Luzon Phil.
94 B3 **San Fernando** Luzon Phil.
65 C4 **San Fernando** Spain
45 C2 **San Fernando** Trinidad and Tobago
34 C4 **San Fernando** Venez.
45 D3 **San Fernando de Apure** Venez.
45 C3 **San Fernando de Atabapo** Venez.
34 D5 **San Filipe Creek** r. U.S.A.
29 D6 **Sanford** FL U.S.A.
33 H3 **Sanford** ME U.S.A.
29 E5 **Sanford** NC U.S.A.
30 E4 **Sanford Lake** l. U.S.A.
47 D1 **San Francisco** Arg.
25 D6 **San Francisco** Mex.
34 A3 **San Francisco** U.S.A.
35 H5 **San Francisco** r. U.S.A.
44 **San Francisco, Paso de** pass Arg.
34 A3 **San Francisco Bay** in. U.S.A.
37 K5 **San Francisco de Macorís** Dom. Rep.
44 C7 **San Francisco de Paula, C.** pt Arg.
65 G3 **San Francisco Javier** Spain
45 A4 **San Gabriel** Ecuador
25 D6 **San Gabriel, Punta** pt Mex.
34 C4 **San Gabriel Mts** mts U.S.A.
42 C4 **Sangai, Parque Nacional** nat. park Ecuador
84 C6 **Sangamner** India
30 C6 **Sangamon** r. U.S.A.
84 B3 **Sangar** r. Pak.
77 O3 **Sangar** Rus. Fed.
66 C5 **San Gavino Monreale** Italy
94 B5 **Sangboy Islands** is Phil.
88 B1 **Sangejing** China
34 C3 **Sanger** U.S.A.
88 E1 **Sanggan** r. China
88 B3 **Sanggarmai** China
88 G2 **Sanggou Wan** b. China
102 B4 **Sangha** r. Congo
84 B4 **Sanghar** Pak.
45 B3 **San Gil** Col.
66 G5 **San Giovanni in Fiore** Italy
66 F4 **San Giovanni Rotondo** Italy
94 B4 **Sangir** i. Indon.
93 G6 **Sangir, Kepulauan** is Indon.
92 □ **Sangkapura** Indon.
95 B2 **Sângke, Stœng** r. Cambodia
93 F6 **Sangkulirang** Indon.
83 D7 **Sangli** India
84 B1 **Sanglich** Afgh.
100 D4 **Sangmélima** Cameroon
84 D3 **Sangnam** India
85 H3 **Sangngagqoiling** China
103 D6 **Sango** Zimbabwe
34 D4 **San Gorgonio Mt** mt U.S.A.
62 D7 **San Gottardo, Passo del** pass Switz.
25 F4 **Sangre de Cristo Range** mts U.S.A.
45 E2 **Sangre Grande** Trinidad and Tobago
84 C3 **Sangrur** India
85 F3 **Sangsang** China
20 G4 **Sangudo** Can.
43 G6 **Sangue** r. Brazil
105 K2 **Sangutane** r. Moz.
89 D4 **Sangzhi** China
36 B3 **San Hipólito, Pta** pt Mex.
80 C1 **Sanhûr** Egypt
42 E6 **San Ignacio** Beni Bol.
42 F7 **San Ignacio** Santa Cruz Bol.
27 C7 **San Ignacio** Mex.

22 E2 **Sanikiluaq** Can.
94 B2 **San Ildefonso, Cape** c. Phil.
94 B2 **San Ildefonso Peninsula** pen. Phil.
94 C4 **San Isidro** Phil.
94 B3 **San Jacinto** Phil.
34 D5 **San Jacinto** U.S.A.
34 D5 **San Jacinto Peak** summit U.S.A.
85 F5 **Sanjai** r. India
47 E1 **San Javier** Arg.
47 B2 **San Javier de Loncomilla** Chile
84 B3 **Sanjawi** Pak.
103 D4 **Sanje** Tanz.
45 A3 **San Jerónimo, Serranía de** mts Col.
89 C5 **Sanjiang** China
91 F6 **Sanjō** Japan
34 B3 **San Joaquin** U.S.A.
34 B3 **San Joaquin** r. U.S.A.
34 B3 **San Joaquin Valley** v. U.S.A.
47 E1 **San Jorge** Arg.
45 B2 **San Jorge** r. Col.
44 C7 **San Jorge, Golfo de** g. Arg.
37 H7 **San José** Costa Rica
94 B3 **San Jose** Phil.
94 B3 **San Jose** Phil.
34 B3 **San Jose** U.S.A.
47 D4 **San José, Golfo** g. Arg.
36 B4 **San José, Isla** i. Mex.
47 C2 **San José, Vol.** vol. Chile
45 E2 **San José de Amacuro** Venez.
94 B4 **San Jose de Buenavista** Phil.
42 F7 **San José de Chiquitos** Bol.
47 E1 **San José de Feliciano** Arg.
25 E6 **San José de Gracia** Mex.
45 D2 **San José de Guanipa** Venez.
47 C1 **San Jose de Jáchal** Arg.
47 D1 **San José de la Dormida** Arg.
47 B3 **San José de la Mariquina** Chile
36 C4 **San José del Cabo** Mex.
45 B4 **San José del Guaviare** Col.
47 F2 **San José de Mayo** Uru.
45 C3 **San José de Ocuné** Col.
25 E6 **San José de Primas** Mex.
47 C1 **San Juan** Arg.
47 C1 **San Juan** div. Arg.
45 A3 **San Juan** r. Col.
37 H6 **San Juan** r. Costa Rica/Nic.
27 C7 **San Juan** Mex.
94 C4 **San Juan** Phil.
37 L5 **San Juan** Puerto Rico
34 B4 **San Juan** r. CA U.S.A.
35 H3 **San Juan** r. UT U.S.A.
45 D3 **San Juan** Venez.
42 E3 **San Juan Bautista** Para.
65 G3 **San Juan Bautista** Spain
36 E5 **San Juan Bautista Tuxtepec** Mex.
47 B4 **San Juan dela Costa** Chile
45 C2 **San Juan de los Cayos** Venez.
45 D2 **San Juan de los Morros** Venez.
25 F4 **San Juan Mts** mts U.S.A.
84 D1 **Sanju He** watercourse China
44 C7 **San Julián** Arg.
47 E1 **San Justo** Arg.
85 F5 **Sankh** r. India
Sankt-Peterburg see St Petersburg
80 G3 **Şanlıurfa** Turkey
47 E2 **San Lorenzo** Arg.
42 F8 **San Lorenzo** Bol.
42 C3 **San Lorenzo** Ecuador
25 F6 **San Lorenzo** Mex.
65 E1 **San Lorenzo** mt Spain
44 B7 **San Lorenzo, Cerro** mt Arg./Chile
42 C6 **San Lorenzo, I.** i. Peru
65 C4 **Sanlúcar de Barrameda** Spain
36 C4 **San Lucas** Mex.
47 C4 **San Luis** Arg.
47 C2 **San Luis** div. Arg.
35 E5 **San Luis** AZ U.S.A.
35 G5 **San Luis** AZ U.S.A.
25 D6 **San Luisito** Mex.
34 B4 **San Luis Obispo** U.S.A.
34 B4 **San Luis Obispo Bay** b. U.S.A.
36 D4 **San Luis Potosí** Mex.
34 B3 **San Luis Reservoir** resr U.S.A.
36 D4 **San Luis Río Colorado** Mex.
66 D5 **San Marco, Capo** c. Italy
27 D6 **San Marcos** U.S.A.
48 **San Marino** country Europe
66 E3 **San Marino** San Marino
44 C3 **San Martín** Catamarca Arg.
47 C2 **San Martín** Mendoza Arg.
42 F6 **San Martín** r. Bol.
44 B7 **San Martín, L.** l. Arg./Chile

47 B4 **San Martín de los Andes** Arg.
34 A3 **San Mateo** U.S.A.
47 D4 **San Matías, Golfo** g. Arg.
45 D2 **San Mauricio** Venez.
89 D4 **Sanmen** China
89 F4 **Sanmen Wan** b. China
88 D3 **Sanmenxia** China
42 F6 **San Miguel** r. Bol.
45 B4 **San Miguel** r. Col.
36 G6 **San Miguel** El Salvador
35 G6 **San Miguel** AZ U.S.A.
34 B4 **San Miguel** CA U.S.A.
35 H2 **San Miguel** r. U.S.A.
94 B3 **San Miguel Bay** b. Phil.
47 E2 **San Miguel del Monte** Arg.
44 C3 **San Miguel de Tucumán** Arg.
34 B4 **San Miguel I.** i. U.S.A.
94 A5 **San Miguel Islands** is Phil.
89 E5 **Sanming** China
94 B3 **San Narciso** Phil.
66 F4 **Sannicandro Garganico** Italy
47 E2 **San Nicolás de los Arroyos** Arg.
34 C5 **San Nicolas I.** i. U.S.A.
105 F3 **Sannieshof** S. Africa
100 B4 **Sanniquellie** Liberia
63 L6 **Sanok** Pol.
94 B3 **San Pablo** Phil.
47 E2 **San Pedro** Buenos Aires Arg.
44 D2 **San Pedro** Jujuy Arg.
42 F7 **San Pedro** Bol.
94 B3 **San Pedro** Phil.
35 G5 **San Pedro** r. U.S.A.
65 C3 **San Pedro, Sierra de** mts Spain
34 C5 **San Pedro Channel** U.S.A.
45 C3 **San Pedro de Arimena** Col.
45 E3 **San Pedro de las Bocas** Venez.
36 D3 **San Pedro de las Colonias** Mex.
25 D6 **San Pedro Mártir, Sierra** mts Mex.
36 G5 **San Pedro Sula** Honduras
66 C5 **San Pietro, Isola di** i. Italy
57 E5 **Sanquhar** U.K.
42 C3 **Sanquianga, Parque Nacional** nat. park Col.
47 C2 **San Rafael** Arg.
34 A3 **San Rafael** U.S.A.
35 G2 **San Rafael** r. U.S.A.
45 C2 **San Rafael** Venez.
35 G2 **San Rafael Knob** summit U.S.A.
34 C4 **San Rafael Mts** mts U.S.A.
42 F6 **San Ramón** Bol.
66 B3 **San Remo** Italy
45 C1 **San Román, C.** pt Venez.
65 B1 **San Roque** Spain
27 D6 **San Saba** U.S.A.
47 E1 **San Salvador** Arg.
36 G6 **San Salvador** El Salvador
37 K4 **San Salvador** i. Bahamas
42 □ **San Salvador, Isla** i. Ecuador
44 C3 **San Salvador de Jujuy** Arg.
65 F1 **San Sebastián** Spain
65 E2 **San Sebastián de los Reyes** Spain
66 E3 **Sansepolcro** Italy
66 F4 **San Severo** Italy
89 F5 **Sansha** China
89 D6 **Sanshui** China
66 G2 **Sanski Most** Bos.-Herz.
89 C5 **Sansui** China
42 E7 **Santa Ana** Bol.
36 G6 **Santa Ana** El Salvador
25 E6 **Santa Ana** Mex.
111 G3 **Santa Ana** i. Solomon Is
34 D5 **Santa Ana** U.S.A.
27 D6 **Santa Ana** U.S.A.
45 B3 **Sta Bárbara** Col.
36 C3 **Santa Bárbara** Mex.
34 C4 **Santa Bárbara** Mex.
34 B4 **Santa Barbara Channel** chan. U.S.A.
34 C5 **Santa Barbara I.** i. U.S.A.
44 C3 **Sta Catalina** Chile
34 C5 **Santa Catalina, Gulf of** b. U.S.A.
65 B1 **Santa Catalina de Armada** Spain
34 C5 **Santa Catalina I.** i. U.S.A.
25 D6 **Santa Catarina** Baja California Norte Mex.
27 C7 **Santa Catarina** Nuevo León Mex.
42 F4 **Santa Clara** Bol.
37 J4 **Santa Clara** Cuba
25 F6 **Santa Clara** Mex.
34 A3 **Santa Clara** CA U.S.A.
35 F3 **Santa Clara** UT U.S.A.
47 F2 **Santa Clara de Olimar** Uru.
34 C4 **Santa Clarita** U.S.A.
66 F6 **Sta Croce, Capo** c. Italy
44 C8 **Santa Cruz** r. Arg.
42 F7 **Sta Cruz** Bol.
47 B3 **Sta Cruz** Chile
25 E6 **Santa Cruz** Mex.

94 B3 **Santa Cruz** Luzon Phil.
94 B2 **Santa Cruz** Luzon Phil.
94 A3 **Sta Cruz** Phil.
34 A3 **Santa Cruz** U.S.A.
25 E5 **Santa Cruz** r. U.S.A.
42 □ **Santa Cruz, Isla** i. Ecuador
44 C8 **Santa Cruz, Pto** Arg.
46 E2 **Santa Cruz Cabrália** Brazil
65 F3 **Santa Cruz de Moya** Spain
100 A2 **Santa Cruz de Tenerife** Canary Is
44 F3 **Santa Cruz do Sul** Brazil
34 C4 **Santa Cruz I.** i. U.S.A.
111 G3 **Santa Cruz Islands** is Solomon Is
47 E1 **Sta Elena** Arg.
42 B4 **Sta Elena, B. de** b. Ecuador
36 G6 **Sta Elena, C.** hd Costa Rica
66 C5 **Sta Eufemia, Golfo di** g. Italy
47 E1 **Santa Fé** Arg.
47 E1 **Santa Fé** div. Arg.
25 F5 **Santa Fe** U.S.A.
46 B2 **Santa Helena de Goiás** Brazil
88 B4 **Santai** China
44 B8 **Santa Inés, Isla** i. Chile
47 C3 **Santa Isabel** Arg.
111 F2 **Santa Isabel** i. Solomon Is
47 F2 **Sta Lucia** r. Uru.
25 B4 **Santa Lucia Range** mts U.S.A.
46 A2 **Santa Luisa, Serra de** h. Brazil
100 □ **Santa Luzia** i. Cape Verde
36 B4 **Santa Margarita, Isla** i. Mex.
44 C3 **Santa María** Arg.
43 G4 **Santa Maria** Amazonas Brazil
44 F3 **Santa Maria** Rio Grande do Sul Brazil
47 F1 **Santa Maria** r. Brazil
100 □ **Santa Maria** Cape Verde
25 F6 **Santa María** r. Mex.
36 C2 **Santa María** r. Mex.
42 D4 **Santa María** Peru
34 B4 **Santa María** Peru
105 K3 **Santa Maria, Cabo de** pt Moz.
65 C4 **Santa María, Cabo de** c. Port.
47 B3 **Santa María, I.** i. Chile
42 □ **Santa María, Isla** i. Ecuador
43 J5 **Santa Maria das Barreiras** Brazil
46 D1 **Santa Maria da Vitória** Brazil
45 C3 **Sta María de Ipire** Venez.
67 H5 **Sta Maria di Leuca, Capo** c. Italy
111 G3 **Santa María I.** i. Vanuatu
29 F7 **Santa Marie, Cape** c. Bahamas
45 B2 **Santa Marta** Col.
45 B2 **Santa Marta, Sierra Nevada de** mts Col.
34 C4 **Santa Monica** U.S.A.
34 C5 **Santa Monica Bay** b. U.S.A.
43 K6 **Santana** Brazil
46 B2 **Santana** r. Brazil
47 G1 **Santana da Boa Vista** Brazil
47 F1 **Santana do Livramento** Brazil
45 A4 **Santander** Col.
65 E1 **Santander** Spain
35 G5 **Santan Mt** mt U.S.A.
66 C5 **Sant'Antioco** i. Italy
66 C5 **Sant'Antioco, Isola di** i. Italy
34 C4 **Santa Paula** U.S.A.
43 K4 **Santa Quitéria** Brazil
43 H4 **Santarém** Brazil
65 B3 **Santarém** Port.
27 C7 **Sta Rita** Venez.
45 C2 **Sta Rita** Venez.
46 B2 **Sta Rita do Araguaia** Brazil
34 B3 **Santa Rita Park** U.S.A.
47 D3 **Santa Rosa** La Pampa Arg.
47 C4 **Santa Rosa** Rio Negro Arg.
42 D5 **Santa Rosa** Brazil
34 A2 **Santa Rosa** CA U.S.A.
25 F5 **Santa Rosa** NM U.S.A.
36 G6 **Santa Rosa de Copán** Honduras
47 D1 **Sta Rosa del Río Primero** Arg.
34 B3 **Santa Rosa I.** i. U.S.A.
36 B3 **Sta Rosalía** Mex.
25 C6 **Sta Rosa Ra.** mts U.S.A.
35 G5 **Santa Rosa Wash** r. U.S.A.
47 G2 **Sta Vitória do Palmar** Brazil
34 D5 **Santee** U.S.A.
29 E5 **Santee** r. U.S.A.
25 C6 **San Telmo** Mex.
44 F3 **Santiago** Brazil
47 B2 **Santiago** Chile
47 B2 **Santiago** div. Chile

94 B3 **Santa Cruz** Luzon Phil.
94 B2 **Santa Cruz** Luzon Phil.
37 K5 **Santiago** Dom. Rep.
37 H7 **Santiago** Panama
94 B2 **Santiago** Phil.
65 B1 **Santiago de Compostela** Spain
37 J4 **Santiago de Cuba** Cuba
47 F2 **Santiago Vazquez** Uru.
21 N2 **Santianna Point** pt Can.
45 C2 **San Timoteo** Venez.
65 G2 **Sant Jordi, Golf de** g. Spain
46 E1 **Santo Amaro** Brazil
46 C4 **Sto Amaro, I. de** i. Brazil
46 C4 **Santo Amaro de Campos** Brazil
46 C3 **Santo André** Brazil
44 F3 **Santo Angelo** Brazil
100 □ **Santo Antão** i. Cape Verde
46 E1 **Sto Antônio, Cabo** c. Brazil
46 B3 **Santo Antônio da Platina** Brazil
46 E1 **Sto Antônio de Jesus** Brazil
42 E4 **Santo Antônio do Içá** Brazil
46 D3 **Santo Antônio do Monte** Brazil
43 G7 **Santo Corazón** Bol.
37 L5 **Santo Domingo** Dom. Rep.
25 D6 **Santo Domingo** Mex.
45 C3 **Sto Domingo** r. Venez.
65 E1 **Santoña** Spain
46 D1 **Sto Onofre** r. Brazil
67 L6 **Santorini** i. Greece
46 C3 **Santos** Brazil
46 C3 **Santos Dumont** Brazil
25 F6 **Santo Tomás** Mex.
25 C6 **Santo Tomás** Nic.
42 D6 **Santo Tomás** Peru
44 C3 **Santo Tomé** Arg.
35 F3 **Sanup Plateau** plat. U.S.A.
44 B7 **San Valentín, Cerro** mt Chile
36 G6 **San Vicente** El Salvador
25 C6 **San Vicente** Mex.
94 B2 **San Vicente** Phil.
42 C6 **San Vicente de Cañete** Peru
45 B4 **San Vicente del Caguán** Col.
66 D3 **San Vincenzo** Italy
66 E5 **San Vito, Capo** c. Italy
89 E5 **Sanya** China
88 C3 **Sanyuan** China
102 B4 **Sanza Pombo** Angola
46 C3 **São Bernardo do Campo** Brazil
44 E3 **São Borja** Brazil
46 C1 **São Carlos** Brazil
46 C3 **São Domingos** Brazil
46 B2 **São Domingos** r. Brazil
43 H6 **São Félix** Mato Grosso Brazil
43 H5 **São Félix** Pará Brazil
46 C3 **São Fidélis** Brazil
100 □ **São Filipe** Cape Verde
46 D1 **São Francisco** Brazil
43 L5 **São Francisco** r. Brazil
44 G3 **São Francisco do Sul** Brazil
47 F1 **São Gabriel** Brazil
46 C3 **São Gonçalo** Brazil
46 D2 **São Gotardo** Brazil
46 C1 **São João da Aliança** Brazil
46 C3 **São João da Barra** Brazil
46 C3 **São João da Boa Vista** Brazil
65 B2 **São João da Madeira** Port.
46 D1 **São João do Paraíso** Brazil
46 D3 **São João Nepomuceno** Brazil
46 C3 **São Joaquim da Barra** Brazil
45 D5 **São José** Brazil
46 E3 **São José do Calçado** Brazil
47 G2 **São José do Norte** Brazil
46 C3 **São José do Rio Preto** Brazil
46 D3 **São José dos Campos** Brazil
46 C4 **São José dos Pinhais** Brazil
46 D3 **São Lourenço** Brazil
46 A2 **São Lourenço** r. Brazil
47 G1 **São Lourenço do Sul** Brazil
43 K4 **São Luís** Brazil
46 C3 **São Manuel** Brazil
46 C3 **São Marcos** r. Brazil
43 K4 **São Marcos, Baía de** b. Brazil
46 E2 **São Mateus** Brazil
46 E2 **São Mateus** r. Brazil
46 C2 **São Miguel** r. Brazil
64 G3 **Saône** r. France
100 □ **São Nicolau** i. Cape Verde
46 C3 **São Paulo** Brazil
46 C3 **São Paulo** div. Brazil
12 H5 **São Pedro e São Paulo** is Atlantic Ocean
43 K5 **São Raimundo Nonato** Brazil
44 F3 **São Romão** Brazil
43 L5 **São Roque, Cabo de** pt Brazil

46 D3 **São Sebastião** Brazil
46 D3 **São Sebastião, Ilha do** i. Brazil
46 C3 **São Sebastião do Paraíso** Brazil
47 G1 **São Sepé** Brazil
46 B2 **São Simão** Brazil
46 B2 **São Simão, Barragem de** resr Brazil
93 H6 **Sao-Siu** Indon.
100 □ **São Tiago** i. Cape Verde
100 C4 **São Tomé** i. Sao Tome and Principe
46 D1 **São Tomé, Cabo de** c. Brazil
100 C4 **São Tomé and Príncipe** country Africa
46 C3 **São Vicente** i. Cape Verde
100 □ **São Vicente** i. Cape Verde
65 B4 **São Vicente, Cabo de** c. Port.
80 C1 **Sapanca** Turkey
93 H7 **Saparua** Indon.
80 C2 **Şaphane Dağı** mt Turkey
100 B4 **Sapo National Park** nat. park Liberia
90 G3 **Sapporo** Japan
66 F4 **Sapri** Italy
27 D4 **Sapulpa** U.S.A.
81 L3 **Sarā** Iran
81 L3 **Sarāb** Iran
81 L5 **Sarābe Meymeh** Iran
95 B2 **Sara Buri** Thai.
Saragossa see Zaragoza
42 C3 **Saraguro** Ecuador
67 H3 **Sarajevo** Bos.-Herz.
116 C4 **Saraji** Austr.
85 H4 **Saramati** mt India
33 G2 **Saranac** r. U.S.A.
33 F2 **Saranac Lake** U.S.A.
22 E5 **Saranac Lakes** lakes U.S.A.
67 J5 **Sarandë** Albania
47 F2 **Sarandí del Yí** Uru.
47 F2 **Sarandí Grande** Uru.
94 C5 **Sarangani** Phil.
94 C5 **Sarangani Bay** b. Phil.
94 C5 **Sarangani Islands** is Phil.
94 C5 **Sarangani Str.** chan. Phil.
68 F3 **Saransk** Rus. Fed.
76 G4 **Sarapul** Rus. Fed.
45 C3 **Sarare** r. Venez.
29 D7 **Sarasota** U.S.A.
84 B5 **Saraswati** r. India
69 D6 **Sarata** Ukr.
24 F3 **Saratoga** U.S.A.
33 G3 **Saratoga Springs** U.S.A.
92 E6 **Saratok** Malaysia
69 H5 **Saratov** Rus. Fed.
69 H5 **Saratovskaya Oblast'** div. Rus. Fed.
68 J4 **Saratovskoye Vdkhr.** resr Rus. Fed.
79 J4 **Saravan** Iran
95 C2 **Saravan** Laos
95 A2 **Sarawa** r. Myanmar
92 E6 **Sarawak** div. Malaysia
80 A1 **Saray** Turkey
80 B3 **Sarayköy** Turkey
80 D2 **Sarayönü** Turkey
66 D2 **Sarca** r. Italy
81 M3 **Sarcham** Iran
84 E3 **Sarda** r. India/Nepal
85 E3 **Sarda** r. Nepal
84 B1 **Sardab Pass** pass Afgh.
84 C3 **Sardarshahr** India
81 M5 **Sardasht** Iran
81 K3 **Sar Dasht** Iran
Sardegna i. see Sardinia
45 B2 **Sardinata** Col.
66 C4 **Sardinia** i. Italy
81 L3 **Sardrūd** Iran
54 P3 **Sareks Nationalpark** nat. park Sweden
54 P3 **Sarektjåkkå** mt Sweden
79 K2 **Sar-e Pol** Afgh.
81 K4 **Sar-e Pol-e Zahāb** Iran
12 E4 **Sargasso Sea** sea Atlantic Ocean
84 C2 **Sargodha** Pak.
101 D4 **Sarh** Chad
79 G2 **Sārī** Iran
67 M7 **Saria** i. Greece
93 L3 **Sarigan** i. N. Mariana Is
84 D2 **Sarigh Jilganang Kol** salt l. China/Jammu and Kashmir
80 B2 **Sarıgöl** Turkey
81 J1 **Sarıkamış** Turkey
80 D3 **Sarıkavak** Turkey
84 D4 **Sarila** India
95 □ **Sarimbun Res.** resr Sing.
116 C3 **Sarina** Austr.
80 E2 **Sarıoğlan** Turkey
84 A2 **Sar-i-Pul** Afgh.
101 D2 **Sarīr Tibesti** des. Libya
81 J2 **Sarısu** Turkey
80 C2 **Sarıyar Barajı** resr Turkey
80 B1 **Sarıyer** Turkey
80 F2 **Sarız** Turkey
84 E4 **Sarju** r. India
82 E1 **Sarkand** Kazak.
84 B4 **Sarkāri Tala** India
80 C2 **Şarkikaraağaç** Turkey
80 F2 **Şarkışla** Turkey
69 C7 **Şarköy** Turkey
64 E4 **Sarlat-la-Canéda** France
93 K7 **Sarmi** Indon.
55 N6 **Särna** Sweden
81 L5 **Sarneh** Iran
66 C1 **Sarnen** Switz.
31 F4 **Sarnia** Can.

69 C5 Sarny Ukr.
92 C7 Sarolangun Indon.
90 H2 Saroma-ko l. Japan
67 K6 Saronikos Kolpos g. Greece
69 C7 Saros Körfezi b. Turkey
84 C4 Sarotra India
68 G4 Sarova Rus. Fed.
84 B2 Sarowbī Afgh.
69 H6 Sarpa, Ozero l. Kalmykiya Rus. Fed.
69 H5 Sarpa, Ozero l. Volgograd. Rus. Fed.
55 M7 Sarpsborg Norway
64 H2 Sarrebourg France
61 F5 Sarreguemines France
65 C1 Sarria Spain
65 F2 Sarrión Spain
66 C4 Sartène France
81 M4 Saruq Iran
81 K2 Sārur Azer.
81 L4 Šarvābād Iran
62 H7 Sárvár Hungary
79 H1 Sarykamyshskoye Ozero salt l. Turkm.
82 E2 Saryozek Kazak.
82 D1 Saryshagan Kazak.
79 L2 Sary-Tash Kyrgyzstan
35 G6 Sasabe U.S.A.
85 F4 Sasaram India
91 A8 Sasebo Japan
21 H4 Saskatchewan div. Can.
21 J4 Saskatchewan r. Can.
21 H4 Saskatoon Can.
77 N2 Saskylakh Rus. Fed.
105 G3 Sasolburg S. Africa
68 G4 Sasovo Rus. Fed.
33 F5 Sassafras U.S.A.
100 B4 Sassandra Côte d'Ivoire
66 C4 Sassari Italy
62 F3 Sassnitz Ger.
86 D2 Sasykkol', Oz. l. Kazak.
69 H6 Sasykoli Rus. Fed.
100 A3 Satadougou Mali
91 B9 Sata-misaki c. Japan
84 C5 Satana India
83 D7 Satara India
105 J2 Satara S. Africa
69 G4 Satinka Rus. Fed.
85 G5 Satkhira Bangl.
84 E4 Satna India
82 C1 Satpayev Kazak.
84 C5 Satpura Range mts India
91 B9 Satsuma-hantō pen. Japan
95 B2 Sattahip Thai.
84 D2 Satti Jammu and Kashmir
63 L7 Satu Mare Romania
95 B4 Satun Thai.
47 L1 Sauce Arg.
27 C7 Sauceda Mex.
35 F5 Sauceda Mts mts U.S.A.
27 B6 Saucillo Mex.
55 K7 Sauda Norway
54 □4 Sauðárkrókur Iceland
70 Saudi Arabia country Asia
30 D4 Saugatuck U.S.A.
33 G3 Saugerties U.S.A.
Saūjbolāgh see Mahābād
26 C4 Sauk Center U.S.A.
30 C4 Sauk City U.S.A.
64 G3 Saulieu France
31 E2 Sault Ste Marie Can.
30 E2 Sault Ste Marie U.S.A.
76 H4 Saumalkol' Kazak.
93 J8 Saumlakki Indon.
64 D3 Saumur France
119 C1 Saunders I. i. Atlantic Ocean
85 F4 Saura r. India
103 C4 Saurimo Angola
84 D5 Sausar India
67 J2 Sava r. Europe
115 F8 Savage River Austr.
111 J3 Savai'i i. Samoa
69 G5 Savala r. Rus. Fed.
100 C4 Savalou Benin
30 B4 Savanna U.S.A.
29 D6 Savannah GA U.S.A.
29 B5 Savannah TN U.S.A.
29 D5 Savannah r. U.S.A.
29 E7 Savannah Sound Bahamas
95 C1 Savannakhét Laos
37 J5 Savanna-la-Mar Jamaica
22 B3 Savant Lake l. Can.
54 R5 Sävar Sweden
67 M5 Savaştepe Turkey
100 C4 Savè Benin
103 D6 Save r. Moz.
54 V5 Saviaho Fin.
76 F3 Savinskiy Rus. Fed.
66 E4 Savoie reg. France
66 C2 Savona Italy
55 V6 Savonlinna Fin.
54 V5 Savonranta Fin.
Savoy reg. see Savoie
81 J1 Savşat Turkey
55 O8 Sävsjö Sweden
93 G9 Savu i. Indon.
54 V3 Savukoski Fin.
81 H3 Savur Turkey
84 D4 Sawai Madhopur India
95 A1 Sawankhalok Thai.
25 H4 Sawatch Mts mts U.S.A.
57 A6 Sawel Mt h. U.K.
95 A3 Sawi, Ao b. Thai.
115 K3 Sawtell Austr.
30 B2 Sawtooth Mountains h. U.S.A.
Sawu i. see Savu
93 G8 Sawu Sea g. Indon.
59 G4 Saxilby U.K.

59 J5 Saxmundham U.K.
54 O4 Saxnäs Sweden
86 F1 Sayano-Shushenskoye Vdkhr. resr Rus. Fed.
79 G6 Sayhūt Yemen
69 H5 Saykhin Kazak.
102 E2 Sāylac Somalia
87 K3 Saynshand Mongolia
65 H1 Sayoa mt Spain
90 E2 Sayon Rus. Fed.
86 D3 Sayram Hu salt l. China
27 D5 Sayre OK U.S.A.
32 E4 Sayre PA U.S.A.
20 D4 Sayward Can.
84 C2 Sazin Pak.
68 E3 Sazonovo Rus. Fed.
100 B2 Sbaa Alg.
100 C1 Sbeitla Tunisia
58 D3 Scafell Pike mt U.K.
57 B4 Scalasaig U.K.
66 F5 Scalea Italy
57 □ Scalloway U.K.
60 C5 Scalp h. Rep. of Ireland
57 C3 Scalpay i. Scot. U.K.
57 B3 Scalpay i. Scot. U.K.
57 A5 Scalp Mountain h. Rep. of Ireland
115 H8 Scamander Austr.
57 E2 Scapa Flow in. U.K.
57 C4 Scarba i. U.K.
31 H4 Scarborough Can.
45 E2 Scarborough Trinidad and Tobago
58 G3 Scarborough U.K.
94 A3 Scarborough Shoal sand bank Phil.
57 C4 Scarp i. U.K.
Scarpanto i. see Karpathos
62 D7 Schaffhausen Switz.
61 C2 Schagen Neth.
61 C2 Schagerbrug Neth.
104 B3 Schakalskuppe Namibia
62 F6 Schärding Austria
61 B3 Scharendijke Neth.
61 E4 Scharteberg h. Ger.
23 G3 Schefferville Can.
61 C3 Schelde r. Belgium
35 E2 Schell Creek Range mts U.S.A.
33 G3 Schenectady U.S.A.
57 D4 Schiehallion mt U.K.
61 E1 Schiermonnikoog i. Neth.
61 E1 Schiermonnikoog Nationaal Park nat. park Neth.
61 E1 Schildmeer l. Neth.
61 D4 Schinnen Neth.
66 D2 Schio Italy
61 E4 Schleiden Ger.
62 D3 Schleswig Ger.
61 E4 Schneifel reg. Ger.
62 D2 Schneverdingen Ger.
33 G3 Schodack Center U.S.A.
30 C3 Schofield U.S.A.
34 □1 Schofield Barracks U.S.A.
62 E4 Schönebeck Ger.
33 J2 Schoodic Lake l. U.S.A.
30 E4 Schoolcraft U.S.A.
61 C3 Schoonhoven Neth.
115 H9 Schouten I. i. Austr.
110 E2 Schouten Islands is P.N.G.
30 D1 Schreiber Can.
33 G3 Schroon Lake l. U.S.A.
35 F5 Schuchuli U.S.A.
60 B6 Schull Rep. of Ireland
21 K2 Schultz Lake l. Can.
34 C2 Schurz U.S.A.
33 G3 Schuylerville U.S.A.
62 D5 Schwäbisch Hall Ger.
62 E6 Schwabmünchen Ger.
62 F6 Schwandorf Ger.
61 E4 Schwarzer Mann h. Ger.
104 B2 Schwarzrand mts Namibia
62 F7 Schwaz Austria
62 G4 Schwedt an der Oder Ger.
62 E5 Schweinfurt Ger.
105 F3 Schweizer-Reneke S. Africa
62 D6 Schwenningen Ger.
62 E4 Schwerin Ger.
62 D7 Schwyz Switz.
66 E6 Sciacca Italy
59 A8 Scilly, Isles of is U.K.
32 B5 Scioto r. U.S.A.
35 F2 Scipio U.S.A.
24 F1 Scobey U.S.A.
59 J5 Scole U.K.
115 J4 Scone Austr.
18 Scoresby Sound sound Greenland
12 F9 Scotia Ridge sea feature Atlantic Ocean
12 F9 Scotia Sea sea Atlantic Ocean
31 G4 Scotland Can.
56 E3 Scotland div. U.K.
20 D4 Scott, C. c. Can.
119 B5 Scott Base N.Z. Base Antarctica
105 J5 Scottburgh S. Africa
26 C4 Scott City U.S.A.
119 B5 Scott Coast coastal area Antarctica
32 D4 Scottdale U.S.A.
119 A5 Scott Island i. Antarctica
21 H3 Scott Lake l. Can.
119 D4 Scott Mts mts Antarctica
26 C3 Scottsbluff U.S.A.
29 C5 Scottsboro U.S.A.

28 C4 Scottsburg U.S.A.
115 G8 Scottsdale Austr.
25 E5 Scottsdale U.S.A.
34 A3 Scotts Valley U.S.A.
30 D4 Scottville U.S.A.
34 D3 Scotty's Junction U.S.A.
57 C2 Scourie U.K.
57 □ Scousburgh U.K.
57 □ Scrabster U.K.
33 F4 Scranton U.S.A.
57 B4 Scridain, Loch in. U.K.
58 G4 Scunthorpe U.K.
59 H7 Seaford U.K.
33 F5 Seaford U.S.A.
116 C3 Seaforth Austr.
31 G4 Seaforth Can.
94 A4 Seahorse Bank sand bank Phil.
21 K3 Seal r. Can.
104 E7 Seal, Cape pt S. Africa
114 E5 Sea Lake Austr.
33 J3 Seal I. i. U.S.A.
23 H3 Seal Lake l. Can.
104 F7 Seal Point pt S. Africa
35 E3 Seaman Range mts U.S.A.
58 G3 Seamer U.K.
35 E4 Searchlight U.S.A.
27 F5 Searcy U.S.A.
34 D4 Searles Lake l. U.S.A.
30 E4 Sears U.S.A.
33 J2 Searsport U.S.A.
34 B3 Seaside CA U.S.A.
24 B2 Seaside OR U.S.A.
58 D3 Seaton U.K.
24 B2 Seattle U.S.A.
116 A2 Seaview Ra. mts Austr.
33 F5 Seaville U.S.A.
33 H3 Sebago Lake l. U.S.A.
36 B3 Sebastián Vizcaíno, Bahía b. Mex.
33 J2 Sebasticook r. U.S.A.
94 A5 Sebatik i. Indon.
80 C1 Seben Turkey
67 K2 Sebeş Romania
92 □ Sebesi i. Indon.
31 H4 Sebewaing U.S.A.
68 D3 Sebezh Rus. Fed.
80 G1 Sebinkarahisar Turkey
33 J2 Šeboeis Lake l. U.S.A.
33 J2 Seboomook U.S.A.
33 J2 Seboomook Lake l. U.S.A.
29 D7 Sebring U.S.A.
69 G5 Sebrovo Rus. Fed.
42 B5 Sechura Peru
42 B5 Sechura, Bahía de b. Peru
33 H2 Second Lake l. U.S.A.
100 □ Secos, Ilhéus i. Cape Verde
117 A6 Secretary Island i. N.Z.
105 H3 Secunda S. Africa
83 E7 Secunderabad India
26 E4 Sedalia U.S.A.
114 C5 Sedan Austr.
64 G2 Sedan France
117 E4 Seddon N.Z.
117 C4 Seddonville N.Z.
33 J2 Sedgwick U.S.A.
100 A3 Sédhiou Senegal
62 D6 Sedlčany Czech Rep.
80 E6 Sedom Israel
35 G4 Sedona U.S.A.
66 B6 Sédrata Alg.
55 S9 Seduva Lith.
60 D5 Seefin h. Rep. of Ireland
103 B6 Seeheim Namibia
35 E5 Seeley U.S.A.
119 B3 Seelig, Mt mt Antarctica
64 E2 Sées France
100 A4 Sefadu Sierra Leone
105 G1 Sefare Botswana
67 M5 Seferihisar Turkey
105 G1 Sefophe Botswana
55 M6 Segalstad Norway
94 A5 Segama r. Malaysia
92 C6 Segamat Malaysia
68 E2 Segezha Rus. Fed.
65 F3 Segorbe Spain
100 B3 Ségou Mali
45 B3 Segovia Col.
Segovia r. see Coco
65 D2 Segovia Spain
68 E2 Segozerskoye, Oz. resr Rus. Fed.
65 G1 Segre r. Spain
101 D2 Séguédine Niger
100 B4 Séguéla Côte d'Ivoire
27 D6 Seguin U.S.A.
47 D1 Segundo r. Arg.
65 F3 Segura r. Spain
103 C6 Sehithwa Botswana
105 H4 Sehlabathebe National Park nat. park Lesotho
84 D5 Sehore India
54 S1 Seiland i. Norway
27 D4 Seiling U.S.A.
54 S5 Seinäjoki Fin.
22 B4 Seine r. Can.
64 E2 Seine r. France
64 E2 Seine, Baie de b. France
64 F2 Seine, Val de v. France
63 L3 Sejny Pol.
92 C7 Sekayu Indon.
104 E2 Sekoma Botswana
100 B4 Sekondi Ghana
95 D5 Sekura Indon.
24 B2 Selah U.S.A.
93 J8 Selaru i. Indon.
92 E7 Selatan, Tanjung pt Indon.
95 □ Selat Johor chan. Malaysia/Sing.
95 □ Selat Jurong chan. Sing.
95 □ Selat Pandan chan. Sing.

54 L5 Selbekken Norway
54 M5 Selbu Norway
58 F4 Selby U.K.
26 C2 Selby U.S.A.
103 C6 Selebi-Phikwe Botswana
80 B2 Selendi Turkey
64 H2 Sélestat France
95 □ Seletar Sing.
95 □ Seletar, P. i. Sing.
95 □ Seletar Res. resr Sing.
Seleucia Pieria see Samandağı
26 C2 Selfridge U.S.A.
68 J2 Selib Rus. Fed.
100 A3 Sélibabi Maur.
68 E3 Seliger, Oz. l. Rus. Fed.
35 F4 Seligman U.S.A.
101 E2 Selima Oasis oasis Sudan
31 J5 Selinsgrove U.S.A.
63 Q2 Selishche Rus. Fed.
69 H6 Selitrennoye Rus. Fed.
63 Q2 Selizharovo Rus. Fed.
55 L7 Seljord Norway
21 K4 Selkirk Can.
57 F5 Selkirk U.K.
20 F4 Selkirk Mountains mts Can.
58 D3 Sellafield U.K.
116 B3 Sellheim r. Austr.
35 G6 Sells U.S.A.
29 C5 Selma AL U.S.A.
34 C3 Selma CA U.S.A.
29 B5 Selmer U.S.A.
59 G7 Selsey Bill hd U.K.
95 C4 Seluan i. Indon.
40 Selvas reg. Brazil
21 J3 Selwyn Lake l. Can.
20 C2 Selwyn Mountains mts Can.
113 D4 Selwyn Range h. Austr.
92 □ Semarang Indon.
92 D6 Sematan Malaysia
94 A6 Semabakung r. Indon.
95 □ Sembawang Sing.
102 B3 Sembé Congo
81 K3 Şemdinli Turkey
69 K4 Semenivka Ukr.
68 H3 Semenov Rus. Fed.
69 G6 Semikarakorsk Rus. Fed.
69 F5 Semiluki Rus. Fed.
24 F3 Seminoe Res. resr U.S.A.
27 C5 Seminole U.S.A.
29 C6 Seminole, L. l. U.S.A.
86 D1 Semipalatinsk Kazak.
94 B3 Semirara i. Phil.
94 B4 Semirara Islands is Phil.
79 G2 Semnān Iran
61 D5 Semois r. Belgium
61 C5 Semois, Vallée de la v. Belgium/France
93 F6 Semporna Malaysia
92 □ Sempu i. Indon.
95 C2 Sên, Stœng r. Cambodia
94 A5 Senaja Malaysia
69 G7 Senaki Georgia
42 E5 Sena Madureira Brazil
103 C5 Senanga Zambia
91 B9 Sendai Japan
90 G5 Sendai Japan
Sêndo see Chido
95 B5 Senebui, Tanjung pt Indon.
35 G2 Seneca AZ U.S.A.
30 C5 Seneca IL U.S.A.
24 C3 Seneca OR U.S.A.
32 E3 Seneca Falls U.S.A.
32 E3 Seneca Lake l. U.S.A.
32 D5 Seneca Rocks U.S.A.
32 C5 Senecaville Lake l. U.S.A.
96 Senegal country Africa
100 A3 Sénégal r. Maur./Senegal
105 G4 Senekal S. Africa
30 E2 Seney U.S.A.
62 G5 Senftenberg Ger.
84 D4 Sengar r. India
102 D4 Sengerema Tanz.
68 J4 Sengiley Rus. Fed.
43 K6 Senhor do Bonfim Brazil
66 E3 Senigallia Italy
66 F2 Senj Croatia
54 P2 Senja i. Norway
81 J1 Şenkaya Turkey
84 D2 Senku Jammu and Kashmir
104 E2 Senlac S. Africa
90 B3 Senlin Shan mt China
61 F5 Senlis France
95 C2 Senmonorom Cambodia
78 C7 Sennar Sudan
59 B7 Sennen U.K.
31 J1 Senneterre Can.
105 G5 Senqu r. Lesotho
64 F2 Sens France
36 G6 Sensuntepeque El Salvador
67 J2 Senta Yugo.
84 D3 Senthal India
35 H5 Sentinel U.S.A.
20 E3 Sentinel Pk summit Can.
95 □ Sentosa i. Sing.
81 H3 Şenyurt Turkey
84 D5 Seoni India
85 E5 Seorinarayan India
87 N4 Seoul S. Korea
117 D4 Separation Pt N.Z.
81 L4 Separ Shāhābād Iran
46 D3 Sepetiba, Baía de b. Brazil
110 E2 Sepik r. P.N.G.
23 G3 Sept-Îles Can.
34 C3 Sequoia National Park nat. park U.S.A.
69 G5 Serafimovich Rus. Fed.
93 H7 Seram i. Indon.
93 J7 Seram Sea g. Indon.

92 □ Serang Indon.
95 □ Serangoon, P. i. Sing.
95 □ Serangoon Harbour chan. Sing.
95 D5 Serasan i. Indon.
95 D5 Serasan, Selat chan. Indon.
95 □ Seraya i. Indon.
95 □ Seraya, P. i. Sing.
67 J3 Serbia div. Yugo.
Serbija div. see Serbia
27 B6 Serdán Mex.
Serdar see Kaypak
102 E2 Serdo Eth.
69 H4 Serdoba r. Rus. Fed.
69 H4 Serdobsk Rus. Fed.
80 D3 Seredka Rus. Fed.
80 C3 Şereflikoçhisar Turkey
92 C6 Seremban Malaysia
102 D4 Serengeti National Park nat. park Tanz.
103 D5 Serenje Zambia
68 H4 Sergach Rus. Fed.
90 C3 Sergeyevka Rus. Fed.
68 F3 Sergiyev Posad Rus. Fed.
92 E6 Seria Brunei
92 E6 Serian Malaysia
67 L6 Serifos i. Greece
23 G2 Sérigny, Lac l. Can.
80 C3 Serik Turkey
114 C3 Serle, Mt h. Austr.
93 H8 Sermata, Kepulauan is Indon.
68 J3 Sernur Rus. Fed.
69 H6 Seroglazka Rus. Fed.
76 H4 Serov Rus. Fed.
103 D4 Serowe Botswana
65 C4 Serpa Port.
45 E2 Serpent's Mouth chan. Trinidad/Venez.
69 F4 Serpukhov Rus. Fed.
46 C3 Serra da Canastra, Parque Nacional da nat. park Brazil
43 H3 Serra do Navio Brazil
45 D4 Serrania de la Neblina, Parque Nacional nat. park Venez.
46 C3 Serranópolis Brazil
61 B5 Serre r. France
67 K4 Serres Greece
47 D3 Serrezuela Arg.
43 L6 Serrinha Brazil
46 D2 Sêrro Brazil
47 B4 Serrucho mt Arg.
66 C6 Sers Tunisia
46 C3 Sertãozinho Brazil
61 D5 Sertolovo Rus. Fed.
95 A4 Seruai Indon.
93 K7 Serui Indon.
92 □ Seruyan r. Indon.
82 J4 Sêrxu China
94 A6 Sesayap Indon.
95 □ Sesayap r. Indon.
22 B3 Seseganaga L. l. Can.
31 □ Sesekinika Can.
103 B5 Sesfontein Namibia
103 C5 Sesheke Zambia
66 E4 Sessa Aurunca Italy
65 H3 Ses Salines, Cap de pt Spain
66 C2 Sestri Levante Italy
68 C2 Sestroretsk Rus. Fed.
95 C2 Set, P. mt Laos
90 F3 Setana Japan
64 F5 Sète France
46 D2 Sete Lagoas Brazil
54 Q2 Setermoen Norway
55 K7 Setesdal v. Norway
84 E3 Seti r. Gandakhi Nepal
84 E3 Seti r. Seti Nepal
100 C1 Sétif Alg.
91 F7 Seto Japan
100 B1 Settat Morocco
58 E3 Settle U.K.
65 B3 Setúbal Port.
65 B3 Setúbal, Baía de b. Port.
22 B3 Seul, Lac l. Can.
30 E3 Seul Choix Pt pt U.S.A.
81 K1 Sevan Armenia
Sevana Lich l. see Lake Sevan
69 E6 Sevastopol' Ukr.
23 H2 Seven Islands Bay b. Can.
59 H6 Sevenoaks U.K.
64 F4 Sévérac-le-Château France
115 J2 Severn r. Austr.
22 B3 Severn r. Can.
104 E3 Severn S. Africa
59 E6 Severn r. U.K.
68 G2 Severnaya Dvina r. Rus. Fed.
69 H7 Severnaya Osetiya, Respublika div. Rus. Fed.
77 M1 Severnaya Zemlya is Rus. Fed.
22 B3 Severn L. l. Can.
76 L3 Severnyy Rus. Fed.
68 F1 Severodvinsk Rus. Fed.
77 R4 Severo-Kuril'sk Rus. Fed.
54 X2 Severomorsk Rus. Fed.
76 L3 Severo-Yeniseyskiy Rus. Fed.
69 F6 Severskaya Rus. Fed.
35 F2 Sevier r. U.S.A.
35 G2 Sevier Bridge Reservoir resr U.S.A.
35 F2 Sevier Desert des. U.S.A.
35 F2 Sevier Lake salt l. U.S.A.
45 B3 Sevilla Col.
Sevilla see Seville
65 D4 Seville Spain
67 L3 Sevlievo Bulg.

84 C3 Sewāni India
26 D3 Seward U.S.A.
77 V3 Seward Peninsula pen. Alaska
20 L3 Sexsmith Can.
76 J2 Seyakha Rus. Fed.
96 Seychelles country Indian Ocean
80 C3 Seydişehir Turkey
54 L4 Seyðisfjörður Iceland
81 K2 Seydvān Iran
Seyhan see Adana
80 E3 Seyhan r. Turkey
69 E5 Seym r. Rus. Fed.
77 R3 Seymchan Rus. Fed.
114 F6 Seymour Austr.
105 G6 Seymour S. Africa
28 C4 Seymour IN U.S.A.
27 D5 Seymour TX U.S.A.
84 B2 Seyyedābād Afgh.
64 F2 Sézanne France
67 L7 Sfakia Greece
67 L2 Sfântu Gheorghe Romania
100 D1 Sfax Tunisia
67 K4 Sfikia, Limni resr Greece
61 D2 's-Graveland Neth.
's-Gravenhage see The Hague
57 B3 Sgurr Alasdair h. U.K.
57 C3 Sgurr Dhomhnuill h. U.K.
57 C3 Sgurr Mor mt U.K.
88 E2 Sha r. China
88 C3 Shaanxi div. China
81 K2 Shabestar Iran
67 N3 Shabla, Nos pt Bulg.
23 J3 Shabogamo Lake l. Can.
102 C4 Shabunda Dem. Rep. Congo
82 E3 Shache China
119 B4 Shackleton Coast coastal area Antarctica
119 D6 Shackleton Ice Shelf ice feature Antarctica
119 C3 Shackleton Ra. mts Antarctica
84 A4 Shadadkot Pak.
81 M6 Shādegān Iran
84 A4 Shadikhak Pass pass Pak.
30 D5 Shafer, Lake l. U.S.A.
119 B5 Shafer Pk summit Antarctica
34 C4 Shafter U.S.A.
59 E6 Shaftesbury U.K.
117 C6 Shag Pt pt N.Z.
84 A4 Shahabad India
84 C5 Shahada India
95 M5 Shah Alam Malaysia
84 A4 Shahbandar Pak.
85 G5 Shahbazpur chan. Bangl.
84 E5 Shahdol India
81 K3 Shāhedān Iraq
84 A2 Shah Fuladi mt Afgh.
84 B4 Shahgarh India
81 K3 Shahi Pen. pen. Iran
84 D4 Shahjahanpur India
Shāhpūr see Salmās
84 B3 Shahpur Pak.
84 E5 Shahpura Madhya Pradesh India
84 C4 Shahpura Rajasthan India
79 J3 Shahr-e Kord Iran
81 M3 Shāhrūd, Rūdkhāneh-ye r. Iran
81 L3 Shakar Bolāghī Iran
105 J4 Shakaville S. Africa
68 E3 Shakhovskaya Rus. Fed.
79 K2 Shakhrisabz Uzbek.
69 G6 Shakhty Rus. Fed.
68 H3 Shakhun'ya Rus. Fed.
26 E2 Shakopee U.S.A.
90 G3 Shakotan-hantō pen. Japan
90 G3 Shakotan-misaki c. Japan
68 G2 Shalakusha Rus. Fed.
82 J4 Shaluli Shan mts China
85 J3 Shaluni mt India
21 L3 Shamattawa Can.
89 □ Sham Chun r. China
32 E4 Shamokin U.S.A.
27 C5 Shamrock U.S.A.
103 D5 Shamva Zimbabwe
60 B6 Shanacrane Rep. of Ireland
88 A2 Shandan China
81 M3 Shānderman Iran
88 E1 Shandian r. China
34 B4 Shandon U.S.A.
88 E2 Shandong div. China
88 F2 Shandong Bandao pen. China
81 K5 Shandrūkh Iraq
84 C1 Shandur Pass pass Pak.
103 D5 Shangani r. Zimbabwe
88 E3 Shangcai China
88 E3 Shangcheng China
85 G3 Shang Chu r. China
89 D6 Shangchuan Dao i. China
88 D1 Shangdu China
88 E3 Shangdundu China
88 E4 Shanggao China
88 F4 Shanghai China
88 F4 Shanghai div. China
88 F4 Shanghe China
88 D3 Shangjin China
89 C6 Shanglin China
88 D3 Shangnan China
88 E3 Shangqiu Henan China
88 E3 Shangqiu Henan China
89 E4 Shangrao Jiangxi China
89 E4 Shangrao Jiangxi China

88 E3 Shangshui China
89 C6 Shangsi China
89 E4 Shangtang China
88 D1 Shangyi China
89 E5 Shangyou China
89 F4 Shangyu China
87 N2 Shangzhi China
88 C3 Shangzhou China
60 C5 Shannon est.
　Rep. of Ireland
60 C4 Shannon r. Rep. of Ireland
60 B5 Shannon, Mouth of the
　est. Rep. of Ireland
18 Shannon Island i.
　Greenland
82 H2 Shanshan China
89 □ Shan Tei Tong h. China
85 G5 Shāntipur India
89 E6 Shantou China
89 E6 Shanwei China
88 D2 Shanxi div. China
88 E3 Shanxian China
88 C3 Shanyang China
88 D2 Shanyin China
89 D5 Shaodong China
89 D5 Shaoguan China
89 E5 Shaowu China
89 F4 Shaoxing China
89 D5 Shaoyang Hunan China
89 D5 Shaoyang Hunan China
58 E3 Shap U.K.
89 D6 Shapa China
57 F1 Shapinsay i. U.K.
78 F4 Shaqrā' Saudi Arabia
81 J6 Sharaf w. Iraq
80 E6 Sharāh, Jibāl ash mts
　Jordan
84 B3 Sharan Jogizai Pak.
69 D5 Sharhorod Ukr.
81 K4 Shārī, Buḥayrat l. Iraq
90 J3 Shari-dake vol. Japan
79 H4 Sharjah U.A.E.
63 N3 Sharkawshchyna
　Belarus
112 B5 Shark Bay b. Austr.
33 G4 Sharon CT U.S.A.
32 C4 Sharon PA U.S.A.
89 □ Sharp Peak h. China
80 E6 Sharqī, Jabal ash mts
　Lebanon/Syria
68 H3 Shar'ya Rus. Fed.
103 C6 Shashe r.
　Botswana/Zimbabwe
102 D3 Shashemenē Eth.
24 B3 Shasta, Mt vol. U.S.A.
24 B3 Shasta L. l. U.S.A.
89 □ Sha Tin China
68 H4 Shatki Rus. Fed.
81 M7 Shaṭṭ al 'Arab r. Iran/Iraq
81 K6 Shaṭṭ al Hillah r. Iraq
68 F4 Shatura Rus. Fed.
21 H5 Shaunavon Can.
32 D5 Shavers Fork r. U.S.A.
33 F4 Shawangunk Mts
　h. U.S.A.
30 C3 Shawano U.S.A.
30 C3 Shawano Lake l. U.S.A.
22 F4 Shawinigan Can.
80 F4 Shawmarīyah, Jabal ash
　mts Syria
27 C4 Shawnee U.S.A.
89 F5 Sha Xi r. China
89 E5 Shaxian China
89 D4 Shayang China
112 D4 Shay Gap Austr.
81 L5 Shaykh Jūwī Iraq
81 L5 Shaykh Sa'd Iraq
68 F4 Shchekino Rus. Fed.
69 F5 Shchigry Rus. Fed.
69 D5 Shchors Ukr.
68 C4 Shchuchyn Belarus
69 F5 Shebekino Rus. Fed.
79 K2 Sheberghān Afgh.
30 D4 Sheboygan U.S.A.
100 D4 Shebshi Mountains mts
　Nigeria
23 H4 Shediac Can.
20 D3 Shedin Pk summit Can.
60 D4 Sheelin, Lough l.
　Rep. of Ireland
60 D2 Sheep Haven b.
　Rep. of Ireland
105 J3 Sheepmoor S. Africa
35 E3 Sheep Peak summit
　U.S.A.
59 H6 Sheerness U.K.
23 H5 Sheet Harbour Can.
115 G8 Sheffield Austr.
117 D5 Sheffield N.Z.
59 F4 Sheffield U.K.
29 C5 Sheffield AL U.S.A.
30 C5 Sheffield IL U.S.A.
32 D4 Sheffield PA U.S.A.
27 C6 Sheffield TX U.S.A.
31 G3 Sheguiandah Can.
88 B4 Shehong China
84 C3 Shekhupura Pak.
89 □ Shek Kwu Chau i. China
89 □ Shekou China
89 □ Shek Pik resr China
68 F3 Sheksna Rus. Fed.
89 □ Shek Uk Shan mt China
77 T2 Shelagskiy, Mys pt
　Rus. Fed.
30 A6 Shelbina U.S.A.
23 G5 Shelburne N.S. Can.
31 G3 Shelburne Ont. Can.
33 G3 Shelburne Falls U.S.A.
30 D4 Shelby MI U.S.A.
24 E1 Shelby MT U.S.A.
29 D5 Shelby NC U.S.A.
32 B4 Shelby OH U.S.A.
28 C4 Shelbyville IN U.S.A.
30 A6 Shelbyville MO U.S.A.

29 C5 Shelbyville TN U.S.A.
35 H5 Sheldon AZ U.S.A.
30 D5 Sheldon IL U.S.A.
33 G2 Sheldon Springs U.S.A.
23 H3 Sheldrake Can.
77 R3 Shelikhova, Zaliv g.
　Rus. Fed.
21 H4 Shellbrook Can.
24 D3 Shelley U.S.A.
115 J5 Shellharbour Austr.
34 A1 Shell Mt mt U.S.A.
20 F4 Shelter Bay Can.
34 A1 Shelter Cove U.S.A.
33 G4 Shelter I. i. U.S.A.
117 B7 Shelter Pt pt N.Z.
86 D1 Shemonaikha Kazak.
26 E3 Shenandoah IA U.S.A.
33 G2 Shenandoah PA U.S.A.
32 D5 Shenandoah VA U.S.A.
32 D5 Shenandoah r. U.S.A.
32 D5 Shenandoah Mountains
　mts U.S.A.
32 D5 Shenandoah National
　Park nat. park U.S.A.
32 D5 Shenango River Lake
　l. U.S.A.
100 C4 Shendam Nigeria
90 C1 Shending Shan h. China
82 E2 Shengel'dy Kazak.
88 G4 Shengsi China
89 F4 Shengzhou China
68 G2 Shenkursk Rus. Fed.
88 D2 Shenmu China
88 D4 Shennongjia China
88 E3 Shenqiu China
90 A1 Shenshu China
88 G1 Shenyang China
89 □ Shenzhen China
89 □ Shenzhen Wan b. China
69 C5 Shepetivka Ukr.
111 G3 Shepherd Is i Vanuatu
115 F6 Shepparton Austr.
59 H6 Sheppey, Isle of i. U.K.
59 E7 Sherborne U.K.
23 H4 Sherbrooke N.S. Can.
23 F4 Sherbrooke Que. Can.
33 F3 Sherburne U.S.A.
60 E4 Shercock Rep. of Ireland
84 B2 Sher Dahan Pass pass
　Afgh.
101 F3 Shereiq Sudan
84 C4 Shergarh India
27 E5 Sheridan AR U.S.A.
24 F2 Sheridan WY U.S.A.
114 A4 Sheringa Austr.
59 J5 Sheringham U.K.
27 D5 Sherman U.S.A.
33 J2 Sherman Mills U.S.A.
35 E1 Sherman Mtn mt U.S.A.
85 G4 Sherpur Bangl.
21 J3 Sherridon Can.
61 D3 's-Hertogenbosch Neth.
59 F4 Sherwood Forest reg.
　U.K.
20 C3 Sheslay Can.
56 F1 Shetland is U.K.
76 G5 Shetpe Kazak.
89 □ Sheung Shui China
89 □ Sheung Sze Mun
　sea chan. China
89 F4 Shexian China
89 F3 Sheyang China
26 D2 Sheyenne U.S.A.
26 D2 Sheyenne r. U.S.A.
57 B3 Shiant Islands is U.K.
77 R5 Shiashkotan, O. i.
　Rus. Fed.
31 E4 Shiawassee r. U.S.A.
78 F6 Shibām Yemen
84 B2 Shibar Pass pass Afgh.
91 F6 Shibata Japan
90 J3 Shibetsu Japan
90 H2 Shibetsu Japan
80 C6 Shibîn el Kôm Egypt
91 F6 Shibukawa Japan
89 E5 Shicheng China
33 E4 Shickshinny U.S.A.
80 G6 Shidād al Mismā' h.
　Saudi Arabia
88 C3 Shidao China
88 G2 Shidao Wan b. China
57 C4 Shiel, Loch l. U.K.
88 B4 Shifang China
68 J4 Shigony Rus. Fed.
88 D1 Shiguai China
82 B2 Shihezi China
88 E2 Shijiazhuang China
84 B4 Shikarpur Pak.
84 D4 Shikohabad India
91 C8 Shikoku i. Japan
91 C8 Shikoku-sanchi mts
　Japan
90 G3 Shikotsu-Tōya National
　Park Japan
58 F3 Shildon U.K.
85 H1 Shilega Rus. Fed.
85 G4 Shiliguri India
84 D2 Shilipu China
84 D2 Shilla mt India
60 E5 Shillelagh Rep. of Ireland
31 G1 Shillington Can.
85 G4 Shillong India
69 J5 Shil'naya Balka Kazak.
33 E4 Shiloh U.S.A.
88 D2 Shilou China
68 F4 Shilovo Rus. Fed.
91 B8 Shimabara Japan
91 F7 Shimada Japan
87 N1 Shimanovsk Rus. Fed.
89 D4 Shimen China
89 B4 Shimian China
91 F7 Shimizu Japan
84 D3 Shimla India
91 F7 Shimoda Japan

83 E8 Shimoga India
102 D4 Shimoni Kenya
91 B8 Shimonoseki Japan
84 C1 Shimshal
　Jammu and Kashmir
68 D3 Shimsk Rus. Fed.
57 D2 Shin, Loch l. U.K.
89 C6 Shinan China
79 J3 Shīndand Afgh.
84 B3 Shinghar Pak.
84 C1 Shinghshal Pass pass Pak.
30 D2 Shingleton U.S.A.
89 □ Shing Mun Resr resr
　China
91 E8 Shingū Japan
105 J1 Shingwedzi S. Africa
105 J1 Shingwedzi r. S. Africa
59 E4 Shining Tor h. U.K.
31 G2 Shining Tree Can.
90 G5 Shinjō Japan
84 A3 Shīnkāy Afgh.
91 E6 Shinminato Japan
33 J1 Shin Pond U.S.A.
102 D4 Shinyanga Tanz.
90 G5 Shiogama Japan
91 D8 Shiono-misaki c. Japan
91 H6 Shioya-zaki pt Japan
89 B6 Shiping China
84 D3 Shipki Pass pass
　China/India
58 F4 Shipley U.K.
23 H4 Shippegan Can.
32 E4 Shippensburg U.S.A.
35 H3 Shiprock U.S.A.
35 H3 Shiprock Peak summit
　U.S.A.
89 F4 Shipu China
89 C5 Shiqian China
88 C3 Shiquan China
84 E2 Shiquan He r. China
88 C3 Shiquan Sk. resr China
81 M2 Shīrābād Iran
91 G6 Shirakawa Japan
91 F6 Shirane-san vol. Japan
79 H4 Shīrāz Iran
80 C5 Shirbīn Egypt
90 J2 Shiretoko-misaki c.
　Japan
90 G4 Shiriya-zaki c. Japan
33 G4 Shirley U.S.A.
33 J2 Shirley Mills U.S.A.
91 E7 Shirotori Japan
84 C5 Shirpur India
89 D3 Shishou China
89 E4 Shitai China
89 F4 Shiyang China
81 J5 Shithāthah Iraq
84 B4 Shiv India
77 S4 Shiveluch, Sopka mt
　Rus. Fed.
28 C4 Shively U.S.A.
84 D4 Shivpuri India
35 F3 Shivwits Plateau plat.
　U.S.A.
89 C6 Shiwan Dashan mts
　China
89 E5 Shixing China
88 D3 Shiyan China
89 C4 Shizhu China
89 B5 Shizong China
90 G5 Shizugawa Japan
88 C2 Shizuishan China
91 F7 Shizuoka Japan
68 D4 Shklow Belarus
67 H3 Shkodër Albania
76 K1 Shmidta, Ostrov i.
　Rus. Fed.
116 B4 Shoalwater B. b. Austr.
91 C7 Shōbara Japan
90 G3 Shokanbetsu-dake mt
　Japan
68 J2 Shomvukva Rus. Fed.
57 C4 Shona, Eilean i. U.K.
84 D2 Shor India
81 K3 Shor Gol Iran
84 C2 Shorkot Pak.
90 G2 Shosanbetsu Japan
34 D4 Shoshone CA U.S.A.
24 D3 Shoshone ID U.S.A.
24 E2 Shoshone r. U.S.A.
24 E2 Shoshone L. l. U.S.A.
25 C4 Shoshone Mts mts U.S.A.
105 G1 Shoshong Botswana
24 D3 Shoshoni U.S.A.
69 E5 Shostka Ukr.
88 F2 Shouguang China
89 F5 Shouning China
88 E3 Shouxian China
88 D2 Shouyang China
88 D2 Shouyang Shan mt China
35 G4 Show Low U.S.A.
66 G6 Shpakovskoye Rus. Fed.
69 D5 Shpola Ukr.
27 E5 Shreveport U.S.A.
59 E5 Shrewsbury U.K.
85 G5 Shrirampur India
88 F3 Shu r. China
82 D2 Shu Kazak.
81 L6 Shu'ba Iraq
89 A5 Shuangbai China
84 C4 Shuanghechang China
83 J6 Shuangjiang China
88 G1 Shuangliao China
89 D5 Shuangpai China
90 B1 Shuangyashan China
88 E4 Shucheng China
89 F5 Shuiji China
89 D5 Shuikou China
88 A2 Shuanglujtai China
84 B3 Shujaabad Pak.
88 D1 Shulinzhao China
90 H2 Shumarinai-ko l. Japan

103 C5 Shumba Zimbabwe
67 M3 Shumen Bulg.
68 M4 Shumerlya Rus. Fed.
63 O3 Shumilina Belarus
35 G4 Shumway U.S.A.
68 E4 Shumyachi Rus. Fed.
89 E5 Shunchang China
89 D6 Shunde China
88 E1 Shunyi China
89 C6 Shuolong China
88 D2 Shuozhou China
78 F7 Shuqrah Yemen
103 D5 Shurugwi Zimbabwe
81 K6 Shuruppak Iraq
81 M5 Shūsh Iran
81 M5 Shushtar Iran
20 F4 Shuswap L. l. Can.
80 F6 Shuwaysh, Tall ash h.
　Jordan
68 J2 Shuya Rus. Fed.
88 F3 Shuyang China
83 J6 Shwebo Myanmar
95 A1 Shwegun Myanmar
83 J7 Shwegyin Myanmar
82 C7 Shymkent Kazak.
84 D2 Shyok r. India
84 D2 Shyok Jammu and Kashmir
69 F5 Shypuvate Ukr.
69 E6 Shyroke Ukr.
93 J8 Sia Indon.
84 D2 Siachen Gl. gl. India
79 J4 Siahan Range mts Pak.
81 K2 Sīāh Chashmeh Iran
84 C2 Sialkot Pak.
95 C1 Siantan i. Indon.
45 D4 Siapa r. Venez.
94 C3 Siargao i. Phil.
94 B5 Siasi Phil.
94 B5 Siasi i. Phil.
94 B4 Siaton Phil.
55 S9 Šiauliai Lith.
105 J1 Sibasa S. Africa
94 B4 Sibay i. Phil.
105 K3 Sibayi, Lake l. S. Africa
66 F3 Šibenik Croatia
92 B7 Siberut i. Indon.
84 A3 Sibi Pak.
102 D3 Siboli National Park
　nat. park Kenya
90 C2 Sibirtsevo Rus. Fed.
67 L2 Sibiu Romania
92 B6 Sibolga Indon.
95 A5 Siborongborong Indon.
85 H4 Sibsagar India
92 E6 Sibu Malaysia
94 B5 Sibuco Phil.
94 B5 Sibuguey r. Phil.
94 B5 Sibuguey Bay b. Phil.
102 B3 Sibut C.A.R.
94 A5 Sibutu i. Phil.
94 A5 Sibutu Passage chan.
　Phil.
94 B3 Sibuyan i. Phil.
94 B3 Sibuyan Sea sea Phil.
94 B2 Sicapoo mt Phil.
95 A3 Sichon Thai.
89 B4 Sichuan div. China
89 B4 Sichuan Pendi basin
　China
64 G5 Sicié, Cap c. France
　Sicilia i. see Sicily
66 E6 Sicilian Channel chan.
　Italy/Tunisia
66 E6 Sicily i. Italy
42 D6 Sicuani Peru
90 D2 Sidatun Rus. Fed.
84 C5 Siddhapur India
67 M7 Sideros, Akra pt Greece
104 E6 Sidesaviwa S. Africa
65 H5 Sidi Aïssa Alg.
65 G4 Sidi Ali Alg.
100 B1 Sidi Bel Abbès Alg.
66 C7 Sidi Bouzid Tunisia
66 D7 Sidi El Hani, Sebkhet de
　salt pan Tunisia
100 A2 Sidi Ifni Morocco
100 B1 Sidi Kacem Morocco
95 A4 Sidikalang Indon.
57 E4 Sidlaw Hills h. U.K.
119 A4 Sidley, Mt mt Antarctica
59 D7 Sidmouth U.K.
20 E5 Sidney Can.
24 F2 Sidney MT U.S.A.
26 D3 Sidney NE U.S.A.
33 F3 Sidney NY U.S.A.
32 A4 Sidney OH U.S.A.
29 D5 Sidney Lanier, L. l. U.S.A.
92 □ Sidoarjo Indon.
85 H5 Sidoktaya Myanmar
80 B5 Sidon Lebanon
68 G3 Sidorovo Rus. Fed.
46 A3 Sidrolândia Brazil
105 J3 Sidvokodvo Swaziland
64 F5 Sié, Col de pass France
64 D5 Siedlce Pol.
61 F4 Sieg r. Ger.
62 D5 Siegen Ger.
95 B2 Siĕmréab Cambodia
66 D3 Siena Italy
63 H3 Sieradz Pol.
47 D4 Sierra, Punta pt Arg.
27 C4 Sierra Blanca U.S.A.
47 C4 Sierra Colorada Arg.
47 D4 Sierra Grande Arg.
96 Sierra Leone country
　Africa
12 H5 Sierra Leone Basin
　sea feature Atlantic Ocean
12 H5 Sierra Leone Rise
　sea feature Atlantic Ocean
34 C4 Sierra Madre Mts mts
　U.S.A.

27 C7 Sierra Mojada Mex.
45 C2 Sierra Nevada, Parque
　Nacional nat. park
　Venez.
45 B2 Sierra Nevada de Santa
　Marta, Parque Nacional
　nat. park Col.
34 B2 Sierraville U.S.A.
35 G6 Sierra Vista U.S.A.
62 C7 Sierre Switz.
54 T5 Sievi Fin.
89 C5 Sifang Ling mts China
67 L6 Sifnos i. Greece
65 F5 Sig Alg.
63 L7 Sighetu Marmației
　Romania
63 M7 Sighişoara Romania
95 □ Siglap Sing.
92 B5 Sigli Indon.
54 □ Siglufjörður Iceland
94 B4 Sigma Phil.
62 D6 Sigmaringen Ger.
61 E4 Signal de Botrange h.
　Belgium
35 □ Signal Peak summit
　U.S.A.
30 A5 Sigourney U.S.A.
67 L5 Sigri, Akra pt Greece
65 E2 Sigüenza Spain
100 B3 Siguiri Guinea
55 T8 Sigulda Latvia
95 Sihanoukville Cambodia
88 F3 Sihong China
84 E5 Sihora India
89 D5 Sihui China
54 T4 Siikajoki Fin.
54 U5 Siilinjärvi Fin.
81 H3 Siirt Turkey
92 C7 Sijunjung Indon.
84 B5 Sika India
84 B2 Sikaram mt Afgh.
20 E3 Sikanni Chief Can.
20 E3 Sikanni Chief r. Can.
84 D4 Sikar India
84 B2 Sikaram mt Afgh.
100 B3 Sikasso Mali
27 F4 Sikeston U.S.A.
87 P2 Sikhote-Alin' mts
　Rus. Fed.
67 L6 Sikinos i. Greece
85 G4 Sikkim div. India
54 U5 Siksjö Sweden
94 A5 Sikuati Malaysia
65 C1 Sil r. Spain
94 C3 Silago Phil.
55 S9 Šilalė Lith.
36 D2 Silao Mex.
94 B4 Silay Phil.
85 H4 Silchar India
80 B1 Şile Turkey
76 J4 Şiletiteniz, Ozero salt l.
　Kazak.
84 E3 Silgarhi Nepal
66 C6 Siliana Tunisia
80 B2 Silifke Turkey
85 G3 Siling Co salt l. China
　Silistat see Bozkır
67 M2 Silistra Bulg.
80 B1 Silivri Turkey
55 O6 Siljan l. Sweden
55 L8 Silkeborg Denmark
116 B1 Silkwood Austr.
55 U7 Sillamäe Estonia
84 C5 Sillod India
105 J3 Silobela S. Africa
85 G3 Silong China
27 C6 Silsbee U.S.A.
54 U3 Siltaharju Fin.
55 R9 Šilutė Lith.
81 H2 Silvan Turkey
84 C5 Silvassa India
30 B2 Silver Bay U.S.A.
25 F4 Silver City U.S.A.
30 C1 Silver Islet Can.
34 C4 Silver Lake l. CA U.S.A.
30 D2 Silver Lake l. MI U.S.A.
60 C5 Silvermine Mts h.
　Rep. of Ireland
34 D3 Silver Peak Range mts
　U.S.A.
32 E5 Silver Spring U.S.A.
34 C2 Silver Springs U.S.A.
114 D3 Silverton Austr.
59 D7 Silverton U.K.
31 F3 Silver Water Can.
94 B3 Simara i. Phil.
31 H2 Simàrd, Lac l. Can.
81 L5 Şīmareh, Rūdkhāneh-ye
　r. Iran
85 F4 Simaria India
80 B2 Simav Turkey
80 B2 Simav Dağları mts Turkey
102 C3 Simba Dem. Rep. Congo
　Simbirsk see Ul'yanovsk
31 G4 Simcoe Can.
31 H3 Simcoe, Lake l. Can.
85 F5 Simdega India
102 D2 Simēn Mountains mts
　Eth.
92 B6 Simeuluë i. Indon.
69 E6 Simferopol' Ukr.
85 E3 Simikot Nepal
45 B3 Simití Col.
34 C4 Simi Valley U.S.A.
25 F4 Simla U.S.A.
67 L2 Şimleu Silvaniei Romania
61 F5 Simmern (Hunsrück) Ger.
35 F4 Simmler U.S.A.
35 F4 Simmons U.S.A.
29 F7 Simm's Bahamas
55 U3 Simojärvi l. Fin.
20 F4 Simonette r. Can.
21 J4 Simonhouse Can.
62 D7 Simplon Pass pass Switz.

113 G5 Simpson Desert des.
　Austr.
113 G5 Simpson Desert National
　Park nat. park Austr.
30 D1 Simpson I. i. Can.
34 D2 Simpson Park Mts mts
　U.S.A.
55 O9 Simrishamn Sweden
94 A5 Simunul i. Phil.
77 R5 Simushir, O. i. Rus. Fed.
95 A5 Sinabung vol. Indon.
78 C4 Sinai pen. Egypt
61 C5 Sinai, Mont h. France
66 D3 Sinalunga Italy
89 C5 Sinan China
85 H5 Sinbyugyun Myanmar
80 F2 Sincan Turkey
45 B2 Sincé Col.
45 B2 Sincelejo Col.
29 D5 Sinclair, L. l. U.S.A.
20 E4 Sinclair Mills Can.
104 B2 Sinclair Mine Namibia
57 E2 Sinclair's Bay b. U.K.
84 D4 Sind r. India
94 B4 Sindañgan Phil.
92 □ Sindangbarang Indon.
84 B4 Sindari India
62 D6 Sindelfingen Ger.
84 B4 Sindh div. India
80 B2 Sındırgı Turkey
84 D6 Sindkhed India
84 C5 Sindkheda India
68 J2 Sindor Rus. Fed.
85 F5 Sindri India
84 B3 Sind Sagar Doab
　lowland Pak.
68 J3 Sinegor'ye Rus. Fed.
67 M4 Sinekçi Turkey
65 B4 Sines Port.
65 B4 Sines, Cabo de pt Port.
100 B4 Sinfra Côte d'Ivoire
101 F3 Singa Sudan
84 E3 Singahi India
84 D2 Singa Pass pass India
70 Singapore country Asia
95 □ Singapore Sing.
95 B5 Singapore, Strait of
　chan. Indon./Sing.
92 □ Singaraja Indon.
95 B2 Sing Buri Thai.
31 G3 Singhampton Can.
102 D4 Singida Tanz.
93 G7 Singkang Indon.
92 D6 Singkawang Indon.
95 A5 Singkil Indon.
115 J4 Singleton Austr.
　Singora see Songkhla
66 C4 Siniscola Italy
66 G3 Sinj Croatia
93 G8 Sinjai Indon.
81 H3 Sinjar Iraq
81 H3 Sinjār, Jabal mt Iraq
81 K3 Sinjī Iran
101 F3 Sinkat Sudan
　Sinkiang Uighur Aut.
　Region div. see Xinjiang
　Uygur Zizhiqu
43 H2 Sinnamary Fr. Guiana
　Sinneh see Sanandaj
67 N2 Sinoie, Lacul lag.
　Romania
69 E7 Sinop Turkey
27 D6 Sinton U.S.A.
45 B2 Sinú r. Col.
87 M3 Sinŭiju N. Korea
94 B5 Siocon Phil.
62 J7 Siófok Hungary
62 C7 Sion Switz.
60 D3 Sion Mills U.K.
26 D3 Sioux Center U.S.A.
26 D3 Sioux City U.S.A.
26 D3 Sioux Falls U.S.A.
22 B3 Sioux Lookout Can.
94 B4 Sipalay Phil.
87 M3 Siping China
21 K3 Sipiwesk Can.
21 K3 Sipiwesk L. l. Can.
84 C5 Sipra r. India
29 C5 Sipsey r. U.S.A.
92 B7 Sipura i. Indon.
37 H6 Siquia r. Nic.
94 B4 Siquijor Phil.
94 B4 Siquijor i. Phil.
84 B5 Sir r. Pak.
88 E3 Sira India
55 K7 Sira r. Norway
95 B2 Si Racha Thai.
　Siracusa see Syracuse
20 E4 Sir Alexander, Mt mt
　Can.
81 G1 Şiran Turkey
81 M3 Sīrdān Iran
113 G3 Sir Edward Pellew Group
　is Austr.
30 A3 Siren U.S.A.
95 B1 Siri Kit Dam dam Thai.
84 B3 Siritoi r. Pak.
20 D2 Sir James McBrien, Mt
　mt Can.
79 H4 Sīrjān Iran
114 B5 Sir Joseph Bank's Group
　is Austr.
84 E4 Sirmour India
81 J3 Şırnak Turkey
82 B2 Širohi India
84 D3 Sironj India
34 C4 Sirretta Peak summit
　U.S.A.
84 C3 Sirsa Haryana India
85 E4 Sirsa Uttar Pradesh India
20 F4 Sir Sanford, Mt mt Can.
84 D3 Sirsi India
101 D1 Sirte Libya

101 D1 Sirte, Gulf of g. Libya
81 J2 Sirvan Turkey
55 T9 Širvintos Lith.
81 K4 Sīrwān r. Iraq
20 F4 Sir Wilfred Laurier, Mt mt Can.
66 G2 Sisak Croatia
95 C2 Sisaket Thai.
104 E3 Sishen S. Africa
81 L2 Sisian Armenia
30 C2 Siskiwit Bay b. U.S.A.
95 B2 Sisŏphŏn Cambodia
34 B4 Sisquoc r. U.S.A.
26 D2 Sisseton U.S.A.
33 K1 Sisson Branch Reservoir resr Can.
79 J3 Sīstan, Daryācheh-ye marsh Afgh.
118 F5 Sisters Beach Austr.
84 C5 Sitamau India
94 A5 Sitangkai Phil.
84 E4 Sitapur India
67 M7 Siteia Greece
105 J3 Siteki Swaziland
67 K4 Sithonia pen. Greece
46 C1 Sítio da Abadia Brazil
46 D1 Sítio do Mato Brazil
20 B3 Sitka U.S.A.
84 B3 Sitpur Pak.
61 D4 Sittard Neth.
85 H4 Sittaung Myanmar
59 H6 Sittingbourne U.K.
83 H6 Sittwe Myanmar
89 □ Siu A Chau i. China
85 F5 Siuri India
80 F2 Sivas Turkey
80 B2 Sivaslı Turkey
81 J3 Siverek Turkey
81 G2 Sivrice Turkey
80 C2 Sivrihisar Turkey
61 C4 Sivry Belgium
105 H3 Sivukile S. Africa
78 B4 Siwa Egypt
84 D3 Siwalik Range mts India/Nepal
85 F4 Siwan India
84 C4 Siwana India
64 G5 Six-Fours-les-Plages France
88 E3 Sixian China
30 E4 Six Lakes U.S.A.
60 D3 Sixmilecross U.K.
105 H2 Siyabuswa S. Africa
88 F3 Siyang China
81 M1 Siyäzän Azer.
88 C1 Siyitang China
Siziwang Qi see Ulan Hua
Sjælland i. see Zealand
55 N9 Sjenica Yugo.
55 N9 Sjöbo Sweden
54 P2 Sjøvegan Norway
45 E2 S. Juan r. Venez.
69 E6 Skadovs'k Ukr.
54 E4 Skaftafell nat. park Iceland
54 E5 Skaftarós est. Iceland
54 D3 Skagafjörður in. Iceland
55 M8 Skagen Denmark
55 L8 Skagerrak str. Denmark/Norway
24 K1 Skagit r. Can./U.S.A.
20 B3 Skagway U.S.A.
54 T1 Skaidi Norway
54 P2 Skaland Norway
54 O4 Skalmodal Sweden
55 M8 Skanderborg Denmark
33 E3 Skaneateles Lake l. U.S.A.
30 C2 Skanee U.S.A.
67 L5 Skantzoura i. Greece
55 N7 Skara Sweden
79 M2 Skardu Jammu and Kashmir
55 R7 Skärgårdshavets Nationalpark nat. park Fin.
55 M6 Skarnes Norway
63 K5 Skarżysko-Kamienna Pol.
54 R3 Skaulo Sweden
63 J6 Skawina Pol.
20 D3 Skeena r. Can.
20 D3 Skeena Mountains mts Can.
59 H4 Skegness U.K.
54 Q4 Skellefteå Sweden
54 Q4 Skellefteälven r. Sweden
54 R4 Skelleftehamn Sweden
60 A6 Skellig Rocks is Rep. of Ireland
58 E4 Skelmersdale U.K.
60 E4 Skerries Rep. of Ireland
55 M7 Ski Norway
67 K5 Skiathos i. Greece
60 B6 Skibbereen Rep. of Ireland
54 R2 Skibotn Norway
58 D3 Skiddaw mt U.K.
55 L7 Skien Norway
63 K5 Skierniewice Pol.
100 C1 Skikda Alg.
58 G4 Skipsea U.K.
114 E6 Skipton Austr.
58 E4 Skipton U.K.
55 L8 Skive Denmark
54 E4 Skjálfandafljót r. Iceland
55 L9 Skjern Denmark
55 K6 Skjolden Norway
55 K5 Skodje Norway
54 T2 Skoganvare Norway
60 F6 Skokholm Island i. Wales
30 D4 Skokie U.S.A.
54 E4 Skomer Island i. U.K.
67 K5 Skopelos i. Greece
68 F4 Skopin Rus. Fed.
67 J4 Skopje Macedonia

69 F5 Skorodnoye Rus. Fed.
55 N7 Skövde Sweden
87 M1 Skovorodino Rus. Fed.
33 J2 Skowhegan U.S.A.
55 S8 Skrunda Latvia
20 B2 Skukum, Mt mt Can.
105 J2 Skukuza S. Africa
34 D3 Skull Peak summit U.S.A.
30 B5 Skunk r. U.S.A.
55 R8 Skuodas Lith.
55 N9 Skurup Sweden
55 P6 Skutskär Sweden
69 D5 Skvyra Ukr.
57 B3 Skye i. U.K.
67 L5 Skyros Greece
67 L5 Skyros i. Greece
55 M9 Slagelse Denmark
54 Q4 Slagnäs Sweden
92 □ Slamet, Gunung vol. Indon.
60 E4 Slane Rep. of Ireland
60 E5 Slaney r. Rep. of Ireland
68 D3 Slantsy Rus. Fed.
69 G5 Slashchevskaya Rus. Fed.
116 B2 Slashers Reefs rf Austr.
30 D1 Slate Is i. Can.
66 G2 Slatina Croatia
67 L2 Slatina Romania
21 G2 Slave r. Can.
100 C4 Slave Coast coastal area Africa
20 G3 Slave Lake Can.
63 O2 Slavkovichi Rus. Fed.
67 H2 Slavonija reg. Croatia
67 H2 Slavonski Brod Croatia
69 C5 Slavuta Ukr.
69 D5 Slavutych Ukr.
90 B3 Slavyanka Rus. Fed.
69 F6 Slavyansk-na-Kubani Rus. Fed.
68 D4 Slawharad Belarus
62 H3 Sławno Pol.
59 G4 Sleaford U.K.
114 A5 Sleaford B. b. Austr.
60 A5 Slea Head hd Rep. of Ireland
57 C3 Sleat pen. U.K.
57 C3 Sleat, Sound of chan. U.K.
22 V2 Sleeper Islands is Can.
30 D3 Sleeping Bear Dunes National Lakeshore res. U.S.A.
30 D3 Sleeping Bear Pt pt U.S.A.
69 H7 Sleptsovskaya Rus. Fed.
119 C3 Slessor Glacier gl. Antarctica
27 F6 Slidell U.S.A.
60 A5 Slievanea h. Rep. of Ireland
60 D3 Slieve Anierin h. Rep. of Ireland
60 D5 Slieveardagh Hills h. Rep. of Ireland
60 C4 Slieve Aughty Mts h. Rep. of Ireland
60 D3 Slieve Beagh h. Rep. of Ireland/U.K.
60 C5 Slieve Bernagh h. Rep. of Ireland
60 D3 Slieve Bloom Mts h. Rep. of Ireland
60 B5 Slievecallan h. Rep. of Ireland
60 B3 Slieve Car h. Rep. of Ireland
60 F3 Slieve Donard h. U.K.
60 B4 Slieve Elva h. Rep. of Ireland
60 C3 Slieve Gamph h. Rep. of Ireland
60 C3 Slieve League h. Rep. of Ireland
60 B5 Slieve Mish Mts h. Rep. of Ireland
60 B6 Slieve Miskish Mts h. Rep. of Ireland
60 A4 Slieve More h. Rep. of Ireland
60 D4 Slieve na Calliagh h. Rep. of Ireland
60 D5 Slievenamon h. Rep. of Ireland
60 D2 Slieve Snaght mt Rep. of Ireland
57 B3 Sligachan U.K.
60 C3 Sligo Rep. of Ireland
60 C3 Sligo Bay b. Rep. of Ireland
55 Q8 Slite Sweden
67 M3 Sliven Bulg.
68 H2 Sloboda Rus. Fed.
68 J2 Slobodchikovo Rus. Fed.
67 M2 Slobozia Romania
20 F5 Slocan Can.
68 C4 Slonim Belarus
111 F2 Slot, The chan. Solomon Is
61 D2 Slotermeer l. Neth.
59 G6 Slough U.K.
48 Slovakia country Europe
48 Slovenia country Europe
66 F1 Slovenj Gradec Slovenia
69 F5 Slov"yans'k Ukr.
62 H3 Słupsk Pol.
54 P4 Slussfors Sweden
68 C4 Slutsk Belarus
60 A4 Slyne Head hd Rep. of Ireland
86 H1 Slyudyanka Rus. Fed.
33 J3 Small Pt pt U.S.A.

23 H3 Smallwood Reservoir resr Can.
68 D4 Smalyavichy Belarus
63 N3 Smarhon' Belarus
104 E5 Smartt Syndicate Dam resr S. Africa
21 J4 Smeaton Can.
67 J2 Smederevo Yugo.
67 J2 Smederevska Palanka Yugo.
32 D4 Smethport U.S.A.
69 D5 Smila Ukr.
55 T8 Smiltene Latvia
20 G3 Smith Can.
34 C2 Smith U.S.A.
32 C6 Smith r. U.S.A.
20 D4 Smithers Can.
105 G5 Smithfield S. Africa
29 E5 Smithfield NC U.S.A.
24 E3 Smithfield UT U.S.A.
33 E5 Smith I. i. MD U.S.A.
33 F6 Smith I. i. VA U.S.A.
32 D6 Smith Mountain Lake l. U.S.A.
20 D3 Smith River Can.
31 J3 Smiths Falls Can.
115 F8 Smithton Austr.
34 C1 Smoke Creek Desert des. U.S.A.
20 F4 Smoky r. Can.
115 K3 Smoky C. hd Austr.
22 D3 Smoky Falls Can.
26 D3 Smoky Hill r. U.S.A.
26 D3 Smoky Hills h. U.S.A.
20 D4 Smoky Lake Can.
54 K5 Smøla i. Norway
68 E4 Smolensk Rus. Fed.
68 E4 Smolenskaya Oblast' div. Rus. Fed.
67 L4 Smolyan Bulg.
90 C3 Smolyoninovo Rus. Fed.
22 D3 Smooth Rock Falls Can.
22 C3 Smoothrock L. l. Can.
21 H4 Smoothstone Lake l. Can.
54 T1 Smørfjord Norway
33 F5 Smyrna DE U.S.A.
29 C5 Smyrna GA U.S.A.
32 C4 Smyrna OH U.S.A.
33 J1 Smyrna Mills U.S.A.
54 F4 Snæfell mt Iceland
58 C3 Snaefell h. U.K.
20 A2 Snag Can.
24 D3 Snake r. U.S.A.
35 E2 Snake Range mts U.S.A.
24 D3 Snake River Plain plain U.S.A.
20 G2 Snare Lake Can.
111 G6 Snares Is is N.Z.
54 N4 Snåsa Norway
61 D1 Sneek Neth.
61 D1 Sneekermeer l. Neth.
60 B6 Sneem Rep. of Ireland
104 F6 Sneeuberge mts S. Africa
23 H3 Snegamook Lake l. Can.
59 H5 Snettisham U.K.
76 K3 Snezhnogorsk Rus. Fed.
66 F2 Snežnik mt Slovenia
63 K4 Śniardwy, Jezioro l. Pol.
69 E6 Snihurivka Ukr.
57 B3 Snizort, Loch b. U.K.
24 C2 Snohomish U.S.A.
24 B2 Snoqualmie Pass pass U.S.A.
54 N3 Snøtinden mt Norway
21 J2 Snowbird Lake l. Can.
59 C4 Snowdon mt U.K.
59 D5 Snowdonia National Park U.K.
35 G4 Snowflake U.S.A.
33 F5 Snow Hill MD U.S.A.
29 E5 Snow Hill NC U.S.A.
21 J4 Snow Lake Can.
114 C4 Snowtown Austr.
24 D3 Snowville U.S.A.
115 H6 Snowy r. Austr.
115 H6 Snowy Mts mts Austr.
115 G9 Snug Austr.
23 J3 Snug Harbour Nfld Can.
31 G3 Snug Harbour Ont. Can.
95 C2 Snuol Cambodia
27 D5 Snyder OK U.S.A.
27 C5 Snyder TX U.S.A.
103 E5 Soalala Madag.
103 E5 Soanierana-Ivongo Madag.
45 B3 Soata Col.
57 B3 Soay i. U.K.
101 F4 Sobat r. Sudan
93 L7 Sobger r. Indon.
91 B8 Sobo-san mt Japan
43 K6 Sobradinho, Barragem de resr Brazil
43 K4 Sobral Brazil
69 F7 Sochi Rus. Fed.
46 B3 Socorro Brazil
45 B3 Socorro Col.
25 D5 Socorro U.S.A.
36 B5 Socorro, I. i. Mex.
79 G7 Socotra i. Yemen
95 C3 Soc Trăng Vietnam
34 D4 Socuéllamos Spain
54 U3 Sodankylä Fin.
84 D2 Soda Plains plain China/Jammu and Kashmir
24 E3 Soda Springs U.S.A.
55 P6 Söderhamn Sweden
55 P7 Söderköping Sweden
55 P7 Södertälje Sweden
101 E3 Sodiri Sudan
102 D3 Sodo Eth.
55 Q6 Södra Kvarken str. Fin./Sweden
105 H1 Soekmekaar S. Africa

61 D3 Soerendonk Neth.
115 H4 Sofala Austr.
67 K3 Sofia Bulg.
Sofiya see Sofia
54 W4 Sofporog Rus. Fed.
91 G10 Sōfu-gan i. Japan
85 H3 Sog China
45 B2 Sogamoso Col.
81 G1 Soğanlı Dağları mts Turkey
68 H2 Sogra Rus. Fed.
88 A1 Sogo Nur l. China
88 A3 Sogruma China
80 C1 Söğüt Turkey
78 C1 Sohâg Egypt
84 D5 Sohagpur India
59 H5 Soham U.K.
84 B2 Sohan r. Pak.
111 F2 Sohano P.N.G.
85 E5 Sohela India
84 D3 Sohna India
90 A4 Sŏho-ri N. Korea
61 C4 Soignes, Forêt de forest Belgium
61 C4 Soignies Belgium
54 T5 Soini Fin.
64 F2 Soissons France
84 C4 Sojat India
94 B4 Sojoton Point pt Phil.
69 C5 Sokal' Ukr.
91 A5 Sokch'o S. Korea
67 M6 Söke Turkey
81 L4 Sokhumi Georgia
69 G7 Sokodé Togo
89 □ Soko Islands is China
68 G3 Sokol Rus. Fed.
63 L4 Sokół Pol.
100 B3 Sokolo Mali
90 B3 Sokolovka Rus. Fed.
63 L4 Sokołów Podlaski Pol.
100 C3 Sokoto Nigeria
100 C3 Sokoto r. Nigeria
69 C5 Sokyryany Ukr.
84 D3 Solan India
117 A7 Solander I. i. N.Z.
83 E7 Solāpur India
45 B2 Soledad Col.
34 B3 Soledad U.S.A.
45 E2 Soledad Venez.
69 G6 Solenoye Rus. Fed.
54 N3 Solfjellsjøen Norway
81 H2 Solhan Turkey
68 G3 Soligalich Rus. Fed.
59 F5 Solihull U.K.
76 G4 Solikamsk Rus. Fed.
76 G4 Sol'-Iletsk Rus. Fed.
61 F3 Solingen Ger.
104 A1 Solitaire Namibia
81 M1 Sollar Azer.
55 P5 Sollefteå Sweden
68 F3 Solnechnogorsk Rus. Fed.
92 C7 Solok Indon.
106 Solomon Islands country Pac. Oc.
110 F2 Solomon Sea sea P.N.G./Solomon Is
30 D3 Solon Springs U.S.A.
93 G8 Solor, Kepulauan is Indon.
62 C7 Solothurn Switz.
68 E1 Solovetskiye Ostrova is Rus. Fed.
68 H3 Solovetskoye Rus. Fed.
66 G3 Šolta i. Croatia
68 D3 Sol'tsy Rus. Fed.
33 E3 Solvay U.S.A.
55 O8 Sölvesborg Sweden
57 E6 Solway Firth est. U.K.
103 C5 Solwezi Zambia
91 G6 Sōma Japan
80 A2 Soma Turkey
96 Somalia country Africa
13 H4 Somali Basin sea feature Indian Ocean
103 C4 Sombo Angola
67 H2 Sombor Yugo.
84 C4 Somdari India
33 J2 Somerest Junction U.S.A.
55 S6 Somero Fin.
28 C4 Somerset KY U.S.A.
30 E4 Somerset MI U.S.A.
32 D5 Somerset PA U.S.A.
116 E6 Somerset, L. l. Austr.
105 F6 Somerset East S. Africa
118 B2 Somerset Island i. Can.
33 G3 Somerset Reservoir resr U.S.A.
104 C7 Somerset West S. Africa
33 H3 Somersworth U.S.A.
27 D6 Somerville Res. resr U.S.A.
81 L5 Someydeh Iran
55 O7 Sommen l. Sweden
23 G3 Sommet, Lac du l. Can.
84 B5 Somnath India
30 C5 Somonauk U.S.A.
47 C4 Somuncurá, Mesa Volcánica de plat. Arg.
85 F4 Son r. India
85 G5 Sonamukhi India
85 E5 Sonapur India
84 D4 Sonar r. India
68 E2 Sondaly Rus. Fed.
55 M8 Sønderborg Denmark
62 E5 Sondershausen Ger.
66 C1 Sondrio Italy
84 B5 Songadh India
88 E4 Songbu China
95 D2 Sông Cau Vietnam
103 D5 Songea Tanz.

90 B1 Songhua Jiang r. China
88 F4 Songjiang China
89 C4 Songkan China
95 B4 Songkhla Thai.
87 M2 Songling China
88 F1 Song Ling mts China
102 B4 Songo Angola
103 D5 Songo Moz.
88 B3 Songpan China
85 G4 Songsak India
88 D3 Song Shan mt China
89 C4 Songtao China
89 F5 Songxi China
88 D3 Songxian China
87 M2 Songyuan China
89 D4 Songzi China
95 D2 Son Ha Vietnam
Sonid Youqi see Saihan Tal
Sonid Zuoqi see Mandalt
84 D3 Sonīpat India
54 U5 Sonkajärvi Fin.
89 B6 Son La Vietnam
46 D2 Sono r. Minas Gerais Brazil
43 J6 Sono r. Tocantins Brazil
35 F6 Sonoita i. Mex.
35 G6 Sonoita U.S.A.
35 G6 Sonora div. Mex.
36 B3 Sonora r. Mex.
34 B3 Sonora CA U.S.A.
27 C6 Sonora TX U.S.A.
35 F6 Sonoyta Mex.
81 L4 Songor Iran
45 B3 Sonsón Col.
36 G6 Sonsonate El Salvador
89 B6 Sơn Tây Vietnam
105 H5 Sonwabile S. Africa
47 F1 Sopas r. Uru.
101 E4 Sopo watercourse Sudan
67 L3 Sopot Bulg.
63 J3 Sopot Pol.
62 H7 Sopron Hungary
82 D4 Sopur Jammu and Kashmir
66 E4 Sora Italy
85 E4 Sorada India
55 P5 Söråker Sweden
22 F4 Sorel Can.
115 G9 Sorell Austr.
115 G9 Sorell L. l. Austr.
80 E2 Sorgun Turkey
65 E2 Soria Spain
76 C2 Sørkappøya i. Svalbard
54 N4 Sørli Norway
85 F5 Soro India
69 D5 Soroca Moldova
46 C3 Sorocaba Brazil
76 G4 Sorochinsk Rus. Fed.
93 L5 Sorol i. Micronesia
93 J7 Sorong Indon.
102 D3 Soroti Uganda
54 S1 Sørøya i. Norway
65 B3 Sorraia r. Port.
54 O2 Sørreisa Norway
114 F7 Sorrento Austr.
66 F4 Sorrento Italy
103 B6 Sorris Sorris Namibia
54 P4 Sorsele Sweden
94 C3 Sorsogon Phil.
68 D2 Sortavala Rus. Fed.
54 O2 Sortland Norway
68 J2 Sortopolovskaya Rus. Fed.
68 J3 Sorvizhi Rus. Fed.
105 H2 Soshanguve S. Africa
69 H4 Sosna r. Rus. Fed.
47 C2 Sosneado mt Arg.
68 K2 Sosnogorsk Rus. Fed.
68 H2 Sosnovka Arkhangel. Rus. Fed.
68 G4 Sosnovka Tambov. Rus. Fed.
76 F2 Sosnovka Rus. Fed.
55 V7 Sosnovyy Bor Rus. Fed.
63 J5 Sosnowiec Pol.
69 F6 Sosyka r. Rus. Fed.
45 H2 Sotara, Volcán vol. Col.
54 V4 Sotkamo Fin.
47 D1 Soto Arg.
36 F4 Soto la Marina Mex.
102 B3 Souanké Congo
100 B4 Soubré Côte d'Ivoire
33 F4 Souderton U.S.A.
67 M4 Soufli Greece
64 E4 Souillac France
100 C3 Souk Ahras Alg.
Sŏul see Seoul
65 H4 Sour el Ghozlane Alg.
21 J5 Souris Man. Can.
23 H4 Souris P.E.I. Can.
21 J5 Souris r. Can./U.S.A.
43 L5 Sousa Brazil
100 D1 Sousse Tunisia
64 D5 Soustons France
96 South Africa, Republic of country Africa
31 J3 Southampton Can.
59 F7 Southampton U.K.
33 G4 Southampton U.S.A.
21 M2 Southampton Island i. Can.
92 A4 South Andaman i. Andaman and Nicobar is
32 E5 South Anna r. U.S.A.
59 F4 South Anston U.K.
23 H2 South Aulatsivik Island i. Can.
113 F5 South Australia div. Austr.

13 N6 South Australian Basin sea feature Indian Ocean
27 F5 Southaven U.S.A.
25 F5 South Baldy mt U.S.A.
58 F3 South Bank U.K.
32 B4 South Bass I. i. U.S.A.
21 N2 South Bay b. Can.
31 F3 South Baymouth Can.
30 D5 South Bend IN U.S.A.
24 B2 South Bend WA U.S.A.
29 E7 South Bight chan. Bahamas
32 B4 South Boston U.S.A.
117 D5 Southbridge N.Z.
33 G3 Southbridge U.S.A.
South Cape c. see Ka Lae
29 D5 South Carolina div. U.S.A.
33 J2 South China U.S.A.
92 E4 South China Sea sea Pac. Oc.
26 C2 South Dakota div. U.S.A.
33 G3 South Deerfield U.S.A.
59 G7 South Downs h. U.K.
105 F2 South East div. Botswana
115 G9 South East Cape c. Austr.
15 N10 Southeast Pacific Basin sea feature Pac. Oc.
115 G7 South East Point c. Austr.
21 J3 Southend Can.
57 C5 Southend U.K.
59 H6 Southend-on-Sea U.K.
30 A5 South English U.S.A.
117 D5 Southern Alps mts N.Z.
112 C6 Southern Cross Austr.
21 K3 Southern Indian Lake l. Can.
101 E4 Southern National Park nat. park Sudan
110 B6 Southern Ocean
29 E5 Southern Pines U.S.A.
119 C1 Southern Thule I. i. Atlantic Ocean
57 D5 Southern Uplands reg. U.K.
57 F4 South Esk r. U.K.
30 B6 South Fabius r. U.S.A.
25 F4 South Fork U.S.A.
30 E3 South Fox I. i. U.S.A.
119 C5 South Geomagnetic Pole Antarctica
57 A3 South Harris i. U.K.
85 G5 South Hatia I. i. Bangl.
30 D4 South Haven U.S.A.
21 K2 South Henik Lake l. Can.
33 G2 South Hero U.S.A.
32 D6 South Hill U.S.A.
14 E4 South Honshu Ridge sea feature Pac. Oc.
21 K3 South Indian Lake Can.
33 G4 Southington U.S.A.
117 C6 South Island i. N.Z.
94 A4 South Islet rf Phil.
85 H4 South Koel r. India
71 South Korea country Asia
34 B2 South Lake Tahoe U.S.A.
103 D5 South Luangwa National Park nat. park Zambia
119 B6 South Magnetic Pole Antarctica
30 D3 South Manitou I. i. U.S.A.
29 D7 South Miami U.S.A.
59 H6 Southminster U.K.
31 J4 South Moose L. l. Can.
32 E5 South Mtns h. U.S.A.
20 D2 South Nahanni r. Can.
57 □ South Nesting Bay b. U.K.
119 B1 South Orkney Is is Atlantic Ocean
33 J2 South Paris U.S.A.
24 G3 South Platte r. U.S.A.
119 B4 South Pole Antarctica
31 G1 South Porcupine Can.
115 K1 Southport Austr.
58 E4 Southport U.K.
33 H3 South Portland U.S.A.
31 H3 South River Can.
57 F2 South Ronaldsay i. U.K.
33 G3 South Royalton U.S.A.
105 J5 South Sand Bluff pt S. Africa
119 C1 South Sandwich Islands is Atlantic Ocean
12 H9 South Sandwich Trench sea feature Atlantic Ocean
21 H4 South Saskatchewan r. Can.
21 K3 South Seal r. Can.
119 B2 South Shetland Is is Antarctica
58 F2 South Shields U.K.
58 G4 South Skirlaugh U.K.
30 A5 South Skunk r. U.S.A.
117 E3 South Taranaki Bight b. N.Z.
35 G2 South Tent summit U.S.A.
85 E4 South Tons r. India
58 E3 South Twin I. i. Can.
58 E3 South Tyne r. U.K.
57 A3 South Uist i. U.K.
115 G9 South West C. hd Austr.
117 A7 South West Cape c. N.Z.
13 H6 South West Indian Ridge sea feature Indian Ocean
116 C1 South West Island i. Coral Sea Islands
115 G9 South West Nat. Park nat. park Austr.
Southwest Peru Ridge sea feature see Nazca Ridge
115 K3 South West Rocks Austr.
30 E5 South Whitley U.S.A.
33 H3 South Windham U.S.A.

59 J5 Southwold U.K.
105 H1 Soutpansberg mts S. Africa
66 G5 Soverato Italy
68 B4 Sovetsk Kaliningrad. Rus. Fed.
68 J3 Sovetsk Kirovsk. Rus. Fed.
87 Q2 Sovetskaya Gavan' Rus. Fed.
68 D2 Sovetskiy Leningrad. Rus. Fed.
68 J3 Sovetskiy Mariy El. Rus. Fed.
76 H3 Sovetskiy Rus. Fed.
105 G5 Soweto S. Africa
90 G2 Sōya-misaki c. Japan
63 P4 Sozh r. Belarus
67 Sozopol Bulg.
48 Spain country Europe
59 G5 Spalding U.K.
59 D6 Span Head h. U.K.
31 F2 Spanish Can.
31 Spanish r. Can.
35 G1 Spanish Fork U.S.A.
37 J5 Spanish Town Jamaica
34 C2 Sparks U.S.A.
32 C6 Sparta NC U.S.A.
30 B4 Sparta WV U.S.A.
29 D5 Spartanburg U.S.A.
67 K6 Sparti Greece
66 G6 Spartivento, Capo c. Italy
20 G5 Sparwood Can.
68 E4 Spas-Demensk Rus. Fed.
68 E2 Spasskaya Guba Rus. Fed.
87 O3 Spassk-Dal'niy Rus. Fed.
67 K7 Spatha, Akra pt Greece
20 D3 Spatsizi Plateau Wilderness Provincial Park res. Can.
26 C2 Spearfish U.S.A.
27 C4 Spearman U.S.A.
33 F3 Speculator U.S.A.
26 E3 Spencer IA U.S.A.
24 D2 Spencer ID U.S.A.
32 C2 Spencer WV U.S.A.
114 B5 Spencer, C. hd Austr.
20 A3 Spencer, Cape c. U.S.A.
114 B5 Spencer Gulf est. Austr.
20 E4 Spences Bridge Can.
58 F3 Spennymoor U.K.
60 D3 Sperrin Mountains h. U.K.
32 D5 Sperryville U.S.A.
62 D5 Spessart reg. Ger.
67 K6 Spetses i. Greece
57 E3 Spey r. U.K.
62 D6 Speyer Ger.
61 F1 Spiekeroog i. Ger.
62 C7 Spiez Switz.
61 C3 Spijkenisse Neth.
66 E1 Spilimbergo Italy
59 H4 Spilsby U.K.
84 B3 Spintangi Pak.
20 F3 Spirit River Can.
30 C3 Spirit River Flowage resr U.S.A.
21 H4 Spiritwood Can.
84 A2 Spirsang P. pass Afgh.
63 K6 Spišská Nová Ves Slovakia
81 K1 Spitak Armenia
84 D3 Spiti r. India
76 C2 Spitsbergen i. Svalbard
62 F7 Spittal an der Drau Austria
66 G3 Split Croatia
21 K3 Split Lake Can.
21 K3 Split Lake l. Can.
24 C2 Spokane U.S.A.
66 E3 Spoleto Italy
95 C2 Spong Cambodia
30 B3 Spooner U.S.A.
24 F2 Spotted Horse U.S.A.
23 J3 Spotted Island Can.
31 F2 Spragge Can.
20 E4 Spranger, Mt mt Can.
24 C2 Spray U.S.A.
62 G5 Spree r. Ger.
31 F3 Spring Bay Can.
104 B4 Springbok S. Africa
23 J4 Springdale Can.
27 E4 Springdale U.S.A.
25 F4 Springer U.S.A.
35 H4 Springerville U.S.A.
27 C7 Springfield CO U.S.A.
30 C6 Springfield IL U.S.A.
33 G3 Springfield MA U.S.A.
33 J2 Springfield ME U.S.A.
26 E2 Springfield MN U.S.A.
27 E4 Springfield MO U.S.A.
32 B5 Springfield OH U.S.A.
27 C4 Springfield OR U.S.A.
33 G3 Springfield VT U.S.A.
32 D5 Springfield WV U.S.A.
30 C6 Springfield, Lake l. U.S.A.
105 F5 Springfontein S. Africa
30 B4 Spring Green U.S.A.
30 B4 Spring Grove U.S.A.
23 H4 Springhill Can.
29 D6 Spring Hill U.S.A.
30 D4 Spring Lake U.S.A.
35 E3 Spring Mountains mts U.S.A.
117 D5 Springs Junction N.Z.
116 C5 Springsure Austr.
30 A4 Spring Valley U.S.A.
32 A3 Springville NY U.S.A.
35 G1 Springville UT U.S.A.
59 J5 Sprowston U.K.
20 G4 Spruce Grove Can.
32 D5 Spruce Knob-Seneca Rocks National Recreation Area res. U.S.A.

24 D3 Spruce Mt. mt U.S.A.
58 H4 Spurn Head c. U.K.
20 E5 Spuzzum Can.
20 E5 Squamish Can.
33 H3 Squam Lake l. U.S.A.
33 J1 Squapan Lake l. U.S.A.
33 J1 Square Lake l. U.S.A.
66 G5 Squillace, Golfo di g. Italy
36 A2 S. Quintín, C. pt Mex.
95 B3 Srê Âmběl Cambodia
67 H2 Srebrenica Bos.-Herz.
67 M3 Sredets Bulg.
77 R4 Sredinnyy Khrebet mts Rus. Fed.
67 K3 Sredna Gora mts Bulg.
77 R3 Srednekolymsk Rus. Fed.
68 E4 Sredne-Russkaya Vozvyshennost' reg. Rus. Fed.
54 W4 Sredneye Kuyto, Oz. l. Rus. Fed.
67 L3 Srednogorie Bulg.
95 C2 Srêpôk, T. r. Cambodia
87 L1 Sretensk Rus. Fed.
92 E6 Sri Aman Malaysia
83 Sri Jayewardenepura Kotte Sri Lanka
83 F7 Srikakulam India
84 D3 Sri Kanta mt India
70 Sri Lanka country Asia
84 D3 Srinagar India
84 C2 Srinagar Jammu and Kashmir
83 Sri Pada mt Sri Lanka
95 B1 Sri Thep Thai.
83 D7 Srivardhan India
113 H3 Staaten River National Park nat. park Austr.
62 E6 Stade Ger.
61 E2 Stadskanaal Neth.
57 B4 Staffa i. U.K.
59 E5 Stafford U.K.
32 E5 Stafford U.S.A.
29 E7 Stafford Creek Bahamas
58 T8 Staicele Latvia
59 G6 Staines U.K.
69 F5 Stakhanov Ukr.
59 E7 Stalbridge U.K.
59 J5 Stalham U.K.
20 E3 Stalin, Mt mt Can.
Stalingrad see Volgograd
63 L5 Stalowa Wola Pol.
67 L3 Stamboliyski Bulg.
59 G5 Stamford U.K.
33 G4 Stamford CT U.S.A.
33 F3 Stamford NY U.S.A.
Stampalia i. see Astypalaia
103 B6 Stampriet Namibia
54 N2 Stamsund Norway
26 E3 Stanberry U.S.A.
61 C3 Standdaarbuiten Neth.
105 H3 Standerton S. Africa
24 D3 Standish U.S.A.
28 C4 Stanford U.S.A.
105 J4 Stanger S. Africa
115 F8 Stanley Austr.
33 K1 Stanley Can.
89 Stanley China
44 E8 Stanley Falkland Is
53 F3 Stanley U.K.
24 D2 Stanley ID U.S.A.
26 C1 Stanley ND U.S.A.
30 B3 Stanley WV U.S.A.
102 C3 Stanley, Mount mt Uganda/Dem. Rep. Congo
115 F8 Stanley, Mt h. Austr.
58 F2 Stannington U.K.
77 R3 Stanovaya Rus. Fed.
77 N4 Stanovoye Nagor'ye mts Rus. Fed.
77 Stanovoy Khrebet mts Rus. Fed.
115 J2 Stanthorpe Austr.
59 H5 Stanton U.K.
32 B6 Stanton KY U.S.A.
30 E4 Stanton MI U.S.A.
26 C3 Stapleton U.S.A.
116 B2 Star r. Austr.
63 K5 Starachowice Pol.
Stara Planina mts see Balkan Mountains
68 H4 Staraya Kulatka Rus. Fed.
69 H5 Staraya Poltavka Rus. Fed.
68 D3 Staraya Russa Rus. Fed.
63 P2 Staraya Toropa Rus. Fed.
68 J4 Staraya Tumba Rus. Fed.
67 L3 Stara Zagora Bulg.
62 G2 Stargard Szczeciński Pol.
68 E3 Staritsa Rus. Fed.
29 D6 Starke U.S.A.
27 F5 Starkville U.S.A.
62 E7 Starnberger See l. Ger.
59 F5 Starobil's'k Ukr.
63 Q4 Starodub Rus. Fed.
63 J4 Starogard Gdański Pol.
69 C5 Starokostyantyniv Ukr.
69 F6 Starominskaya Rus. Fed.
69 F6 Staroshcherbinovskaya Rus. Fed.
34 C1 Star Peak mt U.S.A.
59 D7 Start Point pt U.K.
63 O4 Staryya Darohi Belarus
77 M2 Staryy Kayak Rus. Fed.
69 H5 Staryy Oskol Rus. Fed.
32 E4 State College U.S.A.
29 D5 Statesboro U.S.A.
29 D5 Statesville U.S.A.
54 J7 Stavanger Norway
59 F4 Staveley U.K.

69 G6 Stavropol' Rus. Fed.
69 G6 Stavropol'skaya Vozvyshennost' reg. Rus. Fed.
69 G6 Stavropol'skiy Kray div. Rus. Fed.
114 E4 Stawell Austr.
105 H4 Steadville S. Africa
34 C2 Steamboat U.S.A.
24 F3 Steamboat Springs U.S.A.
32 E4 Steelton U.S.A.
61 E2 Steenderen Neth.
105 J2 Steenkampsberge mts S. Africa
20 E3 Steen River Can.
24 C3 Steens Mt. mt U.S.A.
61 E2 Steenwijk Neth.
62 E6 Steigerwald forest Ger.
21 K5 Steinbach Can.
61 F2 Steinfurt Ger.
103 B6 Steinhausen Namibia
54 M4 Steinkjer Norway
104 B4 Steinkopf S. Africa
35 H5 Steins U.S.A.
54 M4 Steinsdalen Norway
104 F3 Stella S. Africa
29 F7 Stella Maris Bahamas
104 C6 Stellenbosch S. Africa
66 C3 Stello, Monte mt France
62 E4 Stendal Ger.
55 M7 Stenungsund Sweden
Stepanakert see Xankändi
69 H7 Step'anavan Armenia
21 K5 Stephen U.S.A.
114 D4 Stephens watercourse Austr.
117 D5 Stephens, Cape c. N.Z.
114 D3 Stephens Creek Austr.
30 D3 Stephenson U.S.A.
20 C3 Stephens Passage chan. U.S.A.
23 J4 Stephenville Can.
27 D5 Stephenville U.S.A.
69 F5 Stepnoye Rus. Fed.
105 H4 Sterkfontein Dam resr S. Africa
105 G5 Sterkstroom S. Africa
104 D5 Sterling S. Africa
24 G3 Sterling CO U.S.A.
30 C5 Sterling IL U.S.A.
26 C2 Sterling ND U.S.A.
35 G2 Sterling UT U.S.A.
27 C6 Sterling City U.S.A.
31 F4 Sterling Hgts U.S.A.
20 G4 Stettler Can.
30 D2 Steuben U.S.A.
32 C4 Steubenville U.S.A.
59 G6 Stevenage U.K.
21 K4 Stevenson L. l. Can.
30 C3 Stevens Point U.S.A.
20 D3 Stewart Can.
20 B2 Stewart r. Can.
20 B2 Stewart Crossing Can.
117 A7 Stewart Island i. N.Z.
111 G2 Stewart Islands is Solomon Is
57 D5 Stewarton U.K.
30 A4 Stewartville U.S.A.
105 F5 Steynsburg S. Africa
62 G6 Steyr Austria
104 F6 Steytlerville S. Africa
20 C3 Stikine r. Can./U.S.A.
20 C3 Stikine Plateau mts Can.
104 D7 Stilbaai S. Africa
30 A3 Stillwater MN U.S.A.
34 C2 Stillwater NV U.S.A.
27 D4 Stillwater OK U.S.A.
25 C4 Stillwater Ra. mts U.S.A.
59 G5 Stilton U.K.
67 K4 Štip Macedonia
114 C5 Stirling Austr.
57 E4 Stirling U.K.
34 B2 Stirling City U.S.A.
114 B4 Stirling North Austr.
54 M5 Stjørdalshalsen Norway
62 H6 Stockerau Austria
55 Q7 Stockholm Sweden
33 J1 Stockholm U.S.A.
59 E4 Stockport U.K.
34 B3 Stockton CA U.S.A.
26 D4 Stockton KS U.S.A.
35 F1 Stockton UT U.S.A.
30 B2 Stockton I. l. U.S.A.
27 E4 Stockton L. l. U.S.A.
58 F3 Stockton-on-Tees U.K.
33 J2 Stockton Springs U.S.A.
55 P5 Stöde Sweden
95 C2 Stœng Trêng Cambodia
57 C2 Stoer, Point of pt U.K.
59 E4 Stoke-on-Trent U.K.
58 F3 Stokesley U.K.
115 E8 Stokes Pt pt Austr.
54 C5 Stokkseyri Iceland
54 N3 Stokkvågen Norway
54 O2 Stokmarknes Norway
67 G3 Stolac Bos.-Herz.
69 C5 Stolin Belarus
59 E5 Stone U.K.
31 J2 Stonecliffe Can.
33 H5 Stone Harbor U.S.A.
57 F4 Stonehaven U.K.
20 E3 Stone Mountain Prov. Park res. U.S.A.
35 H4 Stoner U.S.A.
33 F4 Stone Ridge U.S.A.
21 K4 Stonewall Can.
32 C5 Stonewall Jackson Lake l. U.S.A.
31 F4 Stoney Point Can.
33 J2 Stonington U.S.A.
34 A2 Stonyford U.S.A.

33 E3 Stony Pt pt U.S.A.
21 H3 Stony Rapids Can.
54 Q3 Stora Lulevatten l. Sweden
54 P3 Stora Sjöfallets Nationalpark nat. park Sweden
54 Q4 Storavan l. Sweden
55 M9 Store Bælt chan. Denmark
54 M5 Støren Norway
54 O3 Storforshei Norway
54 O3 Storjord Norway
115 G9 Storm Bay b. Austr.
105 G5 Stormberg S. Africa
105 G5 Stormberge mts S. Africa
26 E3 Storm Lake U.S.A.
55 K6 Stornosa mt Norway
57 B2 Stornoway U.K.
68 K2 Storozhevsk Rus. Fed.
69 C5 Storozhynets' Ukr.
61 D1 Stortemelk chan. Neth.
54 P4 Storseleby Sweden
54 P4 Storuman Sweden
54 P4 Storuman l. Sweden
55 P6 Storvik Sweden
55 M8 Storvorde Denmark
54 P7 Storvreta Sweden
59 D5 Stotfold U.K.
30 C4 Stoughton U.S.A.
59 E7 Stour r. Eng. U.K.
59 J6 Stour r. Eng. U.K.
59 J6 Stour r. Eng. U.K.
59 H6 Stour r. Eng. U.K.
59 E5 Stourbridge U.K.
59 E5 Stourport-on-Severn U.K.
21 L4 Stout L. l. Can.
68 C4 Stowbtsy Belarus
33 F4 Stowe U.S.A.
59 H5 Stowmarket U.K.
60 D3 Strabane U.K.
60 D4 Stradbally Rep. of Ireland
59 J5 Stradbroke U.K.
66 C2 Stradella Italy
115 F9 Strahan Austr.
35 G3 Straight Cliffs cliff U.S.A.
62 F6 Strakonice Czech Rep.
62 F3 Stralsund Ger.
104 C7 Strand S. Africa
54 K5 Stranda Norway
29 F7 Strangers Cay i. Bahamas
60 F3 Strangford U.K.
60 F3 Strangford Lough l. U.K.
57 D6 Stranraer U.K.
64 H2 Strasbourg France
32 D5 Strasburg U.S.A.
115 G4 Stratford Austr.
31 G4 Stratford Can.
117 E3 Stratford N.Z.
27 C4 Stratford TX U.S.A.
30 B3 Stratford WV U.S.A.
59 F5 Stratford-upon-Avon U.K.
114 C5 Strathalbyn Austr.
57 D5 Strathaven U.K.
57 G3 Strathbeg, Loch of l. U.K.
57 D3 Strathcarron v. U.K.
20 D5 Strathcona Prov. Park res. Can.
57 D3 Strathconon v. U.K.
57 D3 Strath Dearn v. U.K.
57 D2 Strath Fleet v. U.K.
20 E4 Strathmore Can.
20 E4 Strathnaver Can.
57 D2 Strathnaver v. U.K.
57 E2 Strath of Kildonan v. U.K.
31 G4 Strathroy Can.
57 E3 Strathspey v. U.K.
57 E2 Strathy U.K.
57 D2 Strathy Point pt U.K.
33 H2 Stratton U.S.A.
24 C4 Straubing Ger.
54 B3 Straumnes pt Iceland
30 B4 Strawberry Point U.S.A.
35 G1 Strawberry Reservoir resr U.S.A.
113 F6 Streaky Bay Austr.
113 F6 Streaky Bay b. Austr.
30 C5 Streator U.S.A.
59 E6 Street U.K.
67 K2 Strehaia Romania
77 R3 Strelka Rus. Fed.
55 T8 Strenči Latvia
59 E5 Strichen U.K.
93 L8 Strickland r. P.N.G.
67 K4 Strimonas r. Greece
47 C4 Stroeder Arg.
60 C4 Strokestown Rep. of Ireland
57 E2 Stroma, Island of i. U.K.
66 F5 Stromboli, Isola i. Italy
57 F4 Stromness U.K.
26 D3 Stromsburg U.S.A.
54 M7 Strömstad Sweden
54 O5 Strömsund Sweden
32 C2 Strongsville U.S.A.
57 F1 Stronsay i. U.K.
115 J4 Stroud Austr.
59 E6 Stroud U.K.
115 J4 Stroud Road Austr.
33 F4 Stroudsburg U.S.A.
55 L8 Struer Denmark
67 J4 Struga Macedonia
68 D3 Strugi-Krasnyye Rus. Fed.
104 D7 Struis Bay S. Africa
67 K4 Struma r. Bulg.
59 B5 Strumble Head hd U.K.

67 K4 Strumica Macedonia
67 L3 Stryama r. Bulg.
104 E4 Strydenburg S. Africa
55 K6 Stryn Norway
69 B5 Stryy Ukr.
114 D2 Strzelecki Cr. watercourse Austr.
115 H8 Strzelecki Pk h. Austr.
116 D6 Stuart r. Austr.
29 D7 Stuart FL U.S.A.
32 C6 Stuart VA U.S.A.
20 E4 Stuart Lake l. Can.
32 D5 Stuarts Draft U.S.A.
115 H4 Stuart Town Austr.
117 C6 Studholme Junction N.Z.
54 Q5 Studsviken Sweden
27 C6 Study Butte U.S.A.
21 L4 Stull L. l. Can.
68 F4 Stupino Rus. Fed.
119 A6 Sturge I. i. Antarctica
30 D2 Sturgeon r. U.S.A.
21 K4 Sturgeon Bay b. Can.
30 D3 Sturgeon Bay U.S.A.
30 E3 Sturgeon Bay U.S.A.
30 D3 Sturgeon Bay Canal chan. U.S.A.
31 H2 Sturgeon Falls Can.
22 D3 Sturgeon L. l. Can.
28 C5 Sturgis KY U.S.A.
30 E5 Sturgis MI U.S.A.
26 C2 Sturgis SD U.S.A.
114 D2 Sturt, Mt h. Austr.
114 B5 Sturt Bay b. Austr.
112 E3 Sturt Creek r. Austr.
114 D2 Sturt Nat. Park nat. park Austr.
114 D2 Sturt Stony Desert des. Austr.
105 G6 Stutterheim S. Africa
62 D6 Stuttgart Ger.
27 F5 Stuttgart U.S.A.
54 B4 Stykkishólmur Iceland
63 M5 Styr r. Ukr.
46 D2 Suaçuí Grande r. Brazil
101 F3 Suakin Sudan
89 F5 Suao Taiwan
25 E6 Suaqui Gde Mex.
45 B3 Suárez r. Col.
63 M3 Subačius Lith.
92 Subang Indon.
85 H4 Subansiri r. India
85 Subarnarekha r. India
81 G6 Şubayḥah Saudi Arabia
95 D5 Subi Besar i. Indon.
67 H1 Subotica Yugo.
63 N7 Suceava Romania
90 Suchan r. Rus. Fed.
60 C4 Suck r. Rep. of Ireland
42 E7 Sucre Bol.
45 B2 Sucre Col.
45 Sucuaro Col.
46 B3 Sucuriú r. Brazil
69 E6 Sudak Ukr.
96 Sudan country Africa
68 G3 Suday Rus. Fed.
81 K6 Sudayr, Sha'ib watercourse Iraq
31 G2 Sudbury Can.
59 H5 Sudbury U.K.
101 E4 Sudd swamp Sudan
62 H5 Sudety mts Czech Rep./Pol.
33 F3 Sudlersville U.S.A.
68 G4 Sudogda Rus. Fed.
80 D7 Sudr Egypt
54 Suðuroy i. Faroe Is
101 E4 Sue watercourse Sudan
65 F3 Sueca Spain
78 C4 Suez Egypt
78 C4 Suez, Gulf of g. Egypt
78 C3 Suez Canal canal Egypt
32 E6 Suffolk U.S.A.
81 K2 Sūfiān Iran
30 C4 Sugar r. U.S.A.
33 H2 Sugarloaf Mt. mt U.S.A.
115 K4 Sugarloaf Pt pt Austr.
94 C4 Suguhan Point pt Phil.
94 A5 Sugut r. Malaysia
94 A5 Sugut, Tg pt Malaysia
88 B2 Suhait China
79 H5 Şuḥār Oman
86 J1 Sühbaatar Mongolia
62 E5 Suhl Ger.
80 C2 Şuhut Turkey
84 B3 Şui Pak.
90 B1 Suibin China
89 E5 Suichang China
89 E5 Suichuan China
88 D2 Suide China
87 O3 Suifenhe China
84 B4 Suigam India
87 N2 Suihua China
89 B4 Suijiang China
89 D5 Suining Hunan China
88 D3 Suining Jiangsu China
89 B4 Suining Sichuan China
88 E3 Suiping China
60 D5 Suir r. Rep. of Ireland
88 E3 Suixian China
88 E3 Suixi China
89 C5 Suiyang China
88 F1 Suizhong China
89 D4 Suizhou China
88 C1 Suj China
84 C4 Sujangarh India
84 B3 Sujawal Pak.
92 Sukabumi Indon.
92 Sukadana Indon.
91 G6 Sukagawa Japan
94 A5 Sukau Malaysia
90 C1 Sukhanovka Rus. Fed.

68 E4 Sukhinichi Rus. Fed.
68 H2 Sukhona r. Rus. Fed.
95 A1 Sukhothai Thai.
68 E2 Sukkozero Rus. Fed.
84 B4 Sukkur Pak.
84 D1 Sukri r. India
68 F3 Sukromny Rus. Fed.
91 C8 Sukumo Japan
55 J6 Sula i. Norway
93 H7 Sula, Kepulauan is Indon.
84 Sulaiman Ranges mts Pak.
69 H7 Sulak r. Rus. Fed.
57 Sula Sgeir i. U.K.
93 Sulawesi i. Indon.
81 K4 Sulaymän Beg Iraq
57 Sule Skerry i. U.K.
57 Sule Stack i. U.K.
80 F1 Süleymanlı Turkey
100 A4 Sulima Sierra Leone
54 P3 Sulitjelma Norway
55 V6 Sulkava Fin.
42 B4 Sullana Peru
26 F4 Sullivan U.S.A.
21 C2 Sullivan L. l. Can.
33 J1 Sully Can.
66 E3 Sulmona Italy
27 E6 Sulphur U.S.A.
27 E5 Sulphur Springs U.S.A.
31 F2 Sultan Can.
Sultanabad see Arāk
80 C2 Sultan Dağları mts Turkey
80 D2 Sultanhanı Turkey
85 E4 Sultanpur India
94 B5 Sulu Archipelago is Phil.
80 F2 Sulusaray Turkey
94 A4 Sulu Sea sea Phil.
119 A4 Sulzberger Bay b. Antarctica
44 D3 Sumampa Arg.
45 B4 Sumapaz, Parque Nacional nat. park Col.
81 K5 Sūmār Iran
92 C6 Sumatera i. Indon.
Sumatra i. see Sumatera
62 F4 Šumava mts Czech Rep.
93 G8 Sumba i. Indon.
93 F8 Sumba, Selat chan. Indon.
93 F8 Sumbawa i. Indon.
93 F8 Sumbawabesar Indon.
103 D4 Sumbawanga Tanz.
103 B5 Sumbe Angola
57 Sumburgh U.K.
57 Sumburgh Head hd U.K.
84 D2 Sumdo China/Jammu and Kashmir
92 Sumedang Indon.
81 M3 Sume'eh Sarā Iran
92 Sumenep Indon.
Sumgait see Sumqayıt
91 F9 Sumisu-jima i. Japan
81 J3 Summēl Iraq
22 Summer Beaver Can.
23 H4 Summerford Can.
30 D3 Summer I. i. U.S.A.
57 Summer Isles is U.K.
23 H4 Summerside Can.
32 C5 Summersville U.S.A.
32 C5 Summersville Lake l. U.S.A.
20 E4 Summit Lake Can.
30 E5 Summit Lake l. U.S.A.
34 D2 Summit Mt mt U.S.A.
84 D2 Sumnal China/India
117 D5 Sumner N.Z.
30 A4 Sumner U.S.A.
117 D5 Sumner, L. l. N.Z.
20 C3 Sumner Strait chan. U.S.A.
91 F6 Sumon-dake mt Japan
91 D7 Sumoto Japan
62 H6 Šumperk Czech Rep.
81 M1 Sumqayıt Azer.
81 M1 Sumqayıt r. Azer.
84 B4 Sumrahu Pak.
29 D5 Sumter U.S.A.
69 E5 Sumy Ukr.
24 D2 Sun r. U.S.A.
68 J3 Suna Rus. Fed.
90 Sunagawa Japan
85 G4 Sunamganj Bangl.
57 Sunart, Loch in. U.K.
84 B3 Sunbula Kuh mts Iran
24 E1 Sunburst U.S.A.
114 F6 Sunbury Austr.
32 B4 Sunbury OH U.S.A.
32 E4 Sunbury PA U.S.A.
47 E1 Sunchales Arg.
105 G2 Sun City S. Africa
33 H3 Suncook U.S.A.
92 C8 Sunda, Selat chan. Indon.
24 F2 Sundance U.S.A.
85 F5 Sundargarh India
84 D3 Sundarnagar India
Sunda Trench sea feature see Java Trench
58 F3 Sunderland U.K.
80 C2 Sündiken Dağları mts Turkey
31 H3 Sundridge Can.
55 P5 Sundsvall Sweden
105 J4 Sundumbili S. Africa
84 D4 Sunel India
95 Sungaikabung Indon.
92 Sungailiat Indon.
92 C7 Sungaipenuh Indon.
92 Sungei Petani Malaysia
95 Sungei Seletar Res. resr Sing.
80 E1 Sungurlu Turkey

85 F4 Sun Kosi r. Nepal
55 K6 Sunndal Norway
54 L5 Sunndalsøra Norway
55 N7 Sunne Sweden
24 C2 Sunnyside U.S.A.
34 A3 Sunnyvale U.S.A.
30 C4 Sun Prairie U.S.A.
34 □1 Sunset Beach U.S.A.
35 G4 Sunset Crater National Monument res. U.S.A.
77 N3 Suntar Rus. Fed.
24 D3 Sun Valley U.S.A.
100 B4 Sunyani Ghana
54 U3 Suolijärvet l. Fin.
30 C1 Suomi Fin.
54 V4 Suomussalmi Fin.
91 B8 Suō-nada b. Japan
54 U5 Suonenjoki Fin.
95 C5 Suong Cambodia
89 B7 Suong r. Laos
68 E2 Suoyarvi Rus. Fed.
35 H3 Supai U.S.A.
45 E3 Supamo r. Venez.
85 F4 Supaul India
35 G5 Superior AZ U.S.A.
26 D3 Superior NE U.S.A.
30 A2 Superior WV U.S.A.
30 B2 Superior, Lake l. Can./U.S.A.
95 B2 Suphan Buri Thai.
81 J2 Süphan Dağı mt Turkey
68 E4 Suponovo Rus. Fed.
81 L6 Sūq ash Shuyūkh Iraq
88 F3 Suqian China
Suqutrā i. see Socotra
79 H5 Şūr Oman
34 B3 Sur, Pt pt U.S.A.
47 F3 Sur, Pta pt Arg.
68 H4 Sura Rus. Fed.
68 H4 Sura r. Rus. Fed.
81 M1 Suraabad Azer.
79 K4 Şūrab Pak.
92 □ Surabaya Indon.
92 □ Surakarta Indon.
115 H1 Surat Austr.
84 C5 Surat India
84 C3 Suratgarh India
95 A3 Surat Thani Thai.
68 E4 Surazh Rus. Fed.
116 B4 Surbiton Austr.
81 K4 Sürdäsh Iraq
67 K3 Surdulica Yugo.
61 D5 Sûre r. Lux.
84 B5 Surendranagar India
34 B4 Surf U.S.A.
76 J3 Surgut Rus. Fed.
83 E7 Suriapet India
94 C4 Surigao Phil.
94 C4 Surigao Str. chan. Phil.
95 B2 Surin Thai.
38 Suriname country S. America
84 B1 Surkhab r. Afgh.
85 E3 Surkhet Nepal
81 H1 Sürmene Turkey
69 G5 Surovikino Rus. Fed.
32 E6 Surry U.S.A.
68 H4 Sursk Rus. Fed.
Surt see Sirte
Surt, Khalīj g. see Sirte, Gulf of
54 C5 Surtsey i. Iceland
80 G3 Sürüç Turkey
91 F7 Suruga-wan b. Japan
92 □ Surulangun Indon.
94 C5 Surup Phil.
81 L2 Şuşa Azer.
91 B7 Susa Japan
91 C8 Susaki Japan
81 M6 Süsangerd Iran
68 G3 Susanino Rus. Fed.
34 B1 Susanville U.S.A.
80 G1 Suşehri Turkey
95 A4 Suso Thai.
89 E4 Susong China
33 E4 Susquehanna r. U.S.A.
32 D4 Susquehanna, West Branch r. U.S.A.
23 G4 Sussex Can.
33 F4 Sussex U.S.A.
94 A5 Susul Malaysia
77 Q3 Susuman Rus. Fed.
80 B2 Susurluk Turkey
84 D2 Sutak Jammu and Kashmir
34 C2 Sutcliffe U.S.A.
104 D6 Sutherland S. Africa
26 C3 Sutherland U.S.A.
84 C3 Sutlej r. Pak.
34 B2 Sutter Creek U.S.A.
59 G5 Sutterton U.K.
33 G2 Sutton Can.
22 D3 Sutton r. Can.
59 H5 Sutton U.K.
32 C5 Sutton U.S.A.
59 F5 Sutton Coldfield U.K.
59 F4 Sutton in Ashfield U.K.
22 D3 Sutton L. l. Can.
32 C5 Sutton Lake l. U.S.A.
116 B3 Suttor r. Austr.
90 G3 Suttsu Japan
90 D1 Sutungu Rus. Fed.
111 H3 Suva Fiji
68 F4 Suvorov Rus. Fed.
91 F6 Suwa Japan
63 L3 Suwałki Pol.
95 B2 Suwannaphum Thai.
29 D6 Suwannee r. U.S.A.
81 K5 Suwayqīyah, Hawr as l. Iraq
81 H5 Suwayr w. Saudi Arabia
91 F6 Suzaka Japan
68 G3 Suzdal' Rus. Fed.
88 E3 Suzhou Anhui China

88 F4 Suzhou Jiangsu China
91 E6 Suzu Japan
91 E7 Suzuka Japan
91 E6 Suzu-misaki pt Japan
54 U1 Sværholthalvøya pen. Norway
76 C2 Svalbard terr. Arctic Ocean
69 F5 Svatove Ukr.
95 C3 Svay Riêng Cambodia
55 O5 Sveg Sweden
55 U8 Sveki Latvia
55 J6 Svelgen Norway
54 L5 Svellingen Norway
55 T9 Švenčionėliai Lith.
55 U9 Švenčionys Lith.
55 M9 Svendborg Denmark
54 Q2 Svensby Norway
54 O5 Svenstavik Sweden
Sverdlovsk see Yekaterinburg
69 F5 Sverdlovs'k Ukr.
67 J4 Sveti Nikole Macedonia
87 P2 Svetlaya Rus. Fed.
87 Q2 Svetlodarskoye Rus. Fed.
76 K3 Svetlogorsk Rus. Fed.
68 B4 Svetlogorsk Belarus
69 G6 Svetlograd Rus. Fed.
68 B4 Svetlyy Rus. Fed.
69 H5 Svetlyy Yar Rus. Fed.
69 D2 Svetogorsk Rus. Fed.
54 E4 Svíahnúkar vol. Iceland
67 M4 Svilengrad Bulg.
67 K2 Svinecea Mare, Vârful mt Romania
68 C4 Svir Belarus
68 E2 Svir' r. Rus. Fed.
67 L3 Svishtov Bulg.
62 H6 Svitava r. Czech Rep.
62 H6 Svitavy Czech Rep.
69 E5 Svitlovods'k Ukr.
68 J4 Sviyaga r. Rus. Fed.
87 N1 Svobodnyy Rus. Fed.
54 O2 Svolvær Norway
67 K3 Svrljiške Planine mts Yugo.
69 D4 Svyetlahorsk Belarus
59 F5 Swadlincote U.K.
59 H5 Swaffham U.K.
116 E3 Swain Reefs rf Austr.
29 D5 Swainsboro U.S.A.
103 B6 Swakopmund Namibia
58 F3 Swale r. U.K.
111 G3 Swallow Is is Solomon Is
21 J4 Swan r. Can.
59 F7 Swanage U.K.
114 E5 Swan Hill Austr.
20 F4 Swan Hills Can.
37 H5 Swan Islands is Honduras
21 J4 Swan L. l. Can.
59 H6 Swanley U.K.
114 C5 Swan Reach Austr.
21 J4 Swan River Can.
115 J4 Swansea N.S.W. Austr.
115 H9 Swansea Tas. Austr.
59 D6 Swansea U.K.
59 D6 Swansea Bay b. U.K.
33 J2 Swans I. i. U.S.A.
33 G2 Swanton U.S.A.
105 G2 Swartruggens S. Africa
35 F2 Swasey Peak summit U.S.A.
31 G1 Swastika Can.
84 B2 Swat r. Pak.
Swatow see Shantou
96 Swaziland country Africa
48 Sweden country Europe
24 B2 Sweet Home U.S.A.
29 C5 Sweetwater TN U.S.A.
27 C5 Sweetwater TX U.S.A.
24 E3 Sweetwater r. U.S.A.
104 D7 Swellendam S. Africa
62 H5 Świdnica Pol.
62 G4 Świdwin Pol.
62 G4 Świebodzin Pol.
63 J4 Świecie Pol.
33 H2 Swift r. U.S.A.
21 H4 Swift Current Can.
21 H5 Swiftcurrent Cr. r. Can.
20 C2 Swift River Can.
60 D2 Swilly, Lough in. Rep. of Ireland
59 F6 Swindon U.K.
60 C4 Swinford Rep. of Ireland
62 G4 Świnoujście Pol.
57 F5 Swinton U.K.
48 Switzerland country Europe
60 E4 Swords Rep. of Ireland
90 D1 Syain Rus. Fed.
68 D2 Syamozero, Oz. l. Rus. Fed.
68 G2 Syamzha Rus. Fed.
63 O3 Syanno Belarus
68 H3 Syava Rus. Fed.
30 C5 Sycamore U.S.A.
115 J4 Sydney Austr.
23 H4 Sydney Can.
21 L4 Sydney Mt. mt Can.
23 H4 Sydney Mines Can.
69 F5 Syeverodonets'k Ukr.
68 J2 Syktyvkar Rus. Fed.
29 C5 Sylacauga U.S.A.
54 N5 Sylarna mt Norway/Sweden
85 G4 Sylhet Bangl.
62 D3 Sylt i. Ger.
29 D5 Sylvania GA U.S.A.
32 A4 Sylvania OH U.S.A.
20 G4 Sylvan Lake Can.
29 D6 Sylvester U.S.A.

20 E3 Sylvia, Mt mt Can.
67 M6 Symi i. Greece
69 E5 Synel'nykove Ukr.
119 D4 Syowa Japan Base Antarctica
66 F6 Syracuse Italy
26 C4 Syracuse KS U.S.A.
33 E3 Syracuse NY U.S.A.
82 C2 Syrdar'ya r. Kazak.
70 Syria country Asia
83 J7 Syriam Myanmar
78 D3 Syrian Desert des. Asia
67 M6 Syrna i. Greece
67 L6 Syros i. Greece
55 T6 Sysmä Fin.
68 J2 Sysola r. Rus. Fed.
68 J4 Syzran' Rus. Fed.
62 H4 Szczecin Pol.
62 H4 Szczecinek Pol.
63 K4 Szczytno Pol.
63 K7 Szeged Hungary
63 J7 Székesfehérvár Hungary
63 J7 Szekszárd Hungary
63 K7 Szentes Hungary
62 H7 Szentgotthárd Hungary
66 G1 Szigetvár Hungary
63 K7 Szolnok Hungary
62 H7 Szombathely Hungary

T

94 B3 Taal, L. l. Phil.
94 B3 Tabaco Phil.
105 H5 Tabankulu S. Africa
80 C4 Ţabaqah Syria
110 F2 Tabar Is is P.N.G.
80 E4 Tabarja Lebanon
66 C6 Tabarka Tunisia
79 H3 Ţabas Iran
42 E4 Tabatinga Col.
94 B2 Tabayoo, Mt mt Phil.
115 F5 Tabbita Austr.
100 B2 Tabelbala Alg.
21 G5 Taber Can.
85 F3 Tabia Tsaka salt l. China
111 H2 Tabiteuea i. Kiribati
55 U7 Tabivere Estonia
94 B3 Tablas i. Phil.
94 B3 Tablas Strait chan. Phil.
117 F3 Table Cape c. N.Z.
27 E4 Table Rock Res. resr U.S.A.
116 A2 Tabletop, Mount h. Austr.
46 A2 Tabocó r. Brazil
62 G6 Tábor Czech Rep.
102 D4 Tabora Tanz.
100 B4 Tabou Côte d'Ivoire
81 L2 Tabrīz Iran
78 D4 Tabūk Saudi Arabia
115 K2 Tabulam Austr.
111 J3 Tabwémasana, Mount mt Vanuatu
55 Q7 Täby Sweden
45 A2 Tacarcuna, Cerro mt Panama
82 F1 Tacheng China
62 F6 Tachov Czech Rep.
94 C4 Tacloban Phil.
42 D7 Tacna Peru
24 B2 Tacoma U.S.A.
47 F1 Tacuarembó Uru.
47 G2 Tacuarí r. Uru.
25 E6 Tacupeto Mex.
45 E4 Tacutu r. Brazil
58 F4 Tadcaster U.K.
100 C2 Tademaït, Plateau du plat. Alg.
111 G4 Tadine New Caledonia
102 E2 Tadjoura Djibouti
80 G4 Tadmur Syria
21 K3 Tadoule Lake l. Can.
23 G4 Tadoussac Can.
87 N4 Taegu S. Korea
87 N4 Taejôn S. Korea
91 A6 T'aepaek S. Korea
59 C6 Taf r. U.K.
111 J3 Tafahi i. Tonga
65 F1 Tafalla Spain
100 B4 Tafiré Côte d'Ivoire
44 C3 Tafí Viejo Arg.
34 C4 Taft U.S.A.
69 F6 Taganrog Rus. Fed.
69 F6 Taganrog, Gulf of b. Rus. Fed./Ukr.
94 C3 Tagapula i. Phil.
94 B3 Tagaytay City Phil.
94 B4 Tagbilaran Phil.
85 E2 Tagchagpu Ri mt China
60 E5 Taghmon Rep. of Ireland
66 E1 Tagliamento r. Italy
65 J4 Tagma, Col de pass Alg.
94 C4 Tagoloan r. Phil.
94 B4 Tagolo Point pt Phil.
111 F3 Tagula I. i. P.N.G.
94 C5 Tagum Phil.
65 B3 Tagus r. Port./Spain
20 F4 Tahaetkun Mt. mt Can.
95 B4 Tahan, Gunung mt Malaysia
100 C2 Tahat, Mt mt Alg.
47 F2 Tala Uru.
87 M1 Tahe China
117 D1 Taheke N.Z.
27 E5 Tahlequah U.S.A.
34 B2 Tahoe, Lake l. U.S.A.
34 B2 Tahoe City U.S.A.
27 C5 Tahoka U.S.A.
100 C3 Tahoua Niger
20 D4 Tahtsa Pk summit Can.
94 C6 Tahuna Indon.

100 B4 Taï, Parc National de nat. park Côte d'Ivoire
89 □ Tai A Chau i. China
88 E2 Tai'an China
88 C3 Taibai Shan mt China
Taibus Qi see Baochang
89 F5 T'aichung Taiwan
117 C6 Taieri r. N.Z.
88 D2 Taigu China
88 D2 Taihang Shan mts China
88 D2 Taihang Shan mts China
117 E3 Taihape N.Z.
88 E3 Taihe Anhui China
88 E5 Taihe Jiangxi China
89 □ Tai Ho Wan China
89 E4 Taihu China
87 M5 Tai Hu l. China
89 C5 Taijiang China
88 E3 Taikang China
114 C5 Tailem Bend Austr.
89 □ Tai Long Wan b. China
89 F5 T'ailuko Taiwan
89 □ Tai Mo Shan h. China
57 D1 Tain U.K.
89 F6 T'ainan Taiwan
89 F6 T'ainan Taiwan
67 K6 Tainaro, Akra pt Greece
89 E5 Taining China
89 □ Tai O China
89 □ Tai Pak Wan b. China
89 □ Tai Pang Wan b. China
89 F5 T'aipei Taiwan
89 D6 Taiping China
92 C6 Taiping Malaysia
88 A2 Taipingpu China
89 □ Tai Po China
89 □ Tai Po Hoi b. China
90 H3 Taisetsu-zan National Park Japan
91 C7 Taisha Japan
89 C7 Taishan China
89 E5 Taishun China
89 □ Tai Siu Mo To is China
117 D5 Taitanu N.Z.
44 B7 Taitao, Península de pen. Chile
89 □ Tai Tung Shan h. China
54 V4 Taivalkoski Fin.
54 T2 Taivaskero h. Fin.
89 F5 T'aitung Taiwan
89 □ Taiwan country Asia
89 F5 Taiwan Shan mts Taiwan
89 F5 Taiwan Strait str. China/Taiwan
88 F3 Taixing China
88 D2 Taiyuan China
88 D2 Taiyue Shan mts China
88 F3 Taizhou China
89 E4 Taizhou China
89 F4 Taizhou Wan b. China
78 E7 Ta'izz Yemen
84 B3 Tajamulco, Volcán de vol. Guatemala
36 F5 Tajamulco, Volcán de vol. Guatemala
66 C7 Tajerouine Tunisia
70 Tajikistan country Asia
25 D6 Tajitos Mex.
Tajo r. see Tagus
95 A1 Tak Thai.
81 L3 Takāb Iran
91 C7 Takahashi Japan
117 B7 Takaka N.Z.
84 D5 Takal India
91 E6 Takamatsu Japan
91 E6 Takaoka Japan
117 F4 Takapau N.Z.
117 E2 Takapuna N.Z.
91 F6 Takasaki Japan
91 F6 Takayama Japan
95 B4 Tak Bai Thai.
91 E7 Takefu Japan
91 B8 Takeo see Liancourt Rocks
91 B9 Take-shima i. Japan
81 M3 Takestän Iran
91 B8 Taketa Japan
95 C3 Takêv Cambodia
81 K7 Takhādīd w. Iraq
95 C3 Ta Khmau Cambodia
81 M5 Takht Apān, Küh-e mt Iran
84 B3 Takht-i-Sulaiman mt Pak.
21 G1 Takijuq Lake l. Can.
90 D3 Takikawa Japan
90 H2 Takinoue Japan
117 A6 Takitimu Mts mts N.Z.
20 D3 Takla Landing Can.
74 Taklimakan Desert des. China
Taklimakan Shamo des. see Taklimakan Desert
85 H3 Takpa Shiri mt China
95 A3 Takua Pa Thai.
100 C4 Takum Nigeria
68 D4 Talachyn Belarus
79 L3 Talagang Pak.
84 D5 Talaja India
42 B4 Talara Peru
93 H6 Talaud, Kepulauan is Indon.
65 D3 Talavera de la Reina Spain
77 R3 Talaya Rus. Fed.

94 C5 Talayan Phil.
115 H4 Talbragar r. Austr.
47 B2 Talca Chile
47 B3 Talcahuano Chile
85 F5 Talcher India
82 E2 Taldykorgan Kazak.
81 M5 Taleh Zang Iran
81 M3 Tälesh Iran
59 D6 Talgarth U.K.
114 A4 Taliabu i. Indon.
93 G7 Taliabu i. Indon.
94 C4 Talibon Phil.
81 J1 T'alin Armenia
94 B4 Talisay Phil.
94 C4 Talisayan Phil.
81 M2 Talış Dağları mts Azer./Iran
68 H3 Talitsa Rus. Fed.
92 F8 Taliwang Indon.
29 C5 Talladega U.S.A.
81 J3 Tall 'Afar Iraq
29 C6 Tallahassee U.S.A.
115 G6 Tallangatta Austr.
29 C5 Tallassee U.S.A.
81 H3 Tall Baydar Syria
55 T7 Tallinn Estonia
80 F4 Tall Kalakh Syria
81 J3 Tall Kayf Iraq
81 J3 Tall Küjik Syria
60 C5 Tallow Rep. of Ireland
27 F5 Tallulah U.S.A.
81 J3 Tall 'Uwaynāt Iraq
64 D3 Talmont-St-Hilaire France
69 D5 Tal'ne Ukr.
101 F3 Talodi Sudan
23 G2 Talon, Lac l. Can.
84 B1 Tāloqān Afgh.
69 G5 Talovaya Rus. Fed.
84 C2 Tal Pass pass Pak.
58 S8 Talsi Latvia
44 B3 Taltal Chile
21 G2 Taltson r. Can.
81 M4 Talvār, Rūdkhāneh-ye r. Iran
54 S1 Talvik Norway
115 H2 Talwood Austr.
69 G5 Taly Rus. Fed.
114 E4 Talyawalka r. Austr.
30 A4 Tama U.S.A.
45 B2 Tamalameque Col.
100 B4 Tamale Ghana
45 A3 Tamana mt Col.
111 H2 Tamana i. Kiribati
91 C7 Tamano Japan
100 C2 Tamanrasset Alg.
85 H4 Tamanthi Myanmar
33 F4 Tamaqua U.S.A.
59 C7 Tamar r. U.K.
105 G1 Tamasane Botswana
27 D7 Tamaulipas div. Mex.
36 E4 Tamazunchale Mex.
102 D3 Tambacounda Senegal
84 Tamba Kosi r. Nepal
92 D6 Tambelan, Kepulauan is Indon.
94 A5 Tambisan Malaysia
116 B5 Tambo Austr.
115 G6 Tambo r. Austr.
115 G6 Tamboritha mt Austr.
68 G4 Tambov Rus. Fed.
68 G4 Tambovskaya Oblast' div. Rus. Fed.
65 B1 Tambre r. Spain
94 A5 Tambunan, Bukit h. Malaysia
101 F4 Tambura Sudan
94 A5 Tambuyukon, Gunung mt Malaysia
100 A3 Tâmchekkeţ Maur.
45 C2 Tame Col.
65 C2 Tâmega r. Port.
85 H4 Tamenglong India
66 B7 Tamerza Tunisia
84 D5 Tamia India
36 E4 Tamiahua, Lag. de lag. Mex.
95 A4 Tamiang, Ujung pt Indon.
83 E8 Tamil Nadu div. India
68 F1 Tamitsa Rus. Fed.
80 C7 Tâmîya Egypt
95 D2 Tam Ky Vietnam
29 D7 Tampa Fla. U.S.A.
29 D7 Tampa Bay b. U.S.A.
55 T6 Tampere Fin.
36 E4 Tampico Mex.
95 □ Tampines Sing.
87 L2 Tamsagbulag Mongolia
88 B1 Tamsag Muchang China
62 F7 Tamsweg Austria
85 F4 Tamu Myanmar
85 F4 Tamur r. Nepal
115 J3 Tamworth Austr.
59 F5 Tamworth U.K.
102 D4 Tana r. Kenya
102 D2 Tana, Lake l. Eth.
91 D8 Tanabe Japan
54 V1 Tana Bru Norway
54 V1 Tanafjorden chan. Norway
92 □ Tanah, Tanjung pt Indon.
T'ana Hāyk' l. see Tana, Lake
93 G8 Tanahjampea i. Indon.
94 A6 Tanahmerah Indon.
95 B4 Tanah Merah Malaysia
112 F3 Tanami Desert des. Austr.
95 C3 Tân An Vietnam
66 C2 Tanaro r. Italy
94 C4 Tanauan Phil.
88 F3 Tancheng China
90 A4 Tanch'ŏn N. Korea
100 B4 Tanda Côte d'Ivoire

85 E4 Tanda India
94 C4 Tandag Phil.
67 M2 Tăndărei Romania
94 A5 Tandek Malaysia
84 D2 Tandi India
47 E3 Tandil Arg.
47 E3 Tandil, Sa del h. Arg.
84 B4 Tando Adam Pak.
84 B4 Tando Bago Pak.
114 E4 Tandou L. l. Austr.
60 E3 Tandragee U.K.
83 E7 Tandur India
117 F3 Taneatua N.Z.
91 B9 Tanega-shima i. Japan
95 A1 Tanen Taunggyi mts Thai.
32 E5 Taneytown U.S.A.
100 B2 Tanezrouft reg. Alg./Mali
102 D4 Tanga Tanz.
117 E2 Tangaehe N.Z.
85 G4 Tangail Bangl.
111 F2 Tanga Is is P.N.G.
102 C4 Tanganyika, Lake l. Africa
89 B5 Tangdan China
Tanger see Tangier
92 □ Tangerang Indon.
88 B3 Tanggor China
85 G3 Tanggula Shan mts China
85 G2 Tanggula Shankou pass China
88 D3 Tanghe China
84 B2 Tangi Pak.
100 B1 Tangier Morocco
33 E6 Tangier I. i. U.S.A.
85 G4 Tangla India
95 □ Tanglin Sing.
85 H3 Tangmai China
85 F3 Tangra Yumco salt l. China
88 F2 Tangshan China
94 B4 Tangub Phil.
100 C3 Tanguieta Benin
90 A1 Tangwang r. China
89 □ Tangyan He r. China
88 E3 Tangyin China
90 A1 Tangyuan China
54 U3 Tanhua Fin.
95 C3 Tani Cambodia
85 H3 Taniantaweng Shan mts China
93 J8 Tanimbar, Kepulauan is Indon.
94 B3 Tanjay Phil.
95 A5 Tanjungbalai Indon.
92 D8 Tanjungkarang-Telukbetung Indon.
92 D7 Tanjungpandan Indon.
92 C6 Tanjungpinang Indon.
95 A5 Tanjungpura Indon.
93 F6 Tanjungredeb Indon.
93 F6 Tanjungselor Indon.
84 B2 Tank Pak.
84 D2 Tankse Jammu and Kashmir
85 F4 Tankuhi India
111 J3 Tanna i. Vanuatu
57 F4 Tannadice U.K.
55 N5 Tännäs Sweden
116 D4 Tannum Sands Austr.
86 F1 Tannu-Ola, Khrebet mts Rus. Fed.
84 B4 Tanot India
100 C3 Tanout Niger
85 E4 Tansen Nepal
89 F5 Tanshui Taiwan
78 C2 Tanta Egypt
100 A2 Tan-Tan Morocco
114 D6 Tantanoola Austr.
36 E4 Tantoyuca Mex.
55 M7 Tanumshede Sweden
114 C5 Tanunda Austr.
91 A6 Tanyang S. Korea
96 Tanzania country Africa
95 A3 Tao, Ko i. Thai.
88 B3 Tao He r. China
89 D2 Taojiang China
88 C2 Taole China
87 M2 Taonan China
95 □ Tao Payoh Sing.
66 F6 Taormina Italy
25 F4 Taos U.S.A.
100 B2 Taoudenni Mali
100 B1 Taourirt Morocco
89 F5 Taoxi China
89 D4 Taoyuan China
89 F5 T'aoyüan Taiwan
55 T7 Tapa Estonia
94 □ Tapaan Passage chan. Phil.
36 F6 Tapachula Mex.
43 G4 Tapajós r. Brazil
95 A5 Tapaktuan Indon.
44 C4 Tapalqué Arg.
95 A5 Tapanuli, Teluk b. Indon.
42 F5 Tapauá Brazil
42 F5 Tapauá r. Brazil
100 B4 Tapeta Liberia
84 C5 Tāpi r. India
94 B5 Tapiantana i. Phil.
30 C2 Tapiola U.S.A.
95 A5 Tapis mt Malaysia
85 F4 Taplejung Nepal
89 □ Tap Mun Chau i. China
32 E6 Tappahannock U.S.A.
32 C4 Tappan Lake l. U.S.A.
117 D4 Tapuaenuku mt N.Z.
94 B5 Tapul Phil.
94 B5 Tapul Group is Phil.
45 D5 Tapurucuara Brazil
81 K4 Ţāqtaq Iraq
46 B1 Taquaral, Serra do h. Brazil
46 B2 Taquari Brazil

43 G7 Taquarí r. Brazil
46 A2 Taquarí, Serra do h. Brazil
46 C3 Taquaritinga Brazil
46 B3 Taquaruçu r. Brazil
60 D5 Tar r. Rep. of Ireland
115 J1 Tara Austr.
60 E4 Tara, Hill of h. Rep. of Ireland
100 D4 Taraba r. Nigeria
42 E7 Tarabuco Bol.
Ţarābulus see Tripoli
45 C4 Taracua Brazil
84 B4 Tar Ahmad Rind Pak.
84 E4 Tarahuwan India
85 G4 Tarai reg. India
93 F6 Tarakan Indon.
94 A6 Tarakan i. Indon.
80 C1 Taraklı Turkey
115 H5 Taralga Austr.
63 J3 Taran, Mys pt Rus. Fed.
115 H4 Tarana Austr.
84 D5 Tarana India
84 C3 Tārānagar India
117 E3 Taranaki, Mt vol. N.Z.
65 E2 Tarancón Spain
57 A3 Taransay i. U.K.
66 G4 Taranto Italy
66 G4 Taranto, Golfo di g. Italy
42 C5 Tarapoto Peru
117 E4 Tararua Range mts N.Z.
63 P6 Tarashcha Ukr.
42 D5 Tarauacá Brazil
42 E5 Tarauacá r. Brazil
117 F3 Tarawera N.Z.
117 F3 Tarawera, Mt mt N.Z.
82 D2 Taraz Kazak.
65 F2 Tarazona Spain
65 F3 Tarazona de la Mancha Spain
82 F1 Tarbagatay, Khrebet mts Kazak.
57 E3 Tarbat Ness pt U.K.
84 C2 Tarbela Dam dam Pak.
60 B5 Tarbert Rep. of Ireland
57 B3 Tarbert Scot. U.K.
57 C5 Tarbert Scot. U.K.
64 E5 Tarbes France
29 E5 Tarboro U.S.A.
114 A3 Tarcoola Austr.
115 G3 Tarcoon Austr.
115 G5 Tarcutta Austr.
87 P2 Tardoki-Yani, Gora mt Rus. Fed.
115 K3 Taree Austr.
114 E3 Tarella Austr.
76 L2 Tareya Rus. Fed.
24 E2 Targhee Pass pass U.S.A.
67 L2 Târgovişte Romania
67 K2 Târgu Jiu Romania
63 M7 Târgu Mureş Romania
63 N7 Târgu Neamţ Romania
63 N7 Târgu Secuiesc Romania
81 L5 Tarhān Iran
93 L8 Tari P.N.G.
88 C2 Tarian Gol China
65 D4 Tarifa Spain
42 F8 Tarija Bol.
93 K7 Tariku r. Indon.
79 F6 Tarīm Yemen
Tarim Basin basin see Tarim Pendi
82 F3 Tarim Pendi basin China
93 K7 Taritatu r. Indon.
81 K4 Tarjīl Iraq
105 F6 Tarka r. S. Africa
105 G6 Tarkastad S. Africa
26 E3 Tarkio U.S.A.
76 J3 Tarko-Sale Rus. Fed.
100 B4 Tarkwa Ghana
94 B3 Tarlac Phil.
64 F4 Tarn r. France
54 O4 Tärnaby Sweden
84 A3 Tarnak r. Afgh.
63 M7 Târnăveni Romania
63 K5 Tarnobrzeg Pol.
68 G2 Tarnogskiy Gorodok Rus. Fed.
63 K5 Tarnów Pol.
85 E3 Taro Co salt l. China
116 C5 Taroom Austr.
100 B1 Taroudannt Morocco
114 D6 Tarpeena Austr.
29 E7 Tarpum Bay Bahamas
66 D3 Tarquinia Italy
65 G2 Tarragona Spain
54 Q3 Tårrajaur Sweden
115 G9 Tarraleah Austr.
115 G4 Tarran Hills h. Austr.
117 B6 Tarras N.Z.
65 G2 Tàrrega Spain
80 E3 Tarsus Turkey
44 D2 Tartagal Arg.
81 L1 Tärtär Azer.
81 L1 Tärtär r. Azer.
64 D5 Tartas France
55 U7 Tartu Estonia
80 E4 Ţarţūs Syria
46 E2 Tarumirim Brazil
69 H6 Tarumovka Rus. Fed.
95 A5 Tarutung Indon.
66 E1 Tarvisio Italy
22 E4 Taschereau Can.
Tashio Chho see Thimphu
81 K1 Tashir Armenia
79 G3 Tashk, Daryācheh-ye salt pan Iran
79 K1 Tashkent Uzbek.
82 D2 Tash-Kömür Kyrgyzstan
22 F2 Tasiat, Lac l. Can.
92 □ Tasikmalaya Indon.
23 G2 Tasiujaq Can.
82 F1 Taskesken Kazak.
80 E1 Taşköprü Turkey
81 J2 Taşlıçay Turkey
14 F8 Tasman Basin sea feature Pac. Oc.
117 D4 Tasman Bay b. N.Z.
115 G9 Tasman Head hd Austr.
115 F9 Tasmania div. Austr.
117 D4 Tasman Mountains mts N.Z.
115 H9 Tasman Pen. pen. Austr.
14 E9 Tasman Plateau sea feature Pac. Oc.
111 F5 Tasman Sea sea Pac. Oc.
80 F1 Taşova Turkey
34 B3 Tassajara Hot Springs U.S.A.
23 F2 Tassialujjuaq, Lac l. Can.
100 C2 Tassili du Hoggar plat. Alg.
100 C2 Tassili n'Ajjer plat. Alg.
81 K2 Tasūj Iran
77 N3 Tas-Yuryakh Rus. Fed.
93 G7 Tataba Indon.
63 J7 Tatabánya Hungary
69 D6 Tatarbunary Ukr.
76 J4 Tatarsk Rus. Fed.
87 Q1 Tatarskiy Proliv str. Rus. Fed.
68 J4 Tatarstan, Respublika div. Rus. Fed.
81 K3 Tatavi r. Iran
116 A1 Tate r. Austr.
91 F7 Tateyama Japan
91 E6 Tate-yama vol. Japan
20 F2 Tathlina Lake l. Can.
78 E5 Tathlīth, W. watercourse Saudi Arabia
115 H6 Tathra Austr.
21 K2 Tatinnai Lake l. Can.
69 H5 Tatishchevo Rus. Fed.
24 A1 Tatla Lake Can.
20 D3 Tatlatui Prov. Park res. Can.
93 H8 Tat Mailau, G. mt Indon.
115 G6 Tatong Austr.
63 J6 Tatry reg. Pol.
20 B3 Tatshenshini r. Can.
69 G5 Tatsinskiy Rus. Fed.
91 D7 Tatsuno Japan
84 A4 Tatta Pak.
46 C3 Tatuí Brazil
20 E4 Tatuk Mtn mt Can.
27 C5 Tatum U.S.A.
114 F6 Tatura Austr.
81 J2 Tatvan Turkey
55 J7 Tau Norway
43 K5 Taua Brazil
46 D3 Taubaté Brazil
104 F3 Taung S. Africa
83 J6 Taunggyi Myanmar
95 A2 Taungnyo Range mts Myanmar
84 B3 Taunsa Barrage barrage Pak.
59 D6 Taunton U.K.
33 H4 Taunton U.S.A.
117 F3 Taupo N.Z.
117 E3 Taupo, Lake l. N.Z.
55 S9 Tauragė Lith.
117 F2 Tauranga N.Z.
66 G5 Taurianova Italy
117 D1 Tauroa Pt pt N.Z.
Taurus Mountains mts see Toros Dağları
111 F2 Tauu Islands is P.N.G.
80 B3 Tavas Turkey
59 J5 Taverham U.K.
65 C4 Tavira Port.
59 C7 Tavistock U.K.
95 A2 Tavoy Myanmar
95 A2 Tavoy Pt pt Myanmar
90 B3 Tavrichanka Rus. Fed.
80 B2 Tavşanlı Turkey
59 C6 Taw r. U.K.
31 F3 Tawas Bay b. U.S.A.
31 F3 Tawas City U.S.A.
94 A5 Tawau Malaysia
59 D6 Tawe r. U.K.
42 C2 Tawi r. India
94 A5 Tawitawi i. Phil.
89 F6 Tawu Taiwan
36 E5 Taxco Mex.
82 E3 Taxkorgan China
20 C2 Tay r. Can.
57 E4 Tay r. U.K.
57 E4 Tay, Firth of est. U.K.
57 D4 Tay, Loch l. U.K.
94 B3 Tayabas Bay b. Phil.
54 X2 Taybola Rus. Fed.
57 C5 Tayinloan U.K.
20 E3 Taylor Can.
35 G4 Taylor AZ U.S.A.
31 F4 Taylor MI U.S.A.
30 B6 Taylor MO U.S.A.
26 D3 Taylor NE U.S.A.
27 D6 Taylor TX U.S.A.
33 E5 Taylors Island U.S.A.
28 B4 Taylorville U.S.A.
78 D4 Taymā' Saudi Arabia
77 L3 Taymura r. Rus. Fed.
77 M2 Taymyr, Ozero l. Rus. Fed.
77 L2 Taymyr, Poluostrov pen. Rus. Fed.
95 C3 Tây Ninh Vietnam
94 A4 Taytay Phil.
94 B3 Taytay Phil.
94 A4 Taytay Bay b. Phil.
92 □ Tayu Indon.
77 K2 Taz r. Rus. Fed.
100 B1 Taza Morocco
81 K4 Tāza Khurmātū Iraq
81 L2 Tazeh Kand Azer.
32 B6 Tazewell TN U.S.A.
32 C6 Tazewell VA U.S.A.
21 H2 Tazin r. Can.
21 H3 Tazin Lake l. Can.
101 E2 Tāzirbū Libya
65 J4 Tazmalt Alg.
76 J3 Tazovskaya Guba chan. Rus. Fed.
69 H7 T'bilisi Georgia
69 G6 Tbilisskaya Rus. Fed.
102 B4 Tchibanga Gabon
101 D2 Tchigaï, Plateau du plat. Niger
101 D4 Tcholliré Cameroon
63 J3 Tczew Pol.
117 A6 Te Anau N.Z.
117 A6 Te Anau, L. l. N.Z.
36 F5 Teapa Mex.
117 G2 Te Araroa N.Z.
117 E2 Te Aroha N.Z.
117 E3 Te Awamutu N.Z.
58 E3 Tebay U.K.
21 K2 Tebesjuak Lake l. Can.
100 C1 Tébessa Alg.
66 B7 Tébessa, Monts de mts Alg.
44 E3 Tebicuary r. Para.
92 C7 Tebingtinggi Indon.
92 B6 Tebingtinggi Indon.
66 C6 Tébourba Tunisia
66 C6 Téboursouk Tunisia
69 H7 Tebulos Mt'a mt Georgia/Rus. Fed.
34 D5 Tecate Mex.
100 B4 Techiman Ghana
44 B6 Tecka Arg.
61 F2 Tecklenburger Land reg. Ger.
36 D5 Tecomán Mex.
34 D4 Tecopa U.S.A.
25 E6 Tecoripa Mex.
63 N7 Tecuci Romania
31 F5 Tecumseh U.S.A.
79 J2 Tedzhen Turkm.
35 H3 Teec Nos Pos U.S.A.
86 F1 Teeli Rus. Fed.
58 F3 Tees r. U.K.
58 E3 Teesdale reg. U.K.
42 E4 Tefé r. Brazil
80 B3 Tefenni Turkey
92 □ Tegal Indon.
59 D5 Tegid, Llyn l. U.K.
36 G6 Tegucigalpa Honduras
100 C3 Teguidda-n-Tessoumt Niger
34 C4 Tehachapi U.S.A.
25 C5 Tehachapi Mts mts U.S.A.
34 C4 Tehachapi Pass pass U.S.A.
21 K2 Tehek Lake l. Can.
Teheran see Tehrān
100 B4 Téhini Côte d'Ivoire
79 G2 Tehrān Iran
84 D3 Tehri India
Tehri see Tikamgarh
36 F5 Tehuantepec, Golfo de g. Mex.
36 F5 Tehuantepec, Istmo de isth. Mex.
59 C5 Teifi r. U.K.
59 D7 Teign r. U.K.
59 D7 Teignmouth U.K.
Tejo r. see Tagus
34 C4 Tejon Pass pass U.S.A.
117 D1 Te Kao N.Z.
117 C5 Tekapo, L. l. N.Z.
85 F4 Tekari India
36 G4 Tekax Mex.
102 D2 Tekezē Wenz r. Eritrea/Eth.
84 E1 Tekiliktag mt China
80 A1 Tekirdağ Turkey
81 H2 Tekman Turkey
85 H5 Teknaf Bangl.
30 E4 Tekonsha U.S.A.
117 E3 Te Kuiti N.Z.
85 E5 Tel r. India
69 H7 T'elavi Georgia
80 E5 Tel Aviv-Yafo Israel
62 G6 Telč Czech Rep.
36 G4 Telchac Puerto Mex.
20 C3 Telegraph Creek Can.
46 B4 Telêmaco Borba Brazil
47 D3 Telén Arg.
67 L2 Teleorman r. Romania
34 D3 Telescope Peak summit U.S.A.
43 G5 Teles Pires r. Brazil
59 E5 Telford U.K.
100 A3 Télimélé Guinea
20 D4 Telkwa Can.
77 V3 Teller Alaska
81 L6 Telloh Iraq
95 □ Telok Blangah Sing.
47 C4 Telsen Arg.
55 S9 Telšiai Lith.
95 B4 Teluk Anson Malaysia
31 H2 Temagami Can.
31 G2 Temagami Lake l. Can.
92 □ Temanggung Indon.
105 H2 Temba S. Africa
77 L3 Tembenchi r. Rus. Fed.
105 H3 Tembisa S. Africa
102 B4 Tembo Aluma Angola
59 E5 Teme r. U.K.
34 D5 Temecula U.S.A.
80 D2 Temelli Turkey
92 C6 Temerloh Malaysia
81 M5 Temīleh Iran
86 B1 Temirtau Kazak.
31 H2 Temiscaming Can.
31 H2 Témiscamingue, Lac l. Can.
23 G4 Témiscouata, L. l. Can.
115 F8 Temma Austr.
54 T4 Temmes Fin.
68 G4 Temnikov Rus. Fed.
115 G5 Temora Austr.
25 F6 Temósachic Mex.
35 G5 Tempe U.S.A.
66 C4 Tempio Pausania Italy
30 E3 Temple MI U.S.A.
27 D6 Temple TX U.S.A.
59 C5 Temple Bar U.K.
60 D5 Templemore Rep. of Ireland
94 A4 Templer Bank sand bank Phil.
58 E3 Temple Sowerby U.K.
69 F6 Temryuk Rus. Fed.
47 B3 Temuco Chile
117 C6 Temuka N.Z.
42 C4 Tena Ecuador
34 D1 Tenabo, Mt mt U.S.A.
83 F7 Tenali India
95 A2 Tenasserim Myanmar
95 A2 Tenasserim r. Myanmar
59 E5 Tenbury Wells U.K.
59 C6 Tenby U.K.
31 F2 Tenby Bay Can.
102 E2 Tendaho Eth.
64 H4 Tende France
83 H9 Ten Degree Channel chan. Andaman and Nicobar Is
90 G5 Tendō Japan
81 J2 Tendürek Dağı mt Turkey
100 B3 Ténenkou Mali
100 D3 Ténéré reg. Niger
100 D2 Ténéré du Tafassâsset des. Niger
100 A2 Tenerife i. Canary Is
65 G4 Ténès Alg.
93 F8 Tengah, Kepulauan is Indon.
95 □ Tengeh Res. resr Sing.
88 B2 Tengger Shamo des. China
95 B4 Tenggul i. Malaysia
89 C7 Tengqiao China
100 B3 Tengréla Côte d'Ivoire
89 D6 Tengxian China
88 E3 Tengzhou China
119 B2 Teniente Jubany Arg. Base Antarctica
119 B2 Teniente Rodolfo Marsh Chile Base Antarctica
103 C5 Tenke Dem. Rep. Congo
77 Q2 Tenkeli Rus. Fed.
100 B3 Tenkodogo Burkina
113 F3 Tennant Creek Austr.
32 B6 Tennessee div. U.S.A.
29 C5 Tennessee r. U.S.A.
25 F4 Tennessee Pass pass U.S.A.
54 P2 Tennevoll Norway
47 B2 Teno r. Chile
54 U2 Tenojoki r. Fin./Norway
36 F5 Tenosique Mex.
24 F2 Ten Sleep U.S.A.
93 G7 Tenteno Indon.
59 H6 Tenterden U.K.
115 K2 Tenterfield Austr.
29 D7 Ten Thousand Islands is U.S.A.
65 C3 Tentudia mt Spain
46 B3 Teodoro Sampaio Brazil
46 E2 Teófilo Otôni Brazil
93 H8 Tepa Indon.
25 E6 Tepache Mex.
117 D1 Te Paki N.Z.
36 D4 Tepatitlán Mex.
81 H3 Tepe Turkey
81 J3 Tepe Gawra Iraq
36 C3 Tepehuanes Mex.
67 J4 Tepelenë Albania
45 E4 Tepequem, Serra mts Brazil
36 D4 Tepic Mex.
117 C5 Te Pirita N.Z.
62 F5 Teplice Czech Rep.
68 K2 Teplogorka Rus. Fed.
68 F4 Teploye Rus. Fed.
25 D6 Tepoca, Cabo c. Mex.
117 F2 Te Puke N.Z.
65 H1 Ter r. Spain
84 D2 Teram Kangri mt China/Jammu and Kashmir
66 E3 Teramo Italy
114 E7 Terang Austr.
84 B3 Teratani r. Pak.
69 F4 Terbuny Rus. Fed.
81 H2 Tercan Turkey
63 M6 Terebovlya Ukr.
69 H7 Terek Rus. Fed.
69 H7 Terek r. Rus. Fed.
68 J4 Teren'ga Rus. Fed.
46 A3 Terenos Brazil
45 C2 Terepaima, Parque Nacional nat. park Venez.
68 H4 Tereshka r. Rus. Fed.
43 K5 Teresina Brazil
46 D3 Teresópolis Brazil
61 B5 Tergnier France
80 F1 Terme Turkey
79 K2 Termez Uzbek.
66 E6 Termini Imerese Italy
36 F5 Términos, Lag. de b. Mex.
66 F4 Termoli Italy
59 E5 Tern r. U.K.
93 H6 Ternate Indon.
61 B3 Terneuzen Neth.
90 E2 Terney Rus. Fed.
66 E3 Terni Italy
69 C5 Ternopil' Ukr.
114 C4 Terowie Austr.
87 Q2 Terpeniya, Mys c. Rus. Fed.
87 Q2 Terpeniya, Zaliv g. Rus. Fed.
20 D4 Terrace Can.
30 D1 Terrace Bay Can.
104 E2 Terra Firma S. Africa
54 N4 Terråk Norway
66 C5 Terralba Italy
23 K4 Terra Nova Nat. Pk nat. park Can.
27 F6 Terrebonne Bay b. U.S.A.
28 C4 Terre Haute U.S.A.
23 K4 Terrenceville Can.
24 F2 Terry U.S.A.
69 G5 Tersa r. Rus. Fed.
61 D1 Terschelling i. Neth.
86 C3 Terskey Ala-Too mts Kyrgyzstan
66 C5 Tertenia Italy
65 F2 Teruel Spain
95 A4 Terutao i. Thai.
54 T3 Tervola Fin.
66 G2 Tešanj Bos.-Herz.
102 D2 Teseney Eritrea
68 G4 Tesha r. Rus. Fed.
90 J3 Teshikaga Japan
90 G2 Teshio Japan
90 H3 Teshio-dake mt Japan
90 G2 Teshio-gawa r. Japan
20 C2 Teslin Can.
20 C2 Teslin r. Can.
20 C2 Teslin Lake l. Can.
46 B1 Tesouras r. Brazil
46 B2 Tesouro Brazil
100 C3 Tessaoua Niger
59 F6 Test r. U.K.
66 C6 Testour Tunisia
44 B2 Tetas, Pta pt Chile
103 D5 Tete Moz.
117 F3 Te Teko N.Z.
63 P5 Teteriv r. Ukr.
62 F4 Teterow Ger.
63 O6 Tetiyiv Ukr.
58 G4 Tetney U.K.
24 E2 Teton r. U.S.A.
24 E3 Teton Ra. mts U.S.A.
100 B1 Tétouan Morocco
67 J3 Tetovo Macedonia
84 B5 Tetpur India
68 J4 Tetyushi Rus. Fed.
44 D2 Teuco r. Arg.
104 B1 Teufelsbach Namibia
90 G2 Teuri-tō i. Japan
55 R5 Teuva Fin.
Tevere r. see Tiber
Teverya see Tiberias
57 F5 Teviot r. U.K.
57 F5 Teviotdale v. U.K.
117 A7 Te Waewae Bay b. N.Z.
105 G1 Tewane Botswana
116 E6 Tewantin Austr.
117 E4 Te Wharau N.Z.
59 E6 Tewkesbury U.K.
88 B3 Têwo China
20 E5 Texada I. i. Can.
27 E5 Texarkana U.S.A.
115 J2 Texas Austr.
27 D6 Texas div. U.S.A.
27 E6 Texas City U.S.A.
61 C1 Texel i. Neth.
27 C4 Texhoma U.S.A.
27 D5 Texoma, Lake l. U.S.A.
105 G4 Teyateyaneng Lesotho
68 G3 Teykovo Rus. Fed.
68 G3 Teza r. Rus. Fed.
85 H4 Tezpur India
85 J4 Tezu India
21 K2 Tha-anne r. Can.
105 H4 Thabana-Ntlenyana mt Lesotho
105 G4 Thaba Nchu S. Africa
105 G4 Thaba Putsoa mt Lesotho
105 H4 Thaba-Tseka Lesotho
105 G2 Thabazimbi S. Africa
95 B1 Tha Bo Laos
105 G3 Thabong S. Africa
95 A2 Thagyettaw Myanmar
89 C6 Thai Binh Vietnam
70 Thailand country Asia
95 B3 Thailand, Gulf of g. Asia
95 A3 Thai Muang Thai.
89 B6 Thai Nguyên Vietnam
84 E5 Thakurtola India
84 B2 Thal Pak.
66 C7 Thala Tunisia
95 A3 Thalang Thai.
84 B3 Thal Desert des. Pak.
95 B4 Thale Luang lag. Thai.
95 B1 Tha Li Thai.
115 H2 Thallon Austr.
105 F2 Thamaga Botswana
78 F7 Thamar, J. mt Yemen
79 G6 Thamarīt Oman
59 G5 Thame r. U.K.
117 E2 Thames N.Z.
59 H6 Thames est. U.K.
59 G6 Thames r. U.K.
31 G4 Thamesville Can.
95 A2 Thanbyuzayat Myanmar
84 C5 Thandla India
83 D7 Thāne India
84 B5 Thangadh India
95 D2 Thăng Binh Vietnam
116 D5 Thangool Austr.
95 C1 Thanh Hoa Vietnam
83 E8 Thanjavur India
95 B1 Tha Pla Thai.
95 A3 Thap Put Thai.
95 A3 Thap Sakae Thai.
84 B4 Tharad India
84 B4 Thar Desert des. India/Pak.
114 E1 Thargomindah Austr.
83 J7 Tharrawaddy Myanmar
81 J5 Tharthār, Buḩayrat ath l. Iraq
81 J4 Tharthār, Wādī ath r. Iraq
67 L4 Thasos i. Greece
35 H5 Thatcher U.S.A.
89 C6 Thât Khê Vietnam
95 A1 Thaton Myanmar
85 H4 Thaungdut Myanmar
95 A1 Thaungyin r. Myanmar/Thai.
95 C1 Tha Uthen Thai.
117 F2 The Aldermen Islands is N.Z.
35 F5 Theba U.S.A.
16 Bahamas country Caribbean Sea
29 E7 The Bluff Bahamas
58 E2 The Cheviot h. U.K.
114 C5 The Coorong in. Austr.
24 B2 The Dalles U.S.A.
26 C3 Thedford U.S.A.
57 □ The Faither pt U.K.
59 G5 The Fens reg. U.K.
96 The Gambia country Africa
78 C5 The Great Oasis oasis Egypt
79 G4 The Gulf g. Asia
61 C2 The Hague Neth.
117 C6 The Hunters Hills h. N.Z.
95 A3 Theinkun Myanmar
117 A6 The Key N.Z.
21 H2 Thekulthili Lake l. Can.
21 J2 Thelon r. Can.
21 J2 Thelon Game Sanctuary res. Can.
116 A2 The Lynd Junction Austr.
104 F6 Thembalesizwe S. Africa
105 H3 Thembalihle S. Africa
57 C2 The Minch str. U.K.
59 F7 The Needles stack U.K.
65 H4 Thenia Alg.
65 H5 Theniet El Had Alg.
116 D5 Theodore Austr.
42 F5 Theodore Roosevelt r. Brazil
35 G5 Theodore Roosevelt Lake l. U.S.A.
26 C2 Theodore Roosevelt Nat. Park nat. park U.S.A.
60 B5 The Paps h. Rep. of Ireland
21 J4 The Pas Can.
115 H6 The Pilot mt Austr.
60 B6 The Pocket h. Rep. of Ireland
33 F2 Theresa U.S.A.
116 B4 Theresa Cr. r. Austr.
67 K4 Thermaïkos Kolpos g. Greece
34 B2 Thermalito U.S.A.
24 E3 Thermopolis U.S.A.
115 G5 The Rock Austr.
114 E3 The Salt Lake salt flat Austr.
59 F7 The Solent str. U.K.
31 F2 Thessalon Can.
67 K4 Thessaloniki Greece
57 B3 The Storr h. U.K.
59 H5 Thet r. U.K.
94 A4 The Teeth mt Phil.
59 H5 Thetford U.K.
23 F4 Thetford Mines Can.
57 D4 The Trossachs reg. U.K.
114 A2 The Twins Austr.
95 C1 Theun r. Laos
105 G4 Theunissen S. Africa
59 H5 The Wash b. U.K.
59 H6 The Weald reg. U.K.
27 F6 Thibodaux U.S.A.
21 K3 Thicket Portage Can.
26 D1 Thief River Falls U.S.A.
64 F4 Thiers France
100 A3 Thiès Senegal
102 D4 Thika Kenya
83 D9 Thiladhunmathee Atoll atoll Maldives
85 G4 Thimphu Bhutan
64 H2 Thionville France
Thira i. see Santorini
67 L6 Thirasia i. Greece
58 F3 Thirsk U.K.
Thiruvananthapuram see Trivandrum
55 L8 Thisted Denmark
114 B5 Thistle I. i. Austr.
67 K5 Thiva Greece
21 K2 Thlewiaza r. Can.
21 H2 Thoa r. Can.
95 B3 Thô Chu, Đao i. Vietnam
105 J1 Thohoyandou S. Africa
32 D5 Thomas U.S.A.
29 C5 Thomaston GA U.S.A.
33 J2 Thomaston ME U.S.A.
33 K2 Thomaston Corner Can.
60 D5 Thomastown Rep. of Ireland
29 D6 Thomasville U.S.A.
61 E4 Thommen Belgium
21 K3 Thompson Can.
20 E4 Thompson r. Can.
30 D3 Thompson MI U.S.A.
33 F4 Thompson PA U.S.A.
26 E3 Thompson r. U.S.A.
24 D2 Thompson Falls U.S.A.
116 A4 Thomson watercourse Austr.
29 D5 Thomson U.S.A.
95 C1 Thôn Cư Lai Vietnam
62 C7 Thonon-les-Bains France
95 D3 Thôn Sơn Hai Vietnam
25 E5 Thoreau U.S.A.
115 F2 Thorlindah, L. salt flat Austr.
61 D3 Thorn Neth.
58 F3 Thornaby-on-Tees U.K.
30 E4 Thornapple r. U.S.A.

59 E6 Thornbury U.K.
31 H2 Thorne Can.
58 G4 Thorne U.K.
34 C2 Thorne U.S.A.
20 C3 Thorne Bay U.S.A.
30 D5 Thorntown U.S.A.
30 B3 Thorp U.S.A.
119 D3 Thorshavnheiane mts Antarctica
105 G4 Thota-ea-Moli Lesotho
64 D3 Thouars France
33 E2 Thousand Islands is Can.
35 G2 Thousand Lake Mt mt U.S.A.
34 C4 Thousand Oaks U.S.A.
67 L4 Thrakiko Pelagos sea Greece
24 E2 Three Forks U.S.A.
20 G4 Three Hills Can.
115 F8 Three Hummock I. i. Austr.
117 D1 Three Kings Is is N.Z.
30 C3 Three Lakes U.S.A.
30 D5 Three Oaks U.S.A.
95 A2 Three Pagodas Pass pass Myanmar/Thai.
100 B4 Three Points, Cape
30 E5 Three Rivers MI U.S.A.
27 D6 Three Rivers TX U.S.A.
24 B2 Three Sisters mt U.S.A.
Thrissur see Trichur
27 D5 Throckmorton U.S.A.
21 G2 Thubun Lakes l. Can.
95 C3 Thu Dâu Môt Vietnam
61 C4 Thuin Belgium
103 C6 Thuli Zimbabwe
62 C7 Thun Switz.
30 C1 Thunder Bay Can.
30 C1 Thunder Bay b. Can.
31 F3 Thunder Mount Can.
95 A3 Thung Song Thai.
95 A4 Thung Wa Thai.
60 D3 Thurles Rep. of Ireland
32 E5 Thurmont U.S.A.
62 F7 Thurn, Paß pass Austria
33 F2 Thurso Can.
57 E2 Thurso U.K.
57 E2 Thurso r. U.K.
119 A3 Thurston I. i. Antarctica
58 E3 Thwaite U.K.
55 L8 Thyborøn Denmark
88 A1 Tiancang China
88 F3 Tianchang China
89 C6 Tiandeng China
89 C6 Tiandong China
89 C5 Tian'e China
43 K4 Tianguá Brazil
88 E2 Tianjin China
88 E2 Tianjin div. China
82 J3 Tianjun China
89 C5 Tianlin China
89 D4 Tianmen China
89 F4 Tianmu Shan mts China
90 A3 Tianqiaoling China
89 B4 Tianquan China
87 M3 Tianshan China
88 B3 Tianshui China
84 D2 Tianshuihai China/Jammu and Kashmir
89 F4 Tiantai China
88 E1 Tiantaiyong China
89 C6 Tianyang China
88 B2 Tianzhu Gansu China
89 C5 Tianzhu Guizhou China
100 C1 Tiaret Alg.
116 E5 Tiaro Austr.
100 B4 Tiassalé Côte d'Ivoire
46 B4 Tibagi r. Brazil
81 J5 Tibal, Wâdi watercourse Iraq
101 D4 Tibati Cameroon
66 E3 Tiber r. Italy
80 E5 Tiberias Israel
Tiberias, Lake l. see Galilee, Sea of
24 E1 Tiber Res. resr U.S.A.
101 D2 Tibesti mts Chad
Tibet, Plateau of plat. see Qing Zang Gaoyuan
Tibet Aut. Region div. see Xizang Zizhiqu
114 E2 Tibooburra Austr.
85 E3 Tibrikot Nepal
55 O7 Tibro Sweden
36 B3 Tiburón, Isla i. Mex.
94 B3 Ticao i. Phil.
59 H6 Ticehurst U.K.
31 J3 Tichborne Can.
100 B3 Tichît Maur.
100 A3 Tichla Western Sahara
62 D7 Ticino r. Switz.
33 G3 Ticonderoga U.S.A.
36 G4 Ticul Mex.
55 N7 Tidaholm Sweden
85 H5 Tiddim Myanmar
100 C2 Tidikelt, Plaine du plain Alg.
100 A3 Tidjikja Maur.
61 D3 Tiel Neth.
90 A1 Tieli China
88 G1 Tieling China
84 D2 Tielongtan China/Jammu and Kashmir
61 B4 Tielt Belgium
100 B4 Tiémé Côte d'Ivoire
61 C4 Tienen Belgium
74 Tien Shan mts China/Kyrgyzstan
Tientsin see Tianjin
55 P6 Tierp Sweden
25 F4 Tierra Amarilla U.S.A.
28 E5 Tierra Blanca Mex.

44 C8 Tierra del Fuego, Isla Grande de i. Arg./Chile
65 D2 Tiétar r. Spain
65 D2 Tiétar, Valle de v. Spain
46 C3 Tietê Brazil
46 B3 Tietê r. Brazil
32 B4 Tiffin U.S.A.
Tiflis see T'bilisi
29 D6 Tifton U.S.A.
67 L3 Tigheciului, Dealurile h. Moldova
69 D6 Tighina Moldova
85 F5 Tigiria India
101 D4 Tignère Cameroon
23 H4 Tignish Can.
42 C4 Tigre r. Ecuador/Peru
45 E2 Tigre r. Venez.
81 L5 Tigris r. Iraq/Turkey
80 D7 Tîh, Gebel el plat. Egypt
78 E6 Tihāmah reg. Saudi Arabia
36 A2 Tijuana Mex.
46 C2 Tijuco r. Brazil
84 D4 Tikamgarh India
69 G6 Tikhoretsk Rus. Fed.
68 E3 Tikhvin Rus. Fed.
68 E3 Tikhvinskaya Gryada ridge Rus. Fed.
117 F3 Tikokino N.Z.
111 G3 Tikopia i. Solomon Is
81 J4 Tikrīt Iraq
54 W3 Tiksheozero, Oz. l. Rus. Fed.
77 O2 Tiksi Rus. Fed.
85 E3 Tila r. Nepal
85 F4 Tilaiya Reservoir resr India
115 F1 Tilbooroo Austr.
61 D3 Tilburg Neth.
59 H6 Tilbury U.K.
44 C2 Tilcara Arg.
114 D2 Tilcha Austr.
85 H5 Tilin Myanmar
100 C3 Tillabéri Niger
24 A2 Tillamook U.S.A.
57 E4 Tillicoultry U.K.
31 G4 Tillsonburg Can.
57 F3 Tillyfourie U.K.
67 M6 Tilos i. Greece
114 F3 Tilpa Austr.
59 F5 Tilt r. U.K.
68 K1 Timanskiy Kryazh ridge Rus. Fed.
81 J2 Timar Turkey
117 C6 Timaru N.Z.
69 F6 Timashevsk Rus. Fed.
100 B3 Timbedgha Maur.
112 F3 Timber Creek Austr.
34 D3 Timber Mt mt U.S.A.
32 D5 Timberville U.S.A.
114 E7 Timboon Austr.
100 B3 Timétrine reg. Mali
100 C2 Timimoun Alg.
67 J2 Timişoara Romania
31 G1 Timmins Can.
68 F3 Timokhino Rus. Fed.
43 K5 Timon Brazil
93 H8 Timor i. Indon.
110 C3 Timor Sea sea Austr./Indon.
68 H3 Timoshino Rus. Fed.
47 D2 Timote Arg.
55 P5 Timrå Sweden
29 C5 Tims Ford L. l. U.S.A.
84 D5 Timurni Muafi India
45 C2 Tinaco Venez.
116 E5 Tin Can Bay Austr.
83 E8 Tindivanam India
100 B2 Tindouf Alg.
95 C5 Tinggi i. Malaysia
115 J2 Tingha Austr.
89 E5 Ting Jiang r. China
85 F3 Tingri China
55 O8 Tingsryd Sweden
47 B2 Tinguiririca, Vol. vol. Chile
54 L5 Tingvoll Norway
57 E1 Tingwall U.K.
46 E1 Tinharé, Ilha de i. Brazil
95 C1 Tinh Gia Vietnam
93 L4 Tinian i. N. Mariana Is
92 □ Tinjil i. Indon.
44 C3 Tinogasta Arg.
67 L6 Tinos i. Greece
100 C2 Tinrhert, Plateau du plat. Alg.
85 H4 Tinsukia India
59 C7 Tintagel U.K.
114 D5 Tintinara Austr.
57 E5 Tinto h. U.K.
32 E4 Tioga r. U.S.A.
95 C5 Tioman i. Malaysia
31 F1 Tionaga Can.
32 D4 Tionesta Lake l. U.S.A.
33 E3 Tioughnioga r. U.S.A.
65 H4 Tipasa Alg.
30 D5 Tippecanoe r. U.S.A.
30 E5 Tippecanoe Lake l. U.S.A.
60 C5 Tipperary Rep. of Ireland
85 F4 Tiptala Bhanjyang pass Nepal
30 B5 Tipton IA U.S.A.
30 D5 Tipton IN U.S.A.
35 E4 Tipton, Mt mt U.S.A.
30 E1 Tip Top Hill h. Can.
59 H6 Tiptree U.K.
45 C4 Tiquié r. Brazil
43 J4 Tiracambu, Serra do h. Brazil
67 H4 Tirana Albania
Tiranë see Tirana
66 D1 Tirano Italy
69 D6 Tiraspol Moldova
104 B3 Tiraz Mts mts Namibia

80 A2 Tire Turkey
57 B4 Tiree i. U.K.
84 B1 Tirich Mir mt Pak.
83 E8 Tiruchchirāppalli India
83 E8 Tirupati India
83 E8 Tiruppattur India
83 E8 Tiruppur India
21 J4 Tisdale Can.
65 G5 Tissemsilt Alg.
85 G4 Tista r. India
77 O2 Tit-Ary Rus. Fed.
42 E7 Titicaca, Lago l. Bol./Peru
85 E5 Titlagarh India
66 G2 Titov Drvar Bos.-Herz.
31 E4 Tittabawassee r. U.S.A.
67 L2 Titu Romania
29 D6 Titusville FL U.S.A.
32 D4 Titusville PA U.S.A.
89 □ Tiu Chung Chau i. China
31 G3 Tiverton Can.
59 D7 Tiverton U.K.
66 E4 Tivoli Italy
65 H4 Tizi El Arba h. Alg.
36 G4 Tizimín Mex.
65 J4 Tizi Ouzou Alg.
45 D2 Tiznados r. Venez.
100 B2 Tiznit Morocco
27 C7 Tizoc Mex.
105 J2 Tjaneni Swaziland
54 Q4 Tjappsåive Sweden
61 D2 Tjeukemeer l. Neth.
55 K7 Tjorhom Norway
27 C7 Tlahualilo Mex.
36 E5 Tlaxcala Mex.
100 B1 Tlemcen Alg.
104 E4 Tlhakalatlou S. Africa
105 H4 Tlholong S. Africa
105 F2 Tlokweng Botswana
20 D3 Toad River Can.
103 E6 Toamasina Madag.
47 D3 Toay Arg.
91 E7 Toba Japan
95 A5 Toba, Danau l. Indon.
84 A3 Toba and Kakar Ranges mts Pak.
42 F1 Tobago i. Trinidad and Tobago
93 H6 Tobelo Indon.
31 G3 Tobermory Can.
57 B4 Tobermory U.K.
34 D1 Tobin, Mt mt U.S.A.
21 J4 Tobin L. l. Can.
33 K1 Tobique r. Can.
91 E7 Tobi-shima i. Japan
92 D7 Toboali Indon.
76 H4 Tobol r. Kazak./Rus. Fed.
76 H4 Tobol'sk Rus. Fed.
95 D2 Tô Bong Vietnam
43 J5 Tocantinópolis Brazil
43 J4 Tocantins r. Brazil
46 C1 Tocantinzinha r. Brazil
29 D5 Toccoa U.S.A.
84 B2 Tochi r. Pak.
55 M7 Töcksfors Sweden
44 B2 Tocopilla Chile
115 F5 Tocumwal Austr.
45 C2 Tocuyo r. Venez.
93 G7 Todeli Indon.
66 E3 Todi Italy
62 D7 Todi mt Switz.
90 H5 Todoga-saki pt Japan
90 G4 Todohokke Japan
42 E7 Todos Santos Bol.
34 D6 Todos Santos, Bahía de b. Mex.
20 G4 Tofield Can.
20 D5 Tofino Can.
57 □ Toft U.K.
30 B2 Tofte U.S.A.
111 J3 Tofua i. Tonga
93 G7 Togian, Kepulauan is Indon.
96 Togo country Africa
30 A2 Togo U.S.A.
88 D1 Togrog Ul China
88 D1 Togtoh China
35 H4 Tohatchi U.S.A.
88 B1 Tohom China
85 G3 Toiba China
55 S6 Toijala Fin.
91 B9 Toi-misaki pt Japan
55 U5 Toivakka Fin.
34 D2 Toiyabe Range mts U.S.A.
91 F6 Tōkamachi Japan
117 B7 Tokanui N.Z.
101 F3 Tokar Sudan
87 N6 Tokara-rettō is Japan
80 F1 Tokat Turkey
106 Tokelau terr. Pac. Oc.
82 E2 Tokmak Kyrgyzstan
69 E6 Tokmak Ukr.
117 E5 Tokomaru Bay N.Z.
117 E3 Tokoroa N.Z.
105 H3 Tokoza S. Africa
82 G2 Toksun China
91 D7 Tokushima Japan
91 B7 Tokuyama Japan
91 F7 Tōkyō Japan
91 F7 Tōkyō-wan b. Japan
117 G3 Tolaga Bay N.Z.
103 E6 Tôlañaro Madag.
46 B4 Toledo Brazil
65 D3 Toledo Spain
30 A5 Toledo IA U.S.A.
32 B4 Toledo OH U.S.A.
65 D3 Toledo, Montes de mts Spain
27 E6 Toledo Bend Reservoir resr U.S.A.
116 A1 Tolga Austr.
47 B3 Tolhuaca, Parque Nacional nat. park Chile
103 E6 Toliara Madag.

45 B3 Tolima, Nev. del vol. Col.
93 G6 Tolitoli Indon.
76 K3 Tol'ka Rus. Fed.
68 C4 Tolmachevo Rus. Fed.
66 E1 Tolmezzo Italy
65 E1 Tolosa Spain
31 F3 Tolsmaville Can.
57 B2 Tolsta Head hd U.K.
45 B2 Tolú Col.
36 E5 Toluca Mex.
54 W3 Tolvand, Oz. l. Rus. Fed.
54 J4 Tol'yatti Rus. Fed.
30 A4 Tomah U.S.A.
30 C3 Tomahawk U.S.A.
90 G2 Tomakomai Japan
90 G2 Tomamae Japan
111 H3 Tomanivi mt Fiji
45 E4 Tomar Brazil
65 B3 Tomar Port.
80 E2 Tomarza Turkey
47 F1 Tomás Gomensoro Uru.
63 L5 Tomaszów Lubelski Pol.
63 K5 Tomaszów Mazowiecki Pol.
57 E3 Tomatin U.K.
29 B6 Tombigbee r. U.S.A.
102 B4 Tomboco Angola
46 D3 Tombos Brazil
100 B3 Tombouctou Mali
35 H6 Tombstone U.S.A.
103 B5 Tombua Angola
105 H1 Tom Burke S. Africa
47 B3 Tomé Chile
105 L1 Tome Moz.
55 N9 Tomelilla Sweden
65 E3 Tomelloso Spain
82 C2 Tomenaryk Kazak.
31 H2 Tomiko Can.
115 H4 Tomingley Austr.
93 G7 Tomini, Teluk g. Indon.
100 B3 Tominian Mali
57 D3 Tomintoul U.K.
66 G3 Tomislavgrad Bos.-Herz.
55 O8 Tomma i. Norway
77 O4 Tommot Rus. Fed.
45 D4 Tomo Col.
45 C3 Tomo r. Col.
88 D1 Tomortei China
77 P3 Tompo Rus. Fed.
112 C4 Tom Price Austr.
76 K4 Tomsk Rus. Fed.
55 O8 Tomtabacken h. Sweden
77 Q3 Tomtor Rus. Fed.
90 H3 Tomuraushi-yama mt Japan
69 G6 Tomuzlovka r. Rus. Fed.
36 F5 Tonalá Mex.
35 G3 Tonalea U.S.A.
42 E4 Tonantins Brazil
24 C1 Tonasket U.S.A.
59 H6 Tonbridge U.K.
93 G6 Tondano Indon.
55 L9 Tønder Denmark
59 E4 Tone r. U.K.
114 E3 Tonga Austr.
106 Tonga country Pac. Oc.
105 J4 Tongaat S. Africa
114 F6 Tongala Austr.
89 C5 Tong'an China
117 E3 Tongariro National Park nat. park N.Z.
111 J4 Tongatapu Group is Tonga
14 H7 Tonga Tr. sea feature Pac. Oc.
88 D3 Tongbai China
88 D3 Tongbai Shan mts China
88 E4 Tongcheng Anhui China
89 D4 Tongcheng Hubei China
88 C3 Tongchuan China
89 C5 Tongdao China
88 A3 Tongde China
61 D4 Tongeren Belgium
89 E4 Tonggu China
89 D2 Tonggu Jiao pt China
91 A6 Tonghae S. Korea
89 B5 Tonghai China
90 A2 Tonghe China
87 N3 Tonghua China
87 O2 Tongjiang Heilongjiang China
88 C4 Tongjiang Sichuan China
92 D2 Tongking, Gulf of g. China/Vietnam
89 C4 Tongliang China
88 G1 Tongliao China
88 E4 Tongling China
89 F4 Tonglu China
91 A7 Tongnae S. Korea
89 B4 Tongnan China
114 E3 Tongo Lake salt flat Austr.
94 B5 Tongquil i. Phil.
89 C5 Tongren Guizhou China
88 A3 Tongren Qinghai China
89 E4 Tongshan China
89 C7 Tongshi China
85 H2 Tongtian He r. China
57 D2 Tongue U.K.
24 F2 Tongue r. U.S.A.
29 E7 Tongue of the Ocean chan. Bahamas
88 B3 Tongwei China
88 E2 Tongxian China
88 B2 Tongxin China
88 E4 Tongyanghe China
91 A7 T'ongyŏng S. Korea
87 M3 Tongyu China
89 C4 Tongzi China
30 C5 Tonica U.S.A.
25 E6 Tónichi Mex.
84 C4 Tonk India
89 B6 Tonkin reg. Vietnam
68 H3 Tonkino Rus. Fed.
95 C2 Tônlé Repou r. Laos

95 B2 Tônlé Sab l. Cambodia
90 G5 Tōno Japan
34 D2 Tonopah U.S.A.
45 E2 Tonoro r. Venez.
84 D3 Tons r. India
55 M7 Tønsberg Norway
55 K7 Tonstad Norway
35 Tonto National Monument res. U.S.A.
85 H5 Tonzang Myanmar
115 H2 Toobeah Austr.
24 D3 Tooele U.S.A.
115 K1 Toogoolawah Austr.
114 E5 Tooleybuc Austr.
114 A4 Tooligie Austr.
115 H6 Tooma r. Austr.
115 G7 Toora Austr.
115 H1 Tooraweenah Austr.
104 F6 Toorberg mt S. Africa
115 J1 Toowoomba Austr.
35 G4 Topawa U.S.A.
34 C2 Topaz U.S.A.
26 E4 Topeka U.S.A.
20 D4 Topley Landing Can.
47 D2 Topocalma, Pta pt Chile
35 E4 Topock U.S.A.
62 J6 Topol'čany Slovakia
36 C3 Topolobampo Mex.
67 M3 Topolovgrad Bulg.
54 W4 Topozero, Oz. l. Rus. Fed.
24 B2 Toppenish U.S.A.
33 K2 Topsfield U.S.A.
35 G3 Toquerville U.S.A.
102 D3 Tor Eth.
67 M5 Torbalı Turkey
79 H2 Torbat-e Heydarīyeh Iran
79 J2 Torbat-e Jām Iran
68 G4 Torbeyevo Rus. Fed.
30 E3 Torch Lake l. U.S.A.
65 D2 Tordesillas Spain
54 S4 Töre Sweden
65 H1 Torelló Spain
62 F5 Torgau Ger.
69 H5 Torgun r. Rus. Fed.
Torino see Turin
91 G9 Tori-shima i. Japan
101 F4 Torit Sudan
46 B2 Torixoreu Brazil
81 L3 Torkamān Iran
68 G3 Tor'kovskoye Vdkhr. resr Rus. Fed.
65 D2 Tormes r. Spain
54 S3 Torneälven r. Fin./Sweden
54 Q2 Torneträsk Sweden
54 Q2 Torneträsk l. Sweden
23 H2 Torngat Mountains mts Can.
54 T4 Tornio Fin.
Tornionjoki r. see Torneälven
47 D3 Tornquist Arg.
65 D2 Toro Spain
115 J4 Toronto Austr.
31 H4 Toronto Can.
68 D3 Toropets Rus. Fed.
34 D5 Toro Pk summit U.S.A.
102 D3 Tororo Uganda
80 D3 Toros Dağları mts Turkey
57 F3 Torphins U.K.
59 D7 Torquay U.K.
34 C5 Torrance U.S.A.
65 B3 Torrão Port.
65 C2 Torre mt Port.
65 G2 Torreblanca Spain
66 F4 Torre del Greco Italy
65 D1 Torrelavega Spain
65 D4 Torremolinos Spain
114 B3 Torrens, Lake salt flat Austr.
116 A3 Torrens Cr. watercourse Austr.
116 A3 Torrens Creek Austr.
65 F3 Torrent Spain
36 D3 Torreón Mex.
25 E6 Torres Mex.
44 B8 Torres del Paine, Parque Nacional nat. park Chile
111 G3 Torres Islands is Vanuatu
65 B3 Torres Novas Port.
110 E2 Torres Strait str. Austr.
65 B3 Torres Vedras Port.
65 G3 Torreta, Sa h. Spain
65 F4 Torrevieja Spain
35 G2 Torrey U.S.A.
59 C7 Torridge r. U.K.
57 C3 Torridon, Loch in. U.K.
65 D3 Torrijos Spain
115 J2 Torrington Austr.
33 G4 Torrington CT U.S.A.
24 F3 Torrington WY U.S.A.
65 H1 Torroella de Montgrí Spain
55 N6 Torsby Sweden
54 □ Tórshavn Faroe Is
66 C5 Tortolì Italy
66 C2 Tortona Italy
65 G2 Tortosa Spain
81 H1 Tortum Turkey
81 G1 Torul Turkey
63 J4 Toruń Pol.
60 C2 Tory Island i. Rep. of Ireland
60 C2 Tory Sound chan. Rep. of Ireland
68 E3 Torzhok Rus. Fed.
91 C8 Tosa Japan
91 C8 Tosashimizu Japan
54 N4 Tosbotn Norway
104 C3 Tosca S. Africa
66 C2 Toscano, Arcipelago is Italy
90 A2 Tōshima-yama mt Japan
68 H3 Tosno Rus. Fed.
44 D3 Tostado Arg.

91 B8 Tosu Japan
80 E1 Tosya Turkey
68 G3 Tot'ma Rus. Fed.
59 F7 Totton U.K.
91 D7 Tottori Japan
100 B4 Touba Côte d'Ivoire
100 A3 Touba Senegal
100 B1 Toubkal, Jbel mt Morocco
88 B2 Toudaohu China
100 B3 Tougan Burkina
100 C1 Touggourt Alg.
100 A3 Tougué Guinea
64 G2 Toul France
89 F6 Touliu Taiwan
64 G5 Toulon France
64 G5 Toulouse France
100 B4 Toumodi Côte d'Ivoire
83 J7 Toungoo Myanmar
89 D5 Toupai China
100 C1 Tourcoing France
61 B4 Tournai Belgium
64 Tournon-sur-Rhône France
64 G3 Tournus France
43 L5 Touros Brazil
64 E3 Tours France
104 D6 Touwsrivier S. Africa
45 C2 Tovar Venez.
59 F5 Tove r. U.K.
81 K1 Tovuz Azer.
91 E7 Towada Japan
90 G5 Towada-Hachimantai National Park Japan
90 G5 Towada-ko l. Japan
117 E1 Towai N.Z.
33 H3 Towanda U.S.A.
35 H3 Towaoc U.S.A.
59 G5 Towcester U.K.
60 C6 Tower Rep. of Ireland
30 A2 Tower U.S.A.
116 A3 Towerhill Cr. watercourse Austr.
21 J5 Towner U.S.A.
34 B3 Townes Pass pass U.S.A.
24 E2 Townsend U.S.A.
115 H6 Townsend, Mt mt Austr.
116 D4 Townshend I. i. Austr.
116 B2 Townsville Austr.
93 G7 Towori, Teluk b. Indon.
32 E5 Towson U.S.A.
90 G3 Tōya-ko l. Japan
91 E6 Toyama Japan
91 E6 Toyama-wan b. Japan
91 E7 Toyohashi Japan
91 E7 Toyokawa Japan
91 D7 Toyonaka Japan
91 D7 Toyooka Japan
91 E7 Toyota Japan
100 C1 Tozeur Tunisia
69 G7 Tqibuli Georgia
69 G7 Tqvarch'eli Georgia
67 K4 Trabotivište Macedonia
81 G1 Trabzon Turkey
33 K2 Tracy Can.
34 B3 Tracy CA U.S.A.
26 E2 Tracy MN U.S.A.
30 A4 Traer U.S.A.
65 C4 Trafalgar, Cabo pt Spain
47 B3 Traiguén Chile
20 F5 Trail Can.
55 T9 Trakai Lith.
68 J2 Trakt Rus. Fed.
60 B5 Tralee Rep. of Ireland
60 B5 Tralee Bay b. Rep. of Ireland
45 E3 Tramán Tepuí mt Venez.
60 D5 Tramore Rep. of Ireland
55 O7 Tranås Sweden
44 C3 Trancas Arg.
55 N8 Tranemo Sweden
57 F5 Tranent U.K.
95 A4 Trang Thai.
93 J8 Trangan i. Indon.
115 G4 Trangie Austr.
47 F1 Tranqueras Uru.
119 B5 Transantarctic Mountains mts Antarctica
21 G4 Trans Canada Highway Can.
21 K5 Transcona Can.
66 E5 Trapani Italy
115 G7 Traralgon Austr.
85 H4 Trashigang Bhutan
66 E3 Trasimeno, Lago l. Italy
65 E3 Trasvase, Canal de canal Spain
95 B2 Trat Thai.
62 F7 Traunsee l. Austria
62 F7 Traunstein Ger.
114 E4 Travellers L. l. Austr.
117 D5 Travers, Mt mt N.Z.
119 C1 Traversay Is is Atlantic Ocean
30 E3 Traverse City U.S.A.
95 C3 Tra Vinh Vietnam
27 D6 Travis, L. l. U.S.A.
66 F1 Travnik Bos.-Herz.
66 F1 Trbovlje Slovenia
111 F2 Treasury Is is Solomon Is
62 G6 Třebíč Czech Rep.
67 H3 Trebinje Bos.-Herz.
63 K6 Trebišov Slovakia
66 F2 Trebnje Slovenia
116 B2 Trebonne Austr.
30 B3 Trego U.S.A.
116 D1 Tregrosse Islets and Reefs is Coral Sea Is Terr.
57 D4 Treig, Loch l. U.K.
47 F2 Treinta-y-Tres Uru.
44 C6 Trelew Arg.
55 N9 Trelleborg Sweden
59 C5 Tremadog Bay b. U.K.

22 F4 Tremblant, Mt h. Can.
66 F3 Tremiti, Isole is Italy
24 D3 Tremonton U.S.A.
65 G1 Tremp Spain
30 B3 Trempealeau r. U.S.A.
59 B7 Trenance U.K.
62 J6 Trenčín Slovakia
47 D2 Trenque Lauquén Arg.
58 G4 Trent r. U.K.
66 D1 Trento Italy
31 J3 Trenton Can.
26 E3 Trenton MO U.S.A.
33 F4 Trenton NJ U.S.A.
59 D6 Treorchy U.K.
23 K4 Trepassey Can.
47 F2 Tres Arboles Uru.
47 E3 Tres Arroyos Arg.
59 A8 Tresco i. U.K.
46 D3 Três Corações Brazil
45 B4 Tres Esquinas Col.
57 B4 Treshnish Isles is U.K.
46 B3 Três Lagoas Brazil
44 B7 Tres Lagos Arg.
47 D3 Tres Lomas Arg.
46 D2 Três Marias, Represa resr Brazil
47 B4 Tres Picos mt Arg.
47 E3 Tres Picos, Cerro mt Arg.
25 F4 Tres Piedras U.S.A.
46 D3 Três Pontas Brazil
44 C7 Tres Puntas, C. pt Arg.
46 D3 Três Rios Brazil
55 M6 Tretten Norway
55 L7 Treungen Norway
66 C2 Treviglio Italy
66 E2 Treviso Italy
59 B7 Trevose Head hd U.K.
115 G9 Triabunna Austr.
67 M6 Tria Nisia i. Greece
67 N6 Trianta Greece
84 B2 Tribal Areas div. Pak.
67 H5 Tricase Italy
83 E8 Trichur India
115 F4 Trida Austr.
62 C6 Trier Ger.
66 E2 Trieste Italy
66 E1 Triglav mt Slovenia
67 J5 Trikala Greece
80 D4 Trikomon Cyprus
93 K7 Trikora, Pk mt Indon.
60 E4 Trim Rep. of Ireland
83 F9 Trincomalee Sri Lanka
46 C2 Trindade Brazil
12 G7 Trindade, Ilha da i. Atlantic Ocean
42 F6 Trinidad Bol.
45 C3 Trinidad Col.
37 J4 Trinidad Cuba
42 F1 Trinidad i. Trinidad and Tobago
47 F2 Trinidad Uru.
25 F4 Trinidad U.S.A.
38 Trinidad and Tobago country Caribbean Sea
116 A1 Trinity Bay b. Austr.
23 K4 Trinity Bay b. Can.
34 C1 Trinity Range mts U.S.A.
29 C5 Trion U.S.A.
67 K6 Tripoli Greece
Tripoli see Trâblous
101 D1 Tripoli Libya
85 G5 Tripura div. India
84 D3 Trisul mt India
85 F4 Trisul Dam dam Nepal
83 E9 Trivandrum India
66 F4 Trivento Italy
62 H6 Trnava Slovakia
110 F2 Trobriand Islands is P.N.G.
54 N4 Trofors Norway
66 G3 Trogir Croatia
66 F4 Troia Italy
62 C5 Troisdorf Ger.
23 F4 Trois-Rivières Can.
69 H6 Troitskoye Rus. Fed.
55 N7 Trollhättan Sweden
43 G3 Trombetas r. Brazil
13 H5 Tromelin, Île i. Indian Ocean
47 B3 Tromen, Volcán vol. Arg.
105 F5 Trompsburg S. Africa
54 Q2 Tromsø Norway
34 D4 Trona U.S.A.
47 B4 Tronador, Monte mt Arg.
54 M5 Trondheim Norway
54 M5 Trondheimsfjorden chan. Norway
85 G4 Trongsa Chhu r. Bhutan
80 D4 Troödos Cyprus
80 D4 Troödos, Mount mt Cyprus
57 D5 Troon U.K.
46 D1 Tropeiros, Serra dos h. Brazil
35 F3 Tropic U.S.A.
60 E2 Trostan h. U.K.
57 F3 Troup Head hd U.K.
20 E2 Trout r. Can.
31 H3 Trout Creek Can.
35 F2 Trout Creek U.S.A.
22 B3 Trout L. l. Can.
20 G3 Trout Lake Alta. Can.
20 E2 Trout Lake N.W.T. Can.
20 E3 Trout Lake l. Can.
30 E2 Trout Lake U.S.A.
30 C2 Trout Lake l. U.S.A.
24 E2 Trout Peak summit U.S.A.
32 E4 Trout Run U.S.A.
59 E6 Trowbridge U.K.
115 F8 Trowutta Austr.
29 C6 Troy AL U.S.A.
24 D2 Troy MT U.S.A.
33 G3 Troy NH U.S.A.
33 G3 Troy NY U.S.A.
32 A4 Troy OH U.S.A.
32 E4 Troy PA U.S.A.
67 L3 Troyan Bulg.
64 G2 Troyes France
34 D4 Troy Lake l. U.S.A.
35 E2 Troy Peak summit U.S.A.
67 J3 Trstenik Yugo.
69 E4 Trubchevsk Rus. Fed.
65 C1 Truchas Spain
68 E3 Trud Rus. Fed.
90 C3 Trudovoye Rus. Fed.
37 G5 Trujillo Honduras
42 C5 Trujillo Peru
65 D3 Trujillo Spain
45 C2 Trujillo Venez.
33 G4 Trumbull U.S.A.
35 F3 Trumbull, Mt mt U.S.A.
95 A5 Trumon Indon.
115 G4 Trundle Austr.
95 C2 Trưng Hiệp Vietnam
89 C6 Trung Khanh China
23 H4 Truro Can.
59 B7 Truro U.K.
60 C3 Truskmore h. Rep. of Ireland
20 E3 Trutch Can.
25 F5 Truth or Consequences U.S.A.
62 G5 Trutnov Czech Rep.
67 L7 Trypiti, Akra pt Greece
55 N6 Trysil Norway
62 G3 Trzebiatów Pol.
86 E2 Tsagaannuur Mongolia
69 H6 Tsagan Aman Rus. Fed.
69 H6 Tsagan-Nur Rus. Fed.
69 G7 Ts'ageri Georgia
81 K1 Tsalka Georgia
103 E5 Tsaratanana, Massif du mts Madag.
67 M3 Tsarevo Bulg.
104 B2 Tsaris Mts mts Namibia
69 H5 Tsatsa Rus. Fed.
104 A3 Tsaukaib Namibia
102 D4 Tsavo East National Park nat. park Kenya
69 G6 Tselina Rus. Fed.
103 B6 Tses Namibia
103 C6 Tsetseng Botswana
86 H2 Tsetserleg Mongolia
103 C6 Tshabong Botswana
103 C6 Tshane Botswana
69 F6 Tshchikskoye Vdkhr. resr Rus. Fed.
102 B4 Tshela Dem. Rep. Congo
102 C4 Tshibala Dem. Rep. Congo
102 C4 Tshikapa Dem. Rep. Congo
102 C4 Tshikapa r. Dem. Rep. Congo
105 G3 Tshing S. Africa
105 J1 Tshipise S. Africa
103 C4 Tshitanzu Dem. Rep. Congo
102 C4 Tshofa Dem. Rep. Congo
105 J2 Tshokwane S. Africa
102 C4 Tshuapa r. Dem. Rep. Congo
69 G6 Tsimlyansk Rus. Fed.
69 G6 Tsimlyanskoye Vdkhr. resr Rus. Fed.
104 E3 Tsineng S. Africa
89 □ Tsing Shan h. China
89 □ Tsing Shan Wan b. China
Tsingtao see Qingdao
89 □ Tsing Yi i. China
103 E6 Tsiombe Madag.
103 E5 Tsiroanomandidy Madag.
104 E7 Tsitsikamma Forest and Coastal National Park nat. park S. Africa
20 D4 Tsitsutl Pk summit Can.
68 H4 Tsivil'sk Rus. Fed.
69 G7 Ts'khinvali Georgia
68 G4 Tsna r. Rus. Fed.
84 D2 Tsokr Chumo l. India
105 H5 Tsolo S. Africa
105 G6 Tsomo S. Africa
84 D2 Tso Morari L. l. India
69 G7 Tsqaltubo Georgia
91 E7 Tsu Japan
91 G6 Tsuchiura Japan
89 □ Tsuen Wan China
90 G4 Tsugarū-kaikyō str. Japan
103 B5 Tsumeb Namibia
103 B6 Tsumis Park Namibia
103 C5 Tsumkwe Namibia
85 G4 Tsunthang India
91 E7 Tsuruga Japan
91 D8 Tsurugi-san mt Japan
90 F5 Tsuruoka Japan
91 A7 Tsushima i. Japan
Tsushima-kaikyō str. see Korea Strait
91 D7 Tsuyama Japan
104 D1 Tswaane Botswana
105 F4 Tswaraganang S. Africa
105 F3 Tswelelang S. Africa
63 M4 Tsyelyakhany Belarus
54 X2 Tsyp-Navolok Rus. Fed.
69 E6 Tsyurupyns'k Ukr.
93 J8 Tual Indon.
60 C4 Tuam Rep. of Ireland
117 D4 Tuamarina N.Z.
89 B6 Tuân Giao Vietnam
95 A5 Tuangku i. Indon.
69 F6 Tuapse Rus. Fed.
95 □ Tuas Sing.
117 A7 Tuatapere N.Z.
35 G3 Tuba City U.S.A.
92 □ Tuban Indon.
44 G3 Tubarão Brazil
94 A4 Tubbataha Reefs rf Phil.
60 C3 Tubbercurry Rep. of Ireland
62 D6 Tübingen Ger.
100 A4 Tubmanburg Liberia
94 B4 Tubod Phil.
101 E1 Tubruq Libya
25 E6 Tubutama Mex.
43 L6 Tucano Brazil
47 B3 Tucapel, Pta pt Chile
43 G7 Tucavaca Bol.
20 D2 Tuchitua Can.
33 F5 Tuckerton U.S.A.
35 G5 Tucson U.S.A.
35 G5 Tucson Mts mts U.S.A.
45 B2 Tucuco r. Venez.
25 G5 Tucumcari U.S.A.
45 E2 Tucupita Venez.
43 J4 Tucuruí Brazil
43 J4 Tucuruí, Represa resr Brazil
81 M5 Tū Dār Iran
65 F1 Tudela Spain
65 C2 Tuela r. Port.
89 □ Tuen Mun China
85 H4 Tuensang India
105 J4 Tugela r. S. Africa
94 C4 Tugnug Point pt Phil.
94 B2 Tuguegarao Phil.
77 P4 Tugur Rus. Fed.
88 F2 Tuhai r. China
95 A5 Tuhemberua Indon.
65 B1 Tui Spain
45 A2 Tuira r. Panama
93 G8 Tukangbesi, Kepulauan is Indon.
22 E2 Tukarak Island i. Can.
117 F3 Tukituki r. N.Z.
55 S8 Tukums Latvia
68 F4 Tula Rus. Fed.
85 H1 Tulagt Ar Gol r. China
36 E4 Tulancingo Mex.
34 C3 Tulare U.S.A.
34 C4 Tulare Lake Bed l. U.S.A.
25 F5 Tularosa U.S.A.
104 C6 Tulbagh S. Africa
42 C3 Tulcán Ecuador
67 N2 Tulcea Romania
69 D5 Tul'chyn Ukr.
34 C3 Tule r. U.S.A.
45 B2 Tulé Venez.
85 G4 Tule-la Pass pass Bhutan
21 J2 Tulemalu Lake l. Can.
27 C5 Tulia U.S.A.
20 D2 Tulit'a Can.
80 E5 Ţūlkarm West Bank
60 C5 Tulla Rep. of Ireland
115 F8 Tullah Austr.
29 C5 Tullahoma U.S.A.
115 G4 Tullamore Austr.
60 D4 Tullamore Rep. of Ireland
64 E4 Tulle France
54 O5 Tulleråsen Sweden
115 G4 Tullibigeal Austr.
27 E6 Tullos U.S.A.
60 E5 Tullow Rep. of Ireland
116 B1 Tully Austr.
116 A1 Tully r. Austr.
60 D3 Tully U.K.
33 E3 Tully U.S.A.
116 A1 Tully Falls waterfall Austr.
68 D2 Tulos Rus. Fed.
27 D4 Tulsa U.S.A.
68 F4 Tul'skaya Oblast' div. Rus. Fed.
45 A3 Tuluá Col.
77 V3 Tuluksak Alaska
47 C1 Tulum, Valle de v. Arg.
77 M4 Tulun Rus. Fed.
92 □ Tulungagung Indon.
85 H4 Tulung La pass China
94 A4 Tuluran i. Phil.
45 A4 Tumaco Col.
105 G3 Tumahole S. Africa
69 J6 Tumak Rus. Fed.
55 P7 Tumba Sweden
102 B4 Tumba, Lac l. Dem. Rep. Congo
94 C5 Tumbao Phil.
113 J7 Tumbarumba Austr.
42 B4 Tumbes Peru
20 E3 Tumbler Ridge Can.
114 B5 Tumby Bay Austr.
54 W3 Tumcha r. Fin./Rus. Fed.
87 N3 Tumen China
90 A3 Tumen Jiang r. China/N. Korea
88 B2 Tumenzi China
42 F2 Tumereng Guyana
94 A5 Tumindao i. Phil.
83 E8 Tumkur India
85 G3 Tum La pass China
57 E4 Tummel, Loch l. U.K.
87 Q2 Tumnin r. Rus. Fed.
79 J4 Tump Pak.
95 B4 Tumpat Malaysia
100 B3 Tumu Ghana
43 G3 Tumucumaque, Serra h. Brazil
115 H5 Tumut Austr.
115 H5 Tumut r. Austr.
59 H6 Tunbridge Wells, Royal U.K.
81 G2 Tunceli Turkey
89 D7 Tunchang China
115 K4 Tuncurry Austr.
84 D4 Tundla India
103 D5 Tunduru Tanz.
67 M3 Tundzha r. Bulg.
85 H3 Tunga Pass pass China/India
94 B5 Tungawan Phil.
89 □ Tung Lung Chau i. China
54 D4 Tungnaá r. Iceland
20 D2 Tungsten Can.
68 E1 Tunguda Rus. Fed.
89 □ Tung Wan b. China
100 D1 Tunis Tunisia
66 D6 Tunis, Golfe de g. Tunisia
96 Tunisia country Africa
45 B3 Tunja Col.
88 D2 Tunliu China
54 N4 Tunnsjøen l. Norway
59 J5 Tunstall U.K.
54 V3 Tuntsa Fin.
23 H2 Tunungayualok Island i. Can.
47 C2 Tunuyán Arg.
47 C2 Tunuyán r. Arg.
88 E3 Tuo He r. China
88 F2 Tuoji Dao i. China
95 C3 Tuŏl Khpos Cambodia
34 B3 Tuolumne U.S.A.
34 C3 Tuolumne Meadows U.S.A.
89 B5 Tuoniang Jiang r. China
85 H2 Tuotuo He r. China
85 H2 Tuotuoheyan China
46 B3 Tupã Brazil
46 C2 Tupaciguara Brazil
81 L3 Tūp Āghāj Iran
43 F3 Tupanciretã Brazil
45 C3 Tuparro r. Col.
27 F5 Tupelo U.S.A.
42 E8 Tupiza Bol.
33 F2 Tupper Lake U.S.A.
33 F2 Tupper Lake l. U.S.A.
47 C2 Tupungato Arg.
47 C2 Tupungato, Cerro mt Arg./Chile
81 K7 Tuqayyid w. Iraq
45 A4 Túquerres Col.
89 C7 Tuqu Wan b. China
85 G4 Tura India
77 M3 Tura Rus. Fed.
78 E5 Turabah Saudi Arabia
45 D3 Turagua, Serranía mt Venez.
117 E4 Turakina N.Z.
87 O1 Turana, Khrebet mts Rus. Fed.
117 E3 Turangi N.Z.
79 H1 Turan Lowland lowland Asia
82 D2 Turar-Ryskulova Kazak.
80 G6 Turayf Saudi Arabia
55 T7 Turba Estonia
45 B2 Turbaco Col.
79 J4 Turbat Pak.
45 A2 Turbo Col.
63 L7 Turda Romania
81 M4 Tūreh Iran
Turfan see Turpan
76 H5 Turgay Kazak.
67 M3 Tŭrgovishte Bulg.
80 C2 Turgut Turkey
80 A2 Turgutlu Turkey
80 F1 Turhal Turkey
55 T7 Türi Estonia
65 F3 Turia r. Spain
45 D2 Turiamo Venez.
66 B2 Turin Italy
90 B2 Turiy Rog Rus. Fed.
69 C5 Turiys'k Ukr.
86 J1 Turka Rus. Fed.
102 D3 Turkana, Lake salt l. Eth./Kenya
67 M4 Türkeli Adası i. Turkey
82 C2 Turkestan Kazak.
70 Turkey country Asia.
30 B4 Turkey r. U.S.A.
69 G5 Turki Rus. Fed.
79 G2 Turkmenbashi Turkm.
80 C2 Türkmen Dağı mt Turkey
70 Turkmenistan country Asia
80 F3 Türkoğlu Turkey
37 K4 Turks and Caicos Islands terr. Caribbean
37 K4 Turks Islands is Turks and Caicos Is
55 S6 Turku Fin.
102 D3 Turkwel watercourse Kenya
34 B3 Turlock U.S.A.
34 B3 Turlock L. l. U.S.A.
117 F4 Turnagain, Cape c. N.Z.
57 D5 Turnberry U.K.
35 G5 Turnbull, Mt mt U.S.A.
36 G5 Turneffe Is is Belize
31 F3 Turner U.S.A.
61 C3 Turnhout Belgium
21 H3 Turnor Lake l. Can.
67 L3 Turnu Măgurele Romania
115 H4 Turon r. Austr.
68 G3 Turovets Rus. Fed.
82 G2 Turpan China
82 G2 Turpan Pendi depression China
57 F3 Turriff U.K.
81 K5 Tursāq Iraq
79 J1 Turtkul' Uzbek.
30 B2 Turtle Flambeau Flowage resr U.S.A.
21 H4 Turtleford Can.
116 D1 Turtle I. i. Coral Sea Is Terr.
30 A3 Turtle Lake U.S.A.
82 E2 Turugart Pass pass China/Kyrgyzstan
46 B2 Turvo r. Goiás Brazil
46 B2 Turvo r. Goiás Brazil
46 C3 Turvo r. São Paulo Brazil
35 F4 Tusayan U.S.A.
29 C5 Tuscaloosa U.S.A.
32 C4 Tuscarawas r. U.S.A.
32 E4 Tuscarora Mts h. U.S.A.
30 C6 Tuscola IL U.S.A.
27 D5 Tuscola TX U.S.A.
29 C5 Tuskegee U.S.A.
32 D4 Tussey Mts h. U.S.A.
81 J2 Tutak Turkey
68 F3 Tutayev Rus. Fed.
83 E9 Tuticorin India
26 D4 Tuttle Creek Res. resr U.S.A.
62 D7 Tuttlingen Ger.
111 J3 Tutuila i. Pac. Oc.
103 C6 Tutume Botswana
54 W5 Tuupovaara Fin.
54 V5 Tuusniemi Fin.
106 Tuvalu country Pac. Oc.
36 E4 Tuxpan Mex.
36 F5 Tuxtla Gutiérrez Mex.
45 D2 Tuy r. Venez.
95 C2 Tuy Đưc Vietnam
89 B6 Tuyên Quang Vietnam
95 D2 Tuy Hoa Vietnam
81 M4 Tūysarkān Iran
Tuz, Lake salt l. see Tuz Gölü
80 D2 Tuz Gölü salt l. Turkey
35 F4 Tuzigoot National Monument res. U.S.A.
81 K4 Tuz Khurmātū Iraq
67 H2 Tuzla Bos.-Herz.
81 H2 Tuzla r. Turkey
69 F6 Tuzlov r. Rus. Fed.
55 L7 Tvedestrand Norway
68 E3 Tver' Rus. Fed.
68 E3 Tverskaya Oblast' div. Rus. Fed.
31 J3 Tweed Can.
57 F5 Tweed r. U.K.
115 K2 Tweed Heads Austr.
20 D4 Tweedsmuir Prov. Park res. Can.
104 C6 Tweefontein S. Africa
104 C2 Twee Rivier Namibia
61 E2 Twente reg. Neth.
34 D4 Twentynine Palms U.S.A.
23 K4 Twillingate Can.
24 D2 Twin Bridges U.S.A.
27 C6 Twin Buttes Res. resr U.S.A.
23 H3 Twin Falls Can.
24 D3 Twin Falls U.S.A.
20 F3 Twin Lakes Can.
33 H2 Twin Mountain U.S.A.
32 C6 Twin Oaks U.S.A.
34 B2 Twin Peak summit U.S.A.
115 H6 Twofold B. b. Austr.
35 G4 Two Guns U.S.A.
30 B2 Two Harbors U.S.A.
21 G4 Two Hills Can.
24 D1 Two Medicine r. U.S.A.
30 D3 Two Rivers U.S.A.
85 H5 Tyao r. India/Myanmar
54 M5 Tydal Norway
32 D5 Tygart Lake l. U.S.A.
32 D5 Tygart Valley v. U.S.A.
87 N1 Tygda Rus. Fed.
27 E5 Tyler U.S.A.
27 F6 Tylertown U.S.A.
77 O4 Tynda Rus. Fed.
20 A2 Tyndall Gl. gl. U.S.A.
57 F4 Tyne r. U.K.
58 F2 Tynemouth U.K.
55 M5 Tynset Norway
80 E5 Tyre Lebanon
21 H2 Tyrrell Lake l. Can.
87 O1 Tyrma Rus. Fed.
54 T4 Tyrnävä Fin.
67 K5 Tyrnavos Greece
32 D4 Tyrone U.S.A.
114 E5 Tyrrell r. Austr.
114 E5 Tyrrell, L. l. Austr.
52 Tyrrhenian Sea sea France/Italy
77 Q3 Tyubelyakh Rus. Fed.
76 J4 Tyukalinsk Rus. Fed.
76 H4 Tyumen' Rus. Fed.
77 N3 Tyung r. Rus. Fed.
Tyuratam see Baykonur
59 C6 Tywi r. U.K.
59 C5 Tywyn U.K.
105 J1 Tzaneen S. Africa

U

103 C5 Uamanda Angola
45 E4 Uatatás r. Brazil
43 L5 Uauá Brazil
45 D5 Uaupés Brazil
45 C4 Uaupés r. Brazil
81 J7 U'aywij, W. watercourse Saudi Arabia
46 D3 Ubá Brazil
46 D2 Ubaí Brazil
46 E1 Ubaitaba Brazil
102 B4 Ubangi r. C.A.R./Dem. Rep. Congo
45 B3 Ubate Col.
81 J5 Ubayyiḍ, Wādī al watercourse Iraq/S. Arabia
91 B8 Ube Japan
65 E3 Úbeda Spain
46 C2 Uberaba Brazil
43 G7 Uberaba, Lagoa l. Bol./Brazil
46 C2 Uberlândia Brazil
95 □ Ubin, Pulau i. Sing.
95 B1 Ubolratna Res. resr Thai.
105 K3 Ubombo S. Africa
95 C2 Ubon Ratchathani Thai.
102 C4 Ubundu Dem. Rep. Congo
81 L1 Ucar Azer.
42 D5 Ucayali r. Peru
84 B3 Uch Pak.
82 F1 Ucharal Kazak.
90 G3 Uchiura-wan b. Japan
77 P4 Uchur r. Rus. Fed.
59 H7 Uckfield U.K.
20 D5 Ucluelet Can.
35 H3 Ucolo U.S.A.
24 F2 Ucross U.S.A.
77 P4 Uda r. Rus. Fed.
69 H6 Udachnoye Rus. Fed.
77 N3 Udachnyy Rus. Fed.
83 E8 Udagamandalam India
84 C4 Udaipur Rajasthan India
85 G5 Udaipur Tripura India
85 E5 Udanti r. India/Myanmar
55 M7 Uddevalla Sweden
57 D5 Uddingston U.K.
54 P4 Uddjaure l. Sweden
61 D3 Uden Neth.
82 E4 Udhampur Jammu and Kashmir
68 H2 Udimskiy Rus. Fed.
66 E1 Udine Italy
23 J2 Udjuktok Bay b. Can.
68 E3 Udomlya Rus. Fed.
95 B1 Udon Thani Thai.
77 P4 Udskaya Guba b. Rus. Fed.
83 D8 Udupi India
77 P4 Udyl', Ozero l. Rus. Fed.
62 G4 Ueckermünde Ger.
91 F6 Ueda Japan
93 G7 Uekuli Indon.
102 C3 Uele r. Dem. Rep. Congo
62 E4 Uelzen Ger.
102 C3 Uere r. Dem. Rep. Congo
76 G4 Ufa Rus. Fed.
103 B6 Ugab watercourse Namibia
102 D4 Ugalla r. Tanz.
96 Uganda country Africa
105 H5 Ugie S. Africa
87 Q2 Uglegorsk Rus. Fed.
90 C3 Uglekamensk Rus. Fed.
68 F3 Uglich Rus. Fed.
66 F2 Ugljan i. Croatia
68 E3 Uglovka Rus. Fed.
90 C3 Uglovoye Rus. Fed.
77 Q3 Ugol'noye Rus. Fed.
77 T3 Ugol'nyye Kopi Rus. Fed.
68 E4 Ugra Rus. Fed.
62 H6 Uherské Hradiště Czech Rep.
32 C4 Uhrichsville U.S.A.
57 B3 Uig U.K.
102 B4 Uíge Angola
54 W5 Uimaharju Fin.
35 F3 Uinkaret Plateau plat. U.S.A.
103 B6 Uis Mine Namibia
60 D4 Uisneach h. Rep. of Ireland
91 A6 Ŭisŏng S. Korea
105 F6 Uitenhage S. Africa
61 E1 Uithuizen Neth.
23 H2 Uivak, Cape hd Can.
91 D7 Uji Japan
91 A9 Uji-guntō is Japan
84 C5 Ujjain India
93 F8 Ujung Pandang Indon.
81 J5 Ukhaydir Iraq
85 H4 Ukhrul India
68 K2 Ukhta Rus. Fed.
68 K2 Ukhta r. Rus. Fed.
115 K2 Uki Austr.
34 A2 Ukiah CA U.S.A.
24 C2 Ukiah OR U.S.A.
55 T9 Ukmergė Lith.
49 Ukraine country Europe
68 J2 Uktym Rus. Fed.
91 A8 Uku-jima i. Japan
104 D1 Ukwi Botswana
104 D1 Ukwi Pan salt pan Botswana
86 J2 Ulaanbaatar Mongolia
86 F2 Ulaangom Mongolia
115 H4 Ulan Austr.
82 J3 Ulan China
88 C2 Ulan China
Ulan Bator see Ulaanbaatar
88 C1 Ulan Buh Shamo des. China
69 H6 Ulan Erge Rus. Fed.
87 M2 Ulanhot China
88 D1 Ulan Hua China
69 H6 Ulan-Khol Rus. Fed.
88 C1 Ulansuhai Nur l. China
88 A1 Ulan Tohoi China
86 J1 Ulan-Ude Rus. Fed.
85 G2 Ulan Ul Hu l. China
80 F2 Ulaş Turkey
111 G2 Ulawa I. i. Solomon Is
87 N4 Ulchin S. Korea
55 L7 Ulefoss Norway
114 E2 Ulenia, Lake salt flat Austr.
55 U7 Ülenurme Estonia
87 L2 Uliastai China
86 G2 Uliastay Mongolia
54 X2 Ulita r. Rus. Fed.
93 K4 Ulithi i. Micronesia
115 J5 Ulladulla Austr.
57 C3 Ullapool U.K.
54 S5 Ullava Fin.
58 E3 Ullswater l. U.K.
87 O4 Ullŭng-do i. S. Korea
62 D6 Ulm Ger.
115 K2 Ulmarra Austr.
55 N8 Ulricehamn Sweden
91 A7 Ulsan S. Korea
54 L5 Ulsberg Norway
60 D3 Ulster Canal canal Rep. of Ireland/U.K.
114 E5 Ultima Austr.
80 B1 Ulubat Gölü l. Turkey
80 C2 Uluborlu Turkey
80 B1 Uludağ mt Turkey

95 B5 Ulu Kali, Gunung mt Malaysia
80 E3 Ulukışla Turkey
105 J4 Ulundi S. Africa
82 G1 Ulungur Hu l. China
95 □ Ulu Pandan Sing.
112 F5 Uluru h. Austr.
112 F5 Uluru National Park nat. park Austr.
80 D1 Ulus Turkey
57 B4 Ulva i. U.K.
61 C3 Ulvenhout Neth.
58 D3 Ulverston U.K.
115 G8 Ulverstone Austr.
55 O6 Ulvsjön Sweden
68 J4 Ul'yanovsk Rus. Fed.
68 H4 Ul'yanovskaya Oblast' div. Rus. Fed.
27 C4 Ulysses U.S.A.
69 D5 Uman' Ukr.
84 E5 Umaria India
84 D4 Umarkhed India
85 E6 Umarkot India
84 B4 Umarkot Pak.
24 C2 Umatilla U.S.A.
76 E3 Umba Rus. Fed.
32 H2 Umbagog Lake l. U.S.A.
110 E2 Umboi i. P.N.G.
54 B4 Umeå Sweden
54 Q4 Umeälven r. Sweden
105 K4 Umfolozi r. S. Africa
81 L7 Umgharah Kuwait
105 J4 Umhlanga S. Africa
22 E2 Umiujaq Can.
105 J5 Umkomaas S. Africa
105 J4 Umlazi S. Africa
81 K6 Umma Iraq
101 E3 Umm Keddada Sudan
81 L6 Umm Qaşr Iraq
101 F3 Umm Ruwaba Sudan
124 A3 Umpqua r. U.S.A.
103 B5 Umpulo Angola
84 D5 Umred India
84 C5 Umreth India
105 H5 Umtata S. Africa
105 J5 Umtentweni S. Africa
100 C4 Umuahia Nigeria
46 B3 Umuarama Brazil
105 H5 Umzimkulu S. Africa
105 J5 Umzinto S. Africa
66 G2 Una r. Bos.-Herz./Croatia
46 E1 Una Brazil
80 F6 'Unāb, W. al watercourse Jordan
46 C2 Unaí Brazil
84 B2 Unai Pass pass Afgh.
57 C2 Unapool U.K.
45 D2 Unare r. Venez.
80 E6 'Unayzah Jordan
78 E4 'Unayzah Saudi Arabia
81 G5 'Unayzah, Jabal h. Iraq
25 E4 Uncompahgre Plateau plat. U.S.A.
105 H4 Underberg S. Africa
114 B5 Underbool Austr.
26 C2 Underwood U.S.A.
68 E4 Unecha Rus. Fed.
115 G4 Ungarie Austr.
114 B5 Ungarra Austr.
22 F1 Ungava, Péninsule d' pen. Can.
23 G2 Ungava Bay b. Can.
87 O3 Unggi N. Korea
69 C6 Ungheni Moldova
68 J3 Uni Rus. Fed.
46 B3 União da Vitória Brazil
45 B4 Unilla r. Col.
42 F4 Unini r. Brazil
46 A4 Unión Para.
33 J2 Union ME U.S.A.
29 D5 Union SC U.S.A.
32 C6 Union WV U.S.A.
35 F4 Union, Mt U.S.A.
30 E5 Union City OH U.S.A.
32 D4 Union City PA U.S.A.
29 B4 Union City TN U.S.A.
104 E6 Uniondale S. Africa
29 C5 Union Springs U.S.A.
32 D5 Uniontown U.S.A.
31 F4 Unionville U.S.A.
24 E3 Unita Mts. mts U.S.A.
70 United Arab Emirates country Asia
48 United Kingdom country Europe
16 United States of America country North America
21 H4 Unity Can.
33 J2 Unity ME U.S.A.
24 C2 Unity OR U.S.A.
84 C5 Unjha India
84 E4 Unnao India
57 □ Unst i. U.K.
85 G2 Unuli Horog China
85 F5 Upar Ghat reg. India
45 E2 Upata Venez.
103 C4 Upemba, Lac l. Dem. Rep. Congo
94 C5 Upi Phil.
45 B3 Upía r. Col.
104 D4 Upington S. Africa
84 B5 Upleta India
54 W3 Upoloksha Rus. Fed.
111 J3 Upolu i. Samoa
24 B3 Upper Alkali Lake l. U.S.A.
32 B4 Upper Arlington U.S.A.
20 F4 Upper Arrow L. l. Can.
Upper Chindwin see Mawlaik
117 E4 Upper Hutt N.Z.
30 B4 Upper Iowa r. U.S.A.

33 K1 Upper Kent Can.
24 B3 Upper Klamath L. l. U.S.A.
34 A2 Upper Lake U.S.A.
20 D2 Upper Liard Can.
60 D3 Upper Lough Erne l. U.K.
32 E5 Upper Marlboro U.S.A.
95 □ Upper Peirce Res. resr Sing.
23 J4 Upper Salmon Reservoir resr Can.
32 B4 Upper Sandusky U.S.A.
33 F2 Upper Saranac Lake l. U.S.A.
117 D4 Upper Takaka N.Z.
55 P7 Uppsala Sweden
22 B4 Upsala Can.
116 B2 Upstart, C. hd Austr.
116 B2 Upstart B. b. Austr.
33 H2 Upton U.S.A.
81 L7 Uqlat al 'Udhaybah w. Iraq
81 L6 Ur Iraq
45 A2 Urabá, Golfo de b. Col.
Uracas i. see Farallon de Pajaros
Urad Qianqi see Xishanzui
88 C1 Urad Zhongqi China
90 H3 Urakawa Japan
115 G4 Ural h. Austr.
115 J3 Uralla Austr.
76 G4 Ural'sk Kazak.
102 D4 Urambo Tanz.
115 G5 Urana Austr.
115 G5 Urana, L. l. Austr.
46 D1 Urandi Brazil
21 H3 Uranium City Can.
115 G5 Uranquity Austr.
45 E4 Uraricoera Brazil
45 E4 Uraricoera r. Brazil
45 E4 Uraricuera r. Brazil
45 E3 Uraucaima, Sa mt Brazil
35 H2 Uravan U.S.A.
69 F5 Urazovo Rus. Fed.
30 C5 Urbana IL U.S.A.
32 B4 Urbana OH U.S.A.
115 K2 Urbenville Austr.
66 E3 Urbino Italy
42 D6 Urcos Peru
69 H5 Urda Kazak.
68 J2 Urdoma Rus. Fed.
58 F3 Ure r. U.K.
68 H3 Uren' Rus. Fed.
76 J3 Urengoy Rus. Fed.
111 G3 Uréparapara i. Vanuatu
117 F3 Urewera National Park nat. park N.Z.
68 H4 Urga r. Rus. Fed.
79 J1 Urgench Uzbek.
80 E2 Ürgüp Turkey
54 V2 Urho Kekkonen Kansallispuisto nat. park Fin.
45 B2 Uribia Col.
114 E2 Urisino Austr.
55 S6 Urjala Fin.
69 H7 Urkarakh Rus. Fed.
67 M5 Urla Turkey
60 D5 Urlingford Rep. of Ireland
Urmia see Orūmīyeh
Urmia, Lake salt l. see Orūmīyeh, Daryācheh-ye
89 □ Urmston Road sea chan. China
67 J3 Uroševac Yugo.
79 K2 Ùroteppa Tajik.
85 F3 Urru Co salt l. China
88 A1 Urt Mongolia
25 E7 Uruáchic Mex.
46 C1 Uruaçu Brazil
36 D5 Uruapan Mex.
42 D6 Urubamba r. Peru
43 G4 Urucara Brazil
43 K5 Uruçuí Brazil
46 D2 Urucuia r. Brazil
43 K5 Uruçuí Preto r. Brazil
43 G4 Urucurituba Brazil
44 E3 Uruguaiana Brazil
44 E4 Uruguay r. Arg./Uru.
38 Uruguay country S. America
Uruk see Erech
Urumchi see Ürümqi
82 G2 Ürümqi China
115 K3 Urunga Austr.
69 G6 Urup r. Rus. Fed.
77 R5 Urup, O. i. Rus. Fed.
69 H7 Urus-Martan Rus. Fed.
69 G5 Uryupinsk Rus. Fed.
68 J3 Urzhum Rus. Fed.
67 M2 Urziceni Romania
91 B8 Usa Japan
68 J4 Usa r. Rus. Fed.
80 B2 Uşak Turkey
103 B6 Usakos Namibia
119 B5 Usarp Mts mts Antarctica
44 E8 Usborne, Mt h. Falkland Is
76 J1 Ushakova, O. i. Rus. Fed.
91 B8 Ushibuka Japan
82 E1 Ushtobe Kazak.
44 C8 Ushuaia Arg.
76 G3 Usinsk Rus. Fed.
59 E6 Usk U.K.
59 E6 Usk r. U.K.
85 E4 Uska India
68 C4 Uskhodni Belarus
64 F4 Usman' Rus. Fed.
55 S8 Usmas ezers l. Latvia
68 J2 Usogorsk Rus. Fed.
86 H1 Usol'ye-Sibirskoye Rus. Fed.
64 F4 Ussel France

90 D1 Ussuri r. China/Rus. Fed.
87 O3 Ussuriysk Rus. Fed.
68 H3 Usta r. Rus. Fed.
87 J1 Ust'-Barguzin Rus. Fed.
69 G5 Ust'-Buzulukskaya Rus. Fed.
69 G6 Ust'-Donetskiy Rus. Fed.
66 C4 Ustica, Isola di i. Italy
77 M4 Ust'-Ilimsk Rus. Fed.
76 G3 Ust'-Ilych Rus. Fed.
62 G5 Ústí nad Labem Czech Rep.
Ustinov see Izhevsk
62 H3 Ustka Pol.
77 S4 Ust'-Kamchatsk Rus. Fed.
86 D2 Ust'-Kamenogorsk Kazak.
77 M4 Ust'-Kut Rus. Fed.
77 P2 Ust'-Kuyga Rus. Fed.
69 F6 Ust'-Labinsk Rus. Fed.
55 V7 Ust'-Luga Rus. Fed.
77 P3 Ust'-Maya Rus. Fed.
76 G3 Ust'-Nem Rus. Fed.
77 O2 Ust'-Nera Rus. Fed.
68 J2 Ust'-Ocheya Rus. Fed.
77 N2 Ust'-Olenek Rus. Fed.
77 Q3 Ust'-Omchug Rus. Fed.
86 H1 Ust'-Ordynskiy Rus. Fed.
76 K3 Ust'-Port Rus. Fed.
68 G2 Ust'-Shonosha Rus. Fed.
76 G3 Ust'-Tsil'ma Rus. Fed.
68 H2 Ust'-Ura Rus. Fed.
68 G2 Ust'-Vayen'ga Rus. Fed.
68 H2 Ust'-Vyyskaya Rus. Fed.
68 G2 Ust'ya r. Rus. Fed.
68 F3 Ust'ye Rus. Fed.
68 F3 Ust'ye Rus. Fed.
76 G5 Ustyurt Plateau plat. Kazak./Uzbek.
68 F3 Ustyuzhna Rus. Fed.
91 B8 Usuki Japan
68 D4 Usvyaty Rus. Fed.
35 G2 Utah div. U.S.A.
35 G1 Utah Lake l. U.S.A.
54 U4 Utajärvi Fin.
55 T9 Utena Lith.
95 B2 Uthai Thani Thai.
95 A2 U Thong Thai.
95 C2 Uthumphon Phisai Thai.
73 F3 Utica U.S.A.
65 F3 Utiel Spain
20 F3 Utikuma Lake l. Can.
105 F3 Utlwanang S. Africa
85 E4 Utraula India
61 D2 Utrecht Neth.
105 J3 Utrecht S. Africa
65 D4 Utrera Spain
54 U2 Utsjoki Fin.
91 F6 Utsunomiya Japan
69 H6 Utta Rus. Fed.
95 B1 Uttaradit Thai.
84 D4 Uttar Pradesh div. India
59 F5 Uttoxeter U.K.
111 G3 Utupua i. Solomon Is
54 T5 Uurainen Fin.
55 R6 Uusikaupunki Fin.
45 C4 Uva r. Col.
27 D6 Uvalde U.S.A.
69 G5 Uvarovo Rus. Fed.
102 D4 Uvinza Tanz.
105 J5 Uvongo S. Africa
86 F1 Uvs Nuur salt l. Mongolia
91 C8 Uwajima Japan
101 E2 Uweinat, Jebel mt Sudan
59 G6 Uxbridge U.K.
88 C2 Uxin Ju China
L4 Uyar Rus. Fed.
88 C1 Üydzin Mongolia
77 Q3 Uyega Rus. Fed.
100 C4 Uyo Nigeria
42 E8 Uyuni, Salar de salt flat Bol.
68 H4 Uza r. Rus. Fed.
81 K4 'Uẓaym, Nahr al r. Iraq
70 Uzbekistan country Asia
64 G4 Uzès France
69 B5 Uzhhorod Ukr.
79 F4 Uzice Yugo.
68 F4 Uzlovaya Rus. Fed.
68 G3 Uzola r. Rus. Fed.
80 C3 Üzümlü Turkey
81 L3 Üzün Darreh r. Iran
69 C7 Uzunköprü Turkey
69 D5 Uzyn Ukr.

V

55 T5 Vaajakoski Fin.
104 F4 Vaal r. S. Africa
54 U4 Vaala Fin.
104 F4 Vaalbos National Park nat. park S. Africa
105 H3 Vaal Dam dam S. Africa
105 H2 Vaalwater S. Africa
54 R5 Vaasa Fin.
63 J7 Vác Hungary
44 F3 Vacaria Brazil
46 A3 Vacaria r. Mato Grosso do Sul Brazil
46 D2 Vacaria r. Minas Gerais Brazil
46 A3 Vacaria, Serra h. Brazil
34 B2 Vacaville U.S.A.
68 G4 Vad r. Rus. Fed.
84 C6 Vada India
55 K7 Vadla Norway
84 C5 Vadodara India
54 V1 Vadsø Norway
62 D7 Vaduz Liechtenstein
54 N3 Værøy i. Norway
68 G2 Vaga r. Rus. Fed.
55 L6 Vågåmo Norway

66 F2 Vaganski Vrh mt Croatia
54 □ Vágar i. Faroe Is
54 Q4 Vägsele Sweden
54 □ Vágur Faroe Is
55 S5 Vähäkyrö Fin.
111 H2 Vaiaku Tuvalu
111 H2 Vaitupu i. Tuvalu
31 K2 Val-Barrette Can.
55 P6 Valbo Sweden
47 C4 Valcheta Arg.
66 D2 Valdagno Italy
68 E3 Valdayskaya Vozvyshennost' reg. Rus. Fed.
65 D3 Valdecañas, Embalse de resr Spain
55 S8 Valdemārpils Latvia
55 P7 Valdemarsvik Sweden
64 G2 Val-de-Meuse France
65 E3 Valdepeñas Spain
64 E2 Val-de-Reuil France
47 D4 Valdés, Península pen. Arg.
31 K3 Val-des-Bois Can.
47 B3 Valdivia Chile
31 J1 Val-d'Or Can.
29 D6 Valdosta U.S.A.
55 L6 Valdres v. Norway
81 J1 Vale Georgia
24 C2 Vale U.S.A.
20 F4 Valemount Can.
46 E1 Valença Brazil
64 G4 Valence France
65 F3 Valencia Spain
65 D2 Valencia Venez.
65 G3 Valencia, Golfo de g. Spain
65 C3 Valencia de Alcántara Spain
65 D1 Valencia de Don Juan Spain
60 A6 Valencia Island i. Rep. of Ireland
64 F1 Valenciennes France
90 D3 Valentin Rus. Fed.
35 F4 Valentine AZ U.S.A.
26 C3 Valentine NE U.S.A.
27 B6 Valentine TX U.S.A.
94 B3 Valenzuela Phil.
55 M6 Våler Norway
45 C2 Valera Venez.
67 H2 Valjevo Yugo.
61 C4 Val Joly, Lac du l. France
55 U8 Valka Latvia
55 T6 Valkeakoski Fin.
61 D3 Valkenswaard Neth.
69 E5 Valky Ukr.
119 C4 Valkyrie Dome ice feature Antarctica
36 G4 Valladolid Mex.
65 D2 Valladolid Spain
65 F3 Vall de Uxó Spain
55 K7 Valle Norway
45 B2 Valle de la Pascua Venez.
45 B2 Valledupar Col.
47 C1 Valle Fértil, Sa de mts Arg.
42 E7 Valle Grande Bol.
34 A2 Vallejo U.S.A.
66 F7 Valletta Malta
59 C4 Valley U.K.
26 C2 Valley City U.S.A.
24 B3 Valley Falls U.S.A.
32 C5 Valley Head U.S.A.
73 F3 Valleyview Can.
65 G2 Valls Spain
21 H5 Val Marie Can.
55 T8 Valmiera Latvia
65 E1 Valnera mt Spain
22 E4 Valognes Can.
83 E8 Valparai India
46 B3 Valparaíso Brazil
47 B3 Valparaíso Chile
30 D5 Valparaiso U.S.A.
47 B3 Valparaíso div. Chile
64 G4 Valréas France
55 M6 Vals r. S. Africa
104 F3 Valspan S. Africa
68 H1 Val'tevo Rus. Fed.
54 V5 Valtimo Fin.
69 G6 Valuyevka Rus. Fed.
69 F5 Valuyki Rus. Fed.
65 C4 Valverde del Camino Spain
95 C3 Vam Co Tay r. Vietnam
55 S6 Vammala Fin.
81 J2 Van Turkey
Van, Lake salt l. see Van Gölü
81 K1 Vanadzor Armenia
27 C4 Van Buren AR U.S.A.
33 K1 Van Buren ME U.S.A.
33 K2 Vanceboro U.S.A.
33 B5 Vanceburg U.S.A.
20 E5 Vancouver Can.
24 B2 Vancouver U.S.A.
20 A2 Vancouver, Mt mt Can./U.S.A.
20 D5 Vancouver Island i. Can.
28 B4 Vandalia IL U.S.A.
32 A5 Vandalia OH U.S.A.
105 G3 Vanderbijlpark S. Africa
30 E3 Vanderbilt U.S.A.
32 D4 Vandergrift U.S.A.
20 E4 Vanderhoof Can.
104 F5 Vanderkloof Dam resr S. Africa

113 G3 Vanderlin I. i. Austr.
35 H4 Vanderwagen U.S.A.
112 F2 Van Diemen Gulf b. Austr.
55 T7 Vändra Estonia
55 N7 Vänern l. Sweden
55 N7 Vänersborg Sweden
32 N Van Etten U.S.A.
103 E6 Vangaindrano Madag.
81 J2 Van Gölü salt l. Turkey
27 B6 Van Horn U.S.A.
31 K3 Vanier Can.
111 G3 Vanikoro Is is Solomon Is
110 E2 Vanimo P.N.G.
77 Q5 Vanino Rus. Fed.
77 V3 Vankarem Rus. Fed.
33 F2 Vankleek Hill Can.
54 R1 Vanna i. Norway
54 Q3 Vännäs Sweden
64 C3 Vannes France
93 K7 Van Rees, Pegunungan mts Indon.
104 C5 Vanrhynsdorp S. Africa
55 O6 Vansbro Sweden
55 T6 Vantaa Fin.
111 G3 Vanua Lava i. Vanuatu
111 H3 Vanua Levu i. Fiji
106 Vanuatu country Pac. Oc.
32 A4 Van Wert U.S.A.
104 D3 Vanwyksvlei S. Africa
104 D5 Vanwyksvlei r. S. Africa
89 B6 Văn Yên Vietnam
104 E3 Van Zylsrus S. Africa
55 U8 Varakļāni Latvia
85 E4 Varanasi India
54 V1 Varangerfjorden chan. Norway
54 V1 Varangerhalvøya pen. Norway
66 G1 Varaždin Croatia
55 N8 Varberg Sweden
67 K4 Vardar r. Macedonia
55 L9 Varde Denmark
54 W1 Vardø Norway
47 C2 Varela Arg.
55 T9 Varena Lith.
66 C2 Varese Italy
90 C2 Varfolomeyevka Rus. Fed.
55 N7 Vårgårda Sweden
46 D3 Varginha Brazil
61 D3 Varik Neth.
54 U5 Varkaus Fin.
67 M3 Varna Bulg.
55 O8 Värnamo Sweden
55 N6 Värnäs Sweden
68 H3 Varnavino Rus. Fed.
80 D4 Varosia Cyprus
54 U5 Varpaisjärvi Fin.
62 J7 Várpalota Hungary
84 B1 Varsaj Afgh.
81 H2 Varto Turkey
85 E4 Varuna r. India
32 D3 Varysburg U.S.A.
46 D2 Várzea da Palma Brazil
68 H2 Vashka r. Rus. Fed.
Vasht see Khāsh
68 H2 Vasilevo Rus. Fed.
55 U7 Vasknarva Estonia
63 N7 Vaslui Romania
31 F4 Vassar U.S.A.
55 P7 Västerås Sweden
56 N6 Västerdalälven r. Sweden
54 P3 Västerfjäll Sweden
55 Q7 Västerhaninge Sweden
55 P8 Västervik Sweden
66 F3 Vasto Italy
69 D5 Vasyl'kiv Ukr.
64 E3 Vatan France
57 A4 Vatersay i. U.K.
67 M6 Vathy Greece
48 Vatican City country Europe
54 E4 Vatnajökull ice cap Iceland
63 M7 Vatra Dornei Romania
55 O7 Vättern l. Sweden
25 F5 Vaughn U.S.A.
45 C4 Vaupés r. Col.
64 G5 Vauvert France
111 J3 Vava'u Group is Tonga
100 B4 Vavoua Côte d'Ivoire
68 C4 Vawkavysk Belarus
55 O8 Växjö Sweden
95 B3 Vây, Đao i. Vietnam
68 H1 Vazhgort Rus. Fed.
103 E5 Vazobe mt Madag.
95 B2 Veal Vêng Cambodia
61 E2 Vechte r. Ger.
58 N8 Veddige Sweden
67 L3 Vedea r. Romania
69 H7 Vedeno Rus. Fed.
81 K2 Vedi Armenia
47 E2 Vedia Arg.
67 E2 Vedozero Rus. Fed.
30 D5 Veedersburg U.S.A.
61 E1 Veendam Neth.
61 D2 Veenendaal Neth.
54 M4 Vega i. Norway
27 C5 Vega U.S.A.
21 G4 Vegreville Can.
55 U6 Vehkalahti Fin.
84 B3 Vehoa r. Pak.
84 B4 Veirwaro Pak.
65 D4 Vejer de la Frontera Spain
55 L9 Vejle Denmark
67 K3 Velbŭzhdki Prokhod pass Macedonia
104 C6 Velddrif S. Africa
66 F2 Velebit mts Croatia
61 E3 Velen Ger.
66 F1 Velenje Slovenia
67 J4 Veles Macedonia
45 B3 Vélez Col.

65 D4 Vélez–Málaga Spain
65 E4 Vélez–Rubio Spain
46 D2 Velhas r. Brazil
69 H6 Velichayevskoye Rus. Fed.
66 G2 Velika Gorica Croatia
67 G2 Velika Plana Yugo.
68 J3 Velikaya Rus. Fed.
68 E2 Velikaya r. Rus. Fed.
77 T3 Velikaya r. Rus. Fed.
68 E2 Velikaya Guba Rus. Fed.
90 E2 Velikaya Kema Rus. Fed.
67 M3 Veliki Preslav Bulg.
68 D3 Velikiy Novgorod Rus. Fed.
68 H2 Velikiy Ustyug Rus. Fed.
63 Q2 Velikooktyabr'skiy
67 L3 Veliko Türnovo Bulg.
68 F3 Velikoye l. Rus. Fed.
68 F3 Velikoye, Oz. l. Rus. Fed.
68 G2 Velikoye, Oz. l. Rus. Fed.
66 F2 Veli Lošinj Croatia
100 A3 Vélingara Senegal
63 P3 Velizh Rus. Fed.
62 H7 Veľký Meder Slovakia
111 F2 Vella Lavella i. Solomon Is
83 E8 Vellore India
68 G3 Vel'sk Rus. Fed.
62 F4 Velten Ger.
61 D2 Veluwe reg. Neth.
61 D2 Veluwemeer l. Neth.
61 D2 Veluwezoom, Nationaal Park nat. park Neth.
21 J5 Velva U.S.A.
12 G5 Vema Fracture sea feature Atlantic Ocean
13 J4 Vema Trench sea feature Indian Ocean
57 D4 Venachar, Loch l. U.K.
47 C2 Venado Tuerto Arg.
66 F4 Venafro Italy
45 E3 Venamo r. Guyana/Venez.
45 E3 Venamo, Co mt Venez.
46 C3 Venceslau Bráz Brazil
64 E3 Vendôme France
68 F4 Venev Rus. Fed.
Venezia see Venice
38 Venezuela country S. America
45 C2 Venezuela, Golfo de g. Venez.
83 E7 Vengurla India
66 E2 Venice Italy
29 D7 Venice U.S.A.
66 E2 Venice, Gulf of g. Europe
64 G4 Vénissieux France
61 E3 Venlo Neth.
55 K7 Vennesla Norway
61 E3 Venray Neth.
55 R8 Venta r. Latvia/Lith.
55 S8 Venta Lith.
105 G4 Ventersburg S. Africa
105 G3 Ventersdorp S. Africa
105 F5 Venterstad S. Africa
59 F7 Ventnor U.K.
64 G4 Ventoux, Mont mt France
55 R8 Ventspils Latvia
45 C3 Ventuari r. Venez.
34 C4 Ventucopa U.S.A.
34 C4 Ventura U.S.A.
114 F7 Venus B. b. Austr.
27 C7 Venustiano Carranza Mex.
27 C7 Venustiano Carranza, Presa l. Mex.
44 D3 Vera Arg.
65 F4 Vera Spain
36 E5 Veracruz Mex.
84 B5 Veraval India
66 C2 Verbania Italy
66 C2 Vercelli Italy
54 M5 Verdalsøra Norway
47 E4 Verde r. Arg.
46 B2 Verde r. Goiás Brazil
46 B2 Verde r. Goiás Brazil
46 C2 Verde r. Goiás/Minas Gerais Brazil
46 B3 Verde r. Mato Grosso do Sul Brazil
44 E2 Verde r. Para.
35 G4 Verde r. U.S.A.
47 D3 Verde, Pen. pen. Arg.
46 D1 Verde Grande r. Brazil
94 B3 Verde Island Pass. chan. Phil.
62 D4 Verden (Aller) Ger.
27 E4 Verdigris r. U.S.A.
64 H5 Verdon r. France
64 G2 Verdun France
105 G3 Vereeniging S. Africa
47 G2 Vergara Uru.
33 G2 Vergennes U.S.A.
65 C2 Verín Spain
69 F6 Verkhnebakanskiy Rus. Fed.
63 Q3 Verkhnedneprovskiy Rus. Fed.
76 K3 Verkhneimbatsk Rus. Fed.
54 W2 Verkhnetulomskiy Rus. Fed.
77 O3 Verkhnevilyuysk Rus. Fed.
68 H2 Verkhneye Kuyto, Oz. l. Rus. Fed.
69 H5 Verkhniy Baskunchak Rus. Fed.
69 J5 Verkhniy Kushum Rus. Fed.
68 H2 Verkhnyaya Toyma Rus. Fed.
68 G2 Verkhovazh'ye Rus. Fed.
68 F4 Verkhov'ye Rus. Fed.
69 C5 Verkhovyna Ukr.

77 P3 **Verkhoyansk** Rus. Fed.
77 O3 **Verkhoyanskiy Khrebet** *mts* Rus. Fed.
46 B1 **Vermelho** *r.* Brazil
21 G4 **Vermilion** Can.
30 C7 **Vermilion** *r.* U.S.A.
35 F3 **Vermilion Cliffs** *cliff* U.S.A.
30 A2 **Vermilion Lake** *l.* U.S.A.
30 A2 **Vermilion Range** *h.* U.S.A.
26 D3 **Vermillion** U.S.A.
21 L5 **Vermillion Bay** Can.
33 G3 **Vermont** *div.* U.S.A.
24 E3 **Vernal** U.S.A.
31 G2 **Verner** Can.
104 D4 **Verneuk Pan** *salt pan* S. Africa
20 F4 **Vernon** Can.
35 H4 **Vernon** *AZ* U.S.A.
33 G4 **Vernon** *CT* U.S.A.
27 D5 **Vernon** *TX* U.S.A.
35 F1 **Vernon** *UT* U.S.A.
29 D7 **Vero Beach** U.S.A.
67 K4 **Veroia** Greece
66 D2 **Verona** Italy
47 F2 **Verónica** Arg.
114 B4 **Verran** Austr.
64 F2 **Versailles** France
64 D3 **Vertou** France
105 J4 **Verulam** S. Africa
61 D4 **Verviers** Belgium
64 F2 **Vervins** France
66 C3 **Vescovato** France
76 G4 **Veselaya, G.** *mt* Rus. Fed.
69 E6 **Vesele** Ukr.
69 G6 **Veselovskoye Vdkhr.** *resr* Rus. Fed.
69 G5 **Veshenskaya** Rus. Fed.
61 B5 **Vesle** *r.* France
64 H3 **Vesoul** France
90 D7 **Vesselyy Yar** Rus. Fed.
61 D3 **Vessem** Neth.
54 O2 **Vesterålen** *is* Norway
54 N2 **Vesterålsfjorden** *chan.* Norway
119 C3 **Vestfjella** *mts* Antarctica
55 L7 **Vestfjorddalen** *v.* Norway
54 N3 **Vestfjorden** *chan.* Norway
54 ▫ **Vestmanna** Faroe Is
54 C5 **Vestmannaeyjar** Iceland
54 C5 **Vestmannaeyjar** *is* Iceland
54 K5 **Vestnes** Norway
54 F4 **Vesturhorn** *hd* Iceland
Vesuvio *vol. see* Vesuvius
66 F4 **Vesuvius** *vol.* Italy
68 F3 **Ves'yegonsk** Rus. Fed.
62 H7 **Veszprém** Hungary
55 S5 **Veteli** Fin.
55 O8 **Vetlanda** Sweden
68 H3 **Vetluga** Rus. Fed.
68 H3 **Vetluga** *r.* Rus. Fed.
66 E3 **Vettore, Monte** *mt* Italy
61 A3 **Veurne** Belgium
62 C7 **Vevey** Switz.
55 F3 **Veyo** U.S.A.
81 M6 **Veys** Iran
64 E4 **Vézère** *r.* France
80 E1 **Vezirköprü** Turkey
43 K4 **Viana** Brazil
65 B2 **Viana do Castelo** Port.
Viangchan *see* Vientiane
46 C2 **Vianópolis** Brazil
66 D3 **Viareggio** Italy
55 L8 **Viborg** Denmark
66 G5 **Vibo Valentia** Italy
65 H2 **Vic** Spain
119 B2 **Vicecomodoro Marambio** *Arg. Base* Antarctica
34 C5 **Vicente, Pt** *pt* U.S.A.
25 C6 **Vicente Guerrero** Mex.
66 D2 **Vicenza** Italy
42 D3 **Vichada** *r.* Col.
45 C3 **Vichada** *r.* Col.
68 G3 **Vichuga** Rus. Fed.
47 B2 **Vichuquén** Chile
64 F3 **Vichy** France
35 F5 **Vicksburg** *AZ* U.S.A.
27 F5 **Vicksburg** *MS* U.S.A.
46 D3 **Viçosa** Brazil
30 A5 **Victor** U.S.A.
114 C5 **Victor Harbor** Austr.
47 E2 **Victoria** Arg.
114 F6 **Victoria** *div.* Austr.
112 F3 **Victoria** *r.* Austr.
20 E5 **Victoria** Can.
47 B3 **Victoria** Chile
Victoria *see* Labuan
66 F6 **Victoria** Malta
27 D6 **Victoria** U.S.A.
102 D4 **Victoria, Lake** *l.* Africa
114 D4 **Victoria, Lake** *l.* Austr.
115 G6 **Victoria, Lake** *l.* Austr.
85 H5 **Victoria, Mt** *mt* Myanmar
110 E2 **Victoria, Mt** P.N.G.
103 C5 **Victoria Falls** *waterfall* Zambia/Zimbabwe
118 B2 **Victoria Island** *i.* Can.
23 J4 **Victoria Lake** *l.* Can.
119 B5 **Victoria Land** *reg.* Antarctica
101 F4 **Victoria Nile** *r.* Sudan/Uganda
117 D5 **Victoria Range** *mts* N.Z.
112 F3 **Victoria River** Austr.
112 F3 **Victoria River Downs** Austr.
23 F4 **Victoriaville** Can.
104 E5 **Victoria West** S. Africa
47 D3 **Victorica** Arg.
34 D4 **Victorville** U.S.A.
47 D2 **Vicuña Mackenna** Arg.

35 E4 **Vidal Junction** U.S.A.
67 L2 **Videle** Romania
63 K3 **Vidin** Bulg.
84 D5 **Vidisha** India
57 ▫ **Vidlin** U.K.
68 E2 **Vidlitsa** Rus. Fed.
63 N3 **Vidzy** Belarus
68 J2 **Vidz'yuyar** Rus. Fed.
47 D4 **Viedma** Arg.
44 B7 **Viedma, L.** *l.* Arg.
25 D6 **Viejo, Cerro** *mt* Mex.
61 D4 **Vielsalm** Belgium
62 H6 **Vienna** Austria
28 B4 **Vienna** *IL* U.S.A.
33 F5 **Vienna** *MD* U.S.A.
32 C5 **Vienna** *WV* U.S.A.
64 G4 **Vienne** France
64 E3 **Vienne** *r.* France
95 B1 **Vientiane** Laos
47 B3 **Viento, Cordillera del** *mts* Arg.
37 L5 **Vieques** *i.* Puerto Rico
54 U5 **Vieremä** Fin.
61 E3 **Viersen** Ger.
62 D7 **Vierwaldstätter See** *l.* Switz.
64 F3 **Vierzon** France
27 C7 **Viesca** Mex.
55 T8 **Viesīte** Latvia
66 G4 **Vieste** Italy
54 Q3 **Vietas** Sweden
70 **Vietnam** *country* Asia
89 B6 **Viêt Tri** Vietnam
94 B2 **Vigan** Phil.
66 C2 **Vigevano** Italy
64 D5 **Vignemale** *mt* France
66 D2 **Vignola** Italy
65 B1 **Vigo** Spain
65 E1 **Vigy** France
54 T4 **Vihanti** Fin.
84 C3 **Vihari** Pak.
55 T6 **Vihti** Fin.
54 T5 **Viitasaari** Fin.
84 C3 **Vijainagar** India
83 F7 **Vijayawada** India
54 J5 **Vík** Iceland
21 G4 **Viking** Can.
54 M4 **Vikna** *i.* Norway
55 K6 **Vikøyri** Norway
100 ▫ **Vila da Ribeira Brava** Cape Verde
100 ▫ **Vila de Sal Rei** Cape Verde
100 ▫ **Vila do Tarrafal** Antarctica
65 B3 **Vila Franca de Xira** Port.
65 B3 **Vilagarcía de Arousa** Spain
105 K2 **Vila Gomes da Costa** Moz.
65 C1 **Vilalba** Spain
103 E5 **Vilanandro, Tanjona** *pt* Madag.
65 G2 **Vila Nova de Gaia** Port.
65 G2 **Vilanova i la Geltrú** Spain
100 ▫ **Vila Nova Sintra** Cape Verde
65 C2 **Vila Real** Port.
65 C2 **Vilar Formoso** Port.
46 E3 **Vila Velha** Brazil
46 D6 **Vilcabamba, Cordillera** *mts* Peru
54 P4 **Vilhelmina** Sweden
42 F6 **Vilhena** Brazil
55 T7 **Viljandi** Estonia
105 G3 **Viljoenskroon** S. Africa
55 S9 **Vilkaviškis** Lith.
55 S9 **Vilkija** Lith.
77 L2 **Vil'kitskogo, Proliv** *str.* Rus. Fed.
25 F6 **Villa Ahumada** Mex.
42 E6 **Villa Bella** Bol.
65 C1 **Villablino** Spain
47 E2 **Villa Cañás** Arg.
65 E3 **Villacañas** Spain
62 F7 **Villach** Austria
66 C5 **Villacidro** Italy
47 E2 **Villa Constitución** Arg.
47 D1 **Villa del Rosario** Arg.
47 D1 **Villa del Totoral** Arg.
47 D1 **Villa Dolores** Arg.
47 F3 **Villa Gesell** Arg.
47 E1 **Villaguay** Arg.
36 F5 **Villahermosa** Mex.
47 D2 **Villa Huidobro** Arg.
36 B3 **Villa Insurgentes** Mex.
47 D3 **Villa Iris** Arg.
65 F3 **Villajoyosa** Spain
27 C7 **Villaldama** Mex.
47 D2 **Villálonga** Arg.
47 D2 **Villa María** Arg.
47 E1 **Villa María Grande** Arg.
42 F8 **Villa Montes** Bol.
105 H1 **Villa Nora** S. Africa
45 B2 **Villanueva** Col.
65 D3 **Villanueva de la Serena** Spain
65 E3 **Villanueva de los Infantes** Spain
44 B3 **Villa Ocampo** Arg.
27 B7 **Villa Ocampo** Mex.
27 B7 **Villa Orestes Pereyra** Mex.
66 C5 **Villaputzu** Italy
47 D3 **Villa Regina** Arg.
44 B3 **Villarrica** Chile
44 E3 **Villarrica** Para.
47 B3 **Villarrica, L.** *l.* Chile
47 B3 **Villarrica, Parque Nacional** *nat. park* Chile
47 B3 **Villarrica, Volcán** *vol.* Chile

65 E3 **Villarrobledo** Spain
66 F5 **Villa San Giovanni** Italy
47 E2 **Villa San José** Arg.
47 C1 **Villa Santa Rita de Catuna** Arg.
44 C3 **Villa Unión** Arg.
27 C6 **Villa Unión** Mex.
47 D2 **Villa Valeria** Arg.
45 B3 **Villavicencio** Col.
42 E8 **Villazon** Bol.
64 F4 **Villefranche-de-Rouergue** France
64 G4 **Villefranche-sur-Saône** France
31 H2 **Ville-Marie** Can.
65 F3 **Villena** Spain
64 E4 **Villeneuve-sur-Lot** France
64 F2 **Villeneuve-sur-Yonne** France
27 E6 **Ville Platte** U.S.A.
61 B5 **Villers-Cotterêts** France
64 G4 **Villeurbanne** France
105 H3 **Villiers** S. Africa
62 D6 **Villingen** Ger.
21 G4 **Vilna** Can.
55 T9 **Vilnius** Lith.
69 E6 **Vil'nyans'k** Ukr.
55 T5 **Vilppula** Fin.
83 E8 **Viluppuram** India
61 C4 **Vilvoorde** Belgium
68 C4 **Vilyeyka** Belarus
77 O3 **Vilyuy** *r.* Rus. Fed.
77 M3 **Vilyuyskoye Vdkhr.** *resr* Rus. Fed.
55 O8 **Vimmerby** Sweden
34 A2 **Vina** U.S.A.
47 B2 **Viña del Mar** Chile
33 J2 **Vinalhaven** U.S.A.
65 G2 **Vinaròs** Spain
28 C4 **Vincennes** U.S.A.
54 Q4 **Vindelälven** *r.* Sweden
54 Q4 **Vindeln** Sweden
84 C5 **Vindhya Range** *h.* India
33 F5 **Vineland** U.S.A.
33 H4 **Vineyard Haven** U.S.A.
95 C1 **Vinh** Vietnam
95 C1 **Vinh Linh** Vietnam
95 C3 **Vinh Long** Vietnam
89 B6 **Vinh Yên** Vietnam
27 E4 **Vinita** U.S.A.
67 H2 **Vinkovci** Croatia
69 D5 **Vinnytsya** Ukr.
119 B3 **Vinson Massif** *mt* Antarctica
55 L6 **Vinstra** Norway
30 A4 **Vinton** U.S.A.
83 E7 **Vinukonda** India
66 D1 **Vipiteno** Italy
94 C3 **Virac** Phil.
84 C5 **Viramgam** India
81 G3 **Viranşehir** Turkey
84 B4 **Virawah** Pak.
21 J5 **Virden** Can.
64 D2 **Vire** France
103 B5 **Virei** Angola
46 D2 **Virgem da Lapa** Brazil
35 F3 **Virgin** *mts* U.S.A.
31 H1 **Virginatown** Can.
60 D4 **Virginia** Rep. of Ireland
105 G4 **Virginia** S. Africa
30 A2 **Virginia** U.S.A.
32 D6 **Virginia** *div.* U.S.A.
33 G6 **Virginia Beach** U.S.A.
34 C2 **Virginia City** U.S.A.
37 M5 **Virgin Islands (U.K.)** *terr.* Caribbean
37 M5 **Virgin Islands (U.S.A.)** *terr.* Caribbean
55 T6 **Virkkala** Fin.
95 C2 **Virôchey** Cambodia
30 B4 **Viroqua** U.S.A.
66 G2 **Virovitica** Croatia
55 S5 **Virrat** Fin.
61 D5 **Virton** Belgium
55 S7 **Virtsu** Estonia
83 E9 **Virudunagar** India
102 C3 **Virunga, Parc National des** *nat. park* Dem. Rep. Congo
66 G3 **Vis** *i.* Croatia
55 U9 **Visaginas** Lith.
34 C3 **Visalia** U.S.A.
84 B5 **Visavadar** India
94 B4 **Visayan Sea** *sea* Phil.
55 Q8 **Visby** Sweden
76 J2 **Vise, O.** *i.* Rus. Fed.
67 H3 **Višegrad** Bos.-Herz.
43 J4 **Viseu** Brazil
65 C2 **Viseu** Port.
83 F7 **Vishakhapatnam** India
55 U8 **Viški** Latvia
84 C5 **Visnagar** India
66 B2 **Viso, Monte** *mt* Italy
67 H3 **Visoko** Bos.-Herz.
62 C7 **Visp** Switz.
34 D5 **Vista** U.S.A.
46 A2 **Vista Alegre** Brazil
67 L4 **Vistonida, Limni** *lag.* Greece
45 D3 **Vita** *r.* Col.
84 B3 **Vitakri** Pak.
66 F3 **Viterbo** Italy
66 G2 **Vitez** Bos.-Herz.
42 E8 **Vitichi** Bol.
65 C2 **Vitigudino** Spain
111 H3 **Viti Levu** *i.* Fiji
87 L1 **Vitim** *r.* Rus. Fed.
87 K1 **Vitimskoye Ploskogor'ye** *plat.* Rus. Fed.
46 E3 **Vitória** Brazil
Vitoria *see* Vitoria-Gasteiz

46 E1 **Vitória da Conquista** Brazil
65 E1 **Vitoria-Gasteiz** Spain
64 D2 **Vitré** France
64 G2 **Vitry-le-François** France
68 C3 **Vitsyebsk** Belarus
54 R3 **Vittangi** Sweden
66 E2 **Vittoria** Italy
66 E2 **Vittorio Veneto** Italy
14 F3 **Vityaz Depth** *depth* Pac. Oc.
65 C1 **Viveiro** Spain
105 H1 **Vivo** S. Africa
114 B6 **Vivonne B.** *b.* Austr.
25 D7 **Vizcaíno, Desierto de** *des.* Mex.
36 B3 **Vizcaíno, Sierra** *mts* Mex.
69 B3 **Vize** Turkey
83 F7 **Vizianagaram** India
68 J2 **Vizinga** Rus. Fed.
61 C3 **Vlaardingen** Neth.
63 L7 **Vlădeasa, Vârful** *mt* Romania
69 H7 **Vladikavkaz** Rus. Fed.
90 D3 **Vladimir** Rus. Fed.
68 G3 **Vladimir** Rus. Fed.
90 C3 **Vladimiro-Aleksandrovskoye** Rus. Fed.
68 G4 **Vladimirskaya Oblast'** *div.* Rus. Fed.
87 O3 **Vladivostok** Rus. Fed.
105 H2 **Vlakte** S. Africa
67 K3 **Vlasotince** Yugo.
104 D7 **Vleesbaai** *b.* S. Africa
61 C1 **Vlieland** *i.* Neth.
61 B3 **Vlissingen** Neth.
67 H4 **Vlorë** Albania
66 G6 **Vltava** *r.* Czech Rep.
62 F6 **Vöcklabruck** Austria
68 F2 **Vodlozero, Ozero** *l.* Rus. Fed.
57 ▫ **Voe** U.K.
61 D4 **Voerendaal** Neth.
66 C2 **Voghera** Italy
103 E6 **Vohimena, Tanjona** *c.* Madag.
55 T7 **Võhma** Estonia
102 D4 **Voi** Kenya
100 B4 **Voinjama** Liberia
64 G4 **Voiron** France
55 L9 **Vojens** Denmark
67 H2 **Vojvodina** *div.* Yugo.
68 H3 **Vokhma** Rus. Fed.
68 D1 **Voknavolok** Rus. Fed.
24 F2 **Volborg** U.S.A.
47 B1 **Volcán, Co del** *mt* Chile
Volcano Bay *b. see* Uchiura-wan
Volcano Is *is see* Kazan-rettō
55 K5 **Volda** Norway
55 H6 **Volga** *r.* Rus. Fed.
30 A4 **Volga** U.S.A.
69 G6 **Volgodonsk** Rus. Fed.
69 H5 **Volgograd** Rus. Fed.
69 H5 **Volgogradskaya Oblast'** *div.* Rus. Fed.
62 G7 **Völkermarkt** Austria
68 D3 **Volkhov** Rus. Fed.
68 D3 **Volkhov** *r.* Rus. Fed.
61 E5 **Völklingen** Ger.
105 H3 **Volksrust** S. Africa
90 B3 **Vol'no-Nadezhdinskoye** Rus. Fed.
69 F6 **Volnovakha** Ukr.
77 L2 **Volochanka** Rus. Fed.
69 F6 **Volochys'k** Ukr.
69 F6 **Volodars'ke** Ukr.
69 J6 **Volodarskiy** Rus. Fed.
63 O5 **Volodars'k-Volyns'kyy** Ukr.
63 N5 **Volodymyrets'** Ukr.
69 C5 **Volodymyr-Volyns'kyy** Ukr.
68 F3 **Vologda** Rus. Fed.
68 G3 **Vologodskaya Oblast'** *div.* Rus. Fed.
69 F5 **Volokonovka** Rus. Fed.
67 K5 **Volos** Greece
68 D3 **Volosovo** Rus. Fed.
63 P2 **Volot** Rus. Fed.
69 F4 **Volovo** Rus. Fed.
69 H4 **Vol'sk** Rus. Fed.
100 B4 **Volta, Lake** *resr* Ghana
46 D3 **Volta Redonda** Brazil
66 F4 **Volturno** *r.* Italy
67 K4 **Volvi, L.** *l.* Greece
64 J4 **Volzhsk** Rus. Fed.
69 H5 **Volzhskiy** Rus. Fed.
103 E6 **Vondrozo** Madag.
68 B2 **Vôrå** Fin.
68 M3 **Voranava** Belarus
68 J3 **Vorchanka** Rus. Fed.
68 E2 **Vorenzha** Rus. Fed.
76 H3 **Vorkuta** Rus. Fed.
55 S7 **Vormsi** *i.* Estonia
69 F5 **Vorona** *r.* Rus. Fed.
69 F5 **Voronezh** Rus. Fed.
69 F5 **Voronezh** *r.* Rus. Fed.
69 G5 **Voronezhskaya Oblast'** *div.* Rus. Fed.
68 G3 **Voron'ye** Rus. Fed.
Voroshilovgrad *see* Luhans'k
63 O7 **Vorot'kovo** Rus. Fed.
69 O3 **Vorskla** *r.* Rus. Fed.
55 T7 **Võrtsjärv** *l.* Estonia
55 U8 **Võru** Estonia
104 E5 **Vosburg** S. Africa
64 H2 **Vosges** *mts* France

55 K6 **Voss** Norway
Vostochno-Sibirskoye More *sea see* East Siberian Sea
86 G1 **Vostochnyy Sayan** *mts* Rus. Fed.
90 D1 **Vostok** Rus. Fed.
90 E2 **Vostretsovo** Rus. Fed.
76 G4 **Votkinsk** Rus. Fed.
46 C3 **Votuporanga** Brazil
61 C5 **Vouziers** France
64 E2 **Voves** France
68 J3 **Voya** *r.* Rus. Fed.
28 A1 **Voyageurs Nat. Park** *nat. park* U.S.A.
54 W4 **Voynitsa** Rus. Fed.
68 F2 **Vozhe, Ozero** *l.* Rus. Fed.
68 G2 **Vozhega** Rus. Fed.
69 D6 **Voznesens'k** Ukr.
90 C2 **Vrangel'** Rus. Fed.
77 T2 **Vrangelya, O.** *i.* Rus. Fed.
67 J3 **Vranje** Yugo.
67 M3 **Vratnik** *pass* Bulg.
63 K3 **Vratsa** Bulg.
66 G2 **Vrbas** *r.* Bos.-Herz.
67 H2 **Vrbas** Yugo.
105 H3 **Vrede** S. Africa
105 G3 **Vredefort** S. Africa
104 B6 **Vredenburg** S. Africa
104 C5 **Vredendal** S. Africa
61 C5 **Vresse** Belgium
83 E8 **Vriddhachalam** India
55 O8 **Vrigstad** Sweden
67 J2 **Vršac** Yugo.
104 F3 **Vryburg** S. Africa
105 J3 **Vryheid** S. Africa
68 D2 **Vsevolozhsk** Rus. Fed.
67 J3 **Vučitrn** Yugo.
67 H2 **Vukovar** Croatia
76 G3 **Vuktyl'** Rus. Fed.
105 H3 **Vukuzakhe** S. Africa
66 F5 **Vulcano, Isola** *i.* Italy
35 F5 **Vulture Mts** *mts* U.S.A.
95 C3 **Vung Tau** Vietnam
54 U6 **Vuohijärvi** Fin.
54 U4 **Vuolijoki** Fin.
54 V3 **Vuollerim** Sweden
54 U3 **Vuostimo** Fin.
68 H4 **Vurnary** Rus. Fed.
104 D4 **Vwawa** Tanz.
84 C5 **Vyara** India
68 J3 **Vyatka** Rus. Fed.
68 J4 **Vyaz'ma** Rus. Fed.
68 G3 **Vyazniki** Rus. Fed.
68 D2 **Vyborg** Rus. Fed.
68 J2 **Vychegda** *r.* Rus. Fed.
68 J2 **Vychegodskiy** Rus. Fed.
68 C4 **Vyerkhnyadzvinsk** Belarus
68 C4 **Vyetryna** Belarus
68 E2 **Vygozero, Ozero** *l.* Rus. Fed.
68 G2 **Vyksa** Rus. Fed.
69 D6 **Vylkove** Ukr.
63 L6 **Vynohradiv** Ukr.
68 E3 **Vypolzovo** Rus. Fed.
68 D3 **Vyritsa** Rus. Fed.
59 D5 **Vyrnwy, Lake** *l.* U.K.
68 G4 **Vyselki** Rus. Fed.
68 G4 **Vysha** Rus. Fed.
69 D5 **Vyshhorod** Ukr.
68 E3 **Vyshnevolotskaya Gryada** *ridge* Rus. Fed.
68 E3 **Vyshniy-Volochek** Rus. Fed.
66 H5 **Vyškov** Czech Rep.
69 D5 **Vystupovychi** Ukr.
68 F2 **Vytegra** Rus. Fed.

W

100 B3 **Wa** Ghana
61 D3 **Waal** *r.* Neth.
22 D3 **Waabakimi L.** *l.* Can.
20 G3 **Wabasca** *r.* Can.
20 G3 **Wabasca-Desmarais** Can.
30 E5 **Wabash** U.S.A.
30 E5 **Wabash** *r.* U.S.A.
30 A3 **Wabasha** U.S.A.
31 E1 **Wabatongushi Lake** *l.* Can.
102 E3 **Wabē Gestro** *r.* Eth.
102 E3 **Wabē Shebelē Wenz** *r.* Eth.
21 K4 **Wabowden** Can.
22 C2 **Wabuk Pt** *pt* Can.
23 G3 **Wabush** Can.
23 G3 **Wabush L.** *l.* Can.
34 C2 **Wabuska** U.S.A.
29 D6 **Waccasassa Bay** *b.* U.S.A.
27 D6 **Waco** U.S.A.
79 K4 **Wad** Pak.
115 H6 **Wadbilliga Nat. Park** *nat. park* Austr.
101 D2 **Waddān** Libya
61 C1 **Waddeneilanden** *is* Neth.
61 D1 **Waddenzee** *chan.* Neth.
114 B4 **Waddikee** Austr.
20 D4 **Waddington, Mt** *mt* Can.
104 C2 **Waddnixveen** Neth.
116 E5 **Waddy Pt** *pt* Austr.
59 C7 **Wadebridge** U.K.
21 J4 **Wadena** Can.
26 E2 **Wadena** U.S.A.
101 F2 **Wadi Halfa** Sudan
101 F3 **Wad Medani** Sudan
34 C2 **Wadsworth** U.S.A.
88 G2 **Wafangdian** China
115 G5 **Wagga Wagga** Austr.
112 C6 **Wagin** Austr.

84 C2 **Wah** Pak.
34 ▫' **Wahiawa** U.S.A.
26 D3 **Wahoo** U.S.A.
26 D2 **Wahpeton** U.S.A.
35 F2 **Wah Wah Mts** *mts* U.S.A.
34 ▫' **Waialee** U.S.A.
34 ▫' **Waialua** U.S.A.
34 ▫' **Waialua Bay** *b.* U.S.A.
34 ▫' **Waianae** U.S.A.
34 ▫' **Waianae Ra.** *mts* U.S.A.
117 D5 **Waiau** *r.* N.Z.
62 G7 **Waidhofen an der Ybbs** Austria
93 J6 **Waigeo** *i.* Indon.
117 E2 **Waiheke Island** *i.* N.Z.
117 E2 **Waihi** N.Z.
117 E2 **Waihou** *r.* N.Z.
93 F8 **Waikabubak** Indon.
117 B6 **Waikaia** N.Z.
34 ▫' **Waikane** U.S.A.
117 D5 **Waikari** N.Z.
117 E2 **Waikato** *r.* N.Z.
117 F2 **Waikawa Pt** *pt* N.Z.
114 C5 **Waikerie** Austr.
34 ▫' **Waikiki Beach** *beach* U.S.A.
117 C6 **Waikouaiti** N.Z.
34 ▫' **Wailuku** U.S.A.
117 D5 **Waimakariri** *r.* N.Z.
34 ▫' **Waimanalo** U.S.A.
117 C4 **Waimangaroa** N.Z.
117 C6 **Waimate** N.Z.
34 ▫' **Waimea** *HI* U.S.A.
84 D5 **Waimanganga** *r.* India
93 G8 **Waingapu** Indon.
59 C7 **Wainhouse Corner** U.K.
21 G4 **Wainwright** Can.
117 E3 **Waiouru** N.Z.
117 E3 **Waipa** *r.* N.Z.
117 B7 **Waipahi** N.Z.
34 ▫' **Waipahu** U.S.A.
117 F3 **Waipaoa** *r.* N.Z.
117 F2 **Waipapa Pt** *pt* N.Z.
117 D5 **Waipara** N.Z.
117 F3 **Waipawa** N.Z.
117 F3 **Waipukurau** N.Z.
117 F3 **Wairakei** N.Z.
117 E4 **Wairarapa, L.** *l.* N.Z.
117 D4 **Wairau** *r.* N.Z.
117 F3 **Wairoa** N.Z.
117 F3 **Wairoa** *r.* Hawke's Bay N.Z.
117 F1 **Wairoa** *r.* Northland N.Z.
117 F3 **Waitahanui** N.Z.
117 B6 **Waitahuna** N.Z.
117 E2 **Waitakaruru** N.Z.
117 C6 **Waitaki** *r.* N.Z.
117 E3 **Waitara** N.Z.
117 E2 **Waitoa** N.Z.
117 E2 **Waiuku** N.Z.
117 B7 **Waiwera South** N.Z.
89 F5 **Waiyang** China
91 E6 **Wajima** Japan
102 E3 **Wajir** Kenya
91 D7 **Wakasa-wan** *b.* Japan
117 B6 **Wakatipu, Lake** *l.* N.Z.
21 H4 **Wakaw** Can.
91 D7 **Wakayama** Japan
26 D4 **WaKeeney** U.S.A.
31 K3 **Wakefield** Can.
117 D4 **Wakefield** N.Z.
58 F4 **Wakefield** U.K.
30 C2 **Wakefield** *MI* U.S.A.
33 H4 **Wakefield** *RI* U.S.A.
32 E6 **Wakefield** *VA* U.S.A.
90 G4 **Wakinosawa** Japan
90 G2 **Wakkanai** Japan
105 J3 **Wakkerstroom** S. Africa
114 F5 **Wakool** Austr.
114 F5 **Wakool** *r.* Austr.
23 G2 **Wakuach, Lac** *l.* Can.
62 H5 **Wałbrzych** Pol.
115 J3 **Walcha** Austr.
62 F7 **Walchensee** *l.* Ger.
62 H4 **Wałcz** Pol.
33 F4 **Walden** U.S.A.
62 F6 **Waldkraiburg** Ger.
59 C7 **Waldon** *r.* U.K.
32 E5 **Waldorf** U.S.A.
56 E5 **Wales** *div.* U.K.
114 D4 **Walgett** Austr.
102 C4 **Walikale** Dem. Rep. Congo
30 B4 **Walker** *IA* U.S.A.
26 E2 **Walker** *MN* U.S.A.
34 C2 **Walker** *r.* U.S.A.
104 C7 **Walker Bay** *b.* S. Africa
29 E7 **Walker Cay** *i.* Bahamas
34 C2 **Walker Lake** *l.* U.S.A.
34 C4 **Walker Pass** *pass* U.S.A.
31 G3 **Walkerton** Can.
26 C2 **Wall** U.S.A.
24 C2 **Wallace** U.S.A.
31 F4 **Wallaceburg** Can.
115 J2 **Wallangarra** Austr.
114 B4 **Wallaroo** Austr.
59 D4 **Wallasey** U.K.
116 D5 **Wallaville** Austr.
115 G5 **Walla Walla** Austr.
24 C2 **Walla Walla** U.S.A.
104 B5 **Walkkraal** S. Africa
115 H5 **Wallendbeen** Austr.
33 F4 **Wallenpaupack, Lake** *l.* U.S.A.
59 F6 **Wallingford** U.K.
33 G4 **Wallingford** U.S.A.
111 J3 **Wallis, Iles** *is* Pac. Oc.
111 J3 **Wallis and Futuna Is** *terr.* Pac. Oc.
115 K4 **Wallis L.** *b.* Austr.
33 F6 **Wallops I.** *i.* U.S.A.

24 C2 Wallowa Mts *mts* U.S.A.
57 □ Walls U.K.
116 C6 Wallumbilla Austr.
21 H2 Walmsley Lake *l.* Can.
58 D3 Walney, Isle of *i.* U.K.
30 C5 Walnut U.S.A.
35 G4 Walnut Canyon National Monument *res.* U.S.A.
27 F4 Walnut Ridge U.S.A.
85 J3 Walong India
112 C6 Walpole–Nornalup National Park *nat. park* Austr.
59 F5 Walsall U.K.
25 F4 Walsenburg U.S.A.
116 A1 Walsh *r.* Austr.
29 D5 Walterboro U.S.A.
29 C6 Walter F. George Res. *resr* U.S.A.
114 F2 Walter's Ra. *h.* Austr.
31 J3 Waltham Can.
28 C4 Walton *KY* U.S.A.
33 F3 Walton *NY* U.S.A.
103 B6 Walvis Bay Namibia
12 K7 Walvis Ridge *sea feature* Atlantic Ocean
102 C3 Wamba Dem. Rep. Congo
93 K7 Wamena Indon.
84 B2 Wana Pak.
114 F2 Wanaaring Austr.
117 B6 Wanaka N.Z.
117 B6 Wanaka, L. *l.* N.Z.
89 E5 Wan'an China
31 G2 Wanapitei Lake *l.* Can.
33 F4 Wanaque Reservoir *resr* U.S.A.
114 D5 Wanbi Austr.
117 C6 Wanbrow, Cape *c.* N.Z.
114 D2 Wancoocha, Lake *salt flat* Austr.
90 C2 Wanda Shan *mts* China
118 B4 Wandel Sea Greenland
82 J6 Wanding China
116 C6 Wandoan Austr.
95 A1 Wang, Mae Nam *r.* Thai.
117 E3 Wanganui N.Z.
117 E3 Wanganui *r.* N.Z.
115 G6 Wangaratta Austr.
114 A5 Wangary Austr.
88 C3 Wangcang China
89 D4 Wangcheng China
88 F1 Wanghai Shan *h.* China
89 E4 Wangjiang China
89 C5 Wangmo China
87 N3 Wangqing China
84 B5 Wankaner India
102 E3 Wanlaweyn Somalia
89 E4 Wannian China
89 D7 Wanning China
88 E1 Wanquan China
61 D3 Wanroij Neth.
89 D6 Wanshan Qundao *is* China
117 F4 Wanstead N.Z.
59 F6 Wantage U.K.
31 G2 Wanup Can.
89 C4 Wanxian China
89 C4 Wanxian China
88 C3 Wanyuan China
89 E4 Wanzai China
32 A4 Wapakoneta U.S.A.
30 B5 Wapello U.S.A.
22 C3 Wapikopa L. *l.* Can.
20 E4 Wapiti *r.* Can.
27 F4 Wappapello, L. *resr* U.S.A.
30 A5 Wapsipinicon *r.* U.S.A.
88 B3 Waqên China
84 A4 Warah Pak.
83 E7 Warangal India
114 F6 Waranga Reservoir *resr* Austr.
84 E5 Waraseoni India
115 F8 Waratah Austr.
115 F7 Waratah B. *b.* Austr.
112 E5 Warburton Austr.
114 B1 Warburton *watercourse* Austr.
21 G2 Warburton Bay *l.* Can.
116 B5 Ward *watercourse* Austr.
117 A6 Ward, Mt *mt* Southland N.Z.
117 B5 Ward, Mt *mt* West Coast N.Z.
114 B5 Wardang I. *i.* Austr.
105 H3 Warden S. Africa
84 D5 Wardha India
84 D6 Wardha *r.* India
20 D3 Ware Can.
33 G3 Ware U.S.A.
59 E7 Wareham U.K.
33 H4 Wareham U.S.A.
61 D4 Waremme Belgium
62 F4 Waren Ger.
62 C5 Warendorf Ger.
115 J2 Warialda Austr.
95 C2 Warin Chamrap Thai.
117 E2 Warkworth N.Z.
58 F2 Warkworth U.K.
21 H4 Warman Can.
104 C4 Warmbad Namibia
105 H2 Warmbad S. Africa
59 E6 Warminster U.K.
33 F4 Warminster U.S.A.
61 C2 Warmond Neth.
34 D2 Warm Springs *NV* U.S.A.
32 D5 Warm Springs *VA* U.S.A.
104 D6 Warmwaterberg *mts* S. Africa
33 H4 Warner U.S.A.
24 B3 Warner Mts *mts* U.S.A.
29 D5 Warner Robins U.S.A.
42 F7 Warnes Bol.
115 K2 Warning, Mt *mt* Austr.
84 D5 Warora India

115 J1 Warra Austr.
114 E6 Warracknabeal Austr.
115 J5 Warragamba Reservoir *resr* Austr.
115 F7 Warragul Austr.
114 C2 Warrakalanna, Lake *salt flat* Austr.
114 A4 Warramboo Austr.
115 G2 Warrambool *r.* Austr.
112 D4 Warrawagine Austr.
112 D4 Warrawagine Austr.
113 J5 Warrego *r.* Austr.
114 A5 Warrego Ra. *h.* Austr.
115 G3 Warren Austr.
31 G2 Warren Can.
27 E5 Warren *AR* U.S.A.
31 F4 Warren *MI* U.S.A.
26 D1 Warren *MN* U.S.A.
32 C4 Warren *OH* U.S.A.
32 D4 Warren *PA* U.S.A.
32 C4 Warrendale U.S.A.
60 E3 Warrenpoint U.K.
26 E4 Warrensburg *MO* U.S.A.
33 G3 Warrensburg *NY* U.S.A.
104 F4 Warrenton S. Africa
32 E5 Warrenton U.S.A.
100 C4 Warri Nigeria
117 C6 Warrington N.Z.
59 E4 Warrington U.K.
29 C6 Warrington U.S.A.
114 C3 Warriota *watercourse* Austr.
114 E7 Warrnambool Austr.
26 E1 Warroad U.S.A.
114 A5 Warrow Austr.
115 H3 Warrumbungle Ra. *mts* Austr.
114 D2 Warry Warry *watercourse* Austr.
84 B2 Warsak Dam *dam* Pak.
63 K4 Warsaw Pol.
30 E5 Warsaw *IN* U.S.A.
26 E4 Warsaw *MO* U.S.A.
32 D3 Warsaw *NY* U.S.A.
32 E6 Warsaw *VA* U.S.A.
Warszawa *see* Warsaw
62 G4 Warta *r.* Pol.
115 K2 Warwick Austr.
59 F5 Warwick U.K.
33 F4 Warwick *NY* U.S.A.
33 H4 Warwick *RI* U.S.A.
25 E4 Wasatch Range *mts* U.S.A.
105 J4 Wasbank S. Africa
34 C4 Wasco U.S.A.
26 E2 Waseca U.S.A.
30 C5 Washburn *IL* U.S.A.
33 J1 Washburn *ME* U.S.A.
26 C2 Washburn *ND* U.S.A.
30 B2 Washburn *WI* U.S.A.
84 D5 Wāshīm India
32 E5 Washington *DC* U.S.A.
29 D5 Washington *GA* U.S.A.
30 B5 Washington *IA* U.S.A.
30 C5 Washington *IL* U.S.A.
28 C4 Washington *IN* U.S.A.
26 F4 Washington *MO* U.S.A.
29 E5 Washington *NC* U.S.A.
33 F4 Washington *NJ* U.S.A.
32 C4 Washington *PA* U.S.A.
35 F3 Washington *UT* U.S.A.
24 B2 Washington *div.* U.S.A.
119 B5 Washington, C. *c.* Antarctica
33 H2 Washington, Mt *mt* U.S.A.
32 C4 Washington Court House U.S.A.
30 D2 Washington Island *i.* U.S.A.
27 D5 Washita *r.* U.S.A.
81 L5 Wasit Iraq
22 E3 Waskaganish Can.
21 K3 Waskaiowaka Lake *l.* Can.
104 C3 Wasser Namibia
34 C2 Wassuk Range *mts* U.S.A.
22 E4 Waswanipi, Lac *l.* Can.
93 G7 Watampone Indon.
33 G4 Waterbury *CT* U.S.A.
33 G3 Waterbury *VT* U.S.A.
21 H3 Waterbury Lake *l.* Can.
60 D5 Waterford Rep. of Ireland
32 D4 Waterford U.S.A.
60 E5 Waterford Harbour *harbour* Rep. of Ireland
60 C5 Watergrasshill Rep. of Ireland
21 H4 Waterhen *r.* Can.
31 G4 Waterloo Can.
30 A4 Waterloo *IA* U.S.A.
33 H3 Waterloo *ME* U.S.A.
32 E3 Waterloo *NY* U.S.A.
30 C4 Waterloo *WI* U.S.A.
59 F7 Waterlooville U.K.
105 H1 Waterpoort S. Africa
30 C2 Watersmeet U.S.A.
20 G5 Waterton Lakes Nat. Park *nat. park* Can.
33 E3 Watertown *NY* U.S.A.
26 D2 Watertown *SD* U.S.A.
30 C4 Watertown *WI* U.S.A.
105 J2 Waterval-Boven S. Africa
114 C4 Watervale Austr.
33 J2 Waterways Can.
21 G3 Waterways Can.
31 G4 Watford Can.
59 G6 Watford U.K.
26 C2 Watford City U.S.A.
21 J3 Wathaman *r.* Can.
32 E3 Watkins Glen U.S.A.
Watling *i. see* San Salvador
27 D5 Watonga U.S.A.
21 H4 Watrous Can.

102 C3 Watsa Dem. Rep. Congo
30 D5 Watseka U.S.A.
102 C4 Watsi Kengo Dem. Rep. Congo
21 J4 Watson Can.
20 D2 Watson Lake Can.
34 B3 Watsonville U.S.A.
20 F3 Watt, Mt *h.* Can.
57 E2 Watten U.K.
57 E2 Watten, Loch *l.* U.K.
21 J2 Watterson Lake *l.* Can.
114 A2 Wattiwarriganna *watercourse* Austr.
59 H5 Watton U.K.
30 C2 Watton U.S.A.
93 J7 Watubela, Kepulauan *is* Indon.
110 E4 Wau P.N.G.
101 E4 Wau Sudan
30 D3 Waucedah U.S.A.
115 K3 Wauchope Austr.
29 D7 Wauchula U.S.A.
30 D4 Waukegan U.S.A.
30 C4 Waukesha U.S.A.
30 B4 Waukon U.S.A.
30 C3 Waupaca U.S.A.
30 C4 Waupun U.S.A.
27 D5 Waurika U.S.A.
30 C3 Wausau U.S.A.
32 A4 Wauseon U.S.A.
30 C3 Wautoma U.S.A.
30 C4 Wauwatosa U.S.A.
59 J5 Waveney *r.* U.K.
30 A4 Waverly *IA* U.S.A.
32 B5 Waverly *OH* U.S.A.
29 C4 Waverly *TN* U.S.A.
32 E6 Waverly *VA* U.S.A.
30 E1 Wawa Can.
100 C4 Wawa Nigeria
30 E5 Wawasee, Lake *l.* U.S.A.
93 L8 Wawoi *r.* P.N.G.
34 C3 Wawona U.S.A.
27 D5 Waxahachie U.S.A.
29 D6 Waycross U.S.A.
32 B6 Wayland *KY* U.S.A.
30 B5 Wayland *MO* U.S.A.
26 D3 Wayne U.S.A.
29 D5 Waynesboro *GA* U.S.A.
27 F6 Waynesboro *MS* U.S.A.
32 E5 Waynesboro *PA* U.S.A.
32 D5 Waynesboro *VA* U.S.A.
32 C5 Waynesburg U.S.A.
27 E4 Waynesville U.S.A.
27 D4 Waynoka U.S.A.
101 D3 Waza, Parc National de *nat. park* Cameroon
84 C2 Wazirabad Pak.
100 C3 W du Niger, Parcs Nationaux du *nat. park* Niger
22 B3 Weagamow L. *l.* Can.
58 E3 Wear *r.* U.K.
113 J3 Weary B. *b.* Austr.
27 D5 Weatherford U.S.A.
24 B3 Weaverville U.S.A.
31 G2 Webbwood Can.
22 C3 Webequie Can.
20 D3 Weber, Mt *mt* Can.
102 E3 Webi Shabeelle *r.* Somalia
33 H3 Webster *MA* U.S.A.
26 D2 Webster *SD* U.S.A.
30 A3 Webster *WV* U.S.A.
26 E3 Webster City U.S.A.
32 C5 Webster Springs U.S.A.
44 D8 Weddell I. *i.* Falkland Is
119 B2 Weddell Sea *sea* Antarctica
114 E6 Wedderburn Austr.
24 B3 Weed U.S.A.
32 D4 Weedville U.S.A.
115 H2 Weemelah Austr.
105 J4 Weenen S. Africa
61 F1 Weener Ger.
61 D3 Weert Neth.
115 G4 Weethalle Austr.
115 H5 Wee Waa Austr.
63 K3 Węgorzewo Pol.
82 B2 Wei *r.* Henan China
88 D3 Wei *r.* Shaanxi China
88 E1 Weichang China
88 F2 Weifang China
88 G2 Weihai China
88 E3 Weihui China
115 G2 Weilmoringle Austr.
62 E5 Weimar Ger.
88 C3 Weinan China
89 B5 Weining China
113 H2 Weipa Austr.
115 H2 Weir *r.* Austr.
21 L3 Weir River Can.
32 C4 Weirton U.S.A.
24 C2 Weiser U.S.A.
88 E3 Weishan U.S.A.
88 E3 Weishan Hu *l.* China
88 E3 Weishi China
62 E6 Weißenburg in Bayern Ger.
29 C5 Weiss L. *l.* U.S.A.
104 C2 Weissrand Mts *mts* Namibia
89 B5 Weixin China
88 B3 Weiyuan *Gansu* China
89 B4 Weiyuan *Sichuan* China
62 G7 Weiz Austria
89 C6 Weizhou Dao *i.* China
62 J3 Wejherowo Pol.
21 K4 Wekusko Can.
21 K4 Wekusko Lake *l.* Can.
32 C6 Welch U.S.A.
33 H2 Weld U.S.A.
102 D2 Weldiya Eth.
34 C4 Weldon U.S.A.
102 D3 Welk'īt'ē Eth.

105 G3 Welkom S. Africa
31 H4 Welland Can.
59 G5 Welland *r.* U.K.
31 H4 Welland Canal *canal* Can.
31 G4 Wellesley Can.
113 G3 Wellesley Is *is* Austr.
20 B2 Wellesley Lake *l.* Can.
33 H4 Wellfleet U.S.A.
59 G5 Wellingborough U.K.
115 H4 Wellington *N.S.W.* Austr.
114 C5 Wellington *S.A.* Austr.
117 E4 Wellington N.Z.
104 C6 Wellington S. Africa
59 E5 Wellington *Eng.* U.K.
59 D7 Wellington *Eng.* U.K.
24 F3 Wellington *CO* U.S.A.
27 D4 Wellington *KS* U.S.A.
34 C2 Wellington *NV* U.S.A.
32 B4 Wellington *OH* U.S.A.
27 C5 Wellington *TX* U.S.A.
35 G2 Wellington *UT* U.S.A.
44 A7 Wellington, I. *i.* Chile
115 G7 Wellington, L. *l.* Austr.
30 B5 Wellman U.S.A.
20 E4 Wells Can.
59 E6 Wells U.K.
24 D3 Wells *NV* U.S.A.
33 F3 Wells *NY* U.S.A.
112 D5 Wells, L. *salt flat* Austr.
32 E4 Wellsboro U.S.A.
117 E2 Wellsford N.Z.
20 E4 Wells Gray Prov. Park *res.* Can.
59 H5 Wells-next-the-Sea U.K.
32 B5 Wellston U.S.A.
32 E3 Wellsville U.S.A.
35 E5 Wellton U.S.A.
62 G6 Wels Austria
33 K2 Welshpool Can.
59 D5 Welshpool U.K.
59 G6 Welwyn Garden City U.K.
59 E5 Wem U.K.
105 H4 Wembesi S. Africa
20 F3 Wembley Can.
22 E3 Wemindji Can.
29 E7 Wemyss Bight Bahamas
88 F3 Wen *r.* China
24 B2 Wenatchee U.S.A.
89 D7 Wenchang China
89 F5 Wencheng China
100 B4 Wenchi Ghana
88 B4 Wenchuan China
35 F5 Wenden U.S.A.
88 G2 Wendeng China
102 D3 Wendo Eth.
24 D3 Wendover U.S.A.
31 F2 Wenebegon Lake *l.* Can.
89 C5 Weng'an China
89 E5 Wengyuan China
88 B4 Wenjiang China
89 F4 Wenling China
42 C2 Wenman, Isla *i.* Ecuador
30 C5 Wenona U.S.A.
89 B6 Wenshan China
59 H5 Wensum *r.* U.K.
114 D5 Wentworth Austr.
33 H3 Wentworth U.S.A.
88 B3 Wenxian China
89 F5 Wenzhou China
105 G4 Wepener S. Africa
104 E2 Werda Botswana
62 F4 Werder Ger.
20 C2 Wernecke Mountains *mts* Can.
114 D4 Werrimull Austr.
115 J3 Werris Creek Austr.
62 D6 Wertheim Ger.
62 C5 Wesel Ger.
62 D4 Weser *r.* Ger.
26 C4 Weskan U.S.A.
31 J3 Weslemkoon Lake *l.* Can.
33 K2 Wesley U.S.A.
23 K4 Wesleyville Can.
113 G2 Wessel, C. *c.* Austr.
113 G2 Wessel Is *is* Austr.
105 H3 Wesselton S. Africa
26 D2 Wessington Springs U.S.A.
30 C4 West Allis U.S.A.
119 A4 West Antarctica *reg.* Antarctica
13 L5 West Australian Basin *sea feature* Indian Ocean
13 L6 West Australian Ridge *sea feature* Indian Ocean
84 B4 West Banas *r.* India
80 E5 West Bank *terr.* Asia
23 J3 West Bay Can.
27 F6 West Bay *b.* U.S.A.
30 C4 West Bend U.S.A.
85 F5 West Bengal *div.* India
31 E3 West Branch U.S.A.
59 F5 West Bromwich U.K.
33 H3 Westbrook U.S.A.
115 G8 Westbury Austr.
59 E6 Westbury U.K.
115 G5 Westby Austr.
30 B4 Westby U.S.A.
33 F5 West Chester U.S.A.
33 G2 West Danville U.S.A.
31 F3 West Duck Island *i.* Can.
29 E7 West End Bahamas
34 D4 West End U.S.A.
29 E7 West End Pt *pt* Bahamas
62 D3 Westerland Ger.
33 H4 Westerly U.S.A.
21 H1 Western *r.* Can.
112 D4 Western Australia *div.* Austr.
104 D6 Western Cape *div.* S. Africa
78 B4 Western Desert *des.* Egypt

83 D8 Western Ghats *mts* India
114 F7 Western Port *b.* Austr.
96 Western Sahara *terr.* Africa
61 B3 Westerschelde *est.* Neth.
44 D8 West Falkland *i.* Falkland Is
26 D2 West Fargo U.S.A.
30 D5 Westfield *IN* U.S.A.
33 G3 Westfield *MA* U.S.A.
33 K1 Westfield *ME* U.S.A.
32 D3 Westfield *NY* U.S.A.
61 E1 Westgat *chan.* Neth.
116 B6 Westgate Austr.
119 D5 West Ice Shelf *ice feature* Antarctica
32 B5 West Lancaster U.S.A.
117 B5 Westland National Park *nat. park* N.Z.
59 J5 Westleton U.K.
34 B3 Westley U.S.A.
32 B5 West Liberty *KY* U.S.A.
32 B4 West Liberty *OH* U.S.A.
57 E5 West Linton U.K.
57 B2 West Loch Roag *b.* U.K.
20 G4 Westlock Can.
31 G4 West Lorne Can.
27 F5 West Memphis U.S.A.
32 E5 Westminster *MD* U.S.A.
29 D5 Westminster *SC* U.S.A.
32 C5 Weston U.S.A.
59 E6 Weston-super-Mare U.K.
33 F5 Westover U.S.A.
29 D7 West Palm Beach U.S.A.
27 F4 West Plains U.S.A.
114 A5 West Point *pt S.A.* Austr.
115 F8 West Point *pt Tas.* Austr.
27 F5 West Point *MS* U.S.A.
33 F4 West Point *NY* U.S.A.
31 J3 Westport Can.
117 C4 Westport N.Z.
60 B4 Westport Rep. of Ireland
34 A2 Westport U.S.A.
21 J4 Westray Can.
57 E1 Westray *i.* U.K.
31 G2 Westree Can.
61 F5 Westrich *reg.* Ger.
20 E4 West Road *r.* Can.
115 G7 West Sister I. *i.* Austr.
33 H2 West Stewartstown U.S.A.
61 D1 West-Terschelling Neth.
33 H4 West Tisbury U.S.A.
33 G2 West Topsham U.S.A.
33 G3 West Townshend U.S.A.
30 B4 West Union *IA* U.S.A.
32 B5 West Union *OH* U.S.A.
32 C5 West Union *WV* U.S.A.
30 D5 Westville U.S.A.
32 C5 West Virginia *div.* U.S.A.
34 C2 West Walker *r.* U.S.A.
116 D4 Westwood Austr.
34 B1 Westwood U.S.A.
115 G4 West Wyalong Austr.
24 E2 West Yellowstone U.S.A.
61 C2 Westzaan Neth.
93 H8 Wetar *i.* Indon.
20 G4 Wetaskiwin Can.
30 D2 Wetmore U.S.A.
62 D5 Wetzlar Ger.
110 E2 Wewak P.N.G.
60 E5 Wexford Rep. of Ireland
21 H4 Weyakwin Can.
30 C3 Weyauwega U.S.A.
59 G6 Weybridge U.K.
21 J5 Weyburn Can.
59 E7 Weymouth U.K.
33 H3 Weymouth U.S.A.
117 E2 Whakatane N.Z.
117 F3 Whakatane *r.* N.Z.
95 A3 Whale B. *b.* Myanmar
20 B3 Whale B. *b.* U.S.A.
29 E7 Whale Cay *i.* Bahamas
21 L2 Whale Cove Can.
56 F1 Whalsay *i.* U.K.
57 □ Whalsay *i.* U.K.
117 E2 Whangamata N.Z.
117 E3 Whangamomona N.Z.
117 E1 Whangarei N.Z.
22 E2 Whapmagoostui Can.
58 F4 Wharfe *r.* U.K.
31 F2 Wharncliffe Can.
21 J2 Wharton Lake *l.* Can.
30 A5 What Cheer U.S.A.
20 F2 Wha Ti Can.
24 F3 Wheatland U.S.A.
30 C5 Wheaton U.S.A.
25 F4 Wheeler Peak *summit NM* U.S.A.
35 E2 Wheeler Peak *summit NV* U.S.A.
32 C4 Wheeling U.S.A.
47 A2 Wheelwright Arg.
58 E3 Whernside *h.* U.K.
114 A5 Whidbey, Point *pt* Austr.
24 B3 Whiskeytown–Shasta–Trinity Nat. Recreation Area *res.* U.S.A.
57 E5 Whitburn U.K.
58 F3 Whitby Can.
58 G3 Whitby U.K.
59 E5 Whitchurch U.K.
20 A2 White *r.* Can./U.S.A.
27 E4 White *r.* AR U.S.A.
35 G5 White *r.* AZ U.S.A.
24 E3 White *r.* CO U.S.A.
28 C4 White *r.* IN U.S.A.
30 D1 White *r.* MI U.S.A.
35 E2 White *r.* NV U.S.A.
26 C3 White *r.* SD U.S.A.

30 B2 White *r.* WV U.S.A.
112 E4 White, L. *salt flat* Austr.
23 J3 White Bay *b.* Can.
26 C2 White Butte *mt* U.S.A.
114 E3 White Cliffs Austr.
30 E4 White Cloud U.S.A.
20 F4 Whitecourt Can.
30 A2 Whiteface Lake *l.* U.S.A.
33 H2 Whitefield U.S.A.
31 G2 Whitefish Can.
24 D1 Whitefish U.S.A.
30 D3 Whitefish *r.* U.S.A.
21 H2 Whitefish Lake *l.* Can.
30 E2 Whitefish Pt *pt* U.S.A.
60 D5 Whitehall Rep. of Ireland
57 F1 Whitehall U.K.
33 H3 Whitehall *NY* U.S.A.
30 B3 Whitehall *WI* U.S.A.
58 D3 Whitehaven U.K.
60 F3 Whitehead U.K.
59 G6 Whitehill U.K.
20 B2 Whitehorse Can.
59 F6 White Horse, Vale of *v.* U.K.
35 E1 White Horse Pass *pass* U.S.A.
117 F2 White I. *i.* N.Z.
27 E6 White L. *l.* LA U.S.A.
30 D4 White L. *l.* MI U.S.A.
115 H7 Whitemark Austr.
113 J8 Whitemark Austr.
33 H2 White Mountains *mts* U.S.A.
34 C3 White Mt Peak *summit* U.S.A.
78 C7 White Nile *r.* Sudan/Uganda
104 C1 White Nossob *watercourse* Namibia
35 E2 White Pine Range *mts* U.S.A.
33 G4 White Plains U.S.A.
22 C4 White River Can.
35 H5 Whiteriver U.S.A.
33 G3 White River Junction U.S.A.
35 E2 White River Valley *v.* U.S.A.
116 A1 White Rock Austr.
35 E2 White Rock Peak *summit* U.S.A.
25 F5 White Sands Nat. Mon. *res.* U.S.A.
32 B6 Whitesburg U.S.A.
76 E3 White Sea *g.* Rus. Fed.
21 K4 Whiteshell Prov. Park *res.* Can.
24 E2 White Sulphur Springs *MT* U.S.A.
32 C6 White Sulphur Springs *WV* U.S.A.
29 E5 Whiteville U.S.A.
100 B4 White Volta *r.* Ghana
30 C4 Whitewater U.S.A.
35 H5 Whitewater Baldy *mt* U.S.A.
22 C3 Whitewater L. *l.* Can.
21 J4 Whitewood Can.
115 G6 Whitfield Austr.
59 J6 Whitfield U.K.
57 D6 Whithorn U.K.
117 E2 Whitianga N.Z.
33 K2 Whiting U.S.A.
59 C6 Whitland U.K.
58 F2 Whitley Bay U.K.
29 D5 Whitmire U.S.A.
31 H3 Whitney Can.
34 C3 Whitney, Mt *mt* U.S.A.
33 K2 Whitneyville U.S.A.
59 J6 Whitstable U.K.
116 C3 Whitsunday Group *is* Austr.
116 C3 Whitsunday I. *i.* Austr.
116 C3 Whitsunday Pass. *chan.* Austr.
114 F6 Whittlesea Austr.
59 G5 Whittlesey U.K.
115 G5 Whitton Austr.
21 H2 Wholdaia Lake *l.* Can.
35 F5 Why U.S.A.
114 B4 Whyalla Austr.
95 A1 Wiang Phran Thai.
95 B1 Wiang Sa Thai.
31 G2 Wiarton Can.
61 B3 Wichelen Belgium
27 D4 Wichita U.S.A.
27 D5 Wichita Falls U.S.A.
27 D5 Wichita Mts *mts* U.S.A.
57 E2 Wick U.K.
35 F5 Wickenburg U.S.A.
59 H6 Wickford U.K.
115 E7 Wickham, C. *pt* Austr.
60 E5 Wicklow Rep. of Ireland
60 F5 Wicklow Head *hd* Rep. of Ireland
60 E5 Wicklow Mountains *mts* Rep. of Ireland
60 E4 Wicklow Mountains National Park *nat. park* Rep. of Ireland
116 B3 Wide B. *b.* Austr.
115 G2 Widgeegoara *watercourse* Austr.
59 E4 Widnes U.K.
61 F4 Wiehl Ger.
63 J5 Wieluń Pol.
Wien *see* Vienna
62 H7 Wiener Neustadt Austria
61 C2 Wieringermeer Polder *reclaimed land* Neth.
62 D5 Wiesbaden Ger.
62 J3 Wieżyca *h.* Pol.
58 E4 Wigan U.K.

27 F6 Wiggins U.S.A.
59 F7 Wight, Isle of i. U.K.
21 H2 Wignes Lake l. Can.
59 F5 Wigston U.K.
58 D3 Wigton U.K.
57 D6 Wigtown U.K.
57 D6 Wigtown Bay b. U.K.
61 D3 Wijchen Neth.
61 C3 Wijnegem Belgium
35 F4 Wikieup U.S.A.
31 G3 Wikwemikong Can.
24 C2 Wilbur U.S.A.
114 E3 Wilcannia Austr.
21 J4 Wildcat Hill Wilderness Park res. Can.
34 D2 Wildcat Peak summit U.S.A.
105 H5 Wild Coast coastal area S. Africa
30 C1 Wild Goose Can.
20 F4 Wildhay r. Can.
30 A2 Wild Rice Lake l. U.S.A.
62 E7 Wildspitze mt Austria
29 D6 Wildwood FL U.S.A.
33 F5 Wildwood NJ U.S.A.
105 H3 Wilge r. Free State S. Africa
105 H2 Wilge r. Gauteng/Mpumalanga S. Africa
114 A3 Wilgena Austr.
32 C4 Wilhelm, Lake l. U.S.A.
110 E2 Wilhelm, Mt mt P.N.G.
62 D4 Wilhelmshaven Ger.
33 F4 Wilkes-Barre U.S.A.
119 B6 Wilkes Land reg. Antarctica
21 H4 Wilkie Can.
119 B2 Wilkins Ice Shelf ice feature Antarctica
20 D3 Will, Mt mt Can.
24 B2 Willamette r. U.S.A.
59 D7 Willand U.K.
114 E3 Willandra Billabong watercourse Austr.
24 B1 Willapa B. b. U.S.A.
32 B4 Willard U.S.A.
33 F5 Willards U.S.A.
35 H5 Willcox U.S.A.
61 C3 Willebroek Belgium
37 L6 Willemstad Neth. Ant.
21 H3 William r. Can.
114 E6 William, Mt mt Austr.
114 B2 William Cr. Austr.
35 H4 Williams AZ U.S.A.
34 A2 Williams CA U.S.A.
30 A5 Williamsburg IA U.S.A.
32 A6 Williamsburg KY U.S.A.
30 E3 Williamsburg MI U.S.A.
32 E6 Williamsburg VA U.S.A.
29 E7 Williams I. i. Bahamas
20 E4 Williams Lake Can.
23 H1 William Smith, Cap c. Can.
32 E3 Williamson NY U.S.A.
32 B6 Williamson WV U.S.A.
30 D5 Williamsport IN U.S.A.
32 E4 Williamsport PA U.S.A.
29 E5 Williamston U.S.A.
33 G3 Williamstown MA U.S.A.
33 F3 Williamstown NY U.S.A.
32 C5 Williamstown WV U.S.A.
33 G4 Willimantic U.S.A.
116 D1 Willis Group atolls Coral Sea Is Terr.
104 D5 Williston S. Africa
29 D6 Williston FL U.S.A.
26 C1 Williston ND U.S.A.
20 E3 Williston Lake l. Can.
59 D6 Williton U.K.
34 A2 Willits U.S.A.
26 E2 Willmar U.S.A.
20 F4 Willmore Wilderness Prov. Park res. Can.
114 B3 Willochra watercourse Austr.
20 E4 Willow r. Can.
21 H5 Willow Bunch Can.
32 E4 Willow Hill U.S.A.
20 F2 Willow Lake l. Can.
104 E6 Willowmore S. Africa
30 C3 Willow Reservoir resr U.S.A.
34 A2 Willows U.S.A.
27 F4 Willow Springs U.S.A.
115 J3 Willow Tree Austr.
105 H6 Willowvale S. Africa
112 E4 Wills, L. salt flat Austr.
33 G2 Willsboro U.S.A.
114 C5 Willunga Austr.
114 C4 Wilmington Austr.
33 F5 Wilmington DE U.S.A.
29 E5 Wilmington NC U.S.A.
32 B5 Wilmington OH U.S.A.
33 G3 Wilmington VT U.S.A.
59 E4 Wilmslow U.K.
114 C3 Wilpena watercourse Austr.
26 D4 Wilson KS U.S.A.
29 E5 Wilson NC U.S.A.
25 F4 Wilson, Mt mt CO U.S.A.
35 E2 Wilson, Mt mt NV U.S.A.
26 D4 Wilson Res. resr U.S.A.
33 H2 Wilsons Mills U.S.A.
115 G7 Wilson's Promontory pen. Austr.
115 G7 Wilson's Promontory Nat. Park nat. park Austr.
30 B5 Wilton IA U.S.A.
33 H2 Wilton ME U.S.A.
61 D5 Wiltz Lux.
112 D5 Wiluna Austr.
59 J7 Wimereux France

114 E6 Wimmera r. Austr.
30 D5 Winamac U.S.A.
116 A6 Winbin watercourse Austr.
105 G4 Winburg S. Africa
59 E6 Wincanton U.K.
33 G3 Winchendon U.S.A.
22 E4 Winchester Can.
59 F6 Winchester U.K.
30 B6 Winchester IL U.S.A.
30 E5 Winchester IN U.S.A.
32 A6 Winchester KY U.S.A.
33 G3 Winchester NH U.S.A.
29 C5 Winchester TN U.S.A.
32 D5 Winchester VA U.S.A.
24 E3 Wind r. U.S.A.
114 B3 Windabout, L. salt flat Austr.
26 C3 Wind Cave Nat. Park nat. park U.S.A.
58 E3 Windermere U.K.
58 E3 Windermere l. U.K.
103 B6 Windhoek Namibia
26 E3 Windom U.S.A.
113 H5 Windorah Austr.
35 H4 Window Rock U.S.A.
30 A4 Wind Pt pt U.S.A.
24 E3 Wind River Range mts U.S.A.
59 F6 Windrush r. U.K.
115 H4 Windsor Austr.
23 J4 Windsor Nfld Can.
23 H5 Windsor N.S. Can.
31 F4 Windsor Ont. Can.
23 F4 Windsor Que. Can.
59 G6 Windsor U.K.
33 G4 Windsor CT U.S.A.
29 E5 Windsor NC U.S.A.
33 F3 Windsor NY U.S.A.
32 E6 Windsor VA U.S.A.
33 G3 Windsor VT U.S.A.
33 G4 Windsor Locks U.S.A.
37 M5 Windward Islands is Caribbean Sea
37 K5 Windward Passage chan. Cuba/Haiti
29 C5 Winfield AL U.S.A.
30 B5 Winfield IA U.S.A.
27 D4 Winfield KS U.S.A.
58 F3 Wingate U.K.
115 J3 Wingen Austr.
115 K3 Wingham Austr.
31 G4 Wingham Can.
22 C2 Winisk Can.
22 C2 Winisk r. Can.
22 C3 Winisk L. l. Can.
22 C3 Winisk River Provincial Park res. Can.
95 A4 Winkana Myanmar
21 K5 Winkler Can.
33 J2 Winn U.S.A.
100 B4 Winneba Ghana
30 C3 Winnebago, Lake l. U.S.A.
30 C3 Winneconne U.S.A.
24 C3 Winnemucca U.S.A.
34 C1 Winnemucca Lake l. U.S.A.
26 D3 Winner U.S.A.
27 E6 Winnfield U.S.A.
26 E2 Winnibigoshish L. l. U.S.A.
21 K5 Winnipeg Can.
21 K4 Winnipeg, Lake l. Can.
21 J4 Winnipegosis Can.
21 J4 Winnipegosis, Lake l. Can.
33 H3 Winnipesaukee, L. l. U.S.A.
27 F5 Winnsboro U.S.A.
35 G4 Winona AZ U.S.A.
30 C2 Winona MI U.S.A.
30 B3 Winona MN U.S.A.
27 F5 Winona MS U.S.A.
33 G2 Winooski U.S.A.
33 G2 Winooski r. U.S.A.
61 F1 Winschoten Neth.
59 E4 Winsford U.K.
35 G4 Winslow AZ U.S.A.
33 G4 Winsted U.S.A.
29 D4 Winston-Salem U.S.A.
29 D6 Winter Haven U.S.A.
33 J2 Winterport U.S.A.
34 B2 Winters U.S.A.
61 E3 Winterswijk Neth.
62 D7 Winterthur Switz.
105 H4 Winterton S. Africa
33 J1 Winterville U.S.A.
33 J2 Winthrop U.S.A.
113 H4 Winton Austr.
117 B7 Winton N.Z.
59 G5 Winwick U.K.
114 C4 Wirrabara Austr.
59 D4 Wirral pen. U.K.
114 B3 Wirraminna Austr.
114 D6 Wirrega Austr.
114 A4 Wirrulla Austr.
59 H5 Wisbech U.K.
30 C3 Wiscasset U.S.A.
30 C3 Wisconsin div. U.S.A.
30 B4 Wisconsin r. U.S.A.
30 C4 Wisconsin, Lake l. U.S.A.
30 C4 Wisconsin Dells U.S.A.
30 C3 Wisconsin Rapids U.S.A.
32 B6 Wise U.S.A.
57 F5 Wishaw U.K.
63 J4 Wisła r. Pol.
62 E4 Wismar Ger.
59 J7 Wissant France
30 B3 Wissota L. l. U.S.A.
20 D4 Wistaria Can.
105 H2 Witbank S. Africa
104 C2 Witbooisvlei Namibia
59 H6 Witham U.K.

59 G4 Witham r. U.K.
33 G2 Witherbee U.S.A.
58 H4 Withernsea U.K.
113 G5 Witjira National Park nat. park Austr.
59 F6 Witney U.K.
105 J2 Witrivier S. Africa
105 G4 Witteberg mts S. Africa
30 C3 Wittenberg U.S.A.
62 E4 Wittenberge U.S.A.
62 E4 Wittenburg Ger.
64 H3 Wittenheim France
62 D5 Wittlich Ger.
61 F1 Wittmund Ger.
62 F4 Wittstock Ger.
110 E2 Witu Is is P.N.G.
103 B6 Witvlei Namibia
115 K1 Wivenhoe, Lake l. Austr.
23 J3 Władysławowo Pol.
63 J4 Włocławek Pol.
33 H2 Woburn Can.
115 G6 Wodonga Austr.
61 D5 Wœvre, Forêt de forest France
93 J8 Wokam i. Indon.
90 B1 Woken r. China
85 H4 Wokha India
59 G6 Woking U.K.
59 G6 Wokingham U.K.
30 D5 Wolcott IN U.S.A.
32 E3 Wolcott NY U.S.A.
20 C3 Wolf r. Can.
30 C3 Wolf r. U.S.A.
42 □ Wolf, Volcán vol. Ecuador
24 D2 Wolf Creek U.S.A.
25 F4 Wolf Creek Pass pass U.S.A.
33 H3 Wolfeboro U.S.A.
31 J3 Wolfe I. i. Can.
62 E4 Wolfenbüttel Ger.
20 C2 Wolf Lake l. Can.
24 F1 Wolf Point U.S.A.
62 G7 Wolfsberg Austria
62 E4 Wolfsburg Ger.
23 H4 Wolfville Can.
62 F3 Wolgast Ger.
62 G4 Wolin Pol.
44 C9 Wollaston, Islas is Chile
21 J3 Wollaston Lake Can.
21 J3 Wollaston Lake l. Can.
115 J5 Wollongong Austr.
105 F3 Wolmaransstad S. Africa
114 D6 Wolseley Austr.
104 C6 Wolseley S. Africa
61 E2 Wolsingham U.K.
59 E5 Wolverhampton U.K.
30 E3 Wolverine U.S.A.
61 F5 Wolwrather Höhe h. Ger.
116 D6 Wondai Austr.
114 F3 Wongalarroo Lake salt l. Austr.
115 H4 Wongarbon Austr.
85 G4 Wong Chhu r. Bhutan
89 □ Wong Chuk Hang China
89 □ Wong Leng h. China
89 □ Wong Wan Chau i. China
87 N4 Wŏnju S. Korea
113 J7 Wonnangatta Moroka National Park nat. park Austr.
114 F3 Wonominta watercourse Austr.
87 N4 Wŏnsan N. Korea
114 F7 Wonthaggi Austr.
114 B3 Woocalla Austr.
113 G2 Woodah, Isle i. Austr.
59 J5 Woodbridge U.K.
32 E5 Woodbridge U.S.A.
20 G3 Wood Buffalo National Park nat. park Can.
115 K2 Woodburn Austr.
24 B2 Woodburn U.S.A.
30 E4 Woodbury MI U.S.A.
33 F5 Woodbury NJ U.S.A.
32 A6 Wood Creek Lake l. U.S.A.
34 C2 Woodfords U.S.A.
34 C3 Woodlake U.S.A.
34 B2 Woodland U.S.A.
25 F4 Woodland Park U.S.A.
95 □ Woodlands Sing.
111 F2 Woodlark I. i. P.N.G.
112 F5 Woodroffe, Mt mt Austr.
24 E3 Woodruff U.S.A.
113 F3 Woods, L. salt flat Austr.
21 L5 Woods, Lake of the l. Can./U.S.A.
32 C5 Woodsfield U.S.A.
115 G7 Woodside U.S.A.
115 G6 Woods Pt Austr.
116 B2 Woodstock Austr.
23 G4 Woodstock N.B. Can.
31 G4 Woodstock Ont. Can.
30 C4 Woodstock IL U.S.A.
32 D5 Woodstock VA U.S.A.
33 F5 Woodstown U.S.A.
117 E4 Woodville N.Z.
32 E4 Woodville NY U.S.A.
27 E6 Woodville TX U.S.A.
27 D4 Woodward U.S.A.
58 E2 Wooler U.K.
115 K3 Woolgoolga Austr.
115 K2 Wooli Austr.
114 C3 Wooltana Austr.
114 B3 Woomera Austr.
114 A3 Woomera Prohibited Area res. Austr.
33 H4 Woonsocket U.S.A.
116 A6 Woorabinda Austr.
32 C4 Wooster U.S.A.
104 C6 Worcester S. Africa

59 E5 Worcester U.K.
33 H3 Worcester U.S.A.
62 F7 Wörgl Austria
58 D3 Workington U.K.
59 F4 Worksop U.K.
24 F2 Worland U.S.A.
61 C2 Wormerveer Neth.
59 C6 Worms Head hd U.K.
104 B1 Wortel Namibia
59 G7 Worthing U.K.
26 E3 Worthington U.S.A.
93 G7 Wotu Indon.
61 D3 Woudrichem Neth.
26 C3 Wounded Knee U.S.A.
116 D4 Wowan Austr.
93 G7 Wowoni i. Indon.
Wrangel I. i. see Vrangelya, O.
20 C3 Wrangell U.S.A.
20 C3 Wrangell I. i. U.S.A.
57 C2 Wrath, Cape c. U.K.
26 C3 Wray U.S.A.
59 F5 Wreake r. U.K.
104 B4 Wreck Point pt S. Africa
59 E4 Wrexham U.K.
94 C4 Wright Phil.
24 F3 Wright U.S.A.
27 E5 Wright Patman L. l. U.S.A.
35 G6 Wrightson, Mt mt U.S.A.
20 E2 Wrigley Can.
62 H5 Wrocław Pol.
62 H4 Września Pol.
88 E2 Wu'an China
88 D2 Wubu China
89 E4 Wuchang China
89 D6 Wuchuan Guangdong China
89 C4 Wuchuan Guizhou China
88 D1 Wuchuan Nei Monggol Zizhiqu China
88 C2 Wuda China
88 F1 Wudan China
88 D3 Wudang Shan mt China
88 D3 Wudang Shan mts China
85 H2 Wudaoliang China
88 D2 Wudi China
89 B5 Wuding China
88 D2 Wuding r. China
114 A4 Wudinna Austr.
88 B3 Wudu China
89 D4 Wufeng China
89 D5 Wugang China
88 C3 Wugong China
88 C2 Wuhai China
89 E4 Wuhan China
88 E3 Wuhe China
88 F4 Wuhu China
89 E6 Wuhua China
84 D2 Wüjiang China
89 C6 Wujia China
89 C4 Wu Jiang r. China
100 C4 Wukari Nigeria
85 H3 Wulang China
84 C2 Wular L. l. India
88 F2 Wuleidao Wan l. China
88 F3 Wulian China
89 B4 Wulian Feng mts China
82 K6 Wuliang Shan mts China
93 J8 Wuliaru i. Indon.
89 C5 Wuling Shan mts China
89 C4 Wulong China
89 B5 Wumeng Shan mts China
89 C6 Wuming China
88 A4 Wungda China
89 E4 Wuning China
83 J6 Wuntho Myanmar
35 G4 Wupatki National Monument res. U.S.A.
89 E5 Wuping China
62 C5 Wuppertal Ger.
104 C6 Wuppertal S. Africa
88 C2 Wuqi China
88 E2 Wuqiao China
88 E2 Wuqing China
62 D6 Würzburg Ger.
88 B3 Wushan Gansu China
88 C4 Wushan Sichuan China
88 D4 Wu Shan mts China
89 C4 Wusheng China
88 C6 Wushi China
Wusuli Jiang r. see Ussuri
88 D2 Wutai China
88 D2 Wutai Shan mt China
110 E2 Wuvulu I. i. P.N.G.
88 E4 Wuwei Anhui China
88 B2 Wuwei Gansu China
88 F4 Wuxi Jiangsu China
88 C4 Wuxi Sichuan China
Wuxing see Huzhou
89 C6 Wuxu China
89 E4 Wuxuan China
89 D3 Wuyang China
89 F4 Wuyi China
87 N2 Wuyiling China
89 F5 Wuyishan China
89 E5 Wuyi Shan mts China
89 E4 Wuyuan Jiangxi China
88 C1 Wuyuan Nei Monggol Zizhiqu China
88 D2 Wuzhai China
88 D4 Wuzhen China
88 C2 Wuzhong China
89 D6 Wuzhou China
30 B5 Wyaconda r. U.S.A.
115 G4 Wyalong Austr.
31 F4 Wyandotte U.S.A.
116 A6 Wyandra Austr.
30 C5 Wyanet U.S.A.
115 H4 Wyangala Reservoir resr Austr.

114 F2 Wyara, Lake salt flat Austr.
114 C6 Wycheproof Austr.
59 E6 Wye r. U.K.
59 F6 Wylye r. U.K.
59 J5 Wymondham U.K.
112 D3 Wyndham Austr.
114 F6 Wyndham-Werribee Austr.
27 F5 Wynne U.S.A.
115 F8 Wynyard Austr.
21 J4 Wynyard Can.
30 C5 Wyoming IL U.S.A.
30 E4 Wyoming MI U.S.A.
24 E3 Wyoming div. U.S.A.
24 E3 Wyoming Peak summit U.S.A.
115 J4 Wyong Austr.
114 D5 Wyperfeld Nat. Park nat. park Austr.
58 E4 Wyre r. U.K.
59 F5 Wysox U.S.A.
63 K4 Wyszków Pol.
59 F5 Wythall U.K.
32 C6 Wytheville U.S.A.
33 J2 Wytopitlock U.S.A.

X

102 F2 Xaafuun Somalia
81 M1 Xaçmaz Azer.
104 E1 Xade Botswana
85 H3 Xagquka China
84 D1 Xaidulla China
85 G3 Xainza China
103 D6 Xai-Xai Moz.
88 C1 Xamba China
92 C2 Xam Hua Laos
95 B1 Xan r. Laos
95 C2 Xan, Xé r. Vietnam
103 C6 Xanagas Botswana
88 B1 Xangd China
88 D1 Xangdin Hural China
103 B3 Xangongo Angola
81 L2 Xankändi Azer.
67 L4 Xanthi Greece
42 E6 Xapuri Brazil
81 M2 Xaraba Şähär Sayı i. Azer.
81 M2 Xärä Zirä Adası is Azer.
85 F3 Xarba La pass China
88 F1 Xar Moron r. Nei Monggol Zizhiqu China
88 D1 Xar Moron r. Nei Monggol Zizhiqu China
65 F3 Xàtiva Spain
103 C6 Xau, Lake l. Botswana
43 J6 Xavantes, Serra dos h. Brazil
95 C3 Xa Vo Đat Vietnam
32 B5 Xenia U.S.A.
81 H1 Xi r. China
90 B2 Xiachengzi China
89 D6 Xiachuan Dao i. China
88 B3 Xiahe China
89 E5 Xiajiang China
88 E2 Xiajin China
89 F5 Xiamen China
88 C3 Xi'an China
88 C2 Xiancheng China
88 C2 Xianchengbu China
89 C4 Xianfeng China
88 D3 Xiangcheng China
88 D3 Xiangfan China
Xianghuang Qi see Xin Bulag
95 B1 Xiangkhoang Laos
84 D3 Xiangquan He r. China
89 F4 Xiangshan China
89 D5 Xiangtan China
Xianguan see Dali
89 D5 Xiangxiang China
89 D4 Xiangyin China
89 F4 Xianju China
89 D4 Xianning China
89 D4 Xiantao China
89 E5 Xianxia Ling mts China
88 E2 Xianxian China
89 C3 Xianyang China
89 D4 Xianyou China
89 D4 Xianyuan China
89 D4 Xiaochang China
89 C6 Xiaodong China
89 D4 Xiaogan China
87 N2 Xiao Hinggan Ling mts China
88 B4 Xiaojin China
88 B3 Xiaonan China
88 H2 Xiaonanchuan China
89 F4 Xiaoshan China
88 D2 Xiaotao China
88 E2 Xiaowutai Shan mt China
89 B3 Xiaoxian China
89 B4 Xiaoxiang Ling mts China
88 D2 Xiaoyi China
88 F5 Xiapu China
88 D3 Xiayukou China
88 B4 Xichang China
88 C2 Xichong China
89 B6 Xichou China
88 D3 Xichuan China
89 B4 Xide China
45 D4 Xié r. Brazil
89 D6 Xieyang Dao i. China
88 E3 Xifei He r. China
88 C1 Xifeng China
88 C3 Xifeng China
88 G5 Xigazê China
88 C3 Xihan Shui r. China
88 B3 Xihe China
88 A1 Xi He watercourse China

88 B3 Xiji China
89 D1 Xi Jiang r. China
85 G2 Xijir China
85 G2 Xijir Ulan Hu salt l. China
88 B2 Xijishui China
88 D1 Xil China
88 G1 Xiliao r. China
89 B5 Xilin China
88 E1 Xilinhot China
88 A1 Ximiao China
88 C2 Xin China
89 F4 Xin'anjiang China
89 F4 Xin'anjiang Sk. resr China
105 K2 Xinavane Moz.
88 D1 Xin Bulag China
88 E3 Xincai China
89 F4 Xinchang China
88 A2 Xincheng Gansu China
89 C5 Xincheng Guangxi China
88 C2 Xincheng Ningxia China
88 C2 Xinchengbu China
89 D6 Xindu Guangxi China
88 B4 Xindu Sichuan China
89 E5 Xinfeng Guangdong China
89 E5 Xinfeng Jiangxi China
89 E6 Xinfengjiang Sk. resr China
89 D5 Xing'an China
89 E5 Xingan China
88 F1 Xingcheng China
89 E5 Xingguo China
82 J3 Xinghai China
88 D1 Xinghe China
88 F3 Xinghua China
89 F5 Xinghua Wan b. China
90 C2 Xingkai China
Xingkai Hu l. see Khanka, Lake
89 E5 Xingning China
89 D4 Xingou China
88 C3 Xingping China
89 B5 Xingren China
89 D4 Xingsagoinba China
88 B4 Xingshan China
88 E2 Xingtai China
43 H4 Xingu r. Brazil
43 H6 Xingu, Parque Indígena do nat. park Brazil
89 B4 Xingwen China
88 D2 Xingxian China
88 D3 Xingyang China
89 B5 Xingyi China
88 E1 Xin Hot China
89 D5 Xinhua China
88 B2 Xinhuacun China
89 C5 Xinhuang China
88 F1 Xinhui China
89 D6 Xinhui China
88 E2 Xining China
88 D3 Xinjiang China
85 D1 Xinjiang Uygur Zizhiqu div. China
86 D3 Xinjiang Uygur Zizhiqu div. China
88 C3 Xinjie China
88 B4 Xinjin China
88 G1 Xinkai r. China
88 G1 Xinmin China
89 C5 Xinning China
89 A5 Xinping China
89 E5 Xinquan China
88 E3 Xinshao China
88 E3 Xintai China
88 D5 Xintian China
88 D3 Xinxian China
89 D4 Xinxiang China
88 D6 Xinxing China
89 D4 Xinyang Henan China
88 D3 Xinyang Henan China
88 D3 Xinye China
89 D4 Xinye China
89 D6 Xinyi Guangdong China
88 F3 Xinyi Jiangsu China
89 C7 Xinying China
89 E5 Xinyu China
82 F2 Xinyuan China
88 D2 Xinzhou Shanxi China
88 D2 Xinzhou China
65 C1 Xinzo de Limia Spain
89 C4 Xiqing Shan mts China
43 K6 Xique Xique Brazil
88 C4 Xishanzui China
89 C4 Xishui Guizhou China
89 C4 Xishui Hubei China
Xi Ujimqin Qi see Bayan Ul Hot
89 F4 Xiuning China
89 C4 Xiushan China
89 E4 Xiushui China
89 E4 Xiu Shui r. China
89 C5 Xiuwen China
89 D3 Xiuwu China
88 G1 Xiuyan China
89 D6 Xiuying China
85 F3 Xixabangma Feng mt China
88 D3 Xixia China
88 E3 Xixian Henan China
88 D2 Xixian Shanxi China
88 D3 Xixiang China
89 F5 Xiyang Dao i. China
89 B5 Xiyang Jiang r. China
86 D5 Xizang Zizhiqu div. China
88 F2 Xizhong Dao i. China
85 H3 Xoka China
95 C3 Xom An Lôc Vietnam

95 C3 **Xom Đưc Hanh** Vietnam
89 C4 **Xuan'en** China
88 C4 **Xuanhan** China
88 B2 **Xuanhepu** China
88 E1 **Xuanhua** China
95 C3 **Xuân Lôc** Vietnam
89 B5 **Xuanwei** China
88 F4 **Xuanzhou** China
88 D3 **Xuchang** *Henan* China
87 K5 **Xuchang** *Henan* China
81 M1 **Xudat** Azer.
102 E3 **Xuddur** Somalia
89 C5 **Xuefeng Shan** *mts* China
85 H2 **Xugui** China
85 E2 **Xungba** China
85 F3 **Xungru** China
88 C3 **Xun He** *r.* China
89 D6 **Xun Jiang** *r.* China
89 E5 **Xunwu** China
88 C3 **Xunxian** China
88 C3 **Xunyang** China
88 C3 **Xunyi** China
89 D5 **Xupu** China
85 F3 **Xuru Co** *salt l.* China
88 E2 **Xushui** China
89 D6 **Xuwen** China
88 F3 **Xuyi** China
89 B4 **Xuyong** China
88 E3 **Xuzhou** China

Y

116 D4 **Yaamba** Austr.
89 B4 **Ya'an** China
114 E5 **Yaapeet** Austr.
100 C4 **Yabassi** Cameroon
102 D3 **Yabêlo** Eth.
87 K1 **Yablonovyy Khrebet** *mts* Rus. Fed.
88 B2 **Yabrai Shan** *mts* China
88 B2 **Yabrai Yanchang** China
80 F5 **Yabrūd** Syria
90 A2 **Yabuli** China
45 C2 **Yacambu, Parque Nacional** *nat. park* Venez.
89 C7 **Yacheng** China
89 C5 **Yachi He** *r.* China
42 E6 **Yacuma** *r.* Bol.
82 G5 **Yadong** China
68 H4 **Yadrin** Rus. Fed.
90 G2 **Yagishiri-tō** *i.* Japan
101 D3 **Yagoua** Cameroon
85 E3 **Yagra** China
85 H2 **Yagradagzê Shan** *mt* China
47 F2 **Yaguari** *r.* Uru.
Yaguarón *r. see* **Jaguarão**
95 B4 **Yaha** Thai.
80 D2 **Yahşihan** Turkey
80 E2 **Yahyalı** Turkey
84 B3 **Yahya Wana** Afgh.
91 F6 **Yaita** Japan
91 F7 **Yaizu** Japan
89 A4 **Yajiang** China
80 F3 **Yakacık** Turkey
24 B2 **Yakima** U.S.A.
24 B2 **Yakima** *r.* U.S.A.
100 B3 **Yako** Burkina
20 B3 **Yakobi I.** *i.* U.S.A.
90 C2 **Yakovlevka** Rus. Fed.
90 G3 **Yakovo** China
91 B9 **Yaku-shima** *i.* Japan
20 B3 **Yakutat** U.S.A.
20 B3 **Yakutat Bay** *b.* U.S.A.
77 O3 **Yakutsk** Rus. Fed.
69 E6 **Yakymivka** Ukr.
95 B4 **Yala** Thai.
31 F4 **Yale** U.S.A.
116 A5 **Yalleroi** Austr.
115 G7 **Yallourn** Austr.
89 A5 **Yalong Jiang** *r.* China
80 B1 **Yalova** Turkey
69 F6 **Yalta** *Donets'k* Ukr.
69 E7 **Yalta** *Krym* Ukr.
80 C2 **Yalvaç** Turkey
90 G5 **Yamada** Japan
90 G5 **Yamagata** Japan
91 B9 **Yamaga** Japan
91 B7 **Yamaguchi** Japan
76 H2 **Yamal, Poluostrov** *pen.* Rus. Fed.
115 K2 **Yamba** Austr.
115 E7 **Yambacoona** Austr.
21 G2 **Yamba Lake** *l.* Can.
45 C4 **Yambi, Mesa de** *h.* Col.
101 E4 **Yambio** Sudan
67 M3 **Yambol** Bulg.
76 J3 **Yamburg** Rus. Fed.
88 A2 **Yamenzhuang** China
83 J6 **Yamethin** Myanmar
91 G1 **Yamizo-san** *mt* Japan
55 V7 **Yamm** Rus. Fed.
100 B4 **Yamoussoukro** Côte d'Ivoire
24 L3 **Yampa** *r.* U.S.A.
69 D5 **Yampil'** Ukr.
84 E4 **Yamuna** *r.* India
84 D3 **Yamunanagar** India
85 G3 **Yamzho Yumco** *l.* China
88 D2 **Yan** *r.* China
77 P3 **Yana** *r.* Rus. Fed.
114 D6 **Yanac** Austr.
86 D4 **Yanam** India
88 C2 **Yan'an** China
42 D6 **Yanaoca** Peru
89 A5 **Yanbian** China
78 D5 **Yanbu' al Baḥr** Saudi Arabia
88 F3 **Yancheng** China
112 C6 **Yanchep** Austr.

88 C2 **Yanchi** China
88 D2 **Yanchuan** China
115 G5 **Yanco** China
114 D3 **Yanco Glen** Austr.
115 F3 **Yanda** *watercourse* Austr.
114 D3 **Yandama Cr.** *watercourse* Austr.
116 E6 **Yandina** Austr.
100 B3 **Yanfolila** Mali
88 E1 **Yang** *r.* China
85 H3 **Ya'ngamdo** China
85 G3 **Yangbajain** China
88 D3 **Yangcheng** China
89 D6 **Yangchun** China
88 D1 **Yanggao** China
88 E2 **Yanggu** China
79 K1 **Yangiyul'** Uzbek.
89 D6 **Yangjiang** China
83 J7 **Yangôn** Myanmar
88 D4 **Yangping** China
88 D2 **Yangquan** China
89 D5 **Yangshan** China
89 D5 **Yangshuo** China
Yangtze *r. see* **Tongtian He**
89 E4 **Yangtze** *r.* China
88 F4 **Yangtze, Mouth of the** *est.* China
102 E2 **Yangudi Rassa National Park** *nat. park* Eth.
89 D6 **Yangxi** China
88 C3 **Yangxian** China
91 A6 **Yangyang** S. Korea
88 E1 **Yangyuan** China
88 F3 **Yangzhou** China
89 C4 **Yanhe** China
85 E2 **Yanhuqu** China
114 A4 **Yaninee, Lake** *salt flat* Austr.
87 N3 **Yanji** China
89 B4 **Yanjin** China
100 C4 **Yankara National Park** *nat. park* Nigeria
26 D3 **Yankton** U.S.A.
89 D5 **Yanling** China
77 P2 **Yano-Indigirskaya Nizmennost'** *lowland* Rus. Fed.
82 G2 **Yanqi** China
88 E1 **Yanqing** China
88 E2 **Yanshan** *Hebei* China
89 E4 **Yanshan** *Jiangxi* China
89 B6 **Yanshan** *Yunnan* China
88 E1 **Yan Shan** *mts* China
85 H2 **Yanshiping** China
90 A2 **Yanshou** China
77 P2 **Yanskiy Zaliv** *g.* Rus. Fed.
115 F2 **Yantabulla** Austr.
88 E2 **Yanzhou** China
114 E2 **Yantara Lake** *salt flat* Austr.
63 J3 **Yantarnyy** Rus. Fed.
89 A5 **Yanyuan** China
88 E2 **Yanzhou** China
100 D4 **Yaoundé** Cameroon
88 C2 **Yaoxian** China
95 A3 **Yao Yai, Ko** *i.* Thai.
93 K5 **Yap** *i.* Micronesia
45 D4 **Yapacana, Co** *mt* Venez.
93 K7 **Yapen** *i.* Indon.
93 K7 **Yapen, Selat** *chan.* Indon.
14 E5 **Yap Tr.** *sea feature* Pac. Oc.
36 C3 **Yaqui** *r.* Mex.
45 C2 **Yaracuy** *r.* Venez.
113 H4 **Yaraka** Austr.
68 H3 **Yaransk** Rus. Fed.
114 A4 **Yardea** Austr.
80 C3 **Yardımcı Burnu** *pt* Turkey
81 M2 **Yardımlı** Azer.
59 J5 **Yare** *r.* U.K.
68 K2 **Yarega** Rus. Fed.
111 G2 **Yaren** Nauru
68 J2 **Yarensk** Rus. Fed.
45 B5 **Yari** *r.* Col.
91 E6 **Yariga-take** *mt* Japan
45 C2 **Yaritagua** Venez.
31 J3 **Yarker** Can.
84 C1 **Yarkhun** *r.* Pak.
Yarlung Zangbo *r. see* **Brahmaputra**
23 G5 **Yarmouth** Can.
59 F7 **Yarmouth** U.K.
33 H4 **Yarmouth Port** U.S.A.
35 F4 **Yarnell** U.S.A.
68 F3 **Yaroslavl'** Rus. Fed.
68 F3 **Yaroslavskaya Oblast'** *div.* Rus. Fed.
90 C2 **Yaroslavskiy** Rus. Fed.
114 F6 **Yarra** *r.* Austr.
115 G7 **Yarram** Austr.
115 J1 **Yarraman** Austr.
116 A3 **Yarrowmere** Austr.
85 H3 **Yartö Tra La** *pass* China
76 K3 **Yartsevo** Rus. Fed.
68 E4 **Yartsevo** Rus. Fed.
45 B3 **Yarumal** Col.
85 F5 **Yasai** *r.* India
111 H3 **Yasawa Group** *is* Fiji
69 F6 **Yasenskaya** Rus. Fed.
69 G6 **Yashalta** Rus. Fed.
69 H6 **Yashkul'** Rus. Fed.
90 E2 **Yasnaya Polyana** Rus. Fed.
95 C2 **Yasothon** Thai.
115 H5 **Yass** Austr.
115 H5 **Yass** *r.* Austr.
80 B2 **Yatağan** Turkey
111 G4 **Yaté** New Caledonia
27 E4 **Yates Center** U.S.A.
21 K2 **Yathkyed L.** *l.* Can.
91 F7 **Yatsuga-take** *vol.* Japan
91 B8 **Yatsushiro** Japan
59 E6 **Yatton** U.K.

42 D5 **Yavari** *r.* Brazil/Peru
84 D5 **Yavatmāl** India
81 H2 **Yavi** Turkey
45 D3 **Yaví, Co** *mt* Venez.
65 D5 **Yavoriv** Ukr.
91 C8 **Yawatahama** Japan
85 E1 **Yawatongguz He** *r.* China
85 H5 **Yaw Ch.** *r.* Myanmar
79 G3 **Yazd** Iran
80 G2 **Yazıhan** Turkey
27 F5 **Yazoo** *r.* U.S.A.
27 F5 **Yazoo City** U.S.A.
55 L9 **Yding Skovhøj** *h.* Denmark
67 K6 **Ydra** *i.* Greece
95 A2 **Ye** Myanmar
114 F6 **Yea** Austr.
59 D7 **Yealmpton** U.K.
82 E3 **Yecheng** China
25 E6 **Yécora** Mex.
29 D7 **Yeehaw Junction** U.S.A.
114 A5 **Yeelanna** Austr.
68 F4 **Yefremov** Rus. Fed.
81 K2 **Yeghegnadzor** Armenia
69 G6 **Yegorlyk** *r.* Rus. Fed.
69 G6 **Yegorlykskaya** Rus. Fed.
90 E2 **Yegorova, Mys** *pt* Rus. Fed.
68 F4 **Yegor'yevsk** Rus. Fed.
101 F4 **Yei** Sudan
88 E4 **Yeji** China
76 H4 **Yekaterinburg** Rus. Fed.
69 G5 **Yelan'** Rus. Fed.
69 G5 **Yelan'** *r.* Rus. Fed.
115 J2 **Yelarbon** Austr.
69 F4 **Yelets** Rus. Fed.
100 A3 **Yélimané** Mali
57 □ **Yell** *i.* U.K.
30 B3 **Yellow** *r.* U.S.A.
32 D4 **Yellow Creek** U.S.A.
115 G4 **Yellow Mt** *h.* Austr.
Yellow River *r. see* **Huang He**
87 N4 **Yellow Sea** *sea* Pac. Oc.
24 E2 **Yellowstone** *r.* U.S.A.
24 E2 **Yellowstone L.** *l.* U.S.A.
24 E2 **Yellowstone Nat. Park** *nat. park* U.S.A.
24 E2 **Yellowtail Res.** *resr* U.S.A.
57 □ **Yell Sound** *chan.* U.K.
69 D5 **Yel'sk** Belarus
70 **Yemen** *country* Asia
68 G2 **Yemetsk** Rus. Fed.
68 G2 **Yemtsa** Rus. Fed.
68 J2 **Yemva** Rus. Fed.
54 W3 **Yena** Fin.
69 F5 **Yenakiyeve** Ukr.
85 H5 **Yenangyat** Myanmar
85 H5 **Yenangyaung** Myanmar
85 H6 **Yenanma** Myanmar
89 B6 **Yên Bai** Vietnam
115 G5 **Yenda** Austr.
100 B4 **Yendi** Ghana
102 B4 **Yénéganou** Congo
81 L3 **Yengejeh** Iran
80 D1 **Yeniçağa** Turkey
67 M5 **Yenice** Turkey
80 E3 **Yenice** Turkey
80 D2 **Yeniceoba** Turkey
80 B1 **Yenişehir** Turkey
76 L4 **Yenisey** *r.* Rus. Fed.
76 L4 **Yeniseysk** Rus. Fed.
76 L4 **Yeniseyskiy Kryazh** *ridge* Rus. Fed.
76 J2 **Yeniseyskiy Zaliv** *in.* Rus. Fed.
89 B6 **Yên Minh** Vietnam
69 H6 **Yenotayevka** Rus. Fed.
84 C5 **Yeola** India
Yeotmal *see* **Yavatmāl**
115 H4 **Yeoval** Austr.
59 E7 **Yeovil** U.K.
Yeo Yeo *r. see* **Bland**
25 E6 **Yepachi** Mex.
116 D4 **Yeppoon** Austr.
77 M3 **Yerbogachen** Rus. Fed.
81 K1 **Yerevan** Armenia
76 J4 **Yereymentau** Kazak.
69 H6 **Yergeni** *h.* Rus. Fed.
34 C2 **Yerington** U.S.A.
80 E2 **Yerköy** Turkey
27 B7 **Yermo** Mex.
34 D4 **Yermo** U.S.A.
87 M1 **Yerofey Pavlovich** Rus. Fed.
69 J5 **Yershov** Rus. Fed.
69 G2 **Yertsevo** Rus. Fed.
Yerushalayim *see* **Jerusalem**
69 H5 **Yeruslan** *r.* Rus. Fed.
76 H4 **Yesil'** Kazak.
80 E2 **Yeşilhisar** Turkey
80 F1 **Yeşilırmak** *r.* Turkey
80 D2 **Yeşilova** Turkey
69 G6 **Yessentuki** Rus. Fed.
77 M3 **Yessey** Rus. Fed.
115 J2 **Yetman** Austr.
83 J6 **Yeu** Myanmar
64 C3 **Yeu, Île d'** *i.* France
81 L1 **Yevlax** Azer.
69 E6 **Yevpatoriya** Ukr.
88 D3 **Yexian** China
88 E1 **Yeyik** China
69 F6 **Yeysk** Rus. Fed.
68 H1 **Yezhuga** *r.* Rus. Fed.
69 D4 **Yezyaryshcha** Belarus
88 D3 **Yi** *r. Henan* China
88 D3 **Yi** *r. Shandong* China
47 F2 **Yi** *r.* Uru.
88 D3 **Yibin** China
85 F2 **Yibug Caka** *salt l.* China
89 D4 **Yichang** *Hubei* China
89 D4 **Yichang** *Hubei* China

88 D4 **Yicheng** *Hubei* China
88 D3 **Yicheng** *Shanxi* China
88 D3 **Yichuan** China
87 N2 **Yichun** *Heilongjiang* China
89 E5 **Yichun** *Jiangxi* China
89 E4 **Yifeng** China
89 E5 **Yihuang** China
88 C3 **Yijun** China
90 A1 **Yilan** China
80 F2 **Yılan** Turkey
67 M4 **Yıldız Dağları** *mts* Turkey
80 F2 **Yıldızeli** Turkey
89 B5 **Yiliang** *Yunnan* China
89 B5 **Yiliang** *Yunnan* China
89 C4 **Yilong** China
89 B5 **Yilong Hu** *l.* China
89 B5 **Yimen** China
90 A2 **Yiminpo** China
88 C2 **Yinan** China
88 C2 **Yinchuan** China
88 C3 **Yingde** China
89 C7 **Yinggehai** China
88 C3 **Ying He** *r.* China
88 G1 **Yingkou** China
88 B2 **Yingpanshui** China
89 C4 **Yingshan** *Hubei* China
88 C4 **Yingshan** *Sichuan* China
88 E3 **Yingshang** China
89 E4 **Yingtan** China
88 D2 **Yingxian** China
82 E3 **Yining** China
89 C5 **Yinjiang** China
89 H5 **Yinmabin** Myanmar
88 C1 **Yin Shan** *mts* China
85 H3 **Yi'ong Zangbo** *r.* China
89 A5 **Yipinglang** China
102 D3 **Yirga Alem** Eth.
88 F2 **Yi Shan** *mt* China
89 F3 **Yishui** China
95 □ **Yishun** Sing.
82 H2 **Yiwu** China
88 F1 **Yixian** *Anhui* China
88 F1 **Yixian** *Liaoning* China
89 E4 **Yixing** China
89 D4 **Yiyang** *Hunan* China
89 E4 **Yiyang** *Jiangxi* China
89 D5 **Yizhang** China
89 C5 **Yizhou** China
55 S6 **Yläne** Fin.
54 S5 **Ylihärmä** Fin.
54 T4 **Yli-Ii** Fin.
54 T4 **Yli-Kärppä** Fin.
54 U4 **Ylikiiminki** Fin.
54 V3 **Yli-Kitka** *l.* Fin.
54 S5 **Ylistaro** Fin.
54 T4 **Ylitornio** Fin.
54 T4 **Ylivieska** Fin.
55 S6 **Ylöjärvi** Fin.
27 D6 **Yoakum** U.S.A.
90 G3 **Yobetsu-dake** *vol.* Japan
92 □ **Yogyakarta** Indon.
92 □ **Yogyakarta** *div.* Indon.
20 F4 **Yoho Nat. Park** *nat. park* Can.
101 D4 **Yokadouma** Cameroon
91 E7 **Yokkaichi** Japan
101 D4 **Yoko** Cameroon
91 F7 **Yokohama** Japan
91 F7 **Yokosuka** Japan
90 G5 **Yokote** Japan
90 G4 **Yokotsu-dake** *mt* Japan
101 D4 **Yola** Nigeria
95 B2 **Yom, Mae Nam** *r.* Thai.
100 B4 **Yomou** Guinea
91 G6 **Yonezawa** Japan
114 C4 **Yongala** Austr.
89 E5 **Yong'an** China
88 A2 **Yongchang** China
88 C2 **Yongcheng** China
91 A7 **Yŏngch'ŏn** S. Korea
88 B2 **Yongchun** China
88 B2 **Yongdeng** China
89 E5 **Yongding** China
89 D5 **Yongding** *r.* China
91 A6 **Yŏngdŏk** S. Korea
88 C6 **Yongfu** China
85 H3 **Yonggyap** *pass* India
88 B3 **Yongjia** China
88 B3 **Yongjing** China
91 A6 **Yŏngju** S. Korea
88 E2 **Yongkang** China
88 C6 **Yongnian** China
89 A5 **Yongren** China
89 F5 **Yongshun** China
91 A6 **Yŏngwŏl** S. Korea
89 E5 **Yongxing** China
89 E4 **Yongxiu** China
89 D5 **Yongzhou** China
33 G4 **Yonkers** U.S.A.
64 F2 **Yonne** *r.* France
45 B3 **Yopal** Col.
112 C6 **York** Austr.
58 F4 **York** U.K.
26 D3 **York** *NE* U.S.A.
32 E5 **York** *PA* U.S.A.
29 C5 **York** *SC* U.S.A.
113 H2 **York, C.** *c.* Austr.
58 F3 **York, Vale of** *v.* U.K.
114 B5 **Yorke Peninsula** *pen.* Austr.
114 B5 **Yorketown** Austr.
58 G4 **Yorkshire Dales National Park** *nat. park* U.K.
58 G4 **Yorkshire Wolds** *reg.* U.K.
21 J4 **Yorkton** Can.
100 B3 **Yorosso** Mali
34 C3 **Yosemite National Park** *nat. park* U.S.A.
34 C3 **Yosemite Village** U.S.A.
100 B3 **Yorosso** Mali
88 D6 **Yunwu Shan** *mts* China
89 C8 **Yoshino-gawa** *r.* Japan

91 D7 **Yoshino-Kumano National Park** Japan
68 H3 **Yoshkar-Ola** Rus. Fed.
80 E7 **Yotvata** Israel
60 D6 **Youghal** Rep. of Ireland
32 D5 **Youghiogheny River Lake** *l.* U.S.A.
89 C6 **You Jiang** *r.* China
115 H5 **Young** Austr.
47 F2 **Young** Uru.
114 B3 **Younghusband, L.** *salt flat* Austr.
114 C5 **Younghusband Pen.** *pen.* Austr.
119 A6 **Young I.** *i.* Antarctica
32 A6 **Youngstown** U.S.A.
89 D4 **You Shui** *r.* China
100 B3 **Youvarou** Mali
89 C5 **Youxi** China
89 D5 **Youxian** China
90 B1 **Youyang** China
88 D2 **Youyi** China
88 D2 **Youyu** China
115 F1 **Yowah** *watercourse* Austr.
80 E2 **Yozgat** Turkey
46 A3 **Ypané** *r.* Para.
46 A3 **Ypé-Jhú** Para.
24 B3 **Yreka** U.S.A.
Yr Wyddfa *mt see* **Snowdon**
55 N9 **Ystad** Sweden
59 C6 **Ystwyth** *r.* U.K.
Ysyk-Köl *see* **Balykchy**
82 E2 **Ysyk-Köl** *salt l.* Kyrgyzstan
57 F3 **Ythan** *r.* U.K.
77 P3 **Ytyk-Kyuyel'** Rus. Fed.
95 A1 **Yuam, Mae** *r.* Myanmar/Thai.
88 D4 **Yuan'an** China
89 C5 **Yuanbao Shan** *mt* China
89 D4 **Yuanjiang** *Hunan* China
89 A6 **Yuanjiang** *Yunnan* China
89 D4 **Yuan Jiang** *r. Hunan* China
89 B6 **Yuan Jiang** *r. Yunnan* China
89 F5 **Yuanli** Taiwan
89 D4 **Yuanling** China
89 A5 **Yuanmou** China
88 D2 **Yuanping** China
89 B6 **Yuanyang** China
34 B2 **Yuba** *r.* U.S.A.
34 B2 **Yuba City** U.S.A.
90 G3 **Yūbari** Japan
89 C4 **Yubei** China
36 F5 **Yucatán** *pen.* Mex.
36 G4 **Yucatan Channel** *str.* Cuba/Mex.
35 E4 **Yucca** U.S.A.
34 D3 **Yucca L.** *l.* U.S.A.
34 D4 **Yucca Valley** U.S.A.
88 E2 **Yucheng** China
88 D2 **Yuci** China
77 P4 **Yudoma** *r.* Rus. Fed.
89 E5 **Yudu** China
89 C4 **Yuechi** China
112 F4 **Yuendumu** Austr.
89 □ **Yuen Long** China
89 F4 **Yueqing** China
89 E4 **Yuexi** *Anhui* China
89 A4 **Yuexi** *Sichuan* China
89 D4 **Yueyang** China
89 E4 **Yugan** China
76 H3 **Yugorsk** Rus. Fed.
49 **Yugoslavia** *country* Europe
77 R3 **Yugo-Tala** Rus. Fed.
68 K2 **Yugydtydor** Rus. Fed.
89 E2 **Yuhuan** China
88 E2 **Yuhuang Ding** *mt* China
89 E4 **Yujiang** China
89 D6 **Yu Jiang** *r.* China
77 R3 **Yukagirskoye Ploskogor'ye** *plat.* Rus. Fed.
80 E2 **Yukarısarıkaya** Turkey
102 B4 **Yuki** Dem. Rep. Congo
18 **Yukon** *r.* Can./U.S.A.
20 E2 **Yukon Territory** *div.* Can.
81 K3 **Yüksekova** Turkey
112 F5 **Yulara** Austr.
116 C6 **Yuleba** Austr.
29 C6 **Yulee** U.S.A.
89 F6 **Yüli** Taiwan
89 D6 **Yulin** *Guangxi* China
89 C7 **Yulin** *Hainan* China
88 C2 **Yulin** *Shaanxi* China
35 E5 **Yuma** U.S.A.
35 E5 **Yuma Desert** *des.* U.S.A.
45 A4 **Yumbo** Col.
86 G4 **Yumen** China
80 C2 **Yumurtalık** Turkey
80 C2 **Yunak** Turkey
89 D6 **Yunan** China
88 E3 **Yuncheng** *Shandong* China
88 D3 **Yuncheng** *Shanxi* China
89 D6 **Yunfu** China
89 B5 **Yun Gui Gaoyuan** *plat.* China
89 F4 **Yunhe** China
89 D6 **Yunkai Dashan** *mts* China
88 D4 **Yunmeng** China
89 A5 **Yunnan** *div.* China
89 C4 **Yun Shui** *r.* China
114 C4 **Yunta** Austr.
89 D6 **Yunwu Shan** *mts* China
88 D3 **Yunxi** China
89 D3 **Yunxian** China
89 E6 **Yunxiao** China
88 D4 **Yunyang** *Henan* China
88 C4 **Yunyang** *Sichuan* China

89 C5 **Yuping** China
88 E1 **Yuqiao Sk.** *resr* China
89 C5 **Yuqing** China
76 K4 **Yurga** Rus. Fed.
42 C5 **Yurimaguas** Peru
45 E3 **Yuruán** *r.* Venez.
45 E3 **Yuruari** *r.* Venez.
45 C2 **Yurubí, Parque Nacional** *nat. park* Venez.
84 E1 **Yurungkax He** *r.* China
68 J3 **Yur'ya** Rus. Fed.
68 G3 **Yur'yevets** Rus. Fed.
68 F3 **Yur'yev-Pol'skiy** Rus. Fed.
89 F6 **Yü Shan** *mt* Taiwan
88 D2 **Yushe** China
68 E1 **Yushkozero** Rus. Fed.
82 J4 **Yushu** China
68 J3 **Yushut** *r.* Rus. Fed.
96 H6 **Yusta** Rus. Fed.
81 H1 **Yusufeli** Turkey
88 E3 **Yutai** China
85 E1 **Yutian** China
88 C2 **Yuwang** China
89 B5 **Yuxi** China
88 E2 **Yuxian** *Hebei* China
88 D2 **Yuxian** *Shanxi* China
89 F4 **Yuyao** China
90 G5 **Yuzawa** Japan
68 G3 **Yuza** Rus. Fed.
87 Q2 **Yuzhno-Sakhalinsk** Rus. Fed.
69 H6 **Yuzhno-Sukhokumsk** Rus. Fed.
69 D6 **Yuzhnoukrayinsk** Ukr.
90 H1 **Yuzhnoye** Rus. Fed.
69 G6 **Yuzhnyy** Rus. Fed.
88 B3 **Yuzhong** China
88 D3 **Yuzhou** China
62 C7 **Yverdon** Switz.
64 E2 **Yvetot** France
95 A1 **Ywathit** Myanmar

Z

61 C2 **Zaandam** Neth.
81 J3 **Zāb al Kabīr, Nahr az** *r.* Iraq
81 J4 **Zāb aş Şaghīr, Nahr az** *r.* Iraq
87 L2 **Zabaykal'sk** Rus. Fed.
81 K4 **Zab-e Kuchek** *r.* Iran
78 E7 **Zabīd** Yemen
79 J3 **Zābol** Iran
36 G5 **Zacapa** Guatemala
36 D5 **Zacapu** Mex.
36 D4 **Zacatecas** Mex.
67 J6 **Zacharo** Greece
66 F2 **Zadar** Croatia
95 A3 **Zadetkale Kyun** *i.* Myanmar
95 A3 **Zadetkyi Kyun** *i.* Myanmar
85 H3 **Zadoi** China
69 F4 **Zadonsk** Rus. Fed.
81 L4 **Zafarābād** Iran
67 M6 **Zafora** *i.* Greece
65 C3 **Zafra** Spain
78 C3 **Zagazig** Egypt
81 M5 **Zāgheh** Iran
66 D6 **Zaghouan** Tunisia
66 F2 **Zagreb** Croatia
81 L4 **Zagros, Kūhhā-ye** *mts* Iran
85 G3 **Za'gya Zangbo** *r.* China
79 J4 **Zāhedān** Iran
84 B2 **Zahidabad** Afgh.
80 E5 **Zahlé** Lebanon
Zaire *country see* **Congo, Democratic Republic of**
98 **Zaire Basin** *basin* Africa
67 K3 **Zaječar** Yugo.
81 J3 **Zākhō** Iraq
101 D3 **Zakouma, Parc National de** *nat. park* Chad
67 J6 **Zakynthos** Greece
Zakynthos *i. see* **Zante**
62 H7 **Zalaegerszeg** Hungary
62 H7 **Zalai-domsag** *h.* Hungary
65 D3 **Zalamea de la Serena** Spain
63 L7 **Zalău** Romania
68 F3 **Zales'ye** Rus. Fed.
101 E3 **Zalingei** Sudan
63 M6 **Zalishchyky** Ukr.
68 D3 **Zaluch'ye** Rus. Fed.
80 E2 **Zamanti** *r.* Turkey
94 B3 **Zambales Mts** *mts* Phil.
103 D5 **Zambeze** *r.* Moz.
Zambezi *r. see* **Zambeze**
103 C5 **Zambezi** Zambia
96 **Zambia** *country* Africa
94 B5 **Zamboanga** Phil.
94 B5 **Zamboanga Peninsula** *pen.* Phil.
42 C4 **Zamora** Ecuador
65 D2 **Zamora** Spain
36 D5 **Zamora de Hidalgo** Mex.
63 L5 **Zamość** Pol.
88 A3 **Zamtang** China
45 C2 **Zamuro, Pta** *pt* Venez.
45 E3 **Zamuro, Sierra del** *mts* Venez.
84 D3 **Zanda** China
105 L2 **Zandamela** Moz.
61 C3 **Zandvliet** Belgium
32 C5 **Zanesville** U.S.A.
84 D2 **Zangla** Jammu and Kashmir
81 M3 **Zanjān** Iran
81 L3 **Zanjān Rūd** *r.* Iran

67 J6 **Zante** *i.* Greece
102 D4 **Zanzibar** Tanz.
102 D4 **Zanzibar I.** *i.* Tanz.
89 D4 **Zaoshi** China
100 C2 **Zaouatallaz** Alg.
88 D3 **Zaoyang** China
77 L4 **Zaozernyy** Rus. Fed.
88 E3 **Zaozhuang** China
81 J3 **Zap** *r.* Turkey
68 E3 **Zapadnaya Dvina** Rus. Fed.
68 D4 **Zapadnaya Dvina** *r.* Rus. Fed.
67 K4 **Zapadni Rodopi** *mts* Bulg.
87 Q1 **Zapadno–Sakhalinskiy Khrebet** *mts* Rus. Fed.
76 K3 **Zapadno-Sibirskaya Ravnina** *plain* Rus. Fed.
54 Y2 **Zapadnyy Kil'din** Rus. Fed.
86 F1 **Zapadnyy Sayan** *reg.* Rus. Fed.
47 B3 **Zapala** Arg.
27 D7 **Zapata** U.S.A.
45 B3 **Zapatoca** Col.
54 W2 **Zapolyarnyy** Rus. Fed.
69 E6 **Zaporizhzhya** Ukr.
90 D2 **Zapovednik** *mt* Rus. Fed.
84 E2 **Zapug** China
81 L1 **Zaqatala** Azer.
85 H2 **Zaqên** China
85 H2 **Za Qu** *r.* China
80 F2 **Zara** Turkey
45 B3 **Zaragoza** Col.
25 F6 **Zaragoza** *Chihuahua* Mex.
27 C6 **Zaragoza** Mex.
65 F2 **Zaragoza** Spain
79 H3 **Zarand** Iran
79 J3 **Zaranj** Afgh.
80 E6 **Zararikh Reserve** *res.* Egypt
55 U9 **Zarasai** Lith.
47 E2 **Zárate** Arg.
45 D2 **Zaraza** Venez.
81 L1 **Zärdab** Azer.
54 W3 **Zarechensk** Rus. Fed.
81 M4 **Zäreh** Iran
20 C3 **Zarembo I.** *i.* U.S.A.
84 A3 **Zargun** *mt* Pak.
100 C3 **Zaria** Nigeria
69 C5 **Zarichne** Ukr.
81 K3 **Zarîneh Rûd** *r.* Iran
81 L5 **Zarneh** Iran
67 L2 **Zärneşti** Romania
90 B3 **Zarubino** Rus. Fed.
62 G5 **Žary** Pol.
45 A3 **Zarzal** Col.
101 D1 **Zarzis** Tunisia
54 W3 **Zasheyek** Rus. Fed.
84 D2 **Zaskar** *r.* India
84 D2 **Zaskar Mts** *mts* India
68 C4 **Zaslawye** Belarus
105 G5 **Zastron** S. Africa
67 H2 **Zavidovići** Bos.-Herz.
87 N1 **Zavitinsk** Rus. Fed.

88 A2 **Zawa** China
63 J5 **Zawiercie** Pol.
82 F1 **Zaysan** Kazak.
82 F1 **Zaysan, Ozero** *l.* Kazak.
82 J5 **Zayü** China
62 G6 **Žďár nad Sázavou** Czech Rep.
69 C5 **Zdolbuniv** Ukr.
55 M9 **Zealand** *i.* Denmark
81 K3 **Zêbâr** Iraq
61 B3 **Zeebrugge** Belgium
115 F8 **Zeehan** Austr.
105 G2 **Zeerust** S. Africa
61 B3 **Zeeuwsch-Vlaanderen** *reg.* Neth.
80 E5 **Zefat** Israel
112 F4 **Žeil, Mount** *mt* Austr.
88 A3 **Zêkog** China
54 X3 **Zelenoborskiy** Rus. Fed.
68 J4 **Zelenodol'sk** Rus. Fed.
55 V6 **Zelenogorsk** Rus. Fed.
68 F3 **Zelenograd** Rus. Fed.
68 B4 **Zelenogradsk** Rus. Fed.
69 G6 **Zelenokumsk** Rus. Fed.
68 H3 **Zelentsovo** Rus. Fed.
62 F7 **Zell am See** Austria
88 A3 **Zêmdasam** China
68 G4 **Zemetchino** Rus. Fed.
102 C3 **Zémio** C.A.R.
76 F1 **Zemlya Aleksandry** *i.* Rus. Fed.
　　Zemlya Frantsa-Iosifa *is see* **Franz Josef Land**
76 F2 **Zemlya Georga** *i.* Rus. Fed.
76 H1 **Zemlya Vil'cheka** *i.* Rus. Fed.
65 G5 **Zemmora** Alg.
89 D6 **Zengcheng** China
90 A3 **Zengfeng Shan** *mt* China
34 A1 **Zenia** U.S.A.
67 G2 **Zenica** Bos.-Herz.
59 B7 **Zennor** U.K.
34 C2 **Zephyr Cove** U.S.A.
69 G6 **Zernograd** Rus. Fed.
69 G7 **Zestap'oni** Georgia
85 G3 **Zêtang** China
62 D4 **Zeven** Ger.
61 E3 **Zevenaar** Neth.
87 N1 **Zeya** Rus. Fed.
77 O4 **Zeya** *r.* Rus. Fed.
77 O4 **Zeyskoye Vdkhr.** *resr* Rus. Fed.
65 C3 **Zêzere** *r.* Port.
63 J5 **Zgierz** Pol.
85 F3 **Zhabdün** China
68 C4 **Zhabinka** Belarus
76 H4 **Zhaltyr** Kazak.
76 G5 **Zhanaozen** Kazak.
88 E2 **Zhang** *r.* China
88 E1 **Zhangbei** China
87 N2 **Zhangguangcai Ling** *mts* China
88 E1 **Zhangjiakou** China
88 B3 **Zhangla** China

89 E5 **Zhangping** China
89 E5 **Zhangpu** China
88 G1 **Zhangqiangzhen** China
89 E4 **Zhangshu** China
88 E2 **Zhangwei Xinhe** *r.* China
88 G1 **Zhangwu** China
88 B3 **Zhangxian** China
89 E5 **Zhangye** China
89 E5 **Zhangzhou** China
88 D2 **Zhanhe** China
88 B5 **Zhanyi** China
89 D6 **Zhanjiang** China
89 E6 **Zhao'an** China
87 N2 **Zhaodong** China
89 B4 **Zhaojue** China
89 D5 **Zhaoping** China
89 D6 **Zhaoqing** China
82 F2 **Zhaosu** China
89 B5 **Zhaotong** China
88 E2 **Zhaoxian** China
89 D6 **Zhapo** China
85 F3 **Zhari Namco** *salt l.* China
82 F2 **Zharkent** Kazak.
68 E4 **Zharkovskiy** Rus. Fed.
82 F1 **Zharma** Kazak.
69 D5 **Zhashkiv** Ukr.
88 C3 **Zhashui** China
85 F2 **Zhaxi Co** *salt l.* China
84 D2 **Zhaxigang** China
89 F4 **Zhecheng** China
89 F4 **Zhejiang** *div.* China
76 H2 **Zhelaniya, M.** *c.* Rus. Fed.
69 E4 **Zheleznogorsk** Rus. Fed.
88 C3 **Zhen'an** China
88 C3 **Zhenba** China
89 C4 **Zheng'an** China
89 F5 **Zhengding** China
89 F5 **Zhenghe** China
　　Zhenglan Qi *see* **Dund Hot**
88 C3 **Zhengning** China
　　Zhengxiangbai Qi *see* **Qagan Nur**
88 E3 **Zhengyang** China
88 D3 **Zhengzhou** China
89 F4 **Zhenhai** China
88 F3 **Zhenjiang** China
88 B3 **Zhenjiangguan** China
88 D3 **Zhenning** China
88 D3 **Zhenping** China
89 B5 **Zhenxiong** China
88 C3 **Zhenyuan** *Gansu* China
89 C5 **Zhenyuan** *Guizhou* China
89 G5 **Zherdevka** Rus. Fed.
89 F5 **Zherong** China
68 J2 **Zheshart** Rus. Fed.
89 D4 **Zhexi Sk.** *resr* China
82 C1 **Zhezdy** Kazak.
82 C1 **Zhezkazgan** Kazak.
89 D4 **Zhicheng** China
88 C2 **Zhidan** China
85 H2 **Zhidoi** China
77 O3 **Zhigansk** Rus. Fed.

85 G3 **Zhigung** China
89 D4 **Zhijiang** *Hubei* China
89 C5 **Zhijiang** *Hunan* China
89 B5 **Zhijin** China
　　Zhi Qu *r. see* **Tongtian He**
69 H5 **Zhirnovsk** Rus. Fed.
76 H4 **Zhitikara** Kazak.
69 H5 **Zhitkur** Rus. Fed.
81 L4 **Zhîvâr** Iran
68 D4 **Zhlobin** Belarus
69 D5 **Zhmerynka** Ukr.
79 K3 **Zhob** Pak.
84 B3 **Zhob** *r.* Pak.
77 R2 **Zhokhova, O.** *i.* Rus. Fed.
82 J5 **Zhongdian** China
88 B4 **Zhongjiang** China
88 B2 **Zhongning** China
119 D5 **Zhongshan** China Base Antarctica
89 D6 **Zhongshan** *Guangdong* China
89 D5 **Zhongshan** *Guangxi* China
88 D3 **Zhongtiao Shan** *mts* China
88 B2 **Zhongwei** China
89 C4 **Zhongxian** China
89 E5 **Zhongxin** China
89 B5 **Zhongyicun** China
89 D7 **Zhongyuan** China
89 C4 **Zhou He** *r.* China
88 B2 **Zhoujiajing** China
88 E3 **Zhoukou** China
89 F5 **Zhouning** China
89 G4 **Zhoushan** China
89 E5 **Zhovti Vody** Ukr.
88 G2 **Zhuanghe** China
88 B3 **Zhuangliang** China
88 F3 **Zhucheng** China
88 B3 **Zhugqu** China
89 D6 **Zhuhai** China
89 F4 **Zhuji** China
68 E4 **Zhukovka** Rus. Fed.
88 E2 **Zhulong** *r.* China
88 E3 **Zhumadian** China
88 E1 **Zhuolu** China
88 D2 **Zhuozang** *r.* China
88 E2 **Zhuozhou** China
88 D1 **Zhuozi** China
88 D3 **Zhushan** China
88 C3 **Zhuxi** China
89 D5 **Zhuzhou** *Hunan* China
89 D5 **Zhuzhou** *Hunan* China
69 C5 **Zhydachiv** Ukr.
69 C4 **Zhytkavichy** Belarus
69 D5 **Zhytomyr** Ukr.
88 F2 **Zi** *r.* China
63 J6 **Žiar nad Hronom** Slovakia
81 J3 **Zîbâr** Iraq
82 F2 **Zibo** China
88 C2 **Zichang** China
84 B2 **Zidig Pass** *pass* Pak.
62 G5 **Zielona Góra** Pol.
80 C6 **Zifta** Egypt

85 G3 **Zhigung** China
89 D4 **Zhijiang** *Hubei* China
89 C5 **Zhijiang** *Hunan* China
89 B5 **Zhijin** China
81 M1 **Zığ** Azer.
85 H5 **Zigaing** Myanmar
85 G2 **Zigê Tangco** *l.* China
89 B4 **Zigong** China
89 D4 **Zigui** China
100 A3 **Ziguinchor** Senegal
55 U8 **Ziguri** Latvia
89 E6 **Zijin** China
61 E2 **Zijpenberg** *h.* Neth.
80 E5 **Zikhron Ya'aqov** Israel
80 E1 **Zile** Turkey
63 J6 **Žilina** Slovakia
86 H1 **Zima** Rus. Fed.
36 E4 **Zimapán** Mex.
103 C5 **Zimba** Zambia
96 **Zimbabwe** *country* Africa
81 K4 **Zimkän, Rüdkhäneh-ye** *r.* Iran
100 A4 **Zimmi** Sierra Leone
67 L3 **Zimnicea** Romania
69 G6 **Zimovniki** Rus. Fed.
80 E4 **Zimrin** Syria
100 C3 **Zinder** Niger
100 B3 **Ziniaré** Burkina
88 B2 **Zinihu** China
35 F3 **Zion Nat. Park** *nat. park* U.S.A.
22 B3 **Zionz L.** *l.* Can.
45 B3 **Zipaquirá** Col.
85 B3 **Ziqudukou** China
85 H4 **Ziro** India
89 D4 **Zi Shui** *r.* China
62 **Zistersdorf** Austria
36 E5 **Zitácuaro** Mex.
62 G5 **Zittau** Ger.
81 K3 **Zîveh** Iran
85 E5 **Zixi** China
89 D5 **Zixing** China
88 E2 **Ziya** *r.* China
89 B4 **Ziyang** *Shaanxi* China
89 B4 **Ziyang** *Sichuan* China
89 D5 **Ziyuan** China
89 C5 **Ziyun** China
89 B3 **Zizhong** China
62 H6 **Zlín** Czech Rep.
69 F5 **Zmiyiv** Ukr.
68 E4 **Znamenka** Rus. Fed.
69 E5 **Znam''yanka** Ukr.
62 H6 **Znojmo** Czech Rep.
104 D6 **Zoar** S. Africa
81 L4 **Zobeyrî** Iran
81 K4 **Zôhâb** Iran
88 B3 **Zoigê** China
84 C2 **Zoji La** *pass* India
105 G6 **Zola** S. Africa
69 E5 **Zolochiv** *Kharkiv* Ukr.
69 C5 **Zolochiv** *L'viv* Ukr.
69 E5 **Zolotonosha** Ukr.
69 F4 **Zolotukhino** Rus. Fed.
103 D5 **Zomba** Malawi
　　Zongga *see* **Gyirong**
102 B3 **Zongo** Dem. Rep. Congo
80 C1 **Zonguldak** Turkey
85 G3 **Zongxoi** China

89 E4 **Zongyang** China
66 C4 **Zonza** France
100 B3 **Zorgho** Burkina
100 B4 **Zorzor** Liberia
101 D2 **Zouar** Chad
88 E3 **Zoucheng** China
100 A2 **Zouérat** Maur.
88 E2 **Zouping** China
89 D4 **Zoushi** China
67 J2 **Zrenjanin** Yugo.
45 D2 **Zuata** *r.* Venez.
47 D3 **Zubillaga** Arg.
68 G4 **Zubova Polyana** Rus. Fed.
100 B4 **Zuénoula** Côte d'Ivoire
62 D7 **Zug** Switz.
69 G7 **Zugdidi** Georgia
62 E7 **Zugspitze** *mt* Austria/Ger.
　　Zuider Zee *l. see* **IJsselmeer**
61 C2 **Zuid-Kennemerland Nationaal Park** *nat. park* Neth.
61 E1 **Zuidlaardermeer** *l.* Neth.
65 D3 **Zújar** *r.* Spain
45 B2 **Zulia** *r.* Col.
61 E4 **Zülpich** Ger.
103 D5 **Zumbo** Moz.
30 A3 **Zumbro** *r.* U.S.A.
30 A3 **Zumbrota** U.S.A.
100 C4 **Zungeru** Nigeria
88 F1 **Zunhua** China
35 H4 **Zuni** U.S.A.
35 H4 **Zuni Mts** *mts* U.S.A.
89 C5 **Zunyi** *Guizhou* China
89 C5 **Zunyi** *Guizhou* China
89 C6 **Zuo Jiang** *r.* China/Vietnam
88 D2 **Zuoquan** China
88 D2 **Zuoyun** China
81 K2 **Züräbäd** Iran
81 L5 **Zurbätïyah** Iraq
62 D7 **Zürich** Switz.
61 E2 **Zutphen** Neth.
105 F6 **Zuurberg National Park** *nat. park* S. Africa
101 D3 **Zuwärah** Libya
68 J3 **Zuyevka** Rus. Fed.
68 J4 **Zvenigovo** Rus. Fed.
69 D5 **Zvenyhorodka** Ukr.
103 D6 **Zvishavane** Zimbabwe
63 J6 **Zvolen** Slovakia
67 H2 **Zvornik** Bos.-Herz.
61 E2 **Zwartewater** *l.* Neth.
100 B4 **Zwedru** Liberia
61 E2 **Zweeloo** Neth.
61 F5 **Zweibrücken** Ger.
105 G6 **Zwelitsha** S. Africa
62 G6 **Zwettl** Austria
62 F5 **Zwickau** Ger.
61 E2 **Zwolle** Neth.
77 R3 **Zyryanka** Rus. Fed.
86 D2 **Zyryanovsk** Kazak.

SYMBOLS

RELIEF

METRES		FEET
6000		19686
5000		16404
4000		13124
3000		9843
2000		6562
1000		3281
500		1640
200		656
SEA		LEVEL
200		656
2000		6562
4000		13124
6000		19686

Additional bathymetric contour layers are shown at scales greater than 1:2 million. These are labelled on an individual basis.

213
△ Summit
height in metres

BOUNDARIES

- International
- International disputed
- Ceasefire line
- Main administrative (U.K.)
- Main administrative
- Main administrative through water

COMMUNICATIONS

- Motorway
- Motorway tunnel

Motorways are classified separately at scales greater than 1:5 million. At smaller scales motorways are classified with main roads.

- Main road
- Main road under construction
- Main road tunnel
- Other road
- Other road under construction
- Other road tunnel
- Track
- Main railway
- Main railway under construction
- Main railway tunnel
- Other railway
- Other railway under construction
- Other railway tunnel
- ⊕ Main airport
- ⊥ Other airport

PHYSICAL FEATURES

- Freshwater lake
- Seasonal freshwater lake
- Saltwater lake *or* Lagoon
- Seasonal saltwater lake
- Dry salt lake *or* Salt pan
- Marsh
- River
- Waterfall
- Dam *or* Barrage
- Seasonal river *or* Wadi
- Canal
- Flood dyke
- Reef
- Volcano
- Lava field
- Sandy desert
- Rocky desert
- Oasis
- Escarpment
- Mountain pass *height in metres* 923
- Ice cap *or* Glacier

OTHER FEATURES

- National park
- Reserve
- Ancient wall
- ∴ Historic or Tourist site

STYLES OF LETTERING

Country name	**FRANCE**	Island	*Gran Canaria*
	BARBADOS	Lake	*LAKE ERIE*
Main administrative name	HESSEN	Mountain	*ANDES*
Area name	*ARTOIS*	River	*Zambeze*

SETTLEMENTS

POPULATION	NATIONAL CAPITAL	ADMINISTRATIVE CAPITAL	CITY OR TOWN
Over 5 million	▣ **Beijing**	◉ **Tianjin**	◉ **New York**
1 to 5 million	▣ **Seoul**	◉ **Lagos**	◉ **Barranquilla**
500000 to 1 million	▣ **Bangui**	◎ **Douala**	◉ **Memphis**
100000 to 500000	▢ Wellington	○ Mansa	○ Mara
50000 to 100000	▢ Port of Spain	○ Lubango	○ Tuzla
10000 to 50000	▫ Malabo	○ Chinhoyi	○ El Tigre
Less than 10000	▫ Roseau	○ Ati	○ Soledad

Urban area